Vietnam

Nick Ray, Benedict Walker

PLAN YOUR TRIP

HUYTHOAI/GETTY IMAGES ©

HA GIANG PROVINCE P148

PETER ADAMS/GETTY IMAGES ©

FLOWER HMONG PEOPLE, BAC HA P145

ON THE ROAD

Contents

BRUNO DE HOGUES/GETTY IMAGES ©

HOI AN P203

UNDERSTAND

SURVIVAL GUIDE

SPECIAL FEATURES

Welcome to Vietnam

Astonishingly exotic and utterly compelling, Vietnam is a country of breathtaking natural beauty with a unique heritage, where travel quickly becomes addictive.

Sensory Overload

Unforgettable experiences are everywhere in Vietnam. There's the sublime: gazing over a surreal seascape of limestone islands from the deck of a traditional junk in Halong Bay. The ridiculous: taking 10 minutes just to cross the street through a tsunami of motorbikes in Hanoi. The inspirational: exploring the world's most spectacular cave systems in Phong Nha-Ke Bang National Park. The comical: watching a moped loaded with honking pigs weave a wobbly route along a country lane. And the contemplative: witnessing a solitary grave in a cemetery of thousands of war victims.

War, Peace & Progress

Forty years after the carnage and destruction of an epoch-defining conflict, Vietnam is resolutely a nation, not a war, in the eyes of the world. Self-confident and fast-developing, its progress is all-evident in the country's booming metropolises. Vietnam's allure is easy to appreciate (and something of a history lesson) as ancient, labyrinthine trading quarters of still-thriving craft industries are juxtaposed with grand colonial mansions from the French era, all overseen from the skybars of 21st-century glass-and-steel highrises.

A Culinary Superpower

The Thais may grumble, but in Southeast Asia nothing really comes close: Vietnamese food is *that* good. Incredibly subtle in its flavours and outstanding in its diversity, Vietnamese cooking is a fascinating draw for travellers – myriad street-food tours and cooking schools are testament to this. Geography plays a crucial role, with Chinese flavours influencing the soups of the north, spices sparking up southern cuisine, and herbs and complex techniques typifying the central coastline, rightly renowned as Vietnam's epicurean epicentre. And up and down the country you can mingle with villagers, sample local dishes and sip rice wine in Vietnam's many regional markets.

Thrills & Chills

If you've got the bills, Vietnam's got the thrills and chills. Some require a little physical effort, such as motorbiking switchback after switchback up the jaw-dropping Hai Van Pass in central Vietnam. Others require even more sweat: kitesurfing the tropical oceanic waters off Mui Ne or hiking the evergreen hills around Bac Ha or Sapa. And when you're done with all that adrenaline stuff, there's plenty of horizontal 'me' time to relish. Vietnam has outstanding spas – from marble temples of treatments, to simple family-run massage salons with backpacker-friendly rates.

Why I Love Vietnam

By Iain Stewart, Writer

I find myself returning to Vietnam for the same reasons: to feast on the best seafood in the world, ride a lonely mountain pass I've not yet experienced, and search for that perfect cove beach I've not yet found. The country has changed immeasurably since I first arrived in 1991 (when the nation was still shell-shocked from the war with the USA and Hanoi was a city of bicycles) but I continue to be astounded by the spirit, determination and sheer lust for life of the Vietnamese people.

For more about our writers, see page 520

Above: Terraced rice fields, Sapa (p136)

Vietnam

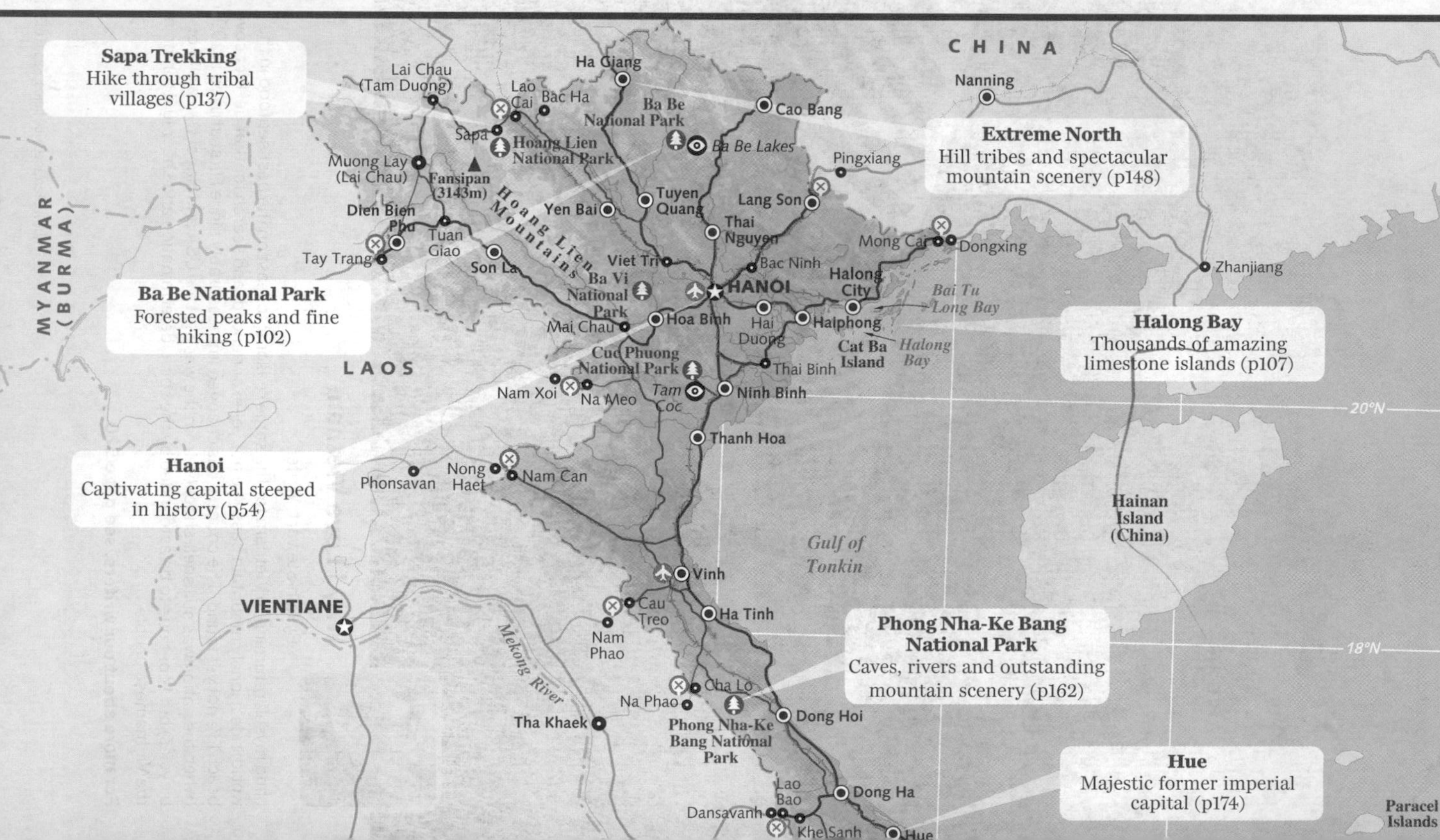

0
0
200 km
120 miles
Sapa Trekking
Hike through tribal villages (p137)
Extreme North
Hill tribes and spectacular mountain scenery (p148)
Ba Be National Park
Forested peaks and fine hiking (p102)
Halong Bay
Thousands of amazing limestone islands (p107)
Hanoi
Captivating capital steeped in history (p54)
Phong Nha-Ke Bang National Park
Caves, rivers and outstanding mountain scenery (p162)
Hue
Majestic former imperial capital (p174)
CHINA
LAOS
MYANMAR (BURMA)
Nanning
Pingxiang
Zhanjiang
Dongxing
Mong Cai
Lai Chau (Tam Duong)
Lao Cai
Bac Ha
Ha Giang
Cao Bang
Ba Be National Park
Ba Be Lakes
Sapa
Hoang Lien National Park
Muong Lay (Lai Chau)
Fansipan (3143m)
Hoang Lien Mountains
Dien Bien Phu
Tuan Giao
Tay Trang
Son La
Yen Bai
Tuyen Quang
Lang Son
Thai Nguyen
Bac Ninh
Viet Tri
Ba Vi National Park
HANOI
Halong City
Bai Tu Long Bay
Mai Chau
Hoa Binh
Hai Duong
Haiphong
Cat Ba Island
Halong Bay
Cuc Phuong National Park
Thai Binh
Nam Xoi
Na Meo
Tam Coc
Ninh Binh
Thanh Hoa
20°N
Phonsavan
Nong Haet
Nam Can
Hainan Island (China)
Gulf of Tonkin
Vinh
VIENTIANE
Cau Treo
Nam Phao
Ha Tinh
Mekong River
18°N
Cha Lo
Na Phao
Tha Khaek
Phong Nha-Ke Bang National Park
Dong Hoi
Lao Bao
Dong Ha
Dansavanh
Khe Sanh
Hue
Paracel Islands

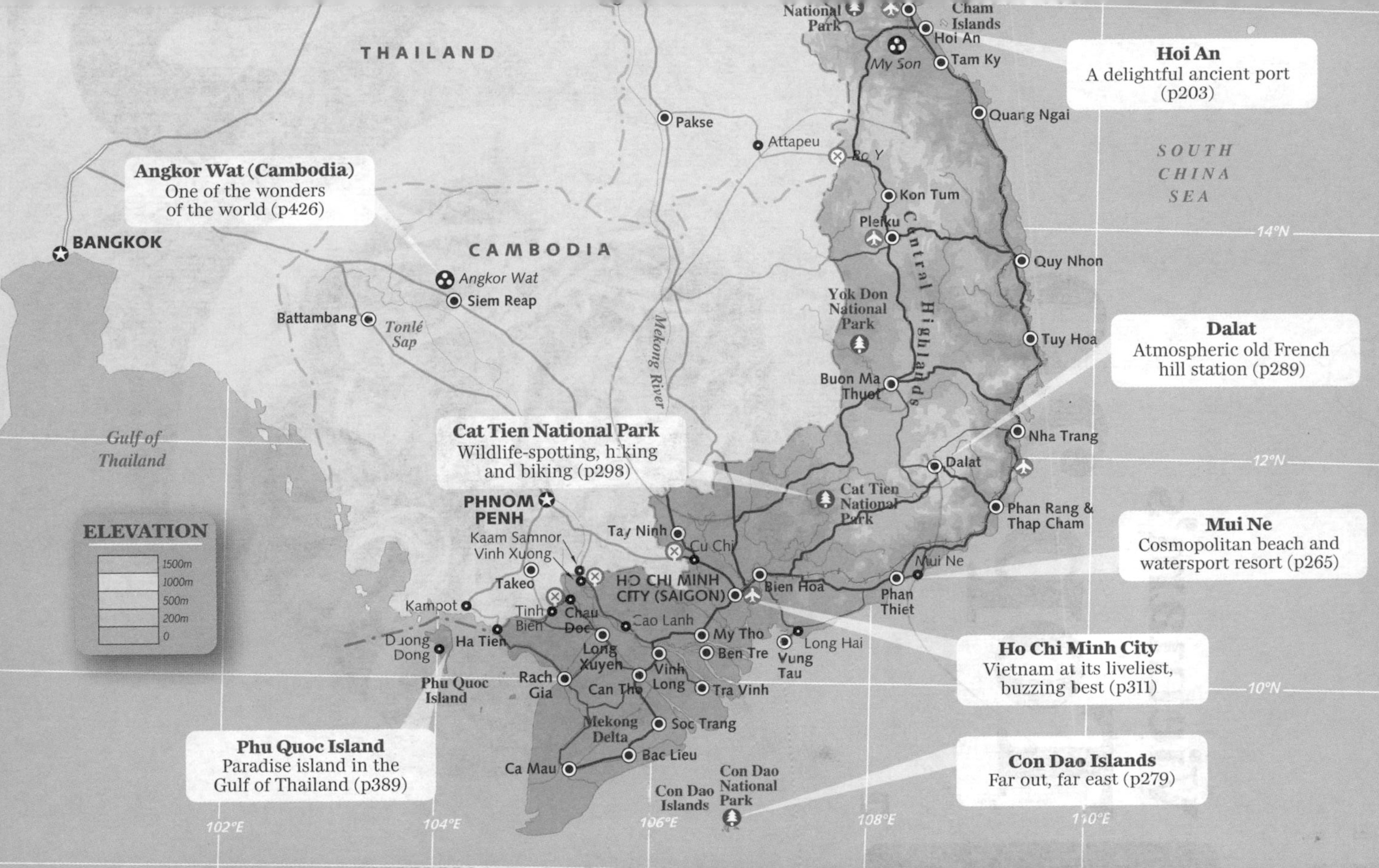

THAILAND
CAMBODIA
BANGKOK
PHNOM PENH
SOUTH CHINA SEA
Gulf of Thailand
Hoi An
A delightful ancient port (p203)
Angkor Wat (Cambodia)
One of the wonders of the world (p426)
Dalat
Atmospheric old French hill station (p289)
Cat Tien National Park
Wildlife-spotting, hiking and biking (p298)
Mui Ne
Cosmopolitan beach and watersport resort (p265)
Ho Chi Minh City
Vietnam at its liveliest, buzzing best (p311)
Phu Quoc Island
Paradise island in the Gulf of Thailand (p389)
Con Dao Islands
Far out, far east (p279)
ELEVATION
1500m
1000m
500m
200m
0
Central Highlands
Mekong River
Tonlé Sap
Angkor Wat
Siem Reap
Battambang
Pakse
Attapeu
Kon Tum
Pleiku
Yok Don National Park
Buon Ma Thuot
Cat Tien National Park
Dalat
Nha Trang
Phan Rang & Thap Cham
Mui Ne
Phan Thiet
Bien Hoa
Long Hai
Vung Tau
HO CHI MINH CITY (SAIGON)
Cu Chi
Tay Ninh
Kaam Samnor
Vinh Xuong
Takeo
Kampot
Tinh Bien
Chau Doc
Cao Lanh
My Tho
Ben Tre
Tra Vinh
Long Xuyen
Vinh Long
Can Tho
Rach Gia
Ha Tien
Duong Dong
Phu Quoc Island
Mekong Delta
Soc Trang
Bac Lieu
Ca Mau
Con Dao Islands
Con Dao National Park
Cham Islands
Hoi An
My Son
Tam Ky
Quang Ngai
Quy Nhon
Tuy Hoa
National Park
14°N
12°N
10°N
102°E
104°E
106°E
108°E
110°E

Vietnam's Top 20

1

Food

1 Locally sourced and seasonal, complex and refined, Vietnamese food (p464) is perhaps Asia's greatest culinary secret. Essentially it's all about the freshness of the ingredients – chefs shop twice daily to collect just-picked herbs from the market. The result? Incomparable texture and flavour combinations. For the Vietnamese, a meal should balance sour and sweet, crunchy and silky, fried and steamed, soup and salad. Wherever you are, you'll find exquisite local specialities – the 'white rose' of Hoi An, the *canh chua* (a fish and vegetable soup) of the Mekong Delta or the good ol' *pho* of the north.

Hoi An

2 Vietnam's most cosmopolitan and civilised town, this beautiful ancient port is bursting with gourmet restaurants, hip bars and cafes, quirky boutiques and expert tailors. Immerse yourself in history in the warren-like lanes of the Old Town, and tour the temples and pagodas. Dine like an emperor on a peasant's budget (and even learn how to cook like the locals). Then hit glorious An Bang Beach, wander along the riverside and bike the back roads. Yes, Hoi An (p203) has it all.

IAIN BAGWELL/LONELY PLANET ©

MEOGIAPHOTO/GETTY IMAGES ©

Phong Nha-Ke Bang National Park

3 With hills shrouded in rainforest, and mountain rivers coursing through ravines, above ground the Phong Nha-Ke Bang region (p162) is one of Vietnam's most spectacular national parks. Head underground for proof that this area should be part of any Vietnamese itinerary. A fortunate selection of travellers can experience Hang Son Doong, the world's largest cave, but more accessible are the ziplining and kayaking thrills of Hang Toi, and the ethereal beauty of Paradise Cave. Hang En (p163)

Halong Bay

4 Halong Bay's (p107) stunning combination of karst limestone peaks and sheltered, shimmering seas is one of Vietnam's top tourist draws, but with more than 2000 different islands, there's plenty of superb scenery to go around. Definitely book an overnight cruise and make time for your own special moments on this World Heritage wonder – rise early for an ethereal misty dawn, or pilot a kayak into grottoes and lagoons. If you're hankering for more karst action, move on to the less touristy but equally spectacular Lan Ha Bay.

3

ROBERT MUCKLEY/GETTY IMAGES ©

THUC NGUYEN/EYEEM/GETTY IMAGES ©

Ho Chi Minh City

5 Increasingly international but still unmistakably Vietnamese, the former Saigon's visceral energy will delight big-city devotees. HCMC (p311) doesn't inspire neutrality: you'll either be drawn into its thrilling vortex and hypnotised by the perpetual whir of its orbiting motorbikes, or you'll find the whole experience overwhelming. Dive in and you'll be rewarded with a wealth of history, delicious food and a vibrant nightlife that sets the standard for Vietnam. The heat is always on in Saigon; loosen your collar and enjoy.

Hue

6 The capital of the nation for 150 years in the 19th and early 20th centuries, Hue (p174) is perhaps the easiest Vietnamese city to love and spend time in. Its situation on the banks of the Perfume River is sublime, its complex cuisine justifiably famous, and its streets are relatively traffic free. And that's without the majesty of the Hue Citadel, its royal residences and elegant temples, formidable walled defences and gateways to explore. On the city's fringes are some of Vietnam's most impressive pagodas and royal tombs, many in wonderful natural settings.

Hanoi

7 Ancient but dynamic, the nation's capital hurtles toward modernity, cautiously embracing visitors. Sample Hanoi's (p54) heady mix of history and ambition by wandering the streets of the Old Quarter, sipping drip-coffee, slurping on a hearty bowl of *bun rieu cua* (hearty crab broth) and scoring souvenirs for next to nothing. When you're done, check out the crumbling decadence of the French Quarter then zip up to cosmopolitan Tay Ho for finer dining and the lowdown on Hanoi's burgeoning art scene.

Extreme North

8 The extreme north of Vietnam is all about raw adventure travel. Ha Giang province (p148) is Vietnam's spectacular emerging destination for the intrepid, with dizzying ascents up the Quan Ba Pass (Heaven's Gate), towering karsts and granite outcrops, and jaw-dropping vistas on the epic trip between Dong Van and Meo Vac. And with improved roads, new trekking routes, minority markets and a wider choice of guesthouses, Vietnam's final frontier – now a Unesco-listed geopark – is really opening up. Ha Giang province (p148)

Phu Quoc Island

9 Lapped by azure waters and edged with the kind of white-sand beaches that make sun seekers sink to their weak knees, Phu Quoc (p389) – way down in the south of Vietnam – is ideal for slipping into low gear, reaching for a seaside cocktail and toasting a blood-orange sun as it dips into the sea. And if you want to notch it up a tad, grab a motorbike and hit the red-dirt roads: the island's the size of Singapore.

Markets

10 From the floating markets of the Mekong Delta, souvenir-rich streets of Hoi An, urban affairs of Ho Chi Minh City and the tribal gatherings in the highlands, Vietnamese markets are a riot of colour and commerce. For photographers, markets are ideal for getting shots of Vietnamese villagers and their perfectly arranged pyramids of fruit or glistening seafood displays. The region around the town of Bac Ha (p145) is particularly market-rich and should not be missed if you're anywhere in the north. Lacquered bowls, Bac Ha Market (p145)

Con Dao Islands

11 The furious energy that characterises Vietnamese cities can be intoxicating, but when you need an urban detox, these idyllic tropical islands make the perfect escape. Once hell on earth for a generation of political prisoners, Con Dao (p279) is now a heavenly destination of remote beaches, pristine dive sites and diverse nature. It's a wonderful place to explore by bike in search of that dream beach, while the main settlement of Con Son is one of Vietnam's most charming towns.

Cat Tien National Park

12 An accessible and impressive protected area, Cat Tien (p298) lies conveniently midway between Ho Chi Minh City and Dalat. It is set on a bend in the Dong Nai River, and there is something vaguely *Apocalypse Now* about arriving here. Popular activities include trekking, cycling and wildlife spotting: the Wild Gibbon Trek is a must. The park is also home to a primate centre, where gibbons and langurs are coaxed back into their natural environment. Bar-bellied Pitta

11

12

13

ANDREW BAIN/GETTY IMAGES ©

14

15

INGRAM PUBLISHING/GETTY IMAGES ©

Coffee Time

13 Starbucks may have opened its first branch here in 2013, but in Vietnam, coffee culture (p469) runs deep. Virtually every neighbourhood in every town (and most villages) will have a little cafe where locals go to de-stress from the office, the family or simply the traffic (most are located on quiet side streets with copious greenery to promote relaxation). Vietnamese coffee can be served hot or iced (a real treat in summer), either treacle-thick, or with milk (usually sweetened and condensed) for a double-whammy caffeine-sugar kick.

Dalat

14 Dalat (p289) is the queen of the southwest highlands and has been popular with international tourists since the days of the French colonialists. Grand Gallic villas are dotted amid pine groves and the whole town is centred on a pretty lake, with numerous nearby waterfalls adding to its natural appeal. Dalat is also fast becoming one of Vietnam's key adventure-sport hubs, with abseiling, canyoning, mountain-biking, hiking and rafting all on off er. The temperate climate here will be quite a relief if you've been suffering in Saigon.

Ba Be National Park

15 Detour off the regular Vietnam tourist trail in Ba Be National Park (p102), an essential destination for adventurous travellers, with towering limestone mountains, plunging valleys and evergreen forests. Waterfalls, caves and lakes combine in a landscape that sustains over 550 different plants and hundreds of different bird and animal species. Explore Ba Be's natural spectacle by boat or on trekking and mountain-biking excursions, before relaxing and recharging in the rustic homestays and village guesthouses of the local Tay ethnic minority.

NIGEL KILLEEN/GETTY IMAGES ©

Battle Sites

16 In the centre of Vietnam, the Demilitarised Zone (DMZ; p169) has the greatest concentration of battle sites from the American War (and some excellent tour operators to get you around them). Down south the Cu Chi Tunnels are a very popular day trip from Ho Chi Minh City, while there are numerous war sites around Vung Tau, which was a big ANZAC base. In the far north, Dien Bien Phu should not be missed: there's a good new museum here to explain the significance of the battle that precipitated the French expulsion from Indochina. Hien Luong Bridge over the Ben Hai River (p171), DMZ

Mui Ne

17 Perhaps the adventure sport epicentre of Vietnam, the relaxed, prosperous beach resort of Mui Ne (p265) is a kitesurfing capital with world-class wind and conditions, and excellent schools for professional training. For those who prefer dry land, sandboarding and golf are popular alternatives. The resort itself has more than 20km of palm-fringed beachfront that stretches invitingly along the shores of the South China Sea. From guesthouses to boutique resorts, boho bars to fine-value spas, Mui Ne has a broad appeal.

Bia Hoi

18 One of the great pleasures of travelling in Vietnam, *bia hoi* – fresh draught beer (p84) – is brewed daily, without additives or preservatives, to be drunk within hours. Incredibly cheap and widely available, *bia hoi* is said to have been introduced to Hanoi by Czech brewers over 40 years ago. Every town has a *bia hoi* place, often with a street terrace, offering a very local experience. Park (or attempt to park) your rear on one of the tiny plastic stools and get stuck in. Snacks to eat are often sold too.

Sapa Trekking

19 Undulating rice terraces cascade down to valleys inhabited by Hmong, Red Dzao and Giay villages. Up above, the sinuous ridges of the Hoang Lien Mountains (dubbed the Tonkinese Alps by the French) touch the sky. Brushed with every shade of green in the palette, the countryside surrounding Sapa (p136) is a showcase of northern Vietnam's most superb rural vistas and a fascinating glimpse into the country's astounding cultural diversity. This is prime territory for digging out your walking boots and hitting the trails.

Temples of Angkor

20 Over the border in Cambodia, the temples of Angkor (p426) form one of the world's most magnificent sights. Choose from Angkor Wat itself, the world's largest religious building; Bayon, with its immense stone faces; or Ta Prohm, where nature runs amok. Siem Reap is the base for exploring Angkor and is a buzzing destination with a superb selection of restaurants and bars. Beyond the temples await activities like quad biking and ziplining, and cultured pursuits such as cooking classes and birdwatching. Angkor Thom (p427)

19

20

Need to Know

For more information, see Survival Guide (p477)

Currency

Dong (d)

Language

Vietnamese

Visas

Complicated and fast-changing: some nationalities need a visa in advance for all visits, some don't (for 15-day stays).

Money

ATMs can be found throughout the country, even in small towns, though charges for withdrawls can be quite steep. In general cash is king in Vietnam, though credit and debit cards can be used in many hotels.

Mobile Phones

To avoid roaming charges, local SIM cards can be used in most European, Asian and Australian (and many North American) phones.

Time

Vietnam is seven hours ahead of GMT/UTC.

When to Go

High Season

(Jul & Aug)

➡ Prices increase by up to 50% by the coast; book hotels well in advance.

➡ All Vietnam, except the far north, is hot and humid, with the summer monsoon bringing downpours.

Shoulder

(Dec–Mar)

➡ During the Tet festival, the whole country is on the move and prices rise.

➡ North of Nha Trang can get cool weather. Expect cold conditions in the very far north.

➡ In the south, clear skies and sunshine are the norm.

Low Season

(Apr–Jun, Sep–Nov)

➡ Perhaps the best time to tour the whole nation.

➡ Typhoons can lash the central and northern coastline until November.

Useful Websites

Vietnam Coracle (http://vietnamcoracle.com) Excellent independent travel advice from a long-term resident.

Thanh Nien News (www.thanhniennews.com) Government-approved news, but includes diverse and interesting content.

Lonely Planet (www.lonelyplanet.com/vietnam) Destination information, hotel bookings, traveller forum and more.

The Word (www.wordhcmc.com) Based in HCMC, this magazine has excellent coverage.

Vietnam Online (www.vietnamonline.com) Good all-rounder.

Rusty Compass (www.rustycompass.com) Useful online travel guide.

Important Numbers

To call Vietnam from outside the country, drop the initial 0 from the area code. Mobile numbers begin with ☎09 or ☎01.

Country Code	☎84
International Access Code	☎00
Directory Assistance	☎116
Police	☎113
General Information Service	☎1080

Exchange Rates

Australia	A$1	16,041d
Canada	C$1	17,005d
Euro	€1	24,495d
Japan	¥100	18,640d
New Zealand	NZ$1	17,676d
UK	£1	34,341d
US	US$1	22,316d

For current exchange rates, see www.xe.com.

Daily Costs

Budget: Less than US$40

- Glass of *bia hoi*: from US$0.50
- One hour on a local bus: US$1–1.50
- Cheap hotel: US$10–15 a night, dorms less
- Local meal of noodles: US$1.50–2.50

Midrange: US$40–100

- Comfortable double room: US$25–50
- Meal in a smart restaurant: from US$8
- One-hour massage: US$6–20
- Ten-minute taxi ride: US$4

Top End: More than US$100

- Luxury hotel room: from US$80
- Gourmet restaurant: from US$20
- Internal flight: US$30–100

Opening Hours

Hours vary very little throughout the year.

Banks 8am to 3pm weekdays, to 11.30am Saturday

Offices and museums 7am or 8am to 5pm or 6pm; museums generally close on Monday and some take a lunch break

Restaurants 11.30am to 9pm

Shops 8am to 6pm

Temples and pagodas 5am to 9pm

Arriving in Vietnam

Tan Son Nhat International Airport (Ho Chi Minh City; p357) Taxis to central districts (around 190,000d) take about 30 minutes. There's also an air-conditioned Route 152 bus (6000d, every 15 minutes, 6am to 6pm, around 40 minutes).

Noi Bai Airport (Hanoi; p94) Taxis to the centre cost 400,000d and take around 50 minutes. Jetstar shuttles (35,000d) and Vietnam Airlines minibuses (50,000d) run hourly. The Route 17 public bus to Long Bien bus station is 5000d.

Getting Around

Buses are the main mode of transport for locals in Vietnam, but travellers tend to prefer planes, trains and automobiles.

Train Reasonably priced and comfortable enough in air-conditioned carriages (and sleepers). But note there are no real express trains.

Plane Cheap if you book ahead and the network is pretty comprehensive. However, cancellations are not unknown.

Car Very useful for travelling at your own pace or for visiting regions with minimal public transport. Cars always come with a driver.

Bus On the main highways services are very frequent, although it's not a particularly relaxing way to travel. In the sticks things deteriorate rapidly. Open-tour buses are very inexpensive and worth considering.

For much more on **getting around**, see p491

First Time Vietnam

For more information, see Survival Guide (p477)

Checklist

➡ Check out the visa situation; you may need to apply in advance

➡ Make sure your passport is valid for at least six months past your arrival date

➡ Check your immunisation history

➡ Arrange appropriate travel insurance

➡ Pre-book internal flights and trains

➡ Inform your debit-/credit-card company

What to Pack

➡ Good footwear – Vietnam's streets are bumpy and lumpy

➡ Mosquito repellent with DEET

➡ Rain jacket

➡ Electrical adapter

➡ Torch (flashlight)

➡ Flip-flops or sandals

➡ Binoculars

Top Tips for Your Trip

➡ Prepare yourself for the crazy driving: traffic can come at you every which way, and in the cities swarms of motorbikes reach biblical proportions. Try to keep calm and consider arranging a massage after a long journey.

➡ Be aware that Vietnam has more than its fair share of scams; most concern overcharging. Though very rare, there are some more serious dangers (like unexploded ordnance) to also be aware of.

➡ In towns like Hue and Sapa, and beaches popular with tourists, expect plenty of hustle from street vendors, *cyclo* (pedicab cycle rickshaw) drivers and the like. Off the beaten track there's little or no hassle.

➡ Load your bargaining head before you arrive.

What to Wear

There are no serious cultural concerns about wearing inappropriate clothing in Vietnam. In religious buildings and government offices (or if attending a formal dinner), legs should be covered and sleeveless tops avoided.

Yes, Vietnam is in the tropics, but visit anywhere north of Hoi An between October and March and it can be cool, so pack some layers (a fleece or two). The rest of the year, and in the south, flip-flops or sandals, a T-shirt and shorts are likely to be your daily uniform.

Sleeping

Tourism is booming in Vietnam so it's usually best to book your accommodation a day or two in advance, or several weeks ahead in the high season (the Tet holiday, July to August, and around Christmas).

➡ **Hotels** Range from simple functional minihotels to uber-luxurious spa resorts.

➡ **Hostels** Popular in the main tourism centres, but rare elsewhere.

➡ **Guesthouses** Usually family-run and less formal than hotels.

Tours

Vietnam can be a culture shock for many travellers. Taking a tour can really help you understand the nation better. Cities including Hanoi, Hoi An, Danang and Nha Trang have street food tours, while motorbike tours are also very popular.

Bargaining

Bargaining is essential in Vietnam, but not for everything. Sharpen your haggling skills when shopping in marketplaces and in some small shops (that sell souvenirs and the like), and when arranging local transport like *cyclos* and *xe om* (motorbike taxi).

Many hotels will also offer a discount if you ask for one. In restaurants, prices are fixed.

Some bus drivers try to overcharge foreigners. Bargain if you're certain the fare is overpriced.

Tipping

➡ **Hotels** Not expected. Leave a small gratuity for cleaning staff if you like.

➡ **Restaurants** Not expected; 5% to 10% in smart restaurants or if you're very satisfied. Locals don't tip.

➡ **Guides** A few dollars on day trips is sufficient, more for longer trips if the service is good.

➡ **Taxis** Not necessary, but a little extra is appreciated, especially at night.

➡ **Bars** Never expected.

SOFT_LIGHT/GETTY IMAGES ©

Enjoy stunning views over Vietnam's verdant bays

Etiquette

➡ **Meals** When dining with Vietnamese people, it's customary for the most senior diner to pay for everyone.

➡ **Homes** Remove your shoes when entering a private house.

➡ **Heads** Don't pat or touch an adult (or child) on the head.

➡ **Feet** Avoid pointing your feet at people or sacred objects.

Eating

It's rarely necessary to reserve a table in advance in Vietnam. Exceptions include national park restaurants and upmarket, select places in Hanoi and Ho Chi Minh City.

➡ **Local restaurants** Vietnamese restaurants tend to have purely functional decor and even look scruffy, but if they're busy the food will usually be fresh and delicious.

➡ **International restaurants** In tourist areas many restaurants serve up Western and Asian food. Often the local food is toned down and not that authentic.

➡ **Street food** Pavement kitchens offer cheap, often incredibly tasty, local grub.

➡ **Cafes** May have a snack or two available, but rarely meals.

Language

English is not widely spoken in Vietnam. In the tourist areas, most staff in hotels and restaurants will speak a little, but communication problems are very common. A few key phrases of Vietnamese go a long way.

What's New

Bai Xep

A cool beach scene is developing fast on this lovely bay south of Quy Nhon, now home to three great beachside guesthouses. (p238)

More Cave Trips

Phong Nha-Ke Bang National Park continues to be an essential destination. New trips include the exciting zipline, swimming and kayaking combo to Hang Toi (Dark Cave) and the subterranean wonders of Hang Va. (p162)

Villa Vista

This intimate hilltop mansion with amphitheatrical views of Dalat has lashings of 19th-century French opulence. It's undoubtedly the southwest highlands' most atmospheric stay. (p294)

Craft Beer in Ho Chi Minh City

Pasteur Street Brewing Company (p347) infuses local ingredients like lemongrass and Dalat coffee; travelling hopheads will find more local brews at BiaCraft (p351) in Saigon's emerging District 2 neighbourhood.

Vespa Adventures

There's no better way to explore the rural lanes, craft villages and riverside scenery around Hoi An than on the back of a vintage scooter. This new outfit has great tours. (p212)

Dien Bien Phu Museum

The important collection commemorating the seminal 1954 battle has found a new home in this upgraded, modern museum building, designed to showcase the exhibits at their best. (p133)

Lotte Tower, Hanoi

The best place to gauge the voracity of Hanoi's growth relative to the Old Quarter is from the observation deck of this spectacular new landmark; it's also home to myriad bars and restaurants. (p71)

Mui Ne Backpacker Village

Travellers have never had it so good with the opening of this chic new pool-blessed hostel just a few steps from the beach. (p269)

Con Dao Cafe Scene

New places including Bar200 Con Dao (p285) and Infinity Cafe & Lounge (p285) have injected life and a little cosmopolitan elan to sleepy old Con Son town.

Aqua Expeditions

This sleek, waterborne five-star hotel, complete with deckside pool and gourmet meals, traverses the Mekong Delta's waterways in style. (p376)

Amanoi

Built into the cliffs on a gorgeous stretch of coastline, this uber-luxurious resort has drop-dead gorgeous pavilions and a tip-top spa, and offers real tranquility and relaxation. (p265)

SUP, Cat Ba Island

Stand-up paddleboarding has hit Cat Ba Island with all-new SUP tours of Lan Ha Bay being pioneered by Asia Outdoors. (p116)

For more recommendations and reviews, see **lonelyplanet.com/vietnam**

If You Like...

Fine Dining

Hoi An Try unique regional specialities, then take a cooking course. (p215)

Ho Chi Minh City Gourmet restaurants, to-die-for Vietnamese eateries and international cuisine. (p340)

Hue Famous for its complex imperial cuisine tradition. (p184)

Pots 'n Pans Innovative Viet-fusion cuisine in a chic Hanoi setting. (p83)

Ganh Hao Dine by the water's edge at this outstanding Vung Tau seafood restaurant. (p277)

Hill Station Signature Restaurant The traditional flavours of the Hmong. (p141)

Bassac Restaurant International classics meet delicate Vietnamese dishes. (p408)

Markets

Bac Ha Head north to one of the most colourful markets in Southeast Asia. (p145)

Mekong Delta's Floating Markets Catch the delta waterworld's river markets, selling everything from durian to dog meat. (p383)

Ben Thanh Market HCMC's central market is a hive of activity. (p352)

Hang Da Check out the basement of this lesser-known Hanoi market for recycled threads. (p89)

Dong Ba Market Cross the Perfume River in Hue to the compelling sensory overload of this market. (p186)

Remote & Hidden

Ha Giang Crammed with jaw-dropping scenery, this rugged area abuts China. (p148)

Tam Hai Island Idyllic isle that features a whale graveyard, Cham ruins and no crowds. (p235)

Pirate Island Descendants of pirates take you night-fishing for squid. (p403)

HCMC Tours Sample food from the backstreets and dig out the city's hidden pockets. (p333)

Ganh Da Dia Coastline boasting empty beaches, lonely fishing villages and impressive sand dunes. (p241)

Phu Dien This small Cham temple was buried in sand dunes for centuries. (p191)

Tombs & Temples

Hue Vietnamese emperors constructed dazzling monuments around this city. Don't miss **Tu Duc** (p187) and **Minh Mang** (p188).

My Son The most impressive Cham site; the hilltop location is very special too. (p224)

Hanoi Come face-to-face with history in Ho Chi Minh's austere mausoleum. (p64)

Cao Dai Great Temple A magnificent hybrid of Chinese temple, mosque and cathedral near HCMC. (p363)

Cholon Discover the Chinese heritage of HCMC amid gilded and incense-infused temples. (p324)

Vo Thi Sau Evocative Con Son resting place of a national heroine. (p281)

Beautiful Beaches

Phu Quoc Island Picture-perfect white crescents and sandy bays sheltered by rocky headlands. (p389)

Con Dao Islands We suggest a self-imposed exile of at least three nights. (p279)

Mui Ne Squeaky sands along the shore, towering sand dunes nearby and empty beaches up the coast. (p265)

An Bang Ride a bicycle from Hoi An to An Bang's combo of sun, sand and seafood. (p220)

Nha Trang Flop on the inviting sands, then explore the bay's islands by boat. (p247)

Road Trips

Mai Pi Leng Pass Negotiate this mountainous route from Dong Van to Meo Vac, cut through a narrow pass. (p151)

Highway 6 Rural vistas of paddy-field patchworks and rolling hills between Mai Chau and Son La. (p129)

Hue to Hoi An Travel by motorcycle taking in the Hai Van Pass and China Beach. (p193)

Ho Chi Minh Highway Light on traffic, big on scenery and ideal for cyclists. (p304)

Spectacular Treks

Phong Nha-Ke Bang National Park Hike through pristine mountain and valley trails, or to the world's largest cave. (p162)

Sapa Join Hmong guides to explore the ethnic minority villages around Sapa. (p136)

Yok Don National Park Trek and camp in the hope of spotting wild elephants. (p303)

Cuc Phuong National Park Hike through wildlife-rich forests and up to tribal villages. (p160)

Quirky Tipples

Highland homebrew Head to **Sapa** (p136) or **Bac Ha** (p145) markets to knock back hill-tribe rice and corn wines.

Pasteur Street Brewing Company Lemongrass and Phu Quoc peppercorns are both used in the excellent Saigon Saison beer. (p347)

K'Ho Coffee Locally roasted coffee grown by K'Ho minority farmers at an 1860s coffee farm. (p292)

Quan Ly Sample traditional *ruou* (rice wine) liquor in this atmospheric watering hole. (p86)

Top: Citadel (p175), Hue

Bottom: Flower Hmong women, Bac Ha Market (p145)

Month by Month

TOP EVENTS

Tet, January–February

Hue Festival, April (Biennial)

Wandering Souls Day, August

Danang Fireworks Festival, April

Buddha's Birth, Enlightenment and Death, May

January

Winter temperatures can be bitterly cold in the far north, with snow possible. The further south you go, the milder the weather. Tet celebrations occur at the end of the month (or in February).

Dalat Flower Festival

Held early in the month, this is always a wonderful occasion, with huge elaborate displays. It's become an international event, with music and fashion shows and a wine festival.

February

North of Danang, chilly 'Chinese winds' usually mean grey, overcast conditions. Conversely, sunny hot days are the norm in the southern provinces.

Tet (Tet Nguyen Dan)

The Big One! Falling in late January or early February, Vietnamese Lunar New Year is like Christmas, New Year and birthdays all rolled into one. Travel is difficult at this time, as transport is booked up and many businesses close.

Quang Trung

Wrestling competitions, lion dances and human chess take place in Hanoi on the fifth day of the first lunar month at Dong Da Mound, site of the uprising against the Chinese led by Emperor Quang Trung (Nguyen Hué) in 1788.

March

Grey skies and cool temperatures can affect anywhere north of Hoi An, but towards the end of the month the thermometer starts to rise. Down south, the dry season is ending.

Buon Ma Thuot Coffee Festival

Caffeine cravers should make for the highlands during March, as Buon Ma Thuot plays host to an annual coffee festival. Growers, grinders, blenders and addicts rub shoulders in the city's main park, and local entertainment is provided.

Saigon Cyclo Challenge

On your marks...get pedalling. Ho Chi Minh City's fastest rickshaw drivers battle it out in their three-wheeled chariots to raise funds for charity. Takes place in mid-March every year.

April

Generally an excellent time to cover the nation, as the winter monsoon rains should have subsided and there are some excellent festivals. Flights are usually moderately priced (unless Easter falls in this month).

Holiday of the Dead (Thanh Minh)

It's time to honour the ancestors with a visit to graves of deceased relatives to tidy up and sweep tombstones. Offerings of flowers, food and paper are presented. It's held on the first three days of the third moon.

Hue Festival (Biennial)

Vietnam's biggest cultural event (www.huefestival.com) is held every two years, with events in 2016 and 2018. Most of the art, theatre, music, circus and dance performances are held inside Hue's Citadel.

Danang Fireworks Festival

Danang's riverside explodes with sound, light and colour during this spectacular event, which features competing pyrotechnic teams from the USA, China, Europe and Vietnam. Held in the last week of the month.

May

A fine time to tour the centre and north, with a good chance of clear skies and warm days. Sea temperatures are warming up nicely and it's a pretty quiet month for tourism.

Buddha's Birth, Enlightenment and Death (Phong Sinh)

A big celebration at Buddhist temples with street processions, and lanterns used to decorate pagodas. Complexes including Chua Bai Dinh (p158) near Ninh Binh and HCMC's Jade Emperor Pagoda (p318) host lavish celebrations. Fifteenth day of the fourth lunar month.

Nha Trang Sea Festival

Falls at the end of May (and the beginning of June) and includes a street festival, photography exhibitions, embroidery displays and kite-flying competitions.

Top: Danang Fireworks Festival

Bottom: Dragon parade at Tet (Tet Nguyen Dan)

June

A great time to tour Vietnam as it's just before the peak domestic season. Humidity can be punishing at this time of year, so plan to spend some time by the coast.

Summer Solstice Day (Tet Doan Ngo)

Keep epidemics at bay with offerings to the spirits, ghosts and the God of Death on the fifth day of the fifth moon. Sticky rice wine *(ruou nep)* is consumed in industrial quantities.

August

The peak month for tourism with domestic and international tourists. Book flights and accommodation well ahead. Weather-wise it's hot, hot, hot.

Wandering Souls Day (Trung Nguyen)

Second in the pecking order to Tet is this ancient Vietnamese tradition. Huge spreads of food are left out for lost spirits who, it's believed, wander the earth on this day. Held on the 15th day of the seventh moon.

Children's (or Mid-Autumn) Festival, Hoi An

This is a big event in Hoi An and Hanoi, when citizens celebrate the full moon, eat mooncakes and beat drums. The lion, unicorn and dragon dance processions are enacted, and children are fully involved in the celebrations.

September

Excellent time to tour the whole nation. The coastal resorts are less crowded and there are fewer people on the move. Temperatures and humidity levels drop.

Vietnam National Day (Sep 2)

Big parades and events are held across Vietnam on September 2. Celebrated with a rally and fireworks at Ba Dinh Square, Hanoi (in front of Ho Chi Minh's Mausoleum) and there are also boat races on Hoan Kiem Lake.

October

A good time to visit the far north, with a strong chance of clear skies and mild temperatures. Winter winds and rain begin to affect the centre, but down south it's often dry.

Mid-Autumn Festival (Trung Thu)

A fine time for foodies, with moon cakes of sticky rice filled with lotus seeds, watermelon seeds, peanuts, the yolks of duck eggs, raisins and other treats. It's celebrated across the nation on the 15th day of the eighth moon and can fall in September or October.

Cham New Year (Kate)

This is celebrated at Po Klong Garai Cham Towers in Thap Cham on the seventh month of the Cham calendar. The festival commemorates ancestors, Cham national heroes and deities, such as the farmers' goddess Po Ino Nagar. (p263)

Khmer Oc Bom Boc Festival

The Mekong Delta's Khmer community celebrates on the 15th day of the 10th moon of the lunar calendar (late October or November) with colourful boat races at Ba Dong Beach in Tra Vinh province and on the Soc Trang River.

December

The month begins quietly, but from mid-December the popular tourist resorts get increasingly busy. Book well ahead to secure a room over the Christmas break. Steamy in the south, but can get chilly up north.

Christmas Day (Giang Sinh)

Not a national holiday, but is celebrated throughout Vietnam, particularly by the sizeable Catholic population. It's a special time to be in places such as Phat Diem and HCMC, where thousands attend midnight Mass.

MATT MUNRO/LONELY PLANET ©

Plan Your Trip
Itineraries

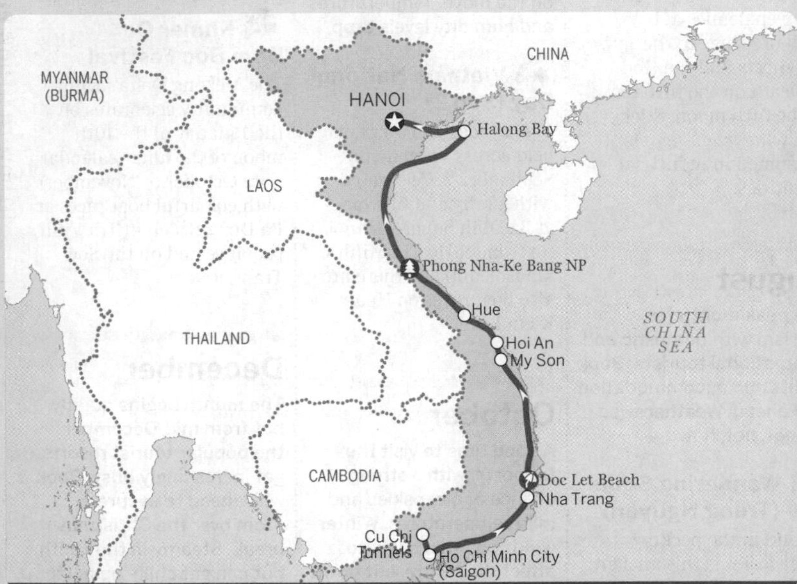

From South to North

Making the most of Vietnam's spectacular coastline, this route hugs the shore and is bookended by the country's two greatest cities. You'll have ample opportunity to indulge in some serious beach time, and be able to hit the cultural sights. Consider taking an internal flight or two to save time.

The adventure begins in the cauldron of commerce that is **Ho Chi Minh City (HCMC)**. Spend two days hitting the markets, browsing museums and eating some of the globe's best cuisine. Take a daytrip to discover wartime history at the **Cu Chi Tunnels**.

Then it's a plane, train or bus trip up the coast to the big brash resort of **Nha Trang** for a couple of days by the sea. Party people will love the city's hedonistic bar scene, while spa lovers can indulge in a gooey, blissful session in one of the area's three mud bath resorts. Nha Trang's beach is a fine one, but for a less-developed base head up to the largely-undeveloped coastline to the north, where you'll find **Doc Let Beach**, or south to the near-infinite sands of Bai Dai beach.

Halong Bay (p107)

Cultured charmer and culinary mecca **Hoi An** is the next essential stop. This town certainly warrants three days, such is its allure. Spend a couple of days enjoying Hoi An's unique ambience, touring the town's temples, pagodas and museums, and feasting on delectable Central Vietnamese cuisine. Consider a motorbike trip around the town's rural hinterland, or an excursion to the terrific Cham ruins of **My Son**. Then it's on to the old imperial capital of **Hue** for a night to explore its citadel, tombs and pagodas. From here head up to the truly remarkable **Phong Nha-Ke Bang National Park**, the world's greatest caving region, with towering limestone mountains and cobalt jungle rivers.

Next it's a long journey by road or train towards **Halong Bay**, with more than 2000 limestone outcrops dotting the ocean. Budget for at least a couple of days in **Hanoi** to sample its evocative Old Quarter and to view the city's elegant architecture and memorable museums. Make the most of your last day, perhaps munching street food and sampling *bia hoi* (draught beer).

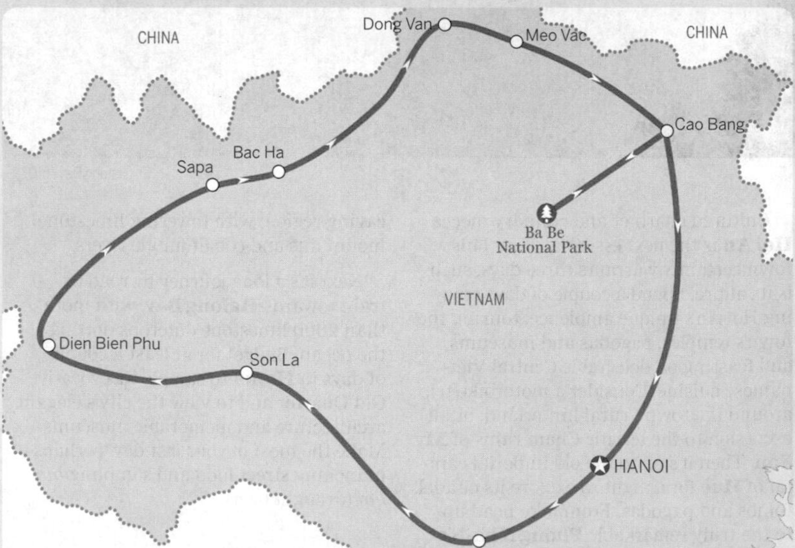

CHINA
Dong Van
Meo Vac
CHINA
Cao Bang
Bac Ha
Sapa
Ba Be
National Park
VIETNAM
Dien Bien Phu
Son La
HANOI
LAOS
Mai Chau

WALTER BIBIKOW/GETTY IMAGES ©

LYNN GAIL/GETTY IMAGES ©

Top: Dien Bien Phu (p131)

Bottom: Flower Hmong women at Bac Ha Market (p145)

3 WEEKS

Northern Mountains

Northern Vietnam is a world unto itself: a land of brooding mountains, overwhelming beauty and a mosaic of ethnic minorities. It's ideal terrain to cover on two wheels, with light traffic and breathtaking views, though, with a patient attitude, most of the region can be tackled by public transport.

Leaving **Hanoi**, head west to **Mai Chau**, home to the White Thai people, for your first two nights; it's a perfect introduction to ethnic minority life. Northwest, where the road begins to climb into the Tonkinese Alps, a logical overnight stop is **Son La**.

Continue on for two nights at **Dien Bien Phu**, a name that resonates with history as it was here that the French colonial story ended in defeat. Tour the military sights and impressive new museum then continue north through stunning scenery up the Tram Ton Pass.

Sapa is the premier destination in the northwest, thanks to the infinite views (on a clear day!), and an amazing array of minority peoples. Explore the area on two feet or two wheels for around four days before heading to **Bac Ha** for three nights to experience the best of the region's markets. Most colourful are the Flower Hmong people.

From Bac Ha, move east to Ha Giang province, taking it slowly through stunning scenery and towns including Yen Minh, Dong Van and Meo Vac. Explore remote destinations like the Lung Cu flag tower and the Vuong Palace from **Dong Van**. Onwards towards the vertiginous Mai Pi Leng Pass and **Meo Vac**, there's no public transport (so you'll need to hire a *xe om* (motorbike taxi) or car). The route then loops down to the riverside junction town of Bao Lac.

Local buses run from Bao Lac to **Cao Bang** and on to **Ba Be National Park**. Spend about three nights around Ba Be, staying at local Tay ethnic minority homestays, and exploring the park by trekking or kayaking. From Ba Be travel back to Cao Bang for the trip back south to Hanoi.

2 WEEKS Deep South

This itinerary takes in a lovely offshore island, the nation's main watersport centre and a waterworld of floating villages. If tropical sunsets and white-sand beaches are high on your agenda it's probably best not to plan this trip during the southern rainy season. There's frequent public transport to virtually all the main centres.

After a couple of days enjoying the urban delights and compelling energy of **HCMC**, head into the Mekong Delta, stopping at **Ben Tre** to explore canal-side lanes by bike and islands by boat. Then hop on board a cargo ship for a slow, scenic journey to **Tra Vinh** and take in the town's colourful pagodas. Next it's a short trip to **Can Tho** where it's worth lingering a couple of days to visit the bustling floating markets, the city museum and a temple or two. Further north, by the Cambodian border, **Chau Doc** is surrounded by beautiful countryside, begging for two-wheeled trips. Head to **Phu Quoc Island** for three days of well-earned beachtime on some of Vietnam's best sandy shores.

From Phu Quoc, fly (or bus it) back to HCMC, then head north into the Southcentral Highlands via a night in **Cat Tien National Park**, home to gibbons, crocodiles and bountiful birdlife. Next up it's the romantic hill station of **Dalat** for a tour of its quirky sights, and the opportunity to get stuck into some adventure sports like canyoning, mountain biking or kayaking.

The road trip from Dalat down to **Mui Ne** is one of the nation's finest, negotiating highland ridges and plunging through valleys and pine forests; it's ideally done on the back of a motorbike (consider hiring an Easy Rider). You can then rest up by the beach in Mui Ne for two or three days, a tropical idyll with towering sand dunes and a laid-back vibe – or for those with the stamina, get stuck into some crazy kitesurfing or a sailing course.

Round the trip off in style with a night in HCMC, perhaps with an ale or two at the Paster Street Brewing Company and dining out somewhere really special like the Racha Room.

Top: Dinh Cau Beach, Phu Quoc Island (p389)
Bottom: Temple in Tra Vinh (p373)

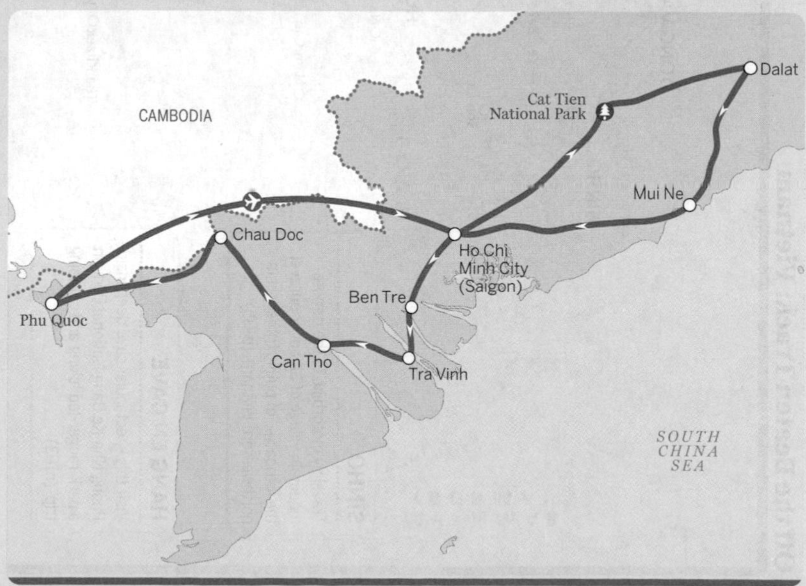
Dalat
Cat Tien
National Park
CAMBODIA
Mui Ne
Chau Doc
Ho Chi
Minh City
(Saigon)
Ben Tre
Phu Quoc
Can Tho
Tra Vinh
SOUTH
CHINA
SEA

Off the Beaten Track: Vietnam

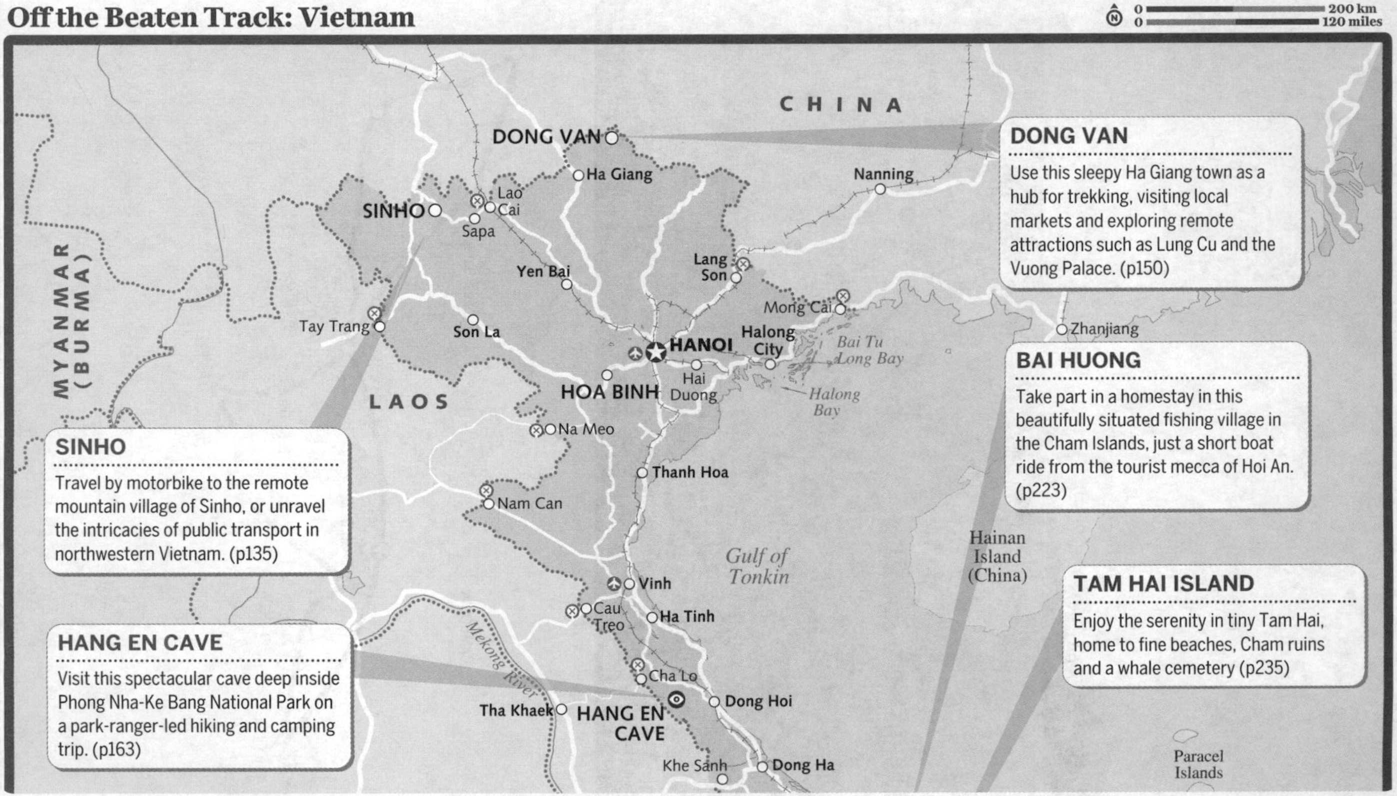

DONG VAN

Use this sleepy Ha Giang town as a hub for trekking, visiting local markets and exploring remote attractions such as Lung Cu and the Vuong Palace. (p150)

SINHO

Travel by motorbike to the remote mountain village of Sinho, or unravel the intricacies of public transport in northwestern Vietnam. (p135)

BAI HUONG

Take part in a homestay in this beautifully situated fishing village in the Cham Islands, just a short boat ride from the tourist mecca of Hoi An. (p223)

HANG EN CAVE

Visit this spectacular cave deep inside Phong Nha-Ke Bang National Park on a park-ranger-led hiking and camping trip. (p163)

TAM HAI ISLAND

Enjoy the serenity in tiny Tam Hai, home to fine beaches, Cham ruins and a whale cemetery (p235)

0 — 200 km
0 — 120 miles
CHINA
LAOS
MYANMAR (BURMA)
DONG VAN
Ha Giang
Nanning
SINHO
Lao Cai
Sapa
Lang Son
Yen Bai
Mong Cai
Tay Trang
Son La
Zhanjiang
HANOI
Halong City
Bai Tu Long Bay
Hai Duong
HOA BINH
Halong Bay
Na Meo
Thanh Hoa
Nam Can
Gulf of Tonkin
Hainan Island (China)
Vinh
Cau Treo
Ha Tinh
Mekong River
Cha Lo
Dong Hoi
Tha Khaek
HANG EN CAVE
Khe Sanh
Dong Ha
Paracel Islands

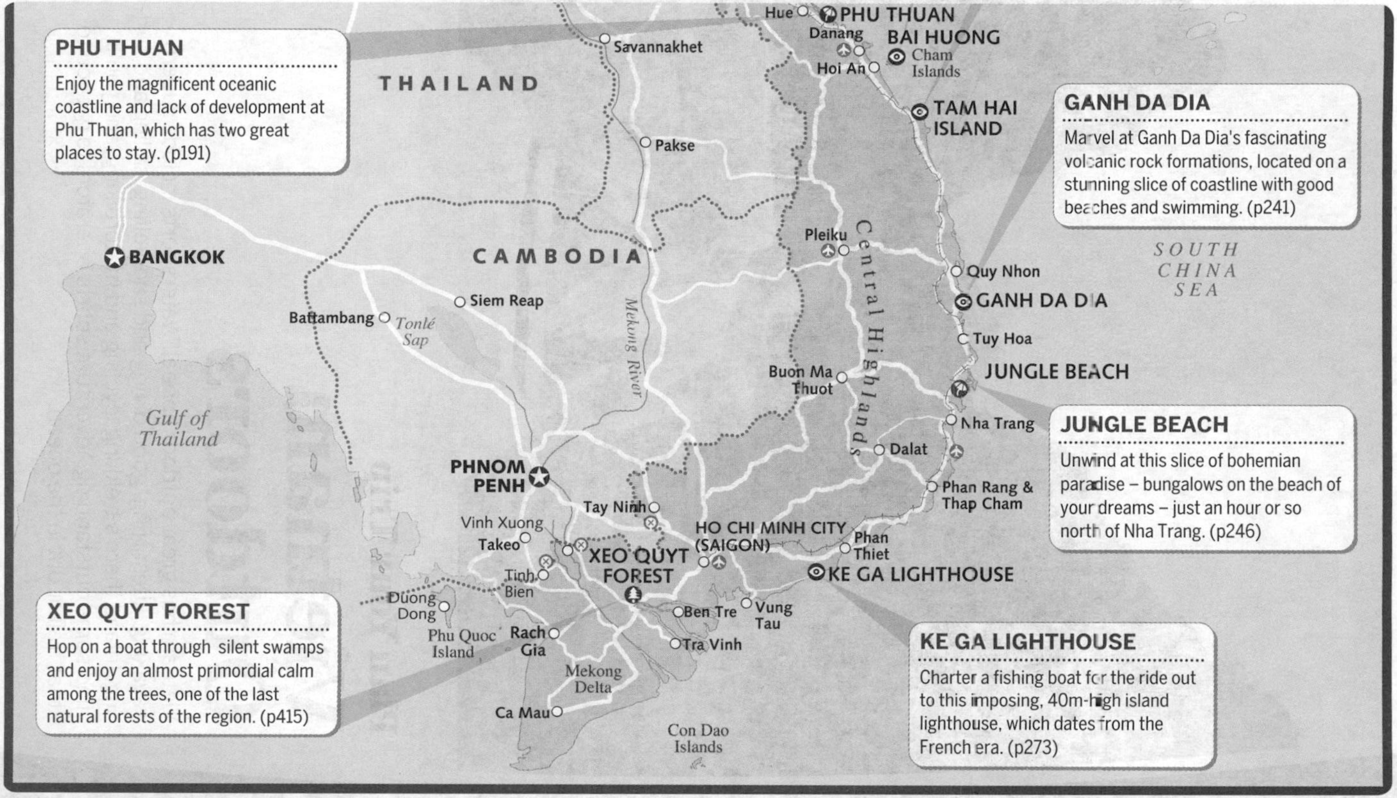

PHU THUAN

Enjoy the magnificent oceanic coastline and lack of development at Phu Thuan, which has two great places to stay. (p191)

GANH DA DIA

Marvel at Ganh Da Dia's fascinating volcanic rock formations, located on a stunning slice of coastline with good beaches and swimming. (p241)

JUNGLE BEACH

Unwind at this slice of bohemian paradise – bungalows on the beach of your dreams – just an hour or so north of Nha Trang. (p246)

XEO QUYT FOREST

Hop on a boat through silent swamps and enjoy an almost primordial calm among the trees, one of the last natural forests of the region. (p415)

KE GA LIGHTHOUSE

Charter a fishing boat for the ride out to this imposing, 40m-high island lighthouse, which dates from the French era. (p273)

Hue
PHU THUAN
Danang
BAI HUONG
Cham Islands
Hoi An
TAM HAI ISLAND
Savannakhet
THAILAND
Pakse
Pleiku
Central Highlands
Quy Nhon
GANH DA DIA
SOUTH CHINA SEA
BANGKOK
CAMBODIA
Siem Reap
Battambang
Tonlé Sap
Mekong River
Tuy Hoa
Buon Ma Thuot
JUNGLE BEACH
Nha Trang
Gulf of Thailand
Dalat
PHNOM PENH
Phan Rang & Thap Cham
Tay Ninh
Vinh Xuong
Takeo
HO CHI MINH CITY (SAIGON)
Phan Thiet
XEO QUYT FOREST
KE GA LIGHTHOUSE
Tinh Bien
Duong Dong
Ben Tre
Vung Tau
Phu Quoc Island
Rach Gia
Tra Vinh
Mekong Delta
Ca Mau
Con Dao Islands

Kayaking, Halong Bay (p107)

Plan Your Trip

Vietnam Outdoors

Vietnam has great outdoor appeal. Watersports include superb kayaking, kitesurfing, good diving and snorkelling, sailing and surfing. Inland there's trekking, cycling and motorbiking, and you'll find some outstanding adventure sports operators to get you to that trail or out in the ocean.

Best Outdoors

Best Trekking

Sapa Superlative views but can be crowded.

Dong Van Trails through dramatic mountain scenery.

Bac Ha Spectacular highland hiking incorporating village homestays.

Mai Chau Sublime landscapes and tribal villages.

Best Diving & Snorkelling

Con Dao Islands Remote, but the best.

Phu Quoc Visibility can be a challenge, but some nice coral gardens.

Nha Trang Professional scuba schools and many dive sites.

Best Cycling

Dalat Base camp for the dramatic two-day descent to Mui Ne.

Hoi An Flat terrain to explore craft villages and cut across rice paddies.

Mekong Delta Back roads beside waterways under the shade of coconut palms.

Planning

When to Go

Whether you're a committed kitesurfer or a warm-water diver, some careful planning is essential – Vietnam's climate is extremely variable and monsoon-dependent.

Best

Surfers should be aware that the wave action peaks in winter (November to April). Kitesurfing also excels at this time of year. Divers take note that water visibility is best in the calm months of June, July and August.

Avoid

It would be foolish to attempt an ascent of Fansipan in the height of the rainy season, from May to September. Snorkelling and diving is not that rewarding between November and April when visibility drops.

Trekking

Vietnam offers excellent trekking and less strenuous walks. The scenery is often remarkable – think plunging highland valleys, tiers of rice paddies and soaring limestone mountains. Anything is possible, from half-day hikes to assaults on Fansipan, Vietnam's highest mountain.

Generally, northern Vietnam is your best bet: its dramatic mountain paths and fascinating minority culture are a huge draw. Elsewhere, national parks and nature reserves have established trails (and usually guides available to keep you on them).

Northern Vietnam

The region north of Hanoi is truly spectacular. Sapa (p136) is Vietnam's trekking hub, full of hiking operators and hire stores (renting out sleeping bags, boots and waterproof gear). Maps detailing trails are available, as are guides. The scenery is spectacular, with majestic mountains, impossibly green rice paddies and some fascinating tribal villages. But prepare yourself – the main trails are incredibly popular and some villages see hiking groups on an hourly basis. To trek remote paths you'll have to find an expert local guide.

At a lower elevation is Bac Ha (p145), less rainy and the trails are not heavily trampled. It's very picturesque, but it lacks

SAFETY FOR HIKERS

➡ Don't stray from established paths – Vietnam is full of unexploded ordnance.

➡ Guides are usually worth hiring; they're inexpensive, speak the language and understand indigenous culture.

➡ Boots with ankle support are a great investment.

Sapa's jaw-dropping mountain scenery. However, you will find great hikes to Flower Hmong and Nung villages.

High altitude Ha Giang province (p148), in the extreme north of Vietnam, is the nation's Tibet. Hikers can hook up with guides in Ha Giang city, or head out to Dong Van where there are exciting trekking opportunities.

The Moc Chau plateau (p130) is famous for its limestone karsts, plum orchards, tea plantations and dairy products. It's an emerging region, and hiking routes are steadily being developed here. Nearby Mai Chau is more established, offering great walking in an idyllic valley setting.

Elsewhere, Ba Be National Park (p102) has a network of rugged trails through spectacular karst scenery to minority villages and Cat Ba (p112) boasts a popular 18km-hike (and shorter alternatives like Butterfly Valley).

Central Vietnam

Some outstanding treks and numerous new trails are being developed between the limestone hills of Phong Nha-Ke Bang National Park (p162) by outfits like Jungle Boss Trekking (p164). Many routes combine trekking with some caving, including, most famously, the hike to the world's largest cave, Hang Son Doong.

You'll find excellent trails inside Cuc Phuong National Park (p160) through superb forest and past ancient trees and caves to a minority village.

Close to Danang, Bach Ma National Park (p190) has some good trails while the Ba Na Hill Station (p193) has short trails and awesome views. Adventure tours operators in Hoi An also offer some intriguing treks in the tribal areas west of town.

Southern Vietnam

With a bit of luck you might glimpse one of the dozens of mammals present in Yok Don National Park (p303) near Buon Ma Thuot. You'll need to hire a guide to see the best of Cat Tien National Park (p298), where crocodiles can be seen and night hikes are possible; the Wild Gibbon Trek here is highly popular. Over in Dalat, several adventure tour operators offer hikes: one rewarding area is the Bidoup Nui Ba National Park (p292).

Rice terraces, Northern Vietnam

Further south there's little for hikers to get excited about – the climate is perennially hot and humid and the landscape largely flat. Con Son (p281) is one curious exception, an island with cooling sea breezes and hikes through rainforest and mangroves.

Cycling

Bikes are a popular mode of transport in Vietnam, so cycling is an excellent way to experience the country. Basic bicycles can be rented for US$1 to US$3 per day, and good-quality mountain bikes for US$6 to US$15.

The flat lands of the Mekong Delta region are ideal for long-distance rides down back roads. Good routes include the country lanes around Chau Doc, and the quiet road that runs along the Cambodian border from Chau Doc to Ha Tien (with a possible detour to Ba Chuc). There's also some nice cycling on the islands off Vinh Long.

Avoid Hwy 1 as insane traffic makes it tough going and dangerous. Consider the

Explore Vietnam by motorbike

inland Ho Chi Minh Highway (Hwys 14, 15 and 8), which offers some stunning scenery and little traffic. Hoi An is an excellent base for exploring craft villages and rural lanes. Hue is also a great place for cycling, with temples, pagodas and the Perfume River.

In the Southwest highlands, Dalat has lots of dirt trails and is the base camp for the dramatic two-day descent to Mui Ne.

Motorbiking

Motorbiking through Vietnam is an unforgettable way to experience the nation. It's the mode of transport for most Vietnamese, and there are repair shops everywhere. Two wheels put you closer to the countryside – its smells, people and scenery – compared with getting around by car or bus. For those seeking true adventure, there is no better way to go.

If you're not confident riding a motorbike, it's comparatively cheap to hire someone to drive one for you. Easy Riders (p295) is one such scheme.

Unless you relish getting high on exhaust fumes and barged by trucks, avoid too much time on Hwy 1. The inland Ho Chi Minh Highway running the spine of the country from north to south is one alternative, though of course you miss out on the ocean. The stretch from Duc Tho to Phong Nha offers wonderful karst scenery, forests, little traffic and an excellent paved road.

ALT HIGHWAY 1

Hwy 1's heavy traffic and trucks don't make for great motorbiking or bicycling. It's possible, with some careful planning, to loop off Hwy 1 at regular intervals and use coastal back roads:

- east of Hue between Thuan An and Vin Hien
- between Chi Thanh and the Hon Gom peninsula
- south of Nha Trang to the Cam Ranh airport
- between Phan Thiet and Vung Tau

Two of the most dramatic rides in the southern half of the country are the Hai Van Pass, featuring hairpin after hairpin and oceanic views, and the spectacular road between Nha Trang and Dalat which cuts through forests and takes in a 1700m pass.

Further north, there's glorious mountain scenery, river valleys and tribal villages around Sapa and Dien Bien Phu. The route through Ha Giang province through Ha Giang, Dong Van and Bao Lac is the ultimate, with superlative vistas and stupendous mountain roads.

Surfing

There's surf most times of year in Vietnam, though it isn't an acclaimed destination – the wave scene in *Apocalypse Now* was shot in the Philippines. Dedicated surf shops are rare; though the odd guesthouse and adventure sport tour operator have boards for hire.

Surf's up between November and April when the winter monsoon blows from the north. Several typhoons form in the South China Sea each year, and these produce the biggest wind swells.

The original GI Joe break, China Beach is a 30km stretch of sand, which can produce clean peaks of over 2m, though watch out for pollution after heavy rains.

In season, head to Bai Dai beach, 27km south of Nha Trang, where's there's a good left-hand break.

Beginners can head to Mui Ne, with multiple breaks around the bay, including short right- and left-handers. Further south, Vung Tau is inconsistent, but offers some of Vietnam's best waves when conditions are right.

Anyone searching for fresh waves in remote locations should be extremely wary of unexploded ordnance. Garbage, stormwater run-off and industrial pollution are other hazards.

Kitesurfing, Windsurfing & Sailing

Windsurfing and kitesurfing are taking off. Mui Ne Beach is fast becoming a windchasers' hotspot in Asia with competitions and a real buzz about the place. Nha Trang and Vung Tau are other possibilities.

Two-hour beginner lessons start at US$100; it's tough to get your head around all the basics (and also tough on your body!).

The best conditions in Mui Ne are between November to April. Mornings are ideal for beginners, while in the afternoon wind speeds regularly reach 35 knots.

Also based in Mui Ne, Manta Sail Training Centre (p268) is a professional new sailing outfit offering training and boat rentals.

BEST BEACHES

Drawing up a list of Vietnam's best beaches is a near-impossible task (there are a dozen idyllic coves in Phu Quoc alone) but here are our picks:

Sao Beach, Phu Quoc (p391)

Bai Dat Doc, Con Dao Islands (p283)

Long Beach, Phu Quoc (p391)

Doc Let Beach (p245)

Bai Mon, Vung Ro Bay (p246)

An Bang Beach, Hoi An (p220)

Thuan An Beach, Hue (p191)

Mui Ne (p265)

Minh Chau Beach, Quan Lan Island (p121)

Bai Dai (p262)

Nha Trang Beach (p247)

My Khe, Danang (p202)

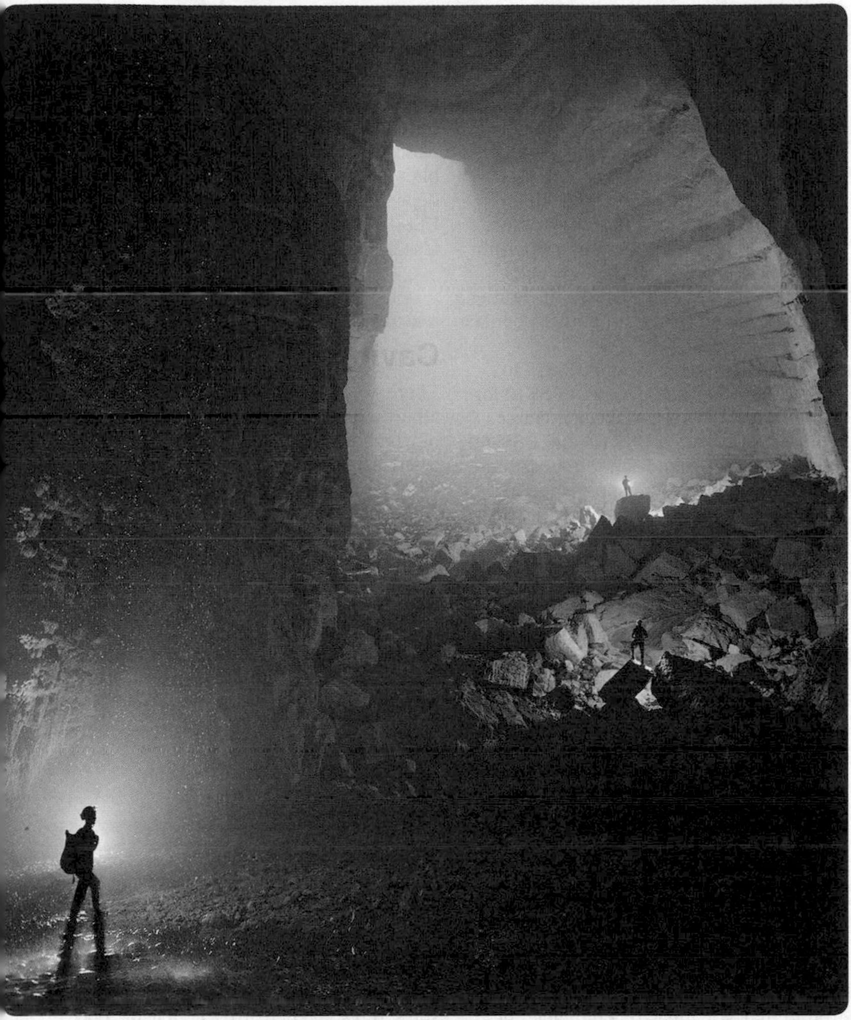

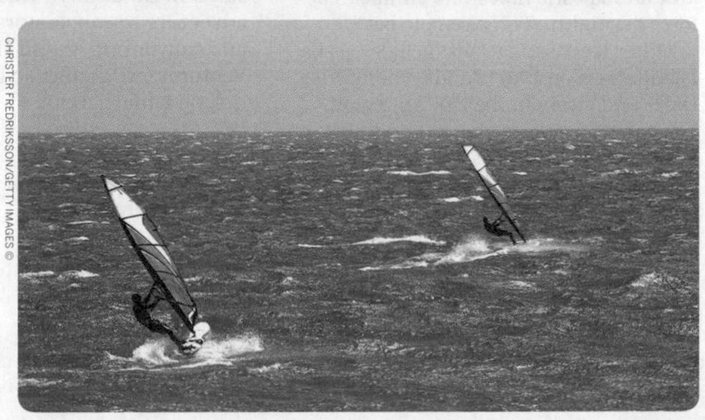

Top: Caving, Phong Nha-Ke Bang National Park (p162)

Bottom: Windsurfing, Mui Ne (p265)

CHRISTER FREDRIKSSON/GETTY IMAGES ©

Diving & Snorkelling

Vietnam is not a world-class dive mecca but it does have some fascinating dive sites. If you've experienced reefs in Indonesia or Australia, prepare yourself for less sea life and reduced visibility. The most popular scuba-diving and snorkelling is around Nha Trang (p247), where there are several reputable dive operators. Hoi An's dive schools head to the Cham Islands (p223), where macro life can be intriguing. Phu Quoc Island (p389) is another popular spot.

Two fun dives cost around US$70 to US$80; expect to pay US$25 to US$40 for snorkelling daytrips. PADI Open Water courses cost between US$325 and US$500.

The Con Dao Islands offer unquestionably the best diving and snorkelling in Vietnam, with bountiful marine life, fine reefs and even a wreck dive. However, prices are higher (around US$160 for two fun dives).

Note that Vietnam is home to several dodgy dive shops, some of which have fake PADI credentials. Nha Trang in particular has an excess of such places. Stick to reputable, recommended dive schools with good safety procedures, qualified instructors and well-maintained equipment.

Whitewater Rafting

Rafting is in its infancy in Vietnam. Several outfits in Dalat offer trips around the town, including Phat Tire Ventures (p293), which runs a day trip down the Langbian River with Class II, III or IV rapids, depending on the season; prices start at US$67. Companies based in Nha Trang also offer trips.

Caving

There are stupendous cave trips at Phong Nha-Ke Bang National Park (p162), many of which involve some hiking, swimming (there are a lot of river caves) and a short climb or two.

Specialist Oxalis (p164) is the only operator licensed to take you to the wonders of Hang Son Doong, the world's largest cave. But if your budget won't stretch to this, other excellent options include Hang Toi (Dark Cave) and Hang Va (both recently opened up to visitors). You can trek 7km inside Paradise Cave and do a remarkable two-day hike to Hang En Cave and Ban Doong village, and there's the lovely swim-through Tu Lan cave system.

Kayaking & SUP

Kayaking has exploded in popularity around Halong Bay. Many tours now include a spot of kayaking or stand up paddle-boarding through the karst islands, or you can choose a specialist and paddle around majestic limestone pinnacles before overnighting on a remote bay.

Other key destinations include Cat Ba Island, the Con Dao Islands, Phong Nha, Dalat and rivers in the Hoi An region. You can also rent sea kayaks and SUPs on beaches including Nha Trang.

Operators include Asia Outdoors (p116), Cat Ba Ventures (p116), Hoi An Kayak Center (p212) and SUP Monkey (p212).

Rock Climbing

The pioneers and acknowledged rock climbing specialists are Asia Outdoors (p116), a highly professional outfit based in Cat Ba Town that has instruction for beginners and dedicated trips for rock stars. In Dalat there are a couple of good adventure tour operators offering climbing and canyoning. And in Hoi An, Phat Tire Ventures (p212) offers climbing and rappelling on a marble cliff.

Pho bo (beef noodle soup)

Plan Your Trip

Eat & Drink Like a Local

Showcasing fresh and vibrant flavours, excellent street food and elegant restaurants in restored colonial architecture, Vietnam is packed with superb opportunities for eating and drinking. Cookery classes, market visits and walking tours make it easy to discover the country's culinary heritage.

A Day in Hanoi

Surrounded by eating and drinking opportunities, this is how a resident of the Vietnamese capital might fill a tasty day.

Early Morning

A local breakfast speciality is *bun rieu cua*, noodle soup made with a hearty broth using tiny crabs from rice paddies.

Mid-Morning

Simple cafes and coffee stalls dot Hanoi, and catching up with friends over deliciously strong *caphe* is virtually mandatory. During summer, *tra chanh* (iced lemon tea) is popular.

Lunch

Bun cha (grilled pork with crab spring rolls, fresh herbs and vermicelli) is the classic Hanoi midday meal.

Mid-Afternoon

Popular on-the-go snacking options include *banh ghoi*, deep-fried pastries with pork and mushrooms.

Evening

Hanoi's footpaths come alive with simple *bia hoi* (fresh draught beer) stalls; popular drinking snacks include roast duck and dried squid.

Food & Drink Experiences

Plan your travel around these tasty recommendations and understand the essence of Vietnamese cuisine.

Introducing Vietnamese Food

Welcome to your first night in Vietnam. Here's where to go to get up to speed with the country's cuisine.

Secret Garden (p340) Vietnamese classics served amid a rooftop garden in Ho Chi Minh City.

Vy's Market (p215) The country's diverse dishes are served around lively open kitchens in Hoi An.

Quan An Ngon (p81) Bustling Hanoi showcases of Vietnamese food in colonial buildings in the nation's capital.

Street-Food Tours

Pull up a squat plastic stool and enjoy discovering what makes Vietnam's street food exceptional.

Saigon Street Eats (p334), Ho Chi Minh City

Eat Hoi An (p212), Hoi An

Danang Unplugged (p196), Danang

Hue Flavor (p182), Hue

Hanoi Street Food Tours (p72), Hanoi

Dalat Happy Tours (p293), Dalat

Best Fusion Restaurants

Discover the culinary intersection between Western flavours and Vietnamese cuisine at these elegant restaurants.

La Badiane (p82) French flavours blend with Vietnamese in this leafy colonial villa in Hanoi.

Xu (p342) Stylish HCMC restaurant-lounge with an inventive Vietnamese-inspired fusion menu.

Nu Eatery (p216) Down a Hoi An laneway and delivering Vietnamese and global flavours with a modern accent.

Spice House at Cassia Cottage (p396) Subtle flavours served beachside with sunset views on Phu Quoc Island.

Vegetarian & Vegan Food

Com Chay (vegetarian) restaurants serving vegan food can be found across Vietnam, often adjacent to Buddhist temples. Around the first and 15th days of the Buddhist calendar month, some food stalls substitute tofu in their dishes.

Chay Nang Tam (p82) Tasty variations on tofu and tempeh; Hanoi.

Hum Vegetarian Cafe & Restaurant (p345) Excellent salads in an elegant HCMC space.

Com Chay Vi Dieu (p271) Around five different daily dishes feature at this simple roadside spot in Mui Ne.

Lien Hoa (p184) Featuring flavour-packed dishes with aubergine and jackfruit; Hue.

Viet Chay Sala (p235) Excellent selection of tempting dips and sauces in Quang Ngai.

Minority Flavours

Curious travellers should seek out the food of Vietnam's ethnic minority groups. Look forward to occasionally challenging, but always interesting dishes.

Chim Sao (p82) Try the ethnic minority sausages, served with a mint and coriander dipping sauce; Hanoi.

Quan Kien (p83) Dishes inspired by Hmong, Thai and Muong cuisine, also in Hanoi.

Hill Station Signature Restaurant (p141) Modern decor combines with dishes influenced by traditional Hmong cuisine in Sapa.

Pleiku (p305) Popular local street foods include *pho kho* (two-dish noodle) and *thit bo nuong ong* (beef cooked in bamboo pipe).

Vietnamese Coffee

Try these places to get your caffeine fix.

Café Duy Tri (p83) Dripping with heritage, and virtually unchanged for more than 75 years; Hanoi.

Cafe Pho Co (p83) Negotiate your way to a hidden balcony overlooking Hanoi's Hoan Kiem Lake.

Cafe Xua & Nay (p242) Ocean breezes and a traditional wooden house built in 1832; Quy Nhon.

K'Ho Coffee (p292) Sample coffee and buy freshly roasted beans at this highland plantation near Dalat.

Cooking Courses

Cooking courses can range from a simple set-up in someone's backyard to purpose-built schools.

Green Bamboo Cooking School (p211) An accomplished chef offers personalised cooking courses in Hoi An.

Hanoi Cooking Centre (p72) Excellent cooking classes in Hanoi that include a visit to the market and cooking classes for kids.

GRAIN Cooking Classes (p332) HCMC classes coordinated by Australian-Vietnamese chef Luke Nguyen.

MATT MUNRO/LONELY PLANET ©

Street-food stalls, Hoi An (p215)

Regional Specialities

Travelling north to south is a Vietnamese journey that, geographically and gastronomically, begins in China and ends in Southeast Asia. Differences in history, culture and geography combine for many techniques, ingredients and tastes, all linked by the Vietnamese love for vibrant flavours, fresh herbs, noodles and seafood.

Northern Vietnam

Northern Vietnamese food bears the imprint of centuries of Chinese occupation. Comforting noodle dishes, generally mild flavours and rustic elegance are all hallmarks of the region's cuisine. Soy is used as frequently as fish sauce, vinegar adds sourness rather than lime juice or tamarind, chillies give way to black pepper, and long cooking times coax maximum flavour from unpretentious ingredients.

Banh Cuon These rolls are made from rice-flour batter that's poured onto a piece of muslin cloth stretched over a steamer; once firm, the noodle sheet is scattered with chopped pork, mushrooms and dried shrimp, then rolled up, sprinkled with

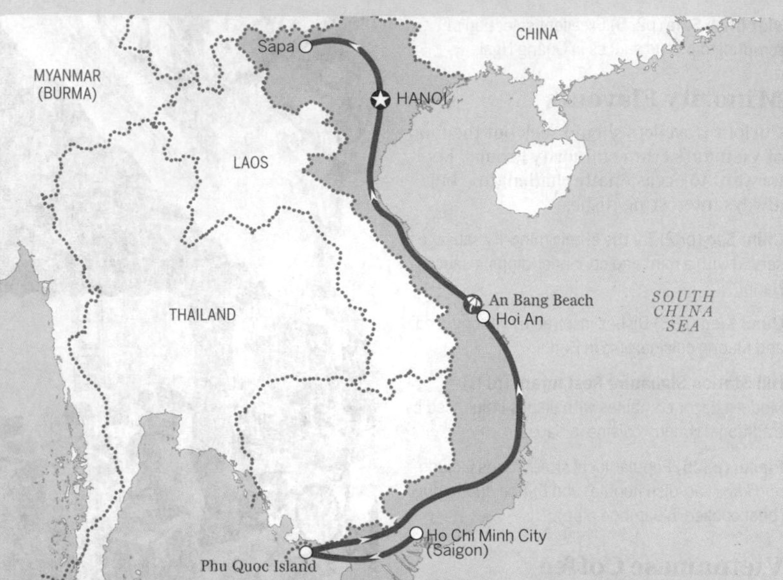

The Ultimate Vietnamese Food Tour

Start in **Ho Chi Minh City**, Vietnam's energetic southern hub, and negotiate the city's street-food scene on two wheels with Vespa Adventures (p333) or XO Tours (p334). Discover local dishes like *banh xeo* (savoury Vietnamese crêpes) before exploring markets and trying a cooking class with Cyclo Resto (p344). Adjourn to the Pasteur Street Brewing Company (p347) for craft beers infused with local ingredients like lemongrass and rambutan.

Consider a southern sojourn on **Phu Quoc Island**, taking in grilled seafood at the Dinh Cao Night Market (p396), before heading north to **Hoi An**. Once one of Asia's most cosmopolitan ports with traders from around the world, Hoi An now hosts international visitors at the town's many cookery schools. Learn the secrets of local cuisine at the Morning Glory Cooking School (p211) or Red Bridge Cooking School (p211), and uncover street food secrets with the Eat Hoi An (p212) food tour.

Detour to nearby **An Bang Beach** for more seafood at Sea Shell (p222), and try Hoi An's signature dish *cao lau* (Japanese-style noodles with herbs, salad greens, bean sprouts and roast pork) at Mermaid Restaurant (p215). Continue north to **Hanoi**, and negotiate the bustling labyrinth of the Old Quarter with Hanoi Street Food Tours (p72). Iconic Hanoi dishes to try include *cha ca* (grilled fish with turmeric and dill) at Cha Ca Thang Long (p80), and *pho bo* (beef noodle soup) at Pho Thin (p79).

Learn about northern Vietnamese cuisine at the Hanoi Cooking Centre (p72), try dishes inspired by Vietnam's ethnic minorities at Quan Kien (p83) or Chim Sao (p82), and then head north to **Sapa**, the heartland region of minority groups including the Hmong and the Red Dzao. Experience Hmong-inspired dishes at Hill Station Signature Restaurant (p141), book in for its cooking class, and toast your new knowledge of Vietnamese cuisine with a *ruou* (rice wine) tasting set.

Bun bo Hue (spicy beef soup)

crispy shallots, and served alongside a tangle of bean sprouts, slivered cucumber and chopped fresh herbs, with a saucer of *nuoc cham* (dipping sauce) for drizzling.

Bun Cha This street favourite features barbecued sliced pork or pork patties served with thin rice vermicelli, fresh herbs and green vegetables, and a bowl of lightly sweetened *nuoc mam* (fish sauce) with floating slices of pickled vegetables. The Hanoi version combines sliced pork belly and pork patties formed from chopped pork shoulder.

Pho Bo A northern culinary highlight is *pho bo* (beef noodle soup). A good *pho* hinges on the broth, which is made from beef bones boiled for hours with shallot, ginger, fish sauce, black cardamom, star anise and cassia. Hardcore northern *pho* lovers frown upon adding lime, basil, and bean sprouts to their bowls.

Central Vietnam

Positioned between culinary extremes, the food of central Vietnam combines moderation and balance – except where it concerns the locals' love of chilli. People cook from the land, transforming modest resources into fare fit for an emperor. Everything seems smaller; baguettes and herbs are miniature versions of their southern selves, while Hue's imperial cuisine showcases dainty, delicate dishes. One edible legacy of the royal court is easily found on the street: *banh beo*, delicate steamed cakes made from rice flour. The central Vietnamese like gutsy and spicy flavours, including briny shrimp sauce and spritely lemongrass.

Banh Khoai These hearty, dessert-plate-sized crepes are made with rice-flour batter and cooked with oil in special long-handled pans. With a filling of shrimp, pork, egg and bean sprouts, they are encased with fresh herbs in lettuce, and then dunked in a sauce based on earthy fermented soybeans.

Bun Bo Hue This punchy rice-noodle soup with beef and pork exemplifies the central Vietnamese proclivity for spicy food. Tinged yellow-orange by chillies and annatto, the broth is laden with lemongrass notes and anchored by savoury shrimp sauce (*mam tom*). Like most Vietnamese noodle soups, it's accompanied by herbs and leafy greens.

Com Hen Rice is served with the flesh of tiny clams, their cooking broth, and garnishes including roasted rice crackers, crisp pork

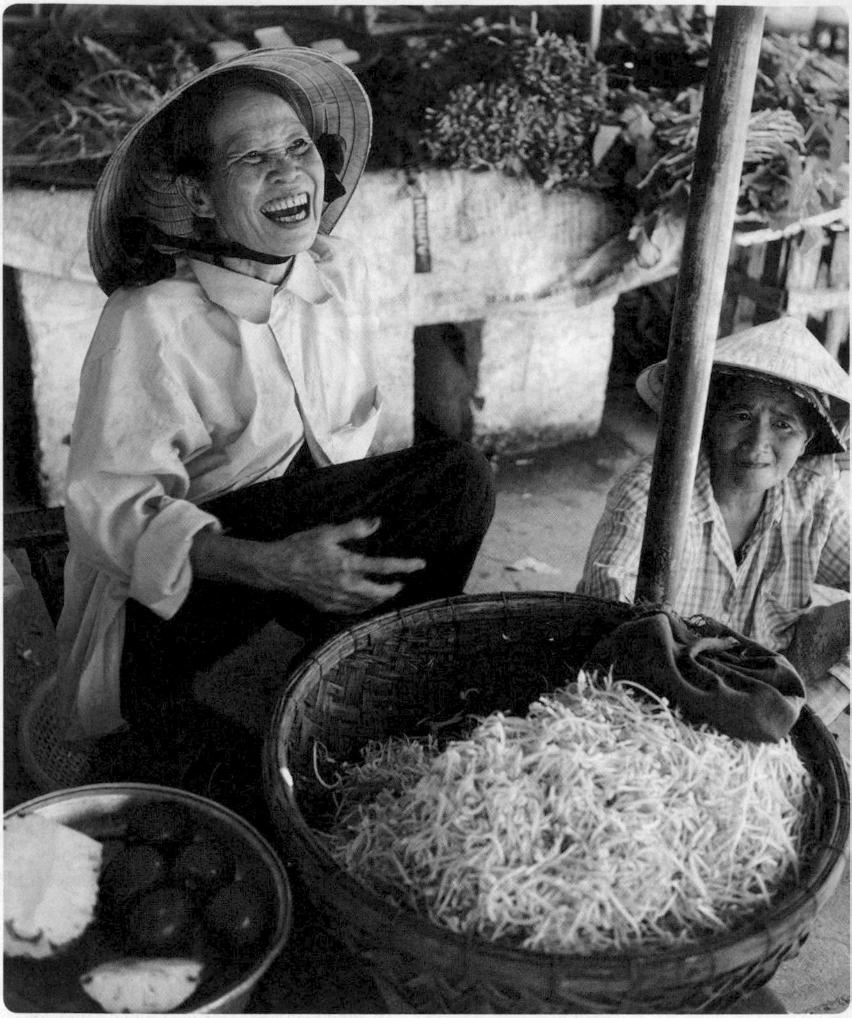

BHOFACK2/GETTY IMAGES ©

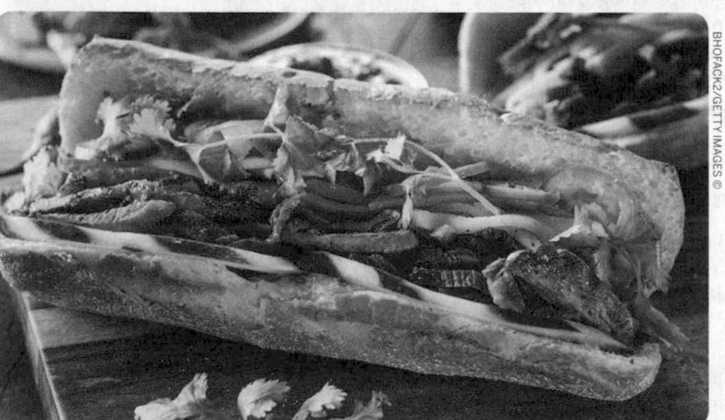

Top: Market stall in Hoi An (p215)

Bottom: Pork *banh mi* (filled baguettes)

crackling, peanuts, sesame seeds, fresh herbs and vegetables. Adding broth and sauce to the other ingredients, the liquid components moisten, season and harmonise.

Southern Vietnam

Southern cuisine emphasises the region's abundance and tends to be on the sweet side. Vendors at southern markets display lush, big-leafed herbs, colourful fruits, and the freshest fish. Coconut milk infuses mild curries and lends richness to sweets. The southern love of fresh herbs, fruit and vegetables comes to the fore in refreshing *goi* (salads), of green papaya, grapefruit-like pomelo, or lotus stems.

Canh Chua Ca This soup is the Mekong Delta in a bowl: plentiful snakehead fish or catfish; fruits like tomato and pineapple; and vegetables including bean sprouts, okra and *bac ha* (taro stem), all in a broth that's tart with tamarind and salty with *nuoc mam*, and finally topped with vivid green herbs and golden fried garlic.

Banh Mi This sandwich is a legacy of French and Chinese colonialism, but it's 100% Vietnamese. The baguette merely encases the filling, which might be a smearing of pâté or a few slices of silky sausage and a sprinkling of pepper. Mayonnaise moistens the bread and a sprinkling of soy sauce imparts *umami* (savoury) goodness.

Banh Xeo This giant crispy, chewy rice crepe is made in 12- or 14-inch skillets or woks and crammed with pork, shrimp, mung beans and bean sprouts. Take a portion and encase it in lettuce or mustard leaf, add some fresh herbs, then dunk it in *nuoc cham*.

How to Eat & Drink

When to Eat

Generally Vietnamese eat three meals per day, beginning with a bowl of noodles or *chao* (rice porridge) for breakfast. Lunch is usually a social affair with workmates in a local restaurant or food stall, and dinner is a leisurely occasion shared with friends and family. Throughout the day, snacking opportunities abound in bigger cities.

TABLE ETIQUETTE

Have your bowl on a small plate, chopsticks and a soup spoon at the ready. Each place setting will include a small bowl at the top right-hand side for *nuoc nam* (fish sauce) and other dipping sauces. Don't dip your chopsticks into the central bowls of shared food, but use the communal serving spoons instead. Pick up your bowl with your left hand, bring it close to your mouth and use the chopsticks to manoeuvre the food. If you're eating noodles, lower your head till it hangs over the bowl and slurp away. If you're dining in a private home, it is polite for the host to offer more food than the guests can eat, and it's also polite for guests not to eat everything. Also, remember not to leave chopsticks standing in a V-shape in your bowl as this is a sign of death.

Where to Eat

Food stalls often specialise in just one dish; simple *com* (literally 'rice') restaurants serve the staple along with vegetables and meat or seafood. Vietnamese-style food courts like Quan An Ngon (p81) in Hanoi serve dishes from around the country, and more expensive eateries offer Vietnamese classics and Vietnamese-French fusion food.

Regions at a Glance

Occupying a slender slice of the east Asian landmass, Vietnam combines jagged alpine peaks in the north, a pancake-flat river delta in the south, cave-riddled limestone hills in its central provinces and dense rainforest along its western border with some of the world's most productive rice-growing terrain. And that's just the countryside.

Climatically the northern half of the nation experiences a much cooler winter, and the cuisine, lifestyle and character of the people reflect this. As you head south, the country has more of a tropical feel, with coconut trees outnumbering bamboo plants and fish sauce replacing soy sauce on the menu. The southern provinces are always humid, hot and sticky, their food sweet, spicy, aromatic and complex.

Hanoi

Food
Temples
Culture

Spectacular Street Food

Dine in elegant colonial villas, or pull up a stool and chow down on street food classics like *pho bo* (beef noodle soup) or *bun cha* (barbecued pork with rice vermicelli).

Religion before Communism

A millennium of history including periods of Chinese and French occupation has left a legacy of religious and spiritual tradition evident in Hanoi's many temples and churches.

Artistic Awakenings

Under the watchful eye of a government which restricts creative expression, Hanoi's budding, highly skilled artists are cautiously finding their voice and a place on the international stage. If you're an art-lover, the time to visit is now.

p54

Northern Vietnam

Landscapes
Culture
Adventure

Soaring Limestone Peaks

Halong Bay's majesty is best observed shrouded in ethereal morning mist. To the north, the sublime mountainous scenery of Ha Giang province is arguably even more spectacular.

Local Life

The cascading rice paddies around Sapa and Bac Ha are a spectacular hub for trekking and homestays with ethnic minorities, including the colourful Dzao and Flower Hmong people.

Active Adventures

Adventurous detours in northern Vietnam include rock climbing on Cat Ba Island or kayaking to hidden coves and sandy beaches in nearby Lan Ha Bay.

p99

Central Vietnam

Food
History
Landscapes

Local Flavours

Partner with local foodies to discover tasty street food unique to Hoi An and Hue – including Hue's famed Imperial cuisine – before dining at sophisticated restaurants helmed by international chefs crafting innovative menus.

Historic Gems

At Hue's citadel, you'll see palaces, temples, gateways and towers, despite wartime bombing. Other gems include the Perfume River's royal tombs and pagodas, and Hoi An's Old Town.

Stunning Scenery

The area around Ninh Binh is typified by sublime limestone mountains. Further south, Phong Nha-Ke Bang National Park offers more of the same, plus many cave systems.

p152

Southeast Coast

Beaches
Temples
Food

Empty Coastlines

Vietnam's coastline at its most voluptuous. Mui Ne and Nha Trang are the big hitters, but there are hundreds of kilometres of empty beaches to discover, including several in the Con Dao Islands.

Ancient Temples

The Kingdom of Champa once held sway over much of this region. The legacy is still visible in ancient temples, including the Po Nagar towers (Nha Trang) and the Po Klong Garai towers (Thap Cham).

Fresh Seafood

Vietnamese cuisine is always a delight, but in this region fresh seafood stands out. Choose from succulent prawns, grilled squid or juicy crabs, prepared on a barbecue at your table.

p233

Southwest Highlands

Adventure
Wildlife
Culture

Ride Around

Get off the trail on a motorbike trip into the hinterlands. Self-drive on a Vespa or Honda Cub, or hook up with the Easy Riders to experience a Vietnam less travelled on the back roads between Dalat and Hoi An.

National Parks

Explore some of Vietnam's leading national parks where the wild things are. Cat Tien is home to endangered primates and the innovative Gibbon Trek. Yok Don, easily accessible from Buon Ma Thuot, is where elephants roam.

Meet the Locals

Leave the lowlanders behind on the coast and meet the high-ground minority people. Get to know them better with a traditional village homestay around Kon Tum.

p287

Ho Chi Minh City

Urban Tours
History
Nightlife

Metropolitan Buzz

From an after-dark street food exploration on two wheels to quirky walking tours uncovering street art and hip cafes hidden in heritage apartments, HCMC has a growing array of fun and informative tours revealing the best of this vibrant city.

Military History

The fall/liberation of Saigon was one of the late 20th century's defining moments. Explore sites associated with the American War, from the tunnels at Cu Chi to the War Remnants Museum and Reunification Palace.

Bars & Clubs

From late-night bars to full-on clubs, Saigon's sizzling nightlife keeps things buzzing till the wee hours. The tireless Pham Ngu Lao backpacker strip is virtually 24/7.

p311

Mekong Delta

Beaches
Boat Trips
Pagodas

White Sands

The white sands of gorgeous Sao Beach and graceful Long Beach on Phu Quoc Island are Mekong Delta trump cards. The island's a world away from the muddy riverbanks of the delta. Don't forget your beach gear.

Floating Markets

Boat trips are essential for understanding how water defines this part of Vietnam, a region where children don life preservers to swim all day and the river can get so wide that you almost lose sight of either bank.

Sacred Sites

The delta's religious undercurrent percolates most visibly in its Vietnamese Buddhist sites, such as Sam Mountain, and a wealth of Khmer temples, where monks in saffron robes read sutras.

p366

Siem Reap & the Temples of Angkor

Temples
Dining
Activities

Khmer Kingdoms

It's not all about Angkor Wat. True, the 'city that is a temple' is one of the world's most iconic buildings, but nearby are the enigmatic faces of the Bayon, the jungle temple of Ta Prohm and the inspirational carvings of Banteay Srei.

Foodie Heaven

Contemporary Khmer, spiced-up street food, fine French and a whole host more, plus legendary Pub St – Siem Reap is where it's happening.

Cultural Immersion

Take to the skies by hot-air balloon, microlight or helicopter to see Angkor from a different angle. Or learn the secrets of Cambodia's intricate national cuisine on a cooking class.

p417

On the Road

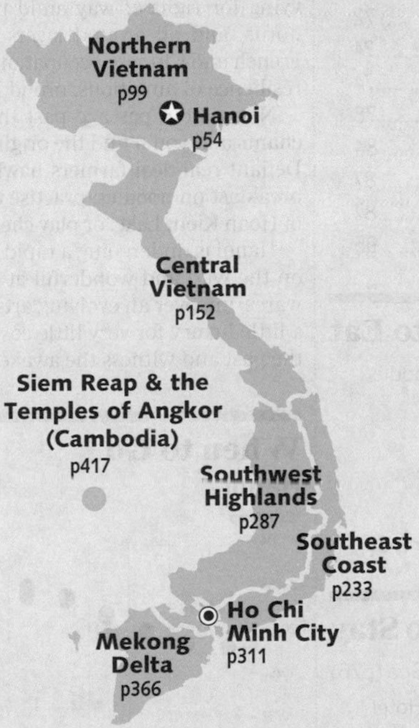

Northern Vietnam
p99

Hanoi
p54

Central Vietnam
p152

Siem Reap & the Temples of Angkor (Cambodia)
p417

Southwest Highlands
p287

Southeast Coast
p233

Ho Chi Minh City
p311

Mekong Delta
p366

Hanoi

☎04 / POP 7.1 MILLION

Includes ➡

Best Places to Eat

- Moto-san Uber Noodle (p82)
- Minh Thuy's (p81)
- Tim Ho Wan (p83)
- La Badiane (p82)
- Maison de Tet Decor (p83)

Best Places to Stay

- La Siesta Hotel & Spa (p76)
- Conifer Boutique Hotel (p77)
- Somerset Grand Hanoi (p77)
- Fraser Suites Hanoi (p78)
- Sofitel Metropole Hotel (p78)

Why Go?

Vietnam's capital races to make up for time lost to the ravages of war and a government that as recently as the 1990s kept the outside world at bay. Its streets surge with scooters vying for right of way amid the din of constantly blaring horns, and all around layers of history reveal periods of French and Chinese occupation – offering a glimpse into the resilience of ambitious, proud Hanoians.

Negotiate a passage past the ubiquitous knock-off merchants and you'll find the original streets of the Old Quarter. Defiant real-deal farmers hawk their wares, while city folk breakfast on noodles, practise t'ai chi at dawn on the shores of Hoan Kiem Lake, or play chess with goateed grandfathers.

Hanoi is undergoing a rapid transformation. You can dine on the wild and wonderful at every corner, sample market wares, uncover an evolving arts scene, then sleep soundly in a little luxury for very little cost. Meet the people, delve into the past and witness the awakening of a Hanoi on the move.

When to Go

Hanoi

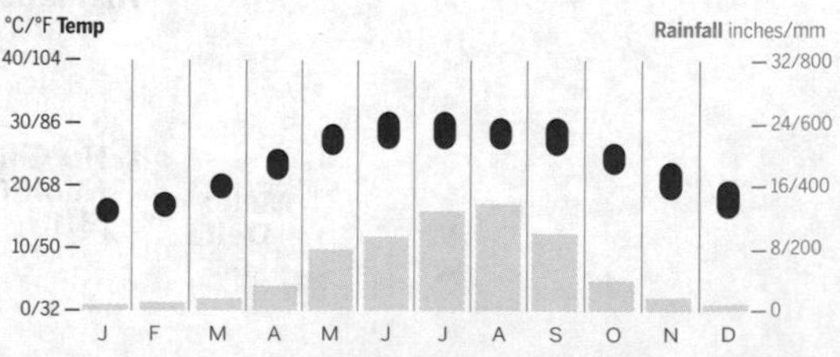

Jan–Apr Cooler days collide with the energy and colour of the Tet festival.

Jun–Aug Heavy heat and humidity signal low season in Hanoi: bargains on hotel suites abound.

Oct–Dec Clear, sunny days and cooler temperatures make this the ideal time to visit Hanoi.

History

The site where Hanoi stands today has been inhabited since the Neolithic Period. Emperor Ly Thai To moved his capital here in AD 1010, naming it Thang Long (Ascending Dragon).

The decision by Emperor Gia Long, founder of the Nguyen dynasty in 1802, to rule from Hue relegated Hanoi to the status of a regional capital for a century. The city was named Hanoi by Emperor Tu Duc in 1831, from the words 'Ha' meaning 'river' and 'Noi' meaning 'interior', referring to its position alongside Song Hong (Red River).

From 1902 to 1953, Hanoi served as the capital of French Indochina and was proclaimed capital of the Democratic Republic of Vietnam by Ho Chi Minh during the August Revolution of 1945. The French restored control and the First Indochina War ensued until 1954. Following the Geneva Accords of the same year, the Viet Minh, having driven the French from the city, were able to return.

During the American War heavy US bombing destroyed parts of Hanoi and killed hundreds of civilians. One of the prime targets was the 1682m-long Long Bien Bridge. US aircraft repeatedly bombed this strategic point, yet after each attack the Vietnamese managed to improvise replacement spans and return road and rail services. It is said that the US military ended the attacks when US POWs were put to work repairing the structure. Today the bridge is renowned as a symbol of the tenacity and strength of the people of Hanoi.

It's hard to believe that Hanoi's millions of motorbikes and scooters would have been an uncommon sight as recently as the early 1990s, when most people got around on bicycles and the occasional Soviet era bus. Today Hanoi's conservationists fight to save historic structures, as the city struggles to cope with a booming population, soaring pollution levels and an inefficient public transport system. It's a case of 'get in quick' before the voracious growth and hasty modernisation spurned on by Vietnam's 'free-market-friendly' brand of communism drowns out history-rich Hanoi's vibrant palette of Vietnamese, French, Russian and American influences.

Sights

Note that some museums are closed on Mondays and take a two-hour lunch break on other days of the week. Check opening hours carefully before setting off.

HANOI IN...

One Day

Rise early for a morning walk around misty **Hoan Kiem Lake** (p61) before a classic Hanoi breakfast of *pho bo* (beef noodle soup) at **Pho Thin** (p79). Get up to speed on Uncle Ho with a visit to the **Ho Chi Minh Mausoleum Complex** (p64) and nearby **Ho Chi Minh Museum** (p65). Wander back down P Dien Bien Phu to the **Vietnam Military History Museum** (p66). Have a strong Vietnamese coffee at **Cong Caphe** (p83) before visiting the cultural treasures of the Fine Arts Museum of Vietnam. Grab a cab to lunch at **La Badiane** (p82) before continuing to the peaceful **Temple of Literature** (p63). Catch another cab to immerse yourself in the organised chaos of the **Old Quarter** (p58), with its market-like lanes, shops and galleries, or, if time permits, contemplate Vietnam's history through the eyes of its women at the **Vietnamese Women's Museum** (p63). Make time to stop for a well-earned and refreshing glass of *bia hoi* (draught beer) and catch a performance of the **water puppets** (p87) before heading south of the lake to the Hanoi branch of the atmospheric **Nha Hang Ngon** (p82) for dinner.

Two Days

Head into the suburbs to the excellent **Vietnam Museum of Ethnology** (p69) to discover the ethnic mosaic that makes up modern Vietnam. Back in the city have lunch at **Chim Sao** (p82) before exploring the **Museum of Vietnamese Revolution** (p62) and the adjacent **National Museum of Vietnamese History** (p61). The architecture at the latter is stunning, and the contents a fine introduction to 2000 years of highs and lows. After dinner at **Cha Ca Thang Long** (p80) or **Old Hanoi** (p82) head for drinks at **Cama ATK** (p85) or the **Summit Lounge** (p85).

Hanoi Highlights

1 Experiencing Asia at its raw, pulsating best in the labyrinthine streets of the **Old Quarter** (p58).

2 Celebrating the strength and sensuality of women at the unique **Vietnamese Women's Museum** (p63).

3 Piecing together the country's ethnic mosaic at the wonderful **Vietnam Museum of Ethnology** (p69).

4 Stepping into history, and a spiritual retreat from the busy streets, at the **Temple of Literature** (p63).

5 Getting an authentic taste of the city while exploring Hanoi's intoxicating **street food scene** (p79).

6 Escaping the hustle and bustle around lake **Ho Tay** (p69) with walking/cycling path and three pagodas.

7 Waking at dawn to ease peacefully into another Hanoi day with the t'ai chi buffs along **Hoan Kiem Lake** (p61).

8 Contemplating the atrocities of war and the resilience of the Vietnamese along the **Long Bien Bridge** (p61).

9 Marvelling at the scope and pace of Hanoi's growth from the **Lotte Tower Observation Deck** (p69).

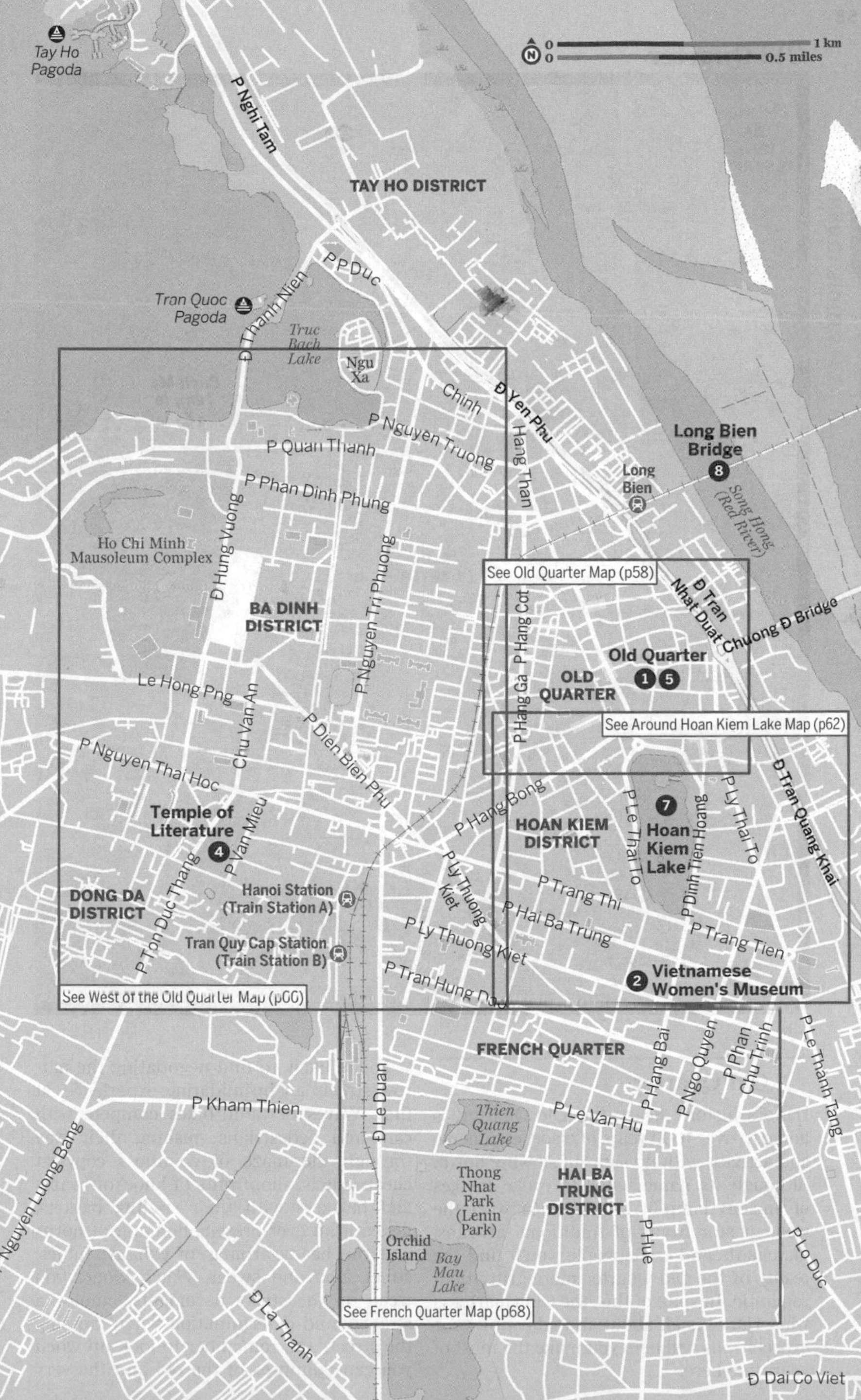

0 1 km
0 0.5 miles
Tay Ho Pagoda
P Nghi Tam
TAY HO DISTRICT
P P Duc
Tran Quoc Pagoda
Đ Thanh Nien
Truc Bach Lake
Ngu Xa
Chinh
Đ Yen Phu
P Nguyen Truong
P Quan Thanh
Hang Than
P Phan Dinh Phung
Long Bien Bridge
8
Long Bien
Song Hong (Red River)
Ho Chi Minh Mausoleum Complex
Đ Hung Vuong
P Nguyen Tri Phuong
See Old Quarter Map (p58)
Đ Tran Nhat Duat
Chuong Đ Bridge
BA DINH DISTRICT
P Hang Cot
Old Quarter
1 5
OLD QUARTER
P Hang Ga
Le Hong Png
Chu Van An
P Dien Bien Phu
See Around Hoan Kiem Lake Map (p62)
P Nguyen Thai Hoc
Đ Tran Quang Khai
P Le Thai To
P Ly Thai To
7
P Hang Bong
Temple of Literature
4
P Van Mieu
HOAN KIEM DISTRICT
Hoan Kiem Lake
P Dinh Tien Hoang
P Ly Thuong Kiet
DONG DA DISTRICT
P Ton Duc Thang
Hanoi Station (Train Station A)
P Trang Thi
P Hai Ba Trung
Tran Quy Cap Station (Train Station B)
P Ly Thuong Kiet
P Trang Tien
P Tran Hung Dao
2
Vietnamese Women's Museum
See West of the Old Quarter Map (p66)
FRENCH QUARTER
P Hang Bai
P Ngo Quyen
P Phan Chu Trinh
P Le Thanh Tang
P Kham Thien
Đ Le Duan
P Le Van Hu
Thien Quang Lake
P Nguyen Luong Bang
Thong Nhat Park (Lenin Park)
HAI BA TRUNG DISTRICT
P Hue
P Lo Duc
Orchid Island
Bay Mau Lake
See French Quarter Map (p68)
Đ La Thanh
Đ Dai Co Viet

Old Quarter

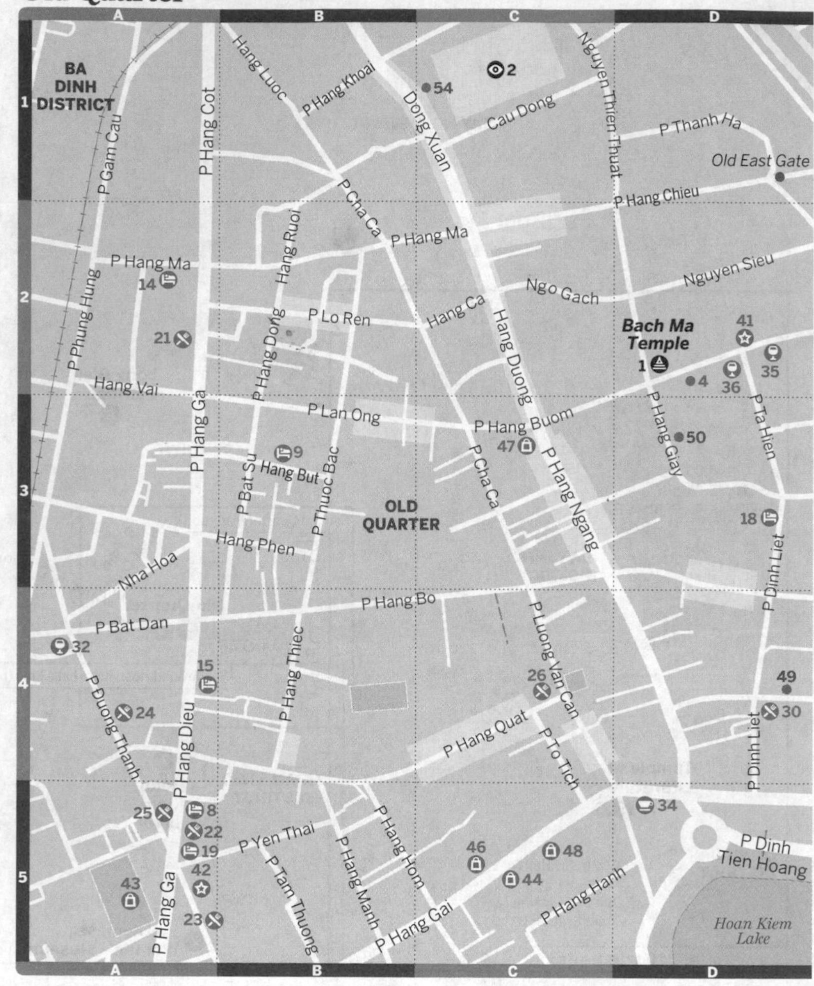

Old Quarter

Hanoi's historic heart, the 'Old Quarter', is home to over 1000 years of trade, commerce and activity, with no signs of slowing down. Although its name tends to evoke images of ancient lamp-lit streets lined with the wooden storefronts of traditional artisans, merchants and craftspeople, you'll find the reality of the Old Quarter more gritty than romantic. In spite of this, the Old Quarter is what Hanoi is all about and adjusting your expectations will help you make the most of your time here.

You're likely to find negotiating the narrow streets an intimidating experience, at first. Waves of motorbikes compete with cars and pedestrians pushing their way through the maze of countless copy-cat cheap hotels, shopfronts of knockoff wares and hawkers with their sizzling baskets, beneath an ever-present honking of horns and the heady aromas of exhaust fumes, street food and sweat. Watch where you tread on the sticky pavements, employ a strategy and determination when crossing the street, and remember to look up when you can: glimpses of the old and the very

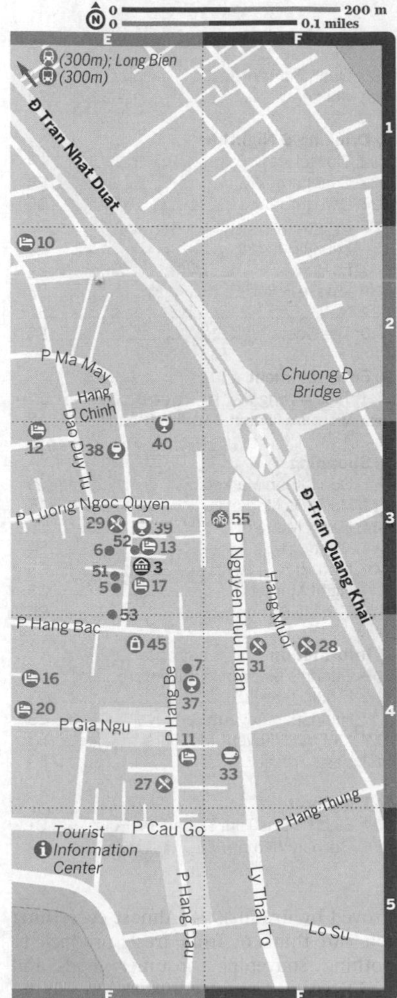

old indeed peek out occasionally from behind garish, modern facades. You'll gain your confidence soon enough, and when you do, there's no better way to spend time here than to wander, soaking up the sights, sounds and smells, and immersing yourself in the unique flavours of Hanoi's streetside kitchens. Carry your hotel's calling card, and if you get lost, it'll be a cheap cab or *xe om* (motorbike taxi) ride back.

The Old Quarter evolved between the Song Hong and the smaller To Lich River, which once flowed through the city centre in an intricate network of canals and waterways. Waters could rise as high as 8m during the monsoon. Dykes, which can still be seen along Tran Quang Khai, were constructed to protect the city. In the 13th century, Hanoi's 36 guilds established themselves here, each taking a different street – hence the Vietnamese '36 Pho Phuong' (36 Guild Sts). There are more than double that many streets in the area today, typically named Pho Hang (Merchandise St) followed by the word for the product traditionally sold there. Some of the specialised streets include **P Hang Quat**, with its red candlesticks, funeral boxes, flags and temple items; and the more glamorous **P Hang Gai**, with its silk, embroidery, lacquerware, paintings and water puppets. Street names today do not always reflect the type of businesses in operation.

Exploring the maze of backstreets is fascinating: some open up while others narrow into a warren of alleys. The area is known for its tunnel (or tube) houses, so called because of their narrow frontages and long rooms, developed to avoid taxes based on the width of their street frontage. By feudal law, houses were also limited to two storeys and, out of respect for the king, could not be taller than the royal palace. Today, as Old Quarter real estate prices are at a premium, most of the streets are lined with narrow, hastily constructed, six- to 10-storey buildings.

A stroll through the historic Old Quarter can last from an hour to a day, depending on your pace and demeanour, during which opportunities to dispense your fistfuls of Vietnamese dong are endless.

★Bach Ma Temple BUDDHIST TEMPLE

(Den Bach Ma; Map p58; cnr P Hang Buom & P Hang Giay; ⌚8-11am & 2-5pm Tue-Sun) FREE In the heart of the Old Quarter, the small Bach Ma Temple is said to be the oldest temple in the city, though much of the current structure dates from the 18th century and a shrine to Confucius was added in 1839. It was originally built by Emperor Ly Thai To in the 11th century to honour a white horse that guided him to this site, where he chose to construct his city walls.

Pass through the wonderful old wooden doors of the pagoda to see a statue of the legendary white horse, as well as a beautiful red-lacquered funeral palanquin.

Old Quarter

Top Sights
1 Bach Ma Temple ... D2

Sights
2 Dong Xuan Market ... C1
3 Memorial House ... E3

Activities, Courses & Tours
4 Blue Butterfly Cooking Class ... D2
5 Buffalo Tours ... E3
6 Handspan Adventure Travel ... E3
7 Vietnam Awesome Travel ... E4

Sleeping
8 Art Hotel ... A5
9 Art Trendy Hotel ... B3
10 Camel City Hotel ... E2
11 Classic Street Hotel ... E4
12 Hanoi Elite ... E3
13 Hanoi Guesthouse ... E3
14 Hanoi Hostel ... A2
15 Hanoi Rendezvous Hotel ... A4
16 La Beaute de Hanoi ... E4
17 La Siesta Hotel & Spa ... E3
18 May De Ville Backpackers ... D3
19 Nova Hotel ... A5
20 Tirant Hotel ... E4

Eating
21 Banh Cuon ... A2
22 Bun Bo Nam Bo ... A5
23 Bun Cha Nem Cua Be Dac Kim ... A5
24 Cha Ca Thang Long ... A4
25 Che ... A5
26 Green Mango ... C4
27 Green Tangerine ... E4
28 Highway 4 ... F4
Mien Xao Luon ... (see 19)
29 New Day ... E3
30 Quan Bia Minh ... D4
31 Xoi Yen ... F4

Drinking & Nightlife
32 Bia Hoi Ha Noi ... A4
33 Cafe Lam ... F4
34 Cafe Pho Co ... D5
35 Dragonfly ... D2
36 Funky Buddha ... D2
37 Le Pub ... E4
38 Moose & Roo ... E3
39 Nola ... E3
40 The Doors ... E3

Entertainment
41 Thang Long Ca Tru Theatre ... D2
42 Vietnam National Tuong Theatre ... A5

Shopping
Dong Xuan Market ... (see 2)
43 Hang Da Market ... A5
44 Hanoi Moment ... C5
45 Mekong+ ... E4
46 Metiseko ... C5
47 Night Market ... C3
48 Tan My Design ... C5

Information
49 Cuong's Motorbike Adventure ... D4
50 Ethnic Travel ... D3
51 Handspan Adventure Travel ... E3
52 Mr Linh's Adventure Tours ... E3
53 Vega Travel ... E3

Transport
54 Electric Bus Tour Departure Point ... C1
55 Offroad Vietnam ... F3

Memorial House HISTORIC BUILDING
(Ngoi Nha; Map p58; 87 P Ma May; admission 5000d; ⏲9am-noon & 1-5pm) One of the Old Quarter's best-restored properties, this traditional merchants' house is sparsely but beautifully decorated, with rooms set around two courtyards and filled with fine furniture. Note the high steps between rooms, a traditional design incorporated to stop the flow of bad energy around the property.

There are crafts for sale here, including silver jewellery, basketwork and Vietnamese tea sets, and there's usually a calligrapher or other craftsperson at work too.

Dong Xuan Market MARKET
(Cho Dong Xuan; Map p58; cnr P Hang Khoai & P Dong Xuan; ⏲7am-9pm) The largest covered market in Hanoi was originally built by the French in 1889 and almost completely destroyed by fire in 1994. Almost everything you can think of from fresh produce to clothing, souvenirs, consumer goods and traditional arts and crafts can be found inside.

Hanoi Ceramic Road SCULPTURE
(Con Duong Gom Su; Map p70) Spanning almost 4km along the Song Hong dyke, from its terminus at the Long Bien Bridge, this ceramic mosaic mural project was commenced in 2007 and completed in 2010 for Hanoi's 1000th-birthday celebrations. Made from ceramics produced at nearby Bat Trang, the colourful mural depicts different periods in Vietnam's history and is the combined work of many local and international artists. It retains its Guinness World Record for being the largest ceramic mosaic on the planet.

Long Bien Bridge BRIDGE

(Cau Long Bien; Map p70) A symbol of the tenacity and resilience of the Hanoian people, the Long Bien Bridge (built between 1899 and 1902) was bombed on several occasions during the American War, and on each, quickly repaired by the Vietnamese. Designed by Gustave Eiffel (of Eiffel Tower fame) the bridge, used by trains, mopeds and pedestrians, is undergoing reconstruction to restore its original appearance. It's colourfully illuminated at night.

Around Hoan Kiem Lake

★Hoan Kiem Lake LAKE

(Map p62) Legend claims in the mid-15th century Heaven sent Emperor Ly Thai To a magical sword, which he used to drive the Chinese from Vietnam. After the war a giant golden turtle grabbed the sword and disappeared into the depths of this lake to restore the sword to its divine owners, inspiring the name Ho Hoan Kiem (Lake of the Restored Sword). Every morning at 6am local residents practise traditional t'ai chi on the shore.

The ramshackle **Thap Rua** (Turtle Tower; Map p62), on an islet near the southern end, is topped with a red star and is often used as an emblem of Hanoi.

★National Museum of Vietnamese History MUSEUM

(Bao Tang Lich Su Quoc Gia; Map p62; ☎04-3824 2433; http://baotanglichsu.vn; 1 P Trang Tien; adult/student 40,000/15,000d; ⊙8am-noon & 1.30-5pm, closed 1st Mon of the month) Built between 1925 and 1932, this architecturally impressive museum was formerly home to the École Française d'Extrême Orient. Its architect, Ernest Hebrard, was among the first in Vietnam to incorporate a blend of Chinese and French design elements. Exhibit highlights include bronzes from the Dong Son culture (3rd century BC to 3rd century AD), Hindu statuary from the Khmer and Champa kingdoms, jewellery from imperial Vietnam, and displays relating to the French occupation and the Communist Party.

★Hoa Lo Prison Museum HISTORIC BUILDING

(Map p62; ☎04-3824 6358; cnr P Hoa Lo & P Hai Ba Trung; admission 30,000d; ⊙8am-5pm) This thought-provoking site is all that remains of the former Hoa Lo Prison, ironically nicknamed the 'Hanoi Hilton' by US POWs during the American War. Most exhibits relate to the prison's use up to the mid-1950s, focusing on the Vietnamese struggle for independence from France. A gruesome relic is the ominous French guillotine, used to behead Vietnamese revolutionaries. There are also displays focusing on the American pilots who were incarcerated at Hoa Lo during the American War.

These pilots include Pete Peterson (the first US ambassador to a unified Vietnam in 1995), and Senator John McCain (the Republican nominee for the US presidency in 2008). McCain's flight suit is displayed,

HANOI FOR CHILDREN

Hanoi is a fun and eye-opening city for most kids, but language barriers, the organised chaos of the Old Quarter and the raw, earthy nature of Hanoi's street food can pose some challenges; however, the friendliness of the Vietnamese people generally helps to diffuse any stresses you might encounter. There's no shortage of things to keep youngsters engaged as you wander around the Old Quarter, with plenty of ice-cream vendors and fruit markets for treats along the way. Most kids love the chance to get hands-on at the special Kids' Club sessions at the Hanoi Cooking Centre (p71), and a tour with the gang at Hanoi Kids (p72) is a great cross-cultural opportunity.

Boating is a fun family activity; you have the choice of bigger boats on Ho Tay (p69) or pedal-powered boats in Thong Nhat Park. Ho Tay Water Park (p71), open April to November, and Royal City (p71), open year-round, have plenty of fun activities for the youngsters, and a trip to the Lotte Tower Observation Deck (p69) should also be on the menu. Come evening, it's essential to catch a water-puppet show at the Municipal Water Puppet Theatre (p87) – a *Punch and Judy* pantomime on water.

If you're in town for a few days and travelling as a family, you can't go past the Somerset Grand Hanoi (p77) apartments for price, location and value.

Around Hoan Kiem Lake

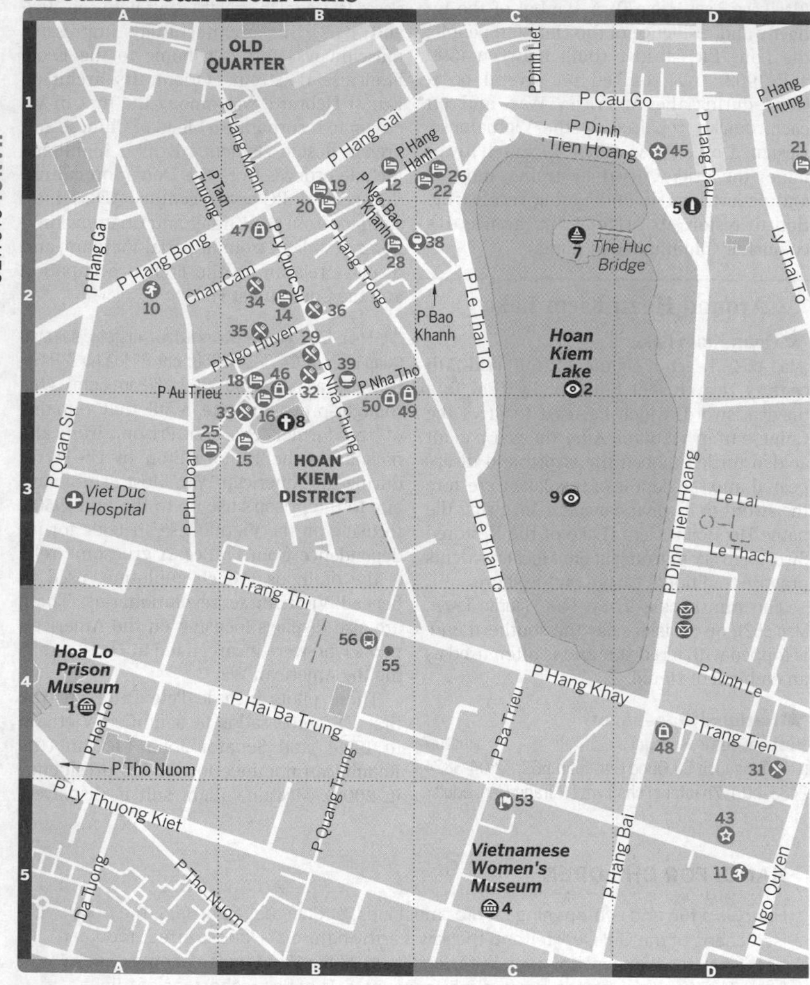

along with a photograph of Hanoi locals rescuing him from Truc Bach Lake after being shot down in 1967.

The prison complex was built by the French in 1896. Originally intended to house 450 inmates, records indicate that by the 1930s there were close to 2000 prisoners. Hoa Lo was never a very successful prison, and hundreds escaped its walls over the years.

Museum of Vietnamese Revolution MUSEUM

(Bao Tang Cach Mang Viet Nam; Map p62; ☎04-3825 4151; 216 Đ Tran Quang Khai; adult/student 20,000/10,000d; ⏲8am-noon & 1.30-5pm, closed first Mon of the month) Inaugurated in 1959 and housing over 40,000 exhibits, the histories of conflict and revolution within Vietnam, from the liberation movements against the French occupation, to the establishment of the Communist Party and the Socialist Republic of Vietnam, are enthusiastically presented here.

Ngoc Son Temple BUDDHIST TEMPLE

(Den Ngoc Son; Map p62; Hoan Kiem Lake; adult/student 20,000/10,000d; ⏲7.30am-5.30pm) Meaning 'Temple of the Jade Mountain',

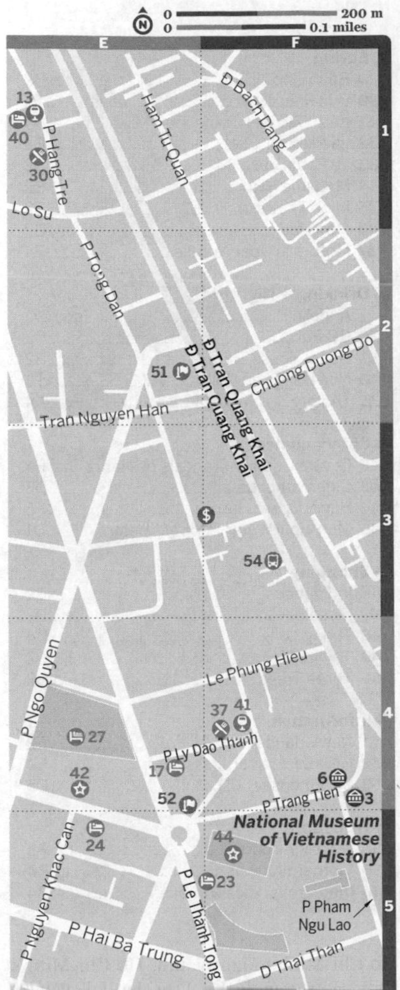

Hanoi's most visited temple sits on a small island in the northern part of Hoan Kiem Lake, connected to the lakeshore by an elegant scarlet bridge, constructed in classical Vietnamese style. The temple is dedicated to General Tran Hung Dao (who defeated the Mongols in the 13th century), La To (patron saint of physicians) and the scholar Van Xuong.

Martyrs' Monument MONUMENT

(Map p62) This photogenic monument, which depicts a woman with a sword and two men holding guns and a torch, was erected as a memorial to those who died fighting for Vietnam's independence.

★Vietnamese Women's Museum MUSEUM

(Map p62; ☎04-3825 9936; www.baotangphunu.org.vn; 36 P Ly Thuong Kiet; admission 30,000d; ⌚8am-5pm) This excellent museum showcases women's role in Vietnamese society and culture. Labelled in English and French, it's the memories of the wartime contribution by individual heroic women that are most poignant. There is a stunning collection of propaganda posters, as well as costumes, tribal basketware and fabric motifs from Vietnam's ethnic minority groups. Check the website for special exhibitions.

St Joseph Cathedral CHURCH

(Nha To Lon Ha Noi; Map p62; P Nha Tho; ⌚8am-noon & 2-6pm) Hanoi's neo-Gothic St Joseph Cathedral was inaugurated in 1886, and boasts a soaring facade that faces a little plaza. Its most noteworthy features are its twin bell towers, elaborate altar and fine stained-glass windows. Entrance via the main gate is only permitted during Mass: times are listed on a sign on the gates to the left of the cathedral.

At other times, enter via the Diocese of Hanoi compound, a block away at 40 P Nha Chung. When you reach the side door to the cathedral, to your right, ring the small bell high up on the right-hand side of the door.

West of the Old Quarter

★Temple of Literature CONFUCIAN TEMPLE

(Van Mieu Quoc Tu Giam; Map p66; ☎04-3845 2917; P Quoc Tu Giam; adult/student 30,000/15,000d; ⌚8am-5pm) Founded in 1070 by Emperor Ly Thanh Tong, the Temple of Literature is dedicated to Confucius (Khong Tu). Inside you'll find a pond known as the 'Well of Heavenly Clarity', a low-slung pagoda and statues of Confucius and his disciples. A rare example of well-preserved traditional Vietnamese architecture, the complex honours Vietnam's finest scholars and those of literary accomplishment. It is the site of Vietnam's first university, established here in 1076, when entrance was only granted to those of noble birth.

After 1442 a more egalitarian approach was adopted and gifted students from all over the nation headed to Hanoi to study the principles of Confucianism, literature and poetry. In 1484 Emperor Ly Thanh Tong ordered that stelae be erected to record the

Around Hoan Kiem Lake

Top Sights

1 Hoa Lo Prison Museum A4
2 Hoan Kiem Lake C2
3 National Museum of Vietnamese History F4
4 Vietnamese Women's Museum C5

Sights

Hanoi Opera House .... (see 44)
5 Martyrs' Monument D2
6 Museum of Vietnamese Revolution F4
7 Ngoc Son Temple C2
8 St Joseph Cathedral B3
9 Thap Rua C3

Activities, Courses & Tours

10 Annam Foot Spa & Massage A2
11 Hash House Harriers D5

Sleeping

12 Artisan Boutique Hotel B1
13 B&B Hanoi Hostel E1
14 Central Backpackers Hanoi B2
15 Cinnamon Hotel B3
16 Cinnamon Hotel Cathedral B3
17 Conifer Boutique Hotel E4
18 Especen Hotel B2
19 Golden Lotus Hotel B1
20 Golden Lotus Luxury Hotel B2
21 Hanoi Elegance Diamond Hotel D1
22 Heart Hotel C1
23 Hilton Hanoi Opera F5
24 Hotel de l'Opera E5
25 Impressive Hotel A3
Joseph's Hotel .... (see 15)
26 Madame Moon Guesthouse C1
27 Sofitel Metropole Hotel E4
28 The Palmy Hotel & Spa B2

Eating

29 Banh Ghoi B2
30 Bun Rieu Cua E1
31 Kem Dac Diet Trang Tien D4
32 La Place B2
33 Le Petit Bruxelles B3
34 Madame Hien B2
35 Minh Thuy's B2
36 Mon Hue B2
37 Moto-san Uber Noodle F4

Drinking & Nightlife

Angelina .... (see 27)
38 GC Pub C2
39 Hanoi House B2
40 Nha Hang Lan Chin E1
41 Tadioto F4

Entertainment

42 Centre Culturel Français de Hanoi E4
43 Cinematheque D5
44 Hanoi Opera House F5
45 Municipal Water Puppet Theatre D1

Shopping

46 Indigenous B2
47 Mosaique B2
48 Thang Long D4
49 Things of Substance B2
50 Three Trees B3

Information

51 Netherlands Embassy E2
52 New Zealand Embassy E4
53 UK Embassy C5

Transport

54 Jetstar Airport Bus F3
55 Vietnam Airlines B4
56 Vietnam Airlines Minibus B4

names, places of birth and achievements of exceptional scholars: 82 of 116 stelae remain standing. Paths lead from the imposing tiered gateway on P Quoc Tu Giam through formal gardens to the Khue Van pavilion, constructed in 1802.

★ Ho Chi Minh Mausoleum Complex — HISTORIC SITE

(Map p66; ☎04-3845 5128; www.bqllang.gov.vn; entrance cnr P Ngoc Ha & P Doi Can) The Ho Chi Minh Mausoleum Complex is an important place of pilgrimage for many Vietnamese. A traffic-free area of **botanical gardens**, monuments, memorials and pagodas, it's usually crowded with groups of Vietnamese who come from far and wide to pay their respects to 'Uncle Ho'. Within the complex are Ho Chi Minh's Mausoleum, Ho Chi Minh's Stilt House and the Presidential Palace, Ho Chi Minh Museum and the One Pillar Pagoda.

➡ Ho Chi Minh's Mausoleum

(Lang Chu Tich Ho Chi Minh; Map p66; ☎04-3845 5128; www.bqllang.gov.vn; ⊙8-11am Tue-Thu, Sat & Sun Dec-Sep, last entry 10.15am, closed 4 Sep-4 Nov) **FREE** In the tradition of Lenin, Stalin and Mao, Ho Chi Minh's Mausoleum is a monumental marble edifice. Contrary to his desire for a simple cremation, the mausoleum was constructed from materials gathered from all over Vietnam between 1973 and 1975. Set deep in the building in a glass sarcophagus is the frail, pale body of Ho Chi Minh. The mausoleum is usually closed from 4 Sep to 4 Nov while his embalmed body goes to Russia for maintenance.

Dress modestly: wearing shorts, tank tops or hats is not permitted. You may be requested to store day packs, cameras and phones before you enter. Talking, putting your hand in your pockets and photography are strictly prohibited in the mausoleum. The queue snakes for several hundred metres to the mausoleum entrance and inside, filing past Ho's body at a slow but steady pace. If you're lucky, you'll catch the changing of the guard outside Ho's mausoleum – the ceremony displayed here rivals the British equivalent at Buckingham Palace.

➡ Ho Chi Minh's Stilt House

(Nha San Bac Ho & Phu Chu Tich Tai; Map p66; admission 25,000d; ⏲8-11.30am daily & 2-4pm Tue-Thu, Sat & Sun) This humble, traditional stilt house where Ho lived intermittently from 1958 to 1969 is set in a well-tended garden adjacent a carp-filled pond and has been preserved just as Ho left it. From here, you look out on to Hanoi's most opulent building, the beautiful, beaux-arts **Presidential Palace** (Map p66), constructed in 1906 for the Governor General of Indochina. It's now used for official receptions and isn't open to the public. Visitors may wander the grounds if you stick to the paths.

There is a combined entrance gate to the stilt house and Presidential Palace grounds located on P Ong Ich Kiem inside the Ho Chi Minh Mausoleum Complex. When the main entrance is closed, enter from Đ Hung Vuong.

➡ Ho Chi Minh Museum

(Bao Tang Ho Chi Minh; Map p66; ☎04-3845 5435; www.baotanghochiminh.vn; admission 25,000d; ⏲8-11.30am daily & 2-4pm Tue-Thu, Sat & Sun) The huge concrete Soviet-style Ho Chi Minh Museum is a triumphalist monument dedicated to the life of the founder of modern Vietnam and to the onward march of revolutionary socialism. Mementoes of Ho's life are showcased, and there are some fascinating photos and dusty official documents relating to the overthrow of the French and the rise of communism. Photography is forbidden and you may be asked to check your bag at reception. An English-speaking guide costs around 100,000d, and given the quite surreal nature of the exhibition it's a worthwhile investment.

➡ One Pillar Pagoda

(Chua Mot Cot; Map p66; P Ong Ich Kiem; admission 25,000d; ⏲8-11.30am daily & 2-4pm Tue-Thu, Sat & Sun) The One Pillar Pagoda was originally built by the Emperor Ly Thai Tong who ruled from 1028 to 1054. According to the annals, the heirless emperor dreamed that he met Quan The Am Bo Tat, the Goddess of Mercy, who handed him a male child. Ly Thai Tong then married a young peasant girl and had a son and heir by her. As a way of expressing his gratitude for this event, he constructed a pagoda here in 1049.

ART IN HANOI

Modern Vietnamese artists are highly technically trained – many could copy a photographic portrait by hand with remarkable detail and accuracy, in a short space of time. Prior to the Communist Party takeover, Vietnam had over 900 years of artistic heritage, which to this day provides many young Vietnamese with an exceptional creative skill set. That said, the Communist Party still curbs freedom of expression, forcing some artists and artisans to work underground. However, with an influx of tourism and interest from the West in recent years, Hanoi's art scene in particular is gaining attention from the outside world. Ever so slowly, talented Vietnamese artists are getting the chance to expand their horizons and broaden their skills.

For visitors interested in art, this means a burgeoning art scene begging for appreciation. Keen shoppers can pick up an original work on canvas by a local artist from as little as US$40 in any one of the Old Quarter's many private galleries – Mai Gallery (p89) is a good start. Kick back and check out the vibe at Tadioto (p85), Manzi Art Space (p85), Bar Betta (p85), or all three: you'll lock in with like-minded arty folk in no time at all. For the low-down on the scene, visit the informative local art blog, www.andofotherthings.com. Better still, take one of Sophie's Art Tours (p72), which began operations in Hanoi in 2015, after enjoying great success in Ho Chi Minh City.

West of the Old Quarter

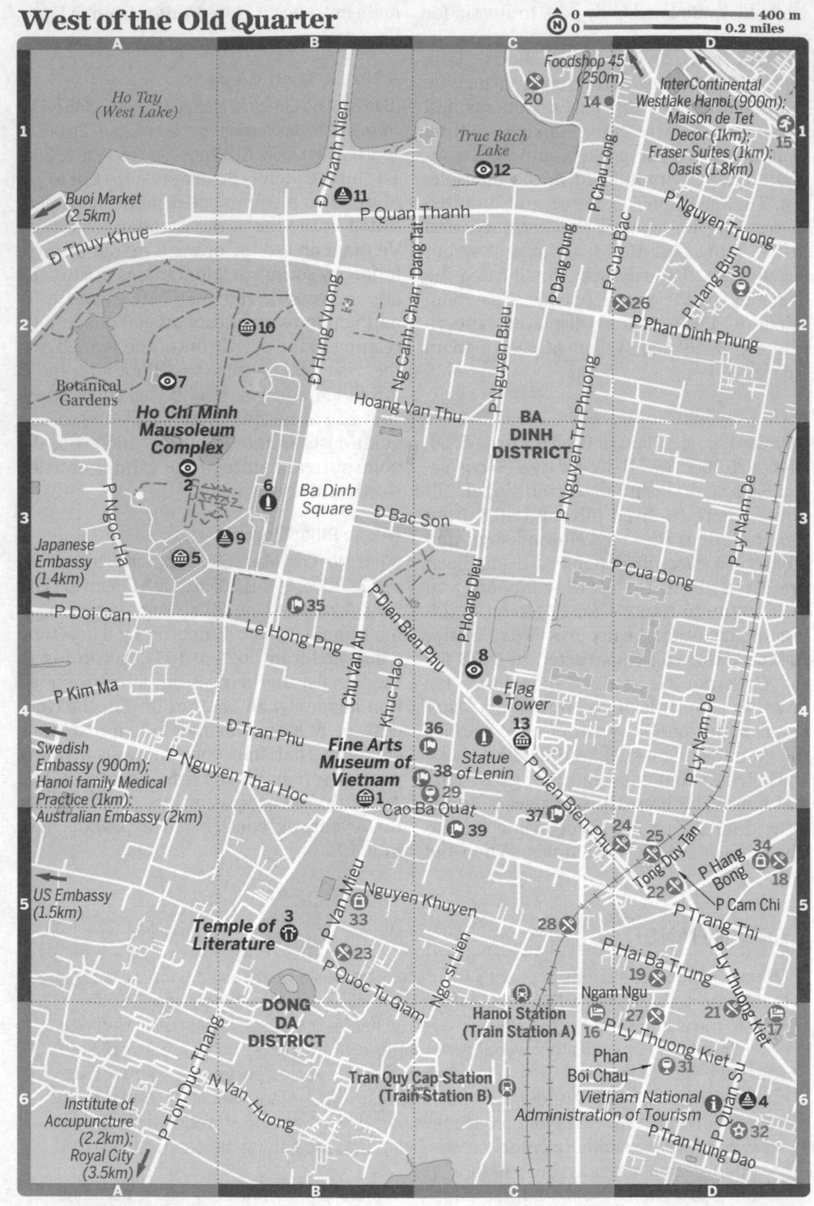

Built of wood on a single stone pillar, the pagoda is designed to resemble a lotus blossom, the symbol of purity, rising out of a sea of sorrow. One of the last acts of the French before quitting Hanoi in 1954 was to destroy the original One Pillar Pagoda; the structure was rebuilt by the new government.

Vietnam Military History Museum MUSEUM
(Bao Tang Lich Su Quan Su Viet Nam; Map p66; ☎04-733 6453; www.btlsqsvn.org.vn; 28a P Dien

West of the Old Quarter

Top Sights
1 Fine Arts Museum of Vietnam B4
2 Ho Chi Minh Mausoleum Complex....... A3
3 Temple of Literature............................. B5

Sights
4 Ambassadors' Pagoda......................... D6
5 Ho Chi Minh Museum........................... A3
6 Ho Chi Minh's Mausoleum.................... B3
7 Ho Chi Minh's Stilt House..................... A2
8 Imperial Citadel of Thang Long C4
9 One Pillar Pagoda B3
10 Presidential Palace.............................. B2
11 Quan Thanh Temple...............................B1
12 Truc Bach Lake C1
13 Vietnam Military History Museum C4

Activities, Courses & Tours
14 Hanoi Cooking Centre............................C1
Hanoi Language Tours.................(see 33)
15 Huong Sen D1

Sleeping
16 Mercure La Gare C6
17 Somerset Grand Hanoi D6

Eating
18 Hanoi Social Club................................. D5
19 La Badiane D5
20 Mau Dich 37 .... C1
21 Namaste D6
22 Net Hue..D5
23 Nha Hang Koto Van Mieu B5
24 Old Hanoi...D5
25 Puku D5
26 Quan An Ngon...D2
27 Quan An Ngon...D6
28 Ray Quan C5

Drinking & Nightlife
29 Bar Betta C4
30 Manzi Art Space D2
31 Rooftop Bar...D6

Entertainment
32 Jazz Club By Quyen Van Minh...............D6

Shopping
Bookworm ....(see 14)
33 Craft Link...B5
34 Mai Gallery..D5

Information
35 Canadian Embassy B3
36 Chinese Embassy....................................C4
37 German Embassy....................................C5
38 Singaporean Embassy............................C4
39 Thai Embassy...C5

Bien Phu; admission 30,000d, camera fee 20,000d; ⌚8-11.30am daily & 2-4pm Tue-Thu, Sat & Sun) Easy to spot thanks to a large collection of weaponry at the front, the Military Museum displays Soviet and Chinese equipment alongside French- and US-made weapons captured during years of warfare. The centrepiece is a Soviet-built MiG-21 jet fighter, triumphant amid the wreckage of French aircraft downed at Dien Bien Phu, and a US F-111.

Adjacent is the hexagonal **Flag Tower**, one of the symbols of Hanoi. Access is possible to a terrace overlooking a rusting collection of war *matériel* (equipment and supplies used by soldiers). Opposite the museum is a small park with a commanding **statue of Lenin**.

★Fine Arts Museum of Vietnam — MUSEUM

(Bao Tang My Thuat Viet Nam; Map p66; ☎04-3733 2131; www.vnfam.vn; 66 P Nguyen Thai Hoc; adult/concession 30,000/15,000d; ⌚8.30am-5pm) This excellent Fine Arts Museum is housed in two buildings that were once the French Ministry of Information. Treasures abound, including ancient Champa stone carvings and some astonishing effigies of Guan Yin, the thousand-eyed, thousand-armed goddess of compassion. Look out for the lacquered statues of Buddhist monks from the Tay Son dynasty and the substantial collection of contemporary art and folk-naive paintings. Guided tours are available for 150,000d.

Imperial Citadel of Thang Long — HISTORIC SITE

(Hoang Thanh Thang Long; Map p66; www.hoangthanhthanglong.vn; 19c P Hoang Dieu; admission 30,000d; ⌚8-11.30am daily & 2-4pm Tue-Thu, Sat & Sun) Added to Unesco's World Heritage List in 2010 and reopened in 2012, Hanoi's Imperial Citadel was the hub of Vietnamese military power for over 1000 years. Ongoing archaeological digs of ancient palaces, grandiose pavilions and imperial gates are complemented by fascinating military command bunkers from the American War – complete with maps and 1960s communications equipment – used by the legendary Vietnamese General Vo Nguyen Giap.

The leafy grounds are also an easygoing and quiet antidote to Hanoi's bustle.

French Quarter

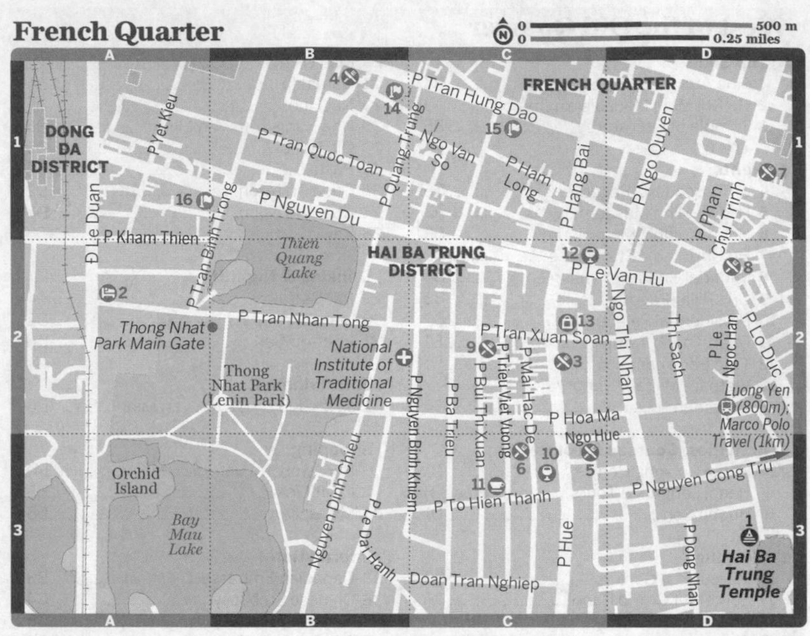

French Quarter

Top Sights
1 Hai Ba Trung Temple D3

Sleeping
2 Hotel Nikko Hanoi A2

Eating
3 Banh My Pho Hue C2
4 Chay Nang Tam B1
5 Chim Sao C3
6 Izakaya Yancha C3
7 Nha Hang Ngon D1
8 Pho Thin D2
9 Pots 'n Pans C2

Drinking & Nightlife
10 Cama ATK C3
11 Cong Caphe C3
12 Quan Ly C2

Shopping
13 Hom Market C2

Information
14 Cambodian Embassy B1
15 French Embassy C1
16 Laotian Embassy A1

Ambassadors' Pagoda BUDDHIST TEMPLE
(Chua Quan Su; Map p66; ☎04-3825 2427; 73 P Quan Su) FREE The official centre of Buddhism in Hanoi, the well maintained and otherwise peaceful Ambassadors' Pagoda attracts quite a crowd on holidays. During the 17th century there was a guesthouse here for the ambassadors of Buddhist countries; today about a dozen monks and nuns are based here. Located next to the pagoda is a shop that sells Buddhist ritual objects.

Quan Thanh Temple BUDDHIST TEMPLE
(Map p66; P Quan Thanh; admission 10,000d) Shaded by huge trees, Quan Thanh Temple was established during the Ly dynasty (1010–1225) and was dedicated to Tran Vo (God of the North), whose symbols of power were the tortoise and the snake. A bronze statue and bell date from 1677. The temple is situated on the shores of Truc Bach Lake, which is near the intersection of Đ Thanh Nien and P Quan Thanh.

French Quarter

Despite its evocative moniker, today's French Quarter lacks the style and elegance of days past. Its once-glamorous villas, annexed by the Communist Party for government offices and repatriation housing, stand in disrepute, desperate for restoration. Many, occupying some of Hanoi's prime development sites, have already been demolished in favour of taller, shinier things. Those that have been best maintained serve as the offices for Hanoi's foreign embassies and diplomatic outposts. In a way, there's some sense of a cycle completing itself here: in creating a Parisian-style city befitting their new area of governance, the French Colonialists appropriated and razed whatever traditional Vietnamese dwellings and monuments stood in their way.

Occupying an area south of Hoan Kiem Lake, west of the Song Hong as far as Hanoi train station (depending on who you talk to) and south of Thong Nhat Park (Lenin Park), it's well worth a visit to this quieter part of town for a stroll among the embassies and crumbling villas, contemplating what once was and what once could have been.

★Hai Ba Trung Temple BUDDHIST TEMPLE

(Map p68; P Tho Lao) Two kilometres south of Hoan Kiem Lake, this temple was founded in 1142. A statue shows the two Trung sisters (from the 1st century AD) kneeling with their arms raised in the air. Some say the statue shows the sisters, who had been proclaimed the queens of the Vietnamese, about to dive into a river. They are said to have drowned themselves rather than surrender in the wake of their defeat at the hands of the Chinese.

Hanoi Opera House HISTORIC BUILDING

(Map p62; ☎04-3993 0113; http://hanoiopera house.org.vn; 1 P Trang Tien) This French-colonial 900-seat venue was built in 1911. On 16 August 1945 the Viet Minh–run Citizens' Committee announced that it had taken over the city from a balcony on this building.

Greater Hanoi

★Vietnam Museum of Ethnology MUSEUM

(☎04-3756 2193; www.vme.org.vn; Đ Nguyen Van Huyen; adult/concession 40,000/15,000d, guide 100,000d; ⏲8.30am-5.30pm Tue-Sun) This fabulous collection relating to Vietnam's ethnic minorities features well-presented tribal art, artefacts and everyday objects gathered from across the nation, and examples of traditional village houses. Displays are well labelled in Vietnamese, French and English. If you're into anthropology, it's well worth the approximately 200,000d each-way taxi fares to the Cau Giay district, about 7km from the city centre, where the museum is located.

Local bus 14 (4000d) departs from P Dinh Tien Hoang on the east side of Hoan Kiem Lake and passes within 600m of the museum – get off at the Nghia Tan bus stop and head to Đ Nguyen Van Huyen.

Ho Tay LAKE

(West Lake; Map p70) The city's largest lake, known as both Ho Tay and West Lake, is 15km in circumference and ringed by upmarket suburbs, including the predominantly expat Tay Ho district. On the south side, along Đ Thuy Khue, are seafood restaurants, and to the east, the Xuan Dieu strip is lined with restaurants, cafes, boutiques and luxury hotels. A pathway circles the lake, making for a great bicycle ride.

Tay Ho Pagoda BUDDHIST TEMPLE

(Phu Tay Ho; Map p70; Đ Thai Mai) Jutting into Ho Tay, beautiful Tay Ho Pagoda is perhaps the most popular place of worship in Hanoi. Throngs of people come here on the first and 15th day of each lunar month in the hope of receiving good fortune from the Mother Goddess, to whom the temple is dedicated.

Tran Quoc Pagoda BUDDHIST TEMPLE

(Chua Tran Quoc; Map p70; P Thanh Nien) One of the oldest pagodas in Vietnam, Tran Quoc Pagoda is on the eastern shore of Ho Tay, just off Đ Thanh Nien, which divides this lake from Truc Bach Lake. A stela here, dating from 1639, tells the history of this site. The pagoda was rebuilt in the 15th century and again in 1842.

Truc Bach Lake LAKE

(Ho Truc Bach; Map p66) Separated from Ho Tay only by Đ Thanh Nien, this lake is lined with flame trees. During the 18th century the Trinh lords built a palace on the lakeside; it was later transformed into a reformatory for wayward royal concubines, who were condemned to spend their days weaving pure white silk.

Greater Hanoi

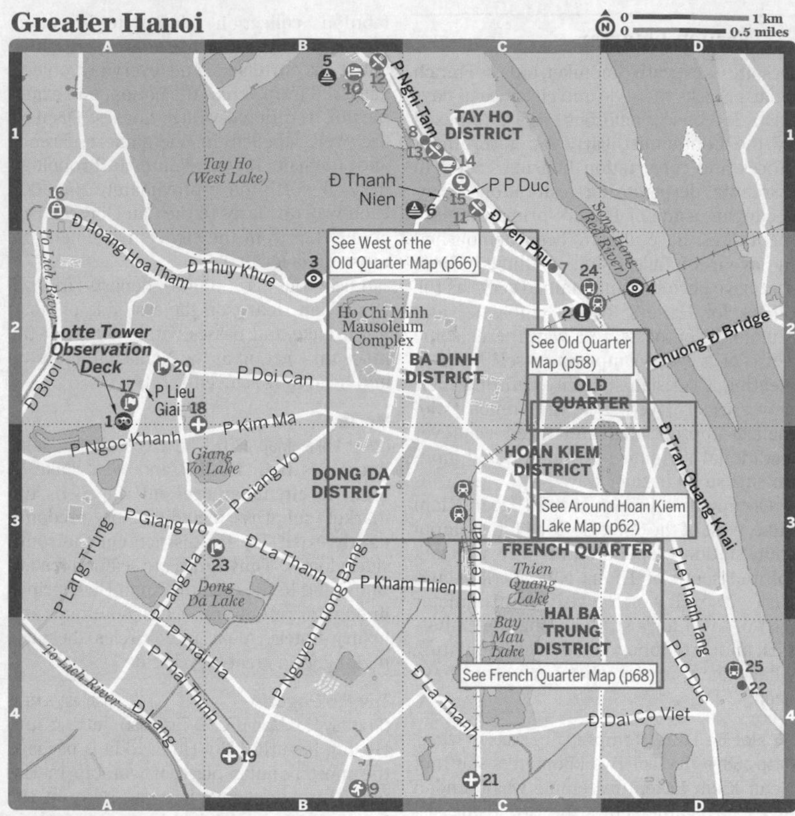

Greater Hanoi

Top Sights
1 Lotte Tower Observation Deck A2

Sights
2 Hanoi Ceramic Road C2
3 Ho Tay B2
4 Long Bien Bridge D2
5 Tay Ho Pagoda B1
6 Tran Quoc Pagoda C1

Activities, Courses & Tours
7 Free Wheelin' Tours C2
8 Hidden Hanoi C1
9 NGO Resource Centre B4
Yakushi Center .... (see 12)

Sleeping
10 InterContinental Westlake Hanoi B1
Lotte Hotel .... (see 1)

Eating
11 Foodshop 45 .... C1
12 Oasis B1
13 Quan Kien C1
Tim Ho Wan .... (see 1)

Drinking & Nightlife
14 Café Duy Tri C1
15 Summit Lounge C1

Shopping
16 Buoi Market A1

Information
17 Australian Embassy A2
18 Hanoi Family Medical Practice A2
19 Institute of Acupuncture B4
20 Japanese Embassy A2
21 L'Hopital Français de Hanoi C4
22 Marco Polo Travel D4
23 US Embassy B3

Transport
24 Long Bien Bus Station C2
25 Luong Yen Bus Station D4

★ Lotte Tower Observation Deck

VIEWPOINT

(Map p70; ☎04-3333 6016; www.lottecenter.com.vn/eng/observation/visit_information.asp; 54 Lieu Giai, Ba Dinh; adult/concession day 230,000/170,000d, night 130,000/110,000d; ⏲9am-10pm) The city's best views can be found on the 65th floor of the landmark Lotte building, opened in 2014, in the western corner of Hanoi's Ba Dinh district. From this uninterrupted vantage point, high above Hanoi's hustle and bustle, one can consider the size of the Old Quarter relative to the sheer scale of Hanoi's voracious growth. The tower also houses a hotel, all manner of restaurants, a rooftop bar and a department store on its lower floors. Lotte Tower is around 20 minutes by taxi to the Old Quarter.

Activities

Sports & Swimming

Hash House Harriers

RUNNING

(Map p62; www.hanoih3.com; ⏲from 1.30pm Sat) For the uninitiated, these are drinkers with a running problem. Check the website for details.

Ho Tay Water Park

SWIMMING

(Cong Vien Ho Tay; ☎04-3718 4222; www.congvienhotay.vn; under 130cm/over 130cm 80,000/150,000d; ⏲9am-9pm Wed-Mon Apr-Nov) If you're desperate for a swim, this water park 5km north of the Old Quarter on the northern edge of Ho Tay has pools, slides and a lazy river. It gets extremely busy here on hot summer afternoons and might not satisfy everyone's standards for safety and hygiene.

Royal City

SWIMMING, SKATING

(☎04-3974 3550; http://royalcity.com.vn; 72a P Nguyen Trai, Thanh Xuan; water park & skating, under 130cm/over 130cm 100,000/170,000d; ⏲11am-9pm) Opened in 2013 as part of the Royal City Mega Mall complex (Vietnam's largest shopping and entertainment complex), the Vinpearl Water Park and Vinpearl Ice Rink are among a bunch of attractions appealing to travelling families. There's also a bowling alley, cinema complex, games area and, of course, shopping for Mum and Dad. Royal City is situated about 7km southwest of the Old Quarter.

FANCY A MASSAGE?

You might be overwhelmed by the countless promises of mind-blowing massages as you wander the streets of the Old Quarter. For something a little different and likely to please even the most discerning of clients, try our top picks for Hanoi's best massage places.

Omamori Spa (☎04-3773 9919; www.blindlink.org.vn/spa; 102 B1, Alley 5, P Huỳnh Thúc Kháng, Dong Da; massage 60min from 170,000d) You'll need a taxi to get to this wonderful little spa, operated by a not-for-profit that provides training and employment opportunities for the blind. Masseuses here are vision impaired and speak excellent English. If you haven't received a massage by a trained blind therapist before, it's quite an experience: there's a level of gentleness and body awareness that differs from traditional practitioners. Tips are not accepted, and the pricing and quality of services is excellent.

Yakushi Center (Map p70; ☎04-3719 1971; http://sites.google.com/site/yakushicenter/; 20 P Xuan Dieu, Quang An, Tay Ho; treatments from 210,000d; ⏲9am-7.30pm) In the fashionable expat-centric suburb of Tay Ho, you'll find this fabulous clinic that specialises in a range of Traditional Vietnamese and Chinese Medicine practices, as well as therapeutic and relaxing massages. Bookings are essential: your English-speaking practitioner will conduct a brief consultation with you prior to commencing your treatment.

Huong Sen (Map p66; ☎04-3825 4911; www.huongsenhealthcare.com; 78 Đ Yen Phu; massage from 250,000d; ⏲9.30am-10.30pm) A wide range of beauty treatments and services, including jacuzzi and steam baths, are available at this professional outfit with good facilities and English-speaking staff. A full menu is available on the website.

Annam Foot Spa & Massage (Map p62; ☎091-321 1558; 71 P Hang Bong; massage from 250,000d; ⏲10am-10pm) In the heart of the Old Quarter, this multilevel establishment is well priced and easy to find.

Courses

Hanoi Cooking Centre COOKING
(Map p66; ☎04-3715 0088; www.hanoicooking centre.com; 44 P Chau Long; per class from 1,330,000d) Excellent interactive classes, including market visits and a special Kids' Club – handy if your children are aspiring chefs. The Hanoi Cooking Centre also runs a highly recommended walking tour exploring Hanoi's street-food scene, and cookery classes conclude with a shared lunch in its elegant restaurant.

Hidden Hanoi COOKING, LANGUAGE
(Map p70; ☎0912 254 045; www.hiddenhanoi.com.vn; 147 P Nghi Tam, Tay Ho; per class with/without market tour US$55/45; ⊙11am-2pm Mon-Sat) Offers cooking classes from its kitchen near the eastern side of Ho Tay (West Lake). Options include seafood and village-food menus. Walking tours (per person US$20 to US$25) exploring the Old Quarter and Hanoi street food are available. Hidden Hanoi also offers a language-study program (per person from US$200), including two field trips.

Blue Butterfly Cooking Class COOKING
(Map p58; ☎04-3926 3845; http://bluebutterfly restaurant.com; 61 P Hang Buom; per class from 735,000d; ⊙daily from 9am) In this popular cooking class, you'll meet your chef/teacher in the restaurant kitchen and be accompanied on a shopping trip to Dong Xuan Market, before returning to the kitchen where you'll be instructed in the preparation and cooking of three dishes. Once the class is over, enjoy the fruits of your labour in the restaurant.

Hanoi Language Tours LANGUAGE
(Map p66; ☎04-3556 1146; www.hanoilan guagetours.com; 31 P Van Mieu, Dong Da; per person from US$150) Courses from two to 10 days focusing on language and cultural essentials for travellers, expats and businesspeople.

Tours

Hidden Hanoi and the Hanoi Cooking Centre also offer interesting tours with a food slant, visiting markets and street food stalls.

★**Hanoi Free Tour Guides** WALKING TOUR
(☎0974 596 895; http://hanoifreetourguides.com) There's no better way to experience the real Hanoi than with this not-for-profit social organisation run by a team of over 400 volunteer staff and guides comprising students and ex-students, speaking a multitude of languages. A variety of suggested tours are available, or work with your guide to tailor your own itinerary. Book online.

Bloom Microventures CULTURAL TOUR
(☎0164 387 6594; www.bloom-microventures.org/vietnam; tours adult/concession from US$75/60) Tours an ethnic minority village in Hoa Binh province, around 70km west of Hanoi. It's a good opportunity to see how micro-loans are funding rural entrepreneurs, and offers an excellent insight into Vietnamese rural life. Most tours run on a Saturday. Check the website for timings.

Vietnam Awesome Travel WALKING TOUR
(Map p58; ☎04-3990 1733; www.vietnam awesometravel.com; 19b P Hang Be; tours from US$15) A wide range of good-value walking tours, including the popular Food on Foot (US$25) street-food walking tours around the Old Quarter. An array of day trips and longer guided tours are also available. See the website for details.

Hanoi Kids WALKING TOUR
(☎0976 217 886; www.hanoikids.org; by donation) This volunteer organisation partners visitors with Hanoi teens and young adults wishing to improve their English-language skills. Tours are customised to the needs of visitors and can include Hanoi sights like the Temple of Literature and Hoa Lo Prison Museum, or street-food and market visits. It's best to arrange tours online a couple of weeks before you arrive in Hanoi.

Hanoi Street Food Tours WALKING TOUR
(☎0904 517 074; www.streetfoodtourshanoi.blog spot.com.au; tours from US$75) There's a local company running tours under the same name, but we continue to recommend this pricier, private option, run by Tu and Mark, a couple of passionate Hanoi foodies. Tours can be customised to different interests.

Sophie's Art Tour CULTURAL TOUR
(☎0168 796 2575; www.sophiesarttour.com; tours from US$55) These fascinating tours are based on the lives of artists who studied, fought, witnessed and documented major changes in 20th- and 21st-century Vietnam, and will be appreciated not only by art lovers, but those who want to gain a deeper understanding of the complexities of Vietnam's unique history and culture.

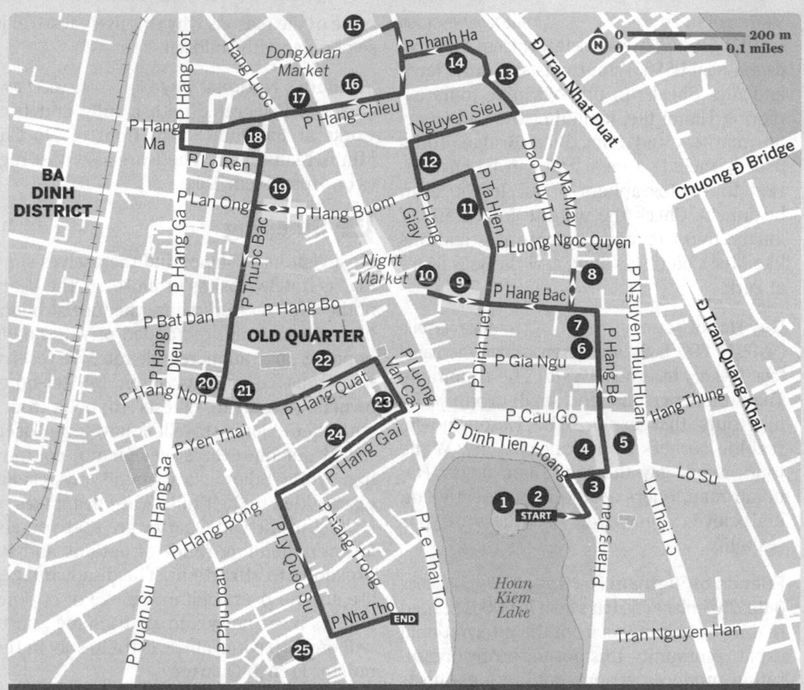

Walking Tour Old Quarter

START NGOC SON TEMPLE
END P NHA THO
LENGTH 3.5KM; MINIMUM TWO HOURS

Start at the ❶ **Ngoc Son Temple** (p62) on Hoan Kiem Lake. Return over the ❷ **Huc Bridge** to the photogenic ❸ **Martyrs' Monument** (p63). Follow P Dinh Tien Hoang to the ❹ **Municipal Water Puppet Theatre** (p87). Head north on P Hang Dau, but don't get too tempted by all the cheap shoes in the ❺ **shoe shops**. Cross P Cau Go to P Hang Be for the ❻ **market** on P Gia Ngu.

Back on P Hang Be, continue north to P Hang Bac: look out for artisans hand carving intricate ❼ **gravestones**. Next head up to the ❽ **Memorial House** (p60) on P Ma May, the street to come to for nightlife.

Return to P Hang Bac, passing ❾ **jewellery shops**, to ❿ **house 102**, which includes a fully functioning temple. Retrace your steps and head up narrow ⓫ **P Ta Hien**, popular for more after-dark bars. Turn left on P Hang Buom to the ⓬ **Bach Ma Temple** (p59), and continue to ⓭ **Cua O Quan Chuong**, the well-preserved Old East Gate, for an obligatory photograph. Continue north to the ⓮ **street market** on P Thanh Ha, then veer right to ⓯ **Dong Xuan Market** (p89).

Backtrack south on Nguyen Thien Thuat and turn right on to P Hang Chieu, past ⓰ **shops** selling straw mats and rope. This becomes ⓱ **P Hang Ma** where imitation 'ghost money' is sold for burning in Buddhist ceremonies. Follow your ears to the ⓲ **blacksmiths** near the corner of P Lo Ren and P Thuoc Bac. Continue along P Lan Ong to the pungent fragrances of ⓳ **herb merchants**.

Double back to P Thuoc Bac and head south past the ⓴ **tin-box makers**, opposite the ㉑ **mirror shops** on P Hang Thiec. Continue left towards shops selling ㉒ **Buddhist altars and statues** along P Hang Quat.

Head south past P Luong Van Can's ㉓ **toy shops**, and continue along P Hang Gai for elegant ㉔ **silk shops**. Head south on P Ly Quoc Su to ㉕ **St Joseph Cathedral** (p63), and the cafes on P Nha Tho and P Au Trieu.

Vietnam in Focus PHOTOGRAPHY TOUR
(☎0121 515 0522; www.vietnaminfocus.com; per person from US$60) Journalists Colm Pierce and Alex Sheal run photographic tours exploring Hanoi life, including the Old Quarter, markets and Long Bien Bridge. Tours usually include a meal and can be customised to photographers of all levels, even beginners. Check the website for details of longer tours to more remote destinations like Moc Chau, Ha Giang and Ba Be National Park.

Gay Hanoi Tours WALKING TOUR
(☎0947 600 602; www.facebook.com/gayhanoitour; half-day tours from US$75) The inimitable Tuan offers personal and small group walking tours that explore the lesser-known, real-life corners of the ancient city. While tours aren't gay themed, Tuan, a gay Hanoian man, offers a unique perspective on his beloved hometown, regardless of your sexuality.

Friends of Vietnam Heritage WALKING TOUR
(http://fvheritage.org; tours from 70,000d) Staffed mainly by volunteers from the international expat community, this not-for-profit organisation produces various publications, hosts events, and conducts fun and informative walking tours aimed at preserving Hanoi's heritage and culture.

Festivals & Events

Tet CULTURAL
(Tet Nguyen Dan, Vietnamese Lunar New Year; late Jan or early Feb) During the week preceding Tet, there is a flower market held on P Hang Luoc. There's also a colourful, two-week flower exhibition and competition, beginning on the first day of the new year, that takes place in Thong Nhat Park (Lenin Park) near Bay Mau Lake.

Quang Trung Festival CULTURAL
(Feb/Mar) Wrestling competitions, lion dances and human chess take place on the 5th day of the first lunar month at Dong Da Mound, site of the uprising against the Chinese led by Emperor Quang Trung (Nguyen Hué) in 1788.

Full Moon Festival CULTURAL
(from 15 Aug) This festival, also known as the Mid-Autumn Festival, begins on 15 August. Singing, dragon dances, and the giving and receiving of moon cakes and money, are some of the reasons why this lively festival is so popular with children.

Vietnam's National Day CULTURAL
(2 Sep) Celebrated with a rally and fireworks at Ba Dinh Sq, in front of Ho Chi Minh's Mausoleum. There are also boat races on Hoan Kiem Lake.

Sleeping

Most visitors to Hanoi find themselves staying, as hotel websites promise, in 'the heart of the Old Quarter', where the tourist boom has seen new and rebranded private hotels popping up at an incredible rate. We receive numerous complaints about budget-hotel owners pressuring guests to book tours with them. Some travellers have even been turfed out onto the street for not complying, while others have found mysterious taxes added to their bills. The advantages of staying in the Old Quarter are that you get an overwhelming range of options and its proximity to attractions. The disadvantages are also an overwhelming range of options and it's busy, noisy and gritty. Some guests will prefer paying a little extra to stay in the quieter French Quarter.

Backpacker accommodation in Hanoi is plentiful, with a whole street of hostels and service providers lining either side of the Old Quarter's P Ngo Huyen. Rooms and dorms in this popular destination see a high turnover of guests (read, wear and tear) and facilities are basic at best. Dorm beds cost US$5 to US$9. Hanoi is one city where, if travelling on a budget, an extra US$10 to US$20 can make a big difference: splurge if you can.

Expect to pay US$25 to US$30 for a compact budget room. For around US$30 to US$50 you'll get a little more space, and usually satellite TV, wi-fi and minibar. A cost of US$75 to US$100 per night should get you a 'junior suite' in a contemporary boutique hotel with proportions closer to a standard Western hotel room, stylish appointments, bath-tub and balcony. Anything over US$100 should be of an international four- to five-star standard and will be located outside the Old Quarter. Almost all hotels include a generic buffet breakfast with some items cooked to order: there's generally not much difference between establishments. Always check whether tax and service is included in the rate.

Old Quarter

May De Ville Backpackers HOSTEL $
(Map p58; ☎04-3935 2468; www.maydevillebackpackershostel.com; 1 Hai Tuong, P Ta Hien; dm/d from US$6/25; ❄@📶) A short walk from Ta Hien's bars, May De Ville is one of Hanoi's best hostels. Dorms are spotless and there's also a movie room. Doubles are also good value.

Hanoi Hostel HOSTEL $
(Map p58; ☎0972 844 804; www.vietnam-hostel.com; 91c P Hang Ma; dm/d/tr US$6/16/21; 📶) This small, quiet, privately owned hostel is nicely located away from Hanoi's conglomeration of hostels. It's well run and clean, with tours on tap and plenty of information available about onward travel to China or Laos.

Hanoi Rendezvous Hotel HOTEL $
(Map p58; ☎04-3828 5777; www.hanoirendezvoushotel.com; 31 P Hang Dieu; dm/s/d/tr US$8/25/30/40; ❄@📶) Deliciously close to several brilliant street-food places, Hanoi Rendezvous features spacious rooms, friendly staff, and organises well-run tours to Halong Bay, Cat Ba Island and Sapa.

Camel City Hotel GUESTHOUSE $
(Map p58; ☎04-3935 2024; www.camelcityhotel.com; 8/50 Dao Duy Tu; d/tw US$17/30; ❄@📶) A family owned operation in a quiet lane just a short walk from the after-dark attractions on P Ta Hien. Rooms are trimmed with Asian design touches and service is friendly.

★**La Beaute de Hanoi** HOTEL $$
(Map p58; ☎04-3935 1626; http://la-beautehanoihotel.com; 15 Ngo Trung Yen; d from US$40; ❄📶) Opened in 2014, this 18-room hotel has a fresh white and cream palette with red accents, cable TV, fast wi-fi, and the larger suites and family rooms have small private balconies. It's in an excellent location on a quiet lane just a hop, skip and a jump from all the action on P Ma May.

★**Art Trendy Hotel** HOTEL $$
(Map p58; ☎04-3923 4294; www.arttrendyhotel.com; 6 Hang But; d/tw US$30/70; 🚭❄@📶) Art Trendy enjoys a quiet location on the western edge of the Old Quarter. Rooms are stylish and relatively spacious, and there's a real can-do attitude from the exceptional and friendly staff. Each room has a laptop, and breakfast includes warm baguettes, omelettes and fresh fruit.

Hanoi Elite HOTEL $$
(Map p58; ☎04-3828 1711; www.hanoielitehotel.com; 10/50 Dao Duy Tu Lane; s/d from US$45/50; ❄@📶) It's surprising what you can find in the most narrow and hidden-away of lanes in the Old Quarter. Hanoi Elite features cool and classy decor, top-notch staff and the kind of touches – rainforest showerheads, breakfasts cooked to order and in-room computers – you would expect from more expensive accommodation.

DO THE HUSTLE

Hanoi is not only the political capital of Vietnam, it is also the capital of hotel hustles. Copycat and fly-by-night hotels abound. These will rent a building, appropriate the name of another hotel, and then work with touts to bring unwitting tourists to their 'chosen' accommodation. Visitors who question the alternative location are told the hotel has moved and it is not until they check the next day that they realise they have been conned. These hotels overcharge on anything they can, often giving a price for the room on check-in and a price per person on check out. The best way to avoid this is to prebook a room by phone or email. This way, you know the hotel is still open, still in the same location and not full.

Airport taxis and minibuses often work in partnership with these copycat hotels, as they give the biggest commissions, and there have even been reports of desperate Westerners working in tandem with these hotels, steering backpackers their way. Confirm an airport transfer with your first night's accommodation to avoid this hassle.

If you come across any dodgy hotels, guesthouses, travel companies or other businesses, report them to the **Vietnam National Administration of Tourism** (Map p66; ☎04-3942 3760; www.vietnamtourism.gov.vn; 80 Quan Su) to hopefully pressure the cowboys into cleaning up their act.

Art Hotel HOTEL $$
(Map p58; ☎04-3923 3868; www.hanoiarthotel.com; 65 P Hang Dieu; s/d from US$25/30; ❄@📶) The young, friendly and welcoming crew at the Art Hotel make this well-located spot really stand out. Rooms are spacious with spotless bathrooms and wooden floors, and within a 30m radius you'll find some of Hanoi's best opportunities for partaking in the city's great street food.

Classic Street Hotel HOTEL $$
(Map p58; ☎04-3825 2421; http://classicstreethotel.com.vn; 41 P Hang Be; d/ste from US$30/70; ❄📶) This place on ever-busy Hang Be has cosy rooms with large beds and satellite TV. Plenty of paintings and ceramics brighten up the communal spaces and corridors.

Hanoi Guesthouse HOTEL $$
(Map p58; ☎04-3935 2571; www.hanoiguesthouse.com; 85 P Ma May; d/tr from US$26/40; ❄@📶) Recently relocated to bustling P Ma May, the Hanoi Guesthouse has newly decorated rooms, and a very central location right in the middle of the action, with bars, restaurants, travel agencies and shopping right outside.

Nova Hotel HOTEL $$
(Map p58; ☎04-3923 3366; www.hanoinovahotel.com; 75 P Hang Dieu; d/tr from US$23/42; ❄@📶) On the western edge of the Old Quarter, P Hang Dieu has good-value mid-range hotels. The Nova exemplifies what any place in this part of town needs to offer: spacious bedrooms, balcony views and spotless modern bathrooms.

★ **La Siesta Hotel & Spa** BOUTIQUE HOTEL $$$
(Map p58; ☎04-3926 3641; www.hanoilasiestahotel.com; 94 P Ma May; d/ste from US$70/125; ❄📶) La Siesta scores points not only for excellence in service and the quality of its rooms, which come in a variety of sizes (including some snazzy bilevel duplex configurations), but for its cracker location on P Ma May with scores of restaurants, bars and things to do on your very doorstep. If that's all a bit too hectic for you, chill out in the day spa.

Tirant Hotel HOTEL $$$
(Map p58; ☎04-6269 8899; www.tiranthotel.com; 38 P Gia Ngu; d/ste from US$75/145; ❄@📶🏊) Trendy decor, switched-on staff who speak excellent English and spacious bedrooms all conspire to make this, one of the largest Old Quarter hotels, a worthy choice. The buffet breakfast is worth lingering for and the oversized suites are impressive. Oh, did we mention it's one of the few hotels with a little rooftop pool?

Around Hoan Kiem Lake

Although the 'Old Quarter' is often referred to specifically as the area north of Hoan Kiem Lake, the area to the west of the lake has a high concentration of hotels and is still consdered the Old Quarter. Here you'll find P Ngo Huyen with its glut of cheap dorms, and nearby, the quieter, atmospheric streets around St Joseph Cathedral.

Especen Hotel HOTEL $
(Map p62; ☎04-3824 4401; www.especen.vn; 28 P Tho Xuong; d US$12-22; ❄@📶) This budget hotel near St Joseph Cathedral has spacious and light rooms, excellent rates and an almost tranquil location (by Old Quarter standards). There are two annexes within walking distance.

B&B Hanoi Hostel HOSTEL $
(Map p62; ☎04-3935 2266; www.bbhanoihostel.com; 16 Hang Trung; d from US$20; ❄📶) This clean hostel has friendly, hard-working staff and is located a short walk to the northeastern shore of Hoan Kiem Lake. Fresh flowers, fruit and Vietnamese coffee give the place a homey feel.

Central Backpackers Hanoi HOSTEL $
(Map p62; ☎04-3938 1849; www.centralbackpackershostel.com; 16 P Ly Quoc Su; dm US$5; @📶) This well-run hostel is in close proximity to good cafes and street eats. Not for the withdrawn, reclusive traveller, it's an easily excitable, social spot, with a nightly free beer happy hour from 7pm. Note that this operator has similarly named hotels at three locations.

★ **Golden Lotus Luxury Hotel** HOTEL $$
(Map p62; ☎04-382 85888; www.goldenlotushotel.com.vn; 53-55 P Hang Trong; d/ste from US$65/100; ❄@📶🏊) Rooms at this stylish, atmospheric hotel boast wooden finishes, fine silk trims, local art and high technology. Standard rooms lack natural light, but oversized suites have generous terraces. There's a rooftop pool! Its older, sister property, the **Golden Lotus Hotel** (Map p62; ☎04-3938 0901; 32 P Hang Trong; d/ste from US$45/80; ❄📶🏊) is marginally cheaper, and you can still use the pool.

Artisan Boutique Hotel BOUTIQUE HOTEL $$
(Map p62; ☎04-3938 1900; www.artisanboutiquehotel.com; 24 P Hang Hanh; d/ste from US$28/110; ❄📶) One of the best features of this joint Australian and Vietnamese co-production a stone's throw from Hoan Kiem Lake is its on-the-ball staff: they're friendly, accommodating but not overbearing. Although some rooms could do with some love, all have great walk-in showers and tasteful design elements. The Penthouse, if available, is a steal. A winner for location, service and price.

Madame Moon Guesthouse GUESTHOUSE $$
(Map p62; ☎04-3938 1255; www.madammoonguesthouse.com; 17 P Hang Hanh; d US$26-45; ❄@📶) Keeping it simple just one block from Hoan Kiem Lake, Madame Moon has surprisingly chic rooms and a (relatively) traffic-free location in a street filled with local cafes and bars. Note that there are three guesthouses belonging to Madame Moon. This review is for the Hang Hanh property.

The Palmy Hotel & Spa HOTEL $$
(Map p62; ☎04-3828 6622; http://thepalmyhotel.vn; 4 Ngo Bao Khanh; d from US$70; ❄📶) The Palmy's stylish, new-in-2014 rooms are compact at best, but junior suites offer good value. Although the top-floor breakfast spread is average, the views are impressive and the on-site spa is a bonus. Note that studio rooms have what is best described as a 'Juliet balcony' and junior suites are the only rooms with a proper balcony, albeit, without furniture.

Cinnamon Hotel BOUTIQUE HOTEL $$
(Map p62; ☎04-3938 0430; www.cinnamonhotel.net; 26 P Au Trieu; d US$58-65; ⊖❄@📶) A hip hotel overlooking St Joseph Cathedral in the Old Quarter's smartest enclave. The design combines the historic features of the building – wrought iron and window shutters – with Japanese-influenced interiors and modern gadgetry. Rooms are equipped with balcony and shower. The theme extends to the neighbouring sister property, **Cinnamon Hotel Cathedral** (Map p62; ☎04-3938 6761; 38 P Au Trieu; d/ste from US$60/85; ❄📶).

Joseph's Hotel HOTEL $$
(Map p62; ☎04-3938 1048; www.josephshotel.com; 5 P Au Trieu; d from US$35; ❄@📶) Tucked away in a quiet lane behind St Joseph Cathedral, this compact 10-room hotel features pastel tones, mod-Asian decor and breakfasts cooked to order. Try to secure a room with views of the church's nearby towers. Balconies are available.

Hanoi Elegance Diamond Hotel HOTEL $$
(Map p62; ☎04-3935 1632; www.elegancehospitality.com; 32 Lo Su; d from US$55; ❄@📶) One of a small local chain that prides itself on maintaining a consistently high level of service and comfort across its properties, the Elegance Diamond boasts great rates, large, stylish rooms and an on-the-pulse location.

Impressive Hotel BOUTIQUE HOTEL $$
(Map p62; ☎04-3938 1590; www.impressivehotel.com; 54-56 P Au Trieu; d from US$40; ❄@) Fortunately, this little property with a cute name that promises the world comes up with the goods, at least in terms of value. It offers great service, clean, cosy rooms and a location that is close to the hustle and bustle but set back from the noise.

Heart Hotel HOTEL $$
(Map p62; ☎04-3928 6682; www.heart-hotel.com; 11b P Hang Hanh; d from 580,000d; ❄@) This popular no-frills hotel has 10 neat rooms in a great spot just 100m from Hoan Kiem Lake. Rooms on higher floors have lake views: an uncommon bonus.

French Quarter

We define the French Quarter as the area just south of Hoan Kiem Lake, west of the Song Hong as far as Hanoi train station and south of Thong Nhat Park.

★**Conifer Boutique Hotel** HOTEL $$
(Map p62; ☎04-3266 9999; www.coniferhotel.com.vn; 9 Ly Dao Thanh; d from US$60; ❄📶) This is a fantastic little hotel tucked away on a pleasant side street in the French Quarter opposite a wonderfully dilapidated French-colonial mansion. Rooms are on the smaller side, but functional and well thought out. Be sure to pay the extra for a street-facing room with a generous, enclosed balcony: perfect for watching afternoon storms.

★**Somerset Grand Hanoi** APARTMENT $$
(Map p66; ☎04-3934 2342; www.somerset.com; 49 P Hai Ba Trung; apt from US$75; ❄📶🏊👪) Rates vary dramatically due to the nature and location of this sprawling apartment-hotel tower, but if you book ahead bargains can be found. For the location and amenities alone, the selection of studio to

three-bedroom apartments with full kitchen and laundry facilities can't be beat: perfect for travelling families.

Mercure La Gare HOTEL **$$**
(Map p66; ☎04-3944 7766; www.mercure.com; 94 P Ly Thuong Kiet; d from US$70;) Opposite Hanoi train station, this international chain hotel's larger-than-average, recently renovated rooms feature fresh, clean lines and neutral tones. It's perfect if you're arriving and departing by rail.

★**Sofitel Metropole Hotel** HOTEL **$$$**
(Map p62; ☎04-3826 6919; www.sofitel.com; 15 P Ngo Quyen; r from US$220;) Hanoi's finest hotel is a slice of colonial history, with its restored French colonial facade, mahogany-panelled reception rooms and haute cuisine. Rooms in the Heritage Wing offer unmatched colonial style, while the modern Opera Wing has sumptuous levels of comfort but not quite the same heritage character. Even if you're not staying here, pop in for a drink at the Bamboo Bar.

Hotel Nikko Hanoi HOTEL **$$$**
(Map p68; ☎04-3822 3535; www.hotelnikkohanoi.com.vn; 84 P Tran Nhan Tong; d from US$90;) This 16-storey luxury property has rooms that are substantially larger than the mainstay of Hanoi hotels, but although spotlessly clean, those picky about design might think they're looking a little dated. The outdoor pool and leafy location opposite Thong Nhat Park are welcome bonuses.

Hotel de l'Opera HOTEL **$$$**
(Map p62; ☎04-6282 5555; www.mgallery.com; 29 P Trang Tien; r from US$155;) The Hotel de l'Opera effortlessly combines French colonial style with a sophisticated design aesthetic. Rooms are trimmed in silk and Asian textiles, and splurge-worthy features include a spa and the hip late-night vibe of the La Fée Verte (Green Fairy) bar. If you're wondering, Green Fairy is a reference to absinthe, the infamous alcoholic beverage.

Hilton Hanoi Opera HOTEL **$$$**
(Map p62; ☎04-3933 0500; www.hanoi.hilton.com; 1 P Le Thanh Tong; r from US$135;) Built in 1998, and refurbished periodically, the oversized rooms and common areas of this luxury property are due for an overhaul to stay at the top of the Hanoi Hotel game. This will likely be underway by the time you read this. Otherwise, service levels are excellent, the grounds and location adjacent the Opera House are lovely, and the pool a welcome oasis.

Greater Hanoi

★**Fraser Suites Hanoi** APARTMENT **$$$**
(☎04-3719 8877; http://hanoi.frasershospitality.com; 51 Xuan Dieu, Tay Ho; apt from US$185;) These sumptuous, fully equipped serviced apartments in buzzing lakeside Ho Tay are the perfect choice for the discerning traveller staying a few days or more. The gorgeous, landscaped outdoor pool is the city's most alluring.

InterContinental Westlake Hanoi HOTEL **$$$**
(Map p70; ☎04-6270 8888; www.intercontinental.com/hanoi; 1a P Nghi Tam, Tay Ho; d from US$175;) Featuring a contemporary Asian-design theme and true five-star service, the Intercontinental is an oasis situated on the shores of Ho Tay. All rooms have balconies and the pick of the bunch are set on stilts above the water. The hotel's signature Sunset Bar celebrates some of the city's best cocktails, sitting on its own manmade island.

Crowne Plaza West Hanoi HOTEL **$$$**
(☎04-6270 6688; www.crowneplaza.com; 36 P Le Duc Tho, My Dinh; d/ste from US$90/160;) This popular chain hotel in an up-and-coming suburb of Hanoi offers excellent value, despite its location about 30 minutes' drive from the Old Quarter. Large, stylish rooms with good views are well priced in comparison with downtown offerings, the buffet breakfast is one of Hanoi's best and there's a good chance you'll have the pleasant outdoor pool to yourself. Enormous junior suites are well worth the splurge.

Lotte Hotel HOTEL **$$$**
(Map p70; ☎04-3333 1000; www.lottehotel.com/hanoi/en; 54 Lieu Giai, Ba Dinh; d from US$144;) Located a 20-minute drive from the Old Quarter, Hanoi's highest hotel rooms are lauded by pretty young things for their design chic, spaciousness and that sense of being above it all. In general, there's a feeling of being the biggest and the boldest, but not necessarily the best. Think young money.

Eating

Hanoi is an international city, and whatever your budget (or tastes), it's available

LOCAL KNOWLEDGE

HANOI STREET EATS: OUR TOP 10

Deciphering Hanoi's street-food scene can be bewildering, but it's worth persevering and diving in. The city's best food definitely comes from the scores of vendors crowding the city's pavements with smoking charcoal burners, tiny blue plastic stools and expectant queues of canny locals. Many of the stalls have been operating for decades, and often they offer just one dish. After that long perfecting their recipes, it's little wonder the food can be sensational. Note that opening hours may change and prices vary. Expect to pay 25,000d to 70,000d, depending on what you devour.

Bun Rieu Cua (Map p62; 40 P Hang Tre; ⏲7-10.30am) Get to this incredibly popular spot early, as its sole dish of *bun rieu cua* (noodle soup with beef in a spicy crab broth) is only served for a few hours from 7am. A Hanoi classic.

Bun Cha Nem Cua Be Dac Kim (Map p58; 67 P Duong Thanh; ⏲11am-7pm) Visiting Hanoi and not eating *bun cha* (barbecued pork with rice vermicelli) with a side of *nem cua be* (sea-crab spring rolls) should be classed as a capital offence. This is an excellent spot to try this street-food classic.

Banh My Pho Hue (Map p68; 118 P Hue; ⏲8am-9pm) *Banh mi* (sandwich) vendors abound in Hanoi, although the phenomenon is less popular than in Ho Chi Minh City. This place is usually packed with locals, which is always a good sign.

Pho Thin (Map p68; 13 P Lo Duc; ⏲6am-3pm) Negotiate your way to the rear of this narrow, rustic establishment and sit down to some excellent *pho bo* (beef noodle soup). A classic Hanoi experience that hasn't changed in decades.

Banh Cuon (Map p58; 14 P Hang Ga; ⏲8am-3pm) Don't even bother ordering here; just squeeze in and a plate of gossamer-light *banh cuon* (steamed rice crêpes filled with minced pork, mushrooms and shrimp) will be placed in front of you.

Banh Ghoi (Map p62; 52 P Ly Quoc Su; ⏲10am-7pm) Nestled under a banyan tree near St Joseph Cathedral, this humble stall turns out *banh ghoi*, moreish deep-fried pastries crammed with pork, vermicelli and mushrooms.

Bun Bo Nam Bo (Map p58; 67 P Hang Dieu; ⏲11am-10pm) *Bun bo nam bo* (dry noodles with beef) is a dish from southern Vietnam, but it's certainly travelled north well. Mix in bean sprouts, garlic, lemongrass and green mango for a filling treat.

Xoi Yen (Map p58; cnr P Nguyen Huu Huan & P Hang Mam; ⏲7am-11pm) Equally good for breakfast or as a hangover cure, Xoi Yen specialises in sticky rice topped with goodies, including sweet Asian sausage, gooey fried egg and slow-cooked pork.

Mien Xao Luon (Map p58; 87 P Hang Dieu; ⏲7am-2pm) Head to this humble stall trimmed with mini-mountains of fried eels for three different ways of eating the crisp little morsels. Try them stir-fried in vermicelli with egg, bean sprouts and shallots.

Che (Map p58; 76 P Hang Dieu; ⏲7am-3pm) In winter try *che banh troi tau*, sweet mung beans with sesame and ginger, or in summer *che thap nam* with coconut milk, crushed peanuts, lotus seeds and dried apples.

here. If you've just flown in, get stuck into the local cuisine, which is tasty, fragrantly spiced and inexpensive. And don't miss the essential experience of dining on Hanoi's street food.

If you've been up in the hills of northern Vietnam subsisting on noodles and rice, the capital's cosmopolitan dining, including Japanese, French, Italian and Indian, will be a welcome change.

Old Quarter

New Day VIETNAMESE $

(Map p58; ☎04-3828 0315; http://newdayrestaurant.com; 72 P Ma May; meals 50,000-100,000d; ⏲8am-late) Clean and tidy New Day attracts locals, expats and travellers with its broad menu. The staff always find space for new diners, so look forward to sharing a table with some like-minded fans of Vietnamese food.

Mon Hue VIETNAMESE $

(Map p62; ☎0986 981 369; 37 P Ly Quoc Su; meals 40,000-80,000d; ⊙10am-10pm;) While this simple, somewhat grubby little restaurant is by no means a member of the famous Ho Chi Minh–based chain whose name it has appropriated, it does have genuinely friendly staff, good food in the style of Hue (adopted by a Hanoian family to local tastes) and a picture menu to ease you into the almost-street-food experience.

Namaste INDIAN $$

(Map p66; ☎04-3935 2400; www.namastehanoi.com; 46 P Tho Nuom; meals 85,000-225,000d; ⊙11am-2.30pm & 6-10pm;) This sprawling restaurant serves delicious Indian cuisine from a huge menu with a decent selection of vegetarian options. Thali set meals (105,000d to 225,000d) are both filling and excellent value. There's also free wi-fi!

Highway 4 VIETNAMESE $$

(Map p58; ☎04-3926 0639; www.highway4.com; 3 P Hang Tre; meals 120,000-275,000d; ⊙noon-late) This is the original location of a restaurant family famed for adapting Vietnamese cuisine for Western palates, although with increasing popularity it beccomes harder to please everybody. There are now four other branches in Hanoi: check the website for locations. Come for small plates to share, cold beer and funky decor.

Cha Ca Thang Long VIETNAMESE $$

(Map p58; ☎04-3824 5115; www.chacathanglong.com; 19-31 P Duong Thanh; cha ca fish 180,000d; ⊙10am-3pm & 5-10pm) Bring along your DIY cooking skills and grill your own succulent fish with a little shrimp paste and plenty of herbs. *Cha ca* is an iconic Hanoi dish, and while another nearby more-famous *cha ca* eatery gets all the tour-bus traffic, the food here is actually better.

Green Mango MEDITERRANEAN $$

(Map p58; ☎04-3928 9917; www.greenmango.vn; 18 P Hang Quat; meals 200,000-250,000d; ⊙noon-late) This hip restaurant-cum-lounge has a real vibe as well as great cooking. The

SPECIALITY FOOD STREETS

To combine eating with exploration, head to these locations crammed with interesting restaurants and food stalls.

Pho Cam Chi This narrow lane is packed with local eateries turning out cheap, tasty food for a few dollars. Cam Chi translates as 'Forbidden to Point' and dates from centuries ago. It is said that the street was named as a reminder for the local residents to keep their curious fingers in their pockets when the king and his entourage went through the neighbourhood. Cam Chi is about 500m northeast of Hanoi train station. Adjoining Tong Duy Tan is also crammed with good eating.

Đuong Thuy Khue On the southern bank of Ho Tay, Đ Thuy Khue features dozens of outdoor seafood restaurants with a lakeside setting. The level of competition is evident by the daredevil touts who literally throw themselves in front of oncoming traffic to steer people towards their tables. You can eat well here for about 150,000d per person.

Truc Bach A quieter waterfront scene is around the northeast edge of Truc Bach Lake. Many *lau* (hotpot) restaurants are huddled together in an almost continuous strip for a few hundred metres. Grab a few friends and settle in at one of the dinky lakeside tables for a DIY session of fresh seafood, chicken or beef. It's perfect on a cool Hanoi night.

Pho Nghi Tam About 10km north of central Hanoi, P Nghi Tam has a 1km-long stretch of about 60 dog-meat restaurants: keep an eye out for the words *thit cho* (dog meat). Hanoians believe that eating dog meat in the first half of the month brings bad luck, so the restaurants are deserted. On the last day of the lunar month, however, they're packed with locals.

Cho Am Thuc Ngoc Lam Across the Song Hong (Red River), in Long Bien, this sprawling riverfront food street is popular with locals and heavy on seafood. There are excellent views of the Chuong Duong and Long Bien bridges. Beware the cluster of *thit cho* dog-meat restaurants at the start of the strip.

stunning dining rooms, complete with rich silk drapes, evoke the feel of an opium den, while the huge rear courtyard comes into its own on summer nights. Menu-wise there's everything from pizza and pasta to mod-Asian fusion creations.

Green Tangerine FUSION $$
(Map p58; ☎04-3825 1286; www.greentangerinehanoi.com; 48 P Hang Be; meals US$12-20; ⊙noon-late; ⊜) Experience the mood and flavour of 1950s Indochine at this elegant restaurant located in a beautifully restored French colonial house with a cobbled courtyard. The fusion French-Vietnamese cuisine is not always entirely successful, but it's still worth popping in for coffee or a drink. Two-course lunches (218,000d) arc good value.

Around Hoan Kiem Lake

★Minh Thuy's VIETNAMESE $
(Map p62; ☎04-3200 7893; 2a Duong Thanh; meals 45,000-155,000d; ⊙11am-10pm; ✎) Masterchef Vietnam contestant Minh Thuy's eponymous restaurant is tucked away in backpacker central and worth your attention. It's cheap, clean and serves mouth-watering Vietnamese food with some very original European twists and plenty of vegetarian options. Highly recommended.

La Place CAFE $
(Map p62; ☎04-3928 5859; www.laplacehanoi.com; 4 P Au Trieu; meals from 70,000d; ⊙7.30am-10.30pm; ☎) This stylish, popular little cafe adjacent to St Joseph Cathedral has walls covered in propaganda art and an East-West menu. Plenty of wine by the glass is on offer and the coffee has a real kick. Good for breakfast also.

Kem Dac Diet Trang Tien ICE CREAM $
(Map p62; 35 P Trang Tien; ice cream from 10,000d; ⊙8am-10pm) It's barely possible to walk down the road to get to this parlour on hot summer nights, such is its popularity.

Le Petit Bruxelles BELGIAN $$
(Map p62; ☎04-3938 1769; www.le-petit-bruxelles.com; 1 P Au Trieu; set lunch 149,000d, meals 115,000-435,000d; ⊙11am-2pm & 5-10pm) For a little taste of Europe, visit this spotless Belgian restaurant on a quiet side street for mussels, frites, fondue and beef bourguignon. The balcony is a great spot to sit and ponder your next move over a cold Belgian beer.

Hanoi Social Club CAFE $$
(Map p66; ☎04-3938 2117; www.facebook.com/thehanoisocialclub; 6 Hoi Vu; meals 95,000-175,000d; ⊙8am-11pm) On three funky levels with retro furniture, the Hanoi Social Club is the city's most cosmopolitan cafe. Dishes include potato fritters with chorizo for breakfast, and pasta, burgers and wraps for lunch or dinner. Vegetarian options feature a mango curry, and the quiet laneway location is a good spot for an end-of-day coffee, beer or wine. The Hanoi Social Club also hosts regular gigs and events. Check its Facebook page for what's on.

Madame Hien VIETNAMESE $$$
(Map p62; ☎04-3938 1588; www.facebook.com/madamehienrestaurant; 15 Chan Cam; set menus from 365,000d, meals 95,000-350,000d; ⊙11am-10pm) Housed in a restored 19th-century villa, Madame Hien is a tribute to French chef Didier Corlu's Vietnamese grandmother. Look forward to more elegant versions of traditional Hanoi street food; the '36 Streets' fixed menu (535,000d) is a good place to kick off your culinary knowledge of the city.

West of the Old Quarter

Ray Quan VIETNAMESE $
(Map p66; ☎0913 578 588; 8a Nguyen Khuyen; dishes from 30,000-120,000d) Popular with expats in the know, this quirky spot directly on the train tracks won't be for everyone, but those who like it, will love it. A wide range of Vietnamese cuisine is cooked to order by the eccentric owner-chef who ferments her own rice wine: it's strong and delicious.

Net Hue VIETNAMESE $
(Map p66; ☎04-3938 1795; http://nethue.com.vn; cnr P Hang Bong & P Cam Chi; snacks & meals from 35,000d; ⊙11am-9pm) One of a small chain, Net Hue is well priced for such comfortable surroundings. Head to the top floor for the nicest ambience and enjoy Hue-style dishes like *banh nam* (steamed rice pancake with minced shrimp).

Quan An Ngon VIETNAMESE $
(Map p66; ☎04-3942 8162; www.ngonhanoi.com.vn; 18 Phan Boi Chau; dishes 70,000-150,000d; ⊙7am-11pm) This branch of a number of small same-named kitchens turns out street-food specialities from across Vietnam. Try to visit just outside the busy lunch and dinner periods, or consider Quan An Ngon's newest branch in a lovely French villa just north of

the Old Quarter (Map p66; ☎04-3734 9777; 34 P Phan Đinh Phung; dishes 70,000-150,000d; ⏰11am-11pm).

Nha Hang Koto Van Mieu CAFE $$
(Map p66; ☎04-3747 0338; www.koto.com.au; 59 P Van Mieu; meals 120,000-160,000d; ⏰7.30am-10pm, closed dinner Mon;) Stunning, four-storey, modernist cafe-bar-restaurant overlooking the Temple of Literature, where the interior design has been taken very seriously, from the stylish seating to the fresh flowers by the till. Daily specials are chalked up on a blackboard, and the short menu has everything from excellent Vietnamese food to yummy pita wraps and beer-battered fish and chips. Koto is a not-for-profit project providing career training and guidance to disadvantaged children and teens.

Puku CAFE $$
(Map p66; ☎04-3938 1745; http://pukukafe.com; 18 Tong Duy Tan; meals 90,000-140,000d; ⏰24hr;) One of Hanoi's few 24/7 establishments, a five-minute walk from Hanoi train station (ideal for a restorative brunch after the overnight train back from Sapa), does excellent coffee, all-day breakfasts and decent burgers and wraps. A little slice of Kiwi cafe culture – Puku means 'stomach' in New Zealand's indigenous Maori language.

★**Old Hanoi** VIETNAMESE $$$
(Map p66; ☎04-3747 8337; www.oldhanoi.com; 4 Ton That Thiep; meals 90,000-179,000d; ⏰11am-2pm & 5-10pm) This sophisticated eatery in a restored French Colonial villa with a courtyard outside and starched white tablecloths inside was once host to celebrity chef Gordon Ramsay. Serving traditional Hanoian and Vietnamese specialities with aplomb, you'll enjoy the selection and find the best value for money if you dine in a group.

French Quarter

★**Moto-san Uber Noodle** NOODLES $
(Map p62; ☎04-6680 9124; 4 Ly Dao Thanh; meals 45,000-70,000d) Brainchild of Hanoi artist, journalist and designer Nguyen Qui Duc (of Tadioto fame), this wonderful noodle stall seats eight eager eaters. The menu is simple: miso, shōyu (soy) or *shio* (salty) ramen, and spicy *banh mi thit ko* (stewed pork) sandwiches with killer hot sauce (optional) *a la* central Vietnam. Sake and beer are, of course, readily available.

★**Chim Sao** VIETNAMESE $$
(Map p68; ☎04-3976 0633; www.chimsao.com; 63-65 Ngo Hue; meals 75,000-180,000d; ⏰11am-11pm) Sit at tables downstairs or grab a more traditional spot on the floor upstairs and discover excellent Vietnamese food, with some dishes inspired by the ethnic minorities of Vietnam's north. Definite standouts are the hearty and robust sausages, zingy and fresh salads, and duck with starfruit. Try to come with a group so you can explore the menu fully.

Nha Hang Ngon VIETNAMESE $$
(Map p68; ☎04-3933 6133; 26a P Tran Hung Dao; meals 80,000-130,000d; ⏰7am-9.30pm) With a focus on authentic flavours from around Vietnam, this joint gets popular with locals and visitors alike. It's street food taken off the street and presented in a delightful restored French villa and courtyard.

Izakaya Yancha JAPANESE $$
(Map p68; ☎04-3974 8437; 121 P Trieu Viet Vuong; meals 120,000-250,000d; ⏰1am-11pm) Surrounded by local cafes on 'Coffee St', Izakaya Yancha serves *izakaya* – think Japanese tapas – in a buzzy and friendly atmosphere. Secure a spot near the open kitchen and work your way through lots of Osaka-style goodies, including excellent tuna sashimi and miso with udon noodles.

Chay Nang Tam VEGETARIAN $$
(Map p68; ☎04-3942 4140; 79a P Tran Hung Dao; items from 100,000d; ⏰11am-8pm;) Dishes of vegetables that look like meat, reflecting an ancient Buddhist tradition designed to make carnivore guests feel at home.

★**La Badiane** INTERNATIONAL $$$
(Map p66; ☎04-3942 4509; www.labadiane-hanoi.com; 10 Nam Ngu; meals from 265,000d; ⏰noon-11pm) This stylish bistro is set in a restored whitewashed French villa arrayed around a breezy central courtyard. French cuisine underpins the menu – La Badiane translates as 'star anise' – but Asian and Mediterranean flavours also feature. Menu highlights include the sea bass tagliatelle with smoked paprika, and prawn bisque with wasabi tomato bruschetta. Three-course lunches priced from 325,000d are excellent value.

Pots 'n Pans FUSION $$$

(Map p68; ☎04-3944 0204; www.potsnpans.vn; 57 P Bui Thi Xuan; meals 300,000-650,000d; ⏲11.30am-late) In a chic modern space, Pots 'n Pans specialises in innovative fusion dishes blending Vietnamese and European influences. An excellent wine list partners dishes like crispy skin sea bass with a prawn and ginger boudin, black sesame noodles, mushrooms, chilli jam and tamarind-and-coconut sauce.

Greater Hanoi

★Tim Ho Wan DIM SUM $

(Map p70; ☎04-3333 1725; 36th fl, Lotte Tower, 54 Lieu Giai, Ba Dinh; dim sum 59,000-95,000d) Do yourself a favour and reserve a window table at the Hanoi branch of this legendary Hong Kong dim sum chain, high above the city on the 36th floor of the Lotte Tower. Bring a friend or six and an empty stomach, and we guarantee you won't regret it.

Oasis DELI $

(Map p70; ☎04-3719 1196; www.oasishanoi.net; 24 P Xuan Dieu; ⏲8am-6pm) Italian-owned deli with excellent bread, cheese and salami, as well as homemade pasta and sauces. It's north of central Hanoi in the Tay Ho restaurant strip on P Xuan Dieu.

★Maison de Tet Decor CAFE $$

(☎0966 611 383; http://tet-lifestyle-collection.com; 36 Tua Hoa, Nghi Tam, Tay Ho; meals from 180,000d; ⏲7am-11pm) Sumptuous, healthy and organic (wherever possible) wholefoods are presented with aplomb in this, one of Hanoi's loveliest settings, an expansive, airy villa overlooking Ho Tay.

Quan Kien VIETNAMESE $$

(Map p70; ☎0983 430 136; www.quankien.com; 143 P Nhgi Tam; meals 80,000-130,000d; ⏲11am-11pm)

HANOI'S COFFEE CULTURE

Western-style cafes and coffee shops are becoming increasingly common in Vietnamese cities, but most of them pale in comparison to the traditional cafes dotted around central Hanoi. Here's where to go and what to order for an authentic local experience. Most cafes are open from around 7am to 7pm, but hours sometimes vary. On the eastern edge of the Old Quarter, P Nguyen Huu Huan is lined with good cafes, most with free wi-fi.

Café Duy Tri (Map p70; ☎04-3829 1386; 43a P Yen Phu) In the same location since 1936, this caffeine-infused labyrinth is a Hanoi classic. You'll feel like Gulliver as you negotiate the tiny ladders and stairways to reach the 3rd-floor balcony. Order the delicious *caphe sua chua* (iced coffee with yoghurt), and you may have discovered your new favourite summertime drink. You'll find P Yen Phu a couple of blocks east of Truc Bach Lake north of the Old Quarter.

Cafe Pho Co (Map p58; 4th fl, 11 P Hang Gai) One of Hanoi's best-kept secrets, this place has plum views over Hoan Kiem Lake. Enter through the silk shop, and continue through the antique-bedecked courtyard up to the top floor for the mother of all vistas. You'll need to order coffee and snacks before tackling the final winding staircase. For something deliciously different, try the *caphe trung da*, coffee topped with a silky-smooth beaten egg white.

Cafe Lam (Map p58; ☎04-3824 5940; www.cafelam.com; 60 P Nguyen Huu Huan) A classic cafe that's been around for years – long enough to build up a compact gallery of paintings left behind by talented patrons who couldn't afford to pay their tabs during the American War. These days you're just as likely to spy Converse-wearing and Vespa-riding bright young things refuelling on wickedly strong *caphe den* (black coffee).

Cong Caphe (Map p68; http://congcaphe.com; 152 P Trieu Viet Vuong) Settle in to the eclectic beats and kitsch Communist memorabilia at Cong Caphe with a *caphe sua da* (iced coffee with condensed milk). You'll notice a bunch of branches around the city – a full list appears on its website.

Hanoi House (Map p62; ☎04-2348 9789; www.thehanoihouse.com; 2nd fl, 47a P Ly Quoc Su; ⏲8.30am-11pm; 📶) A chic cafe with superb upstairs views of St Joseph Cathedral. Chill out on the impossibly slim balcony with excellent juices and Hanoi's best ginger tea.

An interesting spot for cuisine from the Hmong, Muong and Thai ethnic minorities – try the grilled chicken with wild pepper – traditional Vietnamese *ruou* (wine) made from apricots or apples, and more challenging snacks like grilled ants' eggs and crickets. If insects aren't your thing, it's still a fun night sitting at the low tables eating excellent Vietnamese dishes.

Mâu Dich 37 VIETNAMESE **$$**

(Map p66; ☎ 04-3715 4336; 37 Nam Trang, Truc Bach; snacks 35,000-55,000d, meals 90,000-180,000d; ⏲ 10am-10pm) Styled after a government-run food shop from the impoverished period after 1976, Mâu Dich 37 is a unique exercise in nostalgia. Waiters are dressed as state workers, and diners queue to 'purchase' coupons that can be exchanged for food. The menu focuses on robust northern flavours, and features a few challenging dishes like braised frog and snails with ginger leaves.

Foodshop 45 INDIAN **$$**

(Map p70; ☎ 04-3716 2959; www.foodshop45.com; 59 P Truc Bach; meals 100,000-250,000d; ⏲ 10am-10.30pm) Hanoi's best Indian flavours feature at this cosy lakeside spot sandwiched between the *lau* (hotpot) restaurants on Truc Bach Lake. The ambience is more authentic at the rustic downstairs tables, and menu standouts include a superb *kadhai* chicken that will definitely have you ordering a second beer.

Kitchen CAFE **$$**

(☎ 04-3719 2679; 30 To Ngoc Van, Tay Ho; meals 100,000-210,000d; ⏲ 7am-9.30pm; 📶) This Tay Ho terrace cafe with a Mexican tinge ticks all the right boxes with a mellow buzz and a creative, healthy menu of delicious sandwiches and salads sourced from organic ingredients. Also great for breakfast or a juice (try the ginger and watermelon tonic) if you've been cycling around the lake.

Drinking

Hanoi's eclectic drinking scene features grungy dive bars, a Western-style pub or two, sleek lounge bars, cafes and hundreds of *bia hoi* joints.

However, as the no-fun police supervise a strict curfew, and regularly show up to enforce the closure of places that flout this law, there's minimal action after midnight. Lock-in action after midnight does occur, though; ask around in Hanoi's hostels to find out which bars are currently staying open beyond the witching hour.

The best places for a bar crawl include traveller-friendly P Ta Hien in the Old Quarter, and Ngo Bao Khanh near the northwest edge of Hoan Kiem Lake. An alternative

DON'T MISS

BIA AHOY!

'Tram phan tram!' Remember these words, as all over Vietnam, glasses of *bia hoi* are raised and emptied, and cries of *tram phan tram* ('100%' or 'bottoms up') echo around the table.

Bia hoi is Vietnam's very own draught beer or microbrew. This refreshing, light-bodied pilsener was first introduced to Vietnam by the Czechs in a display of Communist solidarity. Brewed without preservatives, it is meant to be enjoyed immediately and costs as little as 5000d a glass.

Hanoi is the *bia hoi* capital of Vietnam and there are microbars on many Old Quarter street corners. A wildly popular place unofficially known as 'Bia Hoi junction' is at the corner of P Ta Hien and P Luong Ngoc Quyen, in the heart of the Old Quarter. It's now packed with backpackers and travellers though, and has lost most of its local charm. Did you really come all this way to drink Heineken and talk to boozed neighbours from Jersey City or Johnsonville?

An alternative, more local *bia hoi* junction is where P Nha Hoa meets P Duong Thanh on the western edge of the Old Quarter. For something to go with the beer, **Bia Hoi Ha Noi** (Map p58; 2 P Duong Thanh) also does the best spare ribs in town; **Nha Hang Lan Chin** (Map p62; cnr P Hang Tre & P Hang Thung) is famed for *vit quay* (roast duck); and you can't go past **Quan Bia Minh** (Map p58; 7a P Dinh Liet; mains 90,000-130,000d; ⏲ 8am-late) for well-priced Vietnamese food and excellent service led by the eponymous Mrs Minh.

scene, popular with expats, is in the Ha To lake area on P Xuan Dieu.

Hanoi is definitely not a clubbers' paradise, and the often-enforced midnight curfew means dancing is pretty much confined to the bar-clubs in and around the Old Quarter.

Tadioto BAR

(Map p62; ☎04-6680 9124; www.tadioto.com; 24b P Tong Dan; ⏰7am-midnight) Nguyen Qui Duc's unofficial clubhouse for the underground arts scene's latest incarnation is this dark and quirky colonial bar in the French Quarter. Obligatory red accents (seat covers, wrought-iron grill on the doors), reworkings of art deco furniture and plenty of recycled ironwork feature heavily. The highlight of the cool cocktail list is the sweet mojito.

Moose & Roo PUB

(Map p58; ☎04-3200 1289; www.mooseandroo.com; 42b P Ma May; ⏰11am-midnight) This jovial Canadian-Aussie-themed pub and grill serves excellent homestyle comfort food (burgers, pulled pork, wings, fish and chips) in a fun and friendly environment. One for the homesick or those looking to hook up with fellow travellers.

Nola BAR

(Map p58, 89 P Ma May; ⏰9am-midnight) Retro furniture is mixed and matched in this bohemian labyrinth tucked away from Ma May's tourist bustle. Pop in for a coffee and banana bread, or return after dark for one of Hanoi's best little bars.

Bar Betta BAR

(Map p66; ☎0165 897 9073; www.facebook.com/barbetta34; 34 Cao Ba Quat; ⏰9am-midnight) Retro decor and a jazz-age vibe combine with good cocktails, coffee and cool music in this breezy French colonial villa. Two-for-one beers are available from 3pm to 7pm, and the rooftop terrace (from 8pm) is essential on a sultry Hanoi night.

Manzi Art Space BAR

(Map p66; ☎04-3716 3397; www.facebook.com/manzihanoi; 14 Phan Huy Ich; ⏰cafe 9am-midnight, shop 10am-6pm) Part cool art gallery, part chic cafe and bar, Manzi is worth seeking out north of the Old Quarter. A restored French villa hosts diverse exhibitions of painting, sculpture and photography, and the compact courtyard garden is perfect for a coffee or glass of wine. There's also a shop selling works by contemporary Vietnamese artists.

Summit Lounge BAR

(Map p70; 20th fl, Sofitel Plaza, 1 Đ Thanh Nien; ⏰4.30pm-late) Enjoy fabulous views from this 20th-floor lounge bar. Order a (pricey) cocktail or beer, grab a spot on the outside deck, and take in Truc Bach Lake and the city beyond.

Cama ATK BAR

(Map p68; www.cama-atk.com; 73 P Mai Hac De; ⏰6pm-midnight Wed-Sat) Make the trek south of Hoan Kiem Lake to this bohemian bar run by Hanoi's Club for Art and Music Appreciation (CAMA). Check the website for what's on, which includes everything from Japanese funk and dancehall DJs through to experimental short films and reggae sound systems.

The Doors BAR

(Map p58; ☎0983 029 010; 11 Hang Chinh; ⏰6pm-midnight) Open daily with live music from Tuesday to Sunday, strong cocktails and happy staff. It can be chilled and quiet as a mouse or rowdy and raucous depending on the day.

LGBT HANOI

There are very few gay venues in Hanoi, but plenty of places that are gay-friendly. However, official attitudes are still fairly conservative and Hanoi is home to these official attitudes. Police raids in the name of 'social reform' aren't unknown, which tends to ensure the gay and lesbian community keeps a low profile. A great way to experience the city and find out about gay life in Hanoi is on a Gay Hanoi Tour (p74): Tuan will happily field any questions you might have.

The GC Pub (p86) is one of the more-established gay bars in Hanoi, and it's a good place to find out about the most happening new places in town. Accommodation-wise, the Art Hotel (p75), Art Trendy Hotel (p75) and Artisan Boutique Hotel (p77) are gay-friendly.

The website www.utopia-asia.com has up-to-date information about gay Hanoi.

Le Pub PUB

(Map p58; ☎04-3926 2104; 25 P Hang Be; ⏲7am-late) Le Pub is a great place to hook up with others, as there's always a good mix of travellers and Hanoi expats. There's a cosy, tavern-like interior (with big screens for sports fans), a street-facing terrace and a rear courtyard. Bar snacks are served, the service is slick and the music usually includes tunes you can sing along to.

Funky Buddha BAR

(Map p58; ☎0936 377 375; 2 P Ta Hien; ⏲noon-late) Crowd around the L-shaped bar and enjoy some of Hanoi's better cocktails. Once the techno and house beats kick in, it's more of a nightclub than a bar. Cheap drinks make it a favourite for travellers from nearby backpacker hostels.

Angelina BAR

(Map p62; Sofitel Metropole Hotel, 15 P Ngo Quyen; ⏲noon-2am) Flash hotel bar with glitzy decor and a late licence. DJs spin funky house and chill-out tunes here on weekend nights. Also in the Sofitel Metropole is the poolside Bamboo Bar, dripping in chic, heritage cool.

Dragonfly BAR

(Map p58; ☎04-3926 2177; 15 P Hang Buom; ⏲4pm-late) Bar-club with a handy Old Quarter location, it draws a (very) young crowd and the music is pretty mainstream.

Rooftop Bar BAR

(Map p66; ☎0913 706 966; http://therooftop.vn; 19th fl, Pacific Place, 83b P Ly Thuong Kiet; ⏲noon-midnight) For views of the city, pop in for an expensive beer or cocktail and enjoy the vista. It's very popular with a glittering array of Hanoi's bright young things.

GC Pub PUB

(Map p62; ☎04-3825 0499; 7 P Bao Khanh; ⏲noon-midnight) Hanoi's unofficial and long-standing gay HQ is a tad dingy but gets very lively on weekend nights. It's popular with locals and usually checked out by most gay visitors, especially those fond of playing pool.

Quan Ly BAR

(Map p68; 82 P Le Van Hu; ⏲10am-9pm) Owner Pham Xuan Ly has lived on this block since 1950, and now runs one of Hanoi's most traditional *ruou* (Vietnamese liquor) bars. Kick

DON'T MISS

PUNCH & JUDY IN A POOL

The ancient art of water puppetry *(roi nuoc)* was virtually unknown outside of northern Vietnam until the 1960s. It originated with rice farmers who worked the flooded fields of the Red River Delta. Some say they saw the potential of the water as a dynamic stage; others say they adapted conventional puppetry during a massive flood. Whatever the real story, the art form is at least 1000 years old. Performances take place at the Municipal Water Puppet Theatre.

The farmers carved the human and animal puppets from water-resistant fig-tree timber *(sung)* and staged performances in ponds, lakes or flooded paddy fields. Today a tank of waist-deep water is used for the 'stage'. The glossy, painted puppets are up to 50cm long and weigh as much as 15kg. Some puppets are simply attached to a long pole, while others are set on a floating base, in turn attached to a pole. In the darkened auditorium, it appears as if they are walking on water. If used continually, each puppet has a lifespan of about four months: puppet production provides several villages outside Hanoi with a full-time livelihood.

Eleven puppeteers, each trained for a minimum of three years, are involved in the performance. Their considerable skills were traditionally passed only from father to son, for fear that daughters would marry outside the village and take the secrets with them.

Traditional live music is as important as the action on stage. Each memorable performance consists of a number of vignettes depicting pastoral scenes and legends. One scene tells of the battle between a fisherman and his prey, which is so electric it is as if a live fish were being used. There's also fire-breathing dragons (complete with fireworks) and a flute-playing boy riding a buffalo.

The water puppets are both amusing and graceful, appearing and disappearing as if by magic. Spectators in front-row seats can expect a bit of a splash!

off with the ginseng one, and work your way up. An English-language menu makes it easy to choose, and there's also cheap beer and good Vietnamese food on offer.

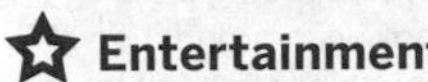

Entertainment

Cinemas

Centre Culturel Français de Hanoi CINEMA
(Map p62; www.ifhanoi-lespace.com; 24 P Trang Tien) Situated in the sublime L'Espace building near the Opera House, it offers a regular program of French films. Musical events are also staged here; check the website for what's on.

Cinematheque CINEMA
(Map p62; ☎04-3936 2648; 22a P Hai Ba Trung) This Hanoi institution is a hub for art-house film lovers, and there's a great little cafe-bar here too. It's nominally 'members only', but a 50,000d one-off membership usually secures visitors an always-interesting themed double bill.

Music

Traditional music is usually performed daily at the Temple of Literature.

Hanoi Opera House OPERA
(Map p62; ☎04-3993 0113; www.ticketvn.com; 1 P Trang Tien) Performances of classical music and opera are periodically held here in the evenings. Check the website for upcoming performances.

Thang Long Ca Tru Theatre LIVE MUSIC
(Map p58; ☎0122 326 6897; www.catruthanglong.com; 28 P Hang Buom; admission 210,000d; ⊙8pm Tue, Thu & Sat) Concerts of traditional Vietnamese music are held in this intimate restored house in the Old Quarter. *Ca tru* is indigenous to the north of Vietnam, and concerts feature a selection of the 100 or so *ca tru* melodies. The art form has also been recognised as an endangered 'intangible cultural heritage' by Unesco.

Hanoi Rock City LIVE MUSIC
(www.hanoirockcity.com; 27/52 To Ngoc Van, Tay Ho) Hanoi Rock City is tucked away down a residential lane about 7km north of the city near Tay Ho, but it's a journey well worth taking for an eclectic mix, including reggae, Hanoi punk and regular electronica nights. A few international acts swing by, so check the website or www.newhanoian.xemzi.com for listings.

Jazz Club By Quyen Van Minh LIVE MUSIC
(Map p66; www.minhjazzvietnam.com; 65 Quan Su; ⊙performances 9-11.30pm) This atmospheric venue is the place in Hanoi to catch live jazz. There's a bar, food menu and high-quality gigs featuring father-and-son team Minh and Dac, plus other local and international jazz acts. Check the website for listings.

Theatre

Municipal Water Puppet Theatre THEATRE
(Map p62; ☎04-3824 9494; www.thanglongwaterpuppet.org/?/en/home/; 57b P Dinh Tien Hoang; admission 60,000-100,000d, camera fee 20,000d, video fee 60,000d; ⊙performance times vary) Water puppetry shows are a real treat for children. Multilingual programs allow the audience to read up on each vignette as it's performed. Although there are multiple performances daily, book well ahead, especially from October to April.

Vietnam National Tuong Theatre OPERA
(Map p58; ☎04-837 0046; www.vietnamtuongtheatre.com; 51 P Duong Thanh; admission 100,000d; ⊙6.30pm Thu-Sun) *Hat tuong* is a uniquely Vietnamese variation of Chinese opera that enjoyed its greatest popularity under the Nguyen dynasty in the 19th century. Until 2007, performances at this theatre were by invitation only. Now performances are open to locals and visitors, and a night watching *hat tuong* is an interesting traditional alternative to Hanoi's wildly popular water puppets.

Expect highly stylised acting, elaborate costumes, and comedy and tragedy with characters from Vietnamese folklore.

Shopping

For Vietnamese handicrafts, including textiles and lacquerware, head to the stores along P Hang Gai, P To Tich, P Hang Khai and P Cau Go. P Hang Gai and its continuation, P Hang Bong, are good places to look for embroidered tablecloths, T-shirts and wall hangings. P Hang Gai is also a fine place to buy silk and have clothes custom-made.

In the historic Old Quarter, you'll find clothes, cosmetics, fake sunglasses, bootleg DVDs and software, T-shirts, musical instruments, plumbing supplies, herbal medicines, jewellery, religious offerings, spices, coffee and much more. Assume that almost all brand-label merchandise you see here is fake.

NEGOTIATING HANOI'S TRAVEL AGENCY MAZE

Hanoi has hundreds of travel agencies and plenty are of ill-repute, operating with pushy staff out of budget Old Quarter hotels. Some hotels have been known to evict guests who book tours elsewhere: it's all about commission. When you book accommodation at properties, check there are no strings attached and that it's not mandatory to book tours at the same business also.

The agencies that we recommend have professional, knowledgeable staff and coordinate well-organised trips with a high-rate of guest satisfaction: most run small groups, use their own vehicles and guides, and offer trips away from the main tourist trail.

If you choose to book elsewhere, beware of clones of popular agencies. It's common for shysters to set up shop close to a respected agency and attempt to cream off a slice of their business. Visit online forums like the Thorn Tree (www.lonelyplanet.com/thorntree) to check the latest travellers' buzz.

Vega Travel (Map p58; ☎04-3926 2092; www.vegatravel.vn; cnr P Ma May & 24a P Hang Bac; ⏰8am-8pm) Family-owned-and-operated company offering well-run tours around the north and throughout Vietnam. Excellent guides and drivers, and it also financially supports ethnic minority kindergartens and schools around Sapa and Bac Ha. Halong bay tours on a private boat are excellent value and bespoke touring is available.

Ethnic Travel (Map p58; ☎04-3926 1951; www.ethnictravel.com.vn; 35 P Hang Giay; ⏰9am-6pm Mon-Sat, 10am-5pm Sun) Off-the-beaten-track trips across the north in small groups. Some trips are low-impact using public transport and homestays, others are activity-based (including hiking, cycling and cooking). Offers Bai Tu Long Bay tours and also has an office in Sapa.

Handspan Adventure Travel (Map p58; ☎04-3926 2828; www.handspan.com; 78 P Ma May; ⏰9am-8pm) Sea-kayaking trips in Halong Bay and around Cat Ba Island, and jeep tours, mountain biking and trekking. Other options include remote areas such as Moc Chau and Ba Be National Park, community-based tourism projects in northern Vietnam, and the *Treasure Junk*, the only true sailing craft cruising Halong Bay. Handspan also has offices in Sapa and Ho Chi Minh City.

Free Wheelin' Tours (Map p70; ☎04-3926 2743; www.freewheelin-tours.com; 62 Đ Yen Phu, Ba Dinh; ⏰10am-7pm) Offers motorbike and 4WD tours around the north, including an eight-day trip to the northeast on Minsk bikes.

Marco Polo Travel (Map p70; ☎04-3997 5136; www.marcopoloasia.com; Room 107b, N14-49 Nguyen Khoai; ⏰9am-5pm) Runs kayaking trips around Halong Bay and Ba Be Lakes. Also mountain-biking trips and hiking expeditions around the north of Vietnam.

Mr Linh's Adventure Tours (Map p58; ☎04-642 5420; www.mrlinhadventure.com; 83 P Ma May) A professional outfit, specialising in off-the-beaten-track and adventure travel in Vietnam's remote north. Ba Be Lakes homestay trips are recommended.

Cuong's Motorbike Adventure (Map p58; ☎0913 518 772; www.cuongs-motorbike-adventure.com; 46 P Gia Ngu; ⏰8am-6pm) This highly recommended operator conducts motorbike tours all around the north. Look out for the bright pink Minsk motorbike.

Bookworm BOOKS
(Map p66; www.bookwormhanoi.com; 44 P Chau Long; ⏰9am-7pm) Stocks over 10,000 new and used English-language books. There's plenty of fiction and it's good on South Asian history and politics.

Thang Long BOOKS
(Map p62; 53-55 P Trang Tien; ⏰9am-6pm) One of the biggest bookshops in town with English and French titles, international newspapers and magazines, and a good selection of titles on the history of Hanoi.

Hanoi Moment HANDICRAFTS
(Map p58; ☎04-3926 3630; www.hanoimoment.vn; 101 P Hang Gai; ⊙8am-9pm) An oasis of classier Vietnamese souvenirs, including lacquerware and jewellery, amid the T-shirt overkill of nearby stores. Bamboo, stone and porcelain are also used to great effect.

Tan My Design CLOTHING
(Map p58; ☎04-3938 1154; www.tanmydesign.com; 61 P Hang Gai; ⊙8am-8pm) Stylish clothing, jewellery and accessories, with the added bonus of a funky cafe when you need a break from shopping. The homewares and bed linen are definitely worth a look.

Metiseko CLOTHING, ACCESSORIES
(Map p58; ☎04-3935 2645; www.metiseko.com; 71 P Hang Gai; ⊙8am-9pm) Lots of stylish, organic and ecofriendly spins on clothing, homewares and accessories. Both cotton and silk are harnessed for Metiseko's chic collections.

Things of Substance CLOTHING
(Map p62; ☎04-3828 6965; 5 P Nha Tho; ⊙9am-6pm) Tailored fashions and some off-the-rack items at moderate prices. The staff are professional and speak decent English.

Three Trees ACCESSORIES
(Map p62; ☎04-3928 8725; www.threetreesdesigns.com; 15 P Nha Tho; ⊙9am-7pm) Stunning, very unusual designer jewellery, including many delicate necklaces, which make special gifts.

Mai Gallery ART
(Map p66; ☎04-3828 5854; www.maigallery-vietnam.com; 113 P Hang Bong; ⊙9am-7pm) Run by resident artist Mai, this is a good place to learn more about Vietnamese art before making a purchase.

Mekong+ HANDICRAFTS
(Map p58; ☎04-3926 4831; http://mekong-plus.com; 13 P Hang Bac; ⊙8am-8pm) Beautiful quilts handcrafted by rural women working in a not-for-profit community development program.

Craft Link HANDICRAFTS
(Map p66; ☎04-3843 7710; www.craftlink.com.vn; 43 P Van Mieu; ⊙9am-6pm) A not-for-profit organisation near the Temple of Literature that sells quality tribal handicrafts and weavings at Fairtrade prices.

Mosaique HOMEWARES
(Map p62; ☎04-3971 3797; www.mosaiquedecoration.com; 6 P Ly Quoc Su; ⊙9am-8pm) Modern and chic updates of traditional lacquerware and silk. The ideal spot to pick up stylish cushion covers, linen and accessories.

Indigenous HANDICRAFTS
(Map p62; ☎04-3938 1263; 36 P Au Trieu; ⊙9am-6pm) A top spot for quirky ethnic-style gifts and excellent Fairtrade coffee. There's a great little cafe too, so you can choose your favourite Vietnamese java before you buy.

Markets

Buoi Market MARKET
(Map p70; cnr P Duong Buoi & Lac Long Quan; ⊙6am-2pm) Located near the southwest edge of Ho Tay at the intersection of P Duong Buoi and Lac Long Quan, this market sells live animals like chickens, ducks and pigs, but also features ornamental plants.

Dong Xuan Market MARKET
(Map p58; Dong Xuan; ⊙6am-7pm) A large, non-touristy market located in the Old Quarter of Hanoi, 900m north of Hoan Kiem Lake. There are hundreds of stalls here, and it's a fascinating place to explore if you want to catch a flavour of Hanoian street life. The area around it also has loads of bustling shops.

Hom Market MARKET
(Map p68; cnr P Hué & P Tran Xuan Soan; ⊙6am-5pm) Situated on the northeast corner of P Hué and P Tran Xuan Soan, this is a good general-purpose market and excellent for local fabric, if you plan to have clothes made.

Night Market MARKET
(Map p58; P Hang Giay; ⊙7pm-midnight Fri-Sun) This market runs north to south through the Old Quarter, from P Hang Giay to P Hang Dao. Content-wise it's something of a spill-over for the area's shops, but at least the streets are closed to traffic. Watch out for pickpockets.

Hang Da Market MARKET
(Map p58; cnr P Hang Da & P Yen Thai; ⊙7am-6pm) In the basement level of this covered complex, you'll find the mother lode of second-hand clothing, albeit largely catering to Vietnamese tastes and sizes. If you've got patience and are into recycled threads, it's worth a look.

Information

DANGERS & ANNOYANCES

First the good news: Hanoi is generally a safe city to explore, and serious crimes against tourists are extremely rare, but it's pertinent to exercise some caution. While it's generally safe to walk around the streets of the Old Quarter at night, it's best to avoid the darker lanes after around 10pm and sensible for solo female travellers to take a metered taxi with a reputable company when travelling across the city at night. Watch out for pickpockets around market areas and unwanted baggage 'helpers' in crowded transport terminals – particularly when boarding night trains.

Traffic and pollution are other irritants. The city's traffic is so dense and unrelenting that simply crossing the street can be a real headache, and weaving a path through a tide of motorbikes (two million and counting) can be a hairy experience. Our advice is to walk slowly and at a constant pace, allowing motorcyclists sufficient time to judge your position and avoid you. Don't try to move quickly as you'll just confuse them. Keep your wits about you as you explore the Old Quarter, as motorbikes come at you from all directions and pavements are obstructed by cooking stalls and more parked motorbikes. Pollution levels are punishing and air quality is poor, with levels of some contaminants higher than in Bangkok.

AIRPORT TAXI SCAMS

It's sad to say, but many of the drivers who hang out at Noi Bai International Airport are working in cahoots with hotels and travel agencies in Hanoi; they know every trick in the book and usually carry the cards of all the popular budget hotels. 'It's full today' is popular, as is 'They have a new place, much nicer, number two'. To avoid any drama, it's a good idea to book your first night's accommodation in advance and arrange an arrival transfer with your hostel/hotel. As there's no effective public transport from the airport, this usually works out cheaper than a taxi and you can arrive into Hanoi's organised chaos without any stress: someone will be waiting with a name board and you can wave goodbye to the taxi scammers as you exit the airport.

Scams

While there's no need to be paranoid, Hanoi is riddled with scams, many of them linked. Most problems involve budget hotels and tours, and occasionally things can get nasty. We've received reports of verbal aggression and threats of physical violence towards tourists who've decided against a hotel room or a tour. Stay calm and back away or things could quickly flare up.

The taxi and minibus mafia at the airport shuttle unwitting tourists to the wrong hotel. Invariably, the hotel has copied the name of another popular property and will then attempt to appropriate as much of your money as possible. Taxi swindles are also becoming increasingly common. Try to avoid the taxis loitering at Hanoi's bus stations: many have super-fast meters.

Some shoeshine boys and *cyclo* drivers attempt to add a zero or two to an agreed price for their services; stick to your guns and give them the amount you originally agreed.

Watch out for friendly, smooth-talking strangers approaching you around Hoan Kiem Lake. There are many variations, but sometimes these con artists pose as students and suggest a drink or a meal. Gay men are also targeted in this way. Your new friend may then suggest a visit to a karaoke bar, snake-meat restaurant or some other venue and before you know it you're presented with a bill for hundreds of dollars. Be careful and follow your instincts, as these crooks can seem quite charming.

We've also heard reports of male travellers being approached by women late at night in the Old Quarter, and then being forced at gunpoint by the women's male accomplices to visit multiple ATMs and empty their accounts. Keep your wits about you, and try to stay in a group if you're returning from a bar late at night.

EMERGENCY

The emergency services should be able to transfer you to an English speaker.

Ambulance ☎115
Fire ☎114
Police ☎113

INTERNET ACCESS

➡ Most budget and midrange hotels offer free access to a computer and the internet: at fancier places in the rooms, at cheaper places in the lobby.

➡ Free wi-fi access is virtually ubiquitous in the city's cafes and bars, but dedicated internet cafes are largely a thing of the past, so pack a tablet or smartphone.

MAPS

➡ Hanoi city maps come in every size and scale. Some are freebies subsidised by advertising and others are precise works of cartography.

➡ Leading maps include detailed versions at a scale of 1:10,000 or 1:17,500. Covit produces a couple of hand-drawn 3D maps of Hanoi, including a detailed Old Town map, which make nice souvenirs. Various maps, including those produced by Covit, are available at leading bookshops in Hanoi.

➡ There is an excellent bus map available: *Xe Buyt Ha Noi* (5000d).

MEDICAL SERVICES

Hanoi Family Medical Practice (Map p70; ☎04-3843 0748; www.vietnammedicalpractice.com; Van Phuc Diplomatic Compound, 298 P Kim Ma; ⏰24hr) Located a few hundred metres west of the Ho Chi Minh Mausoleum Complex, this practice includes a team of well-respected international physicians and dentists, and has 24-hour emergency cover. Prices are high, so check that your medical travel insurance is in order.

L'Hopital Français de Hanoi (Map p70; ☎04-3577 1100, emergency 04-3574 1111; www.hfh.com.vn; 1 Phuong Mai; ⏰24hr) Long-established, international-standard hospital with accident and emergency, intensive care, dental clinic and consulting services. It's located around 3km southwest of Hoan Kiem Lake.

SOS International Clinic (☎04-3826 4545; www.internationalsos.com/locations/asia-pacific/vietnam; 51 Xuan Dieu; ⏰24hr) English, French, German and Japanese are spoken and there is a dental clinic. It's 5km north of central Hanoi near Ho Tay lake.

Viet Duc Hospital (Benh Vien Viet Duc; Map p62; ☎04-3825 3531; 40 P Trang Thi; ⏰24hr) Old Quarter unit for emergency surgery; the doctors here speak English, French and German.

Traditional Medicine

Institute of Acupuncture (Map p70; ☎04-3853 3881; 49 P Thai Thinh; ⏰8-11.30am & 2-4.30pm) Offers effective holistic medicine; located 4km southwest of Hoan Kiem Lake.

National Institute of Traditional Medicine (Map p68; ☎04-3826 3616; 29 P Nguyen Binh Khiem; ⏰7.30-11.30am & 1.30-4pm) For Vietnamese-style medical solutions.

MONEY

Hanoi has many ATMs, and on the main roads around Hoan Kiem Lake are international banks where you can change money and get cash advances on credit cards. Some ATMs limit the amount you can withdraw to only 3,000,000d. ANZ and HSBC ATMs are usually more generous.

ℹ CATCHING THE BUS TO CHINA

Two daily services (at 7.30am and 9.30am) to Nanning, China (480,000d, nine hours) leave from 206 Đ Tran Quang Khai. Tickets should be purchased in advance, through a reputable travel agency. Be sure you have the correct Chinese visa.

The bus runs to the border at Dong Dang, where you pass through Chinese immigration. You then change to a Chinese bus, which continues to the Lang Dong bus station in Nanning. Reports from Nanning-bound travellers indicate that this route is less hassle and quicker than travelling by train.

POST

Domestic Post Office (Buu Dien Trung Vong; Map p62; ☎04-3825 7036; 75 P Dinh Tien Hoang; ⏰7am-9pm) For internal postal services in Vietnam; also sells philatelic items.

International Postal Office (Map p62; ☎04-3825 2030; cnr P Dinh Tien Hoang & P Dinh Le; ⏰7am-8pm) The entrance is to the right of the domestic post office.

TOURIST INFORMATION

In the cafes and bars of the Old Quarter, look for the excellent local magazine *The Word*.

Tourist Information Center (Map p58; ☎04-3926 3366; P Dinh Tien Hoang; ⏰9am-7pm) City maps and brochures, but privately run with an emphasis on selling tours.

USEFUL WEBSITES

And of Other Things (www.andofotherthings.com) Interesting, up-to-date, online magazine for all things arty.

Hanoi Grapevine (www.hanoigrapevine.com) Information about concerts, art exhibitions and cinema.

Lonely Planet (www.lonelyplanet.com/hanoi)

Sticky Rice (www.stickyrice.typepad.com) Foodie website, with the low-down on everything from gourmet Vietnamese to Hanoi street kitchens.

The Word (www.wordhanoi.com) Online version of the free monthly magazine *The Word*.

TNH Vietnam (http://tnhvietnam.xemzi.com) Formerly dubbed The New Hanoian, TNH Vietnam is the premier online resource for visitors and expats; good for restaurant and bar reviews.

ℹ Getting There & Away

AIR

Hanoi has fewer direct international flights than Ho Chi Minh City, but with excellent connections through Singapore, Hong Kong or Bangkok you can get almost anywhere easily.

Jetstar Airways (☎1900 1550; www.jetstar.com) Operates low-cost flights to Danang, Ho Chi Minh City and Nha Trang.

VietJet Air (☎1900 1886; www.vietjetair.com) Launched in 2012, this low-cost airline has flights to Hanoi, Nha Trang, Danang, Dalat and Bangkok.

Vietnam Airlines (Map p62; ☎1900 545 486; www.vietnamair.com.vn; 25 P Trang Thi; ⊙8am-5pm Mon-Fri) Links Hanoi to destinations throughout Vietnam. Popular routes include Hanoi to Dalat, Danang, Dien Bien Phu, Ho Chi Minh City, Hue and Nha Trang, all served daily.

BUS & MINIBUS

Hanoi has four main long-distance bus stations of interest to travellers. They are fairly well organised, with ticket offices, fixed prices and schedules, though can be crowded and at times chaotic. Consider buying tickets the day before you plan to travel on the longer distance routes to ensure a seat. It's often easier to book through a travel agent, but you'll obviously be charged a commission.

Tourist-style minibuses can be booked through most hotels and travel agents. Popular destinations include Halong Bay and Sapa. Prices are usually about 30% to 40% higher than the regular public bus, but include a hotel pick-up.

Many open-ticket tours through Vietnam start or finish in Hanoi.

Giap Bat Bus Station (☎04-3864 1467; Đ Giai Phong) Serves points south of Hanoi, and offers more comfortable sleeper buses. It is 7km south of Hanoi train station.

Gia Lam Bus Station (☎04-3827 1569; Đ Ngoc Lam) Has buses to the northeast of Hanoi. It's located 3km northeast of the city centre across the Song Hong (Red River).

Luong Yen Bus Station (Map p70; ☎04-3942 0477; cnr Tran Quang Khai & Nguyen Khoai) Located 3km southeast of the Old Quarter, it operates services to the east. Transport to Cat Ba Island is best organised here. Note that the taxis at Luong Yen are notorious for dodgy meters. Walk a couple of blocks and hail one on the street.

My Dinh Bus Station (☎04-3768 5549; Đ Pham Hung) This station 7km west of the city provides services to the west and the north, including sleeper buses to Dien Bien Phu for onward travel to Laos. It's also the best option for buses to Ha Giang and Mai Chau.

CAR

Car rental is best arranged via a travel agency or hotel. Rates almost always include a driver, a necessity as many roads and turnings are not signposted. The roads in the north are in OK shape, but narrow lanes, potholes and blind corners equate to an average speed of 35km/h to 40km/h. During the rainy season, expect serious delays as landslides are cleared and bridges repaired. You'll definitely need a 4WD.

Rates start at about US$110 a day (including a driver and petrol). Make sure the driver's expenses are covered in the rate you're quoted.

MOTORBIKE

Offroad Vietnam (Map p58; ☎0913 047 509; www.offroadvietnam.com; 36 P Nguyen Huu Huan; ⊙8am-6pm Mon-Sat) For reliable Honda trail bikes (from US$20 daily) and road bikes (US$17). The number of rental bikes is limited, so booking ahead is recommended. Offroad's main business is running excellent tours, mainly dealing with travellers from English-speaking countries. Tours are either semi-guided, excluding meals and accommodation, or all-inclusive fully-guided tours.

TRAIN

Rail travel in Vietnam can seem quite complicated to the uninitiated. Before you set out, check out the excellent, up-to-date blog at www.seat61.com for the latest information on all trains in Vietnam, or have a chat with a reputable local travel agent. Note that train prices increase by 10% over Tet festival dates.

As of late 2014, the Vietnam Railways website (www.dsvn.vn) began to accept online bookings. The site can be a little clunky, however, and we've had reports of credit card payments not being processed. If you'd like to give it a go, click on the English flag icon at the top right of the screen.

Better still, check out the excellent online train and bus booking agency Bao Lau (www.baolau.vn), which handles bookings for virtually all trains in Vietnam, at the official Vietnam Railways fares. A small service fee of 40,000d per ticket is charged, plus a fee equal to 3.3% of the total purchase price for payment by credit card. Collect tickets from your departure station. It's a relatively new service, but general feedback has been excellent.

Southbound Trains to Hue, Danang, Nha Trang & HCMC

Trains to southern destinations go from the main **Hanoi train station** (Ga Hang Co; Train Station A; ☎04-3825 3949; 120 Đ Le Duan; ⊙ticket office 7.30am-12.30pm & 1.30-7.30pm) at the western end of P Tran Hung Dao on Đ Le Duan. To the left of the main entrance is the ticket office with adjacent posters displaying train departure times and fares. Take a ticket and look out for your booth number on the screens. It's a good idea to write down your train number, departure time and preferred class in Vietnamese. Southbound trains depart at 6.15am, 9am, 1.15pm, 7pm and 11pm.

We recommend buying your tickets a few days before departure to ensure a seat or sleeper. Tickets can also be purchased from most travel

BUSES FROM HANOI

Giap Bat Bus Station

DESTINATION	DURATION (HR)	COST (D)	FREQUENCY
Dalat	35	450,000	9am, 11am
Danang	12	365,000	frequent sleepers noon-6.30pm
Dong Ha	8	380,000	frequent sleepers noon-6.30pm
Dong Hoi	8	380,000	frequent sleepers noon-6.30pm
Hue	10	380,000	frequent sleepers noon-6.30pm
Nha Trang	32	700,000	10am, 3pm, 6pm
Ninh Binh	2	70,000	frequent 7am-6pm

Gia Lam Bus Station

DESTINATION	DURATION (HR)	COST (D)	FREQUENCY
Ba Be	5	150,000	noon
Bai Chay (Halong City)	3½	120,000	every 30min
Haiphong	2	70,000	frequent
Lang Son	5	90,000	every 45min
Lao Cai	9	300,000	6.30pm, 7pm (sleeper)
Mong Cai	9	230,000	hourly (approx)
Sapa	10	250,000	6.30pm, 7pm (sleeper)

Luong Yen Bus Station

DESTINATION	DURATION (HR)	COST (D)	FREQUENCY
Cat Ba Island	5	240,000	5.20am, 7.20am, 11.20am, 1.20pm
Haiphong	2	70,000	frequent
HCMC	40	920,000	7am, 10am, 2pm, 6pm
Lang Son	4	80,000	frequent

My Dinh Bus Station

DESTINATION	DURATION (HR)	COST (D)	FREQUENCY
Cao Bang	10	120,000	every 45min
Dien Bien Phu	8	350,000	11am, 6pm
Ha Giang	8	200,000	frequent
Hoa Binh	2	40,000	frequent
Son La	7	190,000	frequent

TRAINS FROM HANOI

Eastbound & Northbound Trains

DESTINATION	STATION	DURATION (HR)	HARD SEAT/ SLEEPER	SOFT SEAT/ SLEEPER	FREQUENCY
Beijing	Tran Quy Cap	18	US$240	US$352	6.30pm Tue & Fri
Haiphong	Gia Lam	2	60,000d	70,000d	6am
Haiphong	Long Bien	2½-3	60,000d	70,000d	9.20am, 3.30pm, 6.10pm
Nanning	Gia Lam	12	US$28	US$42	9.40pm

Southbound Trains

DESTINATION	HARD SEAT	SOFT SEAT	HARD SLEEPER	SOFT SLEEPER
Danang	from 430,000d	from 630,000d	from 782,000d	from 954,000d
HCMC	from 790,000d	from 1,160,000d	from 1,340,000d	from 1,692,000d
Hue	from 374,000d	from 545,000d	from 675,000d	from 894,000d
Nha Trang	from 692,000d	from 998,000d	from 1,240,000d	from 1,647,000d

agencies, and their commission for booking usually offsets the language hassle of buying tickets directly from the train station. They also often have preferential access to tickets to popular destinations like Hue, Ho Chi Minh City and Lao Cai (for Sapa).

Approximate journey times from Hanoi are as follows, but check when you book, as some trains are quicker than others: Hue (11 hours), Danang (13½ hours), Nha Trang (24½ hours), Ho Chi Minh City (31 hours). Note that different departures have different fare structures and available classes; check www.baolau.vn for ticket costs.

Northbound Trains to Lao Cai (for Sapa) & China

All northbound trains leave from a separate station (just behind Station A and known as Station B) called **Tran Quy Cap Station** (Train Station B; ☎04-3825 2628; P Tran Quy Cap; ⏰ticket office 4-6am & 4-10pm). This is accessed by an entrance on P Tran Quy Cap. Cross the tracks north of Station A and turn left to reach this station. There are separate ticket offices for northbound trains to Lao Cai (for Sapa) and China. If you've already booked for one of the private carriages to Sapa, you'll need to exchange your voucher for a ticket at the appropriate tour desk.

Once you're in China the train to Beijing is a comfortable, air-conditioned service with four-bed sleeper compartments and a restaurant.

Eastbound trains to Haiphong & China

Eastbound (Haiphong) trains depart from Gia Lam Train Station on the eastern side of the Song Hong (Red River), or Long Bien on the western (city) side of the river. Be sure to check which station. Trains to Nanning, China, also depart from here. Note that you cannot board international Nanning-bound trains in Lang Son or Dong Dang.

ℹ Getting Around

TO/FROM THE AIRPORT

Hanoi's Noi Bai International Airport is about 35km north of the city, taking around 45 minutes along a modern highway. If you're planning to use public buses or the airline buses listed following to get to the airport, be sure to allow *plenty* of time before your flight.

Bus

Public bus 17 departing from outside the arrivals hall runs to/from **Long Bien bus station** (Map p70; tickets 5000d; ⏰5am-9pm) on the northern edge of the Old Quarter. Luggage may be charged separately. Allow around 90 minutes' travelling time.

Taxi

Airport Taxi (☎04-3873 3333) charges US$20 for a taxi ride door-to-door to or from Noi Bai International Airport. From the terminal, look out for the official taxi drivers who wear bright-yellow jackets. They do not require that you pay the toll for the bridge you cross en route. Some other taxi drivers do require that you pay the toll, so ask first. There are numerous airport scams involving taxi drivers and dodgy hotels. Don't use freelance taxi drivers touting for business – the chances of a rip-off are too high. If you've already confirmed accommodation, you're well advised to book an arrival transfer through your hotel.

Jetstar Airport Bus

Goes to/from Noi Bai International Airport (30,000d) from 206 Đ Tran Quang Khai. Passengers must be at the city stop *at least* 2½ hours before their flight's scheduled departure time.

Vietnam Airlines Minibus

These minibus services link Hanoi and Noi Bai (5000d), leaving hourly to/from the Vietnam Airlines office on P Trang Thi.

BICYCLE

Many Old Quarter guesthouses and cafes rent bikes for about US$3 per day. Good luck with that traffic – be safe!

The Hanoi Bicycle Collective (☎ 04-3718 3156; www.thbc.vn; Shop 29, Nhat Chieu, Tay Ho; bike rental per day from 100,000d; ⌚8am-8pm Tue-Sun) Vietnamese bikes and mountain bikes (phone ahead one day prior to book) can be rented at this spot that also doubles as a cafe and gin bar. Grab a Spanish-style *bocata* sandwich before setting off on the 15km lakeside path around Ho Tay. Check the website for regular rides around the city hosted by the Collective.

BUS

Hanoi has an extensive public bus system, though few tourists take advantage of the rock-bottom fares (3000d). If you're game, pick up the *Xe Buyt Ha Noi* (Hanoi bus map; 5000d) from the Thang Long (p88) bookshop.

CAR & MOTORBIKE

Getting around Hanoi by motorbike means relentless traffic, nonexistent road manners and inadequate street lighting. Factor in possible theft, parking hassles and bribe-happy police, and it's not for the timid. Intrepid types can arrange mopeds for around US$5 per day in the Old Quarter.

CYCLO

A few *cyclo* drivers still frequent the Old Quarter, and if you're only going a short distance, it's a great way to experience the city (despite the fumes). Settle on a price first and watch out for overcharging – a common ploy when carrying two passengers is to agree on a price, and then *double* it upon arrival, gesturing 'no, no, no...that was per person'.

Aim to pay around 50,000d for a shortish journey; night rides are more. Few *cyclo* drivers speak English so take a map and your hotel calling card with you.

ELECTRIC BUS

Hanoi's golf-buggy-esque ecofriendly **Electric Bus** (Dong Xuan; per buggy 6 passengers per hour 250,000d; ⌚8.30am-10pm) tour is actually a pretty good way to get your bearings in the city. It traverses a network of 14 stops in the Old Quarter and around Hoan Kiem Lake, parting the flow of motorbikes and pedestrians like a slow-moving white dragon. Nothing really beats haphazardly discovering the nooks and crannies of the Old Quarter by foot, but if you're feeling a tad lazy, the electric bus is worth considering. The main departure point is the northern end of Hoan Kiem Lake, and there's another departure point outside Dong Xuan Market. A full journey around the Old Quarter takes around an hour, with a recorded English-language commentary as you ride.

MOTORBIKE TAXI

You won't have any trouble finding a *xe om* (motorbike taxi) in Hanoi. An average journey in the city centre costs around 15,000d to 20,000d, while a trip further to Ho Chi Minh's Mausoleum is around 35,000d to 40,000d. For two or more people, a metered taxi is usually cheaper than a convoy of *xe om*.

TAXI

Several reliable companies offer metered taxis. All charge fairly similar rates. Flag fall is around 20,000d, which takes you 1km to 2km; every kilometre thereafter costs around 15,000d. Some dodgy operators have high-speed meters, so use these more reliable companies.

Hanoi Taxi (☎ 04-3853 5353)
Mai Linh (☎ 04-3822 2666)
Thanh Nga Taxi (☎ 04-3821 5215)
Van Xuan (☎ 04-3822 2888)

AROUND HANOI

The fertile soils along the Red River Delta nurture a rich rice crop, and many of the communities surrounding Hanoi are still engaged in agriculture. The contrast between modern Hanoi and the rural villages is stark.

In recent decades, numerous villages surrounding Hanoi specialised in cottage industries, but many seem to have been swallowed up by Hanoi's urban sprawl. There are two working villages in particular that remain a rewarding day trip, though having a good guide helps make the journey really worthwhile. Most Hanoi tour operators can take you there.

WORTH A TRIP

THAY & TAY PHUONG PAGODAS

Stunning limestone outcrops loom up from the emerald-green paddy fields, and clinging to the cliffs are the Thay and Tay Phuong pagodas, about 20 minutes from each other by road.

The pagodas are located about 30km west of Hanoi in Ha Tay province. Hanoi travel agents and tour operators offer day trips that take in both pagodas, from US$45 per person.

Tay Phuong Pagoda (Pagoda of the West; admission 5000d) Tay Phuong Pagoda, also known as Sung Phuc Pagoda, consists of three single-level structures built in descending order on a hillock that is said to resemble a buffalo. Figures representing 'the conditions of man' are the pagoda's most celebrated feature – carved from jackfruit wood, many date from the 18th century. The earliest construction dates from the 8th century.

Take the steep steps up to the main pagoda building, then find a path at the back that loops down past the other two pagodas and wander through the adjacent hillside village.

Thay Pagoda (Master's Pagoda; admission 5000d) Also known as Thien Phuc (Heavenly Blessing), Thay Pagoda is dedicated to Thich Ca Buddha (Sakyamuni, the historical Buddha). To the left of the main altar is a statue of the 12th-century monk Tu Dao Hanh, the master in whose honour the pagoda is named. To the right is a statue of King Ly Nhan Tong, who is believed to have been a reincarnation of Tu Dao Hanh.

In front of the pagoda is a small stage built on stilts in the middle of a pond where water-puppet shows are staged during festivals. Follow the path around the outside of the main pagoda building and take a steep 10-minute climb up to a beautiful smaller pagoda perched high on the rock. Thay Pagoda is a big and confusing complex for non-Buddhists – consider hiring a guide.

The pagoda's **annual festival** is held from the fifth to the seventh days of the third lunar month (approximately March). Visitors enjoy watching water-puppet shows, hiking and exploring caves in the area.

Bat Trang is known as the 'ceramic village'. Here, artisans mass-produce ceramic vases and other pieces in their kilns. It's hot, sweaty work, but the results are superb and very reasonably priced compared with the boutiques in town. There are masses of ceramic shops, but poke around down the lanes and behind the shops to find the kilns. Bat Trang is 13km southeast of Hanoi. Public bus 47 runs here from Long Bien bus station.

Van Phuc specialises in silk. Silk cloth is produced here on looms and lots of visitors like to buy or order tailor-made clothes. Many of the fine silk items you see on sale in Hanoi's P Hang Gai are made in Van Phuc. There's also a pretty village pagoda with a lily pond. Van Phuc is 8km southwest of Hanoi; take city bus 1 from Long Bien bus station. Look out for the well-signposted gate.

Sights

Ho Chi Minh Trail Museum MUSEUM

(☎034-382 0889; Hwy 6, towards Hoa Binh; admission 20,000d; ⏰7.30-11.30am & 1.30-2.30pm Mon-Sat) A throwback to the 1980s, this graphic museum, about 13km southwest of the Old Quarter, is dedicated to the famous supply route from the Communist north to the occupied south of Vietnam. The displays, including an abundance of American ammunition and weaponry as well as some powerful photography, document all too clearly the horrors of the American War, from a distinctly Vietnamese viewpoint. Put simply, defeat was not an option for the Viet Cong.

If you have an interest in the American War, you're best advised to hire a local guide from a reputable travel agency to bring you here on a half-day tour.

Co Loa Citadel HISTORIC SITE

(Co Loa Thanh; admission per person/car 10,000/20,000d; ⌚7.30am-5.30pm) Located 16km north of the Old Quarter and dating from the 3rd century BC, Co Loa Citadel was the first fortified citadel in Vietnamese history and became the national capital during the reign of Ngo Quyen (AD 939–44). Only vestiges of the ancient ramparts, which enclosed an area of about 5 sq km, remain.

In the centre of the citadel are temples dedicated to the rule of King An Duong Vuong (257–208 BC), who founded the legendary Thuc dynasty, and his daughter My Nuong (Mi Chau). Legend tells that My Nuong showed her father's magic crossbow trigger (which made him invincible in battle) to her husband, the son of a Chinese general. He stole it and gave it to his father. With this not-so-secret weapon, the Chinese defeated An Duong Vuong, beginning 1000 years of Chinese occupation.

Public bus 46 (5000d) runs here every 15 minutes from My Dinh bus station in Hanoi. Buses run regularly from Hanoi's Luong Yen bus station to My Dinh. From the Co Loa bus station, cross the bridge, turn left and walk for around 500m.

Perfume Pagoda BUDDHIST COMPLEX

(Chua Huong; Huong Son, My Duc; admission incl return boat trip 100,000d) About 60km southwest of Hanoi lies this striking complex of pagodas and Buddhist shrines built into the karst cliffs of Huong Tich Mountain (Mountain of the Fragrant Traces). Among the better-known sites here are Thien Chu (Pagoda Leading to Heaven); Giai Oan Chu (Purgatorial Pagoda), where the faithful believe deities purify souls, cure sufferings and grant offspring to childless families; and Huong Tich Chu (Pagoda of the Perfumed Vestige). It's extremely popular with Vietnamese tourists from February to April, but remarkably peaceful during other times.

Getting to the pagodas requires a journey first by road, then by river, then on foot or by cable car. The journey is half the fun, but don't try and do it without a guide: most tour operators offer day-return trips here from US$20 to US$30.

Travel from Hanoi by car for two hours to My Duc, then take a small boat, rowed by women from the local village, for one hour to the foot of the mountain. This entertaining boat trip travels along scenic waterways between limestone cliffs. Allow a couple more hours to climb to the top and return. The path to the summit is steep in places and if it's raining the ground can get very slippery. There's also a cable car to the summit (one way/return 80,000/120,000d), and a smart combination is to catch the cable car up and then walk down.

Activities

Many tour operators in Hanoi offer cycling tours to villages near Hanoi – a great way to discover a different world.

Lotussia CYCLING

(☎04-2249 4668; www.vietnamcycling.com; 4th fl, 2/62 Nguyen Chi Thanh, Hanoi) Lotussia specialises in cycling tours from Hanoi, some taking in the Thay and Tay Phuong pagodas and nearby handicraft villages, as well as venturing into central and northern Vietnam.

These tours also avoid having to struggle through Hanoi's ferocious traffic, as a minibus takes the strain through the suburbs.

Ba Vi National Park

☎034

Formerly a French hill station, the triple-peaked Ba Vi Mountain (Nui Ba Vi) has been attracting visitors for decades and remains a popular weekend escape for Hanoians. The limestone mountain is now part of the **Ba Vi National Park** (☎034-388 1205; per person/motorbike 10,000/5000d), which has several rare and endangered plants in its protected forest, as well as mammals, including two species of rare 'flying' squirrel and bountiful bird life.

There's an orchid garden and a bird garden, and hiking opportunities through the forested slopes. A **temple** dedicated to Ho Chi Minh sits at the mountain's summit (1276m) – it's a difficult but beautiful 30-minute climb up 1229 steps through the trees. Fog often shrouds the peak, but despite the damp and mist it's eerily atmospheric – visit between April and December for the best chance of clear views down to the Song Hong valley and Hanoi in the distance.

Getting There & Away

Ba Vi National Park is about 65km west of Hanoi, and the most practical option is to visit on a day return trip with a guide and/or hired vehicle from Hanoi, which should cost around US$60. There has been some confusion between attractions near Ba Vi town – which is well away from the park boundaries – and Ba Vi National Park. Make sure your driver/tour operator knows you want the national park.

Tam Dao Hill Station

☎0211 / ELEV 930M

Nestling below soaring forest-clad peaks, Tam Dao is a former French hill station in a spectacular setting northwest of Hanoi. Today it's a popular summer resort – a favoured weekend escape for Hanoians, who come here to revel in the temperate climate and make merry in the extensive selection of restaurants and bars. Founded in 1907 by the French, most of its colonial villas were destroyed during the Franco–Viet Minh War, only to be replaced with brutalist concrete architecture. Tam Dao is a useful base for hiking, but the town itself is an unattractive sprawl of hotel blocks.

Remember that it is cool up in Tam Dao, and this part of Vietnam has a distinct winter. Don't be caught unprepared.

The best time to visit is between late April and mid-October, when the mist sometimes lifts and the weather can be fine. Weekends can be packed but weekdays are less busy.

Sights & Activities

Tam Dao National Park NATURE RESERVE

(admission 20,000d) Tam Dao National Park was designated in 1996 and covers much of the area around the town. Tam Dao means 'Three Islands', and the three summits of Tam Dao Mountain, all about 1400m in height, are sometimes visible to the northeast of the hill station, floating like islands in the mist.

There are at least 64 mammal species (including langurs) and 239 bird species in the park, but you'll need a good local guide and be prepared to do some hiking to find them. Illegal hunting remains a big problem.

Hikes vary from half an hour return to the waterfall, to day treks taking in bamboo forest and primary tropical forest. A guide is essential for the longer hikes and can be hired from 400,000d; ask at the Mela Hotel.

Sleeping & Eating

The town is easy to navigate, so look around and negotiate. There are also plenty of hotel restaurants and good *com pho* (rice-noodle soup) places. Try to avoid eating the local wildlife; you'll frequently see civet, squirrel, porcupine, fox and pheasant advertised, but most of these are endangered species.

Huong Lien Hotel HOTEL $

(☎0211-382 4282; r weekday/weekend 250,000/350,000d;) Offering decent value for the price, most of the rooms here have balconies to make the most of those misty mountain views. There's a little restaurant as well (mains 120,000d to 200,000d).

Nha Khach Ngan Hang GUESTHOUSE $

(☎0989 152 969; r 180,000-200,000d;) Situated opposite the Phuong Nam Quan restaurant, this spotless guesthouse sits beside a plot of *xu xu,* the local green vegetable. Try it with garlic when you ask about accommodation.

Getting There & Away

Tam Dao is 85km northwest of Hanoi in Vinh Phuc province. Buses to the town of Vinh Yen (55,000d, frequent 6am to 4pm) leave from Hanoi's Gia Lam bus station. From Vinh Yen hire a *xe om* (one way around 170,000d) or a taxi (320,000d) to travel the 24km road up to Tam Dao.

On a motorbike from Hanoi, the journey takes around three hours, and the last part of the ride into the national park is beautiful.

Northern Vietnam

Includes ➡

Best Places to Eat

- Hill Station Signature Restaurant (p141)
- Nam Giao (p106)
- Thanh Lan Com Binh Dan (p124)

Best Local Markets

- Dong Van Market (p150)
- Bac Ha Market (p145)
- Na Giang Market (p126)
- Sin Cheng Market (p146)
- Sinho Market (p135)

Why Go?

Vistas. This is Vietnam's big-sky country; a place of rippling mountains, cascading rice terraces and the winnowed-out karst topography for which the region is famed.

Halong Bay's seascape of limestone towers is the view everyone's here to see, but the karst connection continues inland, to Ba Be's sprawling lakes and the knobbly topped peaks of Ha Giang, until it segues into the evergreen hills of the northwest highlands.

Not to be outdone by the scenery, northern Vietnam's cultural kaleidoscope is just as diverse. In this heartland of hill-tribe culture, villages snuggle between paddy-field patchworks outside of Sapa and the scarlet headdresses of the Dzao and the Black Hmong's indigo fabrics add dizzying colour to chaotic highland markets.

The twisting ribbon-roads winding north from Hanoi reveal a rural world far removed from Vietnam's horns-a-honking big-city streets. If you're up for some road-tripping, this is the place to do it.

When to Go

Halong City

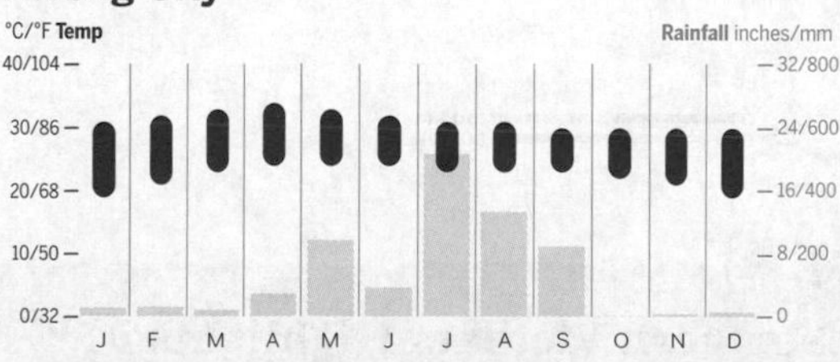

May The month before high season begins to hit has sunny days aplenty yet few crowds.

Late Aug–Sep Hike Sapa and Bac Ha during harvest season.

Nov Blue skies, calm seas; the perfect time for Halong Bay.

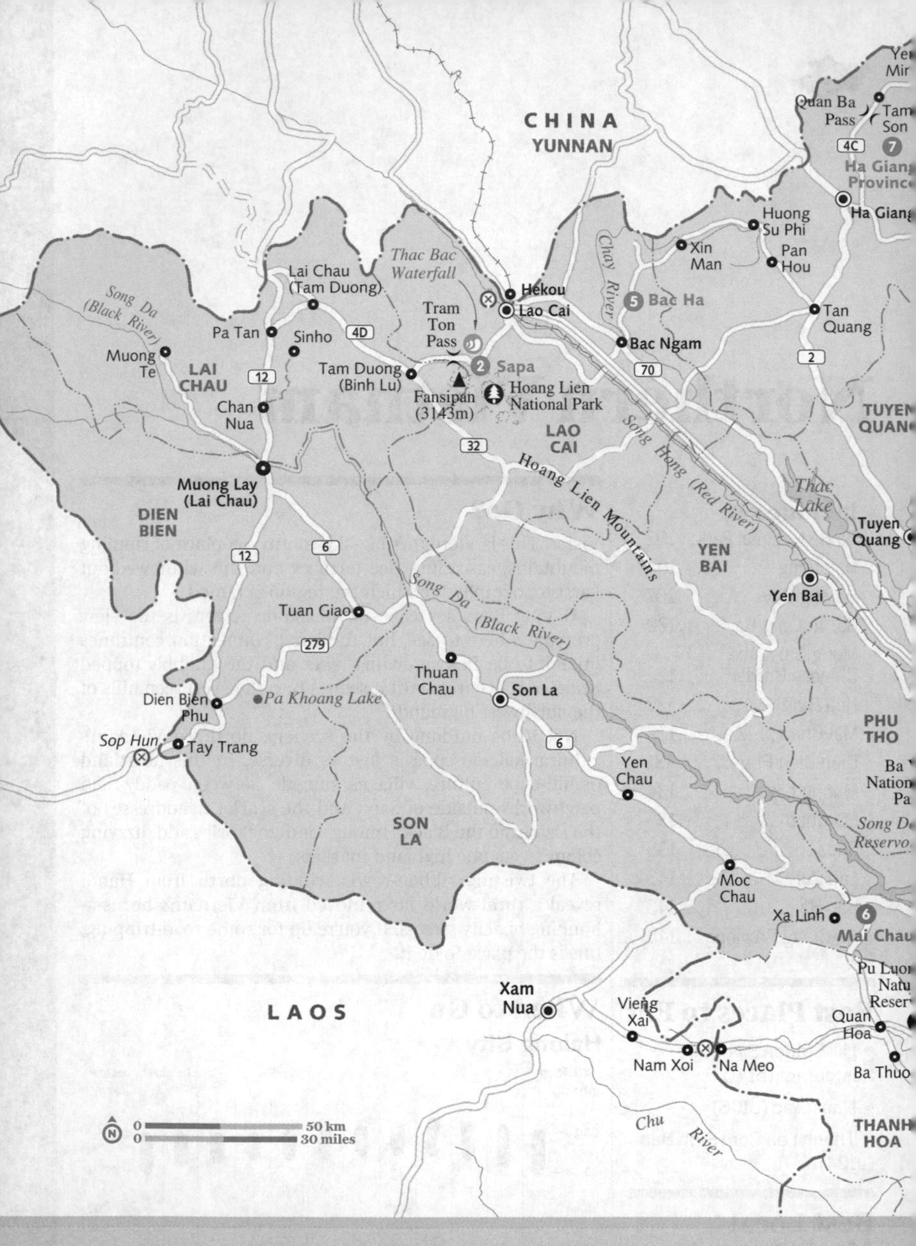

Northern Vietnam Highlights

1 Kayaking within the karsts, into lagoons and grottoes in **Halong Bay** (p107).

2 Trekking mountain trails to the hill-tribe villages around **Sapa** (p136).

3 Gliding across the tranquil lakes of **Ba Be National Park** (p102), soaking up the serene scenery of shoreline village huddles and soaring mountain peaks.

4 Diving into northern Vietnam's action-adventure centre, hiking, biking and climbing your way around **Cat Ba Island** (p112).

5 Exploring a lesser-seen slice of the north, trekking the lush countryside speckled with hill-tribe villages from **Bac Ha** (p145).

6 Resetting your travel batteries after the Hanoi hustle by meandering through green checkerboards of rice paddies in **Mai Chau** (p129).

7 Twisting and turning your way across scenic mountain passes on the north's greatest road trip in **Ha Giang province** (p148).

NORTHEAST VIETNAM

History

Dominated by the Red River basin and the sea, the fertile northeast is the cradle of Vietnamese civilisation. Until very recently, Vietnam has had challenging relations with the neighbouring Chinese. China occupied the country in the 2nd century BC, and was not vanquished until the 10th century.

Any time the Chinese wanted to advance upon Vietnam's affairs, they could do so through the northeast. The most recent occurrence was in a 1979 attempt to punish the Vietnamese for their occupation of Cambodia. Thousands of ethnic Chinese also fled this region in the 1970s and 1980s during the war between Vietnam and China.

More than three decades on, border trade is surging ahead and Chinese tourists flock to the region during summer.

Getting There & Away

Hanoi is the gateway to the northeast. Road connections are fast and buses frequent in the lowlands, but as the terrain gets more mountainous, things slow down considerably and buses get creakier. There are also slow rail links to Haiphong and Lang Son.

Ba Be National Park

☎ 0281

Often referred to as the Ba Be Lakes, **Ba Be National Park** (☎ 0281-389 4014; admission 25,000d) was established in 1992 as Vietnam's eighth national park. The scenery here swoops from towering limestone mountains peaking at 1554m down into plunging valleys wrapped in dense evergreen forests, speckled with waterfalls and caves, with the lakes themselves dominating the very heart of the park.

The park is a rainforest area with more than 550 named plant species, and the government subsidises the villagers not to cut down the trees. The hundreds of wildlife species here include 65 (mostly rarely seen) mammals, 353 butterflies, 106 species of fish, four kinds of turtle, the highly endangered Vietnamese salamander and even the Burmese python. Ba Be bird life is equally prolific, with 233 species recorded, including the spectacular crested serpent eagle and the oriental honey buzzard. Hunting is forbidden, but villagers are permitted to fish.

The region is home to 13 tribal villages, most belonging to the Tay minority plus smaller numbers of Dzao and Hmong.

The park entrance fee is payable at a checkpoint on the road into the park, about 15km before the park headquarters, just beyond the town of Cho Ra.

Sights & Activities

Homestay owners as well as park staff can help organise activities. Boat trips (around 650,000d, up to 12 passengers) are the most popular activity but there's also opportunities for kayaking, cycling and trekking.

Trekking routes can take in Hmong, Tay and Dzao villages scattered through the park. Trekking costs depend on the number of people, starting at about US$30 per day for a solo traveller, less for a group.

Ba Be Lake — LAKE

Rimmed by limestone peaks that swoop down to the shoreline, Ba Be (meaning Three Bays) is in fact three linked lakes, with a total length of 8km and a width of about 400m.

Most boat excursions around the lakes visit the **An Ma Pagoda**, on an islet in the middle of the lake, and the 300m-long tunnel-like **Hang Puong** (Puong Cave), full of stalactites and stalagmites and home to as many as 7000 bats (belonging to 18 species).

Other Ba Be Lake stops can include the pretty Tay village of **Cam Ha** (where every timber house has a satellite dish) and the startling, circular, jungle-rimmed lagoon of **Ao Tien**.

More than a hundred species of freshwater fish inhabit the lake and plentiful bird life is easily spotted – keep an eye out for kingfishers and raptors. Two of the lakes are separated by a 100m-wide strip of water called Be Kam, sandwiched between high walls of chalk rock.

Hua Ma Cave — CAVE

(admission 22,000d; 9am-5pm) One of Ba Be's most popular off-the-water sights is this 800m-long cave complex with a pathway leading down into a soaring cavern (up to 50m high) full of stalactites and stalagmites. Bring a torch (flashlight) to illuminate the darker recesses.

Dau Dang Waterfall — WATERFALL

(Thac Dau Dang) The Dau Dang Waterfall (also called the Ta Ken Waterfall) is a series of spectacular cascades between sheer walls of rock.

Tours

Most travellers come to Ba Be on pre-arranged private tours organised through Hanoi-based travel agencies.

Ba Be Tourism Centre ADVENTURE TOUR
(☎0989 587 400; www.babenationalpark.com.vn; Bo Lu village) This enthusiastic local office, dealing in everything Ba Be, can arrange kayaking, boating, hiking and cycling trips (or a combo of all four) for around US$30 per day. Hires kayaks for US$5 per hour. Specialises in multiday treks and camping trips in the further reaches of the national park.

Sleeping & Eating

Ba Be has a well-established homestay program allowing travellers to experience lakeside village life in typical stilted houses. Most of the homestays are in Pac Ngoi village. All have hot water and can provide meals (50,000d to 80,000d) as long as they are ordered in advance. The even quieter lake villages of Bo Lu and Coc Toc also have a couple of options.

The Ba Be National Park office can organise homestays for independent travellers but you can also just show up and check in.

Another option is to use the nearby town of Cho Ra as a base.

Mr Linh's Homestay GUESTHOUSE $
(☎0989 587 400; www.mrlinhhomestay.com; Coc Toc village; dm/s/d incl breakfast US$5/20/25; ❄📶) A step up in amenities to Ba Be's homestays, this lakeside place in Coc Toc village is run by the same crew behind Ba Be Tourism Centre. Small, spick-and-span wood-panelled private rooms, and a dorm, all share bathrooms. Kayaks can be hired, and pre-ordered set menu meals cost 120,000d.

Hoa Son Guesthouse HOMESTAY $
(☎0168 962 3971, 0281-389 4065; Pac Ngoi village; per person 70,000d) The very-well-kept Hoa Son Guesthouse is one of the best Ba Be homestay options, with a huge balcony and lake views. Meals (30,000d to 60,000d) are available, and can include fresh fish from the lake.

Thuy Dung Guesthouse GUESTHOUSE $
(☎0281-387 6354; 5 Tieu Khu, Cho Ra; r 400,000d; ❄📶) This friendly, family-run spot has basic, clean rooms with balconies and views of the nearby rice paddies. There's a good restaurant, and the staff can arrange onward transport from Cho Ra into the heart of Ba Be National Park.

Information

There is no bank or ATM in Ba Be National Park. Bring all the cash you'll need with you.

Getting There & Away

Ba Be National Park is 240km from Hanoi, 61km from Bac Kan and 18km from Cho Ra.

Most people visit Ba Be as part of a tour, or by chartered vehicle from Hanoi (a 4WD is not necessary).

BUS

From Hanoi, the most direct route to Ba Be's lakeside homestay villages of Pac Ngoi, Bo Lu and Coc Toc is the local bus to Cho Don, via Thai Nguyen, run by Thuong Nga bus company. It leaves My Dinh bus station at 10am (130,000d, four hours). At Cho Don, you hop on a connecting minibus (run by the same company) to Pac Ngoi, Bo Lu and Coc Toc (40,000d).

A more roundabout route is to head into the park via Cho Ra. To Cho Ra directly, there is a daily bus at noon from Hanoi's Gia Lam bus station (180,000d, six hours). A direct bus (90,000d, five hours) also departs from Cao Bang for Cho Ra at noon. There are also regular bus services from both Thai Nguyen and Cho Don to Cho Ra. Once in Cho Ra you can arrange a *xe om* (motorbike taxi; about 100,000d) to cover the last 18km into the park.

Departing Ba Be's lakeside villages there are minibuses to Cho Don at 6am and 1.30pm. If you're heading northeast from Ba Be, you can get a local bus from Cho Ra to Na Phac, from where there are services to Cao Bang.

Con Son & Den Kiep Bac

Although most appealing to domestic travellers, Con Son and Den Kiep Bac are potential diversions en route to Haiphong or Halong City.

Con Son was home to Nguyen Trai (1380–1442), the famed Vietnamese poet, writer and general who assisted Emperor Le Loi in his successful battle against the Chinese Ming dynasty in the 15th century. **Con Son Pagoda** (Con Son; admission per person/vehicle 5000/15,000d) has a temple honouring Nguyen Trai. It's a strenuous 600-step climb. Alternatively, loop past a spring through pine forests and return down the steps.

Nearby, **Kiep Bac Temple** (Den Kiep Bac; admission per person/vehicle 5000/15,000d) is dedicated to Tran Hung Dao (1228–1300).

Founded in 1300, the temple sits where the legendary general is said to have died. Within the complex there's an exhibition on his exploits, but you'll need someone to translate. The annual **Tran Hung Dao Festival** here is held on the 20th day of the eighth lunar month, usually in October.

Den Kiep Bac and Con Son are in Hai Duong province, about 80km east of Hanoi. With your own wheels, it's easy to detour en route to Haiphong or Halong Bay.

Haiphong

☎031 / POP 816,000

Northern Vietnam's most approachable city has a distinctly laid-back air with its tree-lined boulevards host to a bundle of graceful colonial-era buildings. Caffeine-aficionado heaven, the central area buzzes with dinky cafes where tables spill out onto the pavements – perfect for people watching.

Apart from the cafe culture, there's not actually much to do and most travellers only use Haiphong as a transport hop between the bus from Hanoi and the ferry to Cat Ba Island. If you do decide to linger, you'll find a friendly town with minimal hassles that makes a relaxing change from Vietnam's main tourism centres.

History

The French took possession of Haiphong in 1874 and the city developed rapidly, becoming a major port. Heavy industry evolved through the proximity to coal supplies.

The French bombardment of Haiphong in 1946 killed thousands and was a catalyst for the ensuing Franco–Viet Minh War. Between 1965 and 1972 Haiphong came under air and naval attack from the US, and the city's harbour was mined to disrupt Soviet military supplies. In the late 1970s and the 1980s Haiphong experienced a mass exodus that included many ethnic Chinese refugees, who left taking much of the city's fishing fleet with them.

Today Haiphong is a fast-growing city, attracting investment from multinational corporations lured by its port facilities and transport links.

Sights & Activities

Haiphong Museum MUSEUM
(66 P Dien Bien Phu; admission 5000d; ⏲8-11am Tue-Sun & 7.30-9.30pm Wed & Sun) In a splendid colonial building, this small museum concentrates on the city's history with English translations on displays. The front hall's taxidermy collection is rather creepy but there's good exhibits of finds from the Trang Kenh and Viet Khe Tombs archaeological sites and some beautiful ceramic pieces. The museum's garden harbours a diverse collection of war detritus.

Queen of the Rosary Cathedral CATHEDRAL
(P Hoang Van Thu; ⏲24hr) Haiphong's elegant Roman Catholic cathedral was built in the 19th century and comprehensively restored in 2010. The building's grey towers are a local landmark, although the actual interior of the church is rather plain.

Opera House HISTORIC BUILDING
(P Quang Trung) With a facade embellished with white columns, Haiphong's neoclassical Opera House dates from 1904. Unfortunately it's usually not possible to view the interior.

Du Hang Pagoda BUDDHIST TEMPLE
(121 P Chua Hang; ⏲7am-10pm) Du Hang Pagoda was founded three centuries ago. It's been rebuilt several times, but remains a fine example of traditional Vietnamese architecture and sculpture. P Chua Hang leading to the pagoda is a narrow thoroughfare, bustling with Haiphong street life. The pagoda is around 1.5km southwest of Haiphong's main street, P Dien Bien Phu.

Navy Museum MUSEUM
(P Dien Bien Phu; ⏲8-11am Tue, Thu & Sat) FREE The Navy Museum is interesting for visiting sailors and US Vietnam veterans.

Sleeping

Bao Anh Hotel HOTEL $
(☎031-382 3406; www.hotelbaoanh.com; 20 P Minh Khai; r incl breakfast 400,000-600,000d; ❄📶) Refurbished with lots of white paint and new white linen, the Bao Anh has a great location in a leafy street framed by plane trees and buzzy cafes. It's a short walk to good beer places if you're after something stronger. The friendly English-speaking reception is definitely open to negotiation.

Monaco Hotel HOTEL $$
(☎031-374 6468; www.haiphongmonacohotel.com; 103 P Dien Bien Phu; r incl breakfast US$30-50; P❄📶) Modern and central, the Monaco features a smart lobby with helpful staff that speak a little English. The spacious, spotless

Haiphong

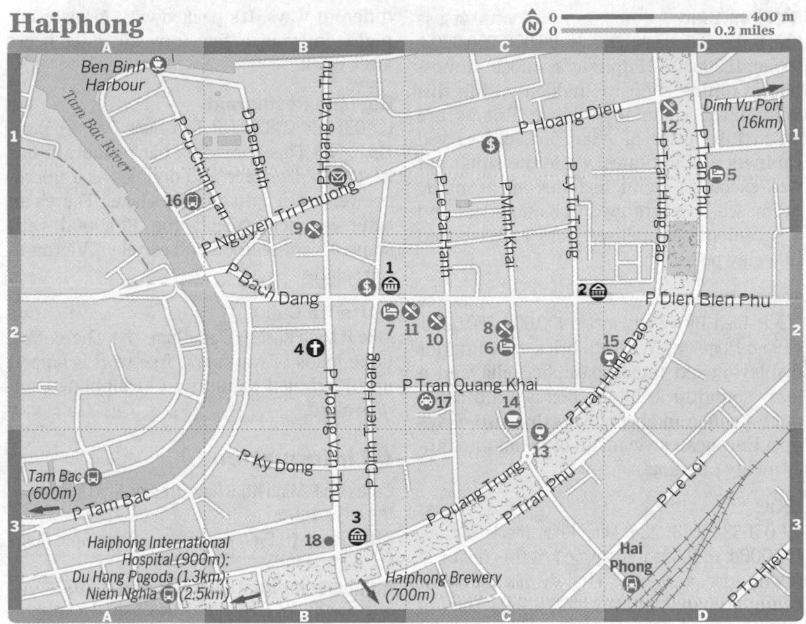

Haiphong

Sights
1 Haiphong Museum ... B2
2 Navy Museum ... C2
3 Opera House ... B3
4 Queen of the Rosary Cathedral ... B2

Sleeping
5 AVANI Hai Phong Harbour View Hotel ... D1
6 Bao Anh Hotel ... C2
7 Monaco Hotel ... B2

Eating
8 BKK ... C2
9 Com Vietnam ... B1
10 Nam Giao ... C2
11 Phono Box ... C2
12 Van Tue ... D1

Drinking & Nightlife
13 Big Man Restaurant ... C3
14 Caffe Tra Cuc ... C2
15 Vuon Dua ... D2

Transport
16 Lac Long Bus Station ... A1
17 Taxi Rank ... C2
18 Vietnam Airlines ... B3

rooms have rather uninspired decor but come with attractive bathrooms.

Avani Hai Phong Harbour View Hotel HOTEL $$$
(031-382 7827; www.avanihotels.com; 12 P Tran Phu; r incl breakfast US$125-140; P ❄ 📶 🏊) Built in replica-colonial style in 1998, this hotel has classically styled rooms and good facilities, including a gym, spa and the excellent Nam Phuong Restaurant. The super-friendly team on reception can arrange tours around Haiphong in a vintage Citroën car. Be sure to try for a substantial discount off rack rates.

Eating

Haiphong is noted for its fresh seafood. Visit P Quang Trung for seafood restaurants with point-and-cook tanks, as well as *bia hoi* (beer) joints. For more stylish cafes and restaurants, take a wander along P Minh Khai.

Com Vietnam VIETNAMESE $
(031-384 1698; 4a P Hoang Van Thu; meals 40,000-60,000d; 11am-9pm) This restaurant hits the spot for its affordable local seafood and Vietnamese specialities. Diminutive, unpretentious and with a small patio.

★Nam Giao VIETNAMESE $$
(22 P Le Dai Hanh; meals 90,000-250,000d; 7am-11.30pm) Haiphong's most atmospheric dining choice is hidden within this dilapidated colonial building. Rooms are an artful clutter of Asian art, old carved cabinets and antiques, while the small but well-executed menu includes an aromatic herby sea bass wrapped in banana leaf and a succulent caramelised pork belly cooked in a clay pot.

Phono Box CAFE $$
(79 P Dien Bien Phu; meals 100,000-250,000d; 9am-11pm;) With its brick-wall interior displaying old music paraphernalia and a jazzy soundtrack, Phono Box is a hip hangout for coffee and beer lovers that also serves up a European-style menu of steaks and other meaty offerings.

BKK THAI $$
(031-382 1018; 22 P Minh Khai; meals 80,000-150,000d; 11.30am-10pm;) At this restored townhouse, authentic Thai dishes are beautifully prepared and presented – try the *lab moo* (pork salad) or pepper squid; there are good vegetarian options too. Leave room for dessert, which includes delicious coconut ice cream.

Van Tue SEAFOOD $$
(031-374 6338; 1 P Hoang Dieu; meals 100,000-250,000d; 11am-11pm) This elegant French colonial villa is renowned for seafood, including an amazing selection of crab dishes. More exotic dishes featuring deer and goat are also on the menu. A favourite with local well-to-do families.

Drinking & Entertainment

P Minh Khai is the heart of Haiphong's caffeine action, where most cafes have street terraces, serve beer and have a snack menu.

Haiphong Brewery BIA HOI
(16 Đ Lach Tray; 10am-8pm) The local brew is deservedly renowned around Vietnam, and the best place to try it is at the brewery's bustling beer hall. Lunchtimes get very crowded – the food is cheap and very good – but staff can always find room for a few more drinkers. The brewery is a short cab ride to the southeast of the city centre.

Vuon Dua BIA HOI
(5 P Tran Hung Dao; 11am-11pm) Boisterous beer garden with lots of cheap brews, and squid, chicken and pork prepared in many different ways. It's packed with locals every night enjoying a few (not so) quiet beers after work.

Big Man Restaurant BAR
(031-384 2383; 7 P Tran Hung Dao; 11am-11pm;) This sprawling bar-restaurant has an outdoor terrace and doubles as a microbrewery with light and dark lager. There's an extensive menu (meals from 100,000d) with some decent seafood and excellent Vietnamese salads.

Caffe Tra Cuc CAFE
(46c P Minh Khai; 7am-11pm;) The coffee, done loads of ways, and free wi-fi is lapped up by grizzled regulars and Haiphong trendies alike.

Information

Cafes on P Minh Khai have free wi-fi. ATMs dot the city centre.

BIDV Bank (P Dien Bien Phu; 8am-3pm Mon-Fri, 8am-11am Sat, ATM 24hr)

Haiphong International Hospital (031-395 5888; 124 P Nguyen Duc Canh) Recently built and modern, with some English-speaking doctors.

Getting There & Away

AIR

Cat Bi airport is 6km southeast of central Haiphong. Daily flights to Ho Chi Minh City and Danang are offered by **Jetstar Pacific Airways** (1900 1550; www.jetstar.com), **Vietnam Airlines** (031-381 0890; www.vietnamair.com.vn; 30 P Hoang Van Thu) and **VietJet** (1900 1886; www.vietjetair.com).

BOAT

Ben Binh Harbour (Đ Ben Binh) Boats leave from the ferry pier, 10 minutes' walk from the city centre. Hydrofoils depart for Cat Ba Town (220,000d, around one hour depending on sea conditions) at 7am, 9am, 1pm and 3pm.

Note that due to a new bridge being built between Haiphong and Cat Hai Island, Ben Binh ferry pier may move to Cat Hai Island after the bridge is finished (with bridge completion pegged for summer 2017).

BUS

Haiphong has three long-distance bus stations:

Lac Long Bus Station (P Cu Chinh Lan) The closest bus station to Haiphong city centre and very convenient for those connecting with the Cat Ba boats at nearby Ben Binh Harbour. Operates services heading north from Haiphong and to Hanoi.

BUSES FROM HAIPHONG'S LAC LONG BUS STATION

DESTINATION	DURATION (HR)	COST (D)	FREQUENCY
Bai Chay (Halong City)	2	60,000	frequent 5am-5pm
Cai Rong (Van Don Island)	3	70,000	frequent 5am-6pm
Hanoi (Giap Bat bus station)	2	70,000	frequent 5am-6pm
Lang Son	7	80,000	5.30am
Mong Cai	5¾	160,000	8am, 10am, 1pm, 7.30pm, 8pm, 8.30pm, 9pm, 10.30pm

Niem Nghia Bus Station (Đ Tran Nguyen Han) Serves destinations south of Haiphong, such as to Ninh Binh (120,000d, 3½ hours, every 30 minutes).

Tam Bac Bus Station (P Tam Bac) Buses to Hanoi (70,000d, two hours, every 10 minutes).

CAR & MOTORBIKE

Haiphong is 103km from Hanoi on the expressway, Hwy 5.

TRAIN

A slow spur-line service travels daily to Hanoi's Long Bien station (48,000d, 2½ hours, 6.05am, 8.55am, 2.55pm, 6.40pm).

Getting Around

A taxi from central Haiphong to Cat Bi airport should be around 150,000d. Try **Haiphong Taxi** (031-383 8383) or **Taxi Mai Linh** (031-383 3833).

A xe om from the bus stations to the hotels should be around 30,000d.

Halong Bay

033

Towering limestone pillars and tiny islets topped by forest rise from the emerald waters of the Gulf of Tonkin. Halong translates as 'where the dragon descends into the sea' and legend tells that this mystical seascape was created when a great mountain dragon charged towards the coast, its flailing tail gouging out valleys and crevasses. As the creature plunged into the sea, the area filled with water leaving only the pinnacles visible. The geological explanation of karst erosion may be more prosaic, but doesn't make this seascape any less poetic.

Designated a World Heritage site in 1994, Halong Bay's spectacular scatter of islands, dotted with wind- and wave-eroded grottoes, is a vision of ethereal beauty and, unsurprisingly, northern Vietnam's number one tourism hub. Sprawling Halong City is the bay's main gateway but its dowdy high-rises are a disappointing doorstep to this site. Most visitors sensibly opt for cruise-tours that include sleeping on board within the bay, while a growing number are deciding to eschew the main bay completely, heading straight for Cat Ba Island from where trips to less-visited but equally alluring Lan Ha Bay are easily set up.

Halong Bay attracts visitors year-round with peak season between late May and early August. January to March is often cool and drizzly, and the ensuing fog can make visibility low, but adds bags of eerie atmosphere. From May to September tropical storms are frequent, and year-round tourist boats sometimes need to alter their itineraries, depending on the weather. November's sunny blue-sky days and lack of crowds make it the best time to make a beeline here.

Sights & Activities

Most cruises and day-tripper boats include at least a couple of caves, an island stop-off, and a visit to one of Halong Bay's **floating villages**. The villagers here farm fish, which are caught offshore and fattened up in netted enclosures.

Caves

Halong Bay's islands are peppered with caves, many now illuminated with technicolor lighting effects. Sadly, litter and trinket-touting vendors are also part of the experience.

Which of the caves you'll visit depends on factors, including the weather and the number of other boats in the vicinity.

Hang Dau Go CAVE

(Cave of Wooden Stakes) This huge cave consists of three chambers reached via 90 steps. Inside, ceilings soar up to 25m high while

Halong Bay & Bai Tu Long Bay

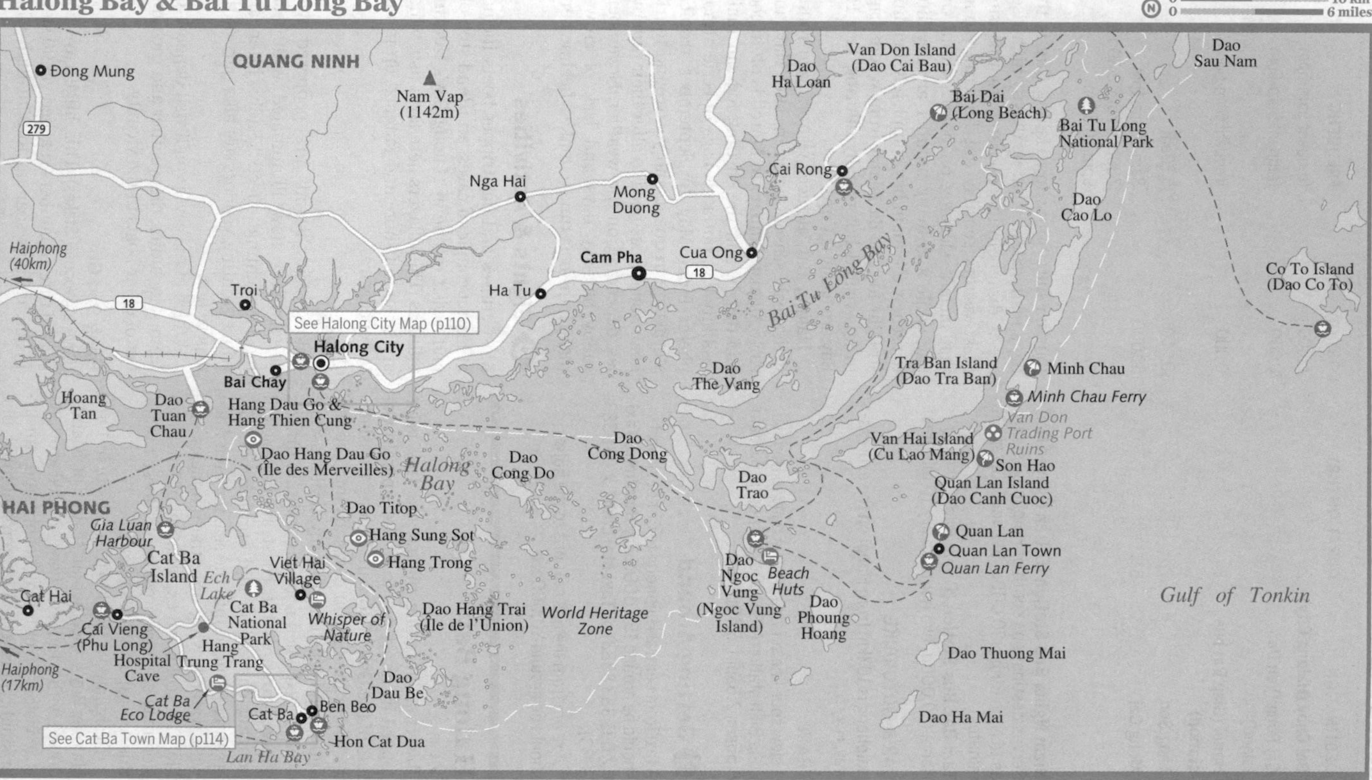

some rather disco-festive lighting illuminates a wacky array of stalactites. Among the stalactites of the first hall, scores of gnomes appear to be holding a meeting. The cave derives its name from the role it played during the 13th-century battles with the Mongolians when locals stored wooden stakes, used to destroy invading ships, in the third chamber here.

Hang Thien Cung CAVE

Part of the same cave system as Hang Dau Go, nearby Hang Thien Cung has 'cauliflower' limestone growths as well as stalactites and stalagmites.

Hang Sung Sot CAVE

(Surprise Cave) The popular Hang Sung Sot has three vast chambers; in the second there's a pink-lit rock phallus unsurprisingly regarded as a fertility symbol. Even less surprisingly, some guides refer to it as the 'Cock Rock'.

Hang Trong CAVE

(Drum Grotto) Hang Trong has wide-arched entrances on either side and a ceiling clustered with stalactites. It's named because when the wind blows through its stalactites, the effect resembles the sound of distant drumbeats.

Islands & Islets

Cat Ba Island is the most developed of Halong Bay's islands with Cat Ba Town the launching pad for the Lan Ha Bay region. Some Halong Bay cruise operators include Cat Ba and Lan Ha Bay on their itineraries.

Dao Titop ISLAND

(Titop Island) This small island (complete with a scruffy beach) is a popular boat stop for superb panoramic views across Halong Bay from its summit.

Dao Ga Choi ISLAND

(Fighting Cockerel Islet) One of Halong Bay's most photographed sites, these two jagged rocks jutting 10m out of the water look like two fighting cockerels having a face-off.

Kayaking

A kayak among the karsts is an option on most Halong Bay tours. Count on about an hour's paddling, often including negotiating your way through karst grottoes and around lagoons, or to a **floating village** in the bay.

If you're really keen on kayaking, contact Handspan Adventure Travel (p88) in Hanoi or Blue Swimmer (p116) on Cat Ba Island, both of which run professionally organised trips and have qualified guides. Trips are operated in less-touristed Lan Ha Bay.

WATCH THOSE VALUABLES!

Take real care with your valuables when cruising the waters of Halong Bay on day-trip boats. Do not leave them unattended as they might grow legs and walk. When it comes to overnight cruises, most boats have lockable cabins.

Information

All visitors must purchase entry tickets for the **national park** (admission 120,000d) and there are also separate admission tickets for attractions in the bay, such as caves and fishing villages (30,000d to 50,000d). Most admission fees are included with organised cruises, but check when booking.

Halong Bay Tourist Information Centre (033-384 7481; www.halong.org.vn; Bai Chay Tourist Wharf, Đ Halong; 7am-4pm) The official Halong Bay Tourist Information Centre is at Bai Chay Tourist Wharf in Halong City. Here you'll find English-speaking staff and excellent maps (20,000d) of the Halong Bay area.

Getting There & Around

Most travellers elect to experience Halong Bay on a cruise-tour prearranged in Hanoi, which usually includes transfers to/from the bay.

It's also possible to head to Halong City (Bai Chay) independently and book a boat trip at Bai Chay Tourist Wharf.

Alternatively, head directly to Cat Ba Island from Hanoi and arrange a boat trip from there to explore Lan Ha Bay.

Bai Chay Tourist Wharf (Đ Halong, Halong City; 7am-6pm) From always bustling Bai Chay Tourist Wharf there are two main boat trips. Route One (100,000d, four hours) potters around the waters of nearby islands visiting the caves of Hang Dau Go and Hang Thien Cung. Route Two (150,000d, six hours) heads further into the bay to Hang Sung Sot and Dao Titop.

On these trips you also have to factor in the separate admission costs to the national park and to each attraction. These day-trip tours are an entirely local tourist experience. Expect a packed boat and boisterous Vietnamese karaoke tunes pumping from the stereo as your soundtrack.

If there's a group of you to share costs, there's the option of hiring a complete boat and creating your

Halong City

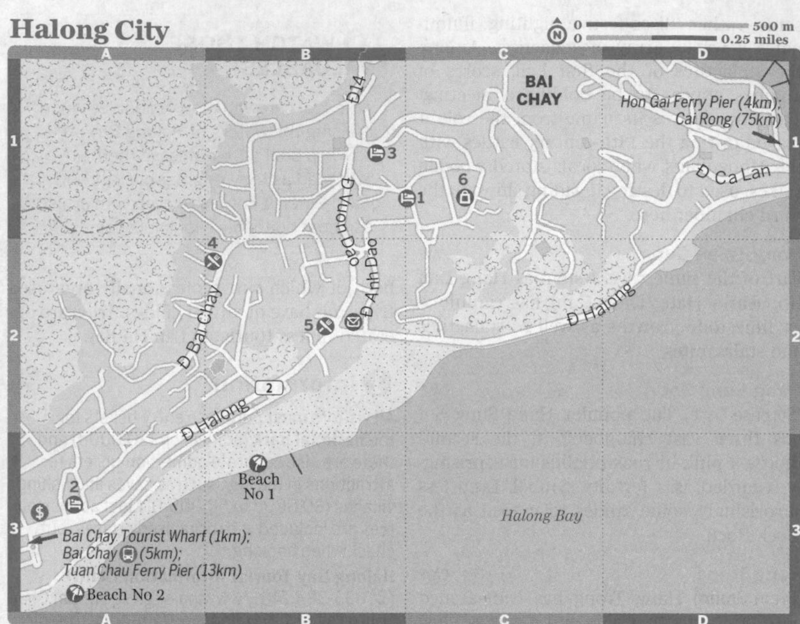

Halong City

Sleeping
1 Halong Backpacker Hostel C1
2 Novotel A3
3 The Light Hotel B1

Eating
4 Linh Dan Restaurant B2
5 Tuan Huong B2

Shopping
6 Bai Chay Market C1

own itinerary (per hour Monday to Friday 400,000d, per hour Saturday and Sunday 500,000d).

Bai Chay Tourist Wharf prices are officially regulated.

Halong City

033 / POP 201,990

Development has not been kind to Halong City (Bai Chay). Despite enjoying a stunning position on the cusp of Halong Bay, this is a gritty town with pockets of bland high-rise hotel development dotting the shoreline.

Many travellers opt to skip Halong City completely, preferring to spend a night out in Halong Bay itself. Increased competition for a dwindling clientele means budget hotel rates are some of the cheapest in Vietnam. Chinese and Korean visitors are now more prevalent, preferring to enjoy terra firma attractions like casinos and karaoke after a day exploring the bay.

Sleeping

Budget accommodation is on, and around, the hotel road of Đ Vuon Dao, home to around 50 identikit minihotels. Midrange and top-end hotels are scattered along Đ Halong and around the harbour area.

Prices are very reasonable outside of the peak season (June to July) or during the Tet festival.

The Light Hotel HOTEL $

(033-384 8518; www.thelighthalong.vn; 108a Đ Vuon Dao; r 350,000d;) The good-sized, modern and super-clean rooms here are excellent value. Chuck in the fact that some of the helpful staff speak English and you've got Halong City's best budget find.

Halong Backpacker Hostel HOSTEL $

(033-361 9333; www.halongbackpackerhostel.com; 41 Đ Anh Dao; dm US$5;) This new hostel (don't confuse it with the 'Halong Backpacker's Hostel' on Đ Vuon Dao) has small, light-filled six-bed dorms and a lively downstairs bar.

DON'T MISS

CRUISING THE KARSTS

The most popular way to experience Halong Bay's karst scenery is on a cruise. Luckily everyone, their grandmother and their friendly family dog wants to sell you a Halong Bay tour in Hanoi. Unluckily, shoddy operators abound.

Every year we receive complaints from travellers about poor service, bad food and rats running around boats on ultra-budget cruises, and more expensive trips where itinerary expectations didn't meet what was delivered.

Tours sold out of Hanoi start from a rock-bottom US$60 per person for a dodgy day trip, and can rise to around US$220 for two nights. For around US$110 to US$130, you should get a worthwhile overnight cruise.

At the other end of the scale, cruising the karsts aboard a luxury Chinese-style junk is hard to beat. But be aware that paying top dollar doesn't necessarily compute into heading away from the crowds.

If you want to experience less-crowded karst views, consider cruises focussed on Lan Ha Bay, near Cat Ba Island.

Most cruise-tours include return transport from Hanoi, Halong Bay entrance fees and meals. A decent overnight tour usually includes kayaking. Drinks are extra.

This is one destination where it definitely pays to do your homework beforehand. Here are some suggestions to help make Halong Bay memorable for the right, rather than wrong, reasons:

➡ It can be a false economy to sign up for an ultra-cheapie tour. Spend a little more and enjoy the experience a whole lot more.

➡ At the very least, check basic on-board safety standards. Life jackets should be provided. If kayaking is included, make sure it's guided. Currents close to the karst formations are surprisingly strong. Accidents can occur when visitors are left to paddle off themselves.

➡ Realise that most Halong Bay cruises follow a strict itinerary, with stops at caves often at the same time as other boats. On an overnight trip there's simply not the time to stray far from Halong City.

➡ Make sure you know what you're paying for to avoid disappointment later. Many cruises (including luxury options) are marketed as 'two-day' trips but are actually overnight tours, some involving less than 24 hours on board.

➡ Ascertain in advance what the tour company's refund policy is if the cruise is cancelled due to bad weather.

Cruise operators to consider:

Cat Ba Ventures (p116) Overnight tours set out from Cat Ba Island and concentrate on the Lan Ha Bay area.

Handspan Adventure Travel (p355) Operates the only true sailing ship on the bay; meander peacefully through the karsts without the constant hum of a diesel engine.

Indochina Sails (☎04-3984 2362; www.indochinasails.com; overnight tour with d cabin from US$478) Cruise Halong on a traditional junk with great viewing decks and cabins kitted out to a three-star standard.

Vega Travel (p88) Good-value overnight tours of Halong Bay, with comfortable cabins. Two-night tours also explore Lan Ha Bay and Cat Ba Island, including kayaking, cycling and hiking.

Novotel HOTEL **$$$**
(☎033-384 8108; www.novotelhalongbay.com; 160 Đ Halong; r from US$95;) The Novotel fuses Asian and Japanese influences with contemporary details. The rooms are simply stunning, with teak floors, marble bathrooms and sliding screens to divide living areas. Facilities include an oval infinity pool and a great restaurant.

BUSES FROM HALONG CITY

DESTINATION	COST (D)	DURATION (HR)	FREQUENCY
Cai Rong (Van Don Island)	35,000	1½	every 30 minutes between 8am & 6pm
Haiphong	60,000	2	frequent 6.20am-5pm
Hanoi	90,000	4	frequent 5.45am-6pm
Lang Son	110,000	5½	6am, 11.45am, 12.15pm
Mong Cai	80,000	4	every 40 minutes between 6.20am & 3pm
Ninh Binh	100,000	4	5.30am, 11.30am
Sapa	400,000	12	7am, 6pm

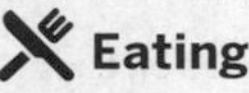

Eating

Halong City is not foodie heaven. Restaurants (many focused on seafood) rim the stretch of Đ Halong west of Bai Chay Tourist Wharf (a 40,000d taxi ride from Đ Vuon Dao).

For cheap, filling food, there are modest eating joints with English menus at the bottom of Đ Vuon Dao, and hole-in-the-wall *pho* places along Đ Bai Chay.

Linh Dan Restaurant VIETNAMESE **$**
(☎033-384 6025; 104 Đ Bai Chay; meals US$3-5; ⏱11am-9pm) Linh Dan has a novella-length menu conjuring up pretty much every stir-fried variation on pork, chicken, seafood and vegetables.

Tuan Huong VIETNAMESE **$**
(☎033-384 4651; 1 Đ Vuon Dao; meals from 80,000d; ⏱10am-10pm) A simple place with a small menu (in English and French) that specialises in fresh seafood. You can also pick your fish or crab from the tanks outside, but make sure you check the price (worked out by weight) first.

Information

Main Post Office (Đ Halong; ⏱7am-6pm Mon-Fri)

Vietcombank (Đ Halong; ⏱8am-3pm Mon-Fri, 8-11.30am Sat)

Getting There & Away

BUS

All buses leave from **Bai Chay bus station** (off Hwy 18), 6km south of central Bai Chay. For Tam Coc, hop on the Ninh Binh–bound bus.

There are regular services to Cai Rong on Van Don Island, where ferries depart for the islands of Bai Tu Long Bay from Cai Rong Pier (Cai Rong Pha).

Note that many buses to Halong City will be marked 'Bai Chay' rather than 'Halong City'.

BOAT

Day-tripping boats leave from Bai Chay Tourist Wharf (p109).

Hon Gai Ferry Pier (Đ Le Thanh Tong) From Hon Gai Ferry Pier (across the suspension bridge from Halong City) there is one daily speedboat service to Quan Lan Island at 1.30pm (160,000d, 1½ hours).

Tuan Chau Ferry Pier (Tuan Chau Island) From Tuan Chau Ferry Pier, 13km southwest of central Bai Chay, there are two car ferries to Cat Ba Island's Gia Luan Harbour at 8am and 3pm (per person/motorbike 70,000/10,000d, one hour) throughout the year with hourly services during the peak period of June to early August.

Gia Luan Harbour is on the other side of the island from Cat Ba Town, so unless you're travelling by motorbike, it's more convenient to catch a ferry to Cat Ba from Haiphong.

CAR & MOTORBIKE

Halong City is 160km from Hanoi and 55km from Haiphong. The one-way trip from Hanoi takes about three hours by private vehicle.

Getting Around

Bai Chay is quite spread out; **Mai Linh** (☎033-382 2226) is a reliable taxi option. A taxi from central Halong City to Tuan Chau Ferry Pier costs around 130,000d.

Cat Ba Island

☎031 / POP 13,500

Rugged, craggy and jungle-clad Cat Ba, the largest island in Halong Bay, has experienced a tourism surge in recent years. The central hub of Cat Ba Town is now framed by a chain of low-rise concrete hotels along its once-lovely bay, but the rest of the island is largely untouched and as wild as ever. With idyllic Lan Ha Bay just offshore you'll soon overlook Cat Ba Town's overdevelopment.

Cat Ba is a pretty laid-back place most of the year and for climbers, kayakers and hikers it's the launching pad for a swag of sweat-inducing activities. Between June and early August (and particularly on summer weekends) the energy level gets dialled up significantly as Cat Ba Town transforms into a roaring resort, filled with vacationing Vietnamese. This is peak season and hotel prices during this period can skyrocket.

Almost half of Cat Ba Island (with a total area of 354 sq km) and 90 sq km of the adjacent waters were declared a national park in 1986 to protect the island's diverse ecosystems. Most of the coastline consists of rocky cliffs, but there are some sandy beaches and tiny fishing villages hidden away in small coves.

Lakes, waterfalls and grottoes dot the spectacular limestone hills, the highest rising 331m above sea level. The island's largest body of water is Ech Lake (3 hectares). Almost all of the surface streams are seasonal. Most of the island's rainwater flows into caves and follows underground streams to the sea, creating a shortage of fresh water during the dry season.

Ho Chi Minh paid a visit to Cat Ba Island on 1 April 1951 and there is an annual festival to commemorate the event. During this time, expect lots of waterfront karaoke and techno beats from 8am to midnight.

Sights

First impressions of Cat Ba Town are not great, but the mediocre vision of a low-rent mini-Manhattan only extends for a street or two behind the promenade. A **Ho Chi Minh monument** (off Đ Nui Ngoc) stands up on Mountain No 1, the hillock opposite the pier in Cat Ba Town. The **market** (7am-7pm) at the northern end of the harbour is a great local affair with twitching crabs, jumbo shrimps and pyramids of fresh fruit. Head out of town for the island's best sights.

★Lan Ha Bay BAY

(admission 30,000d) Lying south and east of Cat Ba Town, the 300 or so karst islands and limestone outcrops of Lan Ha are just as beautiful as those of Halong Bay and have the additional attraction of numerous white-sand beaches.

Due to being a fair way from Halong City, not so many tourist boats venture here, meaning Lan Ha Bay has a more isolated appeal. Sailing and kayak trips here are best organised in Cat Ba Town.

Geologically, Lan Ha is an extension of Halong Bay but sits in a different province of Vietnam. Around 200 species of fish, 500 species of mollusc, 400 species of arthropod, and numerous hard and soft coral live in the waters here, while larger marine animals in the area include seals and three species of dolphin.

The bay's admission fee is often incorporated into the cost of tours.

Cat Ba National Park NATIONAL PARK

(031-216 350; admission 30,000d; sunrise-sunset) Cat Ba's beautiful national park is home to 32 types of mammal, including most of the world's 65 remaining golden-headed langur, the world's most endangered primate. There are some good hiking trails here, including a hard-core 18km route up to a mountain summit.

To reach the **park headquarters** at Trung Trang, hop on the green QH public bus from the docks at Cat Ba Town, hire a *xe om* (around 80,000d one way), or rent a motorbike for the day.

A guide is not mandatory but is definitely recommended to help you make sense of the verdant canopy of trees. Most visitors opt to visit the park on an organised tour – Cat Ba Ventures (p116) runs good day-trips here – but you can also arrange guides with the rangers at the park headquarters. Within the park the multi-chambered **Hang Trung Trang** (Trung Trang Cave) is easily accessible, but you will need to contact a ranger to make sure it's open. Bring a torch (flashlight).

The challenging **18km hiking trail** in the park takes six hours and is best done with a guide. Boat or bus transport to the trailhead and a boat to get back to town also need to be arranged. Again, rangers at the headquarters can help with this or speak to Cat Ba Ventures or Asia Outdoors in Cat Ba Town. Take proper hiking shoes, a raincoat and a generous supply of water for this hike. Independent hikers can buy basic snacks at the kiosks in **Viet Hai**, which is where many hiking groups stop for lunch. This is not an easy walk, and is much harder and more slippery after rain. There are shorter hiking options that are less strenuous.

Many hikes end at Viet Hai, a remote minority village just outside the park boundary, from where taxi boats shuttle back to Ben Beo Pier (about 200,000d per boat). A

Cat Ba Town

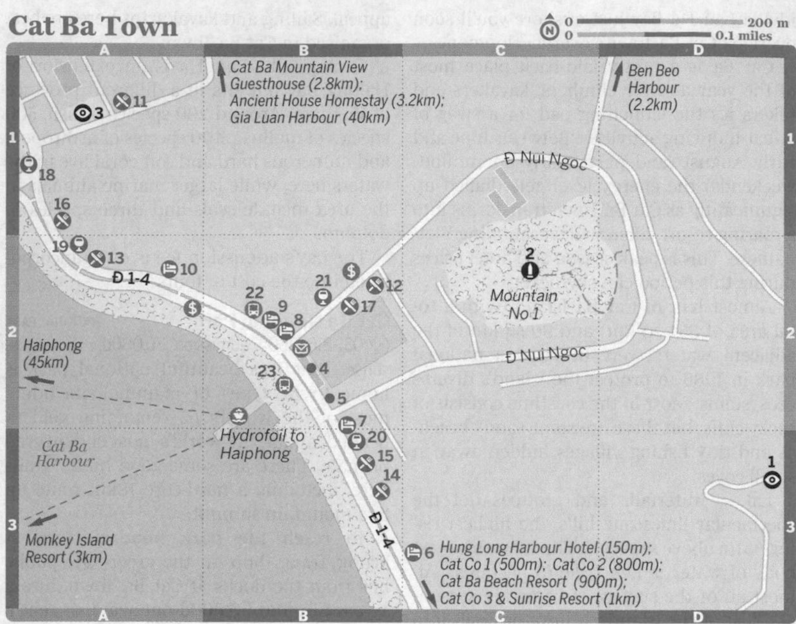

Cat Ba Town

Sights

1 Cannon Fort D3
2 Ho Chi Minh Monument C2
3 Market A1

Activities, Courses & Tours

4 Asia Outdoors B2
5 Cat Ba Ventures B2

Sleeping

6 Cat Ba Central Hostel C3
7 Cat Ba Dream B2
8 Cat Ba Sea View B2
9 Sea Pearl Hotel B2
10 Thu Ha A2

Eating

11 Buddha Belly A1
12 CT Mart B2
13 Family Bakery A2
14 Green Bamboo Forest B3
15 Green Mango B3
16 Phuong Nhung A1
17 Vien Duong B2

Drinking & Nightlife

18 Bia Hoi Stalls A1
19 Flightless Bird Café A2
Good Bar .... (see 4)
20 Oasis Bar B3
21 Rose Bar B2

Transport

22 Hoang Long Bus Company B2
23 QH Green Bus to Gia Luan & National Park B2

shared public boat (50,000d per person) departs from Ben Beo at 6am on weekdays and 7am on weekends.

Of the mammals present in the park, the more commonly seen include macaques, deer, civets and several species of squirrel, including the giant black squirrel. Seventy bird species have been spotted here, including hawks, hornbills and cuckoos. Cat Ba also lies on a major migration route for waterfowl that feed and roost on the beaches in the mangrove forests. Over a thousand species of plants have been recorded in the park, including 118 trees and 160 plants with medicinal value.

Cat Co Cove — BEACH

A 10-minute walk southeast from Cat Ba Town, the three Cat Co Cove beaches boast the nearest sand to town, although rubbish in the water can be problematic some days. **Cat Co 3** is the closest, with a blink-and-you'll-miss-it sliver of sand. From there a walking trail, cut into the cliff, offering gorgeous sea views, winds its way to **Cat Co 1** dominated by a rather ugly resort, then onward to the pretty white-sand swath of **Cat Co 2**.

You can also walk straight up the hill to Cat Co 1 and 2, or take the tourist 'train' (basically an oversized golf cart; 10,000d) that trundles over the hill during the summer months.

Water-sport gear like kayaks and windsurfers are available to rent at Cat Co 1 and 2. Note that on summer weekends the beaches get packed and litter can be a problem.

Other beaches located on Cat Ba Island include Cai Vieng, Hong Xoai Be and Hong Xoai Lon.

Hospital Cave HISTORIC SITE

(☎031-368 8215; admission 15,000d; ⏰7am-4.30pm) Hospital Cave served both as a secret, bombproof hospital during the American War and as a safe house for VC leaders. Built between 1963 and 1965 (with assistance from China), this incredibly well-constructed three-storey feat of engineering was in constant use until 1975. The cave is about 10km north of Cat Ba Town on the road to the Cat Ba National Park entrance.

A guide (most know a few words of English) will show you around the 17 rooms, point out the old operating theatre and take you to the huge natural cavern that was used as a cinema (and even had its own small swimming pool).

Activities

Mountain Biking

Hotels can arrange Chinese mountain bikes (around US$6 per day). Blue Swimmer (p116) rents better-quality mountain bikes for US$15 per day.

One possible route traverses the heart of the island, past Hospital Cave down to the west coast's mangroves and crab farms, and then in a loop back to Cat Ba Town past tidal mud flats and deserted beaches.

Kayaking

Plenty of hotels in Cat Ba Town and travel companies rent kayaks (half-day around US$8) ideal for exploring the Cat Ba coast independently. Due to shifting, strong currents, exploring the karst formations of Lan Ha Bay

DON'T MISS

CLIMBING THE KARSTS

If you've ever been tempted to climb, Cat Ba Island is a superb place to go for it – the karst cliffs here offer exceptional climbing amid stunning scenery. Most climbers in Cat Ba are complete novices, but as the instruction is excellent, many leave Cat Ba completely bitten by the bug.

You don't need great upper-body strength to climb, as you actually use your legs far more. The karst limestone here is not too sharp and quite friendly on the hands, and as many of the routes are sheltered by natural overhangs that prevent the climbable portion of the rock from getting wet, climbing is almost always possible, rain or shine.

A few inexperienced locals may offer climbing excursions to new arrivals on Cat Ba, but beginners should sign up with the experienced crew at Asia Outdoors (p116), who pioneered climbing here.

Climbing opportunities are located on walls inland on Cat Ba Island or out on beautiful Lan Ha Bay. You'll be kitted up with a harness and climbing shoes, given instruction and taught the fundamentals of the climbing and belaying techniques, then given a demonstration. Then it's over to you (with your climbing instructor talking you through each move and anchoring you, of course!). Most people are able to complete a couple of climbs at Hai Pai and Moody's Beach, which are both ideal for beginners.

The vertical cliffs of Halong and Lan Ha Bays are also perfect for deep-water soloing, which is basically climbing alone, without ropes or a harness, and using the ocean as a water bed in case you fall. This is obviously only for experienced climbers, and it's essential to know the depth of water and tidal patterns. We've heard reports of some climbers being injured falling into shallow waters, so it's vital to attempt deep-water soloing only with an experienced crew like Asia Outdoors. It's customary to finish a solo climb with a controlled freefall (or 'tombstone') into the sea and a swim back to the shore, or your boat.

WORTH A TRIP

CANNON FORT

For one of the best views in Vietnam – no, we're not kidding – head to **Cannon Fort** (admission 40,000d; ⊙sunrise-sunset) where there are astounding panoramas of Cat Ba Island's jungle-clad hills rolling down to colourful tangles of fishing boats in the harbour and out to the karst-punctuated sea beyond.

Well-labelled paths guide visitors past underground tunnels, and two well-preserved gun emplacements (one 'manned' by life-size Viet Minh mannequins), out to two viewpoints overlooking the island. There's even a cafe (with more great views) and a tiny museum.

The tunnels and gun emplacements here were first installed by the Japanese in WWII, but were also utilised by the French and Vietnamese during subsequent conflicts.

The entrance gate is a steep 10-minute walk from Cat Ba Town and from the gate it's another stiff 20-minute walk to the fort, or take a *xe om* from Cat Ba Town (15,000d).

by kayak is best done with a guide, particularly if you're not an experienced kayaker.

Trekking

Most of Cat Ba Island consists of protected tropical forest. Cat Ba National Park has the most hiking opportunities.

Tours

Boat trips around Lan Ha Bay are offered by nearly every hotel on Cat Ba Island. Typical prices start at around US$80 for overnight tours, but it is usually worth spending a bit more. We receive unfavourable feedback – cramped conditions and dodgy food – about some of these trips.

★ **Asia Outdoors** ROCK CLIMBING
(☎031-368 8450; www.asiaoutdoors.com.vn; Noble House, Đ 1-4, Cat Ba Town; half/full-day climbing US$66/84; ⊙8am-7.30pm) The pioneer of climbing in Vietnam, Asia Outdoors is a one-stop shop for adventurous travellers. Climbing is its real expertise, with fully licensed and certified instructors leading trips, but it also offers climbing and kayaking packages with an overnight on its boat (US$130). It's also just launched stand-up paddle-boarding (SUP) trips (US$36).

Advanced climbers can hire gear here, talk shop and pick up a copy of *Vietnam: A Climber's Guide* (US$20) by Asia Outdoors' Erik Ferjentsik, which describes climbs and has some great tips about Cat Ba too.

Cat Ba Ventures BOAT TOUR
(☎031-388 8755, 0912 467 016; www.catbaventures.com; 223 Đ 1-4, Cat Ba Town; overnight boat tour per person US$128; ⊙8am-7pm) Locally owned and operated company offering boat trips around Lan Ha and Halong Bays, one-day kayaking trips (US$29) and guided hikes in Cat Ba National Park. Excellent service from Mr Tung is reinforced by multiple reader recommendations. These guys are a font of knowledge on everything Cat Ba and a great source of information on onward transport options.

Blue Swimmer ADVENTURE TOUR
(☎031-368 8237, 0915 063 737; www.blueswimmersailing.com; Ben Beo Harbour; overnight sailing trip per person from US$161; ⊙8am-6pm) This environmentally conscious outfit was established by Vinh, one of the founders of respected tour operator Handspan Adventure Travel. Superb sailing and kayaking trips, trekking and mountain-biking excursions (some with overnight homestay accommodation) are offered. Check it out at Ben Beo Harbour or at its booking office in Cat Ba Town at the Green Bamboo Forest restaurant.

Sleeping

Most basic hotels are clustered on (or just off) the waterfront in Cat Ba Town. There are also some interesting options on other parts of Cat Ba Island and offshore on isolated islands in Lan Ha Bay.

Room rates fluctuate wildly; from June to July they can double. In August some hotels continue to hike prices while others just raise rates on Friday and Saturday nights.

We're using the rates for low season, as during busy periods many hotel owners tend to pick a price out of their heads depending on demand. Note that from May to July, it's definitely worth booking ahead.

Cat Ba Town

If the seafront hotels in Cat Ba Town are full, detour to Đ Nui Ngoc, which is lined with good-value accommodation.

Cat Ba Sea View HOTEL $
(☎031-388 8201; www.catbaseaviewhotel.com; 220 Đ 1-4; r US$15, with sea view US$25; ❄📶) Neat-as-a-pin, light-coloured rooms are further spruced up by snazzy fake-flower decor. All are good-sized, though the seafront ones are by far the most spacious. Each floor has a teensy communal balcony so you can take in the harbour vistas without shelling out extra for your room.

Cat Ba Central Hostel HOSTEL $
(☎0913 311 006; www.catbacentralhostel.com; 240 Đ 1-4; dm US$5; ⊖❄📶) Owner Kong is your host at this friendly hostel that's fast becoming the heart of Cat Ba's backpacker action. Beds in dorms (one 28-bed, one 14-bed and two six-bed, including a female-only room) come with individual storage locker and power point.

Cat Ba Dream HOTEL $
(☎031-388 8274; www.catbadream.com.vn; 226 Đ 1-4; r US$12, with sea view US$15; ❄📶) Service may be a bit lacklustre, but Cat Ba Dream has smart, small rooms at the back, and larger sea-facing ones with killer views of the bay (room 606 is the best).

Thu Ha HOTEL $
(☎031-388 8343; Đ 1-4, Cat Ba Town; r US$12-15; ❄📶) This small family-run place has basically furnished, clean rooms. Negotiate hard for a front room and wake up to sea views.

Sea Pearl Hotel HOTEL $$
(☎031-368 8567; www.seapearlcatbahotel.com.vn; 219 Đ 1-4; r 730,000-1,030,000d; ❄📶) Although we'd like to see the bathrooms be refurbished at this price, the Sea Pearl is a solid choice. Classically styled rooms are decent-sized and comfortable, and staff are professional and helpful.

Hung Long Harbour Hotel HOTEL $$
(☎031-626 9269; www.hunglonghotel.vn; 268 Đ 1-4; d 1,575,000d; P❄📶) At the quieter southeastern end of Cat Ba Town, the Hung Long Harbour has very spacious rooms, many with excellent views. Don't bother upgrading to a superior room: the standards are the ones with balconies.

Cat Ba Island & Around

Cat Ba Mountain View Guesthouse BUNGALOW $
(☎031-368 8641; 452 Đ Ha Sen, Ang Soi village; dm/d US$5/15) One step removed from the hustle of town, this new hostel has a collection of cute bungalows (both private and dorm options), backed by a cliff. The spacious, thatch-roofed restaurant area is a great social spot for hanging out and meeting fellow travellers. It's on the main road, 3km from Cat Ba Town.

Note that the roadside sign outside says 'Mountain View Hostel'.

Ancient House Homestay HOMESTAY $
(☎0915 063 737, 0916 645 858; www.catbahomestay.com; Ang Soi village; shared house per person US$15, private house per 2 people US$50; 📶) Located around 3km from Cat Ba Town, down an unmarked alley in the village of Ang Soi, this heritage house was carefully moved here from the outskirts of Hanoi. Antiques fill the high-ceilinged interior and outside are well-tended gardens. It's not set up to receive independent travellers and is best booked through Blue Swimmer.

Lunch and dinner set menus (US$10 per person) are available on request.

Whisper of Nature BUNGALOW $$
(☎031-265 7678; www.vietbungalow.com; Viet Hai village; dm/d incl breakfast US$15/28; ❄📶) Whisper of Nature is a simple place for nature lovers to kick back and enjoy some downtime. Little concrete-and-thatch bungalows are set on the edge of the forest, surrounded by trees and vegetable gardens. Getting here is an adventure in itself, with the final stage a bicycle ride through lush scenery. Ask about transport when you book.

Cat Ba Eco Lodge RESORT $$
(☎031-368 8966; www.catbaecolodge.com; Xuan Dam village; s/d 735,000/945,000d; ❄@📶) This small resort celebrates a wonderfully quiet village location 12km from Cat Ba Town. Spacious wooden stilt-houses sit around a breezy bar and restaurant, and activities include riding bicycles to a beach 2km away, as well as trekking. It runs two daily shuttles to/from Cat Ba Town (confirm your pick-up when booking).

Monkey Island Resort RESORT $$
(☎04-3926 0572; www.monkeyislandresort.com; Cat Dua Island; d US$60-100; ❄) Although the wood-and-thatch standard bungalows are tiny for the asking price, the strip of beach here is truly lovely. There's a nice social vibe, with a nightly seafood buffet, a bar playing R&B beats, and kayaking and hiking activities offered. Free transfers from Cat Ba Town are provided.

Cat Ba Sandy Beach Resort RESORT $$
(☎0989 555 773; www.catbasandybeachresort.com; Nam Cat Island; d from US$45; ❄) This island's prescription for relaxation includes simple wood-clad bungalows located under looming limestone cliffs. Spend your days swimming and kayaking, and kick back with seafood barbecues and beach bonfires after dark. Free transfers from Ben Beo Harbour provided.

Cat Ba Beach Resort RESORT $$$
(☎031-388 8686; www.catbabeachresort.com; Cat Co 2; bungalow from around US$80; ❄📶) Rimming the furthest sandy edge of Cat Co 2 beach, the dinky stone-and-thatch bungalows of this resort sit within a manicured lawn dotted with palm trees. Windsurfing and a sauna are both on tap, and there's a breezy open-sided bar-restaurant with water views.

Sunrise Resort RESORT $$$
(☎031-388 7360; www.catbasunriseresort.com; Cat Co 3; r from US$145; ❄@📶🏊) This beachfront resort is tastefully planned, with low-rise tiled-roofed blocks sitting below green cliffs. Rooms are spacious and smart (more expensive rooms come with sea-view balconies), and facilities include a swimming pool and kiddies' playground.

Eating

For a cheap feed, head to the food stalls in front of the market, or one block back from the waterfront on the cross street that links the loop of Đ Nui Ngoc.

Green Bamboo Forest VIETNAMESE $
(Đ 1-4; meals 50,000-150,000d; ⏲7am-11pm; 📶) Friendly and well-run waterfront eatery that also acts as a booking office for Blue Swimmer. There's some good seafood on offer and myriad rice and noodle dishes. The quieter location is also a bonus.

Buddha Belly VEGETARIAN $
(Đ 1-4; meals 30,000-80,000d; ⏲10am-9pm; 🌶) Right next to Cat Ba market, this bamboo-clad place serves up lots of vegetable and tofu goodness, and doesn't use any dairy or eggs so is a top choice for vegans as well. Its 30,000d daily-changing set menu is excellent value.

Family Bakery BAKERY $
(196 Đ 1-4, Cat Ba Town; pastries 10,000-15,000d, sandwiches 30,000-40,000d; ⏲7am-4pm) This friendly spot opens early for goodies, such as *pain au chocolat* and almond pastries. Pop in for a coffee, crème caramel or croissant before the bus-ferry-bus combo back to Hanoi.

Phuong Nhung VIETNAMESE $
(184 Đ 1-4, Cat Ba Town; meals 45,000d; ⏲7-10am) Bustling breakfast spot that's a popular place for a hearty bowl of *pho bo* (beef noodle soup) – just the thing you need before a day of climbing or kayaking.

CT Mart SUPERMARKET $
(18 Đ Nui Ngoc, Cat Ba Town; ⏲8am-8pm) Handy supermarket for stocking up before heading off trekking or for the boat trip back to the mainland.

Green Mango INTERNATIONAL $$
(☎031-388 7151; Đ 1-4, Cat Ba Town; meals 110,000-220,000d; ⏲8am-10pm; 📶) With a menu traipsing from steaks to seafood and over to Italy for pasta and pizza (with a small selection of Asian dishes as well), Green Mango is a great dinner choice, with friendly staff. It's also a chilled-out spot for a glass of wine or cocktail.

Vien Duong VIETNAMESE $$
(12 Đ Nui Ngoc, Cat Ba Town; meals from 120,000d; ⏲11am-11pm) One of the most popular of the seafood spots lining Đ Nui Ngoc, and often heaving with Vietnamese tourists diving into local crab, squid and steaming seafood hotpots. Definitely not the place to come if you're looking for a quiet night.

Drinking

For cheap, local-style drinking, head to the **bia hoi stalls** (Đ 1-4) near the entrance to the fishing harbour.

Rose Bar BAR
(15 Đ Nui Ngoc; ⏲noon-3am; 📶) With cheap (US$2) cocktails, loads of happy-hour specials and *shisha* (water pipes), Rose Bar ticks all the boxes for backpacker fun a long way from home. It often stays open after midnight in the busy season.

Oasis Bar BAR
(Đ 1-4; ⏲noon-11pm; 📶) A pool table, smiley staff and a location slap in the centre of the seafront strip make Oasis a popular spot to plonk yourself down for a beer or two. The menu is pretty decent if you're feeling peckish.

LOCAL KNOWLEDGE

FEASTING AT THE FLOATING RESTAURANTS

You can't beat the ambience-factor for feasting on seafood at a floating restaurant, but a few pointers will make sure your experience isn't a washout.

➡ There are numerous 'floating' seafood restaurants just offshore in Cat Ba Harbour, but we've heard reports of overcharging so it's essential to confirm the price of the food in advance, as well as the cost of a boat to get you out there and back.

➡ Locals advise heading around the bay to the floating restaurants in Ben Beo Harbour instead. They're less touristy and less likely to rip you off, but still check on the price of food upfront. A boat ride there and back, including waiting time, should cost around 140,000d.

➡ Hold off paying your boat fare until the return journey is completed, as we've also had reports of diners being left stranded on the restaurants. Ask your hotel to recommend a boat or catch a *xe om* (around 30,000d) over the hill to the harbour.

➡ One recommended place at Ben Beo Pier is **Quang Anh** (☎031-388 8485; Ben Beo; meals from around 200,000d). Choose your dinner from the floating pens and it will be grilled, fried or steamed for your table in no time. Prices go by weight and type of seafood, you can eat your fill of a selection of fish for around 200,000d per person. Just make sure you establish the estimated price before you eat.

Flightless Bird Café BAR
(☎031-388 8517; Đ 1-4; ⊙noon-11pm; 📶) Discover your inner Kiwi at this friendly bar decorated with New Zealand memorabilia. For those who always need to multitask, you can also get your nails painted while you drink, with well-priced massage and manicure services on offer.

Good Bar BAR
(Noble House, Đ 1-4, Cat Ba Town; ⊙noon-late) This upper-floor bar has a real vibe and goes on until late most nights. It comes fully equipped with pool tables and terrific harbour views.

ℹ Information

Most accommodation and restaurants offer wi-fi access.

For tourist information, the best impartial advice is at Asia Outdoors. Cat Ba Ventures is also very helpful. Both companies have websites with local information.

Agribank (Đ Nui Ngoc; ⊙8am-3pm Mon-Fri, 8-11.30am Sat)

ℹ Getting There & Away

Cat Ba Island is 45km east of Haiphong and 50km south of Halong City. Various boat and bus combinations make the journey from Hanoi, or there are ferries from Haiphong and Halong City.

HAIPHONG

A fast hyrdofoil departs Haiphong's Ben Binh Harbour at 7am, 9am, 1pm and 3pm, and goes straight to Cat Ba Town Pier (220,000d, one hour). Haiphong-bound hydrofoils depart Cat Ba Town Pier at 8am, 10am, 2pm and 4pm.

HALONG CITY

Ferries from Halong City's Tuan Chau Ferry Pier terminate at Cat Ba Island's Gia Luan Harbour on the north side of the island, which means you're still 40km from Cat Ba Town. The local QH Green bus between Gia Luan and Cat Ba Town is the only public transport linking the two.

For years this ferry route was blighted by a taxi mini-mafia at Gia Luan Harbour who did their best to make sure you couldn't catch this bus, but a recent crackdown on the culprits has made it more doable.

Due to frequent ferry schedule changes along this route, the Haiphong ferry remains the easier alternative for foot passengers. If you're travelling by motorbike, this is a great option too.

The car ferry from Halong City's Tuan Chau Ferry Pier leaves for Cat Ba Island's Gia Luan Harbour at 8am and 3pm throughout the year (per person/motorbike 70,000/10,000d, one hour), with the number of daily sailings rising to hourly in busy periods. From Gia Luan, throughout the year, the QH Green bus departs for Cat Ba Town at 9am and 4pm (20,000d, 30 minutes). If the ferry is late, the bus waits for the boat to arrive. From approximately May to September there are extra bus services at 1pm and 5pm.

From Gia Luan Harbour to Halong City's Tuan Chau Ferry Pier, car ferries leave at 9am and 4pm. Catch the 7.40am or 3pm QH Green bus from Cat Ba Town to connect with the boat. Again, the ferry timetable from Gia Luan is beefed up according to demand and there are usually hourly sailings from late May to early August.

HANOI

Hoang Long Bus Company (☎031-268 8008; Đ 1-4; tickets 250,000d) Departing from Hanoi's Luong Yen bus station, Hoang Long operates an efficient bus-boat-bus combo to Cat Ba Town. A bus takes you to Haiphong, followed by a minibus to nearby Dinh Vu port, then a 40-minute ferry to Cai Vieng Harbour (also known as Phu Long) on Cat Ba Island. From there, another minibus whisks passengers to Cat Ba Town.

Between May and September buses depart Hanoi at 5.20am, 7.20am, 11.20am and 1.20pm, and return from Cat Ba Town at 7.15am, 9.15am, 1.15pm and 3.15pm. From October to April buses leave Hanoi at 7.20am and 11.20am, and depart Cat Ba Town at 9.15am and 1.15pm.

If you're travelling from Hanoi, this is the most hassle-free way.

Getting Around

A *xe om* from Cat Ba Town to Cat Co 2 beach or Ben Beo Harbour is around 10,000d, and in summer a tourist train (basically oversized golf carts) whizz between Cat Ba Town and Cat Co 1 and 2 (10,000d per person).

BICYCLE & MOTORBIKE

Bicycle and motorbike rentals are available from most Cat Ba hotels (both around US$5 per day). If you're heading out to the beaches or national park, pay the parking fee for security.

BUS

Cat Ba's public QH Green Bus (20,000d) trundles between Cat Ba Harbour and Gia Luan Harbour in the north of the island, passing the national park headquarters en route.

From Cat Ba Town, throughout the year, services leave at 7.40am and 3pm with an 11am and 1pm service added from approximately May to September. During the peak holiday period of June to July, more departures are sometimes added.

Bai Tu Long Bay

☎033

There's way more to northeast Vietnam than Halong Bay. The sinking limestone plateau, which gave birth to the bay's spectacular islands, continues for some 100km to the Chinese border. The area immediately northeast of Halong Bay is part of **Bai Tu Long National Park** (admission 100,000d).

Bai Tu Long Bay is every bit as beautiful as its famous neighbour. In some ways it's actually more stunning, since it's only in its initial stages as a destination for travellers. Improved boat transport to the scattering of resorts here means the area is quickly growing in popularity with domestic tourists, but the bay and its islands are still unpolluted and relatively undeveloped. For Western travellers, it's a laid-back alternative to the touristy bustle of Halong Bay.

As with Halong Bay, the best way to experience the full gamut of limestone pinnacles scattered along the seascape is by cruise. Hanoi travel agencies, including Ethnic Travel (p88), run boat trips into the Bai Tu Long area. Charter boats can also be arranged to Bai Tu Long Bay from Halong City's Bai Chay Tourist Wharf; rates start at around 300,000d per hour and the trip there takes about five hours.

To experience a slice of slow island life, independent travellers can head to Quan Lan Island.

Van Don Island

Van Don is the largest (around 30 sq km), most populated and most developed island in the Bai Tu Long archipelago. Now linked to the mainland by a series of bridges, it has a few places to stay, but you won't want to linger. It's chiefly useful as the jumping-off point to other islands.

Bai Dai (Long Beach) runs along much of the island's southern side and has hard-packed sand with some mangroves. Just offshore there are stunning limestone **rock formations**.

Van Don's main town is scruffy **Cai Rong** (pronounced Cai Zong), about 8km north of the bridge to the mainland. It's a bustling place full of karaoke bars and motorbikes. Here, Cai Rong Pier (Cai Rong Pha) is the key port for boats to other Bai Tu Long islands. If you're forced to overnight before catching a morning ferry, there are a couple of decent hotels.

Hung Toan Hotel (☎033-387 4220; r 250,000d; ❄) is good value, while **Viet Linh Hotel** (☎033-379 3898; r 400,000d; ❄) is fancier. Both are around 300m north of the pier. Just opposite the Viet Linh Hotel is a simple, unnamed restaurant that does great seafood and pork dishes – try the pork with ginger, chilli and lemongrass.

Buses run every 30 minutes between Bai Chay bus station (Halong City) and Cai Rong (35,000d, 1¾ hours). From the Cai Rong bus stop catch a *xe om* for the three-minute trip to the pier.

To head north from Cai Rong, take the Bai Chay–bound bus to the Cua Ong turn-off, where buses to Mong Cai and Lang Son pick up passengers.

Quan Lan Island

If you want to slide right off the typical traveller trail, Quan Lan Island ticks the boxes. The island's only real hub is the sleepy three-street settlement of **Quan Lan Town**, separated from the sea by a hem of mangroves. A handful of simple guesthouses, restaurants and places to rent bicycles (US$4 per day) and motorbikes (US$6 per day) line the main street. Out of town, Minh Chau beach is the island's main attraction with the tiny settlement of **Minh Chau** just a short hop from the sand.

Apart from hanging out on Minh Chau's sand and tootling around this slender island by bicycle or motorbike, there really is very little to do, which is its very charm if that's what you're looking for. There's no ATM on Quan Lan Island, so come armed with cash.

Sights

Minh Chau Beach BEACH

The beautiful 1km-long crescent-moon sweep of Minh Chau beach, located on the northeastern coast, is Quan Lan Island's big drawcard. The water is clear blue and the waves are suitable for surfing. Watersports action includes kayaks for hire, and there are lots of cheap eateries for beer and seafood. Note that most of Minh Chau's beachfront restaurants are only open from May to October, and that June and July are more expensive with the influx of domestic tourists.

There are several other blissful beaches on the eastern seaboard.

Quan Lan Pagoda BUDDHIST TEMPLE

The only attraction within Quan Lan Town itself is this beautiful 200-year-old pagoda.

Van Don Ruins HISTORIC SITE

The northeastern part of the island has some battered ruins of the old Van Don Trading Port.

Sleeping

Ngan Ha Hotel HOTEL $

(☎033-387 7296; Quan Lan Town; r 350,000d; ❄ 📶) This corner-front establishment in the heart of town has redecorated rooms and a good restaurant dishing up lots of local seafood, downstairs. It rents bikes and motorbikes.

Ann Hotel HOTEL $$

(☎033-387 7889; www.annhotel.com.vn; Quan Lan Town; d US$22-31; ❄ 📶) The Ann Hotel offers spacious rooms with gleaming bathrooms. The more expensive rooms at the back have balconies with great ocean views.

Minh Chau Resort RESORT $$$

(☎0904 081 868; www.minhchauresort.vn; Minh Chau; r from US$80; ❄ 📶 🏊) The flashest accommodation on Quan Lan Island is this resort upon the white sands of Minh Chau beach. Light-filled rooms have lots of beachy appeal, there's a good restaurant and a tempting pool. Outside of peak season (June to July) you can often find excellent value packages.

Eating & Drinking

Tuan Thuy Restaurant VIETNAMESE $

(Quan Lan Town; meals from about 100,000d; ⏰8am-8pm) A decent selection of all the usual noodle and rice dishes is available at this simple family-run outfit, which also rents out bikes. It's on Quan Lan Town's main street.

Cafe Mu CAFE

(Quan Lan Town; ⏰9am-9pm) This little cafe has friendly owners and serves up the best Vietnamese coffee and fresh fruit juices in town. It's directly opposite Tuan Thuy Restaurant.

Getting There & Away

CAI RONG

Boats from Cai Rong dock at two places: the Quan Lan Pier, 3km from the main township on the island's southern tip, and near Minh Chau Beach, on the island's northeastern coast.

Fast boats to Minh Chau (120,000d, 45 minutes) depart Cai Rong at 7.30am and 1pm. Returning to Cai Rong, boat schedules change frequently so check locally.

Fast boats to Quan Lan Pier (150,000d, 1½ hours) depart Cai Rong at 7.30am and 1.30pm. A slower wooden boat (50,000d, 2½ hours) departs Cai Rong to Quan Lan Pier at 7am and 1pm. From Qan Lan Pier fast boats make the return journey to Cai Rong at 7am and 1pm, with the slow boat also leaving at 1pm.

HALONG CITY

An alternative route to Quan Lan Pier is from the Hon Gai ferry terminal, across the suspension bridge from Halong City. A speedboat leaves at 2pm (160,000d, 1½ hours).

From Quan Lan Pier the speedboat makes the return journey to Hon Gai ferry terminal at 7am.

Getting Around

Most of Quan Lan is pretty flat, but it's a surprisingly large island, and if you're staying in Quan Lan Town you'll definitely need some kind of transport to get to the beach.

There are many bicycles (US$4 per day) and motorbikes (US$6 per day) for hire in Quan Lan Town.

Quan Lan still uses xe Lam (three-wheeled motorised vehicles) for transport. Xe Lam drivers whiz between Qan Lan Pier and Quan Lan Town (20,000d) and can also be hired to do tours of the island.

Tra Ban & Dao Ngoc Vung Islands

One of Bai Tu Long's largest islands, **Tra Ban** offers some of the bay's most dramatic karsts. The southern part is blanketed in thick jungle and provides a habitat for many colourful butterflies. Boats leave from Van Don's Cai Rong Pier at 7am and 2pm (40,000d, one hour). There's no accommodation, so check on times for return boats.

Dao Ngoc Vung borders Halong Bay and has some dramatic limestone cliffs and a great beach on its southern shore with basic **beach huts** (r 200,000d). Bring along your own food. Daily boats link Cai Rong to Ngoc Vung (60,000d, 2½ hours, 7am and 1.30pm).

GETTING TO CHINA: MONG CAI TO DONGXING

Getting to the border Rarely used by travellers, the Chinese border at the **Mong Cai/Dongxing border crossing** is around 3km from the Mong Cai bus station; around 20,000d on a *xe om* or 40,000d in a taxi.

At the border The border is open daily between 7am and 10pm Vietnam time. Note that China is one hour ahead of Vietnam. You'll need to have a pre-arranged visa for China.

Moving on Across the border in Dongxing, frequent buses run to Nanning in China's Guangxi province.

Co To Island

In the northeast, Co To Island is the furthest inhabited island from the mainland. Its highest peak reaches a respectable 170m. There are numerous other hills, and a large lighthouse. The coastline is mostly cliffs and large rocks, but there's at least one sandy beach.

Unfortunately, due to the military presence on Co To, non-Vietnamese travellers require a permit to visit, which must be procured before travel. Independent travellers should be able to contact a hotel on the island, or one of the bigger travel agencies in Hanoi, to help issue the permit.

There are a couple of small hotels and guesthouses on Co To, including the friendly **Coto Lodge Hotel** (☎0904 701 661; www.coto.vn; Coto Town; d incl breakfast 500,000d; ❄@📶), with a great attached restaurant and friendly staff that can arrange island tours.

A fast speedboat departs Cai Rong Pier daily at 1pm (155,000d, 1½ hours), with an extra morning departure on Saturdays at 6am.

Slow ferries bound for Co To depart Cai Rong Pier at 7am daily (70,000d, three hours).

Mong Cai & the Chinese Border

Huge industrial zones are rising around Mong Cai city with plots being snapped up by Chinese and foreign corporations. Elsewhere in this border region, travellers' highlights include the stunning karst scenery around Cao Bang, historical caves and the thundering Ban Gioc Waterfall.

Mong Cai

☎033 / POP 103,000

A bustling border city, Mong Cai thrives on trade with China. For the Vietnamese, the big draw is the chance to purchase low-priced (and low-quality) Chinese-made consumer goods. For the Chinese, the attraction is two huge casinos and new golf courses. But other than as a border crossing, Mong Cai holds no interest for tourists.

Sleeping & Eating

There are plenty of food stalls on P Hung Vuong, including several good spots near the Nam Phong Hotel.

Nam Phong Hotel HOTEL $
(033-388 7775; P Hung Vuong; r 385,000-450,000d;) Spacious, well-equipped rooms come with satellite TV and surprisingly powerful wi-fi. There's a restaurant downstairs serving good Chinese and Vietnamese dishes.

Nha Nghi Thanh Tam GUESTHOUSE $
(033-388 1373; 71 Đ Trieu Duong; r 280,000d;) Among similar options on this street, this is a solid budget choice with comfortable rooms. Đ Trieu Duong runs south from Đ Tran Phu, two blocks before Mong Cai's main market.

Getting There & Away

Mong Cai is located 340km from Hanoi.

The **bus station** (Hwy 18) is about 3km from the border. To Hanoi there are frequent services until 1pm (230,000d, eight hours); to Halong City buses leave every 30 minutes until around 6pm (100,000d, four hours); and to Lang Son there are buses at 8.30am, 9.30am, 10.30am and 12.30pm (110,000d, 5½ hours).

Lang Son

025 / POP 148,000

Lang Son is a booming city set next to tranquil Phai Loan Lake and surrounded by green karst peaks. Most travellers pull through town on their way to or from China (the border is 18km north, just outside Dong Dang). If you need to spend the night, there are two interesting caves nearby and Lang Son's sprawl of market streets – which radiate outwards from the night market – are a lively jumble of squawking chickens, fresh produce and grilled meat stalls.

The area is populated largely by Tho, Nung, Man and Dzao tribal people, though their influence is not evident in the city. Lang Son was partially destroyed in February 1979 by Chinese forces, and the ruins of the town and the devastated frontier village of Dong Dang were shown to foreign journalists as evidence of Chinese aggression. Although the border is still heavily fortified, both towns have been rebuilt and Sino-Vietnamese trade is in full swing again.

Sights

Lang Son's caves are around 1200m from the central city. Both are illuminated and have Buddhist altars inside.

Tam Thanh Cave CAVE
(combined admission with Nhi Thanh Cave 5000d; 6am-6pm) Tam Thanh Cave is vast and seductive. There's an internal pool and natural 'window' offering a sweeping view of the surrounding rice fields. A few hundred metres up a stone staircase are the ruins of the **Mac Dynasty Citadel**. It's a lovely, deserted spot, with stunning rural views.

Nhi Thanh Cave CAVE
(combined admission with Tam Thanh Cave 5000d; 6am-6pm) The Ngoc Tuyen River flows through Nhi Thanh Cave, 700m beyond Tam Thanh Cave. The entrance has a series of carved poems written by the cave's 18th-century discoverer, a soldier called Ngo Thi San. There's also a carved stone plaque commemorating an early French resident of Lang Son, complete with his silhouette in European clothing.

GETTING TO CHINA: LANG SON TO NANNING

Getting to the border The Friendship Pass at the **Dong Dang/Pingxiang border crossing** is the most popular crossing in the far north. The border post itself is at Huu Nghi Quan (Friendship Pass), 3km north of Dong Dang town. Frequent minibuses travel between Lang Son and Dong Dang. From Dong Dang a *xe om* to Huu Nghi Quan is around 30,000d and a taxi around 60,000d. From Lang Son count on about 140,000d for a taxi and 70,000d for a *xe om*.

At the border The border is open from 7am to 7pm daily Vietnam time. Note that China is one hour ahead of Vietnam. To cross 500m to the Chinese side you'll need to catch one of the electric cars (10,000d). You'll also need a prearranged visa for China.

Moving on On the Chinese side, it's a 20-minute drive to Pingxiang by bus or shared taxi. Pingxiang is connected by train and bus to Nanning (three hours).

Lang Son Market MARKET
(6am-6pm) Lang Son's market area sprawls over about three blocks, just off P Tran Dang Ninh. It's a colourful and hectic place stuffed to the brim with hawkers and stalls selling produce, and plentiful food stalls.

Sleeping & Eating

Van Xuan Hotel HOTEL $
(025-371 0440; lsvanxuanhotel@yahoo.com.vn; 147 P Tran Dang Ninh; r 360,000-500,000d;) By far the best place to bed down in Lang Son, the Van Xuan has friendly, English-speaking staff and neat rooms that lead out to a communal balcony overlooking the eastern edge of the lake. It's around 50m from Lang Son's market.

Hoa Binh Hotel HOTEL $
(025-870 807; 127 Đ Thanh Tam; r 280,000d;) A reliable cheapie close to the Lang Son market, with cane furniture, spacious rooms and clean bathrooms.

★ **Thanh Lan Com Binh Dan** VIETNAMESE $
(Tran Quoc Tran; meals 50,000-70,000d; 11am-10pm) One block south of the market, the delightful Miss Lan serves around 20 different dishes for lunch and dinner. It's a point-and-pick affair – all seasonal and all local.

New Dynasty Restaurant VIETNAMESE $$
(025-389 8000; Phai Loan Lake; hotpots 150,000d; noon-11pm) This bar-restaurant juts out into the lake. Everyone is here for the hotpots, but there's also a draught-beer emporium.

Information

Vietin Bank (51 Đ Le Loi; 8am-3pm Mon-Fri, 8am-11.30am Sat) has an ATM and changes money; the **post office** (Đ Le Loi; 7am-6pm Mon-Fri) is adjacent. Both are around 300m from the lake on the road heading east towards Mong Cai. There are ATMs along P Tran Dang Ninh.

Getting There & Away

BUS

Buses to Hanoi (90,000d, three hours, frequent until 6pm) leave from the bus station on Đ Le Loi, around 500m east of the post office. From the Vietin Bank and post office, turn right into P Tran Dang Ninh, and continue for 200m to the market, hotels and restaurants.

Buses to Mong Cai (100,000d, 5½ hours, 7.30am, 9.30am and 11.30am) and Cao Bang (85,000d, four hours, five departures between 5.15am and 1.45pm) leave from a separate northern bus terminal around 3km north of the town centre.

TRAIN

There are only very slow trains between Lang Son and Hanoi (100,000d, 5½ hours).

Cao Bang

026 / POP 51,386

Mountainous Cao Bang province is one of the most beautiful regions in Vietnam. Cao Bang itself is more prosaic, but it is a useful base to explore the surrounding countryside. The climate is mild here, and winter days can get chilly when a thick fog clings to the banks of the Bang Giang River.

Sights

War Memorial MONUMENT
There's not a whole load to do in Cao Bang town itself, but there are great 360-degree views from the town's hill-summit war memorial. Head up the second lane off Đ Pac Bo, go under the entrance to a primary school and you'll see the steps leading up the hill.

Sleeping

Thanh Loan Hotel HOTEL $
(026-385 7026; ThanhLoan_hotel@yahoo.com; 131 P Vuon Cam; d/tr incl breakfast 400,000/550,000d;) This spotless place features wood panelling in abundance and spacious rooms with high ceilings, dark-wood furniture and bathrooms with tubs.

Duc Trung Hotel HOTEL $$
(026-385 3424; www.ductrunghotel.com.vn; 85 P Be Van Dan; d 520,000-630,000d) A solid option with business-bland-style rooms just a short walk from Cao Bang's main drag. There are good *banh mi* (filled baguettes) and *pho* stalls just across the road.

Eating & Drinking

You'll find cheap food stalls around the **night market** (P Vuon Cam; meals from 15,000d; 5-11pm).

Men Quyen Restaurant VIETNAMESE $
(026-385 6433; Đ Kim Dong; meals 45,000-70,000d) Tucked away behind the market, this modest place has a buffet-style set-up – just point to the dishes you want. Be sure to try the delicious *cha la lot* (cabbage rolls).

Cao Bang

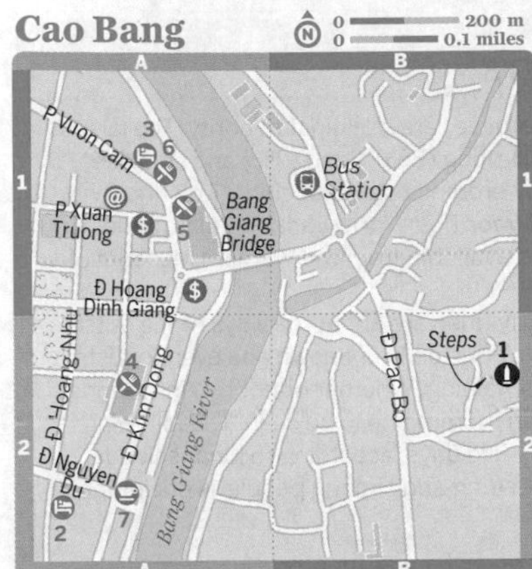

Cao Bang

Thu Ngan VIETNAMESE $
(21 P Vuon Cam; meals 40,000-60,000d; 8am-9pm) Good-value local diner owned by a friendly family.

Cafe 88 CAFE
(cnr Đ Kim Dong & Đ Nguyen Du; 9am-10pm) This simple cafe, with a raised terrace fronting the street, does some of the best Vietnamese coffee in town.

Information

There are a couple of internet cafes on P Xuan Truong and P Vuon Cam.

Bank for Foreign Investment & Development (Đ Kim Dong; 8am-3pm Mon-Fri, 8-11.30am Sat, ATM 24hr)

Getting There & Away

Cao Bang is 272km north of Hanoi, along Hwy 3. It's a fully sealed road, but a full day's drive through mountainous terrain.

Bus schedules at **Cao Bang bus station** (Đ Pac Bo) have a tendency to change frequently so check times the day before if possible. In particular, the direct bus to Ban Gioc Waterfall doesn't always run outside of the summer months.

If you're travelling to Ba Be Lakes (p103), the direct bus to Cho Ra is a good option, but from Cho Ra you'll need to hire a *xe om* for the final stretch into the national park.

If you are endeavouring to venture into the mountainous Ha Giang region from the east, note that there is no public transport between Bao Lac and Meo Vac. You would have to rustle up a local driver in Bao Lac to continue.

Hang Pac Bo (Water-Wheel Cave)

Hang Pac Bo HISTORIC SITE
(Water-Wheel Cave) After 30 years of exile, Ho Chi Minh re-entered Vietnam in January 1941 and took shelter in this small cave in one of the most remote regions of Vietnam, 3km from the Chinese border. The cave and surrounding area are sacred ground for Vietnamese revolutionaries – this is the base from which Ho launched the revolution he'd long been planning.

BUSES FROM CAO BANG

DESTINATION	COST (D)	DURATION (HR)	FREQUENCY
Ban Gioc Waterfall (direct)	75,000	2½	7.30am, 9am
Bao Lac	100,000	4	1pm, 2pm
Cho Ra (Ba Be National Park)	90,000	5	noon
Hanoi	150,000	7	12 daily 6am-5pm
Lang Son	80,000	3	4 daily 7am-2pm
Trung Khanh (for Ban Gioc Waterfall)	70,000	2	12 daily 7am-4pm

OFF THE BEATEN TRACK

HEADING TO THE MINORITY MARKETS

In the province of Cao Bang, Kinh (ethnic Vietnamese) are a distinct minority. The largest ethnic groups are the Tay (46%), Nung (32%), Hmong (8%), Dzao (7%) and Lolo (1%). Intermarriage and mass education are gradually eroding tribal and cultural distinctions. Check out Tim Doling's *Mountains and Ethnic Minorities: North East Vietnam* for detailed accounts of tribal people in the region. It's available from the Vietnam Museum of Ethnology and bookshops in Hanoi.

Most of Cao Bang's minorities remain blissfully unaware about the ways of the outside world. Cheating in the marketplace, for example, is virtually unknown and even tourists are charged the same price as locals without bargaining. Whether or not this innocence can withstand the onslaught of even limited tourism remains to be seen. The following big markets in Cao Bang province are held every five days, according to lunar calendar dates. The Na Giang market, which attracts Tay, Nung and Hmong people, is one of the best and busiest in the provinces.

Nuoc Hai 1st, 6th, 11th, 16th, 21st and 26th day of each lunar month.

Na Giang 1st, 6th, 11th, 16th, 21st and 26th day of each lunar month.

Tra Linh 4th, 9th, 14th, 19th, 24th and 29th day of each lunar month.

Trung Khanh 5th, 10th, 15th, 20th, 25th and 30th day of each lunar month.

Hang Pac Bo is 58km northwest of Cao Bang. For a return half-day trip by *xe om*, expect to pay around 200,000d.

Even if you have little interest in the history of Vietnamese communism, the cave is in a beautiful location surrounded by evergreen forests filled with butterflies and birdsong, and overlooked by limestone mountains.

Ho Chi Minh lived in the cave for a few weeks in 1941, writing poetry and translating key texts by the fathers of socialism. He stuck close to China so that he would be able to flee across the border if French soldiers discovered his hiding place. Ho named the stream in front of his cave Lenin Creek and the jungle-clad mountain that overlooks this stream Karl Marx Peak.

There's a modest **Uncle Ho Museum** (admission 20,000d; ⏲7.30-11.30am & 1.30-5pm Wed-Sun) at the entrance to the Pac Bo area. About 2km beyond this is a parking area. The cave is a 10-minute walk away along a shady stone path that follows the riverbank. You can step inside the mouth of the small cave, but not enter. The path then loops past various other points of interest, including a **rock table** that Ho is said to have used as a kind of jungle office for his translations and writing.

In a patch of forest about a 15-minute walk in the opposite direction is a **jungle hut**, another of Ho's hideouts. On the way to the hut is a **rock outcrop** used as a 'dead-letter box', where he would leave and pick up messages.

No permits are currently needed to visit this area, despite the proximity to the Chinese border.

Ban Gioc Waterfall & Nguom Ngao Cave

Ban Gioc Waterfall is one of Vietnam's best-known waterfalls, and its image adorns the lobby of many a cheap guesthouse. The falls, fed by the Quay Son River that marks the border with China, are an impressive sight and in a highly scenic location.

Boat owners here will punt you on bamboo rafts (100,000d) close enough to the waterfall so you can feel the spray on your hair (bring shampoo!) and skin. Rafts on the Vietnamese side have green canopies, and on the Chinese side canopies are blue. You're allowed to swim in the large natural pool on the Vietnamese side, but not in the river or close to the main waterfall.

It's a picturesque 10-minute stroll through rice paddies to reach the base of the falls from the parking area. If you're here at harvest time in September or October, the farmers may encourage you to try out their pedal-powered threshing machines.

A police permit (200,000d for up to 10 people) is required to visit this region but the permit can be purchased at the police station here beside the waterfall. You'll need to show your passport.

There are snack and drink stalls by the cave and waterfall, but the nearest accommodation is in Cao Bang.

Sights

Ban Gioc Waterfall WATERFALL
(admission 15,000d; 7.30am-5pm) Ban Gioc is the largest waterfall in the country, though not the highest. Its vertical drop is only around 30m, but it has an impressive 300m span; one side of the falls is in China, the other is in Vietnam. Water volume varies considerably between the dry and rainy seasons, and the sight is most impressive from May to September.

Nguom Ngao Cave CAVE
(admission incl guide 30,000d; 7.30am-4.30pm) About 4km from Ban Gioc Waterfall, Nguom Ngao Cave is one of the most spectacular cave systems in Vietnam. Created by an underground river, it extends for several kilometres underground; villagers sheltered here during the 1979 war with China. Visitors are permitted in one section, where a 1km-long concrete path and excellent lighting have been installed.

A guide (no English) accompanies you on an hour-long cave tour, past huge stalagmite and stalactite outcrops and through a vast 100m chamber.

The 10-minute walk from the parking lot to the cave is also very beautiful, threading through the limestone hills that characterise Cao Bang province, past fields of soya beans.

A second, even bigger branch of the cave system is said to extend almost all the way back to Ban Gioc Waterfall, though there's currently no visitor access to this section.

Getting There & Away

The journey to the falls and cave is absolutely stunning; the road follows a beautiful river valley and weaves through soaring karst peaks for much of the trip. It's an 87km journey along a decent paved road, and takes about 2½ hours.

Buses (70,000d, two hours, 12 daily) connect Cao Bang with Trung Khanh, 27km short of the falls. Negotiate for a *xe om* in Trung Khanh to take you onward, which should come to around 200,000d, including a two-hour wait. Another option is the direct bus (75,000d, 2½ hours) departing Cao Bang at 7.30am and 9am.

NORTHWEST VIETNAM

History

The history of the northwest differs to lowland Vietnam. The Vietnamese traditionally avoided mountains, believing the terrain was not suitable for large-scale rice production. For many centuries the area remained inhabited by scatterings of minority people, joined in the 19th century by migrants from Yunnan, China and Tibet. This was the 'badlands', a buffer zone of bandits between China and Vietnam. During Ho Chi Minh's leadership, the North Vietnamese experimented with limited autonomy in 'special zones', but these were abolished after reunification.

Life for the minorities has always been difficult. Their most profitable crop was opium, but the authorities have clamped down and very little is now produced. Educational opportunities were limited, but new schools in remote areas now provide most children with education. Economic prospects remain limited, so many highlanders move to cities in search of work.

Getting There & Away

The main airport is at Dien Bien Phu, but most travellers take the train from Hanoi to Lao Cai, the gateway to Sapa. On a public bus, the mountain roads can be unforgiving. Consider renting a private 4WD and driver, or riding a motorbike.

To undertake the northwest loop, most travellers head for Mai Chau, then Son La and Dien Bien Phu. Continue north to Sapa and back to Hanoi. Allow a week for this journey, and more time if using local buses.

Travellers can cross from Laos into Vietnam at the Tay Trang–Sop Hun border crossing, 34km from Dien Bien Phu.

Hoa Binh

0218 / POP 112,000

A handy pit stop en route to Mai Chau, Hoa Binh means 'peace' and this easygoing town is a relief after the traffic-plagued suburbs of Hanoi. The area is home to many hill-tribe people, including the Hmong and Thai.

Sights

Muong Cultural Museum CULTURAL CENTRE
(Khong Gian Van Hoa Muong; 0913 553 937; www.muong.vn; 202 Tay Tien; admission 50,000d; 7.30am-5pm Tue-Sun) Founded by Hanoi artist Vu Duc Hieu, this establishment showcases the culture of the local Muong ethnic

THE HIGH ROADS ON TWO WHEELS

With spectacular scenery and relatively minimal traffic, more travellers are choosing to motorcycle around the northwest loop from Hanoi up to Lao Cai, over to Dien Bien Phu and back to the capital. For the more intrepid, the roads venturing north towards China into the spectacular provinces of Ha Giang and Cao Bang are the newest frontier for travel in Vietnam.

Hanoi is the place to start making arrangements. Consider joining a tour or hiring a guide who knows the roads and can help with mechanical and linguistic difficulties. Be sure to get acquainted with your bike first and check current road conditions and routes.

Most motorbikes in Vietnam are small capacity (under 250cc). For years the sturdy Minsk was the bike of choice for travellers. Today numbers have dwindled, as mopeds and Chinese off-road bikes have proliferated. Honda road bikes (such as the Honda GL 160) and trail bikes are other good choices. These bikes have a good reputation for reliability and have decent shock absorbers.

Rental agencies will provide checklists, but essentials include a good helmet, a local SIM card in your mobile phone for emergencies, rain gear, a spare parts and repair kit (including spark plugs, spanners, inner tube and tyre levers), air pump and decent maps. Knee and elbow pads and gloves are also a good idea.

Highways can be hell in Vietnam, so let the train take the strain on the long route north to Lao Cai. Load your bike into a goods carriage while you sleep in a berth. You'll have to (almost) drain your bike of petrol.

Take it slowly, particularly in the rain: smooth paved roads can turn into muddy tracks in no time. Do not ride during or immediately after heavy rainstorms as this is when landslides might occur; many mountain roads are quite new and the cliff embankments can be unstable. Expect to average about 35km/h. Only use safe hotel parking. Fill up from petrol stations where the petrol is less likely to have been watered down.

If running short on time or energy, remember that many bus companies will let you put your bike on the roof of a bus, but get permission first from your bike-rental company.

Recommended specialists in Hanoi include Cuong's Motorbike Adventure (p88) and Offroad Vietnam (p92).

minority and the quirky art and sculpture of the owner. Unfortunately, a fire in 2013 destroyed the building holding the collection of Muong artefacts, but the sprawling five-hectare complex is worth visiting for the relaxed vibe and beautiful surroundings.

A *xe om* from Hoa Binh to the museum is around 50,000d and a taxi around 100,000d.

There's also shared accommodation here in simple stilt houses, and treks with local Muong ethnic minority guides can be arranged (300,000d).

Hoa Binh Dam LANDMARK
(Đ Hoa Binh; dam tunnel admission 30,000d; ⌚8-11am & 2-5pm) To view the huge dam wall of Hoa Binh's Russian-built hydroelectric station up close, head across Hoa Binh's bridge and follow the riverside road to the lookout platform right beside the wall. Engineering fans can also enter the tunnels underneath. On the way to the dam there's a memorial to the 161 workers who died during its construction.

Museum MUSEUM
(⌚8-10.30am & 2-4.30pm Mon-Fri) **FREE** A small museum showcases war memorabilia, including an old French amphibious vehicle. It's on Hwy 6, after the turn-off to Cu Chinh Lan.

Sleeping & Eating

You'll find *com pho* (rice-noodle soup) places lining Hwy 6.

Phu Gia Hotel HOTEL $
(☎0218-625 5999; www.phugiahotel.com.vn; Đ Le Thanh Tong; r 350,000-400,000d; ❄📶) Your best bet in Hoa Binh is this shiny new hotel just over Hoa Binh bridge. Modern rooms decked out in cream and beige come with flat-screen TVs, kettles and even a bit of kitsch art on the walls.

Muong Cultural Museum Homestay HOMESTAY $
(☎0913 553 937; www.muong.vn; 202 Tay Tien; per person 100,000d) Simple shared accommodation in ethnic minority stilt houses.

Breakfast is an additional 30,000d and other meals cost around 80,000d to 100,000d. Longer term residencies by artists are possible. A *xe om*/taxi from Hoa Binh costs around 50,000/100,000d.

Thap Vang Hotel HOTEL $
(☎0218-385 2864; 810a Đ Cu Chinh Lan; r 250,000-400,000d; P ❄ ☎) Set just off the main street, this decent budget choice has spotlessly clean rooms with fridge and satellite TV. It's worth paying slightly more for the larger rooms.

ℹ Information

There are ATMs along Hwy 6.

Hoa Binh Tourism Company (☎0218-385 4374; www.hoabinhtourism.com; Hoa Binh Hotel, 367 P An Duong Vuong) Has an office at the government-run Hoa Binh Hotel, off Hwy 6. Organises regional tours.

ℹ Getting There & Away

Hoa Binh is 74km southwest of Hanoi. With private transport you can visit Ba Vi National Park en route from Hanoi, and follow a riverbank road to Hoa Binh.

Hoa Binh Bus Station (Đ Tran Hung Dao) There are frequent services to Hanoi (50,000d, two hours) between 5am and 5.45pm. Buses to Mai Chau (50,000d, 1½ hours) leave at 6am, 8.20am, 10.40am, noon and 2pm.

Mai Chau

☎0218 / POP 12,000

Set in an idyllic valley, hemmed in by hills, the Mai Chau area is a world away from Hanoi's hustle. The small town of Mai Chau itself is unappealing, but just outside a patchwork of rice fields rolls out, speckled by tiny Thai villages where visitors doss down for the night in traditional stilt houses and wake up to a rural soundtrack defined by gurgling irrigation streams and birdsong.

The villagers are mostly White Thai, distantly related to tribes in Thailand, Laos and China. Most no longer wear traditional dress, but the Thai women are masterful weavers producing plenty of traditional-style textiles. Locals do not employ strong-arm sales tactics here: polite bargaining is the norm.

Mai Chau is a successful grassroots tourism project and the village homestays here are firmly stamped on the tour-group agenda, as well as being an extremely popular weekend getaway for locals from Hanoi – try to come midweek if possible. Due to its popularity, some find the experience too sanitised. If you're looking for hard-core exploration, this is not the place, but for biking, hiking and relaxation, Mai Chau fits the bill nicely.

Sights & Activities

Most visitors come simply to sleep in a stilt house and to stroll (or cycle) the paths through the rice fields to the separate minority villages. Most stilt house homestays rent bikes to explore the valley at your own pace and can organise a local guide for about US$10.

A popular 18km trek is from **Lac village** (Ban Lac) in Mai Chau to **Xa Linh village**, near a mountain pass (elevation 1000m) on Hwy 6. Lac village is home to White Thai, while the inhabitants of Xa Linh are

DON'T MISS

SLEEPING ON STILTS

Thai Stilt Houses (Mai Chau; per person 80,000-200,000d) Virtually every visitor to Mai Chau stays in one of the numerous Thai stilt house homestays in the villages of Lac or Pom Coong, a five-minute stroll apart. Overnighting in these minority villages is a civilised experience with electricity, Western-style toilets, hot showers, and roll-up mattresses with mosquito nets provided. Plan on one night plus dinner and breakfast costing around 250,000d.

It's all exceedingly comfortable, so don't arrive expecting a rustic hill-tribe encounter. Despite – or maybe because of – the modern amenities, it's still a memorable experience. The surrounding area is beautifully lush, the Thai villages are attractive and tidy, and locals are exceedingly friendly. Even with a TV on and the hum of the refrigerator, it is a peaceful place, and you're still sleeping in a thatched-roof stilt house on split-bamboo floors.

Reservations are not necessary. Just show up, but try and arrive before dark so you can get your bearings.

Hmong. The trek is strenuous in one day, so most people spend a night in a village. Arrange a guide, and a car to meet you at the mountain pass for the journey back to Mai Chau. Note there's a 600m climb in altitude, and the trail is slippery after rain.

Ask around in Mai Chau about longer treks of three to seven days. Other options include **kayaking** and **mountain-biking excursions**; enquire at Mai Chau Lodge.

Many travel agencies in Hanoi run inexpensive trips to Mai Chau.

Sleeping & Eating

For most visitors, Mai Chau is all about the stilt house homestays in the villages of Lac or Pom Coong.

Most people eat where they stay. Establish the price of meals first as some places charge up to 200,000d for dinner. Everything from fried eggs to French fries is available, but the local food is best and shouldn't be missed.

★ **Mai Chau Nature Lodge** BUNGALOW **$$**
(0946 888 804; www.maichaunatureplace.com; Lac village; dm US$5, d with fan US$30;) For a little more privacy than the neighbourhood homestays, this friendly operation in Lac village offers nine bungalows with rickety bamboo furniture. Dorms are also available. Grab a bungalow at the back to wake up to verdant rice-field views. There are free bikes to explore the surrounding countryside.

Mai Chau Lodge HOTEL **$$$**
(0218-386 8959; www.maichaulodge.com; Mai Chau; r US$145;) This tour-group favourite has contemporary rooms with wooden floors and designer lighting, and trimmed with local textiles. The thatched-roof restaurant overlooks a small lake and the pool. Activities on offer include visits to caves, cookery classes, and guided walking, kayaking and mountain-biking excursions.

Getting There & Away

Direct buses to Mai Chau (100,000d, 3¾ hours) leave Hanoi's My Dinh bus station at 6am, 8.30am and 11am. If you want to stay in Lac or Pom Coong villages, just ask the bus driver to drop you off there. You'll be dropped off at

OFF THE BEATEN TRACK

CHOW DOWN IN MOC CHAU & YEN CHAU

Many travellers enjoy the beautiful scenery around Mai Chau then head back to Hanoi before kicking on north to Sapa. But if you've got some time up your sleeve, or are heading west to Laos, the winding route of Hwy 6 to Dien Bien Phu is a scenic road trip packed with rural vistas. For foodies with a hankering for local flavours, especially if you've got a sweet tooth, it's worth stopping off at a couple of towns along this road.

Around 200km west of Hanoi, **Moc Chau** boasts a pioneering dairy industry launched in the late 1970s with Australian and UN assistance. The dairy provides Hanoi with fresh milk, sweetened condensed milk and little tooth-rotting bars called *banh sua*, and the town is a good place to sample fresh milk and yoghurt. Moc Chau also produces some of Vietnam's best tea, and the surrounding area is home to ethnic minorities, including Green Hmong, Dzao, Thai and Muong.

Vietnam in Focus (p72) offers photographic trips from Hanoi to Moc Chau's fascinating Hmong Love Market in late August/early September.

Handspan Adventure Travel (p88) runs two- and three-day trips to the area, staying in a Black Thai homestay in Ban Doi village.

A further 60km west, the agricultural **Yen Chau district** is known for its abundant fruit production. Apart from bananas, all fruits grown here are seasonal. Mangoes, plums and peaches are harvested from April to June, longans in July and August, and custard apples from August to September.

Yen Chau mangoes are renowned as Vietnam's tastiest, although travellers may initially find them disappointing, as they are small and green, rather than big, yellow and juicy like those of the tropical south. Most Vietnamese actually prefer the tart flavour of the green ones, especially dipped in *nuoc mam* (fish sauce) and sugar.

Both Moc Chau and Yen Chau can be reached on departures to either Son La or Dien Bien Phu from Hanoi's My Dinh bus station. Once on the road, travellers should find it relatively easy to flag down onward transport along Hwy 6.

the crossroads, just a short stroll from both villages. You may have to pay a 7000d entry fee to Mai Chau, but the toll booth is often unattended.

Heading back to Hanoi, buses leave at 9am, 11am and 1pm. Homestay owners can book these buses for you and arrange for you to be picked up from the village.

Son La

022 / POP 66,500

Son La has prospered as a logical transit point between Hanoi and Dien Bien Phu. It's not a must-see destination, but the surrounding scenery is impressive, and there are a few interesting diversions.

The region is one of Vietnam's most ethnically diverse and home to more than 30 different minorities, including Black Thai, Meo, Muong and White Thai. Vietnamese influence was minimal until the 20th century, and from 1959 to 1980 the region was part of the Tay Bac Autonomous Region.

Sights & Activities

You'll find woven shoulder bags, scarves, silver buttons and necklaces, and other hill-tribe crafts at **Son La's market**.

Old French Prison & Museum MUSEUM
(admission 30,000d; 7-11am & 1-4pm) Son La's Old French Prison & Museum was a French penal colony where anticolonial revolutionaries were incarcerated. It was destroyed by the 'off-loading' of unused ammunition by US war planes after bombing raids, but is now partially restored. Rebuilt turrets stand guard over crumbling cells and a famous lone surviving peach tree, planted by To Hieu, a 1940s inmate.

Next door, upstairs in the People's Committee office, is a tiny museum with some fine displays of local hill-tribe textiles.

Lookout Tower VIEWPOINT
For an overview of Son La, follow the stone steps to the left of the Trade Union Hotel. Look forward to a 20-minute walk to reach the lookout.

Thuan Chau Craft Market MARKET
Thuan Chau is about 35km northwest of Son La. Take a local bus or *xe om* here early in the morning, when its daily market is full of colourful hill-tribe women.

Sleeping

Sao Xanh Hotel HOTEL $
(022-378 9999; www.saoxanh.vn; 1 P Quyet Thang; d/tw 290,000/320,000d) Excellent value with spotless, colourful rooms and a friendly vibe at reception. The hotel is just a short walk to good cafes and restaurants.

Hanoi Hotel HOTEL $$
(022-375 3299; 228 Đ Truong Chinh; r US$40-50;) This gleaming main-drag edifice has modern rooms trimmed with colourful art, wooden furniture and surprisingly comfortable beds. Bring along your negotiation A-game to get a good walk-in rate.

Eating & Drinking

Long Phuong Restaurant VIETNAMESE $
(022-385 2339; P Thinh Doi; meals 40,000-70,000d; 11am-10pm) Located at one of the busier junctions in town, this restaurant features local minority dishes. Try sour *mang dang* (bamboo shoots) soup with sticky rice dipped in sesame-seed salt.

Trung Nguyen Cafe CAFE
(P Quyet Thang; 8am-10pm) Next door to the Sao Xanh Hotel, this smart cafe-bar has a relaxing, tree-shaded garden at the front and serves up some of Son La's best coffee.

Information

Agribank (8 Đ Chu Van Thinh; 8am-3pm Mon-Fri, 8-11am Sat, ATM 24hr)

Getting There & Away

Son La is 340km from Hanoi and 140km from Dien Bien Phu.

From the bus station, 5km southwest of town, there are frequent buses between 5am and 1pm to Hanoi (155,000d, 8½ hours) and services to Dien Bien Phu (105,000d, four hours) at 5am, 7am, 8am, 12.30pm and 4pm. There are also two morning buses at 5am and 5.30am to Ninh Binh (165,000d, nine hours).

Dien Bien Phu

0230 / POP 72,700

Dien Bien Phu (DBP) plays a star role in Vietnam's modern history. It was in the surrounding countryside here, on 7 May 1954, that the French colonial forces were defeated by the Viet Minh in a decisive battle, and the days of their Indochina empire became numbered.

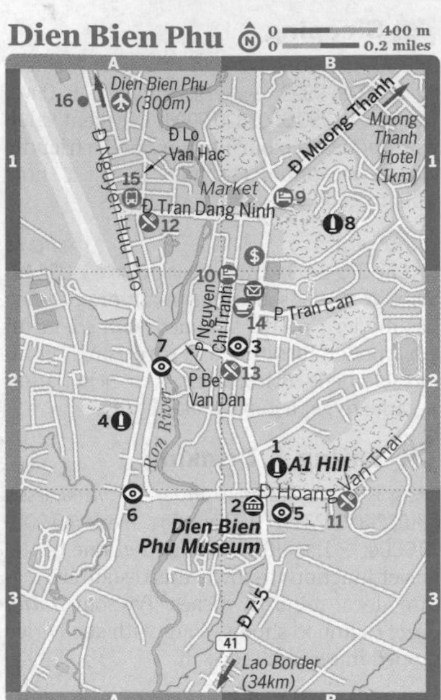

Dien Bien Phu

Top Sights

1 A1 Hill ... B2
2 Dien Bien Phu Museum ... B3

Sights

3 Bunker of Chief Artillery Commander Pirot ... B2
4 Bunker of Colonel de Castries ... A2
5 Dien Bien Phu Cemetery ... B3
6 French War Memorial ... A3
7 Muong Thanh Bridge ... A2
8 Victory Monument ... B1

Sleeping

9 Binh Long Hotel ... B1
10 Ruby Hotel ... B2

Eating

11 Bia Hoi ... B3
12 Pho Stalls ... A1
13 Yen Ninh ... B2

Drinking & Nightlife

14 The Coffee Shop ... B2

Transport

15 Bus Station ... A1
16 Vietnam Airlines ... A1

The town sits in the heart-shaped Muong Thanh Valley, surrounded by heavily forested hills. The scenery along the way here is stunning, with approach roads scything through thick forests and steep terrain. The city itself lies more prosaically on a broad dry plain. Thai, Hmong and Si La people live in the surrounding mountains, but the city and valley are mainly inhabited by ethnic Vietnamese.

Previously just a minor settlement, DBP only achieved town status in 1992. It became a city in 2003, and a year later was elevated to provincial capital. Expansive boulevards and civic buildings have been constructed, and the airport now receives daily flights from Hanoi.

History is DBP's main attraction with the clutch of bunkers, museums and war memorials attracting mostly domestic tourists. With the nearby Tay Trang–Sop Hun Vietnam–Laos border open to foreigners, more travellers are now passing through the city too.

History

In early 1954 General Henri Navarre, commander of the French forces in Indochina, sent 12 battalions to occupy the Muong Thanh Valley in an attempt to prevent the Viet Minh from crossing into Laos and threatening the former Lao capital of Luang Prabang. The French units, of which 30% were ethnic Vietnamese, were soon surrounded by Viet Minh forces under General Vo Nguyen Giap. The Viet Minh outnumbered the French by five to one, and were equipped with artillery pieces and anti-aircraft guns, painstakingly carried by porters through jungles and across rivers. The guns were placed in carefully camouflaged and concealed places overlooking the French positions.

When the guns opened up, French Chief Artillery Commander Pirot committed suicide. He'd assumed there was no way the Viet Minh could get heavy artillery to the area. A failed Viet Minh human-wave assault against the French was followed by weeks of intense artillery bombardments. Six battalions of French paratroopers were parachuted into DBP as the situation worsened, but bad weather and the impervious Viet Minh artillery prevented sufficient French reinforcements from arriving. An elaborate system of trenches and tunnels allowed Viet Minh soldiers to reach French positions without coming under fire. The trenches and bunkers were overrun by the

Viet Minh after the French decided against the use of US conventional bombers, and the Pentagon's proposal to use tactical atomic bombs. All 13,000 French soldiers were either killed or taken prisoner, and Viet Minh casualties were estimated at 25,000.

Just one day before the Geneva Conference on Indochina was set to begin in Switzerland, Viet Minh forces finally overran the beleaguered French garrison after a 57-day siege. This shattered French morale, and the French government abandoned all attempts to re-establish colonial control of Vietnam.

Sights

★Dien Bien Phu Museum MUSEUM
(☎0230-382 4971; Đ 7-5; admission 15,000d; ⏱7-11am & 1.30-4.30pm) This well-laid-out museum, contained in a space-agey modern structure, features an eclectic collection that commemorates the 1954 battle. Alongside weaponry and guns, there's a bathtub that belonged to the French commander Colonel de Castries, a bicycle capable of carrying 330kg of ordnance, and photographs and documents, some with English translations.

★A1 Hill MONUMENT
(Đ 7-5; admission 3000d; ⏱7-11am & 1.30-5pm) There are tanks and a monument to Viet Minh casualties on this former French position, known to the French as Eliane and to the Vietnamese as A1 Hill. The elaborate trenches at the heart of the French defences have also been recreated.

Bunker of Colonel de Castries MONUMENT
(admission 5000d; ⏱7-11am & 1.30-5pm) Across the Ron River, the command bunker of Colonel Christian de Castries has been recreated. A few discarded tanks linger nearby, and you'll probably see Vietnamese tourists mounting the bunker and waving the Vietnamese flag, re-enacting an iconic photograph taken at the battle's conclusion.

Dien Bien Phu Cemetery CEMETERY
(Đ 7-5) The immaculately maintained Dien Bien Phu Cemetery commemorates the Vietnamese dead, each gravestone bearing the gold star of the Vietnamese flag and a clutch of incense sticks.

French War Memorial MEMORIAL
The formal French War Memorial, erected on the 30th anniversary of the 1954 battle, commemorates the 3000 French troops buried under the rice paddies.

Muong Thanh Bridge BRIDGE
The old Muong Thanh Bridge is preserved and closed to four-wheeled traffic.

Bunker of Chief Artillery Commander Pirot MEMORIAL
Though not much more than an overgrown crater, this is the bunker where Chief Artillery Commander Pirot committed suicide.

Sleeping

★Ruby Hotel HOTEL $
(☎091 365 5793; www.rubyhoteldienbien.com; off Đ Nguyen Chi Thanh; s/d/tr 400,000/500,000/600,000d) The best deal in Dien Bien Phu is this friendly hotel, down a signposted alleyway. Rooms are comfortably fitted out with new beds, flat-screen TVs and bathrooms featuring rain shower heads. If you're travelling solo, treat yourself to a double room as the singles are quite small.

GETTING TO LAOS: DIEN BIEN PHU TO MUANG KHUA

Getting to the border Buses from Dien Bien Phu to Muang Khua (110,000d) leave daily at 5.30am. It's advisable to book your ticket the day prior to travelling. This bus takes you through the **Tay Trang/Sop Hun border crossing** and drops you off in Muang Khua in Laos. The journey typically takes between seven and eight hours, but can be longer depending on the roads and border formalities. Other destinations in Laos from DBP include Luang Prabang (495,000d, 6am), Nam Tha (350,000d, 6.30am) and Udomxai (230,000d, 7.30am).

At the border The Tay Trang/Sop Hun border, 34km from Dien Bien Phu, is open daily between 7am and 7pm. Crossing into Laos most travellers can get a 30-day visa on arrival (US$30 to US$42). Have two passport photos, and additional cash (around US$5) on hand for occasional local administrative fees.

Moving on From Muang Khua there are buses to Udomxai.

BUSES FROM DIEN BIEN PHU

DESTINATION	COST (D)	DURATION (HR)	FREQUENCY
Hanoi	270,000-300,000	11½	frequent 4.30am-9pm
Lai Chau	130,000	6-7	6.15am, 7am, 8am, 9am, 10am, 12.30pm, 1.15pm
Muang Khua (Laos)	110,000	7-8	5.30am
Muong Lay	62,000	3-4	2.30pm, 3pm, 4pm
Son La	105,000	4	4.30am, 8am, noon, 2pm

Binh Long Hotel GUESTHOUSE $
(0230-382 4345; 429 Đ Muong Thanh; d 200,000d;) This small, family-run place is squeezed between shops, right in the thick of things on the main road. The small rooms are very worn, but kept in better shape than the rest of DBP's cheapies.

Muong Thanh Hotel HOTEL $$
(0230-381 0043; www.muongthanh.vn; Đ Muong Thanh; r incl breakfast US$50-80;) Midrange hotels are not DBP's forte and the Muong Thanh is the best of a bad bunch. Business-style rooms include big beds and marble bathrooms but carpets are covered in cigarette burns and someone forgot to clean the corners of the rooms. Still, the pool complete with kitsch concrete dragon is amusing.

Eating & Drinking

Dining options are limited in DBP but there is a line of good-value, simple restaurants along P Nguyen Chi Tranh, all with pick-and-choose counters where you can tuck into everything from chicken to fried locusts, and a row of cheap and cheerful **pho stalls** (dishes around 30,000d; 8am-10pm) opposite the bus station; some serve delicious fresh sugar-cane juice.

Yen Ninh VIETNAMESE $
(P Be Van Dan; meals 50,000-80,000d; 11am-9pm;) This modest fully vegetarian diner dishes up tasty noodle and rice plates with plenty of tofu.

Bia Hoi VIETNAMESE $
(Đ Hoang Van Thai; meals 30,000-50,000d; noon-10pm) You're probably only in town for a night so meet the locals at the *bia hoi* gardens along Đ Hoang Van Thai. There's decent and cheap grilled food also if you're tired of rice and noodles.

The Coffee Shop CAFE
(P Tran Can; 10am-10pm) One of a row of modern cafes on this street, we like the smiling staff and brick-and-wood decor here. It serves Vietnamese coffee and good fruit shakes, as well as ice cream.

Information

Agribank (0230-382 5786; Đ 7-5; 8am-3pm Mon-Fri, 8-11.30am Sat, ATM 24hr)
Main Post Office (Đ 7-5; 8am-6pm Mon-Fri)

Getting There & Away

AIR

Dien Bien Phu Airport (DIN) is 1.5km from the town centre along the road to Muong Lay. **Vietnam Airlines** (0230-382 4948; www.vietnamairlines.com; Đ Nguyen Huu Tho; 7.30-11.30am & 1.30-4.30pm) operates two flights daily to Hanoi and has an office near the airport.

BUS

DBP's **bus station** (Hwy 12) is at the corner of Đ Tran Dang Ninh.

CAR & MOTORCYCLE

The 480km drive from Hanoi to Dien Bien Phu on Hwys 6 and 279 takes around 11 hours.

Muong Lay

0231 / POP 8800

Formerly known as Lai Chau, the small township of Muong Lay, en route from Dien Bien Phu to Sapa, used to perch on the banks of the spectacular Da River valley until it was flooded as part of the mammoth Song Da Reservoir hydroelectricity scheme. Today, renamed and moved up to the bank of the newly formed lake, the couple of scruffy streets that make up Muong Lay are a listless place.

The scenery here, though, dominated by the expansive lake rimmed by rippling mountains, is absolutely gorgeous. Situated just out of town, on a cliff above the lake, a couple of hotels make good use of the dramatic views, but unless you need a slightly surreal stopover on the long road north or south, there's really no point in staying.

Sleeping & Eating

Lan Anh Hotel HOTEL **$$**
(0989 673 888, 0230-350 9577; www.lananhhotel.com; r US$20-45;) Located on a ridge overlooking Muong Lay's lake, the Lan Anh has basic wooden rooms at the back and decent-sized midrange options complete with time-warp 1970s furniture in the main building. Service is haphazard at best and the complex can seem hilariously *Twilight Zone*–like if you're the sole guest.

Getting There & Away

From Muong Lay's small bus station there are buses to Dien Bien Phu (80,000d, four hours) at 6.30am and 7.30am; and a service to Sinho (80,000d, 2½ hours) at 8am. To Lai Chau (55,000d, three hours) you can jump on any of the buses from Dien Bien Phu, which all stop here.

Note that due to a dire lack of facilities this is not a good overnight stop for those using public transport. Taking the through-bus between Dien Bien Phu and Lai Chau is a better option.

Lai Chau

0231 / POP 37,000

After passing through one of Vietnam's remotest regions, the new eight-lane boulevards and monumental government buildings of Lai Chau appear like some kind of bizarre mirage.

Formerly known as Tam Duong, this isolated town was renamed Lai Chau when the decision was made to flood 'old' Lai Chau (now known as Muong Lay). 'New' Lai Chau is split between the old town, with its **market** full of hill-tribe people, and the concrete new town located 3km to the southeast.

Despite its grandiose streets and upgrade to provincial capital status, Lai Chau is still something of a one-horse town. Fortunately,

OFF THE BEATEN TRACK

SINHO VILLAGE

Sinho is a scenic mountain village, home to a large number of ethnic minorities. It should attract more tourists, but when you visit, there is a 'you ain't from around here' look on the faces of many locals.

However, a decent hotel and improving road access means it's an interesting detour if you're keen to see an authentic local market very different from those at Sapa and Bac Ha, which are now firmly on the tour-bus route.

Sinho has **markets** (6am-2pm) on Saturday and Sunday; the wildly colourful Sunday market is the more impressive of the two. Just don't expect trendy ethnic handicrafts: you're more likely to be confronted with a full-on mix of bovine moos and porcine squeals.

The best (only!) place in town that accepts foreign travellers is the **Thanh Binh Hotel** (0231-387 0366; Zone 5, Sinho; r incl breakfast US$25-30;), a surprisingly comfortable spot comprised of 17 decent rooms. Meals (120,000d) are available, and treks can be arranged to nearby White Hmong and Red Dzao villages.

Note there are no ATMs or banks in Sinho.

It's definitely slow getting to Sinho by public transport, but achievable with a flexible attitude. A bus to Sinho leaves Dien Bien Phu daily (120,000d, six hours) at around 5.30am, transiting through Muong Lay around 8am. These times can be flexible, so check at the Dien Bien Phu bus station the day before you want to leave. From Sinho, buses then trundle downhill to Lai Chau (45,000d, three hours) at 7am and 1pm. Heading south from Lai Chau to Sinho, there are four buses per day and a daily departure from Sinho to Dien Bien Phu (120,000d, six hours). Note that the road linking Sinho to Lai Chau was not in great shape at the time of writing.

If you're travelling on two wheels, the turn-off uphill to Sinho is 1km north of Chan Nua on the main road from Muong Lay to Lai Chau. Definitely ask about the state of the road from Sinho to Lai Chau before you leave Hanoi.

the surrounding scenery of verdant conical peaks is as beguiling as ever.

Most visitors only dally long enough for a lunch break between Dien Bien Phu and Sapa. The drive from Lai Chau to Sapa along Hwy 4D, threading through the Fansipan Mountain Range near the Chinese border, is a beautiful stretch of road.

Sleeping

Phuong Tanh HOTEL $
(0231-387 5235; 31 Đ Tran Hung; r 300,000-350,000d) The Phuong Tanh overcomes a drab reception area with well-lit rooms offering clean bedding and nice views from the open-to-air corridors. On the 2nd floor, Café Phan Xi Pan is a brightly coloured oasis with wi-fi, cold beer, and tasty variations on rice and noodles.

Muong Phat Hotel HOTEL $
(0231-379 1386; Đ 30-4; r 250,000d) Directly opposite Lai Chau bus station, the Muong Phat has small colourful rooms (pink walls and red carpets, no less) and enthusiastic staff, making it a good option if you want to roll out of town on an early-morning bus.

Information

There are ATMs along Đ Tran Hung in the central town.

Getting There & Away

Lai Chau bus station (Đ 30-4) is 1km from the town centre. A *xe om* from the bus station into the town centre is around 10,000d and a taxi around 20,000d.

Buses south to Dien Bien Phu (130,000d, seven hours) via Muong Lay (55,000d, three hours) leave at 5am, 6.30am, hourly between 8am and 1pm, and 5pm. To Hanoi (from 280,000d, 12 hours) there are services at 6.30am, 9.15am, 9.45am, 10pm and 10.15pm.

Heading to Sapa (75,000d, 2½ hours), get on any Lao Cai–bound bus. They leave at least hourly between 5am and 5pm. For Sinho (45,000d, three hours) there are services at 6am, 7am, 9am and 1.30pm.

Sapa

020 / POP 36,200 / ELEV 1650M

Established as a hill station by the French in 1922, Sapa today is the tourism centre of the northwest.

Sapa is orientated to make the most of the spectacular views emerging on clear days, overlooking a plunging valley, with mountains towering above on all sides. Views of this epic scenery are often subdued by thick mist rolling across the peaks, but even when it's cloudy, local hill-tribe people fill the town with colour.

If you were expecting a quaint alpine town, recalibrate your expectations. Sapa's French colonial villas fell into disrepair during successive wars with the French, Americans and Chinese, and modern tourism development has mushroomed haphazardly. Sapa today is undergoing a construction boom and, thanks to rarely enforced building height restrictions, the skyline is continually thrusting upwards.

But you are not here to hang out in the town. This is northern Vietnam's premier trekking base from where hikers launch themselves into a surrounding countryside filled with cascading rice terraces and tiny hill-tribe villages that seem a world apart. Once you have stepped out into the lush fields you will understand the Sapa area's real charm.

Sights & Activities

★**Sapa Museum** MUSEUM
(103 Đ Xuan Vien; 7.30-11.30am & 1.30-5pm) FREE Excellent showcase of the history and ethnology of the Sapa area, including the colonial times of the French. Exhibitions demonstrate the differences between the various ethnic minority people of the area, so it's definitely worth visiting the museum when you first arrive in town.

Sapa Market MARKET
(Đ Ngu Chi Son; 6am-2pm) Unfortunately turfed out of central Sapa, and now in a purpose-built modern building near the bus station, Sapa Market is still a hive of colourful activity with fresh produce, a butcher's section not for the squeamish and hill-tribe people from surrounding villages heading here most days to sell handicrafts. Saturday is the busiest day.

Tram Ton Pass VIEWPOINT
The road between Sapa and Lai Chau crosses the Tram Ton Pass on the northern side of Fansipan, 15km from Sapa. At 1900m this is Vietnam's highest mountain pass, and acts as a dividing line between two weather fronts. The lookout points here have fantastic views. Most people also stop at 100m-high **Thac Bac** (Silver Waterfall), 12km from Sapa.

On the Sapa side, it's often cold and foggy, but drop a few hundred metres onto the Lai Chau side, and it can be sunny and warm. Surprisingly, Sapa is the coldest place in Vietnam, but Lai Chau can be one of the warmest.

Victoria Spa SPA
(☎020-387 1522; www.victoriahotels-asia.com; Victoria Sapa Resort, P Hoang Dieu; ⏰8am-10pm) After a few days of trekking, treat yourself with a bit of pampering. This upmarket spa complex at the Victoria Sapa Resort has gorgeous massage and treatment rooms. The spa's pool area (with sauna and shower facilities) is open to people not staying at the resort for US$10 per person.

Hiking

You won't step too far out of your hotel in Sapa before being accosted with offers to guide you on hikes.

For longer treks with overnight stays in villages, it's important to hook up with someone who knows the terrain and culture and speaks the language. We recommend using minority guides, as this offers them a means of making a living. Note it's illegal to stay overnight in villages that are not officially recognised as homestays. Ignoring this could cause significant problems for your hosts and yourself.

The surrounding landscape is now part of Hoang Lien National Park and all the villages that can be visited have admission fees from 20,000d to 40,000d.

Cat Cat HIKING
(admission 40,000d) The nearest village within walking distance is Cat Cat, 3km south of Sapa. It's a steep and beautiful hike down, and there are plenty of *xe om* for the return uphill journey.

Sa Seng & Hang Da HIKING
For spectacular valley views (if the mist and cloud gods relent), there's a beautiful hike along a high ridge east of Sapa through the Black Hmong settlements of Sa Seng and Hang Da down to the Ta Van River, where you can get transport back to Sapa.

Ta Phin HIKING
(admission 20,000d) A very popular hike from Sapa is to Ta Phin village, home to Red Dzao and about 10km from Sapa. Most people take a *xe om* to a starting point about 8km from Sapa, and then make a 14km loop through the area, passing through Black Hmong and Red Dzao villages.

Fansipan HIKING
Surrounding Sapa are the Hoang Lien Mountains, dubbed the Tonkinese Alps by the French. These mountains include the often cloud-obscured Fansipan (3143m), Vietnam's highest peak. Fansipan is accessible year-round to sensibly equipped trekkers in good shape, but don't underestimate the challenge. It is very wet, and can be perilously slippery and generally cold.

The summit of Fansipan is 19km by foot from Sapa. The terrain is rough and adverse weather is frequent. The round trip usually takes three days; some experienced hikers do it in two days, but you'll need to be fit. After walking through hill-tribe villages on the first morning, it's just forest, mountain vistas and occasional wildlife, including monkeys, mountain goats and birds. Weather-wise the best time is from mid-October to mid-December, and in March, when wildflowers are in bloom. Don't attempt an ascent if Sapa's weather is poor, as limited visibility on Fansipan can be treacherous.

BUILDING A STRONGER HMONG FUTURE

Inherent in Sapa's burgeoning prosperity is cultural change for the hill-tribe people.

Traditionally, the Hmong have been employees of Vietnamese-owned trekking companies, restaurants and accommodation, with many Hmong children kept out of school to sell handicrafts or act as trekking guides, often walking up to 10km daily from their villages to Sapa to earn money. A new generation, though, is now focused on securing a more independent and positive future for their people.

Sapa O'Chau (p139), meaning 'thank you Sapa' in the Hmong language, is focused on providing training and opportunities to Hmong children. The organisation is run by former handicraft peddler Shu Tan, who created the Sapa O'Chau Learning Centre, a live-in school where up to 20 Hmong children can learn English and Vietnamese. The organisation also runs excellent walks and treks.

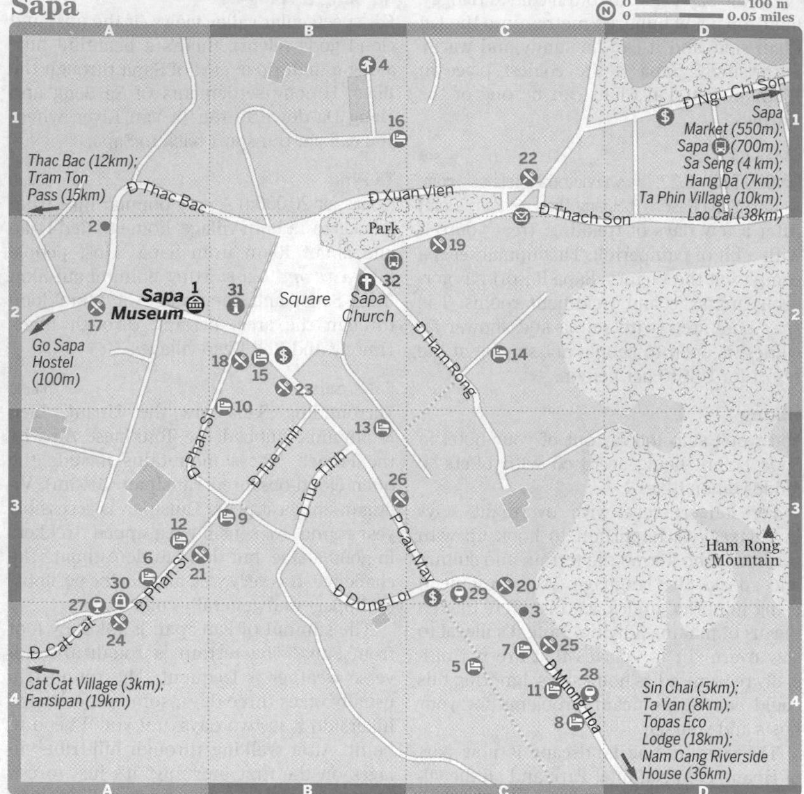

No ropes or technical climbing skills are needed, just endurance. There are a few rudimentary shelters at a couple of base camps en route, but it's better to be self-sufficient with sleeping bag, waterproof tent, food, stove, raincoat, compass and other miscellaneous survival gear. It's important to carry out all your garbage, as some of the camps are now impacted by trash. Hiring a reputable guide is vital, and porters are also recommended.

Through local operators, count on an all-inclusive rate of around US$150 per person for a couple, US$125 per person for a group of four, and US$100 per person for the sensible maximum group size of six.

Fansipan's wild, lonesome beauty has been somewhat shattered with the opening of a 6282m-long cable car, taking people across the Muong Hoa Valley and up to the summit in 15 minutes.

Courses

Indigo Cat CRAFTS

(☎0982 403 647; www.facebook.com/indigocatsapa; 46 Đ Phan Si; class 100,000-200,000d; ⊙9am-7pm) Craft shop Indigo Cat runs afternoon workshops where you can learn traditional Hmong weaving and embroidery skills. Workshops take place in the village of Ta Ven. Call into its Sapa shop for details.

Hill Station Signature Restaurant COOKING

(☎020-388 7112; 37 Đ Phan Si; per person US$29; ⊙from 9am) Excellent three-hour cooking classes with an English-speaking Hmong chef starting with a 30-minute market tour and featuring five local dishes, including homemade tofu, smoked buffalo and Hmong-style black pudding, as well as the chance to taste local rice wine. Book the evening before.

Sapa

Top Sights
1 Sapa Museum A2

Activities, Courses & Tours
Hill Station Signature Restaurant .... (see 21)
Indigo Cat .... (see 6)
2 Sapa O'Chau A2
Sapa Sisters .... (see 10)
3 Topas Travel C4
4 Victoria Spa B1

Sleeping
5 Botanic Sapa C4
6 Cat Cat View Hotel A3
7 Holiday Sapa C4
8 Luong Thuy Family Guesthouse C4
9 Phuong Nam Hotel B3
10 Sapa Graceful Hotel B2
11 Sapa Lodge C4
12 Sapa Luxury Hotel A3
13 Sapa Paradise View B3
14 Thai Binh Hotel C2
15 U Sapa B2
16 Victoria Sapa Resort B1

Eating
17 Baguette & Chocolat A2
18 Barbecue Restaurants B2
19 Gecko C2
20 Hill Station Deli & Boutique C3
21 Hill Station Signature Restaurant A3
22 Hotpot Stalls C1
23 Little Sapa B2
24 Nature View A4
25 Sapa Memories C4
Sapa O'Chau .... (see 2)
26 Viet Emotion B3

Drinking & Nightlife
27 Color Bar A4
28 Hmong Sisters C4
29 Mountain Bar & Pub C3

Shopping
30 Hemp & Embroidery A3
Indigo Cat .... (see 6)

Information
31 Sapa Tourism B2

Transport
32 Minibuses to Lao Cai B2

Tours

Many visitors arrive on tour packages prearranged in Hanoi but there's a couple of standout local operators in town that are well worth looking into.

As well as hiking tours, many companies offer more culturally focused trips such as community-based tours to the nearby Hmong village of **Sin Chai**, with an overnight in the village to learn about textiles or music. Other popular communities to visit include the Giay village of **Ta Van** and the Hmong village of **Matra**.

★ Sapa O'Chau HIKING
(☎020-377 1166; www.sapaochau.com; 8 Đ Thac Bac; ⏲6.30am-6.30pm) Excellent local company offering day walks, longer homestay treks, Bac Ha market trips and Fanispan hikes. It also runs culturally immersive tours that focus on handicrafts and farmstays. Profits provide training to Hmong children in a learning centre.

Sapa Sisters HIKING
(☎020-377 3388; www.sapasisters.com; Sapa Graceful Hotel, 9 Đ Phan Si; ⏲8am-5pm) Run by a group of savvy and knowledgeable Hmong women, Sapa Sisters offers fully customised private day hikes and longer village homestay treks. Excellent English is spoken, and some French, Spanish and Japanese.

Topas Travel HIKING
(☎020-387 1331; www.topastravel.vn; 21 Đ Muong Hoa) High-quality trekking, biking and village encounters. Options include a stay in Topas Ecolodge or the Nam Cang Riverside House.

Sleeping

Many hotels raise rates on Fridays and Saturdays with the weekend influx of domestic tourists.

A lot of hotels give a much better walk-in rate than what is advertised on hotel booking websites. Sapa does get busy, though, so if there's somewhere in particular you want to stay, prebook directly with the hotel itself for a better rate.

Sapa Graceful Hotel HOSTEL $
(☎020-377 3388; www.gracefulhotel.com; 9 Đ Phan Si; dm/d US$5/18; 📶) This bijoux hostel has bags of homey charm and knows how to pull backpackers in, with two-for-one beer happy hours every evening. The dorm is a squeeze, but the foyer has comfy sofas

and stacks of books, and as it's the base for Sapa Sisters, there's a ton of trekking info on offer.

Go Sapa Hostel HOSTEL $
(☎020-387 1198; www.gosapahostel.com; 25 Đ Thac Bac; dm 110,000-150,000d, d 400,000d; @📶) Up the hill from central Sapa, this set-up has a multitude of eight-bed dorms (with lockers) set around a communal courtyard. More expensive dorm options come with private bathroom and some have tiny balconies. There are washing machines, free computers and bike rentals.

Luong Thuy Family Guesthouse GUESTHOUSE $
(☎020-387 2310; www.familysapa.com; 28 Đ Muong Hoa; dm US$5, d US$15-20, tw US$25; @📶) This friendly guesthouse has a decent, though dark, dorm and snug private rooms. Motorcycles and bikes can be rented, trekking and transport arranged, and there are valley views from front balconies.

Phuong Nam Hotel HOTEL $
(☎020-387 1286; www.phuongnamhotelsapa.com; 33 Đ Phan Si; dm/r incl breakfast US$7/20; 📶) Inside this nondescript concrete hotel there's a decent budget deal to be had, with two four-bed dorms with large beds. Private rooms are basic but spick-and-span, though don't bother on weekends when the room price is hiked to a ridiculous US$35.

★**Nam Cang Riverside House** HOMESTAY $$
(www.namcangriversidelodge.com; Nam Cang village; d US$60) Located in a valley, on the outskirts of teensy Nam Cang village, 36km from Sapa, this stylish wooden house with nine rooms is a collaboration between a Red Dzao family and Topas Travel. This is a Sapa stay replete with stunning scenery and local hill-tribe life. The house is right beside a trickling river and backed by lush green forest.

Botanic Sapa HOTEL $$
(☎020-387 3879; www.botanicsapa.com; 8a Cau May Alley; r US$25-30) The cosy Botanic stands out mostly due to friendly owners Minh and his wife Van, who are wonderful hosts. Decent-sized rooms, brightened with local textiles, come with fresh white linen and modern bathrooms, and everything is kept spotlessly clean. The location, down a steep staircase off P Cau May, won't suit everyone.

Thai Binh Hotel HOTEL $$
(☎020-387 1212; www.thaibinhhotel.com; 45 Đ Ham Rong; d incl breakfast US$28-35; 📶) The Thai Binh enjoys a quiet location near Sapa's church. Rooms are spacious and clean, decked out with crisp pine furniture and cosy bedspreads, and boasting some of the nicest bathrooms you'll see for this price in Sapa.

Sapa Paradise View HOTEL $$
(☎020-387 2683; www.sapaparadiseviewhotel.com; 18 P Xuan Huan; d incl breakfast from US$45; ❄@📶) Despite the name, there's not much of a view but this is more than made up for by well-equipped, large and comfortable rooms with plenty of locally inspired decoration touches. Deluxe options have in-room laptops.

Holiday Sapa HOTEL $$
(☎020-387 3874; www.holidaysapa.com; 16 Đ Muong Hoa; r incl breakfast US$30-50; ❄📶) It's no surprise this hotel is a favourite with tour groups, as the service here is on the ball and there's a wide variety of rooms on offer. You really want to bag one on the top floor for the views. The restaurant serves excellent Vietnamese dishes.

Sapa Lodge HOTEL $$
(☎020-377 2885; www.sapalodgehotel.com; 18 Đ Muong Hoa; r incl breakfast US$30-45; ❄📶) Sapa Lodge is a friendly, well-run place with plenty of small-hotel appeal. Upstairs you'll find smart, light-filled rooms with soaring views of the surrounding mountains. Cheaper US$30 rooms have internal windows only and are a tad claustrophobic.

Cat Cat View Hotel HOTEL $$
(☎020-387 1946; www.catcathotel.com; 46 Đ Phan Si; r incl breakfast US$30-50, f apt US$150-180; ❄@📶) There's plenty of choice at this rambling, family-run spot with comfortable pine-trimmed rooms over nine floors, many opening out onto communal terraces with views. The spacious apartments are a great option for travelling families or groups of friends.

Sapa Luxury Hotel HOTEL $$
(☎020-387 2771; www.sapaluxuryhotel.com; 36 Đ Phan Si; r incl breakfast 600,000-800,000d; @📶) Large rooms may be a tad bland but come with modern bathrooms, wooden floors and their own laptops. The cheaper rooms only have poky windows so can be a bit on the dark side.

Topas Ecolodge ECOLODGE $$$
(☎020-387 2404; www.topasecolodge.com; bungalows US$115-140; @📶) 🍃 Overlooking a plunging valley, 18km from Sapa, this ecolodge has stone-and-thatch bungalows with front balconies to make the most of the magnificent views. The whole project is sustainable and environmentally friendly, with solar energy providing the power. Hiking, biking and market tours are available.

Victoria Sapa Resort RESORT HOTEL $$$
(☎020-387 1522; www.victoriahotels-asia.com; P Hoang Dieu; r US$180, deluxe US$250; ❄@📶🏊) This alpine-style hotel gets top marks for its sublime service and beautifully decorated communal areas that highlight local culture. The rooms themselves, within well-tended manicured lawns, are on the small side but have private balconies and newly renovated bathrooms. Facilities include two bars and a spa.

U Sapa HOTEL $$$
(☎020-387 1996; www.usapavietnam.com; 8 P Cau May; r from US$180; ❄@📶) Slap in the centre of town, U Sapa has taken over the old government-run hotel and converted it into a rather sophisticated place offering contemporary-styled rooms decked out in earthy shades of olive and beige, and featuring all the bells and whistles you'd expect at a top-end place. Some rooms have tiny balconies looking out onto the main street below.

Eating

There are plentiful restaurants along P Cau May serving identikit menus of Vietnamese and Western staples. Look out for hill-tribe specialities utilising Sapa's wild mushrooms and herbs and local fish.

For eating on a budget, humble Vietnamese restaurants huddle on Đ Tue Tinh, and the stalls south of the church can't be beaten for *bun cha* (barbecued pork).

Little Sapa VIETNAMESE $
(18 P Cau May; meals 50,000-80,000d; ⏲8am-10pm) One of the better-value eateries along touristy P Cau May, Little Sapa also lures in locals. Steer clear of the largely mediocre European dishes and concentrate on the Vietnamese menu.

Sapa O'Chau CAFE $
(www.sapaochau.org; 8 Đ Thac Bac; snacks from 20,000d; ⏲6.30am-6.30pm; 📶) 🍃 Don't miss warming up with a cup of ginger tea sweetened with Sapa mountain honey at this simple cafe attached to the Sapa O'Chau tour company. Also does good breakfasts and a few simple snacks.

Barbecue Restaurants VIETNAMESE $
(Đ Phan Si; meals around 70,000-120,000d; ⏲noon-11pm) Several easygoing spots along the northern end of Đ Phan Si specialise in grilled meat and vegetables. Pull up a pew at one of the simple tables and tuck in.

Hotpot Stalls VIETNAMESE $
(Đ Xuan Vien; meals around 50,000d; ⏲11am-11pm) Dig into Vietnamese-style *lau* (hotpot; meat stew cooked with local vegetables, cabbage and mushroom) at these stalls.

★**Hill Station Signature Restaurant** VIETNAMESE $$
(www.thehillstation.com; 37 Đ Phan Si; meals 90,000-180,000d; ⏲7am-11pm; 📶) A showcase of Hmong cuisine with cool Zen decor and superb views. Dishes include flash-cooked pork with lime, ash-baked trout in banana leaves, and traditional Hmong-style black pudding. Tasting sets of local rice and corn wine are also of interest to curious travelling foodies. Don't miss trying the delicate rainbow-trout rolls; think of them as 'Sapa sushi'.

Nature View VIETNAMESE $$
(51 Đ Phan Si; meals 90,000-150,000d; ⏲8am-10pm; 📶✍) You've got to love the photos of the owner's kids on the walls at this friendly spot with great valley views. Look forward to decent Vietnamese and European food and just maybe Sapa's best fruit smoothies. Those who aren't fans of tofu should try the sizzling tofu with lemongrass and be converted. Don't worry – it's not all vegetarian food.

Baguette & Chocolat CAFE $$
(☎020-387 1766; Đ Thac Bac; cakes from 30,000d, snacks & meals 70,000-160,000d; ⏲7am-10pm; 📶) 🍃 Head to this converted villa for a fine breakfast, baguette or tasty slab of lemon tart. Many of the staff are students at the Hoa Sua School for disadvantaged youth and are being trained in the cooking and hospitality industry.

Hill Station Deli & Boutique CAFE $$
(7 Đ Muong Hoa; meals 125,000-165,000d; ⏲7am-10.30pm; 📶) With cheese and charcuterie plates, pork terrine and local smoked trout, the Hill Station Deli & Boutique is a stylish addition to the Sapa dining scene. Factor in some of Sapa's best coffee and an interesting

array of international beers and wines, and you've got the most cosmopolitan option in town.

Viet Emotion INTERNATIONAL $$
(☎020-387 2559; www.vietemotion.com; 27 P Cau May; meals 55,000-230,000d; ⏰7am-11pm; 📶) This intimate bistro features a cosy fireplace for cold mountain nights. The menu rambles from pizza, pasta and steaks to Vietnamese with a couple of Sapa specialities, such as herbal medicine hotpot (with lemongrass and mountain mushrooms).

Sapa Memories VIETNAMESE $$
(29 Đ Muong Hoa; meals 70,000-125,000d; ⏰8am-10.30pm; 📶) You'll find all the usual Vietnamese staples here but there's also more adventurous local dishes, including fried frogs and venison. The dinky terrace at the front is a great place to sit back and watch Sapa daily life go by.

Gecko INTERNATIONAL $$
(☎020-377 1504; Đ Ham Rong; meals 120,000-180,000d; 📶) This French-owned place has a rustic feel and a menu of flavoursome country cooking that jumps from French classics and steak options to local fish served with wild Sapa mushrooms.

Drinking

A bar crawl in Sapa will take in a maximum of three or four venues – this is not a party town.

Mountain Bar & Pub BAR
(2 Đ Muong Hoa; ⏰noon-11pm; 📶) Dangerously strong cocktails, cold beer and ultra-competitive games of table football conspire to make this Sapa's go-to place for a great night out. Even if it's freezing outside, a *shisha* beside the open fire will soon perk up the chilliest of travellers. Try the warm apple wine for some highland bliss.

Color Bar BAR
(www.facebook.com/colorbar; 56 Đ Phan Si; ⏰noon-11pm; 📶) Owned by a Hanoi artist, this atmospheric spot ticks all the boxes with reggae, table football, *shisha* and ice-cold Bia Lao Cai. A great refuelling option on the steep walk up from Cat Cat village.

Hmong Sisters BAR
(Đ Muong Hoa; ⏰noon-late; 📶) This spacious bar with pool tables and an open fire has pretty decent music, but can feel a bit sparse if it's a quiet night. Bar prices are reasonable, though, so it's always worth checking out.

Shopping

Lots of the minority women and girls have gone into the souvenir business, and Sapa's streets are packed with handicraft peddlers. The older women in particular are canny traders and known for their strong-armed selling tactics. When negotiating prices, hold your ground, but avoid aggressive bargaining.

Note that on some cheaper textiles, the dyes used are not set, which can turn anything the material touches (including your skin) a muddy blue-green colour. Wash the fabric separately in cold salted water to stop the dye from running, and wrap items in plastic bags before packing them in your luggage.

If you've arrived in town with insufficient warm clothing, stores along P Cau May sell lots of 'brand-name' walking shoes, parkas and thermals. Some of it might even be authentic, but don't count on it.

Indigo Cat HANDICRAFTS
(www.facebook.com/indigocatsapa; 46 Đ Phan Si; ⏰9am-7pm) This Hmong-owned handicrafts shop offers a wonderful selection of interesting local crafts, including bags, clothing, pillows and belts. Co-owner Pang speaks good English and her small son Sanji is a real charmer.

Hemp & Embroidery CRAFTS
(www.facebook.com/hempandembroidery; 50 Đ Phan Si; ⏰9am-8pm) A super-friendly shop owned by a charming Hmong lady, selling gorgeous textiles all made in the Sapa area. There are some divine bedspreads and cushion covers to browse through and the sales pitch is distinctly low-key, which many travellers will heartily appreciate.

Information

Wi-fi is commonplace in hotels and many restaurants and cafes.

Many hotels and businesses will change euros and US dollars.

The *Sapa Tourist Map* (20,000d) is an excellent 1:75,000 scale map of the walking trails and attractions around Sapa. The *Sapa Trekking Map* is a worthwhile hand-drawn map showing trekking routes and the town.

Agribank (P Cau May; ⏰8am-3pm Mon-Fri, ATM 24hr)

BIDV Bank (☎020-387 2569; Đ Ngu Chi Son; ⏰8am-3pm Mon-Fri, 8-11am Sat, ATM 24hr)

Main Post Office (Đ Ham Rong; ⏰8am-6pm Mon-Fri) International phone calls can also be made here.

Sapa Tourism (☎020-387 3239; www.sapa-tourism.com; 103 Đ Xuan Vien; ⏰7.30-11.30am & 1.30-5pm) Helpful English-speaking staff offering details about transport, trekking and weather. Internet access is free for 15 minutes, and the website is also a mine of useful information.

Getting There & Away

The gateway to Sapa is Lao Cai, 38km away via a well-maintained highway. An even speedier bypass road, which will cut travel time to around 20 minutes, was being built during our last visit. If you're using private transport, stick with the highway – it's got the views.

BICYCLE & MOTORCYCLE

Motorcycling from Hanoi to Sapa is feasible, but it's a long 380km trip. Put your bike on the train to Lao Cai and save yourself the hassle. The 38km between Lao Cai and Sapa is all uphill – hell on a bicycle.

BUS

Sapa's **bus station** (Đ Dien Bien) is located in the north of town, but you can also check schedules at Sapa Tourism. To Hanoi (250,000d, 10 hours) buses leave at 7.30am, 8.30am, 4pm and 5pm; and there are two sleeper services (300,000d, six hours) that take the toll road direct to Hanoi at 9pm and 10pm. Heading to Lai Chau there are 10 buses between 6.30am and 5.15pm.

There is no direct service to Dien Bien Phu, Halong Bay or Bac Ha. You need to take a minibus to Lao Cai and change there.

MINIBUS

Minibuses to Lao Cai (30,000d, 30 minutes) leave every half-hour between 6am and 6pm, from a bus stop near Sapa Church.

Hotels and travel agents offer minibus tours to Bac Ha (from US$20 return) for the Sunday market. It's cheaper, but much slower, to go to Bac Ha by public minibus, changing buses in Lao Cai.

TRAIN

There's no direct train line to Sapa, but there are regular services from Hanoi to Lao Cai. Most hotels and travel agencies can book train tickets back to Hanoi.

Getting Around

The best way to get around compact Sapa is to walk. Bicycles can be hired, but you'll spend half your time pushing them up steep hills.

For excursions, motorbikes are available from about US$5 a day. If you've never ridden a motorbike before, this is not the place to learn. The weather can be wet and treacherous at any time of the year, and roads are steep and regularly damaged by floods and heavy rain.

Consider hiring a *xe om*. Local drivers hang out on the corner of P May Cai and Đ Phan Si. Some sample prices: one way/return to Cat Cat 40,000/70,000d; Sin Chai 60,000/100,000d; Ta Van 80,000/120,000d; and Thac Bac (Silver Waterfall) 70,000/120,000d.

Lao Cai

☎020 / POP 76,836

Lao Cai is squeezed right next to the Vietnam–China border. Razed in the Chinese invasion of 1979, most of the buildings here are modern. The border crossing slammed shut during the 1979 war and only

GETTING TO CHINA: LAO CAI TO KUNMING

Getting to the border The Chinese border at the **Lao Cai/Hekou border crossing** is about 3km from Lao Cai train station, a journey done by *xe om* (around 25,000d) or taxi (around 50,000d).

At the border The border is open daily between 7am and 10pm Vietnam time. Note that China is one hour ahead of Vietnam. You'll need to have a pre-arranged visa for China, and border crossing formalities usually take around one hour. China is separated from Vietnam by a road bridge and a separate rail bridge over the Song Hong (Red River). Note that travellers have reported Chinese officials confiscating Lonely Planet *China* guides at this border, so you may want to try masking the cover.

Moving on The new Hekou bus station is around 6km from the border post. There are regular departures to Kunming, including sleeper buses that leave at 7.20pm and 7.30pm, getting into Kunming at around 7am. There are also four daily trains.

BUSES FROM LAO CAI

DESTINATION	COST (D)	DURATION (HR)	FREQUENCY
Dien Bien Phu	from 235,000	8	6.30am, 5.30pm
Ha Giang	120,000	5	5.30am, 12.30pm
Halong City (Bai Chay)	360,000	12	7.15pm, 7.45pm
Hanoi	230,000	10	7.30am, 8.30am, 9am
Hanoi (sleeper service)	from 300,000	5-6	7.30pm, 8.30pm, 9pm
Lai Chau	90,000	3	11 services between 5.30am & 4.15pm

reopened in 1993. Now it's a bustling spot fuelled by growing cross-border trade.

For travellers, Lao Cai is the jumping-off point when journeying between Hanoi and Sapa by train, and a stop-off when heading further north to Kunming in China. With Sapa just a half-hour hop away, it's no place to linger, but it offers everything China-bound travellers will need for an overnight stay.

Sleeping & Eating

The Nest HOTEL $

(☎0912 356 563; 340 Đ Nguyen Hue; d/tr 200,000/300,000d;) This simple place is opposite Lao Cai train station. The large, high-ceilinged triple rooms, facing the street, are a much better deal than the poky, dark doubles.

Thien Hai Hotel BUSINESS HOTEL $$

(☎020-383 3666; www.thienhaihotel.com; 306 P Khanh Yen; d incl breakfast 600,000d;) A hop-skip-jump to Lao Cai train station right next door, the Thien Hai is a solid option with big business-brisk-style rooms and professional staff.

Viet Emotion CAFE $

(65 Pha Dinh Phung; meals 65,000-180,000d; 7am-10pm;) This branch is an offshoot of the successful Sapa cafe, with a handy location midway between the train and bus stations. It does good breakfasts and decent pizza.

Pineapple CAFE $

(☎020-383 5939; Pha Dinh Phung; meals 80,000-125,000d; 7am-10pm;) A stylish Sapa-esque cafe. Try the full English breakfast or a salad, pizza or baguette. To find it from the train station, cross the main road and head west down the street directly in front of you for around 100m.

Information

Be wary of being short-changed by black-market currency traders, especially on the Chinese side. If you do need to change money, just change a small amount.

There are two ATMs by the train station.

BIDV Bank (Đ Thuy Hoa; 8am-3pm Mon-Fri, 8-11.30am Sat) on the west bank of the river changes cash.

Getting There & Away

Lao Cai is about 340km from Hanoi. Most travellers prefer to take the train rather than the road.

BUS

The new speedway toll road connecting Lao Cai and Hanoi can shave hours off bus journey times, but at the moment is only used by sleeper buses. The bus station, at the end of Đ Pha Dinh Phung, is two blocks west of the train station.

MINIBUS

Minibuses for Sapa (30,000d, 30 minutes) leave at least hourly between 5am and 6pm from the car park in front of Lao Cai train station. Minibuses to Bac Ha (70,000d, 2½ hours) leave from the minibus terminal next to the Song Hong (Red River) bridge; there are seven daily services at 6.30am, 8.15am, 9am, 11.30am, noon, 2pm and 3pm.

TAXI

A taxi to Sapa costs about US$25; it's around US$50 to Bac Ha.

TRAIN

Virtually everyone travelling to and from Hanoi uses the train.

There are four daily services to Hanoi from Lao Cai train station. Cheapest is the LC4 train (hard/soft seat 130,000/215,000d, 10 hours), which leaves at 9.50am. The other three services are all sleepers (425,000d, eight hours); the SP8 leaves at 1.15pm; the SP2 at 8.20pm; and SP4 at 9.10pm.

Hotels and travel agencies in both Hanoi and Sapa can book tickets, or you can book at the station yourself.

Several companies operate special private rail carriages that hitch a ride on the main trains, including **ET Pumpkin** (☎0438-295 571; www.ct-pumpkin.com; sleeper berth US$42), **Livitrans** (☎0437-350 069; www.livitrantrain.com; sleeper berth US$34) and the exclusive **Victoria Express** (www.victoriahotels-asia.com), which is only available to guests at Sapa's Victoria Sapa Resort.

Bac Ha

☎020 / POP 7400

Sleepy Bac Ha wakes up for the riot of colour and commerce that is its Sunday market, when the lanes fill to choking point and villagers flock in from the hills and valleys. Once the barter, buy and sell is done and the day-tripper tourist buses from Sapa have left, the town rolls over and goes back to bed for the rest of the week.

Despite being surrounded by countryside just as lush and interesting as Sapa, Bac Ha has somehow flown under the radar as a trekking base so far. In town, woodsmoke fills the morning air, the main street is completely bereft of hawkers, and chickens and pigs snuffle for scraps in the back lanes where a small clutch of traditional adobe houses valiantly clings on in the age of concrete.

Just out of town, trails meander through swooping verdant valleys with their hillslope rice terraces, connecting the tiny villages of 11 hill-tribe groups. The colourful Flower Hmong are the most visible, but other ethnic minorities in the area include Dzao, Giay (Nhang), Han (Hoa), Xa Fang, Lachi, Nung, Phula, Tay, Thai and Thulao.

If you're not worried about a lack of in-town amenities, and are turned off by Sapa's hustle, Bac Ha may just tick your boxes as an alternative base from where to launch yourself out on highland hikes.

Sights & Activities

★Bac Ha Market — MARKET

(off Đ Tran Bac; ⏲sunrise-2pm Sun) This Sunday market is Bac Ha's big draw. There's an increasing range of handicrafts for sale, but it's still pretty much a local affair. Bac Ha market is a magnet for the local hill-tribe people, above all the exotically attired Flower Hmong. If you can, stay overnight in Bac Ha on Saturday, and get here early before hundreds of day trippers from Sapa start arriving.

Flower Hmong women wear several layers of dazzling clothing. These include an elaborate collar-cum-shawl that's pinned at the neck and an apron-style garment; both are made of tightly woven strips of multicoloured fabric, often with a frilly edge. Highly ornate cuffs and ankle fabrics are also part of their costume, as is a checked headscarf (often electric pink or lime green).

Vua Meo — NOTABLE BUILDING

('Cat King' House; ⏲7.30-11.30am & 1.30-5pm) FREE The outlandish Vua Meo, built in 1921 by the French to keep the Flower Hmong chief Hoang A Tuong happily ensconced in style, is a bizarre palace constructed in a

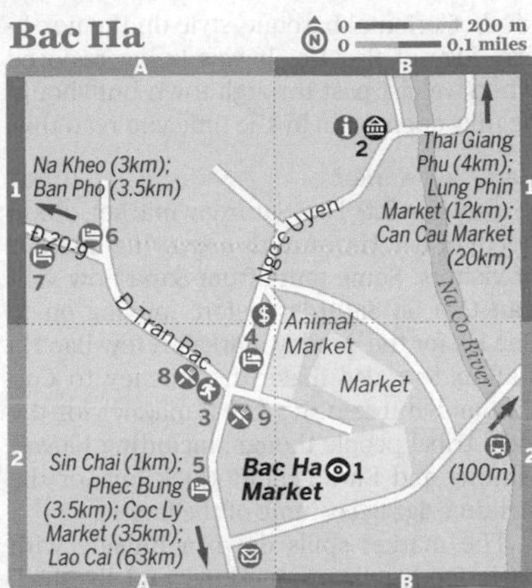

Bac Ha

Top Sights
1 Bac Ha Market B2

Sights
2 Vua Meo B1

Activities, Courses & Tours
3 Green Sapa Tour A2
Ngan Nga Bac Ha .... (see 5)

Sleeping
4 Congfu Hotel A2
5 Ngan Nga Bac Ha A2
6 Sao Mai Hotel A1
7 Toan Thang Hotel A1

Eating
8 Hoang Yen Restaurant A2
9 Restaurant 36 .... A2

kind of 'oriental baroque' style on the northern edge of Bac Ha. It was being restored when we last past through town but should be fully open again by the time you read this.

Can Cau Market MARKET

(⏲6am-1pm Sat) This Saturday market, 20km north of Bac Ha, attracts a growing number of visitors. Some tours from Sapa now visit Can Cau on Saturday before moving on to Bac Ha for the Sunday market. A few Bac Ha stallholders also make the journey to Can Cau on Saturdays. It's still a magnet for the local tribal people though, including Flower Hmong and Blue Hmong (look out for the striking zigzag costume of the latter).

The market spills down a hillside with basic food stalls on one level and livestock at the bottom of the valley, including plenty of dogs. Locals will implore you to drink the local *ruou* with them. Some trips here include the option of an afternoon trek (for those still standing after *ruou* shots) to the nearby village of Fu La.

Hoang Thu Pho Waterfall WATERFALL

FREE There's a waterfall near Huang Thu Pho village, about 12km west of Bac Ha, which has a pool big enough for swimming.

Hiking

There's great hiking to remarkable hill-tribe villages around Bac Ha. The Nung village of **Sin Chai** and Hmong village **Phec Bung** are only a short stroll from town.

Overnights in village homestays are possible on longer treks. Hiking here is best done with a local guide.

Thai Giang Pho to Na Lo HIKING

The looping track that winds from Bac Ha, through the hills and down to the rice terraces that surround the Flower Hmong village of Thai Giang Pho, then onward to the Tay village of Na Lo, is home to some of the finest rural vistas you'll see anywhere in northern Vietnam. It's about an 8km round trip.

Ban Pho to Na Kheo HIKING

The Flower Hmong village of Ban Pho and the Nung settlement of Na Kheo make a good day hike from Bac Ha. The locals of Ban Pho are renowned for their skill in making (extremely potent) corn liquor and the scenery of rolling hillscapes between the villages is superbly verdant.

Nam Det to Nam Khanh HIKING

The hike through rice fields, cinnamon forest and rolling hills to the Black Dzao village of Nam Det and onward to the Dzao village of Nam Khanh is a popular option for an overnight in a village homestay.

Tours

Market trips can be organised in Bac Ha, and also at travel agencies in Sapa.

Green Sapa Tour HIKING

(☎0912 005 952; www.bachatourist.com; Đ Tran Bac; ⏲8am-6pm) Spend any time in Bac Ha and the irrepressible Mr Nghe of Green Sapa Tour will no doubt find you. This one-man cheerleader for the considerable charms of the area offers trekking and day trips to the best of the area's minority markets, and longer two- to six-day adventures integrat-

OFF THE BEATEN TRACK

BAC HA AREA MARKETS

Bac Ha's Sunday market is firmly stamped on the day-trip agenda from Sapa – though it's hardly been trussed up for the tourists and is full of local flavour. But if you want to head further out to other markets, try these on for size:

Coc Ly Market (⏲8.30am-1.30pm Tue) The impressive Coc Ly market attracts Dzao, Flower Hmong, Tay and Nung people from the surrounding hills. It's about 35km southwest of Bac Ha along reasonably good roads. Tour operators in Bac Ha can arrange day trips here.

Lung Phin Market (⏲6am-1pm Sun) Lung Phin market is between Can Cau market and Bac Ha, about 12km from town. It's less busy than other markets, with a really local feel, and is a good place to move on to once the tour buses arrive in Bac Ha from Sapa.

Sin Cheng Market (⏲5am-2pm Wed) This market, in the remote border area of Si Ma Cai, 40km from Bac Ha, is a vibrant and chaotic weekly hub for the local Nung and Thulao ethnic minorities who live in the surrounding villages.

ing village homestays, and more physically challenging mountain hiking.

Ngan Nga Bac Ha HIKING
(☎020-388 0286; www.bachatrip.com; 115-117 P Ngoc Uyen; ⏲8am-9pm) Inside the Ngan Nga Bac Ha hotel, super-organised and highly enthusiastic Mr Dong offers a great range of day hikes and longer treks with village homestay options in the Bac Ha area, as well as one-day buffalo-riding tours. He can also put together motorbike tours, rents motorbikes (US$6 per day) and can organise trips to outlying markets.

Sleeping

Room rates tend to increase by about 20% on weekends due to the Sunday market.

★**Ngan Nga Bac Ha** HOTEL $
(☎020-388 0286; www.nganngabachahotel.com; 117 P Ngoc Uyen; r incl breakfast US$15-20; ❄📶) This friendly place is above a popular restaurant that does a roaring trade in tasty *lau*. Rooms here are the best budget deal in town: decent-sized and decked out with a few homey touches that give them some character. Bag a front room for a balcony.

Toan Thang Hotel HOTEL $
(☎0962 255 410; Đ 20-9; r 150,000-300,000d; ❄📶) This rickety wooden house has barebones basic rooms with fan, while at the front more expensive, rather plain rooms run past a pot-plant-festooned terrace. There's no English spoken but the lovely lady who owns the place tries hard to help.

Congfu Hotel HOTEL $$
(☎020-388 0254; www.congfuhotel.com; 152 P Ngoc Uyen; s US$20, d US$25-30, tr US$30; ❄@📶) This place has freshly painted rooms with white linen, though the bathrooms could do with a spruce up. Book rooms 105, 108, 205 or 208 for their floor-to-ceiling windows overlooking Bac Ha Market. There's a restaurant (meals from 60,000d) downstairs and hiking can be arranged.

Sao Mai Hotel HOTEL $$
(☎020-388 0288; www.saomaibachahotel.com; Đ 20-9; s US$35, d US$40-60; ❄@📶) Although most rooms veer towards the small side, they're well looked after and jazzed up by dark wood furniture. The VIP rooms (US$60) are about as fancy pants as it gets around these parts. Reception staff are usually keen to negotiate.

LOCAL KNOWLEDGE

BAC HA'S TOP TIPPLES

One of Bac Ha's main industries is the manufacture of alcoholic home brews (rice wine, cassava wine and corn liquor). The *ruou* corn hooch produced by the Flower Hmong of Ban Pho village is so potent it can ignite. One of the best places to buy this drink is Bac Ha's Sunday market, where you'll find an entire area devoted to it.

Eating & Drinking

Of Bac Ha's hotel restaurants, the Congfu Hotel has great views of the animal market area through huge plate glass windows, while the Ngan Nga Bac Ha is cosy and has a tasty menu. Both get very busy for Sunday lunch on market day.

Note that tourists are often overcharged at the cafes near the market, so establish the cost of food and drink up front.

Restaurant 36 VIETNAMESE $
(P Ngoc Uyen; meals 30,000-100,000d; ⏲9am-9.30pm) This cute place dishes up lots of *pho* and barbecue options, as well as hotpots for two (from 300,000d). Most travellers come for the great-value set menu of five dishes for 100,000d.

Hoang Yen Restaurant VIETNAMESE $
(Đ Tran Bac; meals 60,000-120,000d; ⏲7am-10pm; 📶) Hoang Yen's menu includes decent breakfast options and a set menu for 200,000d. Cheap beer is also available.

Bia Hoi Stalls BIA HOI
(Đ Tran Bac; ⏲10am-11pm) The cluster of humble drinking dens along Đ Tran Bac is where to head for beer with the locals.

Information

Agribank (P Ngoc Uyen; ⏲8am-3pm Mon-Fri, 8-11am Sat, ATM 24hr)

Getting There & Away

Tours to Bac Ha from Sapa cost from around US$20 per person; on the way back you can bail out in Lao Cai and catch the night train to Hanoi.

BUS

Bac Ha's bus station is just out of the town centre, across the Na Co River. To Hanoi there's a 4.30am service (11 hours), and two sleeper buses at noon and 8.30pm (300,000d, seven hours). Buses run hourly between 6am and 4pm to Lao Cai (70,000d, 2½ hours). Coming into town from Lao Cai, buses usually drop you in the centre of town, near the hotels.

Heading east to Ha Giang, there are two options (we recommend checking the latest information with either Mr Dong at Ngan Nga Bac Ha hotel or Mr Nghe at Green Sapa Tour as Ha Giang schedules change regularly).

Option one is to catch a *xe om* from Bac Ha, 35km northeast to Xin Man (400,000d, 2½ hours). Then the 12.30pm bus (150,000d, four hours) from Xin Man to Ha Giang. Option two is the bus south from Bac Ha to Bac Ngam (70,000d, 30 minutes, 6.30am and noon), followed by another bus from Bac Ngam to Ha Giang (230,000d, five hours, 7am and 12.30pm). The bus from Bac Ngam always waits for the bus from Bac Ha to arrive before leaving.

MOTORCYCLE & TAXI

A *xe om*/taxi to Lao Cai costs US$25/70, or to Sapa US$30/80.

Ha Giang Province

☎0219 / POP 79,000

Ha Giang is the final frontier in northern Vietnam, an amazing landscape of limestone pinnacles and granite outcrops. The far north of the province has some of the most spectacular scenery in the country, and the trip between Yen Minh and Dong Van, and then across the Mai Pi Leng Pass to Meo Vac is quite mind-blowing. Ha Giang should be one of the most popular destinations in this region, but its proximity to the Chinese border still keeps visitor numbers at a low level.

Travel permits (US$10) are required to travel on the road north from Tam Son to Dong Van and Meo Vac, but these are simply paid directly to whichever hotel you choose to overnight in along the way.

The province is best managed with a car and driver or by motorbike. If you're going to splurge on private transport once during your trip, this is the time to do it.

Public transport is improving and it's relatively simple to journey by bus from Ha Giang city to Dong Van, but at the time of writing there was still no public transport from Dong Van onward to Meo Vac. However, there are buses, along the low road, between Meo Vac and Ha Giang city, so by hiring a *xe om* or taxi in Dong Van for the stretch to Meo Vac, it is entirely possible to do a loop back to Ha Giang city. Heading east from Meo Vac to Cao Bang continues to be a headache as there is no public transport from Meo Vac to Bao Lac.

Whichever way you tackle Ha Giang, you'll be among only a handful of travellers to the area and will experience some of Indochina's most jaw-dropping scenery.

WORTH A TRIP

PAN HOU ECOLODGE

Pan Hou Ecolodge (☎0219-383 3535; www.panhou-village.com; Pan Hou village; s/d incl breakfast US$40/50; 📶) is tucked away in a hidden river valley in the High Song Chau mountains. It has simple bungalows, powered by solar, and is set in a riot of tropical gardens and fronted by a thatched restaurant pavilion (meals US$12). Traditional spa treatments and baths, infused with medicinal healing herbs, are available, and day hikes and longer treks to ethnic-minority villages can be arranged.

From Tan Quang village, south of Ha Giang, Pan Hou is 36km west up a gorgeously scenic twisty-turny mountain road.

Ha Giang

Ha Giang is somewhere to recharge the batteries on the long road north. This town, bisected by the broad river Lo, is a provincial capital with clean streets and an understated ambience. The main drag is P Nguyen Trai, which runs north–south paralleling the west bank of the Lo for 3km or so. You'll find hotels, banks and restaurants on this road.

There is little to keep you in the town itself, but the spectacular limestone outcrops that are soaring skywards over the suburbs hint at the amazing scenery in the surrounding hinterland.

☞ Tours

Johnny Nam Tram MOTORBIKING TOUR
(☎0978 159 123, 0917 797 269; info@rockyplateau.com; Group 15, Nguyen Ward) Highly experienced in the back roads and byways of northern Vietnam, Johnny Nam Tram is an excellent contact for motorbike rental or organised bike tours around Ha Giang province. Tours by car and trekking trips can also be arranged.

Sleeping & Eating

You'll find several cheap restaurants scattered along P Nguyen Trai.

Cao Nguyen Hotel HOTEL $
(0219-386 6966; khachsancaonguyen@gmail.com; 297 P Nguyen Thai Hoc; r 400,000-500,000d;) Near the Lo River, this place has 40 spotless and spacious rooms with actual separate shower cubicles in the bathrooms – some even have rain shower heads. There are good *pho* stalls just a short walk away.

Huy Hoan Hotel HOTEL $
(0219-386 1288; P Nguyen Trai; s/d/tr 250,000/350,000/500,000d;) Run by a friendly family, the Huy Hoan offers large, clean, well-kept rooms with (very) firm beds. The communal balcony at the back of each floor looks out over a limestone cliff.

Truong Xuan Resort BUNGALOW $$
(0219-386 2268; www.hagiangresort.com; Km 5, P Nguyen Van Linh; bungalow US$25-30;) A gem of a place sitting alongside the bank of the Lo River, 5km out of town, with bungalows set in a lush garden. You'll want a riverfront bungalow to make the most of the view. Meals (US$5 to $10) are available in the restaurant, herbal baths and Red Dzao massages are offered, and it rents motorbikes (US$10 per day).

From the bus station, count on 40,000d for a *xe om*.

Bien Nho Thanh Thu Restaurant VIETNAMESE $$
(0219-328 2558; 17 P Duong Huu Nghi; meals from 120,000d; 11am-10pm) For something exotic, this place has crocodile, seafood, goose and traditional food from the ethnic minorities of Ha Giang.

Information

Most accommodation in Ha Giang can organise your travel permit (US$10) for the road north from Tam Son – or you can pay the fee at whichever hotel you stay overnight in along the route.

There are a couple of internet cafes on P Nguyen Trai.

Agribank (P Nguyen Trai; 8am-3pm Mon-Fri, 8-11.30am Sat, ATM 24hr)

Getting There & Away

Ha Giang's main **bus station** (Đ 19-5) is centrally located just off P Nguyen Trai, west of the Lo River. Buses to Hanoi (day/sleeper 120,000/220,000d, seven hours, every 30 minutes between 4am and 8.30pm) and Xin Man (to pick up onward transport to Bac Ha; 80,000d to 110,000d, 6am, 11.45am and 12.15pm) leave from here.

A second bus station, 2.5km from the town centre, operates provincial services to Dong Van (via Tam Son, Yen Minh and taking the northern fork along the high pass road); and to Meo Vac (veering off the high road after Yen Minh and taking the southern fork along the low road direct to Meo Vac). Buses to Dong Van (100,000d, 4½ hours) leave at 5am, 6.30am, 10am, 10.30am, 11.30am and noon. To Meo Vac (110,000d, six hours) there are services at 5am, 5.30am, 6am, 10.30am, 11.30am, noon and 1pm.

Quan Ba Pass

Leaving Ha Giang, the road climbs over the Quan Ba Pass (Heaven's Gate) around 40km from the city. Poetic licence is a national pastime in Vietnam, but this time the romantics have it right. The road winds over a saddle and opens up on to an awesome vista of knobbly topped limestone mountains.

At the top of Quan Ba Pass is an **information centre** and lookout with amazing views down into Tam Son. An English-language information board details the 2011 initiative to declare the Dong Van Karst Plateau part of the Unesco Global Network of National Geoparks. It's the first Unesco-recognised geopark in Vietnam and the second one in Southeast Asia, after Langkawi Geological Park in Malaysia.

Tam Son

The small town of Tam Son lies in a valley at the end of the Quan Ba Pass. On Sundays there's a good market with ethnic minorities, including White Hmong, Red Dzao, Tay and Giay.

There's also good accommodation at the guesthouse **Nha Nghi Nui Doi** (0219-651 0789; Tam Son; d/tr 250,000/300,000d;) with seven light-filled, simple rooms. All the buses trundling via the high road to Dong Van and the low road to Meo Vac pass through here (100,000d).

From Tam Son to Dong Van

From Tam Son, Ha Giang province's main mountain pass road connects to Dong Van, first trundling onto the sleepy town of **Yen Minh**. The **Thao Nguyen Hotel** (0219-385 2297; khachsanthaonguyen2011@gmail.com; Yen Minh; r 300,000-400,000d), on the main street through town, opposite the Agribank ATM, has well-kept, colourful rooms, but it's worth pushing on to overnight in Dong Van. There's a great no-name restaurant in Yen Minh that's a popular spot for lunch; coming from Ha Giang, turn left on the corner before the Thao Nguyen Hotel to find it.

Around 5km east of Yen Minh a road meanders southeast to Meo Vac, but the recommended route is the northern fork to Dong Van with the mountain road rubbing shoulders with the Chinese border and vast panoramic vistas of green valleys rolling on below.

If you're travelling by public transport, you can flag down buses to Dong Van (via the northern fork) and Meo Vac (low road) as they pass through.

The northern fork heads past the astounding **Vuong Palace** (admission 20,000d; ⌚8am-5pm), a grandiose two-storey mansion built for a local Hmong king by the French. Set in a hidden valley near a quiet village, the building was renovated in 2006 and is a fascinating sight in such a remote region of the country. The Vuong Palace is at Sa Phin, around 15km west of Dong Van, and the scenery of countless conical peaks through to Dong Van is quite incredible.

Dong Van

Dong Van is the Ha Giang region's most popular overnight stop. The main road through town isn't particularly inspiring, but in the old quarter a clutch of traditional Hmong houses still clings on and timing your visit to be here for the chaotic Sunday market is highly recommended. The town is also a good base for day treks around nearby minority villages and nearby sights such as Lung Cu.

Sights

★Dong Van Market MARKET

(Đ Vao Cho; ⌚6am-2pm Sun) Once a week, local villagers from the surrounding hills, including the Hmong, Tay, Nung and Hoa ethnic minorities, flood into Dong Van for the Sunday market. It's an entirely local affair full of noise, colour, and the hustle and bustle of commerce.

Old Quarter ARCHITECTURE

(off P Co) At the northern end of P Co, just past the old market plaza, a narrow lane, backed by a limestone cliff, meanders into the compact old quarter of Dong Van. The traditional terracotta-coloured adobe houses here, with timber details and slouchy tiled roofs, date from the French colonial period.

Lung Cu MONUMENT

(admission 10,000d; ⌚8am-5pm) Around 25km north of Dong Van and right on the Chinese border, Lung Cu is a massive flag tower erected in 2010 to mark the northernmost point of Vietnam. The summit is reached by almost 300 steps from a midlevel car park, and the views across rural villages are stunning. You'll need to show your passport and Ha Giang permit twice – at the local tourist police and army checkpoint near the base of the tower – before ascending to the top.

Sleeping & Eating

The market halls in Dong Van's old market plaza, in the centre of town, have been turned into open-air cafes, which are great for a coffee or cold drink.

Lam Tung Hotel HOTEL $

(Đ Vao Cho; d/tw/tr 280,000/350,000/380,000d; ❄📶) Just off Dong Van's main road, and overlooking the plaza that hosts the Sunday market, the Lam Tung has surprisingly smart modern rooms and friendly staff. Some of the best food in town is dished up at the restaurant downstairs (meals from 50,000d per person), though unfortunately there's no English menu. It rents motorbikes for 200,000d per day.

Hoang Ngoc Hotel HOTEL $

(☎0219-385 6020; www.hoangngochotel2.blogspot.com; Đ 3-2; d/tr 300,000/370,000d; ❄📶) A solid choice on Dong Van's main road, the Hoang Ngoc features spacious, sparkling-clean rooms, some with balconies. There's a handy map in reception showing trekking trails around the area. Staff can arrange trips to Vuong Palace, Lung Cu and Meo Vac, and can usually rustle up motorbikes to rent.

Quang Dung Restaurant VIETNAMESE

(19 P Co; meals 50,000-120,000d; ⌚7am-10pm; 📖) Opposite the old market plaza, in the centre of town, Quang Dung is a real find with friendly on-the-ball service. There's an English menu featuring good breakfasts and hearty Vietnamese staples, and the titchy balcony at the front is a great place to chill out with a coffee or beer after a long drive.

Information

Dong Van's only ATM is on the main road (Đ 1-3) just past, and opposite, the old market plaza.

Getting There & Away

Buses to Ha Giang (100,000d, 4½ hours) leave at 5am, 7am, 10am and noon. Dong Van's tiny bus station, on the main road at the western end of town, very rarely has anyone in attendance outside of bus departure times, but Dong Van's hotels can all book bus tickets for you and get the bus to pick you up from the hotel.

There is no public transport linking Dong Van to Meo Vac. A *xe om* to Meo Vac should cost around 100,000d and a taxi around 500,000d. Most hotels in Dong Van can arrange this for you and can also help organise private transport to Vuong Palace and Lung Cu.

Meo Vac

Meo Vac is a district capital hemmed in by mountains and, like many towns in the northwest, it is steadily being settled by Vietnamese from elsewhere. The journey here along the spectacular **Mai Pi Leng Pass**, which winds for 22km from Dong Van, is the main attraction. The road has been cut into the side of a cliff with a view of rippling hills tumbling down to the distant waters of the Nho Que River far below. Right at the top of the pass is a lookout point where you can stop to take in the scenery.

Don't be surprised if you're offered a slug of a local speciality, 'bee wine', while you're in town. We're still trying to work out if it's made from bees and honey, or just '100% bees'. Either way, it's a bracing drink on a chilly Meo Vac night.

Meo Vac has a good **Sunday market**. Its proximity and timing with Dong Van's Sunday market means that it's easy enough to combine the two by *xe om*.

Sleeping

Hoa Cuong Hotel HOTEL $

(☎0219-387 2888; d/tr 400,000/500,000d; ❄📶) Centrally located, opposite Meo Vac's Sunday market, this hotel has spacious, neat rooms with beige decor and big TVs. The karaoke places nearby are more active on Saturday and Sunday nights.

Auberge de Meo Vac GUESTHOUSE $$

(☎0219-387 1686; aubergemeovac@gmail.com; dm/d US$15/60) Located in a semirural neighbourhood, around 500m from Meo Vac' Sunday market, this is a unique stay in a lovingly restored ethnic minority house dating from the 19th century. Look forward to clay walls, lots of natural timber and a spacious inner courtyard. Bathroom facilities are shared, and breakfast (US$5) and dinner (US$12) are available.

Getting There & Away

Heading west, Meo Vac has around five services daily between 5am and noon via the low road to Ha Giang. The bus schedule tends to change frequently, so check with the Hoa Cuong Hotel for up-to-date departure times.

There is no public transport southeast to the transport hub of Cao Bang. Instead catch a *xe om* (800,000d) or taxi (1,500,000d) to Bao Lac, where there is accommodation and a daily bus to Cao Bang.

South to Bao Lac & Cao Bang

Foreigners are now permitted to travel from Meo Vac to Bao Lac in Cao Bang province. You must have your Ha Giang permit to do this spectacular trip. The road is now paved, though it's still best on trail bikes or by 4WD.

Heading south from Meo Vac you'll pass through the town of Khau Vai after about 20km, which is famous for its annual **love market**, where the tribal minorities swap wives and husbands. Though it's undoubtedly a fascinating tradition, many busloads of Vietnamese tourists now gatecrash the dating scene, and this unique event has become something of a circus. It takes place on the 27th day of the third lunar month in the Vietnamese calendar, usually from late April to mid-May.

After Khau Vai, a new bridge crosses the Nho Que River, and the road continues south to Bao Lac. In Bao Lac, the **Song Gam** (☎0263-870 269; Bao Lac; s/d from 200,000/250,000d; ❄📶) guesthouse has a riverside location and is popular with motorbike tours. A daily bus service (110,000d) leaves at 6am for Cao Bang, from where there is transport to Hanoi and Ba Be National Park.

Central Vietnam

Includes ➡

Best Places to Eat

- Nu Eatery (p216)
- Morning Glory Restaurant (p216)
- Cargo Club (p216)
- Waterfront (p197)
- Fatfish (p197)

Best for Spectacular Scenery

- Tam Coc (p157)
- Phong Nha-Ke Bang National Park (p162)
- Bach Ma National Park (p190)
- Hai Van Pass (p193)
- Cham Islands (p223)

Why Go?

The geographic heart of the nation, central Vietnam is packed with historic sights and cultural interest, and blessed with ravishing beaches and outstanding national parks. Marvel at Hue and its imperial citadel, royal tombs and excellent street food. Savour the unique heritage grace of riverside jewel Hoi An, and tour the military sites of the Demilitarised Zone (DMZ). Check out Danang, fast emerging as one of the nation's most dynamic cities. Also emerging as a must-visit destination is the extraordinary Phong Nha region, home to three gargantuan cave systems (including the world's largest cave), and a fascinating war history concealed amid stunning scenery. Enjoy well-earned downtime on the golden sands of An Bang beach or learn to cook central Vietnamese cuisine, the nation's most complex. With improving highways, and upgraded international airports at Hue and Danang, access to this compelling and diverse part of Vietnam has never been easier.

When to Go

Hue

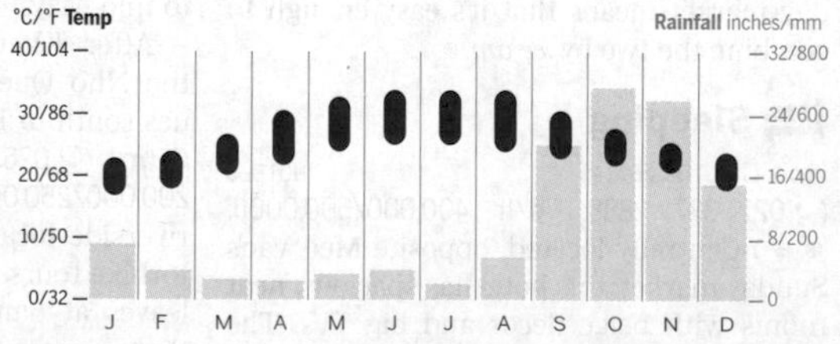

Late Apr Danang's riverfront explodes with colour for the annual fireworks competition.

May Temperatures rise and central Vietnam's beaches come into their own.

Sep Sticky summer heat relents, peak crowds are a memory and sea temperatures are balmy.

History

This region's seen them all: kings and king-makers, warriors and occupiers and a history of warfare and conflict. The ancient kingdom of Champa began here in the 2nd century and flourished for more than a thousand years. Myriad Cham towers and temples dot the landscape; the most renowned are at My Son. The Vietnamese subdued Champa in the 15th century, while in subsequent centuries European, Japanese and Chinese traders established footholds in Hoi An.

In 1802, Vietnam's last royal dynasty, the Nguyens, set up court at Hue, which became the centre of political intrigue, intellectual excellence and spiritual guidance. Later emperors were subdued by expanding French ambitions in Vietnam, and by the time of independence the locus of national power had shifted back to Hanoi.

In 1954, Vietnam was fatefully partitioned into North and South, creating a Demilitarised Zone (DMZ) that saw some of the heaviest fighting of the American War. Thousands of lives were lost in bloody battles as entire cities, including Vinh and most of Hue's imperial enclosure, were flattened. Vast tracts of countryside around Dong Hoi and Dong Ha remain littered with lethal ordnance. Historic Hoi An was one of the few places spared.

Today, tourism drives Hue and Hoi An, and Danang is expanding with energy and investment, but the region's north remains relatively undeveloped.

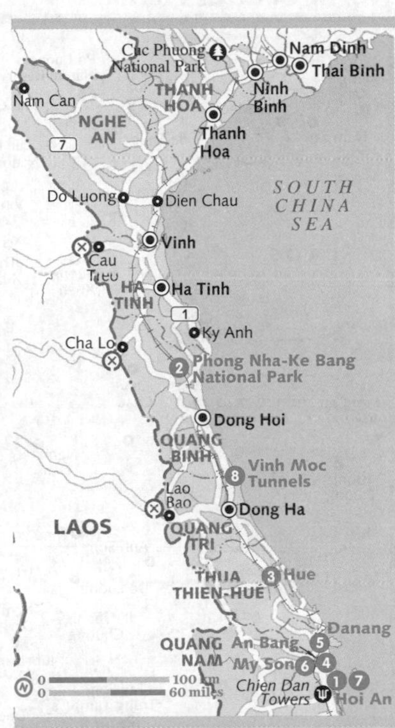

Central Vietnam Highlights

1. Travelling back in time in the historic old port of **Hoi An** (p203).
2. Going underground at the astounding **Phong Nha-Ke Bang National Park** (p162), the world's foremost caving destination.
3. Treading in the footsteps of emperors from the Forbidden Purple City to the imperial tombs of **Hue** (p174).
4. Taking it easy amid the relaxed beach scene at **An Bang** (p220).
5. Experiencing the urban energy and bright lights of exciting **Danang** (p193).
6. Wondering while you wander amid the enigmatic Cham ruins at **My Son** (p224).
7. Testing your two-wheel prowess on a **motorbike tour** (p212) around the idyllic back roads of central Vietnam.
8. Exploring the fascinating **Vinh Moc Tunnels** (p170) in the Demilitarised Zone.

NORTH-CENTRAL VIETNAM

Getting There & Away

The main north–south railway cuts directly through the region, as does Hwy 1 and the Ho Chi Minh Hwy. There are airports at Vinh and Dong Hoi, with flights to Ho Chi Minh City (HCMC) and Hanoi.

Ninh Binh Province

South of Hanoi, Ninh Binh province is blessed with natural beauty, cultural sights and the Cuc Phuong National Park. However, Ninh Binh is very popular with domestic travellers, and many attractions are heavily commercialised. Expect hawkers and a degree of hassle at the main sights.

North-Central Vietnam

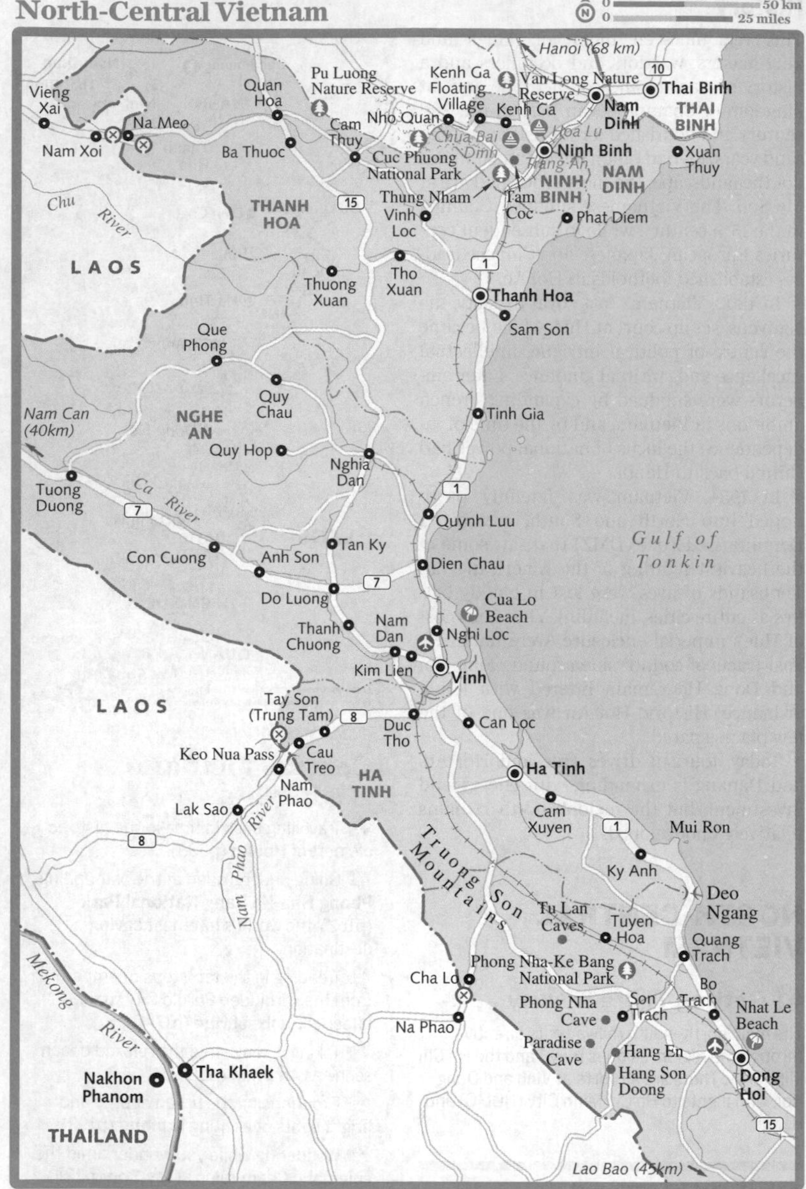

Ninh Binh

☎030 / POP 158,000

Ninh Binh is a good base for exploring quintessentially Vietnamese limestone scenery. A few Western tourists head here, but many Vietnamese flock to nearby sights, including the nation's biggest pagoda and the Unesco World Heritage–listed Trang An grottoes.

The region has significant natural allure, but insensitive development combines giant cement factories next to nature spots.

Tours

Hotels can organise tours around Ninh Binh province.

Truong Nguyen TOUR

(☎091 566 6211, 0165 348 8778; truong_tour@yahoo.com) Freelance guide Truong offers escorted motorbike trips around Ninh Binh using country back roads, and also trekking in Pu Luong Nature Reserve, a forested area across two mountain ridges, where you can stay in Thai and Hmong homestays.

Sleeping

Ninh Binh city has good-value hotels and guesthouses. There's also excellent accommodation around greater Ninh Binh, often conveniently located for cycling to the area's attractions.

Ninh Binh City

Xuan Hoa Hotel 1 HOTEL $

(☎030-388 0970; www.xuanhoahotel.com; 31d P Minh Khai; r US$15-30;) A friendly operation with rooms across two buildings. The original Xuan Hoa Hotel 1 has a room where guests can leave their luggage or have a free shower after checkout. Nearby **Xuan Hoa Hotel 2** (☎030-388 0970; 3d P Minh Khai; r US$6-12;) has balconies overlooking a quiet neighbourhood. Before dining at the Xuan Hoa Hotel 1, have a beer on the edge of the compact lake.

Thanh Thuy's Guest House & New Hotel GUESTHOUSE $

(☎030-387 1811; www.hotelthanhthuy.com; 53 Đ Le Hong Phong; dm US$6, r US$12-30;) This guesthouse's courtyard and restaurant are a great place to meet other travellers. Offers good-value, clean rooms, some with balcony, and also books tours. Cheaper rooms are fan-only.

Thuy Anh Hotel HOTEL $$

(☎030-387 1602; www.thuyanhhotel.com; 55a Đ Truong Han Sieu; r 400,000-700,000d;) Choose between inexpensive, good-value rooms in the old wing or spotless and comfortable rooms in the new wing. You'll also find a top-floor bar and restaurant serving Western-style food (including hearty complimentary breakfasts).

Around Ninh Binh

★**Nguyen Shack** BUNGALOW $$

(☎030-361 8678; www.nguyenshack.com; near Mua Cave, Hoa Lu district; bungalows US$25-55;) With a riverside setting around 5km from Tam Coc, Nguyen Shack's easygoing lazy days thatched bungalows are the perfect antidote to the bustle of Hanoi. Lie in a hammock, drop a fishing rod off your rustic terrace, or grab a bicycle and go exploring. There's an on-site restaurant and bar too.

Mua Cave Ecolodge LODGE $$

(☎030-3618754; www.muacaveecolodge.com; Khe Ha village, Hoa Lu district; s/d 500,000/750,000d;) Surrounded by rice paddies and karst limestone, this ecolodge has spacious rooms and bungalows with a tinge of heritage style. A quirky highlight is the restaurant and bar located within a cave. Half- and full-day tours are available around the area. It's relatively isolated, so you'll need to count on eating at the lodge as well.

Limestone View Homestay GUESTHOUSE $$

(☎091 845 3761; limestoneviewhomestay@gmail.com; Đ Xuan Thanh, Xuan Ang village, Hoa Lu district; s/d US$40/57;) With a village location convenient for Tam Coc (5km), Hoa Lu (5km) or Trang An (2km), Limestone View has four private rooms, and the company of a friendly Dzung family and their school-age kids. When we dropped by, there were plans to transform the rooftop into a restaurant and cafe. Bicycles are available to go exploring.

★**Tam Coc Garden** BOUTIQUE HOTEL $$$

(☎096 603 2555; www.tamcocgarden.com; Hai Nham village, Hoa Lu district; d US$116-152;) The most Zen place to stay around Ninh Binh is this lovely boutique hotel. In a private location and surrounded by a sea of rice paddies, Tam Coc Garden has eight stone and timber bungalows set in a luxuriant garden. Following a day of cycling or exploring nearby attractions, there's the compact pool to look forward to.

Emeralda Resort Ninh Binh HOTEL $$$

(☎030-365 8333; www.emeraldaresort.com; Van Long Nature Reserve; r US$119-140, ste US$184;) Built in a neotraditional style this large resort hotel has comfortable villas with elegant decor, a great pool area and a (pricey) spa. However, staff speak limited English and the location, though in lovely grounds, is 10km north of town and near cement factories.

Eating & Drinking

Plan to eat early as not much is open after 9pm. There's a good restaurant – open to

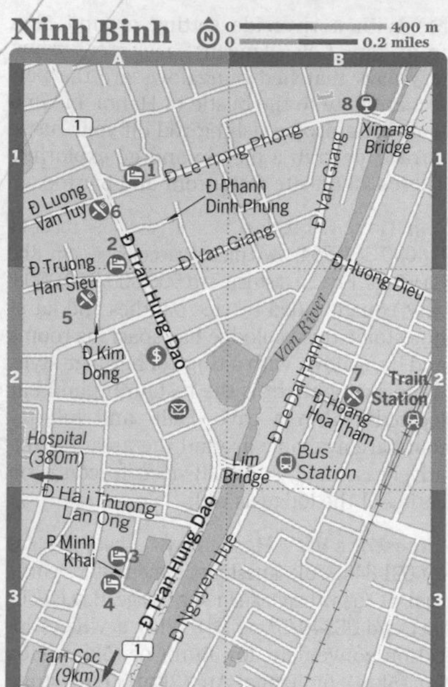

Ninh Binh

Sleeping

1 Thanh Thuy's Guest House & New Hotel A1
2 Thuy Anh Hotel A1
3 Xuan Hoa Hotel 1 .... A3
4 Xuan Hoa Hotel 2 .... A3

Eating

5 Cho Bop market A2
6 Chookie's A1
7 Trung Tuyet B2

Drinking & Nightlife

8 Bia Hoi B1

outside guests – and cold beer at the Xuan Hoa 1 hotel

The local speciality is *de* (goat meat), served with fresh herbs and rice paper. Around 3km out of town, the road to Trang An is lined with **goat meat restaurants**.

Trung Tuyet VIETNAMESE $

(14 Đ Hoang Hoa Tham; meals 40,000-75,000d; 7am–9.45pm) Expect filling portions and a warm welcome from the host family at this busy little place that's popular with travellers. They'll even drop you off at the nearby train station if you're kicking on after your meal.

Chookie's CAFE $

(www.facebook.com/chookiesninhbinh; 17 Đ Luong Van Tuy; meals 30,000-70,000d; 11.30am-10pm;) Good-value Vietnamese and Western food, cheap beer, and plenty of local information about what to do and see around Ninh Binh. Also offers motorbike and car tours around the area.

Snail Restaurants VIETNAMESE $

(meals 30,000-60,000d) The lanes north of Đ Luong Van Tuy, close to the stadium, have snail restaurants serving *oc luoc xa* (snails cooked with lemongrass and chilli). You'll find a few casual bars here too.

Cho Bop Market MARKET $

(Truong Han Sieu; 6am-4pm) For fresh fruit and street food.

Bia Hoi BAR

For drinking *bia hoi* (draught beer), try the riverside places that are located near the local brewery.

Information

Hospital (Benh Vien Da Khoa Tinh; 030-387 1030; Đ Hai Thuong Lan Ong; 24hr) Main city hospital.

Main Post Office (Đ Tran Hung Dao; 7am-6pm Mon-Fri, 8am-1pm Sat)

Vietin Bank & ATM (Đ Tran Hung Dao; 7am-2.30pm Mon-Fri, 7.30am-noon Sat) One of two branches on this street.

Getting There & Away

BUS

Ninh Binh's **bus station** (Đ Le Dai Hanh) is located near Lim Bridge. Public buses leave every 15 minutes until 7pm for the Giap Bat and Luong Yen bus stations in Hanoi (from 65,000d, 2½ hours), and there are regular buses to Haiphong (85,000d, three hours, every 1½ hours) and twice-daily connections to Halong City (120,000d, 3½ hours).

Ninh Binh is also a stop for open-tour buses between Hanoi (US$6, two hours) and Hue (US$14, 10 hours). Hotel pick-up and drop-offs are available.

TRAIN

The **train station** (Ga Ninh Binh; 1 Đ Hoang Hoa Tham) is a scheduled stop on the main north–south line, with destinations including Hanoi (from 85,000d, two to 2½ hours, four daily), Vinh (from 108,000d, six hours, four daily) and Hue (from 301,000d, 12½ to 13½ hours, four daily).

Getting Around

Most hotels rent out bicycles (around US$2 per day) and motorbikes (US$5 to US$8 per day). Motorbike drivers charge around US$10 a day.

Tam Coc

With limestone outcrops amid serene rice paddies, Tam Coc is best appreciated on a languorous row-boat ride with the soundtrack of the river lapping against the oars.

Unfortunately, you'll need to be prepared for a glut of fairly persistent hawkers. The guys photographing you will want to sell you the pix when you return, and overpriced drinks and snacks are sold at the turnaround point for boat trips.

Bring your own refreshments, and combine a polite but firm 'no' and complete lack of interest to combat the hawkers.

Sights & Activities

Tam Coc Boat Trips BOATING

(adult/child 120,000/60,000d, boat 150,000d, maximum 2 per boat; 7am-3.30pm) Tam Coc (meaning 'three caves') boasts surreal beauty along the Ngo Dong River, but it is also immensely popular with domestic tourists. Consider visiting early morning or late afternoon when things are quieter. Rowers use their feet to propel the oars, as the route (around two hours) negotiates Tam Coc's three caves. Unfortunately the area is now overshadowed by giant cement factories. You can't see them from the river, but air quality and pollution are concerns.

Bich Dong Pagoda BUDDHIST TEMPLE

(Jade Grotto) FREE This charming cluster of cave temples is a couple of kilometres north of Tam Coc. The Lower Pagoda is located at the base, from which 100 steps lead to the Middle Pagoda, then a shorter but steep ascent to the Upper Pagoda. Inside each cave temple, looming statues peer from the haze of burning incense. Outside offers incredible countryside views.

Van Lan VILLAGE

Near the entrance to Tam Coc, Van Lan is famous for its embroidery. Local artisans make napkins, tablecloths, pillowcases and T-shirts. Bargain hard.

WORTH A TRIP

PHAT DIEM

Home to a huge cathedral, combining Sino-Vietnamese and European architecture, Phat Diem makes an intriguing half-day excursion.

During colonial times, Phat Diem's bishop ruled the area with his private army, until French troops took over in 1951. The **cathedral** (1891) featured in Graham Greene's novel *The Quiet American* – from the bell tower the author watched battles between the North Vietnamese Army (NVA) and the French.

The entrance can be busy with hawkers, but inside is peaceful. The cathedral's largely wooden interior boasts a vaulted ceiling supported by massive columns. Above the granite altar Vietnamese-looking cherubs swarm, while Chinese-style clouds drift across the blue ceiling. Beneath are icons of the martyrs slaughtered by Emperor Tu Duc during the 1850's anti-Catholic purges.

Opposite the cathedral's main doors is the free-standing **bell tower**, and two enormous stone slabs are where mandarins used to observe the Catholic mass. Between the tower and the cathedral is the tomb of the Vietnamese founder, Father Six, and a Lourdes-style grotto.

Many Vietnamese tourists visit, few of them Catholic, but many curious about Christianity. Mass is celebrated daily at 5am and 5pm, when the massive bell is rung.

Near Phat Diem is a late-19th-century covered bridge. **Dong Huong Pagoda** is the area's largest Buddhist pagoda, and many of its congregation are minority Muong people. Turn right at the canal at the north of town, and continue alongside the water for 3km.

A Gothic counterpoint to Phat Diem is the cathedral at **Ton Dao**, along Route 10 about 5km from Phat Diem. At the rear, a statue of the Virgin Mary keeps unexpected company with porcelain images of Quan Am.

Phat Diem, also known as Kim Son, is 26km southeast of Ninh Binh. Buses run from Ninh Binh (25,000d, one hour), and *xe om* drivers charge about 200,000d for a return trip.

Getting There & Away

Tam Coc is 9km southwest of Ninh Binh. Ninh Binh hotels run tours, or make your own way by bicycle or motorbike. Hotels can advise on beautiful back roads. Hanoi tour operators offer day trips from around US$25.

Mua Cave

Mua Cave CAVE

(Cave of Dance; admission 30,000d; ⏲7am-4pm) Down a sleepy road between rice paddies, this cave is not terribly impressive, but there are panoramic views from the peak above. A stone staircase beside the cave entrance zigzags through the karst (beware the goat droppings) and it's almost 500 steps to a simple altar to Quan Am (the Goddess of Mercy). Look west for the Ngo Dong River winding through Tam Coc.

The climb is paved but steep in sections, so bring water and allow an hour. Mua Cave is 5km from Ninh Binh and is a popular stop on Tam Coc tours.

Hoa Lu

Hoa Lu was the capital of Vietnam during the Dinh (AD 968–80) and early Le (AD 980–1009) dynasties. The Dinh chose the site to distance themselves from China.

Most of the ancient citadel is in ruins, but there are two surviving **temples** (admission 10,000d; ⏲24hr). **Dinh Tien Hoang** is dedicated to the Dinh dynasty and has the stone pedestal of a royal throne. Inside are bronze bells and a statue of Emperor Dinh Tien Hoang with his three sons.

The second temple is dedicated to monarch Le Dai Hanh. It has drums, gongs, weapons and a statue of the king and his queen and son. A modest **museum** features an excavated 10th-century city wall.

For a great perspective of the ruins, hike 20 minutes to the **tomb of Emperor Dinh Tien Hoang**. Access is via the hill opposite the ticket office.

Hoa Lu is 12km northwest of Ninh Binh; turn left 6km north of town on Hwy 1. There is no public transport, but tours leave from Ninh Binh.

Chua Bai Dinh

Completed in 2014, the Buddhist complex of **Chua Bai Dinh** (⏲7am-5.45pm) FREE is hugely popular with Vietnamese tourists. Tours arrive at the main car park where an electric train (per person 30,000d) continues to the main entrance. If you arrive independently by bicycle, you'll still be directed to the car park to catch the train.

The entrance leads to cloistered walkways past 500 stone *arhats* (enlightened Buddhists) lining the route to the main triple-roofed **Phap Chu pagoda**. This contains a 10m, 100-tonne bronze Buddha, flanked by two more gilded Buddha figures.

Steps behind lead to a viewpoint, a **13-storey pagoda** and a **giant Buddha**. The compound's central area features more temples, including one showcasing a 36-tonne bell, the largest in Vietnam. Most structures use natural materials, and the complex's impressive bronzework, lacquerwork and stone-carving was crafted by local artisans.

Chua Bai Dinh is 11km northwest of Ninh Binh, and attracts many Vietnamese visitors. Think twice if you're after a spiritual experience.

Kenh Ga

Kenh Ga (Chicken Canal) is named after the wild chickens that used to live here. Today, a riverine way of life and stunning limestone formations are the main draw.

Locals spend many hours on the water, watching over fish-breeding pens or selling vegetables boat-to-boat. Even the children commute to school by river. This was largely a floating village, but more land-based houses have now been built.

From the pier, hire a motorboat (two people, 200,000d) for a 1½-hour ride around the village. Kenh Ga is best seen in the wet season from June to September. During other months, boats are far less frequent as water levels are lower and there are fewer visitors to the area.

Kenh Ga is 21km from Ninh Binh, off the road to Cuc Phuong National Park. Follow Hwy 1 north for 11km, then it's 10km west to the pier.

Van Long Nature Reserve

Set amid limestone pinnacles, this tranquil **reserve** (admission 15,000d, boat 90,000d; ⏲7am-5pm) comprises a reedy wetland ideal for **birdwatching**. Look for the rare black-faced spoonbill, cotton pygmy goose and white-browed crake. The reserve is also one of the last refuges of the endangered Delacour's langur.

Row-boat rides (90 minutes, maximum two people per boat) are a more relaxed alternative to occasional hawker hassles at Tam Coc. Ninh Binh hotels can arrange tours.

Van Long is 2km east of Tran Me, 23km from Ninh Binh along the road to Cuc Phuong.

Trang An Grottoes

Trang An (⏲7.30am-4pm) offers a similar experience to Tam Coc, though it is very commercial. The sheer number of boats, vast parking lots and weekend traffic jams can make it very busy with local tourists. However, access for hawkers is more tightly controlled, and visitors experience minimum hassle. The area was granted Unesco World Heritage status in 2014, which, despite the numbers visiting, should ensure the stunning landscapes and water quality are protected.

Rowboats bob along the Sao Khe River through limestone caves. It's a relaxing trip, but many caves have also been enlarged to accommodate boats, including the removal of the odd pesky stalactite.

Boat trips (150,000d per person, or 600,000d for your own boat) take two hours, and there are two possible routes, both visiting caves and temples. Bring a hat and sunscreen as the boats lack shade.

Trang An is 7km northwest of Ninh Binh. You'll pass it on the way to the Chua Bai Dinh.

Cuc Phuong National Park

☎030 / ELEVATION 150-656M

With 307 bird species, 133 mammals, 122 reptiles and more than 2000 different plants, this national park is one Vietnam's most important protected areas.

Cuc Phuong spans two limestone mountain ranges and three provinces. Its highest peak is Dinh May Bac (Silver Cloud Peak) at 656m. In 1962, Ho Chi Minh declared this Vietnam's first national park, saying: 'Forest is gold'.

Unfortunately, poaching and habitat destruction plague the park. Improved roads have led to illegal logging, and many native species – the Asiatic black bear, Siamese crocodile, wild dog and tiger – have now vanished from the area. Other wildlife is notoriously elusive, so manage your expectations accordingly.

The park is also home to the minority Muong people, whom the government relocated from the park's central valley to its western edge in the late 1980s.

The best time to visit is in the dry months from November to February. From April to June it becomes increasingly hot, wet and muddy, and from July to October the rains arrive, bringing lots of leeches. Visitors in

SAVING MONKEYS & TURTLES

Cuc Phuong's conservation centres offer a glimpse of the fascinating animals they're helping. Arrange a guide (no charge) from the visitor centre to escort you to these places around 2km from the entrance.

The **Endangered Primate Rescue Center** (☎030-384 8002; admission 30,000d; ⏲9-11am & 1.30-4pm) is supervised by the Frankfurt Zoological Society, and is home to around 150 monkeys: 12 kinds of langur, three species of gibbon and two loris. All the centre's animals were either bred here or rescued from illegal traders.

The centre has bred more than 100 offspring in all, from nine different species, including the world's first captive-born Cat Ba langur and grey-shanked douc langur. Because it's difficult to rehabilitate primates once they've lived in cages, only 30 or so gibbons and langurs have been released into semi-wild areas (one site is adjacent) since the centre opened in 1993.

The **Turtle Conservation Center** (☎030-384 8090; www.asianturtleprogram.org; ⏲9-11am & 2-4.45pm) houses more than 1000 terrestrial, semi-aquatic and aquatic turtles representing 20 of Vietnam's 25 native species. Many have been confiscated from smugglers who have been driven by demand from the domestic and Chinese markets – eating turtle is thought to aid longevity.

Displays include incubation and hatchling viewing areas. The centre successfully breeds and releases turtles from 11 different species, including six native turtles. Around 60 turtles are released back into the wild each year.

April and May might see millions of butterflies. Note, weekends can be busy with Vietnamese families.

The visitor centre has English-speaking staff, and can arrange guides and tours.

Sights & Activities

Cuc Phuong (030-384 8006; www.cucphuongtourism.com; adult/child 40,000/20,000d) offers excellent hiking. Short walks include a 220-step trail up to the **Cave of Prehistoric Man**. Human graves and tools found here date back 7500 years, making it one of Vietnam's oldest sites of human habitation.

Popular hikes include a 6km-return walk to the massive, 1000-year-old **'old tree'** *(Tetrameles nudiflora)* and a longer four-hour walk to **Silver Cloud Peak**. There's also a strenuous 15km (approximately five-hour) hike to **Kanh**, a Muong village. You can stay overnight here with local families and raft on the Buoi River (80,000d).

Park staff can provide basic maps, but a guide is recommended for day trips and mandatory for longer treks. Two-hour escorted **night hikes** to spot nocturnal animals, or the Silver Cloud Peak hike both cost US$25 (for up to five people). The Deep Jungle trek (US$60) gets into remote terrain where you might spot flying squirrels. See the park's website for other one-day and overnight options.

Sleeping & Eating

There is accommodation in the park, and one luxury resort nearby. It's advised to book for weekends and public holidays. Camping (per person US$4) is also available at the visitor centre or Mac Lake.

There are simple restaurants and snack shops at the park headquarters and Mac Lake.

Park Headquarters GUESTHOUSE $
(s US$16-35, d US$27-50, stilt house US$14, bungalow US$23) Beside the park entrance, with accommodation including recently redecorated 'deluxe' rooms, a stilt house and a private bungalow. Non-deluxe rooms are quite dark, but still adequate.

Mac Lake BUNGALOW $
(bungalows US$16-27) Attractive bungalows overlooking Mac Lake are 2km inside the park, though the location is quite isolated and the restaurant often undersupplied.

Bong Sub-Station GUESTHOUSE $
(stilt house per person US$8, bungalows US$23-27) At the reserve's heart, Bong is 18km from the entrance and good for early morning walks and birdwatching. There are simple rooms with no hot water in a stilt house, and more-private bungalows.

Kanh Village Homestays HOMESTAY $
(per person US$10) Simple homestays with Muong families can be organised by park staff.

Cuc Phuong Resort RESORT $$$
(030-384 8886; www.cucphuongresort.com; Dong Tam village; bungalow/villa from US$92/153;) This resort is near a natural spring, enabling mineral-rich water to be pumped into wooden bath-tubs in each room. There are (spring-fed) indoor and outdoor pools, tennis courts and an impressive spa; breakfast is included. It's 2km from the park entrance. Rooms are cheapest from Sunday to Thursday.

Getting There & Away

Cuc Phuong National Park is 45km from Ninh Binh. The turn-off from Hwy 1 is north of Ninh Binh and follows the road that runs to Kenh Ga and Van Long Nature Reserve.

Buses (two hours, 80,000d) from Hanoi's Giap Bat southern bus station depart to the town of Nho Quan near Cuc Phuong regularly from 8am to 4pm, with return buses to Hanoi from 7am to 3pm. From Nho Quan to the park, catch a *xe om* (100,000d) or taxi (200,000d). There's also a direct bus from Giap Bat to Cuc Phuong departing at 3pm, with a return bus to Hanoi at 9am.

From Ninh Binh, catch a *xe om* or taxi to the park.

Hanoi tour companies offer trips to Cuc Phuong, usually combined with other sights in the Ninh Binh area.

Vinh

Practically obliterated during the American War, Vinh was rebuilt with East German aid – hence the brutalist concrete architecture that dominates the downtown area. The only reasons to stop here are if you're a Ho Chi Minh devotee (he was born in a nearby village), or if you're heading to Laos.

Vinh is a major transport hub that has regular bus services to HCMC, Hanoi, Danang and Dien Bien Phu, and trains to all stops north to Hanoi and south to HCMC. Open-tour buses pass through town

GETTING TO LAOS: VINH TO PHONSAVAN & LAK SAO

An alternative crossing is from the Vietnamese city of Thanh Hoa to Sam Neua in Laos, but this route is plagued by reports of rampant overcharging of non-Vietnamese travellers by taxi drivers and bus companies.

Vinh to Phonsavan

Getting to the border The often mist-shrouded **Nam Can/Nong Haet border crossing** is 250km northwest of Vinh. Buses leave at 6am Mondays, Wednesdays, Fridays and Saturdays for Luang Prabang (700,000d, 22 hours) via Phonsavan (410,000d, 12 hours). It's possible to travel independently from Vinh to Muong Xen by bus and then take a motorbike (around 170,000d) uphill to the border, but we strongly recommend you take the direct option due to overcharging and hassle.

At the border The border post's opening hours are from 7am to 5pm. Vietnamese visas aren't available, but Lao visas are available for most nationalities for between US$30 and US$40.

Moving on Travellers not on the direct bus connection face numerous challenges. Firstly you'll have to haggle over a motorbike ride from the border to the nearest town, Muong Xen. The route is breathtaking but only 25km downhill and should cost around 100,000d; drivers may ask for up to 300,000d. From Muong Xen there are irregular buses to Vinh (125,000d, six hours). Note that some buses from Phonsavan claim to continue to Hanoi or Danang, but unceremoniously discharge all their passengers in Vinh.

Transport on the Laos side to Nong Haet is erratic, but once you get there you can pick up a bus to Phonsavan.

Vinh to Lak Sao

Getting to the border The **Cau Treo/Nam Phao border crossing** has a dodgy reputation with travellers on local non-direct buses, who report chronic overcharging and hassle (such as bus drivers ejecting foreigners in the middle of nowhere unless they cough up extra bucks). Stick to direct services. Most transport to Phonsavan in Laos uses the Nong Haet–Nam Can border further north. Buses leave Vinh at 6am (on Mondays, Wednesdays, Fridays and Saturdays) for Vieng Khan in Laos (280,000d). There are also regular local buses from Vinh to Tay Son (70,000d, two hours) and then irregular services from Tay Son on to the border at Cau Treo. Otherwise *xe om* (motorbike taxis) ask for around 170,000d for the ride.

At the border The border is open from 7am to 5pm. Lao visas are available.

Moving on If you're not on a direct bus, expect rip-offs. Upon entering Vietnam bus drivers quote up to US$40 for the ride to Vinh. A metered taxi costs about US$50, a motorbike about 320,000d. Some buses from Lak Sao claim to run to Danang or Hanoi, but in fact terminate in Vinh.

On the Laos side, a jumbo or *songthaew* (truck) between the border and Lak Sao runs to about 50,000 kip (bargain hard).

between Hanoi and Hue, and while it's easy to ask to jump off here, it's difficult to arrange a pick-up.

Most convenient for Lao-bound travellers is the **Thanh An Hotel** (030-384 3478; 156 Nguyen Thai Hoc; r 230,000-350,000d;), with a handy location 300m south of the main bus terminal, and comfortable rooms with attractive wooden furniture and good beds.

Around Vinh

CUA LO BEACH

Cua Lo offers white sand, clean water, pine trees and good seafood restaurants, but the karaoke and massage parlours won't suit all travellers.

Huge government hotels face the beach and behind them are uninspired guesthouses (rooms 300,000d to 400,000d). In summer, rooms can go for triple the usual price.

Cua Lo is 16km northeast of Vinh and can be reached by motorbike (180,000d including waiting time) or taxi (around 140,000d one way).

KIM LIEN

Ho Chi Minh's 1890 birthplace in **Hoang Tru**, and the village of Kim Lien, where he spent some of his formative years, are around 14km northwest of Vinh. For the party faithful, these **pilgrimage spots** (7-11.30am & 2-5pm Mon-Fri, 7.30am-noon & 1.30-5pm Sat & Sun) FREE offer recreated bamboo houses, dressed sparsely with furniture. Not far from the Kim Lien house – around 2km from Hoang Tru – is a shrine-like museum, and a shop with Ho memorabilia.

No English-language information is at either site. From Vinh, *xe om* drivers charge 130,000d (including waiting time), and taxis ask around 250,000d.

Phong Nha-Ke Bang National Park

052

Designated a Unesco World Heritage site in 2003, the remarkable **Phong Nha-Ke Bang National Park** FREE contains the oldest karst mountains in Asia, formed approximately 400 million years ago. Riddled with hundreds of cave systems – many of extraordinary scale and length – and spectacular underground rivers, Phong Nha is a speleologist's heaven on earth.

Serious exploration only began in the 1990s, lead by the British Cave Research Association and Hanoi University. Cavers first penetrated deep into Phong Nha Cave, one of the world's longest systems. In 2005 Paradise Cave was discovered, and in 2009 a team found the world's largest cave – Son Doong. In 2015 public access to two more cave systems was approved.

Above the ground, most of the mountainous 885 sq km of Phong Nha-Ke Bang National Park is near-pristine tropical evergreen jungle, more than 90% of which is primary forest. It borders the biodiverse Hin Namno reserve in Laos to form an impressive, continuous slab of protected habitat. More than 100 types of mammal (including 10 species of primate, tigers, elephants and the saola, a rare Asian antelope), 81 types of reptile and amphibian, and more than 300 varieties of bird have been logged in Phong Nha.

In the past, access to the national park was limited and strictly controlled by the Vietnamese military. Access is still quite tightly controlled for good reason (the park is still riddled with unexploded ordnance). Officially you are not allowed to hike here without a licensed tour operator. You can, however, travel independently (on a motorbike or car) on the Ho Chi Minh Hwy or Hwy 20, which cut through the park.

The Phong Nha region is changing fast. **Son Trach village** (population 3000) is the main centre, with an ATM, a growing range of accommodation and eating options, and improving transport links with other parts of central Vietnam.

The caves are the region's absolute highlights, but the above-ground attractions of forest trekking, the area's war history, and rural mountain biking means it deserves a stay of around three days.

Sights & Activities

The Phong Nha region is exploding in popularity, and it's recommended that overnight caving tours for Tu Lan, Hang Va and Hang En are booked in advance if possible.

★Tu Lan Cave CAVE

(www.oxalis.com.vn; 2-day tour 5,500,000d) The Tu Lan cave trip begins with a countryside hike then a swim (with headlamps and life jackets) through two spectacular river caves before emerging in an idyllic valley. Then there's more hiking through dense forest to a 'beach' where rivers merge that's an ideal campsite. There's more wonderful swimming here in vast caverns. Moderate fitness levels are necessary. Tu Lan is 65km north of Son Trach and can only be visited on a guided tour.

Longer Tu Lan tours are also available. The longer excursions penetrate deeper into the jungle, but as the region is so pristine even day hikes are rewarding. Howard and Deb Limbert, consultants to tour operator Oxalis, discovered these caves in 2010. See the Oxalis website for details and costs of longer tours.

★Hang Toi CAVE

(Dark Cave; per person 350,000d) Incorporating an above-water zipline, followed by a swim into the cave, and then exploration of a pitch-black passageway of oozing mud, it's little wonder Hang Toi is the cave experience you may have already heard about from other travellers. Upon exiting the cave, a leisurely kayak paddle heads to a jetty where there's more into-the-water zipline thrills to be had.

The Dark Cave can be visited independently or on the Farmstay's National Park Tour (p164).

Paradise Cave CAVE

(Thien Dong; adult/child under 1.3m 250,000/125,000d; 7.30am-4.30pm) Surrounded by forested karst peaks, this remarkable cave system extends for 31km, though most people only visit the first kilometre. The scale is breathtaking, as wooden staircases descend into a cathedral-like space with colossal stalagmites and glimmering stalactites. Get here early to beat the crowds, as during peak times (early afternoon), tour guides shepherd groups using megaphones. Paradise Cave is about 14km southwest of Son Trach. Electric buggies (per person one-way/return 15,000/25,000d) ferry visitors from the car park to the entrance.

To explore deep inside Paradise Cave, consider booking Phong Nha Farmstay's (p164) 7km Paradise Cave tour (2,650,000d, minimum two people), which includes a swim through an underground river and lunch under a light shaft.

Phong Nha Cave & Boat Trip CAVE

(adult/child under 1.3m 150,000/25,000d, boat up to 14 people 320,000d; 7am-4pm) The spectacular boat trip through Phong Nha Cave is an enjoyable, though touristy, experience beginning in Son Trach village. Boats cruise along past buffalo, limestone peaks and church steeples to the cave's gaping mouth. The engine is then cut and the boats are negotiated silently through cavern after garishly illuminated cavern. On the return leg there's the option to climb (via 330 steps) up to the mountainside **Tien Son Cave** (admission 80,000d) with the remains of 9th-century Cham altars.

The ticket office and departure jetty are in Son Trach village. Allow two hours to see Phong Nha; add an hour for Tien Son. In November and December seasonal floods may mean Phong Nha Cave is closed. Weekends are extremely popular with Vietnamese visitors, whose presence is amplified by the spectacular echoes and unventilated cigarette smoke. Note the cave was used as a hospital and ammunition depot during the American War and was heavily bombed.

Hang Va CAVE

(www.oxalis.com.vn; per person 9,000,000d) Discovered in 2012, and opened to visitors in 2015, Hang Va is explored on a two-day/one-night excursion that travels firstly along an underground river in Hang Nuoc Nut. Tours overnight in a jungle camp at the entrance to Hang Va, where the cave's highlight is a spectacular stalagmite field partly submerged in crystalline waters. Ropes and harnesses are used extensively.

Hang En CAVE

(per person 6,000,000d) This gigantic cave is very close to Hang Son Doong, and featured in the same *National Geographic* photographic spread in 2011. Getting here involves a trek through dense jungle, valleys and the **Ban Doong minority village**, a very remote tribal settlement (with no electricity or roads). You stay overnight in the cave or a minority village. Tours can be booked via Oxalis or the Phong Nha Farmstay.

Phong Nha Museum MUSEUM

(admission 15,000d; 9am-5pm) Poignant black-and-white photographs of the area's war history – especially the Ho Chi Minh Trail and Hwy 20 – combine with an exhibition about the ongoing work done by MAG (Mine Action Group) in clearing unexploded ordnance around the region.

A RELAXING FORESTED RETREAT

Nuoc Mooc Ecotrail (adult/child 80,000d/free; 7am-5pm) A beautiful riverside retreat inside Phong Nha-Ke Bang National Park, the wooden walkways and paths of the Nuoc Mooc Ecotrail extend over a kilometre through woods to the confluence of two rivers. It's a beautiful place for a swim, where you can wallow hippo-style in turquoise waters with a limestone-mountain backdrop. Recently added attractions include an exciting rope bridge straight from an Indiana Jones movie, and kayaking on a compact weir on the river. Bring a picnic, or order food and drinks and dine in one of Nuoc Mooc's breezy open-air pavilions. Nuoc Mooc is 12km southwest of Son Trach, and is a great place to spend a relaxed day taking your foot off the travel accelerator.

Tours

Tours of Phong Nha are available from Dong Hoi, but as the region offers so much, it's best to stay near the national park. Tours can be set up through most accommodation and the following recommended operators. Don't even consider a day trip from Hue, as you'll spend most of the time on the road.

★ Oxalis Adventure Tours TOUR
(☎091 990 0423; www.oxalis.com.vn; Son Trach) Oxalis is unquestionably *the* expert in caving and trekking expeditions, and is the only outfit licensed to conduct tours to Hang Son Doong. Staff are all fluent English speakers, and trained by world-renowned British cavers Howard and Deb Limbert. All excursions, from day trips to Tu Lan to week-long expeditions to the world's largest cave, are meticulously planned and employ local guides and porters, so the wider community benefits. You can discuss trips at its riverside Expedition Cafe.

Pre-booking Son Doong for the following year is essential, and if possible, booking a few months ahead for expeditions in Tu Lan and Hang En is recommended to avoid disappointment.

Phong Nha Farmstay Tours ADVENTURE TOUR
(☎052-367 5135; www.phong-nha-cave.com; Cu Nam) The Farmstay can book cave tours – in conjunction with Oxalis – but equally interesting is bouncing in a US jeep or Russian Ural motorbike and sidecar exploring the area's scenery and war history. The Farmstay's popular National Park Tour (per person 1,450,000d) travels by minibus to incorporate the Ho Chi Minh Trail with Paradise Cave and Hang Toi.

Jungle Boss Trekking HIKING
(☎094 374 8041; www.jungleboss homestay.com; per person US$75) Originally from the DMZ, Dzung – aka 'Jungle Boss' – has been in Phong Nha for eight years, and is an experienced guide to the area. He speaks excellent English and runs an exciting one-day tour around the Ho Chi Minh Trail and the remote Abandoned Valley area of the national park. You'll need moderate to high fitness levels.

Hai's Eco Conservation Tour HIKING
(☎096 260 6844; www.phong-nha-bamboo-cafe.com; per person 1,000,000d) Interesting day tours combining hiking in the jungle – you'll need to be relatively fit – with a visit to Phong Nha's Wildlife Rescue and Rehabilitation Centre, which rehabilitates rescued animals (mainly macaques from nearby regions, but also snakes and birds). Prices include a barbecue lunch, and there's an opportunity to cool off at the end of the day in a natural swimming hole. Hai is usually at his Bamboo Cafe (p166) in the evenings.

HANG SON DOONG: WORLD'S LARGEST CAVE

Ho Khanh, a hunter from a jungle settlement close to the Vietnam–Laos border, would often take shelter in the caves that honeycomb his mountain homeland. He stumbled across gargantuan **Hang Son Doong** (Mountain River Cave) in the early 1990s, but the sheer scale and majesty of the principal cavern (more than 5km long, 200m high and, in some places, 150m wide) was only confirmed as the world's biggest cave when British explorers returned with him in 2009.

The expedition team's biggest obstacle was to find a way over a vast overhanging barrier of muddy calcite they dubbed the 'Great Wall of Vietnam' that divided the cave. Once they did, its true scale was revealed – a cave big enough to accommodate a battleship. Sections of it are pierced by skylights that reveal formations of ethereal stalagmites that cavers have called the Cactus Garden. Some stalagmites are up to 80m high. Colossal cave pearls have been discovered, measuring 10cm in diameter, formed by millennia of drips, as calcite crystals fused with grains of sand. Magnificent rimstone pools are present throughout the cave.

Hang Son Doong is one of the most spectacular sights in Southeast Asia, and the government only approved (very restricted) access to the cave system in June 2013. The only specialist operator permitted (by the Vietnamese president no less) to lead tours here is Son Trach–based Oxalis. Son Doong is no day-trip destination: it's in an extremely remote area and the only way to visit is by booking a seven-day expedition with around 16 porters. It costs US$3000 per person, with a maximum of 10 trekkers on each trip.

Phong Nha Adventure Cycling MOUNTAIN BIKING
(☎098 555 5827; www.phongnhacycling.jimdo.com; per person US$65-87) Excellent mountain biking tours with the irrepressible Private Shi. Options include biking sections of the Ho Chi Minh Trail, visiting local villages, and lunch at the Chay Lap homestay in the park.

Sleeping

There are simple local hotels in Son Trach town, all charging around 350,000d.

Easy Tiger HOSTEL $
(☎052-367 7844; www.easytigerphongnha.com; Son Trach; dm 160,000d;) In Son Trach town, this hostel has four-bed dorms, a great bar-restaurant area, pool table and excellent travel information. A swimming pool and beer garden makes it ideal for relaxation after trekking and caving. And yes, the bedspreads are actually faux leopard-skin. Don't ask. Do ask about free bicycles and a map to explore the interesting Bong Lai valley.

★**Phong Nha Farmstay** GUESTHOUSE $$
(☎052-367 5135; www.phong-nha-cave.com; Cu Nam; r 900,000-1,200,000d, f 1,300,000-2,000,000d;) The place that really put Phong Nha on the map, the Farmstay has peaceful views overlooking an ocean of rice paddies. Rooms are smallish but neat, with high ceilings and shared balconies. The bar-restaurant serves up Asian and Western meals, and there's a social vibe and occasional movies and live music. Local tours are excellent and there's free bicycle hire.

The Farmstay is in Cu Nam village, 9km east of Son Trach.

Phong Nha Lake House Resort HOTEL $$
(☎052-367 5999; www.phongnhalakehouse.com; Khuong Ha; dm US$10, d US$42-60, f US$70;) Impressive lakeside resort owned by an Australian-Vietnamese couple with an excellent dorm (with quality beds, mosquito nets, en-suite bathroom and high ceilings), and spacious and stylish villas. A pool and newer lake-view bungalows are more proof this is the area's most comfortable place to stay. The wooden restaurant is a traditional structure from Ha Giang province in northern Vietnam.

The Lake House is located 7km east of Son Trach.

Oxalis Home HOTEL $$
(☎052-367 7678; www.oxalis.com.vn; Son Trach; d mountain/river view 1,200,000/1,500,000d;) This new riverside hotel is used by travellers booking cave tours with Oxalis, but is also open to others. Accommodation is in spacious rooms, either with river views, or to equally spectacular karst mountain peaks. Bikes and kayaks – Oxalis Home has its own compact beach – are free for guests, and the on-site Expedition Cafe has elevated river views.

Pepper House GUESTHOUSE $$
(☎016 7873 1560; www.facebook.com/pepperhousehomestay; Khuong Ha; dm 200,000d, villas 1,400,000d;) Run by long-term Aussie expat Dave (aka 'Multi') and his local wife Diem, this welcoming place combines a rural setting and new double rooms in villas arrayed around a compact swimming pool. There are also simpler dorms inside the main house. Look forward to good food and cold beer as well.

Located 6km east of Son Trach.

Jungle Boss Homestay GUESTHOUSE $$
(☎094 374 8041; www.junglebosshomestay.com; Son Trach; d/f US$40/50;) Run by the friendly Dzung – a local trekking guide with excellent English – and his wife Huong, this place has three simple but stylish rooms, and a great edge-of-the-village location with rice paddy views. Rates include breakfast and free use of bicycles, and Dzung also offers caving and jungle trekking trips.

Ho Khanh's Homestay HOMESTAY $$
(☎012 9959 7182; www.phong-nha-homestay.com; Son Trach; r US$45-50;) How often do you get the chance to meet a Vietnamese legend? This homestay belongs to Ho Khanh, who discovered Son Doong, the world's largest cave. He's also a master carpenter, and has four wood-panelled rooms, recently fitted out with air-con and private bathrooms, and also excellent private bungalows. Drop by for a delicious chocolate coffee in the attached cafe.

Phong Nha Homestay Community HOMESTAY $$
(☎094 374 8041; www.phongnhahomestay.com; Son Trach; d/f US$40/50) Numbering three places to stay at the time of writing, this collection of local homestays includes the Jungle Boss Homestay, the Phong Nha Mountain House (a lovely wooden bungalow), and the slightly more rustic Minh's

Homestay in a traditional wooden house. All three have en-suite bathrooms and really welcoming family owners, and rates include breakfast.

Eating & Drinking

At the time of writing, other rustic businesses selling roast duck and local foods were kicking off around the surrounding Bong Lai valley. Easy Tiger can provide you with a map to get there by bike.

Bamboo Cafe CAFE $

(www.phong-nha-bamboo-cafe.com; Son Trach; meals 35,000-70,000d; 7am-10.30pm;) This laid-back haven on Son Trach's main drag has colourful decor, a cool outside deck, and well-priced food and drink, including excellent fresh fruit smoothies. It's also where you'll usually find the friendly Hai who runs eco conservation tours (p164).

Capture Vietnam CAFE $

(www.facebook.com/capturevietnam; Son Trach; snacks & meals 40,000-100,000d; 7am-7pm) Located beside Easy Tiger (p165), this cafe has espresso coffee, homestyle baking, and interesting Western and Vietnamese meals. There's also an attached shop selling local souvenirs – try the Phong Nha beef jerky – and takeaway beer, wine and cider.

The Best Spit Roast Pork & Noodle Shop in the World (Probably...) VIETNAMESE $

(Son Trach; meals 30,000-50,000d; 7am-4pm) Also probably the longest name of any restaurant in Vietnam... sells excellent grilled pork paired with noodles, baguettes or rice. Get ready to smell this place well before you see it as you're wandering Son Trach's sleepy main street.

Mountain Goat Restaurant VIETNAMESE $$

(Son Trach; goat from 150,000d; 11am-9pm) Dine on grilled and steamed *de* (goat) – try the goat with lemongrass – at this riverside spot in Son Trach. Other options include spicy chicken and ice-cold beer. From the Phong Nha Cave boat station, walk 150m along the river, just past the church.

Pub with Cold Beer BARBECUE, BAR $$

(Bong Lai valley; beer 20,000d, meals from 50,000d; 8am-8pm) Up a dirt track in the middle of nowhere (but well signposted), this excellent barn-cum-bar is owned by a local farming family and does what it says on the tin – the beer is ice cold. Hungry? Order roast chicken with peanut sauce (all ingredients are farm-fresh). A kilo of perfectly grilled chicken is 200,000d.

Wild Boar Eco-Farm VIETNAMESE $$

(Bong Lai valley; meals from 100,000d; 11am-6pm) Surprisingly it's roast chicken on offer here, although giant porkers are raised as well. Reached by boat or via a bumpy bike path, the attraction here is relaxing in simple bamboo shelters overlooking a river valley. Service can be leisurely, so ask the team at Easy Tiger or the Farmstay to phone ahead and order. Oh, and for a map...

When we dropped by, Cuong the owner had introduced river-tubing and was also looking at offering tented accommodation.

Vung Hue VIETNAMESE $$

(Son Trach; meals 70,000-130,000d; 11am-9pm) Your best bet for a Vietnamese meal in Son Trach, with good-value multidish menus and a handy location near the car park for departures to the Phong Nha Cave.

Jungle Bar BAR

(Son Trach; 7am-midnight;) The in-house bar-cafe at Easy Tiger is the most happening place in Son Trach, with cheap beer, pool tables, and live music four nights a week. Add to the growing display of national flags if you're feeling patriotic. There's loads of local information on hand, even if you're not staying at Easy Tiger.

Information

Hai at the Bamboo Cafe is a superb source of independent travel information, and the helpful staff at the Phong Nha Farmstay and Easy Tiger can assist with tours, information and transport.

There's a tourist office opposite the jetty in Son Trach, but staff are not well versed regarding independent travel. There's a couple of adjacent ATMs, but occasional power cuts mean they sometimes don't work. It's wise to bring enough Vietnamese dong for your stay.

Getting There & Around

Son Trach town is 50km northwest of Dong Hoi. From Dong Hoi head 20km north on Hwy 1 to Bo Trach, then turn west for another 30km.

Phong Nha-Ke Bang National Park abuts Son Trach and spreads west to the Lao border. Until 2011 access was tightly controlled by the Vietnamese state, and some areas remain off limits to independent travellers.

Hotels can organise lifts in private cars from Dong Hoi (500,000d); they work together so rides can be shared between travellers to cut costs.

BUS

Local buses (35,000d, 90 minutes) shuttle between Dong Hoi's bus station and Son Trach, leaving regularly from 6am to 5pm. Dong Hoi's railway station is around 1.3km from the bus station and the city is on the main north–south line.

From Hue (around 120,000d, five hours), the Hung Thanh open-tour bus leaves 49 Đ Chu Van An at 4.30pm, and the Tan Nha bus leaves from the Why Not? bar on Đ Vo Thi Sau around 6.30am.

Coming from Danang or Hoi An, a local bus (250,000d, seven hours) leaves the Danang bus station for Phong Nha around 1pm. This service has been haphazard so check with the Easy Tiger or Oxalis websites for the latest status.

MOTORCYCLE & BICYCLE

Motorcycling or scootering around the national park is not recommended for inexperienced drivers – the area is not well signposted and every year there's an increasing number of injuries to travellers. A good option is to book a tour with **Thang's Phong Nha Riders** (www.easytigerhostel.com/thangs-phong-nha-riders/; beside Easy Tiger). A day's hire of a bike and driver is around 400,000d, staff are well-versed in the sights of the area, and you'll be providing work for enthusiastic locals. Thang's can also arrange motorbike transfers through absolutely stunning scenery to Hue or Khe Sanh.

Cycling is recommended to explore Phong Nha's rural back roads, especially the quirky collection of rustic local restaurants and activities popping up around the nearby Bong Lai valley. Easy Tiger rent bikes and can supply a handy map.

Dong Hoi & Around

052 / POP 116,000

Dong Hoi is a pleasantly untouristed, port and seaside town. It enjoys an attractive location, clinging to the banks of the Nhat Le River, and has beaches to the north and south.

As the main staging area for the North Vietnamese Army (NVA), Dong Hoi suffered more than most during the American War. The town has since recovered as a bustling provincial capital, and also has excellent transport links to the Phong Nha region.

Sights & Activities

The Nhat Le River, which divides the city from a beautiful sandy spit, boasts a landscaped riverside promenade that includes

Dong Hoi

Top Sights
1 Tam Toa Church A1

Sights
2 Fish Market B3

Activities, Courses & Tours
3 A2Z A1
4 Nam Long Hotel Tours A1
5 Phong Nha Discovery A1

Sleeping
6 Buffalo Hostel A2
7 Nam Long Hotel A1
8 Nam Long Plus A1

Eating
9 7th Heaven A1
10 Tree Hugger Cafe A1
11 Tu Quy B3

Drinking & Nightlife
Buffalo Pub .... (see 6)

the haunting, ruined facade of the **Tam Toa Church** FREE, which was bombed in 1965.

All that remains of **Dong Hoi Citadel** (1825) are two restored gates, one close to the riverbank, the other on Đ Quang Trung.

Get up early and check out the excellent **fish market** (Đ Me Suot; 6am-2pm).

Nam Long Hotel Tours TOUR
(☎091 892 3595; www.namlonghotels.com/attractions-tours/; 22 Đ Ho Xuan Huong) Variety of trips to Phong Nha and exploring the DMZ. Also gives out free local maps with suggested Dong Hoi self-guided walking tours.

Phong Nha Discovery ADVENTURE TOUR
(☎052-385 1660; www.phongnhadiscovery.com; 63 Đ Ly Thuong Kiet; day tours US$50-57) Daily tours from Dong Hoi to Paradise Cave and Hang Toi (Dark Cave); also has multiday tours incorporating Tu Lan and Hang En.

A2Z TOUR
(☎052-384 5868; www.atoztourist.com; 29 Đ Ly Thuong Kiet) Contact for tours to Phong Nha or open-tour bus tickets.

Sleeping & Eating

★Nam Long Hotel HOTEL $
(☎091 892 3595; www.namlonghotels.com; 22 Đ Ho Xuan Huong; dm US$6, r US$20-30;) Simply excellent budget hotel run by Nga and Sy, a welcoming, ever-helpful, English-speaking couple. Rooms are bright and airy with enormous windows - book 301 for a river-view balcony. The eight-bed dorm is superb, with two en-suite bathrooms and its own balcony with great views. Breakfasts are available, and Phong Nha tours and onward transport can be organised.

Nam Long Plus HOTEL $
(☎091 892 3595; www.namlonghotels.com; 28a Đ Phan Chu Trinh; dm US$6, d US$22-25, f US$35;) Fine eight-storey hotel, with 19 comfortable, spacious rooms and dorms, most with city or river views. A free hot breakfast is included, service is good and tours can be arranged.

Buffalo Hostel HOSTEL $
(☎052-381 5599; www.buffalodonghoi.com; 4 Đ Nguyen Du; dm/d 100,000/250,000d;) Dong Hoi's new hostel ticks all the boxes for the thrifty traveller: colourful dorms and private rooms, loads of local information on where to kick on to next, and the promise of a cold beer and company downstairs at the attached Buffalo Pub. The friendly owners can also hook up travellers with various tours.

Tu Quy VIETNAMESE $
(17 Đ Co Tam; meals 20,000–40,000d; ⏲7am-8.30pm) This area is famous for its *banh khoai* (shrimp pancake) restaurants, of which Tu Quy is one of the best. It has street-side tables with the river in sight.

Tree Hugger Cafe CAFE $
(www.treehugger-cafe.com; 30 Đ Nguyen Du; snacks 40,000-60,000d; ⏲7am-10pm;) Operated by a Vietnamese-German couple, Tree Hugger's appealing combo of coffees, juices and Western-style snacks is popular with both travellers and English-speaking Dong Hoi locals. There are also interesting organic and ecofriendly local products for sale, and the information folders and tour listings are really worth investigating for onward travel.

7th Heaven INTERNATIONAL $
(☎052-383 3856; www.7thheavenrestaurant.com; 39 Đ Duong Van An; meals 45,000-155,000d; ⏲10.30am-9pm) Cosy and friendly expat-owned restaurant and bar that offers everything from burgers and steaks to Thai curries.

Buffalo Pub PUB
(www.buffalodonghoi.com; 4 Đ Nguyen Du; ⏲7am-11.30pm;) The best place in town for meeting other travellers over a cold beer is this

BUSES FROM DONG HOI

DESTINATION	COST (D)	DURATION (HR)	FREQUENCY
Danang	200,000	8	7am, 8.30am & 9.30am
Dong Ha	100,000	2	frequent 6am-5pm
Hanoi (via Ninh Binh)	250,000	9	daily, 10pm
Hoi An	250,000	5	daily, 3.30am
Hue	150,000	3½	frequent 6am-5pm
Phong Nha	35,000	1½	frequent 6am-5pm

For Laos, buses leave for Vientiane daily (400,000d) and for Thakhek from Tuesday to Sunday (300,000d). Both nine-hour services run via the Cha Lo–Na Phao border crossing, where Lao visas are available. For all up-to-date transport information, see Sy at the Nam Long Hotel.

chilled spot decked out in lots of natural timber. There's a pool table and occasional live music, or you can hijack the sound system with your own portable music device of choice. Upstairs, sleep comes relatively easy at the attached hostel.

Information

Staff at both Nam Long hotels can organise motorbike and bicycle rentals, provide local maps and book bus and train tickets.

Agribank (2 Đ Me Suot; ⏰7.30am-4pm Mon-Fri, 7.30am-12.30pm Sat) ATM and exchange services.

Getting There & Away

AIR

The airport is 6km north of town.

Vietjet (www.vietjetair.com) To/from HCMC.

Vietnam Airlines (www.vietnamairlines.com) To/from Ho Chi Minh City and Hanoi.

TRAIN

The **train station** (Ga Dong Hoi; Đ Thuan Ly) is located 3km west of the centre. Trains leave for destinations including Hanoi (350,000d, 9½ to 11½ hours, five daily), Hue (150,000d, three to four hours, six daily) and Danang (170,000d, five hours, six daily). All prices quoted are for soft seats on express trains.

SOUTH-CENTRAL VIETNAM

Demilitarised Zone (DMZ)

☎053

Most of the bases and bunkers have long vanished, but this 5km strip of land on either side of the Ben Hai River is still known by its American War moniker: the DMZ. From 1954 to 1975 it acted as a buffer between the North and the South. Ironically,

South-Central Vietnam

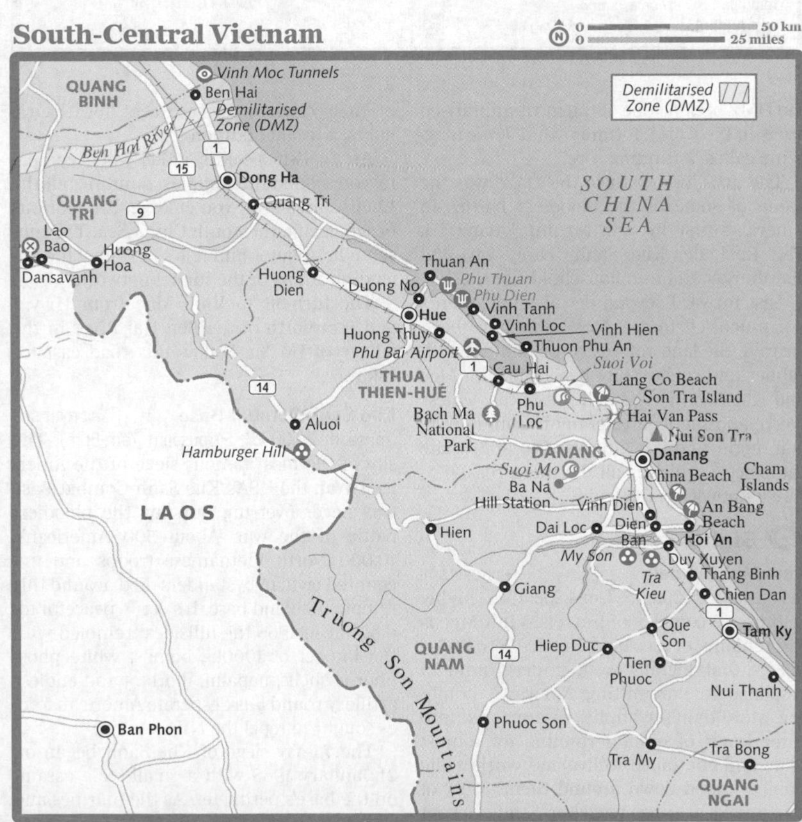

Around the DMZ

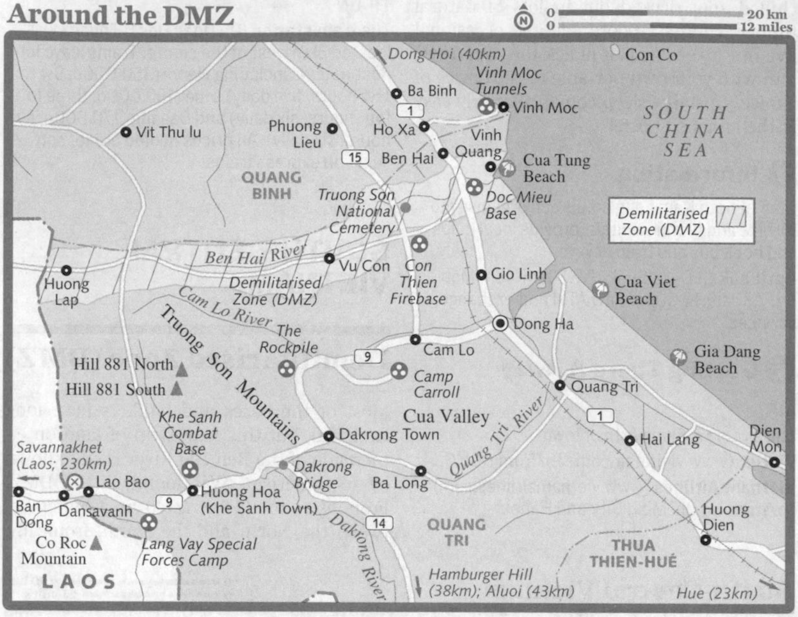

the DMZ became one of the most militarised areas in the world, forming what *Time* magazine called 'a running sore'.

The area just south of the DMZ was the scene of some of the bloodiest battles in America's first TV war, turning Quang Tri, The Rockpile, Khe Sanh, Lang Vay and Hamburger Hill into household names.

Fast forward several decades and there's not much left to see. Most sites have been cleared, the land reforested or planted with rubber and coffee. Only Ben Hai, Vinh Moc and Khe Sanh have small museums. Unless you're an American veteran or military buff, you might find it a little hard to appreciate the place – which is all the more reason to hire a knowledgeable guide.

Sights

Vinh Moc Tunnels HISTORIC SITE

(admission 20,000d; 7am-4.30pm) A highly impressive complex of tunnels, Vinh Moc is the remains of a coastal North Vietnamese village that literally went underground in response to unremitting American bombing. More than 90 families disappeared into three levels of tunnels running for almost 2km, and continued to live and work while bombs rained down around them. Most of the tunnels are open to visitors, and are kept in their original form (except for electric lights, a recent addition).

An English-speaking guide will accompany you around the complex, pointing out the 12 entrances until you emerge at a glorious beach, facing the South China Sea. The museum has photos and relics of tunnel life, including a map of the tunnel network.

The turn-off to Vinh Moc from Hwy 1 is 6.5km north of the Ben Hai River in the village of Ho Xa. Follow this road east for 13km.

Khe Sanh Combat Base HISTORIC SITE

(museum 20,000d; museum 7am-5pm) The site of the most famous siege of the American War, the USA's Khe Sanh Combat Base was never overrun, but saw the bloodiest battle of the war. About 500 Americans, 10,000 North Vietnamese troops and uncounted civilian bystanders died around this remote highland base. It's eerily peaceful today, but in 1968 the hillsides trembled with the impact of 1000kg bombs, white phosphorus shells, napalm, mortars and endless artillery rounds, as desperate American forces sought to repel the NVA.

The 75-day siege of Khe Sanh began on 21 January 1968 with a small-scale assault on the base's perimeter. As the marines and

South Vietnamese rangers braced for a full-scale ground attack, Khe Sanh became the focus of global media attention. It was the cover story for both *Newsweek* and *Life* magazines, and made the front pages of countless newspapers around the world. During the next two months the base was subjected to continuous ground attacks and artillery fire, and US aircraft dropped 100,000 tonnes of explosives in its vicinity. But the expected attempt to overrun the base never came.

On 7 April 1968, after heavy fighting, US troops reopened Hwy 9 and linked up with the marines, ending the siege.

It now seems clear that the siege was an enormous diversion to draw US attention away from the South Vietnamese population centres in preparation for the Tet Offensive, which began a week after the siege started.

Today the site is occupied by a small museum, which contains some fascinating old photographs, plus a few reconstructed bunkers and American aircraft. Most of the area is now planted with coffee, and vendors offer high-grade local arabica beans for sale at the entrance.

Khe Sanh is 3km north of the small town of Huong Hoa.

Truong Son National Cemetery CEMETERY

An evocative memorial to the legions of North Vietnamese soldiers who died along the Ho Chi Minh Trail, this cemetery is a sobering sight. More than 10,000 graves dot these hillsides, each marked by a simple white tombstone headed by the inscription *liet si* (martyr). Many graves lie empty, simply bearing names, representing a fraction of Vietnam's 300,000 soldiers missing in action. It's 27km northwest of Dong Ha; the turn-off from Hwy 1 is close to Doc Mieu.

Ben Hai River RIVER

(museum 20,000d; museum 7am-4.30pm) Once the border between North and South Vietnam, Ben Hai River's southern bank now has a grandiose reunification monument, its stylised palm leaves oddly resembling missiles. Cua Tung Beach's fine golden sands are just east of here. Ben Hai's northern bank is dominated by a reconstructed flag tower and small museum full of war mementoes. Ben Hai is 22km north of Dong Ha on Hwy 1.

Hamburger Hill HISTORIC SITE

FREE Hamburger Hill (Ap Bia) was the site of a tumultuous battle in May 1969 between US forces and the NVA over a 900m-high mountain – resulting in over 600 North Vietnamese and 72 American deaths. Today you need a special permit (US$25 and only obtained in the town of Aluoi) and a guide to see the remaining trenches and bunkers. Hamburger Hill is 8km northwest of Aluoi, about 6km off Hwy 14, and less than 2km from Laos.

There's a rudimentary visitor centre (with a map and information in English) at the base of the hill, from where a 6km trail leads

WATCH YOUR STEP

Millions of tonnes of ordnance were dropped on Vietnam during the American War – it's estimated that about a third did not explode. Death and injury still happen most days. At many places there's still a chance of encountering live mortar rounds, artillery projectiles and mines. Watch where you step and don't leave the marked paths. Never touch any leftover ordnance.

It's not just the DMZ that's affected. It is estimated that as much as 20% of Vietnam remains uncleared, with more than 3.5 million mines and 350,000 to 800,000 tonnes of unexploded ordnance (UXO). In the one-year period between 2012 and 2013, the NGO Mines Advisory Group estimated it cleared 185,639 sq metres of battle-affected areas, and removed and destroyed 16,035 UXO items and 2188 cluster bombs.

Between 1975 and 2007, UXO resulted in 105,000 injuries and over 45,000 deaths. Every year hundreds die and are injured – a disproportionate number of them children or people from the ethnic minority groups.

The People's Army is responsible for most ongoing mine clearance. It's joined by foreign NGOs such as the Mines Advisory Group (www.maginternational.org) and Clear Path International (www.cpi.org), whose efforts are well worth supporting.

Dong Ha has the excellent Mine Action Visitor Centre (p173). Do drop by if you're in the area.

GONE UNDERGROUND

In 1966 the USA began a massive aerial and artillery bombardment of North Vietnam. Just north of the Demilitarised Zone (DMZ), the villagers of Vinh Moc found themselves living in one of the most heavily bombed and shelled strips of land on the planet. Small family shelters could not withstand this onslaught and villagers either fled or began tunnelling by hand and with simple tools into the red-clay earth.

The Viet Cong (VC) found it useful to have a base here and encouraged the villagers to stay. After 18 months of tunnelling, an enormous complex was established, creating new homes on three levels from 12m to 23m below ground, plus meeting rooms and even a maternity unit (17 babies were born underground). Whole families lived here, their longest sojourn lasting 10 days and 10 nights. Later, the civilians and VC were joined by North Vietnamese soldiers, whose mission was to keep communication and supply lines to nearby Con Co Island open.

Other villages north of the DMZ also built tunnel systems, but none was as elaborate as Vinh Moc (p170). The poorly constructed tunnels of Vinh Quang village (at the mouth of the Ben Hai River) collapsed after repeated bombing, killing everyone inside.

US warships stationed off the coast consistently bombarded the Vinh Moc tunnels (craters are still visible), and occasionally the tunnel mouths that faced the sea were struck by naval gunfire. The only ordnance that posed a real threat was the 'drilling bomb'. It scored a direct hit once but failed to explode, and no one was injured; the inhabitants adapted the bomb hole for use as an air shaft.

up the mountain. Bring water and be sure to stick to the main trail. Security is tight around here and you're sure to get your permits inspected by border guards.

Con Thien Firebase HISTORIC SITE

Only one bunker remains of the US Marine Corps base that used to cover the three small hills here. In September 1967 Con Thien was besieged by the NVA, provoking a US response of 4000 bombing sorties. Today the region (though cleared of mines) is still studded with unexploded ordnance – stick to the paths. Con Thien Firebase is 15km west of Hwy 1 and 8km south of Truong Son National Cemetery.

Camp Carroll HISTORIC SITE

Camp Carroll's colossal cannons used to shell targets as far away as Khe Sanh. All that remains now is a Vietnamese memorial. The turn-off to Camp Carroll is 10km west of Cam Lo; it's 3km from Hwy 9.

Rockpile HISTORIC SITE

Visible from Hwy 9, this 230m-high karst outcrop once had a US Marine Corps lookout on top and a base for American long-range artillery nearby. The Rockpile is 29km west of Dong Ha on Hwy 9.

Dakrong Bridge BRIDGE

Crossing the Dakrong River 13km east of the Khe Sanh bus station, this bridge was rebuilt in 2001 and bears a marker hailing its importance as a conduit for the Ho Chi Minh Trail.

Getting There & Around

Virtually everyone explores the DMZ on a tour. Standard tours are cheap (around US$15 for a group day trip) and can be arranged in Hue or Dong Ha. Most take in the Rockpile, Khe Sanh, Vinh Moc and Doc Mieu and leave Hue at 7am, returning by about 5pm. From Hue, much more time is spent driving around 300km than sightseeing.

A superior experience is to see the DMZ independently. Reckon on US$120 for a car and expert guide. Leaving from Dong Ha rather than Hue means less time on the road.

Dong Ha

053 / POP 88,800

Dong Ha is an important transport hub that sits at the intersection of Hwys 1 and 9. Its dusty, traffic-plagued main drag looks pretty dismal – this is because the town was completely flattened during the American War. However, the town does have its attractive aspects, with a string of riverside seafood restaurants. Dong Ha makes a useful base for exploring the DMZ and is the gateway town to the Lao Bao border crossing.

Sights

Mine Action Visitor Centre MUSEUM
(093 521 1281; Đ Ly Thuong Kiet; 8am-5pm Mon-Fri, by appointment Sat & Sun) FREE The Quang Tri province was the most heavily bombed part of Vietnam and it remains the most contaminated with ordnance. This museum – in English and Vietnamese – provides an excellent historical overview, with photographs of the 1972 destruction of Quang Tri Citadel and people attempting to deactivate mines with bamboo sticks. A new display details the tragic legacy of the defoliant Agent Orange. Call an hour ahead and Phu, the excellent English-speaking manager, will show you around the museum.

Information panels detail the grim reality for locals: cluster bombs cause 46% of incidents, of which 80% are fatal. Over 8500 people have died in the province since the war ended. Minority people are particularly vulnerable as they seek scrap metal to sell. Films (from 11 minutes to over an hour) are also available to view.

Bao Tang Quang Tri MUSEUM
(8 Đ Nguyen Hue; 7.30-11am & 1.30-5pm Tue, Thu, Sat & Sun) FREE A modest museum that documents the history of the Quang Tri province, with a focus on its ethnic minorities.

Tours

Dong Ha has several excellent DMZ guides.

Annam Tour MILITARY
(090 514 0600; www.annamtour.com; 207B Đ Nguyen Du) Outstanding tailor-made tours, guided by military historian Mr Vu (who speaks excellent English). Using iPads to show photographs and maps, the sights and battlegrounds come to life. Trips cost around US$120 per day, and can be set up from Hue too.

Tam's Tours MILITARY, FOOD
(090 542 5912; http://tamscafe.jimdo.com; Tam's Cafe, 211 Đ Ba Trieu) Excellent backpacker-priced tours taking in the DMZ sights using English-speaking war veterans. Tours cost around US$30 to US$40 (per person per day) by motorbike, or in a car it's around US$65 to US$80. Tam also offers an excellent evening street-food tour (US$20).

DMZ Tours MILITARY, ADVENTURE
(0914 017 835; www.dmztours.net; 113 Le Loi St) Quality DMZ tours. Prices start at US$118 (two people) for a day's touring around the main war sites in a car.

Sepon Travel MILITARY, TRANSPORT
(385 5289; www.sepontour.com; 189 Đ Le Duan) Tours of the DMZ by car and with English-speaking drivers.

Sleeping

Violet Hotel HOTEL $
(053-358 2959; Đ Ba Trieu; s 200,000d, d & tw 250,000-330,000d;) Represents outstanding value, with inviting modern rooms all with minibar, TV, fan and air-con; some also have rice-paddy views and a balcony. In a quiet location 1km from the centre.

Huu Nghi Hotel HOTEL $
(053-385 2361; www.huunghihotel.com.vn; 68 Đ Tran Hung Dao; r from 450,000d;) Spacious, inviting rooms all with smart furnishings including wardrobe, reading light, bed with comfortable mattress and flat-screen TV – some also have commanding river views. Breakfast is included.

DMZ Hotel HOTEL $
(053-356 0757; 50 Ly Thuong Kiet; r 200,000d; @) Well-priced rooms with cable TV and minibar.

Saigon Quang Binh HOTEL $$
(053-382 2276; www.sgquangbinhtourist.com.vn; 20 Quach Xuan Ky; r 1,600,000-1,900,000d;) The fanciest place in town has a great riverside location, smart rooms and good online specials. The rooftop bar-cafe or the new pool area are top spots for a beer or a coffee even if you're not staying here.

Eating & Drinking

Dong Ha is famous for seafood. Head to the strip of riverside restaurants on Đ Hoang Dieu for wonderful *cua rang me* (crab in tamarind sauce), *vem nuong* (grilled clams) and steamed or roasted squid. There's another group of places opposite the Violet Hotel for Vietnamese meat and seafood. Try the amazing roast suckling pig.

Tam's Cafe CAFE $
(http://tamscafe.jimdo.com; 211 Đ Ba Trieu; meals US$2-3; 7am-6pm;) Vietnamese food and pizza, smoothies and juices. It's run by the ever-helpful Tam, a switched-on, fluent English speaker who works tirelessly to help travellers, offering inexpensive tours and independent travel advice. The cafe employs and supports deaf people. At the time of

GETTING TO LAOS: DONG HA TO SAVANNAKHET

Getting to the border The **Lao Bao/Dansavanh border crossing**, on the Sepon River (Song Xe Pon), is one of the most popular and least problematic border crossings between Laos and Vietnam. Buses to Savannakhet in Laos run from Hue via Dong Ha and Lao Bao. From Hue, there's a 7am air-con bus (350,000d, 9½ hours), on odd days only, that stops in Dong Ha at the Sepon Travel office around 8.30am to pick up more passengers. It's also easy to cross the border on your own; Dong Ha is the gateway. Buses leave the town to Lao Bao (55,000d, two hours) roughly every 15 minutes. From here *xe om* charge 15,000d to the border. You can check schedules and book tickets at Tam's Cafe. Tam's also book tickets to Vientiane (14 hours), Thakhek (10 hours) and Pakse (10 hours). It's not possible to cross on motorbikes from Vietnam at the Lao Bao border.

At the border The border posts (open 7am to 6pm) are a few hundred metres apart. Lao visas are available on arrival, but Vietnamese visas need to be arranged in advance. There are several serviceable hotels on the Vietnamese side. Try not to change currency in Lao Bao: money-changers offer terrible rates.

Moving on *Songthaew* head regularly to Sepon, from where you can get a bus or another *songthaew* to Savannakhet.

writing Tam was looking to add a hostel to his setup in early 2017. Check the website for the latest.

Once his hostel's up and running, he'll pick you up for free if you advise him of your arrival one day prior.

Information

For impartial travel and tourist information and a useful city map, head to Tam's Cafe.

Getting There & Away

BUS

Dong Ha bus station (Ben Xe Khach Dong Ha; 053-385 1488; 68 Đ Le Duan) is near the intersection of Hwys 1 and 9. Buses to Dong Hoi (58,000d, two hours), Hue (46,000d, 1½ hours), Danang (75,000d, 3½ hours), Khe Sanh (30,000d, 1½ hours) and Lao Bao (55,000d, two hours) depart regularly. Buses are advertised to Savannakhet in Laos, but the station won't book tickets for foreigners. **Mekong Travel** (68 Đ Le Duan; 9am-6pm) and Tam's Cafe (p173) will.

For Phong Nha, there are also three daily minibus connections (120,000d) to Son Trach village at noon, 1pm and 5pm. At 6.30pm, the Hung Thanh company runs a sleeper bus service (160,000d) to Easy Tiger hostel, located in Son Trach.

Check all transport schedules at Tam's Cafe.

CAR & MOTORCYCLE

A one-way car trip to the Lao Bao border will set you back US$60. Motorbikes can be hired from US$6 per day.

TRAIN

Dong Ha's **train station** (Ga Dong Ha; 2 Đ Le Thanh Ton), 2km south of the Hwy 1 bridge, has trains to destinations including Hanoi (sleeper from 65,000d, 11 to 14 hours, five daily), Dong Hoi (from 65,000d, 1½ to 2½ hours, six daily) and Hue (from 50,000d, 1½ to 2½ hours, six daily).

Quang Tri

053 / POP 28,600

Quang Tri once boasted an important citadel, but little of its old glory remains. In the Easter Offensive of 1972, North Vietnamese forces laid siege to and then captured the town. This provoked carpet bombing and artillery shelling by the USA and South Vietnamese forces, which all but destroyed Quang Tri.

Remnants of the ancient moat, ramparts and gates of the **citadel** remain. It's off Đ Tran Hung Dao, 1.6km north of Hwy 1.

Outside Quang Tri, along Hwy 1 towards Hue, is the skeleton of **Long Hung Church**. It bears countless bullet holes and mortar damage from the 1972 bombardment.

The **bus station** (Đ Tran Hung Dao) is about 1km from Hwy 1, but buses can also be flagged down on the highway.

Hue

054 / POP 361,000

Pronounced 'Hway', this deeply evocative capital of the Nguyen emperors still resonates with the glories of imperial Vietnam, even though many of its finest buildings were destroyed during the American War.

Hue owes its charm partly to its location on the Perfume River – picturesque on a clear day, atmospheric even in less flattering weather. Today the city blends new and old as sleek modern hotels tower over crumbling century-old Citadel walls.

Journalist Gavin Young's 1997 memoir, *A Wavering Grace*, is a moving account of his 30-year relationship with a family from Hue, and is a fine literary companion to the city.

A few touts are a minor hassle, but Hue remains a tranquil, conservative city, and only a few bars open late.

History

In 1802, Emperor Gia Long founded the Nguyen dynasty, moved the capital from Hanoi to Hue in an effort to unite northern and southern Vietnam, and commenced the building of the Citadel. The city prospered, but its rulers struggled to counter the growing influence of France.

In 1885, French forces responded to a Vietnamese attack by storming the Citadel, burning the imperial library and removing every object of value. The emperors continued to reside in Hue, but were excluded from events of national importance.

In 1968, the attention again shifted to Hue during the Tet Offensive. While the Americans concentrated on holding Khe Sanh, North Vietnamese and Viet Cong (VC) forces seized Hue, an audacious assault that commanded headlines across the globe.

During the 3½ weeks that the North controlled the Citadel, more than 2500 people (ARVN soldiers, wealthy merchants, government workers, monks, priests and intellectuals) were killed. The North called them 'lackeys who owed blood debts'. The USA and South Vietnamese responded by levelling whole neighbourhoods, battering the Citadel and even using napalm on the imperial palace. Approximately 10,000 people died in Hue, including thousands of VC troops, 400 South Vietnamese soldiers and 150 US Marines – but most of those killed were civilians.

Sights

Most of Hue's principal sights lie within the moats of its Citadel and Imperial Enclosure. Other museums and pagodas are dotted around the city. The royal tombs are south of Hue.

Inside the Citadel

Built between 1804 and 1833, the Citadel (Kinh Thanh) is still the heart of Hue. Heavily fortified, it consists of 2m-thick, 10km-long walls, a moat (30m across and 4m deep) and 10 gateways.

The Citadel has distinct sections. The Imperial Enclosure and Forbidden Purple City formed the epicentre of Vietnamese royal life. On the southwestern side were temple compounds. There were residences in the northwest, gardens in the northeast and in the north, the Mang Ca Fortress (still a military base).

Note that if you're planning on also visiting the Royal Tombs, combination tickets including the Citadel and the tombs are available.

★ Imperial Enclosure HISTORIC SITE

(adult/child 150,000/30,000d; ⏲7am-5.30pm)

The Imperial Enclosure is a citadel-within-a-citadel, housing the emperor's residence, temples and palaces and the main buildings of state within 6m-high, 2.5km-long walls. What's left is only a fraction of the original – the enclosure was badly bombed during the French and American wars, and only 20 of its 148 buildings survived. This is a fascinating site easily worth half a day, but poor signage can make navigation a bit difficult. Restoration and reconstruction is ongoing.

Expect a lot of broken masonry, rubble, cracked tiling and weeds as you work your way around. Nevertheless it's enjoyable as a leisurely stroll and some of the less-visited areas are highly atmospheric. There are little cafes and souvenir stands dotted around.

It's best to approach the sights starting from Ngo Mon Gate and moving anticlockwise around the enclosure.

➡ Ngo Mon Gate

The principal entrance to the Imperial Enclosure is Ngo Mon Gate, which faces the Flag Tower. The central passageway with its yellow doors was reserved for the use of the emperor, as was the bridge across the lotus pond. Others had to use the gates to either side and the paths around the pond. On top of the gate is Ngu Phung (Belvedere of the Five Phoenixes); on its upper level is a huge drum and bell.

The emperor appeared here on important occasions, most notably for the promulgation of the lunar calendar. On 30 August

Hue

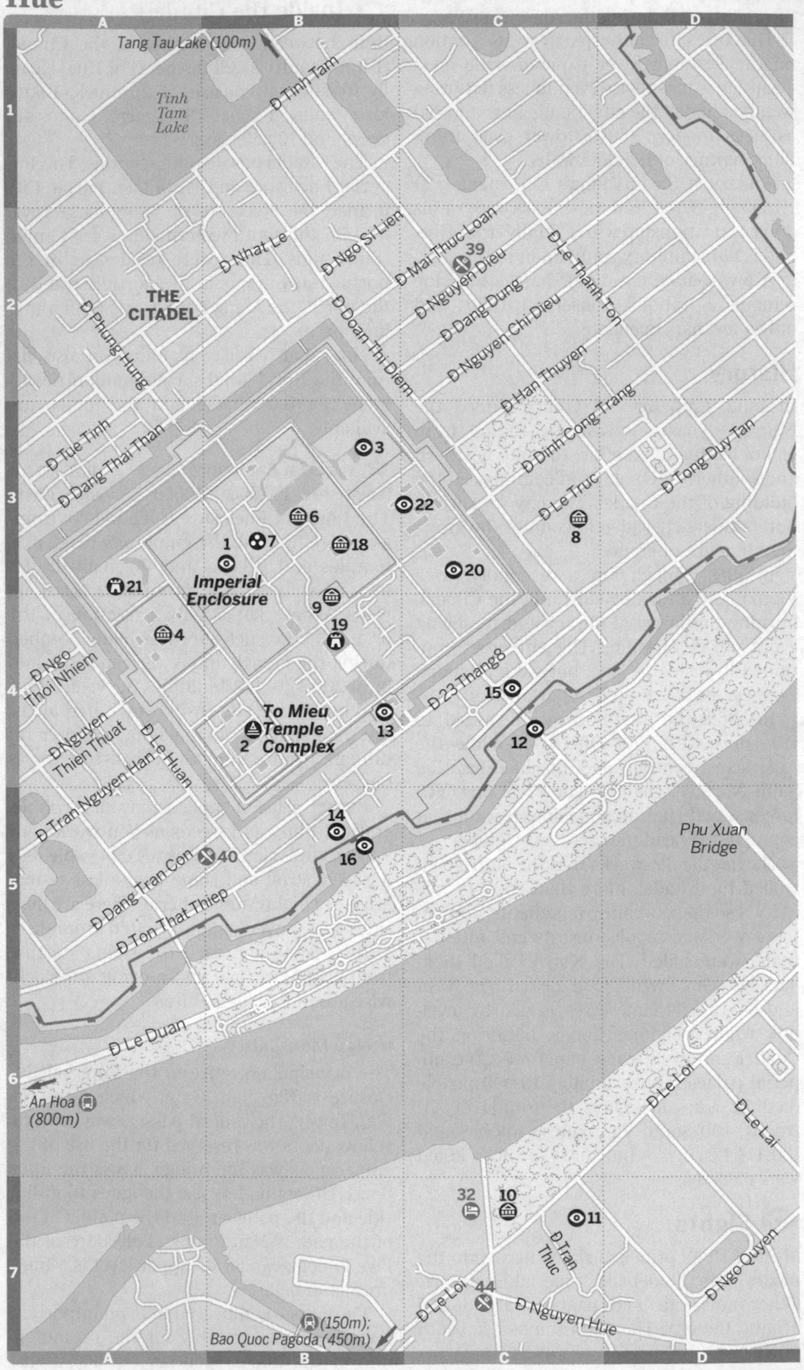

Tang Tau Lake (100m)
Tinh Tam Lake
Đ Tinh Tam
THE CITADEL
Đ Nhat Le
Đ Ngo Si Lien
Đ Mai Thuc Loan
Đ Nguyen Dieu
Đ Le Thanh Ton
Đ Dang Dung
Đ Nguyen Chi Dieu
Đ Doan Thi Diem
Đ Phung Hung
Đ Han Thuyen
Đ Dinh Cong Trang
Đ Tong Duy Tan
Đ Le Truc
Đ Tue Tinh
Đ Dang Thai Than
Imperial Enclosure
To Mieu Temple Complex
Đ Ngo Thoi Nhiem
Đ Nguyen Thien Thuat
Đ Le Huan
Đ Tran Nguyen Han
Đ 23 Thang8
Đ Dang Tran Con
Đ Ton That Thiep
Phu Xuan Bridge
Đ Le Duan
An Hoa (800m)
Đ Le Loi
Đ Le Lai
Đ Tran Thuc
Đ Ngo Quyen
Đ Nguyen Hue
(150m); Bao Quoc Pagoda (450m)

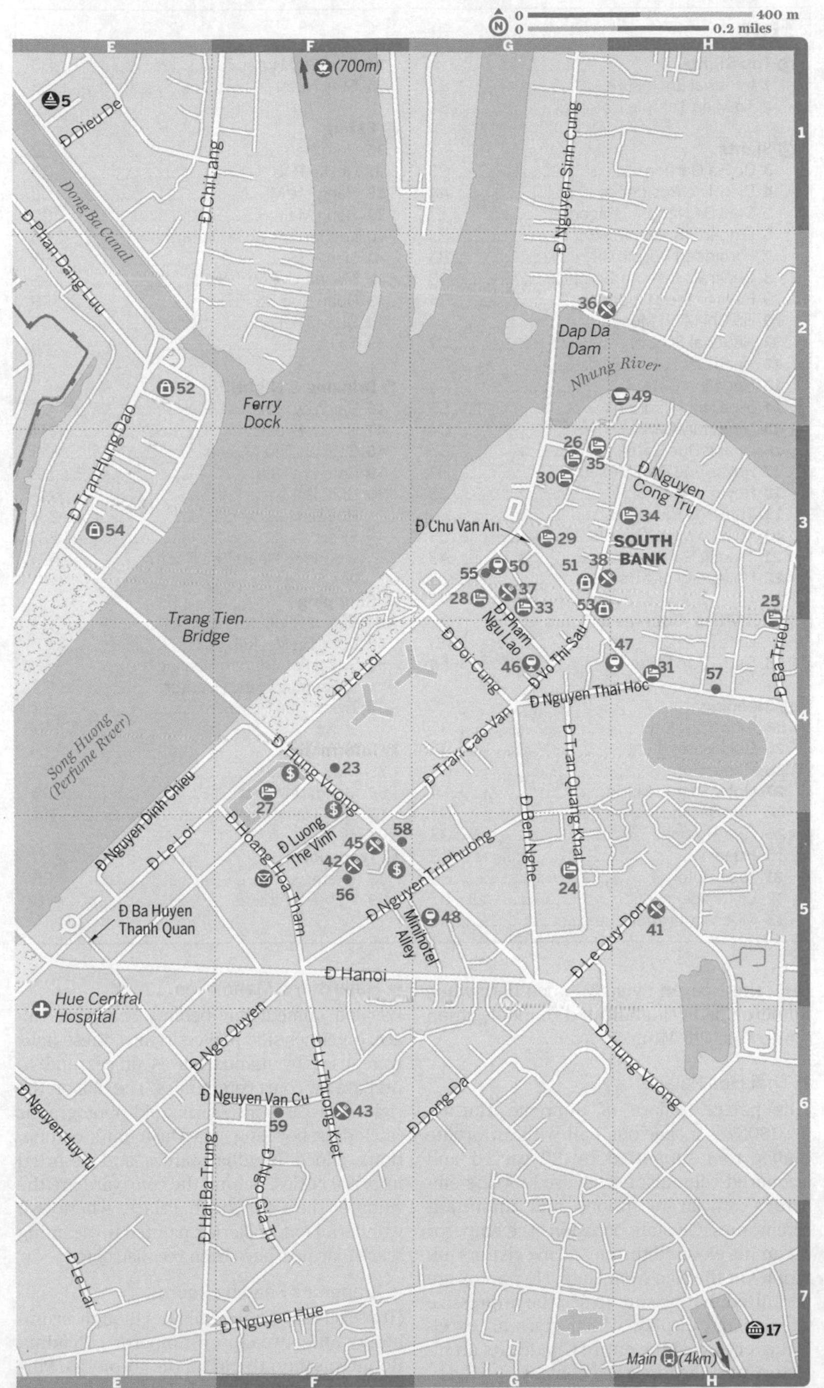

0 400 m
0 0.2 miles
(700m)
Đ Dieu De
Dong Ba Canal
Đ Phan Dang Luu
Đ Chi Lang
Đ Nguyen Sinh Cung
Dap Da Dam
Nhung River
Ferry Dock
Đ Tran Hung Dao
Đ Nguyen Cong Tru
Đ Chu Van An
SOUTH BANK
Trang Tien Bridge
Đ Pham Ngu Lao
Đ Doi Cung
Đ Vo Thi Sau
Đ Le Loi
Đ Nguyen Thai Hoc
Đ Ba Trieu
Song Huong (Perfume River)
Đ Hung Vuong
Đ Tran Cao Van
Đ Tran Quang Khai
Đ Nguyen Dinh Chieu
Đ Le Loi
Đ Hoang Hoa Tham
Đ Luong The Vinh
Đ Ben Nghe
Đ Nguyen Tri Phuong
Minihotel Alley
Đ Ba Huyen Thanh Quan
Đ Le Quy Don
Đ Hanoi
Hue Central Hospital
Đ Ngo Quyen
Đ Hung Vuong
Đ Nguyen Van Cu
Đ Ly Thuong Kiet
Đ Dong Da
Đ Nguyen Huy Tu
Đ Hai Ba Trung
Đ Ngo Gia Tu
Đ Le Lai
Đ Nguyen Hue
Main (4km)

Hue

Top Sights
1 Imperial Enclosure ... B3
2 To Mieu Temple Complex ... B4

Sights
3 Co Ha Gardens ... B3
4 Dien Tho Residence ... A4
5 Dieu De National Pagoda ... E1
6 Emperor's Reading Room ... B3
7 Forbidden Purple City ... B3
8 General Museum Complex ... C3
9 Halls of the Mandarins ... B4
10 Ho Chi Minh Museum ... C7
11 National School ... C7
12 Ngan Gate ... C4
13 Ngo Mon Gate ... B4
14 Nine Holy Cannons ... B5
15 Nine Holy Cannons ... C4
16 Quang Duc Gate ... B5
17 Royal Fine Arts Museum ... H7
18 Royal Theatre ... B3
19 Thai Hoa Palace ... B4
20 Thai To Mieu Temple Complex ... C3
21 Truong San Residence ... A3
22 University of Arts ... C3

Activities, Courses & Tours
Cafe on Thu Wheels ... (see 48)
23 Stop & Go Café ... F4

Sleeping
24 Alba Spa Hotel ... G5
25 Gold Hotel ... H3
26 Home Hotel ... G3
27 Hotel Saigon Morin ... F4
28 Hue Backpackers ... G3
29 Hue Thuong ... G3
30 Huenino ... G3
31 Jade Hotel ... H4
32 La Residence ... C7
33 Moonlight Hotel Hue ... G3
34 Star City Hotel ... H3
35 Stay Hotel ... G3

Eating
36 Com Hen ... G2
37 Gecko Pub ... G3
38 Hang Me Me ... G3
39 Hong Mai ... C2
40 Les Jardins de la Carambole ... B5
41 Lien Hoa ... H5
42 Mandarin Café ... F5
43 Quan Bun Bo Hue ... F6
44 Quan Thai Phu ... C7
45 Ta.ke ... F5

Drinking & Nightlife
46 Bar Why Not? ... G4
47 Brown Eyes ... H4
48 Café on Thu Wheels ... G5
49 Cafe Tre Nga ... H2
50 DMZ Bar ... G3
Hue Backpackers ... (see 28)
Sirius ... (see 28)
Wounded Heart Tea Room ... (see 53)

Shopping
51 Blue de Hue ... G3
52 Dong Ba Market ... E2
53 Spiral Foundation Healing the Wounded Heart Center ... G3
54 Trang Tien Plaza ... E3

Information
55 DMZ Travel ... G3
56 Mandarin Café ... F5
57 Sinh Tourist ... H4

Transport
58 Jetstar ... F5
59 Vietnam Airlines ... F6

1945, the Nguyen dynasty ended here when Emperor Bao Dai abdicated to a delegation sent by Ho Chi Minh.

Thai Hoa Palace

This palace (Palace of Supreme Harmony; 1803) is a spacious hall with an ornate timber roof supported by 80 carved and lacquered columns. It was used for the emperor's official receptions and important ceremonies. On state occasions the emperor sat on his elevated throne, facing visitors entering via the Ngo Mon Gate. No photos are permitted, but be sure to see the impressive audio-visual display, which gives an excellent overview of the entire Citadel, its architecture and the historical context.

Halls of the Mandarins

Located immediately behind Thai Hoa Palace, on either side of a courtyard, these halls were used by mandarins as offices and to prepare for court ceremonies. The hall on the right showcases fascinating old photographs (including boy-king Vua Duya Tan's coronation), gilded Buddha statues and assorted imperial curios. Behind the courtyard are the ruins of the Can Chanh Palace, where two wonderful long galleries, painted in gleaming scarlet lacquer have been reconstructed.

Emperor's Reading Room

(Thai Binh Lau) The exquisite (though crumbling) little two-storey Emperor's Reading Room was the only part of the Forbidden Purple City to escape damage during the French reoccupation of Hue in 1947. It's currently being renovated and not open to visitors, but it's worth checking out the Gaudí-esque roof mosaics.

➡ **Royal Theatre**

(Duyen Thi Duong; ☎054-351 4989; www.nhanhac.com.vn; performances 50,000-100,000d; ⏱performances 9am, 10am, 2.30pm & 3.30pm) The Royal Theatre, begun in 1826 and later home to the National Conservatory of Music, has been rebuilt on its former foundations. Cultural performances here last 45 minutes.

Southeast of here almost nothing remains of the **Thai To Mieu temple complex** (it's now a plant nursery) and former **University of Arts**.

➡ **Co Ha Gardens**

Occupying the northeast corner of the Imperial Enclosure, these delightful gardens were developed by the first four emperors of the Nguyen dynasty but fell into disrepair. They've been beautifully recreated in the last few years, and are dotted with little gazebo-style pavilions and ponds. This is one of the most peaceful spots in the entire Citadel, and was undergoing further careful renovation when we last visited.

➡ **Forbidden Purple City**

(Tu Cam Thanh) In the very centre of the Imperial Enclosure, there's almost nothing left of the once-magnificent Forbidden Purple City. This was a citadel-within-a-citadel-within-a-citadel and was reserved solely for the personal use of the emperor – the only servants allowed into this compound were eunuchs who would pose no threat to the royal concubines. The Forbidden Purple City was almost entirely destroyed in the wars, and its crumbling remains are now overgrown with weeds.

➡ **Truong San Residence**

In 1844, Emperor Thieu Tri described this as one of Hue's most beautiful spots, but it was devastated by war. Check out the entrance gate with prancing dragons and phoenixes, and the oval moat. The exterior has been restored, while the interior remains empty, except for its elaborate columns and tiles.

➡ **Dien Tho Residence**

The stunning, partially ruined Dien Tho Residence (1804) once comprised the apartments and audience hall of the Queen Mothers of the Nguyen dynasty. The audience hall houses an exhibition of photos illustrating its former use, and there is a display of embroidered royal garments. Just outside a pleasure pavilion above a lily pond has been transformed into a cafe worthy of a refreshment stop.

➡ ★ **To Mieu Temple Complex**

Taking up the southwest corner of the Imperial Enclosure, this highly impressive walled complex has been beautifully restored. The imposing three-tiered **Hien Lam Pavilion** sits on the south side of the complex, dating from 1824. On the other side of a courtyard is the solemn **To Mieu Temple**, housing shrines to each of the emperors, topped by their photos. Between these two temples are **Nine Dynastic Urns** *(dinh)*, cast between 1835 and 1836, each dedicated to one Nguyen sovereign.

About 2m in height and weighing 1900kg to 2600kg each, the urns symbolise the power and stability of the Nguyen throne. The central urn, also the largest and most ornate, is dedicated to dynasty founder Gia Long. Also in the courtyard are two dragons, trapped in what look like red phone boxes.

On the north side of the complex, a gate leads into a small walled enclosure that houses the **Hung To Mieu Temple**, a reconstruction of the 1804 original, built to honour Gia Long's parents.

➡ **Nine Holy Cannons**

Located just inside the Citadel ramparts, near the gates to either side of the Flag Tower, are the Nine Holy Cannons (1804), symbolic protectors of the palace and kingdom. Commissioned by Emperor Gia Long, they were never intended to be fired. The **four cannons** near **Ngan Gate** represent the four seasons, while the **five cannons** next to **Quang Duc Gate** represent the five elements: metal, wood, water, fire and earth.

Each brass cannon is 5m long and weighs about 10 tonnes.

Outside the Citadel

Dieu De National Pagoda BUDDHIST TEMPLE

(Quoc Tu Dieu De; 102 Đ Bach Dang) FREE Overlooking Dong Ba Canal, this pagoda was built under Emperor Thieu Tri's rule (1841–47) and is famous for its four low towers, one either side of the gate, and two flanking the sanctuary. The pavilions on either side of the main sanctuary entrance contain the 18 La Ha, whose rank is just below that

Hue's Imperial Enclosure

EXPLORING THE SITE

An incongruous combination of meticulously restored palaces and pagodas, ruins and rubble, the Imperial Enclosure is approached from the south through the outer walls of the Citadel. It's best to tackle the site as a walking tour, winding your way around the structures in an anticlockwise direction.

You'll pass directly through the monumental **Ngo Mon Gateway** ❶ where the ticket office is located. This dramatic approach quickens the pulse and adds to the sense of occasion as you enter this citadel-within-a-citadel. Directly ahead is the **Thai Hoa Palace** ❷ where the emperor would greet offical visitors from his elevated throne. Continuing north you'll step across a small courtyard to the twin **Halls of the Mandarins** ❸, where mandarins once had their offices and prepared for ceremonial occasions.

To the northeast is the Royal Theatre, where traditional dance performances are held several times daily. Next you'll be able to get a glimpse of the Emperor's Reading Room built by Thieu Tri and used as a place of retreat. Just east of here are the lovely Co Ha Gardens. Wander their pathways, dotted with hundreds of bonsai trees and potted plants, which have been recently restored.

Guarding the far north of the complex is the Tu Vo Phuong Pavilion, from where you can follow a moat to the Truong San residence and then loop back south via the **Dien Tho Residence** ❹ and finally view the beautifully restored temple compound of To Mieu, perhaps the most rewarding part of the entire enclosure to visit, including its fabulous **Nine Dynastic Urns** ❺.

TOP TIPS

Allow half a day to explore the Citadel. Drink vendors are dotted around the site, but the best places to take a break are the delightful Co Ha Gardens, the Tu Vo Phuong Pavilion and the Dien Tho Residence (the latter two also serve food).

Dien Tho Residence
This pretty corner of the complex, with its low structures and pond, was the residence of many Queen Mothers. The earliest structures here date from 1804.

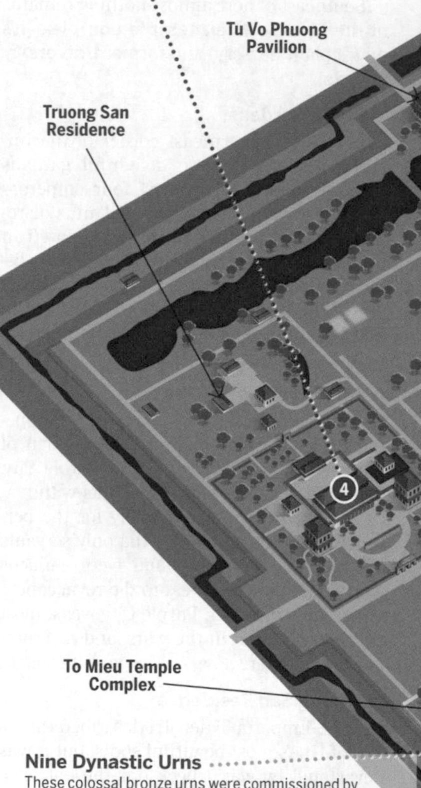

Nine Dynastic Urns
These colossal bronze urns were commissioned by Emperor Minh Mang and cast between 1835 and 1836. They're embellished with decorative elements including landscapes, rivers, flowers and animals.

Tu Vo Phuong Pavilion

The two-storey Tu Vo Phuong Pavilion, elevated above a moat, was once a defense bastion for the northern part of the Imperial Enclosure. It combines both European and Vietnamese architectural styles (note the elaborate roof dragons).

Halls of the Mandarins

Unesco-sponsored conservation work is ongoing in the eastern hall here to preserve the elaborate ceiling and wall murals.

MICHAEL RUNKEL / GETTY IMAGES ©

Emperor's Reading Room

Co Ha Gardens

Royal Theatre

3

2

1

5

Ngo Mon Gateway

A huge, grandiose structure that guards the main approach to the Imperial Enclosure, this gateway has a fortified lower level and a more architecturally elaborate upper part. It dates from 1833.

ANDERS BLOMQVIST / GETTY IMAGES ©

Thai Hoa Palace

Be sure to check out this palace's incredible ironwood columns, painted in 12 coats of brilliant scarlet and gold lacquer. The structure was saved from collapse by restoration work in the 1990s.

SAMI SARKIS / GETTY IMAGES ©

of Bodhisattva, and the eight Kim Cang, protectors of Buddha. In the back row of the main dais is Thich Ca Buddha, flanked by two assistants.

Dieu De was a stronghold of Buddhist and student opposition to the South Vietnamese government and the American War, and many arrests were made here when police stormed the building in 1966.

Royal Fine Arts Museum MUSEUM
(150 Đ Nguyen Hue; 6.30am-5.30pm summer, 7am-5pm winter) FREE This recently renovated museum is located in the baroque-influenced An Dinh Palace, commissioned by Emperor Khai Dinh in 1918 and full of elaborate murals, floral motifs and *trompe l'œil* details. Emperor Bao Dai lived here with his family after abdicating in 1945. Inside, you'll find some outstanding ceramics, paintings, furniture, silverware, porcelain and royal clothing, though information is a little lacking.

Bao Quoc Pagoda BUDDHIST TEMPLE
(Ham Long Hill) FREE Founded in 1670, this hilltop pagoda is on the southern bank of the Perfume River and has a striking triple-gated entrance reached via a wide staircase. On the right is a centre for training monks, which has been functioning since 1940.

General Museum Complex MUSEUM
(Đ 23 Thang 8; admission 15,000d; 7-11am & 1.30-4.30pm Tue-Sun) Formerly a school for princes and the sons of high-ranking mandarins, this slightly rundown complex has a pagoda devoted to archaeology, a small **Natural History Museum** and a building with exhibitions about anticolonial resistance. In the grounds are a variety of military aircraft and vehicles, both Vietnamese and American.

National School NOTABLE BUILDING
(Truong Quoc Hoc; 10 Đ Le Loi; 11.30am-1pm & from 5pm) One of the most famous secondary schools in Vietnam, the National School was founded in 1896. Its former pupils include General Vo Nguyen Giap and Ho Chi Minh (who attended for a year in 1908). You can visit the school during lunch break and after classes finish.

Ho Chi Minh Museum MUSEUM
(7 Đ Le Loi; 7-11am & 1.30-4pm Tue-Sun) FREE The father of the modern Vietnamese nation spent 10 years in Hue, and you'll find some intriguing photographs as well as a collection of certificates and medals here. There's very little information in English though.

Tang Tau Lake LAKE
(Đ Dien Tien Hoang) An island on Tang Tau Lake, which is northeast of Tinh Tam Lake, was once the site of a royal library. It is now occupied by the small **Ngoc Huong Pagoda**.

Tours

Stop & Go Café TOUR
(054-382 7051; www.stopandgo-hue.com; 3 Đ Hung Vuong) Personalised motorbike and car tours. A full-day DMZ car tour guided by a Vietnamese vet costs around US$27 per person for four people, representing a good deal. Guided trips to Hoi An stopping at beaches are also recommended.

Cafe on Thu Wheels TOUR
(054-383 2241; minhthuhue@yahoo.com; 10/2 Đ Nguyen Tri Phuong) Inexpensive cycle hire, and motorbike, minibus and car tours around Hue and the DMZ. Can also arrange transfers to Hoi An by motorbike (US$45) or car (US$55).

Hue Flavor TOUR
(0905 937 006; www.hueflavor.com; per person US$45) Excellent street-food tours exploring

PERFUME RIVER BOAT TRIPS

Many sights around Hue, including Thien Mu Pagoda and several of the Royal Tombs, can be reached by boat via the Perfume River.

Most hotels and travellers' cafes offer shared day tours from US$5 to US$20 per person. Better ones start with a morning river cruise, stopping at pagodas and temples, then after lunch a minibus travels to the main tombs before returning to Hue. On the cheaper options you'll often have to hire a motorbike to get from the moorings to the tombs, or walk in tropical heat.

At the moorings on the south side of the river you can theorectically negotiate your own route. Rates for chartering a boat start at US$10 for an hour's cruise, but these boats are slow. A full day is needed for the more impressive, distant tombs. Be clear on your requirements, preferably in writing.

the delights of Hue cuisine. Transport is by *cyclo* and around 15 different dishes are sampled across four hours.

Ton That Quy TOUR

(☎093 578 2533; www.vietnammotortrail.com) Quy is a friendly and trustworthy motorbike guide who can arrange scenic transfers via the Hai Van Pass to Hoi An, local sightseeing around Hue and the DMZ, and longer trips exploring all parts of Vietnam.

Tran Van Thinh TOUR

(☎0905 731 537; tranvanthinhhue@yahoo.com) Knowledgeable local motorbike guide who can arrange local city tours and explorations of the royal tombs. Thinh is a long-time resident of Hue and speaks excellent English.

Oriental Sky Travel ADVENTURE TOUR

(☎0985 555 827; www.orientalskytravel.com) Helmed by the experienced and friendly Shi, this tour company can arrange active trips including hiking and a zipline in Bach Ma National Park, and also mountain biking, kayaking and caving around Phong Nha National Park and the DMZ. Ask about accommodation at the Chay Lap village homestay near Phong Nha.

Festivals

Festival of Hue FESTIVAL

(www.huefestival.com; ⏲late Apr-early May) Held in even-numbered years (next in 2018), this biennial arts festival features local and international artists and performers.

Sleeping

Hue accommodation rates are well below Hanoi or HCMC. The main tourist enclave is between Đ Le Loi and Đ Vo Thi Sau, and other good options are along Đ Nguyen Cong Tru.

★Home Hotel HOTEL $

(☎054-383 0014; www.huehomehotel.com; 8 Đ Nguyen Cong Tru; r US$16-25; ❄@🛜) Run by a really friendly team, the welcoming Home Hotel has a younger, hip vibe, and spacious rooms arrayed across several levels. Ask to book a room looking over Đ Nguyen Cong Tru for a compact balcony, French doors and views of the river. No lift.

Huenino GUESTHOUSE $

(☎054-625 2171; www.hueninohotel.com; 14 Đ Nguyen Cong Tru; r US$18-25; ⊖❄@🛜) Family-owned, this warm, welcoming guesthouse has an artistic flavour with stylish furniture, artwork and smallish rooms with minibar, cable TV and good-quality beds. A generous breakfast is included.

Stay Hotel HOTEL $

(☎054-3823 999; www.stayhotelhue.com; 7 Đ Nguyen Cong Tru; dm US$7, d US$14-24; ❄@🛜) Stay Hotel is a new opening in the up-and-coming accommodation scene along Đ Nguyen Cong Tru. Rooms are decorated with colourful art, breakast is offered in a stylish dining area, and some rooms have river views.

Jade Hotel GUESTHOUSE $

(☎054-393 8849; http://jadehotelhue.com; 17 Đ Nguyen Thai Hoc; r US$17-30; ⊖❄@🛜) You'll find simply excellent service standards at this fine place; staff are very sweet and welcoming indeed. Rooms enjoy soft comfy mattresses and there's a nice lobby-lounge for hanging out.

Star City Hotel HOTEL $

(☎054-383 1358; http://starcityhotelhue.com; 2/36 Đ Vo Thi Sau; r US$14-18; ❄@🛜) Offering really cheap rates, this five-storey hotel has a lift, and clean, spacious rooms, all with TV and air-con. It's set off the street so traffic noise isn't an issue.

Hue Thuong HOTEL $

(☎054-388 3793; www.huethuonghotel.com; 11 Đ Chu Van An; r US$15-25; ❄@🛜) A great little minihotel, where the rooms, though smallish, have a real sparkle and are very well presented – all come with purple and white linen and attractive furniture.

Hue Backpackers HOSTEL $

(☎054-382 6567; www.vietnambackpackerhostels.com; 10 Đ Pham Ngu Lao; dm US$8-12, r US$18; ❄@🛜) Backpackers' mecca thanks to its central location, eager-to-please staff, good info and sociable bar-restaurant. Dorms are well designed and have air-con and lockers.

★Alba Spa Hotel BOUTIQUE HOTEL $$

(☎054-382 8444; www.albaboutiquehotels.com; 29 Đ Tran Quang Khai; r US$55-85; ❄🛜≋) This lovely new hotel combines cool and classy rooms with a spa centre downstairs. The compact indoor pool is nice for relaxing after a spa treatment, and the breakfast spread – including local Hue culinary specialities – is one of the city's best. The hotel's location is in a quiet backstreet, just a short walk from all the action.

★Tam Tinh Vien BOUTIQUE HOTEL **$$**

(☎054-3519 990; www.huehomestay.wevina.vn; Long Ha village; r US$40; ❄@📶🏊) Around 6km from Hue in Long Ha village, Tam Tinh Vien is called a homestay, but is really a delightful boutique guesthouse. Arrayed around a small pool and verdant garden, spacious villas with four-poster beds are imbued with a chic Asian aesthetic. Borrow a bike to make the 30-minute journey into Hue – a taxi is 100,000d.

Moonlight Hotel Hue HOTEL **$$**

(☎054-397 9797; www.moonlighthue.com; 20 Đ Pham Ngu Lao; r US$50-75, ste US$80-135; 🚭❄@📶🏊) A 'new generation' Hue hotel where the rooms boast a very high spec for the modest bucks charged, all with polished wooden floors, marble-clad bathrooms (with tubs) and lavish furnishings. Pay a bit more for a balcony with a Perfume River view. The pool area is small and covered, and there are good rooftop drinks in the Sirius bar.

Gold Hotel HOTEL **$$**

(☎054-381 4815; www.goldhotelhue.com; 28 Đ Ba Trieu; r US$42-51, ste US$72-92; ❄@📶🏊) Impressive hotel a short walk or *cyclo* (pedicab) ride from the river. It has a main restaurant area and immaculately presented modern rooms with superb bathrooms (all have tubs). It's efficiently run and excellent value, though the pool area is a bit of an afterthought.

La Residence HOTEL **$$$**

(☎054-383 7475; www.la-residence-hue.com; 5 Đ Le Loi; r from US$145; 🚭❄@📶🏊) Once the French governor's residence, this wonderful hotel resonates with art-deco class, with its original features and period detailing. A frangipani-lined path leads down to the 30m pool, from where you can gaze over the Perfume River. Rooms are sumptuously appointed, the restaurants are excellent, and service is polished and professional.

Pilgrimage Village RESORT **$$$**

(☎054-388 5461; www.pilgrimagevillage.com; 130 Đ Minh Mang; r/bungalows from US$155/230; 🚭❄@📶🏊) Designed around a verdant valley that includes a 40m pool, lotus ponds and a spa and yoga space, this is a thoroughly relaxing, luxury eco-retreat. Rooms are all supremely comfortable, but for the ultimate experience book a bungalow with a private plunge pool. There's a fine restaurant, lovely breakfast room and bar. Located about 3km from the centre of Hue.

Hotel Saigon Morin HOTEL **$$$**

(☎054-382 3526; www.morinhotel.com.vn; 30 Đ Le Loi; r/ste from US$100/170; 🚭❄@📶🏊) Built in 1901, this was the first hotel in central Vietnam and once the hub of French colonial life in Hue. The building is very classy, with accommodation set around two inner courtyards and a small pool. Rooms are grand and beautifully presented, with plush carpets and period detail.

Eating

We have the famed fussy eater Emperor Tu Duc to thank for the culinary variety of Hue.

Royal rice cakes, the most common are *banh khoai*, are worth seeking out. Other local variations are *banh beo, banh loc, banh it* and *banh nam*.

Vegetarian food has a long tradition in Hue. Stalls in Dong Ba Market serve it the first and 15th days of the lunar month. Hue also has great street food. Follow our recommendations or join a street-food tour with Hue Flavor (p182).

Hang Me Me VIETNAMESE **$**

(16 Đ Vo Thi Sau; snacks from 20,000d) A top spot to try Hue's dizzying menu of royal rice cakes. Serving portions are pretty big, so rustle up a few friends to try the different variations. Our favourite is the *banh beo*, perfect little mouthfuls topped with scallions and dried shrimp.

Com Hen VIETNAMESE **$**

(17 Đ Han Mac Tu; meals from 10,000d; ⏰7am-11pm) Tuck into bowls of rice *(com hen)* or noodles *(bun hen)* combining fresh herbs and tasty local clams from a nearby island in the middle of the Perfume River. Servings are fairly small, so maybe have a bowl of each.

Lien Hoa VEGETARIAN **$**

(3 Đ Le Quy Don; meals 50,000-75,000d; ⏰6.30am-9.30pm; 🌿) No-nonsense Viet vegetarian restaurant renowned for filling food at bargain prices. Fresh *banh beo*, noodle dishes, crispy fried jackfruit and aubergine with ginger all deliver. The menu has very rough English translations to help you order (staff speak little or no English).

Hong Mai VIETNAMESE **$**

(110 Đ Dinh Tien Toang; snacks from 20,000d; ⏰11am-8pm) After you've admired the Citadel, make your way to this excellent Vietnamese eatery for superior versions of two local street-food classics. The *banh khoai*

(rice crepes filled with pork and shrimp) are light and crammed with bean sprouts, and the *nem lui* (minced pork grilled on lemongrass sticks) go perfectly with a chilled Huda lager.

Quan Thai Phu VIETNAMESE $

(2 Đ Dien Bien Phu; meals 15,000-30,000d; 9am-9pm) Our favourite spot for Hue's famous *bun thit nuong* – grilled pork with vermicelli and a forest of fresh herbs. Don't forget a hearty dollop of the special peanut sauce.

Quan Bun Bo Hue VIETNAMESE $

(17 Đ Ly Thuong Kiet; meals 30,000d; 6am-2pm) Excellent spot for a hearty bowl of *bun bo Hue*, the city's signature noodle dish combining tender beef, vermicelli and lemongrass. Next door at number 19, Ly Thuong Kiet is equally good. Both sell out by early afternoon.

Mandarin Café VIETNAMESE $

(054-382 1281; www.mrcumandarin.com; 24 Đ Tran Cao Van; meals from 25,000d; 6am-10pm;) Owner-photographer Mr Cu, whose inspirational pictures adorn the walls, has been hosting backpackers for years, and his relaxed restaurant has lots of vegetarian and breakfast choices. Also operates as a tour agency.

Gecko Pub CAFE $$

(9 Đ Pham Ngu Lao; meals 30,000-80,000d; 8am-midnight) With a laid-back vibe, this is our favourite of the cafes and restaurants along Pham Ngu Lao. Friendly service and Asian chic decor combine with the best streetside tables in town, and food is a versatile mix of Western and Vietnamese favourites. Look forward to one of central Vietnam's best mojitos too.

Ta.ke JAPANESE $$

(34 Đ Tran Cao Van; meals 60,000-140,000d; 10am-10pm) An authentic Japanese restaurant with tasteful furnishings including lanterns and calligraphy, and a winsome menu with sushi, tempura and yakitori dishes. The interior is a calming haven away from Hue's increasingly busy streets.

Les Jardins de la Carambole FRENCH, VIETNAMESE $$$

(054-354 8815; www.lesjardinsdelacarambole.com; 32 Đ Dang Tran Con; mains from US$5; 7am-11pm;) A memorable dining experience, this classy and refined French restaurant occupies a gorgeous colonial-style building in the Citadel quarter. The menu majors in Gallic classics, and there's a lengthy wine list and informed service. It's just the place for a romantic meal – arrive by *cyclo* and it's easy to roll back the years to Indochine times.

Drinking

Cafe Tre Nga CAFE

(7 Đ Nguyen Cong Tru) Families, courting couples and card players all hang out at this hidden bamboo-shrouded riverside haven that's our favourite place in Hue for a *caphe sua da* (iced coffee with milk). Walk down the lane off Đ Nguyen Cong Tru past the art galleries to find the cafe.

DMZ Bar BAR

(www.dmz.com.vn; 60 Đ Le Loi; 7am-1am;) Ever-popular riverside bar with a free pool table, cold Huda beer, cocktails (try a watermelon mojito) and good craic most nights. Also serves Western and local food till midnight, smoothies and juices. Happy hour is 3pm till 8pm. Check out the upside-down map of the DMZ – complete with a US chopper – on the ceiling of the bar.

Wounded Heart Tea Room TEAHOUSE

(www.hwhshop.com; 23 Đ Vo Thi Sau; tea 40,000d; 8am-6pm) Attached to a Fairtrade gift shop, this little place specialises in Vietnamese tea (including jasmine, ginger and oolong), but it will also rustle up a coffee. Complimentary snacks are served with your drink.

Brown Eyes BAR

(Đ Chu Van An; 5pm-late;) The most popular late-night bar in town, with a good blend of locals and traveller-revellers and a party vibe. DJs drive the dance floor with R&B, hip hop and house anthems, and staff rally the troops with free shots.

Sirius BAR

(www.moonlighthue.com; Moonlight Hotel, 20 Đ Pham Ngu Lao; snacks from 55,000d; 10am-10pm) Atop the Moonlight Hotel, Sirius is the best place in town for sunset drinks. Combine BBQ snacks – beef, squid, prawns – and a few beers or a cocktail and view the arrival of dusk on the Perfume River.

Café on Thu Wheels BAR

(10/2 Đ Nguyen Tri Phuong; 6.30am-11pm;) Graffiti-splattered walls, a sociable vibe, excellent food and smoothies all combine at this welcoming spot owned by a friendly family. They also offer good tours, serve cheap meals and have books and mags to browse.

Hue Backpackers BAR

(10 Đ Pham Ngu Lao; 6am-11pm;) There's always a buzz about this backpackers' drinking den, which packs 'em in with its infused vodkas, cocktail list and regular happy hours. A good bet for the football or big sporting events.

Bar Why Not? BAR

(21 Đ Vo Thi Sau) This place has a more relaxed vibe than some other bars in town, a sensational list of cocktails and a popular street terrace.

Shopping

Hue produces the finest conical hats in Vietnam. The city's speciality is 'poem hats', which, when held up to the light, reveal shadowy scenes of daily life. It's also known for its rice paper and silk paintings.

Spiral Foundation Healing the Wounded Heart Center HANDICRAFTS

(054-383 3694; www.spiralfoundation.org; 23 Đ Vo Thi Sau; 8am-6pm) Generating cash from trash, this store stocks lovely handicrafts – such as quirky bags made from plastic, and picture frames made from recycled beer cans – created by artists with disabilities. Profits aid heart surgery for children in need.

Blue de Hue ANTIQUES

(43 Đ Vo Thi Sau; 7.30am-6.30pm) Well-regarded antiques store selling stonework, ceramics, laquerware and wooden carvings.

Dong Ba Market MARKET

(Đ Tran Hung Dao; 6.30am-8pm) Just north of Trang Tien Bridge, this is Hue's largest market, selling anything and everything.

Trang Tien Plaza SHOPPING CENTRE

(6 Đ Tran Hung Dao; 8am-10pm) A small shopping centre situated between Trang Tien Bridge and Dong Ba Market with a Coopmart supermarket.

Information

MEDICAL SERVICES

Hue Central Hospital (Benh Vien Trung Uong Hue; 054-382 2325; 16 Đ Le Loi; 6am-10pm) Well-regarded local hospital.

MONEY

Vietcombank (30 Đ Le Loi; 7.30am-3.30pm Mon-Sat) At the Hotel Saigon Morin.

Vietin Bank ATM (12 Đ Hung Vuong) Centrally located ATM.

POST

Post Office (8 Đ Hoang Hoa Tham; 7am-5.30pm Mon-Sat) Main post office.

TRAVEL AGENCIES

Most travel agencies and tour operators pool clients on their budget tours, so when you book a (standard) DMZ tour, you'll be on a large bus. Specialist bespoke trips are available but cost far more.

A popular way to travel between Hue and Hoi An – or vice versa – is by motorbike. Trips often stop for a seafood lunch at Lang Co lagoon, and also at the Hai Van pass. Count on around US$45 to US$50 on the back of a bike, or US$25 to US$30 if you're comfortable being in charge of two wheels.

Also see Cafe on Thu Wheels (p182) and Stop & Go Café (p182).

TRANSPORT FROM HUE

DESTINATION	AIR	BUS	CAR/MOTORBIKE	TRAIN
Danang	-	60,000d, 3hr, frequent	2½-4hr	US$3.50-6, 2½-4hr, 7 daily
Dong Hoi	-	85,000d, 4hr, frequent	3½hr	US$5-11, 3-5½hr, 7 daily
Hanoi	from 1,000,000d, 1hr, 3 daily	260,000d, 13-16hr, 9 daily	16hr	US$24-42, 12-15½hr, 6 daily
HCMC	from 480,000d, 1¼hr, 4 daily	490,000d, 19-24hr, 9 daily	22hr	US$32-55, 19½-23hr, 5 daily
Ninh Binh	-	250,000d, 10½-12hr, 8 daily	11hr	US$19-35, 10-13hr, 5 daily
Vinh	-	150,000d, 7½-9hr, frequent to 1pm	7hr	US$23-38, 6½-10hr, 5 daily

DMZ Travel (☎054-224 1904; www.dmz.com.vn; 60 Đ Le Loi) Budget boat trips along the Perfume River and DMZ tours. Also tickets to Laos.

Mandarin Café (☎054-382 1281; www.mrcumandarin.com; 24 Đ Tran Cao Van) Mr Cu offers great information, transport and tours around Hue and beyond.

Sinh Tourist (☎054-384 5022; www.thesinhtourist.vn; 37 Đ Nguyen Thai Hoc; ⏲6.30am-10pm) Books open-tour buses and buses to Laos.

Getting There & Away

AIR

Jetstar (☎1900 1550; Đ Hung Vuong; ⏲closed Sun) To/from HCMC.

Viet Jet (☎1900 1886; www.vietjetair.com) To/from HCMC.

Vietnam Airlines (☎054-382 4709; 23 Đ Nguyen Van Cu; ⏲closed Sun) To/from Hanoi and HCMC.

BUS

The main bus station, 4km southeast of the centre, has connections to Danang and south to HCMC. **An Hoa bus station** (Hwy 1), northwest of the Citadel, serves northern destinations, including Dong Ha (44,000d, two hours, every 30 minutes).

For Phong Nha (around 120,000d, five hours), the Hung Thanh open-tour bus leaves 49 Đ Chu Van An at 4.30pm, and the Tan Nha bus leaves from the Why Not? bar on Đ Vo Thi Sau around 6.30am. One daily bus (look for 'Phuc Vu' in the windscreen) heads for Phong Nha Farmstay and Son Trach at 11.15am (150,000d, four hours) from Hue's An Hoa bus station.

Hue is a regular stop on open-tour bus routes. Most drop off and pick up passengers at central hotels. Expect some hassle from persistent hotel touts when you arrive.

Mandarin, Sinh and Stop & Go Café can arrange bookings for buses to Savannakhet, Laos.

TRAIN

The **Hue train station** (☎054-382 2175; 2 Đ Phan Chu Trinh) is at the southwestern end of Đ Le Loi.

Getting Around

Hue's Phu Bai Airport is 14km south of the city. Metered taxis cost about 220,000d to the centre, or use the minibus service for 50,000d. Vietnam Airlines runs an airport shuttle.

Pedal power is a fun way to tour Hue and the Royal Tombs. Hotels rent bicycles for around US$3 per day. Traffic around Hue can be busy, especially on the bridges crossing the river, so take care when cycling. Motorbikes are from US$5 to US$10. A car with driver costs US$50 to US$55 per day.

Cyclo drivers usually quote extortionate prices in Hue, and a short ride begins at around 40,000d. It's usually cheaper and quicker to get a metered taxi.

For a taxi, try the reliable **Mai Linh** (☎054-389 8989).

Around Hue

South of Hue are the extravagant mausoleums of the rulers of the Nguyen dynasty (1802–1945), spread out along the banks of the Perfume River between 2km and 16km south of the city. There are also fine pagodas and other sights.

Almost all the royal tombs were planned by the emperors during their lifetimes, and some were used as residences while they were still alive.

Most of the mausoleums consist of five essential elements. The first is a stele pavilion dedicated to the accomplishments, exploits and virtues of the emperor. Next is a temple for the worship of the emperor and empress. The third is an enclosed sepulchre, and fourth an honour courtyard with stone elephants, horses, and civil and military mandarins. Finally, there's a lotus pond surrounded by frangipani and pine trees.

Most people visit on an organised tour from Hue, either by boat or combining boat and bus, but it's possible to rent a *xe om* or bicycle and do a DIY tour.

Entrance to the main sites is adult/child 100,000/20,000d per site, but discounted combination tickets including the Citadel are also available.

Sights

Tomb of Tu Duc TOMB

(adult/child 100,000/20,000d) This tomb, constructed between 1864 and 1867, is the most popular and impressive of the royal mausoleums. Emperor Tu Duc designed it himself to use before and after his death. The enormous expense of the tomb and the forced labour used in its construction spawned a coup plot that was discovered and suppressed. Tu Duc's tomb is 5km south of Hue on Van Nien Hill in Duong Xuan Thuong village.

From the entrance, a path leads to **Luu Khiem Lake**. The tiny island to the right, **Tinh Khiem**, is where Tu Duc used to hunt small game. Across the water to the left is

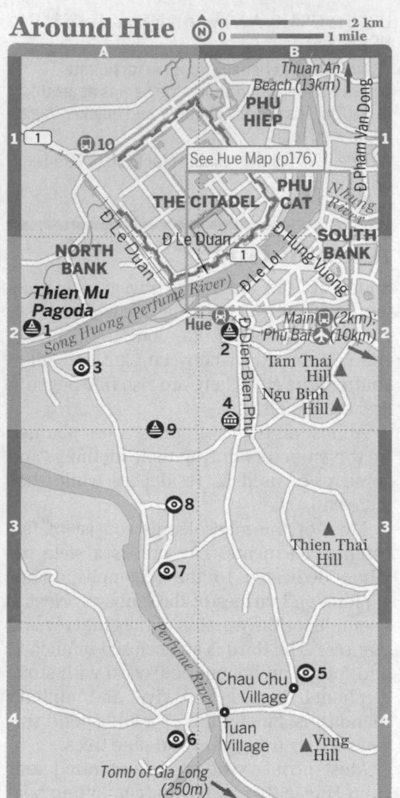

Around Hue

Top Sights

1 Thien Mu Pagoda A2

Sights

2 Bao Quoc Pagoda B2
3 Ho Quyen A2
4 Nam Giao Esplanade B2
5 Tomb of Khai Dinh B4
6 Tomb of Minh Mang A4
7 Tomb of Thieu Tri A3
8 Tomb of Tu Duc A3
9 Tu Hieu Pagoda A2

Transport

10 An Hoa Bus Station A1

Xung Khiem Pavilion, where he would sit with his concubines, composing or reciting poetry. **Hoa Khiem Temple** is where Tu Duc and his wife, Empress Hoang Le Thien Anh, were worshipped – today it houses royal artefacts. The larger throne was for the empress; Tu Duc was only 153cm tall. **Minh Khiem Chamber**, to the right behind Hoa Khiem Temple, was originally meant to be a theatre. Dress-up photo opportunities and cultural performances are available here. Directly behind Hoa Khiem Temple is the quieter **Luong Khiem Temple**, dedicated to Tu Duc's mother, Tu Du. Around the lakeshore is the **Honour Courtyard**.

You pass between a guard of elephants, horses and diminutive mandarins (even shorter than the emperor) before reaching the **Stele Pavilion**, which shelters a 20-tonne stone tablet. Tu Duc drafted the inscriptions himself. He freely admitted he'd made mistakes and named his tomb Khiem ('modest'). The **tomb**, enclosed by a wall, is on the far side of a tiny lagoon. It's a drab monument and the emperor was never interred here; where his remains were buried (along with great treasure) is not known. To keep it secret from grave robbers, all 200 servants who buried the king were beheaded. Tu Duc lived a life of imperial luxury and carnal excess (he had 104 wives and countless concubines), though no offspring.

Tomb of Minh Mang TOMB

(adult/child 100,000/20,000d) This majestic tomb is renowned for its architecture and sublime forest setting. The tomb was planned during Minh Mang's reign (1820–1840) but built by his successor, Thieu Tri.

Minh Mang's tomb is in An Bang village, on the west bank of the Perfume River, 12km from Hue.

The **Honour Courtyard** is reached via three gates on the eastern side of the wall. Three granite staircases lead from the courtyard to the square Stele Pavilion (Dinh Vuong).

Sung An Temple, which is dedicated to Minh Mang and his empress, is reached via three terraces and the rebuilt **Hien Duc Gate**. On the other side of the temple, three stone bridges span **Trung Minh Ho** (Lake of Impeccable Clarity). The central bridge was for the emperor's use only. **Minh Lau Pavilion** (Pavilion of Light) stands on the top of three superimposed terraces that represent the 'three powers': the heavens, the earth and water. To the left is the Fresh Air Pavilion, to the right, the Angling Pavilion.

From a stone bridge across crescent-shaped **Tan Nguyet Lake** (Lake of the New Moon), a monumental staircase with dragon banisters leads to Minh Mang's sepulchre. The gate to the tomb is opened only once a year on the anniversary of the emperor's death.

★Thien Mu Pagoda BUDDHIST TEMPLE

FREE Built on a hill overlooking the Perfume River, 4km southwest of the Citadel, this pagoda is an icon of Vietnam and as potent a symbol of Hue as the Citadel. The 21m-high octagonal tower, **Thap Phuoc Duyen**, was constructed under the reign of Emperor Thieu Tri in 1844. Each of its seven storeys is dedicated to a *manushi-buddha* (a Buddha that appeared in human form). Visit in the morning before tour groups show up.

Thien Mu Pagoda was originally founded in 1601 by Nguyen Hoang, governor of Thuan Hoa province. Over the centuries its buildings have been destroyed and rebuilt several times. Since the 1960s it has been a flashpoint of political demonstrations.

To the right of the tower is a pavilion containing a stele dating from 1715. It's set on the back of a massive marble turtle, a symbol of longevity. To the left of the tower is another six-sided pavilion, this one sheltering an enormous bell (1710), weighing 2052kg and audible from 10km away.

The temple itself is a humble building in the inner courtyard, past the triple-gated entrance where three statues of Buddhist guardians stand at the alert. In the main sanctuary behind the bronze laughing Buddha are three statues: A Di Da, the Buddha of the Past; Thich Ca, the historical Buddha (Sakyamuni); and Di Lac Buddha, the Buddha of the Future.

For a scenic bicycle ride, head southwest (parallel to the Perfume River) on riverside Đ Tran Hung Dao, which turns into Đ Le Duan after Phu Xuan Bridge. Cross the railway tracks and keep going on Đ Kim Long. Thien Mu Pagoda can also be reached by boat.

Tomb of Khai Dinh TOMB

(adult/child 100,000/20,000d) This hillside monument is a synthesis of Vietnamese and European elements. Most of the tomb's grandiose exterior is covered in blackened concrete, creating an unexpectedly Gothic air, while the interiors resemble an explosion of colourful mosaic. Khai Dinh was the penultimate emperor of Vietnam, from 1916 to 1925, and widely seen as a puppet of the French. The construction of his flamboyant tomb took 11 years. The tomb of Khai Dinh is 10km from Hue in Chau Chu village.

Steps lead to the **Honour Courtyard** where mandarin honour guards have a mixture of Vietnamese and European features. Up three more flights of stairs is the stupendous main building, **Thien Dinh**. The walls and ceiling are decorated with murals of the Four Seasons, Eight Precious Objects and Eight Fairies. Under a graceless, gold-speckled concrete canopy is a gilt bronze statue of Khai Dinh. His remains are interred 18m below the statue.

A FIERY PROTEST

Behind the main sanctuary of the Thien Mu Pagoda is the Austin motorcar that transported the monk Thich Quang Duc to the site of his 1963 self-immolation. He publicly burned himself to death in Saigon to protest against the policies of South Vietnamese President Ngo Dinh Diem. A famous photograph of this act was printed on the front pages of newspapers around the world, and his death inspired a number of other self-immolations.

The response of the president's notorious sister-in-law, Tran Le Xuan (Madame Nhu), was to crassly proclaim the self-immolations a 'barbecue party', saying 'Let them burn and we shall clap our hands'. Her statements greatly aggravated the already substantial public disgust with Diem's regime. In November, both President Diem and his brother Ngo Dinh Nhu (Madame Nhu's husband) were assassinated by Diem's military. Madame Nhu was overseas at the time.

Another self-immolation sparked fresh protest in 1993. A man arrived at the pagoda and, after leaving offerings, set himself alight chanting the word 'Buddha'. Although his motivation remains a mystery, this set off a chain of events whereby the pagoda's leading monks were arrested and linked with the independent United Buddhists of Vietnam, the banned alternative to the state-sanctioned Vietnam Buddhists. This led to an official complaint to the UN by the International Federation of Human Rights accusing the Vietnamese government of violating its own constitution, which protects freedom of religion.

Ho Quyen HISTORIC SITE

FREE Wildly overgrown but evocative, Ho Quyen was built in 1830 for the royal pastime of watching elephants and tigers face off in combat. The tigers (and leopards) were usually relieved of their claws and teeth so that the elephants – a symbol of the emperor's power – triumphed every time. Climb up grassy ramparts and imagine the scene in the old arena – the last fight was held in 1904.

The south-facing section was reserved for the royal family, while diametrically opposite are the tiger cages. Ho Quyen is about 3km outside Hue in Truong Da village. Follow Đ Bui Thi Xuan west from the train station, then look out for the blue sign near the market that indicates the turn-off on the left. Follow this lane for about 200m to a fork in the road and go right.

Tu Hieu Pagoda BUDDHIST TEMPLE

FREE Nestled in a pine forest, this popular pagoda was built in 1843 and later co-opted by eunuchs from the Citadel. Today 70 monks reside at Tu Hieu; they welcome visitors to the twin temples (one dedicated to Cong Duc, the other to Buddha). Listen to their chanting daily at 4.30am, 10am, noon, 4pm and 7pm. Tu Hieu Pagoda is about 5km from the centre of Hue, on the way to the tomb of Tu Duc.

Tu Hieu is associated with Zen master Thich Nhat Hanh, who studied at the monastery in the 1940s, but lived in exile for more than 40 years, and was only permitted to return to Vietnam in 2005.

Thanh Toan Bridge BRIDGE

A classic covered Japanese footbridge in picturesque countryside, this makes a lovely diversion from Hue. The bridge is in sleepy Thuy Thanh village, 7km east of Hue. Head north for a few hundred metres on Đ Ba Trieu until you see a sign to the Citadel Hotel. Turn right and follow the bumpy dirt road for another 6km past villages, rice paddies and several pagodas.

Nam Giao Esplanade HISTORIC SITE

This three-tiered esplanade was once the most important religious site in Vietnam, the place where the Nguyen emperors made animal sacrifices and elaborate offerings to the deity Thuong De. Ceremonies (last held in 1946) involved a lavish procession and a three-day fast by the emperor at the nearby Fasting Palace. The Fasting Palace, located at the furthest end of the park, has photographs with English captions.

Since 2006, the ceremony has been re-enacted as part of the Festival of Hue (p183). Nam Giao Esplanade is at the southern end of Đ Dien Bien Phu, about 2km from the railway tracks.

Tomb of Thieu Tri TOMB

(admission 80,000d) The only royal tomb not enclosed by a wall, the monument of Thieu Tri (built 1848) has a similar floor plan to his father Minh Mang's tomb, but is substantially smaller. The tomb is about 7km from Hue.

Tomb of Gia Long TOMB

(admission free) FREE Emperor Gia Long founded the Nguyen dynasty in 1802 and ruled until 1819. Both the emperor and his queen are buried here. The rarely visited tomb is presently in a state of ruin, but careful restoration has begun. It is around 14km south of Hue and 3km from the west bank of the Perfume River.

Bach Ma National Park

A French-era hill station, this **national park** (Vuon Quoc Gia Bach Ma; ☎054-387 1330; www.bachmapark.com.vn; adult/child 40,000/20,000d) reaches a peak of 1450m at Bach Ma mountain, only 18km from the coast. The cool climate attracted the French, who built over a hundred villas here. Not surprisingly the Viet Minh tried hard to spoil the holiday – the area saw some heavy fighting in the early 1950s and again during the American War.

The national park, extended in 2008, stretches from the coast to the Annamite mountain range at the Lao border. More than 1400 species of plants, including rare ferns and orchids, have been discovered in Bach Ma, representing a fifth of the flora of Vietnam. There are 132 kinds of mammals, three of which were only discovered in the 1990s: the antelope-like saola, Truong Son muntjac and the giant muntjac. Nine species of primates are also present, including small numbers of the rare red-shanked Douc langur. It's hoped wild elephants will return from the Lao side of the border.

As most of the park's resident mammals are nocturnal, sightings demand a great deal of effort and patience. Birdwatching is fantastic, but you need to be up at dawn for the best chance of glimpsing some of the 358

OFF THE BEATEN TRACK

TOMBS & DUNES

From the centre of Hue it's only 15km north to the coast, the road shadowing the Perfume River before you hit the sands of **Thuan An Beach**. Southeast from here there's a beautiful, quiet coastal road to follow with very light traffic (so it's ideal for bikers). The route traverses a narrow coastal island, with views of the Tam Giang-Cau Hai lagoon on the inland side and stunning sandy beaches and dunes on the other. This coastal strip is virtually undeveloped, but between September and March, the water's often too rough for swimming.

From Thuan An the road winds past villages alternating with shrimp lagoons and vegetable gardens. Thousands of garishly colourful and opulent graves and family temples line the beach, most the final resting places of Viet Kieu (overseas Vietnamese) who wanted to be buried in their homeland. Tracks cut through the tombs and sand dunes to the beach. Pick a spot and you'll probably have a beach to yourself.

At glorious **Phu Thuan beach** (about 7km southeast of Thuan An), the **Beach Bar Hue** (☎0908 993 584; www.beachbarhue.com; Phu Thuan beach; dm US$12;) has excellent shared four-bed bungalows and sits pretty on a sublime stretch of sand (with no hawkers…for now). There's a funky bamboo-and-thatch bar for drinks and snacks, and next door **Villa Louise** (☎0917 673 656; www.villalouisehue.com; Phu Thuan beach; d US$86-148, villa US$120-244;) has wonderful villas, private rooms and two swimming pools. The villas are lovingly decorated in heritage Vietnamese style. The pools, restaurant and beach can all be used by outside guests, but there's an entrance fee of 100,000d, which can be offset against food and beverage purchases in the beachfront bar. A taxi from Hue to Phu Thuan is around 250,000d and a *xe om* around 125,000d.

Around 8km past Beach Bar Hue, the remains of **Phu Dien**, a small Cham temple, lie protected by a glass pavilion in the dunes just off the beach. There are seafood shacks here too.

Continuing southeast, a narrow but paved road weaves past fishing villages, shrimp farms and giant sand dunes and the settlement of Vinh Hung until you reach the mouth of another river estuary at Thuon Phu An, where there's a row of seafood restaurants. This spot is 40km from Thuan An. Cross the Tu Hien bridge here and you can continue around the eastern lip of the huge Cau Hai lagoon and link up with Hwy 1.

species logged, including the fabulous crested argus pheasant.

Sights & Activities

Bach Ma is the wettest place in Vietnam, with the heaviest of the rain falling in October and November (and bringing out the leeches). It's not out of the question to visit then, but check road conditions first. The best time to visit is from February to September, particularly between March and June.

Hiking HIKING

The **Rhododendron Trail** (from Km 10 on the road) leads to the upper reaches of a spectacular waterfall; it's 689 steps down for a dip. The **Five Lakes Trail** passes pools for swimming before reaching a much smaller waterfall.

The short **Summit Hike** leads to a viewpoint with magnificent views (on a clear day) over the forest, Cau Hai lagoon and the coast. Unexploded ordnance is still around, so stick to the trails.

Zipline ADVENTURE TOUR

(2 to 5 people 800,000d) Bach Ma's newest attraction is a zipline through the Parashorea forest at the 14km mark on the summit road. Fans of aerial action will also appreciate the ropes and ladders forming part of other treks in the park.

Sleeping & Eating

Visitor Centre Accommodation GUESTHOUSE $

(☎054-387 1330; www.bachmapark.com.vn; campsite per person 20,000d, r 300,000d) The park authority has a small camping ground and two guesthouses near the entrance, with basic twin-bed rooms with private bathrooms.

Summit Accommodation GUESTHOUSE $$
(☎054-387 1330; www.bachmapark.com.vn; d 650,000-1,050,0000d) Near the summit are four options, from the simple Kim Giao villa to the more comfortable Phong La villa. All have private bathrooms, but note that not all villas may be available for booking. When you book accommodation, give at least four hours' notice if you're also wanting meals. Karaoke can be a feature of mountain life at the weekend.

Information

At the **visitor centre** (www.bachmapark.com.vn) by the park entrance there's an exhibition on the park's flora and fauna, and hiking booklets are available. You can book village and birdwatching tours and English- or French-speaking guides (between 300,000d and 500,000d per day). Ask whether Mr Cam is available.

Getting There & Around

Bach Ma is 28km west of Lang Co and 40km southeast of Hue. The turn-off is signposted in the town of Cau Hai on Hwy 1. You can also enter from the town of Phu Loc.

Buses from Danang (80,000d, two hours) and Hue (60,000d, one hour) stop at Cau Hai, where *xe om* drivers can ferry you around 3km (25,000d) to the entrance.

From the visitor centre at the park entrance, it's a steep, serpentine 15km ascent, and the road almost reaches the summit. Walking down from the summit takes about three to four hours; you'll need water and sunscreen.

Private transport to the summit is available from the visitor centre, and a return same-day journey is 900,000d for a six-person minibus. At busy times, travellers can usually share the cost with other passengers. For an overnight stay, transport to the summit is 1,300,000d for six people.

Note that cars are allowed in the park, so it's worth considering a tour here from Hue, or arranging a car and driver for around US$50 return. Motorbikes are not allowed in the park, but there is a secure parking area near the visitor centre.

A recommended Hue-based tour company is **Oriental Sky Travel** (☎0985 555 827; www.facebook.com/bachmanationalpark.huevietnam; 2 days/1 night per person US$201), which offers regular overnight explorations of the park.

Lang Co Beach

☎054

Lang Co is an attractive island-like stretch of palm-shaded white sand, with a turquoise lagoon on one side and 10km of beachfront on the other. As a beach resort it's more geared to Vietnamese day trippers than Western travellers, but if the weather's nice the ocean is certainly inviting (if you stay away from the central section, which could be cleaner).

High season is April to July. From late August till November, rains are frequent, and from December to March it can get chilly.

Sleeping & Eating

Most of the accommodation is north of the town along the highway.

Chi Na Guesthouse GUESTHOUSE $
(☎054-387 4597; s/d 200,000/250,000d; ❄📶) One of several clean, basic guesthouses north of the centre, but here the family speaks a little English. Rooms are ageing but serviceable.

Vedana Lagoon RESORT $$$
(☎054-381 9397; www.vedanalagoon.com; Phu Loc; bungalows/villas from US$126/179; 🚭❄@📶🏊) Combining contemporary chic with natural materials, this remote but very comfortable spa hotel has gorgeous villas and bungalows with thatched roofs, modish furnishings and outdoor bathrooms. Some have private pools, others jut over the lagoon to maximise the views. The complex includes a wonderful wellness centre (for t'ai chi and yoga classes). Vedana is 15km north of Lang Co.

Minh Hang SEAFOOD $$
(meals 70,000-130,000d; ⏰7am-9pm) The best seafood restaurant, situated on the north side of Lang Co, and has a lagoon view (instead of the highway and rumbling trucks). Try the lemon pepper squid or spicy clams with lemongrass.

Getting There & Away

Lang Co is on the north side of the Hai Van Tunnel and Danang.

Lang Co's **train station** (☎054-387 4423) is 3km from the beach, in the direction of the lagoon. Getting a *xe om* to the beach shouldn't be difficult. The train journey from here to Danang (50,000d, 1½ to two hours, five daily) is one of the most spectacular in Vietnam. Services also connect to Hue (60,000d, 1½ to two hours, four daily).

Hai Van Pass & Tunnel

The **Hai Van (Sea Cloud) Pass** crosses over a spur of the Truong Son mountain range that juts into the sea. About 30km north of Danang, the road climbs to an elevation of 496m, passing south of the Ai Van Son peak (1172m). It's an incredibly mountainous stretch of highway – you may have seen the spectacular views on the *Top Gear* Vietnam special. The railway track, with its many tunnels, goes around the peninsula, following the beautiful and deserted shoreline.

In the 15th century, this pass formed the boundary between Vietnam and the kingdom of Champa. Until the American War, it was heavily forested. At the summit is a bullet-scarred French fort, later used as a bunker by the South Vietnamese and US armies.

If you cross in winter, the pass is a tangible dividing line between the climates of the north and south, protecting Danang from the fierce 'Chinese winds' that sweep in from the northeast. From November to March the exposed Lang Co side of the pass can be wet and chilly, while just to the south it's often warm and dry.

The top of the pass is the only place you can stop. The view is well worth it, especially if you climb up to the abandoned fort.

In 2005, the 6280m-long **Hai Van Tunnel** opened, bypassing the pass and shaving an hour off the journey between Danang and Hue. Motorbikers and cyclists are not permitted to ride through the tunnel (but you can pay to have your bike transported through in a truck). Sure it saves time, but on a nice day it really is a shame to miss the views from the pass.

Despite the odd hair-raising encounter, the pass road is safer than it used to be. If you can take your eyes off the highway, keep them peeled for the small altars on the roadside – sobering reminders of those who have died in accidents on this winding route.

Ba Na Hill Resort

0511 / ELEV 1485M

A hill resort inherited from the French, lush Ba Na has refreshingly cool weather and gorgeous countryside views. Established in 1919, the resort area once held 200-odd villas, but only a few ruins remain.

Until WWII, the French were carried up the last 20km of rough mountain road by sedan chair, but now a 5.7km (the world's longest) **cable car** system has opened up access. The ride involves a rise of almost 1400m, a truly spectacular trip over dense jungle and waterfalls. At the top, attractions include a **replica French provincial town**, a **funicular railway** ascending even higher, and an exciting and fun downhill **luge**. None of the attractions are vaguely Vietnamese, but the cable car journey is truly spectacular, and if you visit on a weekend or public holiday, it's interesting to mix in with local tourists.

Take an extra layer or two whatever time of year you visit – when it's 36°C on the coast, it could be 15°C on the mountain. Cloud and mist also cling to the hilltop, so if you can, try to visit on a clear day.

Mountain tracks lead to **waterfalls** and **viewing points**. Near the top is the **Linh Ung Pagoda** (2004) and a colossal 24m-high white seated Buddha that's visible for miles around.

As all the hotels are poor value for money, it's best to see Ba Na on a day trip.

See the Ba Na Hill website (www.banahills.com.vn) for more information.

Getting There & Away

Ba Na is 42km west of Danang. From the resort's car park and entrance, the cable car (return 500,000d) ascends to the mountain resort. Travel agencies in Danang or Hoi An can arrange day tours (per person from US$50), or a return taxi from Danang is around US$60.

Danang

0511 / POP 1,070,000

Nowhere in Vietnam is changing as fast as Danang. For decades it had a reputation as a provincial backwater, but big changes are ongoing. Stroll along the Han riverfront and you'll find gleaming new modernist hotels, and apartments and restaurants are emerging. Spectacular new bridges now span the Han River, and in the north of the city, the landmark new D-City is rising from the flatlands. Venture south and the entire China Beach strip is booming with hotel and resort developments.

That said, the city itself still has few conventional sightseeing spots, except for a very decent museum and a stunningly quirky bridge. So for most travellers, a few days enjoying the city's beaches, restaurants and nightlife is probably enough. Book an after-dark tour to see Danang at its shimmering

Danang

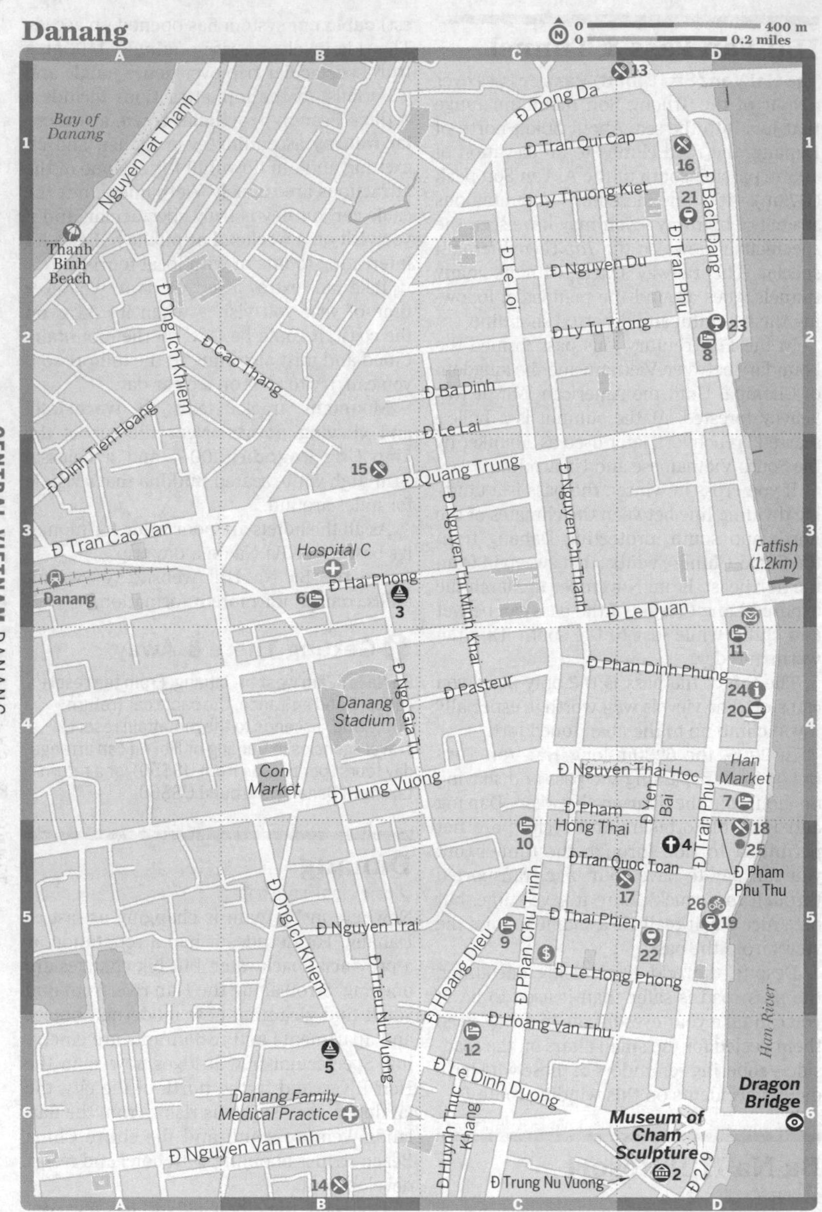

neon-lit best. The city's street-food scene also deserves close investigation.

Danang also makes a great base for day trips. The city is part of a long thin peninsula, at the northern tip of which is Nui Son Tra (called Monkey Mountain by US soldiers). China Beach and the five Marble Mountains lie southwest of the city.

History

Known during French colonial rule as Tourane, Danang succeeded Hoi An as the most

Danang

Top Sights
1 Dragon Bridge D6
2 Museum of Cham Sculpture D6

Sights
3 Cao Dai Temple B3
4 Danang Cathedral D5
5 Phap Lam Pagoda B6

Sleeping
6 Funtastic Danang Hostel B3
7 New Moon Hotel D4
8 Novotel Danang Premier Han River D2
9 Orange Hotel C5
10 Sanouva C5
11 Stargazer Hotel D4
12 Zion Hotel C6

Eating
13 Bread of Life D1
14 Com Tay Cam Cung Dinh B6
15 Le Bambino B3
16 Madame Lan D1
17 Quan Com Hue Ngon D5
18 Waterfront D5

Drinking & Nightlife
19 Bamboo 2 Bar D5
20 Cong Caphe D4
21 Luna Pub D1
22 On the Radio D5
23 Sky 36 .... D2

Information
24 Danang Visitor Centre D4
25 Sinh Tourist D5

Transport
26 Vy Bicycle D5

important port in central Vietnam during the 19th century, a position it retains to this day.

As American involvement in Vietnam escalated, Danang was where American combat troops first landed in South Vietnam – 3500 Marines in March 1965. Memorably, they stormed Nam O Beach in full battle gear, only to be greeted by a bevy of *ao dai*–wearing Vietnamese girls bearing cheerful flower garlands. A decade later, with the Americans and South Vietnamese in full retreat, the scene was very different as desperate civilians fled the city. On 29 March 1975, two truckloads of communist guerrillas, more than half of them women, declared Danang liberated without firing a shot.

Today Danang hosts one of Vietnam's most vibrant economies, and is often dubbed 'Silicon City' due to its booming web sector.

Sights

★Museum of Cham Sculpture — MUSEUM

(Bao Tang; Map p194; 1 Đ Trung Nu Vuong; admission 40,000d; ⏲7am-5pm) This fine museum has the world's largest collection of Cham artefacts, housed in buildings marrying French-colonial architecture with Cham elements. Founded in 1915 by the École Française d'Extrême Orient, it displays more than 300 pieces including altars, lingas, garudas, apsaras, Ganeshas and images of Shiva, Brahma and Vishnu – all dating from the 5th to 15th centuries. To hire an MP3 audio guide (20,000d), you'll need to show ID – passport or drivers licence – or leave a refundable US$50 bond.

The treasures come from Dong Duong (Indrapura), Khuong My, My Son, Tra Kieu and other sites. There are also exhibits focusing on Cham culture today, with contemporary artefacts and photos of the Kate Festival (the Cham New Year).

★Dragon Bridge — BRIDGE

(Map p194; Cau Rong) Welcome to the biggest show in town every Saturday and Sunday night. At 9pm, this graceful golden-hued bridge spouts fire and water from the dragon's head near the Han River's eastern bank. The best places to observe are the various cafes lining the eastern bank to the north of the bridge, and boat trips also depart from Đ Bach Dang on the river's western bank to make the most of Danang's after-dark, neonlit splendour.

Cao Dai Temple — BUDDHIST TEMPLE

(Map p194; 63 Đ Hai Phong; ⏲prayers 5.30am, 11.30am, 5.30pm & 11.30pm) FREE This is Central Vietnam's largest Cao Dai temple, serving about 50,000 followers. A sign reading *van giao nhat ly* (all religions have the same reason) hangs before the main altar. Behind the gilded letters are the founders of five of the world's great religions: Mohammed, Laotse (wearing Eastern Orthodox–style robes), Jesus, a Southeast Asian–looking Buddha and Confucius. Behind the main altar sits an enormous globe with the Cao Dai 'divine eye' symbol.

Ho Chi Minh Museum MUSEUM
(Map p200; 3 Đ Nguyen Van Troi; 7-11am & 1.30-4.30pm) FREE Despite its huge grounds, this museum is typically unenlightening for a site venerating Ho Chi Minh. At the front is a display of the usual US, Soviet and Chinese weaponry. Hidden behind the Party buildings are a replica of Ho Chi Minh's house in Hanoi, and the museum.

Danang Cathedral CHURCH
(Map p194; Đ Tran Phu) FREE Known to locals as Con Ga Church (Rooster Church) because of the weathercock atop the steeple, the candy-pink Danang Cathedral was built for the city's French residents in 1923. Today it serves a Catholic community of over 4000, and is standing room only if you arrive late.

Phap Lam Pagoda BUDDHIST TEMPLE
(Map p194; 574 Đ Ong Ich Khiem; 5-11.30am & 1-9pm) FREE This pagoda has three giant Buddha statues in the courtyard, and an equally imposing large gold one in the temple.

Tours

Danang Unplugged TOUR
(0905 101 930; www.danangunplugged.com; per person US$69-89) These tours – conducted in either a US Army jeep or on the back of a motorbike – explore the city's street-food and after-dark scenes. Other options are sightseeing around town, or a day trip to the Hai Van Pass. Look forward to really interesting street-food discoveries for curious travelling foodies.

Danang Food Tour FOOD
(www.danangfoodtour.com; per person US$45) Excellent morning and evening explorations of the local food scene by a passionate expat foodie. Check the website for his great blog on the best of Danang.

Funtastic Tours TOUR
(0903 561 777; www.funtasticdanang.com; per person US$45) Run by the funky young team behind Danang's Funtastic hostels, with tours including street food and sightseeing. Transport is by car. Check out www.danangcuisine.com for Danang tips by operator Summer Ly, a local food blogger who's been featured in the *NY Times*.

Meet My Danang TOUR
(www.meetmydanang.com; per person US$8-40) Tours exploring Danang ranging from after-dark river cruises to bar-hopping and the city's spooky ghostly past.

Sleeping

Danang has a fast-expanding selection of modern hotels along the riverside, and a couple of much-needed new hostels. For accommodation just across the river, see the China Beach listings.

Funtastic Danang Hostel HOSTEL $
(Map p194; 0511-389 2024; www.funtasticdanang.com; 115 Đ Hai Phong; dm US$9, d & tw US$19;) Danang's first specialist hostel is a goodie, with young and energetic owners, colourful rooms and dorms, and a comfortable lounge area when all you want to do is chill and watch a DVD. Ask about the street-food tours.

Zion Hotel HOTEL $
(Map p194; 0511-382 8333; http://sion.com.vn; 121/7 Đ Hoang Van Thu; s US$15, d US$20-25;) There's a scarlet theme running through this excellent-value hotel from the lobby to the inviting, modern rooms. Boasts a convenient location and staff are eager to please.

Orange Hotel HOTEL $$
(Map p194; 0511-356 6177; www.danangorangehotel.com; 29 Đ Hoang Dieu; d US$52-75;) This family-owned hotel has an outstanding approach to customer service, all instilled by the friendly patriarch/boss who's usually on hand at reception or in the rooftop restaurant. The room decor does veer to chintzy on the style continuum, but any OTT design choices can easily be overlooked because of the spotless rooms and expansive breakfast buffet featuring local dishes.

Sanouva BOUTIQUE HOTEL $$
(Map p194; 0511-382 3468; www.sanouvadanang.com; 68 Đ Phan Chau Trinh; d from US$40;) Boutique meets business at the stylish Sanouva, located in a bustling commercial street just a few blocks from Danang's riverfront. An Asian chic lobby is the introduction to relatively compact but modern rooms, and the in-house S'Spa and S'Ngon restaurant are two good reasons to linger within the Sanouva's chic interior.

New Moon Hotel HOTEL $$
(Map p194; 0511-382 8488; www.newmoonhotel.vn; 126 Đ Bach Dang; r 440,000-900,000d;) Modern minihotel with a selection of inviting rooms in different price catego-

ries, all with flat-screen TV, minibar, wi-fi and en-suite marble bathrooms, while the river-view options enjoy incredible vistas.

Stargazer Hotel HOTEL $$
(Map p194; ☎0511-381 5599; www.stargazer.net; 77 Đ Tran Phu; r 350,000-800,000d; ❄@📶) A welcoming hotel with neat, if smallish, rooms featuring attractive wood furniture, large TVs and comfy beds with duvets. Number 301 has a balcony and river view.

Novotel Danang Premier Han River HOTEL $$$
(Map p194; ☎0511-392 9999; www.novotel-danang-premier.com; 36 Đ Bach Dang; r/ste from US$130/220; ⊖❄@📶🏊) Towering riverside landmark with hip rooms and unmatched views over the Han River towards the beach and ocean. Staff are welcoming and well trained, and facilities include a pool, spa and fitness centre. Those who enjoy the high life should check out the 36th-floor sky bar.

Eating

Danang's restaurant scene is growing more cosmopolitan by the day. Street food is also great here, with copious *bun cha* (barbecued pork), *com* (rice) and *mi quang* (noodle soup) stalls. Dedicated foodies should strongly consider booking a food tour to really explore the Danang scene.

Quan Com Hue Ngon VIETNAMESE $
(Map p194; 65 Đ Tran Quoc Toan; meals 45,000-80,000d; ⏲3-9pm) Fab barbecue place, all charcoal smoke and sizzling meats, where you grill your own. There's a street terrace, and the welcoming English-speaking owner will help with the menu.

Com Tay Cam Cung Dinh VIETNAMESE $
(Map p194; K254/2 Đ Hoang Dieu; meals 20,000-50,000d; ⏲11am-8pm) This simple place is good for local dishes, including *hoanh thanh* (a wonton-like combination of minced pork and shrimp). It's down a little alley.

★**Fatfish** FUSION, PIZZA $$
(Map p200; www.fatfishdanang.com; 439 Đ Tran Hung Dao; meals 70,000-285,000d; ⏲9am-11pm; 📶) This stylish restaurant and lounge bar is leading the eating and drinking charge across the river on the Han's eastern shore. Innovative Asian fusion dishes, pizza and wood-fired barbecue dishes all partner with flavour-packed craft beers from Saigon's Pasteur St Brewing. Fatfish is good for a few snacks or a more leisurely full meal.

Book for before 9pm on a Saturday or Sunday night for front-row seats to see the nearby Dragon Bridge do its fiery party trick. Around Fatfish, a new boating marina and boardwalk is being completed, and the area will no doubt develop into Danang's hottest restaurant precinct.

★**Waterfront** INTERNATIONAL $$
(Map p194; ☎0511-384 3373; www.waterfrontdanang.com; 150-152 Đ Bach Dang; meals 95,000-360,000d; ⏲10am-11pm; 📶) Riverfront lounge-cum-restaurant that gets everything right on every level. It works as a stylish bar for a chilled glass of NZ Sauvignon Blanc or an imported beer and also as a destination restaurant for a memorable meal (book the terrace deck for a stunning river vista). The menu features imported meats, Asian seafood and also terrific 'gourmet' sandwiches.

Le Bambino FRENCH, INTERNATIONAL $$
(Map p194; ☎0511-389 6386; www.lebambino.com; 122/11 Đ Quang Trung; meals 120,000-300,000d; ⏲11.30am-1.30pm & 4.30-10pm Mon-Sat, 4.30-10pm Sun; 📶) Atmospheric place run by a couple (French husband, Vietnamese wife) who have crafted a great menu that takes in French classics, pub food, barbecued meat (try the ribs) and a few Vietnamese favourites. Eat inside or around the pool, and don't neglect the wine list or the cheese selections, both of which are superb.

Madame Lan VIETNAMESE $$
(Map p194; www.madamelan.com; 4 Đ Bach Dang; meals 100,000-250,000d; ⏲10am-10pm; 📶) Huge restaurant in a French colonial-style building where you can eat in an open courtyard or in one of the river-facing dining rooms. The menu has lots of good choices, including squid with chilli and salt, and green papaya salad with shrimp and garlic.

Bread of Life INTERNATIONAL $$
(Map p194; www.breadoflifedanang.com; 4 Đ Dong Da; meals 70,000-180,000d; ⏲10am-10pm Mon-Sat; 📶) Excellent American-style diner-cum-bakery with a good menu of burgers, Mexican food, sandwiches, pizza and pasta. A very good bet for brekkie; the bacon burrito really hits the spot. Run by deaf staff, proceeds go towards training activities for the deaf in Danang.

Drinking

For a lounge-bar-style drink with a view, also check out Waterfront (p197) or Fatfish (p197).

Luna Pub BAR
(Map p194; www.facebook.com/lunapubdanang; 9a Đ Tran Phu; ⏲11.30am-late; 📶) Half-bar, half-Italian restaurant, this hot hang-out is a cool warehouse-sized space with an open frontage, a DJ booth in the cabin of a truck, cool music, an amazing drinks selection and some shisha smoking action. Also popular with the expat crowd for its authentic Italian food (pizza, pasta, salads and more). Check Facebook for regular live gigs.

Sky 36 COCKTAIL BAR
(Map p194; Novotel Danang, 36 Đ Bach Dang; ⏲5pm-midnight) Ubermodern rooftop bar with excellent cocktails, innovative bar snacks and the best after-dark views of Danang's river and neon-lit bridges. Note there is a smart-casual code – including wearing closed-in shoes – this applies to male visitors.

Cong Caphe CAFE
(Map p194; 1 Đ Bach Dang; drinks from 40,000d; ⏲7am-11pm; 📶) The Danang offshoot of Hanoi's quirky Communist-themed cafes is a top spot for a riverside caffeine fix – try the superb coffee with yoghurt – or a well-priced beer or cocktail later in the day. It can get smoky, so try and grab a seat near the windows.

On the Radio BAR
(Map p194; www.facebook.com/ontheradio.bar; 35 Đ Thai Phien; ⏲6pm-late; 📶) Danang's go-to spot for live music and draught beer, and a good place to meet younger residents with a decent grasp of English.

Bamboo 2 Bar BAR
(Map p194; 230 Đ Bach Dang; ⏲10am-midnight; 📶) Sociable, but predictable expat bar with clientele of boozy regulars, cheap beer and a busy pool table. A good place to catch live sport on TV.

Information

Agribank (Map p194; 202 Đ Nguyen Chi Thanh; ⏲7.30am-3.30pm Mon-Sat) With ATM.

Danang Experience (www.danangexperience.com) Comprehensive website with an expat slant but is also good for visitors with eating, drinking and accommodation recommendations.

Danang Family Medical Practice (Map p194; ☎0511-358 2700; www.vietnammedicalpractice.com; 50-52 Đ Nguyen Van Linh; ⏲7am-6pm) With in-patient facilities; run by an Australian doctor.

Danang Visitor Centre (Map p194; ☎0511-386 3595; www.tourism.danang.vn; 32a Đ Phan Dinh Phung; ⏲7.30am-9pm) Really helpful, with English spoken, and good maps and brochures. Danang's official tourism website is one of Vietnam's best.

Hospital C (Benh Vien C; Map p194; ☎0511-382 1483; 122 Đ Hai Phong; ⏲24hr) The most advanced of the four hospitals in town.

In Danang (www.indanang.com) Danang's most established expat/tourist information website.

Main Post Office (Map p194; 64 Đ Bach Dang; ⏲7am-5.30pm) Near the Song Han Bridge.

Sinh Tourist (Map p194; ☎0511-384 3258; www.thesinhtourist.vn; 154 Đ Bach Dang; ⏲7am-10pm) Books open-tour buses and tours, and offers currency exchange.

Getting There & Away

AIR

Danang's busy airport has many domestic connections and popular international flights to Kuala Lumpur, Hong Kong and Singapore.

TRANSPORT FROM DANANG

DESTINATION	AIR	BUS	CAR/MOTORBIKE	TRAIN
Dong Hoi	-	120,000d, 6½hr, 7 daily	6-7hr	US$12-20, 5½-8½hr, 6 daily
Hanoi	from US$42, 1hr 10min, 9 daily	365,000d, 16-19hr, 7 daily	19hr	US$35-50, 14½-18hr, 6 daily
HCMC	from US$47, 1hr 15min, 18 daily	380,000d, 19-25hr, 9 daily	18hr	US$35-55, 17-22hr, 5 daily
Hue	-	55,000d, 3hr, every 20min	2½-4hr	US$4-7, 2½-4hr, 6 daily
Nha Trang	from US$45, 30min, 2 daily	230,000d, 10-13hr, 8 daily	13hr	US$20-35, 9-12hr, 5 daily

There are also a growing number of connections to Laos, China, Taiwan and South Korea.

Domestic services to destinations such as HCMC, Hanoi, Haiphong, Dalat, Nha Trang, Can Tho and Haiphong are operated by regional carriers including Vietnam Airlines, VietJet Air and Jetstar.

BUS

Danang's **intercity bus station** (Map p200; ☎0511-382 1265; Đ Dien Bien Phu) is 3km west of the city centre. A metered taxi to the riverside will cost around 70,000d.

Buses leave for all major centres, including Quy Nhon (130,000d, six hours, six daily).

For Laos, there are daily buses to Savannakhet at 8pm (from 300,000d, 14 hours) and a daily service to Pakse at 6.30am (from 340,000d, 13 hours). Buses to the Lao Bao border alone are 150,000d (six hours); you may have to change buses at Dong Ha.

Yellow public buses to Hoi An (18,000d, one hour, every 30 minutes to 6pm) travel along Đ Bach Dang. The price is usually posted inside the door if any bus drivers attempt to overcharge.

Sinh Tourist open-tour buses pick up from the company office on Đ Bach Dang twice daily to both Hue (89,000d, 2½ hours) and Hoi An (79,000d, one hour), and can advise on travel to Laos.

CAR & MOTORCYCLE

A car to Hoi An costs around 500,000d via your hotel or a local travel agency, while *xe om* will do it for around 150,000d. Bargain hard if you want to stop at the Marble Mountains or China Beach en route.

TRAIN

Danang's **train station** (202 Đ Hai Phong) has services to all destinations on the north–south main line.

The train ride to Hue is one of the best in the country – it's worth taking as an excursion in itself.

Getting Around

TO/FROM THE AIRPORT

Danang's airport is 2km west of the city centre. There is no airport bus and a taxi is around 60,000d.

BICYCLE

Vy Bicycle (Map p194; ☎0914 575 450; www.facebook.com/vy.bicycle; 202 Đ Bach Dang; ⊙8am-8pm) Handy city-side spot if you wish to hire two wheels and explore the beach area east across the river.

CYCLO & XE OM

Danang has plenty of motorbike taxis and *cyclo* drivers. Trips around town shouldn't cost more than 35,000d.

TAXI

Mai Linh (☎0511-356 5656) For metered taxis.

Around Danang

☎0511

Nui Son Tra (Monkey Mountain)

ELEV 850M

Jutting out into the sea like a giant pair of Mickey Mouse ears, the Son Tra peninsula is crowned by the peak that the American soldiers called Monkey Mountain. Overlooking Danang to the south and the Hai Van Pass to the north, it was a prized radar and communications base during the American War. Until recently it was a closed military area, but new roads and beach resorts are opening up the peninsula.

The highlight is the view from the summit, which is stupendous on a clear day. All that remains of the American military presence are a couple of radar domes (still used by the Vietnamese military and a no-go for tourists) next to a helicopter pad, now a lookout point. The steep road to the summit is pretty deserted and road conditions can be iffy. If you're going on a motorbike, you'll need a powerful one to make it to the top. The turn-off to this road is about 3km before Tien Sa Port and marked by a blue sign that reads 'Son Tra Eco-Tourism'.

Most Vietnamese who come here head to one of the beach resorts along the peninsula's southwestern coast. The other big attraction on the peninsula is **Linh Ung** (Map p200), a colossal Buddha statue positioned on a lotus-shaped platform that looks south to Danang city; there's a monastery here too.

On the other side of Nui Son Tra, next to the port, is sheltered **Tien Sa Beach**. A memorial near the port commemorates an unfortunate episode of colonial history. Spanish-led Filipino and French troops attacked Danang in August 1858, ostensibly to end Emperor Tu Duc's mistreatment of Catholics. The city quickly fell, but the invaders were hit by sickness. By the summer of 1859, the number of invaders who had died of illness was 20 times the number who had been killed in combat.

Many of the tombs of Spanish and French soldiers are below a **chapel** (Map p200) that's located behind Tien Sa Port.

Around Danang

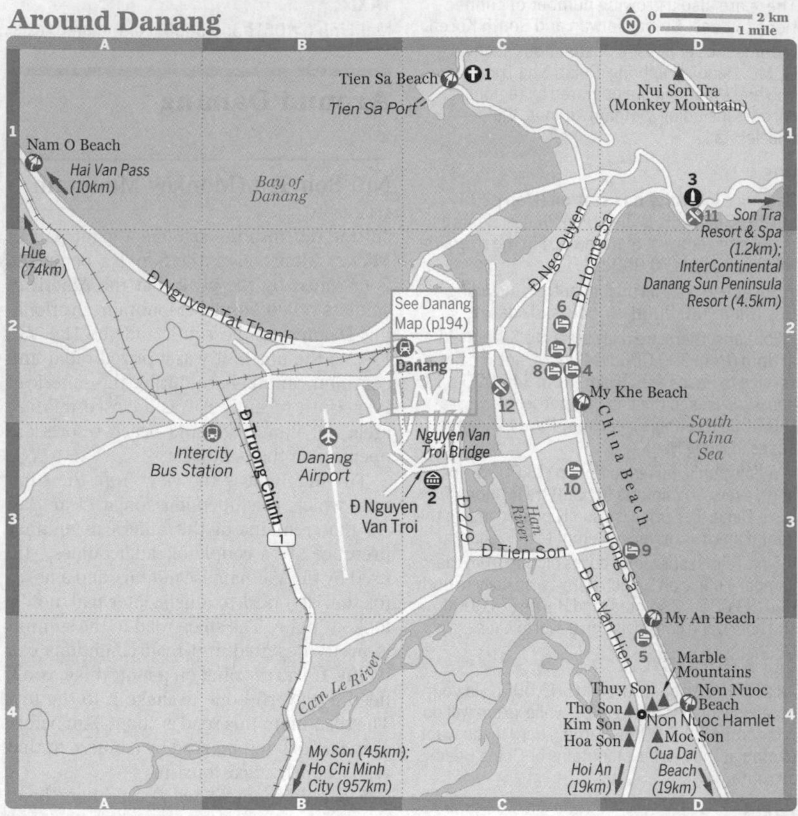

Around Danang

Sights
1 Chapel C1
2 Ho Chi Minh Museum C3
3 Linh Ung D1

Sleeping
4 a la carte C2
5 Bien Nho Hotel D4
6 Eena Hotel C2
7 Frangipani Boutique Hotel C2
8 Funtastic Beach Hostel C2
9 Fusion Maia D3
10 Gold 2 Hotel C3
Sofia Boutique Hotel .... (see 7)

Eating
11 Bay Ban D1
Burger Bros .... (see 10)
12 Fatfish C2

Drinking & Nightlife
Tam's Pub & Surf Shop .... (see 10)
Top Rooftop Lounge .... (see 4)

Sleeping & Eating

There's some construction around the coastline, but Son Tra is largely quiet and a delight to explore by motorbike.

Son Tra Resort & Spa HOTEL $$$
(0511-392 4924; www.sontra.com.vn; Son Tra; villa US$200-250;) Looking directly over a sheltered white-sandy beach, these handsome villas are well maintained, spacious and attractive, and all have kitchens, hardwood floors and sea views. They are ideal for family stays. Make bookings online; deals can be as cheap as US$100 are possible.

InterContinental Danang Sun Peninsula Resort HOTEL $$$
(☎0511-393 8888; http://danang.intercontinental.com; Son Tra; r/ste from US$300/450;) Spilling down a hillside, this huge resort hotel dominates this corner of Son Tra, with golf buggies whisking its pampered guests around the landscaped grounds. There's an impressive spa, fully loaded fitness centre and a huge main pool.

Bay Ban SEAFOOD $$
(Map p200; ☎0511-221 4237; Son Tra; meals 80,000-250,000d; ⏲11am-9.30pm) Seafood restaurant that's very popular with Vietnamese families on weekends and holidays, but usually quiet the rest of the time. Eat right over the water in one of the thatched shelters in the bay. Fresh fish, spider crab, eel and shrimp dishes all feature.

Nam O Beach

Nam O Beach, 15km northwest of Danang, was where the first US combat troops landed in South Vietnam in 1965. There are a few hotels, but the beach is not as attractive as south of Danang.

The villagers make *nuoc mam* (fish sauce) and *goi ca* – raw fish fillets marinated in a special sauce and coated in a spicy powder. It's served with fresh vegetables on rice-paper rolls. You'll find it for sale on the beach in summer or look for it in the village.

Marble Mountains

Just off the China Beach coastal road, the Marble Mountains (Ngu Hanh Son) consist of five craggy marble outcrops topped with pagodas. Each mountain is named for the natural element it's said to represent: Thuy Son (Water), Moc Son (Wood), Hoa Son (Fire), Kim Son (Metal or Gold) and Tho Son (Earth). The villages that have sprung up at the base of the mountains specialise in marble sculpture, though they now astutely use marble from China rather than hacking away at the mountains that bring the visitors in.

Thuy Son (admission 15,000d; ⏲7am-5pm) is the largest and most famous of the five Marble Mountains (and the only one accessible to visitors), with a number of natural caves in which first Hindu and later Buddhist sanctuaries have been created. At the top of the staircase is a gate, **Ong Chon**, which is pockmarked with bullet holes. This leads to **Linh Ong Pagoda**. Behind it, a path heads through two tunnels to caverns that contain several Buddhas and Cham carvings. A flight of steps also leads up to another cave, partially open to the sky, with two seated Buddhas in it. A recently installed elevator is also available to replace the first staircase.

Immediately to the left as you enter Ong Chon Gate is the main path to the rest of Thuy Son, beginning with **Xa Loi Pagoda**, a beautiful stone tower that overlooks the coast. Stairs off the main pathway lead to **Vong Hai Da**, a viewpoint with a panorama of China Beach through scraggly trees. The stone-paved path continues to the right and into a minigorge. On the left is **Van Thong Cave**.

Exit the gorge through a battle-scarred masonry gate. There's a rocky path to the right leading to **Linh Nham**, a tall chimney-shaped cave with a small altar inside. Nearby, another path leads to **Hoa Nghiem**, a shallow cave with a Buddha. Left of here is cathedral-like **Huyen Khong Cave**, lit by an opening to the sky. The entrance to this spectacular chamber is guarded by two administrative mandarins (to the left) and two military mandarins (to the right).

Scattered about the cave are Buddhist and Confucian shrines; note the inscriptions carved into the stone walls. On the right, a door leads to a chamber with two stalactites – during the American War this was used as a VC field hospital. Inside is a plaque dedicated to the Women's Artillery Group, which destroyed 19 US aircraft from a base below the mountains in 1972.

Local buses between Danang and Hoi An (tickets 18,000d) can drop you at Marble Mountains, 10km south of Danang.

China Beach

During the war, the Americans used the name China Beach to refer to the beautiful 30km sweep of fine white sand that starts at Monkey Mountain and ends near Hoi An. Soldiers would be sent here for some R&R from bases all over the country.

The Vietnamese call sections of the beach by different names, including My Khe, My An, Non Nuoc, An Bang and Cua Dai. The northernmost stretch, My Khe, is now basically a suburb of Danang, while in the south An Bang is considered Hoi An's beach. The area between is filled with a growing range of beach resorts.

The best time for swimming is from April to July, when the sea is calmest. At other times the water can get rough. Note that lifeguards only patrol some sections of the beach. The surf can be good from around mid-September to December.

Sights & Activities

My Khe BEACH

Just across the Song Han Bridge, My Khe is fast becoming Danang's easternmost suburb. In the early morning and evening the beach fills up with city folk doing t'ai chi. Tourists emerge during peak sun-tanning hours, while locals prefer the evening. The beach is largely free from hawkers. The water can have a dangerous undertow, especially in winter. However, it's protected by the bulk of Nui Son Tra and is safer than the rest of China Beach.

My An & Non Nuoc BEACH

Much of the central section of China Beach has been parceled off for luxury resort developments. The inland side of the coastal road has a scattering of budget hotels between exclusive golf courses designed by the likes of Greg Norman.

Sleeping

There is a good range of accommodation a short stroll from the sea and good seafood restaurants.

Funtastic Beach Hostel HOSTEL $

(Map p200; ☎0511-392 8789; www.funtastic danang.com; K02/5 Ha Bong; dm/d/apt US$8/24/36;) In the rapidly developing accommodation scene across the river near China Beach, Funtastic Beach Hostel is brightly decorated, has a good rooftop terrace, and a range of rooms from dorms through to a small self-contained apartment that's good for families or friends. Breakfast is included and there's a good chillout area with DVDs and video games on tap.

Eena Hotel HOTEL $

(Map p200; ☎0511-222 5123; www.eenahotel.com; Khu An Cu 3; r 300,000-500,000d;) This Japanese-owned minihotel is a great base in My Khe with its immaculately clean, light, spacious, white rooms. There's a lift, fast wi-fi, friendly English-speaking staff and a good complimentary breakfast.

Bien Nho Hotel HOTEL $

(Map p200; ☎0511-396 7401; biennhohoteldng@gmail.com; 4 Truong Sa, Hoa Hai; r 300,000-400,000d;) Great little minihotel, just across the road from the beach break on My An, so a good option for surfers. Offers well-kept rooms and the jovial owner speaks some English.

Frangipani Boutique Hotel BOUTIQUE HOTEL $$

(Map p200; ☎0511-393 8368; www.frangipani boutiquehotel.com; 8 Nguyen Huu Thong; d US$45;) With just 11 rooms and stylish shared areas, the Frangipani is more like a classy European guesthouse. Rooms are spacious and modern with elegant decor, and it's just a short stroll to the sands of China Beach. A small indoor pool is available downstairs, bicycles are free to use, and there's also a pleasant on-site restaurant with courtyard seating.

Sofia Boutique Hotel HOTEL $$

(Map p200; ☎0511-3941 669; www.sofiahotel danang.com; 111 Đ Pham Van Dong; d US$45;) Handily located a two-minute walk from the beach, the Sofia has spacious and modern rooms decked out in natural timber. There's a good on-site restaurant, a handy cafe downstairs that channels a French ambience, and the friendly staff can arrange tours and transport to Hoi An and beyond.

Gold 2 Hotel HOTEL $$

(Map p200; ☎0511-3958 179; www.gold2hotel.vn; 4-5 Đ Hoang Ke Viem; r 540,000-800,000d, apt from 1,200,000d;) Spotless and modern rooms in one of My Khe's most recently built minihotels. Decor is Asian-inspired and the beach is just across the road. Spacious family apartments are a good option for travelling groups.

a la carte DESIGN HOTEL $$$

(Map p200; www.alacarteliving.com; cnr Đ Vo Nguyen Giap & Đ Duong Dinh Nghe; ste from US$125;) This hotel dominates the beach's skyline with 25 floors of all-suite accommodation, a spa and a fitness centre. Apartment-style suites are spacious and modern, with the best views at the front stretching effortlessly along the coast. An infinity pool sits in front of the hotel's cool rooftop bar, and ground-floor restaurants include a deli and seafood bar.

Fusion Maia HOTEL $$$

(Map p200; ☎0511-396 7999; http://maiadanang.fusion-resorts.com/; Đ Truong Sa, Khue My Beach; villas from US$420;) Contemporary beachfront hotel with an outstanding spa (all guests get a minimum of two treatments per day). And what a wellness zone it is, with treatment rooms, saunas and steam rooms set around a courtyard-style garden. Suites and villas all boast minimalist decor, private pool and gadgets including music-loaded iPods. Free shuttle buses run to/from Hoi An.

Eating & Drinking

Burger Bros BURGERS $

(Map p200; 18 An Thuong 4; burgers 70,000-100,000d; 11am-2pm & 5.30-10pm Tue-Sun) Owned by a hip Japanese surfer, Burger Bros is a cool spot for the best gourmet burgers in central Vietnam, well-priced beer and terrific French fries (try the garlic and rosemary ones with a fruit-packed soda).

Top Rooftop Lounge BAR

(Map p200; a la carte hotel, cnr Đ Vo Nguyen Giap & Đ Duong Dinh Nghe; 11am-late;) Go straight to the Top for the best views of the beach's sprawling arc. Cocktails and imported beers all impress tourists and Danang's smart set as they jostle for position on the sun lounges, funky cane furniture, or in the infinity pool. After dark, the views become even better, as China Beach's glittering necklace of neon and lights sparks up.

Tam's Pub & Surf Shop BAR

(Map p200; 38 An Thuong 5; 7am-11pm;) A stone's throw from China Beach, this is a friendly, popular bar-restaurant with pub grub (think burgers or fish 'n' chips). You can rent boards (US$5 per day, deposit required) and get surfing advice here.

Getting There & Around

The My Khe section of China Beach is just 3km or so east of central Danang and costs around 50,000d by taxi.

Hoi An

0510 / POP 134,000

Graceful, historic Hoi An is Vietnam's most atmospheric and delightful town. Once a major port, it boasts the grand architecture and beguiling riverside setting that befits its heritage, but the 21st-century curses of traffic and pollution are almost entirely absent.

Hoi An owes its easygoing provincial demeanour and remarkably harmonious old-town character more to luck than planning. Had the Thu Bon River not silted up in the late 19th century – so ships could no longer access the town's docks – Hoi An would doubtless be very different today. For a century, the city's allure and importance dwindled until an abrupt rise in fortunes in the 1990s, when a tourism boom transformed the local economy. Today Hoi An is once again a cosmopolitan melting pot, one of the nation's most wealthy towns, a culinary mecca and one of Vietnam's most important tourism centres.

This revival of fortunes has preserved the face of the Old Town and its incredible legacy of tottering Japanese merchant houses, Chinese temples and ancient tea warehouses – though, of course, residents and rice fields have been gradually replaced by tourist businesses. Lounge bars, boutique hotels, travel agents and a glut of tailor shops are very much part of the scene here. And yet, down by the market and over on Cam Nam Island, you'll find life has changed little. Travel a few kilometres further – you'll find some superb bicycle, motorbike and boat trips – and some of central Vietnam's most enticingly laid-back scenery and beaches are within easy reach.

History

The earliest evidence of human habitation here dates back 2200 years: excavated ceramic fragments are thought to belong to the late Iron Age Sa Huynh civilisation, which is related to the Dong Son culture of northern Vietnam. From the 2nd to the 10th centuries, this was a busy seaport of the Champa kingdom, and archaeologists have found the foundations of numerous Cham towers around Hoi An.

In 1307 the Cham king presented Quang Nam province as a gift when he married a Vietnamese princess. When his successor refused to recognise the deal, fighting broke out and chaos reigned for the next century. By the 15th century, peace was restored, allowing commerce to resume. During the next four centuries Hoi An – known as Faifoo to Western traders – was one of Southeast Asia's major ports. Chinese, Japanese, Dutch, Portuguese, Spanish, Indian, Filipino, Indonesian, Thai, French, British and American ships came to call, and the town's warehouses teemed with treasures: high-grade silk, fabrics, paper, porcelain, areca nuts, pepper, Chinese medicines, elephant tusks, beeswax, mother-of-pearl and lacquer.

Chinese and Japanese traders left their mark on Hoi An. Both groups came in the spring, driven south by monsoon winds. They would stay in Hoi An until the summer,

Hoi An

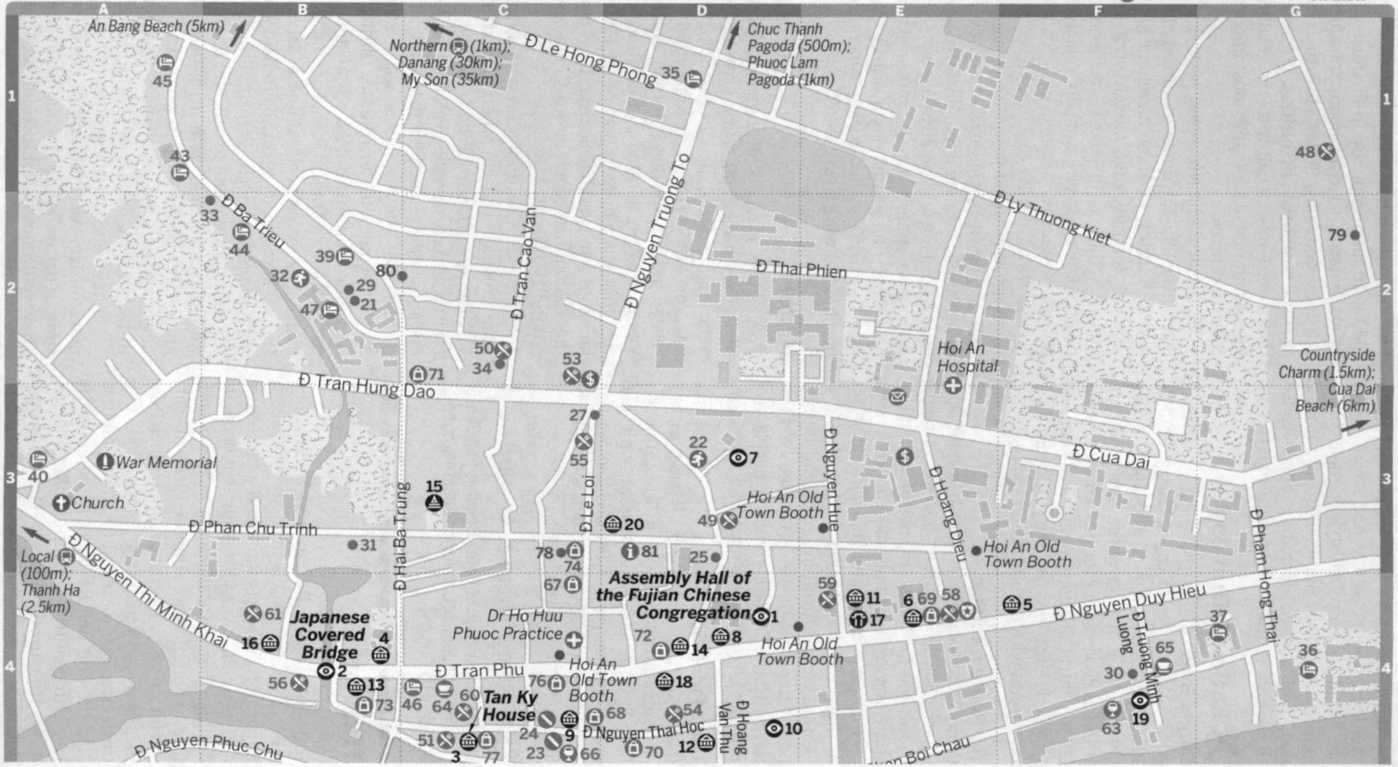

0 200 m
0 0.1 miles
A B C D E F G
1 2 3 4
An Bang Beach (5km)
Northern (1km); Danang (30km); My Son (35km)
Chuc Thanh Pagoda (500m); Phuoc Lam Pagoda (1km)
Đ Le Hong Phong
Đ Ly Thuong Kiet
Đ Ba Trieu
Đ Tran Cao Van
Đ Nguyen Truong To
Đ Thai Phien
Đ Tran Hung Dao
Hoi An Hospital
Countryside Charm (1.5km); Cua Dai Beach (6km)
Đ Cua Dai
War Memorial
Church
Đ Hai Ba Trung
Đ Le Loi
Đ Nguyen Hue
Đ Hoang Dieu
Đ Pham Hong Thai
Đ Phan Chu Trinh
Hoi An Old Town Booth
Local (100m); Thanh Ha (2.5km)
Đ Nguyen Thi Minh Khai
Japanese Covered Bridge
Assembly Hall of the Fujian Chinese Congregation
Dr Ho Huu Phuoc Practice
Đ Tran Phu
Tan Ky House
Đ Nguyen Thai Hoc
Đ Hoang Van Thu
Đ Nguyen Duy Hieu
Đ Truong Minh Luong
Đ Nguyen Phuc Chu
...yen Boi Chau
1 2 3 4 5 6 7 8 9 10 11 12 13 14 15 16 17 18 19 20 21 22 23 24 25 27 29 30 31 32 33 34 35 36 37 39 40 43 44 45 46 47 48 49 50 51 53 54 55 56 58 59 60 61 63 64 65 66 67 68 69 70 71 72 73 74 76 77 78 79 80 81

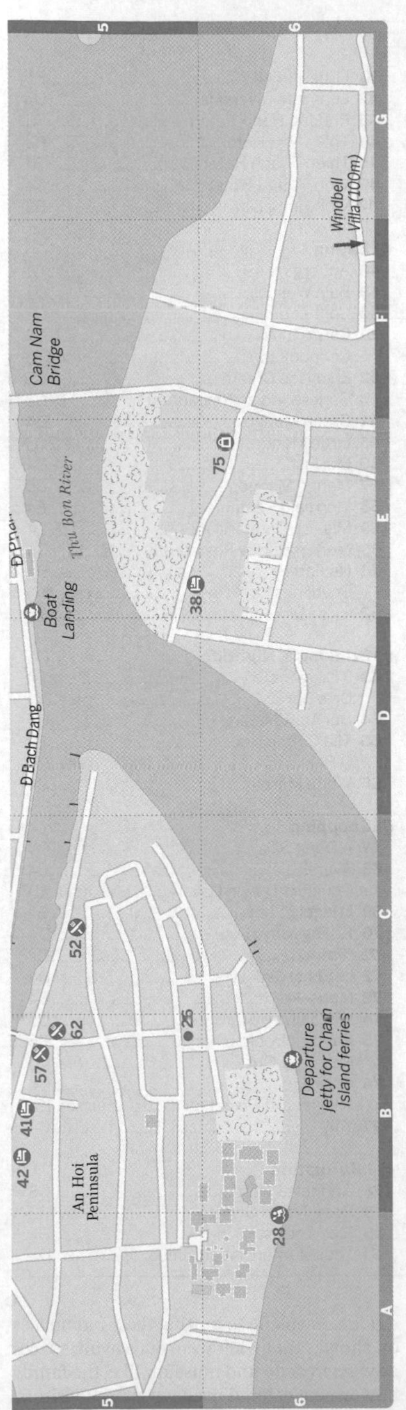

when southerly winds would blow them home. During their four-month sojourn in Hoi An, they rented waterfront houses for use as warehouses and living quarters. Some began leaving full-time agents in Hoi An to take care of their off-season business affairs.

The Japanese ceased coming to Hoi An after 1637 (when the Japanese government forbade contact with the outside world), but the Chinese lingered. The town's Chinese assembly halls still play a special role for southern Vietnam's ethnic Chinese, some of whom come from all over the region to participate in congregation-wide celebrations.

This was also the first place in Vietnam to be exposed to Christianity. Among the 17th-century missionary visitors was Alexandre de Rhodes, who devised the Latin-based *quoc ngu* script for the Vietnamese language.

Although Hoi An was almost completely destroyed during the Tay Son Rebellion, it was rebuilt and continued to be an important port until the late 19th century, when the Thu Bon River silted up. Danang (Tourane) took over as the region's main port.

Under French rule, Hoi An served as an administrative centre. It was virtually untouched in the American War, thanks to the cooperation of both sides. The town was declared a Unesco World Heritage Site in 1999 and there are now very strict rules in place to safeguard the Old Town's unique heritage.

Today Hoi An's economy is booming, and at times the Old Town can struggle to contain the sheer number of visitors. Many accommodation options have opened around the town's periphery, as Hoi An expands to fulfil the ever-hungry tourism sector.

Sights

By Unesco decree, more than 800 historic buildings in Hoi An have been preserved, so much of the **Old Town** (www.hoianworldheritage.org.vn; tickets 120,000d) looks as it did several centuries ago.

The Chinese who settled in Hoi An identified themselves according to their province of origin. Each community built its own assembly hall, known as *hoi quan* in Vietnamese, for social gatherings, meetings and celebrations.

All the old houses, except Diep Dong Nguyen and Quan Thang, offer short guided tours. They are efficient, if a tad perfunctory. You'll be whisked to a heavy wooden chair while your guide recites a scripted

Hoi An

Top Sights

1 Assembly Hall of the Fujian Chinese Congregation D4
2 Japanese Covered Bridge B4
3 Tan Ky House C4

Sights

4 Assembly Hall of the Cantonese Chinese Congregation B4
5 Assembly Hall of the Chaozhou Chinese Congregation F4
6 Assembly Hall of the Hainan Chinese Congregation E4
7 Ba Le Well D3
8 Chinese All-Community Assembly Hall D4
9 Diep Dong Nguyen House C4
10 Handicraft Workshop D4
11 Hoi An Museum of History & Culture E4
12 Museum of Folklore in Hoi An D4
13 Museum of Sa Huynh Culture & Museum of the Revolution B4
14 Museum of Trading Ceramics D4
15 Phac Hat Pagoda C3
16 Phung Hung Old House B4
17 Quan Cong Temple E4
18 Quan Thang House D4
19 Tran Duong House F4
20 Tran Family Chapel D3

Activities, Courses & Tours

21 Active Adventures Vietnam B2
22 Ba Le Beauty Salon D3
23 Blue Coral Diving C4
24 Cham Island Diving Center C4
25 Eat Hoi An D3
26 Heaven & Earth B5
27 Herbs and Spices C3
28 Hoi An Kayak Center A6
29 Hoi An Motorbike Adventures B2
30 Hoi An Photo Tour F4
31 Love of Life B3
Morning Glory Cooking School ..... (see 60)
32 Palmarosa B2
33 Phat Tire Ventures B2
34 Vespa Adventures C2

Sleeping

35 Almanity Hoi An D1
36 Anantara Hoi An Resort G4
37 Ha An Hotel G4
38 Hideout Hostel E5
39 Hoa Binh Hotel B2
40 Hoang Trinh Hotel A3
41 Little Hoi An B5
42 Long Life Riverside B5
43 Phuong Dong Hotel A1
44 Thien Nga Hotel B2
45 Thien Thanh Hotel A1
46 Vinh Hung 1 Hotel C4
47 Vinh Hung Library Hotel B2

Eating

48 Aubergine 49 ..... G1
49 Bale Well D3
50 Cafe Zoom C2
51 Cargo Club C4
Cocobox ..... (see 9)
52 Enjoy Ice Cream C5
53 Ganesh Indian Restaurant C2
54 Green Mango D4
55 Little Menu C3
56 Mai Fish B4
57 Mango Mango B5
58 Mermaid Restaurant E4
59 Miss Ly Cafeteria 22 ..... E4
60 Morning Glory Restaurant C4
61 Nu Eatery B4
Seedlings ..... (see 57)
62 Vy's Market B5

Drinking & Nightlife

63 3 Dragons F4
Dive Bar ..... (see 24)
64 Hoi An Roastery C4
65 Mia Coffee House F4
Q Bar ..... (see 24)
66 White Marble C4

Shopping

67 A Dong Silk C4
68 Avana C4
Couleurs D'Asie Gallery ..... (see 11)
69 Friendly Shop E4
70 Hoang Kim D4
71 Kimmy C2
72 Lotus Jewellery D4
73 Metiseko B4
74 Mosaique Decoration C3
75 Randy's Book Xchange E6
Reaching Out ..... (see 3)
76 Tuoi Ngoc C4
Villagecraft Planet ..... (see 19)
77 Yaly C4

Information

78 Go Travel Vietnam C3
79 Rose Travel Service G2
80 Sinh Tourist B2
81 Tourist Information Office D3

introduction to the house, and gives a souvenir soft sell. You're free to wander around the house after the tour.

One downside to putting these old houses on show is that what were once living spaces now seem dead and museum-like, the family having sequestered itself away from visitors' eyes. Huge tour groups can completely spoil the intimacy of the experience too, as they jostle for photo opportunities.

All four museums are small. Displays are pretty basic and the information provided minimal.

Eighteen of these buildings are open to visitors and require an Old Town ticket for admission; the fee goes towards funding conservation work. Buying a ticket at any of the Old Town booths is easy enough; planning your visit around the byzantine admission options is another matter. Each ticket allows you to visit five different heritage attractions: museums, assembly halls, ancient houses and a traditional music show at the Handicraft Workshop. Tickets are valid for 10 days. Technically, the tickets are for access into the Old Town itself, but you won't normally be checked if you're just dining or shopping in the area. Keep your ticket with you just in case.

Despite the number of tourists who flood into Hoi An, it is still a conservative town. Visitors should dress modestly, especially since some of the old houses are still private homes.

★ Japanese Covered Bridge BRIDGE
(Cau Nhat Ban) FREE This beautiful little bridge is emblematic of Hoi An. A bridge was first constructed here in the 1590s by the Japanese community to link them with the Chinese quarters. Over the centuries the ornamentation has remained relatively faithful to the original Japanese design. The French flattened out the roadway for cars, but the original arched shape was restored in 1986.

The structure is very solidly constructed because of the threat of earthquakes. The entrances to the bridge are guarded by weathered statues: a pair of monkeys on one side, a pair of dogs on the other. According to one story, many of Japan's emperors were born in the years of the dog and monkey. Another tale says that construction of the bridge started in the year of the monkey and was finished in the year of the dog. The stelae, listing all Vietnamese and Chinese contributors to a subsequent restoration of the bridge, are written in *chu nho* (Chinese characters) – the *nom* script had not yet become popular. While access to the Japanese Bridge is free, you have to surrender a ticket to see a small, unimpressive temple built into the bridge's northern side.

★ Assembly Hall of the Fujian Chinese Congregation TEMPLE
(Phuc Kien Hoi Quan; opposite 35 Đ Tran Phu; admission by Old Town ticket; ⏲7am-5.30pm) Originally a traditional assembly hall, this structure was later transformed into a temple for the worship of Thien Hau, a deity from Fujian province. The green-tiled triple gateway dates from 1975. The mural on the right-hand wall depicts Thien Hau, her way lit by lantern light as she crosses a stormy sea to rescue a foundering ship. Opposite is a mural of the heads of the six Fujian families who fled from China to Hoi An in the 17th century.

The penultimate chamber contains a statue of Thien Hau. To either side of the entrance stand red-skinned Thuan Phong Nhi and green-skinned Thien Ly Nhan, deities who alert Thien Hau when sailors are in distress.

In the last chamber, the central altar contains seated figures of the heads of the six Fujian families. The smaller figures below them represent their successors as clan leaders. Behind the altar on the right are three fairies and smaller figures representing the 12 *ba mu* (midwives), each of whom teaches newborns a different skill necessary for the first year of life: smiling, sucking and so forth. Childless couples often come here to pray for offspring and leave fresh fruit as offerings.

★ Tan Ky House HISTORIC BUILDING
(101 Đ Nguyen Thai Hoc; admission by Old Town ticket; ⏲8am-noon & 2-4.30pm) Built two centuries ago by an ethnically Vietnamese family, this gem of a house has been lovingly preserved through seven generations. Look out for signs of Japanese and Chinese influences on the architecture. Japanese elements include the ceiling (in the sitting area), which is supported by three progressively shorter beams, one on top of the other. Under the crab-shell ceiling are carvings of crossed

WATERWORLD

Hoi An's riverside location makes it particularly vulnerable to flooding during the rainy season (October and November). It's common for the waterfront to be hit by sporadic floods of about 1m and a typhoon can bring levels of 2m or more.

HOI AN HOUSES: A CLOSER LOOK

The historical buildings of Hoi An not only survived the 20th century's wars, they also retain features of traditional architecture rarely seen today. As they have been for centuries, some shopfronts are shuttered at night with horizontal planks inserted into grooves that cut into the columns that support the roof.

Some roofs are made up of thousands of brick-coloured *am* and *duong* (yin and yang) roof tiles – so called because of the way the alternating rows of concave and convex tiles fit snugly together. During the rainy season the lichens and moss that live on the tiles spring to life, turning entire rooftops bright green.

A number of Hoi An's houses have round pieces of wood with an *am-duong* symbol in the middle surrounded by a spiral design over the doorway. These *mat cua* (door eyes) are supposed to protect the residents from harm.

Hoi An's historic structures are gradually being sensitively restored. Strict rules govern the colour that houses can be painted and the signs that can be used.

It's not just individual buildings that have survived – it's whole streetscapes. This is particularly true around Đ Tran Phu and waterside promenade Đ Bach Dang. In the former French quarter to the east of Cam Nam Bridge, there's a whole block of colonnaded houses, painted in the mustard yellow typical of French colonial buildings.

sabres wrapped in silk ribbon. The sabres symbolise force, the silk represents flexibility.

The interior is brightened by a beautiful detail: Chinese poems written in inlaid mother-of-pearl hang from some of the columns that hold up the roof. The Chinese characters on these 150-year-old panels are formed entirely of birds gracefully portrayed in various positions of flight.

The courtyard has several functions: to let in light, provide ventilation, bring a glimpse of nature into the home, and collect rainwater and provide drainage. The carved wooden balcony supports around the courtyard are decorated with grape leaves, which are a European import and further evidence of the unique blending of cultures in Hoi An.

The back of the house faces the river and was rented out to foreign merchants. Marks on one wall record recent flood heights, including the 1964 record when the water covered almost the entire ground level. There are two pulleys attached to a beam in the loft – in the past they were used for moving goods into storage, and today for raising furniture for safekeeping from the floods.

The exterior of the roof is made of tiles; inside, the ceiling consists of wood. This design keeps the house cool in summer and warm in winter.

Tran Family Chapel HISTORIC BUILDING

(21 Đ Le Loi; admission by Old Town ticket; ⏲7.30am-noon & 2-5.30pm) Built for worshipping family ancestors, this chapel dates back to 1802. It was commissioned by Tran Tu, one of the clan who ascended to the rank of mandarin and served as an ambassador to China. His picture is to the right of the chapel. The architecture of the building reflects the influence of Chinese (the 'turtle' style roof), Japanese (triple beam) and vernacular (look out for the bow-and-arrow detailing) styles.

The central door is reserved for the dead – it's opened at Tet and on 11 November, the death anniversary of the main ancestor. Traditionally, women entered from the left and men from the right, although these distinctions are no longer observed.

The wooden boxes on the altar contain the Tran ancestors' stone tablets, with chiselled Chinese characters setting out the dates of birth and death, along with some small personal effects. On the anniversary of each family member's death, their box is opened, incense is burned and food is offered.

After a short tour, you'll be shown to the 'antique' room, where there are lots of coins for sale, and a side room full of souvenirs.

Quan Cong Temple CONFUCIAN TEMPLE

(Chua Ong; 24 Đ Tran Phu; admission by Old Town ticket) Founded in 1653, this small temple is dedicated to Quan Cong, an esteemed Chinese general who is worshipped as a symbol of loyalty, sincerity, integrity and justice. His partially gilded statue, made of papier-mâché on a wooden frame, is on the central altar at the back of the sanctuary. When someone makes an offering to the portly looking Quan Cong, the caretaker solemnly strikes a bronze bowl that makes a bell-like sound.

On the left of Quan Cong is a statue of General Chau Xuong, one of his guardians, striking a tough-guy pose. On the right is the rather plump administrative mandarin Quan Binh. The life-sized white horse recalls a mount ridden by Quan Cong.

Check out the carp-shaped rain spouts on the roof surrounding the courtyard. The carp is a symbol of patience in Chinese mythology and is popular in Hoi An.

Shoes should be removed when mounting the platform in front of the statue of Quan Cong.

Phuoc Lam Pagoda BUDDHIST TEMPLE
(Thon 2a, Cam Ha; ⌚8am-5pm) This pagoda (founded in the mid-17th century) is associated with An Thiem, a Vietnamese prodigy and monk from the age of eight. When he was 18, he volunteered for the army so his brothers could escape the draft; he eventually rose to the rank of general. Later he returned to the monkhood, but to atone for his sins of war he volunteered to clean the Hoi An market for 20 years, then joined this pagoda as its head monk.

To reach the pagoda, continue past Chuc Thanh Pagoda for 500m. The path passes an obelisk that was erected over the tomb of 13 ethnic Chinese who were decapitated by the Japanese during WWII for resistance activities.

Museum of Trading Ceramics MUSEUM
(80 Đ Tran Phu; admission by Old Town ticket; ⌚7am-5.30pm) Occupies a restored wooden house and contains artefacts from all over Asia, with oddities from as far afield as Egypt. While this reveals that Hoi An had some rather impressive trading links, it takes an expert's eye to appreciate the display. The exhibition on the restoration of Hoi An's old houses provides a useful crash course in Old Town architecture.

Chinese All-Community Assembly Hall HISTORIC BUILDING
(Chua Ba; ☎0510-861 935; 64 Đ Tran Phu; ⌚8am-5pm) FREE Founded in 1773, this assembly hall was used by Fujian, Cantonese, Hainan, Chaozhou and Hakka congregations in Hoi An. To the right of the entrance are portraits of Chinese resistance heroes in Vietnam who died during WWII. The well-restored main temple is a total assault on the senses, with great smoking incense spirals, demonic-looking deities, dragons and lashings of red lacquer – it's dedicated to Thien Hau.

Assembly Hall of the Chaozhou Chinese Congregation HISTORIC BUILDING
(Trieu Chau Hoi Quan; opposite 157 Đ Nguyen Duy Hieu; admission by Old Town ticket; ⌚8am-5pm) Built in 1752, the highlight in this congregational hall is the gleaming woodcarvings on the beams, walls and altar – absolutely stunning in their intricacy. You could stand here for hours to unravel the stories, but if you're just popping by quickly, look for the carvings on the doors in front of the altar of two Chinese women wearing their hair in an unexpectedly Japanese style.

Chuc Thanh Pagoda BUDDHIST TEMPLE
(Khu Vuc 7, Tan An; ⌚8am-6pm) Founded in 1454 by a Buddhist monk from China, this is the oldest pagoda in Hoi An. Among the antique ritual objects still in use are several bells, a stone gong that is two centuries old and a carp-shaped wooden gong said to be even more venerable. To get to Chuc Thanh Pagoda, go north all the way to the end of Đ Nguyen Truong To and turn left. Follow the lane for 500m.

Handicraft Workshop WORKSHOP
(9 Đ Nguyen Thai Hoc; admission by Old Town ticket) Housed in a 200-year-old Chinese trading house, the Handicraft Workshop has artisans making silk lanterns and practising traditional embroidery in the back. In the front is your typical tourist-oriented cultural show with traditional singers, dancers and musicians. It makes a sufficiently diverting break from sightseeing.

Tran Duong House HISTORIC SITE
(25 Đ Phan Boi Chau; admission 20,000d; ⌚9am-7pm) There's a whole block of colonnaded French colonial buildings on Đ Phan Boi Chau between Nos 22 and 73, among them the 19th-century Tran Duong House. It's still a private home, so a family member will show you around. There's some antique French and Chinese furniture, including a sideboard buffet and a sitting room set with elaborate mother-of-pearl inlay. By contrast, the large, plain wooden table in the front room is the family bed.

Hoi An Museum of History & Culture MUSEUM
(7 Đ Nguyen Hue; admission by Old Town ticket; ⌚7am-5.30pm) Housed in the Quan Am Pagoda, this museum provides a sampling of

pre-Cham, Cham and port-era artefacts, with some huge bells, historic photos, old scales and weights alongside plenty of ceramics.

Quan Thang House HISTORIC BUILDING
(77 Đ Tran Phu; admission by Old Town ticket; ⏲7am-5pm) This house is three centuries old and was built by a Chinese captain. As usual, the architecture includes Japanese and Chinese elements. There are some especially fine carvings of peacocks and flowers on the teak walls of the rooms around the courtyard, on the roof beams and under the crab-shell roof (in the salon beside the courtyard).

Assembly Hall of the Cantonese Chinese Congregation HISTORIC BUILDING
(Quang Trieu Hoi Quan; 176 Đ Tran Phu; admission by Old Town ticket; ⏲8am-5pm) Founded in 1786, this assembly hall has a tall, airy entrance that opens onto a splendidly over-the-top mosaic statue of a dragon and a carp. The main altar is dedicated to Quan Cong. The garden behind has an even more incredible dragon statue.

Assembly Hall of the Hainan Chinese Congregation HISTORIC BUILDING
(Hai Nam Hoi Quan; 10 Đ Tran Phu; ⏲8am-5pm) FREE Built in 1851, this assembly hall is a memorial to 108 merchants from Hainan Island who were mistaken for pirates and killed in Quang Nam province in 1851. The elaborate dais contains plaques to their memory. In front of the central altar is a fine gilded woodcarving of Chinese court life.

Phung Hung Old House HISTORIC BUILDING
(4 Đ Nguyen Thi Minh Khai; admission by Old Town ticket; ⏲8am-7pm) Just a few steps down from the Japanese Covered Bridge, this old house has a wide, welcoming entrance hall decorated with exquisite lanterns, wall hangings and embroidery. There's also an impressive suspended altar.

Diep Dong Nguyen House HISTORIC BUILDING
(58 Đ Nguyen Thai Hoc; ⏲8am-noon & 2-4.30pm) FREE Built for a wealthy Chinese merchant in the late 19th century, this old house looks like an apothecary from another era. The front room was once a dispensary for *thuoc bac* (Chinese medicine); the medicines were stored in the glass-enclosed cases lining the walls.

Museum of Folklore in Hoi An MUSEUM
(33 Đ Nguyen Thai Hoc/62 Đ Bach Dang; admission by Old Town ticket; ⏲7am-5.30pm) Located in a 150-year-old Chinese trading house. The exhibits give some idea of local customs and culture, though it's awfully dusty and decontextualised for a folk-history museum. The view of the river from upstairs is very picturesque.

Phac Hat Pagoda BUDDHIST TEMPLE
(673 Đ Hai Ba Trung) FREE Phac Hat Pagoda has a colourful facade of ceramics and murals and an elaborate roof with snake-like dragons. There's a huge central courtyard containing hundreds of potted plants and bonsai trees.

Museum of Sa Huynh Culture & Museum of the Revolution MUSEUM
(149 Đ Tran Phu; admission by Old Town ticket; ⏲7am-5.30pm) On the lower floor you'll find stone, bronze, gold, glass and agate jewellery, assorted ceramic fragments and burial jars dating from the early Dong Son civilisation of Sa Huynh. The upper floor's revolution museum was closed at the time of research.

Ba Le Well LANDMARK
FREE This square well's claim to fame is that it's the source of water for making authentic *cao lau,* a Hoi An speciality. The well is said to date from Cham times and elderly people make their daily pilgrimage to fill pails here. To find it, turn down the alley opposite 35 Đ Phan Chu Trinh and take the second laneway to the right.

Activities

Diving & Snorkelling

A trip to the Cham Islands is a superb excursion, and Hoi An's two dive schools offer packages including overnight camping and diving trips. The diving is not world class, but can be intriguing.

A PADI Discover Scuba dive costs US$70, two fun dives are US$80, while Open Water courses start at around US$350. Snorkelling costs around US$42, including gear, with an overnight beach camping option adding another US$40.

It's usually only possible to dive or snorkel between February and September; the best conditions and visibility are from June to August.

Cham Island Diving Center DIVING
(☎0510-391 0782; www.vietnamscubadiving.com; 88 Đ Nguyen Thai Hoc) Run by a friendly, experienced team, this dive shop's mantra is 'no troubles, make bubbles'. They've a large boat and also a speedboat for zippy transfers. Also runs one-day and overnight trips to the Cham Islands.

Blue Coral Diving DIVING
(☎0510-627 9297; www.divehoian.com; 77 Đ Nguyen Thai Hoc) A friendly, professional outfit with an 18m dive boat and additional speedboat.

Massage & Spa

There are many massage and treatment centres in Hoi An. Most are average, run by locals with minimal experience or training. A basic massage costs around US$12 an hour – there's a strip along Đ Ba Trieu. At the other end of the scale are indulgent places that offer a wonderful spa experience (with prices to match); these are mostly based in the luxury hotels.

Palmarosa SPA
(☎0510-393 3999; www.palmarosaspa.vn; 90 Đ Ba Trieu; massages & treatments from 220,000d; ⊙10am-9pm) This highly professional spa offers massages (including Thai and Swedish), scrubs, facials, and hand and foot care.

Countryside Charm SPA
(Duyen Que; ☎0510-350 1584; http://spahoian.vn; 512 Đ Cua Dai; 1hr massage from US$20; ⊙8am-11pm) On the beach road, this treatment centre has functional premises, but staff are well trained. It also arranges complimentary pick-up from Hoi An.

Ba Le Beauty Salon SPA
(☎0905 226 974; www.balewellbeautysalon.com; 45 11 Đ Tran Hung Dao; ⊙9am-7pm) Ba Le is run by a fluent English speaker, who has trained in the UK, and offers inexpensive threading, waxing, facials, manicure and pedicures.

Courses

Cooking

Hoi An has become a mecca for Vietnamese cooking courses, with many restaurants offering classes. These range from a simple set-up in someone's backyard to purpose-built schools.

The town does make an ideal place for budding chefs. There are many local specialities unique to the Hoi An region, but most are fiendishly tricky to prepare.

Courses often start with a visit to the market to learn more about key Vietnamese ingredients.

Green Bamboo Cooking School COOKING COURSE
(☎0905 815 600; www.greenbamboo-hoian.com; 21 Đ Truong Minh Hung, Cam An; per person US$40) Directed by Van, a charming local chef and English speaker, these courses are more personalised than most. Groups are limited to a maximum of 10, and take place in Van's spacious kitchen. Choose what to cook from a diverse menu including vegetarian choices. It's 5km east of the centre, near Cu Dai beach, and transport from Hoi An is included.

Herbs and Spices COOKING COURSE
(☎0510-393 6868; www.herbsandspicesvn.com; 2/6 Đ Le Loi; per person US$35-59; ⊙10.30am, 4.30pm & 8pm) Excellent classes with three different menu options, and smaller more hands-on groups than some other cookery classes.

Morning Glory Cooking School COOKING COURSE
(☎0510-224 1555; www.msvy-tastevietnam.com; 106 Đ Nguyen Thai Hoc; half-day course US$25-32) This is the cooking course that launched Hoi An cooking courses. It's directed by Trinh Diem Vy, owner of several restaurants in town, or one of her protégés. Classes concentrate on local recipes including *cao lau* and 'white rose'; they can have up to 30 people and some people feel the whole experience is a little too organised.

Red Bridge Cooking School COOKING COURSE
(☎0510-393 3222; www.visithoian.com/redbridge; Thon 4, Cam Thanh; per person US$32-52) At this school, going to class involves a relaxing 4km cruise down the river. There are half-day and full-day courses, both of which include market visits. The half-day class focuses on local specialities, with rice-paper making and food decoration tips thrown in for good measure. The full-day class instructs participants in the fine art of *pho* (beef noodle soup).

As an added sweetener, there's a 20m swimming pool at the school. It's 4km east of the centre on the banks of the Thu Bon River.

TOURS AROUND HOI AN

The Vietnamese countryside and rural lanes around Hoi An beg to be explored. Motorbike and bicycle trips are popular and there's no better way to appreciate the countryside than on two wheels. Jeep tours are another option, and new water-based options include paddle boarding and kayaking.

The idyllic Cham Islands make another perfect day-trip destination during the March to September season. Both Hoi An dive schools run tours (p210).

Active Adventures Vietnam (☎0905 101 930; www.activeadventures-vietnam.com; 111 Ba Trieu) Heading up into the hills behind Hoi An, this group offers tours in original US jeeps to a Co Tu tribal village. There are hot springs and great hikes in the region.

Hoi An Motorbike Adventures (☎0905 101 930; www.motorbiketours-hoian.com; 111 Ba Trieu) Specialises in tours on cult Minsk motorbikes. The guides really know the terrain and the trips make use of beautiful back roads and riverside tracks.

Phat Tire Ventures (☎0510-653 9839; www.ptv-vietnam.com; 62 Ba Trieu) Offers a terrific mountain bike trip to the My Son ruins that takes in country lanes and temple visits. Also offers adventure thrills via rappelling and rock climbing.

SUP Monkey (☎0935 622 564; www.supmonkey.net; per person US$30-70) Take to a stand-up paddle board to explore the waterways around Hoi An. Options include a sunrise tour and exploring the lagoon beside Tra Que village.

Hoi An Free Tour (☎0905 164 397; www.hoianfreetour.com) Ride on a bike around the fringes of Hoi An with students. You get to meet the locals and see village life, they get to practise their English.

Vespa Adventures (☎0938 500 997; www.vespaadventures.com; 134 Đ Tran Cao Van; per person $US65-76) Quite possibly the most fun and most stylish way to explore around Hoi An, Vespa Adventures offers the opportunity to ride pillion on classic retro two-wheelers with an Italian accent. There are morning and afternoon departures, and a popular after dark 'Streets & Eats' option with lots of good food and cold beer. Tours kick off from Cafe Zoom (p215).

Eat Hoi An (Coconut Tours; ☎0905 411 184; www.eathoian.com; 37 Đ Phan Chau Trinh; per person US$35) Lots of really authentic cuisine and the infectious enthusiasm of host Phuoc make this an excellent choice if you really want to explore the grassroots local street-food scene. Be prepared for *lots* of different foods and flavours; check the website for details of cooking classes held in Phuoc's home village.

Taste of Hoi An (☎0905 382 783; www.tasteofhoian.com) Walk the streets to meet the vendors, then munch your lunch in an ancient (air-conditioned!) Hoi An townhouse.

Heaven & Earth (☎0510-386 4362; www.vietnam-bicycle.com; 57 Đ Ngo Quyen, An Hoi; tours US$12-49) Cycling tours are well thought out and not too strenuous; they explore the Song Thu river delta area. Recently launched mountain bike tours.

Love of Life (☎0510-350 5017; www.hoian-bicycle.com.vn; 95b Đ Phan Chu Trinh; tours US$19) Has good bicycle tours along quiet country lanes past vegetable gardens and fishing villages, and walking tours of Hoi An.

Hoi An Kayak Center (☎0905 056 640; www.hoiankayak.com; 125 Đ Ngo Quyen) Self-paddle rentals for US$10 per hour, or two-hour guided leisure paddles for US$25 per person.

Hoi An Photo Tour (☎0905 671 898; www.hoianphototour.com; 42 Đ Phan Boi Chau; per person US$35) Excellent tours with experienced photographer Etienne Bossot. Sunrise and sunset tours are most popular, harnessing Hoi An's delicate light for images of fishermen and rice paddies. Experienced and newbie photographers are both catered for, and specialist private and night-time workshops are also available.

Hoi An Eco Tour (☎0510-392 8900; www.hoianecotour.com; Phuoc Hai village; tours US$60-75) Offers cultural activities along the river: you can fish, paddle a basket boat, ride a buffalo or learn about wet rice planting.

Yoga

Hoi An Yoga YOGA

(☎0168 874 1406; http://hoianyoga.com) Professional hatha and yin yoga classes either in the operator's home studio in Cam Thanh village, or in a nearby breezy pavilion location dubbed the Field. Check the website for the latest schedule and location details.

Festivals

Full Moon Festival CULTURAL

(⌚5-11pm) Hoi An is a delightful place to be on the 14th day of each lunar month, when the town celebrates a Full Moon Festival. Motorised vehicles are banned from the Old Town, street markets selling handicrafts, souvenirs and food open up, and all the lanterns come out! Traditional plays and musical events are also performed.

Sleeping

Hoi An has good-value accommodation in all price categories. There are only a couple of hotels in the Old Town, but plenty of options close by. Many budget and midrange places are spread out to the northwest around Đ Hai Ba Trung and Đ Ba Trieu. Pretty An Hoi Peninsula and Can Nam island are also very close to the Old Town. The best places book up fast, so plan as far ahead as you can.

Many luxury hotels are a few kilometres from town, on the beach, but all offer shuttle-bus transfers. Another option is staying at An Bang beach.

Hideout Hostel HOSTEL $

(☎0510-392 7359; www.vietnamhideouthostels.com; To 5, Thon Xuyen Trung, Cam Nam; dm US$9-11, d US$25; ❄@🛜🏊) Across the Thu Bon River on Can Nam island, the Hideout is an excellent recent addition to Hoi An's accommodation scene. Dorms and rooms are colourful and spacious, rates include a free beer or soft drink every night, and the centre of town is a 10-minute walk away. Other highlights include a small swimming pool and the popular Hideout Bar.

Hoi An Backpackers Hostel HOSTEL $

(☎0510-391 4400; www.vietnambackpackerhostels.com; 252 Đ Cua Dai; dm/s/tw/d US$7/18/36/36; ❄@🛜) Offering loads of backpacker-friendly attractions, this is the new Hoi An location for a hostel empire spanning Vietnam. Bikes, breakfast and the occasional beer are all free, and accommodation ranges from dorms through to private rooms with en-suite bathrooms. Regular tours take in Hoi An's street-food scene, and there's an exceedingly social bar with regular happy hour deals.

Phuong Dong Hotel HOTEL $

(☎0510-391 6477; www.phuongdonghoian.com; 42 Đ Ba Trieu; s/d/tr US$13/16/20; ❄@🛜) It's nothing fancy, but a safe budget bet: plain, good-value rooms with comfortable mattresses, reading lights, fridge and air-con. The owners rent motorbikes at fair rates too.

Hoang Trinh Hotel HOTEL $

(☎0510-391 6579; www.hoianhoangtrinhhotel.com; 45 Đ Le Quy Don; r US$22-35; ❄@🛜) Well-run hotel with helpful, friendly staff where travellers are made to feel welcome. Rooms are quite 'old school' Vietnamese but spacious and clean. A generous breakfast and pick-up from bus stations are included.

Hoa Binh Hotel HOTEL $

(☎0510-391 6838; www.hoabinhhotelhoian.com; 696 Đ Hai Ba Trung; dm US$8, r US$16-20; ❄@🛜🏊) A good selection of modern rooms, all with minibar, cable TV and air-con, and a reasonable dorm. The inclusive breakfast is good, but the pool is covered by a roof.

Ha An Hotel HISTORIC HOTEL $$

(☎0510-386 3126; www.haanhotel.com; 6-8 Đ Phan Boi Chau; r US$60-109; ❄@🛜) Elegant and refined, the Ha An feels more like a colonial mansion than a hotel. All rooms have nice individual touches – a textile wall hanging or painting – and views over a gorgeous central garden. The helpful, well-trained staff make staying here a very special experience. It's about a 10-minute walk from the centre in the French Quarter.

Thien Nga Hotel HOTEL $$

(☎0510-391 6330; www.thienngahotel.com; 52 Đ Ba Trieu; r US$25-35; ❄@🛜🏊) This place has a fine selection of rooms; most are spacious, light and airy and have a balcony and a minimalist feel (though the bathrooms are more prosaic). Book one at the rear if you can for garden views. Staff are smiley and accommodating, and breakfast is generous. The pool is covered by a roof though.

Vinh Hung Library Hotel HOTEL $$

(☎0510-391 6277; www.vinhhunglibraryhotel.com; 96 Đ Ba Trieu; r US$50-65; ❄@🛜🏊) A fine minihotel with modish rooms that have huge beds, dark-wood furniture, writing desks and satellite TV; some rooms also have balconies. All bathrooms are sleek and inviting, and breakfast is included. The rooftop pool area is perfect for catching some rays or cooling off.

Thien Thanh Hotel HOTEL $$

(Blue Sky Hotel; ☎0510-391 6545; www.hoianthienthanhhotel.com; 16 Đ Ba Trieu; r US$40-70; @) Staff are dressed in traditional *ao dai* at this atmospheric hotel and maintain good service standards. The hotel's spacious, inviting and well-equipped rooms enjoy a few Vietnamese decorative flourishes, DVD players and bath-tubs. At the rear the pool is a small indoor-outdoor affair, but the oasis-like rear garden is a real bonus.

Long Life Riverside HOTEL $$

(☎0510-391 1696; www.longlifehotels.com; 61 Đ Nguyen Phuc Chu; r US$22-105; @) Impressive hotel with a peaceful riverside setting on An Hoi Peninsula where there's virtually zero traffic noise to contend with. Rooms are spacious, all boasting tasteful modern furnishings, a computer and state-of-the-art bathrooms complete with jazzy jacuzzi-style bath-tubs. The pool area, in the centre of the hotel, is a bit of an afterthought, however.

Orchid Garden Hotel GUESTHOUSE $$

(☎0510-386 3720; www.hoianorchidgarden.com; 382 Đ Cua Dai; r US$40-60; @) Between town and beach about 2.5km east of the centre, this little guesthouse has spacious accommodation with hardwood and marble flooring. The inviting bungalows with kitchen are ideal for self-catering and guests get free bike use and breakfast.

Hoi An Garden Villas HOTEL $$

(☎0510-393 9539; www.hoiangardenvillas.com; 145 Đ Tran Nhat Duat; r US$70-110;) Enjoying a tranquil location on a quiet, suburban lane, this eight-roomed hotel has attractive rooms, all with huge beds, bath-tubs, a balcony or terrace with pool views and fine-quality furnishings. It's about 2km east of the centre.

Windbell Villa HOMESTAY $$

(☎0510-393 0888; www.windbellhomestay.com.vn; 127 Nguyen Tri Phuong, Chau Trung, Cam Nam Island; r US$50-80, villas US$95-145; @) A luxury homestay with lovely spacious rooms and villas that either have a pool or garden view and a huge flat-screen TV. The host family is a delight. Located on Cam Nam island, a 10-minute walk from the Old Town, which offers a more local experience.

Almanity Hoi An BOUTIQUE HOTEL $$$

(☎0510-366 6888; www.almanityhoian.com; 326 Đ Ly Thuong Kiet; d from US$140;) Heritage style and modern rooms combine at the Almanity, just maybe the most relaxing hotel in town. Gardens and swimming pools create a laid-back haven despite the central location, happy hour in the bar often runs for three hours, and there's a full menu of spa and massage services on tap. Check online for good-value Spa Journey packages.

Hoi An Chic Hotel HOTEL $$$

(☎0510-392 6799; www.hoianchic.com; Đ Nguyen Trai; r US$95-130; @) Surrounded by rice fields, halfway between town and the beach, Hoi An Chic enjoys a tranquil, near-rural location. The hip design features colourful furnishings, outdoor bathrooms and an elevated pool. Staff are very eager to please, and there's a free shuttle (in an original US jeep!) to town. It's 3km east of the centre.

Little Hoi An HOTEL $$$

(☎0510-386 9999; www.littlehoian.com; 2 Đ Thoai Ngoc Hau; r/ste from US$75/95;) Boasting a superb position opposite the Old Town in tranquil An Hoi, this new hotel has real polish and class. Rooms are very comfortable indeed, with furnishings that are very high grade, and sleek en-suite bathrooms. Staff are welcoming and there's a good restaurant and small spa. The pool is tiny and covered.

Vinh Hung 1 Hotel HISTORIC HOTEL $$$

(☎0510-386 1621; www.vinhhungheritagehotel.com; 143 Đ Tran Phu; r US$80-90; @) For a unique experience, this hotel (occupying a 200-year-old townhouse) is unmatched. The whole timber structure simply oozes history and mystique – you can almost hear echoes of the house's ancestors as they negotiate spice deals with visiting traders from Japan and Manchuria. Rooms at the rear are a little dark. Room 208 featured in *The Quiet American* film (2002).

Anantara Hoi An Resort RESORT $$$

(☎0510-391 4555; www.hoi-an.anantara.com; 1 Đ Pham Hong Thai; r/ste from US$130/155; @) There's a real attention to detail at this large colonial-style resort with beautifully furnished rooms that have a really contemporary look, and wonderful bathrooms. The expansive grounds are immaculately maintained and there's an

Irish pub, fine restaurant, cafe, spa and sublime riverside pool area. It's located in the French Quarter, a short walk from the heart of town.

Eating

Central Vietnamese cuisine is arguably the nation's most complex and flavoursome, combining fresh herbs (which are sourced from organic gardens close by) with culinary influence from centuries of links with China, Japan and Europe.

The beauty of Hoi An is that you can snag a spectacular cheap meal at the central market and in casual eateries – or you can splash out on a fine-dining experience.

Hoi An is also blessed with many international dining choices.

Mermaid Restaurant VIETNAMESE **$**
(0510-386 1527; www.restaurant-hoian.com; 2 Đ Tran Phu; meals 45,000-115,000d; 10.30am-10pm) For local specialities, you can't beat this modest little restaurant, owned by local legend Vy, who chose the location because it was close to the market, ensuring the freshest produce was directly at hand. Hoi An's holy culinary trinity (*cao lau*, white rose and *banh xeo*) are all superb, as are the special fried wontons.

Cocobox CAFE **$**
(www.cocoboxvietnam.com; 94 Đ Le Loi; juices & smoothies 60,000-75,000d; 9am-9pm Mon-Sat) Refreshing cold-press juices are the standout at this compact combo of cafe and deli. Our favourite is the Watermelon Man juice combining watermelon, passion fruit, lime and mint. Coffee, salads and snacks are also good – try the chicken pesto sandwich. The attached 'farm shop' sells Vietnamese artisan produce, including local honey and cider from Saigon.

Bale Well VIETNAMESE **$**
(45-51 Đ Tran Cao Van; meals 100,000d; 11.30am-10pm) Down a little alley near the famous well, this local place is renowned for one dish: barbecued pork, served up satay-style, which you then combine with fresh greens and herbs to create your own fresh spring roll. A global reputation means it can get busy.

Vy's Market VIETNAMESE **$**
(www.msvy-tastevietnam.com/the-market/; Nguyen Hoang, An Hoi; meals 70,000-120,000d; 8am-11pm;) Offering a (sanitised) street-food-style experience for those slightly wary, this huge place has food stations cranking out Vietnamese favourites from all around the country. You sit on benches in a courtyard-like space and the menu is available on electronic tablets. Drinks include beer, lassis, smoothies and juices, and don't leave without trying the cinnamon or lemongrass ice cream.

Cafe Zoom CAFE **$**
(www.facebook.com/cafezoomhoian; 134 Đ Tran Cao Van; meals 70,000-120,000d; 7am-11pm;) Look for the retro Vespas outside this cool cafe and bar that also doubles as the Hoi An location for the friendly Vespa Adventures (p212) crew. Cold beer is well-priced, comfort eats include burgers and tacos, and there's a good mix of classic songs you can hum along to while you're deciding which Vespa trip to sign up for.

Little Menu VIETNAMESE **$**
(www.thelittlemenu.com; 12 Đ Le Loi; meals 45,000-115,000d; 9.30am-11pm;) English-speaking owner Son is a fantastic host at this great little restaurant with an open kitchen and short menu – try the fish in banana leaf or duck spring rolls.

Enjoy Ice Cream ICE CREAM **$**
(www.enjoy-hoian.com; 13 Đ Nguyen Phuc Chu, An Hoi; ice cream from 60,000d; 8am-11pm) More than 50 flavours and Old Town views combine across the river in An Hoi. We're still thinking about the salted caramel flavour.

A HOI AN TASTER

Hoi An is a culinary hot bed and there are some unique dishes you should be sure to sample.

'White rose' or *banh vac* is an incredibly delicate, subtly-flavoured shrimp dumpling topped with crispy onions. *Banh bao* is another steamed dumpling, this time with minced pork or chicken, onions, eggs and mushrooms that's said to be derived from Chinese dim sum. *Cao lau* is an amazing dish – Japanese-style noodles seasoned with herbs, salad greens and bean sprouts and served with slices of roast pork. Other local specialities are fried *hoanh thanh* (wonton) and *banh xeo* (crispy savoury pancakes rolled with herbs in fresh rice paper). Most restaurants serve these items, but quality varies widely.

★Nu Eatery FUSION **$$**
(www.facebook.com/nueateryhoian; 10a Đ Nguyen Thi Minh Khai; mains 80,000d; ⏲noon-9pm Mon-Sat) Don't be deceived by the humble decor at this compact eatery tucked away near the Japanese Bridge. There's a real wow factor to the seasonal small plates at our new favourite Hoi An restaurant. Combine the pork belly steamed buns with a salad of grilled pineapple, coconut and pomelo, and don't miss the homemade lemongrass, ginger or chilli ice cream.

A well-chosen wine list – by the glass or the bottle – showcases Australian, French and South American varietals.

★Cargo Club INTERNATIONAL, VIETNAMESE **$$**
(☎0510-391 1227; www.msvy-tastevietnam.com/cargo-club; 107 Đ Nguyen Thai Hoc; meals 60,000-150,000d; ⏲8am-11pm; 📶) Remarkable cafe-restaurant, serving Vietnamese and Western food, with a terrific riverside location (the upper terrace has stunning views). A relaxing day here munching your way around the menu would be a day well spent. The breakfasts are legendary (try the eggs Benedict), the patisserie and cakes are superb, and fine-dining dishes and good cocktails also deliver.

★Morning Glory Restaurant VIETNAMESE **$$**
(☎0510-224 1555; www.msvy-tastevietnam.com/morning-glory; 106 Đ Nguyen Thai Hoc; meals 60,000-160,000d; ⏲8am-11pm; 📶🖉) An outstanding restaurant in historic premises that concentrates on street food and traditionally prepared dishes (primarily from central Vietnam). Highlights include the pork-stuffed squid, and shrimp mousse on sugarcane skewers. There's an excellent vegetarian selection (try the smoked eggplant), including many wonderful salads. Prices are reasonable given the surrounds, ambience and flavours.

Aubergine 49 FUSION **$$**
(www.facebook.com/aubergine49; 49a Đ Ly Thai Tho; 3 courses 250,000d; ⏲11am-3pm & 6-9.30pm) Three-course menus for 250,000d per person are a fine reason to taxi around five minutes north of central Hoi An to this stylish restaurant crafting interesting fusion combinations of Asian and Western cuisine. There are also à la carte options and a decent wine list; menu standouts include stuffed squid and roast quail.

Seedlings CAFE **$$**
(41 Đ Nguyen Phuc Chu, An Hoi; meals 60,000-190,000d; ⏲10am-10pm) River views and Western and Vietnamese cuisine combine with good deeds at this laid-back restaurant and bar that provides training and career opportunities for disadvantaged youth from the Hoi An area. There's a real verve to the wait staff here, and a more sophisticated ambience compared to other nearby bars.

Ganesh Indian Restaurant INDIAN **$$**
(☎0510-386 4538; www.ganesh.vn; 24 Đ Tran Hung Dao; meals 70,000-155,000d; ⏲11am-10pm; 📶🖉) A highly authentic, fine-value North Indian restaurant where the tandoor oven pumps out perfect naan bread and the chefs' fiery curries don't pull any punches. Unlike many curry houses, this one has atmosphere, and also plenty of vegetarian choices. Slurp a lassi or slug on a beer and you're set.

Mai Fish VIETNAMESE **$$**
(www.themangomango.com; 45 Đ Nguyen Thi; meals 90,000-170,000d; ⏲7am-10pm; 📶) Casual and laid-back eatery owned by well-known Vietnamese–North American chef Duc Tran, which focuses on authentic and tasty versions of homestyle Vietnamese food. It's in a quiet location a short walk from the Japanese Bridge. The red snapper is a standout dish.

Miss Ly Cafeteria 22 VIETNAMESE **$$**
(☎0510-386 1603; 22 Đ Nguyen Hue; meals 45,000-150,000d; ⏲9am-9pm; 📶) A refined little restaurant run by a Vietnamese–North American team with mellow music and antique wall prints. Dishes include tasty *cao lau*, and other Vietnamese favourites are well presented.

Mango Mango FUSION **$$$**
(☎0510-391 0839; www.themangomango.com; 45 Đ Nguyen Phuc Chu, An Hoi; meals US$25-35; ⏲7am-10pm; 📶) Celebrity chef Duc Tran's most beautiful Hoi An restaurant enjoys a prime riverside plot and puts a global spin on Vietnamese cuisine, with fresh, unexpected combinations to the max. Perhaps at times the flavour matches are just a little too out there, but the cocktails are some of the best in town.

Green Mango VIETNAMESE, INTERNATIONAL **$$$**
(www.greenmango.vn; 54 Đ Nguyen Thai Hoc; meals 130,000-300,000d; ⏲11.30am-9.30pm; 📶) The setting, inside one of Hoi An's most impressive traditional wooden houses, is beautiful,

and the accomplished cooking (both Western and Eastern) matches the surrounds. There's also one of the only air-conditioned dining rooms in the Old Town upstairs.

Drinking

Hoi An is not a huge party town as the local authorities keep a fairly strict lid on late-night revelry. The Old Town is a great place to treat yourself to a cocktail or glass of wine.

More raucous action is across the river in An Hoi. Happy hours keep costs down considerably, and most places close around 1am. The most popular spots in An Hoi change on a regular basis. Turn right after crossing the bridge from Hoi An, and you'll soon see (and hear) where the backpacker action is currently happening along Đ Nguyen Phuc Chu.

Mia Coffee House CAFE
(www.facebook.com/miacoffeehouse; 20 Đ Phan Boi Chau; ⌚8am-5pm) Our favourite spot for an espresso, latte or cappuccino features a shaded corner location and good food, including grilled *panini* sandwiches and hearty baguettes. Its own coffee blend sourced from Dalat arabica beans is the standout brew, and be sure to try the coffee *affogato*, a delicious blend of dessert and hot beverage.

Hoi An Roastery CAFE
(www.hoianroastery.com; 135 Đ Tran Phu; ⌚8am-10pm) With single origin brews, excellent cakes, juices and smoothies, this cool little spot wouldn't be out of place in the hipster precincts of Portland or Melbourne. Recharge with one of 200 different caffeine-fuelled variations, and watch the passing promenade on busy Tran Phu.

Dive Bar BAR
(88 Đ Nguyen Thai Hoc; ⌚8am-midnight; 📶) The best bar in town, with a great vibe thanks to the welcoming service, contemporary electronic tunes and sofas for lounging. There's also a cocktail garden and bar at the rear, a pool table and pub grub.

White Marble BAR
(www.visithoian.com; 99 Đ Le Loi; ⌚11am-11pm; 📶) Wine-bar-cum-restaurant in historic premises with an unmatched selection of wines (many are available by the glass, from US$4) and refined ambience. Lunch and dinner set meals cost 230,000d.

Q Bar LOUNGE, BAR
(94 Đ Nguyen Thai Hoc; ⌚noon-midnight; 📶) Q Bar offers stunning lighting, lounge music and electronica, and the best (if pricey at around 120,000d) cocktails and mocktails in town. Draws a cool crowd.

3 Dragons PUB
(51 Đ Phan Boi Chau; ⌚7.30am-midnight; 📶) Half sports bar (where you can watch everything from Aussie Rules to Indian cricket), half restaurant (burgers, steaks and local food).

Shopping

Hoi An has a history of flogging goods to international visitors, and today's residents haven't lost their commercial edge.

Clothes are the biggest lure. Hoi An has long been known for fabric production, and tourist demand has swiftly shoehorned many tailor shops into the tiny Old Town. Shoes, also copied from Western designs, are also popular but quality is variable. Pick up the Live Hoi An (www.livehoianmagazine.com) map for more shopping listings.

Hoi An has over a dozen art galleries too; check out the streets near the Japanese Covered Bridge, along Đ Nguyen Thi Minh Khai. Woodcarvings are a local speciality: Cam Nam village and Cam Kim Island are the places to head for.

Couleurs D'Asie Gallery PHOTOGRAPHY, BOOKS
(www.facebook.com/couleurs.asie; 7 Đ Nguyen Hue; ⌚9am-9pm) Superb images for sale of Vietnam and Asia by Hoi An–based photographer Réhahn. His portraits are particularly stunning, and the best of his images are collected in books also for sale.

Metiseko CLOTHING
(www.metiseko.com; 86 Đ Nguyen Thai Hoc; ⌚9am-9.30pm) Winners of a Sustainable Development award, this eco-minded store stocks gorgeous clothing (including kids' wear), accessories, and homewares such as cushions using natural silk and organic cotton. It is certified to use the Organic Contents Standards label.

★Villagecraft Planet CRAFTS
(www.facebook.com/villagecraftplanet; 37 Đ Phan Boi Chau; ⌚10am-6pm) Shop here for interesting homewares and fashion, often using natural hemp and indigo, and crafted incorporating Fairtrade practices by the Hmong, Black Thai and Lolo ethnic minority people in the north of Vietnam.

GETTING CLOTHES THAT MEASURE UP

Let's face it: the tailor scene in Hoi An is out of control. The estimated number of tailors working here ranges anywhere from 300 to 500. Hotels and tour guides all have their preferred partners – 'We give you good price', they promise before shuttling you off to their aunt/cousin/in-law/neighbour (from whom they'll earn a nice commission).

The first rule of thumb is that while you should always bargain and be comfortable with the price, you also get what you pay for. A tailor who quotes a price much lower than a competitor's is probably cutting corners. Better tailors and better fabrics cost more, as do tighter deadlines.

Hoi An's tailors are master copiers – show them a picture from a magazine, and they'll whip up a near-identical outfit. The shop assistants also have catalogues of many styles.

It helps to know your fabrics and preferences, right down to details such as thread colour, linings and buttons. When buying silk, make sure it's the real thing. The only real test is with a cigarette or match (synthetic fibres melt, silk burns). Similarly, don't accept on face value that a fabric is 100% cotton or wool without giving it a good feel for the quality. Prices currently hover around US$25 for a man's shirt, or US$50 for a cotton dress. If a suit costs around US$100, make sure the fabric and workmanship is up to scratch.

Although many travellers try to squeeze in a clothing order within a 48-hour sojourn, that doesn't leave much time for fittings and alterations. Remember to check the seams of the finished garment; well-tailored garments have a second set of stitches that binds the edge, oversewing the fabric so fraying is impossible.

Shops can pack and ship orders to your home country. Although there are occasional reports of packages going astray or the wrong order arriving, the local post office's service is good.

In such a crowded field, these are places we regularly hear good things about (in alphabetical order): **A Dong Silk** (☎0510-391 0579; www.adongsilk.com; 40 Đ Le Loi; ⏰8am-9.30pm); **Hoang Kim** (☎0510-386 2794; 57 Đ Nguyen Thai Hoc; ⏰8am-9pm); **Kimmy** (☎0510-386 2063; www.kimmytailor.com; 70 Đ Tran Hung Dao; ⏰7.30am-9.30pm); and **Yaly** (☎0510-391 0474; www.yalycouture.com; 47 Đ Nguyen Thai Hoc; ⏰8am-9pm).

A few of Hoi An's tailors have now also diversified into making shoes and bags. See the **Friendly Shop** (www.friendlyshophoian.com; 18 Đ Tran Phu; ⏰9am-9pm) for good work that is guaranteed.

★ **Reaching Out** SOUVENIRS, CLOTHING
(www.reachingoutvietnam.com; 103 Đ Nguyen Thai Hoc; ⏰8.30am-9pm Mon-Fri, 9.30am-8pm Sat & Sun) Excellent Fairtrade gift shop that stocks good-quality silk scarves, clothes, jewellery, hand-painted Vietnamese hats, handmade toys and teddy bears. The shop employs and supports artisans with disabilities, and staff are happy to show visitors through the workshop.

Lotus Jewellery ACCESSORIES
(www.lotusjewellery-hoian.com; 82 Đ Tran Phu; ⏰8am-10pm) Very affordable and attractive hand-crafted pieces loosely modelled on butterflies, dragonflies, Vietnamese sampans, conical hats and Chinese symbols.

Mosaique Decoration HANDICRAFTS
(www.mosaiquedecoration.com; 6 Đ Ly Quoc; ⏰7.30am-8pm) Offers stylish modern lighting, silk, linen and hemp clothing, bamboo matting, hand-embroidered cushion covers, gifts and furniture.

Avana CLOTHING
(www.hoiandesign.com; 57 Đ Le Loi; ⏰8am-8pm) Stylish boutique run by a European fashion designer that stocks fab off-the-peg dresses, blouses, shoes and accessories (including great hats and bags).

Tuoi Ngoc HANDICRAFTS
(103 Đ Tran Phu; ⏰7am-8pm) This family-owned business has been making Chinese-style lanterns for generations.

Randy's Book Xchange BOOKS
(http://bookshoian.com; To 5 Thon Xuyen Trung; ⏰8am-7pm) Head to Cam Nam Island and take the first right to get to this bookshop. Set up like a personal library, it has more than 5000 used books for sale or exchange and offers digital downloads too.

Information

DANGERS & ANNOYANCES

Hoi An is one of Vietnam's safer towns, but there are infrequent stories of late-night bag-snatching, pickpockets, and (very occasionally) assaults on women. If you are a lone female, walk home with somebody. There have also been reports of drinks being spiked in some bars, so keep a close eye on your glass.

Many small-time hustlers peddle tours, boat trips, motorbikes and souvenirs, and using a *xe om* will always be more expensive than a metered taxi.

EMERGENCY

Hoi An Police Station (☎0510-386 1204; 84 Đ Hoang Dieu)

MEDICAL SERVICES

Dr Ho Huu Phuoc Practice (☎0510-386 1419; 74 Đ Le Loi; ⏲11am-12.30pm & 5-9.30pm) English-speaking.

Hoi An Hospital (☎0510-386 1364; 4 Đ Tran Hung Dao; ⏲6am-10pm) For serious problems, go to Danang.

MONEY

Agribank (Đ Cua Dai; ⏲8am-4.30pm Mon-Fri, 8.30am-1pm Sat) Changes cash and has ATMs.

Vietin Bank (☎0510-386 1340; 4 Đ Hoang Dieu; ⏲8am-5pm Mon-Fri, 8.30am-1.30pm Sat) Changes cash and has an ATM.

POST

Main Post Office (6 Đ Tran Hung Dao; ⏲7am-5pm) On the edge of the Old Town.

TOURIST INFORMATION

Hoi An Old Town Booths (⏲7am-5pm) Hoi An Old Town Booths sell Old Town tickets and have limited information and maps. Located at 30 Đ Tran Phu, 10 Đ Nguyen Hue, 5 Đ Hoang Dieu and 78 Đ Le Loi.

Live Hoi An (www.livehoianmagazine.com) Handy free map that is also available to view online.

Tourist Information Office (☎0510-366 633; www.quangnamtourism.com.vn; 47 Đ Phan Chau Trinh; ⏲8am-5pm) Helpful office with good English spoken.

TRAVEL AGENCIES

Competition is strong, so check out your options and negotiate.

Rose Travel Service (☎0510-391 7567; www.rosetravelservice.com; 37-39 Đ Ly Thai To; ⏲7.30am-5.30pm) Tours around the area and Vietnam, plus car rental and buses.

Sinh Tourist (☎0510-386 3948; www.thesinhtourist.vn; 587 Đ Hai Ba Trung; ⏲6am-10pm) Books reputable open-tour buses.

Getting There & Away

AIR

The closest airport is 45 minutes away in Danang.

BUS

Most north–south bus services do not stop at Hoi An, as Hwy 1 passes 10km west of the town, but you can head for the town of Vinh Dien and flag down a bus there.

More convenient open-tour buses offer regular connections for Hue (US$12, four hours) and Nha Trang (regular/sleeper US$14/19, 11 to 12 hours). Most accommodation owners can book tickets.

Buses to Danang (18,000d, one hour) leave from the northern bus station just off Đ Le Hong Phong, and a 15-minute walk from central Hoi An. Bus drivers for Danang sometimes try to charge foreigners more, but the correct fare is posted by the door. Look for the yellow bus. Note the last bus back from Danang leaves around 6pm.

Go Travel Vietnam (☎0510-392 9115; www.gotravel-vietnam.com; 61a Đ Phan Chau Trinh; ⏲9am 9pm) offers shuttle bus transfers between Hoi An and Danang airport and train station five times per day (80,000d, one hour).

CAR & MOTORCYCLE

To get to Danang (30km), head north out of town and join up with Hwy 1, or head east to Cua Dai Beach and follow the China Beach coastal road. Motorbikes charge about 150,000d for the trip to Danang. Taxis cost approximately 400,000d and are cheaper if you *don't* use the meter. Negotiate a price first.

A trip in a car to Hue starts from US$100 (depending on how many stops you plan to make along the way), while a half-day trip around the surrounding area, including My Son, is around US$60.

A popular way to transfer between Hoi An and Hue is on a motorcycle. A bike with driver is around US$45, and around US$25 if you're driving.

Getting Around

Hoi An is best explored on foot; the Old Town is compact and highly walkable. To go further afield, rent a bicycle (25,000d per day). The route east to Cua Dai Beach is quite scenic, passing rice paddies and a river estuary, but is definitely becoming more developed with hotels and guesthouses.

A motorbike without/with a driver will cost around US$6/12 per day. Reckon on about 70,000d for a taxi to An Bang beach.

BOAT

Boat trips on the Thu Bon River can be fascinating. A simple rowboat (with rower) should cost about 90,000d per hour, and one hour is probably long enough. Some My Son tours include a return journey by boat back to central Hoi An.

Motorboats can be hired to visit handicraft and fishing villages for around 200,000d per hour. Boatmen wait between the Cam Nam and An Hoi bridges in central Hoi An.

TAXI

Metered taxis are usually cheaper than *xe om*.

Hoi An Taxi (☎0510-391 9919) Good local operators.

Mai Linh (☎0510-392 5925) Local partners to Vietnam-wide company.

Around Hoi An

Thanh Ha

This small village has long been known for its pottery industry. Most villagers have switched from making bricks and tiles to making pots and souvenirs for tourist trades. The artisans employed in this painstaking work are happy just to show off their work, but prefer it if visitors buy something. There's a 25,000d admission fee to the village. Thanh Ha is 3km west of Hoi An and can be easily reached on bicycle.

Sights

Thanh Ha Terracotta Park MUSEUM
(☎0510-3963 888; www.thanhhaterracotta.com; Thanh Ha village; per person 50,000d; ⊙8.30am-5.30pm) This new museum presents an overview of the history of terracotta in different countries and cultures around the world. Often there are local craftspeople in residence in the museum's workshop.

Cam Kim Island

The master woodcarvers who crafted the intricate detail adorning Hoi An's public buildings and the historical homes of the town's merchants came from Kim Bong village on Cam Kim Island. Most of the woodcarvings on sale in Hoi An are produced here.

Boats to the island leave from the boat landing at Đ Bach Dang in Hoi An (30,000d, 30 minutes). The village and island, quite rural in character, are fun to explore by bicycle.

> **STAY SAFE**
>
> The ocean and waves can get rough east of Hoi An, particularly between October and March. Many local people get into trouble in heavy seas, resulting in regular fatalities. Lifeguards now work the beaches, but be cautious.

Cua Dai Beach

Heading east of Hoi An, new housing and hotels mix with older rice paddies, and the riverbank meanders for around 5km to sandy beaches. This palm-fringed coastline extends north to Danang, and despite the development, there are still a few quieter stretches; it's a good area to explore independently on two wheels.

Nearest to Hoi An, Cua Dai Beach has a few big resorts, and an ongoing and escalating problem with beach erosion exacerbated by the past building of hotels. If you're staying here, your daily swim will need to be in the hotel's pool, because the sandy beach has largely disappeared.

Sleeping

Victoria Hoi An Resort RESORT $$$
(☎0510-392 7040; www.victoriahotels.asia; r/ste from US$120/195;) This handsome hotel adopts a French colonial meets traditional Hoi An design; check out the vintage Citroëns outside. Rooms are modern and immaculately presented, some with teak floors and jacuzzis, and all with balconies. There's a 30m oceanside pool and good in-house dining.

Hoi An Riverside Resort HOTEL $$$
(☎0510-386 4800; www.hoianriverresort.com; 175 Đ Cua Dai; r from US$75;) Offers classy rooms with hardwood floors and tasteful decor, many with balconies right over the river. It's a well-run establishment, about a kilometre from the beach, and has a good restaurant, and massage and fitness facilities. A free shuttle bus connects the hotel with Hoi An.

An Bang Beach

Just 3km north of Cua Dai, An Bang is one of Vietnam's most happening and enjoyable beaches. Not being as impacted by the serious erosion evident at Cua Dai, at present there's a wonderful stretch of fine sand and an enormous horizon, with only the distant Cham Islands interrupting the seaside symmetry.

There's a great selection of beachfront bar-restaurants, and an expanding accommodation scene with several stylish holiday rental houses. Access to Hoi An is easy – just a 20-minute bike ride or a five-minute (70,000d) taxi journey – and staying at the beach and visiting Hoi An on day trips is a good strategy for a relaxing visit to the area.

At the time of research, there was a growing band of vendors selling souvenirs on the beach, but the scene is still pretty laid-back and low-key.

Sleeping

The area is much quieter in the winter months, and excellent rental houses make it a fine alternative for familes and friends travelling together.

Under the Coconut Tree GUESTHOUSE $
(0168 245 5666; www.underthecoconuttreehoian.com; An Bang; dm US$9, d US$30-40;) The funkiest place to stay in An Bang is this ramshackle garden collection of wooden and bamboo lodges and bungalows. For thrifty travellers, the Coconut Dorm House has outdoor showers and simple, shared accommodation in a breezy, open-sided pavilion, while the Bamboo Family house accommodates four, and the cosy Mushroom House is couples-friendly and has a private bathroom.

There's a cool bar-restaurant area to catch up with other travellers.

An Bang Seaside Village BUNGALOW, VILLA $$
(0126 944 4567; www.anbangseasidevillage.com; An Bang; villa US$53-89;) One of *the* best beachside locations in Vietnam, these wonderful cottages and villas are superbly situated between the coastal trees on glorious An Bang Beach, close to restaurants. Each of the six units combines modern (polished concrete) and natural materials beautifully, and boasts stylish furnishings and lots of space. They're serviced daily and breakfast is included.

Friendly Guesthouse GUESTHOUSE $$
(www.hoian-guesthouse.com; Tra Que village; d US$65;) Around 3km from central Hoi An – and 1km from the beach at An Bang – the Friendly Guesthouse has a quiet location in Tra Que village, the source of the organic herbs sold in local markets. Despite the village location, there's a sophistication to the decor, and two of the four rooms have relaxed rice paddy views.

Bikes are provided free of charge, and scooters are US$4 per day.

★ Hoi An Beach Rentals RENTAL HOUSE $$$
(www.hoi-an-beach-rentals.com; An Bang; Temple House US$230, Annam House US$200, CoChin House US$180;) Asian-chic decor is the common theme at these three lovely self-contained rental homes in An Bang village. Annam House (sleeps six) is a converted village home with three bedrooms and a beautiful garden. Nearby, CoChin House (sleeps four) is constructed in wood in heritage Vietnamese style, and has an expansive garden and a private lookout. Temple House (sleeps five) is the most spacious and stunning of all three, and has a lush garden leading to a private pavilion overlooking the beach.

The white-sand expanse of An Bang Beach is close by – along with good bars and restaurants – and the switched-on ownership team of three Vietnamese, Australian and American friends can help with equipping the houses' kitchens with local produce if you're keen to get creative at mealtimes.

Hoi An Beach Bungalows RENTAL HOUSE $$$
(0908 117 533; www.hoianbeachbungalows.com; Lac Long Quan, An Bang; apt US$125-140;) Both of these two rental homes in An Bang village are super-comfortable, surrounded by lush gardens and have been colourfully decorated. Choose from Be's Beach Bungalow with two bedrooms and a stylish self-contained kitchen, or the cosier, one-bedroom Be's Cottage, which is a renovated traditional Vietnamese home. It's also got a kitchen and a breezy verandah with a day bed.

Nam Hai HOTEL $$$
(0510-394 0000; www.thenamhai.com; Dien Duong village; villas from US$637;) About 8km north of An Bang and 15km from Hoi An, this beachfront temple of indulgence has it all: three pools (one is heated), butler service, vast villas kitted out with contemporary gadgets and private plunge pools, excellent fitness facilities and a world-class spa. This all comes at an astonishing cost, but at least service is both thoughtful and excellent.

VISITING THE CO TU

Living high in the mountains inland from Hoi An, the Co Tu people are one of the smallest and most traditional minority groups in Vietnam. Their villages comprise stilt houses set around a *guol*, a community building used for meetings, rituals and performances. Until quite recently, facial tattoos were common, and traditional dress is still worn when cultural performances are given for visitors. In the French and American Wars, the Co Tu were feared and respected fighters, and visitors often get to meet community legends who fought bravely against the Americans.

One Co Tu settlement, **Bho Hoong** (☎0905 101 930; www.bhohoongbungalows.com; Bho Hoong village; 1-night/2-days per person incl meals US$468), has developed a fine community tourism project allowing visitors to stay in the village. Co Tu guides have been trained and income is ploughed back into the area. Accommodation is in very comfortable bungalows with classy Asian decor and spacious bathrooms trimmed with bamboo and river stones.

The village is not set up for random visits, and can only be visited on two-day/one-night tours from Hoi An, which include meals and sightseeing around stunning scenery near the Lao border. Transport is either in a US jeep or an air-con car. Bho Hoong can also be visited by self-drive motorbike tours with Hoi An–based Active Adventures Vietnam (p212). A longer three-day/two-night experience is also available.

Eating

K'Tu Market & Coffee CAFE, DELI $
(An Bang; meals from 60,000d; ⏲8am-6pm) Set back from the beach, this new opening is a relaxed mix of culinary cultures from the Australian-Vietnamese couple who own it. There's excellent coffee, a handy deli section with Euro goodies like sundried tomatoes, pasta sauce and tasty homemade sausages. The funky outdoor tables are a top spot to enjoy K'Tu's barbecues and even the occasional roasted suckling pig.

Soul Kitchen INTERNATIONAL $$
(☎0906 440 320; www.soulkitchen.sitew.com; An Bang; meals 90,000-180,000d; ⏲10am-10pm Tue-Sun, 10am-6pm Mon; 📶) Oceanfront restaurant with a grassy garden and thatched dining area where the daily menu could include tuna carpaccio, seafood salad or calamari. There are good wines and cocktails too, and on Sunday afternoons from around 4pm, it's the place to be for gigs from a crew of talented locals and expats. There's also live music from 5.30pm from Thursday to Saturday.

Sea Shell FRENCH, SEAFOOD $$
(So Bien; An Bang; mains 80,000-140,000d; ⏲noon-2.30pm & 5.30-10pm) In a whitewashed villa with a lovely garden, Sea Shell's food is a mix of Vietnamese and European influences. The charming owner used to live in France, and her touch shines through in Parisian bistro dishes like pâté de maison and quiche. The roast chicken is classic comfort food, and Vietnamese flavours include pork-stuffed squid and fish with tamarind.

White Sail Restaurant & Bar VIETNAMESE, SEAFOOD $$
(www.anbangbeachhideaway.com/white-sails-restaurant/; An Bang; mains 70,000-120,000d) Relocated from Hoi An to the up-and-coming dining scene at An Bang Beach, White Sail offers a good menu of Vietnamese classics, but the real attraction are the regular seafood barbecues. Cocktails are mixed with robust pours; cold beer and ocean and island views come as mandatory side dishes. There's a very laid-back vibe.

La Plage INTERNATIONAL $$
(☎0510-392 8244; www.laplagebeachbar.wordpress.com; An Bang; meals 80,000-140,000d; ⏲8am-10pm; 📶) This beachfront place offers delicious snacks, Gallic-style salads and other French-accented main dishes. Seafood options – usually with a Vietnamese slant – are always strong, and breakfast at La Plage is a great way to start the day. Weekends are very popular with An Bang's growing band of expats.

Luna D'Autunno ITALIAN $$
(www.lunadautunno.vn; An Bang; meals 130,000-230,000d; ⏲11am-10pm; 📶) Fine beachside Italian restaurant with an authentic menu of antipasti, salads, pasta, meat dishes and the best pizza, from a wood-fired oven, in central Vietnam.

Cham Islands

☎0510 / POP 2800

A breathtaking cluster of granite islands, set in aquamarine seas, around 15km directly offshore from Hoi An, the Cham Islands make a wonderful excursion. Once closed to visitors and under close military supervision, day trips, diving or snorkelling the reefs, or overnight stays are now possible.

The serenity of the islands has been compromised – especially on weekends and Vietnamese holidays – by boatloads of tourists from the mainland, so plan your visit accordingly. It'll have to be between March and September, as the ocean is usually too rough at other times. There are also plans afoot to develop the islands more like a central Vietnam version of Phu Quoc, and coastal land has been confirmed for resort development.

Only the main island, **Hon Lao**, is inhabited – the other seven Chams are rocky forested specks. A rich underwater environment features 135 species of soft and hard coral and varied macrolife. The islands are officially protected as a marine park. Fishing and the collection of birds' nests (for soup) are the two key industries here.

Bai Lang, Hon Lao's little port, is the main village (aside from two remote hamlets). A relaxed place with sleepy lanes, its leeward location has long offered protection for mariners from the rough waters of the South China Sea.

Tiny **Bai Huong**, a fishing village 5km southeast of Bai Lang, is an idyllic but isolated spot where an excellent homestay initiative has been established.

At the time of writing, the Vietnamese military had just approved opening up roads that were formerly off limits to tourists. It's now possible to take a bicycle on the public ferry, and ride up to terraced tea plantations and explore other areas of Hon Lao.

Sights & Activities

Unsurprisingly, divers and snorkellers are some of the main visitors to the Cham Islands. While the diving isn't world class (visibility can be poor and overfishing is a problem), it is intriguing: five species of lobster, 84 species of mollusc and some 202 species of fish are endemic to the Chams. Dive trips and overnight stays can be arranged through dive centres in Hoi An, such as Cham Island Diving Center (p211); a full-day trip that includes snorkelling, a short hike, lunch and beach time costs US$44. An overnight option incorporating beach camping is US$82.

Ong Ngu BUDDHIST TEMPLE

Bai Lang's only real sight is a modest temple dedicated to the whales (and whale sharks) once abundant around the Chams. Locals worshipped whales as oceanic deities who would offer them protection at sea. When a carcass washed ashore, they'd clean the bones and perform an elaborate ceremony at the temple before giving the bones a burial. Sadly, whales are very seldom seen around the Chams today.

Bac Beach BEACH

A recently built concrete path heads southwest from Bai Lang for 2km past coves to a fine, sheltered beach, where there's great swimming, powdery sand, and hammocks and thatched parasols beside seafood restaurants. During holiday times the beach is packed with boats coming and going. Trails lead into forested hills behind Bai Lang.

Sleeping & Eating

The Chams only have simple guesthouses (in Bai Lang) or homestays (in Bai Huong).

★Bai Huong Homestays HOMESTAY $

(www.homestaybaihuong.com; per person 120,000d, meals 30,000-70,000d) Live with the locals in Bai Huong village. Visitors are given a bed with a mozzie net, and bathrooms have sit-down toilets and cold-water showers. Delicious home-cooked meals are available. The program works with nine families, generating income from community tourism. Note that little or no English is spoken by locals and there's usually only electricity from 6pm to 10pm.

Local families can take guests fishing or snorkelling (per person 150,000d), and trekking (per person 100,000d). The project has helped fund education for Bai Huong's children, including scholarships and a local library. Also available is a good-value three-day/two-night package (per person 980,000d) including all meals, and snorkelling, fishing and trekking excursions. See the website also for a two-day/one-night package.

Thu Trang GUESTHOUSE $

(☎0510-393 0007; r with shared bathroom 300,000d; Bai Lang village) Right by the whale temple in the main village of Bai Lang, it's tidy, clean and simple. Meals are available (around 200,000d for breakfast, lunch and dinner).

Ngan Ha VIETNAMESE, SEAFOOD $
(☎0510-386 2178; Bai Lang village; mains 70,000-150,000d) Well-priced seafood – including squid dishes and occasionally lobster – feature at this newish Bai Lang eatery with harbour views from the balconies. There are also rooms for rent (300,000d) if the other guesthouse in the village is full.

Cham Restaurant VIETNAMESE $
(☎0510-224 1108; meals 50,000-120,000d; ⊙10am-5pm) About 2km southwest of town, Cham Restaurant sits pretty on a stunning sandy beach and serves wonderful Vietnamese dishes, including lots of seafood. Most of the day-trip boats from Hoi An also stop along this beach.

Getting There & Around

Tour agencies charge US$25 to US$40 for island tours, but most day trips are very rushed and give you little time to enjoy the Chams. Speedboats are often crowded, time for snorkelling limited, and the coral and marine life on display only average.

If possible, we recommend a few nights at the Bai Huong homestay program to experience the best of the islands. For the best one-day experience, book with one of the specialised dive operators in Hoi An. They can also arrange overnight camping stays.

Public boats to Cham Island dock at Bai Lang village. There's a scheduled daily connection from a jetty on Đ Nguyen Hoang in Hoi An (two hours, 7am). Foreigners are routinely charged up to 150,000d. Bring a copy of your passport and visa as the boat captain needs to prepare a permit. Note that boats do not sail during heavy seas. From Bai Lang, a return ferry back to Hoi An leaves around 11am.

Local boatmen and *xe om* offer connections between Bai Lang and Bai Huong; the rate is about 30,000d for a boat and 100,000d for a *xe om*.

My Son

The site of Vietnam's most extensive Cham remains, **My Son** (admission 100,000d; ⊙6.30am-4pm) enjoys an enchanting setting in a lush jungle valley, overlooked by Cat's Tooth Mountain (Hon Quap). The temples are in poor shape – only about 20 structures survive where at least 68 once stood – but the intimate nature of the site, surrounded by gurgling streams, is still enthralling.

My Son was once the most important intellectual and religious centre of the kingdom of Champa and may also have served as a burial place for Cham monarchs. It was rediscovered in the late 19th century by the French, who restored parts of the complex, but American bombing later devastated the temples. Today it is a Unesco World Heritage Site.

The ruins get very busy, so go early or late if you can. By departing from Hoi An at 5am or 6am, you'll arrive for sunrise and should be leaving when tour groups arrive.

Archaeologists have divided My Son's monuments into 10 main groups, uninspiringly named A, A', B, C, D, E, F, G, H and K. Each structure within that group is given a number.

Only a handful of the monuments are properly labelled, but recent ongoing restoration has introduced a range of good information panels outlining the history of the site.

History

My Son (pronounced 'me sun') became a religious centre under King Bhadravarman in the late 4th century and was continuously occupied until the 13th century – the longest period of development of any monument in Southeast Asia. Most of the temples were dedicated to Cham kings associated with divinities, particularly Shiva, who was regarded as the founder and protector of Champa's dynasties.

Because some of the ornamentation work at My Son was never finished, archaeologists know that the Chams first built their structures and only then carved decorations into the brickwork.

During one period in their history, the summits of some of the towers were completely covered with a layer of gold. After the area fell into decline, many of the temples were stripped of their glory. The French moved some of the remaining sculptures and artefacts to the Museum of Cham Sculpture in Danang – fortuitously so, because the VC used My Son as a base during the American War and American bombing destroyed many of the most important monuments.

Sights

Group B HINDU TEMPLE
The main *kalan* (sanctuary), **B1**, was dedicated to Bhadresvara, which is a contraction of the name of King Bhadravarman, who built the first temple at My Son, combined with '-esvara', which means Shiva. The first building on this site was erected in the 4th century, destroyed in the 6th century and rebuilt in

My Son

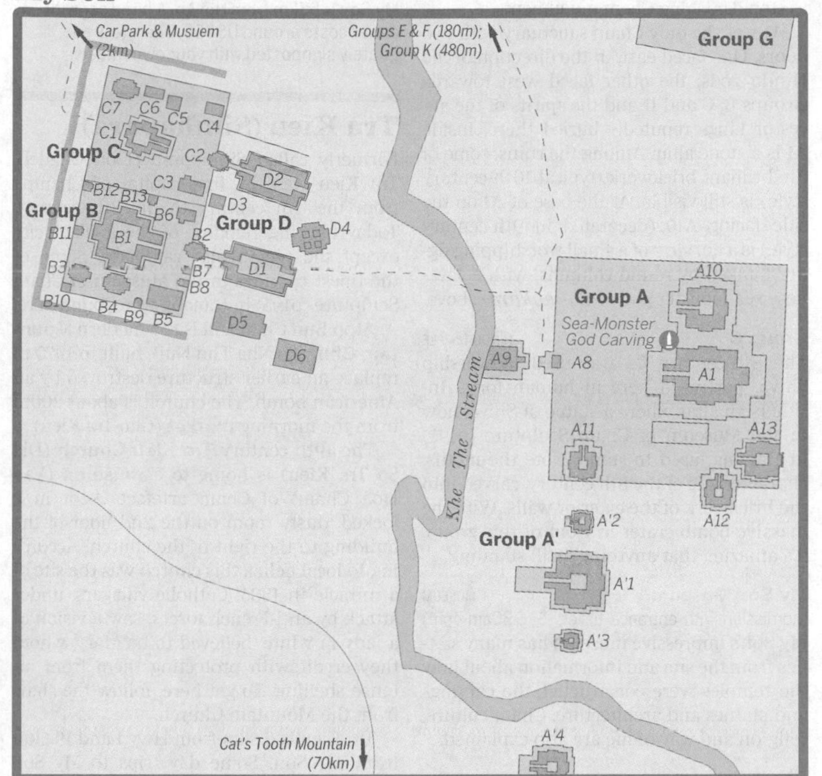

the 7th century. Only the 11th-century base, made of large sandstone blocks, remains.

The niches in the wall were used to hold lamps (Cham sanctuaries had no windows). The linga inside was discovered during excavations in 1985, 1m below its current position.

B5, built in the 10th century, was used for storing sacred books and objects used in ceremonies performed in B1. The boat-shaped roof (the 'bow' and 'stern' have fallen off) demonstrates the Malay-Polynesian architectural influence. Unlike the sanctuaries, this building has windows and the Cham masonry inside is original. Over the window on the outside wall facing B4 is a brick bas-relief of two elephants under a tree with two birds in it.

The ornamentation on the exterior walls of **B4** is an excellent example of a Cham decorative style, typical of the 9th century and said to resemble worms. The style is unlike anything found in other Southeast Asian cultures.

B3 has an Indian-influenced pyramidal roof typical of Cham towers. Inside **B6** is a bath-shaped basin for keeping sacred water that was poured over the linga in B1; this is the only known example of a Cham basin. **B2** is a gate.

Around the perimeter of Group B are small temples, **B7** to **B13**, dedicated to the gods of the directions of the compass *(dikpalaka)*.

Group A
HINDU TEMPLE

Group A was almost completely destroyed by US bombs. According to locals, the massive **A1**, considered the most important monument at My Son, remained impervious to aerial bombing and was intentionally finished off by a helicopter-borne sapper team. All that remains today is a pile of collapsed brick walls. After the destruction of A1, Philippe Stern, an expert on Cham art, wrote a letter of protest to US president Nixon, who ordered US forces to stop damaging Cham monuments.

A1 was the only Cham sanctuary with two doors. One faced east, in the direction of the Hindu gods; the other faced west towards Groups B, C and D and the spirits of the ancestor kings reputedly buried there. Inside A1 is a stone altar. Among the ruins, some of the brilliant brickwork (typical 10th-century style) is still visible. At the base of A1 on the side facing A10 (decorated in 9th-century style) is a **carving** of a small worshipping figure flanked by round columns, with a Javanese sea-monster god *(kala-makara)* above.

Group C HINDU TEMPLE

The 8th-century **C1** was used to worship Shiva, portrayed here in human form. Inside is an altar where a statue of Shiva, now in the Museum of Cham Sculpture (p195) in Danang, used to stand. Note the motifs, characteristic of the 8th century, carved into the brickwork of the exterior walls. With the massive bomb crater in front of this group, it's amazing that anything's still standing.

My Son Museum MUSEUM

(admission with entrance ticket; 6.30am-4pm)

My Son's impressive museum has many statues from the site and information about how the temples were constructed, the carvings and statues and architecture. Cham culture, religion and way of life are also explained.

Other Groups HINDU TEMPLE

Buildings **D1** and **D2** were once meditation halls and now house small displays of Cham sculpture. Dating from the 8th century, **A** is overgrown and inaccessible. Preservation has now been completed at **Group G**, where a roof arches over the 12th-century temples, and there is also a new exhibition space with archaeological findings from the site.

Group E was built between the 8th and 11th centuries, while **Group F** dates from the 8th century; both were badly bombed. Follow the path towards **K** – a stand-alone small tower – to loop back towards the car park.

Getting There & Away

BUS & MINIBUS

Hotels in Hoi An can arrange day trips to My Son (US$5 to US$10). Most minibuses depart at 8am and return between 1pm and 2pm. For the boat-ride option on the return leg, add an extra hour. 'Sunrise' trips do not mean you'll see the first ray of morning light, but they do beat the crowds.

CAR & MOTORCYCLE

My Son is 55km from Hoi An. A hired car with driver costs around US$50. The site is adequately signposted with your own wheels.

Tra Kieu (Simhapura)

Formerly called Simhapura (Lion Citadel), Tra Kieu was the first capital of Champa from the 4th century to the 8th century. Today nothing remains of the ancient city except the rectangular ramparts. Some of the finest carvings in the Museum of Cham Sculpture (p195) in Danang were found here.

Atop Buu Chau Hill is the modern **Mountain Church** (Nha Tho Nui), built in 1970 to replace an earlier structure destroyed by an American bomb. The church is about 200m from the morning **market** (Cho Tra Kieu).

The 19th-century **Tra Kieu Church** (Dia So Tra Kieu) is home to a **museum** (Van Hoa Cham) of Cham artefacts kept in a locked, dusty room on the 2nd floor of the building to the right of the church. According to local belief, this church was the site of a miracle in 1885. Catholic villagers, under attack by anti-French forces, saw a vision of a lady in white, believed to be Mary, whom they credit with protecting them from intense shelling. To get here, follow the signs from the Mountain Church.

Tra Kieu is 6.5km from Hwy 1 and 19.5km from My Son. Some day trips to My Son from Hoi An include a stop-off at Tra Kieu.

Chien Dan

The elegant Cham towers at **Chien Dan** (Chien Dan Cham; Hwy 1; admission 15,000d; 8-11.30am & 1-5.30pm Mon-Fri) are located just outside Tam Ky and the only other building nearby is a small museum. Dating from the 11th or 12th century, each *kalan* faces east. Many decorative friezes remain on the outside walls.

The middle tower was dedicated to Shiva; at the front left-hand edge of its base there are carvings of dancing girls and a fight scene. Look for the grinning faces high up between this and the left tower (honouring Brahma) and the two elephants at the rear. The right-hand tower is dedicated to Vishnu.

Although the towers escaped the bombing that ravaged My Son, bullet holes from the American War are evident.

This rarely visited site is on the right as you approach Tam Ky, 47km south of Hoi An.

Scenes of Vietnam

Towering mountains define the north. Stunning beaches and tropical islands spoil travellers along the country's coast. And French colonial charm and iconic skyscrapers are highlights in the buzzing big cities.

Contents

Above: Hang En (p163), Phong Nha-Ke Bang National Park

CINDYBUG/GETTY IMAGES ©

1. Basket boats on An Bang Beach **2.** Parasailing, Nha Trang **3.** Nha Trang's beachfront skyline **4.** Cat Ba Island

DAVID HANNAH/GETTY IMAGES ©

Islands & Beaches

Vietnam has an incredible coastline that's home to some of Asia's most sublime sandy beaches. Offshore islands – from mountainous Cat Ba in the north to tropical Phu Quoc in the south – also beg to be explored.

An Bang Beach

A short ride from Hoi An, **An Bang** (p220) is a gorgeous expanse of pale sand backed by a protective emerald ribbon of casuarina trees. It's barely developed and very low key, with local families providing sunloungers and serving drinks and snacks. The oceanic horizon is only interrupted by the craggy Cham Islands.

Bai Xep

South of **Quy Nhon** (p238), this lovely sandy bay is drawing more and more travellers. It's one of the few places in Vietnam where you can bag a guesthouse room right on the shore with an ocean view. Bai Xep doubles as a fishing village, so it's also a good spot to interact with locals and enjoy some seriously chilled beach time.

Nha Trang

The city of **Nha Trang** (p247) boasts one of the finest municipal beaches in Asia, a breathtaking strip of fine, golden sand lapped by the balmy waters of the South China Sea. During the day it's a very mellow scene, but on weekends the Sailing Club fires up its legendary sound system to host Vietnam's best beach party.

Cat Ba Island

This rugged, forested **island** (p112), most of which is a national park, is a great base to for hiking, biking and adventure tourism. Trails across the island fringe the habitat of one of the world's rarest primates, the highly endangered Cat Ba langur. And Cat Ba is just a short boat ride from the spectacular karst islets of Lan Ha Bay.

1

ANNAPURNA MELLOR/GETTY IMAGES ©

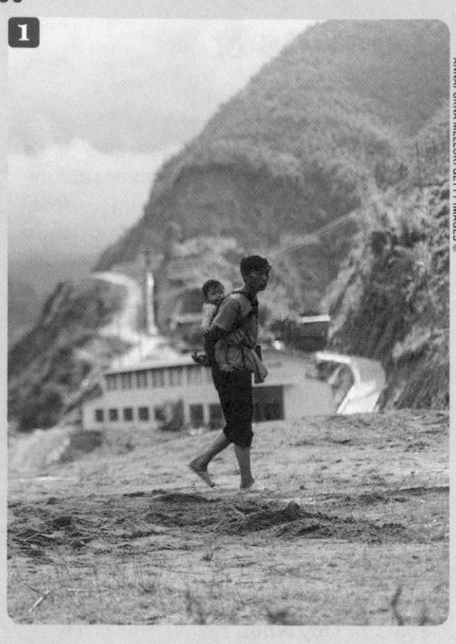

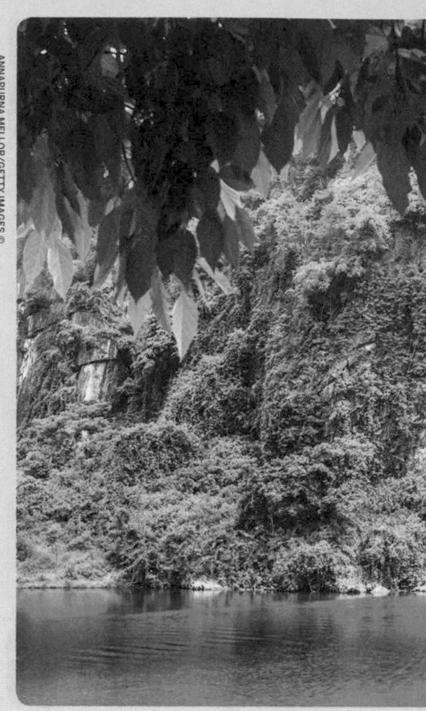

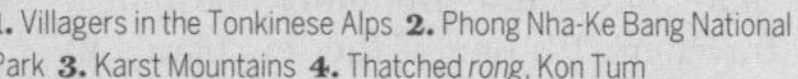

1. Villagers in the Tonkinese Alps **2.** Phong Nha-Ke Bang National Park **3.** Karst Mountains **4.** Thatched *rong*, Kon Tum

3

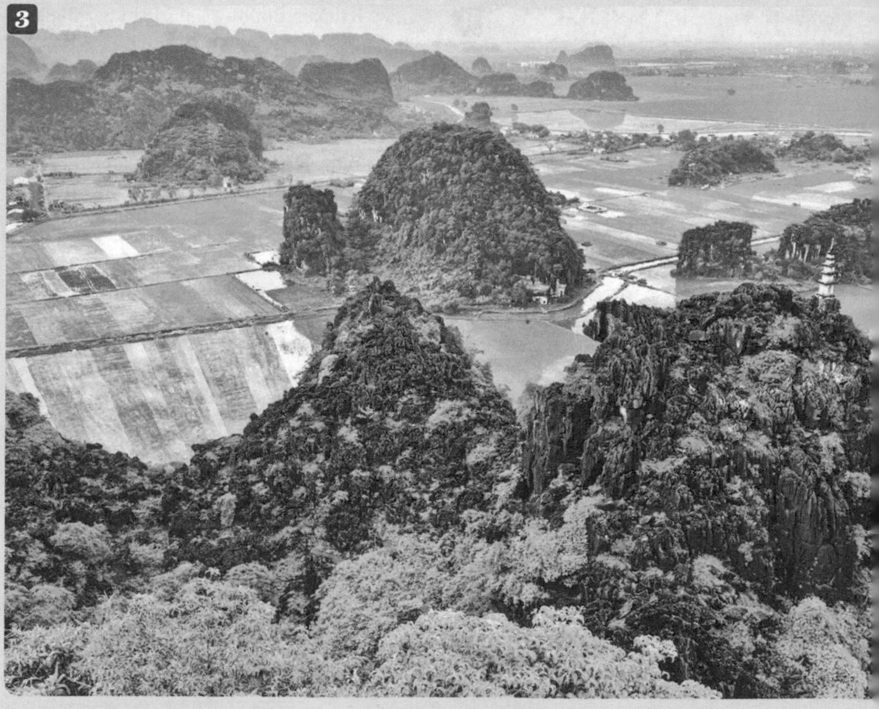

MIHTIANDER/GETTY IMAGES ©

Caves & Highlands

Vietnam is blessed with some of the world's most awe-inspiring cave systems. Its northern and western highlands, topped by ghostly, shape-shifting clouds and mist, form the heartland of the nation's minority people.

Tonkinese Alps

The spectacular Tonkinese Alps soar skywards along the rugged, uncompromising edges of the country and include **Fansipan** (p137), Vietnam's highest peak. From sinuous and spidery ridges, rice terraces cascade down into river valleys home to ethnic minority villages of Hmong, Red Dzao and Giay peoples.

Phong Nha-Ke Bang National Park

The western side of this **national park** (p162) is home to highland jungle that includes the highest concentration of tigers in Vietnam. But Phong Nha is best known for its simply extraordinary cave systems, which include Hang Son Doong, the world's largest cave.

Highland Culture

Dotted around the southwest highlands town of **Kon Tum** (p307), Bahnar villages are wonderful places to experience minority culture. Marvel at the soaring *rongs* (thatched community houses), go fishing with locals and watch kids swim their herds of cattle across rivers.

Karst Mountains

Vietnam's highlands are characterised by spectacular limestone outcrops known as karst formations. These remarkable peaks stretch from the far north-eastern mountains in **Ha Giang** (p148) and Cao Bang provinces down towards the Laos border.

Dragon Bridge (p195), Danang

City Life

Grace and space aren't qualities normally associated with booming Asian metropolises, but Vietnamese cities have a class and heritage of their own. A strong French Colonial architectural influence is evident throughout the country.

Vistas

If you want the full picture, seek out the high life. In Hanoi, the Lotte Tower (p69) offers a terrific perspective of the West Lake and Old Quarter from its 64th floor bar. **Danang** (p193) has many skybars that serve up unmatched views of the bustling Han riverside, while Nha Trang's astonishing new Skylight Bar (p259) sets the standard on the southeastern coast. Down in HCMC, the 48th-floor Saigon Skydeck (p318) reveals the beating heart of the city in all its neon glory.

Parks & Boulevards

Once dubbed the 'Paris of the Orient', Hanoi is Vietnam's greenest and most elegant big city, replete with parks and lakes. For French colonial nostalgia, a stroll along one of **Haiphong's** (p104) boulevards can't be matched, while Dalat's lakeside lanes and Flower Gardens should not be missed.

Riverside

Booming Danang rightly gets rave reviews for the regeneration of its beautiful Han river, which is now spanned by some of the most astonishing bridges in the world (including the fire-breathing Dragon Bridge; p195). In HCMC, it's all about the timeless French-era architecture of buildings like the Majestic Hotel on the Saigon River, while a cruise along Nha Trang's Cai River will reveal city life beyond the touristy beach zone.

Southeast Coast

Includes ➡

Best Places to Eat

- Ganh Hao (p277)
- Lac Canh Restaurant (p258)
- Sandals (p271)
- Kiwami (p259)
- Mix (p258)

Best Beaches

- Doc Let (p245)
- Bai Mon (p246)
- Mui Ne (p265)
- Bai Dai (p262)
- Nha Trang (p247)
- My Khe (p202)

Why Go?

Once the heartland of the Cham civilisation, today this sparkling coastline of ravishing white sands is Vietnam's premier destination for beach holidays.

If your idea of paradise is reclining in front of turquoise waters, weighing up the merits of a massage or a mojito, then you have come to the right place. On hand to complement the sedentary delights are activities to set the pulse racing, including scuba diving, snorkelling, surfing, windsurfing and kitesurfing.

Nha Trang and Mui Ne attract the headlines, but the beach breaks come thick and fast in this part of the country. Set aside a few days to explore more and you'll find hidden coves and lonely lighthouses, and a barefoot vibe is in reach. And for the definitive castaway experience, the fabled Con Dao Islands are the ultimate off-grid destination.

When to Go

Quang Ngai

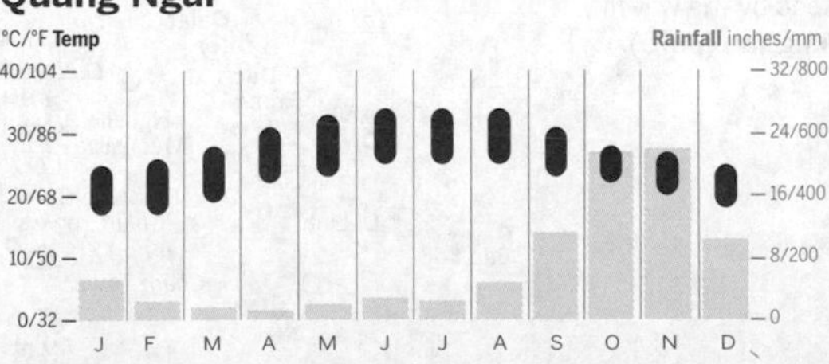

Jul The perfect time to sample the delights and sights of Nha Trang.

Oct See Cham people celebrate *kate*, or new year, at Po Klong Garai temple.

Dec Enjoy Christmas in Mui Ne with the best kitesurfing and windsurfing conditions.

Southeast Coast Highlights

1. Finding beautiful beaches, snorkelling coral reefs and riding motorbikes along empty coastal roads in the **Con Dao Islands** (p279).

2. Kitesurfing by day and chilling at night in the beach-blessed resort of **Mui Ne** (p265).

3. Coming face-to-face with the horrors of war at the poignant **Son My Memorial** (p236).

4. Taking a road trip between Phan Thiet and Long Hai via a spectacular lighthouse and the endless sands of **Ho Tram** (p273) and **Ho Coc** (p273).

5. Combing white-sand beaches for driftwood and seeking out a whale graveyard in **Tam Hai Island** (p235).

6. Soaking up the unique beach scene or exploring offshore islands by boat in the bombastic town of **Nha Trang** (p247).

7. Eating surf-fresh seafood by the waves in **Vung Tau** (p275).

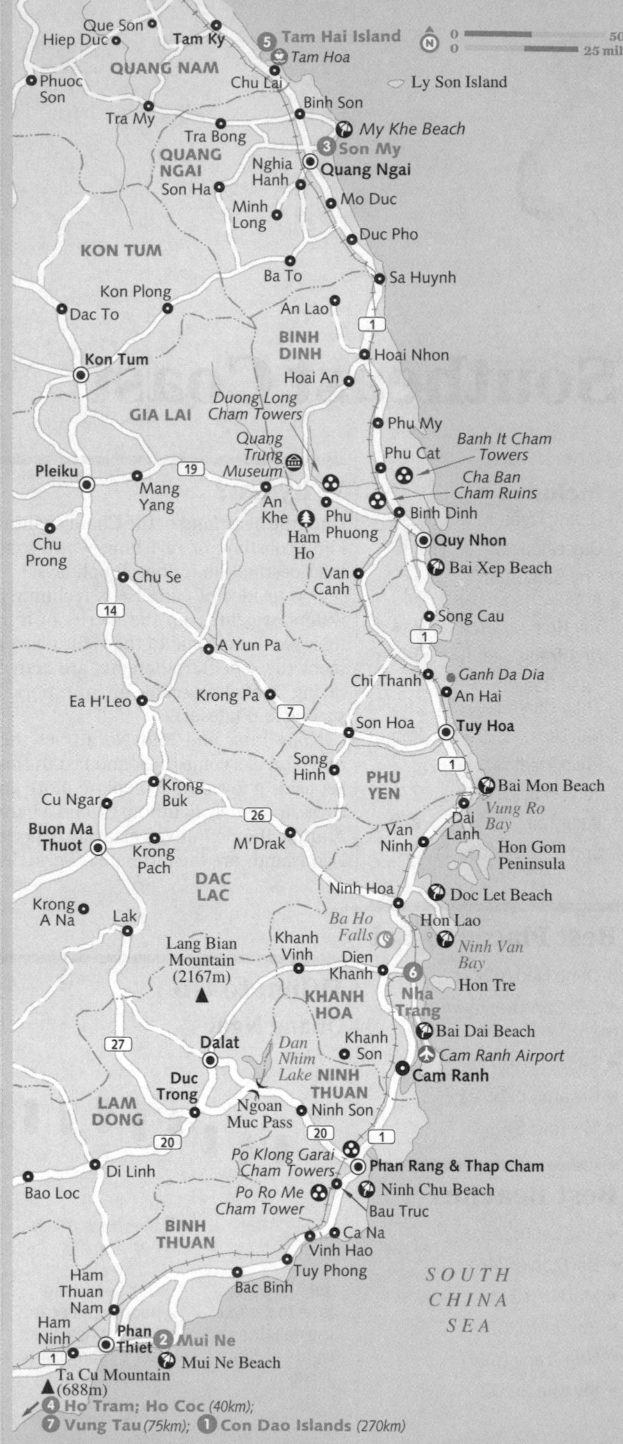

Quang Ngai

☎055 / POP 124,000

The capital of Quang Ngai province is something of an overgrown village with no obvious attractions, so most visitors only drop by for a spot of grazing at lunchtime. The few travellers who venture here come to pay their respects to the victims of the most famous atrocity of the American War at nearby Son My.

Even before WWII, Quang Ngai was a centre of resistance against the French. During the Franco–Viet Minh War, the area was a Viet Minh stronghold. In 1962, the South Vietnamese government introduced its ill-fated Strategic Hamlets Program. Villagers were forcibly removed from their homes and resettled in fortified hamlets, infuriating and alienating the local population and increasing popular support for the Viet Cong (VC or Vietnamese Communists).

Sleeping

The beach at nearby My Khe (p202) is close and has a good accommodation option.

Dong Khanh Hotel HOTEL **$**

(☎055-382 4481; www.khachsandongkhanh.com; 46-48 Ba Trieu; r 220,000-280,000d; ❄📶) This seven-storey block is fine value for money, with clean whitewashed rooms (some with balcony) that have attractive wooden furniture; all have air-con and bathrooms.

Petro Song Tra Hotel HOTEL **$$**

(☎055-382 2665; www.petrosetco.com.vn; 2 Đ Quang Trung; r US$42-68; ❄@📶🏊) A riverside tower that's the town's most luxurious address, complete with an opulent lobby. The rooms, many with sweeping views, could be better maintained, but are spacious.

Eating

Quang Ngai province is famous for *com ga*: boiled chicken over yellow rice (steamed with chicken broth) with mint, egg soup and pickled vegetables.

Viet Chay Sala VEGETARIAN **$**

(83 Đ Cach Mang Thang Tam; meals 30,000-70,000d; ⏲6.30am-8.30pm; 🌿) Inviting, well-run vegetarian restaurant with selection of tempting dishes: noodles, spring rolls, tofu

OFF THE BEATEN TRACK

TAM HAI ISLAND

A tiny (6km-wide), rarely visited island scattered with a handful of fishing villages and coconut-palm-fringed beaches, Tam Hai is mellow, accessible and well worth a visit. Culturally, it's a fascinating place, with some minor Cham ruins, an ancient whale graveyard and some unique festivals.

Tam Hai Island is 43km north of Quang Ngai, connected by boats (5000d, every 20 minutes, 7am to noon and 1.30pm to 10pm) from the mainland port of Tam Hoa. On arrival in Tam Hai you can hire bicycles and motorbikes to tour the island from cafes by the pier.

It's a flat 2km ride northwest to the main village (Tam Hai) where you'll find seafood restaurants and stores. Heading right (north) from the village it's 2km to a whale gravesite. Continuing west from the village you pass Ban Than, a 40m-high black rocky outcrop; below which there's a good snorkelling spot in the calmer summer months (April to August).

Before you make the hike up Ban Than, flag any of the coconut sellers down and ask them to take you to the Cham well and temple ruin, which is hidden down a narrow dirt track under a canopy of coconut trees, almost impossible to find on your own. The well water is considered the most sacred and pure on the island, so the islanders use it to make rice wine that locals believe can cure seasickness.

Ancient traditions run deep in Tam Hai, and islanders regularly gather to host a multitude of festivals connected with the sea. There's an annual whale festival on 20th January, and a large festival, Le Khao Le The Linh, celebrated annually on the March full moon to honour fishermen lost at sea. Village elders build miniature replicas of fishing boats, each with a small mannequin of the deceased, and shamen chant prayers before the boats are cast out to sea along with hundreds of candles to guide the lost souls to safety.

If you like the island so much you want to stay, the peaceful **Le Domaine de Tam Hai** (☎0510-354 5105; www.tamhairesort.com; villa US$100) resort enjoys a romantic, secluded beachside setting.

and soups, all beautifully presented and served with dips and sauces. It's on a side street 300m south of Le Trung Dinh.

Bac Son VIETNAMESE $

(23 Đ Hung Vuong; mains 27,000-80,000d; ⌚7.30am-8.45pm) This ever-popular restaurant on busy Đ Hung Vuong has been in business since 1943. It serves tasty, economical Vietnamese food and has an English menu and a friendly owner.

Getting There & Away

AIR

The nearest airport is Chu Lai (VCL), 36km north of Quang Ngai; it's sometimes still called Tam Ky airport, its old name. Vietnam Airlines, Jetstar and VietJet Air all fly to Ho Chi Minh City, and Vietnam Airlines also has flights to Hanoi. A taxi here from town is around 400,000d.

BUS

Quang Ngai bus station (Đ Le Thanh Ton) is situated to the south of the centre, 50m east of Đ Quang Trung. Regular buses head to all the major stops on Hwy 1, including Danang (from 55,000d, two hours) and Quy Nhon (from 78,000d, four hours). Open-tour buses can drop you off here, but pick-ups are harder to arrange; try contacting Sinh Tourist (p492).

CAR & MOTORBIKE

By road from Quang Ngai, it's 100km to Hoi An, 174km to Quy Nhon and 412km to Nha Trang.

TRAIN

Trains stop at **Quang Ngai train station** (Ga Quang Nghia; ☎055-382 0280; 204 Đ Nguyen Chi Thanh), 1.5km west of the town centre. Destinations include Danang (92,000d, 2½ hours), Dieu Tri, for Quy Nhon (114,000d, three hours) and Nha Trang (259,000d, seven hours).

Around Quang Ngai

Son My (My Lai)

This tranquil rural spot was the setting for one of the most horrific crimes of the American War: a massacre committed by US troops that killed 504 villagers, many of them elderly people and children on 16 March 1968. The deeply poignant **Son My Memorial** (admission 10,000d; ⌚7am-4.30pm) was constructed as a monument to their memory.

The war crime was one of the pivotal moments of the conflict, shaping public perceptions in the USA and across the world. As *Life* magazine put it, 'the American people reacted to the massacre of My Lai with horror, shame and shock, but also with disbelief'.

Centred on a dramatic stone sculpture of an elderly woman holding up her fist in defiance, a dead child in her arms, the monument rises high above the landscape.

Surrounding the main sculpture, scenes have been recreated in peaceful gardens to reflect the aftermath of that fateful day. Burnt-out shells of homes stand in their original locations, each marked with a plaque listing the names and ages of the family that once resided there. The concrete connecting the ruins is coloured to represent a dirt path, and indented with the heavy bootprints of American soldiers and the bare footprints of fleeing villagers.

The massacre was painstakingly documented by a US military photographer, and these graphic images are now the showcase of a powerful museum on-site. Inevitably, the content is incredibly harrowing: villagers are shown cowering from troops, there are corpses of children and limbless victims. The display ends on a hopeful note, chronicling the efforts of the local people to rebuild their lives afterwards. A section honours the GIs who tried to stop the carnage, shielding a group of villagers from certain death, and those responsible for blowing the whistle.

The road to Son My passes through particularly beautiful countryside: rice paddies, cassava patches and vegetable gardens shaded by casuarinas and eucalyptus trees. However, if you look closely you can still make out the odd bomb crater, and the bare hilltops are testimony to the continuing environmental devastation caused by Agent Orange.

The best way to get to Son My is by motorbike (around 140,000d including waiting time) or regular taxi (about 350,000d return). From Quang Ngai, head north on Đ Quang Trung (Hwy 1) and cross the long bridge over the Tra Khuc River. Take the first right (eastward, parallel to the river) where a triangular concrete stela indicates the way and follow the road for 12km.

My Khe Beach

☎055

A world away from the sombre atmosphere of the Son My Memorial, but only a couple of kilometres down the road, My Khe (not to be confused with the other My Khe Beach in Danang) is a superb beach, with fine white sand and clear water. It stretches for kilometres along a thin, casuarina-lined spit of

MY LAI MASSACRE

At about 7.30am on 16 March 1968, the US Army's Charlie Company landed by helicopter in the west of Son My, regarded as a Viet Cong stronghold. The area had been bombarded with artillery, and the landing zone was raked with rocket and machine-gun fire from helicopter gunships. They encountered no resistance during the 'combat-assault', nor did they come under fire at any time during the operation, but as soon as their sweep eastward began, so did the atrocities.

As the soldiers of the 1st Platoon moved through Xom Lang, they shot and bayoneted fleeing villagers, threw hand grenades into houses and bomb shelters, slaughtered livestock and burned dwellings. Somewhere between 75 and 150 unarmed villagers were rounded up and herded to a ditch, where they were executed by machine-gun fire.

In the next few hours, as command helicopters circled overhead and American Navy boats patrolled offshore, the 2nd Platoon, the 3rd Platoon and the company headquarters group also became involved in the attacks. At least half a dozen groups of civilians, including women and children, were assembled and executed. Villagers fleeing towards Quang Ngai were shot. As these massacres were taking place, at least four girls and women were raped or gang-raped by groups of soldiers.

According to the memorial here, a total of 504 Vietnamese were killed during the massacre; US Army sources determined the total number of dead at 347.

Troops who participated were ordered to keep their mouths shut, but several disobeyed orders and went public with the story after returning to the USA, including helicopter pilot Hugh Thompson Jr, who managed to rescue several women and children on that fateful day. When the story broke in the newspapers, it had a devastating effect on the military's morale and fuelled further public protests against the war. It did little to persuade the world that the US Army was fighting on behalf of the Vietnamese people. Unlike WWII veterans, who returned home to parades and glory, soldiers coming home from Vietnam often found themselves ostracised and branded 'baby killers'.

A cover-up of the atrocities was undertaken at all levels of the US Army command, eventually leading to several investigations. Lieutenant William Calley, leader of the 1st Platoon, was court-martialled and found guilty of the murders of 22 unarmed civilians. He was sentenced to life imprisonment in 1971 and spent three years under house arrest at Fort Benning, Georgia, while appealing his conviction.

Calley was paroled in 1974 after the US Supreme Court refused to hear his case. The case still causes controversy – many claim that he was made a scapegoat because of his low rank, and that officers much higher up ordered the massacres. What is certain is that he didn't act alone.

For the full story of this event and its aftermath, pick up a copy of *Four Hours in My Lai* by Michael Bilton and Kevin Sim, a stunning piece of journalism.

sand, separated from the mainland by Song Kinh Giang, a body of water just inland from the beach. If you follow the golden rule (avoiding holidays and weekends), you've a good chance of having this pretty beach largely to yourself. The shoreline's profile is gently shelving so it's great for children.

Sleeping & Eating

Accommodation options are very limited indeed, but you won't go hungry on My Khe beach (particularly if you like seafood). Dozens of seafood shacks are spread along the shore, all in a line, and gallons of beer are guzzled on warm weekends. Settle on prices in advance.

My Khe Hotel HOTEL $
(055-84 3316; khudulichmykhe@gmail.com; My Khe; s/d/tr 360,000/400,000/555,000d;) A great option just off the beach with smart, good-value rooms, all with attractive furnishings, marble floors and flat-screen TVs. There's a restaurant at the front.

Duc Chien SEAFOOD $
(My Khe beach; meals 50,000-120,000d; 9am-8pm;) Seafood place that specialises in delicious prawns in sweet chilli sauce, which you barbecue yourself. It also offers good crab and snapper and has a menu in English.

Quy Nhon

☎056 / POP 298,000

A large, prosperous coastal city, Quy Nhon (pronounced 'hwee ngon') boasts a terrific beach-blessed shoreline and grand boulevards. Its seaside appeal and tidy, litter-free streets make it the kind of place that affluent Vietnamese couples choose to retire to, spending their final days ocean-gazing and promenade-walking.

Quy Nhon is certainly a good spot to sample some fresh seafood, but for most foreign visitors the city's attractions are less obvious. However, growing numbers are being drawn to Bai Xep cove, 12km south of the centre, where a cool little scene has developed around a crop of new guesthouses.

Sights

★ Municipal Beach — BEACH

The long sweep of Quy Nhon's beachfront extends from the port in the northeast to the hills in the south. It's a beautiful stretch of sand and has been given a major facelift in recent years, making it almost as nice as Nha Trang, but with a fraction of the visitors.

Towards the northern end, the nicest section is near the Saigon Quy Nhon Hotel, where a grove of coconut trees lines the road. At dawn and in the evenings this area is packed with locals practising t'ai chi.

South along the shore, the waterfront opens up to a parklike promenade, punctuated by large hotels. Here the beach gets more beautiful and secluded, away from the bustle of town. At night the bright lights of offshore squid boats give the illusion of a floating village far out to sea.

In the distance you can see a giant statue of Tran Hung Dao giving the Chinese the finger on the far headland. It is possible to climb the statue if the door is open and peek out through the eyes. Heading south, a striking socialist-realist war memorial dominates a small square.

Thap Doi Cham Towers — HINDU TEMPLE

(admission 10,000d; ⏲8-11am & 1-6pm) This pair of Cham towers sits within the city limits in a pretty park. Steep steps lead up to the temples, which are open to the sky. Atypically for Cham architecture, they have curved pyramidal roofs rather than the usual terracing. The larger tower (20m tall) retains some of its ornate brickwork and remnants of the granite statuary that once graced its summit. The dismembered torsos of garuda (half-human, half-bird) can be seen at the corners of the roofs. Take Đ Tran Hung Dao west away from the centre and look out for the towers on the right.

Binh Dinh Museum — MUSEUM

(28 Đ Nguyen Hue; ⏲7-11am & 2-5pm Apr-Sep, 7.30-11am & 1.30-4.30pm Oct-Mar) FREE A small museum that concentrates on regional history. The entry hall focuses on local communism, including a silk print (by Zuy Nhat, 1959) showing a fat French colonist sitting aloft mandarins, in turn supported by bureaucrats, and cruel bosses, with the struggling masses supporting the whole ensemble. The room to the left has a small natural-history section and some Cham statues, while the rear room has the bulk of the impressive Cham collection.

The room to the right of the entrance is devoted to the American War, with local relics such as the 'Spittoon of Heroic Vietnamese Mother Huynh Thi Bon'.

Quy Hoa Beach & Leper Hospital — HISTORIC SITE

FREE Leprosy may not conjure up images of fun in the sun, but this really is a lovely spot. As leper hospitals go, this one is highly unusual, a sort of model village near the seafront. There are not so many patients here these days, but the descendants of affected families continue to live together here in a well-kept community.

Fronting the village is Quy Hoa Beach, a lovely stretch of sand and a popular weekend hang-out for the city's expat community.

The hospital grounds are well maintained, complete with numerous busts of distinguished and historically important doctors, both Vietnamese and foreign.

Depending on their abilities, patients work in the rice fields, in fishing, and in

---

WORTH A TRIP

BAI BAU BEACH

Bai Bau (admission 10,000d) Just 2km south of Bai Xep (16km from Quy Nhon), Bai Bau is a beautiful white-sand crescent no more than 150m wide, sheltered by rocky headlands, with mountains for a backdrop. It can get busy on the weekend and during Vietnamese holidays, but midweek you'll likely have the place to yourself.

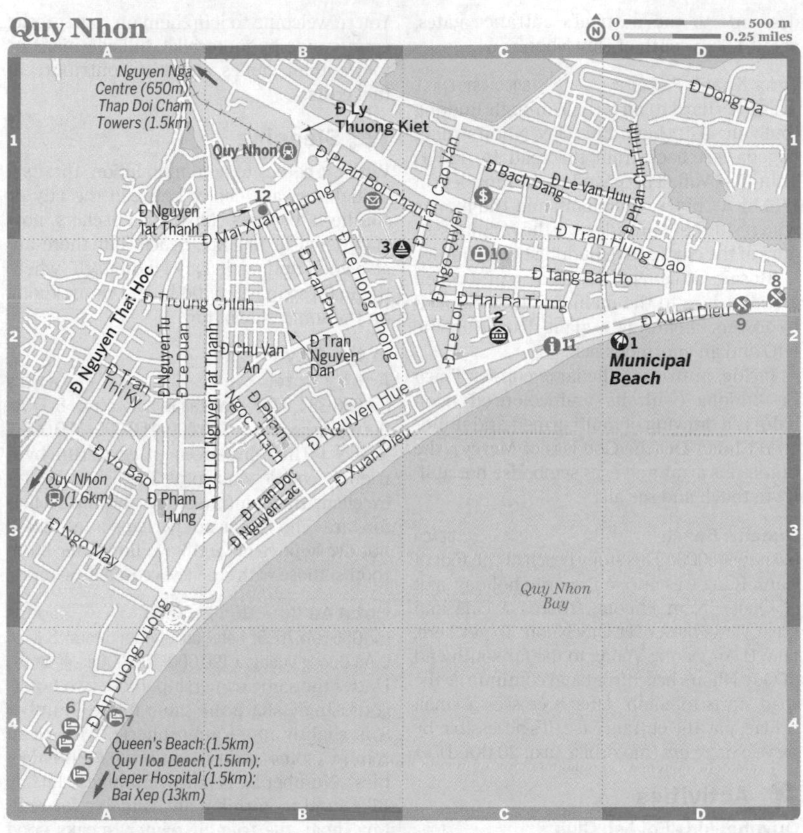

Quy Nhon

Top Sights
1 Municipal Beach D2

Sights
2 Binh Dinh Museum C2
3 Long Khanh Pagoda B2

Sleeping
4 Anh Vy Hotel A4
5 Hoang Yen Hotel A4
6 Hotel Au Co – Ben Bo Bien A4
7 Seagull Hotel A4

Eating
8 C.ine D2
9 Nha Hang Lien Thanh D2

Drinking & Nightlife
Barbara's: The Kiwi Connection .... (see 4)
Cafe Xua & Nay .... (see 5)

Shopping
10 Lon Market C2

Information
Barbara's: The Kiwi Connection .... (see 4)
11 Binh Dinh Tourist C2

Transport
12 Vietnam Airlines B1

repair-oriented businesses. There's also a workshop here where prosthetic limbs and special shoes are crafted, though you'll probably need permission from the director of the institution to visit it.

Just up from the beach, there's a dirt path to the hillside tomb of Han Mac Tu, a mystical poet who died in 1940.

If travelling by foot or bicycle, continue along the road past Queen's Beach until it descends to the hospital's entrance gates, about 1.5km south of Quy Nhon.

Long Khanh Pagoda BUDDHIST TEMPLE

FREE It's hard to miss the 17m-high Buddha (built in 1972) heralding Quy Nhon's main pagoda, set back from the road by 143 Đ Tran Cao Van. The pagoda was founded in 1715 by a Chinese merchant, and the monks who reside here preside over the religious affairs of the city's active Buddhist community.

Mosaic dragons with manes of broken glass lead up to the main building, flanked by towers sheltering a giant drum (on the left) and an enormous bell.

Inside, in front of the large copper Thich Ca Buddha (with its multicoloured neon halo) is a drawing of multi-armed and multi-eyed Chuan De (the Goddess of Mercy); the numerous arms and eyes symbolise her ability to touch and see all.

Queen's Beach BEACH

(admission 5000d This stony beach at the foot of Ganh Rang was once a favourite holiday spot of Queen Nam Phuong. There's a cafe and great views back over Quy Nhon. To get here, take Đ An Duong Vuong to the far south end of Quy Nhon's beachfront and continue as the road starts to climb. After it crosses a small bridge, pay the entrance fee. It's accessible by bicycle or *xe om* (motorbike taxi; 20,000d).

Activities

Quynhonkids English Club TOUR

(☎0122 820 3228; www.facebook.com/quynhonkids) This friendly bunch of locals loves to meet up with foreigners to chat in English. You're welcome to join them on tours of the countryside by motorbike, hillside hikes or for football games and just contribute to fuel costs.

> **WORTH A TRIP**
>
> ### HAM HO NATURE RESERVE
>
> A beautiful nature reserve 55km from Quy Nhon, **Ham Ho** (☎056-388 0860; http://hamhotourist.com.vn; Tay Phu; admission 30,000d; ⊙7am-5pm) can easily be combined with a trip to the **Quang Trung Museum** (p244). Taking up a jungle-lined 3km stretch of clean, fish-filled river, the park is best enjoyed by kayak (two hours 70,000d). The further upriver you travel, the better the swimming spots. Good quality accommodation (325,000d for a twin room) and meals are available.
>
> The road to Ham Ho is signposted to the south of Hwy 19 at Tay Son.

Sleeping

When it comes to accommodation, there's a straightforward choice between the city or southern beaches. Most backpackers now stay down in Bai Xep beach, but there are also good options in Quy Nhon itself (where the main strip is around Đ An Duong Vuong on the south side of town).

In the City

Anh Vy Hotel HOTEL $

(☎056-384 7763; www.anhvyhotel.com; 8 Đ An Duong Vuong; s/d/tr 200,000/250,000/300,000d; ❄@📶) This olive-green place is run by a friendly couple who speak English and offer excellent travel information, and have bikes for hire. The rooms are perhaps a tad dated but are kept clean and have hot-water bathrooms; those with sea views cost a little more.

Hotel Au Co – Ben Bo Bien HOTEL $

(☎056-374 7699; hotel_auco@yahoo.com; 8 & 24 Đ An Duong Vuong; r 190,000-300,000d; ❄@📶) Under the same ownership, these two hotels confusingly share the same name. Number 8 is slightly more atmospheric, with clean rooms (some with sea views and balconies). Number 24 is pure Vietnamese kitsch. Bikes and motorbikes are available for rent. Mr Thoai, the friendly owner, speaks good English.

Seagull Hotel HOTEL $$

(☎384 6377; www.seagullhotel.com.vn; 5 Đ An Duong Vuong; r incl breakfast US$35-50; ❄@📶🏊) A pretty good deal, this grand-looking oceanfront hotel has a three-star wing and slightly better four-star accommodation. All rooms are a little old-fashioned but have generous balconies with panoramic views, and the hotel is located by a beautiful section of beach that's perfect for swimming. Breakfast is a buffet affair with limited Western options.

Hoang Yen Hotel HOTEL $$

(☎056-374 6900; www.hoangyenhotel.com.vn; 5 Đ An Duong Vuong; r 620,000-880,000d incl breakfast; ❄@📶🏊) A 10-storey concrete hotel with a privileged location overlooking the beach. Unfortunately the rooms are past their prime, but if you secure a sea view, the sweeping vistas compensate.

OFF THE BEATEN TRACK

GANH DA DIA

A smaller version of Ireland's Giant's Causeway, Ganh Da Dia is a spectacular outcrop of volcanic rock that juts into the ocean south of Quy Nhon. Half the fun is simply getting there, as the scenery in this coastal region is superb.

Ganh Da Dia is signposted from the small town of Chi Thanh, 68km south of Quy Nhon. Heading down Hwy 1, take the turning just past the river bridge on the northern side of town. The route to the coast meanders for 13km through a delightful pastural landscape of rice paddies and farming villages.

Consisting of hundreds of interlocked columns of volcanic rock, Ganh Da Dia was created millions of years ago as fluid molten basalt cooled. Some of the best sections are formed of incredibly regular pentagonal- and hexagonal-sided horizontal rocks. The Vietnamese call this place 'the cliff of stone plates', and it's regularly used by Buddhist monks for ceremonies.

You can bathe in the tiny rocky cove next to Ganh Da Dia, but the drop-dead gorgeous sandy beach on the south side of the bay, a five-minute walk away, is even more inviting. Overpriced fresh coconuts and snacks are sold by local villagers at the car park.

Continuing south (and avoiding Hwy 1) you can take a lovely coastal road to Tuy Hoa. Head inland (west) from Ganh Da Dia for 3.5km and then a side (paved) road heads south through sand dunes, past cacti and agave to the fishing village of An Hai, where a row of seafood restaurants faces the O Loan estuary and makes an ideal pit stop.

From An Hai, it's 27km south to Tuy Hoa. The route has a few twists and turns, but the kilometre waymarks (which indicate the distance to Tuy Hoa) help guide you the right way.

Southern Beaches

Around 12km south of town, around Bai Xep beach, are some excellent new places.

★Life's a Beach GUESTHOUSE $

(☎096 328 9096, 016 2993 3117; http://lifesabeachvietnam.com; To 2, Khu Vuc 1, Bai Xep; dm 210,000d, r 450,000-750,000d, all incl breakfast; ❄📶) 🍃 A mecca for travellers, this sociable new Western-run place has a hostel vibe and is the perfect spot to share a few tales, meet others and kick back on a lovely sandy bay. There's a choice of digs including dorms, bungalows and a treehouse, as well as family-style dinners (150,000d), barbecues and bonfires.

Big Tree Backpackers and Bistro HOSTEL $

(☎056-384 0000; http://bigtreebackpackers.com; Bai Xep; dm 200,000d; 📶) Geared squarely at backpackers, this beachside place has three dorms (beds have reading lights and power sockets), including a female-only option. There's a great open-air bar and a good vibe but real dong-watchers will perhaps find the bistro's food prices a tad high.

Haven GUESTHOUSE $$

(☎0982 114 906; www.havenvietnam.com; To 2, Khu Vuc 1, Bai Xep; r incl breakfast 660,000-900,000d; ❄📶) On the lovely cove of Bai Xep, this tasteful place has a warm atmosphere and five attractive rooms (four have sea views) with textile wall hangings and stylish touches. It's popular with couples and there's a great dining area for meals. The Aussie owners run a tight ship and can organise boat and waterfall trips.

Avani Quy Nhon Resort & Spa BOUTIQUE HOTEL $$$

(☎056-384 0132; www.avanihotels.com/quynhon; Bai Dai Beach; r/ste incl breakfast from US$156/188; ❄@📶🏊) Recently renovated, this very stylish beachfront resort is set on a lovely private beach 14km south of town. It's well designed, with natural materials and mod cons marrying beautifully in the spacious rooms, which all face the ocean. Staff are sweet, and t'ai chi, yoga, snorkelling and fishing trips are offered.

Eating & Drinking

Quy Nhon is one of the best places in Vietnam to indulge in a seafood session. There's a (kilometre-long) strip of restaurants on the harbourfront road, Đ Xuan Dieu.

★C.ine SEAFOOD $$

(☎056-651 2675; 94 Đ Xuan Dieu; dishes 50,000-150,000d; ⏰11am-10pm) A very popular seafood restaurant with gingham tablecloths and views over the bay. Feast on delectable

TRANSPORT FROM QUY NHON

DESTINATION	AIR	BUS	CAR/MOTORBIKE	TRAIN (SOFT SEAT)
Danang	-	125,000-160,000d, 6½hr, 14-17 daily	7hr	5½hr, from 203,000d, 5 daily
Hanoi	from 700,000d, 1½hr, daily	from 480,000d, 23hr, 7 daily	around 26hr	from 665,000d, 20hr, 4 daily
HCMC	from 620,000d, 1hr, 3 daily	260,000-380,000d, 16hr, 10 daily	18hr	from 393,000d, 11hr, 4 daily

dishes including soft-shell crab, hot and sour fish soup and green-mango prawn salad.

Nha Hang Lien Thanh SEAFOOD **$$**
(104 Đ Xuan Dieu; mains 70,000-130,000d; ⌚11am-9.30pm) This down-to-earth place scores for very fresh, delicious seafood, including huge plates of prawns and marinated or barbecued squid. It's a very local place and there's no English-language menu, so bring your phrasebook.

Cafe Xua & Nay CAFE
(5 Đ An Duong Vuong; drinks from 20,000d; ⌚7am-9pm; 📶) Beachfront cafe based in a traditional Vietnamese wooden house (built in 1832) that serves authentic coffee, teas, snacks and juices. It's a great place to catch the sea breeze.

Barbara's: The Kiwi Connection CAFE
(12 Đ An Duong Vuong; ⌚7am-10pm; 📶) This was a Quy Nhon institution for years but times have changed and the owner has moved on. The Western food is forgettable but it's still an option for an evening beer (15,000d), juice or cup of Earl Grey tea.

Shopping

★**Nguyen Nga Centre** HANDICRAFTS
(www.nguyennga.org; 91 Đ Dong Da; ⌚7.30am-4pm Mon-Fri, 8am-1pm Sat) An excellent centre selling crafts created by people with disabilities and special needs. All the items – silk scarves, bookmarks, hand-painted cards and clothing – are beautifully made. Musical performances are also given by blind students using traditional Vietnamese instruments.

Lon Market MARKET
(Cho Lon, Đ Tang Bat Ho; ⌚6am-4pm) Bustling central market where street-sellers spill over into the surrounding roads. Great for photo opportunities.

Information

Barbara's: The Kiwi Connection (☎056-389 2921; www.barbaraquynhon.weebly.com; 12 Đ An Duong Vuong; ⌚7am-9pm; 📶) Free tourist information including bus and train timetables and tickets, city and countryside tours, bike and motorbike hire, and local maps.

Binh Dinh Tourist (☎056-389 2524; 10 Đ Nguyen Hue; ⌚7.30am-4pm) Government-run tourist office. Don't expect much practical help.

Main Post Office (197 Đ Phan Boi Chau; ⌚6.30am-10pm)

Vietcombank (148 Đ Le Loi; ⌚7.30am-3pm Mon-Sat) With ATM.

Getting There & Away

AIR

Vietnam Airlines (☎056-382 5313; www.vietnamairlines.com; 1 Đ Nguyen Tat Thanh) links Quy Nhon with Hanoi. Vietnam Airlines, VietJet Air and Jetstar all fly daily to Ho Chi Minh City (HCMC).

There's a minibus transfer (45,000d) for airline passengers between the Vietnam Airlines' office and Phu Cat airport, 32km north of the city.

BUS

Quy Nhon bus station (☎056-384 6246; Đ Tay Son) is on the south side of town, with very frequent buses to Quang Ngai (78,000d, four hours, hourly), Nha Trang and towns in the central highlands including Pleiku (85,000d, four hours, six daily).

It's also possible to get a bus all the way to Pakse (from 400,000d, 20 hours, three per week) in Laos, crossing the border at Bo Y.

At the time of research, no open-tour buses were stopping at Quy Nhon.

TRAIN

The nearest mainline station is Dieu Tri, 10km west of the city. Only very slow local trains stop at **Quy Nhon train station** (☎056-382 2036; Đ Le Hong Phong) which is at the end of a spur off the main north–south track.

Destinations include Quang Ngai (114,000d, three hours) and all major towns on the main north–south line.

Getting Around

From central Quy Nhon to Dieu Tri station costs 150,000d in a taxi or about 70,000d on a *xe om*.

Local T9 buses trundle down the coast between Quy Nhon (catch them on Đ An Duong Vuong) and the beach at Bai Xep (8000d, 45 minutes, hourly 5am to 5pm). A taxi to Bai Xep is around 175,000d.

Cha Ban Cham Area

The former Cham capital of Cha Ban (also known as Vijay and Quy Nhon) was located 26km north of Quy Nhon and 5km from Binh Dinh. While of archaeological importance, there's very little to see for the casual visitor. However, there are several interesting Cham structures dotted around the area.

Banh It Cham Towers

The most impressive of the area's Cham sites, this group of four **towers** (Phuoc Hiep, Tuy Phuoc district; admission free; ⌚7-11am & 1.30-4.30pm) sits atop a hill 20km to the north of Quy Nhon and is clearly visible from Hwy 1. The architecture of each tower is distinctly different, although all were built around the turn of the 12th century. The smaller, barrel-roofed tower has the most intricate carvings, although there's still a wonderfully toothy face looking down on it from the wall of the largest tower. A large Buddhist pagoda sits on the side of the hill under the lowest of the towers. There are great views of the surrounding countryside from the top of the hill.

The towers are easily reached by taking Đ Tran Hung Dao out of Quy Nhon for about 30 minutes, when you'll see the towers in the distance to the right of the road. After the traffic lights joining the main highway, cross the bridge and turn right. Take the left turn heading up the hill to reach the entrance.

Duong Long Cham Towers

These **towers** (Binh Hoa, Tay Son district; admission free; ⌚7-11am & 1.30-4.30pm) are hard to find, sitting in the countryside about 50km northwest of Quy Nhon. Dating from the late 12th century, the largest of the three brick towers (24m high) is embellished with granite ornamentation representing *naga* (a mythical serpent-being with divine powers) and elephants (Duong Long means 'Towers of Ivory'). Over the doors are bas-reliefs of women, dancers, monsters and various

THE LOST CITY OF CHAMPA

Cha Ban, which served as the capital of Champa from the year 1000 (after the loss of Indrapura/Dong Duong) until 1471, was attacked and plundered repeatedly by the Vietnamese, Khmers and Chinese.

In 1044, the Vietnamese prince Phat Ma occupied the city and carried off a great deal of booty, along with the Cham king's wives, harem, female dancers, musicians and singers. Cha Ban was under the control of Jayavarman VII and the Khmer empire from 1190 to 1220. In 1377, the Vietnamese were defeated and their king was killed in an attempt to capture Cha Ban. The Vietnamese emperor Le Thanh Ton breached the eastern gate of the city in 1471 and captured the Cham king and 50 members of the royal family. During this, the last great battle fought by the Cham, 60,000 Cham were killed and 30,000 more were taken prisoner by the Vietnamese.

During the Tay Son Rebellion, Cha Ban served as the capital of central Vietnam, and was ruled by the eldest of the three Tay Son brothers. It was attacked in 1793 by the forces of Nguyen Anh (later Emperor Gia Long), but the assault failed. In 1799, they laid siege to the city again, under the command of General Vu Tinh, capturing it at last.

The Tay Son rebels soon reoccupied the port of Thi Nai (modern-day Quy Nhon) and then laid siege to Cha Ban themselves. The siege continued for over a year, and by June 1801, Vu Tinh's provisions were gone. Food was in short supply; all the horses and elephants had long since been eaten. Refusing to consider the ignominy of surrender, Vu Tinh had an octagonal wooden tower constructed. He filled it with gunpowder and, arrayed in his ceremonial robes, went inside and blew himself up. Upon hearing the news of the death of his dedicated general, Nguyen Anh wept.

animals. The corners of the structure are formed by enormous dragon heads.

It is best to visit the towers with a driver or on a tour, as the site is reached by a succession of pretty country lanes through rice paddies and over rickety bridges.

Quang Trung Museum

Nguyen Hue, the second-oldest of the three brothers who led the Tay Son Rebellion, crowned himself Emperor Quang Trung in 1788. In 1789, Quang Trung led the campaign that overwhelmingly defeated a Chinese invasion of 200,000 troops near Hanoi. This epic battle is still celebrated as one of the greatest triumphs in Vietnamese history.

During his reign, Quang Trung was something of a social reformer. He encouraged land reform, revised the system of taxation, improved the army and emphasised education, opening many schools and encouraging the development of Vietnamese poetry and literature. He died in 1792 at the age of 40. Communist literature portrays him as the leader of a peasant revolution whose progressive policies were crushed by the reactionary Nguyen dynasty, which came to power in 1802 and was overthrown by Ho Chi Minh in 1945.

The **Quang Trung Museum** (Phu Phong, Tay Son district; admission 10,000d; ⌚8-11.30am & 1-4.30pm Mon-Fri) is built on the site of the brothers' house and encloses the original well and an ancient tamarind tree said to have been planted by the brothers. Displays include various statues, costumes, documents and artefacts from the 18th century, most of them labelled in English. Especially notable are the elephant-skin battle drums and gongs from the Bahnar tribe. The museum is also known for its demonstrations of *vo binh dinh,* a traditional martial art that is performed with a bamboo stick.

The museum is about 50km from Quy Nhon. Take Hwy 19 west for 40km towards Pleiku. The museum is about 5km north of the highway (the turn-off is signposted) in Phu Phong, Tay Son district.

Tuy Hoa

☎057 / POP 212,000

Steadily being transformed into a vast, sprawling new city, Tuy Hoa is a somewhat soulless place characterised by the requisite vast plaza and multi-laned boulevards. It's a possible overnight stop to break up a longer journey, especially for cyclists brave enough to tackle Hwy 1, but most visitors are just passing through.

Sights

The few sights the town has are all on hilltops visible from the main highway.

Nhan Cham Tower TEMPLE

(off Đ Le Trung Kien) To the south of town, the Nhan Cham Tower is an impressive sight, particularly when illuminated at night. The climb up to the tower takes you through a small botanic garden and you'll be rewarded with great views from the hilltop.

War Memorial MEMORIAL

(off Đ Le Trung Kien) This striking white war memorial in the south of town has been designed with overlapping sails that are vaguely reminiscent of the Sydney Opera House.

Sleeping & Eating

There are plenty of nondescript mini-hotels, and a glut of humble restaurants and street vendors along the main highway and Đ Tran Hung Dao.

The best dining is to be had on the beach, where a stretch of seafood shacks and *bia hoi* (draught beer) joints serve fresh seafood. Many charge by the kilogram, so be sure to agree on prices to avoid an expensive surprise.

Nhiet Doi Hotel HOTEL $

(☎057-382 2424; www.nhietdoihotel.com; 216 Đ Nguyen Hue; r 200,000-350,000d; ❄📶) Modern mini-hotel where the rooms have attractive furnishings; all but the cheapest are quite spacious. Staff speak little English but will help with motorbike rentals. Tasty meals (30,000d to 50,000d) are available.

Cendeluxe Hotel HOTEL $$

(☎057-381 8818; www.cendeluxehotel.com; Đ Hai Duong; r/ste from US$68/135; ❄@📶🏊) This towering landmark dominates the city's skyline and claims most of the business trade. It's the most luxurious address in town, however it is quite a hike from the beach. Rooms are very well equipped and spacious, and the pool area, spa and gym are all impressive. Dining options could be improved, though.

Bob's Cafe American PIZZA $$

(☎021 1975 9159; 43 Đ Nguyen Dinh Chieu; meals from 65,000-160,000d; ⌚3-9pm Tue-Sun; ❄📶) Just inland from the beach on a quiet suburban street, Bob's is an unexpected find in deeply provincial Tuy Hoa. It's an intimate little place serving up pizza (with toppings including pepperoni and seafood), chicken wings and burgers. Check out the Crow's Nest bar upstairs for a beer.

Getting There & Away

AIR

Vietnam Airlines (057-382 6508; www.vietnamairlines.com; 353 Đ Tran Hung Dao) has five flights weekly to Hanoi (from 799,000d) while Jetstar operates daily flights to HCMC (from 360,000d). The airport, sometimes called Dong Tac, is 8km south of town.

BUS

From Tuy Hoa, there are very regular buses to Quy Nhon (48,000d, two hours) and Nha Trang (66,000d, three hours).

TRAIN

Tuy Hoa train station (057-382 3672; Đ Le Trung Kien) is on the road parallel to the highway, north of the main street. Destinations include Danang (275,000d, 7½ hours) and Nha Trang (75,000d, two hours).

Tuy Hoa to Nha Trang

058

The coastal drive between Tuy Hoa and Nha Trang on Hwy 1 provides tantalising glimpses of a number of remote and beautiful spots, while others are hidden away in the jungle along promontories or on secluded islands. Leave behind the guidebook for a day or two and go exploring. Money-changing facilities and ATMs are thin on the ground here, so plan ahead in Nha Trang, Tuy Hoa or Quy Nhon.

Dai Lanh Beach

Crescent-shaped Dai Lanh Beach has a split personality: a scruffy fishing village occupies the northern end, but yields to an attractive beach shaded by casuarina trees. The roar of traffic from Hwy 1 does blight the setting, but when a new tunnel currently under construction is finished (scheduled for late 2016), peace should return to Dai Lanh.

Accommodation options are grouped together in the fishing village. **Binh Lieu** (058-394 9138; Hwy 1; r 220,000-350,000d;) is the best of the mini-hotels with smart, well-equipped rooms. Fresh seafood features prominently at the beachside restaurants.

Dai Lanh is 40km south of Tuy Hoa and 83km north of Nha Trang on Hwy 1.

Whale Island

About a kilometre south of Dai Lanh, a vast sand-dune causeway connects the mainland to the Hon Gom peninsula, which is almost 30km in length.

Boats for Whale Island leave from Hom Gom's main village, Dam Mon, set on a sheltered bay. Whale Island is a tiny speck on the map and home to the romantic and secluded **Whale Island Resort** (058-384 0501; www.whaleislandresort.com; s/d incl breakfast from US$33/45;). It's a fine place for some barefoot living, with snorkelling, kayaking and windsurfing, and a pretty beachside setting. It has rustic bamboo and timber (fan-cooled) bungalows; and compulsory meals (US$28 per person per day) are good if pricey. Bus-boat transfers from Nha Trang cost US$20.

Rainbow Divers (p253) has a permanent base on the island; two dives cost US$80. The scuba season is mid-January to mid-October. Unfortunately whale sharks and whales (which used to be regular visitors) have not been sighted for some years.

Doc Let Beach

Stretching for 18km, the chalk-white sands and shallow turquoise waters of Doc Let rank among Vietnam's best beaches.

This giant bay can be divided into three sections. The northern part is where most of the tourism action is, with a cluster of beachfront hotels and cheaper guesthouses inland. Looming over the central section is the giant Hyundai shipyard and port, an important local employer but a real blight on the landscape. The isolated southern section is backed by a wooded promontory and is the place to really get away from it all.

There's little or no public transport, but with a rented bike it's easy to find your own piece of beachside paradise for the day.

Sleeping

Hoang Khang Hotel HOTEL $
(058-367 2268; quyetthangdoclet@gmail.com; Dong Cat Village; r 300,000-400,000d;) A short stroll from the beach, this new white four-storey hotel has clean, well-presented and good-value rooms and an English-speaking manager. There's a restaurant on-site and full-board packages are available.

Doc Let Resort HOTEL $
(058-384 9152; bungalows incl breakfast 375,000-475,000d;) Pluses here are the

OFF THE BEATEN TRACK

VUNG RO BAY

A spectacular natural harbour ringed by forested peaks, Vung Ro Bay is a remote, wildy beautiful lagoon-like expanse of turquoise water 25km south of Tuy Hoa. It's celebrated as Vietnam's most easterly point on the mainland.

A crooked finger of land protects the bay from the worst South China Sea storms, allowing a floating village and fish farms to flourish in its sheltered waters. On the northeast side of Vung Ro, the coastal road passes an exquisite undeveloped sandy cove, **Bai Mon**, the perfect spot for a swim. From this beach a steep path leads up to a 19th-century lighthouse, built by the French, from where there are oceanic vistas of the Vung Ro coastline.

This part of Vietnam hit the headlines back in February 1965 when a US helicopter detected the movement of a North Vietnamese supply ship in the area. Vung Ro was part of the alternative Ho Chi Minh Sea Trail and was being used to smuggle arms into South Vietnam for Viet Cong forces. The discovery of a sea supply route from north to south confirmed US suspicions and was used as justification to ramp up US involvement in the war.

Today the isolation and raw beauty of the Vung Ro coast is under threat by a plan for a giant oil refinery and billion-dollar resort complex and marina, funded by the US-based Rose Rock Group. This development project was proposed years ago but no construction work had started by late 2015. Get here quick.

stunning beachfront setting, palm-shaded grounds and decent restaurant, which serves up good local dishes at reasonable prices. Minuses are the dated, if spacious, bungalows and lack of atmosphere. All in all it's fair value for the fine setting.

★**Jungle Beach** BUNGALOW **$$**
(☎091 342 9144; www.junglebeachvietnam.com; r per person incl all meals from 500,000d;) Offering a castaway vibe, this Canadian-owned beachside place sits pretty on an idyllic stretch of white sand. Rattan, bamboo and thatch huts are beach-bum basic but adequate. Meals are eaten family-style, so there's a sociable ambience. It *is* very isolated (but that's entirely the point) at the end of lonely road, 7km south of the shipyard.

★**Some Days of Silence** BOUTIQUE HOTEL **$$$**
(☎058-367 0952; www.somedaysresort.com; r US$110-120, bungalows US$170-180, all incl breakfast;) Stunning, artistically designed place that feels more of an in-the-know retreat than a mere hotel. Elegant bungalows and rooms are lovingly decorated with art and feature four-poster beds and bathrooms with pebble detailing. There's a sublime tropical garden, good spa, and service is great. The pagoda-style restaurant and terrace make a great setting for healthy, creative meals (US$12 each).

Getting There & Away

The turn-off for Doc Let is signposted just south of a toll-road section on Hwy 1, around 4km past Ninh Hoa where there's a big sign for Hyundai Vinashin (shipyard). Continue 10km past photogenic salt fields, looking out for the signs to the resorts. Make a left turn through Doc Let village and then a right to the beach. Most of the hotels and resorts also offer some sort of transfer service for a fee.

There's a separate, direct (paved) road to Jungle Beach via the shipyard from the same Hwy 1 turn-off (look out for the signs to 'wild beach').

Ninh Van Bay

Welcome to an alternate reality populated by European royalty, film stars and the otherwise rich and secretive. Sadly for the average punter, this place doesn't exist. Ninh Van Bay is blessed with a sprinkling of exquisite sandy cove beaches that a couple of uber-luxurious hotels have set up camp on.

Six Senses Ninh Van Bay and An Lam Ninh Van Bay Villas are not accessible by road; you arrive by boat from private docks 15km north of Nha Trang.

★**Six Senses Ninh Van Bay** RESORT **$$$**
(☎058-3524 268; www.sixsenses.com; villas US$690-1240;) Occupying a secluded cove abutting a dense jungle-covered peninsula, this resort comprises of drop-dead-gorgeous, traditionally inspired villas, each with its own swimming pool. As you would expect for the price, the detail is superb and the setting is simply magical. Facilities include a wonderful Six Senses Spa and restaurants featuring Western and Asian cuisine.

An Lam Ninh Van Bay Villas RESORT **$$$**
(058-362 4777; www.anlamnvb.com;)
All guests approach this enclave of luxury in a speed boat, skimming across a turquoise bay fringed by forested hills. And on arrival you can quickly settle in to a life of sybaritic tropical living: thatched villas with private plunge pools, personal butler service, complimentary yoga classes, kayaking and hiking.

Nha Trang

058 / POP 386,000

Loud and proud (say it!), the high-rise, high-energy beach resort of Nha Trang enjoys a stunning setting: ringed by a necklace of hills, with a crescent beach, the city's turquoise bay dotted with tropical islands.

The shoreline has been given a huge makeover in recent years, with parks and sculpture gardens spread along the impressive promenade, while the streets inland reveal some quirky boutiques and a cosmopolitan array of dining options.

As the restaurants wind down, the nightlife cranks up – Nha Trang is a party town at heart, like any self-respecting resort should be. Forget the curfews of the capital; people play late in this town.

If cocktails and shooters aren't your flavour, there are some more sedate activities on offer. Try an old-school spa treatment with a visit to a mud bath or explore centuries-old Cham towers still standing in the centre of town.

This part of the country has its very own microclimate and the rains tend to come from October until December, a time best avoided if you are into lazing on the beach or diving in the tropical waters.

Sights

There are several superb black-and-white photographic galleries in Nha Trang.

★**Nha Trang Beach** BEACH
(Map p250) Forming a magnificent sweeping arc, Nha Trang's 6km-long golden-sand beach is the city's trump card. Various sections are roped off and designated for swimmers (where you won't be bothered by jetskis or boats). The turquoise water is fabulously inviting, and the promenade a delight to stroll.

Two popular lounging spots are the Sailing Club and Louisiane Brewhouse. If you head south of here, the beach gets quieter and it's possible to find a stretch of sand to yourself.

The best beach weather is generally before 1pm, as the afternoon sea breezes can whip up the sand.

During heavy rains, run-off from the rivers at each end of the beach flows into the bay, gradually turning it a murky brown. Most of the year, however, the sea is just like it appears in the brochures.

★**Po Nagar Cham Towers** BUDDHIST TEMPLE
(Thap Ba, Lady of the City; Map p248; admission 22,000d, guide 50,000d; 6am-6pm) Built between the 7th and 12th centuries, these four Cham towers are still actively used for worship by Cham, Chinese and Vietnamese Buddhists. Originally the complex had seven or eight towers, but only four towers remain, of which the 28m-high North Tower (Thap Chinh), which dates from AD 817, with its terraced pyramidal roof, vaulted interior masonry and vestibule, is the most magnificent.

The towers stand on a granite knoll 2km north of central Nha Trang, on the banks of the Cai River.

It's thought this site was first used for worship as early as the 2nd century AD. The original wooden structure was razed to the ground by attacking Javanese in AD 774, but was replaced by a stone-and-brick temple (the first of its kind) in 784.

The towers serve as the Holy See, honouring Yang Ino Po Nagar, the goddess of the Dua (Liu) clan, which ruled over the southern part of the Cham kingdom. There are inscribed stone slabs scattered throughout the complex, most of which relate to history or religion and provide insight into the spiritual life and social structure of the Cham.

All of the temples face east, as did the original entrance to the complex, which is to the right as you ascend the hillock. In centuries past, worshippers passed through the pillared meditation hall, 10 pillars of which can still be seen, before proceeding up the steep staircase to the towers.

In 918, King Indravarman III placed a gold *mukha-linga* (carved phallus with a human face painted on it) in the North Tower, but it was taken by Khmer raiders. This pattern of statues being destroyed or stolen and then replaced continued until 965, when King Jaya Indravarman IV replaced the gold *mukha-linga* with the stone figure, Uma (shakti, or female consort of Shiva), which remains to this day.

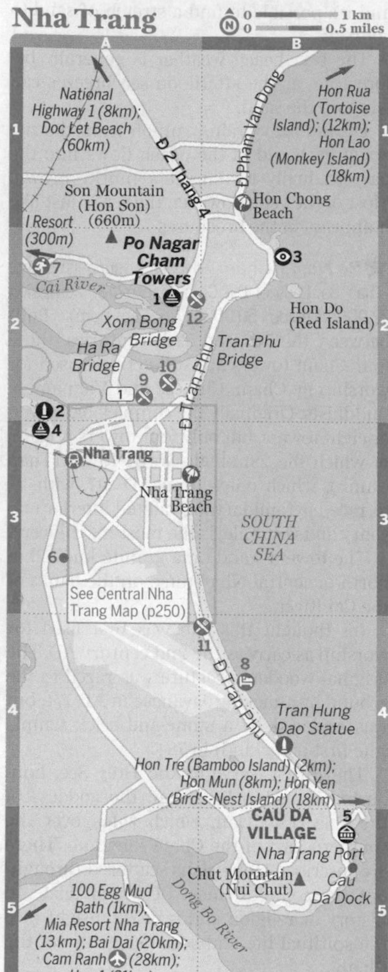

Nha Trang

Top Sights

1 Po Nagar Cham Towers A2

Sights

2 Buddha A2
3 Hon Chong Promontory B2
4 Long Son Pagoda A3
5 National Oceanographic Museum B5

Activities, Courses & Tours

6 Sailing Center Vietnam A3
7 Thap Ba Hot Spring Center A2

Sleeping

8 Evason Ana Mandara Resort & Spa B4

Eating

Banh Xeo stand .... (see 12)
9 Dam Market A2
10 Lac Canh Restaurant A2
11 Lang Nuong Phu Dong Hai San B4
12 Thap Ba A2

Drinking & Nightlife

Hon Chong Cafe .... (see 3)

Above the entrance to the North Tower, two musicians, one of whose feet is on the head of the bull Nandin, flank a dancing four-armed Shiva. The sandstone doorposts are covered with inscriptions, as are parts of the walls of the vestibule. A gong and a drum stand under the pyramid-shaped ceiling of the antechamber. In the 28m-high pyramidal main chamber, there is a black-stone statue of the goddess Uma with 10 arms, two of which are hidden under her vest; she is seated and leaning back against a monstrous beast.

The Central Tower (Thap Nam) was built partly of recycled bricks in the 12th century on the site of a structure dating from the 7th century. It is less finely constructed than the other towers and has little ornamentation; the pyramidal roof lacks terracing or pilasters, although the interior altars were once covered with silver. There is a linga inside the main chamber.

The South Tower (Mieu Dong Nam), at one time dedicated to Sandhaka (Shiva), still shelters a linga, while the richly ornamented Northwest Tower (Thap Tay Bac) was originally dedicated to Ganesh. To the rear of the complex is a less impressive museum with a few examples of Cham stonework.

To get here from central Nha Trang, take Đ Quang Trung (which becomes Đ 2 Thang 4) north across the Ha Ra and Xom Bong Bridges. Po Nagar can also be reached via the Tran Phu Bridge along the beachfront road.

This site has a continuing religious significance, so be sure to remove your shoes before entering.

Long Son Pagoda BUDDHIST TEMPLE

(Map p248; 7.30-11.30am & 1.30-5.30pm) FREE This striking pagoda was founded in the late 19th century. The entrance and roofs are decorated with mosaic dragons constructed of glass and ceramic tile while the main sanctuary is a hall adorned with modern interpretations of traditional motifs.

Behind the pagoda, a huge white **Buddha** (Map p248; Kim Than Phat To) is seated on a lotus blossom. Around the statue's base are fire-ringed relief busts of Thich Quang Duc and six other Buddhist monks who died in self-immolations in 1963.

The platform around the 14m-high Buddha has great views of Nha Trang and nearby rural areas. As you approach the pagoda from the street, the 152 stone steps up the hill to the Buddha begin to the right of the structure. Take some time to explore off to the left, where there's an entrance to another hall of the pagoda.

Beggars congregate within the complex, as do a number of scam artists. There's a persistent scam here, where visitors are approached by children (and adults) with pre-printed name badges claiming to work for the monks. After showing you around the pagoda, whether invited to or not, they will then demand money 'for the monks' or 'for a prayer'. If that fails, they insist that you buy postcards for 200,000d. The best course of action is to ignore them when they first appear; if they persist, tell them you're not going to give them any money. If you do want to make a contribution towards the upkeep of the complex, leave it in the donation boxes as you would in any other pagoda.

The pagoda is located about 400m west of the train station, just off Đ 23 Thang 10.

Nha Trang Cathedral CHURCH

(Map p250; cnr Đ Nguyen Trai & Đ Thai Nguyen) FREE Built between 1928 and 1933 in French Gothic style, complete with stained-glass windows, Nha Trang Cathedral stands on a small hill overlooking the train station. It's a surprisingly elegant building given that it was constructed of simple cement blocks. Some particularly colourful Vietnamese touches include the red neon outlining the crucifix, the pink back-lighting on the tabernacle and the blue neon arch and white neon halo over the statue of St Mary.

In 1988, a Catholic cemetery not far from the church was disinterred to make room for a new railway building. The remains were brought to the cathedral and reburied in the cavities behind the wall of plaques that line the ramp up the hill.

Alexandre Yersin Museum MUSEUM

(Map p250; ☎058-382 2355; 10 Đ Tran Phu; admission 26,000d; ⊙7.30-11am & 2-4.30pm Mon-Fri, 8-11am Sat) Highly popular in Vietnam, Dr Alexandre Yersin (1863–1943) founded Nha Trang's Pasteur Institute in 1895. He learned to speak Vietnamese fluently, introduced rubber- and quinine-producing trees to Vietnam, and discovered the rat-borne microbe that causes bubonic plague.

You can see Yersin's library and office at this small, interesting museum; displays include laboratory equipment (such as astronomical instruments) and a fascinating 3-D photo viewer.

Tours are conducted in French, English and Vietnamese, and a short film on Yersin's life is shown.

Yersin travelled throughout the central highlands and recorded his observations. During this period he came upon the site of what is now Dalat and recommended that a hill station be established there.

Today, the Pasteur Institute in Nha Trang coordinates vaccination and hygiene programs for the country's southern coastal region. The institute produces vaccines and carries out medical research and testing to European standards. Physicians at the clinic here offer medical advice to around 70 patients a day.

Hon Chong Promontory LANDMARK

(Map p248; admission 21,000d) The narrow granite promontory of Hon Chong offers fine views of the mountainous coastline north of Nha Trang and the nearby islands.

The beach here has a more local flavour than Nha Trang Beach (but the accompanying refuse is unpleasant). Still, it's fun to

VINPEARL LAND

Nha Trang's answer to Disneyland (well, sort of), the island resort of **Vinpearl Land** (☎359 0111; www.vinpearlland.com; Hon Tre Island; adult/child 600,000/400,000d; ⊙8am-9pm) has fun-fair rides, an impressive water park, arcade games and plenty of other attractions to keep the kiddies amused. You approach the amusement park via a 3km cable-car ride over the ocean. Note that the Underwater World aquarium costs an extra 60,000/45,000d per adult/child. Note that there are also dolphin shows here, which may not sit well with some visitors – animal welfare groups argue against keeping dolphins in captivity.

Central Nha Trang

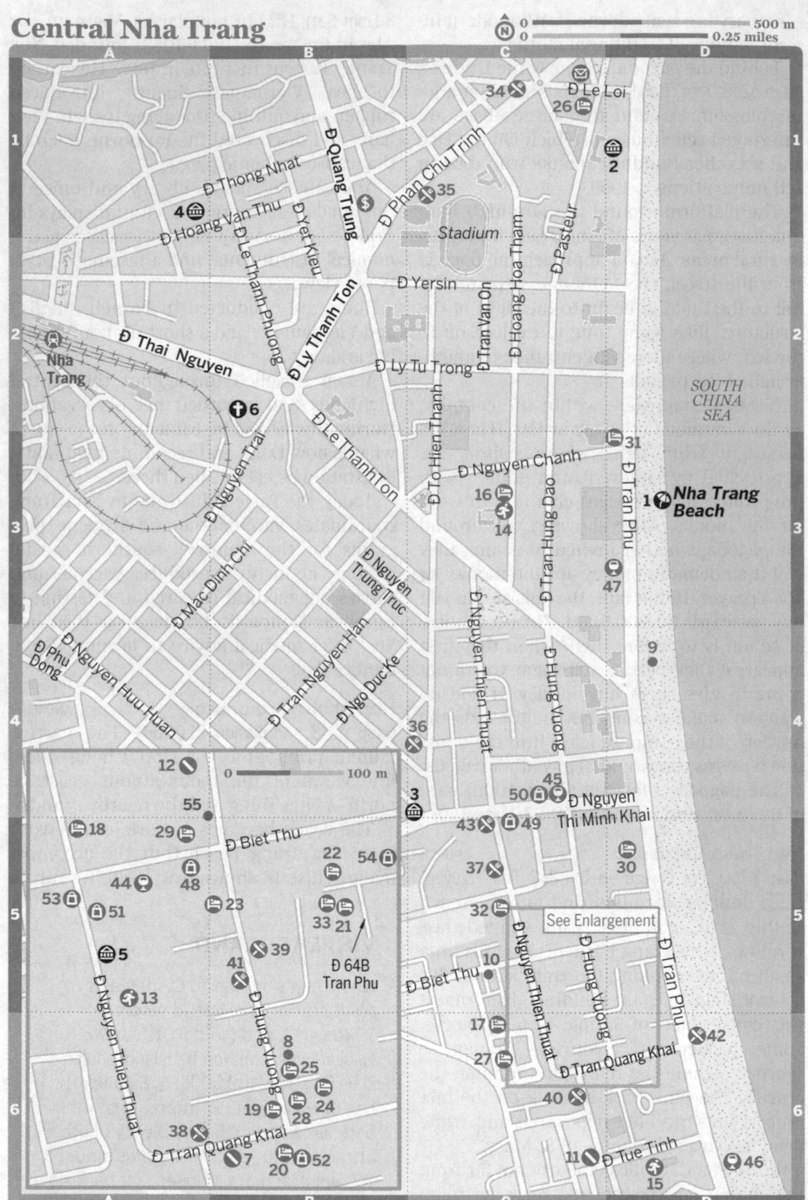

watch local kids do Acapulco-style swandives into the ocean.

There is also a reconstructed traditional Ruong residence and a great cafe (p260). A taxi here from the city centre is around 30,000d.

About 300m south of Hon Chong (towards Nha Trang) and a few dozen metres from the beach is tiny Hon Do (Red Island), which has a Buddhist temple on top. To the northeast is Hon Rua (Tortoise Island), which really does resemble a tortoise. The

Central Nha Trang

Top Sights

1 Nha Trang Beach ... D3

Sights

2 Alexandre Yersin Museum ... D1
3 Do Dien Khanh Gallery ... C4
4 Long Thanh Gallery ... A1
5 Mai Loc Gallery ... A5
6 Nha Trang Cathedral ... B2

Activities, Courses & Tours

7 Angel Dive ... B6
Brewery Tour ... (see 46)
8 Funky Monkey ... B6
9 Khanh Hoa Tourist Information ... D4
Lanterns Tours ... (see 37)
10 Nha Trang Tours ... C5
11 Oceans 5 ... C6
12 Rainbow Divers ... A4
Sailing Club Divers ... (see 42)
Shamrock Adventures ... (see 7)
13 Su Spa ... A5
Vietnam Active ... (see 28)
14 Vietnam Bike Tours ... C3
15 Vy Spa ... D6

Sleeping

16 Binh An Hotel ... C3
17 Carpe DM Hotel ... C6
18 Galliot Hotel ... A5
19 Golden Rain Hotel ... B6
20 Golden Summer Hotel ... B6
21 Ha Tram Hotel ... B5
22 Hotel An Hoa ... B5
23 King Town Hotel ... B5
24 Le Duong ... B6
25 Mai Huy Hotel ... B6
26 Michelia Hotel ... C1
27 Mojzo Inn ... C6
28 Ngoc Thach ... B6
29 Nhi Phi Hotel ... A5
30 Novotel Nha Trang ... D5
31 Sheraton Nha Trang Hotel & Spa ... D3
32 Summer Hotel ... C5
33 Sunny Sea ... B5

Eating

34 15 Le Loi ... C1
35 79 Dung Lin ... C1
Au Lac ... (see 16)
36 Kiwami ... C4
37 Lanterns ... C5
38 Le Petit Bistro ... A6
39 Mix ... B5
40 Nha Hang Yen's ... C6
Omar's Indian Restaurant ... (see 51)
41 Refuge ... B5
42 Sailing Club ... D6
43 Tasty ... C5

Drinking & Nightlife

Altitude ... (see 31)
44 Crazy Kim Bar ... A5
45 ifruit ... C4
46 Louisiane Brewhouse ... D6
Nghia Bia Hoi ... (see 25)
Sailing Club ... (see 42)
47 Skylight Bar ... D3

Shopping

48 Bambou ... A5
49 Cu Meo ... C5
50 Lemongrass House ... C4
51 Peekaboo ... A5
52 Saga du Mekong ... B6
53 Saga Etnik ... A5
54 XQ ... B5

Information

Khanh Hoa Tourist Information ... (see 9)
Pasteur Institute ... (see 2)
55 Sinh Tourist ... A4

Transport

Vietnam Airlines ... (see 13)

two islands of Hon Yen (Bird's-Nest Island) are off in the distance to the east.

National Oceanographic Museum MUSEUM
(Map p248; 058-359 0037; 1 Cau Da; adult/child 30,000/12,000d; 6am-6pm) Housed in a grand French-colonial building in the port district of Cau Da at the far south end of Nha Trang, this poorly maintained museum has 60,000 or so jars of pickled marine specimens, stuffed birds and sea mammals, and displays of local boats and fishing artefacts. There are tanks with reef fish (and sharks) but also live seals kept here in pitiful enclosures.

Long Thanh Gallery GALLERY
(Map p250; 058-382 4875; www.longthanhart.com; 126 Đ Hoang Van Thu; 8am-5.30pm Mon-Sat) FREE Paradise for monochrome aficionados, this gallery showcases the work of Vietnam's most prominent photographer. Long Thanh developed his first photo in 1964 and continues to shoot extraordinary black-and-white images of everyday Vietnamese moments and compelling portraits. The powerful images capture the heart and soul of Vietnam.

Mai Loc Gallery GALLERY
(Map p250; www.mailocphotos.com; 99 Đ Nguyen Thien Thuat; 8-11am & 2.30-10.30pm) FREE

Showcases the powerful, highly accomplished monochrome photography of Mai Loc, a native of Nha Trang. Ask him about his life story (he's an ex-gold miner, *cyclo* driver and tour guide).

Do Dien Khanh Gallery GALLERY

(Map p250; ☎058-351 2202; www.ddk-gallery.com; 126B Đ Hong Bat; ⏱8am-6pm Mon-Fri) FREE Do Dien Khanh is a welcoming host and very talented photographer of Vietnamese landscapes and life – his portraits of surrounding Cham communities are hauntingly beautiful.

Activities

The Nha Trang area is a key diving, surfing, wake-boarding, parasailing, white-water rafting and mountain-biking centre. Boat trips around the bay and up the Cai River are also a great day out.

Islands

Island tours are a big part of the Nha Trang experience.

Hon Yen BOAT TOUR

(Bird's-Nest Island) Also known as Salangane Island, this is the lump-shaped land mass visible from Nha Trang Beach. This and other islands off Khanh Hoa province are the source of Vietnam's finest *salangane* (swiftlet) nests; locals climb up tottering bamboo ladders to fetch them. There is a small, secluded beach here. The 17km trip out to the islands takes three hours or so by small boat from Nha Trang.

Hon Mieu BOAT TOUR

This is billed as an outdoor **aquarium** (Ho Ca Tri Nguyen; admission 90,000d) but it's actually more of a fish-breeding farm, where over 40 species of fish, crustacean and other marine creatures are raised. Surrounding the tanks is an incredibly kitsch concrete collection of giant shrimps, fang-bearing sharks and so on.

Hon Mieu is included in most island boat tours. DIY travellers can catch one of the regular ferries (5000d) that travel here from Cau Da dock.

Hon Mun SNORKELLING

(Ebony Island) Pretty Hon Mun island is Nha Trang's most famous snorkelling and dive site. The coral is in fair condition and visibility usually good, but it can get very crowded as it's on the main day-tripping agenda.

Hon Mot SNORKELLING

Sandwiched neatly between Hon Mun and Hon Tam, or Silkworm Island, is tiny Hon Mot, a popular place for snorkelling.

Diving

Nha Trang is Vietnam's most popular scuba-diving centre, although not necessarily its best. Visibility averages 15m but can be as much as 30m, depending on the season. February to September is considered the best time to dive, while October to December is the worst time of year.

There are around 25 dive sites in the area. There are no wrecks to visit, but some sites have good drop-offs and there are a few small underwater caves to explore. Frankly, it's not world-class diving, but the waters support a good variety of soft and hard corals, and a reasonable number of small reef fish. You can expect to see reef fish including clownfish, pufferfish and trumpetfish, as well as cuttlefish and octopus.

A full-day outing including boat transport, two dives and lunch typically costs between US$65 and US$85 with a professional dive school. Snorkellers can usually tag along for US$15 to US$20.

Most dive operators also offer a range of dive courses, including a 'discover diving' program for uncertified first-time divers to experience the underwater world with the supervision of a qualified dive master. PADI courses start at US$350, SSI cost a little less.

There are a dozen or so dive operators in Nha Trang. We've heard reports about the odd dodgy set-up not following responsible diving practices and even using fake PADI/SSI accreditation. These tend to charge ridiculously cheap prices (as low as US$35 for two dives).

Stick to reputable outfits such as Vietnam Active and recommended schools.

Oceans 5 DIVING

(Map p250; ☎058-381 1969, 058-352 2012; www.oceans5.co; 78 Tue Tinh) SSI school run by two Australian instructors, providing professionally run training courses and well-organised fun dives. Gear is in good condition, and the company also does dive training inside the protected marine area. Two dives are US$75.

Sailing Club Divers DIVING

(Map p250; ☎058-352 2788; www.sailingclubdivers.com; 72-74 Đ Tran Phu) A PADI five-star centre offering professional instruction, modern equipment and multilingual instructors. The dive boat is superb. A Discover Scuba dive is 1,250,000d.

NHA TRANG'S BEST DIVE SITES

Most of the best dive action is around Hon Mun island, which is an officially designated marine park.

Moray Beach On the south side of Hon Mun, with healthy hard and soft corals, including a giant table coral formation. Two species of moray eel, lionfish, leaf fish and scorpionfish can be spotted. Maximum depth is 18m.

Coral Garden An array of impressive hard corals including gorgonians. Expect to see Moorish Idols, nudibranchs and pufferfish. It's on the east side of Hon Mun.

Madonna Rock Off tiny Hon Rom, this site has a resident 1.5m grouper, and barracudas and unicorn fish are encountered. There are great swim-throughs. Also known as Octopus Rock.

Light House A deep dive at the tip of Hon Tre island where barracuda, stingrays, triggerfish and snapper are seen. For experienced divers.

Green Canyon Off the northeast coast of Hon Mun with a steep drop-off suitable for deep diving. It's a good spot to see lionfish, nudibranches and passing snapper.

Angel Dive DIVING
(Map p250; ☎058-352 2461; www.angeldivevietnam.info; 1/27 Đ Tran Quang Khai) Reliable, experienced SSI operator with English, French and German instruction, with good courses for kids. Snorkelling trips cost US$20 per person.

Rainbow Divers DIVING
(Map p250; ☎058-352 4351; www.divevietnam.com; 90A Đ Hung Vuong) Large, well-established PADI dive school, part of a nationwide chain. Here at HQ, there is also a popular restaurant and bar. A boat trip with three dives is 2,050,000d.

Adventure Sports

From mountain biking to white-water rafting, Nha Trang offers lots of activities to get the pulse racing.

★**Vietnam Active** ADVENTURE SPORTS
(Map p250; ☎058-351 5821; www.vietnamactive.com; 115 Đ Hung Vuong) Offers a diverse range of excellent activities including rafting, kayaking, mountain-biking trips and scuba diving (SSI and PADI accredited). Exact prices depend upon numbers. Stretch those aching limbs afterwards at one of the hatha or ashtanga yoga classes. It also rents quality bikes (from US$5 per day).

Vietnam Bike Tours BICYCLE TOUR
(Map p250; ☎0905 779 311; www.vietnambikeurs.com; 17/14 Đ Hoang Hoa Tham) Organises excellent local tours of the countryside and coastline, taking in mud baths and fishing villages with patient, experienced guides. All levels are catered for.

Shamrock Adventures RAFTING
(Map p250; ☎058-352 7548; www.shamrockadventures.vn; Đ Tran Quang Khai; trips per person incl lunch from US$40) This outfit runs white-water rafting excursions (which can be combined with some mountain biking). Kayaking, snorkelling and fishing trips are also on offer.

River Trips

A impressive broad estuary, the Cai River just north of central Nha Trang is best explored as a day trip by boat.

Nha Trang River Tour BOAT TOUR
(☎0914 047 406; www.nhatrangrivertour.com; 120/1/6 Hung Vuong; per person from US$40) Pham is a well-organised, interesting guide and his river tours are worthwhile. Tours concentrate on cultural sights and cottage industries (rice-paper making, mat weavers, embroidery) along the Cai River and include a hot spring and mud bath session.

Spas & Thermal Baths

Locals swear that the only way to get really clean is to get deep down and dirty in a natural mud bath, and there are now several places around Nha Trang where you can get stuck in (the mud). Try to avoid weekends, when Vietnamese families descend en masse.

If you'd prefer a more conventional spa there are plenty that fit the bill nicely.

★**I Resort** THERMAL BATHS
(☎058-383 8838; 19 Xuan Ngoc, Vinh Ngoc; packages from 250,000d; ⏰7am-8pm) Just the place to really indulge, this upmarket thermal spa

is the most attractive of the three mudfests around Nha Trang, with hot mineral mud baths, lovely bathing pools and even waterfalls. The rural setting is gorgeous, with distant mountain views, and there's a decent restaurant and spa/massage centre. Budget spending at least half a day here, it's well worth it. All kinds of mud/spa packages are available. Call for a shuttle (20,000d one way) from your hotel.

It's 7km northwest of the centre.

Thap Ba Hot Spring Center THERMAL BATHS
(Map p248; ☎058-383 5345; www.thapbahotspring.com.vn; 15 Ngoc Son; ⏰7am-7.30pm) Gooey mud heaven, this (the original hot thermal mud centre) remains decent value. A communal mud bath is 150,000d (20 minutes maximum time), while private bathtubs are more costly. There are also mineral water swimming pools and lots of packages. Located 7km northwest of Nha Trang (130,000d in a taxi).

To get here by yourself, follow the signpost on the second road to the left past the Po Nagar Cham Towers and continue along the winding road for 2.5km.

100 Egg Mud Bath THERMAL BATHS
(Tam Bun Tram Trung; ☎058-371 1733; www.tambuntramtrung.vn; Nguyen Tat Thanh, Phuoc Trung; ⏰8am-7pm) This place gets its name from the egg-shaped private pods where couples or kids can indulge in a little mud play. All kinds of mud plastering, wraps and scrubs are offered. You'll also find pools and tubs (which can be filled with herbs and essential oils) scattered around this huge complex, which also has a restaurant and (man-made) waterfall. Full packages that include all facilities cost 500,000d. It's 6km southwest of Nha Trang.

From the Cau Binh Tan bridge on the southwest side of town, head along Đ Nguyen Tat Thanh until you reach the highway at Phuoc Trung; it's just over the road from here and clearly signposted.

HON LAO'S ANIMAL CIRCUS

The island of Hon Lao is home to 1000 or so monkeys that are accustomed to receiving food handouts from the hordes of tourists who descend here. These are wild animals and monkey bites do occur (and are a possible source of rabies). Hon Lao's monkeys are also materialistic and will grab the sunglasses off your face or snatch a pen from your shirt pocket. There are also several circus-style animal acts here, including shows with performing bears, monkeys and dogs. Hon Lao is very popular with locals, though note that travellers have reported seeing animals being abused.

★Xanh Spa SPA
(☎058-398 9666; www.mianhatrang.com/relax; Mia Resort Nha Trang; massages from US$42) With Zen-like treatment rooms high above the ocean, this high-end hotel's spa enjoys a dramatic setting. Staff are superbly trained, and responsive to client requests. Body wraps and scrubs, massages, pedicures and manicures are all superb.

Vy Spa SPA
(Map p250; ☎012 8275 8662; 78B Đ Tue Tinh; ⏰8am-9pm) Run by a friendly couple, this simple place offers fine-value massages and treatments. Chose from Vietnamese, Thai or Swedish massages (from 200,000d per hour), or try a facial or scrub.

Su Spa SPA
(Map p250; ☎058-352 3242; www.suspa.com.vn; 93 Đ Nguyen Thien Thuat; ⏰8am-9.30pm) The pretty little brick gateway and greenery set a welcoming tone at Su Spa, and the relaxed ambience will ease the travel-weary. This stylishly designed place offers good scrubs, rubs, tubs and body massages (from US$25).

Tours

★Lanterns Tours CULTURAL TOUR
(Map p250; ☎058-247 1674; www.lanternsvietnam.com; 34/6 Đ Nguyen Thien Thuat; tour US$25) This non-profit restaurant offers an interesting tour (US$25) of the non-touristy town of Ninh Hoa, taking in a local market and lunch with a local family. Its walking street-food tours (200,000d) of Nha Trang are also highly recommended, featuring seven dishes including *banh tai vac* (shrimp dumplings) and *che chuoi nuong* (banana and sticky rice).

Brewery Tour TOUR
(Map p250; ☎352 1948; www.louisianebrewhouse.com.vn; Louisiane Brewhouse, 29 Đ Tran Phu; tour 200,000d) A highly informative tour, here you can find out how malt and hops become ale and lager, and of course sample the golden nectar.

TRIPPING THE BAY BY BOAT

The 71 offshore islands around Nha Trang are renowned for the remarkably clear water surrounding them. Trips to these islands have been a huge draw for years now, and virtually every hotel and travel company in town books island-hopping boat tours.

Back in the day (well, the 1990s), party boat tours involved a bumpy ride out to sea on a leaky fishing boat, copious joints and rice wine shots in a 'floating bar' (a tube in the ocean). Unsurprisingly local party officials deemed the ganja and drinking games a bit too counter-revolutionary for their tastes.

Today there's more of a choice – with everything from backpacker booze cruises to family-geared outings.

Frankly, most of these trips are extremely touristy, involving whistle-stop visits to the Tri Nguyen Aquarium (admission 90,000d), some snorkelling on a degraded reef, and a bit of beach time (beach admissions 30,000d). The booze cruises feature (very) organised entertainment with a DJ on the deck (or a cheesy boy band) and lots of drinking games. Expect 20 or 30 people packed on a small boat. If this sounds like your idea of hell, well, you've been warned.

In recent years upmarket options have increased, with everything from private charters to cruises on traditional junks now available.

Keep the following tips in mind:

- Choose the right tour. Some are geared towards Asian families, others are booze cruises aimed solely at the backpacker market.
- Remember sunscreen and drink plenty of water.
- Entrance charges to the aquarium and beach are not usually included.
- If you're more interested in snorkelling than drinking, the dive schools' trips will be more appropriate.

There are a few decent boat-trip operators.

Funky Monkey (Map p250; ☎091 3458 950, 058-352 2426; http://funkymonkeytour.com; 75A Đ Hung Vuong; cruise incl pick-up 200,000d) A party-hard, backpacker-geared trip that kicks off at 8.30am. Features live 'entertainment' from the Funky Monkey boy band, as well as the usual stops.

Sailing Center Vietnam (Map p248; ☎058-387 8714; www.sailing.vn; 7 Hien Luong; half-day trips from US$275) These professionals organise bespoke trimaran and catamaran charters to the islands off Nha Trang. Trips include snorkelling, lunch and refreshments.

Nha Trang Tours (Map p250; ☎058-352 4471; www.nhatrangtour.com.vn; 29 Đ Biet Thu) Budget party-themed booze cruises for 200,000d or snorkelling trips for 320,000d.

Emperor Cruises (☎0123 666 8879; http://emperorcruises.com; dinner/day cruise US$79/147) The classiest way to cruise the bay, Emperor offers memorable trips on traditional wooden junks. The cuisine, drinks and service are tip-top, but then so are the rates charged.

Khanh Hoa Tourist Information (Map p250; ☎058-352 8000; khtourism@dng.vnn.vn; Đ Tran Phu; cruise incl lunch 380,000d) For something a little different, consider a boat trip to beautiful Van Phong Bay. The two-hour trip there puts many off, but the remote, secluded bays certainly help compensate. Contact the tourist office for details and bookings.

Sleeping

Nha Trang has hundreds of hotels, from dives to the divine, and most places are within a block or two of the beach. Discounts of 20% to 30% are common in midrange and top-end places when business is slow.

There is a cluster of cheapies on an alleyway at 64 Đ Tran Phu, very close to the beach. All offer similar air-conditioned rooms for around US$10 or so, even less if you go with the flow of a fan. Most budget places don't include breakfast.

Luxury hotels line Đ Tran Phu, the waterfront boulevard. The area's most exclusive resort hotels are out of town, in Ninh Van Bay to the north and there's also a number of new places being constructed on Bai Dai beach, along the airport road.

★Sunny Sea HOTEL $

(Map p250; ☎058-352 2286; sunnyseahotel@gmail.com; 64B/9 Đ Tran Phu; r US$10-15; ❄@📶) A class above the others on 'budget alley' just off the beach, this exceptional place is owned by a welcoming local couple (a doctor and nurse) and their super-helpful staff. The rooms are kept very clean and are in fine shape, with good-quality mattresses, minibar and modern bathrooms; some have a balcony.

Mojzo Inn HOTEL $

(Map p250; ☎0988 879 069; www.facebook.com/MojzoInn; 120/36 Đ Nguyen Thien Thuat; dm US$8, r US$16-20; ❄@📶) OK, the name is more cocktail list than hotel bed, but this funky hostel gets most things right, with well-designed dorms and a lovely cushion-scattered lounge area. Staff really go the extra mile to help here.

Carpe DM Hotel HOTEL $

(Map p250; ☎058-352 7868; www.carpedmhotel.com; 120/62 Đ Nguyen Thien Thuat; r US$16-22; ❄📶) This likeable, well-managed place has excellent, well-scrubbed, bright rooms with a contemporary touch, all very well equipped and attractively furnished with large flat-screen TV. The more expensive options have a balcony. It's a no-smoking hotel.

Binh An Hotel GUESTHOUSE $

(Map p250; www.binhanhotel.com; ☎0128 705 0399; 28H Đ Hoang Hoa Tham; r 350,000-380,000d; ❄@📶) A welcoming place run by an accommodating couple who look after guests with pride. Rooms are spotless, spacious and boast good air-con and fast wi-fi. Say hi to Zon, the chihuahua dog, while you're here.

Hotel An Hoa HOTEL $

(Map p250; ☎058-352 4029; www.anhoahotel.com.vn; 64B/6 Đ Tran Phu; r with fan/air-con US$10/14; ❄@📶) Getting top marks for friendliness, this is a well-run budget hotel. Cleanliness standards are high; its rooms vary from small, fan-cooled and windowless, to bigger and better options with larger bathrooms and a smarter trim.

Ha Tram Hotel HOTEL $

(Map p250; ☎058-352 1819; hatramhotel.weebly.com; 64B/5 Đ Tran Phu; r US$10-14; ❄@📶) The newest hotel on this strip, this smart mini-hotel has light, bright, well-equipped rooms and smart en-suite bathrooms. The very cheapest don't have windows, posher options have a balcony.

Mai Huy Hotel HOTEL $

(Map p250; ☎058-352 7553; maihuyhotel.com; 7H Quan Tran, Đ Hung Vuong; r with fan/air-con from US$8/14; ❄@📶) For a really cheap base, this long-standing backpacking place is certainly worth considering. The rooms (there are five price categories) vary quite a bit, from cramped but doable to fresh and modernised.

Ngoc Thach HOTEL $

(Map p250; ☎058-352 5988; ngocthachhotel@gmail.com; 61 Quan Tran, Đ Hung Vuong; r US$15-20; ❄📶) A pleasant mini-hotel in the thick of things with spacious, modern rooms (some with balcony) that represent decent value. There's a lift.

Michelia Hotel HOTEL $$

(Map p250; ☎058-382 0820; www.michelia.vn; 4 Đ Pasteur; r/ste incl breakfast from 1,150,000/2,550,000d; ❄@📶🏊) One block from the beach towards the north end of the centre, the Michelia has sleek, modern accommodation and helpful staff, and the breakfast buffet is excellent. The pool is big enough for laps.

Golden Summer Hotel HOTEL $$

(Map p250; ☎058-352 6662; www.goldensummerhotel.com.vn; 22-23 Đ Tran Quang Khai; r US$27-50; ❄@📶) Modish hotel, with a super-stylish lobby and inviting, modern rooms all with nice artistic touches such as statement photography on the walls. The location is excellent with myriad restaurants and the beach a short stroll away.

Galliot Hotel HOTEL $$

(Map p250; ☎058-352 8555; http://galliothotel.com; 61A Đ Nguyen Thien Thuat; r 1,300,000-1,800,000d; ❄@📶🏊) This new hotel boasts a convenient location in the heart of the city with a bevy of bars and restaurants just steps away. There's a wide choice of well-presented rooms, avoid the very cheapest, which don't have a window. The rooftop pool is perfect for cooling off.

Summer Hotel HOTEL $$

(Map p250; ☎058-352 2186; www.thesummerhotel.com.vn; 34C Đ Nguyen Thien Thuat; r US$30-117; ❄@📶🏊) Smart three-star hotel with affordable prices, and rooms with high comfort levels and comfortable trim. The pool zone on the rooftop clinches the deal. Booking sites often offer rates well below those on the hotel's website.

Nhi Phi Hotel HOTEL $$
(Map p250; ☎058-352 4585; www.nhiphihotel.vn; 10A Đ Biet Thu; r US$45-75; ❄@📶🏊) Imposing colossus with an amazing lobby atrium, small rooftop pool and well-furnished rooms (those above the 7th floor have fine city views). During quiet times, promotional rates represent a real bargain.

Le Duong HOTEL $$
(Map p250; nhatrangleduonghotel.com; 5 & 6 Quan Tran, Đ Hung Vuong; r 460,000-750,000d; ❄📶) Close to restaurants and nightlife, this modern hotel has 50 light, spacious rooms with pale furniture and white linen, cable TV and fridges. Prices are flexible to a degree, depending on demand.

Golden Rain Hotel HOTEL $$
(Map p250; ☎058-352 7799; www.goldenrainhotel.com; 142 Đ Hung Vuong; r US$29-58; ❄@📶🏊) Conveniently located; rooms are spacious if a little dated and some include large windows. The rooftop pool and gym round things off nicely.

King Town Hotel HOTEL $$
(Map p250; ☎352 5818; www.kingtownhotel.com.vn; 92 Đ Hung Vuong; r US$22-45; ❄@📶🏊) This place discounts heavily during slow periods when it's fine value, considering the spacious rooms and rooftop swimming pool with city views. At other times of year it's still worth considering.

★Mia Resort Nha Trang HOTEL $$$
(☎058-398 9666; www.mianhatrang.com; Bai Dong, Cam Hai Dong; villa from US$230; 🚌❄@📶🏊) This exceptional hotel enjoys a privileged position, occupying a private cove beach and the hillside behind.

Accommodation units are modern, spacious and commodious – freshen up in a vast bathtub or take an al fresco shower. Ocean Villas have private pools, Garden Villas are closer to the shore. Great service, a top spa and a stunning waveside restaurant complete the Mia experience.

First impressions are electric: the open-sided reception is high above the ocean, overlooking a horizon-filling expanse of big blue.

Evason Ana Mandara Resort & Spa RESORT HOTEL $$$
(Map p248; ☎058-352 2522; www.evasonresorts.com; Đ Tran Phu; villa US$240-545; ❄@📶🏊) This fine hotel consists of a charming cluster of spacious oceanside villas that have a colonial feel thanks to the classic furnishings and four-poster beds. It's the only city hotel on the shoreside of the beach, so there's no traffic between you and the delightful sandy shore. Facilities include two swimming pools (one 30m), Western and Vietnamese restaurants and a Six Senses spa.

Novotel Nha Trang HOTEL $$$
(Map p250; ☎058-625 6900; www.novotel.com/6033; 50 Đ Tran Phu; r/ste from US$130/262; ❄@📶🏊) Stylish and very contemporary, this oceanfront hotel features split-level rooms with sunken bathtubs – invest in a sea view on the upper floor to see Nha Trang in all its glory. Staff are very well trained and helpful. The gym is well equipped for a workout, though the pool is on the small side. Book via the group's own website for the best rate.

Fusion Resort Nha Trang RESORT $$$
(☎058-398 9777; http://fusionresortnhatrang.com; Nguyen Tat Thanh; s/d incl breakfast from US$259/518; ❄@📶🏊) For sybaritic living look no further. New in 2015, this new resort's unique selling point is its complimentary spa treatments (two daily per guest are guaranteed). It's a huge complex where the suites and villas all have sea views, and many have private plunge pools. It's located on the ocean road 30km south of Nha Trang, there's a free shuttle bus service from the airport.

Sheraton Nha Trang Hotel & Spa HOTEL $$$
(Map p250; ☎058-388 0000; www.sheraton.com/nhatrang; 26-28 Đ Tran Phu; r/ste from US$155/275; ❄@📶🏊) The Sheraton dominates the oceanfront boulevard, and the views from its cocktail lounge are simply staggering. Rooms are spacious and modern with open-plan bathrooms; book a suite for real luxury (and access to the impressive Club Lounge).

Eating

As a resort town, Nha Trang caters to a decidedly international clientele and there's an array of cosmopolitan flavours to savour – from Cretan to Indian. Đ Tran Quang Khai and Đ Biet Thu are popular hunting grounds, but more authentic Vietnamese grub is found further afield. Seafood-lovers are in for a treat with fresh fish, crab, shrimp and an assortment of exotic shellfish on offer.

For a traditional local experience, try **Dam Market** (Map p248; Đ Trang Nu Vuong;

NHA TRANG STREET FOOD

Rents and real-estate prices are high in central Nha Trang, which is not a great place for cheap local grub. All these street-food experiences are north of the centre.

Banh Xeo stand Almost opposite the Cham towers, this **stand** (Map p248; Đ 2 Thang 4) is worked by a feisty old lady who cooks up great *banh xeo* (savoury riceflour pancakes with shrimp/pork and bean sprouts) on a smoking griddle.

Seafood Street Famous for its evening only seafood places, **Thap Ba** (Map p248; Thap Ba; ⏲5.30-10pm) produces fine steamed or barbecued clams, crab and prawns.

Barbecued Duck Popular **79 Dung Lin** (Map p250; 29 Phan Chu Trinh; ⏲6-9.30pm), just west of the stadium, is famous for its wonderfully flavoursome duck (half a duck with salad, dips and rice is 100,000d).

Pork Meatballs Head to **15 Le Loi** (Map p250; 15 Le Loi; ⏲10.30am-8pm) for superb *nem nuong* (grilled minced pork marinated with shallots and spices) served with dipping sauce, herbs and salad. There are two places here.

⏲6am-4pm), which has a colourful collection of stalls, including *com chay* (vegetarian) options, in the 'food court'.

Tasty CAFE $
(Map p250; 30 Đ Nguyen Thien Thuat; snacks/meals from 22,000/40,000d; ⏲6.30am-10.30pm;) A hip, bustling cafe with real appeal thanks to the bold retro murals (camper vans and vespas), kitsch touches and mismatched seating. You'll find plenty of interest on the menu too, including good *banh mi*, Vietnamese salads, cheap breakfasts, juices and coffee. There's an open kitchen.

Nha Hang Yen's VIETNAMESE $
(Map p250; 093 3766 205; http://yensrestaurantnhatrang.com; 3/2A Đ Tran Quang Khai; dishes 55,000-120,000d; ⏲7am-9.30pm;) Stylish restaurant with a hospitable atmosphere and a winning line-up of flavoursome claypot, curry, noodle, rice and stir-fry dishes. Lilting traditional music and waitresses in *ao dai* (national dress) add to the vibe.

Omar's Indian Restaurant INDIAN $
(Map p250; www.omarsindianrestaurant.com; 89B Đ Nguyen Thien Thuat; mains 55,000-136,000d, set meal 150,000d; ⏲7am-11pm;) Authentic Indian cuisine – you can't go wrong with a set meal (150,000d) which includes a bhaji, popodums, a veggie or chicken curry, rice and a beer.

Au Lac VEGETARIAN $
(Map p250; 28C Đ Hoang Hoa Tham; meals 15,000-30,000d; ⏲10am-7pm;) This long-running, no-frills vegan/vegetarian is near the corner of Đ Nguyen Chanh. A mixed plate (15,000d) is just about the best-value meal you can find in Nha Trang.

★Lac Canh Restaurant VIETNAMESE $$
(Map p248; 44 Đ Nguyen Binh Khiem; dishes 30,000-150,000d; ⏲11am-8.45pm) This bustling, smoky, scruffy and highly enjoyable place is crammed most nights with groups firing up the table-top barbecues (beef, richly marinated with spices, is the speciality, but there are other meats and seafood, too). Closes quite early.

★Mix GREEK $$
(Map p250; 77 Đ Hung Vuong; meals 80,000-150,000d; ⏲11am-10pm) Somehow Christos, the affable, kind-hearted Greek owner, manages to keep the quality high and prices moderate at his ever-busy restaurant, a Herculean effort. Everything is freshly prepared and beautifully presented; highlights include the seafood and meat platters, salads and souvlaki.

Nha Trang Xua VIETNAMESE $$
(Thai Thong, Vinh Thai; dishes 40,000-210,000d; ⏲8am-9pm;) A classic Vietnamese restaurant set in a beautiful old house in the countryside surrounded by rice paddies and a lotus pond, around 7km west of town (100,000d in a taxi). Think: a refined (hand-written) menu, chunky wooden tables and a rustic ambience. Highlights include the hotpots, Vietnamese salads, five-spice beef and fish (try the snakehead fish grilled in banana leaf).

Lanterns VIETNAMESE $$

(Map p250; www.lanternsvietnam.com; 34/6 Đ Nguyen Thien Thuat; dishes 48,000-117,000d; 7.30am-9.30pm;)  This restaurant supports local orphanages and provides scholarships programs. Flavours are predominantly Vietnamese, with specials including curries, claypots and steaming hot pots (210,000d for two). The 'street food' items are not bad and international offerings include pasta. Cooking classes and tours get good feedback. Eat between 2pm and 4pm and 20% is knocked off your bill.

Lang Nuong Phu Dong Hai San SEAFOOD $$

(Map p248; Đ Tran Phu; dishes 45,000-180,000d; 2pm-3am) The decor is basic (think plastic chairs and strip lights) but the seafood is fresh and delicious. Choose from scallops, crab, prawns and lobster, all at market prices.

Refuge INTERNATIONAL $$

(Map p250; 1L Đ Hung Vuong; mains 60,000-175,000d; 7.30am-10pm;) A Swiss-owned log-cabin-style restaurant with great crêpes, salads (try the goat's cheese), cheeses, and grilled beef and lamb steaks (you choose your own sauce). Wine is available by the glass and reasonably priced. Unusually around here, the premises are air-conditioned.

Le Petit Bistro FRENCH $$

(Map p250; 058-352 7201; http://bistronhatrang.com; 34 Đ Tran Quang Khai; mains 90,000-250,000d; 7am-10.30pm;) This well-established French restaurant is highly regarded by the Gallic crowd, and is the place for a steak tartare, a brochette or some serious *fromage* (cheese). There's a daily specials board, and, for those who like to quaff, the wine list is the city's best.

★Kiwami JAPANESE $$$

(Map p250; 095 6130 933, 058-351 6613; www.kiwamirestaurantsushi.info.vn; 136 Bach Dang; meals 250,000-500,000d; noon-10pm Thu-Tue;) An intimate, highly authentic neighbourhood Japanese place that gets everything right. There's a specialist sushi chef – perch on a bar stool and watch him at work or sit in one of the side alcoves. All of your favourite dishes are present and correct, from sashimi to teriyaki. Visit at lunchtime and there are special sushi sets and bentos available.

★Sailing Club INTERNATIONAL $$$

(Map p250; 058-352 4628; www.sailingclubnhatrang.com; 72-74 Đ Tran Phu; mains 130,000-400,000d; 7.30am-11pm;) A beachfront institution. People-watch from elegant seating by day, sip on a cocktail at sundown, dine on gourmet food under the stars and then burn it all off on the dance floor. There are three separate menus – Vietnamese, international and Indian. Standouts include oven-roasted sea bass and beef carpaccio.

Drinking

Nha Trang has historically been renowned for its backpacker party scene, but these days there's a wide choice of places, from sky bars to beachside lounges.

Pay serious attention to your drink and possessions (p260) if you're in the party bars of Nha Trang.

Sailing Club BAR, CLUB

(Map p250; www.sailingclubnhatrang.com; 72-74 Đ Tran Phu; 7am-2am;) This Nha Trang beach club is a city institution with DJs and bands, and draws a beautiful, up-for-it crowd. On Thursdays, Fridays and Saturdays a bonfire is lit and the action moves to the sand (weather permitting!). It draws a good mix of locals and foreigners.

Skylight Bar BAR

(Map p250; http://skylightnhatrang.com; Best Western Premier Havana Nha Trang, 38 Đ Tran Phu; admission incl drink 100,000d; 4.30-11pm;) Soaring above the city on the 43rd floor, this bombastic new place set up by a team from LA boasts mile-high vistas from its rooftop perch, a killer cocktail list (120,000d to 150,000d), shishas, cigars, DJs and pool parties. The only question: is it too ahead of the curve? Is Nha Trang ready for it?

DRINK SPIKING

There has been a number of reports of laced cocktail buckets doing the rounds in popular nightspots. This might mean staff using homemade moonshine instead of legal spirits or could mean the addition of drugs of some sort by other punters. While buckets are fun and communal, take care in Nha Trang and try to keep an eye on what goes into the bucket. You don't want your night to end in paranoia or robbery.

Louisiane Brewhouse BREWERY

(Map p250; ☎058-352 1948; 29 Đ Tran Phu; per glass 40,000d; ⏲7am-midnight; 📶) Microbreweries don't get much more sophisticated than this. Louisiane's copper vats sure have a helluva view, gazing over an inviting swimming pool down to a private strip of sand. There are six brews to try, including a red ale and superb *witbier* (a dark lager brewed Belgian-style).

Hon Chong Cafe CAFE

(Map p248; Hon Chong; drinks 18,000-30,000d; ⏲7am-7pm) With panoramic views of Nha Trang, this lovely shady cafe in Hon Chong is the perfect spot to enjoy a coffee or beer (or even a margarita) and catch the sea breeze. No food is served (other than ice cream).

Crazy Kim Bar BAR

(Map p250; http://crazykimvietnam.wordpress.com; 19 Đ Biet Thu; ⏲9am-late; 📶) This place is home to the commendable 'Hands off the Kids!' campaign, working to prevent paedophilia – part of the profits go towards the cause. Crazy Kim's has regular themed party nights, devilish cocktail buckets (60,000d), shooters, cheap beer and tasty grub. La Rue beer is 2-4-1 during happy hour (noon to 8.30pm).

Altitude BAR

(Map p250; 26-28 Đ Tran Phu; ⏲noon-midnight; 📶) Located on the 28th floor of the Sheraton Nha Trang, this bar has simply out-of-this-world views of the coast – you can pick out every footprint in the sand below (if your eyes are up to it!). The interior is non-smoking. Prices are five-star too, so consider dropping by during happy hour (4pm to 6pm).

Nghia Bia Hoi BIA HOI

(Map p250; 7G/3 Đ Hung Vuong; ⏲11am-10pm) A popular *bia hoi* (draught beer) joint which pulls in a loyal local (and backpacker) crowd. It serves a light lager and a darker brown beer, as well as snacks.

ifruit JUICE BAR

(Map p250; 4 Nguyen Thi Minh Khai; ⏲7am-11pm) On a busy corner plot; head here for a hit-and-run juice or smoothie, as there are 20 different flavours to choose from. It's run by a friendly young team.

Shopping

Nha Trang has some good arts and crafts shops in the blocks around the corner of Đ Tran Quang Khai and Đ Hung Vuong.

Fashion boutiques selling everything from slingbacks to sunglasses are concentrated along Đ Nguyen Thi Minh Khai.

★**Lemongrass House** BEAUTY

(Map p250; https://instagram.com/lemongrasshouse.vn; 38 Đ Nguyen Thi Minh Khai; ⏲10am-10pm) 🌿 A terrific little store selling wonderful face creams (270,000d), masks, hair products, essential oils and some teas. The products are sourced from natural ingredients and made in small batches in Thailand.

Peekaboo CLOTHING

(Map p250; 97 Đ Nguyen Thien Thuat; ⏲10am-10pm) This quirky little place has a well-curated selection of bags, summer dresses, swimming costumes, sunglasses and accessories. It's up a steep flight of stairs.

Saga Etnik CLOTHING

(Map p250; 48 Đ Nguyen Thien Thuat; ⏲9am-10pm) Tropical heat getting you down? Come here for blouses, dresses and hats; some items are based on traditional Vietnamese designs and are in lightweight natural fabrics.

Saga du Mekong CLOTHING

(Map p250; www.sagadumekong.com; 1/21 Đ Nguyen Dinh Chieu; ⏲9am-9pm) This stylish fashion boutique specialises in linen, silk, bamboo and fine cotton clothing. Stocks Western sizes and has its own factory for quality control.

XQ HANDICRAFTS

(Map p250; www.xqvietnam.com; 64 Đ Tran Phu; ⏲8am-8pm) At this place, designed to look like a traditional rural village, you can watch the artisans at work in the embroidery workshop and gallery.

Cu Meo CLOTHING, ACCESSORIES

(Map p250; 37 Đ Nguyen Thi Minh Khai; ⏲8am-7pm) A hip boutique renowned for its modish ladies' shoe designs; also stocks lingerie, swimwear and dresses.

Bambou CLOTHING

(Map p250; www.bamboucompany.com; 15 Đ Biet Thu; ⏲8am-9pm) Specialises in casual clothing for men, women and kids, with Vietnamese motifs. Natural materials including tencel and bamboo are used.

Information

DANGERS & ANNOYANCES

The vast vast majority of visitors experience no troubles at all in Nha Trang. While there's no need to be paranoid, you should take a little extra care here as the town certainly has its share of thieves.

There are many ways for you and your valuables to part company. Young travellers are most frequently targeted. We hear many stories about people getting pickpocketed in bars and clubs: packed dance floors are particularly popular hunting ground for thieves. Do you really need to carry a smartphone and credit card on your night out? It's safest to just to carry the cash you'll need for a good time.

We've also heard reports of thefts on the beach (bags are taken when you've dozed off).

Drive-by bag-snatching is an issue, which can be highly dangerous if you fall victim while on the back of a *xe om*. It's safer to wear bags close to your chest rather than as a backpack.

Keep phones and tablets out of sight, not on restaurant tables. If you're using a map app to find your way around, hold the phone or tablet with two hands.

Some female tourists have reported being photographed by young Vietnamese males when emerging from the water or just lying on the beach. These guys are quite blatant about it and are rather persistent.

At popular tourist sites, and on public boats, unobservant foreigners may be overcharged – check the price on pre-printed tickets, and check your change.

INTERNET ACCESS

Virtually all hotels and most restaurants and cafes have wi-fi. Many places also have a PC or two.

MEDICAL SERVICES

Pasteur Institute (Map p250; ☎058-382 2355; pasteur-nhatrang.org.vn; 8-10 Đ Tran Phu; ⊙7-11am & 1-4.30pm) Offers medical consultations and vaccinations. Located inside the Alexandre Yersin Museum.

MONEY

There are ATMs all over Nha Trang.

Vietcombank (Map p250; 17 Đ Quang Trung; ⊙7.30am-4pm Mon-Fri) Has an ATM.

POST

Main Post Office (Map p250; 4 Đ Le Loi; ⊙6.30am-8pm Mon-Fri, 6.30am-1pm Sat)

TOURIST INFORMATION

Khanh Hoa Tourist Information (Map p250; ☎058-352 8000; khtourism@dng.vnn.vn; Đ Tran Phu) Government-run tourism office on the seafront with various tour programs, including boat trips. Staff speak reasonable English.

TRAVEL AGENCY

Sinh Tourist (Map p250; ☎058-352 2982; www.thesinhtourist.vn; 90C Đ Hung Vuong; ⊙6am-10pm) A reliable, professional company for inexpensive local trips, including a city tour for 259,000d (excluding entrance fees) and island boat cruises, as well as open-tour buses.

Getting There & Away

AIR

Vietnam Airlines (Map p250; ☎058-352 6768; www.vietnamairlines.com; 91 Đ Nguyen Thien Thuat) connects Nha Trang with Hanoi (three daily), HCMC (four daily) and Danang daily. **VietJet Air** (www.vietjetir.com) usually has the cheapest fares if you book well ahead, flying to both Hanoi and HCMC daily. **Jetstar** (www.jetstar.com) offers good connections with both Hanoi and HCMC.

BUS

Phia Nam Nha Trang bus station (Đ 23 Thang 10) is Nha Trang's main intercity bus terminal, 500m west of the train station. Very regular daily buses head north to Danang. Heading south, there are very frequent connections to Phan Rang (46,000d, two hours) and HCMC, including sleeper buses from 7pm. Buses also head west into the central highlands, to Dalat

TRANSPORT FROM NHA TRANG

DESTINATION	AIR	BUS	CAR/MOTORBIKE	TRAIN
Dalat	-	US$7, 5hr, 15 daily	4hr	-
Danang	from US$31, 1hr, 1 daily	US$11-15, 12hr, 13-15 daily	11hr	US$15-21, 9-11hr, 6 daily
HCMC	from US$21, 1hr, 8 daily	US$10-15, 11hr, 13 daily	10hr	US$11-16, 7-9hr, 7 daily
Mui Ne	-	US$7, 5½hr, open-tour buses only	5hr	-
Quy Nhon	-	US$6.50, 6hr, every 2hr	6hr	US$5.50-8, 4hr, 6 daily

and Buon Ma Thuot (110,000d to 130,000d, five hours, seven daily).

Nha Trang is a major stopping point on all of the open-tour buses. These are the best option for accessing Mui Ne, which is not served by standard buses; Sinh Tourist (p261) has two daily buses on this route. There are also regular open-tour buses to Dalat (five hours) and Hoi An (11 hours).

CAR & MOTORBIKE

One of the best trips to experience is the mountain pass from Nha Trang to Dalat, as seen on the BBC *Top Gear* special. It's a stunning journey by car or motorbike. Throw the mountain road back down from Dalat to Mui Ne into the mix and you have a great loop.

There are quite a number of Easy Riders based in Nha Trang. **Easy Rider Trips** (☎090 5384 406; http://easyridertrips.com; 7G/4 Hung Vuong) gets good feedback and charges from US$65 per day for the Nha Trang–Dalat journey, which can be covered in one to three days depending on where you want to stop on the way.

TRAIN

The **Nha Trang train station** (☎058-382 2113; Đ Thai Nguyen; ⊙ticket office 7-11.30am, 1.30-6pm & 7-9pm) is west of the cathedral in the centre of town. It's on the main north–south line with good connections to destinations including Dieu Tri (for Quy Nhon), Danang and HCMC.

Getting Around

TO/FROM THE AIRPORT

Cam Ranh international airport is 35km south of the city via a beautiful coastal road. A shuttle bus runs the route (65,000d), leaving from the site of the old airport (near 86 Đ Tran Phu) two hours and 10 minutes before scheduled departure times (for all airlines), taking about 40 minutes. Returning to Nha Trang, there's an official desk at the airport to buy your bus ticket; buses leave 30 minutes after all flight arrivals.

Departing town, taxis are a convenient option. **Nha Trang Taxi** (☎058-382 6000), the official maroon-coloured cabs, cost 380,000d from the airport to downtown. It's cheaper in the other direction, around 300,000d, if you fix a price ahead rather than use taxi meters, which work out to be more expensive.

BICYCLE

Most of Nha Trang is pretty flat, so it's easy to get around all the sights, including Thap Ba, by bicycle. Hotels have bikes to rent from 30,000d per day, or for a quality mountain bike head to Vietnam Bike Tours (p253). Watch out for the one-way system around the train station, and the chaotic roundabouts.

TAXI & XE OM

It's safer to take a metered taxi with a reputable company, such as **Mai Linh** (☎058-382 2266).

Nha Trang has an excessive number of *xe om* drivers. A motorcycle ride anywhere in the centre shouldn't cost more than 25,000d. Be

WORTH A TRIP

BAI DAI BEACH

South of Nha Trang, a spectacular coastal road leads to Cam Ranh Bay, a gorgeous natural harbour and the airport. Virtually the entire shoreline south of Mia Resort forms Bai Dai (Long Beach), a breathtaking sandy coast.

Until very recently, the Vietnamese military controlled the entire area, restricting access to the odd fishing boat. However times are a-changing and now the entire strip has been earmarked for development. Dozens of giant resort hotels are planned and giant advertising billboards now line the coastal road.

As of late 2015, only a few hotels had been completed, including Fusion Resort Nha Trang (p257), so it should still be possible to find a virgin stretch of sand. Some of the best surf breaks in Vietnam are found along here.

At the northern tip of Bai Dai, **Shack Vietnam** (www.shackvietnam.com) offers one-hour board rental and surf instruction in English for 600,000d (board rental only is 180,000d per hour). It also offers kayak hire. Ice-cold beer, fish tacos (40,000d each), burgers, burritos and fish and chips are are on the menu. Service can be pretty slow, however. The Shack sits in the middle of a strip of 20 or so locally owned seafood restaurants, all with near-identical menus.

A one-way journey in a taxi to the north end of Bai Dai costs around 260,000d, reckon on 300,000d to hit the central stretch. There's no public transport along Bai Dai road. As traffic is very light, this is a region that's ideal to explore on a motorbike.

careful at night, when some less reputable drivers moonlight as pimps and drug dealers.

Around Nha Trang

Thanh Citadel HISTORIC SITE

This citadel dates from the 17th-century Trinh dynasty. It was rebuilt by Prince Nguyen Anh (later Emperor Gia Long) in 1793 during his successful offensive against the Tay Son Rebels. Only a few sections of the walls and gates remain. Thanh Citadel is 11km west of Nha Trang, near Dien Khanh town.

Ba Ho Falls WATERFALL

(Suoi Ba Ho; admission 15,000d, bike parking 2000d; 7am-5.30pm) The three waterfalls and refreshing pools at Ba Ho Falls are in a forested area about 20km north of Nha Trang and about 2km west of Phu Huu village. Turn off Hwy 1 just north of Quyen Restaurant, and you'll find them a 20-minute walk from the parking area. It's fun clambering upstream through the pools, though they are slippery; good footwear is recommended.

Phan Rang & Thap Cham

068 / POP 185,000

This really is a tale of two cities: Phan Rang hugging the shoulders of Hwy 1, and Thap Cham straddling Hwy 20 as it starts its long climb to Dalat. Anyone travelling Vietnam from north to south will notice a big change in the vegetation when approaching the joint capitals of Ninh Thuan province. The familiar lush green rice paddies are replaced with sandy soil supporting only scrubby plants. Local flora includes poinciana trees and prickly-pear cacti with vicious thorns.

With two major highways (1A and 20) intersecting in the town, this area makes a good pit stop on the coastal run. As the twin towns of Phan Rang and Thap Cham are both industrial and not particularly attractive, consider basing yourself at nearby Ninh Chu Beach, 6km to the east.

Sights

The area's best-known sight is the group of Cham towers known as Po Klong Garai, from which Thap Cham (Cham Tower) derives its name. There are many more towers dotted about the countryside in this area and the province is home to tens of thousands of Cham people. There are also several thousand Chinese in the area, many of whom come to worship at the 135-year-old **Quang Cong Pagoda** (Đ Thong Nhat), a colourful Chinese temple in the town centre.

Po Klong Garai Cham Towers HINDU TEMPLE

(Thap Cham; admission 15,000d; 7am-5pm) These four brick towers date from the end of the 13th century. Built as Hindu temples, they stand on a brick platform at the top of Cho'k Hala, an exposed granite hill covered with cacti. It can be furnace-hot here.

Over the entrance to the largest tower (the *kalan*, or sanctuary) is a beautiful carving of a dancing Shiva with six arms. Note the inscriptions in the ancient Cham language on the doorposts. These tell of past restoration efforts and offerings of sacrifices and slaves.

Inside the *kalan*'s vestibule is a statue of the bull Nandin, vehicle of the Hindu god Shiva. Nandin is also a symbol of the agricultural productivity of the countryside. To ensure a good crop, farmers would place an offering of fresh greens, herbs and areca nuts in front of Nandin's muzzle. Under the main tower is a *mukha-linga* (carved phallus with a human face painted on it) sitting

CHAM NEW YEAR

The Cham New Year *(kate)* is celebrated at Po Klong Garai in the seventh month of the Cham calendar (around October). The festival commemorates ancestors, Cham national heroes and deities such as the farmers' goddess Po Ino Nagar.

On the eve of the festival, a procession guarded by the mountain people of Tay Nguyen carries King Po Klong Garai's clothing to the accompaniment of traditional music. The procession lasts until midnight. The following morning the garments are carried to the tower, once again accompanied by music, along with banners, flags, singing and dancing. Notables, dignitaries and village elders follow behind. This colourful ceremony continues into the afternoon.

The celebrations then carry on for the rest of the month, as the Cham attend parties and visit friends and relatives. They also use this time to pray for good fortune.

under a wooden pyramid. Liquor is offered and incense burned here.

Inside the smaller tower opposite the entrance to the sanctuary, you can get a good look at some of the Cham's sophisticated building technology; the wooden columns that support the lightweight roof are visible. The structure attached to it was originally the main entrance to the complex.

Po Klong Garai is just north of Hwy 20, at a point 6km west of Phan Rang towards Dalat. The towers are on the opposite side of the tracks to Thap Cham train station. Some of the open-tour buses running the coastal route make a requisite pit stop here.

Po Ro Me Cham Tower HINDU TEMPLE
(admission free, donations welcome) Po Ro Me is one of the most atmospheric of Vietnam's Cham towers, thanks in part to its isolated setting on top of a craggy hill with sweeping views over the cactus-strewn landscape. The temple honours the last ruler of an independent Champa, King Po Ro Me (r 1629–51); his image and those of his family are found on the external decorations.

The temple is still in active use, with ceremonies taking place twice a year. The rest of the time it's locked up, but the caretakers at the foot of the hill will open the sanctuary for you. Consider leaving a small donation with them, and don't forget to remove your shoes.

The occupants of the temple aren't used to having their rest disturbed, and it can be a little creepy when the bats start chattering and swooping overhead in the confined dark space. Through the gloom you'll be able to make out a blood-red and black centrepiece – a bas-relief representing the deified king in the form of Shiva. Behind the main deity and to the left is one of his queens, Thanh Chanh. Look out for the inscriptions on the doorposts and a stone statue of the bull Nandin.

Note the flame motif repeated around the arches, a symbol of purity, cleansing visitors of any residual bad karma.

The best way to reach the site is with your own motorbike or a *xe om*. The route is tricky. Take Hwy 1 south from Phan Rang for 9km. Turn right at the turn-off to Ho Tan Giang, a narrow sealed road just after the petrol station, and continue for a further 6km. Turn left in the middle of a dusty village at a paddock that doubles as a football field and follow the road as it meanders to the right until the tower comes into sight. A sign points the way cross-country for the last 500m.

Cham Cultural Centre MUSEUM
(Thap Cham; ⏲7am-5pm) FREE At the base of the Po Klong Garai towers, this large modern structure (built in attractive, vaguely Cham style) is dedicated to Cham culture. There's some superb photography of Cham people, village life and customs exhibited here, as well as paintings, pottery, traditional dress and agricultural tools.

It's a good reminder that while the Cham kingdom is long gone, the Cham people are an important minority in this region.

There are also numerous souvenir stalls.

Bau Truc Village NEIGHBOURHOOD
This Cham village is known for its pottery and you'll see several family shops in front of the mud and bamboo houses. On the way to Po Ro Me turn right off Hwy 1 near the war memorial, into the commune with the banner 'Lang Nghe Gom Bau Truc'. Inside the village take the first left for some of the better pottery stores.

Sleeping & Eating

The twin towns are not relaxing places to stay due to traffic congestion and industry. Nearby Ninh Chu Beach, 6km east of Phan Rang, is far more inviting.

Com ga (chicken with rice) is a local speciality, try it at **Phuoc Thanh** (3 Đ Tran Quang Dieu; mains 30,000-55,000d), located just north of Đ 16 Thang 4, the road to Ninh Chu Beach.

Another local delicacy is roasted or baked *ky nhong* (gecko), served with fresh green mango. If you prefer self-catering and have quick reflexes, most hotel rooms in Vietnam have a ready supply.

Phan Rang is the grape capital of Vietnam. Stalls in the market sell fresh grapes, grape juice and dried grapes (too juicy to be called raisins).

Ho Phong Hotel HOTEL $
(☎068-392 0333; 363 Đ Ngo Gia Tu; r 295,000-575,000d; ❄@📶) This hotel is highly visible by night when it's lit up like a Christmas tree. Inside, things are more subdued, with attractive, well-furnished rooms with power showers. Staff rent out motorbikes for 70,000d per day.

Getting There & Away

BUS

Phan Rang bus station (opposite 64 Đ Thong Nhat) is on the northern outskirts of town. Regular buses head north to Nha Trang (50,000d, 2½ hours, every 45 minutes), northwest to

Dalat (77,000d, four hours, hourly), and south to Ca Na (20,000d, one hour, every 45 minutes) and beyond.

CAR & MOTORBIKE

Phan Rang is 344km from HCMC, 147km from Phan Thiet, 104km from Nha Trang and 108km from Dalat.

TRAIN

The **Thap Cham train station** (☎068-388 8029; 7 Đ Phan Dinh Phung) is about 6km west of Hwy 1, within sight of Po Klong Garai Cham Towers, but only slower trains stop here. Destinations include Nha Trang (around 2½ hours) and HCMC (around eight hours).

Ninh Chu Beach

☎068

Southeast of Phan Rang, the giant bite-shaped bay of Ninh Chu is popular with Vietnamese tourists on weekends and holidays, but relatively tranquil the rest of the time. Some litter blights the scene, but the 10km-long beach is attractive and makes a quieter alternative to Phan Rang as a base for visiting the Cham ruins. New resort hotels are springing up around the bay.

Sleeping & Eating

Hotel are scattered along the shoreline. Budget accommodation is concentrated at the north end of the bay, where there's a fishing village and a row of beachfront seafood restaurants.

Nha Nghi Dieu Hien GUESTHOUSE **$**
(☎068-387 3399; s/d 170,000/220,000d; ❄) A stone's throw from the north end of the beach, this guesthouse is run by a friendly (but non-English-speaking) couple. Rooms are clean, all with TV, fan and air-conditioning.

Anh Duong Hotel HOTEL **$**
(☎068-389 0009; hotellananh.com.vn; 66 Yen Ninh; r 255,000-500,000d; ❄ 📶) Away from the shore, this roadside place offers inexpensive, good-value rooms with smart trim and cable TV. It's a short walk to the beach.

Con Ga Vang Resort RESORT **$$**
(☎068-387 4899; www.congavangresort.com; r US$42-75, ste from US$110; ❄ @ 📶 🏊) A dated but decent Vietnamese resort hotel, the Con Ga enjoys a beachfront location and has some tempting room rates given the coconut-palm-fringed swimming pool and tennis courts.

Amanoi RESORT **$$$**
(☎068-377 0777; www.aman.com; Vinh Hy village; r US$757-1136; ❄ @ 📶 🏊) This monument to luxe living boasts attention to detail that makes it rank alongside Vietnam's best hotels. Amanoi enjoys a truly spectacular location on a private cove north of Ninh Chu, its pavilions with ocean or national park views. The trad-hip design echoes Buddhist temple architecture, while the yoga and meditation classes help evoke a Zen spirit.

Getting There & Away

Ninh Chu is 7km east of Phan Rang, local buses are infrequent. *Xe om* charge around 30,000d or a metered taxi is 70,000d.

Ca Na

☎068

During the 16th century, princes of the Cham royal family would fish and hunt tigers, elephants and rhinoceros here. Today Ca Na is better known for its white-sand beaches, which are dotted with huge granite boulders. The best of the beach is just off Hwy 1, a kilometre north of the fishing village. It's a beautiful spot, but it's tough to ignore the constant honking and rumble of trucks.

The terrain is studded with magnificent prickly pear cacti. Bright yellow **Lac Son**, a small pagoda on the hillside, makes for an interesting but steep climb.

There are a few hotels and guesthouses, but if you do stay here, be aware that there are no ATMs.

Ca Na is 32km south of Phan Rang. Most long-haul buses cruising Hwy 1 will drop off or pick up people here. Local buses from Phan Rang (20,000d, one hour) head to Ca Na fishing village – ask to be let out on the highway and catch a *xe om* for the last kilometre.

Mui Ne

☎062 / POP 17,000

Once upon a time, Mui Ne was an isolated stretch of beach where pioneering travellers camped on the sand. Times have changed and it's now a string of beach resorts, which have fused into one long coastal strip. These resorts are, for the most part, mercifully low-rise and set amid pretty gardens by the sea. The original fishing village is still here, but tourists outnumber locals these days. Mui Ne is definitely moving upmarket, as more exclusive places open their doors,

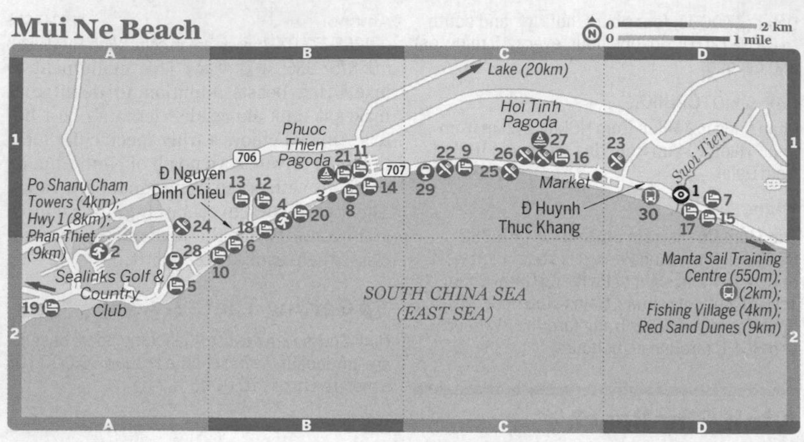

Mui Ne Beach

Sights
1 Fairy Spring D1

Activities, Courses & Tours
Forester Beach Spa .... (see 8)
Jibes .... (see 8)
Sankara Kitesurfing Academy .... (see 3)
2 Sealinks Golf & Country Club A2
Song Huong Spa .... (see 16)
Surfpoint Kiteboarding School .... (see 18)
3 Taste of Vietnam B1
4 Tropical Minigolf Mui Ne B1
Xanh Spa .... (see 10)

Sleeping
5 Allez Boo Resort A2
6 Cham Villas B2
Coco Sand Hotel .... (see 8)
7 Duy An Guesthouse D1
8 Full Moon Beach Hotel B1
9 Hai Yen Resort C1
10 Mia Resort B2
11 Mui Ne Backpacker Village B1
Mui Ne Backpackers .... (see 8)
12 Mui Ne Hills Budget Hotel B1
13 Mui Ne Hills Villa Hotel B1
Rang Garden Bungalow .... (see 9)
14 Sea Winds Resort B1
15 Seaflower Guesthouse D1
16 Song Huong Hotel C1
17 Sun & Sands Beach Hotel D1
18 Sunsea Resort B1
19 Takalau Residence & Resort A2
20 Villa Aria Mui Ne B1
Windflower Beach Boutique Hotel .... (see 17)
21 Xin Chao B1

Eating
22 Bo Ke C1
23 Com Chay Vi Dieu D1
24 Ganesh A1
Lam Tong Quan .... (see 8)
25 Nhu Bao C1
26 Phat Hamburgers C1
Sandals .... (see 10)
27 Sindbad C1
Villa Aria Mui Ne .... (see 20)

Drinking & Nightlife
28 Deja Vu A2
Dragon Beach .... (see 29)
29 Fun Key C1
Joe's Café .... (see 8)
PoGo .... (see 25)

Information
Sinh Tourist .... (see 25)

Transport
30 Phuong Trang D1

complemented by swish restaurants and swanky shops, but there is still a (kite) surfer vibe to the town.

Mui Ne is the adrenaline capital of southern Vietnam. There's no scuba diving or snorkelling to speak of, but when Nha Trang and Hoi An get the rains, Mui Ne gets the waves. Surf's up from August to December. For windsurfers, the gales blow as well, especially from late October to late April, when swells can stir things up big time. Kitesurfing has really taken off and the infinite horizon is often obscured by dozens of kites flapping in the wind. If this all sounds too much like hard work, you can simply lounge around on the beach, watching others take the strain.

Mui Ne sees only about half the rainfall of nearby Phan Thiet. The sand dunes help protect its unique microclimate, and even during the wet season (from June to September) rains tend to be fairly light and sporadic.

One major problem the area faces is the steady creep of coastal erosion. Many resorts east of Km 12 have almost completely lost their beaches and rely on sandbagging to keep the little they have left.

Road safety is another serious issue. There are no traffic-calming measures along the main coastal road, and speeding cars and trucks have little regard for pedestrians.

It's almost impossible to get lost in Mui Ne, as everything is spread out along a 10km stretch of highway. Most accommodation lines the beach side, while restaurants and shops flank the other.

Sights

Sand Dunes SAND DUNES

Mui Ne is famous for its enormous red and white sand dunes. The white dunes are the more impressive, the near-constant oceanic winds sculpting the sands into wonderful Saharaesque formations. But as this is Vietnam (not deepest Mali) there's little chance of experiencing the silence of the desert.

Prepare yourself for the hard sell as children press you to hire a plastic sledge to ride the dunes. Unless you're supermodel-light, it can be tricky to travel for more than a few metres this way.

Quad bikes and dune buggies also destroy the peace. Bizarrely, ostrich riding (from 100,000d) is offered as an activity, but we don't recommend it due to animal cruelty concerns. Expect some litter too; periodically there's a clean-up, but the tide of plastic keeps returning.

You'll need a 4WD to explore the dunes properly, but be careful to agree on an itinerary for the tour, preferably in writing. We hear complaints, particularly about 'sunset tours' that cut short with the sun high in the sky.

Fairy Spring RIVER

(Suoi Tien) This stream flows through a patch of dunes with interesting sand and rock formations. It's a beautiful walk wading up the stream from the sea to its source, a spring. You can do the trek barefoot, but if you're heading out into the big sand dunes after, you'll need proper footwear.

Po Shanu Cham Towers HINDU TEMPLE

(Km 5; admission 5000d; ⏲7.30-11.30am & 1-4.30pm) West of Mui Ne, the Po Shanu Cham Towers occupy a hill near Phan Thiet, with sweeping views of the town and a cemetery filled with candylike tombstones. Dating from the 9th century, this complex consists of the ruins of three towers, none of which are in very good shape. There's a small pagoda on the site, as well as a gallery and shop.

Activities

Golf

Tropical Minigolf Mui Ne MINIGOLF

(97 Đ Nguyen Dinh Chieu; one round 100,000-120,000d; ⏲10am-10.30pm) This attractive palm-shaded minigolf course is dotted with craggy rock formations to challenge your putting skills. Rates include a cold drink.

Sealinks Golf & Country Club GOLF

(☎062-374 1777; www.sealinksvietnam.com; Km 8, Mui Ne; 18 holes 1,350,000d) Fine 7671yd course with ocean views and a challenging layout that includes water hazards. Play a discounted twilight round from 2.30pm. The complex has a resort hotel and driving range.

Spas

There's an excess of spa/massage places, at least 25 or so, along the Mui Ne strip, most

LIZARD FISHING

When most people think of fishing in the mountains they conjure up images of hooking river trout or lake bass. But in the arid foothills of the south-central coast (notably around places such as Ca Na, Phan Rang, Phan Thiet and Mui Ne) there is a whole other kind of angling, and a walk in these hills can yield one of the strangest sights in Vietnam: lizard fishing.

These lizards, called *than lan nui*, are members of the gecko family and good for eating. The traditional way of catching the lizards is by setting a hook on a long bamboo fishing pole and dangling bait from the top of a boulder until the spunky little reptiles strike.

Lizards are served grilled, roasted or fried, and are often made into a pâté (complete with finely chopped bones) and eaten as a dip with rice-paper crackers.

THE MUI NE STRIP

Heading east from Phan Thiet, development is sporadic until the Km 8 mark and the rather splendid-looking University of Phan Thiet. After this, there are several resorts, restaurants and a golf course, as the main strip takes shape. From Km 10 to Km 12, Mui Ne has quite a Russian feel, with souvenir shops and spas galore emblazoned with Cyrillic script. Km 12 to Km 14 is where many of the popular midrange resorts and restaurants are found. From here there is a break in the resorts, with a strip of seafood stalls and some late-night beach clubs before another cluster of backpacker accommodation and restaurant-bars around the Km 16 strip. This is where the village of Ham Tien (the original settlement) starts before giving way to more backpacker accommodation around Km 18. Look out for superb views over the Mui Ne fishing fleet around Km 20 and you've arrived at the end of the strip.

of a low quality offering body massages from as little as US$7 per hour.

★ Forester Beach Spa SPA
(☎062-374 1899; 82 Nguyen Dinh Chieu; 1hr massage 320,000d) A class above the cheapo joints, this well-designed spa has lovely little bamboo massage cabins right by the shore, so you can tune into rolling waves while you're being pampered. Staff are very well trained and discounts are often available.

Xanh Spa SPA
(☎062-384 7440; www.miamuine.com; 24 Đ Nguyen Dinh Chieu; 1hr massage from 710,000d) Located in the Mia Resort, this gorgeous upmarket spa offers the full gamut of massages, facials, body treatments, steam sessions and wraps. Essential oils and natural products are used. Foot massages (45 minutes, 420,000d) are good value here.

Song Huong Spa SPA
(241 Đ Nguyen Dinh Chieu; 1hr massage from US$10; ⏲8am-9pm) Budget spa offering an extensive range of massages, beauty treatments, steam bath and Jacuzzi in clean, orderly surroundings. Staff are professional and welcoming. Located in the grounds of the Son Huong Hotel.

Swimming

Bun Khoang Mui Ne SWIMMING
(www.bunkhoangmuine.com; 133 Đ Nguyen Dinh Chieu; admission 80,000d; ⏲7.30am-6.30pm) When the winds are too strong to make sea swimming pleasant, this hilltop leisure complex comes into its own. The main pool is around 30m, and there's a smaller kids' pool and sunloungers (and pounding music...). There are also hot mineral baths and mud pools here, though the concrete tubs (570,000d for two people) aren't that tempting.

Water Sports

Consider investing in a short kitesurfing lesson before opting for a multiday course, as it's a tricky skill to master. Bear in mind it is an extreme sport and most places will not offer a refund on an immersion course for anyone who drops out.

Manta Sail Training Centre SAILING
(☎0908 400 108; http://mantasailing.org; 108 Đ Huynh Thuc Khang; sailing instruction per hour US$60) Excellent new sailing school offering International Sailing Federation training (from beginner to advanced racing), wakeboarding (US$100 per hour including boat) and stand-up paddle board (SUP) rentals. Staff are very professional and there are also budget rooms available.

Surfpoint Kiteboarding School KITESURFING, SURFING
(☎0167 3422 136; www.surfpoint-vietnam.com; 52A Đ Nguyen Dinh Chieu; 3hr course incl all gear US$150 ; ⏲7am-6pm) With well-trained instructors and a friendly vibe, it's no surprise Surfpoint is one of the best-regarded kite schools in town. A five-hour course costs US$250. Surfing lessons on softboards are also offered (from US$50) when waves permit and there are short boards for rent.

Jibes KITESURFING
(☎062-384 7405; www.windsurf-vietnam.com; 84-90 Đ Nguyen Dinh Chieu; ⏲7.30am-6pm) Mui Ne's original kitesurfing school, Jibes provides safety-conscious and patient instruction (US$60 per hour) and rents gear including windsurfs (US$35 per half-day), SUPs, surfboards, kitesurfs and kayaks.

Sankara Kitesurfing Academy KITESURFING
(☎0914 910 607; www.facebook.com/sankarakitesurfingacademy; 78 Đ Nguyen Dinh Chieu; ⏲9am-5pm) This school is run by experienced IKO-

trained kitesurfers and offers instruction and equipment rentals. Lessons start at US$99 for two hours.

Courses

Taste of Vietnam COOKING
(☎0916 655 241; www.muinecookingschool.com; Sunshine Beach Resort, 82 Đ Nguyen Dinh Chieu; 2½-hr class US$30; ⊙classes 8.45am-12.30pm) Well-regarded Vietnamese cooking classes by the beach. Pay US$35 and a market visit is included (3¼ hours total). Make sure you have a light breakfast first as there's lots of grub to try!

Sleeping

Most accommodation is either right on the coastal road or just off it, with a few good-value places in the hills behind town. Wherever you are, you won't be far from the beach.

Rates have become more flexible in recent years as Russian tour operators have pulled out, so it's always worth requesting a discount.

★Mui Ne Backpacker Village HOSTEL $
(☎062-374 1047; www.muinebackpackervillage.com; 137 Đ Nguyen Dinh Chieu; dm/r from US$7/25;) Cornering the backpacker market, this ambitious, well-designed new construction is proving wildly popular thanks to its inviting pool, bar-restaurant and social vibe. All dorms have air-con, individual beds (no bunks!) and lockers while the 18 private rooms all have a balcony or patio.

Coco Sand Hotel GUESTHOUSE $
(☎0127 364 3446; http://cocosandhotel.com; 119 Đ Nguyen Dinh Chieu; r US$13-18;) Excellent-value rooms are grouped around a shady courtyard garden (with hammocks) at this very hospitable place. It's just off the main drag, down a little lane so it's quiet. The owners rent out motorbikes at fair rates.

Seaflower Guesthouse GUESTHOUSE $
(Hoa Bien; 86 Đ Huynh Thuc Khang; r 250,000-350,000d;) At the eastern end of the Mui Ne bay, this two-storey place is run by a friendly Vietnamese couple. Rooms are at the rear of a compound that stretches down to the shore.

Mui Ne Hills Budget Hotel HOTEL $
(☎062-374 1707; www.muinehills.com; 69 Đ Nguyen Dinh Chieu; dm/r from US$5/15;) This place offers a good bed for your buck, with several air-con dorms that have en-suites while the rooms have quality furnishings and contemporary design touches. It's around 300m north of the main strip, via an incredibly steep access road.

Song Huong Hotel HOTEL $
(☎062-384 7450; www.songhuonghotel.com; 241 Đ Nguyen Dinh Chieu; r US$12-20;) Run by welcoming family owners, this hotel is set well back from the road and boasts spacious, light, airy rooms in a modern house. Breakfast is included.

Duy An Guesthouse GUESTHOUSE $
(☎062-384 7799; 87A Đ Huynh Thuc Khang; s/d US$10/12; @) This traditional guesthouse is run by a friendly soul who looks after guests well (try his wild honey wine). It's located close to the eastern end of the strip in a shady compound, and has a good restaurant.

Sea Winds Resort GUESTHOUSE $
(☎062-384 7018; sea.winds.resort@gmail.com; 139 Đ Nguyen Dinh Chieu; r US$10-21; @) Set back off the road, all the simple, fine-value rooms here have TV, plus aspects over a lovely little garden. Fan rooms are very spacious for this sort of money.

Hai Yen Resort HOTEL $
(☎384 7243; http://haiyenresort.com; 132 Đ Nguyen Dinh Chieu; r US$16-30; @) Boasts a good selection of rooms, including some with three beds, set behind the seafront swimming pool. Spend a little more to enjoy sea views.

Mui Ne Hills Villa Hotel BOUTIQUE HOTEL $$
(☎062-374 1707; www.muinehills.com; 69 Đ Nguyen Dinh Chieu; r US$35-55; @) Formerly Mui Ne Hills 1, this fine villa-style hotel has wonderful vistas from its pool. Rooms are superb value, all with contemporary design touches and full facilities, but it's the personal touch from staff and owners that makes a real difference. It's located up a dusty, very steep lane (but is close to the best section of beach).

Xin Chao BOUTIQUE HOTEL $$
(☎062-374 3086; www.xinchaohotel.com; 129 Đ Nguyen Dinh Chieu; r US$25-50; @) Impressive new hotel (owned by kitesurfers) set well back from the busy coastal road. A lot of thought has gone into the design, with rooms grouped around a pool at the rear. A small lounge area (with pool table) and roadside bar-restaurant add to its appeal.

Full Moon Beach Hotel HOTEL $$
(☎062-384 7008; www.fullmoonbeach.com.vn; 84 Đ Nguyen Dinh Chieu; r incl breakfast from US$52; ❄@📶🏊) An artistically designed place where the committed owners have consistently upgraded the facilities to keep up with the competition. Features a bamboo-shaded pool, rooms with four-poster beds and terracotta tiling, and an oceanfront bar.

Sun & Sands Beach Hotel HOTEL $$
(☎062-384 7979; sunnsandsmuine.com; 62 Đ Huynh Thuc Khang; r/f incl breakfast US$35/70; ❄📶🏊) There's a choice of accommodation at this beachside place, from sleek, contemporary rooms in a three-storey block to older thatched cottages; the hotel's restaurant is between the two. Staff are eager to please.

Mui Ne Backpackers GUESTHOUSE $$
(☎062-384 7047; www.muinebackpackers.com; 88 Đ Nguyen Dinh Chieu; r US$25-55; ❄@📶🏊) Dorms are no more at this beachfront place, which moved upmarket and now has a choice of plain, whitewashed rooms and bungalows, all with air-con, cable TV, minibar and hot-water bathrooms.

Windflower Beach Boutique Hotel HOTEL $$
(☎062-3743 969; http://windflowermuine.com; 76 Đ Huynh Thuc Khang; r 800,000đ; ❄@📶🏊) For clean lines and a contemporary look, the (smallish) rooms, some with sea views, at this hotel are certainly worth considering. There's a lovely rear garden that stretches down to the beach, with pool and bar. Free bikes for guests.

Rang Garden Bungalow HOTEL $$
(☎062-374 3638; 233A Đ Nguyen Dinh Chieu; r US$22-42; ❄@📶🏊) Rooms are set in attractive villas around the generously proportioned swimming pool. The higher-standard rooms enjoy great spec and more space, and there's a small restaurant out front.

★**Mia Resort** BOUTIQUE HOTEL $$$
(☎062-384 7440; www.miamuine.com; 24 Đ Nguyen Dinh Chieu; r US$120, bungalows US$145-200, all incl breakfast; ❄@📶🏊) With recently upgraded accommodation, this seriously stylish beachfront hotel remains top dog in Mui Ne. A calm ambience pervades and the friendly, efficient staff really give the hotel a little extra polish; it's wonderfully relaxing here. The pool is small but it's a great place to chill, facing the ocean. You'll love Sandals, the in-house restaurant, where a magnificent breakfast spread is served.

Cham Villas BOUTIQUE HOTEL $$$
(☎062-374 1234; www.chamvillas.com; 32 Đ Nguyen Dinh Chieu; r incl breakfast US$149-229; ❄@📶🏊) You can really unwind in this fine luxury hotel, where the lovely villas are spaced well apart around a stunning garden. The secuded, partly shaded pool area is particuarly beautiful in the morning, with birdsong in the air and dappled light on the water. Book early during peak periods.

Allez Boo Resort RESORT $$$
(☎062-374 3777; www.allezbooresort.com; 8 Đ Nguyen Dinh Chieu; r US$85-190; ❄@📶🏊) Allez Boo has a very classy ambience thanks to the French Colonial–style building and delightful grounds which spill down to the shore, where you'll find a pool and huge (shaded) Jacuzzi. The beach just beyond the hotel is particularly broad and attractive.

Sunsea Resort BOUTIQUE HOTEL $$$
(☎062-384 7700; www.sunsearesort-muine.com; 50 Đ Nguyen Dinh Chieu; r incl breakfast US$78-150; ❄@📶🏊) Offering good value, this is one of the most attractive hotels in Mui Ne, the elegant accommodation blending natural materials (thatch, lacquerware and rosewood) with modern design. There's an infinity pool and a second (partly shaded) pool fronted by the garden-view rooms.

Takalau Residence & Resort RESORT $$$
(☎062-384 7778; http://takalauresort.com; Nguyen Dinh Chieu, Phuong 5; r/villa from US$135/180; ❄@📶🏊) West of the centre, this new place feels more like a regent's ocean estate than a resort hotel with its wood panelling, antiques and art. Staff are charming and the grounds are magnificent; you'll find the Sealinks golf course just over the road.

Villa Aria Mui Ne BOUTIQUE HOTEL $$$
(☎062-374 1660; www.villaariamuine.com; 60A Đ Nguyen Dinh Chieu; r US$110-170; ❄📶🏊) This modish hotel only occupies a slim strip of land but its hip rooms, gorgeous garden and beachside pool all add up to an inviting package. The restaurant is a wonderful place for breakfast and Villa Aria's location, close to the centre of the action, is very handy.

Eating

Mui Ne is one of the most expensive places to dine out in Vietnam. There's an incredible selection of restaurants, most geared to the cosmopolitan tastes of its visitors, with Russian, Italian, Thai and Indian cuisine all present. Indeed, at times it seems the only thing tricky to find is authentic local food.

Periodically, the famous but illegally-built seafront shacks – collectively known as the **Bo Ke** (Đ Nguyen Dinh Chieu; mains 40,000-120,000d; ⏲5-10pm) restaurants – are closed down by police. There was a big clear-out in 2013, but the owners returned soon after. The nearby town of Phan Thiet has lots of great seafood places.

Try the goat restaurants in Ham Tien around the Km 18 mark for a local experience. Choose from barbecued goat or goat hotpot, herbs and all.

Com Chay Vi Dieu VEGETARIAN $
(15B Đ Huynh Thuc Khang; meals 25,000-40,000d; ⏲7am-9pm;) This simple roadside place scores strongly for inexpensive Vietnamese vegetarian dishes, and serves up great smoothies (20,000d). It's right opposite the Eiffel Tower of the Little Paris resort.

Sindbad MIDDLE EASTERN $
(www.sindbad.vn; 233 Đ Nguyen Dinh Chieu; mains 50,000-85,000d; ⏲11am-1am;) A kind of kebab shack par excellence. Come here for shawarma and shish kebabs and other Med favourites like Greek salads. Very inexpensive, and portions are generous; opens late.

Nhu Bao SEAFOOD $
(146 Đ Nguyen Dinh Chieu; mains 50,000-180,000d; ⏲9am-9.30pm) A classic, no-nonsense Vietnamese seafood place: step past the bubbling tanks and there's a huge covered terrace which stretches down to the ocean. It's renowned for its crab.

Lam Tong Quan VIETNAMESE, SEAFOOD $
(92 Đ Nguyen Dinh Chieu; dishes 30,000-115,000d; ⏲7.30am-10pm) For seafood on a budget, this no-frills seafront place is worth considering. There are tables by the shore, or if it's raining you're eating under a corrugated roof. Staff can be brusque verging on rude but the crab, grilled and steamed fish, and squid dishes are all good.

★**Sandals** INTERNATIONAL $$
(www.miamuine.com/dine; 24 Đ Nguyen Dinh Chieu, Mia Resort; meals 120,000-370,000d; ⏲7am-10pm;) This outstanding hotel restaurant is the most atmospheric place in town. It's particularly romantic at night, with tables set around the shoreside pool or in the elegant dining rooms. Wait staff are knowledgeable, attentive and welcoming. The menu is superb, with everything from pasta dishes to Vietnamese claypots executed and presented beautifully. Consider visiting for the breakfast buffet, which is also wonderful.

Ganesh INDIAN $$
(www.ganesh.vn; 57 Đ Nguyen Dinh Chieu; mains 60,000-160,000d; ⏲11am-10pm;) Excellent, authentic Indian restaurant with a wide selection of dishes from the subcontinent, including plenty of choice for vegetarians (including a generous thali). The garlic naan really is to savour.

Villa Aria Mui Ne INTERNATIONAL $$
(mains 95,000-200,000d; ⏲7am-9.30pm;) The beautiful beachside location, with tables set on a shoreside deck, is the main attraction at this classy hotel restaurant. The menu takes in salads (from 75,000d), soups and pasta, and you'll find staff are attentive and eager to please.

Phat Hamburgers INTERNATIONAL $$
(253 Đ Nguyen Dinh Chieu; burgers 80,000-110,000d; ⏲11am-10pm;) Roadside burger joint with 15 or so options, from gourmet to classic, plus hot dogs and great fries. Sip on a shake while you feast on meat.

Drinking

It wouldn't be a surf centre without a legion of beachside bars, and Mui Ne delivers.

★**PoGo** BAR
(www.thepogobar.com; 138 Đ Nguyen Dinh Chieu; ⏲8.30am-2am, closed Wed) A mighty fine bar with a prime beach location, daybeds for lounging, DJs on weekends and regular movie nights. Staff are very friendly and there's a full menu too.

Joe's Café BAR
(www.joescafegardenresort.com; 86 Đ Nguyen Dinh Chieu; ⏲7am-1am;) If bangin' techno is not your bag, Joe's is worth a try with live music (every night at 7.30pm) and a pub-like vibe. During the day it's a good place to hang too,

DRUNK AND DISORDERLY

Perhaps due in some part to the insane drinks promotions on offer in Mui Ne nightspots, the odd fight breaks out each month. Keep your distance from trouble, especially if it involves local Vietnamese, as you don't know who they are, how many friends they have or what they might be carrying in their pockets.

with a sociable bar area, lots of drinks specials and an extensive food menu.

Fun Key BAR
(124 Đ Nguyen Dinh Chieu; ⏰10am-1am; 📶) With a faintly boho ambience, this bar is popular with the backpacker crowd and has drink promotions to rev things up. Fun Key serves food (try the crepes) and overlooks the ocean.

Dragon Beach BAR, CLUB
(120-121 Đ Nguyen Dinh Chieu; ⏰4pm-2am) Western and local DJs play electronic dance music, house and techno at this shoreside bar-club. There's a chill-out deck with cushions to one side and shishas for puffing. Happy hour is 8pm to 10pm.

Deja Vu BAR
(21 Đ Nguyen Dinh Chieu; ⏰noon-1am; 📶) A hip-ish bar-restaurant at the Phan Thiet end of the strip, offering shishas, cocktails and an international menu – there's a set lunch for 80,000d.

Information

Internet and wi-fi is available at pretty much all hotels and resorts, as well as at many restaurants and bars. There are many ATMs along the main Mui Ne strip.

Main Post Office (348 Đ Huynh Thuc Khang; ⏰7am-5pm) In Mui Ne village.

Sinh Tourist (www.thesinhtourist.vn; 144 Đ Nguyen Dinh Chieu; ⏰7am-10pm) Ever-reliable and trustworthy agency for open-tour buses, trips around Mui Ne and credit-card cash advances.

Getting There & Away

Mui Ne offers both north and south links to Hwy 1. The northern link is a wonderfully scenic stretch, passing giant dunes, deserted beaches and a beautiful lake ringed with water lilies.

BUS

Open-tour buses are the most convenient option for Mui Ne, as most public buses only serve Phan Thiet. Several companies have daily services to/from HCMC (99,000d to 150,000d, six hours), Nha Trang (from 122,000d, 5½ hours) and Dalat (100,000d, four hours). Sleeper open-tour night buses usually cost more – Sinh Tourist's price to HCMC is 169,000d.

Phuong Trang (http://futabus.vn; 97 Đ Nguyen Dinh Chieu) has four comfortable buses a day running between Mui Ne and HCMC (135,000d).

Local buses (9000d, 45 minutes, every 15 minutes) make trips between Phan Thiet bus station and Mui Ne, departing from the Coopmart, on the corner of Đ Nguyen Tat Thanh and Đ Tran Hung Dao.

CAR

It costs around US$100/125 to rent a car/minivan for the run to HCMC (five to six hours). **Saigon 2 Mui Ne** (☎012 6552 0065; www.saigon2muine.com) gets good reports for reliability.

If you've a little more time, consider hiring a car to take you along the scenic coastal road to Vung Tau, perhaps stopping at the Ke Ga lighthouse en route. A one-way trip (five to six hours for a leisurely drive) costs US$100. Very regular buses connect Vung Tau with HCMC. This is a far more relaxing way to travel to central HCMC as it avoids the chaos of Hwy 1.

MOTORBIKE

Easy Riders operate from Mui Ne, although there are not as many riders as in Dalat or Nha Trang. One of the best trips to experience by motorbike is actually the triangle between these three destinations, as the mountain roads from Mui Ne to Dalat and on to Nha Trang are some of the most dramatic in the south.

A *xe om* ride from Phan Thiet to Mui Ne will cost around 75,000d.

Getting Around

CAR & MOTORBIKE

Periodically, the local police clamp down on tourists riding motorbikes in Mui Ne without the correct documentation, and issue fines. However, dozens of visitors still rent scooters, which cost from 120,000d per day.

The area isn't highly populated and it's not on the main highway, but traffic still moves very fast along the main strip. Take care.

TAXI

Mui Ne is so spread out that it's difficult to wander about on foot if it is very hot. There are plenty of *xe om* drivers to take you up and down the strip; short trips should cost 20,000d or so.

Mai Linh (☎062-389 8989) operates metered taxis. Call ahead to book later in the evening, or ask the restaurant or bar to assist.

Phan Thiet

☎062 / POP 186,000

The bustling port city of Phan Thiet is traditionally known for its *nuoc mam* (fish sauce), producing millions of litres of the stinky stuff per annum. There's not so much to see in town, but the riverside fishing harbour is always chock-a-block with brightly painted boats and is worth a look.

Phan Thiet has some excellent seafood restaurants off its seafront promenade, including **Song Bien** (☎062-382 9868; 162 Le Loi; meals 70,000-200,000d; ⏰11am-9pm; 📶).

Phan Thiet bus station (Đ Tu Van Tu) is on the northern outskirts of town. The nearest train station to Phan Thiet is 12km west of town in dusty little Muong Man.

Ta Cu Mountain

The highlight here is the white reclining Buddha (Tuong Phat Nam). At 49m long, it's the largest in Vietnam. The pagoda was constructed in 1861, but the Buddha was only added in 1972. It has become an important pilgrimage centre for Buddhists, who stay overnight in the pagoda's dormitory; foreigners can't do this without police permission.

The mountain is just off Hwy 1, 28km south from Phan Thiet. From the highway it's a beautiful two-hour trek, or a 10-minute cable-car ride (160,000d return) and a short, but steep, hike.

Phan Thiet to Long Hai

☎064

A beautiful road parallels the coast between Phan Thiet and Long Hai, passing some memorable scenery; traffic is light. There are pockets of tourism development, but for now most of the coastline is a beguiling mix of giant sand dunes, fishing villages, wide ocean views and some near-deserted beaches. This region makes a great day trip from Vung Tau or Long Hai, or a rewarding scenic road to enjoy. The most impressive sight is the majestic Ke Ga lighthouse.

There's very limited public transport so a motorbike or car is the way to go. Savvy travellers are now using this road to avoid tackling the nightmarish Hwy 1.

Immediately south of Phan Thiet, the first section of the road is beautiful, with a casuarina-lined shoreline and the ocean to the east, while the inland scenery is dominated by rust-red sand dunes.

Ke Ga Lighthouse

Around 30km south of Phan Thiet, the spectacular **Ke Ga lighthouse** (admission 20,000d; ⏰7am-4.30pm) dates from the French era. Constructed in 1899, it sits on a rocky islet some 300m from the shore, towering almost 40m above the ocean. It's just possible to swim (or even wade) across if the tide is very low, but most visitors hire a boatman (250,000d return) to get across.

A staircase winds up to the top, from where there are magnificent vistas over the ocean and inland hills.

Ke Ga to Ho Coc

South of Ke Ga, the coastal road pushes southwest, passing fields bursting with dragon fruit (the main crop), reaching La Gi, 22km down the road. There's no reason to hang around La Gi, an isolated market town, but it does have hourly bus connections (35,000d, two hours) to Long Hai.

Continuing southwest of La Gi, the coastal road just keeps on snaking its way along the shoreline, with towering sand dunes on the inland side. Chunks of the near-virgin coastline have been parceled off here and there, awaiting future hotel resorts and mass tourism, but it's not hard to park up and find a bit of beach for a revitalising dip. The section around 7km north of Ho Coc is particularly scenic and worth investigating, the lonely (for now) road hugging an undeveloped shore.

Ho Coc Beach

With golden sands, rolling inland dunes and clear waters, this beach makes a tempting place to stop. There's one big hotel resort here, very much geared at the local market, but on weekdays it's still peaceful and you should have the beach largely to yourself.

About 300m inland from the beach, **Hotel Ven Ven** (☎064-379 1121; http://venvenhotel.com; r 700,000-1,000,000d; ❄@📶) is tasteful, with classy, well-appointed rooms in lush gardens. The restaurant here is good, if quite pricey, and strong on seafood (meals 60,000d upwards).

Ho Tram Beach

South of Ho Coc, the coastal road soon unexpectedly becomes a four-lane highway, the construction of which is designed to facilitate access to the gargantuan Grand Ho Tram Strip, a casino resort complex, plus restaurants and shops. A concrete blot on the landscape, this isolated Vegas-style development was originally constructed by the MGM group, but after an on-off saga lasting years, they finally abandoned the project and a local business took over and opened the resort in July 2013. As Vietnamese are not permitted to gamble, the hotel and casino are full of Chinese tourists.

Casino aside, Ho Tram consists of nothing more than a tiny fishing village, scruffy open-air market and a fine beach (though the central section is strewn with rubbish). There are a handful of places to stay.

Sleeping & Eating

Local villagers steam, fry and grill tasty fresh seafood right on the beach in Ho Tram. Make sure you try the delicious steamed clams or mussels served with a topping of peanuts, spring onion, lime and chilli; a portion of six costs around 30,000d.

Hoa Bien Motel HOTEL $
(064-378 2279; http://nhanghihoabien.com; r 300,000-550,000d;) A simple place where the rooms have modern facilities and bathrooms are well presented; the cheapest options are small, though. It's 100m from the beach in the fishing village. The helpful owners speak some English and there's a restaurant for breakfast and seafood.

Ho Tram Beach Resort & Spa BOUTIQUE HOTEL $$$
(064-378 1525; www.hotramresort.com; r/bungalow from US$110/150;) The landscaped grounds here are dotted with bungalows that have a Hoi An–meets-Bali style, each with high ceilings and outdoor bathrooms. There's also a spa, infinity pool and an open-plan restaurant (open to nonguests for a memorable lunch stop). It's a great place for kids with a playground and children's pools.

Sanctuary BOUTIQUE RESORT $$$
(064-378 1631; www.sanctuary.com.vn; villas from US$581;) Now managed by the Mia Resort group, which owns some of Vietnam's best beach hotels, this stunning complex is home to state-of-the-art contemporary villas, each with private pool, open-plan kitchens and contemporary furnishings. It's just off a stunning, broad sandy beach and the resort's cafe-restaurant is great for a healthy Western or local meal.

Long Hai

064

If Vung Tau is all a bit bling for you, then consider Long Hai, a more local seaside retreat and fishing port within a few hours' drive of HCMC. Long Hai has pretty white-sand beaches and the area benefits from a microclimate that brings less rain than other parts of the south. This is why Bao Dai, the last emperor of Vietnam, built a private residence here (now the Alma Oasis Long Hai Resort).

The town can be a peaceful place to visit during the week, but it loses its local character on the weekends when Vietnamese tourists pack the sands. Most of the resort hotels are on the northeast of town, on the road that heads to Ho Tram.

Sights & Activities

The western end of Long Hai's beach is where fishing boats moor and is not so clean. However, the eastern end is pretty, with white sand and swaying palms. For an even prettier beach, keep heading east.

After the Tet holiday, Long Hai hosts an annual major fishermen's pilgrimage festival, where hundreds of boats come from afar to worship at Mo Co Temple.

Sleeping

Thuy Lan Guesthouse GUESTHOUSE $
(064-366 3567; Rte 19; r 250,000-450,000d;) This small, white-and-pink guesthouse has light, airy rooms with firm beds; some rooms with balconies. It's about 150m from the beach; some English is spoken.

Alma Oasis Long Hai RESORT $$$
(064-366 2222; http://almaoasislonghai.com; 44 Tinh Lo; r from US$160;) This large resort's arresting white-and-turquoise colour scheme and classical-inspired architecture evokes images of the Greek islands. The in-house spa and restaurant are excellent, and the staff attentive. It's the perfect spot for a romantic stay by the coast.

Eating

There's a cluster of beachside restaurants called **Can Tin 1, 2, 3 and 4** (An Dieu Duong; mains 30,000-100,000d; 7am-9pm). All with the same opening hours and prices, these restaurants serve reliable Vietnamese cuisine, including fresh seafood dishes.

Getting There & Away

Thanks to improved road connections from HCMC, journey times to Long Hai have dropped. Very regular public buses connect HCMC's Mien Dong terminal (85,000d, 2½ hours, every 30 minutes) with Long Hai.

From Mui Ne, follow the road less travelled along coastal Rte 55. It is very scenic, passing a series of stunning beaches and the Ke Ga lighthouse, and traffic is mercifully light for Vietnam.

Vung Tau

064 / POP 212,000

A popular weekend escape from HCMC, Vung Tau rocks at weekends when beach-starved locals and expats descend in numbers, but it is relatively quiet during the week. The city enjoys a spectacular location on a peninsula, with ocean on three sides; the light and the sea air make it a refreshing break from sultry Saigon.

Oil is big business here, so the horizon is regularly dotted with oil tankers, and petro dollars dominate the economy, inflating prices considerably.

Vung Tau is a remarkably civilised-looking city of broad boulevards and imposing colonial-era buildings, but a slightly seedy bar scene also flourishes here, accommodating the tastes (and wallets) of retired Anzac servicemen, Russian expats and oil workers.

Historically few travellers ever bothered to visit the city, but it makes a good place to start (or end) an intriguing coastal road trip to Mui Ne, and beyond.

Sights

Welcome to Rio di Vietnam, where soaring forested peaks rise over a turquoise bay. There's even a giant Jesus, though few would compare Vung Tau's beaches to Copacabana.

Two museums should open in the next year or two. A new city museum was nearing completion on the seafront boulevard Đ Tran Phu when we passed by; a new home is being sought for the collection of the privately owned Worldwide Arms Museum.

Giant Jesus MONUMENT

(Tuong Dai Chua Kito Vua; parking 2000d; 7.30-11.30am & 1.30-5pm) FREE Atop Small Mountain with his arms outstretched to embrace the South China Sea, this 32m Giant Jesus is one of the biggest in the world – taller than his illustrious Brazilian cousin. It is possible to ascend to the arms for a panoramic view of Vung Tau. Note you cannot enter the actual statue in vest-tops or shorts.

Some 800-odd stairs lead up the mountain, but it is possible to take a short cut by motorbike up a bumpy mountain road if you can find a local who knows the way. It starts from Hem 220, off Đ Phan Chu Trinh.

Lighthouse LIGHTHOUSE

(parking 2000d; 7am-5pm) FREE Built by the French, this 1910 lighthouse boasts a spectacular 360-degree view of Vung Tau. From Cau Da Pier on Đ Ha Long, take a sharp right on the alley north of the Hai Au Hotel, then roll on up the hill. Although Jesus and the lighthouse look temptingly close, it is not possible to walk or drive directly between them, as there is a military base in the hills here.

White Villa MUSEUM

(Bach Dinh, Villa Blanche; Đ Tran Phu; admission 15,000d; 7am-4pm) The weekend retreat of French governor Paul Doumer (later French president), this gorgeous, grand colonial-era residence has extensive gardens and an oddly empty interior (besides the odd piece of furniture and some Ming pottery retrieved from shipwrecks off the coast). It sits about 30m above the road, up a winding lane.

French Field Guns LANDMARK

FREE Further along Tran Phu beyond Mulberry Beach, a pretty but rough road winds up the hillside to some old French field guns. There are six of these massive cannons, all with support trenches, demonstrating how strategically important Cap St Jacques was to the colonial authorities as it guarded the waterways to Saigon. Look out for Hem 444 in the fishing village, about 8km from Vung Tau, and turn right on a small track.

Activities

Vung Tau is not a major water sports centre, but if the weather gods are smiling, some residents surf and kitesurf.

Vung Tau Paradise Golf Course GOLF

(064-385 9697; www.golfparadise.com.vn) On the eastern side of the Vung Tau peninsula, this 27-hole course is quite a challenge, with mature trees lining the fairways and some water hazards.

Surf Station SURFING, WINDSURFING

(0163 2900 040, 064-526 101; www.vungtausurf.com; 8 Đ Thuy Van; 8am-5.30pm) Based at the Vung Tau Beach Club, Surf Station offers board rental, and kitesurfing and surfing classes. The equipment is good and instructors professional.

Seagull & Dolphin Pools SWIMMING

(Đ Thuy Ban, Back Beach) These pools are almost opposite the Imperial Plaza. Both charge 60,000d for the day.

Vung Tau

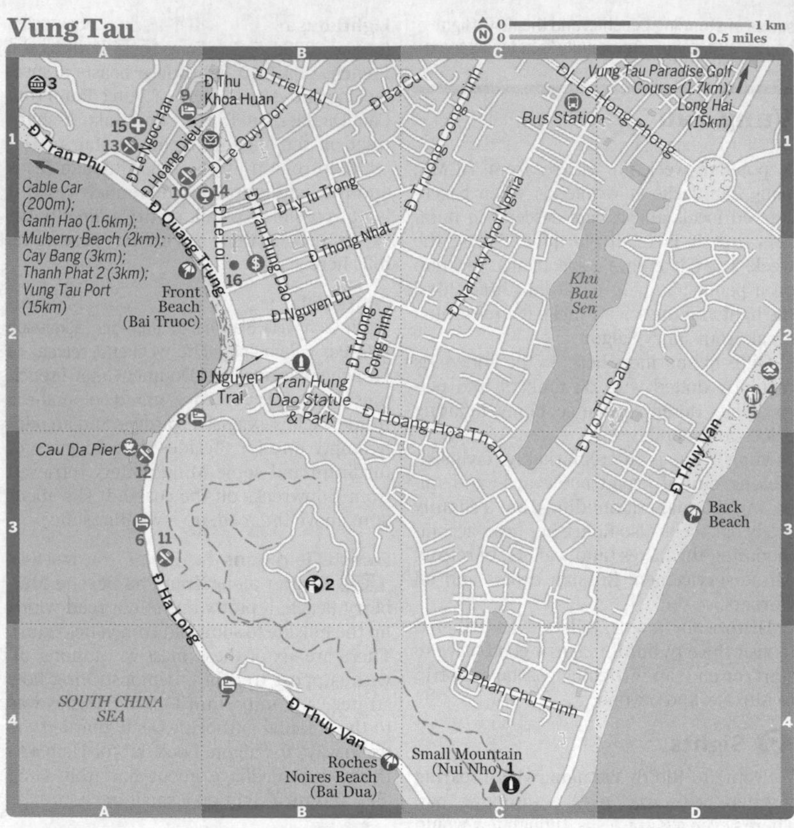

Vung Tau

Sights
1 Giant Jesus ... C4
2 Lighthouse ... B3
3 White Villa ... A1

Activities, Courses & Tours
4 Seagull & Dolphin Pools ... D2
5 Surf Station ... D2

Sleeping
6 Jolie Mod Hotel ... A3
7 Lan Rung Resort & Spa ... B4
8 Lucy's Hotel ... A2
9 Son Ha Hotel ... A1

Eating
10 Bistrot 9 ... A1
11 David Italian Restaurant ... A3
12 Ferry Cafe ... A3
13 Tommy's 3 ... A1

Drinking & Nightlife
Lucy's Sports Bar ... (see 8)
14 Red Parrot ... B1

Information
15 International SOS ... A1
16 OSC Vietnam Travel ... B2

Sleeping

Most foreigners prefer to stay on Front Beach where the restaurants and bars are found, while the majority of Vietnamese visitors head for Back Beach.

On weekends and holidays Vung Tau heaves with local tourists, so book ahead.

Son Ha Hotel HOTEL $
(064-385 2356; 17A Đ Thu Khoa Huan; r US$20;) One of the few budget options near Front Beach, this family-run hotel offers

a homely welcome. Rooms are in good shape, including satellite TV and a fridge.

Jolie Mod Hotel BOUTIQUE HOTEL **$$**
(☎064-362 6666; joliemodhotel@gmail.com; 150 Đ Ha Long; weekdays/weekends from 1,000,000/1,400,000d; ❄📶) Jutting into the bay, this white-and-purple art deco structure is something of a local landmark, and has only recently been converted into a hotel. Rooms are very well presented, all with windows directly overlooking the sea (and some with Jacuzzi). Rates are good value and there's a popular cafe-restaurant downstairs.

Lucy's Hotel HOTEL **$$**
(☎064-385 8896; www.lucyssportsbar.com; 138 Đ Ha Long; r 700,000d; ❄📶) Just across the road from the ferry terminal, these comfortable rooms are above a popular bar. All have a balcony overlooking the bay, and modern bathrooms. Staff are friendly.

Lan Rung Resort & Spa HOTEL **$$$**
(☎064-352 6010; www.lanrungresort.com; 3-6 Đ Ha Long; r from US$80; ❄@📶🏊) One of the few hotels in town with a beachside setting, albeit a rocky one. The rooms are a tad chintzy and include heavy wooden furniture but do have all the facilities you'd expect. There are seafood and Italian restaurants. Service is willing, but expect a few communication issues.

Eating

There's great seafood, and lots of international flavours available in Vung Tau.

Ferry Cafe VIETNAMESE **$**
(Ferry Terminal, Đ Ha Long; mains 38,000-90,000d; ⏲7am-9pm) Inside the ferry terminal building, this large, open-sided place catches the sea breeze and serves up noodles and meat dishes – try steak cooked in a skillet.

★**Ganh Hao** SEAFOOD **$$**
(☎064-355 0909; www.ganhhao.com; 3 Đ Tran Phu; mains 55,000-210,000d; ⏲11.30am-9pm; 📶) Highly impressive seafood restaurant, with tables on terraces by the ocean. It's always packed with locals, so try to get here early. The menu is extensive, with delicious fish, lobster, crab (great with pepper sauce), squid, prawn and mussels (called 'oysters' on the menu try some backed with cheese – it works). It's huge, but somehow everything ticks over efficiently.

Bistrot 9 FRENCH, INTERNATIONAL **$$**
(9 Đ Truong Vinh Ky; snacks/meals from 49,000/100,000d; ⏲6am-10pm; ❄📶) Excellent bistro, perfect for an (all-day) breakfast, crêpe, panini or a full-on splurge (don't neglect the desserts, including great profiteroles). It also sells homemade gourmet chocolates and has the best wine selection in town. Eat on the pavement terrace.

Thanh Phat 2 SEAFOOD **$$**
(121 Đ Tranh Phu; meals 70,000-400,000d; ⏲10.30am-9.30pm) A large, local seafood place with strip lights and blue plastic chairs on a covered terrace right by the sea. Seafood is expertly prepared, with lobster at 1,250,000 per kilo and sea bass for a quarter of that. It's 4km north of central Vung Tau.

Cay Bang SEAFOOD **$$**
(☎064-383 8522; 69 Đ Tran Phu; mains 60,000-280,000d; ⏲11am-10pm) A seafood institution with a great location on the water, Cay Bang is set under the shadow of the Virgin Mary and Baby Jesus. At weekends it draws a huge crowd of Vung Tau faithful for the shellfish, hotpots and grilled fish.

Tommy's 3 INTERNATIONAL **$$**
(www.tommysvietnam.com; 3 Đ Ba Cu; mains 60,000-280,000d; ⏲7am-11pm; 📶) The food is mainly Western and familiar, with big portions of steaks and burgers, plus local food including tasty noodle dishes. There's a prime front terrace that draws a mixed crowd of locals, expats and tourists.

David Italian Restaurant ITALIAN **$$**
(92 Đ Ha Long; mains 60,000-200,000d; ⏲11am-10pm; 📶) This is an authentic Italian-run restaurant with freshly prepared pasta, and the pizzas are the best in town. Quite expensive but has a nice sea-facing terrace

Drinking

Vung Tau nightlife is raucous by Vietnamese standards, with lots of hostess bars. However if you want a quiet beer there are some good options.

Haven BAR
(www.havenbarvungtau.com; 166 Đ Tran Phu; ⏲11am-late; 📶) This lounge-ish bar enjoys a great ocean-facing terrace, has reasonably priced drinks and is a top spot for sunset. Located 2km north of the centre on the coast road.

Lucy's Sports Bar SPORTS BAR
(www.lucyssportsbar.com; 138 Đ Ha Long; ⏰7am-midnight; 📶) Almost opposite the ferry terminal, this non-sleazy bar has a busy pool table, a great sea-facing terrace and a sociable vibe. As the name indicates, there's a viewing diet of sports events – from Test cricket to Aussie Rules football. Also serves pub grub.

Red Parrot PUB
(6 Đ Le Quy Don; ⏰noon-midnight; 📶) One of the better expat joints in town with a heavy-duty clientele of war veterans, oil workers and working girls. Check out the vintage Vespas.

ℹ Information

Consult www.vungtau-city.com for relatively up-to-date information on the city of Vung Tau.

International SOS (☎064-385 8776; www.internationalsos.com; 1 Đ Le Ngoc Han; ⏰24hr) A well-respected clinic with international standards and international prices.

Main Post Office (8 Đ Hoang Dieu; ⏰7am-5.30pm Mon-Sat) Located at the ground level of the Petrovietnam Towers building.

OSC Vietnam Travel (☎064-385 2008; www.oscvietnamtravel.com.vn; 2 Đ Le Loi; ⏰7am-4.30pm) Offers transport booking and a host of local trips.

Vietcombank (27-29 Đ Tran Hung Dao; ⏰7.30am-3.30pm) Exchanges cash and offers credit-card advances.

ℹ Getting There & Away

BUS

Orange air-con Futa Phuong Trang buses (115,000d) leave hourly between 4am and 6pm from Pham Nga Lao in the heart of HCMC's backpacker district to Vung Tau's **bus station** (192A Đ Nam Ky Khoi Nghia); your ticket includes a drop-off in Vung Tau, saving you a taxi.

There are also minibuses from Mien Dong bus station in HCMC (85,000d, frequent) between 5am and 7pm to Vung Tau.

The journey time is around 90 minutes.

BOAT

It's more enjoyable to catch a hydrofoil to/from HCMC, though with the opening of a new expressway, services have been reduced. Boat operators to HCMC (weekday/weekend 200,000/250,000d, 90 minutes) use the same terminals. The best boats are run by **Vina Express** (☎HCMC 08-3825 3333, Vung Tau 064-385 6530) and **Petro Express** (☎HCMC 08-3821 0650, Vung Tau 064-351 5151). Services leave roughly every 90 minutes until 4.45pm and there are additional boats at weekends, when it's important to book ahead. In Vung Tau, the boat leaves from Cau Da Pier.

Two ferries connect Con Son Island with Vung Tau, with sailings every second day. Boats do not leave when seas are rough (and conditions aboard the boats are pretty rough too). Tickets can be purchased from the office at 1007/36 Đ 30/4 which reads **BQL Cang Ben Dam Huyen Con Dao** (bunk bed 270,000d; ⏰7.30-11.30am & 1.30-4.30pm Mon-Fri). The ferry departs at 5pm

ANZAC SITES AROUND VUNG TAU

Nearly 60,000 Australian soldiers were involved in the American War throughout the 1960s and 1970s. The **Long Tan Memorial Cross** commemorates a particularly fierce battle that took place on 18 August 1966 between Australian troops and Viet Cong fighters. Originally erected by Australian survivors of the battle, the current cross is a replica installed by the Vietnamese in 2002. It's located about 18km from Ba Ria town or 55km from Vung Tau, near the town of Nui Dat. Permits to visit the Long Tan memorial are no longer necessary, and can be combined with the seldom-visited **Lon Phuoc tunnels**, an underground network that is a much smaller version of the more famous tunnels at Cu Chi.

At Minh Dam, 5km from Long Hai, there are **caves** with historical connections to the Franco–Viet Minh and American Wars. Although the caves are little more than spaces between the boulders covering the cliff face, VC soldiers bunked here off and on between 1948 and 1975; you can still see bullet holes in the rocks from the skirmishes that took place. Steps hewn into the rock face lead up to the caves, with spectacular views over the coastal plains from the top. Nearby there is a **mountain-top temple** with more great panoramic views of the coastline.

Tommy's (☎064-351 5181; www.tommysvietnam.com; 3 Đ Ba Cu, Vung Tau) operate tours for returning vets that include Long Tan, Long Phuoc and Minh Dam. The cost, including transport and guide, is around US$125 per day for up to three people.

Otherwise hook up with a *xe om* driver and expect to pay US$25 or so for a tour around these sights.

Around Vung Tau

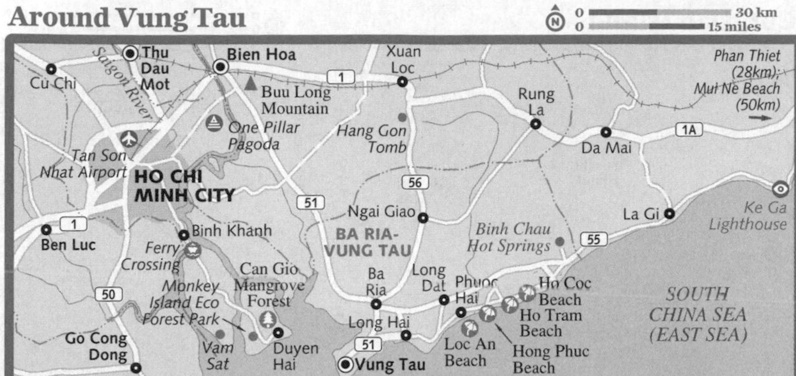

from Vung Tau port, which lies about 15km west of the city; the journey takes 12 hours.

Getting Around

Vung Tau is easily traversed on two wheels or four. Guesthouses and restaurants can arrange bicycle hire (per day US$2) and motorbike hire (from US$6 per day). Metered taxis (which are everywhere) will likely work out cheaper than trying to negotiate with ruthless *cyclo* or *xe om* drivers. **Mai Linh** (064-356 5656) is a reliable operator and has plenty of taxis cruising the streets.

Con Dao Islands

064 / POP 6300

Isolated from the mainland, the Con Dao Islands are one of the star attractions in Vietnam. Long the Devil's Island of Indochina, the preserve of political prisoners and undesirables, this place is now turning heads thanks to its striking natural beauty. Con Son, the largest of this chain of 15 islands and islets, is ringed with lovely beaches, coral reefs and scenic bays, and remains partially covered in thick forests. In addition to hiking, diving and exploring empty coastal roads and deserted beaches, there are some excellent wildlife-watching opportunities such as the black giant squirrel and the endemic bow-fingered gecko.

Although it seems an island paradise, Con Son was once hell on earth for the thousands of prisoners who languished in confinement here in a dozen jails during French rule and the American-backed regime.

Many visitors to Con Son are package-tour groups of former VC soldiers who were imprisoned on the island. The Vietnamese government subsidises these jaunts as a show of gratitude for their sacrifice.

Roughly 80% of the land area in the island chain is part of Con Dao National Park, which protects Vietnam's most important sea-turtle nesting grounds; the main nesting season is June to September. Sadly monitoring operations by park rangers have been scaled right back in recent years and turtle-egg poaching has consequently mushroomed. Other interesting sea life around Con Dao includes the dugong, a rare marine mammal in the same family as the manatee.

The driest time to visit Con Dao is from November to February, although the seas are calmest from March to July. The rainy season lasts from June to September, but there are also northeast and southwest monsoons from September to November that can bring heavy winds. September and October are the hottest months, though even then the cool island breezes make Con Dao relatively comfortable when compared with HCMC or Vung Tau.

Change has been almost glacial, but with the arrival of the uber-luxurious Six Senses Con Dao, the islands are now on the radar of the international jet set. Backpackers are also discovering the islands as transport connections have improved. But with flights still quite expensive (and the islands' cost of living approximately double the mainland's), numbers are still small.

History

Occupied at various times by the Khmer, Malays and Vietnamese, Con Son Island

Con Dao Islands

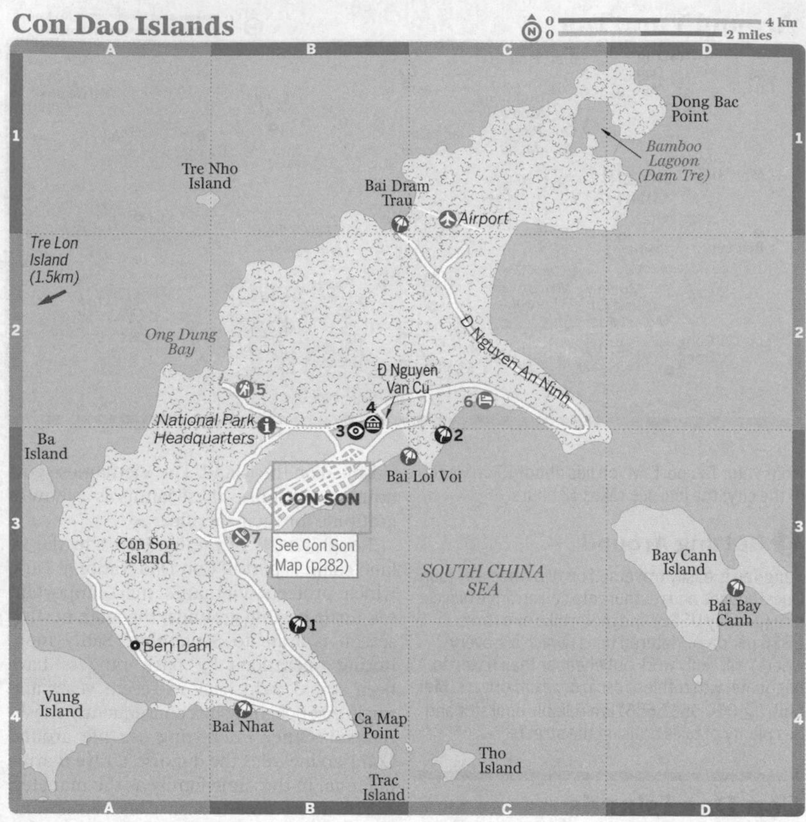

Con Dao Islands

Sights

Activities, Courses & Tours

Sleeping

Eating

also served as an early base for European commercial ventures in the region. The first recorded European arrival was a ship of Portuguese mariners in 1560. The British East India Company maintained a fortified trading post here from 1702 to 1705 – an experiment that ended when the English on the island were massacred in a revolt by the Makassar soldiers they had recruited on the Indonesian island of Sulawesi.

Con Son Island has a strong political and cultural history, and an all-star line-up of Vietnamese revolutionary heroes were incarcerated here. (Many streets are named after them.) Under the French, Con Son was used as a major prison for opponents of colonialism, earning a reputation for the routine mistreatment and torture of prisoners. National heroine Vo Thi Sau was executed here in 1952.

In 1954, the island was taken over by the South Vietnamese government, which continued to utilise its remoteness to hold opponents of the government (including students) in horrendous conditions.

During the American War, the South Vietnamese were joined here by US forces. The US built prisons here and maintained the notorious 'tiger cages' as late as 1970, when news of their existence was broken by a *Life* magazine report.

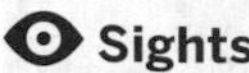

Sights

Con Son Town

There's nowhere quite like it in all Vietnam. This pocket-sized island capital – with its litter-free streets, well-kept municipal buildings and air of calm and prosperity – would make a perfect location for a period film.

The main seafront promenade of Đ Ton Duc Thanh is a delight to stroll, lined with French-era villas, some crumbling, others renovated into hotels. Nearby is the local **market**, busiest between 7am and 9am.

Of course, the town's genteel appearance and character is tempered by the presence of several prisons, cemeteries and reminders of the islands' historic role as a penal colony. There are ghosts everywhere in Con Son.

All the following sights are in Con Son town, share roughly the same hours and are covered by a single ticket costing 20,000d. You can purchase this ticket in the museum, which is the logical place to get some historical context before you start a tour of the prisons.

Bao Tang Con Dao Museum MUSEUM
(7-11am & 1.30-5pm) This impressive new museum has more than 2000 exhibits, including many rare documents, dioramas and excellent photographs, which comprehensively record the islands' history, including the French colonial era and of course the 'prison period'. Modern displays including audiovisuals are used.

Phu Hai Prison HISTORIC BUILDING
(7-11.30am & 1-5pm) The largest of the 11 jails on the island, this prison dates from 1862. Thousands of prisoners were held here, with up to 200 prisoners crammed into each detention building. During the French era, all prisoners were kept naked, chained together in rows, with one small box serving as a toilet for hundreds. One can only imagine the squalor and stench. Today, emaciated mannequins that are all too lifelike recreate the era.

It's a huge complex, where political and criminal classes were mixed together. 'Solitary' rooms (where prisoners considered to be particularly dangerous were held) contained as many as 63 inmates, herded together so tightly that there was no room to lie down. The prison church dates from the US era, but it was never used.

Tiger Cages HISTORIC BUILDING
(7-11.30am & 1-5pm) The notorious cells dubbed 'tiger cages' were built in 1940 by the French to incarcerate nearly 2000 political prisoners. There are 120 chambers with ceiling bars, where guards could poke at prisoners like tigers in a Victorian zoo. Prisoners were beaten with sticks from above, and sprinkled with quicklime and water (which burnt their skin, and caused blindness).

The tiger cages were deliberately constructed away from the main prison, out of sight, and only accessed by an alleyway. They were unknown to the outside world until 1970, when a US congressional aide, Tom Harkin, visited Con Son and saw evidence of brutal torture of the prisoners he met there. Harkin had been tipped off about the cages' existence by a former inmate and managed to break off the pre-arranged tour. Using a map given to him, he discovered the tiger cages behind a vegetable garden, and photographed the cells and prisoners inside. The images were published by *Life* magazine in July 1970.

Hang Duong Cemetery CEMETERY
Some 20,000 Vietnamese prisoners died on Con Son and 1994 of their graves can be seen at the peaceful Hang Duong Cemetery, located at the eastern edge of town. Sadly, only 700 of these graves bear the name of the victims.

Vietnam's most famous heroine, Vo Thi Sau (1933–52) is buried here. She was the first woman executed by a firing squad on Con Son, on 23 January 1952. Today's pilgrims come to burn incense and leave offerings at her tomb, mirrors, combs and lipstick (symbolic because she died so young). You may even encounter fruit, and meals of sticky rice and pork.

In the distance behind the cemetery you'll see a huge monument symbolising three giant sticks of incense.

Phu Binh Camp HISTORIC BUILDING
(7-11.30am & 1-5pm) On the edge of town, this prison was built in 1971 by the Americans, and had 384 chambers. The cells had corrugated-iron roofs, and were infernally hot. The original structures remain in situ, but there's not that much left to see today. It was known as Camp 7 until 1973, when it closed following evidence of torture.

Con Son

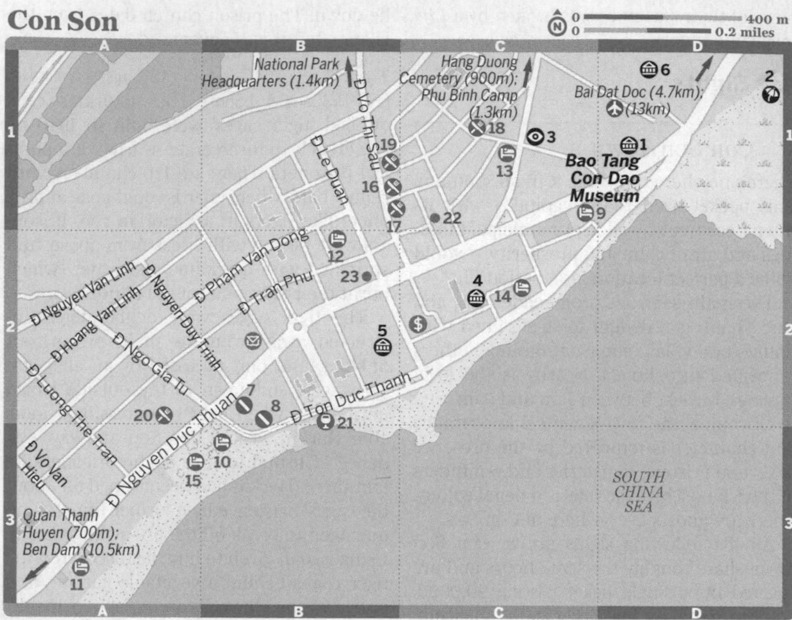

Con Son

Top Sights
1 Bao Tang Con Dao Museum D1

Sights
2 Bai Loi Voi D1
3 Night Market C1
4 Phu Hai Prison C2
5 Revolutionary Museum B2
6 Tiger Cages D1

Activities, Courses & Tours
Con Dao Dive Center .... (see 16)
7 Dive! Dive! Dive! B2
8 Rainbow Divers B2

Sleeping
9 ATC Con Dao Resort & Spa C1
10 Con Dao Camping B3
11 Con Dao Resort A3
12 Hai Nga Mini Hotel B2
13 Red Hotel C1
14 Saigon Con Dao Resort C2
Thien Tan Hotel .... (see 15)
15 Thien Tan Star Hotel A3

Eating
16 Bar200 Con Dao B1
17 Con Son Market B1
18 Infinity Cafe & Lounge C1
19 Thu Ba B1
20 Tri Ky A2

Drinking & Nightlife
21 Con Son Cafe B2

Information
22 Vung Tau Ferry Ticket Office C1

Transport
23 Vasco B2

After the Paris Agreements in 1973, the name was changed to Phu Binh Camp.

Revolutionary Museum MUSEUM
(7-11am & 1.30-5pm) Located in the former French commandant's residence, this museum has exhibits on Vietnamese resistance against the French, communist opposition to the Republic of Vietnam, and the treatment of political prisoners. You'll also find a painting of Vo Thi Sau (facing death with her head held high) and some stuffed wildlife: boas, lizards and monkeys.

Con Dao Beaches

Con Dao has some excellent beaches. Enquire in hotels about snorkelling gear rental for about 100,000d per day or rent new gear through the dive schools. Sandflies can be a big problem on Con Dao beaches, so make sure you bring insect repellent.

Bai Dat Doc BEACH

The best beach on Con Son Island, Bai Dat Doc is a beautiful cove, consisting of a kilometre-long crescent of sand, backed by green hills. It has a gently shelving profile and no pollution, so it's ideal for swimming. Though it's backed by the luxury bungalows of the Six Senses hotel, it's not a private beach and there are access points close to the road.

Very rarely dugongs have been seen frolicking in the water off the nearby cape.

Bai Dram Trau BEACH

Reached via a dirt track 1km before the airport on Con Son Island, Bai Dram Trau is a sublime but remote 700m half-moon crescent of soft sand, fringed by casuarina trees and bookended by forest-topped rocky promontories. It's best visited at low tide.

There's some snorkelling on reefs offshore and three very simple seafood shacks (all open noon till dusk only).

Bai Loi Voi BEACH

On the north side of Con Son town, Bai Loi Voi is a broad beach with lots of seashells and casuarinas for shade. There's a good stretch of sandy beach right in the centre of Con Son town, around the Con Dao Resort.

Bai An Hai BEACH

Bai An Hai on the south side of Con Son town is appealing, but there are a good number of fishing boats moored nearby.

Bay Canh ISLAND

Perhaps the best all-round island to visit is Bay Canh, to the east of Con Son Island, which has lovely beaches, old-growth forest, mangroves, coral reefs and sea turtles (seasonal). There is a fantastic two-hour walk to a functioning French-era lighthouse on Bay Canh's eastern tip, although it involves a steep climb of 325m. Once at the summit, the panoramic views are breathtaking.

Tre Lon ISLAND

Some of the more pristine beaches are on the smaller islands, such as the beautiful white-sand beach on Tre Lon, to the west of Con Son Island.

Activities

For more information on treks and boat trips around the Con Dao Islands, visit www.condaopark.com.vn, the official website for Con Dao National Park. It costs 20,000d to enter the park by day or 40,000d by night.

Note that two of the dive schools in Con Dao were recommending travellers *not* to join turtle tours in protest at what they see as the inaction of national park staff in protecting nesting turtles, and their eggs, from poachers. If you do decide to go overnight, turtle-watching tours cost around 1,500,000d per person if booked via the national park office. Note that nesting turtles are very rarely seen outside the main season (late June to early September).

Diving & Snorkelling

Experienced divers who know the waters of Vietnam have long talked up Con Dao as the most pristine marine environment in the country. The waters around the islands are officially protected, and there's abundant healthy coral (table, staghorn and brain are all in evidence). Marine life includes green and hawksbill turtles, rays, triggerfish and parrotfish, groupers, cuttlefish and the odd shark.

That said, things could be even better, as official protection is weak. Some boatmen still anchor on the reef, and illegal fishing

THE TEENAGE MARTYR

If breeze is blowing from the north, you can probably smell the incense from a specific grave in Con Son's cemetery: the tomb of Vo Thi Sau, a national icon.

Vo Thi Sau, a teenage resistance fighter executed in Con Dao during the French occupation, was politically active from a very early age. She killed a French captain in a grenade attack at the age of 14, and was only captured years later following a second assassination attempt. Vo Thi Sau was taken to Con Dao and executed here, aged 19.

Visit the cemetery at midnight and you'll find crowds of people packed around her grave, saying prayers and making offerings. The Vietnamese believe that this is the most auspicious time to pay respects and venerate the spirit of this national heroine, who was killed in the early hours of 23 January 1952.

affects fish numbers. Every day dive schools clear discarded nets and garbage from reefs.

Diving is possible year-round, but for ideal conditions and good visibility, January to June is considered the best time, while November and December can see big storms. Prices are more expensive than at mainland destinations, but also more rewarding.

Wrecks, including a 65m freighter resting in 30m to 40m with abundant sea life, offer huge potential for more experienced divers.

Cheapo snorkelling trips are offered by some hotels, but we've heard reports of boatmen spearfishing illegally on some of these trips. Dive schools' excursions do cost more, but are environmentally sound.

★Dive! Dive! Dive! DIVING
(☎064-383 0701; www.dive-condao.com; Đ Nguyen Hue; ⏲8am-9pm) Instructor Larry has been in Con Dao since 2011 and has vast experience diving the island reefs. This is a conservation-minded operation, offering RAID courses, and the dive shop is a great source of general information on Con Dao. The company constantly monitors reefs to remove fishing nets and trash from corals.

Con Dao Dive Center DIVING
(☎0903 700 8483; http://divecondao.com; Bar200, Pham Van Dong; ⏲7.30am-10pm) A very friendly and professional PADI dive resort, offering fine instruction and courses (Open Water is US$550), fun dives (two-dive trips US$160), snorkelling and freediving trips. Owner Rhys is happy to chat about diving options and things to do in Con Dao. It's based at Bar200.

Rainbow Divers DIVING
(☎0905 577 671; www.divevietnam.com; 40 Đ Ton Duc Thang; ⏲8am-8pm) Established outfit offering dive lessons and recreational dives.

Trekking

There are lots of treks around Con Son Island, as much of the interior remains heavily forested. It is necessary to take a national park guide when venturing into the forest. Rates range from 180,000d to 300,000d depending on the duration of the trek.

It's a steep uphill climb to the old fruit plantations of So Ray, following a slippery but well-marked trail (lined with information panels about trees and wildlife) through dense rainforest. The plantation is home to a sociable troop of long-tailed macaques, with sweeping views over the main town to the other Con Dao Islands beyond. The return hike takes about 90 minutes.

Bamboo Lagoon HIKING
(Dam Tre) One of the more beautiful walks leads through thick forest and mangroves, past a hilltop stream to Bamboo Lagoon. There's good snorkelling in the bay here. This leisurely two-hour trek starts from near the airport runway, but you'll definitely need a local guide to do this.

Ong Dung Bay HIKING
A hike that you can do yourself is a 1km walk (about 30 minutes each way) through rainforest to Ong Dung Bay. The trail begins a few kilometres north of Con Son town. The bay has only a rocky beach, although there is a good coral reef about 300m offshore.

Ma Thien Lanh Bridge HIKING
Near the trailhead for Ong Dung Bay, you'll find the ruins of the Ma Thien Lanh Bridge, which was built by prisoners under the French occupation.

Sleeping

Accommodation options have greatly improved in Con Dao over the last few years and there are now about 20 guesthouses and mini-hotels in Con Son town. However expect to pay about double the rate for the equivalent place on the mainland.

Thien Tan Hotel HOTEL $
(☎0946 782 468; 4 Đ Nguyen Duc Thuan; r US$16-30; ❄📶) The beachfront location is the main draw at this place, which is located under a patch of pine trees. Rooms are decent value for Con Son, though wi-fi is spotty and near-zero English is spoken.

Red Hotel HOTEL $
(☎064-363 0079; 17B Đ Nguyen An Ninh; r 350,000-650,000d; ❄📶) A good budget option, this new mini-hotel has spotless, spacious rooms and is in the thick of things, close to the night market and plenty of eating options. It's run by a helpful team.

Hai Nga Mini Hotel HOTEL $
(☎064-363 0308; 7 Đ Tran Phu; r 400,000-600,000d; ❄@📶) A tempting option for sharers, some rooms here sleep up to five people, and all have air-con. Run by a family who can speak some English and German.

Con Dao Camping HOTEL $$
(☎064-383 1555; Đ Nguyen Duc Thuan; r 700,000-850,000d; ❄@📶) These two rows

of cute A-frame bungalows enjoy a nice position right by a stretch of beach and are cleaned daily. Frills (if not thrills) include satellite TV, two beds, a porch, minibar and showers with a view of the night sky. They're located very close to the town's new dock.

Thien Tan Star Hotel HOTEL $$
(064-363 0123; http://thientanstarhotel.com; 4 Đ Nguyen Duc Thuan; r 750,000-1,500,000d;) This new hotel occupies a beachfront plot close to everything in Con Son. Rooms are simply presented with whitewashed walls, minibar, flat-screen TV and good bed linen; you can save some dong if you forgo a sea view.

Con Dao Resort HOTEL $$
(064-383 0939; www.condaoresort.com.vn; 8 Đ Nguyen Duc Thuan; r US$62-98;) Facing an inviting sandy beach, this dated resort hotel, complete with extensive manicured gardens and a large swimming pool, certainly enjoys a great location. Rooms are spacious and comfortable enough, but showing their age.

ATC Con Dao Resort & Spa HOTEL $$
(064-383 0111; www.atcvietnam.com; 8 Đ Ton Duc Thang; r US$45-90, ste from US$120;) This is a tale of two cities. ATC's renovated accommodation is some of the most attractive in town, offering smart, inviting and comfortable rooms with terracotta tiling and great ocean-facing balconies. There are also older rooms and bungalows which should be avoided.

★ Six Senses Con Dao BOUTIQUE HOTEL $$$
(064-383 1222; www.sixsenses.com; Dat Doc Beach; villas from US$612;) In a class of its own, the astonishing Six Senses is located on the island's best beach, 4km northeast of Con Son town. One of Vietnam's most exclusive resorts, here are 50 or so ocean-facing timber-clad beach units that fuse contemporary style with rustic chic, each with its own pool, giant bathtub and a couple of bikes. Staff are very well trained indeed.

Eating options include a casual cafe where you can grab a panini, and the magnificent restaurant by the shore. Diving, sailing trips and trekking can all be arranged and the spa has indoor and outdoor rooms for Ayurvedic treatments.

Saigon Con Dao Resort HOTEL $$$
(064-383 0155; www.saigoncondao.com; 18 Đ Ton Duc Thang; r US$75-135, ste from US$186;) Originally set in a cluster of old French buildings on the waterfront, this place has an impressive new wing with a swimming pool which is where most foreign visitors are hosted. The old wing is mostly reserved for visiting veterans. Service is a bit spotty for the rates charged.

Eating & Drinking

The dining scene has changed recently in Con Son and there are now several Western-geared places to eat, but this is still little more than a village so don't expect too wide a selection. Restaurants are scattered around town. Six Senses Con Dao is *the* destination for a sumptuous treat with a virtuoso menu.

If you're on a tight budget, check out the small **night market** around the intersection of Đ Tran Huy Lieu and Đ Nguyen An Ninh for cheap eats.

Bar200 Con Dao CAFE $
(Đ Pham Van Dong; meals from 35,000d; 8am-10.30pm;) Popular place to hang for travellers in town, with a relaxed, sociable vibe; the owners are clued-up when it comes to island info. There's great coffee (including espresso and cappuccino) and Western comfort grub including burgers, pizza, sandwiches and breakfast cereals. After dark the beers and cocktails start flowing.

Con Son Market VIETNAMESE $
(Đ Vo Thi Sau; meals 15,000-25,000d; 6am-5pm) A good spot for breakfast, with ladies churning out delicious noodle dishes and pancakes (for peanuts). You can stock up on fruit and snacks here too.

★ Infinity Cafe & Lounge CAFE $$
(Đ Pham Van Dong; meals 70,000-150,000d;) A lot of effort has gone into this hip cafe-bar with its artistic, reclaimed furnishings and lovely pavement terrace with bench seating. Cocktails are chalked up on a board and you'll find plenty of interest on the menu, including great pizza and pasta.

Thu Ba VIETNAMESE, SEAFOOD $$
(064-3830 255; Đ Vo Thi Sau; meals 75,000-200,000d) Creatively prepared, beautifully presented Vietnamese cuisine – Thu Ba is strong on seafood, hotpots and curries. The gregarious owner speaks great English and is happy to make suggestions based upon what's seasonal and fresh.

Quan Thanh Huyen VIETNAMESE $$
(Khu 3, Hoang Phi Yen; meals 70,000-160,000d; ⏲noon-9pm) South of town by a lake, this lovely little restaurant enjoys a great setting, with little gazebos next to the water and an orchestra of croaking frogs. Offers authentic Vietnamese cuisine including hotpots and snakehead fish straight from the lake.

Tri Ky VIETNAMESE $$
(7 Đ Nguyen Duc Thuan; mains 45,000-200,000d; ⏲10.30am-9pm) Popular for its fresh seafood, particularly grilled squid, grouper and crab. The premises (a huge covered terrace with plastic chairs and strip lights) are very simple but the owners are welcoming.

Con Son Cafe BAR
(Đ Ton Duc Thanh; ⏲7am-9.30pm) Formerly the customs house, this elegant French colonial structure has a lovely breezy, shady terrace from where you can gaze out over the bay's fishing boats. Serves tea, coffee, shakes, beers and cocktails. French composer Camille Saint-Saens lived in this building, writing his opera *Brunhilda* in 1895.

Information

Both Larry of Dive! Dive! Dive! (p284) and the team at Con Dao Dive Center (p284) are great contacts, and very knowledgeable about the islands.

There are several ATMs in Con Dao.

Internet access is available at most hotels in town, including free wi-fi for guests. Many cafes and restaurants also have wi-fi.

National Park Headquarters (☎064-383 0669; www.condaopark.com.vn; 29 Đ Vo Thi Sau; ⏲7-11.30am & 1.30-5pm) A good place to get information. Since the military controls access to parts of the national park, stop here first to learn more about possible island excursions and hikes, plus pick up a useful free handout on walks around the island. Some hiking trails have interpretive signage in English and Vietnamese. The headquarters also has an exhibition hall with displays on the diversity of local forest and marine life, threats to the local environment, and local conservation activities.

Vietin Bank (Đ Le Duan; ⏲8am-2pm Mon-Fri, 8am-noon Sat) With ATM, does not change foreign currency.

Getting There & Away

AIR

There are three to five daily flights between Con Son Island and HCMC jointly operated by **Vasco** (☎064-383 1831; www.vasco.com.vn; 44 Đ Nguyen Hue) and **Vietnam Airlines** (www.vietnamairlines.com). Tickets cost US$60 to US$80 one way. Con Son is also connected to Can Tho in the Mekong Delta via Vasco/Vietnam Airlines; there are four weekly flights, and if you book well ahead tickets can be as low as US$28 one way.

The tiny airport is about 15km from the town centre. All of the big hotels on the island provide free transport both to and from the airport. It's nearly always possible to show up and grab a seat on one of the hotel shuttle vans that meet the planes; drivers charge 50,000d and will usually drop you off at your hotel or in the town centre.

BOAT

There are two ferries connecting Con Son Island with Vung Tau, with sailings three to four times a week, though they don't sail during stormy weather or heavy seas. Facilities are basic and the crossing can be very rough. Ferries depart from Ben Dam port at 5pm, taking around 12 hours. Seats cost 160,000d but it is better to invest in a sleeper berth for 275,000d, with six bunks to a room.

Tickets can be purchased from a small office near the market in town. Look out for the sign at the kiosk on Đ Vo Thi Sau that reads **BQL Cang Ben Dam Huyen Con Dao** (⏲8-11.30am & 1-5pm). A *xe om* to Ben Dam will cost about 110,000d, a taxi about 300,000d.

Getting Around

BOAT

Exploring the islands by boat can be arranged via hotels and the national park office. A 12-person boat costs around 2,000,000d to 5,000,000d per day depending on the destinations. Local fishermen also offer excursions, but be sure to bargain hard.

MOTORBIKE & BICYCLE

This is one of the best places in Vietnam to ride a bike, with little traffic, no pollution and good surfaced roads. There's only one main road, connecting the airport in the north to Ben Dam in the south via Con Son town.

Most hotels rent motorbikes for about US$6 to US$10 per day. Bicycles cost around US$2 per day. There are good coastal cycling routes, such as from Con Son town to Bai Nhat and on to the tiny settlement of Ben Dam. The ups and downs are pretty gentle and, thankfully, there is little motorised traffic. If motorbiking or cycling to Ben Dam, be very careful of the high winds around Mui Ca Map Point. Locals have been blown off their bikes during gales.

TAXI

Con Son Island has many **taxis** (☎064-361 6161). However, as metered rates are very high (around 20,000d per km!) negotiate hard for a fixed-price rate to destinations outside Con Son town.

Southwest Highlands

Includes ➡

Best Places to Eat

- ➡ Le Rabelais (p296)
- ➡ Thanh Tram (p302)
- ➡ Restaurant Ichi (p295)
- ➡ Ming Dynasty (p296)
- ➡ Dakbla's Restaurant (p310)

Best Places to Stay

- ➡ Villa Vista (p294)
- ➡ Ana Mandara Villas Dalat (p294)
- ➡ Forest Floor Lodge (p300)
- ➡ Coffee Tour Resort (p301)
- ➡ Konklor Hotel (p309)

Why Go?

Few parts of Vietnam stir the imagination with the lure of adventure quite like the highlands. The ribbon that is the Ho Chi Minh Hwy winds its scenic way past coffee plantations, pine-studded mountains, rice paddies with their wallowing buffalo, enormous reed-covered lakes and peaceful hill-tribe villages, laying down the challenge of a two-wheeled journey.

Protected jungle hosts singing gibbons, pygmy loris, wild elephants and incredible numbers of birds. Active travellers take to the mountains, forests, waterfalls and rivers in biking, hiking, rafting and abseiling adventures, and the former French hill station of Dalat beguiles with its cool climate, the palaces of the last emperor of Vietnam and bars for after-dark thrills.

As varied as the land, the people of the highlands are a great mix of cultures. If you're lucky, you may sleep in a Bahnar *rong* or watch the Jarai 'feed' the graves of their dead.

When to Go

Dalat

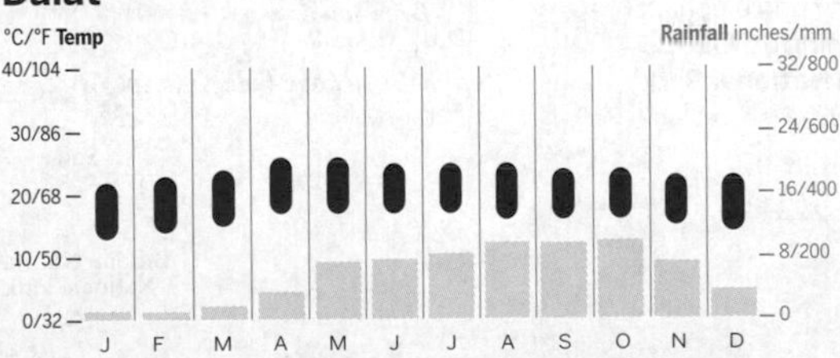

Mar Great for the annual Coffee Festival in Buon Ma Thuot or elephant races in nearby Don.

Oct Autumn in Dalat, the perfect time for exploring or adrenaline-pumping activities.

Dec Trek or cycle through Cat Tien National Park in cooler times, visiting the wild gibbons.

Southwest Highlands Highlights

1 Cranking up the adrenaline rate with a hike, biking trip, white-water rafting, or canyoning or climbing adventure in the hills around **Dalat** (p289).

2 Firing up a motorbike and exploring the twists and turns of the **Ho Chi Minh Highway** (p304).

3 Discovering the hill-tribe customs and culture in Bahnar, Sedang and Jarai villages around **Kon Tum** (p307).

4 Tracking down wild gibbons in the early morning, then seeking out crocodiles by torchlight in **Cat Tien National Park** (p298).

5 Viewing the watery majesty of **Dambri Falls** (p298).

6 Hiking and boating to the minority villages of **Lak Lake** (p300), the biggest lake in the highlands.

7 Going birding, hiking and elephant washing at **Yok Don National Park** (p303).

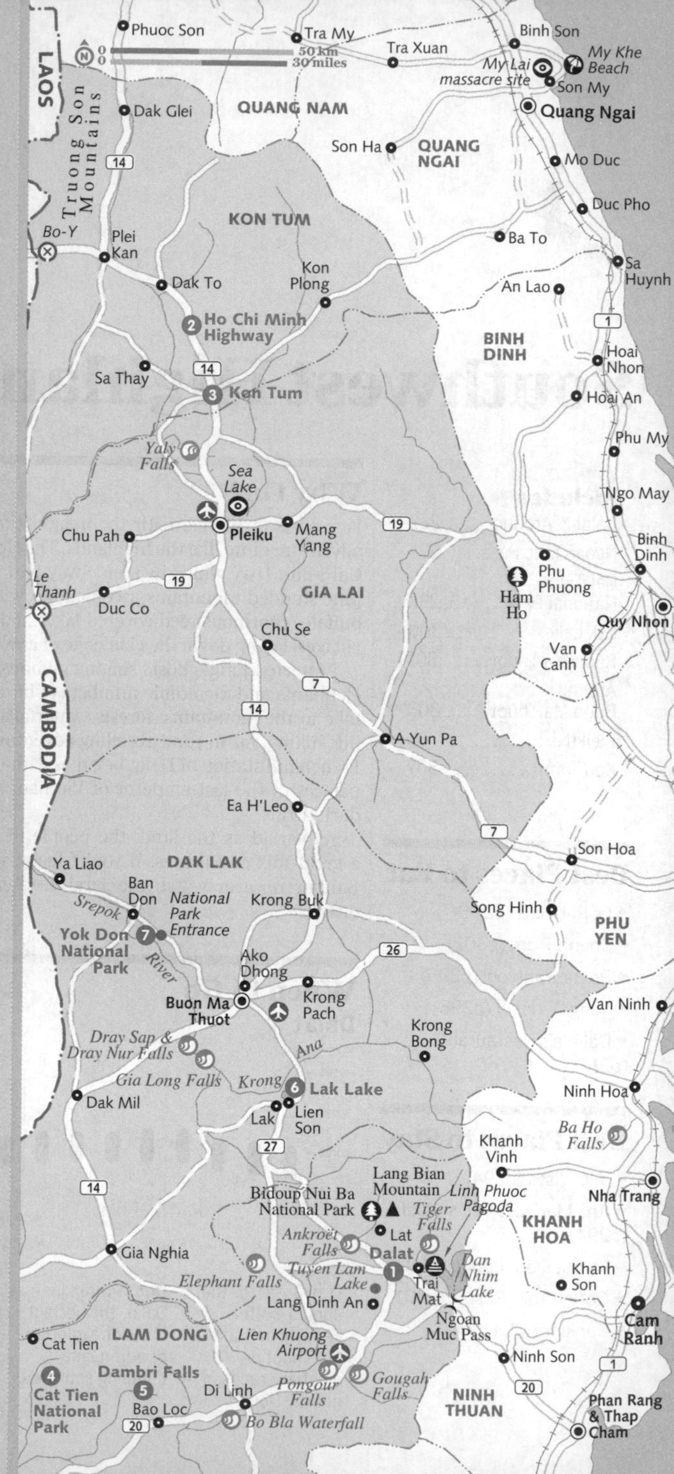

Getting There & Around

AIR

Dalat, Buon Ma Thuot and Pleiku have daily flights to Ho Chi Minh City, Danang and Hanoi. There are also new twice-weekly flights from Dalat to Can Tho.

BUS

Comfortable sleeper buses serve the coastal cities, HCMC and destinations further afield from Dalat, Buon Ma Thuot and Pleiku, while the towns along Hwy 14 are connected to each other by frequent but less comfortable smaller bus services. From Pleiku and Kon Tum there are direct buses to Laos and Cambodia.

CAR & MOTORCYCLE

Exploring the highlands by motorcycle is a popular way to go. There are plenty of scenic stops en route, the traffic isn't heavy even on the main Hwy 14 and you can explore the picturesque back roads. Paved, scenic routes connect the highland towns to the coast.

TOUR

Plenty of motorcycle tours depart Dalat for Buon Ma Thuot, Lak Lake and Kon Tum, for Nha Trang and to Danang and Hoi An, further up the coast. Cycling tours from Dalat head for Mui Ne and Nha Trang.

Dalat & Around

063 / POP 184,755 / ELEV 1475M

Dalat is Vietnam's alter ego: the weather is spring-like cool instead of tropical hot, the town is dotted with elegant French-colonial villas rather than stark socialist architecture, and the farms around are thick with strawberries and flowers, not rice.

The French came first, fleeing the heat of Saigon. They left behind not only their holiday homes but also the vibe of a European town. The Vietnamese couldn't resist adding little touches to, shall we say, enhance Dalat's natural beauty. Whether it's the Eiffel Tower–shaped radio tower, the horse-drawn carriages or the zealously colourful heart-shaped cut-outs at the Valley of Love, this is a town that takes romance very seriously, although it teeters on the brink of kitsch.

Dalat is a big draw for domestic tourists. It's Le Petit Paris, the honeymoon capital and the City of Eternal Spring (daily temperatures hover between 15°C and 24°C) all rolled into one. For travellers, the moderate climate makes it a superb place for all kinds of adrenaline-fuelled activities.

History

Home to hill tribes for centuries, 'Da Lat' means 'river of the Lat tribe' in their language. The city was established in 1912 and quickly became fashionable with Europeans – at one point during the French colonial period, some 20% of Dalat's population was foreign, and grand villas remain scattered around the city.

During the American War, Dalat was spared by the tacit agreement of all parties concerned. Indeed, it seems that while South Vietnamese soldiers were being trained at the city's military academy and affluent officials of the Saigon regime were relaxing in their villas, VC cadres were doing the same thing not far away (also in villas). On 3 April 1975 Dalat fell to the North without a fight.

Sights

Dalat

★Hang Nga Crazy House ARCHITECTURE

(063-382 2070; 3 Đ Huynh Thuc Khang; admission 40,000d; 8.30am-7pm Mon-Fri) A free-wheeling architectural exploration of surrealism, Hang Nga Crazy House is a joyously designed, outrageously artistic private home. Imagine sculptured rooms connected by super-slim bridges rising out of a tangle of greenery, an excess of cascading lava-flow-like shapes, wild colours, spiderweb windows and an almost organic quality to it all, with the swooping hand rails resembling jungle vines. Think Gaudí meeting Tolkien and dropping acid together.

The brainchild of owner Mrs Dang Viet Nga, the Crazy House has been an imaginative work in progress since 1990. Hang Nga, as she's known locally, has a PhD in architecture from Moscow and has designed a number of other buildings around Dalat. One of her earlier masterpieces, the 'House with 100 Roofs', was torn down as a fire hazard because the People's Committee thought it looked antisocialist.

Hang Nga started the Crazy House project to entice people back to nature, and though it's becoming more outlandish every year, she's not likely to have any more trouble with the authorities. Her father, Truong Chinh, was Ho Chi Minh's successor, serving as Vietnam's second president from 1981 until his death in 1988. There's a shrine to him in the ground-floor lounge.

Central Dalat

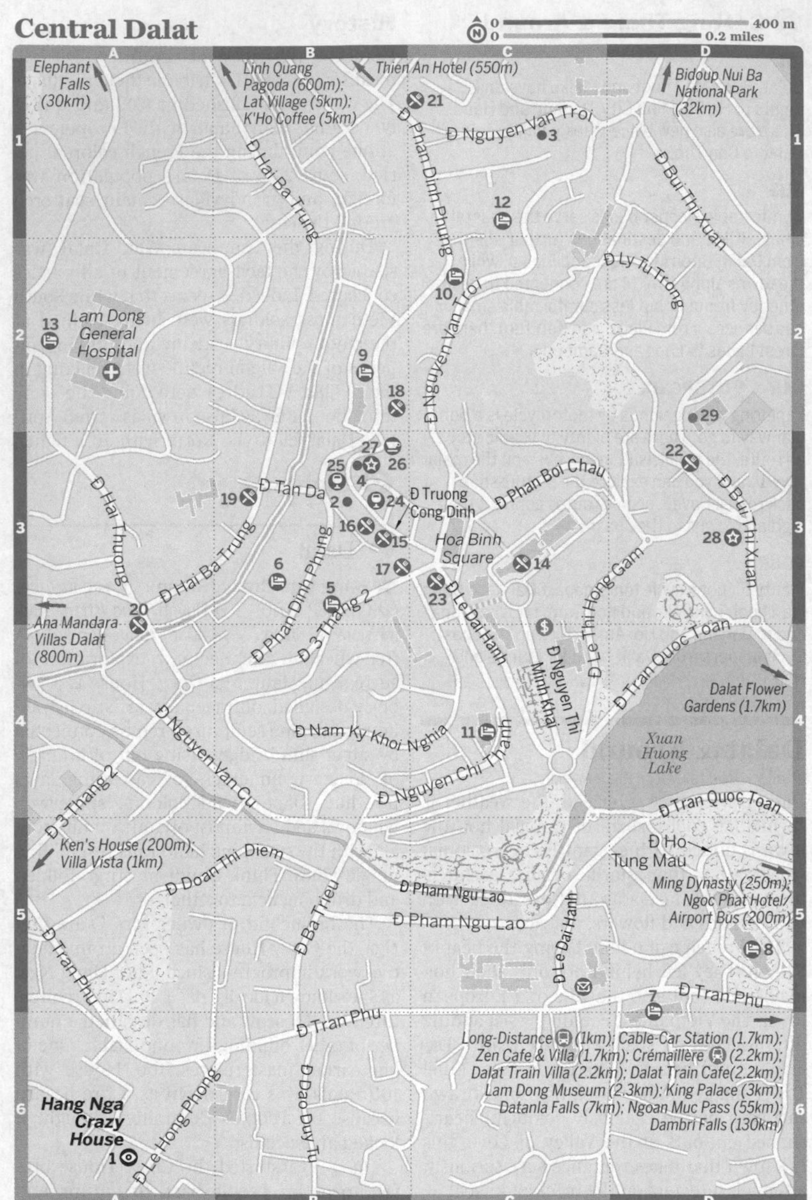

A note of caution for those people who have young kids: the Crazy House's maze of precarious tunnels, high walkways with low guard rails and steep ladders are certainly not child safe.

King Palace PALACE

(Dinh 1; www.dinh1dalat.com; Hung Vuong; adult/child 20,000/10,000d; ⌚7.30am-5pm) Tastefully revamped, the main palace of Bao Dai, Vietnam's last emperor, beckons visitors with its beautiful tree-lined avenue and a surprisingly

Central Dalat

Top Sights
1 Hang Nga Crazy House A6

Activities, Courses & Tours
2 Groovy Gecko Adventure Tours B3
3 Phat Tire Ventures C1
4 Pine Track Adventures B3

Sleeping
5 Dalat Central Hostel B3
6 Dalat Cozy Nook Hostel B3
7 Dalat Hotel du Parc D5
8 Dalat Palace D5
9 Dreams 3 .... B2
10 Dreams Hotel C2
11 Ngoc Lan Hotel C4
12 Sleep In Dalat Hostel C1
13 Villa Pink House A2

Eating
14 Central Market C3
15 Da Quy B3
16 Goc Ha Thanh B3
Le Rabelais .... (see 8)
17 Long Hoa B3
18 Nhat Ly B2
19 One More Cafe B3
20 Restaurant Ichi A4
21 Trong Dong C1
22 V Cafe D3
23 Windmills C3

Drinking & Nightlife
24 13 Cafe-Bar B3
25 Hangout B3
26 La Viet B3

Entertainment
27 Beepub B3
28 Escape Bar D3

Information
29 Sinh Tourist D2

modest royal residence. Its peach-coloured rooms were once home to him, his wife and their five children before being taken over by Prime Minister Ngo Dinh Diem once Bao Dai went into exile in France in 1954.

Highlights are undoubtedly the family photos: Bao Dai playing with a dog, riding a horse, and well-scrubbed royal children with serious faces.

Crémaillère Railway Station HISTORIC BUILDING
(Ga Da Lat; 1 Đ Quang Trung; ⊙6.30am-5pm) FREE From Dalat's wonderful art-deco train station you can ride one of the five scheduled trains that run to Trai Mat (return 124,000d, 30 minutes) daily between 7.45am and 4pm; a minimum of 20 passengers required.

A crémaillère (cog railway) linking Dalat and Thap Cham from 1928 to 1964 was closed due to VC attacks. A Japanese steam train is on display, and the classy waiting room retains a colonial feel.

Lam Dong Museum MUSEUM
(☎063-382 0387; 4 Đ Hung Vuong; admission 10,000d; ⊙7.30-11.30am & 1.30-4.30pm Mon-Sat) This hillside museum is a stampede through Dalat's history, with a side trip into the natural history section, complete with outrageously bad taxidermy (look out for the angry wildcats!). Highlights include the wonderfully evocative photos of the Ma, K'Ho and Churu people and displays of their traditional dress, musical instruments and ceremonial altars. Also, check out the remarkable stone xylophones dating back over 3000 years. Propaganda about the government support for local indigenous groups is hard to swallow, though.

Linh Quang Pagoda BUDDHIST SHRINE
(Chua Linh Quang; 133 Đ Hai Ba Trung; ⊙dawn-dusk) Flanked by enormous dragons and with an outdoor tableau featuring the young Buddha atop a lotus flower, this is Dalat's oldest and most colourful pagoda. Founded in 1931, it had to be extensively restored after the American War.

Xuan Huong Lake LAKE
Created by a dam in 1919, this banana-shaped lake was named after an anti-authoritarian 17th-century Vietnamese poet. The lake can be circumnavigated along a scenic 7km sealed path that passes the flower gardens, the golf club and the Dalat Palace hotel.

Around Dalat

Truc Lam Pagoda & Cable Car BUDDHIST TEMPLE
(Ho Tuyen Lam; cable car one way/return adult 50,000/70,000d, child 30,000/40,000d; ⊙cable car 7.30-11.30am & 1.30-5pm) The Truc Lam Pagoda enjoys a hilltop setting and has splendid gardens. It's an active monastery, though the grounds frequently teem with tour groups. Be sure to arrive by cable car (the terminus is 3km south of the centre), which soars over majestic pine forests.

The pagoda can be reached by road via turn-offs from Hwy 20.

K'Ho Coffee COFFEE PLANTATION

(☎0989 722 184; www.khocoffee.com; Lat Village; ⏲by appointment) This coffee farm has been in the family of Rolan since the 1860s. It's part of a K'Ho coffee-growing cooperative that ensures that profits are directly supporting the K'Ho minority farmers. The beans are arabica, including varieties grown in Africa, which are rarely found in Vietnam even though it's the world's second-biggest coffee producer. If you call Josh and Rolan in advance, you can stop by to see the plantation and pick up some Fairtrade, locally roasted beans.

They also stock beautiful traditional weavings done by the K'Ho women in the community. Predominantly blue and intricately embroidered, each takes weeks to complete; prices start at 1,200,000d.

Bidoup Nui Ba National Park NATURE RESERVE

(☎063-374 7449; www.bidoupnuiba.gov.vn) Occupying a densely forested highland plateau, this national park encompasses evergreen and coniferous woodlands, bamboo groves and grasslands at altitudes between 650m and 2288m. Hill-tribe guides are available to guide you along trails, and there's an impressive visitor centre, 32km north of Dalat, with interactive displays about the flora and fauna and K'Ho hill-tribe crafts and culture.

Bidoup Nui Ba has 96 endemic plants, including the Dalat pine, and nearly 300 species of orchids. Yellow-cheeked gibbons can be heard in the early morning if you're fortunate, while the national park is also home to black bears and the vampire flying frog.

The pleasant 3.5km trail from the visitor centre to a waterfall only fringes the national park; to penetrate deep inside Bidoup Nui Ba consider one of three other options, which include ascents of Lang Biang and Bidoup mountains. The longer trails do not start from the visitor centre itself, but staff there can organise guides and help with logistics.

Elephant Falls WATERFALL

(admission 10,000d; ⏲7am-5pm) Named after a large rock that allegedly resembles an elephant's head, these powerful curved falls are reachable via a steep ascent along uneven, slippery stone steps with intermittent railings. You can also squeeze yourself through a cave to get behind the falls and be doused with bracing spray. The falls are near Nam Ban village, 30km west of Dalat.

THE ONGOING BATTLE FOR THE HIGHLANDS

The uneasy relationship in the central highlands between the hill tribes and the Vietnamese majority dates back centuries, when Vietnamese expansion pushed the tribes up into the mountains. While French-colonial rule recognised the tribes as a separate community, South Vietnam later attempted to assimilate them through such means as abolishing tribal schools and courts, prohibiting the construction of stilt houses and appropriating their land.

In response the minority people formed nationalist guerrilla movements, the best-known of which was the Front Unifié de Lutte des Races Opprimées (FULRO) or the United Front for the Struggle of the Oppressed Races. In the 1960s the hill tribes were courted by the US as allies against North Vietnam, and were trained by the CIA and US Special Forces.

They paid dearly for this after the war, when government policies brought more ethnic Vietnamese into the highlands, along with clampdowns on education in native languages and religious freedom (many hill-tribe people belong to unauthorised churches). Many of these minority people have been relocated to modern villages, partly to discourage slash-and-burn agriculture. It also speeds up assimilation.

In 2001 and 2004 protests erupted, which the government quickly and, according to human rights organisations, violently suppressed. International human rights groups point to more deaths than the government admits to, and thousands of hill tribe people fled to Cambodia or the US afterwards. What happens in the central highlands all too often remains behind closed doors, both for most outsiders and international observers, but also for many ordinary Vietnamese. Talk to any organisation that works with the minority people and you'll hear a story of continuing government surveillance, harassment and religious persecution, with tensions remaining over religious issues (most hill tribe people are Protestant) and land rights.

Datanla Falls WATERFALL

(adult/child 20,000/10,000d, bobsled ride one way/return 40,000/50,000d) This is the closest waterfall to Dalat, so expect lots of tour groups. You can reach the cascade (which is pretty but quite modest) either by walking down or taking the exhilarating **bobsled** on rails instead. Datanla is 7km south of Dalat. Take Hwy 20 and turn right about 200m past the turn-off to Tuyen Lam Lake.

Lat Village VILLAGE

Less than 1km from the base of Lang Bian Mountain is Lat Village (pronounced 'lak'), a fairly unremarkable minority community of about 6000 people spread across nine hamlets. Only five of Lat Village's hamlets are actually Lat; residents of the other four are members of the Chill, Ma and K'Ho tribes. It's worth peeking into the Catholic church for a glimpse of a K'Ho ritual pole alongside the altar.

Activities

Adventure outfits offer trekking, mountain biking, kayaking, canyoning, abseiling and rock climbing, as well as trips to the coast. Compare prices, but make sure that you're comfortable with all the equipment and safety procedures.

★ **Phat Tire Ventures** ADVENTURE TOUR

(☎063-382 9422; www.ptv-vietnam.com; 109 Đ Nguyen Van Troi; ⊙8am-7pm) A highly professional and experienced operator with mountain-biking trips from US$49, trekking from US$39, kayaking from US$39, canyoning (US$75), rappelling (US$57) and white-water rafting (US$67) in the rainy season. Multiday cycling trips are available and it also ventures into Cat Tien National Park.

Groovy Gecko Adventure Tours ADVENTURE TOUR

(☎063-383 6521; www.groovygeckotours.net; 65 Đ Truong Cong Dinh; ⊙8am-7pm) Experienced agency operated by a lively young team with prices starting at US$38 for rock climbing, canyoning or mountain biking, day treks from US$25 and two-day treks from US$65.

Pine Track Adventures ADVENTURE TOUR

(☎063-383 1916; www.pinetrackadventures.com; 72b Đ Truong Cong Dinh; ⊙8am-7pm) Run by an enthusiastic local team, this operator offers canyoning (from US$55), white-water rafting (from US$60), trekking, biking and some excellent multisport packages. A six-day exploration of the area around Dalat and bike ride down to Mui Ne is US$635.

Dalat Happy Tours FOOD TOUR

(☎0912 893 091; www.dalathappytours.com; street-food tour US$4) After all the active exertions around Dalat, replenish your calories by going an an entertaining nightly street-food tour with friendly Lao. Start from the central Hoa Binh cinema at 6pm and proceed to sample *bahn xeo* (filled pancakes), buffalo tail hotpot, delectable grilled skewers, 'Dalat pizza', rabbit curry, hot rice wine and more. Meal price not included.

Sleeping

★ **Ken's House** HOSTEL $

(☎063-383 7119; www.kenhousedalat.com; D59 Hoang Van Thu; r US$12-22; ⊖📶) With walls covered with creeping vines, Parisian scenes and jungle imagery and patterned quilts on beds, this is by far Dalat's most colourful hostel. Join an impromptu hotpot party/communal dinner with the friendly staff.

Sleep In Dalat Hostel HOSTEL $

(☎0913 923 379; www.sleepindalathostel.com; 83/5b Đ Nguyen Van Troi; dm US$7, d US$20-35; 📶) Haunted by Ben the sausage dog, this welcoming hostel is tucked away down a narrow alleyway, insulating you from main street noise. Owner Linh cooks communal dinners so that you can get to know your fellow travellers, and the canyoning tours get rave reviews. Private rooms have their own bathrooms; dorms share (clean) facilities.

Dalat Cozy Nook Hostel HOSTEL $

(☎0949 691 553; 45/5a Đ Phan Dinh Phung; dm US$5; ❄📶) Two spotless mixed dorms with the most comfortable bunks in Dalat attract a constant crowd of international backpackers, and the lively group dinners, organised by helpful owners, give you the perfect opportunity to swap traveller tales.

Dalat Central Hostel HOSTEL $

(Hotel Phuong Hanh; ☎0989 878 879; 80 Đ Ba Thang Hai; dm/d US$5/20; ❄📶) More a budget hotel than a hostel, though it's a popular traveller hub. The vast eight- and 12-bed dorms come with comfy bunks and privacy curtains, a women-only dorm is available and the private rooms are huge, with triangular bath-tubs.

Villa Pink House HOTEL $

(☎063-381 5667; ahomeawayfromhome_dalat@yahoo.com; 7 Đ Hai Thuong; s/d/tr US$16/20/30; @📶) A well-run family-owned place, where many rooms have great views. It's managed by the affable Mr Rot, who can arrange motorbike tours in the countryside around Dalat.

★Villa Vista BOUTIQUE HOTEL $$
(☎063-351 2468; huongdo_82@yahoo.com; 93 Ngo Thi Sy, Phuong 4; r from US$60;) Look down from this mansion on the hill and the whole of Dalat opens up in the valley below you. There are only four exquisite rooms here, decorated in the 19th-century French fashion (albeit with flat-screen TVs and rain showers). Delightful owners Tim and Huong prepare remarkable breakfasts, hook you up with Easy Riders and share their Dalat knowledge.

Dalat Hotel du Parc HOTEL $$
(☎063-382 5777; www.dalatresorts.com; 7 Đ Tran Phu; r 1,700,000-1,900,000d, ste 2,800,000d;) A respectfully refurbished 1932 building that offers colonial-era style at enticing prices. The grand lobby lift sets the tone and the spacious rooms include classy furnishings and polished wooden floors. It's bristling with facilities, from the spa and fitness centre to the excellent restaurant.

Dreams 3 HOTEL $$
(☎063-382 5877, 063-383 3748; dreams@hcm.vnn.vn; 138-140 Đ Phan Dinh Phung; s/d US$32/37;) This commodious venture owned by the amazing 'Dreams Team' offers incredibly tasteful accommodation. All rooms have high-quality mattresses and modish bathrooms, and some have a balcony. On the top floor there's a jacuzzi, a steam room and a sauna. The only downer is the location on a traffic-heavy street.

Dreams Hotel GUESTHOUSE $$
(☎063-383 3748; www.dreamshoteldalat.com; 151 & 164b Đ Phan Dinh Phung; s/d US$22/27;) An incredibly hospitable guesthouse owned by a family that looks after its guests with affection and care. Boasts spotless rooms, a breakfast spread, and hot tub and sauna.

Dalat Train Villa APARTMENT $$
(☎063-381 6365; www.dalattrainvilla.com; 1 Đ Quang Trung; d US$35-45, f US$75;) Three stunning French-era villas that have been sensitively converted into apartments with lounges and kitchens, family rooms perfect for groups, and refined doubles. There's a converted train-carriage cafe on your doorstep for meals. About 2km east of the centre.

Zen Cafe & Villa GUESTHOUSE $$
(☎0994 799 518; www.zencafedalat.com; 27c Pham Hong Thai; r US$21-39;) Lodge in spacious, characterful rooms in a century-old French villa, surrounded by tranquil gardens, sufficiently high up to give you mountain views. Owners Axel and Mai Dung regale you with local anecdotes and the coffee served at their cafe is wonderful.

★Ana Mandara Villas Dalat BOUTIQUE HOTEL $$$
(☎063-355 5888; www.anamandara-resort.com; Đ Le Lai; r US$115-157;) Elegant property spread across seven lovingly restored French colonial villas. Finished in period furnishings, the villas have the option of private dining; most come with a fireplace in the lounge and all have wonderful panoramic views. The spa is glorious. Located in the suburbs.

Dalat Palace HISTORIC HOTEL $$$
(☎063-382 5444; www.dalatpalace.vn; 12 Đ Tran Phu; d/ste from US$135/252;) With unimpeded views of Xuan Huong Lake, this *grande dame* of hotels has vintage Citroën cars in its sweeping driveway, and lashings of wood panelling and period class. The opulence of French-colonial life has been splendidly preserved: claw-foot tubs, fireplaces, chandeliers and paintings. However, it can be empty at times, and consequently lack ambience. Look for online deals.

Ngoc Lan Hotel HOTEL $$$
(☎063-382 2136; www.ngoclanhotel.vn; 42 Đ Nguyen Chi Thanh; r/ste from US$75/143;) Luxury hotel where the rooms have clean white lines with stylish purple accents. The modern decor juxtaposes nicely with the colonial character of the building, including wooden floors and French windows. It's right in the heart of town, so expect some noise.

Eating

Dalat's restaurants make the most of the city's wealth of vegetables, grown in abundance in the temperate climate. Keep an eye out for avocado shakes and ice cream, and artichoke tea, said to lower blood pressure.

Trong Dong VIETNAMESE $
(☎063-382 1889; 220 Đ Phan Dinh Phung; meals 80,000-120,000d; 11.30am-3pm & 5.30-9.30pm;) Intimate restaurant run by a very hospitable team where the creative menu includes such delights as shrimp paste on a sugarcane stick, beef wrapped in *la lut* leaf, and fiery lemongrass and chilli squid.

One More Cafe CAFE $
(77 Đ Hai Ba Trung; cake 25,000d; 8am-9pm, closed Wed;) Comfy chairs to sink into,

eclectically lined peach walls and a glass display full of cakes greet you at this cosy, Aussie-run cafe. Linger over an array of teas, an espresso, an all-day breakfast or a smoothie.

Central Market VIETNAMESE $
(Cho Da Lat; meals from 20,000d; ⏲7am-3pm) For cheap eats in the day, head to the upper level of the Central Market. In the evening, food stalls pop up around the market along Nguyen Thi Minh Khai.

Da Quy VIETNAMESE $
(Wild Sunflower; 49 Đ Truong Cong Dinh; meals from 50,000d; ⏲8am-10pm) Run by Loc, a friendly English speaker, this place has a sophisticated ambience but unsophisticated prices. The traditional clay-pot dishes and hotpots are more exciting than the Western menu.

★**Restaurant Ichi** JAPANESE $$
(☎063-355 5098; 1 Đ Hoang Dieu; meals 100,000-300,000d; ⏲5.30-10pm Tue-Sun) Dalat's only truly genuine Japanese restaurant is compact, with subdued lighting and jazz in the background. Spicy tuna rolls, chicken yakitori and tempura are all fantastic, the bento boxes are a bargain and there's even *natto* for aficionados. Perch in front of the bar (with extensive whisky offerings from around the world) to watch sushi master Tommo at work.

V Cafe INTERNATIONAL $$
(☎063-352 0215; www.vcafedalatvietnam.com; 1/1 Đ Bui Thi Xuan; meals 89,000-145,000d; ⏲7am-10.30pm; 📶✍) Atmospheric bistro-style place that serves international cuisine, such as chicken curry Calcutta, veggie lasagne, Grandma's Hungarian goulash and Mexican-style quesadillas. The interior is decorated with atmospheric photography and there's live music every night from 7.30pm.

Windmills ITALIAN $$
(Đ Le Dai Hanh 1; meals 120,000-200,000d; ⏲11am-10pm; 📶✍) You won't be tilting at windmills at this cute-as-a-button cafe that specialises in Dalat's best pizza and classic pasta dishes such as linguine vongole. But even if you're not tucking into a *quattro*

EASY RIDING IN THE CENTRAL HIGHLANDS

For many travellers, the highlight of their trip to the highlands is an off-the-beaten-track motorcycle tour with an Easy Rider. Besides the romance of cruising down endless highways, the Easy Riders' stock-in-trade is good company and insider knowledge, providing a brief but intimate window into highland life.

The flip side to the popularity of the Easy Riders is that now everyone claims to be one. Some Easy Riders have banded together to protect 'their' brand, donning blue jackets and charging membership fees. Similarly, in Danang, Hoi An and Nha Trang, the Easy Rider moniker applies to other packs of motorcycle guides.

Whether you're speaking to a jacket-wearing chap or an indie-spirited upstart, it's prudent to find out just what they can show you that you can't see on your own. Easy Rider excursions start at US$25 for a day ride close to Dalat, ramping up to US$60 to US$75 per day for extended trips across the highlands and to the coast, or even all the way to Hanoi.

Not every jacketed Easy Rider is a good guide and many freelance riders are perfectly talented guides. Most riders can produce a logbook of glowing testimonials from past clients; also check internet forums for recommendations.

Before you commit to a long-haul trip, it's a good idea to test a rider out with a day trip. Consider the following:

- Is the driver safe?
- How is the driver's command of English?
- Can you spend the next 48 hours or more with the driver?
- Are your bags safely strapped on the bike?
- Is the seat padded and the helmet comfortable (and clean)?
- Are rain ponchos provided?

One more important element to consider is the route. The most beautiful roads in southern Vietnam are the scenic back roads between Dalat, Buon Ma Thuot, Pleiku and Kon Tum (the main road linking the four isn't hugely attractive), plus the coastal highways that link Dalat to Mui Ne and Nha Trang.

NATIONAL HIGHWAY 20: ROADSIDE ATTRACTIONS

Open-tour buses, private cars and Easy Riders with passengers tackle the twists and turns from Ho Chi Minh City to Dalat, and there are several possible stops along the way.

Langa Lake The HCMC–Dalat road (Hwy 20) spans this reservoir, which is traversed by a bridge. Lots of floating houses, where families harvest the fish underneath, can be seen here.

Volcanic Craters Near Dinh Quan on Hwy 20 there are three extinct yet impressive volcanoes. The craters date from the late Jurassic period, about 150 million years ago. You'll have to do a little walking to see the craters. One is on the left-hand side of the road, about 2km south of Dinh Quan, and another on the right-hand side about 8km beyond Dinh Quan, towards Dalat.

Underground Lava Tubes Almost halfway between Ho Chi Minh City and Dalat are rare underground caves that were formed as the surface lava cooled and solidified, while the hotter underground lava continued to flow, leaving a hollow space.

To find the lava tubes, first find the teak forest on Hwy 20 between the Km 120 and Km 124 markers. The children who live around the forest can point you to the entrance of the lava tubes. Take a torch (flashlight) and go with a guide.

formagghi, it's worth stopping by for the excellent cappuccinos and espressos.

Goc Ha Thanh VIETNAMESE **$$**
(53 Đ Truong Cong Dinh; meals 100,000-150,000d; 7am-10pm;) Casual place with attractive bamboo furnishings owned by a welcoming Hanoi couple. Strong on dishes such as coconut curry, hotpots, clay pots, tofu stir fries and noodles.

Nhat Ly VIETNAMESE **$$**
(88 Đ Phan Dinh Phung; meals 55,000-160,000d; 11am-9.30pm) This place serves hearty highland meals on tartan tablecloths including sumptuous hotpots, grilled meats and seafood – try the steamed crab in beer (1kg costs 320,000d). Draws plenty of locals: always a good sign.

Dalat Train Cafe INTERNATIONAL **$$**
(www.dalattrainvilla.com; 1 Đ Quang Trung; mains 79,000-155,000d; 7am-10pm;) Calling all trainspotters! Don't miss the opportunity to step inside this lovingly resorted French-era railway carriage for a snack or meal in a unique setting, surrounded by images of trains worldwide. The blue-cheese burger, spicy tofu and veggie lasagne are all solid choices. From Dalat Train Station, turn right, walk 80m up the hill and look for the sign on the left.

Long Hoa VIETNAMESE **$$**
(063-382 2934; 6 Đ 3 Thang 2; meals 50,000-150,000d; 11am-2.30pm & 5.30-9.30pm) A cosy bistro run by a Francophile owner. Westerners come here for the Vietnamese food; Vietnamese come here to try the steaks. Top off your meal with a glass of Dalat wine.

★**Le Rabelais** FRENCH **$$$**
(063-382 5444; www.dalatresorts.com; 12 Đ Tran Phu; meals 600,000-1,700,000d; 7am-10pm) The signature restaurant at the Dalat Palace is *the* colonial-style destination with the grandest of dining rooms and a spectacular terrace that looks down to the lakeshore. Set dinner menus (1,700,000d) offer the full treatment; otherwise treat yourself to flawless à la carte dishes, such as seared duck breast with orange or roast rack of lamb.

★**Ming Dynasty** CHINESE **$$$**
(063-381 3816; www.khaisilkorp.com; 7 Tran Hung Dao; mains 150,000-850,000d; noon-3pm & 7-10pm) Paintings of mountainous landscapes adorn the walls of this refined Chinese restaurant, with lake views from its terrace. Scroll through the iPad menu to select beautifully executed dishes such as Beijing duck, pork ribs with honey sauce, whole steamed grouper and flower crab with ginger and scallion.

Drinking & Entertainment

Dalat wine is served all over Vietnam. The reds are pleasantly light, while the whites tend to be heavy on the oak. Dalat has a limited but decent night scene.

La Viet COFFEE
(82 Đ Truong Cong Dinh; 7am-10pm) Is it an antique store? Is it a cafe? This cosy corner

beguiles with its riot of plants, old bicycle parts, birdcages, vintage telephones and antique pianos. Find a corner to perch in to sip some seriously good coffee.

Hangout BAR
(71 Đ Truong Cong Dinh; 11am-midnight;) Late-night watering hole popular with some of Dalat's Easy Riders, as well as visiting backpackers, with a relaxed vibe, a pool table and inexpensive beers. The owner, a fluent English speaker, is an excellent source of local information.

13 Cafe-Bar BAR
(13 Đ Tang Bat Ho; noon-11pm) This plant-filled terrace strung with twinkly lights and Chinese lanterns makes for a relaxed beer stop. The mellow soft rock-reggae soundtrack adds to the ambience and its burgers are seriously tasty.

★Escape Bar LIVE MUSIC
(www.escapebardalat.com; Basement, Muong Thanh Hotel, 4 Đ Phan Boi Chau; 4pm-midnight;) Outstanding live-music bar, owned by blues guitarist Curtis King who performs here nightly with a rotating band (from 9pm). Expect covers of Hendrix, The Eagles, The Doors and other classics, but the improvisation is such that each tune takes on a life of its own; travelling musicians are welcome to jam. The bar's decor, all 1970s chic, suits the sonics perfectly.

Beepub LIVE MUSIC
(74 Đ Truong Cong Dinh; 5.30pm-late) On good nights the owner leads the place in a hot jam session, and there are occasional DJ nights. On bad nights the volume is cranked up loud enough to summon the police, and it's set to get even louder when the bar next door starts its own music nights.

Shopping

There's a good selection of Vietnamese coffee in Dalat; check out the shops in and around the Central Market.

Information

Lam Dong General Hospital (063-382 1369; 4 Đ Pham Ngoc Thach; 24hr) Emergency medical care.

Main Post Office (14 Đ Tran Phu; 7am-6pm)

Sinh Tourist (063-382 2663; www.thesinhtourist.vn; 22 Đ Bui Thi Xuan; 8am-7pm) Tours, including city sightseeing trips, and open-tour bus bookings.

Vietcombank (6 Đ Nguyen Thi Minh Khai; 7.30am-3pm Mon-Fri, to 1pm Sat) Changes travellers cheques and foreign currencies.

Getting There & Away

AIR

There are regular flights with Vietnam Airlines, VietJet Air and Jetstar, including a daily service to Danang (1¼ hours), four daily to Hanoi (1¾ hours) and HCMC (45 minutes), and two weekly to Can Tho (1¼ hours).

Lien Khuong Airport The airport is 30km south of Dalat.

BUS

Dalat is a major stop for open-tour buses. The Sinh Tourist has daily buses to Mui Ne, Nha Trang and HCMC.

Long-Distance Bus Station (Ben Xe Lien Tinh Da Lat; Đ 3 Thang 4) Dalat's long-distance bus station is 1.5km south of Xuan Huong Lake, and is dominated by smart Phuong Trang buses that offer free hotel pick-ups and drop-offs and cover all main regional destinations.

CAR & MOTORCYCLE

From Nha Trang, a high road offers spectacular views – a dream for motorbikers and cyclists –

BUSES FROM DALAT

DESTINATION	COST (D)	DURATION (HR)	FREQUENCY	DISTANCE
Buon Ma Thuot	110,000	5	9 daily	200km
Can Tho	320,000	11	2 daily at 7am & 7pm	461km
Danang	270,000	15	3 daily	660km
HCMC	230,000	7-8	every 30min	306km
Kon Tum	280,000	11	2 daily at 4am & 4.30am	272km
Nha Trang	135,000	4-5	17 daily	136km
Pleiku	210,000-230,000	9	3 daily	409km

DON'T MISS

DAMBRI FALLS

Located one hundred and thirty kilometres south of Dalat, en route to Bao Loc and Ho Chi Minh City, **Dambri Falls** (admission 10,000d; 7am-5pm) are one of the highest (90m), most magnificent and easily accessible waterfalls in Vietnam that are worth visiting even in the dry season. For some incredible views, ride the **vertical cable car** (5000d) or trudge up the steep path to the top of the falls.

A second path leads down some steep stairs to the front of the falls for more great views, and carries on down to the smaller **Dasara Falls**.

The road to the falls branches off Hwy 20 18km north of Bao Loc.

hitting 1700m at Hon Giao mountain and following a breathtaking 33km pass.

Hwy 27 to Buon Ma Thuot is scenic but potholed. A major new road is being built between Dalat and Buon Ma Thuot that bypasses the airport.

Getting Around

TO/FROM THE AIRPORT

The Vietnam Airlines bus between Lien Khuong Airport and Dalat (40,000d, 40 minutes) is timed around flights. It leaves from in front of the Ngoc Phat Hotel at 10 Đ Ho Tung Mau two hours before each departure; your lodgings can organise a free shuttle to pick you up.

A transfer company offers taxi services to Dalat from the airport for a fixed 180,000d; fixed-fee taxis from Dalat are 200,000d. Metered taxis cost around 430,000d.

BICYCLE

The hilly terrain makes it sweaty work getting around Dalat. Several hotels rent out bicycles and some provide them free to guests. Cycling tours available.

CAR

Daily rentals (with driver) start at US$50.

MOTORCYCLE

For short trips around town (around 20,000d), *xe om* drivers can be flagged down around the Central Market area. Self-drive motorbikes are 150,000d to 200,000d per day.

TAXI

For reliable taxis try **Mai Linh** (063-352 1111).

Ngoan Muc Pass

The spectacular Ngoan Muc Pass is 43km southeast of Dalat. On a clear day you can see the ocean, 55km away. As the highway winds down the mountain it passes under two gargantuan water pipes that link the lake with the hydroelectric power station at the base of the pass.

South of the road (to the right as you face the ocean) you can see the steep tracks of the crémaillère linking Thap Cham with Dalat. At the top of the pass there's a **waterfall** next to the highway, pine forests and an old train station.

Cat Tien National Park

061 / ELEV 700M

Cat Tien (061-366 9228; www.cattiennationalpark.vn; adult/child 50,000/20,000d; 7am-10pm) comprises an amazingly biodiverse area of lowland tropical rainforest. The 72,000-hectare park is one of the outstanding natural treasures in Vietnam, and the hiking, mountain biking and birdwatching here are the best in the south of the country. Always call ahead for reservations as the park can accommodate only a limited number of visitors. However, a word of caution: visitors have to be really lucky to see any of the larger mammals resident in the park, so don't come expecting to encounter tigers and elephants.

Cat Tien was hit hard by defoliants during the American War, but the large old-growth trees survived and the smaller plants have recovered. In 2001 Unesco added Cat Tien National Park to its list of biosphere reserves. As there are good overnight options, it's worth spending at least two full days here, if possible.

Fauna in the park includes 100 types of mammal including the bison-like guar, 79 types of reptile, 41 amphibian species, plus an incredible array of insects, including 400 or so butterfly species. Of the 350-plus birds, rare species include the orange-necked partridge and Siamese fireback.

Sights & Activities

Cat Tien National Park can be explored on foot, by mountain bike, by 4WD and also by boat along the Dong Nai River. There are 14 well-established **hiking trails** in the park, colour-coded by the level of difficulty and ranging from 2km to 26km in length.

Some are flat and paved, while others are demanding, muddy slogs that require crossing streams. Only the three most difficult trails require the services of a guide, as well as transport to and from the start of the trail.

If you need a guide, be sure to book one in advance; guides charge 800,000d for birdwatching excursions and 1,200,000 per day trek, regardless of group size. Take plenty of insect repellent. Leeches keep you company; you can rent 'leech socks' at the park HQ for a small fee.

★Dao Tien Endangered Primate Species Centre NATURE RESERVE

(www.go-east.org; adult/child incl boat ride 300,000/150,000d; ⏲tours 8.30am & 2pm) This centre, on an island in the Dong Nai River, is a rehabilitation centre hosting golden-cheeked gibbons, pygmy loris (both endemic to Vietnam and Cambodia), black-shanked douc and silvered langur that have been illegally trafficked. The eventual goal is to release the primates back into the forest. You can view gibbons in a semiwild environment and hear their incredible calls.

Hundreds of native fruit-tree saplings were planted on the island to provide the primates with foraging territory, and encourage them to learn the necessary skills to move around the forest canopy.

The centre's current focus is preserving the pygmy loris from extinction. Several of the rescued animals may never be released into the wild, as hunters tore out their poisonous teeth, without which they can't fend for themselves. The Dao Tien website allows you to 'adopt' individual animals.

Crocodile Lake LAKE

(Bau Sau; admission 200,000d, guide fee 500,000d, boat trip 450,000d) Crocodile Lake is one of the park highlights, reachable via two different routes. The more straightforward option involves a 9km drive or bike ride from the park headquarters and a 5km trek to the swamp; the walk takes about three hours return. Alternatively, you can trek all the way with a guide along a tougher jungle route criss-crossed by streams. Night treks are popular, as you've the chance of seeing crocs then, as well as other wildlife.

Cat Tien Bear & Wild Cat Rescue Station WILDLIFE RESERVE

(admission 150,000d; ⏲7.30am-4pm) Inside the national park, near the park headquarters, this rescue centre is home to nine sun bears and 25 black bears, rescued from poachers and/or bear bile farms. Other rescued animals include a small leopard and several yellow-cheeked gibbons. The conditions are not ideal, though the bears space-share a large outdoor area in which they're let loose every morning. The centre is due to relocate into new, larger premises 3km away by mid-2016.

Sleeping & Eating

The national park runs accommodation options that are handy for early morning trekking; you'll also avoid paying for repeat river crossings. There are some good,

WILD GIBBON TREK

Golden-cheeked gibbons have been reintroduced into Cat Tien and this experience offers a rare insight into the lives of these charismatic primates. The trek (US$60 per person, maximum four people) runs daily from the park HQ and involves a 5am start to get out to the gibbons in time for their dawn chorus; you have a chance to watch two separate gibbon families go about their everyday business.

Golden-cheeked gibbons are very territorial, with dominant females, and live in nuclear family groups, with the young staying with their mother for up to eight years. As with most other endangered creatures in Vietnam, they're hunted for the illegal pet trade, with parents killed and babies taken away, and also for dubious traditional medicine purposes.

The trip includes a fully guided tour of the Dao Tien primate centre, typically done at 8.30am, straight after the trek. The wild gibbon trek is now run by the park authorities, with the support of **Go East** (www.go-east.org), and requires you to stay in park-run accommodation the night before, as river crossings in the dark are too dangerous. All proceeds are ploughed back into the national park and assist the rangers in their protection efforts. To avoid disappointment, book in advance through cattienvietnam@gmail.com, or call ahead (☎061-366 9228).

privately run lodges just outside the park entrance that are considerably more comfortable; all have restaurants. Avoid weekends and holidays if possible, when locals descend in large numbers.

★ **Ta Lai Long House** GUESTHOUSE $
(☎0935 160 730; www.talai-adventure.vn; dm 315,000d; ❄ ☎ 👪) Excellent, traditional-style lodge managed by Westerners and locals from the S'Tieng and Ma minorities. Accommodation is in a well-constructed timber longhouse, with good, screened bedding, modern facilities and plenty of activities on offer. It's a 12km bicycle ride from the park HQ in the indigenous village of Ta Lai.

River Lodge LODGE $
(☎0973 346 345; r US$12; ❄ ☎) A 250m walk from the ferry crossing, River Lodge (aka Green Bamboo Lodge) consists of a cluster of thatched bamboo-and-brick bungalows (with plug-in air-con and fan) overlooking the rolling river. It's run by a friendly family and their restaurant serves decent standards.

Cat Tien National Park GUESTHOUSE $
(☎061-366 9228; cattienvietnam@gmail.com; dm/d/tr from 80,000/200,000/680,000d, 2-person tents 200,000d; ❄ ☎) Rooms at the national park's HQ are fairly basic and overpriced but include a bathroom. There are also canvas tents for couples and large tents (sleeping up to 12) that operate on a communal basis. There are two simple places to eat near the park HQ: a canteen and a slightly fancier restaurant.

★ **Forest Floor Lodge** LODGE $$$
(☎061-366 9890; www.forestfloorlodge.com; luxury tents or houses US$125; ❄ ☎) This ecolodge – inside the national park – sets the standard for atmospheric accommodation in Vietnam's protected areas. There are three lovely safari tents overlooking the river rapids, and larger, stylish rooms set in traditional wooden houses. The lodge is located across from the Dao Tien primate centre, so it's often possible to see and hear gibbons on the island.

ℹ Information

Guides and tours are booked and paid for at the park headquarters across the river from the majority of lodgings. A ferry makes frequent crossings of the Dong Nai River between 7am and 7pm. Park entry (which includes river crossings) of 40,000d is paid at the ticket booth by the ferry.

ℹ Getting There & Around

BICYCLE

Guesthouses either rent or provide bicycles free of charge. You can also rent pricey bicycles at park headquarters for 30,000d per hour or 150,000d per day.

BOAT

One approach to Cat Tien National Park is to take a boat across Langa Lake and then go by foot from there. Phat Tire Ventures (p293) is a reputable ecotour operator in Dalat that can offer this option.

BUS

All buses between Dalat and HCMC (every 30 minutes) pass the junction Vuon Quoc Gia Cat Tien on Hwy 20 for the park. The junction is around four hours' travel (190,000d to 200,000d) from both cities. From this junction, you can hire a *xe om* (around 170,000d, but negotiate very hard) to cover the remaining 24km to the park. Lodges can also arrange a transfer to/from the main road.

TOUR

Sinhbalo Adventures (p355) runs recommended tours to Cat Tien from Ho Chi Minh City.

Lak Lake

The largest natural body of water in the central highlands, Lak Lake (Ho Lak) is surrounded by bucolic rural scenery. There are several minority villages scattered around the lake, two of which often receive visitors. You can get paddled out into the blue, reed-covered expanse for around US$15 an hour.

On the south shores near the town of Lien Son lies **Jun village**, a fairly traditional M'nong settlement filled with rattan and wooden stilt houses. **DakLak Tourist** (☎0500-385 2246; www.daklaktourist.com.vn) has a small office by the lake and can organise trekking guides (US$20 per day). It also offers elephant rides, though these are not recommended, since the elephants are saddled with bulky, heavy metal seats and mahouts frequently cram three riders into a single seat (see boxed text, p472).

The second village of **M'lieng** is on the southwestern shore and can be reached by elephant, boat or new dirt road; enquire at DakLak Tourist.

Sleeping & Eating

Accommodation leaves something to be desired. There are some new homestays along the main road through the village, consisting of mattresses and mozzie nets inside rather hot concrete longhouses. There are still no decent restaurants near the lake.

Cafe Duc Mai GUESTHOUSE $
(☎0500-358 6280; 268 Đ Nguyen Tat Thanh; per person US$5) Mr Duc at Cafe Duc Mai speaks a few words of English and can organise a mattress in one of several traditional, thatched stilt longhouses, as well as gong concerts, elephant rides, and kayaking or walking tours.

Getting There & Away

Nine daily buses connecting Dalat (95,000d, four hours) and Buon Ma Thuot (30,000d, one hour) pass the lake. It's also regularly visited on the Easy Rider trail. All the tour agencies in Buon Ma Thuot also offer day tours.

Buon Ma Thuot

☎0500 / POP 211,891 / ELEV 451M

The Ede name translates as 'Thuot's father's village', but Buon Ma Thuot has outgrown its rustic origins without acquiring any real charm. An affluent, modern, but rather characterless city (pronounced 'boon me tote'), it is inundated by traffic from three highways.

Its two saving graces are its museum and its coffee: the region grows some of the best in Vietnam, plenty of which is sold and drunk in town. Buon Ma Thuot plays host to an annual Coffee Festival in March that sees gallons of the black nectar drunk and elephant races held in nearby Don village.

Most travellers stop in Buon Ma Thuot en route to the attractions located around it: Yok Don National Park, a couple of striking waterfalls and heaps of minority villages. The province is home to 44 ethnic groups, the dominant groups being the Ede, Jarai, M'nong and Lao.

Sights & Activities

★Ethnographic Museum MUSEUM
(Bao Tang Tinh Daklak; Đ Y Nong; admission 20,000d; ⏲8am-4pm) This excellent museum takes you through the history of the Dak Lak province, from stone tools and bronze burial drums to the American War and its aftermath, written from the North Vietnamese perspective. Chortle at the natural history section with the wacky taxidermy and a demonic-looking deer! Marvel at the minority culture exhibits, with outstanding photography, displays of traditional clothing, musical instruments, and ritual objects such as the buffalo sacrifice pole, and learn about the seven-year tomb abandoning ceremony.

Victory Monument MONUMENT
This monument commemorates the events of 10 March 1975 when VC and North Vietnamese troops liberated the city. It's an interesting piece of socialist realist sculpture, consisting of a column supporting a central group of figures holding a flag, with a modernist arch forming a rainbow over a concrete replica tank.

Sleeping

Ngoc Mai Mini Hotel HOTEL $
(☎0500-385 3406; ethnictour@gmail.com; B14 Đ So 1/Đ Dien Bien Phu; s/d 180,000/250,000d; ❄📶) The closest thing that Buon Ma Thuot has to a hostel, this cheapie attracts international travellers with its English- and French-speaking staff who can arrange tours of the area.

Eden Hotel HOTEL $
(☎0500-368 5666; www.edenhotelbmt.com.vn; 228 Đ Nguyen Cong Tru; r from 170,000d; ❄@📶) Clean budget joint popular with Easy Riders and their clients. Pluses include location on a fairly quiet street with numerous cafes and restaurants, friendly staff and fellow travellers to share a beer with.

★Coffee Tour Resort DESIGN HOTEL $$
(☎0500-357 5575; www.coffeetour.com.vn; 149-153 Ly Thai To; r incl breakfast 600,000-1,000,000d; ❄📶) It's hard to believe that greenery and silence exist in such close proximity to Buon Ma Thuot city centre, but here it is: an artistic representation of an Ede longhouse set amid landscaped grounds, complete with spotless rooms with bath-tubs and massive TVs. Out back is an adorable cafe in the shape of an actual Ede longhouse, serving great coffee.

Saigon Ban Me Hotel HOTEL $$$
(☎0500-368 5666; www.saigonbanmehotel.com.vn; 1-3 Đ Phan Chu Trinh; r 1,207,000-2,310,000d; ❄📶🏊) This gleaming tower rises above the most central intersection in town, but guests at Buon Ma Thuot's swishest hotel are sufficiently high up and well-insulated from street sounds. Expect spacious, carpeted,

Buon Ma Thuot

Buon Ma Thuot

Top Sights
1 Ethnographic Museum........A4

Sights
2 Victory Monument........B2

Sleeping
3 Eden Hotel........D2
4 Ngoc Mai Mini Hotel........A2
5 Saigon Ban Me Hotel........B2

Eating
6 Thanh Tram........A2

Drinking & Nightlife
7 Cafe Hoa Da Quy........D2

Information
8 DakLak Tourist........A2
9 Vietnam Highland Travel........A2

business-hotel-standard lodgings. Staff are friendly and speak some English.

Eating & Drinking

For a coffee or a beer, Đ Nguyen Cong Tru has scores of atmospheric places.

★ Thanh Tram VIETNAMESE $
(22 Đ Ly Thuong Kiet; meals 30,000d; ⏲10.30am-9pm) There's only one dish here: delicious, roll-your-own *nem nuong* (rice-paper rolls, with salad and herbs, fried pork sausage and raw garlic, served with either peanut sauce or fish sauce and chilli).

King Mark Pizza PIZZA $$
(113 Đ Le Thanh Tong; pizza 119,000-185,000d; ⏲noon-10pm;) Run by Sicilian Marco, whose staff bake their wares in a proper pizza oven, this is your best bet for Western food in town if you're feeling a bit homesick. There's a short and sweet pizza menu and some good fresh fruit juices to accompany it.

BUSES FROM BUON MA THUOT

DESTINATION	COST (D)	DURATION (HR)	FREQUENCY	DISTANCE
Dalat	110,000	4	7 daily	201km
Danang	290,000	11	10 daily	558km
HCMC	215,000	8-9	every 30min	319km
Kon Tum	110,000	5	8 daily	229km
Nha Trang	99,000	4½	15 daily	196km
Pleiku	100,000-150,000	4	every 30min	207km

Cafe Hoa Da Quy COFFEE
(173 Đ Nguyen Cong Tru; 9am-10pm;) Casual, open-sided, three-storey cafe with rattan seating and a rooftop bar. Good spot for a *ca phe sua da* (iced coffee) and an inexpensive collection of cocktails.

Shopping

Stock up on coffee here, as the price is lower and the quality higher than in HCMC or Hanoi. Browse the coffee shop strip on Đ Ly Thuong Kiet before you buy.

Information

Permits are required to visit most minority villages in the area. Local travel agencies can make the arrangements.

Agribank (37 Đ Phan Boi Chau; 7.30am-2.30pm Mon-Sat) Changes currency and travellers cheques.

DakLak Tourist (0500-385 8243; www.daklaktourist.com.vn; 51 Đ Ly Thuong Kiet) On the ground floor of Thanh Cong Hotel; offers tours of villages, waterfalls, Lak Lake and Yok Don National Park.

Vietnam Highland Travel (0500-385 5009; www.vietnamhighlandtravel.com; 24 Đ Ly Thuong Kiet) Experienced guides, homestays and off-the-beaten-track trekking trips.

Getting There & Around

AIR

There are regular flights with Vietnam Airlines, VietJet Air and Jetstar, including five daily flights to HCMC, two daily to Hanoi, and daily flights to Danang and Vinh.

Buon Ma Thuot Airport (Cang Hang Khong Buon Ma Thuot; Hoa Thang) The airport is 8km east of town; a taxi should cost about 140,000d.

BUS

Bus Station (Ben Xe Lien Tinh Dak Lak; 71 Đ Nguyen Chi Thanh) The bus station is about 4km from the centre. Buon Ma Thuot is often called 'Dak Lak' (the province it is located in) on bus timetables.

CAR & MOTORCYCLE

Well-maintained though fairly steep Hwy 26 links the coast with Buon Ma Thuot, intersecting Hwy 1A at Ninh Hoa (157km), 34km north of Nha Trang. Hwy 14 to Pleiku (199km) is in good shape, while Hwy 27 to Dalat is scenic but potholed.

TAXI

For reliable metered fares, use **Mai Linh** (0500-381 9819).

Around Buon Ma Thuot

0500

Yok Don National Park

Yok Don National Park (0500-378 3049; www.yokdonnationalpark.vn; admission 40,000d), the largest of Vietnam's nature reserves, has been gradually expanded and today encompasses 115,000 hectares of mainly dry deciduous forest. The park runs all the way up to the border with Cambodia, with the beautiful Srepok River flowing through it.

Unfortunately, deforestation is a big problem, particularly in the region closest to the entrance, and poaching is an ongoing issue.

Yok Don is home to 89 mammal species including wild elephants, tigers, leopards and rare red wolves. However, these exotica are very rare (and virtually never encountered by visitors). More common wildlife includes muntjac deer, monkeys and snakes. Numerous bird species live in the park, including storks and two types of hornbills.

Within the park's boundaries are four **minority villages**, predominantly M'nong but also with Ede and Lao people. Three villages are accessible (one by boat from the park office) while the fourth is deep inside the park and out of bounds.

The delicate balance between ecological conservation and the preservation of local cultures is a challenge, considering the poverty of the region's people and their traditional means of survival, such as hunting.

HO CHI MINH TRAIL

This legendary route was not one but many paths that formed the major supply link for the North Vietnamese and VC during the American War. Supplies and troops leaving from the port of Vinh headed inland along mountainous jungle paths, crossing in and out of Laos, and eventually arrived near Saigon. With all the secrecy, propaganda and confusion regarding the trail, it's hard to say how long it was in full; estimates range from over 5500km (said the US military) to more than 13,000km (boasted the North Vietnamese).

While elephants were initially used to cross the Truong Son Mountains into Laos, eventually it was sheer human power that shouldered supplies down the trail, sometimes supplemented by ponies, bicycles or trucks. Travelling from the 17th Parallel to the vicinity of Saigon took about six months in the mid-1960s; years later, with a more complex network of paths, the journey took only six weeks but it was still hard going.

Each person started out with a 36kg pack of supplies, as well as a few personal items (eg a tent, a spare uniform and snake antivenom). What lay ahead was a rugged and mountainous route, plagued by flooding, disease and the constant threat of American bombing. At their peak, more than 500 American air strikes hit the trail every day and more ordnance was dropped on it than was used in all the theatres of war in WWII.

Despite these shock-and-awe tactics and the elaborate electronic sensors along the McNamara Line, the trail was never blocked. Most of it has returned to the jungle, but you can still follow sections of the trail today. Note that this is usually the more developed trail from the early 1970s, as the older trail was over the border in Laos. The **Ho Chi Minh Highway** is the easiest way to get a fix; it's a scenic mountain road running along the spine of the country. Starting near Hanoi, it passes through some popular tourist destinations and former battlefields, including the Phong Nha caves, Khe Sanh, Aluoi, Kon Tum and Buon Ma Thuot on its way to Saigon. The most spectacular sections include the roller-coaster ride through the Phong Nha-Ke Bang National Park, where looming karsts are cloaked in jungle.

Travel this route by car (or 4WD), motorbike or even bicycle if you are training for the King of the Mountains jersey; or arrange a tour through the Easy Riders in Dalat or one of the leading motorbike touring companies in Hanoi. **Explore Indochina** (www.exploreindochina.com) specialises in trail tours. **Hoi An Motorbike Adventures** (www.motorbiketours-hoian.com) offers shorter rides along sections between Hoi An and Phong Nha and a loop from Hoi An to Hue via the Hai Van Pass.

To explore the national park, it's best to engage a guide at the park office.

Activities

Book various tours and activities at the national park office inside the park entrance.

Elephant Care ANIMAL ENCOUNTER

(2 people 600,000d) Aimed squarely at foreign visitors who express concern regarding elephant welfare, this tour leaves at 6am and allows visitors to get to know the pachyderms by assisting the mahouts with their daily care, including bathing them in the river. Fifteen-minute bareback ride is included; book the tour the night before.

Visitors should be aware that animal welfare groups advocate that carrying loads is detrimental to the elephant's health.

Trekking TREKKING

There are various hiking trails inside the national park forest and guided treks can be arranged, ranging from two hours to three days (including overnight camping). Expect to pay around 400,000d for a day trek and around 3,000,000d for three days' worth of forest adventure, including food and tents.

Birdwatching BIRDWATCHING

Treks in the jungle can be arranged with an emphasis on birdwatching. Guide prices range from 400,000d for a day's watching to 3,000,000d for a three-day trek with camping.

Cooking Course COOKING COURSE

(per person 400,000d) Immerse yourself in Ede life in Buon Don village by signing up for a four-hour cooking course with a local family before 9am. You'll assist the family with lunch or dinner preparation and share the meal with them afterwards.

Sleeping & Eating

There's a convenient guesthouse inside the park, near the park entrance. Basic stilt houses and bungalows cater overwhelmingly to domestic tourists and are located 5km northwest of the park entrance, by the Buon Don Tourist Centre (also catering to local tourists). There's a restaurant in Buon Don (meals from 40,000d) and a basic canteen by the guesthouse inside the park entrance.

Yok Don Guesthouse GUESTHOUSE **$**
(0500-378 3049; r US$20;) Inside the park, just up the road from the park entrance, this guesthouse offers clean, slightly musty tiled rooms with TVs.

Stilt Houses LONGHOUSE **$$**
(per person 180,000d) A couple of Ede stilt houses near the Buon Don Tourist Centre, 5km from the national park entrance, offer basic mattresses on the floor and mosquito nets.

Information

Yok Don National Park Ecotourism Education Centre (0500-378 3049; www.yokdonnationalpark.vn; 7am-5pm) From the national park entrance, a road runs up to this office and the official national park guesthouse by the river. This is by far the best place for foreign visitors to arrange English-speaking guides in the park. If possible, call Mr Vu Duc Gioi in advance to book tours and guides.

Getting There & Around

Local buses head from Buon Ma Thuot bus station to Yok Don National Park (20,000d, hourly).

Motorbike taxis in Buon Ma Thuot take you to the park for 220,000/350,000d one way/return.

Dray Sap, Gia Long & Dray Nur Falls

Located on the Krong Ana River, there are three **waterfalls** (0500-321 3194; admission 30,000d; 8am-6pm) you can visit; they are particularly splendid during the rainy season. From the ticket booth, the road forks. The right branch takes you to the Gia Long Falls along a gorgeous, forested 7km road. The falls plummet into a green-blue lake; according to legend, Gia Long Emperor and his concubines used to bathe here and you can follow their example by taking a narrow footpath down to a natural swimming pool (get your guide to point it out).

The left branch terminates in a car park after 1km. From the car park, there are two paths to the 100m-wide Dray Sap ('smoky falls' in Ede) waterfall. Steep steps lead down and you can follow a wooded path (600m) to a viewpoint; the other path takes you to the top of the falls, with yet another path branching off towards Nuoc Trang – a clear stream ideal for a cool dip.

The lower path towards the Dray Sap Falls passes by a **suspension bridge** that crosses the river. Since the suspension bridge was broken at research time, the only way to reach the Dray Nur Falls is by taking a circuitous route (25km one way).

Due to the many dams located on the Srepok River, the three sets of falls are reduced to trickles during the dry season.

The falls are signposted from Hwy 14; the turn-off is about 15km southwest of Buon Ma Thuot. Drive for another 11km through a small industrial zone, then farmland, before you arrive at the entrance.

Pleiku

059 / POP 162,051 / ELEV 785M

The rather forgettable capital of Gia Lai province, Pleiku is better known as a strategic American and South Vietnamese base during the American War than for any postwar accomplishments. It makes an adequate pit stop, but there's little to detain a traveller

GETTING TO CAMBODIA: PLEIKU TO BAN LUNG

Getting to the border Remote and rarely used by foreigners, the **Le Thanh/O Yadaw border crossing** is 90km from Pleiku and 64km from Ban Lung, Cambodia. From Pleiku there's a daily Noi Thinh bus at 7am (65,000d, two hours) from the main marketplace on Đ Tran Phu direct to the Cambodian border at Le Thanh, and another from the main bus terminal.

At the border Cambodian visas (US$30) are issued at the border; you may end up overpaying by a few dollars or be made to wait. Vietnamese visas need to be organised in advance.

Moving on From O Yadaw, on the Cambodia side of the border, local buses (around US$10) or motorbikes (around US$25) head to Ban Lung. There are far fewer transport options in the afternoon.

for more than a few hours. Torched by departing South Vietnamese soldiers in 1975, the city was rebuilt in the 1980s with help from the Soviet Union, which thoroughly explains its lack of architectural appeal today.

In 2001 and 2004 Pleiku was the scene of hill-tribe protests against the government. The surrounding area is perfectly safe for travellers but remains sensitive politically, so you'll need a permit to explore the province.

Sights

Gia Lai Museum MUSEUM
(Bao Tang Gia Lai; Đ Tran Hung Dao; 7.30-11am & 1.30-5pm Mon-Fri) FREE The most interesting exhibits here are the Bahnar artefacts, from household utensils, fine weaving and weaponry to a replica traditional grave and longhouse, as well as stone reliefs dating back to the Cham culture. In the natural history section, the taxidermy is hilarious, and there's the obligatory history section dedicated to Pleiku's role during the American War.

Minh Thanh Temple BUDDHIST TEMPLE
(Chua Minh Thanh; Nguyen Viet Xuan; dawn-dusk) FREE Built only a few years ago, this splendid Buddhist temple, surrounded by water features and statues, sits south of the city centre. Its proudest feature is a gorgeous nine-tiered pagoda that's lit up at night, and fearsome dragons curl up from the corners of the roof of the main temple building.

Sleeping & Eating

Local specialities include *pho kho* or *pho hai,* served in two bowls. One contains dry noodles topped with fried ground pork, onion, lettuce, bean sprouts and hot-chilli garlic sauce. The other bowl holds a broth with sliced beef or meatballs. Also look out for *thit bo nuong ong* (grilled beef in bamboo pipe).

Duc Long Gia Lai 1 Hotel HOTEL $
(059-387 6303; 95-97 Đ Hai Ba Trung; d/tr 340,000/485,000d;) Spacious, well-presented, pine-trimmed rooms (some with balconies and bath-tubs) and an elevator make this a popular choice. It also offers foot massages and hot-stone massages.

HAGL Hotel Pleiku HOTEL $$
(059-371 8450; www.haglhotelpleiku.vn; 1 Phu Dong; s/d/ste from US$50/60/180;) The opulent marble-rich lobby of this high-rise hotel sets a luxurious tone and the spacious, well-equipped rooms won't disappoint either, though the location is a short taxi ride from attractions. However, note that the parent company, the HAGL group, has been accused by Global Witness of breaching Cambodian laws related to forest clearing.

Com Ga Hai Nam VIETNAMESE $
(73 Đ Hai Ba Trung; meals 35,000-50,000d; 10am-8.30pm) This busy, simple place specialises in delicious crispy chicken and rice with a side salad of lettuce, tomato and onion.

Acacia Restaurant INTERNATIONAL $$
(1 Đ Phu Dong; mains 120,000-700,000d; 7am-11pm;) Inside the HAGL Hotel, the menu at this welcoming restaurant is a stampede through a vast variety of Asian (read: Chinese), Western and Vietnamese dishes. The latter – from snake-head fish soup to grilled squid with pineapple rice – work best, and there's a good range of veggie accompaniments.

Information

Permits and guide (costs vary) are compulsory to visit Bahnar and Jarai villages in Gia Lai prov-

BUSES FROM PLEIKU

DESTINATION	COST (D)	DURATION (HR)	FREQUENCY	DISTANCE
Attapeu, Laos	120,000	6	daily at 8am	246km
Ban Lung, Cambodia	65,000	3	daily at 7am	147km
Buon Ma Thuot	100,000-150,000	4	every 30min	215km
Dalat	210,000-230,000	9	3 daily	383km
Danang	160,000-200,000	7½	7 daily	340km
HCMC	250,000	11-12	at least 6 daily	509km
Kon Tum	25,000	1	frequent	48km
Nha Trang	145,000-170,000	7	3 daily	297km
Pakse, Laos	220,000	9	daily at 8am	497km

ince. This puts many travellers off, who usually skip Pleiku and head north to Kon Tum. All tourist agencies in town can make the necessary arrangements, though.

Gia Lai Tourist (☎059-350 0126; www.gialaiecotourist.com; 82 Đ Hung Vuong) Multiday tours of Vietnam, including through the highlands, led by English- and French-speaking guides.

Vietin Bank (1 Đ Tran Hung Dao; ⏰7am-3.30pm Mon-Fri, 7am-noon Sat) Foreign exchange and credit-card advances.

Getting There & Around

AIR

There are regular flights with Vietnam Airlines, VietJet Air and Jetstar, including daily flights to Danang (45 minutes), two flights daily to Hanoi (1½ hours) and five flights daily to HCMC (one hour).

Pleiku Airport (www.pleikuairport.vn; Thong Nhat) The airport is about 5km from the town and accessible by taxi (around 120,000d) or *xe om* (around 60,000d).

BUS

Minibuses for Kon Tum pick up passengers along Nguyen Tat Thanh and also depart from the Noi Tinh Bus Station. For buses to Attapeu and Pakse, Laos, see p306.

Gia Lai Bus Station (Ben Xe Duc Long Gia Lai; 45 Đ Ly Nam De) Pleiku's main bus station is located about 2.5km southeast of town. It serves most destinations, including those in Laos, but only a couple of buses run from here to Kon Tum. Pleiku is known as Gia Lai on most bus timetables.

Noi Tinh Bus Station (Ben Xe Noi Tinh; Đ Tran Phu) Some buses to Kon Tum and Noi Tinh buses to Cambodia run from the main marketplace car park in central Pleiku.

Kon Tum

☎060 / POP 86,362 / ELEV 525M

Kon Tum's relaxed ambience, river setting and relatively traffic-free streets make it a worthwhile stop for travellers intent on exploring the surrounding hill-tribe villages, of which there are 700 or so dotting the area – mostly Bahnar, but also Sedang and Jarai. You'll also find a few intriguing sights in town, and Kon Tum is a far better base than Pleiku for delving into indigenous culture.

The region saw its share of combat during the American War. A major battle between the South and North Vietnamese took place in and around Kon Tum in the spring of 1972, when the area was devastated by hundreds of American B-52 raids.

More recently, in the 2004 protests against government policies in the highlands, hill tribes in Kon Tum province clashed with police and soldiers. On the surface things have cooled off, but relations between the hill tribes and the authorities remain fraught.

Sights

Minority Villages

There are several clusters of Bahnar villages on the periphery of Kon Tum. Village life here centres on the traditional *rong (nha rong)*, a tall thatched-roof community house built on stilts. The *rong* is the focal point for festivals and doubles as a village meeting house and court. *Rong* roofs typically have decorations on top, or even woven into them. The stilts were originally there to provide protection from elephants, tigers and other animals. The traditional houses are also on stilts, with livestock residing underneath.

GETTING TO LAOS: KON TUM TO ATTAPEU

Getting to the border The **Bo Y/Phou Keau border crossing** lies 86km northwest of Kon Tum and 119km northeast of Attapeu (Laos). Attapeu- and Pakse-bound buses depart from Pleiku bus station at 8am, passing through Kon Tum around 9am; Kon Tum Tourist or your lodgings can arrange a ticket.

Crossing the border independently can be a challenge. On the Vietnam side, the nearest major town is Ngoc Hoi, 68km west of Kon Tum, which can be reached by bus (56,000d, 1½ hours). You'll have to catch a minibus from Ngoc Hoi to the border (15,000d, 30 minutes). There are also morning buses from Ngoc Hoi directly to Attapeu; get here as early as possible. On the Laos side, things are even quieter and you'll be at the mercy of passing traffic to hitch a ride onwards.

At the border Vietnamese visas aren't available at this border, but Lao visas are available for most nationalities (between US$30 and US$40, depending on your nationality).

Moving on Buses from Pleiku arrive in Attapeu around 2pm, where a free lunch is included as part of your fare if you're travelling with Mai Linh. You'll arrive in Pakse around 7pm.

Kon Tum

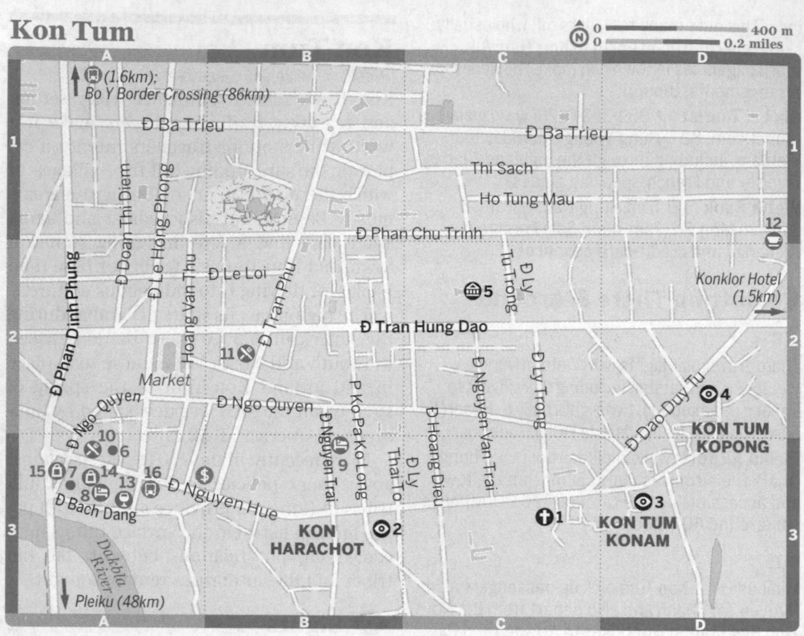

Further away are the more isolated Sedang villages and Jarai villages; the latter still practise traditional customs, such as the feeding of the dead in traditional cemeteries, as do the 'Hilltop' Bahnar. The rest have converted to Catholicism, only bury their dead once and don't 'feed' them.

Generally the local people welcome tourists and it's fine to explore the villages around Kon Tum under your own steam. But ask permission before pointing a camera into people's faces or homes.

Guided day trips to villages are available from about 500,000d for a guide/motorbike driver, depending on the places visited. Permits are included in the price and your guide has to notify the local police if you want to stay in a village overnight.

If you have time to spend several days here, An Nguyen, Highlands Eco Tours and Kon Tum Tourist can arrange village homestays. Because the guides are careful not to intrude too frequently on any one village, visitors are always welcomed and it's possible to participate in daily activities.

Kon Ktu
VILLAGE

Five kilometres southeast of Kon Tum, the village of Kon Ktu is reachable across the suspension bridge and along a potholed road. There's a beautiful *rong* here, near the Catholic church, and you can watch locals transporting crops along the river in rafts made of tyres.

Ya Chim
VILLAGE

This Jarai village, 17km from Kon Tum, has traditional cemeteries complete with wooden mourning figures. If you're lucky, you'll see villagers 'feeding' the dead by putting food down bamboo tubes leading into the graves.

Kon Jodreh
VILLAGE

Six kilometres east of Kon Tum, this village has a small *rong* and you can observe tranquil riverside activities.

Plei Thonghia
VILLAGE

This village is west of Kon Tum; you can watch local boys swimming with the cattle from the pastureland across the river.

Kon Klor
VILLAGE

Near the suspension bridge across the river you'll find a large, immaculate *rong* in the village of Kon Klor.

Kon Harachot
VILLAGE

Kon Harachot's beautiful *rong* sits next to the football field.

Kon Tum Konam
VILLAGE

Near Kon Harachot, this village has a large and appealing *rong*.

Kon Tum Kopong
VILLAGE

You may see villagers weaving baskets out of bamboo along the streets of Kon Tum Kopong village.

Other Sights

Immaculate Conception Cathedral
CHURCH

(Đ Nguyen Hue; ⌚dawn-dusk) Built entirely from wood, this stunning cathedral from the French era has a dark frontage, yellow trim and wide terraces. Inside it's light, airy and elegant, with incredible interlocking beams. Seating on all four sides faces a central altar. The heart of the 160-year-old Kon Tum diocese, it primarily serves the ethnic minority community, and the altar is bedecked in traditional woven fabrics. Local newlyweds tend to pose for photos on the steps.

Seminary & Hill-Tribe Museum
MUSEUM

(Đ Tran Hung Dao; ⌚7.30-11am & 2-5pm, closed Tue) FREE This lovely old Catholic seminary was built in 1934 and is fronted by a sculpture of Mary and baby Jesus; notice that Mary is carrying a Bahnar-style backpack and is dressed in traditional tribal patterns. The 'traditional room' upstairs functions as an absorbing museum of hill-tribe life and the Kon Tum diocese, with English descriptions of rites and excellent examples of funerial 'sorrow sculptures', Jarai coffins, traditional weavings, gongs and other musical instruments, and fishing and hunting paraphernalia.

Tours

★ An Nguyen
CULTURAL TOUR

(☎060-386 2944; evacoffee@ymail.com; 5 Phan Chu Trinh; day tours around US$80) Based at Eva Cafe, local scupltor An is a wonderfully knowledgeable local guide who can arrange anything from day tours of Bahnar villages to multiday in-depth explorations of indigenous culture, complete with local homestays. Contact him in advance, as he's very popular.

Highlands Eco Tours
CULTURAL TOUR

(☎060-391 2788; www.vietnamhighlands.com; 15 Đ Ho Tung Mau) Independently run travel company specialising in minority village trips, homestays in off-the-beaten-track communities, trekking and battlefield visits. From US$35 per day if going by motorbike.

Kon Tum Tourist
CULTURAL TOUR

(☎060-386 1626; www.kontumtourist.com; 2 Đ Phan Dinh Phung) Staff here can arrange tours to Bahnar and Jarai villages, including homestays. However, there isn't always an English speaker at the office.

Sleeping

★ Konklor Hotel
HOTEL $

(☎060-386 1555; www.konklorhotel.vn; d/q 360,000/427,000d; ❄📶) In a little green oasis of its own, this minihotel is 2km or so east of town, with large, wood-trimmed rooms and a shady cafe. Friendly staff speak English and there are bicycles and motorbikes (150,000d) for rent to get you into town. Popular with Easy Riders and their clients.

Thinh Vuon Hotel
HOTEL $

(☎060-391 4729; thinhvuonghotel.kontum@gmail.com; 17 Đ Nguyen Trai; s 200,000-230,000d, d 260,000-320,000d; ❄📶) On a quiet central street, this friendly hotel gets extra points for the helpfulness of its staff and the large, spotless rooms at bargain prices. The beds are strangely low, but that's our only quibble.

BUSES FROM KON TUM

DESTINATION	COST (D)	DURATION (HR)	FREQUENCY	DISTANCE
Buon Ma Thuot (Dak Lak)	140,000	5	7 daily	188km
Dalat	250,000	10	2 daily at 5am & 5.30am	433km
Danang	180,000	6½	16 daily	293km
HCMC	290,000	12	5 daily	550km
Hoi An	154,000	6½	2 daily	285km
Hue	210,000	8½	5 daily	445km
Nha Trang	238,000	8	2 daily	344km
Pleiku (Gia Lai)	25,000	1	every 30min	48km
Quy Nhon	90,000	4½	17 daily	190km

Indochine Hotel HOTEL **$$**
(☎060-386 3335; www.indochinehotel.vn; 30 Đ Bach Dang; s/d from US$25/30; ❄📶) Right on the riverbank, this large concrete hotel's spacious rooms enjoy great views and have all the mod cons. Prices include a breakfast buffet, and tours of the surrounding Bahnar villages are on offer, ranging from one to three days (from US$30 per person).

Eating & Drinking

Nem Ninh Hoa VIETNAMESE **$**
(15 Đ Tran Phu; meals 35,000d; ⏲11am-8pm) The only thing this informal little place serves are delicious *nem nuong* – roll-your-own spring rolls that incorporate Vietnamese pork sausage, green banana, cucumber, star fruit, assorted fresh herbs and lettuce.

★Dakbla's Restaurant VIETNAMESE **$$**
(168 Đ Nguyen Hue; meals 100,000-180,000d; ⏲8am-10pm; 📝) Half-museum and restaurant, this atmospheric place has good Vietnamese and Western menus that include plenty of vegetarian choices. For the anthropologically inclined, its walls are the real attraction, festooned as they are with (mostly) Bahnar artefacts and some superb photos.

★Eva Cafe CAFE
(1 Đ Phan Chu Trinh; ⏲7am-9pm) This neighbourhood cafe is a garden complete with totem poles, sculptures, treehouse-style spaces with gongs hanging overhead and tribal-style masks. A nice place to unwind with a beer, a coffee, or a salted lemonade as you admire the works of local sculptor An.

Indochine Coffee BAR
(30 Đ Bach Dang; ⏲7am-10pm) A highly unexpected find in deepest Kon Tum province, this modernist cafe, shaded by artistically arranged bamboo pillars and roofing, is where the hipsters hang. Join them for a tea, *ca phe sua da* or ice-cold Saigon.

Shopping

If you collect indigenous artefacts, Kon Tum and the surrounding villages are good places to shop. Items may be cheaper in the villages, but there's a better selection overall in Kon Tum.

Shop INDIGENOUS ARTEFACTS
(Đ Phan Dinh Phung; ⏲10am-8pm) This nameless shop next to Daklak Hotel stocks some choice Sedang and Bahnar hunter backpacks (1,000,000d to 1,500,000d), antique drums, crossbows and more.

Long Xanh INDIGENOUS ARTEFACTS
(137a Đ Nguyen Hue; ⏲10am-7pm) Amid touristy tat and replicas of *rong*, you'll also find some antique Sedang hunter backpacks, gongs, fish traps, rattan containers and replica Bahnar funerial masks (80,000d).

Information

BIDV ATM (1 Đ Tran Phu) Bank with ATM.

Getting There & Around

BUS

Buses to Pleiku depart from several locations, including a car park on Đ Nguyen Hue.

Bus Station (Ben Xe Kon Tum; 279 Đ Phan Dinh Phung) Kon Tum's main bus station has most long-distance services, including those to Laos.

TAXI

Mai Linh (☎060-395 5555) Reliable taxi service.

XE OM

Kon Tum is easy to traverse on foot, but *xe om* (20,000d for a short ride) are in ready supply. Drivers hang out by the Daklak Hotel.

Ho Chi Minh City

08 / POP 7.9 MILLION

Includes ➡

Why Go?

Ho Chi Minh City (HCMC) is Vietnam at its most dizzying: a high-octane city of commerce and culture that has driven the country forward with its pulsating energy. A chaotic whirl, the city breathes life and vitality into all who settle here, and visitors cannot help but be hauled along for the ride.

From the finest of hotels to the cheapest of guesthouses, the classiest of restaurants to the tastiest of street stalls, the choicest of boutiques to the scrum of the markets, HCMC is a city of energy and discovery.

Wander through timeless alleys to incense-infused temples before negotiating chic designer malls beneath sleek 21st-century skyscrapers. The ghosts of the past live on in buildings that one generation ago witnessed a city in turmoil, but now the real beauty of the former Saigon's urban collage is the seamless blending of these two worlds into one exciting mass.

Best Places to Eat

- ➡ Nha Hang Ngon (p341)
- ➡ Hum Lounge & Restaurant (p341)
- ➡ The Racha Room (p341)
- ➡ Cuc Gach Quan (p344)
- ➡ Propaganda (p341)

Best Places to Stay

- ➡ Lily's Hostel (p338)
- ➡ Town House 23 (p339)
- ➡ Ma Maison Boutique Hotel (p340)
- ➡ Park Hyatt Saigon (p335)
- ➡ Villa Song (p340)

When to Go

Ho Chi Minh City

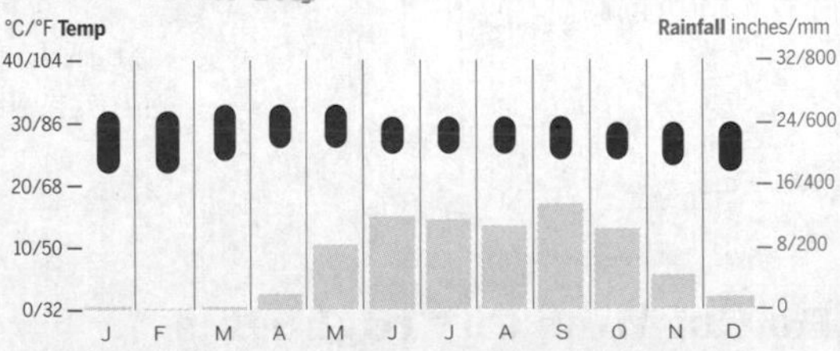

Feb Hardly any rain, the least humidity, and a city filled with blooms for the Tet celebrations.

Mar Low rain and humidity persist, plus the annual *cyclo* challenge.

Dec December is a whisper cooler than normal for HCMC and comparatively dry.

Ho Chi Minh City Highlights

1 Soaking up the city's electric energy from a high-altitude perch in one of its **rooftop bars** (p348).

2 Witnessing the turbulence of conflict in the **War Remnants Museum** (p321).

3 Feasting on an eye-opening selection of **local and international cuisine** (p340) at the city's standout restaurants and street stalls.

4 Smothering yourself in clouds of incense within the mystical world of the **Jade Emperor Pagoda** (p318).

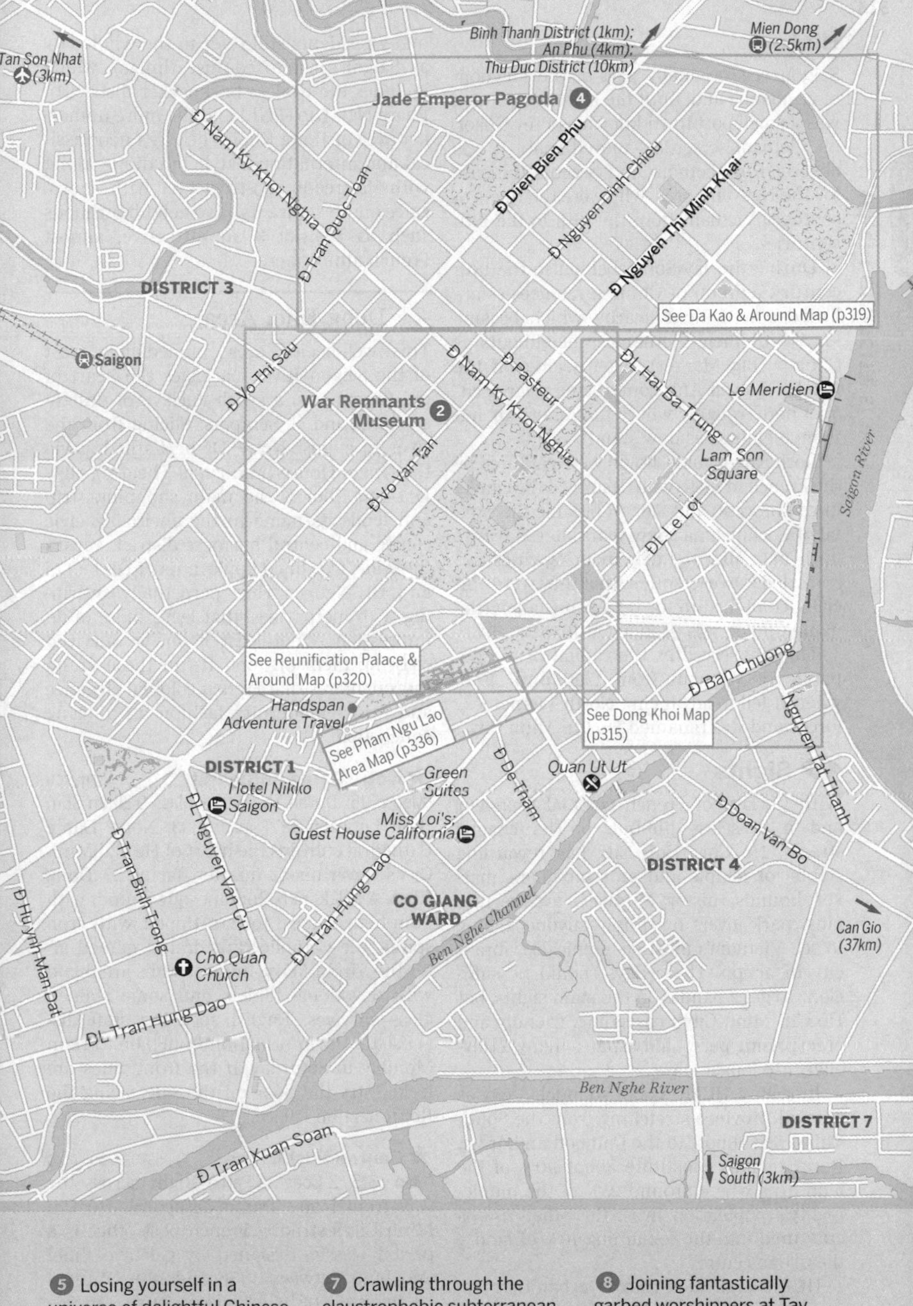

5 Losing yourself in a universe of delightful Chinese temples in **Cholon** (p324).

6 Tagging along with one of the entertaining **tours** (p333) of the city.

7 Crawling through the claustrophobic subterranean warren of the Viet Cong in the **Cu Chi Tunnels** (p361).

8 Joining fantastically garbed worshippers at Tay Ninh's astounding **Cao Dai Great Temple** (p363).

History

Saigon was originally part of the kingdom of Cambodia and, until the late 17th century, was a small port town known as Prey Nokor. As Vietnamese settlers moved south it was absorbed by Vietnam and became the base for the Nguyen Lords, who were the rulers of southern Vietnam from the 16th to the 18th centuries.

During the Tay Son rebellion in the 18th century, a group of Chinese refugees established a settlement nearby, which became known by their Vietnamese neighbours as Cholon (Big Market). After seeing off the rebels, Nguyen Anh constructed a large citadel here (roughly where the American and French embassies now stand).

Both Saigon and Cholon were captured by the French in 1859 (who destroyed the citadel in the process) and Saigon became the capital of Cochinchina a few years later. It wasn't until 1931, after the neighbouring cities had sprawled into each other, that they were officially combined to form Saigon-Cholon (the name Cholon was dropped in 1956).

The city served as the capital of the Republic of Vietnam from 1956 until 1975, when it fell to advancing North Vietnamese forces and was renamed Ho Chi Minh City.

Sights

With pockets of French colonial grandeur and a ceaseless hubbub on its chaotic streets, Ho Chi Minh City has rewarding sights for temple and museum-goers, market hounds, history junkies, architecture fans, park lovers or simply anyone itching to see Vietnam's most economically vibrant city in action. Three days should be sufficient to get a handle on the main sights, but Ho Chi Minh City's easygoing, friendly and enterprising personality snares many a traveller into longer stays.

In reality, HCMC is not so much a city as a small province stretching from the South China Sea almost to the Cambodian border. Rural regions constitute about 90% of the land area where around 25% of the municipality's population lives; the other 75% is crammed into the remaining 10% of land – the urban centre.

HCMC is divided into 19 urban districts (*quan,* derived from the French *quartier*) and five rural districts (*huyen,* derived from the Chinese *xian*). The majority of places and sights converge in District 1, the district still known as Saigon (although many residents still refer to the whole city as Saigon, just to confuse things), which includes the tireless backpacker district of Pham Ngu Lao (PNL) and the more upmarket area of Dong Khoi. The city's neoclassical and international-style buildings, along with its tree-lined streets set with shops, cafes and restaurants, give neighbourhoods such as District 3 an attractive, almost French atmosphere.

Dong Khoi Area

This well-heeled area, immediately west of the Saigon River, packages the heart of old Saigon into a swish enclave of designer stores and skyscrapers. Slicing from the river to august Notre Dame Cathedral via the Opera House (Municipal Theatre), ritzy Đ Dong Khoi is the main shopping strip and lends its name to the encircling civic centre and central business district. Yet it's the wide, tree-lined boulevards of ĐL Le Loi and ĐL Nguyen Hue, perpetually swarming with motorbikes, that leave more of an impression – not least if you've survived crossing them on foot. It's in these grand thoroughfares that French colonial elegance and urban modernity fashion an alluring concoction.

★Notre Dame Cathedral CHURCH
(Map p315; Đ Han Thuyen; Mass 9.30am Sun) Built between 1877 and 1883, Notre Dame Cathedral enlivens the heart of Ho Chi Minh City's government quarter, facing Đ Dong Khoi. A brick, neo-Romanesque church with 40m-high square towers tipped with iron spires, the Catholic cathedral is named after the Virgin Mary. Interior walls are inlaid with devotional tablets and some stained glass survives. English-speaking staff dispense tourist information from 9am to 11am Monday to Saturday. If the front gates are locked, try the door on the side facing the Reunification Palace.

★Central Post Office HISTORIC BUILDING
(Map p315; 2 Cong Xa Paris) Right across the way from Notre Dame Cathedral, Ho Chi Minh City's striking French post office is a period classic, designed by Gustave Eiffel and built between 1886 and 1891. Painted on the walls of its grand concourse are fascinating historic maps of South Vietnam, Saigon and Cholon, while a mosaic of Ho Chi Minh takes pride of place at the end of its barrel-vaulted hall. Note the magnificent

Dong Khoi

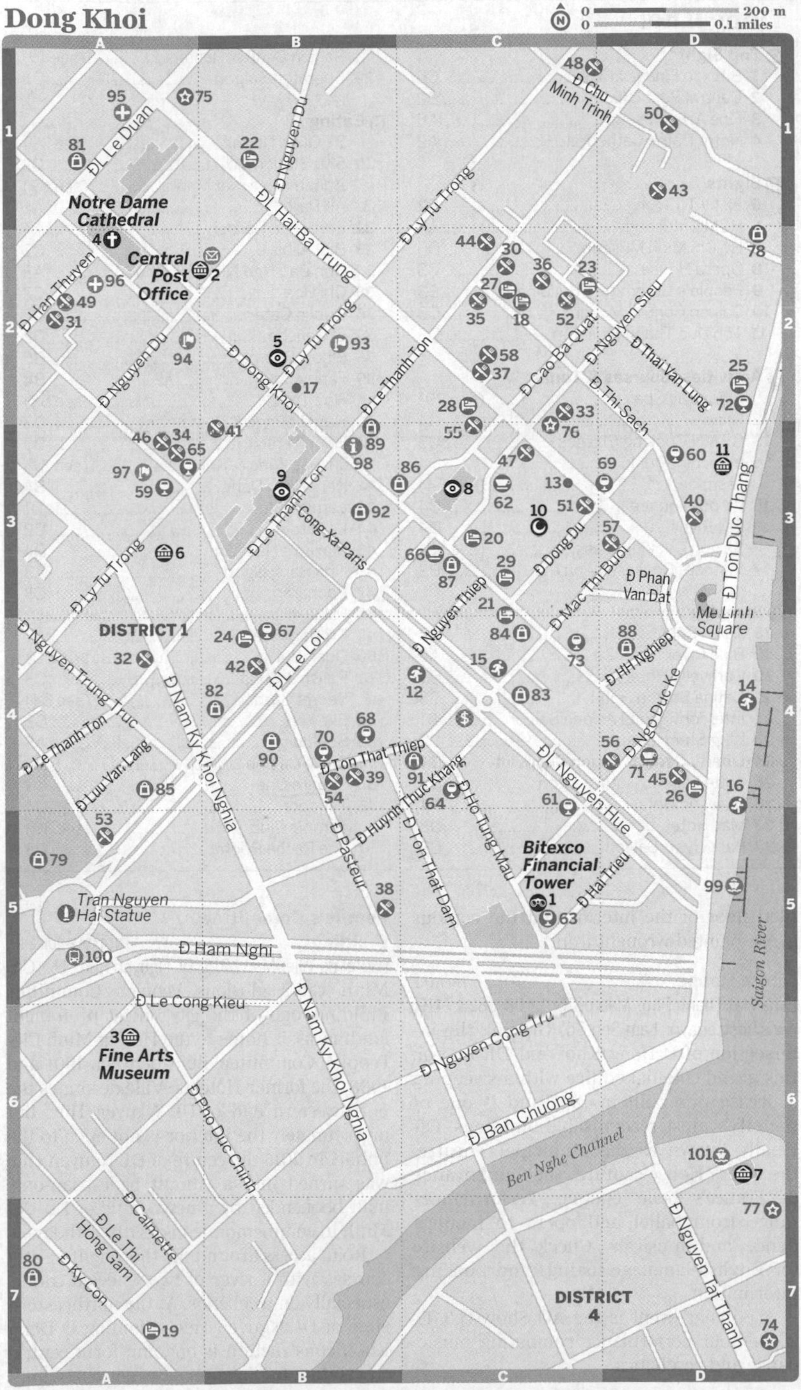

0 200 m
0 0.1 miles

Notre Dame Cathedral
Central Post Office
Bitexco Financial Tower
Fine Arts Museum
Tran Nguyen Hai Statue
Me Linh Square
DISTRICT 1
DISTRICT 4
Saigon River
Ben Nghe Channel

Đ Chu Minh Trinh
ĐL Le Duan
Đ Nguyen Du
ĐL Hai Ba Trung
Đ Ly Tu Trong
Đ Han Thuyen
Đ Dong Khoi
Đ Le Thanh Ton
Đ Cao Ba Quat
Đ Nguyen Sieu
Đ Thai Van Lung
Đ Thi Sach
Cong Xa Paris
Đ Dong Du
Đ Mac Thi Buoi
Đ Phan Van Dat
Đ Ton Duc Thang
Đ Nguyen Thiep
Đ HH Nghiep
Đ Ngo Duc Ke
ĐL Nguyen Hue
Đ Nguyen Trung Truc
Đ Nam Ky Khoi Nghia
ĐL Le Loi
Đ Luu Van Lang
Đ Ton That Thiep
Đ Huynh Thuc Khang
Đ Ho Tung Mau
Đ Pasteur
Đ Ton That Dam
Đ Hai Trieu
Đ Ham Nghi
Đ Le Cong Kieu
Đ Nguyen Cong Tru
Đ Ban Chuong
Đ Pho Duc Chinh
Đ Calmette
Đ Le Thi Hong Gam
Đ Ky Con
Đ Nguyen Tat Thanh

Dong Khoi

Top Sights

1 Bitexco Financial Tower....C5
2 Central Post Office....B2
3 Fine Arts Museum....A6
4 Notre Dame Cathedral....A2

Sights

5 22 Ly Tu Trong....B2
6 HCMC Museum....A3
7 Ho Chi Minh Museum....D6
8 Opera House....C3
9 People's Committee Building....B3
10 Saigon Central Mosque....C3
11 Ton Duc Thang Museum....D3

Activities, Courses & Tours

Aqua Day Spa....(see 29)
12 Glow....C4
13 GRAIN Cooking Classes....C3
14 Indochina Junk....D4
Jasmine....(see 54)
15 L'Apothiquaire....C4
16 Les Rives....D4
Saigon Cooking Class....(see 58)
17 Vietnam Cookery Centre....B2

Sleeping

18 Asian Ruby....C2
19 Blue River Hotel 2....A7
20 Caravelle Hotel....C3
21 Catina Saigon Hotel....C3
22 Intercontinental Asiana Saigon....B1
23 King Star Hotel....C2
24 Liberty Central Saigon Citypoint....B4
25 Lotte Legend Hotel Saigon....D2
26 Majestic Hotel....D4
27 May Hotel....C2
28 Park Hyatt Saigon....C2
Saigon Central Hostel....(see 19)
29 Sheraton Saigon....C3

Eating

3T Quan Nuong....(see 39)
30 5Ku Station....C2
Annam Gourmet Market....(see 69)
31 Au Parc....A2
32 Barbecue Garden....A4
33 Bibi Alibi....C2
34 Bun Dau Ngo Nho Pho Nho....A3
35 Chi Hoa....C2
36 Dublin Gate....C2
37 El Gaucho....C2
38 Elbow Room....B5
39 Fanny....B4
Hoa Tuc....(see 58)
40 Hum Lounge & Restaurant....D3
41 Huong Lai....B3
Jaspas Wine & Grill....(see 37)
42 Kem Bach Dang....B4
43 Lamie Cafe....D1
44 Le Jardin....C2
45 Maxim's Nam An....D4
46 Nha Hang Ngon....A3
47 Pacharan....C3
48 Pizza 4P's....C1
49 Propaganda....A2
50 Quan Bui....D1
51 Relish & Sons....C3
Secret Garden....(see 34)
52 Skewers....C2
53 Soulburger....A5
54 Spice Ca'phe....B4
55 Square One....C3
56 Tandoor....D4
Temple Club....(see 39)
57 The Racha Room....D3

tiled floor of the interior and the copious green-painted wrought iron.

Opera House THEATRE

(Nha Hat Thanh Pho; Map p315; ☎08-3823 7419; www.hbso.org.vn; Lam Son Sq) Gracing the intersection of Đ Dong Khoi and ĐL Le Loi, this grand colonial edifice with a sweeping staircase was built in 1897 and is one of the city's most recognisable buildings. Officially known as the Municipal Theatre, the Opera House captures the flamboyance of France's belle époque. Performances range from ballet and opera to modern dance and musicals. Check the website for English-language listings and booking information.

A popular event is the AO Show (p351), a one-hour performance combining music, dance and acrobatics.

People's Committee Building NOTABLE BUILDING

(Hôtel de Ville; Map p315; ĐL Nguyen Hue) Ho Chi Minh City's glorious People's Committee Building, one of the city's most prominent landmarks, is home to the Ho Chi Minh City People's Committee. Built between 1901 and 1908, the former Hôtel de Ville decorates the northwestern end of ĐL Nguyen Hue, but unfortunately the interior is not open to the public. In 2015 the centre of ĐL Nguyen Hue was turned into a vibrant pedestrian-only mall bookended by a new statue of Ho Chi Minh to commemorate his 125th birthday.

Road access around the thoroughfare still courses with a river of two-wheeled traffic, especially on weekends. At the northeastern edge of ĐL Nguyen Hue adjoining Đ Dong Khoi, construction is ongoing for a central city station for Saigon's new metro system.

HCMC Museum

MUSEUM

(Bao Tang Thanh Pho Ho Chi Minh; Map p315; www.hcmc-museum.edu.vn; 65 Đ Ly Tu Trong; admission 15,000d; ⏲8am-5pm) A grand, neoclassical structure built in 1885 and once known as Gia Long Palace (and later the Revolutionary Museum), HCMC's city museum is a singularly beautiful and impressive building, telling the story of the city through archaeological artefacts, ceramics, old city maps and displays on the marriage traditions of its various ethnicities. The struggle for independence is extensively covered, with most of the upper floor devoted to it.

Deep beneath the building is a network of reinforced concrete bunkers and fortified corridors. The system, branches of which stretch all the way to Reunification Palace, included living areas, a kitchen and a large meeting hall. In 1963 President Diem and his brother hid here before fleeing to Cha Tam Church (p328). The network is not open to the public because most of the tunnels are flooded.

In the gardens are various pieces of military hardware, including the American-built F-5E jet used by a renegade South Vietnamese pilot to bomb the Presidential Palace (now Reunification Palace) on 8 April 1975.

Ho Chi Minh Museum

MUSEUM

(Bao Tang Ho Chi Minh; Map p315; 1 Đ Nguyen Tat Thanh, District 4; admission 10,000d; ⏲7.30-11.30am & 1.30-5pm Tue-Sun) Nicknamed the 'Dragon House' (Nha Rong), this former customs house was built by the French authorities in 1863. The museum houses many of Ho Chi Minh's personal effects, including some of his clothing, his sandals and spectacles. On the waterfront, just across Ben Nghe Channel from District 1, the museum is easily reached on foot by heading south along the river on Đ Ton Duc Thang and crossing the bridge.

Otherwise, it covers the story of the man born Nguyen Tat Thanh – from his childhood to his political awakening, his role in booting out the French and leading North Vietnam, and his death in 1969 – mainly through photographs.

The link between Ho Chi Minh and the museum building is tenuous: 21-year-old Ho, having signed on as a stoker and galley boy on a French freighter, left Vietnam from here in 1911 and began 30 years of exile in France, the Soviet Union, China and elsewhere.

★Bitexco Financial Tower VIEWPOINT
(Map p315; www.saigonskydeck.com; 2 Đ Hai Trieu; adult/child 200,000/130,000d; ⌚9.30am-9.30pm) The 68-storey, 262m-high, Carlos Zapata–designed skyscraper dwarfs all around it. It's reportedly shaped like a lotus bulb, but also resembles a CD rack with a tambourine shoved into it. That tambourine is the 48th-floor **Saigon Skydeck**, with a helipad on its roof. Choose a clear day and aim for sunset, or down a drink in the Eon Heli Bar (p348) instead.

Ton Duc Thang Museum MUSEUM
(Bao Tang Ton Duc Thang; Map p315; ☎08-3829 7542; www.baotangtonducthang.com; 5 Đ Ton Duc Thang; ⌚7.30-11.30am & 1.30-5pm) FREE This small patriotic museum is dedicated to Ton Duc Thang, Ho Chi Minh's successor as president of Vietnam. Born in 1888 in Long Xuyen in the Mekong Delta region, he died in office in 1980. Exhibits celebrate his role in the Vietnamese Revolution, enhanced by some displays on French colonial brutality.

Saigon Central Mosque MOSQUE
(Map p315; 66 Đ Dong Du) Built by South Indian Muslims in 1935 on the site of an earlier mosque, lime-green Saigon Central Mosque is an immaculately clean and well-tended island of calm in the bustling Dong Khoi area. In front of the sparkling white and blue structure, with its four decorative minarets, is a pool for the ritual ablutions required by Islamic law before prayers. Take off your shoes before entering the building.

22 Ly Tu Trong HISTORIC SITE
(Map p315; 22 Đ Ly Tu Trong) The ground floor of this innocuous-looking building on Đ Ly Tu Trong is currently occupied by the Vietnam National Chemical Group. Step across the road to outside the Vincom Center to look up at the roof and you will see a structure (housing the lift shaft) that served as a temporary landing pad for a US helicopter evacuating personnel the day before the fall of Saigon, an image immortalised by Dutch photographer Hubert Van Es. The photograph is commonly misunderstood to depict US citizens leaving the roof of the US embassy, but this building did house CIA staff.

Da Kao & Around

This old District 1 ward, directly north of the city centre, is home to most of the consulates and some beautiful buildings dating from the French colonial period. Hidden within its historic streets (and those bordering it in the eastern corner of District 3) are good new restaurants and bars, along with some of the city's best traditional eateries.

★Jade Emperor Pagoda TAOIST TEMPLE
(Phuoc Hai Tu, Chua Ngoc Hoang; Map p319; 73 Đ Mai Thi Luu; ⌚7am-6pm, on 1st & 15th of lunar month 5am-7pm) FREE Built in 1909 in honour of the supreme Taoist god (the Jade Emperor or King of Heaven, Ngoc Hoang), this is one of the most spectacularly atmospheric temples in Ho Chi Minh City, stuffed with statues of phantasmal divinities and grotesque heroes. The pungent smoke of incense *(huong)* fills the air, obscuring the exquisite woodcarvings. Its roof encrusted with elaborate tile work, the temple's statues, depicting characters from both Buddhist and Taoist lore, are made from reinforced papier mâché.

Inside the main building are two especially fierce and menacing Taoist figures. On the right (as you face the altar) is a 4m-high statue of the general who defeated the Green Dragon (depicted underfoot). On the left is the general who defeated the White Tiger, which is also being stepped on.

Worshippers mass before the ineffable Jade Emperor, who presides – draped in luxurious robes and shrouded in a dense fug of incense smoke – over the main sanctuary. He is flanked by his guardians, the Four Big Diamonds (Tu Dai Kim Cuong), so named because they are said to be as hard as diamonds.

Out the door on the left-hand side of the Jade Emperor's chamber is another

Da Kao & Around

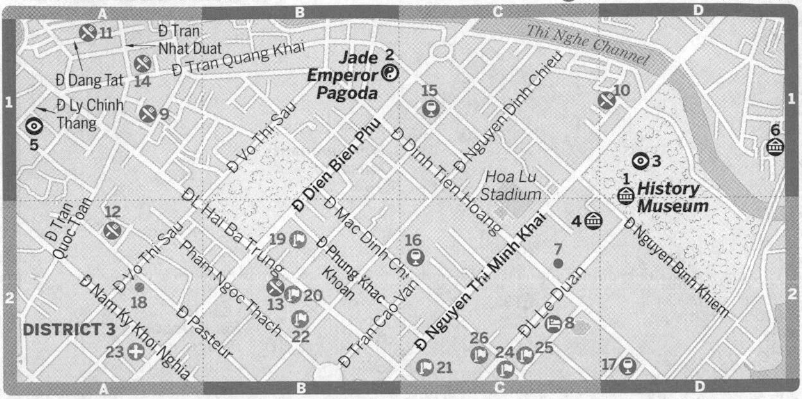

Da Kao & Around

Top Sights
1 History Museum D1
2 Jade Emperor Pagoda B1

Sights
3 Botanic Gardens D1
4 Military Museum C2
5 Pho Binh A1
6 San Art D1

Activities, Courses & Tours
7 University of Social Sciences & Humanities C2

Sleeping
8 Sofitel Saigon Plaza C2

Eating
9 Banh Xeo 46A A1
10 Bloom Saigon D1
11 Cuc Gach Quan A1
12 Pho Hoa A2
13 Tib B2
14 Tib Vegetarian A1

Drinking & Nightlife
15 Decibel C1
16 Hoa Vien C2
17 Lush D2

Information
18 Buffalo Tours A2
19 Cambodian Consulate B2
20 Chinese Consulate B2
21 French Consulate C2
22 German Consulate B2
23 International SOS A2
24 Netherlands Consulate C2
25 UK Consulate C2
26 US Consulate C2

room. The semi-enclosed area to the right (as you enter) is presided over by Thanh Hoang, the Chief of Hell; to the left is his red horse. Other figures here represent the gods who dispense punishments for evil acts and rewards for good deeds. The room also contains the famous Hall of the Ten Hells, carved wooden panels illustrating the varied torments awaiting evil people in each of the Ten Regions of Hell. Women queue up at the seated effigy of the City God, who wears a hat inscribed with Chinese characters that announce 'At one glance, money is given'. In a mesmerising ritual, worshippers first put money into a box, then rub a piece of red paper against his hand before circling it around a candle flame.

On the other side of the wall is a fascinating little room in which the ceramic figures of 12 women, overrun with children and wearing colourful clothes, sit in two rows of six. Each of the women exemplifies a human characteristic, either good or bad (as in the case of the woman drinking alcohol from a jug). Each figure represents a year in the 12-year Chinese astrological calendar. Presiding over the room is Kim Hoa Thanh Mau, the Chief of All Women. Upstairs is a hall to Quan Am, the Goddess of Mercy, opposite a portrait of Dat Ma, the bearded Indian founder of Zen Buddhism.

The multifaith nature of the temple is echoed in the shrine's alternative name Phuoc Hai Tu (福海寺; Sea of Blessing Temple),

Reunification Palace & Around

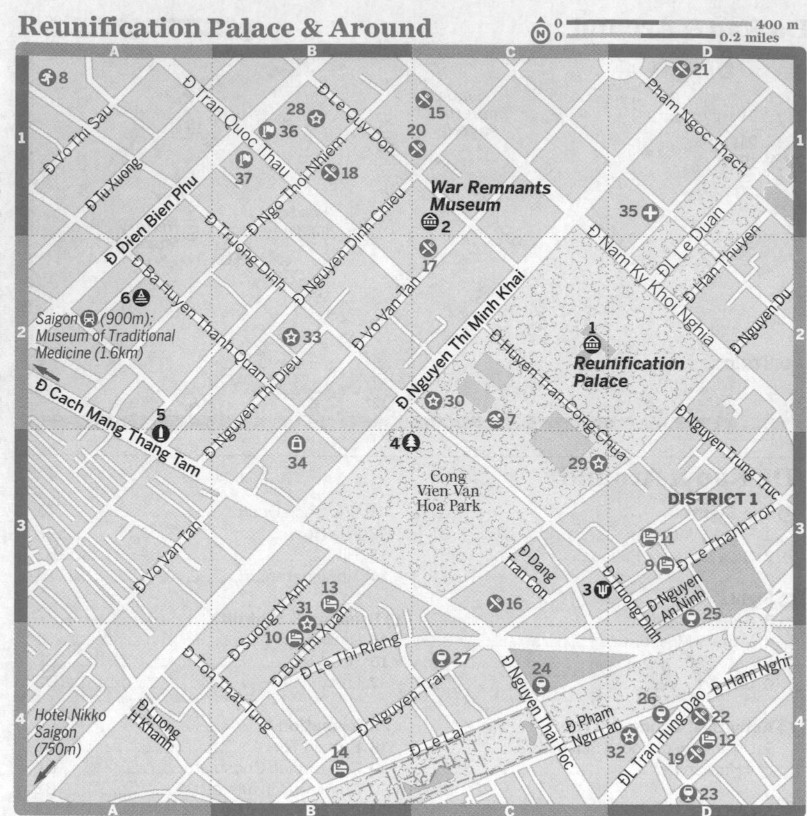

whose message is clearly Buddhist. Similarly, the Chinese characters (佛光普照; Phat Quang Pho Chieu) in the main temple hall mean 'The light of Buddha shines on all'.

Outside, a small pond seethes with turtles, some of which have shells inscribed with auspicious inscriptions.

★History Museum — MUSEUM

(Bao Tang Lich Su; Map p319; Đ Nguyen Binh Khiem; admission 15,000d; ⌚8-11.30am & 1.30-5pm Tue-Sun) Built in 1929 by the Société des Études Indochinoises, this notable Sino-French museum houses a rewarding collection of artefacts illustrating the evolution of the cultures of Vietnam, from the Bronze Age Dong Son civilisation (which emerged in 2000 BC) and the Funan civilisation (1st to 6th centuries AD), to the Cham, Khmer and Vietnamese. The museum is just inside the main gate to the city's botanic gardens and zoo.

Highlights include valuable relics taken from Cambodia's Angkor Wat, a fine collection of Buddha statues, the perfectly preserved mummy of a local woman who died in 1869, excavated from Xom Cai in District 5, and some exquisite stylised mother-of-pearl Chinese characters inlaid into panels.

Botanic Gardens — GARDENS

(Thao Cam Vien; Map p319; 2 Đ Nguyen Binh Khiem; 50,000d incl entry to zoo; ⌚7am-7pm) One of the first projects undertaken by the French after establishing Cochinchina as a colony was founding these fantastic, lush gardens. Once one of the finest such gardens in Asia, they're very agreeable for strolling beneath giant tropical trees, including towering Tung and So Khi trees. Also equipped with a zoo, the gardens are next to the History Museum.

Military Museum — MUSEUM

(Bao Tang Quan Doi; Map p319; 2 ĐL Le Duan; ⌚7.30-11am & 1.30-4.30pm Tue-Sat) FREE A

Reunification Palace & Around

Top Sights
1 Reunification Palace ... C2
2 War Remnants Museum ... C1

Sights
3 Mariamman Hindu Temple ... C3
4 Tao Dan Park ... B3
5 Venerable Thich Quang Duc Memorial ... A3
6 Xa Loi Pagoda ... A2

Activities, Courses & Tours
Cyclo Resto ... (see 16)
7 Labour Culture Palace ... C2
8 L'Apothiquaire ... A1
Saigon Soul Pool Parties ... (see 24)

Sleeping
9 Anpha Boutique Hotel ... D3
10 Family Inn ... B4
Lavender Hotel ... (see 9)
11 Sanouva ... D3
12 Town House 23 ... D4
13 Town House 50 ... B3
14 Vietnam Inn Saigon ... B4

Eating
15 Beefsteak Nam Son ... C1
16 Cyclo Resto ... C3
17 Hum Vegetarian Cafe & Restaurant ... C2
18 Khoi Thom ... B1
19 La Fiesta ... D4
20 Marina ... C1
San Fu Lou ... (see 24)
21 Shri Restaurant & Lounge ... D1
22 Tin Nghia ... D4

Drinking & Nightlife
23 Air 360 ... D4
24 Chill Sky Bar ... C4
25 OMG ... D3
Shri ... (see 21)
26 Vespa Sofar ... D4
27 Vuvuzela Beer Club ... C4

Entertainment
28 Acoustic ... B1
29 Conservatory of Music ... C3
30 Golden Dragon Water Puppet Theatre ... C2
31 MZ Bar ... B4
32 Seventeen Saloon ... D4
33 Yoko ... B2

Shopping
34 Vinh Loi Gallery ... B3

Information
35 Columbia Asia ... D1
36 Japanese Consulate ... B1
37 Thai Consulate ... B1

short distance from the History Museum, this small collection is devoted to Ho Chi Minh's campaign to liberate the south. Interior exhibits are of minor interest but some US, Chinese and Soviet war material is on display outdoors, including a South Vietnamese Air Force Cessna A-37 and a US-built F-5E Tiger with the 20mm nose gun still loaded. The tank on display is one of the tanks that broke into the grounds of Reunification Palace on 30 April 1975.

Pho Binh HISTORIC SITE
(Map p319; 7 Đ Ly Chinh Thang, District 3; noodle soup 60,000d) A humble noodle-soup restaurant may seem an unusual attraction, but there's more to Pho Binh than meets the eye. This was the secret headquarters of the Viet Cong (Vietnamese Communists; VC) in Saigon and from here they planned their attacks on the US embassy and other Saigon targets during the Tet Offensive of 1968. One wonders how many US soldiers ate here, completely unaware. The *pho* (rice-noodle soup) makes it a worthwhile stop for lunch or breakfast.

Reunification Palace & Around

Straddling District 1 and District 3, this grid of busy streets encloses the inviting spaces of Tao Dan Park and the pristine grounds of Reunification Palace. It's here that you'll find some of Ho Chi Minh City's most popular sights and good restaurants.

★War Remnants Museum MUSEUM
(Bao Tang Chung Tich Chien Tranh; Map p320; ☎08-3930 5587; www.baotangchungtichchientranh.vn; 28 Đ Vo Van Tan, cnr Đ Le Quy Don; admission 15,000d; ⊙7.30am-noon & 1.30-5pm) Formerly the Museum of Chinese and American War Crimes, the War Remnants Museum is popular with Western tourists. Few museums anywhere convey the brutality of war and its civilian victims. Many of the atrocities documented here were well publicised but rarely do Westerners hear the victims of US military action tell their own stories. While some displays are one-sided, many of the most disturbing photographs illustrating US atrocities are from US sources, including those of the infamous My Lai Massacre.

HO CHI MINH CITY IN...

One Day

Slurp up a steaming bowl of *pho* (rice-noodle soup) and then take a walk through **old Saigon** (p330). After lunch at nearby **Propaganda** (p341) head to the **War Remnants Museum** (p321), tour **Reunification Palace** (p322) and, if there's still time, the **HCMC Museum** (p317). In the evening, catch the sky-high sunset views from **Air 360** (p350), followed by a meal at **Nha Hang Ngon** (p341) or **The Racha Room** (p341). Have a nightcap of bold craft beer at the **Pasteur Street Brewing Company** (p347), or punchy Asian-inspired cocktails at **Shrine** (p348).

Two Days

Spend the morning in **Cholon** (p324), wandering around the market and historic temples. Catch a taxi up to District 3 for a cheap traditional lunch at **Pho Hoa** (p344) or **Banh Xeo 46A** (p344), and then walk through Da Kao ward to the **Jade Emperor Pagoda** (p318) and **History Museum** (p320). If it's your last night in HCMC, make the most of it. Start your evening at another of the city's good restaurants – perhaps **Quan Bui** (p342), **Cuc Gach Quan** (p344) or **Hum Lounge & Restaurant** (p341) – and then catch a band at **Acoustic** (p351) or **Saigon Ranger** (p351). If you're ready for the evening to descend into a very Saigon state of messiness, continue on to **Cargo** (p351) or **The Observatory** (p351).

US armoured vehicles, artillery pieces, bombs and infantry weapons are on display outside. One corner of the grounds is devoted to the notorious French and South Vietnamese prisons on Phu Quoc and Con Son Islands. Artefacts include that most iconic of French appliances, the guillotine, and the notoriously inhumane 'tiger cages' used to house Viet Cong (Vietnamese Communists; VC) prisoners.

The ground floor of the museum is devoted to a collection of posters and photographs showing support for the antiwar movement internationally. This somewhat upbeat display provides a counterbalance to the horrors upstairs.

Even those who supported the war are likely to be horrified by the photos of children affected by US bombing and napalming. You'll also have the rare chance to see some of the experimental weapons used in the war, which were at one time military secrets, such as the *flechette*, an artillery shell filled with thousands of tiny darts.

Upstairs, look out for the **Requiem Exhibition**. Compiled by legendary war photographer Tim Page, this striking collection documents the work of photographers killed during the course of the conflict, on both sides, and includes works by Larry Burrows and Robert Capa.

The War Remnants Museum is in the former US Information Service building. Captions are in Vietnamese and English.

★Reunification Palace HISTORIC BUILDING
(Dinh Thong Nhat; Map p320; ☎08-3829 4117; www.dinhdoclap.gov.vn; Đ Nam Ky Khoi Nghia; adult/child 30,000/5000d; ⏲7.30-11am & 1-4pm) Surrounded by Royal Palm trees, the dissonant 1960s architecture of this government building and the eerie mood that accompanies a walk through its deserted halls make it an intriguing spectacle. The first Communist tanks to arrive in Saigon rumbled here on 30 April 1975 and it's as if time has stood still since then. The building is deeply associated with the fall of the city in 1975, yet it's the kitsch detailing and period motifs that steal the show.

After crashing through the wrought-iron gates – in a dramatic scene recorded by photojournalists and shown around the world – a soldier ran into the building and up the stairs to unfurl a VC flag from the balcony. In an ornate reception chamber, General Minh, who had become head of the South Vietnamese state only 43 hours before, waited with his improvised cabinet. 'I have been waiting since early this morning to transfer power to you', Minh said to the VC officer who entered the room. 'There is no question of your transferring power', replied the officer. 'You cannot give up what you do not have.'

In 1868 a residence was built on this site for the French governor-general of Cochinchina and gradually it expanded to become Norodom Palace. When the French departed, the palace became home to the

South Vietnamese president Ngo Dinh Diem. So unpopular was Diem that his own air force bombed the palace in 1962 in an unsuccessful attempt to kill him. The president ordered a new residence to be built on the same site, this time with a sizeable bomb shelter in the basement. Work was completed in 1966, but Diem did not get to see his dream house as he was killed by his own troops in 1963.

The new building was named Independence Palace and was home to the successive South Vietnamese president, Nguyen Van Thieu, until his hasty departure in 1975. Designed by Paris-trained Vietnamese architect Ngo Viet Thu, it is an outstanding example of 1960s architecture, with an airy and open atmosphere.

The ground floor is arranged with meeting rooms, while upstairs is a grand set of reception rooms, used for welcoming foreign and national dignitaries. In the back of the structure are the president's living quarters; check out the model boats, horse tails and severed elephants' feet. The 2nd floor contributes a shagadelic card-playing room, complete with a cheesy round leather banquette, a barrel-shaped bar, hubcap light fixtures and groovy three-legged chairs set around a flared-legged card table. There's also a cinema and a rooftop nightclub, complete with helipad: James Bond/Austin Powers – eat your heart out.

Perhaps most fascinating of all is the basement with its telecommunications centre, war room and warren of tunnels, where hulking old fans chop the air and ancient radio transmitters sit impassively. Towards the end are rooms where videos appraise the palace and its history in Vietnamese, English, French, Chinese and Japanese. The national anthem is played at the end of the tape and you are expected to stand up – it would be rude not to.

Reunification Palace is open to visitors as long as official receptions or meetings aren't taking place. English- and French-speaking guides are on duty during opening hours.

Venerable Thich Quang Duc Memorial MONUMENT

(Map p320; cnr Đ Nguyen Dinh Chieu & Đ Cach Mang Thang Tam) This peaceful memorial park is dedicated to Thich Quang Duc, the Buddhist monk who self-immolated in protest at this intersection not far from the Presidential Palace (today's Reunification Palace) in 1963. The memorial was inaugurated in 2010, displaying Thich Quang Duc wreathed in flames before a bas-relief.

Note that Thich Quang Duc has been elevated to the status of a Bo Tat on the memorial, which means a Boddhisattva (an enlightened person who forgoes Nirvana in order to save others).

Mariamman Hindu Temple HINDU TEMPLE

(Chua Ba Mariamman; Map p320; 45 Đ Truong Dinh; ⌚7.30am-7.30pm) Only a small number of Hindus live in HCMC, but this colourful slice of southern India is also considered sacred by many ethnic Vietnamese and Chinese. Reputed to have miraculous powers, the temple was built at the end of the 19th century and dedicated to the Hindu goddess Mariamman. Remove your shoes before stepping onto the slightly raised platform and ignore any demands to buy joss sticks and jasmine. The temple is three blocks west of Ben Thanh Market.

The lion to the left of the entrance used to be carried around the city in a street procession every autumn. In the shrine in the middle of the temple is Mariamman, flanked by her guardians Maduraiveeran (to her left) and Pechiamman (to her right). In front of the Mariamman figure are two *linga* (stylised phalluses that represent the Hindu god Shiva). Favourite offerings placed nearby include joss sticks, jasmine, lilies and gladioli.

Tao Dan Park PARK

(Map p320; Đ Nguyen Thi Minh Khai) One of the city's most attractive green spaces is 10-hectare Tao Dan Park, its bench-lined walks shaded with avenues of towering tropical trees, including flame trees and vast Sao Den and So Khi trees. It's fascinating to visit in the early morning and late afternoon when thousands of locals exercise. Also noteworthy is the daily flocking here of the city's bird lovers (mainly elderly gentlemen), who arrive, cages in hand, at what is universally known as the bird cafe.

The park is split down the middle by Đ Truong Dinh. To the northeast of Đ Truong Dinh is a small contemporary sculpture garden and the old Cercle Sportif, an elite sporting club during the French colonial period and now the Labour Culture Palace with tennis courts, a colonnaded art deco swimming pool and a clubhouse.

Xa Loi Pagoda BUDDHIST TEMPLE

(Chua Xa Loi; Map p320; 89 Đ Ba Huyen Thanh Quan; ⌚7-11am & 2-5pm) Famed as the repository of a sacred relic of the Buddha, this 1956 building is most notable for its dramatic history. In August 1963 truckloads of armed men under the command of Ngo Dinh Nhu, President Ngo Dinh Diem's brother, attacked the temple, which had become a centre of opposition to the Diem government.

The temple was ransacked and 400 monks and nuns, including the country's 80-year-old Buddhist patriarch, were arrested. This raid and others elsewhere helped solidify opposition among Buddhists to the regime, a crucial factor in the US decision to support the coup against Diem. The pagoda was also the site of several self-immolations by monks protesting against the Diem regime and the American War.

The etymology of the temple name points to its significance. The Chinese characters on the front of the temple – 'Sheli Si' (舍利寺; Sheli Temple), pronounced Xa Loi Chua in Vietnamese – mean 'Sarira Temple', from the Sanskrit word for 'Buddhist relic'.

Women enter the main hall of Xa Loi Pagoda, housing a giant golden Sakyamuni (the historical Buddha), by the staircase on the right as you come in the gate; men use the stairs on the left. The walls of the sanctuary are adorned with paintings depicting the Buddha's life. Behind the main hall, a further hall contains a painting of Bodhidharma, an Indian monk celebrated as the father of Zen Buddhism. He stayed at the Shaolin Temple in China, developing the exercises that would become **Shaolin Boxing**. He is depicted here carrying a shoe on a stick (the story goes that when Bodhidharma's coffin was opened after his death, it was empty apart from one shoe).

A monk preaches every Sunday from 8am to 10am. On full- and new-moon days, special prayers are held from 7am to 9am and 7pm to 8pm.

Nguyen Thai Binh & Around

This District 1 ward is a busy workaday neighbourhood nestled between the central city, Ben Thanh Market, the Pham Ngu Lao backpacker strip and Ben Nghe Channel.

★ **Fine Arts Museum** ART GALLERY

(Bao Tang My Thuat; Map p315; 97a Đ Pho Duc Chinh; admission 10,000d; 9am-5pm Tue-Sun)

With its airy corridors and verandas, this elegant 1929 colonial-era yellow-and-white building is stuffed with period details; it is exuberantly tiled throughout and home to some fine (albeit deteriorated) stained glass, as well as one of Saigon's oldest lifts. Hung from the walls is an impressive selection of art, including thoughtful pieces from the modern period. As well as contemporary art, much of it (unsurprisingly) inspired by war, the museum displays historical pieces dating back to the 4th century.

These include elegant Funan-era sculptures of Vishnu, the Buddha and other revered figures (carved in both wood and stone), and Cham art dating from the 7th to the 14th century.

More statuary is scattered around the grounds and in the central courtyard (accessed from the rear of the building). There's a selection of lovely prints for sale at the shop, costing from around 100,000d. Building No 2 alongside hosts lesser-known works and stages exhibitions.

The space on the pavement in front of the impressive old Railway Office, up the road between Đ Ham Nghi and ĐL Le Loi and facing the roundabout, was used for public executions in the early 1960s.

Cholon

Rummage through Cholon (District 5) and lift the lid on a treasure trove of historic temples and Chinese flavours. Ho Chi Minh City's Chinatown is less Chinese than it once was, largely due to the 1978–79 anti-capitalist and anti-Chinese campaign, when many ethnic Chinese fled the country, taking with them their money and entrepreneurial skills. A lot of those refugees have since returned (with foreign passports) to explore investment possibilities. Full-form written Chinese characters (as opposed to the simplified system used in mainland China) decorate shopfronts and temples in abundance, adding to the sensation that you have strayed into a forgotten corner of China. Finding a Mandarin speaker isn't hard, although most Hoa-Kieu (Vietnamese-Chinese) residents chat in southern Chinese dialects.

Cholon means 'big market' and during the American War it was home to a thriving black market. Like much of HCMC, Cholon's historic shopfronts are swiftly disappearing under advertising hoardings or succumbing to developers' bulldozers, but some traditional architecture survives and an atmospheric strip of **traditional herb shops** (Map p325; Đ Hai Thuong Lan Ong) thrives between Đ Luong Nhu Hoc and Đ Trieu Quang Phuc, providing both a visual and an olfactory reminder of the old Chinese city. A taxi from Pham Ngu Lao to Cholon costs around

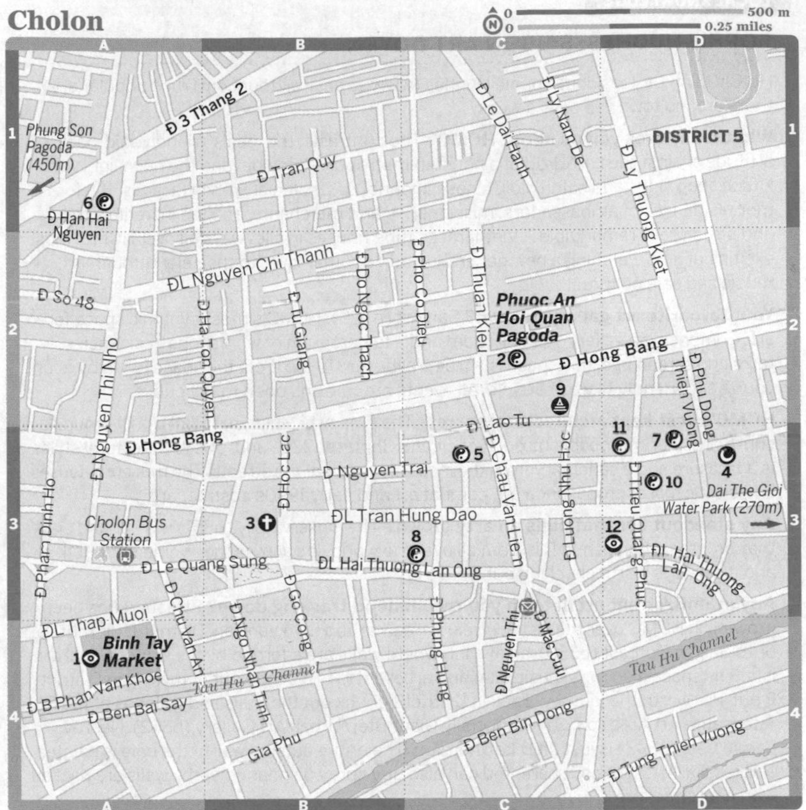

100,000d or hop on bus 1 from Ben Thanh Market. For in-depth tours of Cholon, contact local expert Tim Doling (p334).

★ Binh Tay Market MARKET

(Cho Binh Tay; Map p325; www.chobinhtay.gov.vn; 57a Đl Thap Muoi) Cholon's main market has a great clock tower and a central courtyard with gardens. Much of the business here is wholesale but it's popular with tour groups. The market was originally built by the French in the 1880s; Guangdong-born philanthropist Quach Dam paid for its rebuilding and was commemorated by a statue that is now in the Fine Arts Museum. Expect a friendly welcome when you sit down for breakfast or coffee with the market's street-food vendors.

Thien Hau Pagoda TAOIST TEMPLE

(Ba Mieu, Pho Mieu, Chua Ba Thien Hau; Map p325; 710 Đ Nguyen Trai) FREE This 19th-century temple is dedicated to the goddess Thien Hau, and attracts worshippers and visitors who mingle beneath the coils of incense overhead. It is believed that Thien Hau can travel over the oceans on a mat and ride the clouds to save people in trouble on the high seas.

Cholon

Top Sights

1 Binh Tay Market A4
2 Phuoc An Hoi Quan Pagoda C2

Sights

3 Cha Tam Church B3
4 Cholon Jamail Mosque D3
5 Ha Chuong Hoi Quan Pagoda C3
6 Khanh Van Nam Vien Pagoda A1
7 Nghia An Hoi Quan Pagoda D3
8 Ong Bon Pagoda C3
9 Quan Am Pagoda C2
10 Tam Son Hoi Quan Pagoda D3
11 Thien Hau Pagoda D3
12 Traditional Herb Shops D3

LOCAL KNOWLEDGE

SOPHIE HUGHES: SAIGON ART DOYEN

Ho Chi Minh City resident Sophie Hughes (www.sophiesarttour.com) runs popular art tours around town five days a week.

What really fires you up about HCMC? The contrasts: the locals' friendly, laid-back attitude against the backdrop of a nonstop metropolis. Look beyond the neon lights and kitsch shop signs and catch old Chinese shophouses, colonial French facades, the former residences of ambassadors, missionaries and merchants, and the incredibly thin – and structurally remarkable – Vietnamese tube houses in alleyways all over HCMC. Most exciting of all is watching a new generation add another layer to their city through art, music and cafe culture.

Your favourite art gallery in town? San Art (p329): HCMC's most dynamic space for art. Comprising a gallery, reading room and a full program of workshops, residencies, talks and screenings, this space is a true trailblazer. To top it off, the space is run by a fun, young and friendly team of people. All events are free and open to the public.

HCMC's best-kept architectural secret? The Fine Arts Museum (p324): built around a courtyard, this improbable mix of French and Chinese 1920s and '30s architectural styles is a treasure and a sanctuary from the incessant buzz of the streets. The museum houses an eclectic mix of propaganda art, combat art and early 1990s abstract art.

Any standout bar that pulls an arty crowd? The Observatory (p351) is a bar and club that programs bands and DJs from all over the world. It's across the river in District 4, and it's always worth checking out what's on.

Any graffiti/street art in town you recommend tracking down? Street art has been growing in HCMC over the last few years. Head to 15b Đ Vo Van Tan, District 1, for murals or to Saigon Outcast (p350), an art hub where walls are adorned by the work of local artists. The space also runs music, film and art events – it's a little out of the city in District 2 but well worth the journey. Back in District 1 check out the walls and galleries of the 3A Alternative Art Area (p353) – especially Giant Step Urban Art Gallery (p352). Nearby, Lamie Cafe (p343) is just off Đ Le Than Ton. The entire outside wall of the cafe is painted and local artists hang out here. You can also buy spray paint and nearby walls are packed with cool street art.

There are intricate ceramic friezes above the roof line of the interior courtyard, while the protectors of the pagoda are said to be two land turtles that live here. Near the large braziers stand two miniature wooden structures in which a small figure of Thien Hau is paraded around nearby streets on the 23rd day of the third lunar month. On the main dais are three figures of Thien Hau, one behind the other, all flanked by two servants or guardians. To the right is a scale-model boat and on the far right is the Goddess Long Mau, Protector of Mothers and Newborns.

Khanh Van Nam Vien Pagoda TAOIST TEMPLE
(Map p325; 269/2 Đ Nguyen Thi Nho) Built between 1939 and 1942, this temple is said to be the only pure Taoist temple in Vietnam and is unique for its statues of Taoist disciples. Features to seek out include the unique 150cm-high statue of Laotse – the supreme philosopher of Taoism and author of the *Dao De Jing* – located upstairs.

Laotse's mirror-edged halo is rather surreal, while off to his left are two stone plaques with instructions for Taoist inhalation and exhalation exercises. A schematic drawing represents the human organs as a scene from rural China. The diaphragm, agent of inhalation, is at the bottom; the stomach is represented by a peasant ploughing with a water buffalo. The kidney is marked by four yin and yang symbols, the liver is shown as a grove of trees and the heart is represented by a circle with a peasant standing in it, above which is a constellation. The tall pagoda represents the throat and the broken rainbow is the mouth. Situated at the top are mountains and a seated figure that represent the brain and imagination, respectively.

The temple operates a home for several dozen elderly people. Next door is a free medical clinic also run by the pagoda. Leave a donation with the monks if you wish.

Quan Am Pagoda BUDDHIST TEMPLE
(Chua Quan Am; Map p325; 12 Đ Lao Tu) FREE One of Cholon's most active and colourful temples, this shrine was founded in the early 19th century. It's named after the Goddess of Mercy, whose full name is Quan The Am Bo Tat, literally 'the Bodhisattva who listens to the cries of the world' (觀世音菩薩 in Chinese characters), in reflection of her compassionate mission.

The goddess' name is usually shortened to Quan Am (she is also worshipped in China, Korea and Japan) and her statue lies hidden behind a remarkably ornate exterior. In Tibet, where she is also widely worshipped, the goddess – who was once male – finds earthly form in the Dalai Lama. Fantastic ceramic scenes decorate the roof, depicting figures from traditional Chinese plays and stories. Other unique features of this temple are the gold-and-lacquer panels of the entrance doors.

★Phuoc An Hoi Quan Pagoda TAOIST TEMPLE
(Map p325; 184 Đ Hong Bang) FREE Delightfully fronted by greenery and opening to an interior blaze of red, gold, green and yellow, this is one of the most beautifully ornamented temples in town, dating from 1902. Of special interest are the elaborate brass ritual ornaments and weapons, and the fine woodcarvings on the altars, walls, columns, hanging lanterns and incense coils. From the exterior, look out for the ceramic scenes, each containing innumerable small figurines, that decorate the roof.

To the left of the entrance stands a life-size figure of the sacred horse of Quan Cong. Before departing on a journey, people make offerings to the equine figure, before stroking its mane and ringing the bell around its neck. Behind the main altar, with its stone and brass incense braziers, is a statue of Quan Cong, to whom the temple is dedicated (the other name for the temple is the Quan De Mieu); other shrines are dedicated to Ong Bon and Nam Ba Ngu Hanh.

Tam Son Hoi Quan Pagoda TAOIST TEMPLE
(Chua Ba; Map p325; 118 Đ Trieu Quang Phuc) Retaining much of its original rich ornamentation, this 19th-century temple – a guildhall named after Sanshan (Three Mountains) in China's seaboard Fujian province – is dedicated to Me Sanh, the Goddess of Fertility, entreated by local women praying for children. Thien Hau – the Goddess of Seafarers – is also revered within the main shrine.

Among the striking figures is Quan Cong with his long black beard, to the right of the covered courtyard. Flanking him are two guardians, the Military Mandarin Chau Xuong on the left and the Administrative Mandarin Quan Binh on the right. Next to Chau Xuong is Quan Cong's sacred red horse.

Ong Bon Pagoda TAOIST TEMPLE
(Chua Ong Bon, Nhi Phu Mieu; Map p325; 264 ĐL Hai Thuong Lan Ong) This atmospheric temple is crammed with gilded carvings, smoking incense and the constant hubbub of kids from the large school next door. Built by Chinese immigrants from Fujian province, it's dedicated to Ong Bon, the guardian who presides over happiness and wealth, who is seated in a gilded cabinet sparkling with LED lights, an intricately carved and gilded wooden altar before him.

Other shrines are dedicated to Thien Hau, Quan Am, the Jade Emperor and even the Monkey King. Along the walls of the chamber are murals of five tigers (to the left) and two dragons (to the right).

Nghia An Hoi Quan Pagoda TAOIST TEMPLE
(Map p325; 678 Đ Nguyen Trai) Noteworthy for its gilded woodwork, this temple has a large carved wooden boat hanging over its entrance and inside, to the left of the doorway, an enormous representation of Quan Cong's red horse with its groom. The temple is more accurately a guildhall built in the early 19th century by Chinese from Yian in China's Guangdong province.

Quan Cong – also called Quan De or Quan Vu, a deified Chinese general from the Three Kingdoms Period (184–280) – occupies a position in a glass case behind the main altar, with his assistants flanking him on both sides. Nghia An Hoi Quan celebrates on the 14th day of the first lunar month when various dances are staged in front of the temple.

Ha Chuong Hoi Quan Pagoda TAOIST TEMPLE
(Map p325; 802 Đ Nguyen Trai) This Fujian temple is dedicated to the Goddess of Seafarers, Thien Hau (Thien Hau Thanh Mau), also known as Ma To. The four carved stone pillars, wrapped in painted dragons, were fashioned in China and delivered to Vietnam by boat. The temple – actually a guildhall – becomes extremely active during the Lantern Festival, a Chinese holiday held on the 15th day of the first lunar month (the first full moon of the new lunar year).

Noteworthy murals can be seen either side of the main altar, while impressive ceramic relief scenes decorate the roof. To the right of Thien Hau is Chua Sinh Nuong Nuong, a Taoist fertility goddess; to the left of Thien Hau is the ever-popular Taoist God of Wealth. Blending Buddhism into the mix, a figure of Quan Am looks on mercifully, clothed in white and draped with a pearl necklace. Note the upright fan in the main hall, used for dispelling calamity.

Cha Tam Church CHURCH

(Map p325; 25 Đ Hoc Lac) Built around the turn of the 19th century, this decaying light-caramel painted church exudes a sleepy, tropical feel. A pew in the church is marked with a small plaque identifying the spot where President Ngo Dinh Diem was seized after taking refuge here with his brother Ngo Dinh Nhu on 2 November 1963, after fleeing the Presidential Palace.

When their efforts to contact loyal military officers (of whom there were almost none) failed, Diem and Nhu agreed to surrender unconditionally and revealed where they were hiding. The coup leaders sent an M-113 armoured personnel carrier to the church and the two were taken into custody. However, before the vehicle reached central Saigon the soldiers had killed Diem and Nhu by shooting them at point-blank range and then repeatedly stabbing their bodies.

When news of the deaths was broadcast on radio, Saigon exploded with jubilation. Portraits of the two were torn up and political prisoners, many of whom had been tortured, were set free. The city's nightclubs, which had closed because of the Ngos' conservative Catholic beliefs, were reopened. Three weeks later the US president, John F Kennedy, was assassinated. As his administration had supported the coup against Diem, some conspiracy theorists speculated that Diem's family orchestrated Kennedy's death in retaliation.

The mint-green and white church interior is decorated with images of the Stations of the Cross, while holy water is dispensed from huge clamshells. The statue in the tower is of François Xavier Tam Assou (1855–1934), a Chinese-born vicar apostolic (delegate of the pope) of Saigon. Today the church has a very active congregation of 3000 ethnic Vietnamese and 2000 ethnic Chinese. Masses are held daily.

Cholon Jamail Mosque MOSQUE

(Map p325; 641 Đ Nguyen Trai) The clean lines and minimal ornamentation of this mosque contrast starkly with nearby Chinese and Vietnamese Buddhist temples. Note the pool for ritual ablutions in the courtyard and the tiled mihrab (niche) in the wall of the prayer hall, indicating the direction of Mecca. This mosque was built by Tamil Muslims in 1935 but since 1975 it has served the Malaysian and Indonesian Muslim communities.

Cho Quan Church CHURCH

(133 Đ Tran Binh Trong; ⏲4-7am & 3-6pm Mon-Sat, 4-9am & 1.30-6pm Sun) Originally built by the French and destroyed three times, this 19th-century house of worship is one of the city's largest churches, with good views from the belfry (a steep climb). The church is on the eastern fringe of District 5, between ĐL Tran Hung Dao and Đ Nguyen Trai.

District 11

Immediately west of Cholon, the main enticements of District 11 are a couple of old pagodas and a popular water park.

Giac Vien Pagoda BUDDHIST TEMPLE

(Đ Lac Long Quan, District 11; ⏲7-11.30am & 1.30-7pm) In a land where so many ancient temples have been 'restored' in concrete and neon, it's a joy to discover one that looks its age. The temple was founded by Hai Tinh Giac Vien in the late 1700s and it is said that Emperor Gia Long, who died in 1819, used to worship here.

The temple has an atmosphere of scholarly serenity, and its secluded location down an alley near Dam Sen Lake means it is less visited than other temples in nearby Cholon.

Hidden behind a warren of winding lanes, the approach to the pagoda has many impressive tombs on the right – a popular playground for local kids. The pagoda itself boasts some 100 carvings of divine beings.

The main sanctuary is on the other side of the wall behind the Hai Tinh Giac Vien statue. The dais is set behind a fantastic brass incense basin with fierce dragon heads emerging from each side. The Guardian of the Pagoda is against the wall opposite the dais. Nearby rises a prayer tree similar to the one in Giac Lam Pagoda.

Phung Son Pagoda BUDDHIST TEMPLE

(Phung Son Tu, Chua Go; 1408 ĐL 3 Thang 2, District 11; ⏲prayers three times daily – 4-5am, 4-5pm & 6-7pm) Built between 1802 and 1820 on the site of structures from the Funan period, dating back at least to the early centuries of Christianity, this Buddhist temple is extremely rich in gilded, painted and beautifully fashioned bronze, wood, ceramic and beaten copper statuary. The **main dais**, with its many levels, is dominated by a large gilded A Di Da Buddha (the Buddha of Infinite Light; Amitābha). The main entrances are usually locked most of the time, but the side entrance is open during prayer times.

Once upon a time, it was decided to move Phung Son Pagoda to a different site. The pagoda's ritual objects – bells, drums, statues – were loaded onto the back of a white elephant that slipped under the great weight, sending all the precious objects tumbling into a nearby pond. This event was interpreted as an omen that the pagoda should remain in its original location. Everything was recovered but the bell, which, until about a century ago, locals insist could be heard ringing whenever there was a full or new moon.

Other Neighbourhoods

Giac Lam Pagoda BUDDHIST TEMPLE

(Chua Giac Lam; 118 Đ Lac Long Quan, Tan Binh District; 6am-noon & 2-8.30pm) Believed to be the oldest temple in HCMC (1744), Giac Lam is a fantastically atmospheric place set in peaceful, garden-like grounds. The Chinese characters that constitute the temple's name (覚林寺) mean 'Feel the Woods Temple' and the looming Bodhi tree (a native fig tree, sacred to Buddhists) in the front garden was the gift of a Sri Lankan monk in 1953.

Next to the tree stands a gleaming white statue of compassionate Quan The Am Bo Tat on a lotus blossom, a symbol of purity.

Like many Vietnamese Buddhist temples, aspects of both Taoism and Confucianism can be found. For the sick and elderly, the pagoda is a minor pilgrimage sight, as it contains a bronze bell that, when rung, is believed to answer the prayers posted by petitioners.

The main sanctuary lies in the next room, filled with countless gilded figures. On the dais in the centre of the back row sits the A Di Da Buddha, easily spotted by his colourful halo. The fat laughing fellow, seated with five children climbing all over him, is Ameda, the Buddha of Enlightenment, Compassion and Wisdom.

Prayers are held daily from 4am to 5am, 11am to noon, 4pm to 5pm and 7pm to 9pm.

About 3km from Cholon, Giac Lam Pagoda is best reached by taxi or *xe om* (motorbike taxi).

Le Van Duyet Temple TEMPLE

(Đ Dinh Tien Hoang, Binh Thanh District) Dedicated to Marshal Le Van Duyet (1763–1831), this shrine is also his burial place, alongside that of his wife. The marshal was a South Vietnamese general and viceroy who helped defeat the Tay Son Rebellion and reunify Vietnam. Among the items on display are a portrait of Le Van Duyet, personal effects including European-style crystal goblets, two life-size horse statues and a stuffed, mounted tiger. The temple is reached by heading north from Da Kao on Đ Dinh Tien Hoang.

When the Nguyen dynasty came to power in 1802, Le Van Duyet was elevated by Emperor Gia Long to the rank of marshal. He fell out of favour with Gia Long's successor, Minh Mang, who tried him posthumously and desecrated his grave. Emperor Thieu Tri, who succeeded Minh Mang, restored the tomb, thus fulfilling a prophecy of its destruction and restoration. Le Van Duyet was considered a national hero in the South before 1975 but is disliked by the Communists because of his involvement in the expansion of French influence.

During celebrations of Tet and on the 30th day of the seventh lunar month (the anniversary of Le Van Duyet's death), the tomb throngs with pilgrims. The caged birds for sale in and around the grounds are bought by pilgrims and freed to earn merit. The unfortunate creatures are often recaptured (and liberated again).

Museum of Traditional Vietnamese Medicine MUSEUM

(www.fitomuseum.com.vn; 41 Đ Hoang Du Khuong, District 10; adult/child 50,000/25,000d; 8.30am-5.30pm) A lovely piece of traditional architecture in itself, this absorbing and very well-stocked museum affords fascinating insights into traditional Vietnamese medicine, itself heavily influenced by Chinese philosophy. Delve into the world of Vietnamese potions and remedies through the centuries and don't miss the Cham tower at the top, equipped with a fertility symbol.

San Art GALLERY

(Map p319; www.san-art.org; 3 Me Linh, Binh Thanh District; 10.30am-6.30pm Tue-Sat;) This inspiring, independent, nonprofit gallery was founded by artists, giving other local artists the opportunity to display and develop their intriguing work. There's an excellent open-resource library-reading room on the ground floor, with a great selection of contemporary art books.

Saigon South NEIGHBOURHOOD
Saigon's District 7 is a sleek, fashionable and well-designed retreat for the wealthy within the fringes of the city. Businesspeople, both expats and the local nouveau riche, have embraced this planned neighbourhood of wide streets, fancy shops and manicured parks.

A centrepiece is the **Crescent** (Ho Ban Nguyet), a glitzy promenade of eating and upscale shopping along a scooped-out section of canal. After dark, the 700m-long pedestrian-only **Starlight Bridge** is a colourful attraction. The recently opened SC Vivo City (p354) is also located here.

It's well worth visiting Saigon South for a stroll and a look around. If you're a fitness freak, it's one of the less petrol-fumed places for a jog. Plenty of big-name city restaurants and chains have colonised the area. The Crescent is 7km south of Pham Ngu Lao; it should only take 15 minutes by cab (around 120,000d), outside of peak times.

Activities

River Cruises

There's always someone hanging around the vicinity of **Bach Dang jetty** (Map p315; Đ Ton Duc Thang) looking to charter a boat to tour the Saigon River. Prices should be around US$20 per hour for a small boat or US$25 to US$30 for a larger, faster craft. It's best to set an itinerary and a time limit at the start and ask them to bring the boat to you, rather than going to the boat yourself.

Les Rives DINNER CRUISE
(Map p315; ☎0128 592 0018; www.lesrivesexperience.com; Bach Dang jetty; sunset cruise adult/child 1,278,00/894,000d, Mekong Delta adult/child 2,263,000/1,697,000d) Sunset boat tour (minimum two people) at 4pm along canals beyond the city edges. Les Rives also offers a Mekong Delta cruise, departing at 7.30am and taking seven to nine hours. It can also convey you to the Cu Chi Tunnels (adult/child 1,899,000/1,299,000d) and Can Gio (adult/child 2,263,000/1,697,000d) by boat. Other options include incorporating *cyclo* (pedicab) excursions or cooking classes.

Indochina Junk DINNER CRUISE
(Map p315; ☎08-3895 7438; www.indochinajunk.com.vn) A lunch and dinner cruise, with set menus (US$15 to US$35) in an atmospheric wooden junk.

City Walk
Old Saigon

START 23/9 PARK
END SHRI
DISTANCE 4KM
DURATION 3 HOURS

Ho Chi Minh City may be rapidly modernising, but this tour through District 1 strips back the layers of modern lacquer to reveal the fascinating historic city beneath.

Start at 1 **23/9 Park**, which borders Đ Pham Ngu Lao and the city's unofficial backpacker district. The park owes its long, thin shape to a former tenure as the city's main railway terminus. Wander through the park to 1914 2 **Ben Thanh Market** (p352) – at its bustling best in the morning. The main entrance, with its belfry and clock, has become a symbol of HCMC.

Cross to the massive roundabout (carefully!) with an equestrian 3 **statue of Tran Nguyen Han**, a trusted general of 15th-century leader Le Loi. On a pillar at its base is a small white bust of Quach Thi Trang, a 15-year-old girl who was killed near here during antigovernment protests in 1963.

Muster up the courage and cross the road again, this time to the bus station. On Đ Pho Duc Chinh you'll see the lovely Sino-French 4 **Fine Arts Museum** (p324), stuffed with period details (and art). Turn onto Đ Le Cong Kieu, a short street lined with 5 **antique shops**. At the end turn (in quick succession) left, left again, then right onto Đ Ham Nghi. Before 1870 this wide boulevard was a canal with roads on either side.

Turn left onto Đ Ton That Dam and stroll through the colourful outdoor 6 **street market**. Turn right onto Đ Huynh Thuc Khang and follow it to ĐL Nguyen Hue, another former canal – now a grand boulevard. Turn right, heading past the dramatic and contemporary form of the 7 **Bitexco Financial Tower** (p318).

Turn left onto busy riverside Đ Ton Duc Thang. At the corner of Đ Dong Khoi is the grand 1925 8 **Majestic Hotel** (p335), requisitioned in WWII by the Japanese for use as their military barracks.

Continue along the river to the giant 9 **statue of Tran Hung Dao**, defeater of the Mongols, lording it over a semicircular

plaza with roads radiating out from it. Take the second one, Đ Ho Huan Nghiep, turning right at the end onto Đ Dong Khoi, formerly Rue Catinat and still the city's most famous street.

Further up Đ Dong Khoi stands the 10 **Caravelle Hotel** (p335). The curved corner section was the original 1959 hotel, which, during the American War, housed foreign news bureaux, the Australian and New Zealand embassies, and members of the press corps. In August 1964 a bomb exploded on the 5th floor. No-one was killed but the hotel spent the rest of the war with its corner windows taped up in case of further bombings.

Across the road is the 11 **Municipal Theatre** (p352), still referred to by its former name, the Opera House. On the next corner is perhaps HCMC's most famous hotel, the 12 **Continental**. Built in 1880, it was a favourite of the press corps during the French War. Graham Greene regularly stayed in room 214 and the hotel featured prominently in *The Quiet American*. Key scenes were set in the cafe known as the Continental Shelf, which once occupied the 1st-floor balcony.

Facing the Municipal Theatre, compact 13 **Lam Son Park** is currently in danger of being overwhelmed by construction for Saigon's new metro system. Walk with the construction on your left and turn right into the pedestrian mall of Đ Nguyen Hue. A recently inaugurated 2015 14 **statue of Ho Chi Minh** stands in front of the 15 **People's Committee Building** (p316). At night, the exterior of the beautifully illuminated building is often covered with thousands of geckos.

Turn right, then left again, back onto Đ Dong Khoi. Directly ahead is 16 **Notre Dame Cathedral** (p314), built between 1877 and 1883, sitting behind a large white statue of (namesake) St Mary holding an orb. East of the cathedral is the magnificent French-style 17 **Central Post Office** (p355).

Cross the square in front of the cathedral, turn right and head into 30/4 Park – a lovely formal space providing a grand approach to 18 **Reunification Palace** (p322). Stop to explore the palace or continue north along Pham Ngoc Thach to the large 19 **Turtle Lake** (Ho Con Rua) roundabout, with its concrete walkways and flower-like sculpture.

Backtrack a block and turn left onto Đ Nguyen Thi Minh Khai where you can finish with a drink at 20 **Shri** (p348) on the 23rd floor of the Centec Tower, enjoying views to your starting point and far beyond.

Swimming Pools & Water Parks

Several inner-city hotels offer access to their pools to nonguests for a fee, including the Lotte Legend Hotel Saigon, Park Hyatt Saigon, Majestic Hotel and May Hotel.

Saigon Soul Pool Parties SWIMMING
(Map p320; ☎0122 734 8128; www.facebook.com/SaigonSoul; New World Saigon Hotel, 76 Đ Le Lai; admission 150,000d) Cool beats, cold beers and a fun crowd of locals, expats and visitors all combine at the New World Saigon Hotel on Saturday afternoons from late November to early May. With around 500 pool-going guests, what could possibly go wrong?

The Oasis Saigon SWIMMING
(Map p336; 40/15 Đ Bui Vien; admission US$8; ⏲6.30am-10pm) Cunningly squeezed into a side alley in Pham Ngu Lao, this compact pool is a welcome haven from the city's heat. Drinks and food (40,000d to 90,000d) are available. If you're staying at any of the hotels belonging to the Beautiful group, you can use the pool for free.

Dam Sen Water Park WATER PARK
(www.damsenwaterpark.com.vn; 3 Đ Hoa Binh, District 11; adult/child before 4pm 140,000/90,000d, after 4pm 120,000/80,000d; ⏲9am-6pm Mon-Sat, 8.30am-6pm Sun) Water slides, rivers with rapids (or slow currents) and rope swings.

Labour Culture Palace SWIMMING
(Map p320; 55b Đ Nguyen Thi Minh Khai, District 3; admission 30,000d; ⏲pool 5.30am-7pm) The swimming pool of the old Cercle Sportif still has its colonnades and some art deco charm.

Dai The Gioi Water Park WATER PARK
(www.daithegioiwaterpark.com.vn; Đ Ham Tu, Cholon; admission 45,000-80,000d; ⏲8am-9pm Mon-Fri, 10am-9pm Sat & Sun) Large pool and slides.

Massage & Spa

Ho Chi Minh City offers some truly fantastic hideaways for pampering – the perfect antidote to a frenetic day spent dodging motorbikes. Check out www.spasvietnam.com for extensive reviews and online bookings.

L'Apothiquaire SPA
(La Maison de L'Apothiquaire; Map p320; ☎08-3932 5181; www.lapothiquaire.com; 64a Đ Truong Dinh, District 3; ⏲8.30am-9pm) Long considered the city's most elegant spa, L'Apothiquaire is housed in a beautiful white mansion tucked down a quiet alley, with a pool and sauna. Guests enjoy body wraps, massages, facials, foot treatments and herbal baths, and L'Apothiquaire makes its own line of lotions and cosmetics.

Other branches are located in **District 1** (Artisan Beauté; Map p315; ☎08-3822 2158; 100 Đ Mac Thi Buoi, District 1; ⏲9am-8.30pm) and **Saigon South** (☎08-5413 6638; 103 Đ Ton Dat Thien, District 7; ⏲9.30am-8pm).

Aveda SPA
(☎08-3519 4679; www.facebook.com/avedaherbal; Villa 21/1 Đ Xuan Thuy) Across in District 2, but worth the journey for its intensely soothing Indian-influenced Ayurvedic spa and massage treatments.

Aqua Day Spa SPA
(Map p315; ☎08-3827 2828; www.aquadayspasaigon.com; Sheraton Saigon, 88 Đ Dong Khoi; ⏲10am-11pm) One of HCMC's smartest hotel spas, this beautiful space offers a range of treatments, including warm-stone massage, foot pampering and facials.

Jasmine SPA
(Map p315; ☎08-3827 2737; www.jasminespa.vn; 45 Đ Ton That Thiep, District 1; 1hr massage 506,000d; ⏲9am-8pm) Spa and massage treatments.

Glow SPA
(Map p315; ☎08-3823 8368; www.glowsaigon.com; 129a ĐL Nguyen Hue, District 1; 1hr massage 540,000d; ⏲11am-9pm) Offers an array of aromatherapy facials, hair treatments and therapeutic massage.

Other Activities

Vietnam Golf & Country Club GOLF
(Cau Lac Bo Golf Quoc Te Viet Nam; ☎08-6280 0101; www.vietnamgolfcc.com; Long Thanh My Village, District 9; 18 holes weekday/weekend US$109/143) Playing golf has become a mark of status in Vietnam and this club, about 20km east of central HCMC, caters to the city's would-be high-flyers.

Courses

GRAIN Cooking Classes COOKING COURSE
(Map p315; ☎08-3827 4929; www.grainbyluke.com; Level 3, 71-75 ĐL Hai Ba Trung; per person from US$65; ⏲9am-noon & 2-5pm Mon-Sat) These cooking classes are designed and coordinated by Vietnamese-Australian chef Luke Nguyen. Four-course menus change regularly to reflect seasonal produce, and Luke himself is on hand for some classes throughout the year. Check the website for timings.

Saigon Cooking Class COOKING COURSE
(Map p315; ☎08-3825 8485; www.saigoncookingclass.com; 74/7 ĐL Hai Ba Trung; per adult/child under 12yr US$39/25; ⊙10am & 2pm Tue-Sun) Watch and learn from the chefs at Hoa Tuc (p342) as they prepare three mains (including *pho bo* – beef noodle soup – and some of their signature dishes) and one dessert. A market visit is optional (per adult/child under 12 years US$45/28, including a three-hour class).

Vietnam Cookery Centre COOKING COURSE
(Map p315; ☎08-3827 0349; www.vietnamese-cooking-class-saigon.com; 4th fl, 26 Đ Ly Tu Truong) Offers introductory classes, market visits and VIP premium classes

Cyclo Resto COOKING COURSE
(Map p320; ☎0975 513 011; www.cycloresto.com.vn; 6/28 Đ Cach Mang Thang Tam; per person US$29) Fun and informative three-hour cooking class, including a *cyclo* trip to the Thai Binh Market near Pham Ngu Lao.

Mai Home COOKING COURSE
(Saigon Culinary Arts Center; Map p336; ☎08-3838 6037; www.vietnamsaigoncookingclass.com; 269 Đ Nguyen Trai; per person US$37-45) Market visits and cooking classes near Saigon's Pham Ngu Lao backpacker area. Special vegetarian menus are available.

University of Social Sciences & Humanities LANGUAGE COURSE
(Dai Hoc Khoa Hoc Xa Hoi Va Nhan Van; Map p319; ☎08-3822 5009; www.vns.edu.vn; 12 Đ Dinh Tien Hoang) If you're planning a longer stay in HCMC, the university's group classes are a reasonably priced way to learn the language.

 Tours

Before you sign up for a standard, middle-of-the-road travel-agent tour of the city – the cheapest of which are available from agencies in the Pham Ngu Lao area – consider these far more imaginative and fun tours covering everything from street food and hidden cafes, to Chinatown, the art scene and Saigon after dark. Motorbike/scooter tours usually arrange pick up from your accommodation.

Hiring a *cyclo* for a half-day or full day of sightseeing is an interesting option, but agree on the price before setting out (most drivers charge around US$3 per hour).

Detoured TOUR
(☎0168 597 6136; www.detouredasia.com; per person US$55-65) Excellent walking tours with an inquisitive and fun Saigon expat discovering hidden secrets of the city. Highlights include funky street art, hip cafes and shops concealed in art deco apartment blocks, good street snacks, and lunch in a chic Vietnamese restaurant. Additional transport between walking stops is by taxi or motorbike.

Vietnam Photo Adventures TOUR
(☎0913 236 876; www.vietnamphotoadventures.com; per person US$29-59) Get creative with your camera and produce your own photographic memories on various tours focusing on Saigon landmarks, the street life of Cholon and local neighbourhoods. Tours are conducted by an experienced photographer who is also a long-term resident of Vietnam. Longer one- and two-night trips in the Mekong Delta are also available.

Vespa Adventures TOUR
(Map p336; ☎0122 299 3585; www.vespaadventures.com; 169a Đ De Tham; per person from US$69) Zooming out of Café Zoom (p346), Vespa Adventures offers entertaining, guided city tours on vintage scooters, as well as multiday trips around southern Vietnam. Embracing food, drink and music, the Saigon After Dark tour is brilliant fun.

Saigon Riders TOUR
(☎0913 767 113; www.saigonriders.vn; from US$29) Runs a variety of motorbike tours in and around Saigon, including full-day two-wheeled excursions to Cu Chi and Can Gio. Also longer overnight trips to the Mekong Delta.

HCMC FOR CHILDREN

At first glance, Ho Chi Minh City's hectic streets might not look that child-friendly, but there's the **Saigon Skydeck** (p318) at Bitexco Financial Tower, water parks, swimming pools, water-puppet shows, plenty of leafy parks, family-friendly cafes and ice-cream shops. World Games on the Basement 2 level (unit B2-18) of the **Vincom Center** (p353) (Tower B) is a fun, centrally located amusement arcade. Beyond the city is **Dai Nam Theme Park** (p360), the closest thing to Disneyland in Vietnam. Online, check out Kidz Saigon (www.kidzsaigon.com) for lots of ideas and places to keep children active and entertained in the big city.

Saigon Street Eats TOUR

(☎0908 449 408; www.saigonstreeteats.com; from US$40) Highly entertaining three- to four-hour scooter foodie tours around the streets and backstreets of town with Barbara and her husband, Vu. Select your tour according to taste: morning *pho* tours, lunchtime veggie or evening seafood tours, and prepare for some fun surprises.

XO Tours CULTURAL TOUR

(☎0933 083 727; www.xotours.vn; from US$45) Wearing *ao dai* (traditional dress), these girls run scooter/motorbike foodie, sights and Saigon by night tours: super hospitable and fantastic fun.

Back of the Bike Tours TOUR

(☎08-2221 5591; www.backofthebiketours.com; from US$48) Hop on the back of a motorbike and dine like a local on the wildly popular four-hour Street Food tours, or lasso in the sights of Saigon. Excellent guides.

Sophie's Art Tour TOUR

(☎0121 830 3742; www.sophiesarttour.com; per person US$55; ⌚9am-1pm Tue-Sat) Highly engaging and informative four-hour tour from expert Sophie Hughes, who has her finger on the pulse of the HCMC art scene (p326). Tours visit the Fine Arts Museum, private collections and contemporary art spaces, explaining the influence of recent Vietnamese history on artistic style and technique.

Tim Doling TOUR

(☎0128 579 4800; www.historicvietnam.com; tours 1,250,000d, minimum group size of five) Your Saigon and Cholon (Chinatown) heritage buff, with tours blending walking with minibus travel, bringing the city to life with insightful anecdotes and erudite observations. Tim's website also features his excellent essays on the city's changing face.

Saigon Unseen TOUR

(www.saigonunseen.com; from US$25) Motorbike tours around local markets and off-the-beaten path parts of HCMC and around.

Festivals & Events

Tet NEW YEAR

(⌚first day of first lunar month) The whole city parties and then empties out for family breaks. Đ Nguyen Hue features a huge flower exhibition, blooms fill Tao Dan Park and everyone exchanges lucky money.

Saigon Cyclo Challenge CHARITY RACE

(www.saigonchildren.com; ⌚mid-Mar) Professional and amateur *cyclo* drivers find out who's fastest; money raised is donated to charities supporting disadvantaged children.

Sleeping

District 1 is the obvious lodging choice in Ho Chi Minh City given its proximity to almost everything of interest, its relative closeness to the airport and its tempting array of establishments across all price ranges. Within District 1, you can either head east towards Đ Dong Khoi for smarter options close to the city's best restaurants and bars, west towards Pham Ngu Lao for budget accommodation and cheap tours, or somewhere in between – geographically and price-wise. Around Ben Thanh Market also has decent options.

At the lower end, a few dollars can be the difference between a dank, stuffy, windowless shoebox and a pleasant, well-appointed room with air-conditioning, ventilation and free wi-fi. Needless to say, cheaper places exist but you get what you pay for. For rock-bottom prices, a swift door-to-door around Pham Ngu Lao will turn up dives for US$15 or even less.

Upgrading to a midrange property can seem rather pointless when excellent, comfortable, almost hip rooms with all the bells and whistles are available for US$25 around Pham Ngu Lao and nearby. More discerning budget travellers can book ahead for similar places at slightly lower rates in the surrounding wards, such as the Co Giang and Nguyen Thai Binh wards.

At the top end, some of the city's best hotels occupy period, character-filled buildings where standards are international, as are the prices. The very best hotels, however, are newer, such as the Park Hyatt Saigon and Le Meridien.

Most hotels will pick you up at the airport for US$5 to US$10.

Dong Khoi Area

Home to Ho Chi Minh City's top-notch hotels, the Dong Khoi area is also sprinkled with attractive midrange options.

Asian Ruby HOTEL $$

(Map p315; ☎08-3827 2837; www.asianrubyhotel.com; 26 Đ Thi Sach; d US$70-90; ❄@📶) This comfortable midrange hotel is a gem, with a top location and polite staff, although for space it's worth outlaying an extra US$20 to upgrade to a deluxe room. Ask for a room facing out, not into the adjacent block.

King Star Hotel HOTEL $$

(Map p315; ☎08-3822 6424; www.kingstarhotel.com; 8a ĐL Thai Van Lung; r US$55-90; ❄@☞) Completely refurbished a few years ago, this spruce hotel verges on the boutique-business look. The decoration is contemporary and all rooms have flat-screen TVs and snazzy showers, but the cheapest have no window.

May Hotel HOTEL $$

(Map p315; ☎08-3823 4501; www.mayhotel.com.vn; 28-30 Đ Thi Sach; r US$65-90; ❄@☞≋) The brown-grey marble theme on the floors is weary but rooms, all with bathtub and flat-screen TV, are clean and inviting. Staff are dignified, but it's the top-floor pool (rare at this price) with its fine views that steals the show. Nonguests can take a dip for US$5.

Park Hyatt Saigon HOTEL $$$

(Map p315; ☎08-3824 1234; www.saigon.park.hyatt.com; 2 Lam Son Sq; r from US$310; ❄@☞≋) Following extensive renovations in 2015, this is one of the jewels in Saigon's hotel crown. A prime location opposite the Opera House combines with exemplary service, fastidiously attired staff and lavishly appointed rooms. Relaxation opportunities include an inviting pool and the acclaimed Xuan Spa. Highly regarded (yet affordable) restaurants include Opera (Italian) and Square One (Vietnamese and international).

Le Meridien HOTEL $$$

(☎08-6263 6688; www.starwoodhotels.com/lemeridien; 3c Đ Ton Duc Thang; d from US$210; P⊖❄@☞≋) Le Meridien's opening in mid-2015 caused the city's top-end hotels to enter renovation mode, but they'll need a special makeover to compete with this luxury property. Stellar facilities include a pool, spa, and five different bars, cafes and restaurants. Location-wise, many rooms have excellent river views, and the emerging dining scene on Đ Ngo Van Nam is nearby.

Liberty Central Saigon Citypoint HOTEL $$$

(Map p315; ☎08-3822 5678; www.odysseahotels.com/saigon-city-point-hotel; 59 Đ Pasteur; d from US$86; ⊖❄@☞≋) The newly opened Saigon Citypoint is one of HCMC's most stylish hotels. A classy streetside cafe segues to the modern reception area, and rooms feature chic decor and spacious bathrooms. Relaxation options include a rooftop pool with views to the Saigon River, an excellent spa, and some of the city's best eating and drinking options are nearby.

Lotte Legend Hotel Saigon HOTEL $$$

(Map p315; ☎08-3823 3333; www.legendsaigon.com; 2a-4a Đ Ton Duc Thang; r from US$175; ❄@☞≋) Look beyond the overblown lobby to attractive green- and cream-shaded corridors and lovingly presented, light, bright rooms with a slight deco feel. Standard rooms are actually more tastefully decorated than the executive standard rooms, while river-view standard rooms are the same price as city-view rooms. Visible from the lobby is Saigon's most beautiful resort-style pool.

Majestic Hotel HOTEL $$$

(Map p315; ☎08-3829 5517; www.majesticsaigon.com.vn; 1 Đ Dong Khoi; s/d from US$130/140; ❄@☞≋) Dollar for dollar it may not have the best rooms in town, but the colonial atmosphere of this venerable 1925 riverside hotel makes it a romantic option. Take a dip in the courtyard pool on a hot afternoon or sip a cocktail at the rooftop bar on a breezy evening. Breakfast and fruit basket included.

Intercontinental Asiana Saigon HOTEL $$$

(Map p315; ☎08-3520 9999; www.intercontinental.com; cnr ĐL Hai Ba Trung & ĐL Le Duan; r from US$189; ❄@☞≋) Modern and tasteful without falling into generic blandness, the Intercontintental is a welcome feature of Saigon's range of luxury establishments. Rooms have separate shower cubicles and free-standing baths, and many enjoy supreme views. A neighbouring tower of apartment-style residences caters to longer stayers.

Caravelle Hotel HOTEL $$$

(Map p315; ☎08-3823 4999; www.caravellehotel.com; 19 Lam Son Sq; r from US$180; ❄@☞≋) One of the first luxury hotels to reopen its doors in postwar Saigon, the five-star Caravelle remains a classic operation. Rooms in the modern 24-floor block are quietly elegant, with two rooms bigger than the others on each floor (ask); the priciest rooms and suites are in the historic 'signature' wing. The rooftop Saigon Saigon Bar (p348) is a spectacular spot for a cocktail.

Sheraton Saigon HOTEL $$$

(Map p315; ☎08-3827 2828; www.sheraton.com/saigon; 88 Đ Dong Khoi; r from US$200; ⊖❄@≋) The Sheraton lives up to expectations with luxurious rooms, an excellent spa and an elegant pool.

Pham Ngu Lao Area

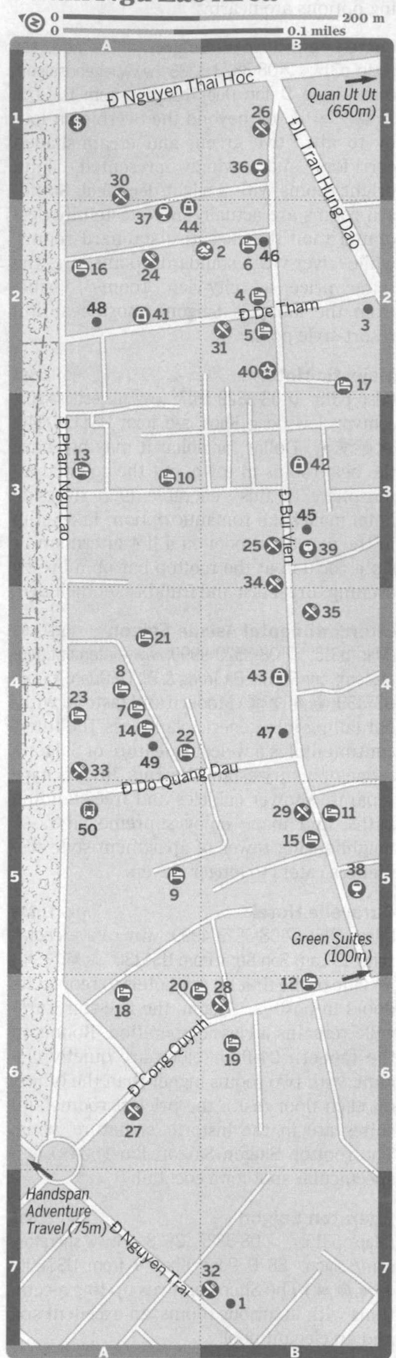

Catina Saigon Hotel HOTEL $$$
(Map p315; ☎08-3829 6296; www.hotelcatina.com.vn; 109 Đ Dong Khoi; d US$60-110;) Accessed through a jewellery shop, this smart, five-floor, 43-room boutique hotel at the heart of town is a good choice, with attractive discounts. Rooms are spacious, but superior and deluxe options are windowless (or have a fake window), so consider opting for premium deluxe.

Da Kao & Around

Sofitel Saigon Plaza HOTEL $$$
(Map p319; ☎08-3824 1555; www.sofitel.com; 17 ĐL Le Duan; d from US$150) Rooms are spiffing at this recently redecorated luxury hotel, and staff are particularly helpful and obliging. Check online for excellent discounts off rack rates.

Reunification Palace & Around

Town House 50 GUESTHOUSE, HOSTEL $
(Map p320; ☎08-3925 0210; www.townhousesaigon.com; 50e Đ Bui Thi Xuan; dm US$11, s/d/tr US$20/35/45;) Part guesthouse and part boutique hotel, Town House 50 offers stylish accommodation down a quiet laneway on a street with good restaurants and cafes. All dorms and rooms are non-smoking, and the decor is clean and modern. Rates include a cooked breakfast, and the team at reception has loads of local information on offer.

Vietnam Inn Saigon HOSTEL $
(Map p320; ☎08-3925 4348; www.vietnaminnsaigon.com; 200 Đ Le Lai; dm US$6, r US$24-30;) Just across the park north of the Pham Ngu Lao backpacker strip, Vietnam Inn Saigon is a sprawling, multistorey hostel that offers good-value and surprisingly spacious private rooms. It's a pretty social spot, and the rooftop bar is a great place to meet other travellers.

Family Inn HOTEL $$
(Map p320; ☎08-3925 7458; www.familyinnsaigon.com; 84a Đ Bui Thi Xuan; r US$45-66;) Yes, it may just have the city's slowest lift, but everything else about the welcoming Family Inn gets two big ticks. The team at reception is unfailingly friendly, rooms clean and spacious, and the central location – on a quiet street with good eateries – is pleasantly removed from the hustle and bustle of nearby Pham Ngu Lao.

Pham Ngu Lao Area

Activities, Courses & Tours

1	Mai Home	B7
2	The Oasis Saigon	B2
3	Vespa Adventures	B2

Sleeping

4	An An 2 Hotel	B2
5	Beautiful Saigon	B2
6	Beautiful Saigon 2	B2
7	Bich Duyen Hotel	A4
8	Blue River Hotel	A4
9	Cat Huy Hotel	A5
10	Diep Anh	A3
11	Duc Vuong	B5
12	Elegant Inn	B6
13	Elios Hotel	A3
14	Giang Son	A4
15	Hong Han Hotel	B5
16	Liberty Hotel Saigon Greenview	A2
17	Lily's Hostel	B2
18	Long Hostel	A6
19	Madame Cuc 127	B6
20	Madame Cuc 184	A6
21	Ngoc Minh Hotel	A4
22	PP Backpackers	A4
23	The Hideout Hostel	A4

Eating

	An Lac Chay	(see 30)
24	Asian Kitchen	A2
25	Baba's Kitchen	B3
	Café Zoom	(see 3)
	Chi's Cafe	(see 2)
26	Coriander	B1
27	Dinh Y	A6
28	Espy	B6
29	Five Oysters	B5
30	Margherita	A1
31	Mon Hue	B2
32	Pho Hung	B7
33	Pho Quynh	A4
34	Sozo	B3
35	Vittorio	B4

Drinking & Nightlife

36	Babylon Pub	B1
37	Le Pub	A2
38	Long Phi	B5
39	Spotted Cow	B3
	The View	(see 11)

Entertainment

40	Universal Bar	B2

Shopping

41	Gingko	A2
42	Hanoi Gallery	B3
43	Orange	B4
44	SahaBook	A2

Information

45	Asiana Travel Mate	B3
46	Go Go Vietnam	B2
47	Innoviet	B4
48	Kim Tran Travel	A2
	Sinh Tourist	(see 41)
49	Sinhbalo Adventures	A4

Transport

50	Sapaco	A5

Sanouva HOTEL **$$**
(Map p320; ☎08-3827 5275; www.sanouvahotel.com; 177 Đ Ly Tu Trong; r US$40-75;) A recent entry in the city's hotel stakes, the Sanouva channels a chic Asian vibe and has a good location just two blocks back from Ben Thanh Market.

Lavender Hotel HOTEL **$$**
(Map p320; ☎08-2222 8888; www.lavenderhotel.com.vn; 208 Đ Le Thanh Ton; r US$55-85;) Eschewing the nanna-ish connotations of its name, Lavender drapes itself stylishly in creamy marble and muted tones. The location, right by Ben Thanh Market, is excellent if potentially noisy.

Anpha Boutique Hotel BOUTIQUE HOTEL **$$$**
(Map p320; ☎08-3823 8890; www.anphaboutiquehotel.com; 202 Đ Le Thanh Ton; d US$60-100;) Close to Ben Thanh Market, Anpha features stylish rooms with comfortable beds, coffee-making facilities and flat-screen TVs. Reception and other staff are helpful and friendly, and don't be surprised if a chatty security guard wants to practise his English with you. Breakfast on the roof terrace could be better, but consolation comes with views of the Bitexco Financial Tower.

Pham Ngu Lao Area

Pham Ngu Lao is Ho Chi Minh City's budget zone and it's easy to hunt for a hotel or guesthouse on foot. Four streets (Đ Pham Ngu Lao, Đ De Tham, Đ Bui Vien and Đ Do Quang Dau) along with a warren of intersecting alleys form the heart of this backpacker ghetto, with more than 100 accommodation choices. Don't let that backpacker tag put you off. Even midrange travellers can find excellent deals here, often at budget prices. Basic breakfasts are usually included.

Among the options are countless family-run guesthouses (US$15 to US$35) and mini-hotels (US$30 to US$55), and even a few dorms (from US$7). We have highlighted some of the better places but there are dozens more, with new places opening all the time.

★Lily's Hostel HOSTEL $
(Map p336; ☎0948 213 181; lilyhostel.hcm@gmail.com; 35/5 Đ Bui Vien; dm/d US$8/26;) One of the new breed of modern hostels popping up in Pham Ngu Lao, Lily's has a warm and welcoming ambience courtesy of the elegant and soothing decor. Located in a quiet lane just off bustling Đ Bui Vien, Lily's easily bridges the gap between hostel and boutique guesthouse. Some private rooms have flat-screen TV and a minibar.

Diep Anh GUESTHOUSE $
(Map p336; ☎08-3836 7920; dieptheanh@hcm.vnn.vn; 241/31 Đ Pham Ngu Lao; r US$20-25;) A step above most PNL guesthouses, figuratively and literally (think thousand-yard stairs), Diep Anh's tall and narrow shape makes for light and airy upper rooms. The staff ensure they're kept in good nick.

Madame Cuc 127 GUESTHOUSE $
(Map p336; ☎08-3836 8761; www.madamcuchotels.com; 127 Đ Cong Quynh; US$20-30;) The original and by far the best of the three hotels run by the welcoming Madame Cuc and her friendly and fantastic staff. Rooms are clean and spacious.

Giang Son GUESTHOUSE $
(Map p336; ☎08-3837 7547; www.guesthouse.com.vn; 283/14 Đ Pham Ngu Lao; r US$20-30;) Tall and thin, with three rooms on each floor, a roof terrace and great service, Giang Son's sole downer is that there's no lift. Consider upgrading to a room with window.

The Hideout Hostel HOSTEL $
(Map p336; ☎08-3838 9147; www.vietnamhideouthostels.com; 281 Đ Pham Ngu Lao; dm US$8;) A new PNL hostel, this time with an emphasis on good times and meeting other travellers. Dorms are spick and span with bright colours; two free beers per day are on offer at the Hideout Bar next door; and the hostel also runs pub crawls three times a week that are free for guests (US$2 for nonguests).

Long Hostel HOSTEL $
(Map p336; ☎08-3836 0184; longhomestay@yahoo.com; 373/10 Đ Pham Ngu Lao; dm/d US$7/18;) This popular 12-room guesthouse tucked away down an alley near Thai Binh Market is run by a pleasant and helpful family. Five- and six-bed dorms available.

Hong Han Hotel GUESTHOUSE $
(Map p336; ☎08-3836 1927; www.honghanhotel.com.vn; 238 Đ Bui Vien; r US$18-30;) A corker guesthouse (seven floors, no lift), Hong Han has front rooms with ace views and smaller, quieter and cheaper rear rooms, plus free breakfast served on the 1st-floor terrace.

Bich Duyen Hotel GUESTHOUSE $
(Map p336; ☎08-3837 4588; bichduyenhotel@yahoo.com; 283/4 Đ Pham Ngu Lao; r US$22-25;) This spruce 15-room guesthouse offers a welcoming stay. The US$25 rooms are worth the extra money for a window. No lift.

PP Backpackers HOSTEL $
(Map p336; ☎0939 815 799; www.ppbackpackers.com.vn; Đ 283/41 Đ Pham Ngu Lao; dm US$7, d US$16-18;) Very helpful and efficient staff at this cheap and welcoming hostel where you can nab a dorm bed or fork out a bit more for an affordable double room.

Madame Cuc 184 HOTEL $
(Map p336; ☎08-3836 1679; www.madamcuchotels.com; 184 Đ Cong Quynh; r US$20-25) Tucked away down an alley off Đ Cong Quynh, this clean and well-managed choice carries Madame Cuc's trademark motifs: friendly, welcoming staff, complimentary tea and coffee, free breakfast and good rooms. No lift.

Elegant Inn HOTEL $
(Map p336; ☎08-6921 2860; www.elegantinnsaigon.com; 140 Đ Cong Quynh; r US$17-20;) Overseen by very helpful staff, this place has spick-and-span and reasonably sized rooms; tasty breakfasts included. As it's off the Đ Bui Vien nightlife drag, it's a bit quieter.

Liberty Hotel Saigon Greenview HOTEL $$
(Map p336; ☎08-3836 9522; www.odysseahotels.com/saigongreenview; 187 Đ Pham Ngu Lao; r from US$47;) Recently refurbished in a cool and classy mix of soothing neutral colours and natural wood, Liberty's Saigon Greenview is one of Pham Ngu Lao's flasher accommodation options. Rooms at the front have views of the 23/9 park on the northern edge of Saigon's backpacker district.

Green Suites HOTEL $$
(☎08-3836 5400; www.greensuiteshotel.com; 102/1 Đ Cong Quynh; s US$20-30, d $US24-35;) Slunk down a quiet alley off Đ Cong Quynh, immediately south of Đ Bui Vien,

this trim, comfy and spacious hotel exudes a pea-green theme, although the tiled rooms are clean and actually not very green at all.

Duc Vuong HOTEL $$
(Map p336; ☎08-3920 6991; www.ducvuonghotel.com; 195 Đ Bui Vien; d US$30-45; ❄@📶) A cut above other hotels in busy Pham Ngu Lao, the Duc Vuong features really friendly staff, good-value rates, and a rooftop restaurant that effortlessly morphs into The View (p350), a top bar for sunset drinks.

Blue River Hotel HOTEL $$
(Map p336; ☎08-3837 6483; www.blueriverhotel.com; 283/2c Đ Pham Ngu Lao; r US$25-50; ❄@📶) This welcoming and well-run 10-room place offers clean, spacious rooms, each with neat furnishings and a safe. A kitchen for guests' use is available, and there are also newer rooms across the lane.

Beautiful Saigon 2 HOTEL $$
(Map p336; ☎08-3920 8929; www.beautifulsaigon2hotel.com; 40/19 Đ Bui Vien; r US$30-45; ❄@📶) This eight-room mini-hotel lurks down a quiet back lane. The ground floor is taken up by a restaurant, giving it more of a guesthouse feel. Rooms have computers and deluxe versions have balconies; no lift.

Cat Huy Hotel HOTEL $$
(Map p336; ☎08-3920 8716; www.cathuyhotel.com; 353/28 Đ Pham Ngu Lao; r US$25-27; ❄📶) Down an alley in Pham Ngu Lao, this lovely 10-room hotel has modern and chic accommodation. The cheapest rooms are windowless, others have balconies. No lift.

Ngoc Minh Hotel GUESTHOUSE $$
(Map p336; ☎08-3837 6407; 283/11 Đ Pham Ngu Lao; r US$24-35; ❄@📶) This bright and friendly guesthouse has 19 clean and well-presented rooms with all mod-cons, a rooftop terrace decorated with blooming orchids, and a lift.

Elios Hotel HOTEL $$
(Map p336; ☎08-3838 5584; www.elioshotel.vn; 233 Đ Pham Ngu Lao; r US$50-80; ❄@📶) The swish entrance to this three-star hotel, with its aquaria and elegant design, is proof of the ongoing gentrification of the PNL area. The dark-wood rooms are clean and modern, with safes and writing desks. For huge views, head to the rooftop Blue Sky Restaurant.

Beautiful Saigon HOTEL $$
(Map p336; ☎08-3836 4852; www.beautifulsaigonhotel.com; 62 Đ Bui Vien; r US$30-45; ❄@📶) A tall and skinny mini-hotel, with a modern reception staffed by staff wearing red *ao dai* (the national dress of Vietnam). A lift ascends to the tidy rooms, the cheaper of which are small and windowless.

An An 2 Hotel HOTEL $$
(Map p336; ☎08-3838 5665; www.anan.vn; 216 Đ De Tham; r US$30-40) The spotlessly clean, comfortable, compact and stylish rooms here are a good-value step into the midrange bracket. The lift-equipped hotel is in the very centre of the Pham Ngu Lao backpacking area.

Nguyen Thai Binh & Around

Saigon Central Hostel HOSTEL $
(Map p315; ☎08-3914 1107; saigoncentralhostel@gmail.com; 54/6 Đ Ky Con; dm/d US$6/20; ❄@📶) Family-owned guesthouse located in a laneway in a more local area of town – still just a short walk to Pham Ngu Lao, Dong Khoi and Ben Thanh Market, though.

Blue River Hotel 2 GUESTHOUSE $
(Map p315; ☎08-3915 2852; www.blueriverhotel.vn; 54/13 Đ Ky Con; r US$12-20; ❄@📶) Fronted by bamboo fronds, and within reach of both Dong Khoi and Pham Ngu Lao but far enough away to flee the tourist buzz, this friendly and quiet guesthouse is excellent. It's down a quiet cul-de-sac, offering a window into local urban life. Cheaper rooms have no window.

Town House 23 HOSTEL, GUESTHOUSE $
(Map p320; ☎08-3915 1491; www.townhousesaigon.com; 23 Đ Dang Thi Nhu; dm $US11, r US$28-37; ⊝❄@📶) Located in a quiet cafe-lined street a short walk from the bustle of Pham Ngu Lao, Town House 23 is a modern and well-designed combination of hostel and guesthouse. Decor is particularly stylish and the team at reception is very helpful. Note that not all rooms have windows.

Co Giang

For a quieter and slightly cheaper alternative to Pham Ngu Lao, there's a string of guesthouses in Co Giang ward (District 1) in a quiet alley connecting Đ Co Giang and Đ Co Bac. To reach the alley, head southwest on ĐL Tran Hung Dao, turn left at Đ Nguyen Kac Nhu and then first right onto Đ Co Bac. The guesthouses are down the first alley to the left.

All of the guesthouses down this lane are popular with long-timers (expat English teachers and the like), so you'll need to book well ahead to nab a place. Preference goes to longer-term bookings.

Guest House California GUESTHOUSE $
(08-3837 8885; guesthousecaliforniasaigon@yahoo.com; 171a Đ Co Bac; r US$15-18;) No mirrors on the ceiling or pink champagne on ice, but friendly and clean California has a guest kitchen, free laundry, a penchant for garden gnomes, a roof garden, and further rooms across the way.

Miss Loi's GUESTHOUSE $
(08-3837 9589; missloi@hcm.fpt.vn; 178/20 Đ Co Giang; s/d US$14/16;) The original Co Giang guesthouse, with a homey atmosphere and helpful staff. Miss Loi is an attentive host and rates include a light breakfast; rooms all have fridge and window.

Other Neighbourhoods

★Ma Maison Boutique Hotel HOTEL $$
(08-3846 0263; www.mamaison.vn; 656/52 Cach Mang Thang Tam, District 3; s US$60-70, d US$70-110;) Down a peaceful lane off a busy arterial route, friendly Ma Maison is halfway between the airport and the city centre, and partly in the French countryside, decor-wise. Wooden shutters soften the exterior of the modern, medium-rise block, while in the rooms, painted French provincial-style furniture and first-rate bathrooms add a touch of panache.

★Villa Song BOUTIQUE HOTEL $$$
(08-3744 6090; www.villasong.com; 187/2 Đ Nguyen Van Huong, District 2; r US$159-220, ste US$350-460;) In a District 2 garden location with river views, this French-inspired boutique hotel is one of Saigon's most relaxing places to stay. Very romantic rooms and suites are filled with heritage Indochine style and contemporary Vietnamese art, and the property's Song Vie bar has an absolute riverside location. The spa is also well regarded and luxury speedboat trips are available. A free minibus shuttle – around 30 minutes – to central Saigon is available.

Hotel Nikko Saigon HOTEL $$$
(08-3925 7777; www.hotelnikkosaigon.com.vn; 235 Đ Nguyen Van Cu, District 1; d from US$150;) The location is a bit stranded for sightseers, but this is one of HCMC's most supreme hotels, with roomy minimalist accommodation, faultless service and an obsessive attention to detail.

Thao Dien Village BOUTIQUE HOTEL $$$
(08-3744 6457; www.thaodienvillage.com; 189-197 Đ Nguyen Van Huong, District 2; r/ste from US$100/160;) Combining restaurants, a bar and a poolside spa centre, this riverside property is a good option if you're keen to escape from the big-city bustle. Verdant surroundings and wooden pavilions create an ambience reminiscent of Bali. Just note that Vietnamese weddings are often held on weekends, and that downtown Saigon is around 30 minutes by taxi from District 2.

Eating

Hanoi may consider itself more cultured, but Ho Chi Minh City is Vietnam's culinary capital. Delicious regional fare is complemented by a well-developed choice of international restaurants, with Indian, Japanese, Thai, Italian and East–West fusions well represented. Unsurprisingly, given its heritage, HCMC has a fine selection of French restaurants, from the casual bistro to haute cuisine.

Good foodie neighbourhoods include the Dong Khoi area, with a high concentration of top-quality restaurants, as well as the bordering sections of District 3. Some of Pham Ngu Lao's eateries, attempting to satisfy every possible culinary whim, are good value but generally less impressive, although others are standout. There are also a few escapes further afield for those willing to explore.

Markets have a good selection of stalls whipping up tasty treats. Ben Thanh's night market is particularly good.

Banh mi – cheap filled baguettes with a French look and very Vietnamese taste – are sold by street vendors. The fresh baguettes are stuffed with something resembling pâté (don't ask), pickled vegetables and various other fillings. To really discover more of the city's great street food, a tour (p333) is an excellent option.

The largest concentration of vegetarian restaurants is around the Pham Ngu Lao area and you'll usually find one within a chopstick's throw of Buddhist temples.

Dong Khoi Area

Secret Garden VIETNAMESE $
(Map p315; 8th fl, 158 Đ Pasteur; meals 55,000-80,000d; 8am-10pm;) Negotiate the stairs in this faded Saigon apartment building to arrive at Secret Garden's wonderful rooftop restaurant. Rogue chickens peck away in the herb garden, Buddhist statues add Asian ambience, and delicious homestyle

dishes are served up with city views. Service can sometimes be a little *too* casual, but it's worth persevering for the great flavours.

5Ku Station BARBECUE $

(Map p315; 29 Đ Le Thanh Thon; meals around 100,000d; ⏲4pm-late) Hopping with evening diners, this chain of makeshift-looking al fresco barbecue restaurants is fun, boisterous, outgoing and tasty. Grab yourself a wooden box seat and a cold beer and chow down on barbecue and hotpot alongside a mix of locals, travellers and expats.

Huong Lai VIETNAMESE $

(Map p315; ☎08-3822 6814; www.huonglai2001saigon.com; 38 Đ Ly Tu Trong; meals 55,000-160,000d; ⏲noon-3pm & 6-10pm) A must for finely presented, traditional Vietnamese food, where the airy and high-ceilinged loft of an old French-era shophouse is the setting for dining with a difference. Staff are from disadvantaged families or are former street children and receive on-the-job training, education and a place to stay.

Spice Ca'phe CAFE $

(Map p315; 47 Đ Ton That Thiep; meals 45,000-80,0000; ⏲8am-9pm; ✎) Located near decent shopping, Spice Ca'phe is a relaxing haven from the buzz of HCMC retail therapy. Healthy teas, smoothies and juices partner with a concise menu of local dishes, many with a healthy vegetarian spin. Happy hour from 2pm to 6pm offers a 20% discount.

Chi Hoa VIETNAMESE $

(Map p315; ☎08-3827 3155; www.chihoacuisine.com; 31a Đ Le Thanh Thon; meals 65,000-100,000d; ⏲8am-10pm) Homestyle Vietnamese food served in simple but attractive surroundings. The menu ranges widely from lots of different *banh mi* sandwiches to salads and rice and noodle bowls.

Fanny ICE CREAM $

(Map p315; www.fanny.com.vn; 29-31 Đ Ton That Thiep; per scoop from 40,000d; ⏲8am-11pm; 📶) On the ground floor of a lavish French villa, Fanny concocts excellent Franco-Vietnamese ice cream in a healthy range of home-grown flavours. Our refreshing favourites are coconut, star anise and green tea.

Bun Dau Ngo Nho Pho Nho VIETNAMESE $

(Map p315; 158 Đ Pasteur; meals 25,000-60,000d; ⏲10am-9pm; ✎) Street-art decor and great-value noodle and tofu dishes make this a favourite of Saigonese students. It's on the right-hand side of the lane – look forward to intense conversations with friendly locals looking to practise their English.

Kem Bach Dang ICE CREAM $

(Map p315; 26-28 ĐL Le Loi, cnr Đ Pasteur; ice creams from 50,000d; ⏲8am-11pm) Take the temperature down with a freshly made coconut ice cream (served in a coconut) or a cooling banana split at this long-standing local ice-cream parlour on the corner of roaring ĐL Le Loi.

★ **The Racha Room** THAI $$

(Map p315; ☎0908 791 412; www.facebook.com/theracharoom; 12-14 Đ Mac Thi Buoi; shared plates 195,000-320,000d; ⏲11.30am-midnight) The Racha Room is one of the city's most hip eateries. Thai street food underpins the diverse menu of bar snacks (40,000d to 150,000d) and shared plates, but effortlessly stretches to include neighbouring countries as well. Asian-inspired cocktails ensure the Racha Room is also one of the city's best bars. Pop in for happy hour from 5pm to 7.30pm.

★ **Propaganda** VIETNAMESE $$

(Map p315; ☎08-3822 9048; www.propagandasaigon.com; Đ 21 Han Thuyen; meals 95,000-185,000d; ⏲7.30am-10.30pm) Colourful murals and retro socialist posters brighten up this popular bistro with park views. The menu focuses on street-food classics from around Vietnam, all enjoyed with a bustling ambience. Salads are particularly good – try the wild pepper and green mango salad with barbecue chicken – and retreat to the 1st floor if downstairs is too crowded.

Nha Hang Ngon VIETNAMESE $$

(Map p315; ☎08-3827 7131; 160 Đ Pasteur; meals 50,000-260,000d; ⏲7am-10pm; 📶) Thronging with locals and foreigners, this is one of HCMC's most popular spots, with a large range of the best street food in stylish surroundings. It's set in a leafy garden ringed by food stalls; each cook serves up a traditional dish, ensuring an authentic taste.

Hum Lounge & Restaurant VEGETARIAN $$

(Map p315; ☎08-3832 8920; www.hum-vegetarian.vn; 2 Đ Thi Sach; meals 80,000-190,000d; ⏲10am-10pm) This new opening brings the excellent Vietnamese-inspired vegetarian cuisine of the city's long-established Hum Vegetarian Cafe & Restaurant (p345) to a central garden location. Settle into the elegant and verdant space and enjoy dishes including papaya and banana flower salads, mushrooms steamed in coconut, and the subtle combination of braised tofu with star anise and cinnamon.

Quan Bui VIETNAMESE $$

(Map p315; ☎08-3829 1545; 17a Đ Ngo Van Nam; meals 80,000-140,000d; ⊙8am-11pm; ❄) Stylish Indochine decor features at this recent opening in up-and-coming Đ Ngo Van Nam. Nearby restaurants offer Japanese flavours, but Quan Bui's focus is on authentic Vietnamese dishes served by hip young waitstaff. Cocktails – delivered from the associated bar across the lane – are among Saigon's best, and upstairs there's an air-conditioned and smoke-free dining room.

Temple Club VIETNAMESE $$

(Map p315; ☎08-3829 9244; www.templeclub.com.vn; 29 Đ Ton That Thiep; meals 120,000-210,000d; ⊙noon-midnight; 📶✎) This classy establishment, housed on the 2nd floor of a beautiful colonial-era villa decorated with spiritual motifs and elegant Chinese characters, offers a huge selection of delectable Vietnamese dishes, including vegetarian specialities, alongside a spectrum of cocktails.

3T Quan Nuong BARBECUE $$

(Map p315; ☎08-3821 1631; 29 Đ Ton That Thiep; meals 85,000-280,000d; ⊙5-11pm) This breezy al fresco Vietnamese barbecue restaurant on the Temple Club's rooftop is in many a Saigon diner's diary: choose your meat, fish, seafood and veggies and flame them up right there on the table.

Xu VIETNAMESE $$

(Map p315; ☎08-3824 8468; www.xusaigon.com; 1st fl, 75 ĐL Hai Ba Trung; 3-course set lunch Mon-Fri 295,000d, meals 115,000-320,000d, 8-course tasting menu 850,000d; ⊙11.30am-midnight) This super-stylish restaurant-lounge serves up a menu of Vietnamese-inspired fusion dishes. It's pricey, but well worth the flutter for top service and a classy wine list. Innovative bar snacks (70,000d to 150,000d) and top-notch cocktails reinforce Xu's status as one of the city's most elegant lounge bars.

Hoa Tuc VIETNAMESE $$

(Map p315; ☎08-3825 1676; www.hoatuc.com; 74/7 ĐL Hai Ba Trung; meals 135,000-310,000d; ⊙10.30am-10.30pm) In the trendy courtyard of the former opium refinery, Hoa Tuc offers atmosphere and style to match the excellence of its food. Signature dishes include mustard leaves rolled with crispy vegetables and shrimp, and spicy beef salad with kumquat, baby white eggplant and lemongrass. Home chefs can pick up tricks at an in-house cooking class (p333).

Au Parc CAFE $$

(Map p315; ☎08-3822 3080; www.auparcsaigon.com; 23 Đ Han Thuyen; meals 125,000-275,000d; ⊙7am-11pm; 📶) The laptop and tablet crowd flocks to this slender two-floor cafe for its Mediterranean and Middle Eastern-inflected selection of salads, quiches, baguettes, pasta, mezze and light grills, from breakfast and brunch to dinner. Many ingredients are homemade, and the smoothies, juices and views of the park are all sublime. There's a nonsmoking lounge upstairs.

Tandoor INDIAN $$

(Map p315; ☎08-3930 4839; www.tandoorvietnam.com; 39b Đ Ngo Duc Ke; meals 69,000-179,000d; ⊙11am-2.30pm & 5-11pm; 📶✎) This restaurant's lengthy menu has vegetarian and South Indian sections, but the focus here is mainly on North Indian dishes. The fruit-packed lassis are very refreshing.

Relish & Sons BISTRO $$

(Map p315; ☎012 0721 4294; www.facebook.com/relishandsons; 44 Đ Dong Du; meals 100,000-170,000d; ⊙8am-midnight; 📶) Relish & Sons brings a versatile Melbourne vibe to Saigon. Kick off with good coffee and eggs lots of ways, before returning for gourmet burgers, bar snacks, and craft beer and cider on tap. Later in the evening, cocktails with an Asian spin become most people's drink of choice. Try the Sugar 'n' Spice with Vietnamese mint and fresh pomelo.

Pacharan SPANISH $$

(Map p315; ☎08-3825 6024; www.pacharansaigon.com; 97 Đ Hai Ba Trung; tapas 80,000-160,000d, meals 220,000-440,000d; ⊙10am-late; 📶) Spread over three floors, Pacharan has bites including succulent chorizo, marinated anchovies and chilli *gambas* (prawns), plus more substantial mains such as an authentic paella (for two). The rooftop terrace is great for sampling Spanish wine, and there's a cosy bar downstairs and live music.

Dublin Gate INTERNATIONAL $$

(Map p315; www.thedublingateirishpub.com; 19 Đ Thai Van Lung; mains 90,000-550,000d; ⊙7am-1am; 📶) Load up on cold beer, Guinness, whisky, sports TV and quality expat comfort food. The menu ranges from steaks and burgers (in Aussie–New Zealand style with beetroot) to pizza, pasta, sandwiches, salads and excellent MSG-free Vietnamese dishes.

The Refinery BISTRO $$

(Map p315; ☎08-3823 0509; www.therefinerysaigon.com; 74/7c ĐL Hai Ba Trung; meals 175,000-345,000d; ⏰11am-late; 📶) With a black-and-red tiled floor and relaxed vibe in the old French opium refinery, this bistro and wine bar has winning cocktails, a top wine list, and appetising food with a French and Mediterranean accent. Menu highlights include very good pasta and risotto, and a lazy brunch in the Refinery's al fresco area is a top way to start another day.

Annam Gourmet Market CAFE $$

(Map p315; www.annam-gourmet.com; 16 Đ Hai Ba Trung; sandwiches from 70,000d, meals from 140,000d; ⏰7am-9pm; 📶🖉) A quiet, relaxing and neat place for breakfast, brunch, a salad, bruschetta or baguette sandwich, this cafe on the upper floor of a delicatessen is stylish, with lime-green sofas, a curved glass window, and snappily dressed snackers and diners. There are goodies on sale if you're planning on a picnic or self-catering.

Elbow Room AMERICAN $$

(Map p315; 52 Đ Pasteur; meals 100,000-350,000d; ⏰8am-10pm Mon-Sat, to 5pm Sun; 📶) If you're a lumberjack, you'll be OK at this upmarket American-style bistro where there's a big breakfast with your name on it (pancakes, bacon, eggs, ham, fries, toast). Otherwise, there's a hefty menu of burgers, burritos, hot dogs, pizza, pasta, sandwiches and, in a concession to the healthy, wraps.

Skewers MEDITERRANEAN $$

(Map p315; ☎08-3822 4798; www.skewers-restaurant.com; 9a Đ Thai Van Lung; meals 250,000-400,000d, set lunch 350,000d; ⏰11.30am-2.30pm Mon-Sat, from 6pm daily; 📶) With a winning line in perfectly-done skewered meats, the Mediterranean menu here takes in all stops from the Maghreb to Marseilles. It's strong on atmosphere with an open-plan kitchen and draws a crowd, so book ahead.

Barbecue Garden VIETNAMESE $$

(Map p315; www.barbecuegarden.com; 135a Đ Nam Ky Khoi Nghia; meals 80,000-180,000d; ⏰11am-11pm) Trees festooned with fairy lights, outdoor tables and a laid-back ambience make this the ideal spot for groups. Fire up the table-top grills to barbecue different meats and seafood, and partner it all with tasty Vietnamese salads and cold beer. Friday nights are popular with locals celebrating the end of the week, and weekday lunch specials are good value.

Soulburger BURGERS $$

(Map p315; www.facebook.com/soulburgersaigon; 4 Đ Phan Boi Chau; burgers 165,000-345,000d; ⏰4.30pm-midnight Tue-Sun; 📶) Head up the narrow staircase for some of Saigon's best burgers. They're all named after music legends like Little Richard and James Brown, and sides of chicken wings, onion rings and poutine complete the North American focus. Grab a balcony table for Ben Thanh Market views, and be surprised by the good range of German and Belgian beers also available.

Jaspas Wine & Grill INTERNATIONAL $$

(Map p315; ☎08-3827 0931; http://jaspas.com.vn; 74/7 ĐL Hai Ba Trung; meals 175,000-485,000d, pizza & burgers 175,000-195,000d) Light, uncomplicated, busy and popular, Jaspas serves up Asian and Western favourites in a relaxed setting with an al fresco aspect. The grilled sea bass on wasabi-infused mashed potato is awesome and, for indulgence, the Mars Bar cheesecake is the way to go.

Bibi Alibi FRENCH $$

(Map p315; www.facebook.com/BibiAlibi; 5a Đ Nguyen Sieu; meals 200,000-400,000d; ⏰11.30am-2.30pm & 6.30-10.30pm; 📶) Formerly a trendy cocktail bar, Alibi has been reborn as a welcoming and good-value French bistro. Standout dishes include Gallic classics like steak tartare and a pear tarte tatin, and a Mediterranean influence underpins the concise menu.

Pizza 4P's ITALIAN $$

(Map p315; www.pizza4ps.com/; 8/15 Đ Le Thanh Ton; pizza & pasta 140,000-330,000d; ⏰10am-11pm) This crisp, modern, chilled-out and unusual Italian-Japanese fusion restaurant has a pizza oven at its hub and a delicious bar to boot. Service is unflappable and prices as tempting as the food. It's tucked away on the left fork of an alley off Đ Le Thanh Ton.

Le Jardin FRENCH $$

(Map p315; ☎08-3825 8465; 31 Đ Thai Van Lung; meals 120,000-200,000d; ⏰11am-11pm Mon-Sat; 📶) This place is popular with French expats seeking an escape from the busier boulevards. It has a wholesome bistro-style menu, with a shaded terrace cafe in the outdoor garden of the French cultural centre, Idecaf.

Lamie Cafe CAFE $$

(Map p315; www.facebook.com/lamiesaigon; 15b/62 Đ Le Thanh Ton; snacks & meals 80,000-130,000d; ⏰8.30am-10pm Mon-Sat, 10.30am-8pm Sun) Good coffee, juices and baguette sandwiches right in the middle of some of Saigon's best street art. It's also a hang-out for the city's best street artists, and the surrounding walls are used as vibrant canvases on a regular basis.

Square One VIETNAMESE $$$
(Map p315; ☎08-3824 1234; www.saigon.park.hyattrestaurants.com/squareOne; Park Hyatt Saigon, 2 Lam Son Sq; meals from 240,000d; ⏰noon-2.30pm & 5.30-10.30pm; 📶) With five open kitchens on the mezzanine level of the Park Hyatt, Square One concocts a faultless formula of style, ambience, good looks, fine food (Vietnamese and Western), crisply fresh ingredients and tip-top service. The Saturday brunch includes a popular free-flow wine and bubbly menu.

El Gaucho ARGENTINIAN $$$
(Map p315; ☎08-3827 2090; www.elgaucho.asia; 74 Đ Hai Ba Trung; meals 390,000-3,050,000d; ⏰11am-late) Nirvana for the serious meat lover, El Gaucho matches hearty serves of fall-apart lamb shanks, tender skewers and juicy steaks to a fine-dining environment. It even make its own chorizo and *salchicha* (spicy sausage). Look forward to a stunning, if pricey, drinks list too.

Maxim's Nam An VIETNAMESE $$$
(Map p315; ☎08-3829 6676; www.maxims.com.vn; 15 Đ Dong Khoi; meals 190,000-400,000d; ⏰7pm-late) Something of a Saigon legend, this supper club is distinguished more for its over-the-top jazz-club ambience and live music than for the food, which is fine if not jaw-dropping. If you're after a memorable experience, though, you could do a lot worse.

Da Kao & Around

Pho Hoa VIETNAMESE $
(Map p319; 260c Đ Pasteur; meals 60,000-75,000d; ⏰6am-midnight) This long-running establishment is more upmarket than most but is definitely the real deal – as evidenced by its popularity with regular local patrons. Tables come laden with herbs, chilli and lime, as well as *gio chao quay* (fried Chinese bread), *banh xu xe* (glutinous coconut cakes with mung-bean paste) and *cha lua* (pork-paste sausages wrapped in banana leaves).

Banh Xeo 46A VIETNAMESE $
(Map p319; ☎08-3824 1110; 46a Đ Dinh Cong Trang; regular/extra large 70,000/110,000d; ⏰10am-9pm; 🌶) Locals will always hit the restaurants that specialise in a single dish, and this renowned spot serves some of the best *banh xeo* in town. These Vietnamese rice-flour pancakes stuffed with bean sprouts, prawns and pork (vegetarian versions available) are legendary. Other dishes available include excellent *goi cuon* (fresh summer rolls with pork and prawn).

Cuc Gach Quan VIETNAMESE $$
(Map p319; ☎08-3848 0144; www.cucgachquan.com.vn/en; 10 Đ Dang Tat; meals 75,000-200,000d; ⏰9am-midnight) When you step into this cleverly renovated old villa it comes as little surprise that the owner is an architect. The decor is rustic and elegant at the same time, which is also true of the food. Despite its tucked-away location in the northernmost reaches of District 1, this is no secret hideaway: book ahead.

Tib VIETNAMESE $$
(Map p319; ☎08-3829 7242; www.tibrestaurant.com.vn; 187 Đ Hai Ba Trung; mains 125,000-285,000d; 📶) Visiting presidents and prime ministers have slunk down this lantern- and fairy-light-festooned alley and into this atmospheric old house to sample Tib's imperial Hue cuisine. Although you could probably find similar food for less money elsewhere, the setting is wonderful. **Tib Vegetarian** (Map p319; www.tibrestaurant.com.vn; 11 Đ Tran Nhat Duat; mains & snacks 40,000-60,000d; ⏰7am-10pm; 🌶) offers a more relaxed alternative with a cheaper and less formal spin on the vegetarian menu.

Bloom Saigon FUSION $$$
(Map p319; ☎08-3910 1277; www.bloom-saigon.com; 3/5 Hoang Sa; meals 100,000-460,000d; ⏰10.30am-10.30pm) In a lovingly restored heritage mansion near the city's recently revitalised Thi Nghe channel, Bloom combines fusion flavours with the good news story of offering culinary training for disadvantaged youth. Meals are firmly based in Vietnam, but tinged with subtle Western influences. Interesting menu options include coconut-crusted salmon with jackfruit and a green apple salad. Vietnamese dishes are cheaper.

Reunification Palace & Around

Cyclo Resto VIETNAMESE $
(Map p320; ☎0975 513 011; www.cycloresto.com.vn; 6.28 Đ Cach Mang Thang Tam; 5 courses US$6; ⏰11am-10pm) This place offers some of the best-value food in town. For US$6 you get five fabulous Vietnamese dishes. The popu-

lar cooking course – incorporating five dishes – is US$29, and US$10 *cyclo* tours of the city are also available.

Beefsteak Nam Son VIETNAMESE **$**

(Map p320; 157 Đ Nam Ky Khoi Nghia; meals from 60,000d; ⊙6am-10pm;) For first-rate, affordable steak in a simple setting, this is a superb choice. Local steak, other beef dishes (such as the spicy beef soup *bun bo Hue*), imported Canadian fillets and even cholesterol-friendly ostrich are on the well-priced menu.

Tin Nghia VEGETARIAN **$**

(Map p320; 9 ĐL Tran Hung Dao; meals 25,000-35,000d; ⊙7.30am-1pm & 4.30-8pm, closed 2nd & 16th of lunar month;) This Cao Dai vegetarian restaurant turns out delicious traditional treats without resorting to fake meat.

Hum Vegetarian Cafe & Restaurant VEGETARIAN **$$**

(Map p320; 08-3930 3819; www.hum-vegetarian.vn; 32 Đ Vo Van Tan; meals 80,000-165,000d; ⊙10am-10pm;) Even if you're not a vegetarian, this serene and elegant restaurant requires your attention. Everything – from the charming service to the delightful Vietnamese dishes and peaceful outside tables – makes dining here an occasion to savour. There's also a new, equally laid-back and more central location (p341).

La Fiesta TEX-MEX **$$**

(Map p320; 0944 291 697; www.facebook.com/lafiestavietnam; 33 Đ Dang Thi Nhu; meals 135,000-210,000d; ⊙11am-10pm Tue-Sun) Tacos, burritos and enchiladas all feature at this colourful restaurant, on a quiet street a short walk south from Pham Ngu Lao. Potted cacti and *lucha libre* (Mexican wrestling) masks provide plenty of hints for what's on offer. Well-crafted margaritas and sangria seal the deal – especially when served by the jug.

San Fu Lou DIM SUM **$$**

(Map p320; 08-3823 9513; www.sanfulou.com; Ground fl, AB Tower, 76a Đ Le Lai; dim sum 45,000-175,000d; ⊙7am-3am) Always bustling, the modern San Fu Lou offers a fine array of Cantonese dim sum shared plates. Highlights include duck and black-truffle dumplings, and beef short ribs with ginger and black pepper. Bring along a few friends so you can sample more of the huge menu, and be ready to linger longer than first planned.

Khoi Thom MEXICAN **$$**

(Map p320; www.khoithom.com; 29 Đ Ngo Thoi Nhiem; meals 115,000-175,000d, set lunch 140,000d; ⊙11am-late) With its breezy al fresco seating area and top-notch menu, this vibrantly coloured and bubbly Vietnamese-Mexican restaurant hits all the right notes, including the splendid tequila cocktails and slammers (delivered by Tequila Girls), and live music on Fridays.

Marina VIETNAMESE, SEAFOOD **$$**

(Map p320; 08-3930 2379; 172 Đ Nguyen Dinh Chieu; meals 100,000-500,000d; ⊙11am-11pm) Ask a sample of well-to-do Saigonese where to go for seafood and the chances are they will recommend this place. It's definitely geared to local tastes (bright lights, TVs playing sports, and bad piped music), but the food is delicious, particularly squid and the soft-shell crabs.

Shri Restaurant & Lounge INTERNATIONAL **$$$**

(Map p320; 08-3827 9631; www.shri.vn; 23rd fl, Centec Tower, 72-74 Đ Nguyen Thi Minh Khai; meals 450,000-900,000d; ⊙11am-midnight Mon-Sat, from 5pm Sun) Perched on an office block, romantic Shri has some of the choicest views in town. Book ahead for a terrace table or settle for the dark, industrial-chic dining room. Look forward to international spins on steak and seafood – with international prices to match – or a cheaper pasta and risotto menu. It's also worth considering for a sunset cocktail.

Pham Ngu Lao Area

Five Oysters VIETNAMESE **$**

(Map p336; www.fiveoysters.com; 234 Đ Bui Vien; meals from 35,000d; ⊙9am-11pm) With a strong seafood slant and friendly service, light and bright Five Oysters in backpackerland is frequently packed with travellers feasting on oysters (30,000d), grilled octopus, seafood soup, snail pie, *pho,* fried noodles, grilled mackerel with chilli oil and more. Bargain-priced beer also makes it a popular spot along the PNL strip.

Margherita INTERNATIONAL **$**

(Map p336; 175/1 Đ Pham Ngu Lao; meals 35,000-100,000d; ⊙8am-10pm) A golden oldie, Margherita cooks up Vietnamese, Italian and Mexican food at a steal. Secure an outdoor table, order a freshly squeezed juice, and watch the world go by on one of PNL's busier side streets.

An Lac Chay VEGETARIAN **$**

(Map p336; Upstairs, 175/1 Đ Pham Ngu Lao; meals 35,000-100,000d; ⊙8am-10pm;) Head upstairs at the rear of the Margherita restaurant to An Lac Chay, a purely vegetarian restaurant offering an eclectic range of tasty choices, from Vietnamese sour soup through to four-cheese pizzas and Mexican dishes.

Café Zoom BURGERS, MEXICAN $

(Map p336; www.facebook.com/cafezoomsaigon; 169a Đ De Tham; meals 40,000-80,000d; ⏲7am-2am) Paying homage to the classic Vespa, this buzzing place has a perfect location for watching the world go by. The menu includes great burgers with original toppings, plus tacos and a mix of Italian and Vietnamese favourites. It's also where Vespa Adventures (p333) launches its excellent tours from.

Coriander THAI $

(Map p336; 16 Đ Bui Vien; meals 50,000-180,000d; ⏲11am-2pm & 5-11pm) The blonde-wood furniture and cheap bamboo wallpaper do Coriander few favours, but the menu is stuffed with authentic Siamese delights. The lovely fried *doufu* (tofu) is almost a meal in itself, the green curry is zesty, and the claypot seafood fried rice is excellent.

Mon Hue VIETNAMESE $

(Map p336; www.nhahangmonhue.vn; 201 Đ De Tham; meals 45,000-120,000d; ⏲6am-11pm) Hue's famous cuisine comes to HCMC's hungry hordes through this chain of eight restaurants. This handy branch offers a good introduction for travellers who don't make it to the old capital.

Dinh Y VEGETARIAN $

(Map p336; 171b Đ Cong Quynh; meals from 30,000d; ⏲6am-9pm; ✎) Run by a friendly Cao Dai family, this humble eatery is in a very 'local' part of PNL near Thai Binh Market. The food is delicious and cheap.

Sozo CAFE $

(Map p336; www.sozocentre.com; 176 Đ Bui Vien; 3 cookies 28,000d; ⏲7am-10.30pm; ᯤ) This charming cafe in the Pham Ngu Lao backpacker ghetto has excellent smoothies, doughy cinnamon rolls, homemade cookies, other sweet treats, bags of style, and trains and employs disadvantaged Vietnamese.

Pho Quynh VIETNAMESE $

(Map p336; 323 Đ Pham Ngu Lao; pho 60,000d; ⏲24hr) Occupying a bustling corner on Pham Ngu Lao, this place is regularly packed out. As well as regular *pho,* it specialises in *pho bo kho,* a stewlike broth.

Espy PIZZA $

(Map p336; www.facebook.com/espypizza; 154 Đ Cong Quynh; pizza slices from 45,000d; ⏲11am-10.30pm) Espy dishes up pretty authentic New York–style pizza by the slice. New flavours emerge piping hot from the oven on a regular basis, and whole pizzas are also available if you want to quickly make new friends at your hostel.

Chi's Cafe INTERNATIONAL, CAFE $

(Map p336; 185/30 Đ Pham Ngu Lao; meals from 60,000d; ⏲7.15am-10.30pm; ᯤ✎) Hung with eye-catching oils, this relaxing spot is one of the better budget cafes in the area. Look forward to big breakfasts, Western favourites like tacos and burgers, and some local dishes.

Asian Kitchen PAN-ASIAN $

(Map p336; ☎08-3836 7397; 185/22 Đ Pham Ngu Lao; meals 50,000-80,000d; ⏲7am-midnight; ᯤ✎) A reliable PNL cheapie, the menu here includes Japanese, Vietnamese, Chinese and Indian.

Pho Hung VIETNAMESE $

(Map p336; 241 Đ Nguyen Trai; meals 40,000-70,000d; ⏲6am-3am) Popular *pho* place near backpackersville, open till the wee hours.

Quan Ut Ut BARBECUE $$

(☎08-3914 4500; www.quanutut.com; 168 Đ Vo Van Kiet; meals 180,000-300,000d; ⏲4-11.30pm) Roughly translating to the 'Oink Oink Eatery', this casual place with river views celebrates everything porcine with an American-style barbecue spin. Huge streetside grills prepare great ribs, spicy sausages and pork belly, and tasty sides include charred sweetcorn and grilled pineapple. Huge burgers are also good, and the owners even make their own craft beers.

Baba's Kitchen INDIAN $$

(Map p336; ☎08-3838 6661; www.babaskitchen.in; 164 Đ Bui Vien; meals 65,000-210,000d; ⏲11am-11pm; ✎) Baba's sets Đ Bui Vien alight with the fine flavours, aromas and spices of India. There's ample vegetarian choice and the atmosphere is as inviting as the cuisine is delectable. If you like your food eye-poppingly spicy, the vindaloo dishes can assist, although the waiter may politely caution you that they are 'rather hot'. Rather excellent service too.

Vittorio ITALIAN $$

(Map p336; www.facebook.com/vittoriovietnam; 137 Đ Bui Vien; pizza & pasta 80,000-180,000d;

9am-10.30pm) One of the better options along bustling Đ Bui Vien, with a friendly atmosphere, decent wood-fired pizza and other Italian-inspired dishes.

Thao Dien (District 2)

East of the Saigon River, the Thao Dien neighbourhood of District 2 is popular with expat diners, and a new tunnel under the river has now made it quicker to get to. A taxi from District 1 should be around 150,000d to 180,000d and take around 20 to 30 minutes. Make sure your driver knows where he's going before you set off.

Boat House BISTRO $$
(08-3744 6790; www.facebook.com/boathousevietnam; 40 Lily Rd, APSC Compound, 36 Đ Thao Dien; bar snacks 65,000-165,000d, meals 145,000-195,0000d; 8am-11pm) This versatile spot features many riverside options. Enjoy a leisurely lunch at the outside tables, sit at the bar for a few beers, or graduate to cocktails on the daybeds. Food runs from bar snacks to burgers, salads and wraps, and weekdays from 4.30pm to 6.30pm there are good happy-hour specials. Look forward to occasional live music too.

The MAD House BISTRO $$
(08-3519 4009; www.facebook.com/madsaigon; 6/1/2 Đ Nguyen U Di; meals 150,000-300,000d; 5-10pm Mon, 11.30am-10pm Tue-Fri, 9am-10pm Sat & Sun;) The MAD House is a popular option for the expat denizens of District 2. Highlights include excellent coffee, robust cocktails, and an innovative menu blending Scandinavian and Vietnamese influences – MAD House translates to Food House in Danish. Look forward to stunning tropical decor and a lovely garden area that's a perfect retreat from the bustle of the city.

Mekong Merchant CAFE, BISTRO $$
(08-3744 6788; www.facebook.com/MMsaigon; 23 Đ Thao Dien; breakfast 70,000-200,000d, meals 95,000-310,000d; 8am-10pm;) Thatched-roof buildings clustered around a courtyard provide an atmospheric setting for this informal but upmarket cafe-bistro-bar. It's worth the trip for the best eggs Benedict and pizza in HCMC, although the speciality is Phu Quoc seafood – delivered directly and chalked up on the blackboard menu daily.

The Deck FUSION $$$
(08-3744 6632; www.thedecksaigon.com; 33 Đ Nguyen U Di; tapas 95,000-330,000d, meals 185,000-680,000d; 8am-midnight;) Housed in an architecturally impressive pavilion set between an elegant garden and the river, and you could happily linger all afternoon, knocking off a few bottles of wine and several dim sum plates along the way. Mains combine European cooking styles with the flavours of Asia. The three-course lunch (525,000d) is good value for lazy afternoon river views.

Trois Gourmands FRENCH $$$
(08-3744 4585; http://3gourmandsaigon.com; 39 Đ Tran Ngoc Dien; meals from 400,000d; noon-3pm & 6-10.30pm Tue-Sun) An elegant villa-with-swimming-pool setting is the venue for this impressive restaurant, overseen by the warm and welcoming Frenchman and former sommelier Gils Brault. Champion of fine food served through indulgent set menus, Trois Gourmands is worth the trek: cheese lovers can come for the selection alone, made in-house, while the wine choice is naturally strong.

If you find yourself immovable after your feast, there's always on-site accommodation (US$40).

Drinking & Nightlife

Happening Ho Chi Minh City is concentrated around the Dong Khoi area, with everything from dives to designer bars. However, places in this area generally close around 1am as they are under the watchful gaze of local authorities. Pham Ngu Lao rumbles on into the wee hours.

Check out **Everyone's a DJ** (www.facebook.com/everyonesadj) for notifications of various gigs and events around town. Other purveyors of fine events worth attending are **The Beats Saigon** (www.facebook.com/pages/The-Beats-Saigon/207148399324751) and Saigon Outcast (p350).

Most of the listed dance clubs don't really warm up until after 10pm; ask around at popular bars about the latest greatest places.

Dong Khoi Area

Many of Dong Khoi's coolest bars double as restaurants or are flung out at the top of hotels.

★Pasteur Street Brewing Company CRAFT BEER
(Map p315; www.pasteurstreet.com; 144 Đ Pasteur; small/large beer from 45,000/95,000d; 11am-10pm;) Proving there's hoppy life beyond

DRINKS WITH A VIEW

There's something madly exciting about gazing over the neon city at night, preferably with a cocktail in hand. It's well worth the extra dong to enjoy the frenetic pace of life on the streets from the lofty vantage point of a rooftop bar. Bars with great sunset and after-dark vistas include **Air 360** (p350), **Chill Sky Bar** (p350), **OMG** (p350) and **The View** (p350).

Our favourite spots:

EON Heli Bar (Map p315; 52nd fl, Bitexco Financial Tower, 2 Đ Hai Trieu; ⏰11.30am-2am) Secure a window seat and catch the sun going down from this snappy 52nd-floor vantage point over town.

Shri (Map p320; ☎08-3827 9631; 23rd fl, Centec Tower, 72-74 Đ Nguyen Thi Minh Khai; ⏰10am-midnight Mon-Sat, from 5pm Sun) On the Centec Tower's 23rd floor, Shri's stylish terrace has a separate area for non-diners reached by stepping stones over a tiny stream.

M Bar (Map p315; www.majesticsaigon.com.vn; 1 Đ Dong Khoi; ⏰4pm-1am) On the 8th floor of the Majestic Hotel, this is a great spot for a sundowner, with panoramic views of the river and a certain colonial-era cachet.

Saigon Saigon Bar (Map p315; www.caravellehotel.com; 19 Lam Son Sq; ⏰11am-2am; 📶) For excellent views in the city centre, stop by Saigon Saigon for a drink around dusk. This fancy bar has live music, cool breezes and a casually upscale feel.

333 lager, Pasteur Street Brewing turns out a fine selection of excellent craft beer. Brews utilise local ingredients, including lemongrass, rambutan and jasmine, and up to six different beers are always available. Great bar snacks – try the spicy Nashville fried chicken – are also served in Pasteur Street's hip upstairs tasting room.

The Workshop COFFEE
(Map p315; www.facebook.com/the.workshop.coffee; 10 Đ Ngo Duc Ke; coffee from 45,000d; ⏰8am-8pm; 📶) Coffee-geek culture comes to HCMC at this spacious upstairs warehouse space that's also perfect if you need to do some writing or other work. Single-origin fair-trade roasts from Dalat feature, and there's a great display of B&W photos of old Saigon to peruse while you're waiting for your Chemex or cold brew.

Vesper BAR
(Map p315; www.facebook.com/vespersaigon; Ground fl, Landmark Bldg, 5b Đ Ton Duc Thang; ⏰11am-late Mon-Sat) From the sinuous curve of the hardwood bar to the smoothly arranged bottles on the shelves, soft chill-out rhythms, funky caramel leather furniture and fine tapas menu, Vesper is a cool spot by the river. There's a roadside terrace, but traffic noise is epic.

Shrine COCKTAIL BAR, BISTRO
(Map p315; ☎0916 806 093; www.shrinebarsaigon.com; 64 Đ Ton That Thiep; ⏰11am-1am Mon-Sat, 4pm-midnight Sun) Decked out with replica Khmer sculptures, Shrine is a chic and sophisticated alternative to more rowdy sports and hostess bars nearby. There's a proud focus on creating interesting – and very potent – cocktails from the team behind the bar, and Pan-Asian flavours infuse a versatile food menu stretching from bar snacks (85,000d to 230,000d) to larger shared plates (220,000d to 460,000d).

2 Lam Son Martini Bar COCKTAIL BAR
(Map p315; www.saigon.park.hyatt.com; Park Hyatt Saigon, 2 Lam Son Sq, enter ĐL Hai Ba Trung; ⏰5pm-late) A chic blend of wood, glass and steel, the Park Hyatt's ground-floor cocktail bar is a super-stylish meeting ground for Saigon's movers and shakers, with an intimate lounge level slung out above.

Plantrip Cha TEAHOUSE
(Map p315; www.facebook.com/PlantripCha; 3a Đ Ton Duc Thang; tea from 30,000d; ⏰9am-9pm) After perusing the galleries and street art of the emerging 3A Alternative Art Area (p353) district, recharge and revive at this funky teahouse with brews from around the planet. Our favourite is the refreshing Tra Mojito iced tea.

L'Usine CAFE
(Map p315; www.lusinespace.com; 151/1 Đ Dong Khoi; ⏰7.30am-10.30pm; 📶) Tucked away in a colonial building with high ceilings, marble-topped tables, photos of old Saigon and an

appetising cafe menu (sandwiches from 95,000d). A designer homewares and clothing store is attached; head through the Art Arcade, turn right along the lane between the buildings and zip upstairs.

2Go JUICE BAR

(Map p315; www.2gosaigon.vn; 91 Đ Pasteur; juices 23,000-39,000d; ⏲7am-11pm) Excellent juices, smoothies and Vietnamese snacks (23,000d to 31,000d) are served up from this funky and colourful shipping container. It's a handy refuelling stop if you're exploring nearby museums and Notre Dame Cathedral. Try the refreshing – non-alcoholic – apple mojito.

Apocalypse Now CLUB

(Map p315; ☎08-3824 1463; www.facebook.com/apocalypsenowsaigon; 2C Đ Thi Sach; ⏲7pm-2am) 'Apo' has been around since 1991 and remains one of the must-visit clubs. A sprawling place with a big dance floor and an outdoor courtyard, the bar's eclectic cast combines travellers, expats, Vietnamese movers and shakers, plus the odd working girl. The music is thumping and it's apocalyptically rowdy. The 150,000d weekend charge gets you a free drink.

Game On SPORTS BAR

(Map p315; www.gameonsaigon.com; 115 Đ Ho Tung Mau; ⏲8am-late) Friendly sports bar that schedules an entire planet's worth of live events across any given week. An essential detour if you're familiar with sporting acronyms from AFL to NBA. Check the website to see what's on.

Broma: Not a Bar BAR

(Map p315; www.facebook.com/bromabar; 41 Đ Nguyen Hue; ⏲5pm-2am) Compact and bohemian rooftop bar overlooking the busy pedestrian mall of Đ Nguyen Hue. Look forward to a good selection of international beers, live gigs, and DJs with a funk, hip-hop and electronica edge.

Lush BAR, NIGHTCLUB

(Map p319; www.lush.vn; 2 Đ Ly Tu Trong; ⏲7.30pm-late) Once you're done chatting in the garden bars, move to the central bar for serious people-watching and ass-shaking. The decor is very manga, with cool graphics plastering the walls. DJs spin most nights, with Fridays devoted to hip-hop.

La Fenetre Soleil BAR

(Map p315; www.facebook.com/lafenetre.soleil.3; 1st fl, 44 Đ Ly Tu Trong; coffee from 40,000d; ⏲9am-midnight; 📶) Making the most of the bones of a French colonial building, this shabby-chic upstairs hang-out has exposed brickwork and beams, chandeliers, frilly mirrors, overhead fans chopping a breeze, and an Inodnesian menu. Live music – blues, Latin, reggae and funk – draws crowds in the evening, and lazy Sunday afternoon sessions slow the weekend down from 1pm to 5pm.

Phatty's SPORTS BAR

(Map p315; www.phattysbar.com; 46-48 Đ Ton That Thiep; ⏲8am-late; 📶) Its convivial atmosphere, good grub and big-screen live sports make Phatty's a solid crowd-puller for after-work expats. AFL, NRL and big rugby matches are all screened on a regular basis, and Phatty's is also growing as a venue for stand-up comedy.

Wine Bar 38 WINE BAR

(Map p315; www.facebook.com/WineBar38DongKhoi; 38 Đ Dong Khoi; ⏲11am-midnight) Slick and smart, this contemporary two-floor wine bar with snappy leather furniture offers a magnificent choice of wines complemented by an outstanding menu.

Fuse CLUB

(Map p315; www.facebook.com/FuseSG; 3a Đ Ton Duc Thang; ⏲7pm-late) Small club playing loud techno.

Da Kao & Around

Decibel BAR

(Map p319; www.decibel.vn; 79/2/5 Đ Phan Kê Bính; ⏲7.30am-midnight Mon-Sat) This small, two-floor restaurant-cafe-bar is a super-relaxed choice for a coffee or cocktail, with a fine cultural vibe, film nights and art events.

Hoa Vien MICROBREWERY

(Map p319; www.hoavien.vn; 18 bis/28 Đ Nguyen Thi Minh Khai; ⏲8am-midnight; 📶) An unexpected find in the backstreets of HCMC, this Czech restaurant brews up fresh pilsner and dark beer daily. The entrance is down a lane off Đ Nguyen Thi Minh Khai.

Reunification Palace & Around

Vespa Sofar BAR

(Map p320; www.vespasofar.com; 99 Đ Pham Ngu Lao; ⏲11am-midnight; 📶) This cool Vespa and Mod-themed cafe-bar combo is a short walk from Pham Ngu Lao. Look forward to good coffee, juice and smoothies, well-priced cocktails, and a decent beer list including a few Belgian brews. Look for the cool VW Kombi van that's the main bar, and the retro Vespas parked outside. Happy hour runs from 6pm to 8pm.

Air 360 BAR
(Map p320; www.air360skybar.com; 21st fl, Ben Thanh Tower, 136-138 Đ Le Thi Hong Gam; ⏲5.30pm-2am) Happy hour runs from 5pm to 8pm at this new sky bar – perfect to make the most of sunset and secure a good discount on the pricey drinks menu. Pâtés, terrines and charcuterie selections underpin the food menu. It's just a short walk from the heaving backpacker bars on Pham Ngu Lao.

Chill Sky Bar COCKTAIL BAR
(Map p320; www.chillsaigon.com; 26 & 27th fl, AB Tower, 76a Đ Le Lai; ⏲5.30pm-late) The most upmarket of Saigon's sky bars – it's very popular with local high rollers working their way through a bottle of Hennessy cognac or Johnnie Walker Blue Label – and the only one to enforce a pretty strict dress code. Dig out your cleanest long trousers and maybe leave the Beer Lao or Vang Vieng rafting T-shirt in your backpack.

OMG BAR
(Map p320; www.facebook.com/OMGSAIGON; Tan Hai Long Hotel, 15-19 Nguyen An Ninh; beer/cocktails from 90,000/160,000d; ⏲11am-1am) Get past the silly name, and OMG is a decent rooftop bar near Ben Thanh Market that's less pretentious than some other sky bars around town. Food-wise, there's an adventurous spirit evident with offerings including crocodile tartare with wasabi and mango.

LGBT HCMC

There are few openly gay venues in town, but most of Ho Chi Minh City's popular bars and clubs are generally gay-friendly. **Apocalypse Now** (p349) sometimes attracts a small gay contingent, and **Centro Cafe** (Map p315; ☎08-3827 5946; 11-13 Lam Son Sq; Wi-Fi) attracts a gay crowd on Saturday night. **Republic** (Map p315; 63/201 Đ Dong Du; ⏲10am-2am) just off Đ Dong Khoi and **Babylon Pub** (Map p336; 24-26 Đ Bui Vien; ⏲noon-2am) in Pham Ngu Lao are also popular.

Vuvuzela Beer Club BEER HALL, CLUB
(Map p320; www.vuvuzela.com.vn; Zen Plaza, 275 Đ Nguyen Trai; ⏲10am-midnight) Welcome to the latest craze in Saigon nightlife, a raucous mash-up of beer bar, American diner and nightclub. At the time of writing, beer clubs were wildly popular with local partygoers, and when the beats kick off around 10pm, you certainly won't mistake a visit to Vuvuzela as a quiet night out. Definitely a subtlety-free zone.

Pham Ngu Lao Area

The View BAR
(Map p336; www.theviewrooftopbar.com; 8th fl, Duc Vuong Hotel, 195 Đ Bui Vien; ⏲10am-midnight Mon-Fri, to 2am Sat & Sun) Not as elevated as other rooftop bars around town, but less pretentious, and a whole lot easier on the wallet. It's still a good escape to look down on the heaving backpacker bustle of Pham Ngu Lao, and the food menu is also good value.

Le Pub PUB
(Map p336; ☎08-3837 7679; www.lepub.org; 175/22 Đ Pham Ngu Lao; ⏲9am-2am; Wi-Fi) The name says it all – British pub meets French cafe-bar – and the pomegranate-coloured result, ranging over three floors, is a hit. An extensive beer list, nightly promotions, cocktail jugs and pub grub draw in the crowds. The surrounding lane is becoming popular with a local after-dark crowd.

Long Phi BAR
(Map p336; 207 Đ Bui Vien; ⏲10am-5am Tue-Sun) One of the PNL originals, this French-run bar has looooong hours and occasionally hosts live bands.

Spotted Cow SPORTS BAR
(Map p336; 111 Đ Bui Vien; ⏲11am-midnight) Fun, Aussie-run, bovine-themed sports bar on Đ Bui Vien with lots of drink specials.

Thao Dien (District 2)

★ **Saigon Outcast** BAR, BEER GARDEN
(www.saigonoutcast.com; 188 Đ Nguyen Van Huong; ⏲10am-11.45pm) Head across to District 2 for this venue's diverse combo of live music, DJs, cinema nights and good times amid funky street art. Cocktails, craft beer and local ciders are available in the raffish garden bar, and there's a cool outdoor market occasionally on Sunday mornings. Check the website for what's on. From District 1, it's around 150,000d in a taxi.

BiaCraft BAR
(www.biacraft.com; 90 Đ Xuan Thuy, Thao Dien; ⊙11am-midnight) Excellent craft-beer bar across the river in the District 2 area. Look forward to locally brewed beers, plus the best of hoppy and distinctive imported brews. Bar snacks complete a tasty offering that may well see you kicking on for 'just one more round'.

Buddha Bar & Grill BAR
(7 Thao Dien; ⊙2am-2pm) Popular expat bar in District 2 that offers live music most Friday nights from 9pm. Check Buddha Bar's Facebook page to see what's on. The barbecue menu (60,000d to 120,000d) daily from 4pm is another fine reason to linger.

☆ Entertainment

Pick up *The Word HCMC, Asialife HCMC* or *The Guide* to find out what's on during your stay in Ho Chi Minh City, or log onto www.anyarena.com or www.thewordhcmc.com. Monthly listings include club nights, live music, art shows and theatre performances.

Live Music

Ho Chi Minh City has an enthusiastic live music scene, with all styles of bands hitting the city's stages. Dublin Gate (p342) has live bands every weekend and Pacharan (p342) is pumping on Wednesday and Friday nights. Most nights you'll find a Cuban band turning up the heat at Saigon Saigon Bar (p348) at the Caravelle Hotel.

Acoustic LIVE MUSIC
(Map p320; ☎08-3930 2239; www.facebook.com/acousticbarpage; 6e1 Đ Ngo Thoi Nhiem; ⊙7pm-midnight; 📶) Don't be misled by the name: most of the musicians are fully plugged and dangerous when they take to the intimate stage of the city's leading live music venue. And judging by the numbers that pack in, the crowd just can't get enough. It's at the end of the alley by the up-ended VW Beetle, and the cocktails are deceptively strong.

Cargo LIVE MUSIC
(Map p315; www.facebook.com/cargosaigon; Đ 7 Nguyen Tat Thanh; ⊙3pm-midnight Wed-Sun) Hugely popular, spacious warehouse venue for up-and-coming local acts, regional bands and DJ events backed up by a great sound system; it's across the river in District 4.

The Observatory LIVE MUSIC
(Map p315; www.facebook.com/theobservatoryhcm; 5 Đ Nguyen Tat Thanh; ⊙6pm-6am Wed-Sun) Happening venue with everything from live bands to DJs from around the globe. Now relocated to just across the river in District 4.

Saigon Ranger LIVE MUSIC
(Map p315; www.facebook.com/saigonranger; 5/7 Đ Nguyen Sieu; ⊙3pm-late Tue-Sun) Centrally located just a short stroll from Lam Son Park, Saigon Ranger is a raffish live music and performance venue with different acts from Tuesday to Sunday. Look forward to an eclectic roster of performers – including rock, blues and Latin sounds – with most gigs kicking off around 9pm.

Yoko LIVE MUSIC
(Map p320; ☎08-3933 0577; www.facebook.com/YokoBar; 22a Đ Nguyen Thi Dieu; ⊙8am-late; 📶) Soulful portraits of John Lennon, Jim Morrison and James Brown look on at this cool shrine to live music. The environment: exposed t-beam joists and concrete floor; the music: anything from funk rock to metal, kicking off around 9.30pm nightly.

Hard Rock Cafe LIVE MUSIC
(Map p315; www.hardrock.com; 39 Đ Le Duan; ⊙11am-midnight; 📶) Live bands or DJs every Friday and Saturday night.

Seventeen Saloon LIVE MUSIC
(Map p320; www.17saloon.vn; 103a Đ Pham Ngu Lao; ⊙7pm-2am) Love-it-or-loathe-it *yeeha*-style Wild West–themed Pham Ngu Lao bar has staff kitted out in boots, denim and cowboy hats with roof-raising rock classics from the resident Filipino band.

AO Show LIVE PERFORMANCE
(Map p315; www.aoshowsaigon.com; Opera House, Lam Son Sq; either 6pm or 8pm most days; ⊙admission from 504,000d) Popular tourist-oriented showcase of Vietnamese music, dance and flying acrobats. Most hotels can book tickets and there is a box office at the Opera House.

Universal Bar LIVE MUSIC
(Map p336; www.facebook.com/UniversalBarSaigon; 90 Đ Bui Vien; ⊙till 2am) This bar sees some great acts for the roof-lifting live music that takes to the floor nightly at 9.30pm. Seats are out the front for people-watching along Đ Bui Vien and multiple sports TVs provide further entertainment within.

Municipal Theatre CONCERT HALL

(Opera House; Map p315; ☎08-3829 9976; Lam Son Sq) The French-era Opera House is home to the HCMC Ballet and **Ballet & Symphony Orchestra** (www.hbso.org.vn) and hosts performances by visiting artists.

Conservatory of Music CONCERT HALL

(Nhac Vien Thanh Pho Ho Chi Minh; Map p320; ☎08-3824 3774; 112 Đ Nguyen Du) Performances of both traditional Vietnamese and Western classical music are held here.

MZ Bar LIVE MUSIC

(Map p320; ☎08-3925 5258; www.m-zing.com; 56a Đ Bui Thi Xuan; ⊙6pm-late) A live cover band blasts out danceable versions of classic songs you know all the words to.

Water Puppets

Although it originates in the north, the art of water puppetry migrated south to Ho Chi Minh City to satiate tourist demands.

Golden Dragon Water Puppet Theatre WATER PUPPETS

(Map p320; ☎08-3930 2196; 55b Đ Nguyen Thi Minh Khai; ticket US$7.50) Saigon's main water-puppet venue, with shows starting at 5pm, 6.30pm and 7.45pm and lasting about 50 minutes.

Cinemas

Tickets are around 90,000d to 150,000d.

CGV Cinemas CINEMA

(Map p315; www.cgv.vn; 59-61 Đ Pasteur) Located on top of the Liberty Central Saigon Citypoint hotel, this centrally located new complex has five compact auditoriums.

Lotte Cinema Diamond CINEMA

(Map p315; http://lottecinemavn.com; 13th fl, Diamond Department Store, 34 Đ Le Duan) Three screens with films in their original language with Vietnamese subtitles.

Shopping

Junk is energetically peddled to tourists on the city's teeming streets, but plenty of great finds can be uncovered in bustling markets, antique stores, silk boutiques and speciality stores selling ceramics, ethnic fabrics, lacquered bamboo and custom-made clothing.

There are plenty of places where you can find chic apparel or custom-made *ao dai*, the couture symbol of Vietnam. This gorgeous outfit of silk tunic and trousers is tailored at shops in and around Ben Thanh Market and at the top end of Đ Pasteur. Male *ao dai* are also available, in a looser fit that comes with a silk-covered head wrap to match.

Dong Khoi Area

Any shopping journey should start along gallery- and boutique-lined Đ Dong Khoi and its intersecting streets, where high-quality handicrafts and gifts can also be found.

Ben Thanh Market MARKET

(Cho Ben Thanh; Map p315; ĐL Le Loi, ĐL Ham Nghi, ĐL Tran Hung Dao & Đ Le Lai) Centrally located, Ben Thanh and its surrounding streets comprise one of Saigon's liveliest areas. Everything that's commonly eaten, worn or used by the Saigonese is piled high, and souvenir items can be found in equal abundance. Vendors are determined and prices usually higher than elsewhere, so bargain vigorously and ignore any 'Fixed Price' signs.

Good food stalls are usually open until mid-afternoon, and it's an area where it pays to be extra vigilant about looking after personal items and smartphones.

Mekong Quilts HANDICRAFTS

(Map p315; ☎08-2210 3110; www.mekong-quilts.org; 1st fl, 68 ĐL Le Loi; ⊙9am-7pm) For beautiful handmade silk quilts, sewn by the rural poor in support of a sustainable income.

Giant Step Urban Art Gallery ARTS

(Map p315; ☎0126 415 4338; 3a Đ Ton Duc Thang; ⊙11am-6pm Mon-Sat) Excellent gallery and retail outlet focusing on street art. Find it on Facebook to see what exhibitions are scheduled. The surrounding laneways are also packed with street art.

Saigon Kitsch SOUVENIRS

(Map p315; 33 Đ Ton That Thiep; ⊙9am-10pm) This colourful store specialises in reproduction propaganda posters, emblazoning its revolutionary motifs on coffee mugs, coasters, jigsaws and T-shirts. Also cool laptop and tablet covers fashioned from recycled Vietnamese packaging.

Mai Lam CLOTHING

(Map p315; www.mailam.com.vn; 132-134 Đ Dong Khoi; ⊙9am-9pm) Vibrant, colourful, creative and highly inspiring, Mai Lam carries beautiful (but pricey) hand-stitched men's and women's clothing and accessories.

L'Usine CLOTHING, HOMEWARES

(Map p315; www.facebook.com/Lusinespace; 151/1 Đ Dong Khoi; ⏲7.30am-10.30pm) Marrying shopping and dining, this smooth upstairs outlet, next to the restaurant-cafe of the same name, has an eye-catching line in stylish threads and colourful bags. There's another L'Usine classy cafe and design combo on **Đ Le Loi** (Map p315; 70b Đ Le Loi; ⏲7.30am-10.30pm).

Annam Gourmet Market MARKET

(Map p315; www.annam-gourmet.com; 16 Đ Hai Ba Trung; ⏲7am-9pm) This large, fabulously stocked deli sells imported cheeses, wines, chocolates and other delicacies over two floors, with a fine restaurant crammed into the corner of the 1st level.

Mystere HANDICRAFTS

(Map p315; 141 Đ Dong Khoi; ⏲9am-10pm) Attractive lacquerware, fabrics and jewellery sourced from ethnic minority peoples and hill tribes.

3A Alternative Art Area ARTS

(Map p315; 3a Đ Ton Duc Thang) Street art, galleries, interesting homeware shops and a growing range of hip cafes and bars make this an essential destination if you're keen to understand how Saigon is evolving. At weekends it's a popular location for edgy fashion shoots and wedding photos.

Sadec HOMEWARES

(Map p315; www.sadecdistrict.com; 3a Đ Ton Duc Thang; ⏲8.30am-8.30pm) This wonderful store in the 3A Alternative Art Area has stylish homeware, clothing, art and fabrics from all around the Mekong River region.

Khai Silk CLOTHING

(Map p315; ☎08-3829 1146; www.khaisilkcorp.com; 107 Đ Dong Khoi; ⏲9.30am-8pm) This is one of several branches in HCMC of the nationwide silk empire. Expensive but high quality.

Vincom Center MALL

(Map p315; 70-72 Le Than Ton & 45a Ly Tu Trong; ⏲9am-10pm; 📶) The Vincom Center is divided into two towers, with upscale shopping, luxury brands (Dior, Hermès, Omega etc) and a popular food court in the basement of Tower B.

Sapa HANDICRAFTS, ACCESSORIES

(Map p315; 7 Đ Ton That Thiep; ⏲8am-9pm) Small store incorporating ethnic fabrics and designs with modern styling; also sells gifts, jewellery, lampshades and handbags.

Art Arcade ARTWORK

(Map p315; 151 Đ Dong Khoi) A passageway leading off Dong Khoi that is lined with art vendors.

Nhu Y Oriental Lacquer Wares HANDICRAFTS

(Map p315; www.nhuylacquer.com; 22 Đ Ho Huan Nghiep; ⏲9am-9.30pm) Gorgeous collection of eye-catching handmade boxes, Chinese lacquered couplets, inscribed pictures and more.

Fahasa Bookshop BOOKS

(Map p315; 40 ĐL Nguyen Hue; ⏲8am-10pm) Government-run bookshop with dictionaries, maps and general books in English and French. Also has a location on **ĐL Le Loi** (Map p315; 60-62 ĐL Le Loi; ⏲8am-10pm).

Diamond Department Store DEPARTMENT STORE

(Map p315; 34 Đ Le Duan; ⏲10am-9.30pm) Four floors of sleek, Western-style shopping topped by a very American level of tenpin bowling, arcade games and a food hall.

Saigon Centre SHOPPING CENTRE

(Map p315; 65 ĐL Le Loi) A tower block with flashy international stores and cafes on its lower floors.

Parkson Plaza DEPARTMENT STORE

(Map p315; 41-45 Đ Le Thanh Ton) Clothing and cosmetics.

Chi Chi CLOTHING

(Map p315; 144/1 Đ Pasteur; ⏲8am-8.30pm) Offers custom tailoring.

Reunification Palace & Around

Vinh Loi Gallery ART

(Map p320; www.galleryvinhloi.com; 41 Đ Ba Huyen Thanh Quan; ⏲9am-6pm) This excellent gallery displays some tantalising artwork by Vietnamese artists.

Pham Ngu Lao Area

For cheap reproductions of famous paintings, visit the art shops along Đ Bui Vien.

Hanoi Gallery POSTERS

(Map p336; 79 Đ Bui Vien; ⏲9am-10pm) Fans of socialist realism should visit this very cool little store selling both original (or so we're told) propaganda posters (US$600) and A3 prints (US$10).

Orange CLOTHING, ACCESSORIES
(Map p336; 180 Đ Bui Vien; ⏲9am-10pm) Funky T-shirts and bags.

Gingko CLOTHING
(Map p336; www.ginkgo-vietnam.com; 254 Đ De Tham; ⏲8am-10pm) With three branches in the PNL area, this fun store sells exuberant, brightly coloured T-shirts and hoodies, some decorated with Chinese characters and ironic English logos.

SahaBook BOOKS
(Map p336; www.sahabook.com; 175/24 Đ Pham Ngu Lao; ⏲9am-5.30pm Mon-Fri) Specialises in guidebooks and travel literature, with authentic Lonely Planet guidebooks with readable maps – unlike the knock-offs you'll see on the street.

Nguyen Thai Binh & Around

Antique hunters can head to Đ Le Cong Kieu, directly across the road from the Fine Arts Museum. There's no guarantee objects for sale are actually old, so purchase with care.

Dan Sinh Market MARKET
(Map p315; 104 Đ Yersin; ⏲7am-6pm) Also known as the War Surplus Market, this is the place for authentic combat boots or rusty (perhaps less authentic) dog tags, among the hardware stalls. There are also handy gas masks, field stretchers, rain gear, mosquito nets, canteens, duffel bags, ponchos, boots and flak jackets.

Other Neighbourhoods

Mai Handicrafts HANDICRAFTS
(☎08-3844 0988; www.facebook.com/maivietnamesehandicrafts; 298 Đ Nguyen Trong Tuyen, Tan Binh District; ⏲9am-5pm Mon-Sat) A fair-trade shop dealing in ceramics, ethnic fabrics and other gift items that, in turn, support disadvantaged families and street children. To get here, head northwest on ĐL Hai Ba Trung, which becomes Đ Phan Dinh Phung, and turn left on Đ Nguyen Trong Tuyen.

Gaya HOMEWARES, CLOTHING
(☎08-3925 1495; www.gayavietnam.com; 3 Đ Tran Ngoc Dien, District 2) Designer homeware and clothing boutique that includes the collection of leading Cambodian-French designer Romyda Keth. Across the river in the expat area of District 2.

SC Vivo City MALL
(www.scvivocity.com.vn; 1058 Nguyen Van Linh; ⏲10am-10pm) Opened in 2015, SC Vivo City is a sprawling international mall for those seeking retail therapy.

Information

DANGERS & ANNOYANCES

Be careful at all times but especially in the Dong Khoi area, around Pham Ngu Lao and the Ben Thanh Market, and along the Saigon riverfront. Motorbike 'cowboys' specialise in bag-, camera-, laptop- and tablet-snatching. It's always best to leave your passport in your hotel room, and try to be prudent and careful when you use your smartphone on the street.

MEDIA

Hotels, bars and restaurants around Ho Chi Minh City carry free city-centric magazines, such as the excellent monthly magazine *The Word HCMC* (www.wordhcmc.com), *Asialife HCMC* (www.asialifehcmc.com) and *The Guide*, a monthly magazine published by the *Vietnam Economic Times* (VET). Keep an eye out also for the compact *Citypass Guide* (www.citypassguide.com).

MEDICAL SERVICES

Columbia Asia (Map p320; ☎08-3823 8888; www.columbiaasia.com/saigon; 8 Alexandre de Rhodes; ⏲emergency 8am-9pm) Centrally located near Notre Dame Cathedral.

FV Hospital (Franco-Vietnamese Hospital; ☎08-5411 3333; www.fvhospital.com; 6 Đ Nguyen Luong Bang, District 7; ⏲24hr) French-, Vietnamese- and English-speaking physicians; superb care and equipment.

HCMC Family Medical Practice (Map p315; ☎24hr emergency 08-3822 7848; www.vietnammedicalpractice.com; Rear, Diamond Department Store, 34 ĐL Le Duan; ⏲24hr) Well-run practice with branches in Hanoi and Danang.

International Medical Centre (Map p315; ☎08-3827 2366; www.cmi-vietnam.com; 1 Đ Han Thuyen; ⏲8.30am-7pm Mon-Fri, 9am-1pm Sat) A nonprofit organisation with English-speaking French doctors.

International SOS (Map p319; ☎08-3829 8520; www.internationalsos.com; 167a Đ Nam Ky Khoi Nghia; ⏲24hr) Has an international team of doctors who speak English, French, Japanese and Vietnamese.

MONEY

There are several exchange counters in the arrivals hall at Tan Son Nhat Airport just after clearing customs; most offer the official rates. Turn right after leaving the terminal for ATMs.

ATMs are widespread in town, although most will only dispense a maximum of 2,000,000d per day. Some ANZ ATMs in the inner city will allow withdrawals up to 4,000,000d; **Citibank** (Map p315; 115 ĐL Nguyen Hue), in the foyer of the Sun Wah Tower, dispenses 8,000,000d, but only for Citibank cards (2,000,000d for other cards). Visa or MasterCard cash advances for larger amounts of dong, as well as US dollars, can be handled at bank counters.

POST

Central Post Office (Map p315; 2 Cong Xa Paris; ⌚7am-9.30pm) Right across from Notre Dame Cathedral is the city's magnificent central post office.

FedEx (☎08-3948 0370; www.fedex.com; 6 Đ Thang Long, Tan Binh District; ⌚7.30am-6pm Mon-Fri, to 4.30pm Sat) Private freight carrier.

TRAVEL AGENCIES

Ho Chi Minh City's official government-run travel agency is **Saigon Tourist** (Map p315; ☎08-3824 4554; www.saigontourist.net; 45 Đ Le Thanh Ton; ⌚8-11.30am & 1-5.30pm). The agency owns, or is a joint-venture partner in, more than 70 hotels, numerous restaurants, a car-rental agency, golf clubs and assorted tourist traps.

There's a plethora of other travel agencies in town, virtually all of them joint ventures between government agencies and private companies. These places can provide cars, book air tickets and extend visas. Competition is keen and you can often undercut Saigon Tourist's tariffs by a reasonable margin if you shop around. Many agencies have multilingual guides.

Most tour guides and drivers are not paid that well, so if you're happy with their service, tipping is common. Many travellers on bus tours to Cu Chi or the Mekong Delta, for example, collect a kitty (say US$1 or US$2 per person) and give it to the guide and driver at the end of the trip.

Plenty of cheap tours – of varying quality – are sold around Pham Ngu Lao.

Another option is a customised private tour with your own car, driver and guide, which allows maximum flexibility and, split between a few people, can be surprisingly affordable.

Asiana Travel Mate (Map p336; ☎0908 689 140; www.asianatravelmate.com; 113c Đ Bui Vien) Top-end travel agency.

Buffalo Tours (Map p319; ☎08-3827 9170; www.buffalotours.com; 157 Đ Pasteur; ⌚8.30am-5pm Mon-Fri, to 2.30pm Sat) Top-end travel agency.

EXO Travel (☎08-3519 4111; www.exotissimo.com; 261-263 Đ Phan Xich Long, District 2; ⌚9am-6pm Mon-Sat) Excellent Indochina specialists.

Go Go Vietnam (Map p336; ☎08-3920 9297; www.gogo-vietnam.com; 40/7 Đ Bui Vien) Well-run tour company and travel agency with excellent credentials in visa extensions and renewals, and good-value day trips.

Handspan Adventure Travel (☎08-3925 7605; www.handspan.com; 10th fl, Central Park Bldg, 208 Nguyen Trai) Excellent, high-quality tours from this HCMC branch of the Hanoi-based travel agency.

Innoviet (Map p336; ☎08-6291 5407; www.innoviet.com; 1st fl, 161 Đ Bui Vien; ⌚8am-9pm) Budget travel agency.

Kim Tran Travel (Map p336; ☎08-3836 5489; www.thekimtourist.com; 270 Đ De Tham; ⌚7am-9pm) Day trips and overnighters around the HCMC and Mekong area.

Sinh Tourist (Map p336; ☎08-3838 9593; www.thesinhtourist.vn; 246 Đ De Tham; ⌚6.30am-10.30pm) Budget travel agency.

Sinhbalo Adventures (Map p336; ☎08-3837 6766; www.sinhbalo.com; 283/20 Đ Pham Ngu Lao; ⌚7.30am-noon & 1.30-6pm Mon-Sat) For customised tours this is a great choice. Sinhbalo specialises in cycling trips, but also arranges innovative special-interest journeys to the Mekong Delta, central highlands and further afield. its most popular package trips

GETTING TO CAMBODIA: HCMC TO PHNOM PENH

Getting to the border The busy **Moc Bai/Bavet border crossing** is the fastest land route between Ho Chi Minh City and Phnom Penh. Pham Ngu Lao traveller cafes sell through-bus tickets (US$10 to US$15) to Phnom Penh; buses leave from Pham Ngu Lao between 6am and 3pm. Reliable bus companies include Mekong Express (www.catmekongexpress.com) and Sapaco (www.sapacotourist.vn). Allow six hours for the entire trip, including time spent on border formalities.

At the border Cambodian visas (US$30) are issued at the border (you'll need a passport-sized photo). Moc Bai is two hours from HCMC by bus and is a major duty-free shopping zone. It's a short walk from Moc Bai to Bavet (the Cambodian border) and its enclave of casinos.

Moving on Most travellers have a through-bus ticket from HCMC to Phnom Penh, a further four-hour bus ride away.

include a two-day Mekong tour and three-day Mekong cycling tour.

Getting There & Away

AIR

Ho Chi Minh City is served by Tan Son Nhat Airport. A number of airlines serve domestic routes from HCMC.

Vietnam Airlines (☎08-3832 0320; www.vietnamairlines.com) Flies to/from Hanoi, Hai Phong, Vinh, Dong Hoi, Hue, Danang, Quy Nhon, Nha Trang, Dalat, Buon Ma Thuot, Pleiku, Rach Gia and Phu Quoc Island.

VietJet Air (☎1900 1886; www.vietjetair.com) Flies to/from Hanoi, Hai Phong, Vinh, Dong Hoi, Hue, Danang, Quy Nhon, Nha Trang, Dalat, Buon Ma Thuot and Phu Quoc Island.

Jetstar Pacific Airlines (☎1900 1550; www.jetstar.com/vn/en/home) Flies to/from Hanoi, Hai Phong, Vinh, Hue, Phu Quoc, Nha Trang, Buon Ma Thuot, Dong Hoi and Danang.

Vietnam Air Service Company (Vasco; ☎08-3845 8017; www.vasco.com.vn) Flies to/from Rach Gia, Con Dao Islands and Ca Mau.

BOAT

Vina Express (Map p315; ☎08-3825 3333; www.vinaexpress.com.vn; 5 Đ Nguyen Tat Thanh, District 4; adult/child Mon-Fri 200,000/100,000d, weekends & public holidays 250,000/120,000d; ⏲departs 8am, 10am, noon, 2pm, 4pm, 6pm daily, additional 9am service Sat) Hydrofoils depart for Vung Tau (around 1¼ hours) from Saigon port near the Ho Chi Minh Museum in District 4.

BUS

Intercity buses operate from three large stations on the city outskirts, all well served by local bus services from Ben Thanh Market. Ho Chi Minh City is one place where the open-tour buses really come into their own, as they depart and arrive in the very convenient Pham Ngu Lao area, saving the extra local bus journey or taxi fare.

Mien Tay bus station (Ben Xe Mien Tay; ☎08-3825 5955; Đ Kinh Duong Vuong) serves all areas south of HCMC, essentially the Mekong Delta. This huge station is about 10km west of HCMC in An Lac, a part of Binh Chanh district (Huyen Binh Chanh). A taxi here from Pham Ngu Lao costs around 200,000d. Buses and minibuses from Mien Tay serve most towns in the Mekong Delta using air-con express buses and premium minibuses.

Buses to locations north of HCMC leave from the huge and busy **Mien Dong bus station** (Ben Xe Mien Dong; ☎08-3829 4056) in Binh Thanh district, about 5km from central HCMC on Hwy 13 (Quoc Lo 13; the continuation of Đ Xo Viet Nghe Tinh). The station is just under 2km north of the intersection of Đ Xo Viet Nghe Tinh and Đ Dien Bien Phu. Note that express buses depart from the east side, and local buses connect with the west side of the complex.

Buses to Tay Ninh, Cu Chi and points northwest of HCMC depart from **An Suong bus station** (Ben Xe An Suong) in District 12, but it's not really worth using them as the Cu Chi Tunnels are off the main highway and a nightmare to navigate. Plus, tourist buses are extremely competitively priced and leave from District 1.

Plenty of international bus services connect HCMC and Cambodia, most with departures from the Pham Ngu Lao area. **Sapaco** (Map p336; ☎08-3920 3623; www.sapacotourist.vn; 325 Đ Pham Ngu Lao) has nine direct daily services to Phnom Penh (230,000d, six hours, departures 6am to 3pm), as well as one to Siem Reap (450,000d, 12 hours, 6am).

CAR & MOTORBIKE

Enquire at almost any hotel, tourist cafe or travel agency to arrange car rental. Just remember that your rental will include a driver as it's illegal for foreigners to drive in Vietnam without a Vietnamese driving licence. The agencies in the Pham Ngu Lao area generally offer the lowest prices.

Motorbikes are available in the Pham Ngu Lao area for around US$10 to US$12 per day, although this is one city where it definitely helps to have experience. Check the quality of the helmet provided.

TRAIN

Trains from **Saigon train station** (Ga Sai Gon; ☎08-3823 0105; 1 Đ Nguyen Thong, District 3; ⏲ticket office 7.15-11am & 1-3pm) head north to various destinations:

Danang (US$27 to US$44, 15½ to 20¾ hours, five daily)

Hanoi (US$47 to US$69, 30 to 41 hours, four daily)

HCMC TRANSPORT CONNECTIONS

DESTINATION	AIR	BUS	TRAIN
Dalat	50min; from US$41	7hr; US$11-15	n/a
Nha Trang	55min; from US$22	12hr; US$10-20	6½hr; US$14-32
Hue	80min; from US$48	29hr; US$26-37	18hr; US$17-44
Hanoi	2hr; from US$62	41hr; US$39-49	30hr; US$47-69

Hue (US$17 to US$44, 18 to 24½ hours, five daily)

Nha Trang (US$14 to US$32, 6½ to nine hours, six daily)

Purchase tickets from travel agents for a small booking fee at the train station.

Getting Around

TO/FROM THE AIRPORT

Tan Son Nhat Airport is 7km northwest of central Ho Chi Minh City. Choose Mai Linh or Vinasun taxis and especially avoid similar-sounding imitations; Mai Linh Taxi has a counter in arrivals. Sasco Taxi has the concession for the domestic terminal. From the arrivals taxi rank, a taxi should cost around 170,000d to Dong Khoi, plus a 15,000d vehicle access ticket to the airport. You can pay in US dollars if you want.

Metered cabs will cost around 160,000d to District 1, so if you're travelling light you can head upstairs to the arrivals area, or into the car park of the domestic terminal, to try to catch a taxi.

To get to the airport from town, ask staff at your hotel to call a trustworthy taxi for you. Some cafes in the Pham Ngu Lao area offer runs to the airport – some have sign-up sheets where you can book share-taxis for around US$5 per person.

Most economical is the air-conditioned bus (route 152; 6000d, plus a variable fee for luggage) to/from the international airport terminal. Buses leave approximately every 15 minutes and make regular stops along Đ De Tham (Pham Ngu Lao area) and international hotels along Đ Dong Khoi, such as the Caravelle and the Majestic. Buses are labelled in English, but you might also look for the words 'Xe Buyt San Bay'. This service only operates between 6am and 6pm.

Consider a motorbike taxi only if you're travelling light. Drivers can't access the airport, so you will need to walk outside and negotiate: 90,000d to the city centre is the going rate.

BICYCLE

A bicycle can be a useful (if sometimes scary) way to get around the city. Bikes can be rented from several outlets, including hotels, cafes and travel agencies.

Bicycle parking lots are usually just roped-off sections of pavement. For about 2000d you can leave your bicycle, bearing in mind that theft is a big problem. Your bicycle will have a number written on the seat in chalk or stapled to the handlebars and you'll be given a reclaim chit. Don't lose it. If you come back and your bicycle is gone, the parking lot is supposedly required to replace it.

> **GOING UNDERGROUND: THE HCMC METRO**
>
> Ho Chi Minh City sorely needs a metro system to help marshal the transport chaos above ground. First proposed in 2001, the system will run to an estimated five or six lines, with the 20km (part-underground, part-elevated) first line – linking Ben Thanh Market with Suoi Tien in the east – currently slated for a 2020 launch. Sandwiched between Đ Dong Khoi and Đ Nguyen Hue, the central station is taking shape near the Opera House. Up to 88% of the scheme is being funded by the Japanese government.

BUS

Local buses are cheap and plentiful, serving more than 130 routes around greater Ho Chi Minh City. A useful, free *Ho Chi Minh Bus Route Diagram* (map to you and me) is available at the **Ben Thanh bus station** (Map p315; ĐL Tran Hung Dao).

Useful lines from Ben Thanh include the 152 to Tan Son Nhat Airport, 149 to Saigon train station, 1 to Binh Tay Market in Cholon, 102 to Mien Tay bus station and 26 to Mien Dong bus station. All buses have air-con and the ticket price is usually 6000d. Buy your ticket on board from the attendant.

CAR & MOTORBIKE

Travel agencies, hotels and tourist cafes all rent cars (with drivers) and motorbikes. Many expats swear that motorbike rental is the fastest and easiest way to get around the city – or to the hospital, if you don't know what you're doing. Note that your travel insurance may not offer cover, so check beforehand as things could get expensive and troublesome in the event of an accident. Even if you're an experienced biker, make sure you've spent some time observing traffic patterns before venturing forth. A 100cc motorbike can be rented for US$10 to US$12 per day, including some sort of helmet, and your passport may be kept as collateral. Before renting a motorbike, make sure it's in good working order.

Saigon Scooter Centre (☎08-6681 2362; www.saigonscootercentre.com; 20 Cong Hoa, Tan Binh District; ⏰noon-5pm Tue-Fri, 10am-4pm Sat) is a reliable source for restored classic Vespa scooters, new scooters and trail bikes. Daily rates start from US$10, with a minimum rental period of four days. For an extra fee it's possible to arrange a one-way service, with a

XE OM OR TAXI?

You'd expect to pay extra for the relative comfort and safety of an air-con taxi as opposed to a white-knuckle motorbike ride, and in theory that's the case. However, overcharging by *xe om* (motorbike taxi) drivers in the tourist areas can make any difference negligible. Until you're familiar with the distances and fares involved, catching a metered taxi can help avoid being ripped off. Plus, if there's more than one of you, taxis will be cheaper. However, weaving through the traffic on the back of a motorbike is often faster, especially in rush hour.

There are still dodgy taxi operators with meters that spin around faster than normal, but the taxi situation in Ho Chi Minh City has definitely improved in recent years. If you catch taxis from the two most trustworthy companies – Vinasun Taxi and Mai Linh Taxi – then you should have no problems.

If catching a *xe om*, agree on a price in advance. A trip from Pham Ngu Lao to Dong Khoi shouldn't cost more than 30,000d. One common trick is for drivers to offer to take you for 15,000d but then insist that they really said 50,000d.

pick up of the bikes anywhere between Ho Chi Minh City and Hanoi.

CYCLO

A vanishing icon of Ho Chi Minh City, the *cyclo* (pedicab or bicycle rickshaw) remains a slow-moving feature along certain streets, particularly along Đ Pham Ngu Lao and around Đ Dong Khoi. Some Vietnamese may still enjoy them, but their use has long been overtaken by motorbike and taxi, and tourists remain the shrinking bedrock of this poorly paid trade. In HCMC, a few of the older riders are former South Vietnamese army soldiers and quite a few know at least basic English, while others are quite fluent. Some drivers weave stories of war, 're-education', persecution and poverty into the pedal-powered experience (and will often gladly regale you with tales over a bowl of *pho* or a beer at the end of the day).

In an effort to control HCMC's traffic problems, there are dozens of streets on which *cyclos* are prohibited. As a result, your driver must often take a circuitous route to avoid these trouble spots (and possible fines levied by the police) and may not be able to drop you at the exact address. Try to have some sympathy as it is not the driver's fault.

Overcharging tourists is de rigueur, so hammer out a price beforehand and have the exact change ready (get familiar with the currency – *cyclo* drivers may exploit ignorance). If more than one person is travelling, make sure you negotiate the price for both and not a per-passenger fee. It sometimes pays to sketch out numbers and pictures with pen and paper so all parties agree. Unfortunately, 'misunderstandings' do happen. Unless the *cyclo* driver has pedalled you to all the districts of HCMC, US$25 is not the going rate. That said, don't just assume the driver is trying to cheat you.

Short hops around the city centre will cost around 30,000d to 40,000d; District 1 to central Cholon costs about 60,000d. You can rent a *cyclo* from around 70,000d per hour – a fine idea if you will be doing a lot of touring. Most *cyclo* drivers around the Pham Ngu Lao area can cook up a sample tour program. If hopping aboard a tour, aim for morning or late afternoon to avoid the hottest part of the day.

Enjoy *cyclos* while you can as the municipal government plans to phase them out, and it won't be too long before the *cyclo* disappears entirely from the city's streets. In the cause of charity, the annual Saigon Cyclo Challenge (p334) pits teams of high-paced riders against each other in a fun spectacle each March.

MOTORBIKE TAXI

For traffic-dodging speed and convenience, the *xe om* (sometimes called a *Honda om*; motorbike taxi) is the way to go for many. *Xe om* drivers usually hang out on their parked bikes on street corners, touting for passengers. You'll rarely have to walk more than 10 steps before being offered a ride. The accepted rate is around 30,000d for short rides (Pham Ngu Lao to Dong Khoi area for instance) or you can charter one for around US$5/20 per hour/day.

TAXI

Metered taxis cruise the streets, but it is worth calling ahead if you are off the beaten path. The flagfall is around 12,000d for the first kilometre; expect to pay around 25,000d (US$1) from Dong Khoi to Pham Ngu Lao. Some companies have dodgy taxi meters, rigged to jump quickly, but both **Mai Linh Taxi** (☎ 08-3838 3838) and **Vinasun Taxi** (☎ 08-3827 2727) can be trusted. Uber is also becoming more popular in the city.

AROUND HO CHI MINH CITY

Rewarding escapes, such as wilderness areas and fascinating historical and cultural sights, are a short journey from town.

Cu Chi

If the tenacious spirit of the Vietnamese can be symbolised by a place, then few sites could make a stronger case than Cu Chi. This district of greater Ho Chi Minh City now has a population of about 350,000, but during the American War it had about 80,000 residents. At first glance there is scant evidence today of the vicious fighting, bombing and destruction that convulsed Cu Chi during the war. To see what went on, you have to dig deeper – underground.

The tunnel network of Cu Chi became legendary during the 1960s for its role in facilitating VC (Viet Cong or Vietnamese Communists) control of a large rural area only 30km to 40km from HCMC. At its peak the tunnel system stretched from the South Vietnamese capital to the Cambodian border; in the district of Cu Chi alone more than 250km of tunnels honeycomb the ground. The network, parts of which were several storeys deep, included countless trapdoors, constructed living areas, storage facilities, weapon factories, field hospitals, command centres and kitchens.

The tunnels facilitated communication and coordination between the VC-controlled enclaves, isolated from each other by South Vietnamese and American land and air operations. They also allowed the VC to mount surprise attacks wherever the tunnels went – even within the perimeters of the US military base at Dong Du – and to disappear suddenly into hidden trapdoors without a trace. After ground operations against the tunnels claimed large numbers of US casualties and proved ineffective, the Americans resorted to massive firepower, eventually turning Cu Chi's 420 sq km into what BBC journalists Tom Mangold and John Penycate, authors of *The Tunnels of Cu Chi*, have called 'the most bombed, shelled, gassed, defoliated and generally devastated area in the history of warfare'.

Cu Chi has become a place of pilgrimage for Vietnamese school children and Communist Party cadres.

History

The tunnels of Cu Chi were built over a period of 25 years, beginning sometime in the late 1940s. They were the improvised

Around Ho Chi Minh City

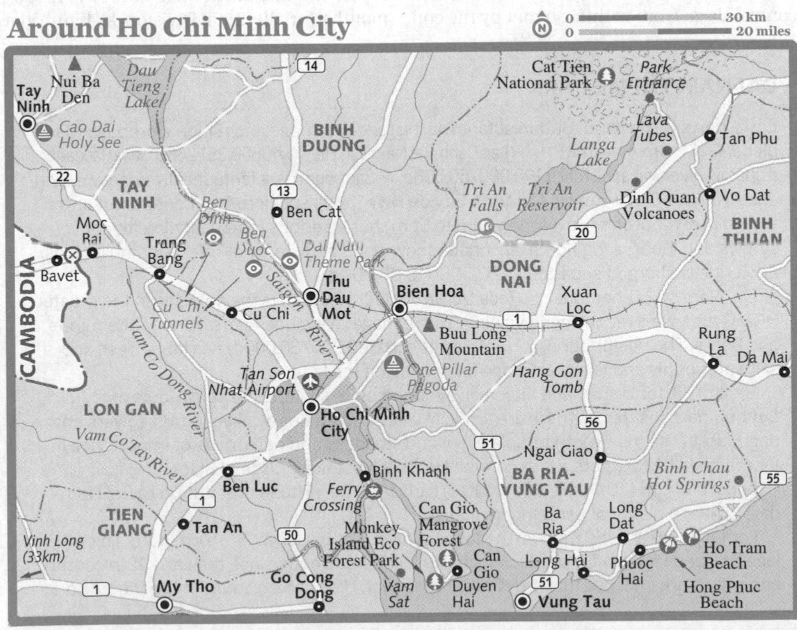

response of a poorly equipped peasant army to its enemy's high-tech ordnance, helicopters, artillery and chemical weapons.

The Viet Minh built the first tunnels in the red earth (soft during the rainy season, rock-hard during dry months) of Cu Chi during the war against the French. The excavations were used mostly for communication between villages and to evade French army sweeps of the area.

When the Viet Cong's National Liberation Front (NLF) insurgency began in earnest in around 1960, the old Viet Minh tunnels were repaired and new extensions were excavated. Within a few years the tunnel system assumed enormous strategic importance, and most of Cu Chi district and the nearby area came under VC control. In addition, Cu Chi was used as a base for infiltrating intelligence agents and sabotage teams into Saigon. The audacious attacks in the South Vietnamese capital during the 1968 Tet Offensive were planned and launched from Cu Chi.

In early 1963 the Diem government implemented the Strategic Hamlets Program, under which fortified encampments, surrounded by many rows of sharp bamboo spikes, were built to house people who had been 'relocated' from Communist-controlled areas. The first strategic hamlet was in Ben Cat district, next to Cu Chi. However, the VC was able to tunnel into the hamlets and control them from within, so that by the end of 1963 the first showpiece hamlet had been overrun.

Over the years the VC developed simple but effective techniques to make their tunnels difficult to detect or disable. Wooden trapdoors were camouflaged with earth and branches; some were booby-trapped. Hidden underwater entrances from rivers were constructed. To cook they used 'Dien Bien Phu kitchens', which exhausted the smoke through vents many metres away from the cooking site. Trapdoors were installed throughout the network to prevent tear gas, smoke or water from moving from one part of the system to another. Some sections were even equipped with electric lighting.

The series of setbacks and defeats suffered by the South Vietnamese forces in the Cu Chi area rendered a complete VC victory by the end of 1965 a distinct possibility. In the early months of that year, the guerrillas boldly held a victory parade in the middle of Cu Chi town. VC strength in and around Cu Chi was one of the reasons the Johnson administration decided to involve US troops in the war.

To deal with the threat posed by VC control of an area so near the South Vietnamese capital, one of the USA's first actions was to establish a large base camp in Cu Chi district. Unknowingly, they built it right on top of an existing tunnel network. It took months for the 25th Division to figure out

DAI NAM THEME PARK

Equal parts Disneyland, Buddhist fantasia, historical homage and national propaganda piece, **Dai Nam Theme Park** (Lac Canh Dai Nam Van Hien; ☎0650 351 2660; www.laccanhdainamvanhien.vn; adult/child 100,000/50,000d; ⊙8am-6pm) is a fantastically cheesy experience. About 30km from Ho Chi Minh City on Hwy 13, it's split into four constituent parts.

The **amusement park** (open 8am to 6pm) has a serious rollercoaster with corkscrews and loops, a log flume, an indoor snow world and plenty of rides for smaller kids. Each ride is charged separately (20,000d to 80,000d).

Dai Nam's 12.5-hectare **zoo** (adult/child 80,000/50,000d) is the only one in the greater HCMC area we'd recommend visiting. The menagerie include tigers, lions, white rhinos and bears. The neighbouring **beach** (adult/child 100,000/60,000d) has large fresh and saltwater pools and is a good place for cooling off the kids.

Best of all, for Disneyland kitsch on a monumental scale, is the **temple complex**. Set behind a vast plaza, there are artificial lakes, mountains, walking paths, towers and pagodas. In the mammoth temple every god, goddess and personage of importance in Vietnamese history gets a look-in, with Ho Chi Minh taking pride of place.

Local bus 616 (50,000d, 90 minutes) runs from Ben Thanh bus station to Dai Nam daily. There's plenty of car parking on-site.

For lacquerware, it's well worth stopping off at **Tuong Binh Hiep** en route. This village has been known for producing quality lacquered goods since the early 18th century and prices are cheaper than in HCMC. Tuong Binh Hiep is 5km south of the theme park.

why they kept getting shot at in their tents at night.

The US and Australian troops tried a variety of methods to 'pacify' the area around Cu Chi, which came to be known as the Iron Triangle. They launched large-scale ground operations involving tens of thousands of troops but failed to locate the tunnels. To deny the VC cover and supplies, rice paddies were defoliated, huge swathes of jungle bulldozed, and villages evacuated and razed. The Americans also sprayed chemical defoliants on the area aerially and a few months later ignited the tinder-dry vegetation with gasoline and napalm. But the intense heat interacted with the wet tropical air in such a way as to create cloudbursts that extinguished the fires. The VC remained safe in their tunnels.

Unable to win this battle with chemicals, the US army began sending men down into the tunnels. These 'tunnel rats', who were often involved in underground firefights, sustained appallingly high casualty rates.

When the Americans began using German shepherd dogs, trained to use their keen sense of smell to locate trapdoors and guerrillas, the VC began washing with American soap, which gave off a scent the canines identified as friendly. Captured US uniforms were put out to confuse the dogs further. Most importantly, the dogs were not able to spot booby traps. So many dogs were killed or maimed that their horrified handlers then refused to send them into the tunnels.

The USA declared Cu Chi a free-strike zone: little authorisation was needed to shoot at anything in the area, random artillery was fired into the area at night, and pilots were told to drop unused bombs and napalm there before returning to base. But the VC stayed put. Finally, in the late 1960s, American B-52s carpet-bombed the whole area, destroying most of the tunnels along with everything else around. The gesture was almost symbolic by then because the USA was already on its way out of the war. The tunnels had served their purpose.

The VC guerrillas serving in the tunnels lived in extremely difficult conditions and suffered serious casualties. Only about 6000 of the 16,000 cadres who fought in the tunnels survived the war. Thousands of civilians in the area were also killed. Their tenacity was extraordinary considering the bombings, the claustrophobia of living underground for weeks or months at a time, and the deaths of countless friends and comrades.

The villages of Cu Chi have since been presented with numerous honorific awards, decorations and citations by the government, and many have been declared 'heroic villages'. Since 1975 new hamlets have been established and the population of the area has multiplied; however, chemical defoliants remain in the soil and water, and crop yields are still poor.

Mangold and Penycate's *Tunnels of Cu Chi* is a powerful book documenting the story of the tunnels and the people involved on both sides.

Sights

Cu Chi Tunnels HISTORIC SITE

(adult/child 110,000/30,000d) Two sections of this remarkable tunnel network (which are enlarged and upgraded versions of the real thing) are open to the public. One is near the village of Ben Dinh and the other is 15km beyond at Ben Duoc. Most tourists visiting the tunnels end up at Ben Dinh, as it's easier for tour buses to reach. Even if you stay above ground, it's still an interesting experience learning about the region's ingenious and brave resistance activities.

Both sites have gun ranges attached where you can shell out a small fortune to fire genuine AK47s and machine guns. You pay per bullet so be warned: if you're firing an automatic weapon, they do come out pretty fast.

➡ Ben Dinh HISTORIC SITE

The most visited of the tunnel sites, this small, renovated section is near the village of Ben Dinh, about 50km from HCMC. In one of the classrooms at the visitors centre a large map shows the extent of the network while another shows cross-section diagrams of the tunnels. The section of the tunnel system presently open to visitors is a few hundred metres south of the visitors centre. It snakes up and down through various chambers along its 50m length.

The tunnels are about 1.2m high and 80cm across, and are unlit. Some travellers find them too claustrophobic for comfort. A knocked-out M-41 tank and a bomb crater are near the exit, which is in a reforested eucalyptus grove.

Be warned that this site tends to get crowded and you can feel like you're on a tourist conveyor belt most days.

Ben Duoc HISTORIC SITE

The tunnels here have been enlarged to accommodate tourists, although they're still a tight squeeze. Inside the underground chambers are bunkers, a hospital and a command centre that played a role in the 1968 Tet Offensive. The set pieces include tables, chairs, beds, lights, and dummies outfitted in guerrilla gear.

The massive Ben Duoc temple, built in 1993 in memory of the Vietnamese killed at Cu Chi, is flanked by a nine-storey tower with a flower garden at the front. You'll only be permitted to enter if you're dressed appropriately – although temple wear (long trousers etc) may not be conducive to clambering through earthen tunnels.

Cu Chi War History Museum MUSEUM

(Nha Truyen Thong Huyen Cu Chi) FREE The small Cu Chi War History Museum is not actually at the tunnel sites but just off the main highway in the central part of Cu Chi town. Like most similar museums, its displays consist mainly of photographs (some quite graphic) and large chunks of rusting military hardware. The subject is covered much more comprehensively in the War Remnants Museum in HCMC and you'll see many of the same photos at the tunnels themselves.

Cu Chi Wildlife Rescue Station WILDLIFE

(www.wildlifeatrisk.org; adult/child US$5/free; 7.30-11.30am & 1-4.30pm) Located just a few kilometres from the Ben Dinh tunnels, this centre is dedicated to the protection of wildlife that has been confiscated from owners or illegal traders. Animals include bears, otters and gibbons. There is an informative display on the rather depressing state of wildlife in Vietnam, including the 'room of death' featuring traps and baits. It's tough to navigate these back roads solo, so talk to a travel agent about incorporating the centre into a Cu Chi Tunnels trip.

Phoning ahead before a visit is recommended to ensure centre staff are on hand.

Getting There & Around

Cu Chi district covers a large area, parts of which are as close as 30km to central Ho Chi Minh City. The Cu Chi War History Museum is closest to the city, while the Ben Dinh and Ben Duoc tunnels are about 50km and 65km, respectively, from central HCMC.

CAR

To visit the rescue centre as well as the tunnels, consider hiring a car and driver, a relatively cheap option if shared between a few people. It is hard to find, so make sure your driver knows where he's going.

PUBLIC TRANSPORT

Requiring several changes of bus, it is very difficult to visit by public transport. Tay Ninh buses pass though Cu Chi, but getting from the town of Cu Chi to the tunnels by public transport is difficult.

TOURS

By far the easiest way to get to the tunnels is by guided tour and, as the competition is stiff, prices are exceptionally reasonable. For something different, hop on a boat to the Cu Chi Tunnels with Les Rives (p330); boats depart twice daily, at 7am and 11am, and include hotel pick-up, meals, refreshments, guide and admission fees. The entire trip takes five hours. Another option is a motorbike tour with Saigon Riders (p333), which costs US$69 per person (minimum two people).

Tay Ninh

POP POP 127,000

Tay Ninh town, the capital of Tay Ninh province, serves as the headquarters of one of Vietnam's most intriguing indigenous religions, Cao Daism. The Cao Dai Great Temple at the sect's Holy See is one of Asia's most unusual and astonishing structures. Built between 1933 and 1955, the temple is a rococo extravaganza blending the dissonant architectural motifs of a French church, a Chinese temple and an Islamic mosque.

Tay Ninh province, northwest of Ho Chi Minh City, is bordered by Cambodia on three sides. The area's dominant geographic feature is Nui Ba Den (Black Lady Mountain), which towers above the surrounding plains. Tay Ninh province's eastern border is formed by the Saigon River. The Vam Co River flows from Cambodia through the western part of the province.

Because of the once-vaunted political and military power of the Cao Dai, this region was the scene of prolonged and heavy fighting during the Franco–Viet Minh War. Tay Ninh province served as a major terminus of the Ho Chi Minh Trail during the American War, and in 1969 the Viet Cong captured Tay Ninh town and held it for several days.

During the period of conflict between Cambodia and Vietnam in the late 1970s, the Khmer Rouge launched a number of cross-border raids into Tay Ninh province and committed atrocities against civilians.

CAO DAISM

A thought-provoking fusion of East and West, Cao Daism (Dai Dao Tam Ky Pho Do) is a syncretic religion born in 20th-century Vietnam that embraces disparate elements of Buddhism, Confucianism, Taoism, native Vietnamese spiritualism, Christianity and Islam – with a dash of secular enlightenment thrown in for good measure. The term 'Cao Dai' (meaning 'high terrace'; 高台) is a euphemism for God; an estimated two to three million followers of Cao Daism exist worldwide.

Cao Daism was founded by the mystic Ngo Minh Chieu (also known as Ngo Van Chieu; born 1878), a civil servant who once served as district chief of Phu Quoc Island. Widely read in Eastern and Western religious works, he became active in seances and in 1919 began receiving revelations in which the tenets of Cao Daism were set forth.

Much of Cao Dai doctrine is drawn from Mahayana Buddhism, mixed with Taoist and Confucian elements (Vietnam's 'Triple Religion'). Cao Dai ethics are based on the Buddhist ideal of 'the good person' but incorporate traditional Vietnamese beliefs as well. The ultimate goal of the Cao Dai disciple is to escape the cycle of reincarnation. This can only be achieved by refraining from killing, lying, luxurious living, sensuality and stealing.

Read more on the official Cao Dai site: www.caodai.org.

Several cemeteries around Tay Ninh are stark reminders of these events.

Sights

Cao Dai Holy See TEMPLE

Home to the **Cao Dai Great Temple** (Thanh That Cao Dai), the Cao Dai Holy See, founded in 1926, is 4km east of Tay Ninh, in the village of Long Hoa. As well as the Great Temple, the complex houses administrative offices, residences for officials and adepts, and a hospital of traditional Vietnamese herbal medicine that attracts people from all over the south for its treatments

Prayers are conducted four times daily in the Great Temple (suspended during Tet). It's worth visiting during prayer sessions (the one at noon is most popular with tour groups from HCMC) but don't disturb the worshippers. Only a few hundred adherents, dressed in splendid garments, participate in weekday prayers but during festivals several thousand may attend.

The Cao Dai clergy have no objection to visitors photographing temple objects, but do not photograph people without their permission, which is seldom granted. However, it is possible to photograph the prayer sessions from the upstairs balcony, an apparent concession to the troops of tourists who come here daily.

It's important that guests wear modest and respectful attire inside the temple, which means no shorts or sleeveless T-shirts.

Set above the front portico of the Great Temple is the divine eye. Lay women enter the Great Temple through a door at the base of the tower on the left. Once inside they walk around the outside of the colonnaded hall in a clockwise direction. Men enter on the right and walk around the hall in an anticlockwise direction. Hats must be removed upon entering the building. The area in the centre of the sanctuary is reserved for Cao Dai priests.

A mural in the front entry hall depicts the three signatories of the 'Third Alliance between God and Man': the Chinese statesman and revolutionary leader Dr Sun Yat-sen (Sun Zhongshan; 1866–1925) holds an ink stone, while the Vietnamese poet Nguyen Binh Khiem (1492–1587) and French poet and author Victor Hugo (1802–85) write 'God and humanity' and 'Love and justice' in Chinese and French (Nguyen Binh Khiem writes with a brush, Victor Hugo uses a quill pen). Nearby signs in English, French and German each give a slightly different version of the fundamentals of Cao Daism.

The main hall is divided into nine sections by shallow steps, representing the nine steps to heaven, with each level marked by a pair of columns. Worshippers attain each new level depending on their years as Cao Dai adherents. At the far end of the sanctuary, eight plaster columns entwined with multicoloured dragons support a dome representing the heavens. Under the dome is a giant star-speckled blue globe with the 'divine eye' on it.

The largest of the seven chairs in front of the globe is reserved for the Cao Dai pope, a position that has remained vacant since 1933. The next three chairs are for the three men responsible for the religion's law books. The remaining chairs are for the leaders of the three branches of Cao Daism, represented by the colours yellow, blue and red.

On both sides of the area between the columns are two pulpits similar in design to the minbar in mosques. During festivals the pulpits are used by officials to address the assembled worshippers. The upstairs balconies are used if the crowd overflows.

Up near the altar are barely discernible portraits of six figures important to Cao Daism: Sakyamuni (Siddhartha Gautama, the founder of Buddhism), Ly Thai Bach (Li Taibai, a fairy from Chinese mythology), Khuong Tu Nha (Jiang Taigong, a Chinese saint), Laotse (the founder of Taoism), Quan Cong (Guangong, Chinese God of War) and Quan Am (Guanyin, the Goddess of Mercy).

Nui Ba Den TEMPLES, MOUNTAIN

(Black Lady Mountain; gondola one way/return adult 80,000/150,000d, child 75,000/40,000d) Fifteen kilometres northeast of Tay Ninh, Nui Ba Den rises 850m above the rice paddies, corn, cassava (manioc) and rubber plantations of the surrounding countryside. Over the centuries it has served as a shrine for various peoples of the area, including the Khmer, Cham, Vietnamese and Chinese, and there are several interesting **cave temples** here.

The summits of Nui Ba Den are much cooler than the rest of Tay Ninh province, most of which is only a few dozen metres above sea level.

Nui Ba Den was used as a staging area by both the Viet Minh and the VC, and was the scene of fierce fighting during the French and American Wars, when it was defoliated and heavily bombed by US aircraft.

Several stories surround the name 'Black Lady Mountain'. One is derived from the legend of Huong, a young woman who married her true love despite the advances of a wealthy Mandarin. While her husband was away doing military service, she would visit a magical statue of Buddha at the mountain's summit. One day Huong was attacked by kidnappers but, preferring death to dishonour, she threw herself off a cliff. She then reappeared in the visions of a monk who lived on the mountain, and he told her story.

The hike from the base of the mountain to the main temple complex and back takes about 1½ hours. Although steep in parts, it's not a difficult walk – plenty of older pilgrims in sandals make the journey to worship at the temple. Around the temple complex are a few stands selling snacks and drinks.

If you need more exercise, a walk to the summit and back takes about six hours. The fastest, easiest way is via the gondola system that shuttles the pilgrims up and down the hill. For a more exhilarating descent, try the 'slideway', a sort of winding track that drops 1700m around the mountain.

Because of crowds, visiting on Sunday or during a holiday or festival is a bad idea.

Nui Ba Den appears prominently in a memoir published by former American soldier Larry Heinemann, *Black Virgin Mountain: A Return to Vietnam*.

Getting There & Away

Tay Ninh is on Hwy 22 (Quoc Lo 22), 96km from HCMC. The road passes through **Trang Bang**, the place where the famous photograph of a severely burnt young girl, Kim Phuc, screaming and running, was taken during a napalm attack in the American War. Read more about her story in *The Girl in the Picture* (1999) by Denise Chong.

BUS & TOURS

The easiest way to get here is via one of the Tay Ninh/Cu Chi tours leaving from District 1. Consider leaving one of the cheaper tours at the Holy See, and then taking a taxi or *xe om* from there to Nui Ba Den (90,000d). You'll need to arrange to meet your bus back at Tay Ninh to get return transport to HCMC.

By public transport from HCMC, bus number 65 travels from the Ben Thanh bus station to the An Suong bus station (7000d). From there catch a bus to the Tay Ninh bus station (70,000d), from where you can arrange a taxi or *xe om* (90,000d) to Nui Ba Den.

One Pillar Pagoda

One Pillar Pagoda of Thu Duc BUDDHIST TEMPLE

(Chua Mot Cot Thu Duc; 1/91 Đ Nguyen Du, Thu Duc District) Officially known as Nam Thien Nhat Tru, most people call this Buddhist temple the One Pillar Pagoda of Thu Duc. Modelled on Hanoi's One Pillar Pagoda, the structure is similar but not identical, consisting of a small, one-room temple hall rising on a pillar above a pond, containing a multi-armed image of Quan Am, Goddess of Mercy. At the rear of the compound are tombs holding urns containing bones of monks and other Buddhist faithful.

The pagoda is 15km northeast of central HCMC. Traveller cafes and travel agencies in HCMC should be able to put together a customised tour to the pagoda or to arrange a car and driver for you.

Can Gio

Notable for its extensive mangrove forest, Can Gio is a low, palm-fringed island sitting at the mouth of the Saigon River, some 25km southeast of Ho Chi Minh City. It was formed from silt washing downstream from the river, so don't expect any white-sand beaches. A few hopeful resorts have sprung up along the murky 10km shoreline.

Of more interest is the forest. This listed Unesco Biosphere Reserve contains a high degree of biodiversity, with more than 200 species of fauna and 150 species of flora. If you're looking for a relatively traffic-free route to explore by motorbike, it's a great day trip.

Sights

Monkey Island Eco Forest Park NATURE RESERVE
(www.cangioresort.com.vn; admission 30,000d)
This island is home to a monkey sanctuary, which houses at least a hundred wild but unafraid simians. Take care: like monkeys everywhere, the line between cheeky charmer, thieving pest and dangerous beast is very fine. Keep a firm hold on your possessions. While this is the most interesting and accessible part of the forest to visit, it's hard to stomach the cruel conditions in which the stars of the island's animal circus (including bears and monkeys) are kept.

The motorboat ride (about 180,000d) through the waterways to the VC's Rung Sac base is the highlight of a visit. At the reconstructed base, dummies portray VC cadres sawing open unexploded American bombs in order to salvage the explosives, and wrestling with crocodiles, which were once common here but are now confined to crocodile farms like the one by the entrance. A small museum has wildlife displays, along with exhibits relating to local war history and archaeological finds.

Coming from HCMC, Monkey Island is to the right of the main road, about 34km past the ferry.

Vam Sat NATURE RESERVE
Located within Can Gio's mangroves, Vam Sat is noted for its crab-angling, a crocodile farm and **Dam Doi** (Bat Swamp), an area where fruit bats nest. Boats to Vam Sat (around 180,000d) depart from under Dan Xay Bridge, which is on the main road, 22km south of the ferry and 12km north of Monkey Island.

Duyen Hai TOWN
Facing Vung Tau at the southeastern tip of Can Gio district, this small town has a **Cao Dai temple** and a large **market**, which is made very conspicuous by some rather powerful odours. Seafood and salt are the local specialities; the vegetables, rice and fruit are all imported by boat from around HCMC. Adjacent to the local shrimp hatchery is a vast **cemetery** and **war memorial** (Nghia Trang Liet Si Rung Sac), 2km from Can Gio Market.

Getting There & Away

CAR & MOTORBIKE

Can Gio is about 60km southeast of central HCMC, and the fastest way to make the journey is by car or motorbike (about two hours). There's a ferry crossing (motorbike/car 2000d/10,000d) 15km from HCMC at Binh Khanh (Cat Lai), a former US naval base. Once you get past the ferry, there is little traffic and the sides of the road are lined with mangrove forests. The motorbike ride is an excellent day out in itself.

TOURS

There are day trips from HCMC offered by Cafe Kim Tourist (US$25) and Saigon Tourist (from US$56). A boat trip to Can Gio is also offered by **Les Rives** (p330), which departs at 7.30am and takes a total of seven to nine hours. The trip includes hotel pick-up, meals, refreshments, guide and admission fees. **Saigon Riders** (p333) operates a fun motorbike trip to Can Gio, costing US$109 per person (all-inclusive, minimum two people), kicking off at 8am.

Mekong Delta

Includes ➡

Best Places to Eat

- Bassac Restaurant (p408)
- Itaca Resto Lounge (p397)
- L'Escale (p382)
- Nem Nuong Thanh Van (p381)
- Spice House at Cassia Cottage (p396)

Best Places to Stay

- Murray Guesthouse (p407)
- Mango Home Riverside (p372)
- Island Lodge (p370)
- Victoria Can Tho Resort (p381)
- Bamboo Cottages & Restaurant (p396)

Why Go?

The 'rice bowl' of Vietnam, the delta is carpeted in a dizzying variety of greens. It's a water world that moves to the rhythms of the mighty Mekong, where boats, houses and markets float upon the innumerable rivers, canals and streams that criss-cross the landscape like arteries.

The bustling commerce of its towns contrasts sharply with the languid, almost soporific pace of life in the countryside. Here buffaloes wallow in rice paddies, coconut- and fruit-laden boats float slowly along the mud-brown waters, and two-wheeled exploration of the narrow lanes is amply rewarded with a true taste of rural hospitality (and delicious river fish).

Elsewhere, mangrove forests teem with a wealth of bird life and bristle with the remains of Viet Cong bunkers, ornate Khmer pagodas and Buddhist temples reach for the sky, while off-coast islands offer white-sand beaches and tropical hideaways to some, pirate havens to others.

When to Go

My Tho

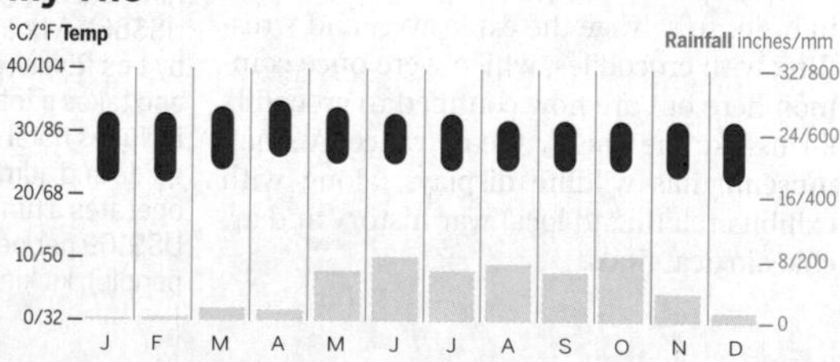

Jan While they shiver up north, Phu Quoc's beaches stay temperate and dry.

Mar A March visit avoids the Tet madness, and the summer heat and rain.

Nov The dry season starts, with Khmer longboat festivals in Tra Vinh and Soc Trang.

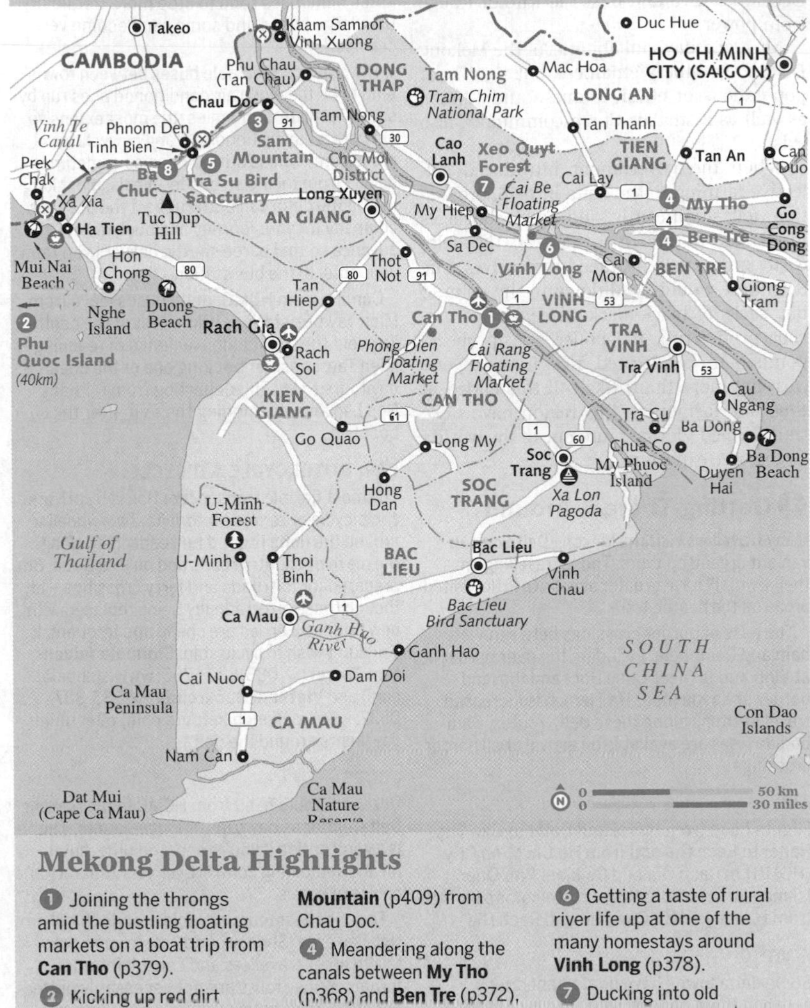

Mekong Delta Highlights

1. Joining the throngs amid the bustling floating markets on a boat trip from **Can Tho** (p379).
2. Kicking up red dirt on a motorbike ride and watching a sunset on **Phu Quoc Island's** (p389) many beaches.
3. Cycling through idyllic countryside to **Sam Mountain** (p409) from Chau Doc.
4. Meandering along the canals between **My Tho** (p368) and **Ben Tre** (p372), then stepping ashore to feast on fresh fish.
5. Watching clouds of storks and egrets at one of the excellent birdwatching sites, such as **Tra Su Bird Sanctuary** (p409).
6. Getting a taste of rural river life up at one of the many homestays around **Vinh Long** (p378).
7. Ducking into old Viet Cong bunkers and boating around enchanted waterways at **Xeo Quyt Forest** (p415).
8. Paying your respects to massacre remains at **Ba Chuc** (p404).

History

Once part of the Khmer kingdom, the Mekong Delta was the last region of modern-day Vietnam to be annexed and settled by the Vietnamese. Cambodians, mindful that they controlled the area until the 18th century, still call the delta Kampuchea Krom (p371), or 'Lower Cambodia'.

The Khmer Rouge attempted to reclaim the area by raiding Vietnamese villages and killing their inhabitants. This provoked the Vietnamese army to invade Cambodia on 25

December 1978 and oust the Khmer Rouge from power.

Most of today's inhabitants of the Mekong Delta are ethnic Vietnamese, but significant populations of ethnic Chinese and Khmer, as well as a smaller Cham community, also exist.

When the government introduced collective farming to the delta in 1975, production fell significantly and food shortages hit Saigon, although farmers in the delta easily grew enough to feed themselves. The Saigonese would head down to the delta to buy sacks of black-market rice, but to prevent profiteering the police set up checkpoints and confiscated rice from anyone carrying more than 10kg. All this ended in 1986 and farmers in this region have since transformed Vietnam into one of the world's largest rice exporters.

Getting There & Around

Many travellers visit the Mekong Delta on convenient organised tours. Those travelling on their own will have greater access to little-visited areas off the beaten track.

The ease of border crossings between Vietnam and Cambodia, including the river border at Vinh Xuong (near Chau Doc) and the land border at Xa Xia (near Ha Tien), has increased traveller traffic along these delta routes. Cambodian visas are available on arrival at all border crossings.

AIR

Flights head from Hanoi and Dalat to Can Tho, Hanoi to Rach Gia and from Ho Chi Minh City (HCMC) to Rach Gia and Ca Mau. Phu Quoc Island's international airport welcomes flights from Hanoi, HCMC, Can Tho and Rach Gia.

BOAT

Some delta towns have boat connections between them, though with road improvement and the building of bridges passenger travel on water is declining. The journey between Ca Mau and Rach Gia is particularly scenic. Fast passenger ferries to Phu Quoc Island leave from Rach Gia and Ha Tien, the latter also served by car ferries. Cargo boats and infrequent passenger boats head to the remote southern islands.

BUS

It's easy to travel the delta using public transport, and bus connections are excellent. Each urban centre has a main bus station for both buses and minibuses – although it's usually located on the edge of town, requiring a short *xe om* (motorbike taxi) or taxi ride to your hotel. Minibuses tend to stop more frequently than large buses and some can become very cramped.

The most comfortable buses between towns tend to be the plush air-conditioned ones run by several private companies; the most extensive network is run by Phuong Trang (www.futaexpress.com). These bus companies sometimes depart from their own bus terminals; most lodgings in the delta can both suggest the best bus company for your journey and book tickets in advance so that a free shuttle delivers you from your hotel to the bus station.

Coming from HCMC, delta buses leave from Mien Tay bus station, 10km west of the centre. To avoid the slight inconvenience of reaching Mien Tay, consider booking one of the cheap day tours to My Tho departing from Đ Pham Ngu Lao and abandoning the tour after the boat trip.

CAR, MOTORCYCLE & BICYCLE

The most flexible transport option is by private car, bicycle or rented motorbike. Two-wheeling around the delta is good fun, especially along the maze of country roads and on Phu Quoc. Be prepared for toll roads and ferry crossings – although these are gradually being replaced with new bridges. Ferries are cheap and frequent. If you don't wish to cycle solo, **Sinhbalo Adventure Travel** (☎ 083-837 6766; www.sinhbalo.com) and **Vietnam Backroads** (☎ 083-837 0532; www.mekongbiketours.com) offer multi-day jaunts around the delta.

TOURS

Dozens of tours head from HCMC to the Mekong Delta, either as day trips or longer jaunts. This is a good option if you're short on time, but it means abdicating control over your itinerary and choice of hotels.

The cheapest tours are sold around the Pham Ngu Lao area. Shop around before you book, talk to other travellers and consult internet forums. Pricey tours are not necessarily better, but often 'rock-bottom' means travelling with dozens of other tourists and being shuffled from one souvenir stall to another. Rewarding motorbike and scooter tours of the Delta are run by Vietnam Vespa Adventure (p333) and Saigon Riders (p333).

My Tho

☎ 073 / POP 140,000

Gateway to the Mekong Delta, My Tho is the capital of Tien Giang province and an important market town – although for the famous floating markets, you'll need to continue on to Can Tho.

My Tho

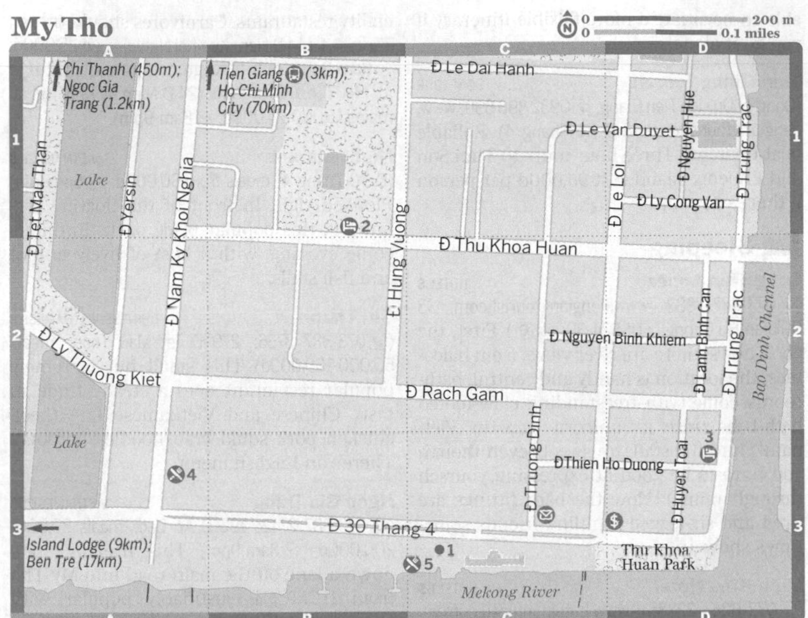

My Tho

Activities, Courses & Tours
1 My Tho Tourist Boat Station C3
Tien Giang Tourist ....(see 1)

Sleeping
2 Minh Kieu Hotel B1
3 Song Tien Annex...............................D3

Eating
4 Hu Tieu 44..A3
Hu Tieu Chay 24 .... (see 4)
5 Night Market...C3

My Tho's proximity to HCMC means it's a popular day-trip destination for a taste of river life – a flotilla of boats tour the local islands and their cottage industries daily, though many bypass the town itself. The riverfront makes for a pleasant stroll and the town, including the lively market (Đ Trung Trac), is easily explored on foot.

My Tho was founded in the 1680s by Chinese refugees fleeing Taiwan after the fall of the Southern Ming dynasty. The economy is based on tourism, fishing and the cultivation of rice, coconuts, bananas, mangoes, longans and citrus fruit.

Sights

Vinh Trang Pagoda BUDDHIST TEMPLE
(60a Đ Nguyen Trung Truc; 9-11.30am & 1.30-5pm) FREE Giant Buddha statues tower over the beautiful grounds of this peaceful temple around 1km east of the city centre, where the monks maintain an ornate sanctuary, decorated with carved and gilded wood. They also provide a home for children in need; donations welcome.

To get here, head north on Le Loi, turn right onto Nguyen Trai and cross the bridge. After 400m turn left onto Nguyen Trung Truc. The entrance is located about 200m from the turn-off, on the right-hand side.

Tours

In a prominent building on the riverfront, the **My Tho Tourist Boat Station** (8 Đ 30 Thang 4) is home to several tour companies offering cruises to the neighbouring islands and through the maze of small canals. Depending on what you book, destinations usually include a coconut-candy workshop, a honey farm (try the banana wine) and an orchid garden. A 2½-hour boat tour costs around 400,000d for one person or 500,000d for two. If you're a day-tripper, it's easiest to book your package (including connecting transport) through a HCMC-based tour operator. Prices are significantly better if you can join a group, although you may be able to negotiate a more flexible itinerary if you go it alone.

Tien Giang Tourist BOAT TOUR
(Cong Ty Du Lich Tien Giang; ☎0932 896 699; www.tiengiangtourist.com; 8 Đ 30 Thang 4) Reliable boat operator. Three-hour tours to Thoi Son and Phoenix island cost 95,000d per person if there's a group.

Sleeping

Song Tien Annex HOTEL $
(☎073-387 7883; www.tiengiangtourist.com; 33 Đ Thien Ho Duong; r US$24-30;) First, the good news: there are river views from balconies, the location is handy and central, bathrooms come with freestanding claw-footed bath-tubs (rare as unicorn eggs in Vietnam!) and the staff are sweet (even though you have to be good at expressing yourself through mime). Now the bad: fittings are tired and six-legged scuttling friends sometimes show up.

Minh Kieu Hotel HOTEL $$
(☎073-626 2288; www.hotelminhkieu.com.vn; 2 Đ Thu Khoa Huan; s/d US$20/25;) It's central, its tiled rooms are spick-and-span and while this multistorey beauty probably won't make your social media posts, the location, value for money, good breakfast and the helpfulness of its staff in spite of Babylonian issues all work in this hotel's favour.

★**Island Lodge** BOUTIQUE HOTEL $$$
(☎073-651 9000; www.theislandlodge.com.vn; 390 Ap Thoi Binh, Xa Thoi Son; r US$150;) It's hard to imagine a more tranquil place than this island hideaway. At this intimate luxury hotel, the occupants of its 12 rooms are cheerfully attended to by professional staff. You can watch the goings-on on the river from the riverside pool, indulge in gourmet cuisine, or retreat to your light, bright room, complete with contemporary art and bamboo-framed beds.

After crossing the bridge from My Tho in the Ben Tre direction, take the turn towards Thoi Son and travel for another 3km or so.

Eating

My Tho is known for its vermicelli soup, *hu tieu My Tho,* richly garnished with fresh and dried seafood, pork, chicken, offal and fresh herbs. It is served either with broth or dry and can also be made vegetarian.

Although *hu tieu* can be found at almost any eatery in town, there's a handful of speciality restaurants. Carnivores should try **Hu Tieu 44** (44 Đ Nam Ky Khoi Nghia; soup 25,000d; ⏲8am-9pm), while vegetarians can indulge at **Hu Tieu Chay 24** (24 Đ Nam Ky Khoi Nghia; mains 15,000-24,000d; ⏲8am-9pm).

Night Market VIETNAMESE $
(Đ 30 Thang 4; meals from 30,000d; ⏲5pm-late) Plonked right in front of the floating restaurant, this popular place packs in diners come evening, with a host of lively hotpot and fish stalls.

Chi Thanh CHINESE, VIETNAMESE $
(☎073-387 3756; 279 Đ Tet Mau Than; meals 50,000-100,000d) This small but extremely popular restaurant does a steady trade in tasty Chinese and Vietnamese fare (beef, chicken, pork, squid, crab, noodles, hotpots). There's an English menu.

Ngoc Gia Trang VIETNAMESE $$
(☎073-387 2742; 196 Đ Ap Bac; meals 80,000-200,000d; ⏲8am-9pm) This friendly spot, down a lane off the main road into My Tho from HCMC, is justifiably popular with tour groups thanks to the excellent, beautifully presented local specialities, such as elephant-ear fish, pork meatballs and a tangy, sour soup.

Getting There & Around

New bridges and freeways have considerably shortened travel distances to My Tho. If heading to Ben Tre, a taxi (around 260,000d) or *xe om* (around 120,000d) are considerably faster than buses. Buses head to Ben Tre (10,000d, 25 minutes, frequent), Can Tho (70,000d, 2½ hours, several daily) and HCMC (80,000d, 1½ hours, hourly).

Tien Giang Bus Station (Ben Xe Tien Giang; 42 Đ Ap Bac) The bus station is 2.3km northwest of town, on the main Hwy 1A towards Ho Chi Minh City. A *xe om* into town should cost around 40,000d.

Around My Tho

Phoenix Island

Until his imprisonment for antigovernment activities and the consequent dispersion of his flock, the Coconut Monk (Dao Dua) led a small community on Phoenix Island (Con Phung), a few kilometres from My Tho. The Coconut Monk left his family to pursue a monastic life and for three years he sat on a stone slab under a flagpole and meditated day and night.

In its heyday the island was dominated by a somewhat trippy open-air **sanctuary** (admission 5000d; ⏲8-11.30am & 1.30-6pm). The dragon-emblazoned columns and quirky tower, with its huge metal globe, must have once been brightly painted, but these days the whole place has become faded, rickety and silent. Nevertheless, it is seriously kitsch, with a model of the *Apollo* rocket set among the Buddhist statues. With some imagination you can almost picture how it all must have appeared as the Coconut Monk presided over his congregation, flanked by enormous elephant tusks and seated on a richly ornamented throne.

Plaques on the 3.5m-high porcelain jar (created in 1972) on the island tell all about the Coconut Monk. He founded a religion, Tinh Do Cu Si, a fusion of Buddhism and Christianity. Representations of Jesus and the Buddha appeared together, as did the Virgin Mary and eminent Buddhist women,

KAMPUCHEA KROM

Visitors to some Mekong provinces may be surprised to find Khmer towns whose inhabitants speak a different language, follow a different brand of Buddhism and have a vastly different history and culture to their Vietnamese neighbours. Though the Khmer are a minority in the Mekong, they were the first inhabitants here, with an ancestry dating back more than 2000 years.

Kampuchea Krom (meaning 'Lower Cambodia') is the unofficial Khmer name for the Mekong Delta region, whose indigenous inhabitants are the Khmer Krom, an ethnic minority living in southern Vietnam. The Khmer Krom trace their origins back to the 1st century AD, to the founding of Funan, a maritime empire that stretched from the Malay peninsula to the Mekong. Archaeologists believe Funan was a sophisticated society that built canals, traded in precious metals and had a high level of political organisation as well as agricultural know-how. Following the Funan came the Chenla empire (630–802 AD) and then the Khmer empire, the mightiest in Southeast Asia, which saw the creation of Angkor Wat among other great achievements. By the 17th century, however, the empire was in ruins, under pressure from the expansionist Thais and Vietnamese. This was a time of rising power for the Vietnamese empire, which began expanding south, conquering first the Cham empire before setting their sights on Khmer lands in the Mekong Delta.

According to some historians, there were around 40,000 Khmer families living around Prey Nokor when the Vietnamese arrived in the 1600s, following the granting of settlement rights by King Chey Chettha in 1623. Prey Nokor was an important port for the Cambodian kingdom and was renamed Saigon in 1698. Waves of Vietnamese settlers populated the city as other colonists continued south. Prior to their arrival there were 700 Khmer temples scattered around south Vietnam. Over the next century the Khmer Krom fought and won some minor victories in the region, expelling the intruders, only to lose their gains in new rounds of attacks.

When the French subjugated Indochina in the 19th century, the hope of an independent Kampuchea Krom would be forever destroyed. Although the ethnic Khmer were a majority in southern Vietnam at that time, the French didn't incorporate the colony with Cambodia but made it a separate protectorate called Cochinchina. On 4 June 1949 the French formally annexed Kampuchea Krom, a day of sorrow for many Cambodians, although the writing had been on the wall centuries earlier as the area was colonised.

Since independence in 1954, the Vietnamese government has adopted a policy of integration and forced assimilation (the Khmer Krom must take Vietnamese family names and learn the Vietnamese language, among other things). According to the Khmer Kampuchea-Krom Federation (KKF; www.khmerkrom.org), the Khmer Krom continue to suffer persecution. They report difficult access to Vietnamese health services, religious discrimination (Khmer Krom are Theravada Buddhists, unlike Vietnam's Mahayana Buddhists) and racial discrimination.

The Khmer are the poorest segment of the population. Even their numbers remain a contentious topic: Vietnam reports one million Khmer Krom, while KKF claims there are seven million Khmer living in southern Vietnam.

together with the cross and Buddhist symbols. Today only the symbols remain, as the Tinh Do Cu Si community has dissolved from the island.

Private boat operators can include the island as part of an organised tour.

Other Islands

Famed for its longan orchards, **Dragon Island** (Con Tan Long) makes for a pleasant stop and stroll, just a five-minute boat trip from My Tho. Some of the residents of the island are shipwrights and the lush, palm-fringed shores are lined with wooden fishing boats. The island has some small restaurants and cafes.

Tortoise Island (Con Qui) and **Unicorn Island** (Thoi Son) are popular stops for the coconut candy and banana wine workshops.

Ben Tre

075 / POP 1.25 MILLION

The picturesque little province of Ben Tre was always one ferry beyond the tourist traffic of My Tho and consequently developed at a more languid pace, although new bridges connecting Ben Tre with My Tho and Tra Vinh funneled more visitors into the area. The town's sleepy waterfront, lined with ageing villas, is easy to explore on foot, as is the rustic settlement across the bridge to the south of the centre. This is also a good place to arrange boat trips in the area, particularly for those wanting to escape the tour bus bustle. Plus, the riverside promenade and the narrow lanes on both sides of the river are ideal for two-wheeled exploration.

The Ben Tre area is famous for its *keo dua* (coconut candy). Many local women work in small factories making these sweets, spending their days boiling cauldrons of the sticky coconut goo before rolling it out and slicing sections off into squares.

Tours

Ho Chi Minh City–based Sinhbalo and Mekong Bike Tours offer cycling trips that take in the best of the narrow lanes around Ben Tre.

★**Mango Cruises** CYCLING, BOAT TOUR
(0902 880 120; www.mangocruises.com) Unlike cookie-cutter tours from HCMC, Mango Cruises focuses on the less-visited back roads and canals around Ben Tre and beyond. Day tours comprise a nice mix of cycling, dining on local specialities and observing how rice paper and other local staples are made. Longer tours include outings on its day cruisers and multiday boat trips in the delta.

Sleeping

All the following options are located near Ben Tre rather than in the town proper; all offer meals.

★**Mango Home Riverside** BOUTIQUE HOTEL $$
(075-351 1958; www.mangohomeriverside.com; d/ste US$45/57;) Set amid coconut and mango trees along the bank of a Mekong tributary, this delightful mango-coloured B&B, run by a Canadian-Vietnamese couple, provides a welcome place to unwind. Spacious rooms have air-con, some have outdoor bathrooms, and there are hammocks for lounging. The food is excellent and at

Ben Tre

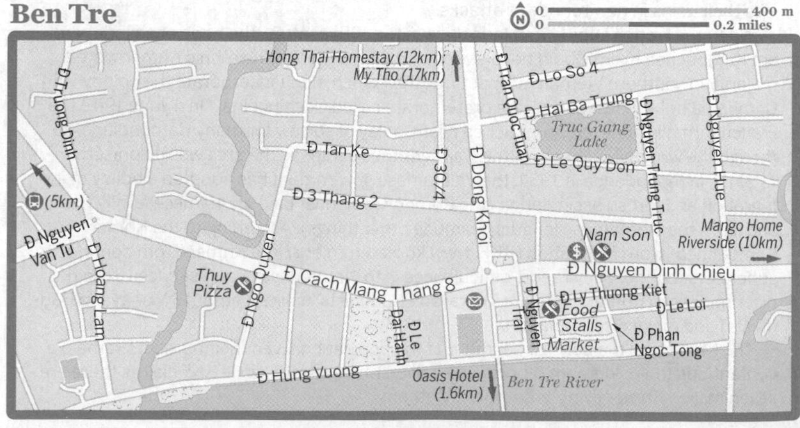

BUSES FROM BEN TRE

DESTINATION	COST (D)	TIME (HR)	FREQUENCY	DISTANCE
Can Tho	70,000	1½	every 30min	78km
HCMC	80,000	2¼	hourly	87km
My Tho	10,000	30min	frequent	16km
Tra Vinh	120,000	2¼	several daily	86km
Vinh Long	20,000	1½	several daily	44km

night there's complete silence. It's 10km out of town; call for pick-up.

Oasis Hotel HOTEL $$
(075-383 8800; http://bentrehoteloasis.com; 151c My An C, My Thanh An; d 720,000-855,000d, f 1,080,000d;) There's always a warm welcome at this popular, bright-yellow, small hotel, run by an affable and very helpful couple. It's in the village south of the river and best reached by taxi. Free bicycles facilitate countryside exploration.

Hong Thai Homestay HOMESTAY $$
(0914 557 386; 16c Ap 2 Quoi Son, Chau Thanh; s/d US$20/32;) Mr Thai and his wife make a formidable team: he arranges excursions for his guests amid the coconut groves around their countryside home, and she cooks veritable mountains of delicious local staples to feed them. Rooms are simple, fan-cooled and tiled. Located around 12km from Ben Tre, across the river from My Tho; arrange pick-up with the owners.

Eating & Drinking

For ultra-cheap eats, head to the market, where plenty of **food stalls** (dishes around 15,000d) await. Ham Luong's rooftop cafe is good for a drink or an ice cream.

Thuy Pizza PIZZA $
(51 Đ Ngo Quyen; mains from 65,000d; noon-10pm) Adding a welcome touch of innovation to Ben Tre's largely uninspiring dining scene, this friendly place attracts a healthy contingent of travellers and curious locals. The pizza is as good as can be expected in a small-town delta place, and owner Thuy is friendly and keen to practise her English.

Nam Son VIETNAMESE $
(075-382 2873; 40 Đ Phan Ngoc Tong; mains 26,000-60,000d; 11am-10pm) Centrally located, this place attracts a lively local crowd thanks to its popular grilled chicken, best washed down with draught beer.

Getting There & Away

BUS

Buses to Vinh Long drop you at Pha Dinh Kao, the ferry port across the river from town; take the ferry across.

Bus Station (Ben Xe Thanh Pho Ben Tre; Đ Dong Khoi) Buses stop at the bus station 2.5km northwest of the town centre. The last buses to HCMC depart between 4pm and 5pm; Thinh Phat are among the most comfortable.

Tra Vinh

074 / POP 91,500

The boulevards of Tra Vinh, one of the prettiest towns in the Mekong Delta, are still lined with shady trees, harking back to an earlier era. With more than 140 Khmer pagodas dotting the province, Tra Vinh is a quiet place for exploring the Mekong's little-touted Cambodian connection. The town itself sees a little more tourist traffic now that it's linked to Ben Tre and beyond by large new bridges.

About 300,000 ethnic Khmer live in Tra Vinh province. They may seem an invisible

DON'T MISS

BEN TRE TO TRA VINH THE SLOW WAY

Every morning around 9am, a cargo boat sets off from Ben Tre's dock for Tra Vinh. The owner is happy to take on a passenger or two (150,000d per person, six hours) and you get to ride in the upstairs 'cabin' or on the roof amid the cargo, unobtrusively observing river life. The boat passes along canals where coconuts are harvested and processed, and where kids swim beneath the stilt houses, occasionally docking in villages to drop off goods. Every bridge built in the delta brings the cargo boats closer to extinction, so catch one while you can.

Tra Vinh

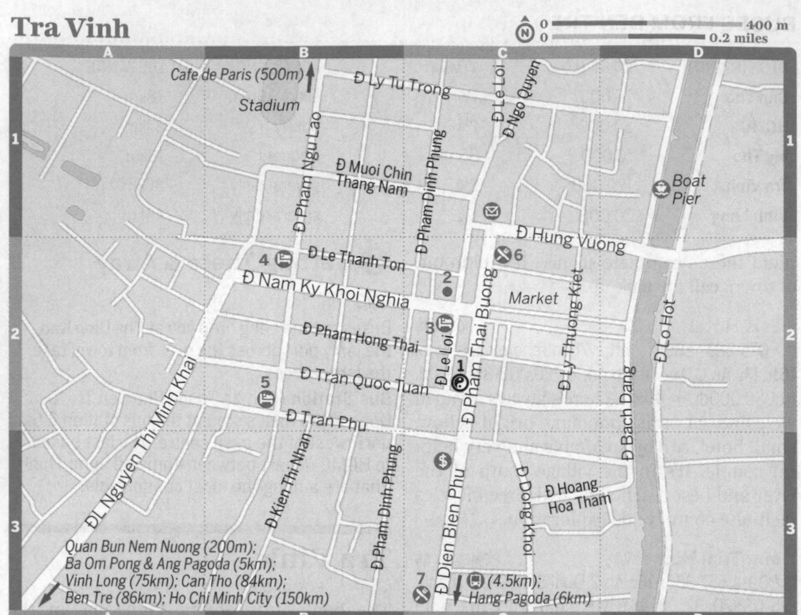

Tra Vinh

Sights
1 Ong Pagoda ... C2

Activities, Courses & Tours
2 Tra Vinh Tourist ... C2

Sleeping
3 Hotel Gia Hoa 2 ... C2
4 Tra Vinh Palace ... B2
5 Tra Vinh Palace 2 ... B2

Eating
6 Thanh Tra Restaurant ... C2
7 Vi Huong ... C3

minority as they all speak fluent Vietnamese and there's nothing outwardly distinguishing about their clothing or lifestyle. Dig a bit deeper and discover that Khmer culture is alive and well in these parts of Vietnam. Many of its numerous pagodas have schools to teach the Khmer language and many Tra Vinh locals can read and write Khmer at least as well as Vietnamese. Vietnam's Khmer minority are almost all followers of Theravada Buddhism. Between the ages of 15 and 20, most boys set aside a few months to live as monks (they decide themselves on the length of service). Khmer monks are allowed to eat meat, but cannot kill animals.

There is also a small but active Chinese community in Tra Vinh, one of the few such communities that remain in the Mekong Delta region.

Sights

Ba Om Pond & Ang Pagoda BUDDHIST TEMPLE
(Ao Ba Om & Chua Ang/Angkor Rek Borei; Square Lake; dawn-dusk) Five kilometres southwest of Tra Vinh, this large, square pond is a favourite with local picnickers, and a spiritual site for the Khmers. It would have once served as a bathing pond for the 10th-century Angkor-era temple that was situated here.

Built on the temple ruins, Ang Pagoda is a venerable Khmer-style pagoda, fusing classic Khmer architecture with French colonial influences. The interior features brightly painted scenes from the Buddha's life and the friendly monks may try chatting to you.

Opposite the pagoda entrance is the nicely presented **Khmer Minority People's Museum** (Bao Tang Van Hoa Dan Tac; 8am-5pm) FREE, which displays photos, costumes and other artefacts of traditional Khmer culture.

Ong Pagoda TAOIST TEMPLE

(Chua Ong & Chua Tau; 44 Đ Dien Bien Phu; ⏲dawn-dusk) The very ornate, brightly painted Ong Pagoda is a fully fledged Chinese pagoda and a very active place of worship. The red-faced god on the altar is deified general Quan Cong, who is believed to offer protection against war and is based on a historical figure, a 3rd-century soldier.

The Ong Pagoda was founded in 1556 by the Fujian Chinese Congregation, but has been rebuilt and restored a number of times, most recently thanks to funds from visitors from Taiwan and Hong Kong.

Hang Pagoda BUDDHIST TEMPLE

(Chua Hang, Kampongnigrodha; Đ Dien Bien Phu; ⏲dawn-dusk) This modern Khmer pagoda is also known as the Stork Pagoda after the birds that nest in the tall trees here. It's a beautiful, peaceful complex and watching dozens of white egrets and storks wheeling overhead is an attraction in itself, but bring a hat. If you're lucky, you'll get to see the orange-robed acolytes beat the heck out of the enormous drum in the courtyard. The pagoda is located 6km south of town, about 300m past the bus station.

Tours

Tra Vinh Tourist BOAT TOUR

(☎074-385 8556, 64 Đ Le Loi; ⏲7.30-11am & 1.30-5pm) Helpful tourist office where some English is spoken. Arranges trips to various sites around the province, including boat cruises to local islands.

Sleeping

Tra Vinh Palace HOTEL $

(☎074-386 4999; www.travinh.lofteight.com; 3 Đ Le Thanh Ton; r 250,000-350,000d; ❄📶) Dominating the corner of a tree-lined backstreet, this four-storey hotel is all pink columns, decorative plasterwork, mother-of-pearl-inlaid wooden furniture (in the lobby) and balconies. The spacious rooms have high ceilings but the air-con struggles to keep them cool.

Tra Vinh Palace 2 HOTEL $

(☎074-386 4999; 48 Đ Pham Ngu Lao; d/tw/tr 220,000/240,000/280,000d; ❄📶) This friendly minihotel has sparkling rooms with tiled floors and either a bath-tub or a shub (shower tub). Double rooms are internal and windowless, so consider upgrading to a triple.

Hotel Gia Hoa 2 HOTEL $$

(☎074-385 8008; www.giahotel.com; 50 Đ Le Loi; r 320,000-580,000d; ❄📶) Hard to miss due to its height and its bright-yellow exterior, this brash hotel is surprisingly pleasant inside. Expect large rooms, separate shower stalls and a lift to haul your luggage up.

Eating & Drinking

Quan Bun Nem Nuong VIETNAMESE $

(12 Đ Nguyen Dang; meals 35,000d; ⏲11am-10pm) South of the centre, this informal joint is justifiably popular with locals for its *nem nuong* – roll-your-own spring rolls filled with pork sausage, green banana, star fruit, cucumber and fresh herbs, with a peanut sauce for dipping.

Vi Huong VIETNAMESE $

(37a Đ Dien Bien Phu; meals 20,000-80,000d; ⏲9am-10pm) Cheap, cheerful hole-in-the-wall with wholesome traditional dishes such as sour soup, fish in claypot and pork with rice.

Thanh Tra Restaurant VIETNAMESE $$

(1 Pham Thai Buong; meals 80,000-180,000d; ⏲6am-9pm) On the top floor of the namesake hotel, the restaurant offers an extensive menu of Vietnamese dishes. The service can be so laid-back that you may catch them taking a nap, but we can vouch for the spring rolls and the grilled squid.

Cafe de Paris CAFE

(200 Đ Pham Ngu Lao; ⏲6am-10pm; 📶) With a stylish interior and upmarket aspirations, this cafe wouldn't look out of place in Ho Chi Minh City. The friendly proprietor speaks some English, the wide range of coffees is

BUSES FROM TRA VINH

DESTINATION	COST (D)	DURATION (HR)	FREQUENCY	DISTANCE
Ben Tre	110,000	2¼	several daily	86km
Can Tho	120,000	2½	hourly	84km
Cao Lanh	130,000	3½	several daily	124km
HCMC	130,000	3¾	hourly	150km
Vinh Long	70,000	1½	several daily	75km

complemented by some seriously good cakes and there are some light bites as well. It's a 1km walk north of the centre.

Getting There & Away

BOAT

A cargo boat still plies its slow way between Tra Vinh and Ben Tre and can take on passengers (p373).

BUS

Most buses leave from the main bus station, though some operators leave from their own departure points. Bear in mind that only the smaller minibuses bound for Vinh Long take you to the Vinh Long central bus station; larger buses from Tra Vinh either use the bus station out of the centre or drop you along the main road outside the centre.

Long-Distance Bus Station (Ben Xe Khach Tra Vinh) The main bus station is about 5km south of the town centre on Hwy 54, which is the continuation of the main street, Đ Dien Bien Phu.

Vinh Long

070 / POP 113,000

The capital of Vinh Long province, plonked about midway between My Tho and Can Tho, Vinh Long is a major transit hub. Flee the mayhem by heading to the riverfront, where a handful of cafes and restaurants afford respite. Vinh Long is the gateway to island life, the Cai Be Floating Market, abundant orchards and rural homestays.

Sights

Vinh Long's main draw are the tranquil islands dotting the river, with houses built on stilts and slow-paced agricultural life.

A NIGHT ON THE MEKONG

Spending the night onboard a boat on the Mekong River is a good way to explore more of the waterways that make up this incredible region and helps bring you closer to life on the river.

In addition to the following options, there are various companies offering luxury cruises between My Tho (including transfers from Ho Chi Minh City) and Siem Reap. **Pandaw Cruises** (www.pandaw.com; 7 nights US$2330-3107) is favoured by high-end tour companies. **Compagnie Fluviale du Mekong** (www.cfmekong.com; 7 nights per person from US$1849) is smaller and is well regarded for its personal service and excellent food. Taking the competition to a new level of lush are **AmaWaterways** (www.amawaterways.com) and **Heritage Line** (www.heritage-line.com; 3 nights from US$1756). The longer cruises mean a lot of time looking at very similar scenery, so it's arguably better just to opt for a shorter sector such as My Tho to Phnom Penh.

There are a number of interesting options for overnighting on the Mekong.

Mango Cruises (0902 880 120; www.mangocruises.com) The overnight and three-day cruises of the Mekong Delta's less explored waterways between My Tho and Can Tho, and Ben Tre and Sa Dec on beautiful, traditional wooden sampans receive a great deal of praise from travellers.

Bassac (0710-382 9540; www.transmekong.com; overnight US$254) Offers a range of beautiful wooden sampans for small groups. The standard itinerary is an overnight between Cai Be and Can Tho, but custom routes are possible.

Mekong Eyes (0710-378 3586; www.mekongeyes.com) Choose from a beautifully converted traditional rice barge *(Mekong Eyes)*, a two-cabin sampan *(Dragon Eyes)* or a private houseboat *(Gecko Eyes)*. The name plays on the ever-present eyes painted on fishing boats throughout Vietnam. These stylish boats do a range of Mekong tours, from one day to two weeks.

Aqua Expeditions (1 866 603 3687; www.aquaexpeditions.com; 3 nights from US$3315) Essentially a sleek, waterborne five-star hotel, *Aqua Mekong* takes care of all the creature comforts, such as spacious cabins, a deckside pool, gourmet meals and even a library and games room. Mekong cruises range between three and seven nights and run from Siep Reap to Ho Chi Minh City, exploring Cambodia and Vietnam's waterways in style and considerable comfort.

Vinh Long

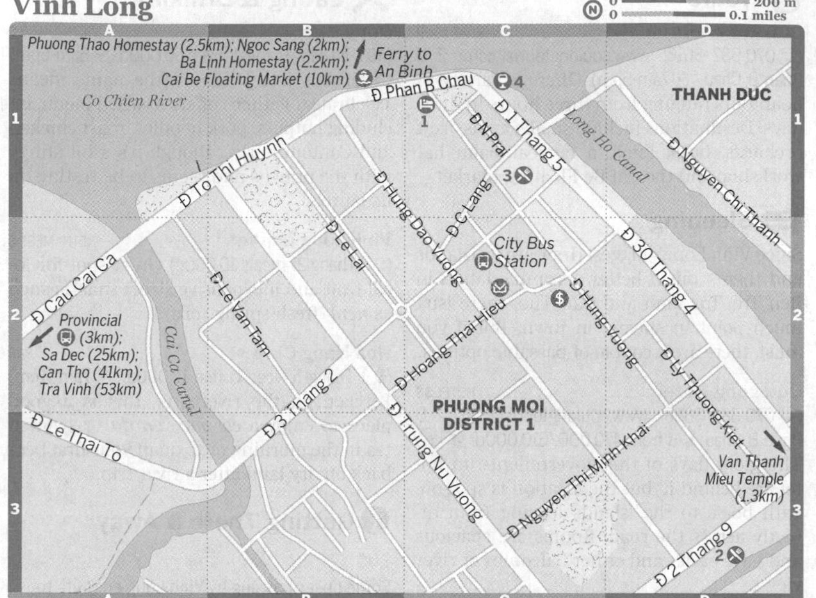

An Binh

ISLAND

The more popular and easiest island to visit is An Binh. You can take the public ferry across and then walk or cycle around on your own. Most island homestays organise half-day cruises along narrow canals for around US$20, taking in the floating market and then slowly floating along the picturesque backwaters.

Cai Be Floating Market

MARKET

(⏲5am-noon) This river market is still the principle attraction on a boat tour from Vinh Long, though it has shrunk considerably due to the building of bridges in the delta and the subsequent transportation of goods by road rather than river. The market is at its best around 6am. Wholesalers on big boats moor here, each specialising in different types of fruit or vegetable, hanging samples of their goods from tall wooden poles. It's an hour by boat from Vinh Long.

A notable sight is the huge and photogenic **Catholic cathedral** on the riverside.

Most people make detours along the way there or back to see the canals or visit orchards. For those who are travelling on an organised tour of the delta, it is customary to board a boat here, explore the islands and moor in Vinh Long before continuing to Can Tho.

Vinh Long

Activities, Courses & Tours

Cuu Long Tourist .... (see 1)

Sleeping

1 Cuu Long Hotel C1

Eating

2 Dong Khanh D3

3 Vinh Long Market C1

Drinking & Nightlife

4 Hoa Nang Cafe C1

Van Thanh Mieu Temple

TEMPLE

(Phan Thanh Gian Temple; Đ Tran Phu; ⏲5-11am & 1-7pm) Sitting in pleasant grounds across from the river, this temple is southeast of town. Confucian temples such as this are rare in southern Vietnam. The front hall honours local hero Phan Thanh Gian, who led an uprising against the French colonists in 1930. When it became obvious that his revolt was doomed, Phan killed himself rather than be captured by the colonial army. The rear hall, built in 1866, has a portrait of Confucius above the altar.

Tours

Cuu Long Tourist BOAT TOUR
(070-382 3616; www.cuulongtourist.com; 2 Đ Phan B Chau; 7am-5pm) Offers a variety of boat tours ranging from three hours to three days. Destinations include small canals, fruit orchards, brick kilns, a conical palm hat workshop and the Cai Be Floating Market.

Sleeping

Since Vinh Long's biggest draw are its islands and there's much better accommodation in Ben Tre, Tra Vinh and Can Tho, there isn't much point in staying in town. But if you must, there are a couple of passable options.

Cuu Long Hotel HOTEL $$
(070-382 3656; www.cuulongtourist.com; 2 Đ Phan B Chau; s/d from 470,000/610,000d;) The glory days of this government-run hotel are behind it, but the location is spot-on, with boats to the islands leaving from directly across the road. Rooms are spacious and have baths, and either balconies or river views.

Eating & Drinking

Dong Khanh VIETNAMESE $
(49 Đ 2 Thang 9; meals from 60,000d; 6am-6pm) Cavernous Dong Khanh (the name means 'celebrate together') offers a varied menu, including hotpots, pork noodles, roast chicken and Cantonese rice, though it's a bit stingy with the prawns and seems to be resting on its laurels.

Vinh Long Market VIETNAMESE $
(Đ 3 Thang 2; meals 10,000d) Great spot for local fruit and inexpensive street snacks, such as *nem* (fresh spring rolls).

Hoa Nang Cafe BAR
(Đ 1 Thang 5; iced coffee 12,000d; 7am-11pm) Perched on the riverbank, this is a good place to enjoy a *ca phe sua da* or scented tea in the morning or to quaff your first beer back on dry land after a river trip.

Getting There & Away

BUS

Some buses passing by Vinh Long en route to HCMC from Tra Vinh may drop you off at the

'HOMESTAYS' AROUND VINH LONG

For many travellers, the chance to experience river life and get to know a local family is a highlight of a Mekong visit. Perhaps 'homestay' is the wrong word: in most cases you will actually be staying in specially constructed rustic hostels and guesthouses.

Some homestays have large communal rooms with bunks, while others offer basic bungalows with shared facilities and some even have rooms with en suites. Breakfast is usually included; in some places you'll share a meal with the family, while in bigger places there are simple restaurants. The only constant is a verdant, rustic setting and a taste of rural life.

Although many tourists book through group tours in HCMC, you can just take the ferry from Vinh Long and then a *xe om* to your preferred choice. Some hosts don't speak much English, but welcome foreign guests just the same.

Ngoc Sang (070-385 8694; 95/8 Binh Luong, An Binh; per person 250,000d;) Most travellers love this friendly, canal-facing rustic homestay. The grandmother cooks up some wonderful local dishes, free bikes are available, the owner runs decent early morning boat tours and there's a languid atmosphere about the place. The family seems shy when it comes to hanging out with the guests, though.

Phuong Thao Homestay (070-383 6854; http://en.phuongthaohomestay.com; An Binh; dm/d US$10/32;) Tucked away by the river, around 1.5km from the An Binh boat landing, this rustic guesthouse is run by the friendly Mr Phu, who speaks very good English and who can lend you bicycles and motorbikes to explore the island. Stay in the large, thatch-walled dorms with mozzie nets or the two concrete doubles. Good ratio of guests per bathroom.

Ba Linh Homestay (070-385 8683, 0939 138 142; balinhhomestay@gmail.com; 95 An Thanh, An Binh; r 500,000d) Run by friendly Mr Truong, this traditional-looking and popular place has six simple, high-roofed, partitioned rooms in a line, all with fan. Breakfast and dinner is included in the price and you may get to try such local specialities as rice-field rat.

corner of Pho Co Dieu and Nguyen Hue as they don't stop at either of the bus stations. Buses leave hourly for Can Tho (50,000d, one hour) and HCMC (105,000, three hours). There are several daily buses to Sa Dec (15,000, one hour) and Tra Vinh (70,000, 1½ hours).

City Bus Station (Ben Xe Thanh Pho Vinh Long; Đ 3 Thang 2) The central bus station has small bus services to Sa Dec and HCMC.

Provincial Bus Station (Ben Xe Khach Vinh Long; Hwy 1A) Long-distance services to HCMC and other delta destinations, excluding Sa Dec. It's 2.5km south of town on the way to Can Tho. A taxi costs around 130,000d.

Can Tho

071 / POP 759,000

The epicentre of the Mekong Delta, Can Tho is the largest city in the region and feels like a metropolis after a few days exploring the backwaters. As the political, economic, cultural and transportation centre of the Mekong Delta, it's a buzzing town with a lively waterfront lined with sculpted gardens, an appealing blend of narrow backstreets and wide boulevards, and perhaps the greatest concentration of foreigners in the delta. It is also the perfect base for nearby floating markets, the major draw for tourists who come here to boat along the many canals and rivers leading out of town.

Sights

Ong Temple TEMPLE

(32 Đ Hai Ba Trung; 6am-8pm) FREE In a fantastic location facing the Can Tho River and decorated with huge incense coils, this Chinese temple is set inside the **Guangzhou Assembly Hall**, and wandering through its interior is very enjoyable. It was originally built in the late 19th century to worship Kuang Kung, a deity symbolising loyalty, justice, reason, intelligence, honour and courage, among other merits.

Approaching the engraved screen, the right side is dedicated to the Goddess of Fortune and the left side is reserved for the worship of General Ma Tien. In the centre of the temple is Kuang Kung flanked by the God of Earth and the God of Finance.

Can Tho Museum MUSEUM

(Bao Tang Can Tho; 1 ĐL Hoa Binh; 8-11am & 2-5pm Tue-Thu, 8-11am & 6.30-9pm Sat & Sun) FREE This large, well-presented museum brings local history to life with manikins and life-size reproductions of buildings, including a Chinese pagoda and a house interior. Displays (with ample English translations) focus on the Khmer and Chinese communities, plant and fish specimens, rice production and, inevitably, the American War.

Munireangsey Pagoda BUDDHIST TEMPLE

(36 ĐL Hoa Binh; 8am-5pm) FREE This pagoda was originally built in 1946 to serve Can Tho's Khmer community. The ornamentation is typical of Khmer Theravada Buddhist pagodas, with none of the multiple Bodhisattvas and Taoist spirits common in Vietnamese Mahayana pagodas.

Tours

★Hieu's Tour CULTURAL TOUR

(0939 666 156; www.hieutour.com; 27a Đ Le Thanh Ton) Young, enthusiastic, English-speaking guide Hieu offers excellent tours around Can Tho – from early morning jaunts to the floating markets (US$23 to Cai Rang, US$30 to both markets) to cycling tours, food tours and even visits to Pirate Island (p403) further afield. Hieu is keen to show visitors true delta culture and a floating homestay is in the works.

Mekong Tours CULTURAL TOUR

(0907 852 927; www.mekongtours.info; 93 Đ Mau Than) Based at Xoai Hotel, this operator offers highly recommended tours of the floating markets, as well as an entertaining nightly street-food tour that departs the hotel at 6.30pm.

WORTH A TRIP

MEKONG RIVERSIDE RESORT & SPA

With a magnificent sense of seclusion, the four-star **Mekong Riverside Resort & Spa** (073-392 4466; www.mekongriversideresort.vn; Hoa Qui Ward, Hoa Khanh, Cai Be district; bungalow US$120-170;) has lovely thatched bungalows and stunning views across the vast river. Angle for fish from your balcony or sit back and watch the river boats cruise the Mekong at night. With free canoes and birdwatching tower, the resort offers the chance to fully experience the riverine world of the Mekong Delta.

It's 2km west of Cai Be along the river; offers pick-up from Saigon.

Can Tho

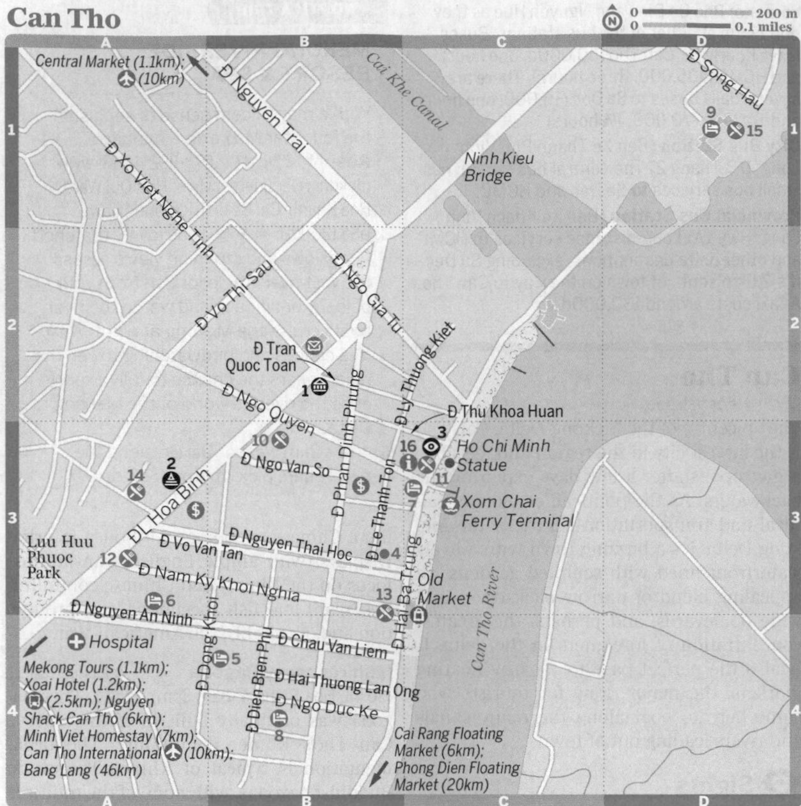

Can Tho

Sights

1 Can Tho Museum B2
2 Munireangsey Pagoda A3
3 Ong Temple C3

Activities, Courses & Tours

4 Hieu's Tour B3

Sleeping

5 Anh Dao Mekong Hotel B4
6 Kim Lan Hotel A3
7 Nam Bo Boutique Hotel C3
8 Thanh Ha B4
9 Victoria Can Tho Resort D1

Eating

10 CoopMart B3
L'Escale .... (see 7)
11 Mekong C3
Nam Bo .... (see 7)
12 Nem Nuong Thanh Van A3
13 Night Market B3
14 Quan Com Chay Cuong A3
15 Spices Restaurant D1

Information

16 Can Tho Tourist C3

Sleeping

Can Tho boasts the best range of accommodation that is available in the Mekong Delta, as well as guesthouses that are located in the nearby countryside.

★ Xoai Hotel HOTEL $

(☎0907 652 927; http://hotelxoai.com; 93 Đ Mau Than; s/d 235,000/293,000d; ❄@📶) Fantastic value at this friendly, efficient hotel with bright, mango-coloured (the hotel name means 'Mango Hotel'), airy rooms. Helpful staff speak excellent English and there's a roof terrace with hammocks.

Thanh Ha GUESTHOUSE $
(☎0918 183 522; mshaguesthouse@gmail.com; 118/14 Đ Phan Dinh Phung; r US$12; ❄📶) You'll find this guesthouse with a clutch of large, sparkling white rooms down a narrow alleyway that bustles quietly with local life. Ms Ha – the proprietor – is a character, and she can help arrange tours and rent you a bicycle or motorbike.

★**Nguyen Shack Can Tho** GUESTHOUSE $$
(☎0966 550 016; www.nguyenshack.com; Ong Tim Bridge, Thanh My, Thuong Thanh; r US$25, bungalow US$49-69; 📶) Not a shack, but rather a clutch of rustic thatched bungalows, this great place overlooks the Ong Tim River, situated 6km from Can Tho. It's the kind of place where backpackers are inspired to linger longer, thanks to the camaraderie between staff and guests. The engaging boat and bicycle tours and the proximity to Cai Rang floating markets are bonuses.

Kim Lan Hotel HOTEL $$
(☎071-0381 7079; www.kimlancantho.com.vn; 138a Đ Nguyen An Ninh; r 630,000-1,750,000d; ❄@📶) This very clean minihotel has chic rooms with contemporary furnishings and artworks on the wall. Even the cheapest, windowless standard rooms are perfectly adequate, and deluxe rooms are lovely. Staff are friendly and helpful.

Minh Viet Homestay GUESTHOUSE $$
(☎0978 123 213; 245/1 Phu Quoi, Cai Rang; s/d/q US$15/25/45; 📶) Situated closer to the Cai Rang floating market than Can Tho, this is a rustic guesthouse consisting of basic rooms with mozzie nets and thatched roofs. Minh and his family are welcoming, congenial hosts, and he's happy to take guests on whirlwind tours of the countryside and the floating markets. Bring earplugs to block out the chugging of early-morning boats.

Anh Dao Mekong Hotel HOTEL $$
(☎071-0381 9501; www.anhdaomekonghotel.com; Chau Van Liem; r 786,000-1,122,000d; ❄📶) A handy central location, spacious, contemporary rooms and very helpful staff define this neon-fronted hotel. Breakfast is extensive and tours get good traveller feedback, even if the staff can sometimes be overly enthusiastic in selling them.

★**Victoria Can Tho Resort** RESORT $$$
(☎071-0381 0111; www.victoriahotels.asia; Cai Khe Ward; r/ste from 2,365,600/3,429,300d; ❄@📶🏊) Designed with a French colonial look, the breezy rooms at this stylish, sophisticated hotel are set amid lush greenery around an inviting pool that looks out over the river. Facilities include an excellent restaurant, an open-air bar and a riverside spa. Activities on offer include cycling tours, cooking classes and cruises on the *Lady Hau*, a converted rice barge.

Nam Bo Boutique Hotel BOUTIQUE HOTEL $$$
(☎071-0381 9139; www.nambocantho.com; 1 Đ Ngo Quyen; ste 2,610,000-5,220,000d) Presiding over a mere eight suites in a colonial-era building, this super-central riverfront hotel revels in traditional presentation and contemporary elegance, although service can be rather flat. The Nam Bo suite is the loveliest, while corner suite No 8 can suffer from noise. Excellent restaurants on the top floor, and at ground level.

Eating & Drinking

'Hotpot Alley' is the place for fish and duck hotpots, with restaurants stuffed into an alley (Hem 1) between Đ Mau Than and Đ Ly Tu Trung east of Xoai Hotel.

★**Nem Nuong Thanh Van** VIETNAMESE $
(cnr Nam Ky Khoi Nghia & 30 Thang 4; meals 45,000d; ⏲8am-9pm) The only dish this locally acclaimed little spot does is the best *nem nuong* in town. Roll your own rice rolls using the ingredients provided: pork sausage, rice paper, green banana, starfruit, cucumber and a riot of fresh herbs, then dip into the peanut-and-something-else sauce, its secret jealously guarded. Simple and fantastic!

Night Market VIETNAMESE $
(Đ Phan Boi Chau; meals around 20,000d; ⏲5-10pm) Every evening the space between Phan Boi Chau and Phan Chu Trinh streets comes alive with dozens of bustling food stalls, selling grilled meats and tofu on skewers, as well as sweet sticky rice, fresh sugarcane juice and more.

Quan Com Chay Cuong VEGETARIAN $
(9 Đ De Tham; meals from 20,000d; ⏲11am-10pm; 🖉) Located around the back of the Munireangsey pagoda, this is one of the better *com chay* (vegetarian) eateries in the city. The vegetable, rice and mock-meat dishes (including mock-chicken hotpot) are nicely prepared and the service is friendly. Order

from the English menu or point at what you like at the buffet.

CoopMart SUPERMARKET $
(Đ Hoa Binh; ⊙9am-9pm) An immense, well-stocked supermarket.

Mekong VIETNAMESE, INTERNATIONAL $
(38 Đ Hai Ba Trung; meals from 60,000d; ⊙7am-8pm; ☑) Looking onto busy Hai Ba Trung, this travellers' favourite has a good blend of local and international food at reasonable prices, though it's a case of quantity over quality. Try the tangy sour soup with fish and the passionfruit crème brûlée.

★**L'Escale** VIETNAMESE, INTERNATIONAL $$
(☎071-381 9139; Nam Bo Boutique Hotel, 1 Đ Ngo Quyen; meals 200,000-500,000d; ⊙6am-10.30pm; ☑) With tantalising river views from the top of the Nam Bo hotel and subdued romantic lighting, this is the place to canoodle with your sweetie over glasses of wine from the strong wine list and beautifully executed dishes such as claypot fish with pineapple, sautéed garlic shrimp with spinach and smoked duck salad.

Nam Bo VIETNAMESE, INTERNATIONAL $$
(☎071-382 3908; http://nambocantho.com; Nam Bo Boutique Hotel, 1 Đ Ngo Quyen; meals 200,000-350,000d; ⊙8am-11pm) With a charming, romantic Mediterranean feel, this restaurant does a good mix of Vietnamese and Western dishes. We're fans of the lemongrass chicken and grilled sea bass in banana leaf; bananas flambéed in rice wine add a rum touch to the meal. The six-dish set menu (280,000d) is a steal.

★**Spices Restaurant** VIETNAMESE, INTERNATIONAL $$$
(Victoria Can Tho Resort, Cai Khe, Ninh Kieu; meals 200,000-680,000d; ⊙6am-10pm; ☑) Go for a table overlooking the river at this fine restaurant, refined without being stuffy, and opt for the beautifully presented trio of salads (green papaya, banana flower, green mango) or the assortment starter for two, and follow up with deep-fried elephant fish or pork-stuffed squid. Lamb shanks and seared duck cater to homesick palates and the desserts are magnificent.

Information

Can Tho Tourist (☎071-382 1852; www.canthotourist.com.vn; 50 Đ Hai Ba Trung; ⊙8am-7pm) Helpful staff speak both English and French here and decent city maps are available, as well as general information on attractions in the area.

Hospital (Benh Vien; ☎071-382 0071; 4 Đ Chau Van Liem) Emergency medical care.

Main Post Office (2 ĐL Hoa Binh; ⊙8am-5pm Mon-Sat)

TO MARKET, TO MARKET

The undisputed highlight of any visit to Can Tho is taking a boat ride to a **floating market**. Yet Can Tho is also the only place in the delta where you may experience hassle from would-be guides who'll accost you as soon as you get off the bus and even turn up at your lodgings after asking your *xe om* or taxi driver where you're headed. To choose who you go with, consider the following:

- What does the tour include? Is it a 40-minute dash to Cai Rang, returning to Can Tho straight away, or a half-day tour taking in smaller waterways?
- How big is the boat? Larger boats come equipped with life jackets, have roofs and get to the markets faster, but you'll be in a large group. Smaller boats make for a more intimate experience, but not all carry life jackets and may have flimsy roofs (or none at all), so you may end up doing a wet rat impression in a downpour.
- When does the tour depart? If you start out after 6.30am, you've missed the best of the action.
- Does the guide speak good English? Small boats along the riverside near the giant statue of Ho Chi Minh offer the cheapest deals, but you won't get a commentary on riverside life.
- Costs range from around 120,000d per hour (depending on your negotiating skills) for a small boat with the operator speaking a few words of English to around US$30 per person for a seven-hour tour taking in both markets, with a fluent English-speaking guide.

BUSES FROM CAN THO

DESTINATION	COST (D)	TIME (HR)	FREQUENCY	DISTANCE
Ben Tre	75,000	3	several daily	123km
Ca Mau	67,000-150,000	3¼-4	hourly	149km
Cao Lanh	50,000	2½	daily	82km
Chau Doc	105,000-245,000	3¼	hourly	120km
HCMC	110,000	3½	every 30min	169km
Long Xuyen	105,000	1½	hourly	61km
Phnom Penh	380,000	7	daily at 6.30am	226km
Soc Trang	100,000	1½	hourly	62km

Getting There & Away

AIR

Can Tho is served by Vietnam Airlines, Veitjet Air and VASCO, with flights to Dalat (one hour, twice weekly), Danang (1½ hours, daily), Hanoi (2¼ hours, three daily) and Phu Quoc (one hour, daily).

Can Tho International Airport (www.canthoairport.com; Đ Le Hong Phong) The airport is 10km northwest of the city centre. A taxi into town will cost around 220,000d.

BOAT

There are several boat services to other cities in the Mekong Delta, including hydrofoils to Ca Mau (300,000d, three to four hours), passing through Phung Hiep.

BUS

Bus Station (Ben Xe 91B; Đ Nguyen Van Linh) All buses now depart from the main bus station, 2.5km northwest of the centre. A *xe om* into town costs around 50,000d.

Getting Around

Short hops on a *xe om* cost around 20,000d.

Around Can Tho

Arguably the biggest drawcards of the delta are its colourful **floating markets**, which hug the banks of wide stretches of river. Most market folk set out early to avoid the daytime heat, so try to visit between 6am and 7am to beat the tourist tide. The real tides, however, are also a factor, as bigger boats must often wait until the water is high enough for them to navigate.

Improved roads and public transport mean that some of the smaller, rural floating markets are disappearing, but the larger markets near urban areas are still going strong.

Rural areas of Can Tho province, renowned for their durian, mangosteen and orange orchards, can be easily reached from Can Tho by boat or bicycle.

Sights

★Cai Rang Floating Market MARKET

(⏰5am-noon) Just 6km from Can Tho in the direction of Soc Trang is Cai Rang, the biggest floating market in the Mekong Delta. There is a bridge here that serves as a great vantage point for photography. The market is best around 6am to 7am, and it's well worth getting here early to beat boatloads of tourists. This is a wholesale market, so look at what's tied to the long pole above the boat to figure out what they're selling to smaller traders.

Cai Rang can be seen from the road, but getting here is far more interesting by boat (US$10 to US$15). From the market area in Can Tho it takes about 45 minutes by river, or you can drive to the Cau Dau Sau boat landing (by the Dau Sau Bridge), from where it takes only about 10 minutes to reach the market.

★Phong Dien Floating Market MARKET

(⏰5am-noon) The Mekong Delta's most intimate and best floating market, Phong Dien has fewer motorised craft and more standup rowing boats, with local vendors shopping and exchanging gossip. Less crowded than Cai Rang, there are also far fewer tourists. It's at its bustling best between 5am and 7am. The market is 20km southwest of Can Tho; you can get there by road but many operators now offer a six-hour combined Cai Rang–Phong Dien tour, returning to Can Tho through quieter backwaters.

Bang Lang BIRD SANCTUARY

(admission 8000d; ⏰5am-6pm) On the road between Can Tho and Long Xuyen, this is a magnificent 1.3-hectare bird sanctuary with astonishing views of thousands of resident storks and snowy egrets. There is a tall viewing platform to see the birds filling the branches; the best times to view this incredible sight are around dawn and dusk.

Bang Lang is 46km northwest of Can Tho; join a tour, or take a *xe om* or a bus to Thoi An hamlet and then a *xe om*.

Soc Trang

☎079 / POP 146,000

It's not the most charming of Mekong towns, but Soc Trang is an important centre for the Khmer people, who constitute 28% of the province's population. It's a useful base for exploring Khmer temples in the area, although you can probably skip these if Cambodia is on your radar.

Sights

Mahatup Pagoda BUDDHIST TEMPLE

(Chua Doi; Đ Van Ngoc Chinh; dawn-dusk) Mahatup Pagoda, also called the Bat Pagoda, is a large, peaceful, Khmer monastery compound with a resident colony of fruit bats. Literally hundreds of these creatures hang from the trees: the largest weigh about 1kg, with a wingspan of about 1.5m. Around dusk hundreds of bats swoop out of the trees to forage in orchards all over the Mekong Delta.

The Bat Pagoda is 2km south of Soc Trang, a 20,000d *xe om* ride away.

The monks don't ask for money, although donations won't hurt. The pagoda is decorated with gilt Buddhas and murals paid for by overseas Vietnamese contributors. In one room there's a life-size statue of the monk who was the former head of the complex.

Buu Son Tu BUDDHIST TEMPLE

(Chua Dat Set; 163 Đ Ton Duc Thang; entry by donation; dawn-dusk) Buu Son Tu (Precious Mountain Temple) was founded over 200 years ago by a Chinese family named Ngo. This temple is highly unusual in that nearly every object inside is made entirely of clay. The hundreds of statues and sculptures that adorn the interior were hand-sculpted by the monk Ngo Kim Tong. The pagoda is an active place of worship, and totally different from the Khmer and Vietnamese pagodas elsewhere in Soc Trang.

From the age of 20 until his death at 62, the ingenious artisan dedicated his life to decorating the pagoda. Entering the pagoda, visitors are greeted by one of Ngo's largest creations – a six-tusked clay elephant, which is said to have appeared in a dream of Buddha's mother. Behind this is the central altar, fashioned from more than 5 tonnes of clay. In the altar are a thousand Buddhas seated on lotus petals. Other highlights include a 13-storey Chinese-style tower over 4m tall. The tower features 208 cubby holes, each

OFF THE BEATEN TRACK

BAC LIEU BIRD SANCTUARY

The **Bac Lieu Bird Sanctuary** (Vuon Chim Bac Lieu; ☎0781-383 5991; admission 20,000d; 7.30am-5pm), 6km southwest of the little-visited town of Bac Lieu, is notable for its 50-odd species of bird, including a large population of graceful white herons. Bird populations peak in the rainy season – approximately May to October – and the birds nest until about January.

Birding guides should be hired at the sanctuary entrance since without them there's a good chance of getting lost; little English is spoken. The **Bac Lieu Tourist Office** (☎0781-382 4273; www.baclieutourist.com; 2 Đ Hoang Van Thu; 7-11am & 1-5pm) also arranges transport and guides (at a mark-up).

The trek is through dense (and often muddy) jungle: bring plenty of repellent, good shoes, water and binoculars. The guides aren't supposed to receive money, so tip them discreetly.

Cong Tu Hotel (☎0781-358 0580; www.congtubaclieu.vn; 13 Đ Dien Bien Phu; r 500,000-2,000,000d;) is by far the most characterful place to stay in town. It's a revamped 1919 colonial gem; the smarter rooms have balconies and high ceilings and are decorated in decadent 19th-century style. The restaurant (mains 40,000d to 100,000d) has an extensive menu and the fish dishes are particularly good.

Bac Lieu is on the bus route between Can Tho via Soc Trang (three hours) and Ca Mau (two hours).

with a mini-Buddha figure inside, and is decorated with 156 dragons.

Kh'leang Pagoda BUDDHIST TEMPLE
(Chua Kh'leang; 68 Đ Ton Duc Thang; ⏲ dawn-dusk) Except for the rather garish paint job, this pagoda could have been transported straight from Cambodia. Originally built from bamboo in 1533, it had a complete concrete rebuild in 1905. Several monks reside in the pagoda, which also serves as a base for over 150 novices who come from around the Mekong Delta to study at Soc Trang's College of Buddhist Education across the street.

There's a small but absorbing **museum** (⏲8am-5pm) across from the pagoda, dedicated to Vietnam's Khmer minority. Also, seven religious festivals are held at the pagoda every year, drawing people from outlying areas of the province.

Festivals & Events

Oc Bom Boc Festival CULTURAL
(Bon Om Touk) Once a year, the Khmer community from all over Vietnam and even Cambodia turns out for this festival, with longboat races on the Soc Trang River. Races are held according to the lunar calendar on the 15th day of the 10th moon (roughly in November). The races start at noon, but things get jumping in Soc Trang the evening before.

Sleeping & Eating

Que Huong Hotel HOTEL $$
(☎079-361 6122; 128 Đ Nguyen Trung Truc; r 320,000d, ste 490,000-680,000d; ❄📶) Rooms here are in much better shape than the no-nonsense exterior might first suggest. The suites include a sunken bath and a full-size bar, although drinks are not included.

Quan Hung VIETNAMESE $
(24/5 Đ Hung Vuong; meals 80,000-170,000d; ⏲11am-10pm) Down a lane off the main road into town, this large, open-sided restaurant is perpetually popular, serving up delicious grilled meat and fish. If there are a few of you, try a hotpot.

Getting There & Away

Buses run hourly from Soc Trang to Bac Lieu (150,000d, three hours), Ca Mau (140,000d, three hours), Can Tho (100,000d, 1½ hours) and HCMC (135,000d, five hours).

Soc Trang Bus Station (Ben Xe Soc Trang; Đ Le Duan) The bus station is 1.3km out of the centre, near the corner of Le Hung Vuong, the main road into town.

WORTH A TRIP

XA LONG PAGODA

Originally built in wood in the 18th century, the magnificent Khmer **Xa Long Pagoda** (Hwy 1A; ⏲ sunrise-sunset) was completely rebuilt in 1923 but proved to be too small. From 1969 to 1985, the present-day large pagoda was slowly built as funds trickled in from donations. The ceramic tiles on the exterior of the pagoda are particularly impressive.

It's located 12km from Soc Trang, towards Bac Lieu.

The monks lead an austere life, eating breakfast at 6am and seeking alms until 11am, when they hold an hour of worship. They eat again just before noon, study in the afternoon and eat no dinner. The pagoda also operates a school for the study of Buddhism and Sanskrit.

Ca Mau

☎0780 / POP 140,000

On the shores of the Ganh Hao River, Ca Mau is the capital and sole city in Ca Mau province, which covers the southern tip of the Mekong Delta. It's a remote and inhospitable area that wasn't cultivated until the late 17th century. Owing to the boggy terrain, the province has the lowest population density in southern Vietnam.

Given that, it's perhaps surprising that Ca Mau city is a relatively pleasant place. With wide boulevards and parks and busy shopping streets, the town has developed rapidly in recent years but sees few visitors.

Improved transport links make for an easy stopover for a slice of delta life untroubled by tourism, such as the **Ca Mau Market** (Đ Le Loi) that sprawls along the streets to the west of Phung Hiep Canal, south of Đ Phan Ngoc Hien. The other noteworthy sight is the riot of colour and ornamentation that is the **Cao Dai Temple** (Đ Phan Ngoc Hien; ⏲ dawn-dusk), though there are more impressive ones elsewhere in the delta.

Dong Anh Hotel (☎0780-357 6666; www.donganhhotel.com.vn; 25 Tran Hung Dao; r 350,000d; ❄📶) provides clean and central rooms, some with terraces overlooking the main street. **Anh Nguyet Hotel** (☎0780-356 7666; www.anhnguyethotel.com; 207 Đ Phan Ngoc

Ca Mau

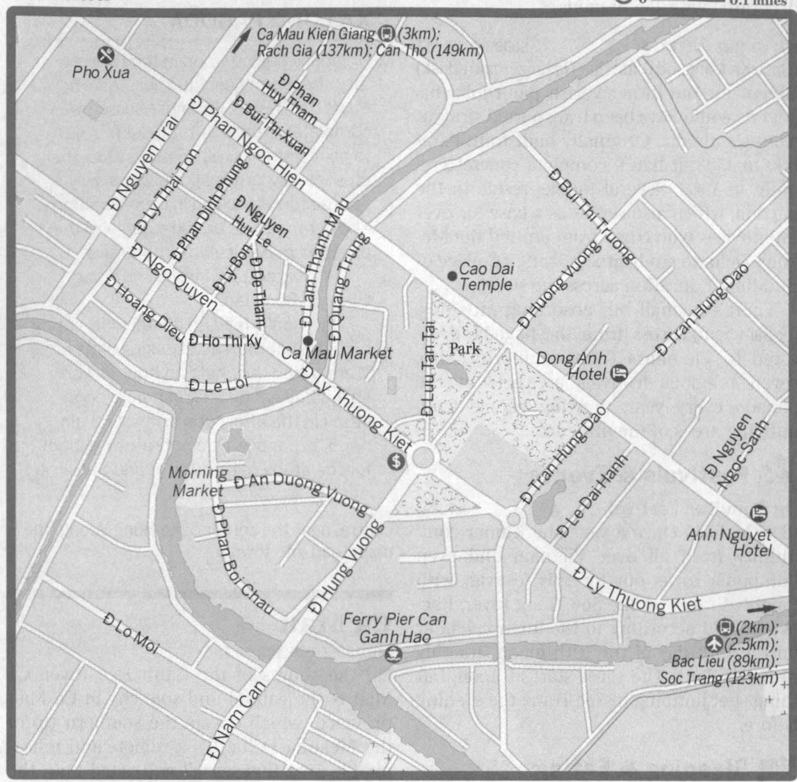

Hien; r US$29-49; ❄🛜) falls short of the glitz it aspires to, though rooms are comfortable enough and there's a good buffet breakfast.

Ca Mau's speciality is shrimp, raised in ponds and mangrove forests; it can be sampled at the seafood-heavy **Pho Xua** (126 Đ Phan Ngoc Hien; mains 60,000-189,000d; ⌚7am-10pm). Some of the best food can be found at the cluster of small, cheap roadside restaurants and *banh mi* stalls in the streets around the market, particularly at the end of Đ Nguyen Huu Le.

ℹ Getting There & Around

AIR

Vietnam Airlines has a daily flight to and from HCMC (one hour). The airport is 3km east of the centre, on Hwy 1A.

BOAT

Three hydrofoils a day travel between Ca Mau and Rach Gia (300,000d, three hours) from **Ferry Pier Can Ganh Hao** (Pha Can Ganh Hao), departing at 6.20am, 8.20am and 9.20am. Boats to Can Tho (250,000d, three to four hours) depart from Cong Ca Mau pier (Đ Quang Trung), 3km east of town.

BUS

There are two bus stations. Phuong Trang offers the most comfortable services to HCMC, Can Tho and even Dalat. Express buses leave for HCMC between 5am and 10.30am.

Ca Mau Bus Station (Đ Ly Thuong Kiet, Ben Xe Ca Mau) The main bus station is 2km east of central Ca Mau. It serves most destinations bar Rach Gia and Ha Tien.

Ca Mau Kien Giang Bus Station (Ben Xe Ca Mau Kien Giang; Đ Nguyen Trai) This small bus station is around 3km northeast of central Ca Mau. Services run to Rach Gia and Ha Tien.

CAR & MOTORBIKE

Hwy 1A now continues to Nam Can (50km), the southernmost town in Vietnam.

BUSES FROM CA MAU

DESTINATION	COST (D)	DURATION (HR)	FREQUENCY	DISTANCE
Bac Lieu	39,000	1¾	every 30min	89km
Ben Tre	109,000	6	daily at 9.20am	283km
Can Tho	67,000-150,000	5	hourly	151km
Chau Doc	109,000	8	3 daily	228km
Dalat	329,000	17	daily at 6pm	604km
Ha Tien	230,000	5½	several daily	221km
HCMC	120,000-200,000	9	hourly	329km
Rach Gia	130,000	3½	several daily	138km

U-Minh Forest

Bordered by Ca Mau, **U-Minh Forest** (admission 10,000d; 6am-5pm, closed Mar-May), the largest mangrove forest beyond the Amazon basin, covers 1000 sq km. Home to endangered mammals – including the hairy-nosed otter and the fishing cat – and 187 bird species, the forest was a hideout for the VC during the American War. Thirty-minute boat trips around the forest cost 140,000d.

Ca Mau Tourist can arrange boat tours (US$180), but you can try to get a speedboat to Thu Bay (two hours), followed by a motorbike for 90,000d.

During the American War, the Americans tried to flush out the VC with chemical defoliation, which caused enormous damage to the forests. The heavy rainfall slowly washed the dioxin out to sea and the forest is returning. Many eucalyptus trees have also been planted here because they have proved to be relatively dioxin-resistant.

Unfortunately today the mangrove forests are being further damaged by clearing for shrimp-farming ponds, charcoal production and woodchipping, although the government has tried to limit these activities. In 2002 an area of 80 sq km was preserved as U Minh Thuong (Upper U-Minh) National Park.

Rach Gia

077 / POP 221,000

A thriving port on the Gulf of Thailand, Rach Gia's population includes significant numbers of both ethnic Chinese and ethnic Khmers, and the lively waterfront and bustling backstreets are worth a stroll.

With its easy access to the sea and the proximity of Cambodia and Thailand, fishing, agriculture and smuggling are profitable trades in this province. The area was once famous for supplying the large feathers used to make ceremonial fans for the Imperial Court.

If you're in town for longer than it takes to catch a boat to Phu Quoc Island, stop by the worthwhile **Kien Giang Museum** (21 Đ Nguyen Van Troi; 7.30-11am & 1.30-5pm Mon-Fri) FREE, housed in an ornate gem of a French colonial-era building and containing war photos and some Oc-Eo artefacts and pottery.

Not far from the fast ferry jetty, **Nguyen Trung Truc Temple** (18 Đ Nguyen Cong Tru; sunrise-sunset) is the other worthwhile sight. It's dedicated to Nguyen Trung Truc, a leader of the resistance campaign of the 1860s against the newly arrived French and features his portrait on the altar.

If overnighting, clean, cheap **An An Hotel** (13-14 Đ Huynh Thuc Khang; r 250,000-350,000d;) is particularly convenient for the central bus station, while **Palace Hotel** (0913 864 730; 16a Đ Hoa Bien; d/tr from

TRAVEL BY HYDROFOIL

If you're tossing up between taking a hydrofoil or a bus, the hydrofoil is less crowded than the basic buses between Ca Mau and Rach Gia and, until more bridges have been built, it's also faster and generally more comfortable, plus the journey is more interesting. The boats are low and long, meaning views are just above the waterline. The trip between Ca Mau and Rach Gia allows you to observe the countryside as it switches from a green, undeveloped section dotted with rattan houses near Ca Mau to a heavily built-up and industrial stretch approaching Rach Gia. If you're cycling around the delta, the hydrofoils can carry your bicycle for an extra fee.

Rach Gia

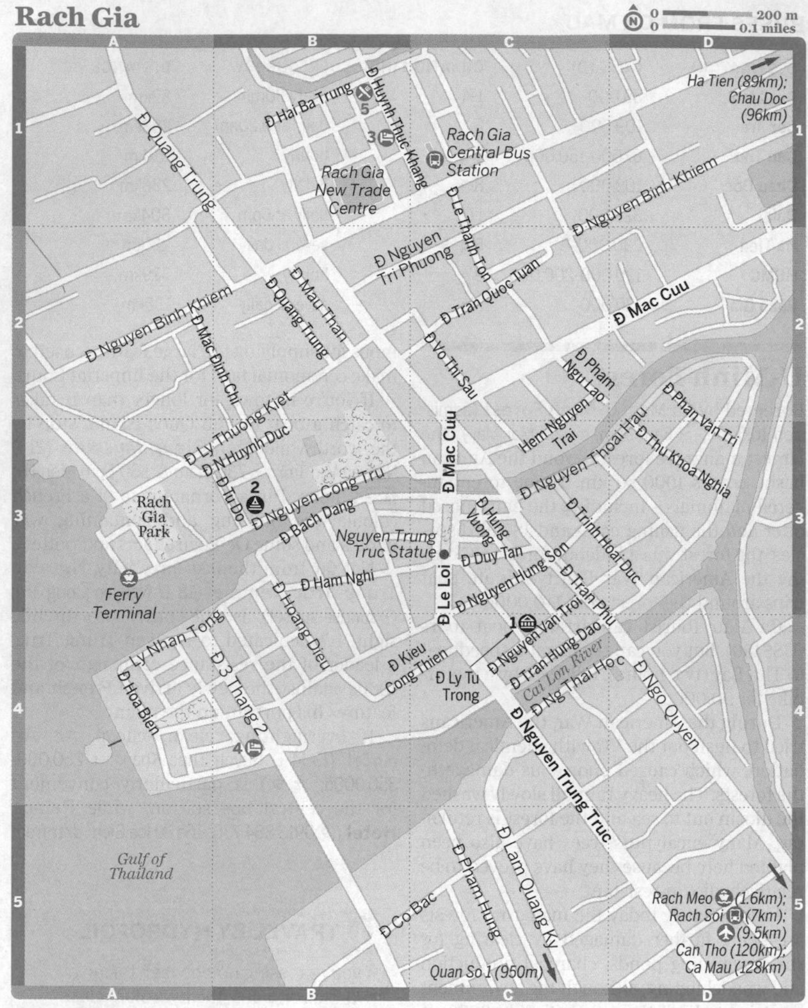

Rach Gia

Sights

1	Kien Giang Museum	C4
2	Nguyen Trung Truc Temple	B3

Sleeping

3	An An Hotel	B1
4	Palace Hotel	B4

Eating

5	Quan F28	B1

US$28/39; ❄️📶) is more refined and just a 10-minute walk from the ferry port.

Rach Gia is big on seafood, and you can get your fill at **Quan F28** (28 Đ Le Thanh Thon; meals from 40,000d; ⏰11am-10pm), near the central bus station, or cook your own on a tabletop barbecue at **Quan So 1** (82 Đ Lac Hong; meals from 50,000d; ⏰8am-10pm).

ℹ Getting There & Away

AIR

Vietnam Airlines has daily flights to and from HCMC and Phu Quoc Island (in high season).

Rach Gia Airport is around 10km southeast of the centre, along Hwy 80; a taxi into town costs around 150,000d.

BUSES FROM RACH GIA

DESTINATION	COST (D)	DURATION (HR)	FREQUENCY	DISTANCE
Ca Mau	130,000	3½	6 daily	128km
Can Tho	150,000	3	every 30min	120km
Chau Doc	55,000	2¾	4 daily	96km
Ha Tien	50,000	2	at least 20 daily	89km
HCMC	210,000	6½	frequent	274km

BOAT

Boats to Phu Quoc Island (p398) leave from the centrally located **ferry terminal** (Ban Tau Rach Gia Phu Quoc) at the western end of Đ Nguyen Cong Tru. Three speedboats leave daily for Ca Mau (300,000d, three hours) from the **Rach Meo ferry terminal** (Ben Tau Rach Meo; ☎077-381 1306; Đ Ngo Quyen), about 2km south of town.

BUS

A taxi into town from the central bus station costs around 30,000d. From the Rach Soi bus station, fares are around 150,000d.

Rach Gia Central Bus Station (Ben Xe Khach Rach Gia) Just north of the city centre, this bus station serves primarily Ha Tien. Trang Ngoc Phat buses are the most comfortable way to go, followed by Mai Linh.

Rach Soi Bus Station (Ben Xe Rach Soi; 78 Đ Nguyen Trung Truc) Ben Xe Rach Soi, 7km south of the city, serves Ho Chi Minh City and the majority of delta destinations (bar Ha Tien).

Phu Quoc Island

☎077 / POP 108,000

Fringed with white-sand beaches and with large tracts still cloaked in dense, tropical jungle, Phu Quoc rapidly morphed from a sleepy island backwater to a must-visit beach escape for Western expats and sun-seeking tourists. Beyond the resorts lining Long Beach and development beginning on the east coast, there's still ample room for exploration and escaping. Dive the reefs, kayak in the bays, eat up the back-road miles on a motorbike, or just lounge on the beach, indulge in a massage and dine on fresh seafood.

The tear-shaped island lies in the Gulf of Thailand, 45km west of Ha Tien and 15km south of the coast of Cambodia. It's no lightweight: at 48km long (with an area of 574 sq km), Phu Quoc is Vietnam's largest island – about the same size as Singapore. It's also politically contentious: Phu Quoc is claimed by Cambodia who call it Koh Tral and this explains why the Vietnamese have built a substantial military base covering much of the northern end of the island. It was only granted to Vietnam by the French in 1949, as part of the formal annexation of the Mekong Delta.

Phu Quoc is not really part of the Mekong Delta and doesn't share the delta's extraordinary ability to produce rice. The most valuable crop is black pepper, but the islanders here have traditionally earned their living from the sea. Phu Quoc is also famed across Vietnam for its production of high-quality fish sauce *(nuoc mam)*.

Despite development (a new international airport, a golf course, new roads and a planned 'casino eco-tourism resort project'), much of this island is still protected since becoming a national park in 2001. Phu Quoc National Park covers close to 70% of the island, an area of 31,422 hectares.

Phu Quoc's rainy season darkens skies from late May to October, when the sea gets rough and a lot of diving stops. The peak season for tourism is midwinter (December and January), when the sky is blue and the sea is calm, but it can get pretty damn hot around April and May.

History

Phu Quoc Island served as a base for the French missionary Pigneau de Behaine during the 1760s and 1780s. Prince Nguyen Anh, who later became Emperor Gia Long, was sheltered here by Behaine when he was being hunted by the Tay Son rebels.

Being a relatively remote and forested island (and an economically marginal area of Vietnam), Phu Quoc was useful to the French colonial administration as a prison.

The Americans took over where the French left off and housed about 40,000 VC prisoners here. The island's main penal colony, which is still in use today, was known as the Coconut Tree Prison (Nha Lao Cay Dua) and is near An Thoi town. Though it's considered a historic site, plans to open a museum here have stalled.

Phu Quoc Island

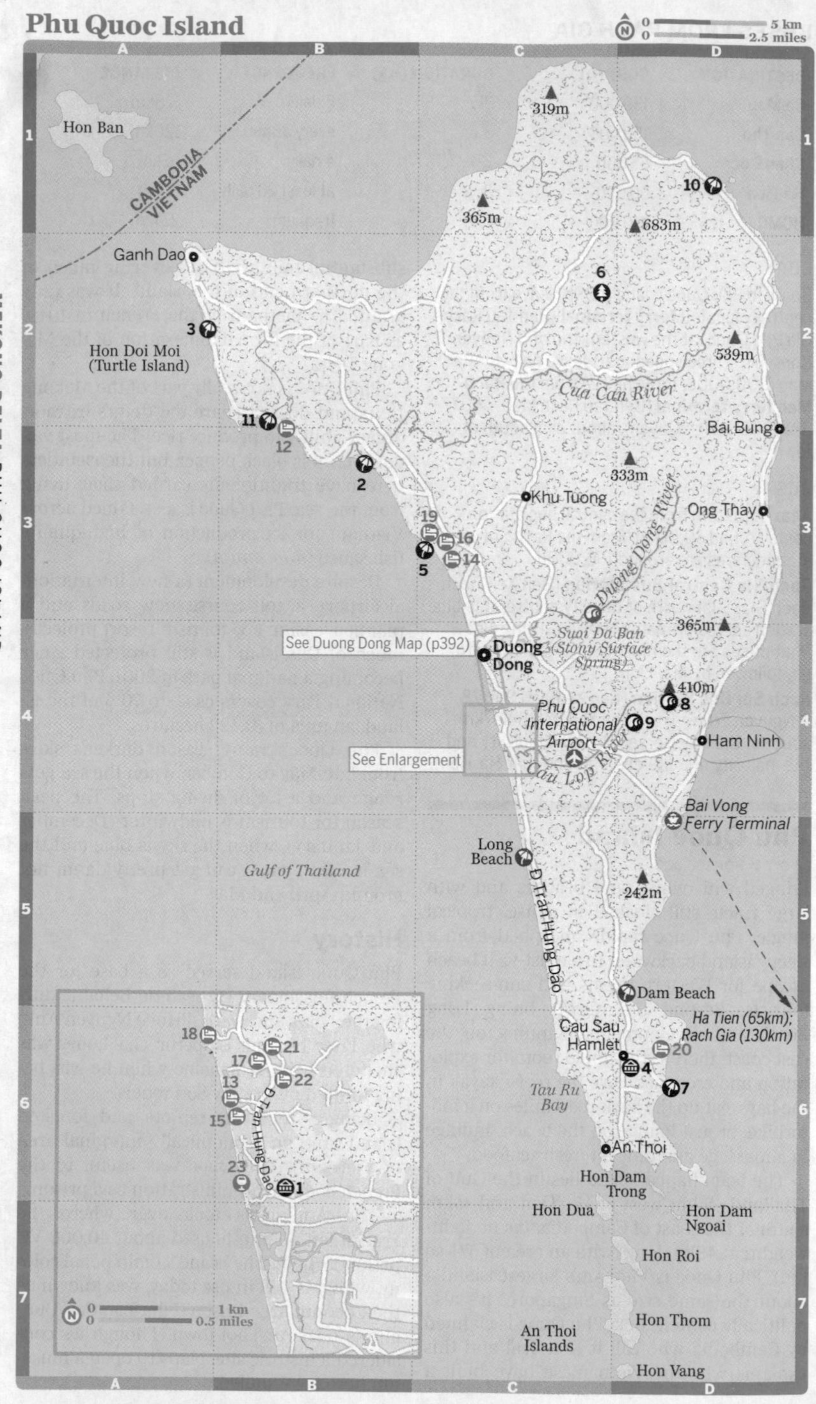

Phu Quoc Island

Sights

1 Coi Nguon Museum B6
2 Cua Can Beach B3
3 Dai Beach A2
4 Nha Tu Phu Quoc D6
5 Ong Lan Beach C3
6 Phu Quoc National Park C2
7 Sao Beach D6
8 Suoi Da Ban D4
9 Suoi Tranh D4
10 Thom Beach D1
11 Vung Bau Beach B2

Sleeping

12 Bamboo Cottages & Restaurant B3
13 Beach Club B6
14 Chen Sea Resort & Spa C3
15 Famiana Resort & Spa B6
16 Freedomland C3
17 Lan Anh Garden Resort B6
18 Lien Hiep Thanh Hotel A6
19 Mango Bay C3
20 Mango Garden D6
21 Mush'rooms Backpacker Hostel B6
22 Nhat Huy Garden Guesthouse B6
Paris Beach .... (see 13)

Eating

Sakura .... (see 16)

Drinking & Nightlife

Lee's Safari Bar .... (see 21)
23 Rory's Beach Bar B6

Sights

Duong Dong TOWN

The island's main town and chief fishing port on the central west coast is a tangle of budget hotels catering to domestic tourists, streetside stalls, bars and shops. The old bridge in town is a great vantage point to photograph the island's scruffy fishing fleet crammed into the narrow channel, and the filthy, bustling produce market makes for an interesting stroll.

Long Beach BEACH

(Bai Truong; Map p392) Long Beach is draped invitingly along the west coast from Duong Dong almost to An Thoi port. Development concentrates in the north near Duong Dong, where the recliners and rattan umbrellas of the various resorts rule; these are the only stretches that are kept garbage-free. With its west-facing aspect, sunsets can be stupendous.

A motorbike or bicycle is necessary to reach some of the remote stretches flung out towards the southern end of the island.

There should be no problem for beachcombers to stretch out their towels on the sand, but you may get moved on quickly if you get too close to the paying guests.

There are several small lanes heading from the main Đ Tran Hung Dao drag down to Long Beach that shelter some of the nicest places to stay and eat. There are a few bamboo huts where you can buy drinks, but bring water if planning a long hike along the beach. Beachside massages are popular, but be clear about what you're paying for: a neck rub can quickly turn into a foot massage, manicure and leg-hair threading – often all simultaneously.

An Thoi Islands ISLAND

(Quan Dao An Thoi) Just off the southern tip of Phu Quoc, these 15 islands and islets can be visited by chartered boat. It's a fine area for sightseeing, fishing, swimming and snorkelling. **Hon Thom** (Pineapple Island) is about 3km in length and is the largest island in the group.

Most boats depart from An Thoi on Phu Quoc, but you can make arrangements through hotels on Long Beach, as well as dive operators. Boat trips generally do not run during the rainy season.

Other islands here include **Hon Dua** (Coconut Island), **Hon Roi** (Lamp Island), **Hon Vang** (Echo Island), **Hon May Rut** (Cold Cloud Island), the **Hon Dams** (Shadow Islands), **Chan Qui** (Yellow Tortoise) and **Hon Mong Tay** (Short Gun Island). As yet, there is no real development on the islands, but expect some movement in future.

Sao Beach BEACH

(Bai Sao; Map p390) With picture-perfect white sand, the delightful curve of beautiful Sao Beach bends out alongside a sea of mineral-water clarity just a few kilometres from An Thoi, the main shipping port at the southern tip of the island. There are a couple of beachfront restaurants, where you can settle into a deckchair or partake in water sports. If heading down to Sao Beach by motorbike, fill up with petrol before the trip.

Cua Can Beach BEACH

(Bai Cua Can; Map p390) The most accessible of the northern beaches, Cua Can is about

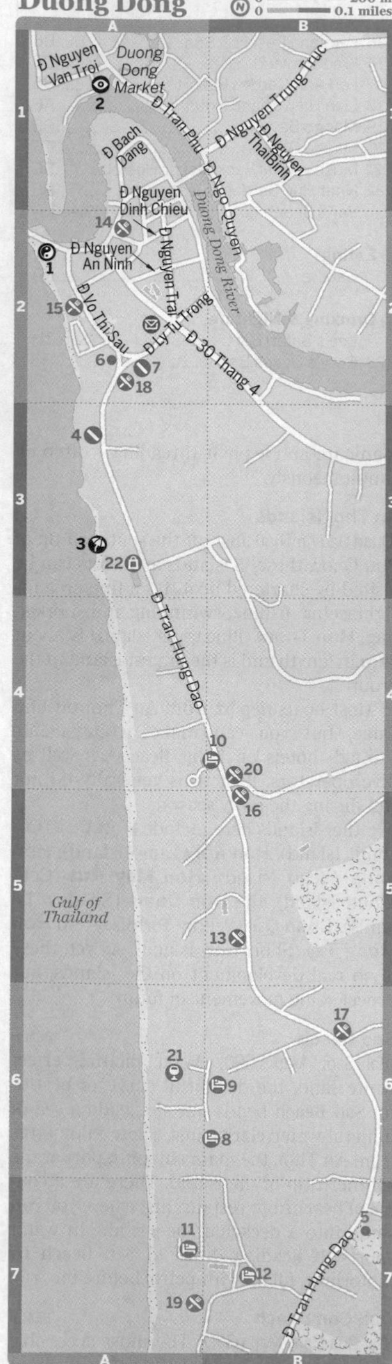

Duong Dong

Sights

1 Cau Castle A2
2 Fish Sauce Factory A1
3 Long Beach A3

Activities, Courses & Tours

4 Flipper Diving Club A3
5 Jerry's Jungle Tours B7
6 John's Tours A2
7 Rainbow Divers A2

Sleeping

8 Cassia Cottage B6
9 La Veranda B6
10 Langchia Hostel B4
11 Phuong Binh House A7
12 Sunshine Bungalow B7

Eating

13 Alanis Deli B5
14 Buddy Ice Cream A2
15 Dinh Cau Night Market A2
16 Ganesh B5
17 Itaca Resto Lounge B6
18 Nha Ghe Phu Quoc Crab House A2
19 Pepper Tree Restaurant A7
20 Pepper's Pizza & Grill B4
Spice House at Cassia Cottage .... (see 8)
Winston's Burgers & Beer .... (see 17)

Drinking & Nightlife

21 Coco Bar A6
Le Bar .... (see 19)

Shopping

22 Phu Quoc Pearls A3

11km from Duong Dong. It remains mercifully quiet during the week, but can get busy at weekends. A ride through the villages around Cua Can is interesting, with the road crossing the river several times on rickety wooden bridges.

Ong Lan Beach BEACH

(Bai Ong Lan; Map p390) Ong Lan Beach has a series of sandy bays sheltered by rocky headlands. Several midrange resorts in this area service those wanting to get away from everything (apart from the comfort of said resorts).

Dai Beach BEACH

(Bai Dai; Map p390) A relatively isolated northern beach that retains its remote tropical charm.

Vung Bau Beach BEACH

(Bai Vung Bau; Map p390) Appealing northern beach reachable via the coastal road.

Thom Beach BEACH

(Bai Thom; Map p390) The road from Dai Beach to Thom Beach via Ganh Dau is very beautiful, passing through dense forest with tantalising glimpses of the coast below.

Suoi Tranh WATERFALL

(Map p390; admission 5000d) Compared with the waterlogged Mekong Delta, Phu Quoc has very little surface moisture, but there are several springs originating in the hills. The most accessible of these is Suoi Tranh; look for the entrance sign and concrete tree from the Duong Dong–Vong Beach road. From the ticket counter it's a 10-minute walk through the forest to the falls.

Phu Quoc National Park NATURE RESERVE

(Map p390) About 90% of Phu Quoc is forested and the trees and adjoining marine environment enjoy official protection. This is the last large stand of forest in the south, and in 2010 the park was declared a Unesco Biosphere Reserve. The forest is densest in northern Phu Quoc, in the Khu Rung Nguyen Sinh forest reserve; you'll need a motorbike or mountain bike to tackle the bumpy dirt roads that cut through it. There are no real hiking trails.

Suoi Da Ban WATERFALL

(Map p390; admission 5000d, motorbike 1000d) Suoi Da Ban is a white-water creek tumbling across some attractive large granite boulders. There are deep pools and it's nice enough for a dip. Bring plenty of mosquito repellent.

For the falls, the best months to visit are between May and September – by the end of the dry season there's little more than a trickle.

Coi Nguon Museum MUSEUM

(Map p390; www.coinguonphuquoc.com; 149 Tran Hung Dao; admission 20,000d; ⏲7am-5pm) With displays on Vietnamese medicines, Stone Age tools, a boatful of barnacle-encrusted ceramics, oddly compelling, shell-covered furniture and a small room devoted to the island prison, this private museum is an oddball introduction to Phu Quoc history and culture. But did the marine fauna section really require the untimely demise of 14 hawksbill turtles?!

Nha Tu Phu Quoc MUSEUM

(Map p390; ⏲7.30-11am & 1.30-4pm) FREE Not far from Sao Beach in the south of the island, Phu Quoc's notorious old prison, built by the French in the late 1940s, contains a small museum that narrates the gruesome history of the jail. A war memorial stands south of the prison on the far side of the road.

Cau Castle TAOIST TEMPLE

(Dinh Cau; Map p392; Đ Bach Dang, Duong Dong) FREE More of a combination temple and lighthouse, Dinh Cau was built in 1937 to honour Thien Hau, the Goddess of the Sea, who provides protection for sailors and fishermen. The 'castle' gives you a good view of the harbour entrance and the promenade is popular with strolling locals around sunset.

Fish Sauce Factory FACTORY

(Map p392; Duong Dong; ⏲8-11am & 1-5pm) FREE The distillery of Nuoc Mam Hung Thanh is the largest of Phu Quoc's fish-sauce makers, a short walk from the market in Duong Dong. At first glance, the giant wooden vats may make you think you've arrived for a wine tasting, but one sniff of the festering *nuoc mam* essence jolts you back to reality.

Most of the sauce produced is exported to the mainland for domestic consumption, though an impressive amount finds its way abroad to kitchens in Japan, North America and Europe. Take a guide along unless you speak Vietnamese.

Activities

Diving & Snorkelling

Although Nha Trang is arguably the best all-round dive destination in Vietnam, there's plenty of underwater action around Phu Quoc, but only during the dry months (from November to May). Two fun dives cost from US$70 to US$90 depending on the location and operator; four-day PADI Open Water courses hover between US$340 and US$380; snorkelling trips are US$30 to US$35.

Flipper Diving Club DIVING

(Map p392; ☎077-399 4924; www.flipperdiving.com; 60 Đ Tran Hung Dao; ⏲9am-9pm) Centrally located (by the Coco Bar), multilingual PADI dive centre for everything from novice dive trips to full instructor courses. Very professional, with plenty of diving experience worldwide, and with instructors who put you at ease if you're a newbie.

Rainbow Divers DIVING, SNORKELLING
(Map p392; ☎0913 400 964; www.divevietnam.com; 11 Đ Tran Hung Dao; ⊙9am-6pm) This reputable PADI outfit was the first to set up shop on the island and offers a wide range of diving and snorkelling trips. As well as the walk-in office, it's well represented at resorts on Long Beach. Some of the equipment is worn and could use replacing.

Kayaking

There are several places to rent kayaks along Sao Beach, and its protected, fairly calm waters make for a smooth ride. In addition to locals who hire out boats, you can ask at the beachside restaurants. The going rate is about 80,000d per hour.

Tours

Your best bet for booking tours is through your hotel or resort. Squid fishing at night is popular, and you'll spot the lights of boats (to lure the cephalopods to the surface) on the evening horizon.

Specialised companies and individuals offer boat excursions and fishing trips.

Jerry's Jungle Tours BOAT TOUR, HIKING
(Map p392; ☎0938 226 021; www.jerrystours.wix.com; 112 Đ Tran Hung Dao; day trips from US$30) Archipelago explorations by boat, snorkelling, fishing, day and multiday trips to islands, motorbike tours, bouldering, birdwatching, hiking and cultural tours around Phu Quoc.

John's Tours BOAT TOUR
(Map p392; ☎0918 939 111; www.johnsislandtours.com; 4 Đ Tran Hung Dao; tours per person US$15-35) Well-represented at hotels and resorts; cruises include snorkelling, island-hopping, sunrise fishing and squid-fishing trips.

Sleeping

Accommodation prices on Phu Quoc yo-yo up and down depending on the season and visitor numbers. Variations are more extreme than anywhere else in Vietnam, but tend to affect budget and midrange places more than the high-end resorts. Some places will treble their prices for the peak season of December and January, when bookings are crucial. Across all of the budget categories, you'll get less for your money than you'd expect for the price.

Long Beach

Some hotels provide free transport to and from the airport; enquire when making a booking.

★ **Langchia Hostel** HOSTEL $
(Map p392; ☎0939 132 613; www.langchia-village.com; 84 Đ Tran Hung Dao; dm/d US$6/15; ❄📶🏊) A favourite with solo travellers, this hostel gets plenty of praise for the friendliness and helpfulness of its staff, the lively bar with pool table and the swimming pool to cool down in. Dorm beds come with mozzie nets and individual fans and it's worth paying extra for the decent breakfast.

Mush'rooms Backpacker Hostel HOSTEL $
(Map p390; ☎0937 942 017; www.mushroomsphuquoc.com; 170 Đ Tran Hung Dao; dm US$7, d US$12-15; ❄📶) Pros? This colourful hostel is a great place to meet fellow backpackers. Cons? The grungy charm wears off when staff forget to clean the rooms and bathrooms and veer between being uncooperative and surly, the plug-in fans struggle to cool the rooms and there's not mush'room to move in the dorms.

Lan Anh Garden Resort RESORT $$
(Map p390; ☎077-398 5985; www.lananhphuquoc.com.vn; KP7 Tran Hung Dao; d US$58-75, f US$115; ❄📶🏊) Enticing little resort hotel with friendly, professional staff, a clutch of rooms arranged around a small pool and motorbikes for rent. Nab an upstairs room if you can for the breezy verandahs.

Sunshine Bungalow HOTEL $$
(Map p392; www.sunshinephuquoc.com; Đ Tran Hung Dao; bungalow US$48-67; ❄📶) Friendly place run by a Vietnamese family, just 80m from the sea and sand. Light, bright, large rooms nestle amid lush vegetation and the owners do their best to help. Some English and German spoken.

Nhat Huy Garden Guesthouse GUESTHOUSE $$
(Map p390; ☎0932 766 809; Đ Tran Hung Dao; d/f US$35/57; ❄📶🏊) Travellers who linger here a few days find themselves treated like family by the gregarious staff and invited to join impromptu barbecues. Your crashpad is a small bungalow in a shady garden setting, with a hammock out front for lazing about. It's on the main road and a short walk from the beach.

Beach Club RESORT **$$**
(Map p390; 077-398 0998; Ap Cua Lap, Xa Duong To; r US$25-45;) Run by an English-Vietnamese couple, this is a great escape from the main-drag bustle, with tightly grouped and well-kept rooms and bungalows on a small plot, plus a breezy beachside restaurant.

Paris Beach RESORT **$$**
(Map p390; 077-399 4548; www.phuquocparisbeach.com; Cau Ba Phong, Cua Lap, Duong To; r US$35-52, bungalows US$70-150;) With some lovely rooms facing the sea, this French-Vietnamese-run resort hotel has a swimming pool and clean and spacious bungalows. There's a tiled terrace where delicious food is served by the congenial hosts.

Lien Hiep Thanh Hotel HOTEL **$$**
(Map p390; 0934 995 882; www.lienhiepthanhresort.com; 118/12 Đ Tran Hung Dao; r US$45-70;) This friendly place has revamped rooms and bungalows amid trees, right on the beach. Splurge on a beachfront bungalow if you can. The downside? The beach is not the cleanest and the restaurant is only so-so.

Phuong Binh House RESORT **$$**
(Map p392; 077-399 4101; www.phuongbinhhouse.com; 118 Đ Tran Hung Dao; r US$30-65;) This small, friendly place is buried away at the end of the road to the beach. Choose from five types of bungalows, ranging from deluxe beachfront with air-con set to Arctic if you so desire, to smaller fan-cooled ones. All come with king-sized beds and all are tiled and spotless, but the fans struggle during the hottest time of year.

★**La Veranda** RESORT **$$$**
(Map p392; 077-398 2988; www.laverandaresort.com; 118/9 Đ Tran Hung Dao; r US$225-410, villa US$445-468, ste US$571-595;) Shaded by palms, this is the most elegant place to stay on the island, designed in colonial style and small enough to remain intimate. There's an appealing pool with a kiddies' area, a stylish spa and all rooms feature designer bathrooms. The beach is pristine and dining options include a cafe on the lawn and the Pepper Tree Restaurant upstairs.

Famiana Resort & Spa RESORT **$$$**
(Map p390; 077-399 3026; www.famiana-resort.com; Đ Tran Hung Dao; r US$172-246, villa US$324-344, ste US$648-690;) This refined 60-room resort has splendid seafront villas with mezzanine floors, a large pool, a spotless stretch of private beach and sea kayaks available for active travellers.

Cassia Cottage RESORT **$$$**
(Map p392; 077-384 8395; www.cassiacottage.com; 100c Đ Tran Hung Dao; r US$215-252, villa US$451;) Set amid flourishing greenery, this seductive boutique-style resort on Long Beach has a sleepy beachside repose, rooms with handsome furnishings, two pools and a pretty garden restaurant with tables overlooking the sea.

Sao Beach

Mango Garden B&B **$$**
(Map p390; 077-629 1339; mangogarden.inn@gmail.com; r US$38-55; Oct-Mar;) Best suited to those with their own (two) wheels, this isolated B&B is reached by a bumpy dirt road (turn left just before Sao Beach and look for the signs) away from the beach. Run by a Vietnamese-Canadian couple, the Western-style, generator-powered B&B is surrounded by gorgeous flower and mango gardens, with solar showers and fishing and snorkelling trips. Book ahead.

Ong Lang Beach

Rockier than Long Beach, Ong Lang, 7km north of Duong Dong, has the advantage of being substantially less crowded and, hence, feels much more like a tropical-island escape. Because of its relative isolation, expect to spend most of your time in and around your resort – although most places can arrange bike or motorbike hire to get you out and about. Definitely book ahead.

Freedomland HOMESTAY **$$**
(Map p390; 077-399 4891; www.freedomlandphuquoc.com; 2 Ap Ong Lang, Xa Cua Duong; bungalow US$30-60; Oct-Jun;) With an emphasis on switching off (no TV) and socialising – fun, communal dinners are a mainstay – Freedomland has 11 basic bungalows (mosquito nets, fans, solar-heated showers) scattered around a shady plot. The beach is a five-minute walk away, or you can slump in the hammocks strung between the trees. Popular with solo budget travellers; call ahead. Shut in the rainy season.

★**Chen Sea Resort & Spa** RESORT **$$$**
(Map p390; 077-399 5895; www.centarahotelsresorts.com; villa US$230-652;) Tranquil and chilled-out Chen Sea has lovely

villas with sunken baths, some with hot tubs, and deep verandahs, designed to resemble ancient terracotta-roofed houses. The large azure rectangle of the infinity pool faces the resort's beautiful sandy beach. The isolation is mitigated by plenty of activities on hand: cycling, kayaking, catamaran outings, in-spa pampering and dining in the open-sided restaurant.

Mango Bay RESORT $$$

(Map p390; ☎077-398 1693; www.mangobayphuquoc.com; bungalow US$185-485;) Situated around a small cove that is accessed from a dusty road through a mango orchard, this ecofriendly resort uses solar panels and organic and recycled building materials, and has its own butterfly garden. Strung out along the beach, airy bungalows come with delightful open-air bathrooms. All in all it's a romantic, if simple, getaway for those who want to get cosy with their sweetheart.

Vung Bau Beach

★Bamboo Cottages & Restaurant RESORT $$

(Map p390; ☎077-281 0345; www.bamboophuquoc.com; r US$95-125;) Run by a friendly family with a coterie of cheeky dogs, Bamboo Cottages has Vung Bau Beach largely to itself. The focal point is an open-sided restaurant and bar, right by the beach. Set around the lawns, the attractive, lemon-coloured villas have private, open-roofed bathrooms with solar-powered hot water. The family supports an education scholarship for local kids in need.

Eating

Many of the recommended resorts have excellent restaurants, often with a beachside location or a sunset view. Guests staying at more remote resorts such as those at Ong Lang Beach tend to eat in, as it is a long way into town.

For something a bit more local, try the seafood restaurants in the fishing village of Ham Ninh; there are several along the pier at the end of the main road.

Duong Dong

Dinh Cau Night Market VIETNAMESE $

(Map p392; Đ Vo Thi Sau; meals from 70,000d; 5pm-midnight) Hands down the most atmospheric, affordable and excellent place to dine on the island, Duong Dong's night market has around a dozen stalls serving a delicious range of Vietnamese seafood, grills and vegetarian options. Look for a local crowd, as they are a discerning bunch.

★Nha Ghe Phu Quoc Crab House SEAFOOD $$

(Map p392; 21 Đ Tran Hung Dao; meals 200,000-780,000d; 11am-10pm;) At this crustacean sensation you won't be crabby once you get your claws into the likes of soft-shell crab with green peppercorn salsa, *com ghe* (jasmine rice with crab meat and fish sauce) or Cajun-style blue crab. Extra hungry? Don't be shellfish and share the mega squid-crab-shrimp-sausage combo with your nearest and dearest.

Buddy Ice Cream INTERNATIONAL $$

(Map p392; www.visitphuquoc.info; 6 Đ Bach Dang; meals 80,000-180,000d; 8am-10pm;) With the coolest music in town, this cafe is excellent for sides of tourist info with its New Zealand ice-cream combos, toasted sandwiches, fish 'n' chips, thirst-busting fruit juices, shakes, smoothies, all-day breakfasts, comfy sofas and a book exchange.

Long Beach

Winston's Burgers & Beer BURGERS $

(Map p392; 121 Đ Tran Hung Dao; burgers from 70,000d; 1-9pm) The name says it all: this bar is all about (really good) burgers, beer and a large selection of cocktails, mixed by the eponymous Winston. Linger for a chat or challenge your drinking companions to a game of Connect 4.

Alanis Deli CAFE $

(Map p392; 98 Đ Tran Hung Dao; pancakes from 80,000d; 8am-10pm;) Fab caramel pancakes, American breakfast combos, plus good (if pricey) coffees and wonderfully friendly service.

★Spice House at Cassia Cottage VIETNAMESE $$

(Map p392; www.cassiacottage.com; 100c Đ Tran Hung Dao; meals 180,000-300,000d; 7-10am & 11am-10pm) Nab a beachside high-table, order a papaya salad, grilled garlic prawns, a cinnamon-infused okra, a delectable fish curry, or grilled beef skewers wrapped in betel leaves and time dinner to catch the sunset at this excellent restaurant.

Ganesh
INDIAN $$

(Map p392; 97 Tran Hung Dao; meals 150,000-300,000d; ⏲11am-10pm; ✎) While the service is lacklustre, by contrast, the Indian dishes here are fantastic: the mango prawn curry is a standout. If extra hungry, go for a vegetarian/meat/seafood *thali* set (from 210,000d).

Pepper's Pizza & Grill
ITALIAN, GERMAN $$

(Map p392; ☎077-384 8773; 89 Đ Tran Hung Dao; meals 90,000-220,000d; ⏲10am-11pm; 📶✎) Pepper's does fine pizzas, including decent veggie options, and it'll even deliver to your resort. The rest of the menu is a mixture of Italian, German and Asian dishes, including steaks, ribs and the like.

★Itaca Resto Lounge
FUSION $$$

(Map p392; www.itacalounge.com; 125 Đ Tran Hung Dao; meals 260,000-700,000d; ⏲4pm-1am, closed May-Oct; 📶) This much-applauded restaurant has a winning Mediterranean-Asian fusion menu (with tapas), a much-enjoyed alfresco arrangement and friendly, welcoming hosts. Don't expect sea views, but do expect wagyu beef burgers, seared tuna with passionfruit, wild mushroom risotto and a charming ambience.

Pepper Tree Restaurant
VIETNAMESE, INTERNATIONAL $$$

(Map p392; www.laverandaresort.com; 118/9 Đ Tran Hung Dao; meals 250,000-700,000d; ⏲6.30am-11pm; 📶✎) The Pepper Tree on an upstairs verandah (appropriately, at La Veranda resort) gives you an exhaustive choice of Vietnamese dishes, such as stuffed squid and lotus salad, as well as a few international classics (seared duck breast, slow-cooked lamb shank), some of which are hit-and-miss.

Ong Lang

Sakura
VIETNAMESE $$

(Map p390; meals from 100,000d; ⏲10am-10pm) This simple wooden restaurant is run by the very fluent English-speaking Kiem. In spite of the name, the dishes are Vietnamese rather than Japanese; standouts include prawns in tamarind sauce and smoked aubergine, and if you're with a group, whole red snapper makes a great addition to the meal. Very friendly service, too.

Drinking & Nightlife

The following are all either on Long Beach or in Duong Dong.

★Le Bar
BAR

(Map p392; 118/9 Đ Tran Hung Dao; ⏲6am-11pm; 📶) With its gorgeous tiled floor, art-deco furniture and colonial charms, this highly elegant and well-poised upstairs lounge-bar at La Veranda is a superb spot for a terrace sundowner.

Rory's Beach Bar
BAR

(Map p390; 118/10 Đ Tran Hung Dao; ⏲9am-late) Phu Quoc's liveliest and most fun beach bar draws a steady torrent of travellers and island residents down the path to its seaside perch. Expect bonfires on the beach, great happy hour specials and staff happy to chat.

Lee's Safari Bar
BAR

(Map p390; 167 Đ Tran Hung Dao; ⏲4-11pm) The welcoming English owner of this otherwise rather uneventful bar is a useful source of local info on all things Phu Quoc. The food also gets good press and it's a relaxed spot to watch a football game.

Coco Bar
BAR

(Map p392; 118 Đ Tran Hung Dao; ⏲10am-late) With chairs and music spilling onto the pavement, Coco is a great place for a roadside bevvy and chat with the mix of travelling folk, Gallic wayfarers, local drinkers and passing pool sharks.

Shopping

Your best bets for souvenirs are the night market in Duong Dong and the pearl farm near the centre of Long Beach.

Phu Quoc Pearls
JEWELLERY

(Map p392; Đ Tran Hung Dao; ⏲8am-5pm) For black, yellow, white, pink or any other colour of pearl, Phu Quoc Pearls is a requisite stop. Displays feature all manner of jewellery made from said pearls.

Avid pearl hunters can find cheaper wares at kiosks that are located in the village of Ham Ninh, but you have a guarantee of authenticity here.

Information

There are ATMs in Duong Dong and in many resorts on Long Beach. A handy one is positioned at the top of the lane at 118 Đ Tran Hung Dao, not far from Oasis.

Post Office (Map p392; Đ 30 Thang 4; ⏲8am-5pm Mon-Fri) Located in the downtown area of Duong Dong.

Getting There & Away

AIR

Demand can be high in peak season, so book ahead. Among the services are daily flights to Can Tho (50 minutes), three daily to Hanoi (2½ hours), 15 daily to HCMC (one hour), daily flights in season to Rach Gia (30 minutes), and two flights per week to Singapore (1¾ hours).

Phu Quoc International Airport (Map p390; www.phuquocairport.com) The airport is 10km southeast of Duong Dong.

BOAT

Fast boats connect Phu Quoc to both Ha Tien (1½ hours) and Rach Gia (2½ hours). Phu Quoc travel agents have the most up-to-date schedules and can book tickets. Five virtually identical operators, including **Duong Dong Express** (Phu Quoc 077-399 0747, Rach Gia 077-387 9765) and Superdong run fast boats from Rach Gia to Phu Quoc's Bai Vong on the east coast, most departing at 8am and making the return journey at 1pm (250,000d). Fast ferries from Ha Tien arrive at the Ham Ninh port, just north of Bai Vong. Seas can be rough between

THE RIVER OF NINE DRAGONS

The Mekong River is one of the world's great rivers and its delta is one of the world's largest. It originates high in the Tibetan plateau, flowing 4500km through China, between Myanmar (Burma) and Laos, through Laos, along the Laos–Thailand border, and through Cambodia and Vietnam on its way to the South China Sea. At Phnom Penh (Cambodia), the Mekong River splits into two main branches: the Hau Giang (Lower River, also called the Bassac River), which flows via Chau Doc, Long Xuyen and Can Tho to the sea; and the Tien Giang (Upper River), which splits into several branches at Vinh Long and empties into the sea at five points. The numerous branches explain the Vietnamese name for the river: Song Cuu Long (River of Nine Dragons).

The Mekong's flow begins to rise around the end of May and reaches its highest point in September. A tributary of the river that empties into the Mekong at Phnom Penh drains Cambodia's Tonlé Sap Lake. When the Mekong is at flood stage, this tributary reverses its direction and flows into Tonlé Sap, acting as one of the world's largest natural flood barriers. Unfortunately, deforestation in Cambodia is disturbing this delicate balancing act, resulting in more flooding in Vietnam's portion of the Mekong River basin.

In recent years seasonal flooding has claimed the lives of hundreds and forced tens of thousands of residents to evacuate their homes. Floods cause millions of dollars' worth of damage and have a catastrophic effect on regional rice and coffee crops.

Living on a flood plain presents some technical challenges. Lacking any high ground to escape flooding, many delta residents build their houses on bamboo stilts to avoid the rising waters. Many roads are submerged or turn to muck during floods; all-weather roads have to be built on raised embankments, but this is expensive. The traditional solution has been to build canals and travel by boat. There are thousands of canals in the Mekong Delta – keeping them properly dredged and navigable is a constant but essential chore.

A further challenge is keeping the canals clean. The normal practice of dumping all garbage and sewage directly into the waterways behind the houses that line them is taking its toll. Many of the more populated areas in the Mekong Delta are showing signs of unpleasant waste build-up. The World Wildlife Foundation (WWF) is one organisation that's working with local and provincial governments to help preserve the environment.

In 2013 Laos declared its intention to build the 260-megawatt Don Sahong Dam on the Mekong, without consulting downstream neighbours, which looks set to go ahead, while its construction of the 1260-megawatt Xayaburi dam continues in the north of the country. Cambodia signed an agreement with China in 2006 to build the Sambor dam, which would cause the displacement of thousands of people and destroy habitats. Dams on the Chinese stretch have already been blamed for reduced water levels, and environmental groups have petitioned the Laos government to put plans on hold after concerns that the target of 11 dams will disrupt the breeding cycles of dozens of fish species. There are also concerns that the reduced flows will cause more salt water to enter the Vietnamese section (a process exacerbated by global warming), which environmentalists fear will have a catastrophic effect on rice production.

June and September. During peak season, fast ferries run extra trips between Ha Tien and Phu Quoc.

Car Ferry From Ha Tien, two car ferries run to Phu Quoc's Da Chong port, in the northeast part of the island. They depart daily at 8am and 8.20am from Ha Tien and 1pm from Phu Quoc (185,000/80,000/700,000d per passenger/motorbike/car). Two more car ferries are due to be added to meet demand.

Superdong (Ha Tien) (☎077-395 5933; www.superdong.com.vn; per passenger 230,000d) Fast ferry from Ha Tien departs at 7.30am, 8am and 1.15pm (1½ hours), returning from Phu Quoc at 8.30am, 9.45am and 1pm.

Superdong (Rach Gia) (☎077-387 7742; per passenger 250,000d) Departs Rach Gia at 8am, 9am, 12.40pm and 1pm (2½ hours). Departures from Phu Quoc run at exactly the same times.

ℹ Getting Around

TO/FROM THE AIRPORT

Expect to pay around 70,000d for a *xe om* to Long Beach and 100,000d for a taxi.

BICYCLE

Bicycle rentals are available through most lodgings from 70,000d per day.

MOTORBIKE

For short *xe om* runs, 20,000d should be sufficient. Otherwise, figure on around 60,000d for about 5km. From Duong Dong to Bai Vong will cost you about 70,000d or so. Agree on a price before setting off.

Motorbikes can be hired from most hotels and bungalows for around 120,000d (semi-automatic) to 150,000d (automatic) per day. Inspect cheaper bikes thoroughly before setting out.

A good paved road now runs south from Duong Dong to An Thoi, the southern tip of the island, and north as far as Cape Ganh Dau, the northwest tip of Phu Quoc. A two-lane highway connects Duong Dong with the car ferry port, but other roads tend to be dirt-and-gravel, potholed and bumpy.

TAXI

Mai Linh (☎077-397 9797) is a reliable operator. It costs about 250,000d from Duong Dong to the dock at Vong Beach.

Ha Tien

☎077 / POP 40,000

Ha Tien may be part of the Mekong Delta but lying on the Gulf of Thailand it feels a world away from the rice fields and rivers that typify the region. There are dramatic limestone formations peppering the area, which are home to a network of caves, some of which have been turned into temples. Plantations of pepper trees cling to the hillsides. On a clear day, Phu Quoc Island is easily visible to the west.

The town itself has a languid charm, with crumbling colonial villas and a colourful riverside market. Already bolstered by the number of Phu Quoc- or Cambodia-bound travellers, visitor numbers are set to soar further with the proposed introduction of two more car ferries to Phu Quoc to join the two already in place.

Oh yes, Ha Tien is on the map. And it's occupying a bigger portion of it thanks to major expansion plans that will see the city spread southwest along the coast. Already a precinct of markets and hotels has sprung up on land reclaimed from the river between the end of Phuong Thanh and the bridge. With development concentrated in this neighbourhood, the charming colonial shopfronts around the old market have thankfully been left to decay in peace, but many changes are still afoot.

History

Ha Tien was a province of Cambodia until 1708. In the face of attacks by the Thai, the Khmer-appointed governor, a Chinese immigrant named Mac Cuu, turned to the Vietnamese for protection and assistance. Mac Cuu thereafter governed this area as a fiefdom under the protection of the Nguyen Lords. He was succeeded as ruler by his son, Mac Thien Tu. During the 18th century the area was invaded and pillaged several times by the Thai. Rach Gia and the southern tip of the Mekong Delta came under direct Nguyen rule in 1798.

During the American War the area around Ha Tien was an important weapon smuggling area for the Viet Cong, who transported guns from the deep harbour in Sihanoukville, Cambodia, to the delta in fishing boats.

During the Khmer Rouge regime, Cambodian forces repeatedly attacked Vietnamese territory and massacred thousands of civilians here. The entire populations of Ha Tien and nearby villages (in fact, tens of thousands of people) fled their homes. Also during this period, areas north of Ha Tien along the Cambodian border were sown with mines and booby traps, some of which have yet to be cleared.

Ha Tien

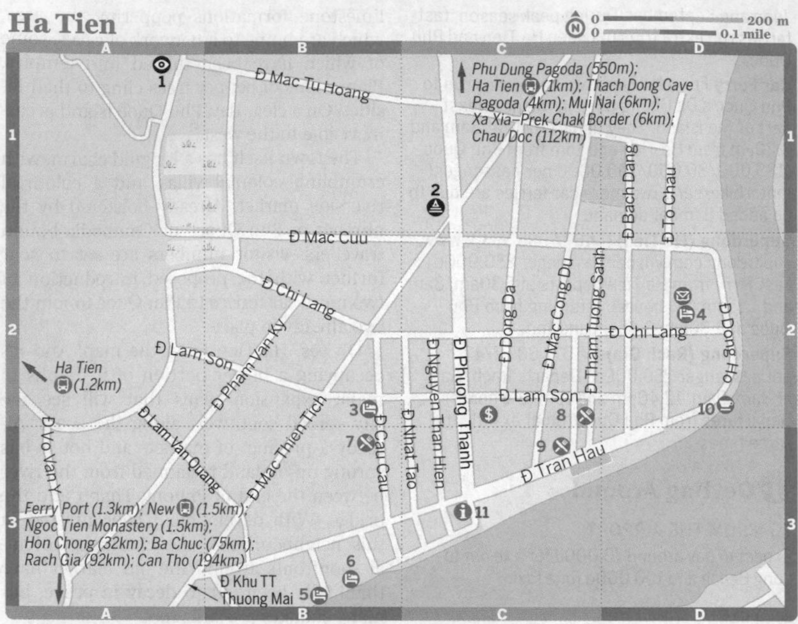

Ha Tien

Sights
1 Mac Cuu Family Tombs A1
2 Tam Bao Pagoda C1

Sleeping
3 Hai Van Hotel B2
4 Hai Yen Hotel D2
5 Long Chau Hotel B3
6 River Hotel B3

Eating
7 Floating Restaurant B3
8 Night Market C2
9 Oasis Bar C3

Drinking & Nightlife
10 Thuy Tien D2

Information
11 Ha Tien Tourism C3

Sights

★Thach Dong Cave Pagoda — BUDDHIST TEMPLE

(Chua Thanh Van; 9am-5pm) Also known as Chua Thanh Van, this Buddhist cave temple is 4km northeast of town. Scramble through the cave chambers to see the funerary tablets and altars to Ngoc Hoang, Quan The Am Bo Tat and the two Buddhist monks who founded the temples of this pagoda.

To the left of the entrance is the Stele of Hatred (Bia Cam Thu), shaped like a raised fist, which commemorates the Khmer Rouge massacre of 130 people here on 14 March 1978.

The wind here creates extraordinary sounds as it funnels through the grotto's passageways. Openings in several branches of the cave afford views of nearby Cambodia.

Mac Cuu Family Tombs — TOMB

(Lang Mac Cuu, Nui Binh San; Đ Mac Cuu; 8am-5pm) FREE Not far from town are the Mac Cuu Family Tombs, known locally as Nui Lang, the Hill of the Tombs. Mac Cuu, a Khmer-appointed 18th-century Chinese governor, and several dozen of his relatives are buried here in traditional Chinese tombs decorated with figures of dragons, phoenixes, lions and guardians. At the bottom of the complex is an ornate shrine dedicated to the Mac family.

Tam Bao Pagoda — BUDDHIST TEMPLE

(Sac Tu Tam Bao Tu; 328 Đ Phuong Thanh; dawn-dusk) Founded by Mac Cuu in 1730, Tam Bao Pagoda is home to a community of Buddhist nuns. In front of the splendid, many-tiered pagoda is a statue of Quan The Am Bo Tat (the Goddess of Mercy) standing on a lotus blossom. Within the sanctuary, the largest statue on the dais represents A Di Da (the Buddha of the Past), made of painted brass.

Outside in the tranquil grounds are the tombs of 16 monks. Near the pagoda is a section of the city wall dating from the early 18th century.

Phu Dung Pagoda BUDDHIST TEMPLE

(Phu Cu Am Tu; Đ Phu Dung; ⊙dawn-dusk) This pagoda was founded in the mid-18th century by Mac Thien Tich's wife, Nguyen Thi Xuan. Her tomb and that of one of her female servants are on the hillside behind the pagoda. Inside the main hall of the pagoda, the most notable statue on the central dais is a bronze Thich Ca Buddha from China.

To get here, continue north past the Mac Cuu Tombs and take the first right onto Đ Phu Dung.

Behind the main hall is a small temple, Dien Ngoc Hoang, dedicated to the Taoist Jade Emperor. Head up the steep blue stairs to the shrine. The figures inside are of Ngoc Hoang (the Jade Emperor) flanked by Nam Tao, the Taoist God of the Southern Polar Star and the God of Happiness (on the right); and Bac Dao, the Taoist God of the Northern Polar Star and the God of Longevity (on the left). The statues are made of papier mâché moulded over bamboo frames.

Ngoc Tien Monastery BUDDHIST TEMPLE

(Tinh Xa Ngoc Tien; ⊙dawn-dusk) From Ha Tien's riverfront, this Buddhist monastery is a striking sight – sprawling up the hill on the other side of the river. The buildings themselves are unremarkable but it's worth making the steep climb up here for the sweeping views of the town and countryside. Follow your nose to the narrow road at its base.

The monastery is reached via a tiny lane at number 48; look for the yellow sign topped with a swastika (symbolising eternity).

Dong Ho INLET

The name translates as East Lake, but Dong Ho is not a lake but an inlet of the sea. Dong Ho is said to be most beautiful on nights when there is a full or almost-full moon. According to legend, on such nights fairies dance here.

The 'lake' is just east of Ha Tien, bounded to the east by a chain of granite hills known as the Ngu Ho (Five Tigers) and to the west by the To Chan hills.

Sleeping

Hai Yen Hotel HOTEL $

(☎077-385 1580; www.kshaiyen.com; 15 Đ To Chau; d/tr/q 300,000/370,000/450,000d; ❄📶) Quite elegantly presented at an empty Ha Tien intersection, this old-timer has a variety of

GETTING TO CAMBODIA: HA TIEN TO KEP

Getting to the border The **Xa Xia/Prek Chak border crossing** connects Ha Tien with Kep and Kampot on Cambodia's south coast, making a trip to Cambodia from Phu Quoc via Ha Tien, or vice versa, that much easier. Several minibus companies leave Ha Tien for Cambodia at around 1pm, heading to Kep (US$9, one hour, 47km), Kampot (US$12, 1½ hours, 75km), Sihanoukville (US$15, four hours, 150km) and Phnom Penh (US$15, four hours, 180km). Bookings can be made through Ha Tien Tourism (p402), which can arrange the Cambodian visa too.

It's a really good idea to have US dollars on you when crossing into Cambodia; you can pay for the Cambodian visa in dong but they'll get you with a really unfavourable exchange rate. On the Cambodian side, you can withdraw dollars from ATMs.

In peak season, when minibuses get booked up way in advance, if you're travelling light you can go all the way to Kep or Kampot on the back of a *xe om* (Oasis Bar, p402, can recommend reputable motorbike drivers). If you make an independent arrangement with a *xe om* driver, do not hand over the money until you reach your destination, or else you risk being abandoned at the border.

At the border Cambodian visas officially cost US$30 at research time but be prepared to overpay by around US$5 at the border to join the 'express line', or be made to wait indefinitely.

Moving on It's possible to take a local bus to the border and then wait for a local bus on the Cambodian side, but since tourist minibuses cost only slightly more and are far comfier, most travellers opt for a through minibus ticket.

decent accommodation from simple doubles to spacious rooms with balcony and river views.

Hai Van Hotel HOTEL $
(☎077-385 2872; www.khachsanhaivan.com; 55 Đ Lam Son; s/d from 200,000/250,000d; ❄📶) A favourite with tour groups and conventions, the Hai Van offers clean, smart (if somewhat featureless) rooms with polished floors. Some English spoken.

Long Chau Hotel HOTEL $
(☎077-395 9189; 36-38 Đ Truong Sa; r 350,000d; ❄📶) At this riverfront hotel rooms are spacious, with views of the water from the balconies. Tell the staff if you want your room cleaned as it won't happen automatically.

River Hotel HOTEL $$$
(☎077-395 5888; www.riverhotelvn.com; Binh San Ward, Đ Tran Ha; r/ste from 1,890,000/4,200,000d; ❄📶🏊) With contemporary, spacious and stylish rooms, a towering and sinuous outline and ample river views, Ha Tien's most glam hotel enjoys an optimum position on the waterfront. The staff are helpful in spite of limited English, and the place is practically deserted midweek, so discounts are negotiable. Karaoke 'entertainment' takes place on the top floor.

Eating & Drinking

Ha Tien's speciality is an unusual variety of coconut – containing no milk, but with delicate and delicious flesh – that can only be found in Cambodia and this part of Vietnam. Restaurants all around the Ha Tien area serve up the coconut flesh in a glass with ice and sugar.

★**Oasis Bar** INTERNATIONAL $
(☎077-370 1553; www.oasisbarhatien.com; Đ Tran Hau; meals 60,000-150,000d; ⏰9am-9pm; 📶) Run by Ha Tien's only resident Western expat and his Vietnamese wife, this friendly little restaurant-bar is a great spot for a cold beer, plunger coffee, impartial travel information and for leafing through copies of the *Evening Standard*, the *Observer* and the *Daily Mail* newspapers. The menu runs to all-day, full-English breakfasts, filled baguettes, Greek salad, mango shakes and plenty more.

Night Market MARKET $
(Đ Lam Son; meals from 20,000d; ⏰5-9pm) Some of Ha Tien's cheapest and best eats; the grilled seafood is particularly good.

Floating Restaurant INTERNATIONAL, VIETNAMESE $$
(Tran Hau Park; meals from 100,000d; ⏰6am-10pm) Smartly refurbished and sitting by the River Hotel, this cheery boat is a good bet on weekends, when a team of chefs is on hand to feed the convention-attending masses. The rest of the week the results can be somewhat hit-and-miss.

Thuy Tien CAFE
(☎077-385 1828; Đ Dong Ho; ⏰6am-9pm) Dotted with fairy lights and glowing with Chinese lanterns at night, this floating cafe is a breezy choice for a sundowner beer or a *cafe sua* overlooking Dong Ho.

ℹ Information

Oasis Bar is an unofficial wanderers' hub that most travellers funnel into when passing through Ha Tien. Owner Andy is happy to share local info and can help arrange tours of the area and onward transport.

Agribank (☎077-385 2055; 37 Đ Lam Son) Located one block from the waterfront and has an ATM.

Ha Tien Tourism (☎077-395 9598; Đ Tran Hau; ⏰8am-5pm) Handles transport bookings, including boats to Phu Quoc and buses to Cambodia. Also arranges Cambodian visas (US$35). Look for the neon 'food & drink' sign.

Main Post Office (☎077-385 2190; 3 Đ To Chau; ⏰7am-5pm)

BUSES FROM HA TIEN

DESTINATION	COST (D)	DURATION (HR)	FREQUENCY	DISTANCE
Ca Mau	160,000	5-6	several daily	219km
Can Tho	180,000	3½	6 daily	194km
Chau Doc	130,000-200,000	3½-4	3 daily	112km
HCMC	200,000	9-10	10 daily	317km
Rach Gia	60,000	2¼	every 30min	92km

OFF THE BEATEN TRACK

PIRATE ISLAND

This small speck of an island, its hill covered in lush vegetation, has a sordid 500-year history as a pirate haven, which only came to an end during the reunification in 1975. Today the inhabitants make their living from the sea. A paved motorbike trail circles the island; you can hike up to the hill temple and visit the tranquil beach, and if you come with a Vietnamese speaker, you can arrange to go out with the fishermen.

Besides the 100 or so inhabitants who reside in the four small, scrappy fishing villages, there's an army base on top of the hill, keeping a vigilant eye out for potential invaders from Cambodia. Rumours of pirate treasure have circulated for years, and in 1983 the army promptly expelled from Vietnam a couple of foreign treasure-seekers who arrived illegally by boat from Cambodia, equipped with metal detectors.

There's limited electricity until 10pm, after which the only light comes from candles and boat lights. Going out on a fishing boat at night, you may see the sparkly shapes of fish shoot through the water, thanks to the phosphorescence phenomenon.

It's reachable either by green cargo boat (40,000d, 1½ hours) that departs Ha Tien at 2.30pm, returning from the island at 9am, or by passenger boat (100,000d, 1¼ hours), departing Ha Tien at 9am and returning at 4pm. The passenger boat sometimes doesn't run; otherwise it's possible to borrow a bicycle in Ha Tien and pop over for the day. If you'd like to stay the night, there are a couple of very simple homestays (60,000d per room) and if you buy some fish or crabs from the fishermen, your hosts can cook you dinner.

Getting There & Away

BOAT

Ferries (p398) stop across the river from the town.

BUS

Trang Ngoc Phat (www.taxihatien.vn) runs the most comfortable buses to Rach Gia.

Ha Tien Bus Station (Ben Xe Ha Tien; Hwy 80) The bus station is due to relocate to larger, purpose-built facilties 1.5km south of the bridge by early 2016. Buses for HCMC depart either between 7am and 10am or 6pm and 10pm.

CAR & MOTORBIKE

The Ha Tien–Chau Doc road is narrow but interesting and with light traffic, following a canal along the border. As you approach Ha Tien, the land turns into a mangrove forest that is infertile and almost uninhabited. The drive takes about three hours, and it's possible to visit Ba Chuc and Tuc Dup en route.

Around Ha Tien

Mui Nai

The best of the Gulf of Thailand beaches, **Mui Nai** (Stag's Head Peninsula; admission person/car 2500/10,000d) is 8km west of Ha Tien. The water is incredibly warm and becalmed, great for bathing and diving. The bay spills over with stalls selling loud-coloured water rings, swimsuits and beach balls, beneath a canopy of lofty palms. On top is a lighthouse and there are beaches on both sides of the peninsula, lined with simple restaurants and guesthouses.

A *xe om* here should set you back around 60,000d.

Hon Giang & Nghe Islands

There are many islands along this coast and some locals make a living gathering swiftlet nests (the most important ingredient of that famous Chinese delicacy, bird's-nest soup) from their rocky cliffs. About 15km from Ha Tien and accessible by small boat, Hon Giang Island has a lovely, secluded beach.

Nghe Island, near Hon Chong, is a favourite pilgrimage spot for Buddhists. The island contains a **cave pagoda** (Chua Hang) next to a large statue of Quan The Am Bo Tat, which faces out to sea.

Hon Chong

You'll pass Khmer pagodas, Cao Dai temples, grandiose churches and karst outcrops en route to Hon Chong, home to stone grottoes, cave shrines and what would be the nicest stretch of sand on the delta's mainland if it weren't for the dirty water, polluted by discharge from the nearby cement factory.

After passing through the scrappy village, the road rounds a headland and follows

Duong Beach (Bai Duong; per person 5000d) for 3km. The entrance fee is charged only at the far end of the beach, where there are food stalls, karaoke bars, and pigs and chickens wandering around. From the beach you can see rocky remnants of **Father & Son Isle** (Hon Phu Tu), several hundred metres offshore. It was said to be shaped like a father embracing his son, but the father was washed away in 2006. Boats can be hired at the shore to row out for a closer look at the orphan remains.

You need to walk through the market at the far end of Duong Beach to reach the **cave pagoda** (Chua Hang; ⊙dawn-dusk), which is set against the base of a stony headland. The entry to the cave containing **Hai Son Tu** (Sea Mountain Temple) is inside the pagoda. Visitors light incense and offer prayers here before entering the cool grotto itself, whose entrance is located behind the altar. Inside are statues of Sakyamuni and Quan The Am Bo Tat, back-lit by neon mandalas, as well as small cabinets enclosing green glass Buddhas. Mind your head on the low-hanging rock roof of the cave leading to the beach. The pagoda is swamped with pilgrims 15 days before and one month after Tet, while another deluge of worshippers arrives in March and April.

Casual seafood-cooking shacks line the beach. Hon Chong is easily visited as a day trip from Ha Tien, but should you wish to linger, well-maintained and friendly **Green Hill Guesthouse** (☎077-385 4369; r US$14-20; ❄), in an imposing villa on the northern headland of Duong Beach, has spacious rooms, including the room of choice on the top floor.

ℹ Getting There & Away

Hon Chong is 32km from Ha Tien towards Rach Gia. The access road branches off the Rach Gia–Ha Tien highway at the small town of Ba Hon. Buses can drop you off at Ba Hon, from where you can hire a motorbike to continue the journey on to Hon Chong (around 80,000d). A motorbike day tour from Ha Tien will cost around US$15.

Tuc Dup Hill

Because of its network of connecting caves, **Tuc Dup Hill** (216m) served as a strategic base of operations during the American War. *Tuc dup* is Khmer for 'water runs at night' and it is also known locally as 'Two Million Dollar Hill', in reference to the amount of money the Americans sank into securing it.

There isn't much to see, but you'll pass near it if you're taking the back road through Ba Chuc to Chau Doc.

Ba Chuc

Ba Chuc's **memorial** (⊙8am-5pm) stands as a ghastly reminder of the horrors perpetrated by the Khmer Rouge. Between 18 April and 30 April 1978, the Khmer Rouge killed 3157 villagers here; only two survived.

The memorial consists of two parts: the **ossuary** housing the skulls and bones of more than 1100 victims, and the **memorial room** next door, displaying wrenching post-massacre photos.

Between 1975 and 1978 Khmer Rouge soldiers regularly crossed the border into Vietnam and slaughtered innocent civilians. Over the border, things were even worse, where nearly two million Cambodians were killed during the period of Pol Pot's Democratic Kampuchea regime.

In the ossuary, resembling either an onion or a lotus flower bud (depending on your outlook), the skulls and bones are divided by age group (including the minute skulls of toddlers and babies) and gender. This collection resembles Cambodia's Choeung Ek killing fields, where thousands of skulls of Khmer Rouge victims are on display, but as it's clean, sterile and well-lit, with a spot to leave offerings in the centre, it appears almost cheerful compared to what confronts you next door.

The memorial room showcases the weapons used by the Khmer Rouge (knives, bayonets and cudgels) and sticks used for torture, particularly of women. Many of the Ba Chuc victims were tortured to death. The photos are for strong stomachs only.

The bottoms of walls at the **Phi Lai Tu Temple** behind the memorial room are still stained dark with the blood of the slain; over 300 villagers were slaughtered inside. The Vietnamese government might have had other motives for invading Cambodia at the end of 1978, but certainly outrage at the Ba Chuc massacre was a major justification.

Ba Chuc is 4km south of the road running parallel to the Cambodian border between Ha Tien and Chau Doc, somewhat closer to Ha Tien (75km). It's possible to organise a tour from Chau Doc (US$30) or a *xe om* from Ha Tien (400,000d).

Chau Doc

☎076 / POP 103,000

Draped along the banks of the Hau Giang River (Bassac River), Chau Doc sees plenty of travellers washing through on the river route between Cambodia and Vietnam. A likeable little town with significant Chinese, Cham and Khmer communities, Chau Doc's cultural diversity – apparent in the mosques, temples, churches and nearby pilgrimage sites – makes it fascinating to explore even if you're not Cambodia-bound. Taking a boat trip to the Cham communities across the river is another highlight, while the bustling market and intriguing waterfront provide fine backdrops to a few days of relaxation.

Sights

Floating Market MARKET
(⌚5am-noon) You need to get up at the crack of dawn to see the best of this floating market. The action is busiest around 5am to 6am, when locals gather to buy fresh produce wholesale.

30 Thang 4 Park PARK
(Đ Le Loi) Stretching from the main market to the Victoria Chau Doc Hotel, this park is the city's main promenading place and a superlative spot for river gazing. Sculptures and a fountain are framed by manicured lawns and paths, and if you're interested in getting river-borne, women may approach you here offering rides in small boats.

Floating Houses HOUSE
These houses, whose floats consist of empty metal drums, are both a place to live and a livelihood for their residents. Under each house, fish are raised in suspended metal nets. The fish flourish in their natural river habitat; the family can feed them whatever scraps are handy. You can get a close-up look by hiring a boat.

Chau Phu Temple BUDDHIST TEMPLE
(Dinh Than Chau Phu; cnr Đ Nguyen Van Thoai & Đ Gia Long; ⌚dawn-dusk) In 1926 this temple was built to worship the Nguyen dynasty official Thoai Ngoc Hau, buried at Sam Mountain. The structure is decorated with both Vietnamese and Chinese motifs; inside are funeral tablets bearing the names of the deceased as well as biographical information about them. There's also a shrine to Ho Chi Minh.

Chau Giang Mosque MOSQUE
Domed, arched Chau Giang Mosque, in the hamlet of Chau Giang, serves the local Cham Muslims. To get there, take the car ferry from Chau Giang ferry landing across the Hau Giang River. From the ferry landing, walk inland from the river for 30m, turn left and walk 50m.

FISH FARMING & BIOFUEL

Fish farming constitutes around 20% of Vietnam's total seafood output and is widely practised in An Giang province, in the region near the Cambodian border. The highest concentration of 'floating houses' with fish cages can be observed on the banks of the Hau Giang River (Bassac River) in Chau Doc.

The fish farmed are two members of the Asian catfish family: basa *(Pangasius bocourti)* and tra *(Pangasius hypophthalmus)*. About 1.1 million tonnes are produced by this method annually and much of it is exported, primarily to European and American markets (as well as Australia and Japan).

The two-step production cycle starts with capturing fish eggs from the wild, usually sourced in the Tonle Sap Lake in Cambodia, followed by raising the fish to a marketable size – usually about 1kg.

One of the more interesting developments affecting fish farming is the move to convert fish fat, a by-product of processing, into biofuel. One kilogram of fish fat can yield 1L of bio-diesel fuel, according to specialists. It is claimed that the biofuel will be more efficient than diesel, is nontoxic and will generate far fewer fumes.

Due to concerns about detrimental environmental effects from fish farming (particularly related to waste management and the use of antibiotics and other chemicals), the World Wildlife Fund (WWF) placed farmed Vietnamese *pangasius* on a red list for environmentally conscious European consumers to avoid. It was subsequently removed in 2011 and the WWF has devised a set of standards and an accreditation agency to certify sustainable Vietnamese producers.

Chau Doc

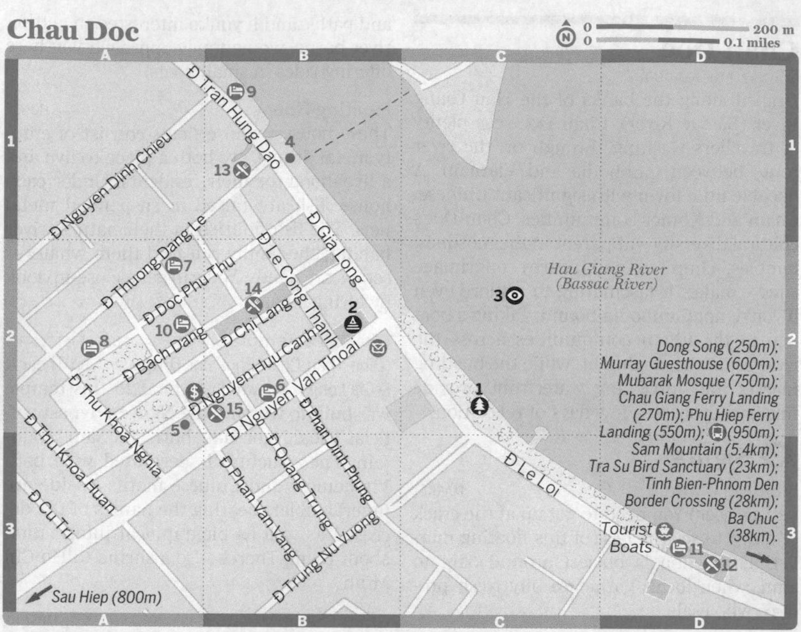

Chau Doc

Sights
- 1 30 Thang 4 Park C2
- 2 Chau Phu Temple B2
- 3 Floating Market C2

Activities, Courses & Tours
- 4 Hang Chau B1
- 5 Mekong Tours A2

Sleeping
- 6 Dai Loi Hotel B2
- 7 Hai Chau A2
- 8 Hotel Hung Cuong A2
- 9 Thuan Loi Hotel B1
- 10 Trung Nguyen Hotel A2
- 11 Victoria Chau Doc Hotel D3

Eating
- 12 Bassac Restaurant D3
- 13 Bay Bong B1
- 14 Chau Doc Covered Market B2
- 15 Memory Delicatessen B2

Drinking & Nightlife
- Bamboo Bar ...... (see 11)
- Tan Chau Salon Bar ...... (see 11)

Mubarak Mosque MOSQUE
(Thanh Duong Hoi Giao; on river bank, opposite Chau Doc) The Mubarak Mosque, where children study the Koran in Arabic script, is also on the river bank opposite Chau Doc. Visitors are permitted, but you should avoid entering during the calls to prayer (five times daily) unless you are a Muslim.

Tours

Xuan Mai CULTURAL TOUR
(0855 8896 11847, 0849 1891 0477; maixuanvn2001@yahoo.com) Friendly English-speaking Mai arranges tours of the area, either on motorbike or by car. She also makes bookings for speedboat transfers to Cambodia.

Mekong Tours CULTURAL TOUR
(076-386 7817; www.mekongvietnam.com; 14 Đ Nguyen Huu Canh; 8am-8pm) Local travel agency for booking boat or bus transport to Phnom Penh, boat trips on the Mekong, cars with drivers and day tours that include the floating market.

Sleeping

Since Chau Doc is on the well-trodden traveller route to Cambodia, some English is spoken at most accommodation options.

Trung Nguyen Hotel HOTEL $
(076-356 1561; www.trungnguyenhotel.com.vn; 86 Đ Bach Dang; s/d US$15/17;) One of the better budget places, with more midrange

trim. Rooms are more decorative than the competition, with balconies overlooking the market. It's situated on a busy corner site, so pack earplugs or ask for a room facing the rear.

Hai Chau HOTEL **$**
(☎076-626 0066; www.haichauhotel.com; 63 Đ Suong Nguyet Anh; s US$15, d US$18-28; ❄📶) A decent, central cheapie, Hai Chau has 16 rooms spread over four floors above a restaurant, with a lift. Well-kept rooms are smartly fitted out with dark wooden furniture; some have a balcony.

Thuan Loi Hotel HOTEL **$**
(☎076-386 6134; hotelthuanloi@gmail.com; 275 Đ Tran Hung Dao; r 200,000-280,000d; ❄📶) The sole cheapie with a riverside location, plus a floating restaurant. Rooms are not so atmospheric, but good value. The cheaper rooms are cold-water only, so consider a mini-splurge.

★ **Murray Guesthouse** GUESTHOUSE **$$**
(☎076-356 2108; www.murrayguesthouse.com; Truong Dinh; s/d US$26/29; ❄📶) Its walls decorated with indigenous art, collected by the Kiwi-Vietnamese owners around the world, this wonderful guesthouse raises the standard of Chau Doc accommodation dramatically. Boons include a guest lounge with snooker table and honour bar, a rooftop terrace drowning in greenery, wonderfully comfortable beds and some of Vietnam's best *pho* for breakfast. Owners are happy to advise and lend bicycles.

Hotel Hung Cuong BUSINESS HOTEL **$$**
(☎076-356 8111; www.hungcuonghotel.com; 96 Đ Dong Da; s/d from US$38/42; ❄📶) Stylish hotel overlooking a peaceful green square. Rooms come with satellite TV and welcome touches of artwork. The Hung Cuong sleeper buses to Ho Chi Minh City conveniently depart from just outside the hotel. Rooms facing the front 'benefit' from the ringing of gongs at the temple.

Dai Loi Hotel BUSINESS HOTEL **$$**
(☎076-356 6619; dailoi.hotel@yahoo.com.vn; 68-72 Đ Nguyen Van Thoai; r from 450,000d; ❄📶) This shiny super-central hotel sparkles with myriad Christmas baubles in the lobby. Rooms are spotless, spacious, tiled affairs and the place attracts a mixed crowd of international travellers and Chinese businessmen. English and French spoken.

★ **Victoria Chau Doc Hotel** HOTEL **$$$**
(☎076-386 5010; www.victoriahotels.asia; 32 Đ Le Loi; r from 4,193,000d, ste from 6,128,000d; ❄📶🏊) Chau Doc's most luxurious option, the Victoria delivers classic colonial charm, overseen by *ao-dai*-clad staff. With a striking location on the riverfront, the grand rooms here have dark-wood floors and furniture, and inviting bath-tubs. The swimming pool overlooks the busy river action and there's a small spa upstairs. A range of tours is available to guests.

Eating

At night, you can try a variety of cool *che* (dessert soups) at *che* stalls on Đ Bach Dang, next to the pagoda. There are also lots of other inexpensive stalls with large whiteboard menus.

Chau Doc Covered Market VIETNAMESE **$**
(Đ Bach Dang; meals 20,000-40,000d; ⏰7am-9pm) Delicious local specialities, such as grilled glutinous rice filled with banana and other stall food.

GETTING TO CAMBODIA: CHAU DOC TO PHNOM PENH BY BUS

Getting to the border Eclipsed by the newer crossing of Xa Xia near Ha Tien, the **Tinh Bien/Phnom Den border crossing** is less convenient for Phnom Penh–bound travellers, but may be of interest to those who savour the challenge of obscure border crossings. A bus to Phnom Penh (US$25, five to six hours) passes through Chau Doc en route from Can Tho at around 7.30am and can be booked through Mekong Tours in Chau Doc; double-check the pick-up point. The roads leading to the border have improved but are still bumpy.

At the border Cambodian visas can be obtained here, although you may wish to pay US$35 rather than the offical (at research time) fee of US$30 to be processed quickly. Yes, it's a mild form of extortion, but your time may be more valuable than your money.

Moving on Most travellers opt for a through bus ticket from Chau Doc.

Bay Bong VIETNAMESE $

(22 Đ Thuong Dang Le; meals 50,000-100,000d; ⏲9am-8pm) Informal spot with metal tables and chairs, but the food is something, with tasty fish-and-vegetable hotpot, stir-fried rice with seafood, snake-head fish soup, garlicky morning glory and more.

Sau Hiep VIETNAMESE $

(398 Đ Nguyen Van Thoai; meals 35,000d; ⏲8am-9pm) On the way to Sam Mountain, 1km out of town, this simple eatery makes a great pit stop for roll-your-own *nem nuong* (spring rolls filled with spiced pork meatballs, cucumber, fresh herbs, pineapple and beansprouts), dipped in a tangy, spicy sauce.

★**Memory Delicatessen** INTERNATIONAL $$

(57 Đ Nguyen Huu Canh; meals 60,000-200,000d; ⏲7am-10pm; ❄📶🖉) This sophisticated cafe-restaurant that attracts local trendies is memorable for its wonderful melange of international dishes, from the excellent pizzas topped with imported ingredients, to the fragrant vegetable curry with coconut milk and lemongrass, accompanied by an array of fresh juices and imaginative shakes. Skip dessert, though, unless it's the homemade ice cream.

Dong Song SEAFOOD $$

(7 Đ Le Loi; mains from 60,000d; ⏲noon-10pm) The atmospheric riverside setting of this cavernous restaurant is complemented by the extensive menu of fish and seafood dishes, such as squid with chilli and lemongrass, tamarind clams, steamed whole red snapper and more. Garlicky morning glory and vats of steamed rice make the ideal supporting cast.

★**Bassac Restaurant** FRENCH, VIETNAMESE $$$

(☎076-386 5010; 32 Đ Le Loi; meals 160,000-450,000d; ⏲6am-10pm; 🖉) Chau Doc's most sophisticated dining experience is at the Victoria Chau Doc Hotel where the menu veers between wonderful international dishes (roast rack of lamb, seared duck breast), dishes with a French accent (Provençale tart, *gratin dauphinois*) and beautifully presented Vietnamese dishes, such as grilled squid with green peppercorns. The apple pie with cinnamon ice cream makes for a sublime ending.

Drinking

Chau Doc is pretty sleepy.

Tan Chau Salon Bar BAR

(www.victoriahotels.asia; Victoria Chau Doc Hotel, 32 Đ Le Loi; ⏲6am-11pm) Sip a cocktail amid elegant Indochine surroundings.

Bamboo Bar BAR

(www.victoriahotels.asia; Victoria Chau Doc Hotel, 32 Đ Le Loi; ⏲noon-10pm) A stylish place for a tipple. Take your drink outside for a sundowner overlooking the river.

Information

Main Post Office (2 Đ Le Loi; ⏲8am-5pm)

Vietinbank (☎076-386 6497; 68-70 Đ Nguyen Huu Canh) Foreign currency can be exchanged.

GETTING TO CAMBODIA: CHAU DOC TO PHNOM PENH BY BOAT

Getting to the border One of the most enjoyable ways to enter Cambodia is via the **Vinh Xuong/Kaam Samnor border crossing** located just northwest of Chau Doc along the Mekong River. Several companies in Chau Doc sell boat journeys from Chau Doc to Phnom Penh via the Vinh Xuong border. **Hang Chau** (☎Chau Doc 076-356 2771, Phnom Penh 855-12-883 542; www.hangchautourist.com.vn; per person US$25) boats depart Chau Doc at 7.30am from a pier at 18 Đ Tran Hung Dao, arriving at 12.30pm. From Phnom Penh they depart at noon. The more upmarket **Blue Cruiser** (☎HCMC 08-3926 0253, Phnom Penh 855-236-333 666; www.bluecruiser.com) leaves the Victoria Hotel pier at 7am, costing US$55 (US$44 in the reverse direction, leaving Phnom Penh at 1.30pm). It takes about five hours, including the border check. The price includes all-you-can-drink beer and a snack. Delta Adventures advertises a boat transfer to Phnom Penh for just US$15; however, it's a slower boat with an imperfect safety record and after you reach the border, you have to switch to a minibus to take you the rest of the way.

At the border If coming from Cambodia, arrange a visa in advance. If leaving Vietnam, Cambodian visas are available at the crossing, but minor overcharging is common (plan on paying around US$35).

Moving on Hang Chau and Blue Cruiser boats take you all the way to Phnom Penh.

BUSES FROM CHAU DOC

DESTINATION	COST (D)	TIME (HR)	FREQUENCY	DISTANCE
Can Tho	105,000-245,000	3½	hourly	120km
Cao Lanh	100,000	3	hourly	90km
Ha Tien	130,000-200,000	2¼	5 daily	88km
HCMC	150,000-350,000	7½	every 30min	245km
Long Xuyen	65,000-100,000	1½	every 30min	62km
Vinh Long	270,000	4	hourly	127km

Getting There & Away

BUS

The most comfortable long-distance buses to Can Tho and HCMC are **Phuong Trang** (www.futaexpress.com), which depart from the main bus station, and **Hung Cuong** (www.hungcuonghotel.com), which depart from in front of Hung Cuong Hotel. Book tickets in advance via your lodgings.

Chau Doc Bus Station (Ben Xe Chau Doc; Đ Le Loi) The bus station is on the eastern edge of town, around 2km out of the centre, where Đ Le Loi becomes Hwy 91. All buses depart from here, with the exception of the Hung Cuong buses to HCMC.

Getting Around

Boats to Chau Giang district (across the Hau Giang River) leave from two docks: vehicle ferries depart from **Chau Giang ferry landing** (Ben Pha Chau Giang), opposite 419 Đ Le Loi; smaller, more frequent boats leave from **Phu Hiep ferry landing** (Ben Pha FB Phu Hiep), a little further southeast.

Private boats (around 100,000d for two hours), which are rowed standing up, can be hired from either of these spots or from 30 Thang 4 Park, and are highly recommended for seeing the floating houses and visiting nearby Cham minority villages and mosques. Motorboats (around 140,000d per hour) can be hired in the same area.

Sam Mountain

A sacred place for Buddhists, Sam Mountain (Nui Sam, 284m) and its environs are crammed with dozens of pagodas and temples. A strong Chinese influence makes it particularly popular with ethnic Chinese but Buddhists of all ethnicities visit here. The views from the top are excellent (weather permitting), ranging deep into Cambodia. There's a military outpost on the summit, a legacy of the days when the Khmer Rouge made cross-border raids and massacred Vietnamese civilians.

Along with the shrines and tombs, the steep path to the top is lined with the unholy clamour of commerce and there are plenty of cafes and stalls in which to stop for a drink or a snack. Walking down is easier than walking up (a not particularly scenic 45-minute climb), so you can get a motorbike to drop you at the summit (about 30,000d from the base of the mountain). The road to the top runs along the east side of the mountain. Veer left at the base of the mountain and turn right after about 1km where the road begins its climb. The mountain is open 24/7, with lights on the road for nocturnal climbs.

Sights

★Cavern Pagoda BUDDHIST TEMPLE
(Chua Hang; 4am-9pm) Also known as Phuoc Dien Tu, this temple is halfway up the western (far) side of Sam Mountain, with

WORTH A TRIP

TRA SU BIRD SANCTUARY FOREST

Twenty-three kilometres west of Chau Doc, the immense 800,000-hectare **Tra Su Bird Sanctuary** (admission 120,000d; boat rides per person 75,000d; 7am-4pm) is home to an astounding number of wading birds. Much of the wetland is off-limits to visitors so that the birds' breeding grounds are not disturbed, but visits include a short speedboat ride and a tranquil 20-minute paddle along narrow channels through the gnarled and green sunken forest. The best time to visit is December to January, when the babies hatch. Motorbike tours from Chau Doc cost around US$20 per person.

amazing views of the surrounding countryside. The lower part of the pagoda includes monks' quarters and two hexagonal tombs in which the founder of the pagoda, a female tailor named Le Thi Tho, and a former head monk, Thich Hue Thien, are buried. The upper section has two parts: the main sanctuary, and an astounding complex of caverns and grottoes.

The main sanctuary features the statues of A Di Da (the Buddha of the Past) and Thich Ca Buddha (Sakyamuni, the Historical Buddha), while in the caverns and grottoes you'll find a host of deities, including a 1000-arm and 1000-eye Quan Am. There's also a mirror room of Buddhas and an effigy of Bodhidharma, the founder of Zen Buddhism.

According to legend, Le Thi Tho came from Tay An Pagoda to this site half a century ago to lead a quiet, meditative life. When she arrived, she found two enormous cobras, one white and the other dark green. Le Thi Tho soon converted the snakes, which thereafter led pious lives. Upon her death, the snakes disappeared, but remain in statue form in one of the dark cavern passages.

Tay An Pagoda BUDDHIST TEMPLE

(Chua Tay An; ⌚4am-10pm) Although founded in 1847 on the site of an earlier bamboo shrine, Tay An's current structure dates from 1958. Aspects of its eclectic architecture, particularly its domed tower, reflect Hindu and Islamic influences.

Its main gate is of traditional Vietnamese design, and on its roofline romp figures of lions and two dragons fighting for possession of pearls, chrysanthemums, apricot trees and lotus blossoms.

If you're coming from Chau Doc on Hwy 91, Tay An Pagoda is located straight ahead at the foot of the mountain.

The temple itself is guarded by statues of a black elephant with two tusks and a white elephant with six tusks. Inside are arrayed fine carvings of hundreds of religious figures, most made of wood and some blinged up with disco-light halos. Statues include Sakyamuni, the 18 *a-la-han* (arhat) and the 12 *muoi hai ba mu* (midwives). The temple's name – Tay An – means 'Western Peace'.

Temple of Lady Xu BUDDHIST TEMPLE

(Mieu Ba Chua Xu; ⌚24hr) Founded in the 1820s to house a statue of Lady Xu that's become the subject of a popular cult, this large temple faces Sam Mountain, on the same road as Tay An Pagoda. Originally a simple affair of bamboo and leaves, the temple has been rebuilt many times, blending mid-20th-century design with Vietnamese Buddhist decorative motifs and plenty of neon.

The statue itself is possibly a relic of the Oc-Eo culture, dating from the 6th century, and is also possibly that of a man – but don't suggest that to one of the faithful.

According to one of several legends, the statue of Lady Xu used to stand at the summit of Sam Mountain. In the early 19th century Siamese troops invaded the area and decided to take it back to Thailand. But as they carried the statue down the hill, it became heavier and heavier, and they were forced to abandon it by the side of the path.

One day some villagers who were cutting wood came upon the statue and decided to bring it back to their village in order to build a temple for it; but it weighed too much for them to budge it. Suddenly, a girl appeared who, possessed by a spirit, declared herself to be Lady Xu. She announced to them that nine virgins were to be brought and that they would be able to transport the statue down the mountainside. The virgins were then summoned and carried the statue down the slope, but when they reached the plain, it became too heavy and they had to set it down. The people concluded that the site where the virgins halted had been selected by Lady Xu for the temple construction and it's here that the Temple of Lady Xu stands to this day.

Offerings of roast whole pigs are frequently presented to the statue, which is dressed in glittering robes and adorned with an astonishing headdress. Once a month a creation of vegetables representing a dragon, tortoise, phoenix and *qilin* is also proffered to the effigy. The Chinese characters in the portal where worshippers pray are 主处聖母, which mean 'the main place of the sacred mother'. A further couplet reads 爲国爲民, which means 'for the country and for the people'. The temple's most important festival is held from the 23rd to the 26th day of the fourth lunar month, usually late May or early June. During this time, pilgrims flock here, sleeping on mats in the large rooms of the two-storey resthouse next to the temple.

Tomb of Thoai Ngoc Hau TOMB

(Lang Thoai Ngoc Hau; ⌚5am-10.30pm) A high-ranking official, Thoai Ngoc Hau (1761–1829) served the Nguyen Lords and, later, the Nguyen dynasty. In early 1829

Thoai Ngoc Hau ordered that a fine tomb be constructed for himself at the foot of Sam Mountain. The site he chose is nearly opposite the Temple of Lady Xu.

The steps are made of red 'beehive' stone *(da ong)* brought from the southeastern part of Vietnam. In the middle of the platform is the tomb of Thoai Ngoc Hau and those of his wives, Chau Thi Te and Truong Thi Miet. There's a shrine at the rear and several dozen other tombs in the vicinity where his officials are buried.

Getting There & Away

Many people get here by rented motorbike or on the back of a *xe om* (about 50,000d one way from Chau Doc). The most rewarding way to get here, however, is to rent a bicycle and to take the new road that runs towards the Cambodian border through peaceful rice paddy scenery.

Long Xuyen

076 / POP 255,000

The capital of An Giang province has little to detain travellers, especially since Can Tho and Chau Doc are an easy bus ride away. Long Xuyen was once a stronghold of the Hoa Hao sect. Founded in 1939, the sect emphasises simplicity in worship and does not believe in temples or intermediaries between humans and the Supreme Being. Until 1956 the Hoa Hao had an army and constituted a major military force in this region.

The town's other claim to fame is being the birthplace of Vietnam's second president, Ton Duc Thang. If you're a scholar of Vietnamese history, you can visit his birthplace and childhood home in My Hoa Hung village on Tiger Island by taking the ferry from **My Hoa Hung ferry port** (Ben Pha O Moi; Đ Nguyen Hue). The **Ton Duc Thang Museum** (Khu Luu Niem Bac Ton Duc Thang; off Đ Nguyen Hue; 7-11am & 1-5pm) FREE showcases the leg irons he wore when serving his 16 years in Con Dao prison for plotting against the French.

The **An Giang Museum** (Nha Bao Tang An Giang; 11 Ton Duc Thang; admission 15,000d; 7.30-11am & 1.30-5pm Tue-Sun) is also well worth a look for its collection of Oc-Eo artefacts, including pottery, fine gold jewellery and a giant phallus.

If overnight you must, large rooms with polished wooden floors, friendly service and a decent breakfast served on the roof terrace make **Hotel Hoa Binh 1** (076-385 7227; 130 Đ Tran Hung Dao; r from 350,000d;) a good option.

Hungry? Try the ultra-fresh fish and seafood served grilled and steamed with a variety of sauces at the professionally run **Lang**

Long Xuyen

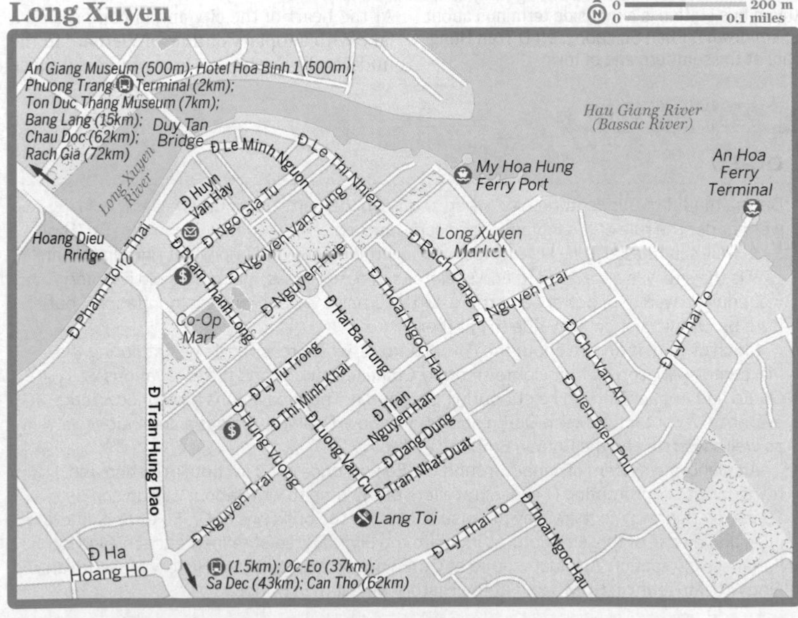

BUSES FROM LONG XUYEN

DESTINATION	COST (D)	DURATION (HR)	FREQUENCY	DISTANCE
Cao Lanh	60,000	1½	hourly	46km
Can Tho	105,000	1½	hourly	62km
Chau Doc	65,000-100,000	1½	hourly	62km
Ho Chi Minh City	125,000	5	hourly	187km
Rach Gia	130,000	2	hourly	72km

Toi (33 Đ Tran Nhat Duat; meals from 90,000d; ⌚11am-10pm).

Getting There & Away

BOAT

All buses bound for Ho Chi Minh City (passing by the Cao Lanh ferry dock) currently cross the river using ferries from the **An Hoa ferry terminal** (Pha An Hoa; Đ Ly Thai To).

BUS

The most comfortable buses to HCMC, Can Tho and Chau Doc are **Phuong Trang** (www.futaexpress.com) and **Hung Cuong** (www.hungcuonghotel.com); both depart from their own respective terminals. Phuong Trang terminal is around 2.5km north of central Long Xuyen; Hung Cuong office is about 1km south of the centre, on the main highway. All HCMC-bound buses take the car ferry across the river and pass by Pha Cao Lanh en route.

Long Xuyen Bus Station (Ben Xe Khach Long Xuyen; opposite 96/3b Đ Tran Hung Dao) Long Xuyen bus station is a roadside terminus about 1.5km down Đ Phan Cu Luong, off Đ Tran Hung Dao, at the southern end of town.

CAR & MOTORCYCLE

To get to Cao Lanh or Sa Dec you'll need to take the car ferry from An Hoa ferry terminal.

Cao Lanh

067 / POP 101,000

A newish town carved from the jungles and swamps of the Mekong Delta region, Cao Lanh is big for business, but draws few tourists; in fact, you may double the foreigner population just by turning up (the only other foreigner when we visited was teaching at the local college). Cao Lanh's main appeal is as a base to explore Rung Tram (Tram Forest) and Tram Chim National Park, both reachable by boat, but it's also a suprisingly walkable, pleasant city that's refreshingly untouristy.

Sights

Van Thanh Mieu PARK

At the heart of the city and encompassing a lake with a topiary outline of Vietnam in the middle, this lush park is a wonderful place

OFF THE BEATEN TRACK

OC-EO

During the 1st to 6th centuries AD, when southern Vietnam and southern Cambodia were under the rule of the Indian-influenced Cambodian kingdom of Funan, **Oc-Eo** (Hwy 943; 37km southwest of Long Xuyen) was a major trading city and important port. In the late 1990s the site was excavated to find skeletons in burial vases, elaborate gold jewellery, weaponry, a wealth of pottery and more. Little remains except building foundations, but it's a beautiful back-country ride to get there.

Much of what is known about the Funan empire, which reached its height during the 5th century AD, comes from contemporary Chinese sources and the excavations at Oc-Eo and Angkor Borei in neighbouring Cambodia. The excavations have uncovered evidence of contact between Oc-Eo and what is now Thailand, Malaysia and Indonesia, as well as Persia and the Roman Empire.

An elaborate system of canals around Oc-Eo was once used for both irrigation and transportation, prompting Chinese travellers of the time to write about 'sailing across Funan' on their way to the Malay peninsula. Most of the buildings of Oc-Eo were built on piles and pieces of these structures indicate the high degree of refinement achieved by Funanese civilisation. Artefacts found at Oc-Eo are on display at the History Museum and Fine Arts Museum in HCMC and at the History Museum in Hanoi.

Cao Lanh

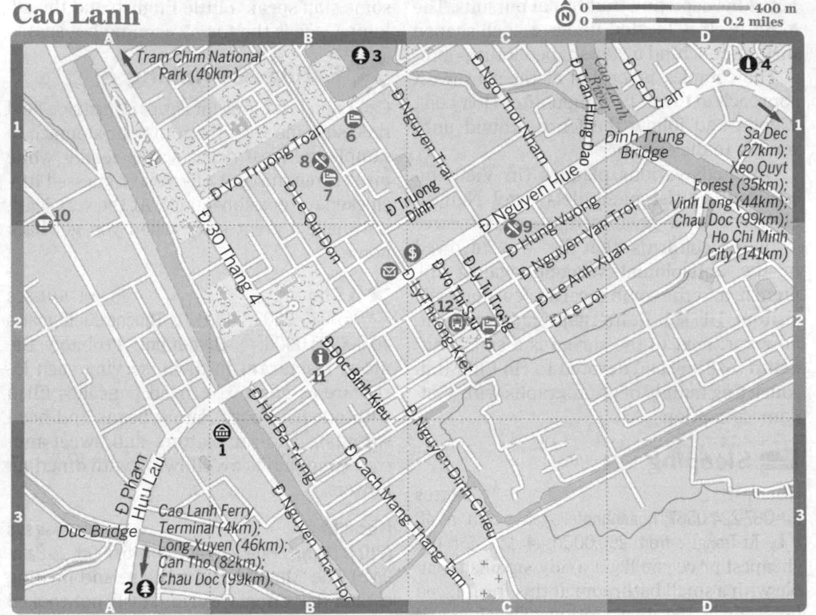

to observe local life: from early-morning exercise on the strange-looking contraptions to the twinkling lights after dark, when local lovers gather on the benches around the lake, staring at the water and keeping physical contact to a minimum.

Dong Thap Museum MUSEUM
(226 Đ Nguyen Thai Hoc; 7.30-11.30am & 1.30-5pm) FREE The Dong Thap Museum is among the Mekong's best museums, despite having no English captions. The ground floor displays an anthropological history of Dong Thap province, with exhibits of tools, sculpture, models of traditional houses and a few stuffed animals and pickled fish. Upstairs is devoted to war history and Ho Chi Minh.

War Martyrs Monument MONUMENT
On the eastern edge of town off Hwy 30, the War Memorial (Dai Liet Si) is Cao Lanh's most prominent landmark, a Socialist Realist–style sculpture featuring a large white concrete statue of a decorated soldier holding flowers in front of a stylised star. The rear of the statue is illustrated with storks, a symbol of the Mekong.

Within the grounds are the graves of 3112 VC who died fighting in the American War.

Cao Lanh

Sights
1 Dong Thap Museum ... B3
2 Tomb of Nguyen Sinh Sac ... A3
3 Van Thanh Mieu ... B1
4 War Martyrs Monument ... D1

Sleeping
5 Hoa Anh ... C2
6 Huong Sen Hotel ... B1
7 Nha Khach Dong Thap ... B1

Eating
8 A Chau ... B1
9 Ngoc Lan ... C2

Drinking & Nightlife
10 Cau Vua Coffee ... A1

Information
11 Dong Thap Tourist ... B2

Transport
12 Cao Lanh Bus Station ... C2

Tomb of Nguyen Sinh Sac PARK
(Lang Cu Nguyen Sinh Sac; off Đ Pham Huu Lau) The tomb of Ho Chi Minh's father, Nguyen Sinh Sac (1862–1929), is the centrepiece of a pretty 9.6-hectare park and model heritage village of wooden houses peopled by

manikins depicting traditional pursuits. The tomb itself is located under a shell-shaped shrine set behind a star-shaped lotus pond.

The complex is located at the southwest approach to town; turn right after Hoa Long Pagoda and follow the fence around until you get to the entrance.

Although various plaques (in Vietnamese) and tourist pamphlets extol Nguyen Sinh Sac as a great revolutionary, scarce evidence confirms that he was involved in the anticolonial struggle against the French, and the tomb receives few domestic visitors. His son more than made up for it, however: next to the shrine is a small **museum** (8am-5pm) devoted to Ho Chi Minh consisting mainly of photographs with Vietnamese captions.

Sleeping

Hoa Anh HOTEL $

(067-224 0567; hoaanhhotel@yahoo.com.vn; 40 Đ Ly Tu Trong; r from 250,000d;) For the cheapest price you'll get a tidy, smallish double with a small bathroom at this fresh-faced hotel near the bus station. The two-bed rooms are spacious, while the pricier rooms would fit a family.

Nha Khach Dong Thap HOTEL $

(067-387 2670; 48 Đ Ly Thuong Kiet; r from 400,000d;) A Communist Party special and a favourite with the army, with large, airy, OK rooms, a reception dripping in marble, and a quiet location, set back from the main street. However, very little English is spoken and it has an institutionalised feel.

Huong Sen Hotel BUSINESS HOTEL $$

(0128 294 5104; www.huongsenhoteldt.com; 18 Đ Vo Truong Toan; r 730,000d;) The smartest of Cao Lanh's lodgings, and the tallest building in town, Huong Sen overlooks the park. Rooms are compact but comfortable, some staff speak a little English and the adjoning cafe is the town's evening hot spot.

Eating & Drinking

Cao Lanh is famous for *chuot dong* (rice-field rats) so come with room in your stomach to sample the local delicacy; the tender white meat is reminiscent of – you've guessed it! – chicken (or possibly quail). At the very least, it'll make a great story when you get back home.

★**A Chau** VIETNAMESE $

(067-385 2202; 42 Đ Ly Thuong Kiet; mains 40,000-95,000d; 11am-10pm) Probably the nicest restaurant in town, serving such local fare as *banh xeo* (fried pancakes filled with crayfish, pork, mung beans and bean sprouts), field-rat platters and sweet-and-sour soup that is overflowing with dingding flowers.

Ngoc Lan VIETNAMESE $

(210 Đ Nguyen Hue; dishes from 45,000d; 8am-9pm) The 'Magnolia' is a bright and inviting choice, that offers fresh and tasty pot-cooked pork and mixed-vegetable soup. It's illuminated with a red-and-green LED sign at night.

Cau Vua Coffee COFFEE

(cnr Nguyen Thi Luu & Thien Ho Duong; 7.30am-9pm) With a leafy courtyard, comfy chairs on the patio and a tranquil water feature, this is one of the nicest cafes to savour a *ca phe sua da* (iced coffee with condensed milk).

Information

Dong Thap Tourist (067-387 3026; www.dongthaptourist.com; 2 Đ Doc Binh Kieu; 7-11.30am & 1.30-5pm) A friendly, helpful outfit that can arrange rather pricey boat and other tours of the surrounding area.

Main Post Office (85 Đ Nguyen Hue)

Vietinbank (067-382 2030; Đ Nguyen Hue) You can also exchange cash here.

BUSES FROM CAO LANH

DESTINATION	COST (D)	DURATION (HR)	FREQUENCY	DISTANCE
Can Tho	50,000	2¼	daily	82km
Chau Doc	100,000	3½	hourly	99km
HCMC	100,000	3½	every 30min	141km
Long Xuyen	60,000	2	hourly	46km
Sa Dec	13,000	45min	several daily	27km
Vinh Long	30,000	1¼	several daily	44km

Getting There & Away

While there are no direct services to Chau Doc from Cao Lanh, comfortable sleeper buses from HCMC to Chau Doc (via Long Xuyen) pass the **Cao Lanh Ferry Terminal** (Pha Cao Lanh) along the main road across the river from the town at least hourly. If possible, reserve your seat in advance with Phuong Trang at the Cao Lanh bus station, take a *xe om* to the passenger ferry, cross the river and wait. Sa Dec–bound services take you as far as the ferry; you connect to a different bus across the river.

BUS

Cao Lanh Bus Station (Ben Xe Cao Lanh; 71/1 Đ Ly Thuong Kiet) Conveniently located in the centre of town.

Around Cao Lanh

Sights

★Xeo Quyt Forest NATURE RESERVE
(Xeo Quyt, Xeo Quit; admission 5000d; 7am-4.30pm) Around 35km southeast of Cao Lanh is the magnificent 52-hectare Xeo Quyt Forest near My Hiep village. One vast swamp beneath a beautiful thick canopy of tall trees and vines, it hides the remains of Viet Cong bunkers, which can be seen both on a canoe tour inside the forest and on foot along the walking trails.

A taxi from Cao Lanh, including waiting time, costs around 800,000d.

For much of the year, a marvellous 20-minute **canoe tour** (15,000d) takes you past old bunkers and former mine fields along a narrow canal loop beneath the forest canopy and choked with water hyacinths *(luc binh)*. It's an exquisite experience but splash on the repellent. A walking trail parallels the canal and allows you to duck into the Z- and L-shaped Viet Cong bunkers (if you're compact enough) and to admire the expertly hidden, tiny trapdoors through which the Viet Cong disappeared underground.

During the American War the VC had a base here, where top-brass VC lived in underground bunkers. Only about 10 VC were here at any given time; they were all generals who directed the war from here, just 2km from a US military base. The Americans never realised that the VC generals were living right under their noses. Naturally, they were suspicious about that patch of forest and periodically dropped some bombs on it to reassure themselves, but the VC remained safe in their hideouts.

Tram Chim National Park NATURE RESERVE
(7am-4pm) Tram Chim National Park is situated around 40km due north of Cao Lanh and is notable for its rare red-headed cranes *(Grus antigone sharpii)*, though more than 220 species of bird live within the reserve.

The cranes nest here from about December to May; from June to November they migrate to northwest Cambodia. Seeing them requires a considerable commitment (time, effort and money), with Dong Thap Tourist organising expensive trips by car and small boat (5,000,000d); it's cheaper to go if you make friends with locals.

Sa Dec

067 / POP 77,000

The drowsy former capital of Dong Thap province, Sa Dec is a comparatively peaceful city of tree-lined streets and fading colonial villas, ringed with orchards and flower markets. You can visit the **nurseries** (Vuon Hoa; 7am-5pm) FREE lining the river and canals a short *xe om* ride (30,000d) out of the centre. The town is particularly famous for its roses; the best time to visit is just before Tet, to watch a riot of flowers loaded onto boats.

The town's biggest attraction (though it'll only take up about 20 minutes of your time) is the **Huynh Thuy Le Old House** (Nha Co Huynh Thuy Le; 0939 533 523; 225a Đ Nguyen Hue; admission 30,000d; 8am-5pm), a wonderfully atmospheric 1895 residence on the riverfront that was once the residence of Huynh Thuy Le, the 27-year-old son of a rich Chinese family who Marguerite Duras had an affair with in 1929 when she was only 15 – she immortalised the romance in the semi-autobiographical novel, *The Lover*, which was eventually made into a film by Jean-Jacques Annaud. The house is a Sino-French design with intricate interior woodwork, mother-of-pearl inlaid doors, heavy wooden furniture and original floor tiles, made in France. In the entrance hall there are photos of the Le family, as well as those of Marguerite Duras herself, and stills from the film.

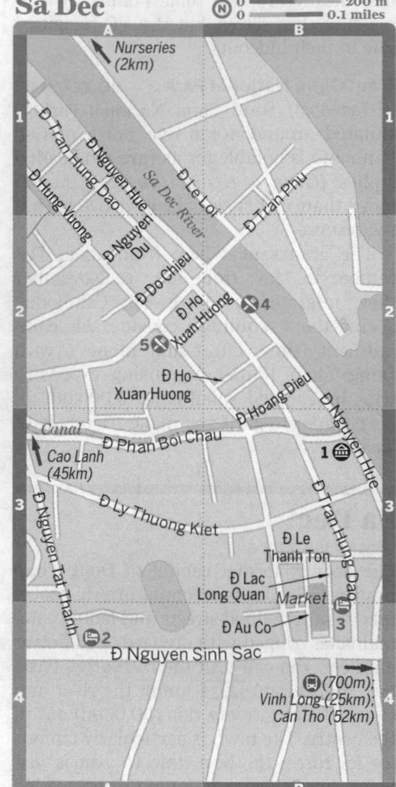

Sa Dec

Sights

1 Huynh Thuy Le Old House.......B3

Sleeping

2 Phuong Nam.......A4

3 Thao Ngan Hotel.......B4

Eating

4 Night Market.......B2

5 Quan Com Thuy.......A2

Sleeping & Eating

Thao Ngan Hotel HOTEL $

(067-377 4255; 4 An Duong Vuong; r 350,000d;) The cleanest and nicest of the local hotels, this one is very centrally located near the market and one of the receptionists speaks good English.

Phuong Nam HOTEL $

(067-386 7867; www.khachsanphuongnam.com; 384a Đ Nguyen Sinh Sac; r 180,000-370,000d;) This decent minihotel is situated on the main road.

Night Market VIETNAMESE $

(Đ Nguyen Hue; meals around 50,000d; 5-10pm) The hopping night market that is situated riverside has a lively string of hotpot restaurants come evening, as well as stalls that sell all manner of grilled things.

Quan Com Thuy VIETNAMESE $

(067-386 1644; 439 Đ Hung Vuong; mains 50,000-90,000d; 9am-9pm) This reputable meat-and-rice joint offers aluminium furniture, bright lights and a menu filled with the local specialities, such as claypot eel with rice.

Getting There & Away

From the **bus station** (Ben Xe Sa Dec; Hwy 80) behind the hospital, frequent buses leave for Ho Chi Minh City (58,000d to 95,000d, 3½ hours, hourly), Vinh Long (15,000d, one hour, several daily) and Cao Lanh (13,000d, 45 minutes, several daily). Some of the latter may drop you at the Cao Lanh ferry port across the river from town.

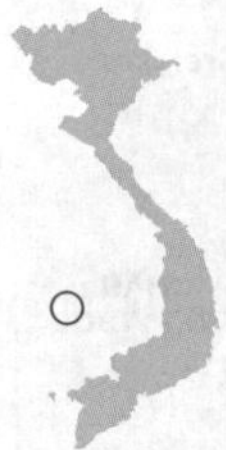

Siem Reap & the Temples of Angkor (Cambodia)

Includes ➡

Best Temples

➡ Angkor Wat (p426)
➡ Bayon (p431)
➡ Ta Prohm (p432)
➡ Banteay Srei (p432)
➡ Beng Mealea (p432)

Best Eating & Drinking

➡ Marum (p422)
➡ Cuisine Wat Damnak (p423)
➡ Haven (p422)
➡ Charlie's (p423)
➡ Laundry Bar (p423)

Why Go?

Where to begin with Angkor? There is no greater concentration of architectural riches anywhere on earth. Choose from the world's largest religious building, Angkor Wat; one of the world's weirdest, Bayon; or the riotous jungle of Ta Prohm. All are global icons and have helped put Cambodia on the map as the temple capital of Asia. Today, the monuments are a point of pilgrimage for all Khmers, and no traveller to the region will want to miss their expressive architecture.

Siem Reap was always destined for great things and offers everything from backpacker party pads to hip hotels, world-class wining and dining, and sumptuous spas.

Despite the headline act that is Angkor and the sophistication of Siem Reap, Cambodia's greatest treasure is its people. The Khmers have been to hell and back, but they have prevailed with a smile and no visitor comes away from this kingdom without a measure of admiration and affection for its inhabitants.

When to Go

Siem Reap

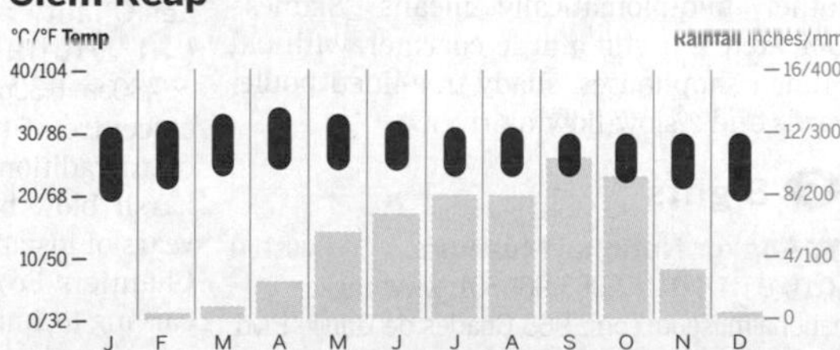

Nov–Feb Humidity is low, there are cool breezes and little rain. Peak season for visitors.

Mar–Jun Temperatures rise and in May or June the monsoon brings rain and humidity.

Jul–Oct The wet season: Angkor is surrounded by lush foliage and the moats are full of water.

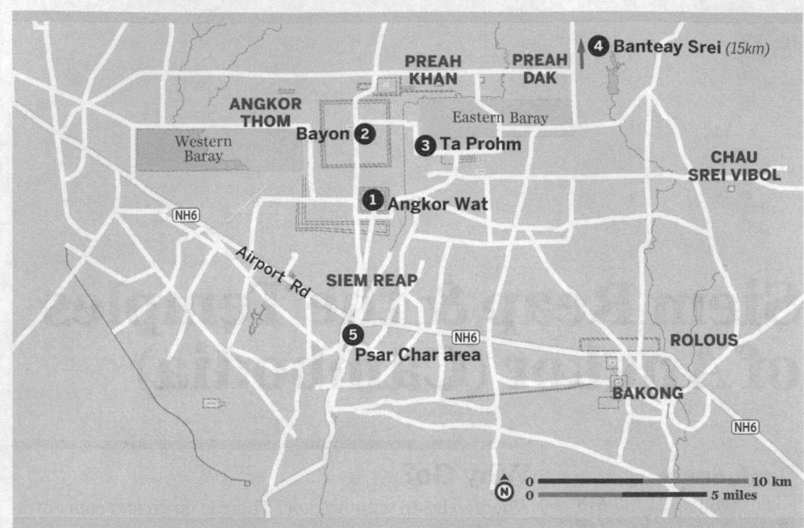

Siem Reap & the Temples of Angkor Highlights

1. Seeing the sun rise over one of the world's most iconic buildings, the one and only **Angkor Wat** (p426).
2. Contemplating the serenity and splendour of **Bayon** (p431), with its 216 enigmatic faces staring out into the jungle.
3. Witnessing nature running riot at the mysterious ruin of **Ta Prohm** (p432), the *Tomb Raider* temple.
4. Staring in wonder at the delicate carvings adorning **Banteay Srei** (p432), the finest seen at Angkor.
5. Exploring the **Psar Chaa** (Old Market) area (p422) of Siem Reap, home to the funkiest restaurants and bars in town.

SIEM REAP

☎063 / POP 175,000

Life-support system for the temples of Angkor, Siem Reap (pronounced see-em ree-ep) is part of the new, cool Cambodia, a pulsating place that's one of the most popular destinations on the planet right now. At its heart though, Siem Reap – whose name rather undiplomatically means 'Siamese Defeated' – is still a little charmer, with old French shophouses, shady tree-lined boulevards and a slow-flowing river.

Sights

★Angkor National Museum MUSEUM

(សារមន្ទីរអង្គរ; ☎063-966601; www.angkornationalmuseum.com; 968 Charles de Gaulle Blvd; adult/child under 1.2m US$12/6; ⏲8.30am-6pm, to 6.30pm Oct-Apr) Looming large on the road to Angkor is the Angkor National Museum, a state-of-the-art showpiece on the Khmer civilisation and the majesty of Angkor. Displays are themed by era, religion and royalty as visitors move through the impressive galleries. After a short presentation, visitors enter the Zen-like 'Gallery of a Thousand Buddhas', which has an excellent collection of images. Other exhibits include the pre-Angkorian periods of Funan and Chenla; the Khmer kings; Angkor Wat; Angkor Thom; and the inscriptions.

Artisans Angkor – Les Chantiers Écoles ARTS CENTRE

(អា ទីសង់អង្គរ; www.artisansdangkor.com; ⏲7.30am-6.30pm) FREE Siem Reap is the epicentre of the drive to revitalise Cambodian traditional culture, which was dealt a harsh blow by the Khmer Rouge and the years of instability that followed its rule. Les Chantiers Écoles teaches wood- and stone-carving techniques, traditional silk painting, lacquerware and other artisan skills to impoverished young Cambodians. Free guided tours explaining traditional techniques are available daily from 7.30am to 6.30pm. Tucked down a side road, the school is well signposted from Sivatha St.

Cambodia Landmine Museum MUSEUM
សារមន្ទីរគ្រាប់មីនកម្ពុជា និងមូលនិធិសង្គ្រោះ;
(☎ 012 598951; www.cambodialandminemuseum.org; donation US$3; ⏲ 7.30am-5pm) Established by DIY de-miner Aki Ra, this museum has excellent displays on the curse of landmines in Cambodia. The collection includes mines, mortars, guns and weaponry, and there is a mock minefield where visitors can attempt to locate the deactivated mines. Proceeds from the museum are ploughed into mine-awareness campaigns. The museum is about 25km from Siem Reap, near Banteay Srei.

Cambodian Cultural Village CULTURAL CENTRE
(☎ 063-963836; www.cambodianculturalvillage.com; Airport Rd; adult/child under 1.1m US$9/free; ⏲ 8am-7pm) It may be kitsch, it may be kooky, but it's very popular with Cambodians and provides a diversion for families travelling with children. This is the Cambodian Cultural Village, which tries to represent all of Cambodia in a whirlwind tour of re-created houses and villages. The visit begins with a wax museum and includes homes of the Cham, Chinese, Kreung and Khmer people, as well as miniature replicas of landmark buildings in Cambodia.

Angkor Centre for Conservation of Biodiversity WILDLIFE RESERVE
(ACCB; www.accb-cambodia.org; donation US$3; ⏲ tours 9am & 1pm Mon-Sat) Conveniently located near the base of the trail to Kbal Spean is the Angkor Centre for Conservation of Biodiversity, committed to rescuing, rehabilitating and reintroducing threatened wildlife to the Cambodian forests. Tours of the centre are available daily at 9am and 1pm, taking about 90 minutes. The 9am tour is the better option as animals are fed at this time and are more lively than during the heat of the day in the afternoon.

Activities

There is an incredible array of activities on offer in Siem Reap, including Flight of the Gibbon Angkor (p422), a zipline adventure through the jungle.

KKO (Khmer for Khmer Organisation) Bike Tours BICYCLE TOUR
(☎ 093 903024; www.kko-cambodia.org; cnr St 20 & Wat Bo Rd; tours US$35-50) Good-cause cycling tours around the paths of Angkor or into the countryside beyond the Western Baray. Proceeds go towards the Khmer for Khmer Organisation, which supports education and vocational training.

Cambodia Vespa Adventures TOUR
(☎ 012 861610; www.cambodiavespaadventures.com; tours per person from US$60-99) The modern Vespa is a cut above the average *moto* and is a comfortable way to explore the temples, learn about local life in the countryside or check out some street food after dark, all in the company of excellent and knowledgeable local guides.

Quad Adventure Cambodia ADVENTURE TOUR
(☎ 092 787216; www.quad-adventure-cambodia.com; sunset ride US$30, full day US$170) The original quad-bike operator in town. Rides around Siem Reap involve rice fields at sunset, pretty temples, and back roads through traditional villages.

Bodia Spa SPA
(☎ 063-761593; www.bodia-spa.com; Pithnou St; ⏲ 10am-midnight) Sophisticated spa near Psar Chaa offering a full range of scrubs, rubs and natural remedies, including its own line of herbal products.

Cooks in Tuk Tuks COOKING COURSE
(☎ 063-963400; www.therivergarden.info; River Rd West; per person US$25) Starts at 10am daily with a visit to Psar Leu market, then returns to the River Garden for a professional class.

Angkor Golf Resort GOLF
(☎ 063-761139; www.angkor-golf.com; green fees US$115) This world-class course was designed by British golfer Nick Faldo. Fees rise to US$175 with clubs, caddies, carts and all.

CAMBODIA FAST FACTS

Area 181,035 sq km

Border Crossings with Vietnam Seven

Capital Phnom Penh

Phone Country Code ☎ 855

Head of State King Sihamoni

Population 16 million

Money US$1 = 4000r (riel)

National Holiday Chaul Chnam or Khmer New Year, mid-April

Phrases *sua s'dei* (hello), *lia suhn hao-y* (goodbye), *aw kohn* (thank you)

Siem Reap

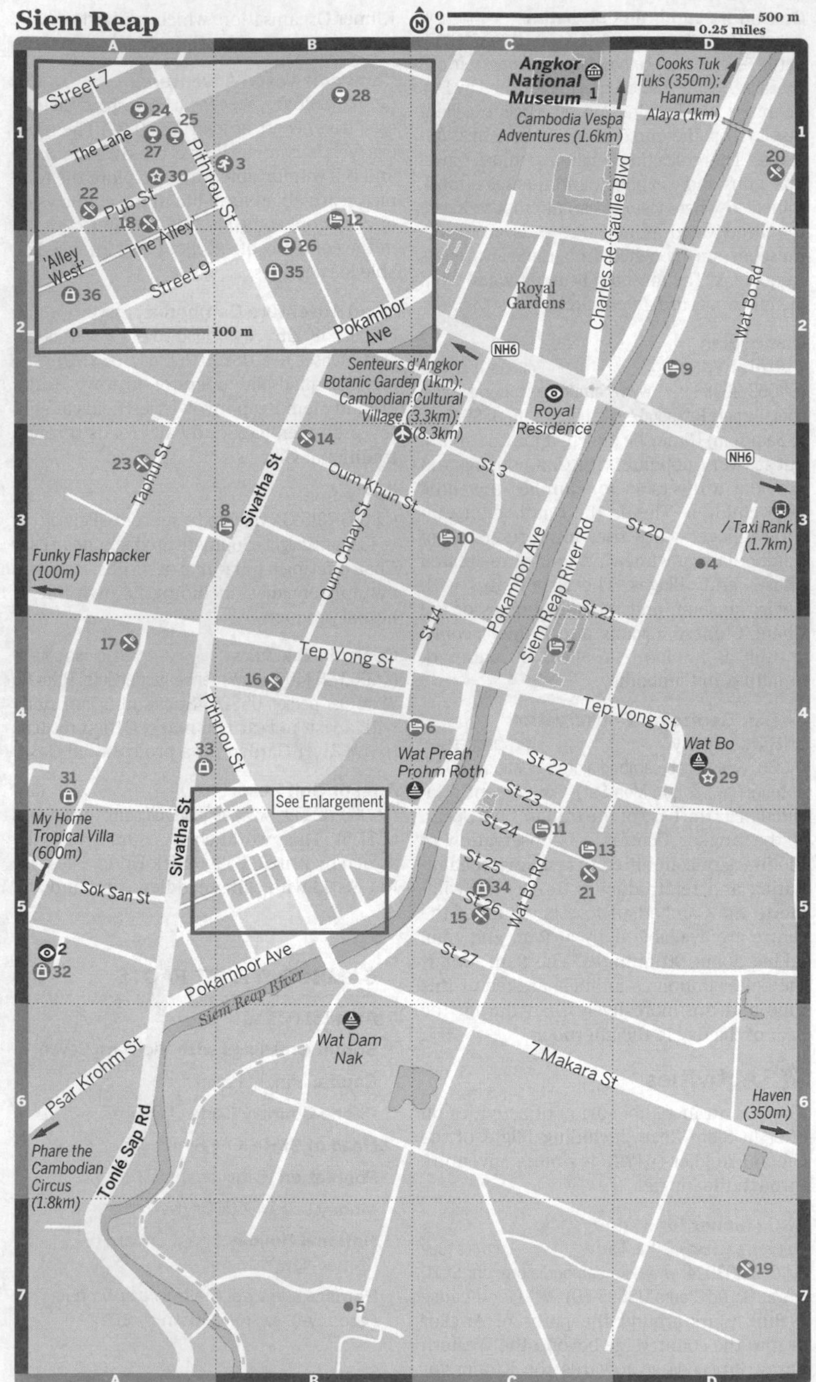
0 500 m
0 0.25 miles
Angkor National Museum
Cambodia Vespa Adventures (1.6km)
Cooks Tuk Tuks (350m); Hanuman Alaya (1km)
Street 7
The Lane
Pithnou St
Pub St
'The Alley'
'Alley West'
Street 9
Pokambor Ave
0 100 m
Royal Gardens
Charles de Gaulle Blvd
Wat Bo Rd
NH6
Senteurs d'Angkor Botanic Garden (1km); Cambodian Cultural Village (3.3km); (8.3km)
Royal Residence
Taphul St
Sivatha St
Oum Khun St
St 3
Oum Chhay St
St 20
/ Taxi Rank (1.7km)
Funky Flashpacker (100m)
Pokambor Ave
Siem Reap River Rd
St 21
St 14
Tep Vong St
Tep Vong St
Wat Preah Prohm Roth
Wat Bo
St 22
St 23
St 24
St 25
St 26
St 27
See Enlargement
My Home Tropical Villa (600m)
Sok San St
Siem Reap River
Wat Dam Nak
Psar Krohm St
7 Makara St
Haven (350m)
Phare the Cambodian Circus (1.8km)
Tonlé Sap Rd

Siem Reap

Top Sights

1 Angkor National Museum C1

Sights

2 Artisans Angkor – Les Chantiers Écoles A5

Activities, Courses & Tours

3 Bodia Spa B1
4 KKO (Khmer for Khmer Organisation) Bike Tours D3
5 Quad Adventure Cambodia B7

Sleeping

6 Ivy Guesthouse 2 .... C4
7 La Résidence d'Angkor C4
8 Mad Monkey B3
9 Rosy Guesthouse D2
10 Shinta Mani C3
11 Soria Moria Hotel C5
12 Steung Siem Reap Hotel B1
13 Viroth's Hotel C5

Eating

14 Angkor Market B3
15 Banllé Vegetarian Restaurant C5
16 Blossom Cafe B4
17 Bugs Cafe A4
18 Cambodian BBQ A1
19 Cuisine Wat Damnak D7
20 Marum D1
21 Pages Cafe C5
22 Red Piano A1
23 Sugar Palm A3

Drinking & Nightlife

24 Asana A1
25 Charlie's A1
26 Laundry Bar B2
27 Miss Wong A1
28 YOLO Bar B1

Entertainment

29 Plae Pakaa D4
30 Temple Club A1

Shopping

31 Angkor Night Market A4
32 Artisans Angkor A5
33 Rajana A4
34 Samatoa C5
35 Senteurs d'Angkor B2
36 Smateria A2

Sleeping

Siem Reap offers everything from cheap shacks with dorms to five-star luxury palaces.

★ Ivy Guesthouse 2 GUESTHOUSE $
(☎012 800860; www.ivy-guesthouse.com; Psar Kandal St; r US$6-15; ❄@☜) An inviting guesthouse with a chill-out area and bar, the Ivy is a lively place to stay. The restaurant is good, with a huge vegetarian selection and US$1 'Tapas Fridays'.

Mad Monkey HOSTEL $
(www.madmonkeyhostels.com; Sivatha St; dm US$7-9, r US$16-26; ❄@☜) The Siem Reap outpost of an expanding Monkey business, this is a classic backpacker crashpad with several dorms, good-value rooms for those wanting privacy, and the obligatory rooftop bar, only this one's a beach bar!

Funky Flashpacker HOSTEL $
(☎070 221524; www.funkyflashpacker.com; Funky Lane; dm US$7, r US$16-35; ❄@☜≋) This upscale backpackers has a funky vibe – the entire downstairs courtyard is taken up with a swimming pool where regular bouts of water polo take place. A great hostel, but not ideal for recovering partyholics as there's always a buzz about the place.

Rosy Guesthouse GUESTHOUSE $
(☎063-965059; www.rosyguesthouse.com; Siem Reap River Rd; r US$9-35; ❄☜) A Brit-run establishment whose 13 rooms come with TV and DVD. The lively pub downstairs has great grub and hosts regular events to support community causes, including a popular quiz night.

★ Soria Moria Hotel BOUTIQUE HOTEL $$
(☎063-964768; www.thesoriamoria.com; Wat Bo Rd; r US$39-63; ❄@☜≋) A hotel with a heart, promoting local causes to help the community, this boutique place has attractive rooms with smart bathroom fittings. There's a fusion restaurant downstairs, sky hot-tub upstairs and a new swimming pool. Half the hotel was transferred to staff ownership in 2011, a visionary move.

Viroth's Hotel BOUTIQUE HOTEL $$
(☎063-766107; www.viroth-hotel.com; St 24; r from US$86; ❄@☜≋) The new Viroth's is an ultra-stylish, retro-chic property with 30 rooms fitted out with classy contemporary furnishings. Behind the impressive facade lies a 30m swimming pool, a gym and a spa. The original seven-bedroom hotel is still operating as Viroth's Villa.

HanumanAlaya BOUTIQUE HOTEL $$
(☎063-760582; www.hanumanalaya.com; 5 Krom 2, Phoum Treang, just off Charles de Gaulle Blvd; r US$60-100; ❄@📶🏊) The most traditionally Cambodian of the boutique hotels in town, HanumanAlaya is set around a lush garden and pretty swimming pool. Rooms are decorated with antiques and handicrafts but include modern touches such as flat-screen TV, minibar and safe.

Steung Siem Reap Hotel HOTEL $$
(☎063-965167; www.steungsiemreaphotel.com; near Psar Chaa; r from US$65; ❄@📶🏊) In keeping with the French colonial-era legacy around Psar Chaa, this hotel has high ceilings, louvre shutters and wrought-iron balconies. Three-star rooms feature smart wooden trim. The location is hard to beat.

★**La Résidence d'Angkor** RESORT $$$
(☎063-963390; www.residencedangkor.com; Siem Reap River Rd; r from US$220; ❄@📶🏊) The 54 wood-appointed rooms, among the most tasteful and inviting in town, come with verandas and huge Jacuzzi-sized tubs. The gorgeous swimming pool is perfect for laps. The newer wing is ultra-contemporary, as is the sumptuous Kong Kea Spa.

Shinta Mani RESORT $$$
(☎063-761998; www.shintamani.com; Oum Khun St; r US$140-305; ❄@📶🏊) 🍃 With a contemporary chic design by renowned architect Bill Bensley, Shinta Mani Resort features an inviting central pool, while Shinta Mani Club offers more exclusive rooms. Shinta Mani has won several international awards for responsible tourism practices and hosts a regular 'Well Made in Cambodia' market.

FLIGHT OF THE GIBBON ANGKOR

Angkor is the ultimate backdrop for a zipline experience in Asia, although you won't actually see the temples while navigating the course. **Flight of the Gibbon Angkor** (☎096 9999101; www.treetopasia.com; near Ta Nei Temple, Angkor; per person US$109; ⏲7am-5pm) is inside the Angkor protected area and the course includes 10 ziplines, 21 treetop platforms, four skybridges and an abseil finish. A conservation element is included in the project with a family of gibbons released in the surrounding forest. The price includes a transfer to/from any Siem Reap hotel, plus a lunch before or after the trip near Sra Srang.

Eating

Noteworthy restaurants are sprinkled all around town but Siem Reap's culinary heart is the Psar Chaa area, whose focal point, the Alley, is literally lined with mellow eateries offering great atmosphere.

There are some good restaurants that support worthy causes or help train Cambodia's future hospitality staff with a subsidised ticket into the tourism industry.

For self-caterers, markets have fresh produce. **Angkor Market** (Sivatha St) has international treats such as olives and cheeses.

★**Marum** INETRNATIONAL $
(www.marum-restaurant.org; Wat Polanka area; mains US$3.25-6.75; ⏲11am-10pm Mon-Sat; 📶🖉) 🍃 Set in a delightful wooden house with a spacious garden, Marum serves up lots of vegetarian and seafood dishes, plus some mouth-watering desserts. Menu highlights include red-tree-ant fritters and ginger basil meatballs. Marum is part of the Tree Alliance group of training restaurants; the experience is a must.

★**Haven** FUSION $
(☎078 342404; www.haven-cambodia.com; Chocolate Rd; mains US$3-7; ⏲11.30am-2.30pm & 5.30-9.30pm Mon-Sat; 📶) 🍃 A culinary haven indeed, dine here for the best of east meets west; the fish fillet with green mango is particularly zesty. Proceeds go towards helping young adult orphans make the step from institution to employment. It recently relocated to the Wat Dam Nak area, just near Angkor High School.

Bugs Cafe INSECTS $
(☎017 764560; www.bugs-cafe.com; Steung Thmei St; US$2-8; ⏲5pm-midnight; 📶) Cambodians were on to insects long before the food scientists started bugging us about the merits of critters. Choose from a veritable feast of crickets, water bugs, silkworms and spiders. Bee cream soup, feta and tarantula samosas, and pan-fried scorpions – you won't forget this menu in a hurry.

Blossom Cafe CAFE $
(www.blossomcakes.org; St 6; cupcakes US$1.50; ⏲10am-5pm Mon-Sat; 📶) 🍃 Cupcakes are elevated to an art form at this elegant cafe, with beautiful creations available in a rotating array of 48 flavours. Creative coffees, teas

HEARTBEAT OF CAMBODIA

The largest freshwater lake in Southeast Asia, Tonlé Sap is an incredible natural phenomenon that provides fish and irrigation water for half of Cambodia's population.

The lake is linked to the Mekong at Phnom Penh by a 100km-long channel, the Tonlé Sap River. From June to October (the wet season), rains raise the level of the Mekong, backing up the Tonlé Sap River and causing it to flow northwest into the Tonlé Sap Lake. During this period, the lake swells from 2500 sq km to 13,000 sq km or more, its maximum depth increasing from about 2.2m to more than 10m. Around the start of October, as the water level of the Mekong begins to fall, the Tonlé Sap River reverses its flow, draining the waters of the lake back into the Mekong.

This extraordinary process makes the Tonlé Sap one of the world's richest sources of freshwater fish and an ideal habitat for waterbirds.

The Tonlé Sap is located just 11km from Siem Reap town. It is possible to visit the floating village of Chong Kneas, and the stilted village and flooded forests of Kompong Pluk, as half-day trips. Or you can visit Prek Toal Bird Sanctuary as a long day trip from Siem Reap.

and juices are also on offer and profits assist Cambodian women in vocational training.

Pages Cafe CAFE $

(☎092 966812; www.pages-siemreap.com; St 24; US$2-6; ⏲6am-10pm; 📶) This hip little hideaway is no longer so hidden with the new Viroth's Hotel opposite. Exposed brickwork and designer decor make it a good place to linger over the excellent breakfasts or light tapas bites. On Saturdays it offers an outdoor grill with and pool access. Rooms also available.

Banllé Vegetarian Restaurant VEGETARIAN $

(☎085 330160; www.banlle-vegetarian.com; St 26; US$2-4; ⏲9am-9.30pm, closed Tue; 📶🖉) Set in a traditional wooden house with its own vegetable garden, this is a great place for a healthy bite. The menu offers international and Cambodian dishes, including a vegetable *amoc*, and zesty fruit and vegetable shakes.

Sugar Palm CAMBODIAN $$

(www.sugarpalmrestaurant.com; Taphul St; mains US$5-9; ⏲11.30am-3pm & 5.30-10pm Mon-Sat; 📶) Set in a beautiful wooden house, the Sugar Palm is the place to sample traditional flavours, including delicious *char kreung* (curried lemongrass) dishes. Owner Kethana showed celebrity chef Gordon Ramsay how to prepare *amoc* (baked fish).

Red Piano ASIAN, INTERNATIONAL $$

(www.redpianocambodia.com; Pub St; mains US$3-10; 📶) Set in a restored colonial gem, Red Piano has a big balcony for watching the action unfold below. The menu has a selection of Asian and international food, all at decent prices. Former celebrity guest Angelina Jolie has a cocktail named in her honour.

Cambodian BBQ BARBECUE $$

(www.restaurant-siemreap.com/html/cambodianbbq.php; The Alley; mains US$5-9; ⏲11am-11pm; 📶) Crocodile, snake, ostrich and kangaroo meat add an exotic twist to the traditional *phnom pleung* (hill of fire) grills. Cambodian BBQ has spawned half a dozen or more copycats in the surrounding streets, many of which offer discount specials.

★**Cuisine Wat Damnak** CAMBODIAN $$$

(www.cuisinewatdamnak.com; Wat Dam Nak village; 5-course menu US$24, 6-course menu US$28; ⏲6.30-10.30pm Tue-Sat, last orders 9.30pm) Set in a traditional wooden house is this highly regarded restaurant from Siem Reap celeb chef Joannes Riviere. The menu delivers a contemporary Khmer dining experience. Seasonal set menus focus on market-fresh ingredients and change weekly; vegetarian options are available with advance notice.

Drinking

Siem Reap is now firmly on Southeast Asia's nightlife map, with many of the most interesting places situated in the vicinity of Psar Chaa, on or near Pub St.

★**Charlie's** BAR

(www.charliessiemreap.com; 98 Pithnou St; ⏲10am-1am; 📶) A cracking retro Americana bar with cheap drinks and a convivial crowd. This is the missing link between the more sophisticated bars around the alleyways and the madness unfolding nightly on Pub St. Food optional, shots obligatory.

★**Laundry Bar** BAR

(St 9; ⏲4pm-late; 📶) One of the most chilled bars in town thanks to low lighting and discerning decor, this is the place to come for electronica and ambient sounds. It heaves on weekends or when guest DJs crank up the volume. Happy hour until 9pm.

Miss Wong BAR
(www.misswong.net; The Lane; 5pm-late;) Miss Wong carries you back to the chic of 1920s Shanghai. The cocktails are a draw here, making it a cool place to while away an evening, with a new menu offering dim sum. Gay-friendly and extremely popular with the well-heeled expat crowd.

Asana BAR
(www.asana-cambodia.com; The Lane; 11am-late;) Also known as the wooden house, this is a traditional Cambodian countryside home dropped into the backstreets of Siem Reap, which makes for an atmospheric place to drink. Lounge on *capok* (fibre)-filled rice sacks over a classic cocktail made with infused rice wine. Khmer cocktail classes with Sombai spirits available at US$15 per person.

YOLO Bar BAR
(Wat Prohm Roth St; 5pm-late;) A popular backpacker bar down a side street, YOLO specialises in cheap cocktails by the bucketload (quite literally) and DIY tunes played through its open table laptop. Give it a try... after all, you only live once.

DON'T MISS

ROLL UP, ROLL UP, THE CIRCUS HAS COME TO TOWN

Cambodia's answer to Cirque du Soleil, **Phare the Cambodian Circus** (015 499480; www.pharecambodiancircus.org; west end of Sok San Rd; adult/child US$18/10, premium seats US$35/18; 8pm daily) is so much more than a conventional circus, with an emphasis on performance art. Phare Ponleu Selpak, Cambodia's leading circus, theatre and performing arts organisation, stages nightly shows at its big top and several past stars have gone on to perform in international shows around the world. It's an inspiring night out for adults and children alike and Phare reinvests all proceeds into Phare Ponleu Selpak activities. Animal lovers will be pleased to note there are no animals used in any performance.

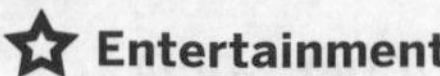

Entertainment

Classical dance shows take place all over town, but only a few are worth considering.

Plae Pakaa PERFORMING ARTS
(099 516580; www.cambodianlivingarts.org; Artisans Angkor - Les Chantiers Écoles; adult/child US$15/6; 7pm Mon-Sat) Plae Pakaa is a series of traditional dance performances hosted by the talented dancers of Cambodian Living Arts. Originating in Phnom Penh, the show now runs at Artisans Angkor during high season from November to the end of March, but there may also be a reduced schedule during the low season.

Temple Club DANCE
(Pub St;) Temple Club stages a free traditional dance show upstairs from 7.30pm, providing punters order some food and drink from the reasonably priced menu.

Shopping

Siem Reap has an excellent selection of Cambodian-made handicrafts. Psar Chaa is well stocked with anything you may want to buy in Cambodia, and lots you don't. There are bargains to be had if you haggle patiently and humorously. **Angkor Night Market** (www.angkornightmarket.com; 4pm-midnight) is packed with silks, handicrafts and souvenirs. Up-and-coming Alley West is also a great strip to browse.

A number of shops support Cambodia's disabled and disenfranchised.

Artisans Angkor ARTS & CRAFTS
(www.artisansdangkor.com; 7.30am-6.30pm) On the premises of Les Chantiers Écoles (p418) is this beautiful shop, which sells everything from stone and wood reproductions of Angkorian-era statues to household furnishings. There's also a second shop opposite Angkor Wat in the Angkor Cafe building, and outlets at Phnom Penh and Siem Reap international airports.

Rajana ARTS & CRAFTS
(063-964744; www.rajanacrafts.org; Sivatha St; 9am-9pm Mon-Sat) Sells quirky wooden and metalwork objects, well-designed silver jewellery and handmade cards. Rajana promotes fair-trade employment opportunities for Cambodians.

Samatoa CLOTHING
(063-965310; www.samatoa.com; St 26; 8am-11pm) If you find yourself in need of a party frock, this designer dress shop offers

original threads in silk, with the option of a tailored fit in 48 hours. Samatoa employs fair-trade practices.

Senteurs d'Angkor HANDICRAFTS
(063-964860; Pithnou St; 8.30am-9.30pm) Opposite Psar Chaa, this shop has an eclectic collection of silk and carvings, as well as a superb range of traditional beauty products and spices, all made locally. It targets rural poor and disadvantaged Cambodians for jobs and training, and sources local products from farmers. Visit its **Botanic Garden** (Airport Rd; 7.30am-5.30pm) on Airport Rd, a sort of Willy Wonka's for the senses, where you can sample infused teas and speciality coffees.

Smateria ACCESSORIES
(www.smateria.com; Alley West; 10am-10pm) Recycling rocks here with bags made from construction nets, plastic bags, motorbike seat covers and more. Fair-trade enterprise employing some disabled Cambodians.

Information

Pick up the free *Siem Reap Angkor Visitors Guide* (www.canbypublications.com) or the handy *Dining & Drinking* and *Out & About* guides produced by Pocket Guide Cambodia (www.cambodia pocketguide.com).

There are ATMs at the airport and in banks and minimarts all over central Siem Reap, especially along Sivatha St. There are also a few internet shops along Sivatha St.

Royal Angkor International Hospital (063-761888; www.royalangkorhospital.com; Airport Rd) This international facility affiliated with the Bangkok Hospital is on the expensive side as it's used to dealing with insurance companies.

Tourist Police (012 402424) Located at the main ticket checkpoint for the Angkor area, this is the place to lodge a complaint if you encounter any serious problems while in Siem Reap.

Getting There & Away

There are two main options for travelling between Vietnam and Cambodia. Air travel is more convenient, with daily flight connections between Ho Chi Minh City (HCMC), Hanoi and Siem Reap, plus less frequent flights from Danang. Road travel is a more daunting prospect as it takes an entire day to travel direct between HCMC and Siem Reap, including a change of bus in Phnom Penh. However, it is easy enough to break the journey in the lively Cambodian capital for a night or two.

AIR

Siem Reap International Airport (063-761261; www.cambodia-airports.com) is 7km west of the town centre. Vietnam Airlines (and its partner airline Cambodia Angkor Air) offers up to six daily connections between Siem Reap and HCMC, up to four daily connections with Hanoi, and one daily flight to/from Danang. There are also three flights a week connecting Siem Reap with the popular island of Phu Quoc.

SIEM REAP & THE TEMPLES ONLINE

ConCERT (www.concertcambodia.org) Siem Reap–based organisation 'connecting communities, environment and responsible tourism'.

Lonely Planet (www.lonelyplanet.com/cambodia) Information on travelling to and within Cambodia, the Thorn Tree Travel Forum and up-to-date travel news.

Angkor – Unesco World Heritage Site (http://whc.unesco.org/en/list/668) Information, images and videos on the world's top temples.

Phnom Penh Post (www.phnompenh post.com) The online version of Cambodia's newspaper of record.

Sam Veasna Center (www.samveasna.org) The best source of information on sustainable bird-watching trips in the Siem Reap and Angkor area.

BUS

Most travellers use international buses between HCMC and Phnom Penh, crossing at the Moc Bai (Vietnam)–Bavet (Cambodia) border. Buses take about six hours or so, including border-crossing formalities. Tickets usually cost US$10 to US$15. Regular services run throughout the day between 6am and about 3pm in both directions. Buses leave from the Pham Ngu Lao area of Ho Chi Minh City. In Phnom Penh, they arrive and depart from various bus offices around the city, including the offices of the following popular operators:

Capitol Tour (023-724104; 14 St 182)

Mekong Express (023-427518; http://cat mekongexpress.com; 2020 NH5)

Sapaco (023-210300; www.sapacotourist.com; 309 Sihanouk Blvd)

It is possible to connect the same day changing buses in Phnom Penh, but it's easier travelling from Ho Chi Minh City to Siem Reap rather than travelling in the other direction, as Phnom Penh to Siem Reap services operate later in the afternoon.

Tickets between Siem Reap and Phnom Penh (six hours) cost US$6 to US$15, depending on the level of service (air-con, leg room, a toilet, a host). There are also several night buses

VISAS FOR CAMBODIA

For most nationalities, one-month tourist visas (US$30) are available on arrival at Siem Reap and Phnom Penh airports, as well as all land border crossings. One passport-sized photo is required. One-month tourist e-visas (US$30 plus a US$5 processing fee) are available at www.mfaic.gov.kh. They take three business days to issue and are valid for entry to Cambodia at the airports and the Bavet–Moc Bai border crossing with Vietnam.

Anyone planning to take a side trip to the temples of Angkor and then return to Vietnam will need a multiple-entry Vietnam visa or will need to arrange another visa while in Cambodia.

between Phnom Penh and Siem Reap, which could be useful for those in a hurry.

In Siem Reap, all buses depart from the **bus station**, which is 3km east of town and about 1km south of NH6. Tickets are available at guesthouses, hotels, bus offices, travel agencies and ticket kiosks. Some bus companies send a minibus around to pick up passengers at their place of lodging. Be prepared for a rugby scrum of eager *moto* (motorbike taxi) drivers when you get off the bus in Siem Reap.

Getting Around

From the airport to the centre of Siem Reap, an official taxi costs US$9, while *remork-motos (tuk tuks)* cost US$7. From the bus station, a *moto* to the city centre should cost about US$1, while a *remork* will be around US$3.

Short *moto* trips around the centre of town cost 2000r or 3000r (US$1 at night). A *remork* should be about double that, more with lots of people.

TEMPLES OF ANGKOR

Angkor is, quite literally, heaven on earth. It is the earthly representation of Mt Meru, the Mt Olympus of the Hindu faith and the abode of ancient gods. Angkor is the perfect fusion of creative ambition and spiritual devotion. The Cambodian 'god-kings' of old each strove to better their ancestors in size, scale and symmetry, culminating in the world's largest religious building, Angkor Wat.

The hundreds of temples surviving today are but the sacred skeleton of the vast political, religious and social centre of the ancient Khmer empire. At its zenith Angkor boasted a population of nearly one million, while London was still an insignificant town of just 50,000. The houses, public buildings and palaces of Angkor were constructed of wood – now long decayed – because the right to dwell in structures of brick or stone was reserved for the gods.

Angkor is one of the most impressive ancient sites on earth, the eighth wonder of the world, with the epic proportions of the Great Wall of China, the detail and intricacy of the Taj Mahal, and the symbolism and symmetry of the Egyptian Pyramids, all rolled into one.

Angkor Wat

The traveller's first glimpse of **Angkor Wat** (អង្គរវត្ត; admission to all of Angkor 1 day/3 days/1 week US$20/40/60; 5am-5.30pm), the ultimate expression of Khmer genius, is staggering, matched by only a few select spots on earth, such as Peru's Machu Picchu or Jordan's Petra.

Soaring skyward and surrounded by a moat that would make its European castle counterparts blush, Angkor Wat is one of the most inspired and spectacular monuments ever conceived by the human mind. It is a sumptuous blend of form and function, a spellbinding shrine to Vishnu, its captivating image replicated in the reflective pools below.

Like the other temple-mountains of Angkor, Angkor Wat replicates the spatial universe in miniature. The central tower is Mt Meru, with its surrounding smaller peaks, bounded in turn by continents (the lower courtyards) and the oceans (the moat). The seven-headed *naga* (mythical serpent) serves as a symbolic rainbow bridge for humans to reach the abode of the gods.

Angkor Wat is surrounded by a moat, 190m wide, which forms a giant rectangle measuring 1.5km by 1.3km. Stretching around the outside of the central temple complex is an 800m-long series of incredible **bas-reliefs** that are designed to be viewed in an anticlockwise direction. Rising 31m above the third level (and situated 55m above the ground) is the central tower, which gives the whole ensemble its sublime unity.

Angkor Wat was built by Suryavarman II (r 1112–52), who unified Cambodia and extended Khmer influence across much of mainland Southeast Asia. He also set himself apart religiously from earlier kings by his devotion to the Hindu deity Vishnu, to whom he consecrated the temple – built, coincidentally,

Temples of Angkor

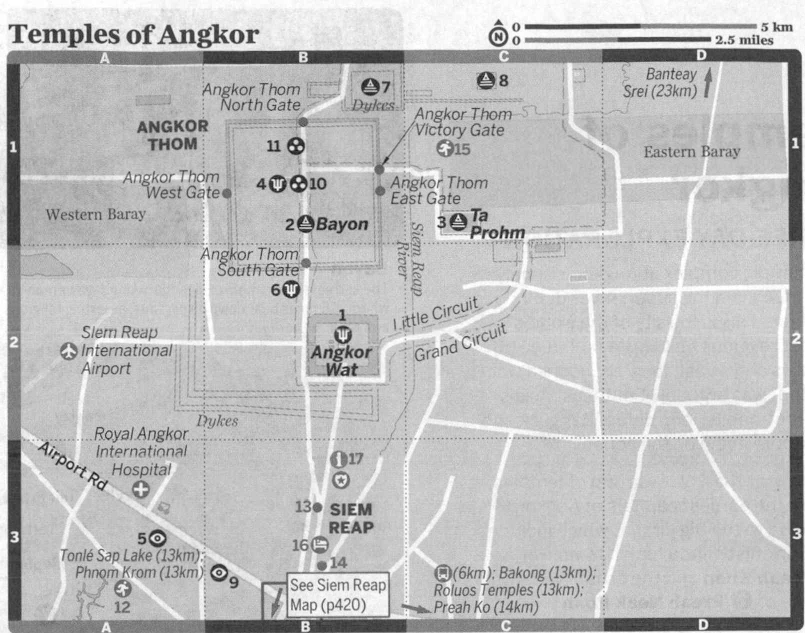

Temples of Angkor

Top Sights
1 Angkor Wat B2
2 Bayon B1
3 Ta Prohm C1

Sights
4 Baphuon B1
5 Cambodian Cultural Village A3
6 Phnom Bakheng B2
7 Preah Khan B1
8 Preah Neak Poan C1
9 Senteurs d'Angkor Botanic Garden B3
10 Terrace of the Elephants B1
11 Terrace of the Leper King B1

Activities, Courses & Tours
12 Angkor Golf Resort A3
13 Cambodia Vespa Adventures B3
14 Cooks in Tuk Tuks B3
15 Flight of the Gibbon Angkor C1

Sleeping
16 HanumanAlaya B3

Information
17 Angkor Ticket Checkpoint B3

around the same time as European Gothic cathedrals such as Notre Dame and Chartres.

The upper level of Angkor Wat, known as **Bakan**, is once again open to modern pilgrims, but visits are strictly timed to 20 minutes.

Angkor Thom

It is hard to imagine any building bigger or more beautiful than Angkor Wat, but at Angkor Thom the sum of the parts add up to a greater whole. It is the gates that grab you first, flanked by a monumental representation of the Churning of the Ocean of Milk, 54 demons and 54 gods engaged in an epic tug of war on the causeway. Each of the gates – **North**, **South**, **East**, **West** and **Victory** – towers above the visitor, the magnanimous faces of the Bodhisattva Avalokiteshvara staring out over the kingdom. Imagine being a peasant in the 13th century approaching the forbidding capital for the first time? It would have been an awe-inspiring yet unsettling experience to enter such a gateway and come face-to-face with the divine power of the god-kings.

The last great capital of the Khmer empire, Angkor Thom – set over 10 sq km – took monumental to a whole new level. It was built in part as a reaction to the surprise

Temples of Angkor

THREE-DAY EXPLORATION

The temple complex at Angkor is simply enormous and the superlatives don't do it justice. This is the site of the world's largest religious building, a multitude of temples and a vast, long-abandoned walled city that was arguably Southeast Asia's first metropolis, long before Bangkok and Singapore got in on the action.

Starting at the Roluos group of temples, one of the earliest capitals of Angkor, move on to the big circuit, which includes the Buddhist-Hindu fusion temple of ❶ **Preah Khan** and the ornate water temple of ❷ **Preah Neak Poan**.

On the second day downsize to the small circuit, starting with an early visit to ❸ **Ta Prohm**, before continuing to the temple pyramid of Ta Keo, the Buddhist monastery of Banteay Kdei and the immense royal bathing pond of ❹ **Sra Srang**.

Next venture further afield to Banteay Srei temple, the jewel in the crown of Angkorian art, and Beng Mealea, a remote jungle temple.

Saving the biggest and best until last, experience sunrise at ❺ **Angkor Wat** and stick around for breakfast in the temple to discover its amazing architecture without the crowds. In the afternoon, explore ❻ **Angkor Thom**, an immense complex that is home to the enigmatic ❼ **Bayon**.

Three days around Angkor? That's just for starters.

TOP TIPS

» **Dodging the Crowds** To avoid the hordes, try dawn at Sra Srang, post sunrise at Angkor Wat, and lunchtime at Banteay Srei.

» **Extended Explorations** Three-day passes can be used on non-consecutive days over the period of a week but be sure to request this.

Bayon
The surreal state temple of legendary king Jayavarman VII, where 216 faces bear down on pilgrims, asserting religious and regal authority.

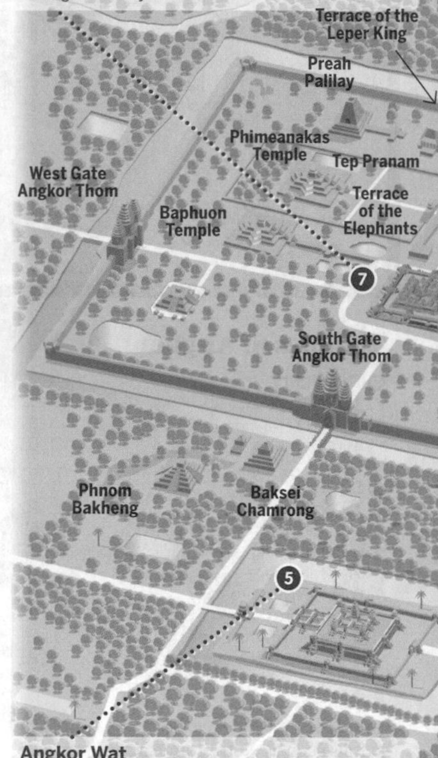

Angkor Wat
The world's largest religious building. Experience sunrise at the holiest of holies, then explore the beautiful bas-reliefs – devotion etched in stone.

CHRISTOPHER GROENHOUT / GETTY IMAGES ©

Angkor Thom

The last great capital of the Khmer empire conceals a wealth of temples and its epic proportions would have inspired and terrified in equal measure.

ANDERS BLOMQVIST / GETTY IMAGES ©

Preah Khan

A fusion temple dedicated to Buddha, Brahma, Shiva and Vishnu; the immense corridors are like an unending hall of mirrors.

ANDERS BLOMQVIST / GETTY IMAGES ©

Preah Neak Poan

If Vegas ever adopts the Angkor theme, this will be the swimming pool; a petite tower set in a lake, surrounded by four smaller ponds.

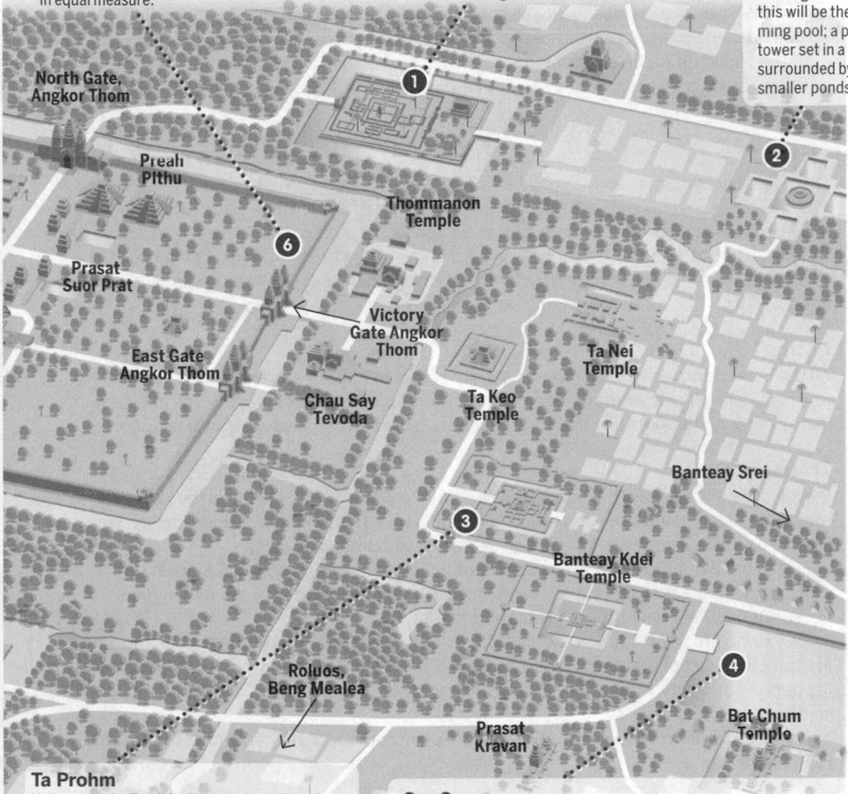

North Gate, Angkor Thom

1

Preah Pithu

2

Thommanon Temple

6

Prasat Suor Prat

Victory Gate Angkor Thom

East Gate Angkor Thom

Ta Nei Temple

Chau Say Tevoda

Ta Keo Temple

Banteay Srei

3

Banteay Kdei Temple

4

Roluos, Beng Mealea

Bat Chum Temple

Prasat Kravan

Ta Prohm

Nicknamed the *Tomb Raider* temple; *Indiana Jones* would be equally apt. Nature has run riot, leaving iconic tree roots strangling the surviving stones.

Sra Srang

Once the royal bathing pond, this is the ablutions pool to beat all ablutions pools and makes a good stop for sunrise or sunset.

ANDERS BLOMQVIST / GETTY IMAGES ©

ARIADNE VAN ZANDBERGEN / GETTY IMAGES ©

EXPLORING THE TEMPLES

Itinerary

If you have only one day to visit Angkor, arrive at Angkor Wat in time for sunrise and then stick around to explore the mighty temple in the post-sunrise quiet. From there continue to the tree roots of Ta Prohm before lunch. In the afternoon, explore the temples within the walled city of Angkor Thom and the beauty of the Bayon in the late-afternoon light.

If you have three days, follow up the first action-packed day by beating the tourists to beautiful Banteay Srei, with a quick stop at Preah Khan along the way. Then make your way to the River of a Thousand Lingas at Kbal Spean. On the third day, head out to the Roluos area and then on to the massive jungle temple of Beng Mealea. Or reverse the order and build up to the biggest temples.

For those with a week, continue the three-day itinerary with a visit to the remote temple of Koh Ker.

Tickets

The ticket checkpoint is on the road from Siem Reap to Angkor. Visitors have the choice of a one-day pass (US$20), a three-day pass (US$40) or a one-week pass (US$60). The three-day passes can be used over three non-consecutive days in a one-week period. Tickets issued after 5pm (for sunset viewing) are valid the next day. Tickets are not valid for Phnom Kulen, Beng Mealea or Koh Ker. Get caught ticketless in a temple and you'll be fined US$100.

Eating

All the major temples have some sort of nourishment near the entrance. The most extensive selection of restaurants is opposite the entrance to Angkor Wat. Some excellent local Khmer restaurants line the northern shore of Sra Srang, the royal bathing pond.

Transport

Bicycles are a great way to get to and around the temples, which are linked by good, flat roads. Various guesthouses and hotels rent out **White Bicycles**, (www.thewhitebicycles.org; per day US$2) proceeds of which go to local development projects.

Motos are a popular form of transport around the temples (around US$10 per day, more for distant sites). Drivers accost visitors from the moment they set foot in Siem Reap, but they're often knowledgeable and friendly.

Remorks (around US$15 a day, more for distant sites) take a little longer than *motos* but offer protection from the rain and sun. Even more protection is offered by cars (about US$30 a day, more for distant sites), though these tend to isolate you from the sights, sounds and smells.

Hiring a car will cost about US$50 to Kbal Spean and Banteay Srei, and about US$70 to Beng Mealea.

Tours

Most visitors are in Siem Reap to tour the temples of Angkor and there are a number of tour operators ready to guide you around. The **Khmer Angkor Tour Guide Association** (☎063-964347; www.khmerangkortourguide.com) can arrange certified tour guides in 10 languages for US$25 to US$50 a day.

Beyond (www.beyonduniqueescapes.com) Responsible operator offering tours to Beng Mealea and Kompong Pluk, plus cycling trips and cooking classes.

Buffalo Trails (☎012 297506; www.buffalotrails-cambodia.com) Ecotours and lifestyle adventures around Siem Reap.

sacking of Angkor by the Chams, Jayavarman VII (r 1181–1219) decided that his empire would never be vulnerable at home. Beyond the walls is a moat that would have stopped all but the hardiest invaders in their tracks.

Sights

Bayon

At the heart of Angkor Thom, the 12th-century **Bayon** (បាយ័ន; 7.30am-5.30pm), the mesmerising, if slightly mind-bending, state temple of Jayavarman VII epitomises the creative genius and inflated ego of Cambodia's most celebrated king. Its 54 Gothic towers are famously decorated with 216 gargantuan smiling **faces of Avalokiteshvara** that bear more than a passing resemblance to the great king himself.

It's known as the 'face temple' thanks to its iconic visages; these huge heads glare down from every angle, exuding power with a hint of humanity – precisely the blend required to hold sway over such a vast empire, ensuring the disparate and far-flung population yielded to the king'smagnanimous will.

The Bayon is decorated with 1.2km of extraordinary **bas-reliefs** incorporating more than 11,000 figures, depicting everyday life in 12th-century Cambodia.

Elsewhere in Angkor Thom

Baphuon HINDU TEMPLE
(បាពួន; 7.30am-5.30pm) Some have called Baphuon the 'world's largest jigsaw puzzle'. Before the civil war the Baphuon was painstakingly taken apart piece-by-piece by a team of archaeologists, but their records were destroyed during the Khmer Rouge regime, leaving experts with 300,000 stones to put back into place. After years of research, this temple has been partially restored. On the western side, the retaining wall of the second level was fashioned, in the 16th century, into a reclining Buddha 60m in length.

Terrace of the Elephants ARCHAEOLOGICAL SITE
(ទីលានជល់ដំរី) The 350m-long Terrace of the Elephants was used as a viewing stand for public ceremonies and served as a base for the king's audience hall. Try to imagine the grandeur of the Khmer empire at its height, with infantry, cavalry, horse-drawn chariots and elephants parading across Central Square in a procession, pennants and standards aloft. Looking on is the god-king, shaded by multi-tiered parasols and attended by mandarins and handmaidens bearing gold and silver utensils.

Terrace of the Leper King ARCHAEOLOGICAL SITE
(ទីលានព្រះគម្លង់) The Terrace of the Leper King is just north of the Terrace of the Elephants. Dating from the late 12th century, it is a 7m-high platform, on top of which stands a nude, though sexless, statue. The front retaining walls of the terrace are decorated with at least five tiers of meticulously executed carvings. On the southern side of the Terrace of the Leper King, there is access to a hidden terrace with exquisitely preserved carvings.

Around Angkor Thom

Sights

Phnom Bakheng HINDU TEMPLE
(ភ្នំបាខែង; 5am-7pm) Located around 400m south of Angkor Thom, the main attraction at Phnom Bakheng is the sunset view over Angkor Wat. For many years the whole affair turned into a circus, with crowds of tourists ascending the slopes of the hill and jockeying for space. Numbers are restricted to just 300 visitors at any one time, so get here early (4pm) to guarantee a sunset spot. The temple, built by Yasovarman I (r 889–910), has five tiers, with seven levels.

Preah Khan BUDDHIST TEMPLE
(ព្រះខ័ន, Sacred Sword; 7.30am-5.30pm) The temple of Preah Khan (Sacred Sword) is one of the largest complexes at Angkor, a maze of vaulted corridors, fine carvings and lichen-clad stonework. It is a good counterpoint to Ta Prohm and generally sees slightly fewer visitors. Like Ta Prohm it is a place of towered enclosures and shoulder-hugging corridors. Unlike Ta Prohm, however, the temple of Preah Khan is in a reasonable state of preservation thanks to the ongoing restoration efforts of the World Monuments Fund (WMF; www.wmf.org).

Preah Neak Poan BUDDHIST TEMPLE
(ព្រះនាគព័ន្ធ, Temple of the Intertwined Nagas; 7.30am-5.30pm) The Buddhist temple of Preah Neak Poan is a petite yet perfect temple constructed by Jayavarman VII in the late 12th century. It has a large square pool surrounded by four smaller square pools. Situated in the central pool is a circular 'island' encircled by the two *nagas* whose intertwined tails give the temple its name.

DON'T MISS

TA PROHM

The ultimate *Indiana Jones* fantasy, **Ta Prohm** (តាព្រហ្ម; ⌚7.30am-5.30pm) is cloaked in dappled shadow, its crumbling towers and walls locked in the slow muscular embrace of vast root systems. If Angkor Wat is testimony to the genius of the ancient Khmers, Ta Prohm reminds us equally of the awesome fecundity and power of the jungle. There is a poetic cycle to this venerable ruin, with humanity first conquering nature to rapidly create, and nature once again conquering humanity to slowly destroy.

Built from 1186 and originally known as Rajavihara (Monastery of the King), Ta Prohm was a Buddhist temple dedicated to the mother of Jayavarman VII. Ta Prohm is a temple of towers, closed courtyards and narrow corridors. Ancient trees tower overhead, their leaves filtering the sunlight and casting a greenish pall over the whole scene. It is the closest most of us will get to the discoveries of the explorers of old. Ta Prohm is at its most impressive at dawn before the crowds arrive. It's located about 2km east of Angkor Thom.

Further Afield

Sights

Bakong HINDU TEMPLE

(បាគង; ⌚7.30am-5.30pm) Bakong is the largest, most interesting of the Roluos group of temples. Built and dedicated to Shiva by Indravarman I, it's a representation of Mt Meru, and it served as the city's central temple. The east-facing complex consists of a five-tier central pyramid of sandstone, 60m square at the base, flanked by eight towers of brick and sandstone, and by other minor sanctuaries. A number of the lower towers are still partly covered by their original plasterwork.

★**Banteay Srei** HINDU TEMPLE

(បន្ទាយស្រី; ⌚7.30am-5.30pm) Considered by many to be the jewel in the crown of Angkorian art, Banteay Srei is cut from stone of a pinkish hue and includes some of the finest stone carving anywhere on earth. Begun in AD 967, it is one of the smallest sites at Angkor, but what it lacks in size it makes up for in stature. Banteay Srei is a Hindu temple dedicated to Shiva; it's wonderfully well preserved and many of its carvings are three-dimensional.

Kbal Spean HINDU SHRINE

(ក្បាលស្ពាន; ⌚7.30am-5.30pm) A spectacularly carved riverbed, Kbal Spean is set deep in the jungle to the northeast of Angkor. More commonly referred to in English as the 'River of a Thousand Lingas', the name actually means 'bridgehead', a reference to the natural rock bridge at the site. *Lingas* have been elaborately carved into the riverbed, and images of Hindu deities are dotted about the area. Kbal Spean was 'discovered' in 1969, when ethnologist Jean Boulbet was shown the area by a hermit.

Phnom Kulen MOUNTAIN

(ភ្នំគូលែន; US$20) Considered by Khmers to be the most sacred mountain in Cambodia, Phnom Kulen is a popular place of pilgrimage on weekends and during festivals. It played a significant role in the history of the Khmer empire, as it was from here in AD 802 that Jayavarman II proclaimed himself a *devaraja* (god-king), giving birth to the Cambodian kingdom. Attractions include a giant reclining Buddha, hundreds of *lingas* carved in the riverbed, an impressive waterfall and some remote temples.

Beng Mealea BUDDHIST TEMPLE

(បឹងមាលា; admission US$5; ⌚7.30am-5.30pm) A sight to behold, Beng Mealea, about 68km northeast of Siem Reap, is one of the most mysterious temples at Angkor, as nature has well and truly run riot. it's built to the same floorplan as Angkor Wat, and exploring this titanic of temples is Angkor's ultimate *Indiana Jones* experience. Built in the 12th century under Suryavarman II, Beng Mealea is enclosed by a massive moat measuring 1.2km by 900m.

Koh Ker HINDU TEMPLE

(កោះកេរ; admission US$10; ⌚7.30am-5.30pm) Abandoned to the forests of the north, Koh Ker, capital of the Angkorian empire from AD 928 to 944, is now in day-trip distance of Siem Reap. Most visitors start at Prasat Krahom where stone carvings grace lintels, and doorposts. The principal monument is Mayan-looking Prasat Thom, a 55m-wide, 40m-high sandstone pyramid whose seven tiers offer spectacular views across the forest. Koh Ker is 127km northeast of Siem Reap.

Understand Vietnam

Vietnam Today

A period of rising, sustained growth has transformed Vietnam. Change is most apparent in the big cities, where steel-and glass highrises define skylines and a burgeoning middle class now has the spending power to enjoy air-conditioned living and overseas travel. Yet, in rural areas the nation's new-found prosperity is less evident, and up the highlands, life remains a day-to-day struggle for millions of minority people.

Best in Print

The Quiet American (Graham Greene) Classic novel set in the 1950s as the French empire is collapsing.

The Sorrow of War (Bao Ninh) The North Vietnamese perspective, retold in novel form via flashbacks.

Vietnam: Rising Dragon (Bill Hayton) A candid, highly insightful assessment of the nation.

Catfish & Mandala (Andrew X Pham) Beautifully written and thought-provoking biographical tale of a Vietnamese-American who returns to his homeland.

Best on Film

Apocalypse Now (1979) The American War depicted as an epic 'heart of darkness' adventure.

The Deer Hunter (1978) Examines the emotional breakdown suffered by small-town servicemen.

Platoon (1986) Based on the first-hand experiences of the director, Oliver Stone, it follows idealistic volunteer Charlie Sheen to 'Nam.

Cyclo (Xich Lo; 1995) Visually stunning masterpiece that cuts to the core of HCMC's underworld.

The Quiet American (2002) Atmospherically set in Saigon during the French colonial period, with rebellion in the air.

The Big Picture

Forty years since the end of the American War, Vietnam has made giant strides. A victorious, though bankrupt, nation has worked around the clock, slogging its way forward, overcoming a series of formidable hurdles (including a 19-year US trade embargo). Per-capita income has grown from US$98 in 1993 to over US$2000 by 2015, and today Vietnam is one of the 10 fastest-growing economies in the world, boosted by strong manufacturing. Start-up business numbers are booming. And yet this rapid development is disjointed. The state sector remains huge, controlling around two-fifths of the economy – 100 of the 200 biggest Vietnamese companies are state owned (including oil production, shipbuilding, cement and coal).

The spectre of corruption casts a shadow over development every step of the way. Transparency International ranked Vietnam the lowest of all the Asia-Pacific countries it measured in 2014. Corruption scandals emerge on a daily basis, such as the nine Vinashin shipbuilding execs jailed following the company's near collapse under US$4.5 billion of debt. For most Vietnamese people corruption is simply a part of day-to-day life, as they have to pay backhanders for everything from securing a civil service job to an internet connection.

Tourism Woes: a Blip or a Trend?

In mid-2015, the Vietnamese government did what its tourism industry had been urging them to do for years – it (partially) relaxed visa regulations, allowing easier access to the country for several European nationalities. After years of exponential growth, tourist arrivals were on the slide, with a knock-on effect for the nation's important service sector. Further visa reforms may or may not boost tourism. The reasons for the downturn, and whether it's a blip or a long-term trend, are complex. Falling visitor numbers from Russia (due to the collapse of the rouble) and China (due to political tensions) were particularly evident.

As tourism chiefs pondered the stats, an EU-funded study found that just 6% of tourists surveyed said they would want to return to Vietnam, provoking a barrage of newspaper headlines. The clearly alarmed Vietnam Tourism authority quickly ordered a counter-survey (which suggested higher approval ratings). But an underlying message was clear: overseas visitors considered road transport dangerous and the nation's infrastructure poor, felt hassled by street vendors and overcharged by shopkeepers, and were frustrated by the lack of reliable travel information. There's clearly work to be done, not least by Vietnam Tourism, which critics allege is far too concerned with pedalling tours for profit than dispensing independent advice to travellers.

Uneasy Neighbours

On the surface, Vietnam and its northern neighbour China have much in common, with a shared heritage, common frontier and all-powerful ruling Communist parties. But for the Vietnamese, China represents something of an overbearing big brother (and 1000 years of subordination). The nations fought a recent on-off border war that rumbled on for years, only ending in 1990, and there are concerns that another conflict could erupt over offshore islands in the South China Sea (always the 'East Sea' in Vietnam). China claims virtually the whole area, and is busy constructing port facilities and airstrips. In May 2014, anti-Chinese riots erupted in several provinces, resulting in at least 21 deaths, in response to China deploying an oil rig in the Paracel Islands. Thousands of Chinese nationals fled the country. By November 2015 tensions remained, but the situation had calmed enough for President Xi Jinping to visit Hanoi as the countries sought to repair ties.

The two nations have plenty of mutual ground. Trade has continued to boom (though more one-way than the Vietnamese would like) reaching US$58 billion in 2014 and Chinese is the second most popular foreign language studied in Vietnam. Ultimately, Presidents Trong and Xi signed various cooperation agreements concerning investment and infrastructure but little progress was evident over territorial disputes.

POPULATION: **94.3 MILLION**

LIFE EXPECTANCY: **71 FOR MEN, 76 FOR WOMEN**

INFANT MORTALITY: **18 PER 1000 BIRTHS**

GDP GROWTH: **6.3%**

INFLATION: **1.3%**

ADULT LITERACY RATE: **93%**

if Vietnam were 100 people

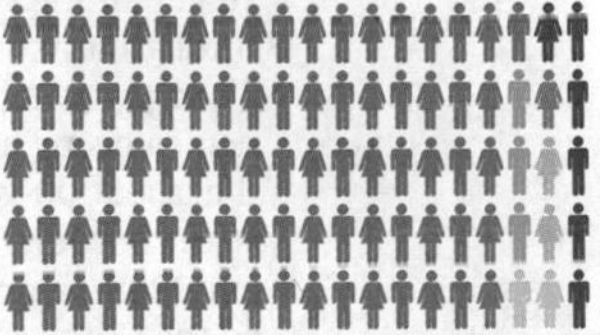

86 would be Kinh
3 would be Thai & Muong
2 would be Khmer Krom
2 would be Tay
1 would be Hoa
6 would be Other

belief systems

(% of population)

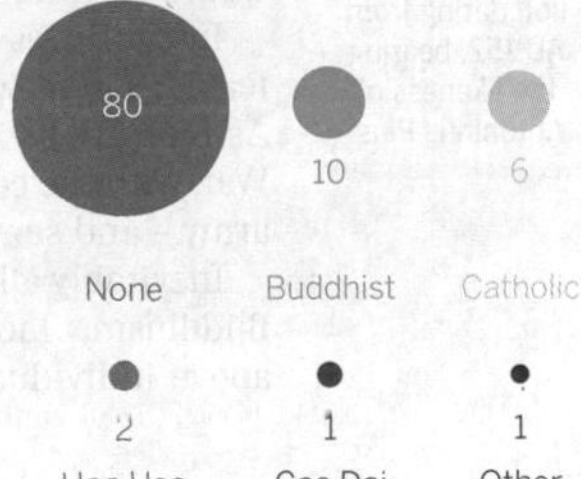

population per sq km

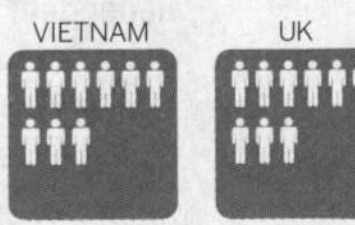

≈ 30 people

History

The Vietnamese trace their roots back to the Red River Delta where farmers first cultivated rice. Millennia of struggle against the Chinese then followed. Vietnam only became a united state in the 19th century, but quickly faced the ignominy of French colonialism and then the devastation of the American intervention. The Vietnamese nation has survived tempestuous, troubled times, but its strength of character has served it well. Today, the signs are it's continuing to grow with some promise.

To get an idea of Vietnam's turbulent history all you have to do is stroll through any town in the country and take at look at the street names. Then try it again somewhere else. You'll soon get déjà vu. The same names occur again and again, reflecting the national heroes who, over the last 2000 years, have repelled a succession of foreign invaders. If the street borders a river, it'll be called Bach Dang (after the battles of 938 and 1288); a principal boulevard will be Le Loi (the emperor who defeated the Chinese in 1427).

The Vietnamese, in the backyard of a giant neighbour, have first and foremost had to deal with China. They've been resisting Chinese domination from as far back as the 2nd century BC and had to endure a 1000-year occupation. The struggle to nationhood has been immense.

Archaeologists conducting excavations at Oc-Eo discovered a Roman medallion dating from AD 152, bearing the likeness of Antoninus Pius.

Sure, the American War in Vietnam captured the attention of the West, but for the Vietnamese the Americans were simply the last in a long line of visitors who had come and gone. As far as Ho Chi Minh was concerned, no matter what was required or how long it took, they too would be vanquished.

In centuries past, the Khmers, the Mongols and Chams were all defeated. There was a humbling period of colonialism under the French. As recently as 1979, just after the cataclysmic horrors of the American War, with the country on its knees, Vietnam took on an invading Chinese army – and sent them home in a matter of weeks.

Inevitably all these invaders have left their mark. The Chinese brought Buddhism, Taoism and the principles of Confucianism (community above individual and a respect for education and family). The French

TIMELINE

2789 BC

The Van Lang kingdom, considered the first independent Vietnamese state, is founded by the Hung Vuong kings. It's referred to by both the Chin and Tang Chinese dynasties.

2000 BC

The Bronze Age Dong Son culture emerges in the Red River Delta around Hanoi, renowned for its rice cultivation and the production of bronzeware, including drums and gongs.

300BC

Vietnamese people of the northern region were culturally divided between Au Viet (highland Vietnamese) and Lac Viet (Vietnamese of the plains) who settled the Red River basin.

IN THE BEGINNING…

Every country has a creation myth and Vietnam is no exception. The Vietnamese are supposed to have descended from a union of Dragon Lord Lac Long Quan and the fairy Au Co. Their relationship was fruitful, producing 100 sons, 50 migrating with their mother to the mountains and the other half travelling with their father to the sea. These sons founded the first Vietnamese dynasty, the Hung, who ruled over the kingdom of Van Lang, whose people were the first to be known as the Lac Viet.

introduced railways, and bequeathed some grand architecture and fabulous cuisine. And though the Americans left a devastated nation, Vietnamese pride remained intact.

In recent years, progress has been remarkable, as Vietnam has become a key member of ASEAN and its economy has boomed – though systemic corruption, creaking infrastructure and an anti-democratic ruling party remain. But the country is united and prospering, its borders secure, and the Vietnamese people can look forward to a lasting period of stability and progress.

The Early Days

Humans first inhabited northern Vietnam about 500,000 years ago, though it took until 7000 BC for these hunter gatherers to practise rudimentary agriculture. The sophisticated Dong Son culture, famous for its bronze moko drums, emerged sometime around the 3rd century BC. The Dong Son period also saw huge advances in rice cultivation and the emergence of the Red River Delta as a major agricultural centre.

From the 1st to 6th centuries AD, southern Vietnam was part of the Indianised Cambodian kingdom of Funan – famous for its refined art and architecture. Based around the walled city of Angkor Borei, it was probably a grouping of feudal states rather than a unified empire. The people of Funan constructed an elaborate system of canals both for transportation and the irrigation of rice. Funan's principal port city was Oc-Eo in the Mekong Delta, and archaeological excavations here suggest there was contact with China, Indonesia, Persia and even the Mediterranean. Later on, the Chenla empire replaced the Funan kingdom, spreading along the Mekong River.

The Hindu kingdom of Champa emerged around present-day Danang in the late 2nd century AD. Like Funan, it adopted Sanskrit as a sacred language and borrowed heavily from Indian art and culture. By the 8th century, Champa had expanded southward to include what is now Nha Trang and Phan Rang. The Cham were a feisty bunch who conducted

The people of the Bronze Age Dong Son period were major traders in the region, and bronze drums from northern Vietnam have been found as far afield as the island of Alor, in eastern Indonesia.

250 BC

Van Lang is conquered by a Chinese warlord and a new kingdom known as Au Lac is established at Co Loa, close to the modern-day capital of Hanoi.

225–248BC

Female warrior, Trieu Thi Trinh, described as a giant who rode war elephants to battle, confronts the Chinese for decades until defeat and her suicide in 248.

111 BC

The Han emperors of China annex the Red River Delta region of Vietnam, heralding 1000 years of Chinese rule. Confucianism prevails as the governing philosophy.

AD 40

The Trung Sisters (Hai Ba Trung) vanquish the Chinese and proclaim themselves queens of an independent Vietnam.

raids along the entire coast of Indochina, and thus found themselves in a perpetual state of war with the Vietnamese to the north and the Khmers to the south. Ultimately this cost them their kingdom, as they found themselves squeezed between these two great powers.

One Thousand Years of Chinese Occupation

The Chinese conquered the Red River Delta in the 2nd century BC. Over the following centuries, large numbers of Chinese settlers, officials and scholars moved south, seeking to impress a centralised state system on the Vietnamese.

For a closer look at China's 1000-year occupation of Vietnam, which was instrumental in shaping the country's outlook and attitude today, try *The Birth of Vietnam* by Keith Weller Taylor.

In the most famous act of resistance, in AD 40, the Trung Sisters (Hai Ba Trung) rallied the people, raised an army and led a revolt against the Chinese. The Chinese counter-attacked, but, rather than surrender, the Trung Sisters threw themselves into the Hat Giang River. There were numerous small-scale rebellions against Chinese rule – which was characterised by tyranny, forced labour and insatiable demands for tribute – from the 3rd to 6th centuries, but all were defeated.

However, the early Vietnamese learned much from the Chinese, including the advancement of dykes and irrigation works – reinforcing the role of rice as the 'staff of life'. As food became more plentiful the population expanded, forcing the Vietnamese to seek new lands. The Truong Son Mountains prevented westward expansion, as the climate was harsh and the terrain unsuited to rice cultivation, so instead the Vietnamese moved south along the coast.

During this era, Vietnam was a key port of call on the sea route between China and India. The Chinese introduced Confucianism, Taoism and Mahayana Buddhism to Vietnam, while the Indian influence brought Theravada Buddhism and Hinduism (to Champa and Funan). Monks carried with them the scientific and medical knowledge of these two great civilisations and Vietnam was soon producing its own doctors, botanists and scholars.

Liberation from China

In the early 10th century, the Tang dynasty collapsed, provoking the Vietnamese to launch a revolt against Chinese rule. In AD 938, popular patriot Ngo Quyen defeated Chinese forces by luring the Chinese fleet up the Bach Dang River in a feigned retreat, only to counter-attack and impale their ships on sharpened stakes hidden beneath the waters. This ended 1000 years of Chinese rule (though it was not to be the last time the Vietnamese would tussle with their mighty northern neighbour).

166

First contact between Rome and China as envoys pass through the Gulf of Tonkin.

446

Relations between the kingdom of Champa and the Chinese deteriorate. China invades Champa, sacks the capital of Simhapura and plunders a 50-tonne golden Buddha statue.

602

Rebellions by leaders including Ly Bon and Trieu Quang Phuc against Chinese rule ultimately fail as the Sui dynasty reconquers Vietnam, with its capital Dai La Thanh (Hanoi).

938

The Chinese are kicked out of Vietnam after 1000 years of occupation, as Ngo Quyen leads his people to victory in the battle of the Bach Dang River.

STREET NAMES IN VIETNAM

All Vietnamese street names are controlled by an intensely patriotic Communist party. These reflect important dates, battles, heroes and heroines.

30 Thang 4 The date (30th April) Communist forces captured Saigon.

Hai Bai Trung Two sisters who lead a revolt against Chinese rule in AD 40.

Le Loi Robin Hood–style rebel leader; vanquished the Chinese in 1426.

Nguyen Thai Hoc Lead the Yen Bai revolt against the French.

Quang Trung Ruthless 18th-century military leader, emperor and reformer.

Tran Hunh Dao Defeated Kublai Khan and invading Mongol forces.

From the 11th to 13th centuries, Vietnamese independence was consolidated under the emperors of the Ly dynasty, founded by Ly Thai To. This was a period of progress that saw the introduction of an elaborate dyke system for flood control and cultivation, and the establishment of the country's first university. During the Ly dynasty, the Chinese, the Khmer and the Cham launched attacks on Vietnam, but all were repelled. Meanwhile, the Vietnamese continued their expansion southwards and slowly but surely began to consolidate control of the Cham kingdom.

The coastal Champa kingdoms were predominantly Hindu, their culture and religion heavily influenced by India. Shiva and the earth goddess Lady Po Nagar were two principal deities.

Bach Dang Again

Mongol warrior Kublai Khan completed his conquest of China in the mid-13th century. For his next trick, he planned to attack Champa and demanded the right to cross Vietnamese territory. The Vietnamese refused, but the Mongol hordes – all 500,000 of them – pushed ahead. They met their match in the revered general Tran Hung Dao. He defeated them at Bach Dang River, utilising acute military acumen by repeating the same tactics (and location) as Ngo Quyen in one of the most celebrated scalps in Vietnamese history.

China Bites Back

The Chinese took control of Vietnam again in the early 15th century, taking the national archives and some of the country's intellectuals back to Nanjing – a loss that was to have a lasting impact on Vietnamese civilisation. Heavy taxation and slave labour were also typical of the era. The poet Nguyen Trai (1380–1442) wrote of this period: 'Were the water of the Eastern Sea to be exhausted, the stain of their ignominy could not be washed away; all the bamboo of the Southern Mountains would not suffice to provide the paper for recording all their crimes'.

1010

Thang Long (City of the Soaring Dragon), known today as Hanoi, is founded by Emperor Ly Thai To and becomes the new capital of Vietnam.

1010–1225

Under the 200-year Ly dynasty Vietnam maintains many institutions and traditions of the Chinese era including Confucianism and its civil service structure. Wet rice cultivation remains vital.

1076

The Vietnamese military, led by General Ly Thuong, attack the Sung Chinese and win a decisive battle near the present-day city of Nanning, and later defeat Cham forces.

1288

The Mongols invade Dai Viet but General Tran Hung Dao repeats history by spearing the Mongol fleet on sharpened stakes on the Bach Dang River.

INDEPENDENT, CIVILISED & HEROIC

Following the successful 15th-century Le Loi rebellion against Chinese rule, poet Nguyen Trai issued a stirring nationalist declaration that is still quoted in Vietnamese school books and used by politicians today. The Great Proclamation *(Binh Ngo Dai Cao)* articulates the country's fierce spirit of independence: 'Our people long ago established Vietnam as an independent nation with its own civilisation. We have our own mountains and our own rivers, our own customs and traditions, and these are different from those of the foreign country to the north...We have sometimes been weak and sometimes powerful, but at no time have we suffered from a lack of heroes'.

Enter Le Loi

In 1418, wealthy philanthropist Le Loi sparked the Lam Son Uprising by refusing to serve as an official for the Chinese Ming dynasty. By 1425, local rebellions had erupted in several regions and Le Loi travelled the countryside to rally the people, and eventually defeat the Chinese.

Le Loi and his successors launched a campaign to take over Cham lands to the south, which culminated in the occupation of its capital Vijaya, near present-day Quy Nhon in 1471. This was the end of Champa as a military power and the Cham people began to migrate southwards as Vietnamese settlers moved into their territory.

Dynasties of Vietnam

- *Ngo 939–965 AD*
- *Dinh 968–980 AD*
- *Early Le 980–1009 AD*
- *Ly 1010–1225*
- *Tran 1225–1400*
- *Ho 1400–1407*
- *Post-Tran 1407–1413*
- *Chinese rule 1414–1427*
- *Later Le 1428–1524*
- *Mac 1527–1592*
- *Trinh Lords of the North 1539–1787*
- *Nguyen Lords of the South 1558–1778*
- *Tay Son 1788–1802*
- *Nguyen 1802–1945*

The Coming of the Europeans

The first Portuguese sailors came ashore at Danang in 1516 and were soon followed by a party of Dominican missionaries. During the following decades the Portuguese began to trade with Vietnam, setting up a commercial colony alongside those of the Japanese and Chinese at Faifo (present-day Hoi An). With the exception of the Philippines, which was ruled by the Spanish for 400 years, the Catholic Church has had a greater impact on Vietnam than on any country in Asia.

Lording It over the People

In a dress rehearsal for the tumultuous events of the 20th century, Vietnam found itself divided in two throughout much of the 17th and 18th centuries. The powerful Trinh Lords (later Le kings), ruled the North. To the South were the Nguyen Lords. The Trinh failed in their persistent efforts to subdue the Nguyen, in part because their Dutch weaponry was matched by the Portuguese armaments supplied to the Nguyen. By this time, several European nations were interested in Vietnam's potential and were jockeying for influence. For their part, the Nguyen expanded southwards again, absorbing territories in the Mekong Delta.

14th century
Cham forces led by king Che Bong Nga kill Viet Emperor Tran Due Tong and lay siege to his capital Thang Long in 1377 and 1383.

1427
Le Loi triumphs over the Chinese, declaring himself emperor, the first in the long line of the Le dynasty. He is revered as one of the nation's greatest heroes.

1471
The Vietnamese inflict a humbling defeat on the kingdom of Champa, killing more than 60,000 Cham soldiers and capturing 36,000, including the king and most of the royal family.

16th century
HCMC begins life as humble Prey Nokor, a backwater Khmer village in what was then the eastern edge of Cambodia.

Tay Son Rebellion

In 1765, a rebellion erupted in the town of Tay Son near Qui Nhon, ostensibly against the punitive taxes of the Nguyen family. The Tay Son Rebels, as they were known, were led by the brothers Nguyen, who espoused a sort of Robin Hood–like philosophy of take from the rich and redistribute to the poor. It was clearly popular and in less than a decade they controlled the whole of central Vietnam. In 1783, they captured Saigon and the South, killing the reigning prince and his family. Nguyen Lu became king of the South, while Nguyen Nhac was crowned king of central Vietnam.

Continuing their conquests, the Tay Son Rebels overthrew the Trinh Lords in the North, while the Chinese moved in to take advantage of the power vacuum. In response, the third brother, Nguyen Hue, proclaimed himself Emperor Quang Trung. In 1789, Nguyen Hue's armed forces overwhelmingly defeated the Chinese army at Dong Da in another of the greatest hits of Vietnamese history.

In the South, Nguyen Anh, a rare survivor from the original Nguyen Lords – yes, know your Nguyens if you hope to understand Vietnamese history! – gradually overcame the rebels. In 1802, Nguyen Anh proclaimed himself Emperor Gia Long, thus beginning the Nguyen dynasty. When he captured Hanoi, his work was complete and, for the first time in two centuries, Vietnam was united, with Hue as its new capital city.

Ho Chi Minh City (HCMC) began life as humble Prey Nokor in the 16th century, a backwater of a Khmer village in what was then the eastern edge of Cambodia.

The Traditionalists Prevail

Emperor Gia Long returned Vietnam to Confucian values in an effort to consolidate his precarious position, a calculated move to win over conservative elements of the elite.

Gia Long's son, Emperor Minh Mang, worked to strengthen the state. He was profoundly hostile to Catholicism, which he saw as a threat to Confucian traditions, and extended this antipathy to all Western influences.

The early Nguyen emperors continued the expansionist policies of the preceding dynasties, pushing into Cambodia and Lao territory. Clashes with Thailand broke out in an attempt to pick apart the skeleton of the fractured Khmer empire.

The return to traditional values may have earned support among the elite at home, but the isolation and hostility to the West ultimately cost the Nguyen emperors as they failed to modernise the country quickly enough to compete with the well-armed Europeans.

One of the most prominent early missionaries was French Jesuit Alexandre de Rhodes (1591–1660), widely lauded for his work in devising *quoc ngu*, the Latin-based phonetic alphabet in which Vietnamese is written today.

The French Takeover

France's military activity in Vietnam began in 1847, when the French Navy attacked Danang harbour in response to Emperor Thieu Tri's imprisonment of Catholic missionaries. Saigon was seized in early 1859

1516

Portuguese traders land at Danang, sparking the start of European interest in Vietnam. They set up a trading post in Faifo (present-day Hoi An) and introduce Catholicism.

1524

A period of instability and warfare ensues as feudal conflicts rage between the Trinh from the north (Thang Long) and the Nguyen from the South (based around Hue).

1651

The first *quoc ngu* (Romanised Vietnamese) dictionary, the *Dictionarium Annamiticum Lusitanum et Latinum*, is produced, following years of work by Father Alexandre de Rhodes.

17th century

Ethnic Vietnamese settlers arrive in the Mekong Delta and Saigon region, taking advantage of Khmer weaknesses, who are torn apart by internal strife and Siamese invasions.

and, in 1862, Emperor Tu Duc signed a treaty that gave the French the three eastern provinces of Cochinchina (the southern part of Vietnam during the French-colonial era). However, over the next four decades the French colonial venture in Indochina faltered repeatedly and, at times, only the reckless adventures of a few mavericks kept it going.

In 1872, Jean Dupuis, a merchant seeking to supply salt and weapons via the Red River, seized the Hanoi Citadel. Captain Francis Garnier, ostensibly dispatched to rein in Dupuis, instead took over where Dupuis left off and began a conquest of the North.

Buddhism flourished during the 17th and 18th centuries and many pagodas were erected across the country. However, it was not pure Buddhism, but a peculiarly Vietnamese blend mixed with ancestor worship, animism and Taoism.

A few weeks after the death of Tu Duc in 1883, the French attacked Hue and the Treaty of Protectorate was imposed on the imperial court. A struggle then began for royal succession that was notable for its palace coups, the death of emperors in suspicious circumstances and heavy-handed French diplomacy.

The French colonial authorities carried out ambitious public works, such as the construction of the Saigon–Hanoi railway and draining of the Mekong Delta swamps. These projects were funded by heavy government taxes which had a devastating impact on the rural economy. Such operations became notorious for the abysmal wages paid by the French and the appalling treatment of Vietnamese workers.

Independence Aspirations

Throughout the colonial period, the desire of many Vietnamese for independence simmered below the surface. Nationalist aspirations often erupted into open defiance of the French. This ranged from the publishing of patriotic periodicals to a dramatic attempt to poison the French garrison in Hanoi.

The imperial court in Hue, although allegedly quite corrupt, was a centre of nationalist sentiment and the French orchestrated a game of musical thrones, as one emperor after another turned against their patronage. This culminated in the accession of Emperor Bao Dai in 1925, who was just 12 years old at the time and studying in France.

Leading patriots soon realised that modernisation was the key to an independent Vietnam. Phan Boi Chau launched the Dong Du (Go East) movement which planned to send Vietnamese intellectuals to Japan for study with a view to fomenting a successful uprising in the future. Phan Tru Chinh favoured the education of the masses, the modernisation of the economy and working with the French towards independence. It was at this time that the Roman script of *quoc ngu* came to prominence, as educators realised this would be a far easier tool with which to educate the masses than the elaborate Chinese-style script of *nom*.

1765

The Tay Son Rebellion erupts near Quy Nhon, led by the brothers Nguyen; they take control of the whole country over the next 25 years.

1802

Emperor Gia Long takes the throne and the Nguyen dynasty is born, ruling over Vietnam until 1945. The country is reunited for the first time in more than 200 years.

1862

Following French attacks on both Danang and Saigon, Emperor Tu Duc signs a treaty ceding control of the Mekong Delta provinces to France, renaming them Cochinchina (Cochinchine).

1883

The French impose the Treaty of Protectorate on the Vietnamese, marking the start of 70 years of colonial control, although active resistance continues throughout this period.

UNCLE OF THE PEOPLE

Father of the nation, Ho Chi Minh (Bringer of Light) was the son of a fiercely nationalistic scholar-official. Born Nguyen Tat Thanh near Vinh in 1890, he was educated in Hue and adopted many pseudonyms during his momentous life. Many Vietnamese affectionately refer to him as Bac Ho ('Uncle Ho') today.

In 1911, he signed up as a cook's apprentice on a French ship, sailing to North America, Africa and Europe. While odd-jobbing in England and France as a gardener, snow sweeper, waiter, photo retoucher and stoker, his political consciousness began to develop.

Ho Chi Minh moved to Paris, where he mastered a number of languages (including English, French, German and Mandarin) and began to promote Indochinese independence. He was a founding member of the French Communist Party in 1920 and later travelled to Guangzhou in China, where he founded the Revolutionary Youth League of Vietnam.

During the early 1930s, the English rulers of Hong Kong obliged the French government by imprisoning Ho for his revolutionary activities. After his release he travelled to the USSR and China. In 1941, he returned to Vietnam for the first time in 30 years, and founded the Viet Minh, the goal of which was the independence of Vietnam. As Japan prepared to surrender in August 1945, Ho Chi Minh led the August Revolution, and his forces then established control throughout much of Victnam.

The return of the French compelled the Viet Minh to conduct a guerrilla war, which led to victory against the colonists at Dien Bien Phu in 1954. Ho then led North Vietnam until his death in September 1969 – he never lived to see the North's victory over the South.

The party has worked hard to preserve the reputation of Bac Ho. His image dominates contemporary Vietnam – no town is complete without a Ho statue, and most cities have a museum in his name. This cult of personality is in stark contrast to the simplicity with which Ho lived his life. For more Ho, check out *Ho Chi Minh,* the excellent biography by William J Duiker.

Rise of the Communists

The most successful of the anti-colonialists were the communists, who were able to tune into the frustrations of the population – especially the peasants – and effectively channel their demands for fairer land distribution.

The story of Vietnamese communism, which in many ways is also the political biography of Ho Chi Minh, is convoluted. The first Marxist grouping in Indochina was the Vietnam Revolutionary Youth League, founded in 1925 by Ho Chi Minh in Canton, China. This was succeeded in February 1930 by the Vietnamese Communist Party. In 1941, Ho formed the Viet Minh, which resisted the Vichy French government, as well as Japanese forces, and carried out extensive political activities during WWII. Despite its nationalist platform, the Viet Minh was, from its inception, dominated by Ho's communists. However, as well as being a communist, Ho appeared pragmatic and populist and understood the need for national unity.

late 19th century	1925	1930–1931	1930s
The Romanised *quoc ngu* alphabet for Vietnamese grows in popularity as a means of eradicating illiteracy and promoting education. Traditional Chinese-style scripts are phased out.	Ho Chi Minh moves towards organised political agitation, establishing the Revolutionary Youth League of Vietnam in southern China, an early incarnation of the Vietnamese Communist Party.	Nghe Tinh rebellion against French rule features strikes and protests by Vietnamese farmers, workers and intellectuals against the French regime and local landowners.	Marxism gains in popularity with the formation of three communist parties, which later unite to form the Vietnamese Communist Party with Tran Phu as the first Secretary General.

WWII & Famine

Between 1944 and 1945, the Viet Minh received funding and arms from the US Office of Strategic Services (OSS; today the CIA). When Ho Chi Minh declared independence in 1945, he had OSS agents at his side and borrowed liberally from the American Declaration of Independence.

When France fell to Nazi Germany in 1940, the Indochinese government of Vichy France–collaborators acquiesced to the presence of Japanese troops in Vietnam. The Japanese left the French administration in charge of the day-to-day running of the country and, for a time, Vietnam was spared the ravages of Japanese occupation. However, as WWII drew to a close, Japanese rice requisitions, combined with floods and breaches in the dykes, caused a horrific famine in which perhaps two million North Vietnamese people starved to death. The only force opposed to both the French and Japanese presence in Vietnam was the Viet Minh, and Ho Chi Minh received assistance from the US government during this period. As events unfolded in mainland Europe, the French and Japanese fell out and the Viet Minh saw its opportunity to strike.

A False Dawn

By the spring of 1945, the Viet Minh controlled large swathes of the country, particularly in the north. In mid-August, Ho Chi Minh called for a general uprising, later known as the August Revolution. Meanwhile in central Vietnam, Bao Dai abdicated in favour of the new government, and in the South the Viet Minh soon held power in a shaky coalition with non-communist groups. On 2 September 1945, Ho Chi Minh declared independence at a rally in Hanoi. Throughout this period, Ho wrote eight letters to US president Harry Truman and the US State Department asking for US aid, but received no replies.

A footnote on the agenda of the Potsdam Conference of 1945 was the disarming of Japanese occupation forces in Vietnam: Chinese Kuomintang would accept the Japanese surrender north of the 16th Parallel and the British would do so in the south.

When the British arrived in Saigon, anarchy ruled with private militia, the remaining Japanese forces, the French, and Viet Minh competing for hegemony. When armed French paratroopers reacted to Ho's declaration of independence by attacking civilians, the Viet Minh began a guerrilla campaign. On 24 September, French general Jacques Philippe Leclerc arrived in Saigon, declaring, 'we have come to reclaim our inheritance'.

The 1945 Potsdam Agreement fails to recognise Vietnam as an independent state but partitions Vietnam at the 16th parallel (just north of Danang).

In the north, Chinese Kuomintang troops were fleeing the Chinese communists and making their way southward towards Hanoi. Ho tried to placate them, but as the months of Chinese occupation dragged on, he decided to accept a temporary return of the French, deeming them less of a long-term threat than the Chinese. The French were to stay for five years in return for recognising Vietnam as a free state within the French Union.

1940
The Japanese occupation of Vietnam begins, as the pro-Vichy France colonial government offers the use of military facilities in return for the continued control over administration.

1941
Ho Chi Minh forms the Viet Minh (short for the League for the Independence of Vietnam), a liberation movement seeking independence from France and fighting the Japanese occupation.

mid-1940s
The combination of Japanese rice requisitions and widespread flooding leads to a disastrous famine in which 10% of North Vietnam's population (around two million people) dies.

1944–1945
The Viet Minh receive funding and arms from the US Office of Strategic Services (OSS; today the CIA).

War with the French

The French had managed to regain control of Vietnam, at least in name. However, following the French shelling of Haiphong in November 1946, which killed hundreds of civilians, the détente with the Viet Minh began to unravel. Fighting soon broke out in Hanoi, and Ho Chi Minh and his forces fled to the mountains to regroup, where they would remain for the next eight years.

In the face of determined Vietnamese nationalism, the French proved unable to reassert their control. Despite massive US aid to halt communism throughout Asia, for the French it was ultimately an unwinnable war. As Ho said to the French at the outset: 'You can kill 10 of my men for every one I kill of yours, but even at those odds you will lose and I will win'.

After eight years of fighting, the Viet Minh controlled much of Vietnam and neighbouring Laos. On 7 May 1954, after a 57-day siege, more than 10,000 starving French troops surrendered to the Viet Minh at Dien Bien Phu. This defeat brought an end to the French colonial adventure in Indochina. The following day, the Geneva Conference opened to negotiate an end to the conflict, but the French had no cards left to bring to the table. Resolutions included an exchange of prisoners; the 'temporary' division of Vietnam into two zones at the Ben Hai River (near the 17th Parallel) until nationwide elections could be held; the free passage of people across the 17th Parallel for a period of 300 days; and the holding of nationwide elections on 20 July 1956. In the course of the Franco–Viet Minh War, more than 35,000 French fighters had been killed and 48,000 wounded; there are no exact numbers for Vietnamese casualties, but they were certainly higher.

In May 1954, the Viet Minh dug a tunnel network under French defences on Hill A1 at Dien Bien Phu and rigged it with explosives. Comrade Sapper Nguyen Van Bach volunteered himself as a human fuse in case the detonator failed. Luckily for him it didn't and he is today honoured as a national hero.

A Separate South Vietnam

After the Geneva Accords were signed and sealed, the South was ruled by a government led by Ngo Dinh Diem, a fiercely anti-communist Catholic. His power base was significantly strengthened by 900,000 refugees, many of them Catholics, who had fled the communist North during the 300-day free-passage period.

Nationwide elections were never held, as the Americans rightly feared that Ho Chi Minh would win with a massive majority. During the first few years of his rule, Diem consolidated power fairly effectively, defeating the Binh Xuyen crime syndicate and the private armies of the Hoa Hao and Cao Dai religious sects. During Diem's 1957 official visit to the USA, President Eisenhower called him the 'miracle man' of Asia. As time went on Diem became increasingly tyrannical, closing Buddhist monasteries, imprisoning monks and banning opposition parties. He also doled

In Hanoi and the North, Ho Chi Minh created a very effective police state. The regime was characterised by ruthless police power, denunciations by a huge network of secret informers, and the blacklisting of dissidents, their children and their children's children.

1945

Ho Chi Minh proclaims Vietnamese independence on 2 September in Ba Dinh Square in central Hanoi, but the French aim to reassert their authority and impose colonial rule once more.

1946

Strained relations between the Viet Minh forces and the French colonialists erupt into open fighting in Hanoi and Haiphong, marking the start of the eight-year Franco–Viet Minh War.

late 1940s

While the Viet Minh retreat to the mountains to regroup, the French attempt to forge a Vietnamese government under Emperor Bao Dai, last ruler of the Nguyen dynasty.

1949

The Communist victory in China sees increased arms supplies flow across the border to Viet Minh forces, who score notable battle successes against the French.

out power to family members (including his sister-in-law Madame Nhu, who effectively became First Lady).

In the early 1960s, the South was rocked by anti-Diem unrest led by university students and Buddhist clergy, which included several highly publicised self-immolations by monks that shocked the world. The US began to see Diem as a liability and threw its support behind a military coup. A group of young generals led the operation in November 1963. Diem was meant to go into exile, but the generals executed both Diem and his brother. Diem was succeeded by a string of military rulers who continued his policies.

The 2002 remake of *The Quiet American*, starring Michael Caine, is a must-see. Beautifully shot, it is a classic introduction to Vietnam in the 1950s, as the French disengaged and the Americans moved in to take their place.

A New North Vietnam

The Geneva Accords allowed the leadership of the Democratic Republic of Vietnam to return to Hanoi and assert control of all territory north of the 17th Parallel. The new government immediately set out to eliminate those elements of the population that threatened its power. Tens of thousands of landlords, some with only tiny holdings, were denounced to security committees by their neighbours and arrested. Hasty trials resulted in between 10,000 and 15,000 executions and the imprisonment of thousands more. In 1956, the party, faced with widespread rural unrest, recognised that things had spiralled out of control and began a Campaign for the Rectification of Errors.

The North–South War

The communists' campaign to liberate the South began in 1959. The Ho Chi Minh Trail reopened for business, universal military conscription was implemented and the National Liberation Front (NLF), later known as the Viet Cong (VC), was formed.

As the NLF launched its campaign, the Diem government quickly lost control of the countryside. To stem the tide, peasants were moved into fortified 'strategic hamlets' in order to deny the VC potential support.

For the South it was no longer just a battle with the VC. In 1964, Hanoi began sending regular North Vietnamese Army (NVA) units down the Ho Chi Minh Trail. By early 1965, the Saigon government was on its last legs. Desertions from the Army of the Republic of Vietnam (ARVN) had reached 2000 per month. The South was losing a district capital each week, yet in 10 years only one senior South Vietnamese army officer had been wounded. The army was getting ready to evacuate Hue and Danang, and the central highlands seemed about to fall.

Viet Cong and VC are both abbreviations for Viet Nam Cong San, which means Vietnamese communist. American soldiers nicknamed the VC 'Charlie', as in 'Victor Charlie'.

Enter the Cavalry

The Americans saw France's war in Indochina as an important element in the worldwide struggle against communist expansion. Vietnam was

1954

French forces surrender to Viet Minh fighters as the siege of Dien Bien Phu comes to a dramatic close on 7 May, marking the end of colonial rule in Indochina.

1955

Vietnam is 'temporarily' divided at the 17th Parallel into North Vietnam and South Vietnam and people are given 300 days to relocate to either side of the border.

1960

The National Liberation Front (better known as the Viet Cong) launch a guerrilla war against the Diem government in the South, sparking the 'American War'.

1962

Cuc Phuong National Park, just west of the city of Ninh Binh is declared Vietnam's first national park as Ho Chi Minh declares 'forest is gold.'

the next domino and could not topple. In 1950, US advisers rolled into Vietnam, ostensibly to train local troops – but American soldiers would remain on Vietnamese soil for the next 25 years. As early as 1954, US military aid to the French topped US$2 billion.

A turning point in US strategy came with the August 1964 Gulf of Tonkin incident. Two US destroyers claimed to have come under unprovoked attack off the North Vietnamese coast. Subsequent research suggests that there was a certain degree of provocation: one ship was assisting a secret South Vietnamese commando raid, and according to an official National Security Agency report in 2005, the second attack never happened.

However, on US president Lyndon Johnson's orders, 64 sorties unleashed bombs on the North – the first of thousands of such missions that would hit every single road and rail bridge in the country, as well as 4000 of North Vietnam's 5788 villages. A few days later, the US Congress overwhelmingly passed the Tonkin Gulf Resolution, which gave the president the power to take any action in Vietnam without congressional control.

As the military situation of the Saigon government reached a new nadir, the first US combat troops splashed ashore at Danang in March 1965. By December 1965, there were 184,300 US military personnel in Vietnam and 636 Americans had died. By December 1967, the figures had risen to 485,600 US soldiers in the country and 16,021 dead. There were 1.3 million soldiers fighting for the Saigon government, including the South Vietnamese and other allies.

The War in Numbers

3689 US fixed-wing aircraft lost

4857 US helicopters downed

15 million tonnes of US ammunition expended

Four million Vietnamese killed or injured

US Strategies

By 1966, the buzz words in Washington were 'pacification', 'search and destroy' and 'free-fire zones'. Pacification involved developing a pro-government civilian infrastructure in each village, and providing the soldiers to guard it. To protect villages from VC raids, mobile search-and-destroy units of soldiers moved around the country hunting VC guerrillas. In some cases, villagers were evacuated so the Americans could use heavy weaponry such as napalm and tanks in areas declared free-fire zones.

These strategies were only partially successful: US forces could control the countryside by day, while the VC usually controlled it by night. Even without heavy weapons, VC guerrillas continued to inflict heavy casualties in ambushes and through extensive use of mines and booby traps. Although free-fire zones were supposed to prevent civilian casualties, plenty of villagers were nevertheless shelled, bombed, strafed or napalmed. These attacks turned out to be a fairly efficient recruiting tool for the VC.

The American War in Vietnam claimed the lives of countless journalists. For a look at the finest photographic work from the battlefront, *Requiem* is an anthology of work from fallen correspondents on all sides of the conflict and a fitting tribute to their trade.

The Turning Point

In January 1968, North Vietnamese troops launched a major attack on the US base at Khe Sanh in the Demilitarised Zone (DMZ). This battle,

1963
South Vietnam's president Ngo Dinh Diem is overthrown and killed in a coup backed by the USA, which brings a new group of young military commanders into power.

1964
Although the US is not officially at war, it launches Operation Pierce Arrow and bombs North Vietnam for the first time in retaliation for the Gulf of Tonkin incident.

1965
To prevent the total collapse of the Saigon regime, US President Lyndon Johnson intensifies bombing of North Vietnam and approves the dispatch of American combat troops to the South.

1967
By the end of the year, there are 1.3 million soldiers fighting for the South – nearly half a million of these are from the US.

the single largest of the war, was in part a massive diversion from the Tet Offensive.

The Tet Offensive marked a decisive turning point in the war. On the evening of 31 January, as the country celebrated the Lunar New Year, the VC broke an unofficial holiday ceasefire with a series of coordinated strikes in more than 100 cities and towns. As the TV cameras rolled, a VC commando team took over the courtyard of the US embassy in central Saigon. However, the communists miscalculated the mood of the population, as the popular uprising they had hoped to provoke never materialised. In cities such as Hue, the VC were not welcomed as liberators and this contributed to a communist backlash against the civilian population.

The poignant wartime diaries of a young doctor who volunteers for the Viet Cong, *Last Night I Dreamed of Peace: The Diary of Dang Thuy Tram* were only published 35 years after her death.

Although the US were utterly surprised – a major failure of military intelligence – they immediately counter-attacked with massive firepower, bombing and shelling heavily populated cities. The counter-attack devastated the VC, but also traumatised the civilian population. In Hue, a US officer bitterly remarked that they 'had to destroy the town in order to save it'.

The Tet Offensive killed about 1000 US soldiers and 2000 ARVN troops, but VC losses were more than 10 times higher.

The VC may have lost the battle, but were on the road to winning the war. The US military had long been boasting that victory was just a matter of time. Watching the killing and chaos in Saigon beamed into their living rooms, many Americans stopped swallowing the official line. While US generals were proclaiming a great victory, public tolerance of the war and its casualties reached breaking point.

Simultaneously, stories began leaking out of Vietnam about atrocities and massacres carried out against unarmed Vietnamese civilians, including the infamous My Lai Massacre. This helped turn the tide and a coalition of the concerned emerged.

Oliver Stone, never one to shy away from political point-scoring, earns a maximum 10 with *Platoon*, the first of his famous trilogy about Vietnam. It is a brutal and cynical look at the conflict through the eyes of rookie Charlie Sheen, with great performances from Tom Berenger and Willem Dafoe.

Nixon & His Doctrine

Once elected president, Richard Nixon released a doctrine that called on Asian nations to be more 'self-reliant' in matters of defence. Nixon's strategy advocated 'Vietnamisation' – making the South Vietnamese fight the war without the support of US troops.

Meanwhile, the first half of 1969 saw the conflict escalate further as the number of US soldiers in Vietnam reached an all-time high of 543,400. While the fighting raged, Nixon's chief negotiator, Henry Kissinger, pursued peace talks in Paris with his North Vietnamese counterpart Le Duc Tho.

In 1969, the Americans began secretly bombing Cambodia in an attempt to flush out Vietnamese communist sanctuaries. In 1970, US ground forces were sent into Cambodia and the North Vietnamese moved deeper into Cambodian territory. By summer 1970, they (together with their Khmer Rouge allies) controlled half of Cambodia, including Angkor Wat.

1968

The Viet Cong launches the Tet Offensive, a surprise attack on towns and cities throughout the South. Hundreds of Vietnamese civilians are killed in the My Lai Massacre.

1969

After a lifetime dedicated to revolution, Ho Chi Minh dies in Hanoi in September 1969, of heart failure. He's succeeded by a 'collective leadership,' headed by Le Duan.

1970

Nixon's national security advisor, Henry Kissinger, and Le Duc Tho, for the Hanoi government, start talks in Paris as the US begins a reduction in troop numbers.

1971

The ARVN's Operation Lam Son, aimed at cutting the Ho Chi Minh trail in Laos, ends in calamitous defeat as half its invading troops are either captured or killed.

TRACKING THE AMERICAN WAR

The American War in Vietnam was the story for a generation. Follow in the footsteps of soldiers, journalists and politicians on all sides with a visit to the sites where the story unfolded.

China Beach The strip of sand near Danang where US soldiers dropped in for some rest and relaxation.

Cu Chi Tunnels The Vietnamese dug an incredible and elaborate tunnel network to evade American forces, just 30km from Saigon and right under the noses of a US base.

Demilitarised Zone (DMZ) The no-man's land at the 17th Parallel, dividing North and South Vietnam. After 1954, it became one of the most heavily militarised zones in the world.

Ho Chi Minh Trail The supply route for the South; the North Vietnamese moved soldiers and munitions down this incredible trail through the Truong Son Mountains in an almost unparalleled logistical feat.

Hue Citadel The ancient Citadel was razed to the ground during street-to-street fighting in early 1968 when the Americans retook the city from the communists after a three-week occupation.

Khe Sanh This was the biggest smokescreen of the war, as the North Vietnamese massed forces around this US base in 1968 to draw attention away from the Tet Offensive.

Long Tan Memorial The Australian contingent who fought in Vietnam, mostly based near Vung Tau in the south, is remembered here with the Long Tan Memorial Cross.

My Lai The village of My Lai is infamous as the site of one of the worst atrocities in the war, when American GIs massacred hundreds of villagers in March 1968.

Vinh Moc Tunnels The real deal: these tunnels haven't been surgically enlarged for tourists and they mark yet another feat of infrastructural ingenuity.

This new escalation provoked violent anti-war protests in the US and elsewhere. A peace demonstration at Kent State University in Ohio resulted in four protesters being shot dead. The rise of organisations such as Vietnam Veterans Against the War demonstrated that it wasn't just those fearing military conscription who wanted the USA out of Vietnam. It was clear that the war was tearing America apart.

In the spring of 1972, the North Vietnamese launched an offensive across the 17th Parallel; the USA responded with increased bombing of the North and by laying mines in North Vietnam's harbours. The 'Christmas bombing' of Haiphong and Hanoi at the end of 1972 was calculated to wrest concessions from North Vietnam at the negotiating table. Eventually, the Paris Peace Accords were signed by the USA, North Vietnam, South Vietnam and the VC on 27 January 1973, which provided for a

1972

The North Vietnamese cross the Demilitarised Zone (DMZ) at the 17th parallel to attack South Vietnam and US forces in what became known as the Easter Offensive.

1973

All sides put pen to paper to sign the Paris Peace Accords on 27 January 1973, stipulating an end to hostilities, but the conflict rumbles on.

1975

On 30 April 1975, Saigon falls to the North Vietnamese, as the last Americans scramble to leave the city.

1976

The Socialist Republic of Vietnam is proclaimed as Saigon is re-named Ho Chi Minh City. Hundreds of thousands flee abroad, including many boat people.

'WE WERE WRONG'

Commentators and historians have since observed that if Washington had allowed Vietnam's long history of successfully repelling invaders to deter it, the extensive tragedy of this war might have been averted, and likewise the resulting social disruption in America, as people sought to come to terms with what had happened in Vietnam. An entire generation of Americans had to assess its conduct. Years later, one of the architects of the war, former Defense Secretary Robert NcNamara, stated in his memoir, 'We were wrong, terribly wrong. We owe it to future generations to explain why'.

ceasefire, the total withdrawal of US combat forces and the release of 590 American POWs. The agreement failed to mention the 200,000 North Vietnamese troops still in South Vietnam.

US teams continue to search Vietnam, Laos and Cambodia for the remains of their fallen comrades. In more recent years, the Vietnamese have been searching for their own MIAs in Cambodia and Laos.

Other Foreign Involvement

Australia, New Zealand, South Korea, the Philippines and Thailand also sent military personnel to South Vietnam as part of what the Americans called the 'Free World Military Forces', whose purpose was to help internationalise the American war effort in order to give it more legitimacy.

The Paris Peace Accords of 1973 included a provision for US reparations to Vietnam totalling US$3.5 billion, and this became the main stumbling block to normalising relations in 1978. No money has ever been paid to Vietnam.

Australia's participation in the conflict constituted the most significant commitment of its military forces since WWII. Of the 46,852 Australian military personnel who served in the war, casualties totalled 496, with 2398 soldiers wounded.

Most of New Zealand's contingent, which numbered 548 at its highest point in 1968, operated as an integral part of the Australian Task Force, which was stationed near Baria, just north of Vung Tau.

The Fall of the South

Most US military personnel departed Vietnam in 1973, leaving behind a small contingent of technicians, advisors and CIA agents. The bombing of North Vietnam ceased and the US POWs were released. Still the war rumbled on, only now the South Vietnamese were fighting alone.

In January 1975, the North Vietnamese launched a massive ground attack across the 17th Parallel using tanks and heavy artillery. The invasion provoked panic in the South Vietnamese army, which had always depended on US support. In March, the NVA occupied a strategic section of the central highlands at Buon Ma Thuot. South Vietnam's president,

1978
Vietnamese forces invade Cambodia on Christmas Day 1978, sweeping through the shattered country and later overthrowing the Khmer Rouge government on 7 January 1979.

1979
China invades northern Vietnam in February in a retaliatory attack against Vietnam's overthrow of the Khmer Rouge, but the Vietnamese emerge relatively unscathed. Thousands of ethnic Chinese flee Vietnam.

1980s
During the decade Vietnam receives nearly $3 billion a year in economic and military aid from the Soviet Union and trades mostly with the USSR and eastern bloc nations.

1986
Doi moi (economic reform), Vietnam's answer to *perestroika* and the first step towards re-engaging with the West, is launched with a rash of economic reforms.

Nguyen Van Thieu, decided on a strategy of tactical withdrawal to more defensible positions. This was to prove a spectacular military blunder.

Whole brigades of ARVN soldiers disintegrated and fled southward, joining hundreds of thousands of civilians clogging Hwy 1. City after city – Hue, Danang, Quy Nhon, Nha Trang – were simply abandoned with hardly a shot fired. The ARVN troops were fleeing so quickly that the North Vietnamese army could barely keep up.

Nguyen Van Thieu, in power since 1967, resigned on 21 April 1975 and fled the country, allegedly carting off millions of dollars in ill-gotten wealth. The North Vietnamese pushed on to Saigon and on the morning of 30 April 1975, their tanks smashed through the gates of Saigon's Independence Palace. General Duong Van Minh, president for just 42 hours, formally surrendered, marking the end of the war.

Just a few hours before the surrender, the last Americans were evacuated by helicopter from the US embassy roof to ships stationed just offshore. Harrowing images of US Marines booting Vietnamese people off their helicopters were beamed around the world. And so more than a quarter of a century of American military involvement came to a close. Throughout the entire conflict, the USA never actually declared war on North Vietnam.

The Americans weren't the only ones who left. As the South collapsed, 135,000 Vietnamese also fled the country; over the next five years, at least half a million of their compatriots would do the same. Those who left by sea would become known to the world as 'boat people'. These refugees risked everything to undertake perilous journeys on the South China Sea, but eventually some of these hardy souls found new lives in places as diverse as Australia and France.

Reunification of Vietnam

On the first day of their victory, the communists changed Saigon's name to Ho Chi Minh City (HCMC). This was just for starters.

The sudden success of the 1975 North Vietnamese offensive surprised the North almost as much as it did the South. Consequently, Hanoi had no detailed plans to deal with the reintegration of the North and South, which had totally different social and economic systems.

The party faced the legacy of a cruel and protracted war that had fractured the country. There was bitterness on both sides, and a daunting series of challenges. Damage from the fighting was extensive, including anything from unmarked minefields to war-focused, dysfunctional economies; from a chemically poisoned countryside to a population who were physically or mentally scarred. Peace may have arrived, but the struggle was far from over.

The majority of Vietnamese 'boat people' who fled the country in the late 1970s were ethnic Chinese whose wealth and business acumen, to say nothing of their ethnicity, made them an obvious target for the revolution.

Neil Sheehan's account of the life of Colonel John Paul Vann, *Bright Shining Lie*, won the Pulitzer Prize and is the portrayal of one man's disenchantment with the war, mirroring America's realisation it could not be won.

1989

Vietnamese forces pull out of Cambodia in September as the Soviet Union scales back its commitment to its communist partners. Vietnam is at peace for the first time in decades.

1991

Vietnam, a hard currency–starved nation, opens its doors to tourism in a bid to boost its finances. The first backpackers arrive, though tough restrictions apply to travel.

1992

A new constitution is drawn up which allows selective economic reforms and freedoms. However, the Communist Party remains the leading force in Vietnamese society and politics.

1994

The US trade embargo on Vietnam, in place in the North since 1964 and extended to the reunified nation since 1975, is revoked as relations begin to normalise.

THE COST OF WAR

In total, 3.14 million Americans (including 7200 women) served in Vietnam. Officially, 58,183 Americans were killed in action or listed as missing in action (MIA). The direct cost of the war was officially put at US$165 billion, though its real cost to the economy was likely to have been considerably more.

By the end of 1973, 223,748 South Vietnamese soldiers had been killed in action; North Vietnamese and VC fatalities have been estimated at one million. Approximately four million civilians (or 10% of the Vietnamese population) were injured or killed during the war. At least 300,000 Vietnamese and 2200 Americans are still listed as MIA.

Until the formal reunification of Vietnam in July 1976, the South was ruled by the Provisional Revolutionary Government. The Communist Party did not trust the South's urban intelligentsia, so large numbers of Northern cadres were sent southward to manage the transition. This fuelled resentment among Southerners who had worked against the Thieu government and then, after its overthrow, found themselves frozen out.

The party opted for a rapid transition to socialism in the South, but it proved disastrous for the economy. Reunification was accompanied by widespread political repression. Despite repeated assurances to the contrary, hundreds of thousands of people who had ties to the previous regime had their property confiscated and were rounded up and imprisoned without trial in forced-labour camps, euphemistically known as re-education camps. Tens of thousands of business people, intellectuals, artists, journalists, writers, union leaders and religious leaders – some of whom had opposed both the Southern government and the war – were held in terrible conditions.

For a human perspective on the North Vietnamese experience during the war, read *The Sorrow of War* by Bao Ninh, a poignant tale of love and loss that suggests the soldiers from the North had the same fears and desires as most American GIs.

Contrary to its economic policy, Vietnam sought a rapprochement with the USA, and by 1978 Washington was close to establishing relations with Hanoi. But the China card was ultimately played: Vietnam was sacrificed for the prize of US relations with Beijing, and Hanoi moved into the orbit of the Soviet Union, on whom it was to rely for the next decade.

China & the Khmer Rouge

Relations with China to the north and its Khmer Rouge allies to the west were rapidly deteriorating. War-weary Vietnam felt encircled by enemies. An anti-capitalist campaign was launched in March 1978, seizing private property and businesses. Most of the victims were ethnic Chinese –

1995

Vietnam joins the Association of South-East Asian Nations (ASEAN), an organisation originally founded as a bulwark against the expansion of communism in the region.

2003

Crime figure Nam Can is sentenced to death for corruption, embezzlement, kidnap and murder; the case implicates dozens of police and politicians.

2004

The first US commercial flight since the end of the American War touches down in Ho Chi Minh City.

2006

Vietnam plays host to the glitzy APEC (Asia-Pacific Economic Cooperation) summit, welcomes US president George W Bush, and prepares to join the World Trade Organization.

hundreds of thousands soon became refugees or 'boat people', and relations with China soured further.

Meanwhile, repeated attacks on Vietnamese border villages by the Khmer Rouge forced Vietnam to respond. Vietnamese forces entered Cambodia on Christmas Day 1978. They succeeded in driving the Khmer Rouge from power on 7 January 1979 and set up a pro-Hanoi regime in Phnom Penh. China viewed the attack on the Khmer Rouge as a serious provocation. In February 1979, Chinese forces invaded Vietnam and fought a brief, 17-day war before withdrawing.

Liberation of Cambodia from the Khmer Rouge soon turned to occupation and a long civil war, which exacted a heavy toll on Vietnam. The command economy was strangling the commercial instincts of Vietnamese rice farmers. Today, one of the world's leading rice exporters, Vietnam was a rice importer back in the early 1980s. War and revolution had brought the country to its knees and a radical change in direction was required.

Vietnam received nearly $3 billion a year in Soviet Union aid throughout the 1980s, and most of its trade was with other socialist countries, from Cuba to Czechoslovakia. Russian and Vietnamese politicans would seal deals at restaurants such as Maxim's in Ho Chi Minh City with Bulgarian wine and Havana cigars.

Opening the Door

In 1985, President Mikhael Gorbachev came to power in the Soviet Union. *Glasnost* (openness) and *perestroika* (restructuring) were in, radical revolutionaries were out. Vietnam followed suit in 1986 by choosing reform-minded Nguyen Van Linh to lead the Vietnamese Communist Party. *Doi moi* (economic reform) was experimented with in Cambodia and introduced to Vietnam. As the USSR scaled back its commitments to the communist world, the far-flung outposts were the first to feel the pinch. The Vietnamese decided to unilaterally withdraw from Cambodia in September 1989, as they could no longer afford the occupation. The party in Vietnam was on its own and needed to reform to survive.

However, dramatic changes in Eastern Europe in 1989 and the collapse of the Soviet Union in 1991 were not viewed with favour in Hanoi. The party denounced the participation of non-communists in Eastern bloc governments, calling the democratic revolutions 'a counter-attack from imperialist circles' against socialism. Politically, things were moving at a glacial pace, but economically the Vietnamese decided to embrace the market. Capitalism has since taken root, and Vietnam joined ASEAN in 1995.

Relations with Vietnam's old nemesis, the USA, have also vastly improved. In early 1994, the USA lifted its economic embargo, which had been in place against the North since the 1960s. Full diplomatic relations were restored and presidents Bill Clinton and George W Bush have subsequently visited Hanoi.

2009

Pro-democracy activists are jailed for 'spreading propaganda against the government' by actions including hanging pro-democracy banners on a road bridge and publishing articles on the internet.

2010

Hanoi celebrates its 1000th birthday in October with exhibitions, and wild celebrations grip the capital; its imperial Citadel is declared a Unesco World Heritage site.

2013

General Giap, architect of the victory at Dien Bien Phu and military commander during the American War, dies at the age of 102. Millions pay their respects across the nation.

2015

Vietnam marks the 40th anniversary of reunification with massive military parades.

People & Culture

Industrious, proud, stubborn and yet mischievous, quick to laugh and fond of a joke, the Vietnamese are a complicated bunch. For Westerners, the national character can be difficult to fathom: direct questions are frequently met with evasive answers. A Vietnamese person would never tell a relative stranger their life story or profound personal thoughts the way people sometimes share feelings in the West. Their deep respect for tradition, family and the state reflects core Confucian principles.

The National Psyche

Historically the national mentality has been to work as a team, in harmony rather than in conflict; but times are changing. If you're on the highway or doing business, it's everyone for themselves. It's these attitudes (towards traffic and commerce) that many outsiders, not just Westerners, find most alien. 'Face' is vital, and Vietnamese people hate giving way, often employing elaborate tactics of bluster and bluff (and cunning) to ensure they get where they want to go.

Shadows and Wind (1999), by journalist Robert Templer, is a snappily written exploration of contemporary Vietnam, from Ho Chi Minh personality cults to Vietnam's rock-and-roll youth.

My Generation

In many ways Vietnam is still a traditional, conservative society, particularly for the older generation, who remember the long, hard years and every inch of the territory for which they fought. Brought up on restraint and moderation, many remain unmoved by 21st-century consumer culture. For the new generation, Vietnam is very different: a place to succeed and to ignore the staid structures set by the Communists. And yes, to show off that gleaming new motorbike, sharp haircut or iPhone.

North–South Divide

The north–south divide lingers on. It's said that Southerners think, then do; while Northerners think, then think some more. Southerners typically reckon Northerners have 'hard faces', that they take themselves too seriously and don't know how to have fun. Northerners are just as likely to think of Southerners as superficial, frivolous and business-obsessed. Caricatures these may be, but they shed light on the real differences be-

BROTHERS OR MATES?

There are few places on earth where terms of address are as important as Vietnam. To use the wrong term can be a gross insult, disrespectful, or just a little too casual depending on the circumstances. Age and status are key factors.

Three men, all strangers, get chatting in a bar. Dzung is in his mid-20s, Vinh in his mid-30s, Huong is in his 40s. They quickly work out they have broadly similar social backgrounds. The correct way for Dzung to refer to Vinh is *anh* (big brother), but he should call Huong *chu* (uncle). He should also refer to himself as *em* (little brother) when speaking to Vinh but *chau* (nephew) to Huong.

Unless they are being very modern (or very merry!) and all decide to use the term *ban* (friend).

tween north and south that reach beyond the (very different) regional dialects.

Climate plays its part too. Life is easier in the south, where the fertile Mekong Delta allows three rice harvests a year. The north endures a long winter of grey skies, drizzle, mist and cool winds. Think of the differences between northern and southern Europe (or Maine and Alabama) and you have a snapshot of how one people can become two. Don't forget that the north has also lived with communism for more than half a century, while the south had more than two decades of free-wheelin' free-for-all with the Americans.

Face

Face is all important in Asia, and in Vietnam it is above all. Having 'big face' is synonymous with prestige, and prestige is particularly important. All families, even poor ones, are expected to have elaborate wedding parties and throw their money around like it's water in order to gain face. This is often ruinously expensive, but far less distressing than 'losing face'.

Foreigners should never lose their tempers with the Vietnamese; this will bring unacceptable 'loss of face' to the individual involved and end any chance of a sensible solution to the dispute. Similarly, it's also not culturally acceptable for Vietnamese traders to shout at, tug or pressure tourists when trying to do a deal. Hustlers can adopt these tactics during a hard sell. Walk on.

Dancing Girl, directed by Le Hoang, caused a major splash with its release in 2003. It tells the story of two HIV-positive prostitutes, and Hoa (played by My Duyen) is seen mainlining heroin.

Lifestyle

Traditionally, Vietnamese life has revolved around family, fields and faith, with the rhythm of rural existence continuing for centuries at the same pace. All this has been disrupted by war, the impact of communism and globalisation. Whilst it's true that several generations may still share the same roof, the same rice and the same religion, lifestyles have changed immeasurably.

Vietnam is experiencing its very own '60s swing, which is creating feisty friction as sons and daughters dress as they like, date who they want and hit the town until all hours. But few live on their own and they still come home to Mum and Dad at the end of the day, where arguments might arise, particularly when it comes to marriage and settling down.

Some things never change. Most Vietnamese despise idleness and are early risers. You'll see parks full of t'ai chi devotees as dawn breaks, and offices are fully staffed by 7am. Indeed the whole nation seems supercharged with energy and vitality, no matter how hot and humid it is.

Family

In Vietnam the status of your family is more important than your salary. A family's reputation commands respect and opens doors.

Extended family is important to the Vietnamese and that includes second or third cousins, the sort of family that many Westerners may not even realise they have. The extended family comes together during times of trouble and times of joy, celebrating festivals and successes, mourning deaths or disappointments. This is a source of strength for many of the older generation.

Vietnamese who have emigrated are called Viet Kieu. They have traditionally been maligned by locals as cowardly, arrogant and privileged. However the official policy is now to welcome them, and their money, back to the motherland.

Business Practices

Western visitors regularly complain about the business practices of many Vietnamese they encounter, which can range from mild price hiking to outright scamming. For many foreigners it's the most off-putting aspect of their visit to the nation. At times it seems impossible to get the local price for anything. A little background is important.

WHEN IN NAM… DO AS THE VIETS

Take your time to learn a little about the local culture in Vietnam. Here are a few tips to help you go native.

Dress code Respect local dress standards: shorts to the knees, women's tops covering the shoulder, particularly at religious sites. Remove your shoes before entering a temple. Topless or nude sunbathing is totally inappropriate.

It's on the cards Exchanging business cards is an important part of even the smallest transaction or business contact. Hand them out like confetti.

Deadly chopsticks Leaving a pair of chopsticks sitting vertically in a rice bowl looks very much like the incense sticks that are burned for the dead. This is not appreciated anywhere in Asia.

Mean feet Remove shoes when entering somebody's home. Don't point the bottom of your feet towards other people. Never, ever point your feet towards anything sacred, such as a Buddha image.

Hats off to them As a form of respect to elderly or other esteemed people, such as monks, take off your hat and bow your head politely when addressing them. The head is the symbolic highest point – never pat or touch a person on the head.

Most of these rapacious individuals work in tourism; chronic overcharging is rare once you're off the main banana pancake trail. The mentality is that Westerners do not bother to learn the real price, don't learn Vietnamese and are only in the country for a week or two. For years, many Vietnamese have only thought about the short term – about making a fast buck. Steadily the concept has grown that good service will bring repeat business (and bad service will be all over internet forums immediately).

It's not an excuse, but Vietnam is a unique country. Famine killed 2 million in the 1940s, and the country was among the poorest of the poor following the American War. Vietnam's tourism industry is still young and the Vietnamese state actually helped forge this overcharging mentality – until relatively recently the government set separate local and foreign rates (which were four to 10 times more) for everything from train fares to hotel rooms.

The People of Vietnam

Vietnamese culture and civilisation have been profoundly influenced by the Chinese, who occupied the country for 1000 years and whose culture deeply permeates Vietnamese society.

Failing businesses often call in a geomancer (feng shui expert). Sometimes the solution is to move a door or a window. If this doesn't do the trick, it might be necessary to move an ancestor's grave.

History has of course influenced the mix of Vietnamese minorities. The steady expansion southwards in search of cultivable lands absorbed first the Kingdom of Champa and later the eastern extent of the Khmer Empire; both the Chams and the Khmers are sizeable minorities today.

Traffic was not only one-way. Many of the 50 or more minority groups that live in the far northwest only migrated to these areas from Yunnan (China) and Tibet in the past few centuries. They moved into the mountains that the lowland Vietnamese considered uncultivable, and help make up the most colourful part of the ethnic mosaic that is Vietnam today.

The largest minority group in Vietnam has always been the ethnic-Chinese community, which makes up much of the commercial class in the cities. The government has traditionally viewed them with suspicion, and many left the country as 'boat people' in the 1970s. But today they play a major part in economic development.

Minorities

Vietnam is home to 53 ethnic minority groups (around 14 million people). Most live in northern Vietnam, carving an existence out of the lush mountain landscapes along the Chinese and Lao borders.

Some groups have lived in Vietnam for millennia, while the Hmong migrated south from China in the past few centuries. Each has its own language, customs, mode of dress and spiritual beliefs.

The government has long encouraged hill tribes to shift to lower altitudes and adopt wet-rice agriculture and the cultivation of cash crops, tea and coffee, with incentives such as subsidised irrigation, better education and health care. But the hill tribes' long history of independence keep many away from the lowlands.

In the far north, many hill-tribe women still wear incredible handwoven costumes – some girls start to learn to embroider before they can walk. In the central highlands attachment to traditional dress is rarer.

Prejudices against hill tribe people endure. Attitudes are changing slowly but the Vietnamese media can still present them as primitive and exotic. It's also not uncommon for Vietnamese people to still see minorities as subversive (some sided with the USA during the American War).

The reality is that minority people remain at the bottom of the educational and economic ladder. Despite improvements in rural schooling and regional healthcare, many hill tribe people marry young, have large families and die early. According to 2015 World Health Organisation figures, poor minority households account for 50% of all Vietnam's poor households (yet only number 14% of the population).

Paradise of the Blind, by Duong Thu Huong, was the first Vietnamese novel to be published in the USA. It is set in a northern village and a Hanoi slum, and recalls the lives of three women and the hardships they faced over some 40 years.

Minority Groups

These are some of the main minority groups in Vietnam:

Tay (population 1.6 million) Live at low elevations between Hanoi and the Chinese border. They adhere closely to Vietnamese beliefs in Buddhism, Confucianism and Taoism, but many also worship genies and local spirits. Tay literature and arts are famous throughout Vietnam.

Thai A large group (population 1.5 million) with origins in southern China, they settled along fertile riverbeds between Hoa Binh and Muong Lay. Villages consist of thatched houses built on bamboo stilts. The Thai minority are usually categorised by colour: Red, Black and White Thai. Black Thai women wear vibrantly coloured blouses and headgear.

Muong Mainly concentrated in Hoa Binh province, the male-dominated Muong (population 1.4 million) live in small stilt-house hamlets and are known for their folk literature, poems and music (performed with gongs, drums, pan pipes, flutes and two-stringed violin).

Hmong Around a million Hmong are spread across the far northern mountains. Most are animists, cultivating dry rice and raising animals. Each Hmong group – Black, White, Red, Green and Flower – has its own dress code.

ETHINIC MINORITY VILLAGES

Vietnam's minorities are spread throughout highland areas in the north and west of the country.

Sapa Red Dzao and Black Hmong live in the dramatic valleys around town.

Bac Ha Famous for its market, which draws Flower Hmong from far and wide.

Mai Chau Beautiful valley base of the White Thai, with many homestays.

Cao Bang Rugged highland region where Hmong, Nung and Tay people live.

Kon Tum Traditional Bahnar settlements and homestays.

Bho Hoong Remote village with homestays that's in Co Tu heartland.

During the American War, many minorities were enrolled in the Civil Irregular Defense Program (CIDG), part of the US Army Special Forces. Some fighters later formed militias and resisted Hanoi rule well into the 1980s.

Nung This tribe (population 800,000) live in small villages in the far northeastern provinces; their culture combines ancestral worship and a talent for handicrafts, including basketry.

Jarai These people (population 350,000) of the south-central highlands still practise animistic rituals, paying respect to their ancestors and nature through a host or *yang* (genie). Jarai cemeteries are elaborate, including carved totem-style effigies of the deceased.

Sedang The 150,000 Sedang of the south-central highlands do not carry family names, and there's said to be complete equality between the sexes. Sedang customs include grave abandonment and giving birth at the forest's edge.

Religion

Many Vietnamese are not very religious and some surveys indicate that only 20% of the population consider themselves to have a faith. That said, over the centuries, Confucianism, Taoism and Buddhism have fused with popular Chinese beliefs and ancient Vietnamese animism to create the Tam Giao (Triple Religion) that many Vietnamese identify with.

Christianity, present in Vietnam for 500 years, and Cao Daism (unique to the region) are other important religions.

Buddhism

The predominant school of Buddhism in Vietnam is Mahayana Buddhism (Dai Thua or Bac Tong, meaning 'From the North'). The largest Mahayana sect in the country is Zen (Dhyana or Thien), also known as the school of meditation. Dao Trang (the Pure Land school), another important sect, is practised mainly in the south.

Theravada Buddhism (Tieu Thua or Nam Tong) is found mainly in the Mekong Delta region, and is mostly practised by ethnic Khmers.

TET: THE BIG ONE

Tet is Christmas, New Year and birthdays all rolled into one. Tet Nguyen Dan (Festival of the First Day) ushers in the Lunar New Year and is the most significant date in the Vietnamese calendar. It's a time when families reunite in the hope of good fortune for the coming year, and ancestral spirits are welcomed back into the family home. And the whole of Vietnam celebrates a birthday; everyone becomes one year older.

The festival falls between 19 January and 20 February, the same dates as Chinese New Year. The first three days after Tet are the official holidays but many people take the whole week off.

Tet rites begin seven days before New Year's Day. Altars, laden with offerings, are prepared to ensure good luck in the coming year. Cemeteries are visited and the spirits of dead relatives invited home for the celebrations. Absent family members return home. It's important that the new year is started with a clean slate; debts are paid and cleaning becomes the national sport. A New Year's tree *(cay neu)* – kumquat, peach or apricot blossom – is displayed to ward off evil spirits.

At the stroke of midnight on New Year's Eve, all problems are left behind and mayhem ensues. The goal is to make as much noise as possible: drums and percussion fill the night air.

The events of New Year's Day are crucial as it's believed they affect the year ahead. People take extra care not to be rude or show anger. Other activities that are believed to attract bad spirits include sewing, sweeping, swearing and breaking things.

It's crucial that the first visitor of the year to each household is suitable – a wealthy married man with several children is ideal. Foreigners may not be considered auspicious!

Apart from New Year's Eve itself, Tet is a quiet family affair – *banh chung* (sticky rice with pork and egg) is eaten at home. Shops are closed, and virtually all transport ceases to run. It's a troublesome time to travel in Vietnam. However you're sure to be invited to join the celebrations. Just remember this phrase: *chuc mung nam moi* – Happy New Year!

Taoism

Taoism (Lao Giao or Dao Giao) originated in China and is based on the philosophy of Laotse (Old One), who lived in the 6th century BC.

Understanding Taoism is not easy. The philosophy values contemplation and simplicity. Its ideal is returning to the Tao (the Way, or the essence of which all things are made), and it emphasises *am* and *duong*, the Vietnamese equivalents of yin and yang.

Confucianism

More a philosophy than an organised religion, Confucianism (Nho Giao or Khong Giao) has been an important force in shaping Vietnam's social system and the lives and beliefs of its people.

Confucius (Khong Tu) was born in China around 550 BC. His code laid down a person's obligations to family, society and the state, which remain the pillars of the Vietnamese nation today.

Cao Daism

Cao Daism is an indigenous Vietnamese religion founded in the 1920s that fuses the secular and religious philosophies of both East and West. Its prophets include Buddha, Confucius, Jesus Christ, Moses and Mohammed, and some wacky choices, such as Joan of Arc, William Shakespeare and Victor Hugo.

There are thought to be between two and three million followers of Cao Daism in Vietnam. Its colourful headquarters are in Tay Ninh, northwest of HCMC.

Hoa Hao Buddhism

The Hoa Hao Buddhist sect (Phat Giao Hoa Hao) was founded in the Mekong Delta in 1939 by Huynh Phu So. His Buddhist philosophies involve simplicity in worship and no intermediaries between humans and the Supreme Being.

In recent years, vast new Buddhist temples have been constructed, including Chua Bai Dinh (near Ninh Binh), while giant new Buddha statues now define the coastline of Danang and Vung Tao.

Christianity

Catholicism was introduced in the 16th century by missionaries. Today, Vietnam has the second-highest concentration of Catholics (8% to 10% of the population) in Asia.

Protestantism was introduced to Vietnam in 1911 and most of the 200,000 or so followers today are hill tribe people in the central highlands.

Islam

Around 70,000 Muslims, mostly ethnic Chams, live in Vietnam, mainly in the south of the country. Traditionally, most Cham Muslims followed a localised adaptation of Islam (praying only on Fridays), though more orthodox Muslim practices have now been adopted.

Hinduism

There are around 60,000 Cham living in Vietnam who identify themselves as Hindus. They predominantly live in the same region as Cham Muslims, concentrated around Phan Rang on the south-central coast.

Arts & Architecture

Vietnam has a fascinating artistic and architectural heritage. Historically, the nation has absorbed influences from China, India and the Khmer kingdoms and fused them with indigenous traditions. Then the French, Americans and Soviet Union left their mark. Today, contemporary artists and architects look across the globe for inspiration.

Arts

Traditional Music

Vietnam's traditional music uses the five note (pentatonic) scale of Chinese origin. Folk tunes are usually sung without any instrumental accompaniment (and have been adapted by the Communist Party for many a patriotic marching song).

Indigenous instruments include the *dan bau,* a single-stringed zither that generates an astounding array of tones, and the *trung,* a large bamboo xylophone. Vietnam's minorities use distinctive instruments: reed flutes, gongs and stringed instruments made from gourds.

Contemporary Music

Vietnam's contemporary music scene is diverse and influenced by trends in the West and east Asia. As all artists are monitored by the government, subjects which could be deemed subversive are largely avoided (or heavily coded). V-pop girl and boy bands like 365 and YO!Girls with heavily stylised looks and choreographed moves are wildly popular with teenagers.

There's a small but growing hip-hop scene, with HCMC-born Suboi (who has over a million Facebook likes and two albums under her belt) acknowledged as Vietnam's leading female artist; she raps to eclectic beats including dubstep rhythms.

Vietnam's electronic scene is dominated by commercial DJs playing EDM. Club DJs are hampered by government policies (such in advance as producing track lists and translated lyrics – not easy for house and techno!). However HCMC's Heart Beat (www.heartbeatsaigon.com) promotes excellent underground events around the city. In the north, the Quest Festival (www.questfestival.net) pioneers electronic music, as well as indie and acoustic acts.

Hot bands include rock band Microwave, metal merchants Black Infinity, the punk band Giao Chi and also alt-roots band 6789.

Trinh Cong Son, who died in 2001, was a prolific writer-composer of anti-war and reconciliation songs; he was once called the Bob Dylan of Vietnam by Joan Baez.

Dance

Traditionally reserved for ceremonies and festivals, Vietnamese folk dance is again mainstream thanks to tourism. The Conical Hat Dance is visually stunning: women wearing *ao dai* (the national dress of Vietnam) spin around, whirling their classic conical hats.

Theatre

Vietnamese theatre fuses music, singing, recitation, dance and mime into an artistic whole. Classical theatre is very formal, employing fixed gestures and scenery and has an accompanying orchestra (dominated by the drum) and a limited cast of characters.

Popular theatre *(hat cheo)* expresses social protest through satire. The singing and verse include many proverbs accompanied by folk melodies. Modern theatre *(cai luong)* shows strong Western influences. Spoken drama *(kich noi* or *kich),* with its Western roots, appeared in the 1920s and is popular among students and intellectuals.

Vietnamese theatre is performed by dozens of state-funded troupes and companies around the country.

Puppetry

Conventional puppetry *(roi can)* and the uniquely Vietnamese art form of water puppetry *(roi nuoc)* draw their plots from the same legendary and historical sources as other forms of traditional theatre.

Water puppetry was first developed by farmers in northern Vietnam, who manipulated wooden puppets and used rice paddies as a stage. There are water-puppet theatres in both Hanoi and HCMC.

Painting

Painting on frame-mounted silk dates from the 13th century. It was originally the preserve of scholar-calligraphers, who painted grand works inspired by nature and realistic portraits for use in ancestor worship.

Much recent work has had political rather than aesthetic or artistic motives – some of this propaganda art is now highly collectable. Some young artists have gone back to the traditional-style silk or lacquer paintings, while others experiment with contemporary subjects. Hanoi and Hoi An have some great galleries.

Literature

Traditional oral literature *(truyen khau)* includes legends, folk songs and proverbs while Sino-Vietnamese literature was dominated by Confucian and Buddhist texts and governed by strict rules of metre and verse. From the late-13th century, *nom* characters began to used: the earliest text written was *Van Te Ca Sau* (Ode to an Alligator).

One of Vietnam's literary masterpieces, *Kim Van Kieu* (The Tale of Kieu) was written by Nguyen Du (1765–1820), a poet, scholar, mandarin and diplomat.

Contemporary writers include Nguyen Huy Thiep, who articulates the experiences of Vietnamese people in *The General Retires and Other Stories* while Duong Van Mai Elliot's memoir, *The Sacred Willow: Four Generations in the Life of a Vietnamese Family* was nominated for a Pulitzer Prize.

A Good Scent from a Strange Mountain by Robert Olen Butler is a compelling collection of short stories focusing on the struggles of Vietnamese emigrants in America

Cinema

One of Vietnam's earliest cinematographic efforts was a newsreel of Ho Chi Minh's 1945 Proclamation of Independence. Prior to reunification, the South Vietnamese movie industry produced a string of sensational, low-budget flicks. Conversely, North Vietnamese film-making efforts were very propagandist.

Contemporary films span a wide range of themes, from warfare to modern romance. In Nguyen Khac's *The Retired General* (1988), the central character copes with adjusting from his life as a soldier to that of a civilian family man.

Dang Nhat Minh is perhaps Vietnam's most prolific film-maker. In *The Return* (1993), he hones in on the complexities of modern relationships,

CONTEMPORARY LGBT FILMS

Important Vietnamese films featuring powerful LGBT narratives have recently been released. Vu Ngoc Dang' s 2011 *Lost In Paradise* is an empathetic portrayal of a country boy seeking a new life in HCMC, while the excellent Hanoi-set 2014 *Flapping in the Middle of Nowhere*, directed by Hoang Diep Nguyen, deals with sexual obsession and features a transgender character. The latter won best film at the Venice International Critics Week.

while *The Girl on the River* (1987) tells the stirring tale of a female journalist who joins an ex-prostitute in search of her former lover, a Viet Cong soldier.

For a look at the impact of *doi moi* (economic reform), Vu Xuan Hung's *Misforutune's End* (1996) tells the tale of a silk weaver who is deserted by her husband for a businesswoman.

Overseas-Vietnamese films include Tran Anh Hung's touching *The Scent of Green Papaya* (1992) which celebrates the coming of age of a young servant girl in Saigon. *Cyclo* (1995), his visually stunning masterpiece, cuts to the core of HCMC's gritty underworld and its violent existence.

Vietnamese-American Tony Bui made a splash with his exquisite feature debut *Three Seasons* (1999); it was set in HCMC and featured Harvey Keitel.

Architecture

Traditional Vietnamese architecture is unusual, as most important buildings are single-storey structures with heavy tiled roofs based on a substantial wooden framework (to withstand typhoons).

In rural parts, houses are chiefly constructed from timber and built in stilted style, so that the home is above seasonal floods (and away from snakes and wild animals). Bamboo and palm leaves (for roofing) are also well suited to the tropical monsoon climate. Homes are usually divided into sections for sleeping, cooking and storage, while livestock live below the house.

Quirky Vietnamese styles include the narrow tube houses of Hanoi's Old Quarter – the government collected tax according to the width of the space, so the slimmer the cheaper. The Nung minority people's homes are also unusual, sometimes built with mud walls and with only one part elevated on stilts.

Consider the Vietnamese saying 'land is gold' as you survey a typical townscape today. Skinny concrete blocks of dubious architectural merit, many up to seven storeys high, soar above empty lots or loom above paddy fields. Planning laws (or the virtual lack of them) allow land owners to build whatever they like, so cement constructions painted lime green or pink, kitted out with mirror windows, and built with vaguely French-inspired ornate balconies or Chinese details are quite common.

Colonial Style

Balconies *Grace important municipal buildings.*

Louvered windows *Usually green or brown.*

Stucco features *Decorative flourishes.*

Colour *Ochre/pale mustard.*

Terracotta roof tiles *Mediterranean-style.*

Colonial Buildings

Vietnam's French legacy is pronounced in the nation's architecture. Stately neoclassical buildings reinforced notions of European hegemony in the colonial era, and many still line grand city boulevards.

After the 1950s, most of these were left to rot as they symbolised an era many Vietnamese wished to forget. However recent renovation programs have led to structures, such as the former Hôtel de Ville (People's Committee Building) in Ho Chi Minh City and the Sofitel Metropole Hotel in Hanoi, being restored to their former glory. In HCMC, stop to admire the spectacular halls and vaulted ceiling of the central post office –

designed by Gustave Eiffel (of tower fame). Haiphong is another city with wonderful French designs.

In Hanoi's French Quarter, many grand villas have fallen on hard times and are today worth a fortune to developers. Meanwhile in Dalat, French villas have been converted into hotels; these include the classy Ana Mandara Villas; stately Dalat Hotel du Parc with its grand facade; and the shock-and-awe colonial magnificence of the Dalat Palace Hotel.

Colonial churches were built in a range of architectural styles. In Hanoi, the sombre neo-Gothic form of St Joseph is enhanced by dark grey stone, whereas all the bricks used to construct Ho Chi Minh City's cathedral were imported from France.

Art deco curiosities built under French rule include Dalat's wonderful train station, with its multicoloured windows, and the sleek La Residence Hotel in Hue.

Soviet architectural influence is deeply evident in Vietnam. Key buildings include Ho Chi Minh's Mausoleum in Hanoi and the Reunification Palace in Ho Chi Minh City.

Pagodas & Temples

Vietnamese religious structures do not follow a specific national prototype. Pagoda styles echo the unique religious make-up of the nation, with strong Chinese content (including Confucian, Tao and Mahayana Buddhist elements), while southern Cham temples reflect influences from India, Hindu culture and the Khmer empire.

Pagodas *(chua)* incorporate Chinese ornamentation and motifs, with buildings grouped around garden courtyards and adorned with statues and stelae. Most have single or double roofs with elevated hip rafters, though there are some with multi-tiered towers *(thap)* like Hue's Thien Mu Pagoda.

Vietnamese pagodas are designed according to feng shui (locally called *dia ly*) to achieve harmony of surroundings. They're primarily Buddhist places of worship, even though they may be dedicated to a local deity. Most are single-storey structures, with three wooden doors at the front. Inside are a number of chambers, usually filled with statues of Buddhas, bodhisattvas and assorted heroes and deities (Thien Hau, Goddess of the Sea, is popular in coastal towns). Flashing fairy lights, giant smoking incense spirals, gongs and huge bells add to the atmosphere. Garden courtyards, many with sculptures and some with a sacred pond (perhaps filled with turtles), connect to other temple structures, and there's often accommodation for monks at the rear.

Check out Hanoi's Temple of Literature for a superb example of a traditional Vietnamese temple or the wonderful pagodas in Hue.

Pagoda Features

Bodhisattvas *Enlightened earthly figures.*

Cheung Huang Yeh *Feared God of the City.*

Quan Am *Goddess of Mercy.*

Swastika *Sacred symbol signifying the heart of the Buddha.*

Thien Hau *Goddess providing protection at sea.*

Cham Style

The Cham primarily practised the Hindu religion, though some elements of Buddhism were also incorporated. Temple-building commenced as early as the 4th century.

Most Cham temples were built from brick, with decorative carvings and detailing probably added later. Principal features included the *kalan* (tower, the home of the deity), saddle-roofed *kosagrha* temples (which housed valuables belonging to the gods) and the *gopura* gateway. Dotting the temple sites are stone statues of deities and numerous stelae with inscriptions listing important events.

Important Cham sights include My Son, Po Nagar, Po Klong Garai and Po Shanu.

Food & Drink

Prepare to be amazed by Vietnam's cuisine. From traditional street stalls to contemporary big-city temples of upscale dining, the country serves up an endless banquet of exquisite eating.

Diverse landscapes – fertile highlands, waterlogged rice paddies, forest-cloaked mountains and sandy coasts – lend the cuisine variety, while a long history of contact with outsiders brings complexity. Over the centuries locals have adapted Chinese, Indian, French and Japanese techniques and specialities to their own palates.

The country's vast range of excellent edibles invites experimentation. Though Vietnam's well-known classics – *pho,* spring rolls and shrimp paste grilled on sugar cane – are all good and tasty, it pays to venture into the backstreets and markets and chow down on the street with the locals, as that's where you'll often find the most authentic food.

Flavours

Vietnamese palates vary from north to south, but no matter where they are, local cooks work to balance hot, sour, salty and sweet flavours in each dish.

Saltiness

Vietnamese food's saltiness comes from, well, salt, but also from the fermented seafood sauces that grace the shelves of every Vietnamese pantry. The most common is *nuoc mam* (fish sauce), which is so elemental to the cuisine that, sprinkled over a bowl of rice, it's considered a meal. *Nuoc mam* is made from small fish (most often anchovies) that are layered with salt in large containers, weighted to keep the fish submerged in their own liquid, and left in a hot place for up to a year. As they ferment, the fish release a fragrant (some might say stinky) liquid. The first extraction, called *nuoc mam cot,* is dark brown and richly flavoured – essentially an 'extra virgin' fish sauce reserved for table use. The second extraction, obtained by adding salted water to the already fermented fish is used for cooking. Phu Quoc Island is famous for its *nuoc mam,* though some cooks prefer the milder version made around coastal Phan Thiet.

The best way to tackle Vietnamese cuisine head-on is to sign up for a cooking course during your stay. Courses have really taken off in recent years, and many courses also incorporate a market visit to purchase essential ingredients.

Sweetness

Sugar's centrality to the cuisine is best illustrated by the ever popular *kho,* a sweet-savoury dish of fish or meat simmered in a clay pot with fish sauce and another oft-used seasoning – bitter caramel sauce made from cane sugar. Vietnamese cooks also use sugar to sweeten dipping sauces, desserts and, of course, coffee.

Sourness

Sweetness is countered with fruity tartness, derived from lime (to squeeze into noodle soups and dipping sauces) and from *kalamansi* (a small, green-skinned, orange-fleshed citrus fruit), the juice of which is combined with salt and black pepper as a delicious dip for seafood, meats and omelettes. In the south, tamarind is added as a souring agent to a fish-and-vegetable soup called *canh chua*, and to a delectable dish of whole prawns coated with sticky, sweet-and-sour sauce called *tom rang me*. Northern cooks who seek sourness are more likely to turn to vinegar. A clear, yellowish vinegar mixed with chopped ginger is often served alongside snail specialities such as *bun oc* (rice noodle and snail soup).

Herbs

Vietnamese food is often described as 'fresh' and 'light' owing to the plates heaped with gorgeous fresh herbs that seem to accompany every meal. Coriander, mint and anise-flavoured Thai basil will be familiar to anyone who's travelled in the region. Look also for green-and-garnet *perilla* leaves; small, pointy, pleasantly peppery, astringent *rau ram* leaves; and *rau om* (rice-paddy herb), which has delicate leaves that hint of lemon and cumin. *Rau om* invariably shows up atop bowls of *canh chua*. Shallots, thinly sliced and slowly fried in oil until caramelised, add a bit of sweetness when sprinkled on salad and noodle dishes.

Chilli & Pepper

Vietnamese cooking uses less hot chilli than Thai cuisine, though it's a key ingredient in central Vietnamese meals. Local chillies vary from the mild-flavoured, long, red, fleshy variety that appears in many southern dishes and is served chopped to accompany noodles, to the smallish pale-chartreuse specimen served as an accompaniment in restaurants specialising in Hue cuisine. Beware: the latter really packs a punch. Dried ground chillies and spicy chilli sauces are tabletop condiments in many a central Vietnamese eatery.

Vietnam is a huge peppercorn exporter, and ground black and white peppercorns season everything from *chao* (rice porridge) to beef stew. Wonderfully pungent, Vietnamese black peppercorns put what's sold in supermarkets back home to shame; if your country will allow it in, a half-kilogram bag makes a fine edible souvenir.

Fish Flavours

When it comes to fermented fish products, *nuoc mam* is only the tip of the iceberg. *Mam tom* is a violet (some would also say violent!) paste of salted, fermented shrimp. It's added to noodle soups, smeared onto rice-paper rolls, and even serves as a dip for sour fruits like green mango. It also lends a pungent salty backbone to specialities like *bun mam* (a southern fish-and-vegetable noodle soup). *Mam tom* has many versions in Vietnam, including ones made from crabs, shrimp of all sizes and various types of fish. Try to get past the odour and sample a range of dishes made with it: the flavour it lends to food is much more subtle than its stench might imply.

HABITS & CUSTOMS

Enter the Vietnamese kitchen and you'll be convinced that good food comes from simplicity. Essentials consist of a strong flame, basic cutting utensils, a mortar and pestle, and a well-blackened pot or two. The kitchen is so sacred that it is inhabited by its own deity, Ong Tao (Kitchen God). Offerings are always left in the kitchen for the spiritual guardian of the hearth, and every kitchen has an Ong Tao altar, considered to be the most important object in the kitchen.

When ordering from a restaurant menu don't worry about the succession of courses. All dishes are placed in the centre of the table as soon as they're ready and diners serve themselves. If it's a special occasion, the host may drop a morsel or two into your rice bowl.

Fish flavours also come from dried seafood. Vietnamese cooks are quite choosy about dried shrimp, with market stalls displaying up to 15 grades. You'll also find all sorts and sizes of dried fish, both whole and in fillets, and dried squid. The latter is often barbecued and sold from roving stalls.

Sauces, Spices & Curries

Kim Fay's *Communion – A Culinary Journey Through Vietnam* offers a real insight into Vietnam's wonderful food scene as the author travels the nation, shifting from street-food stalls to exquisite seafood restaurants. Engaging text is accompanied by recipes and photographs.

Vietnamese cooks use quite a few sauces, such as soy, oyster and fermented soybean – culinary souvenirs of China's almost 1000-year rule over the country's north. Warm spices like star anise and cinnamon are essential to a good *pho*.

Curries were introduced to Vietnam by Indian traders; now they're cooked up using locally made curry powder and paste packed in oil. Vietnamese curries, such as *ca ri ga* (chicken curry cooked with coconut milk and lemongrass) and *lau de* (curried goat hotpot), tend to be more aromatic than fiery.

Staples

Rice

Rice, or *com*, is the very bedrock of Vietnamese cuisine. In imperial Hue, rice with salt was served to distinguished guests by royal mandarins; these days locals eat at least one rice-based meal every day and offer a bowl of rice to departed ancestors.

If a Vietnamese says '*an com*' (literally 'let's eat rice'), it's an invitation to lunch or dinner. You can also get your fill of the stuff, accompanied by a variety of stir-fried meat, fish and vegetable dishes, at specialised, informal eateries called *quan com binh dan*.

Cooked to a soupy state with chicken, fish, eel or duck, rice becomes *chao* (rice porridge); fried in a hot wok with egg, vegetables and other ingredients, it's *com rang;* and 'broken' into short grains, steamed, topped with barbecued pork, an egg, and sliced cucumber, and accompanied by *nuoc cham* (a dipping sauce of sweetened fish sauce), it's *com tam*. Tiny clams called *hen* are sautéed with peppery Vietnamese coriander and ladled over rice to make *com hen*.

Sticky or glutinous rice (white, red and black) is mixed with pulses or rehydrated dried corn, peanuts and sesame seeds for a filling breakfast treat called *xoi* (*ngo* in central Vietnam). It can also be mixed with sugar and coconut milk then moulded into sweet treats, or layered with pork and steamed in bamboo or banana leaves for *banh chung*, a Tet speciality.

Soaked and ground into flour, rice becomes the base for everything from noodles and sweets to crackers and the translucent 'papers' that Vietnamese moisten before using to wrap salad rolls and other specialities.

VEGETARIANS & VEGANS

The good news is that there is now more choice than ever before when it comes to vegetarian dining. The bad news is that you have not landed in Veg Heaven, for the Vietnamese are voracious omnivores. While they dearly love veggies, they also adore much of what crawls on the ground, swims in the sea or flies in the air.

However, there are vegetarian *(com chay)* establishments in most towns, usually near Buddhist temples. Often these are local, simple places popular with observant Buddhists. Many use 'mock meat', tofu and gluten, to create meat-like dishes that can be quite delicious.

In keeping with Buddhist precepts, many vendors and eateries go vegetarian on the 1st and 15th days of each lunar month; this is a great time to scour the markets and sample dishes that would otherwise be off-limits. Otherwise, be wary. Any dish of vegetables may well have been cooked with fish sauce or shrimp paste.

Noodles

Noodles are an anytime-of-day Vietnamese meal or snack. *Pho* is made with *banh pho* (flat rice noodles), and though this northern dish gets all the culinary press, the truth is that truly fine versions, featuring a rich, carefully made broth are hard to come by. Other northern-style noodle dishes worth seeking out include *bun cha,* barbecued sliced pork or pork patties served with thin rice vermicelli, and *banh cuon,* stuffed noodle sheets that recall Hong Kong–style noodle rolls.

If you're a noodle lover, look for dishes featuring *bun,* the round rice noodles that are a central element in *bun bo Hue,* a spicy, beef speciality from central Vietnam. Other characteristically central Vietnamese noodle dishes include *my quang,* a dish of rice noodles tinted yellow with annatto seeds or pale pink (if made from red rice flour) topped with pork, shrimp, slivered banana blossoms, herbs and chopped peanuts, and doused with just enough broth to moisten. It's eaten with rice crackers (crumbled over to add crunch) and sweet hot chilli jam.

Cao lau, a noodle dish specific to the ancient port town of Hoi An, features thick, rough-textured noodles that are said to have origins in the soba noodles brought by Japanese traders. It's moistened with just a smidge of richly flavoured broth, then topped with slices of stewed pork, blanched bean sprouts, fresh greens and herbs, and crispy square 'croutons' made from the same dough as the noodles.

Southerners lay claim to a number of noodle specialities as well, such as the cool salad noodle *bun thit nuong* and *bun mam,* a strong fish-flavoured rice-noodle broth that includes tomatoes, pineapple and *bac ha* (a thick, spongy plant stem). (An identically named but significantly more challenging dish of cool rice noodles, bean sprouts and herbs dressed with straight *nuoc mam* is found in central Vietnam.)

Across Vietnam, keep an eye open also for *banh hoi,* very thin rice-flour noodles that are formed into delicate nests and eaten rolled with grilled meat in leafy greens. Chinese-style egg noodles *(mi)* are thrown into soups or fried and topped with a stir-fried mixture of seafood, meats and vegetables in gravy for a dish called *mi xao. Mien* (bean-thread noodles) made from mung-bean starch are stir-fried with *mien cua* (crab meat) and eaten with steamed fish.

A legacy of the French, *banh mi* refers to the crackly crusted rice- and wheat-flour baguettes sold everywhere (eaten plain or dipped in beef stew and soups), and the sandwiches made with them, stuffed with meats, veggies and pickles. If you haven't tried stuffed *banh mi,* you haven't eaten in Vietnam.

Rice-Paper Rolls

Vietnamese will wrap almost anything in crackly rice paper. Steamed fish and grilled meats are often rolled at the table with herbs, lettuce and slices of sour star fruit and green banana, and dipped in *nuoc cham.* Fat *goi cuon,* a southern speciality popularly known as 'salad' or 'summer' rolls, contain shrimp, pork, rice noodles and herbs and are meant to be dipped in bean paste or hoisin sauce. *Bo pia,* thin rice-paper cigars filled with slices of Chinese sausage, dried shrimp, cooked *jicama* (a crisp root vegetable), lettuce and chilli paste, are usually knocked up to order by street vendors with mobile carts.

Hue has its own version of the spring roll: soft, fresh *nem cuon Hue,* filled with sweet potato, pork, crunchy pickled prawns, water spinach and herbs. And then there's *nem ran ha noi,* northern-style, crispy, deep-fried spring rolls.

Meat, Fish & Fowl

Chicken and pork are widely eaten. In the mornings, the tantalising aroma of barbecuing *nuoc mam*–marinated pork, intended to fill breakfast baguette sandwiches and top broken rice, fills the air of many a city street. Beef is less frequently seen but does show up in bowls of *pho,* in *kho bo* (beef stew with tomato), in *thit bo bit tet* (Vietnamese pan-seared beefsteak), and wrapped in *la lot* (wild pepper leaves) and grilled. Other sources of protein include goat (eaten in hotpots with a curried broth) and frogs.

Thanks to Vietnam's long coastline and plentiful river deltas, seafood is a major source of protein. From the ocean comes fish such as tuna, pomfret, red snapper and sea bass, as well as prawns, crabs and clams. In Vietnam, seafood restaurants always keep their catch live in tanks or bowls, so you can be assured it's ocean fresh.

Flooded rice paddies yield minuscule crabs and golf-ball-sized snails called *oc*. In northern Vietnam, the former go into *bun rieu cua,* thin rice noodles in a crimson-hued broth made from tomatoes and pulverised crab shells; on top floats a heavenly layer of crab fat sautéed with shallots.

Snails can be found in *bun oc*, or chopped with lemongrass and herbs, stuffed into the snail shells and steamed, for *oc nhoi hap la xa* (a sort of Vietnamese escargot). A length of lemongrass leaf protrudes from each snail shell – give it a tug to pull out the meat.

Other favourite freshwater eats include the well-loved *ca loc* (snakehead fish), catfish, and, along the central coast, *hen* (small clams). The latter are eaten with rice in *hen com*, in broth with noodles, or scooped up with rice crackers (*banh da*).

Vegetables & Fruit

Vegetables range from the mundane – tomatoes, potatoes, eggplants (delicious grilled and topped with ground pork and *nuoc mam*), cucumbers, asparagus – to the exotic. Banana blossoms and lotus-flower stems are made into *goi* (salads), a thick, spongy plant stem called *bac ha* is added to soups, and *thien ly,* a wild plant with tender leaves and fragrant blossoms, is eaten stir-fried with garlic. Bunches of sunshine-yellow squash blossoms are a common sight in southern markets; locals like them simply stir-fried with garlic.

Keep an eye out for *sinh to* stalls stocked with a variety of fruits (including avocado, which the Vietnamese treat as a fruit rather than a vegetable) and a blender, where you can treat yourself to a refreshing blended-to-order iced fruit smoothie. It doesn't get much fresher than that.

All sorts of delicious wild mushrooms sprout on forest floors during the rainy season, and if you're off the beaten track, then you might also be treated to tender fern tips, which, like the more common *rau muong* (water spinach), get the stir-fry treatment. Especially loved are leafy greens such as lettuce, watercress and mustard, which Vietnamese use to wrap *banh xeo* (crispy pork and shrimp pancakes) into bite-sized parcels suitable for dipping in *nuoc mam.*

If you're a fruit lover you've come to the right place. Depending on when you're travelling, you'll be able to gorge on mangoes, crispy and sour green or soft and tartly floral pink guavas, juicy lychees and longans, and exotic mangosteen, passionfruit and jackfruit. Hue cooks treat young jackfruit as a vegetable, boiling the flesh (which tastes like a cross between artichoke and asparagus), shredding it, dressing it with fish sauce, scattering the lot with sesame seeds, and serving the dish (called *nom mit non)* with rice crackers. Tamarind is a typically southern ingredient; it also sauces shelled or unshelled prawns in *tom rang me* – a messy but rewarding sweet-tart dish.

Sweets

Do ngot (Vietnamese sweets) and *do trang mieng* (desserts) are popular everywhere, and are especially prevalent during festivals when you'll encounter sweet varieties of *banh* (traditional cakes). Rice flour is the base for many desserts, sweetened with sugar and coconut milk and enriched with lotus seeds, sesame seeds and peanuts. Yellow mung beans are also used, while the French influence is evident in crème caramel. Cold sweets, like *kem* (ice cream), *thach,* lovely layered agar-agar jellies in flavours such as pandan and coffee-and-coconut, and locally made sweetened yoghurt sold in small glass pots, hit the spot on steamy days.

VIETNAMESE COFFEE CULTURE

Enjoying a Vietnamese coffee is a tradition that can't be rushed. A glass tumbler, topped with a curious aluminium top is placed before you while you crouch on a tiny blue plastic chair. A layer of condensed milk on the bottom of the glass is gradually infused with coffee lazily drop, drop, dropping from the aluminium top. Minutes pass, and eventually a darker caffeine-laden layer floats atop the condensed milk. Stir it together purposefully – maybe pouring it over ice in a separate glass – and it's definitely an energising ritual worth waiting for. And while you're waiting, consider the *caphe* variations usually on offer in a Vietnamese cafe.

Caphe sua da Iced coffee with condensed milk

Caphe da Iced coffee without milk

Caphe den Black coffee

Caphe sua chua Iced coffee with yoghurt

Caphe trung da Coffee topped with a beaten egg white

Che are sweet 'soups' that combine ingredients like lotus seeds or tapioca pearls and coconut milk. They're also a scrumptious shaved-ice treat, for which a mound of ice crystals with your choice of toddy palm seeds, bits of agar-agar jelly, white or red beans, corn, and other bits is doused with coconut milk, condensed milk, sugar syrup or all three. The combination of beans, corn and sweet liquid might sound strange, but in addition to being delicious, *che* is surprisingly refreshing.

Drinks

You're unlikely to go thirsty in Vietnam where, thanks to a healthy drinking culture, there exists all manner of beverages, including plenty of beer. Sooner or later every traveller succumbs to *bia hoi* ('fresh' or draught beer) – local brands are served straight from the keg by the glass for a pittance from specialist stands on street corners. If you're looking to pay a little more, Saigon and Huda are decent, and La Rue, brewed on the central coast is quite good. In Ho Chi Minh City, the Pasteur Street Brewing Company (p347) has excellent craft beer often incorporating local ingredients like kaffir lime, jackfruit, and fragrant peppercorns from Phu Quoc Island.

While imported liquor can be expensive, Vietnam brews a number of its own spirits, including a drinkable, dirt-cheap vodka called Ha Noi. Distilled sticky-rice wine called *ruou* is often flavoured with herbs, spices, fruits and even animals. Travel to the northern highlands and you may be offered *ruou can*, sherry-like rice wine drunk through long bamboo straws from a communal vessel. And you'll undoubtedly encounter *ruou ran* (snake wine), supposedly a cure-all elixir. Cobras and many other snakes in Vietnam are officially listed as endangered, a fact that producers rarely heed.

Northerners favour hot green tea, while in the south the same is often served over big chunks of ice. Chrysanthemum and jasmine infusions are also popular. Particularly delicious is a fragrant non-caffeinated tea made from lotus seeds.

In Vietnam, the preparation, serving and drinking of tea (*tra* in the south and *che* in the north) has a social importance seldom appreciated by Western visitors. Serving tea in the home or office is more than a gesture of hospitality; it is a ritual.

Vietnam is also a major coffee producer, and whiling away a morning or an afternoon over glasses of iced coffee, with or without milk (*caphe sua da* or *caphe da*) is something of a ritual for Vietnam's male population.

Other liquid options in Vietnam include *mia da*, a freshly squeezed sugar-cane juice that's especially refreshing served over ice with a squeeze of *kalamansi; sinh to* (fresh-fruit smoothies blended to order); and soy milk.

Environment

Vietnam is one of the most diverse countries on earth, with tropical lowlands, intensely cultivated rice-growing regions, a remarkable coastline and karst mountains. But due to population pressure, poverty and a lack of environmental protection, many regions, and the nation's wildlife, are under threat.

The Landscape

As the Vietnamese are quick to point out, their nation resembles a *don ganh,* the ubiquitous bamboo pole with a basket of rice slung from each end. The baskets represent the main rice-growing regions of the Red River Delta in the north and the Mekong Delta in the south. The country bulges in the north and south and has a very slim waistline – at one point it's only 50km wide. Mountain ranges define most of Vietnam's western and northern borders.

Coast & Islands

Vietnam's extraordinary 3451km-long coastline is one of the nation's biggest draws and it doesn't disappoint, with sweeping sandy beaches, towering cliffs, undulating dunes and countless offshore islands. The largest of these islands is Phu Quoc in the Gulf of Thailand; others include Cat Ba and Van Don, the 2000 or so islets of Halong Bay, a spattering of dots off Nha Trang, and the fabled Con Dao Islands way out in the South China Sea.

River Deltas

The Red River and Mekong River deltas are both pancake-flat and prone to flooding. Silt carried by the Red River and its tributaries, confined to their paths by 3000km of dykes, has raised the level of the river beds above the surrounding plains. The Mekong Delta has no such protection, so when *cuu long* ('the nine dragons', ie the nine channels of the Mekong in the delta) burst their banks, it creates havoc for communities and crops.

RESPONSIBLE TRAVEL

- Consider shunning elephant rides. Working elephants are still illegally trapped and conservation groups have grave concerns about their living conditions, as well as the detrimental effects elephant rides have on the animal's health.
- When snorkelling or diving be careful not to touch coral as this hinders its growth.
- Avoid touching limestone formations as it affects their development and turns the limestone black.
- Most 'exotic' meats such as porcupine and squirrel have been illegally poached from national parks.
- Many civets are kept in appalling conditions to produce 'poo coffee'.
- Before downing snake wine or snake blood consider that the reptiles (sometimes endangered species) are killed without anaesthesia and can carry salmonella.

KARST YOUR EYES

Karsts are eroded limestone hills, the result of millennia of monsoon rains that have shaped towering tooth-like outcrops pierced by fissures, sinkholes, caves and underground rivers. Northern Vietnam contains some of the world's most impressive karst mountains, with stunning landscapes at Halong Bay, Bai Tu Long Bay, around Ninh Binh and in the Phong Nha region. At Halong and Bai Tu Long bays, an enormous limestone plateau has dramatically eroded so that old mountain tops stick out of the sea like bony vertical fingers pointing towards the sky. Phong Nha's cave systems are on an astonishing scale, stretching for tens of kilometres deep into the limestone land mass.

Highlands

Three-quarters of the country consists of rolling hills (mostly in the south) and mighty mountains (mainly in the north), the highest of which is 3143m Fansipan, close to Sapa. The Truong Son Mountains, which form the southwest highlands, run almost the full length of Vietnam along its borders with Laos and Cambodia. The coastal ranges near Nha Trang and those at Hai Van Pass (Danang) are composed of granite, and the giant boulders littering the hillsides are a surreal sight. The western part of the southwest highlands is well known for its fertile, red volcanic soil. However, Northern Vietnam's incredible karst formations are probably the nation's most iconic physical features.

Tram Chim National Park in the Mekong Delta is one of Vietnam's most important wetland reserves, and home to the giant sarus crane, which can measure up to 1.8m in height.

Wildlife

We'll start with the good news. Despite some disastrous bouts of deforestation, Vietnam's flora and fauna is still incredibly exotic and varied. Intensive surveys by the World Wildlife Fund along the Mekong River (including the Vietnamese section) found a total of 1068 new species from 1997 to 2007, placing this area on Conservation International's list of the top five biodiversity hot spots in the world. Numerous areas inside Vietnam remain unsurveyed or poorly known, and many more species are likely to be found.

The other side of the story is that despite this outstanding diversity, the threat to Vietnam's remaining wildlife has never been greater due to poaching, hunting and habitat loss. Three of the nation's iconic animals – the elephant, saola and tiger – are on the brink. It's virtually certain that the last wild Vietnamese rhino was killed inside Cat Tien National Park in 2010.

And for every trophy animal there are hundreds of other less 'headline' species that are being cleared from forests and reserves for the sake of profit (or hunger). Many of the hunters responsible are from poor minority groups who have traditionally relied on the jungle for their survival.

In October 2013 customs officials in Haiphong found more than two tonnes of elephant tusks and marine turtle shells hidden in a consignment labelled 'seashells'.

Animals

Vietnam has plenty to offer those who are wild about wildlife, but in reality many animals live in remote forested areas and encountering them is extremely unlikely.

With a wide range of habitats – from equatorial lowlands to high, temperate plateaus and even alpine peaks – the wildlife of Vietnam is enormously diverse. One recent tally listed 275 species of mammals, more than 800 birds, 180 reptiles, 80 amphibians, hundreds of fish and tens of thousands of invertebrates, but new species are being discovered at such a rapid rate that this list is constantly being revised upward.

Rare and little-known birds previously thought to be extinct have been spotted and no doubt there are more in the extensive forests along the

Lao border. Edwards's pheasant, previously believed to be extinct, was found on a scientific expedition, and other excursions have yielded the white-winged wood duck and white-shouldered ibis.

Even casual visitors will spot a few bird species: swallows and swifts flying over fields and along watercourses; flocks of finches at roadsides and in paddies; and bulbuls and mynas in gardens and patches of forest. Vietnam is on the east-Asian flyway and is an important stopover for migratory waders en route from Siberian breeding grounds to their Australian winter quarters.

William DeBuys' *The Last Unicorn: A Search for One of Earth's Rarest Creatures* is about searching for the saola and written by a Pulitzer Prize finalist.

Endangered Species

Vietnam's wildlife has been in significant decline as forest habitats are destroyed, waterways polluted and hunting continues with minimal checks. Captive-breeding programs may be the only hope for some, but rarely are the money and resources available for such expensive efforts.

Officially, the government has recognised 54 species of mammal and 60 species of bird as endangered. Larger animals at the forefront of the country's conservation efforts include elephant, tiger, leopard, black bear, honey bear, snub-nosed monkey, flying squirrel, crocodile and turtle. In the early 1990s, a small population of Javan rhinoceroses, the world's rarest rhino, was discovered in Cat Tien National Park. Twenty years later they had all been wiped out.

However, there have been some successful stories. The Siamese crocodile, extinct in the wild due to excessive hunting and cross-breeding, has been reintroduced to Cat Tien and is now thriving. Wildlife populations have also re-established themselves in reforested areas, and birds, fish and crustaceans have reappeared in replanted mangroves.

Twitchers with a serious interest in the birdlife of Vietnam should carry a copy of *Birds of South-east Asia* (2005) by Craig Robson, which includes thorough coverage of Vietnam.

National Parks

Vietnam has 31 national parks, from Hoang Lien in the far north to Mui Ca Mau on the very southern tip of Vietnam and over 150 nature reserves. Officially, 9% of the nation's territory is now protected. Levels of infrastructure and enforcement vary widely but every park has a ranger station. You can hire a ranger to guide you in most parks.

The management of national parks is a continuing source of conflict because Vietnam is still figuring out how to balance conservation with the needs of the adjoining rural populations (many of them minority people). Rangers are often vastly outnumbered by villagers who rely on

ON THE BRINK

Vietnam's native elephant species has been listed as endangered since 1976. The government announced the creation of three conservation areas to help protect wild elephants (in Pu Mat, Cat Tien and Yok Don national parks) in June 2013, but as the Forestry department estimates that less than 100 elephants remain in the wild, many see the action as too little, too late.

Only discovered in 1992, the saola is a large antelope-like wild ox and is only found in the Annamite mountains of Vietnam and Laos. Surviving numbers are thought to be in the hundreds. Conservation groups are working with minority people in the area to remove tens of thousands of snares from their forest habitat. For more information, consult www.savethesaola.org.

It's estimated that around 350 Indochinese tigers remain in the region, of which between 30 and 70 are in Vietnam. As they are in isolated pockets, their long-term chances are not great. Tigers are particularly vulnerable because of their value in the illegal trade in tiger parts for 'traditional' medicine.

TOP 10 NATIONAL PARKS

PARK	FEATURES	ACTIVITIES	BEST TIME TO VISIT
Ba Be	lakes, rainforest, waterfalls, towering peaks, caves, bears, langurs	hiking, boating, bird-watching	Apr-Nov
Bai Tu Long	karst peaks, tropical evergreen forest, caves, hidden beaches	swimming, surfing, boating, kayaking, hiking	Apr-Nov
Bach Ma	waterfalls, tigers, primates	hiking, bird-watching	Feb-Sep
Cat Ba	jungle, caves, trails, langurs, boars, deer, waterfowl	hiking, swimming, bird-watching	Apr-Aug
Cat Tien	primates, elephants, birdlife, tigers	jungle exploration, hiking	Nov-Jun
Con Dao	dugongs, turtles, beaches	bird-watching, snorkelling, diving	Nov-Jun
Cuc Phuong	jungle, grottoes, primates, bird-watching centre, caves	endangered-primate viewing, hiking	Nov-Feb
Hoang Lien	mountains, birdlife, minority communities	hiking, cycling, bird-watching, mountain climbing	Sep-Nov, Apr & May
Phong Nha-Ke Bang	caves, karsts	boat trips, caving, kayaking, hiking	Apr-Sep
Yok Don	stilt houses, minority communities	elephant rides, hiking	Nov-Feb

forests for food and income. Some parks now use high-tech mapping software to track poaching and logging activity.

If you can, try to visit the more popular parks during the week. For many locals a trip to a park is all about having a good time, and noise and littering can be a part of the weekend scene.

Many parks have accommodation and a restaurant; you should always call ahead and order food in advance though.

Fauna & Flora International (www.fauna-flora.org) produces the excellent *Nature Tourism Map of Vietnam*, which includes detailed coverage of all the national parks in the country. All proceeds from sales of the map go towards supporting primate conservation in Vietnam.

Environmental Issues

Vietnam's environment is not yet in intensive care, but it's reaching crisis level on several fronts. As a poor, densely populated country, the government's main priorities are job creation and economic growth. There's minimal monitoring of pollution and dirty industries, while loggers and animal traffickers are all too often able to escape trouble through bribery and official inaction. Quite simply, the environment is a low priority despite the government signing up to key conservation treaties.

Deforestation

Deforestation is a key issue. While 44% of the nation was forested in 1943, by 1983 only 24% was left and in 1995 it was down to 20%. Recent reforestation projects have increased cover since then, but these mostly consist of monocultural plantations of trees (like acacia for furniture) in straight rows that have little ecological merit. Plantations accounted for around 16% of all forest cover by 2015.

RHINO HORN & VIETNAM

The international pressure around the use of rhino horn is growing; in 2013, the World Wildlife Fund (WWF) and Traffic (the wildlife trade monitoring network) launched a campaign in Vietnam to counter its sale and consumption, declaring that the country needed to 'clean up its act'.

Demand for rhino horn has increased in recent years in Vietnam, spurred by superstitions and old wives' tales about rhino horn doing everything from increasing libido to curing cancer. Using rhino horn is also considered something of a status symbol for some of the emerging wealthy class. Some utterly deluded individuals even consider it a hangover-cure.

Even the tragic news about the extinction of the rhino in Vietnam has failed to curb demand. With tens of thousands of dollars being paid per kilo of horn, traffickers have simply switched their attention elsewhere.

Vietnamese gangs have stolen dozens of antique rhino horns from museum displays across Europe, sometimes at gunpoint. And in South Africa, home to over 70% of all the world's rhinos, there's been a rhino-poaching crisis. In 2007, 13 rhinos were killed in the country. By 2014 authorities reported a staggering 1215 rhinos had been killed (one every eight hours). According to the Environmental Investigation Agency, groups including Al-Shabaab are selling rhino horn to fund terrorism.

Vietnam is the world's largest user of rhino horn. A media campaign – public-service announcements on national radio, TV and internet lobbying – is ongoing to try to change mindsets and make the consumption of rhino horn unacceptable in Vietnam.

In September 2014, a new campaign called 'Chi' was launched, backed by Save the Rhino International (www.savetherhino.org), Traffic (www.traffic.org) and ENV (Education for Nature-Vietnam; www.envietnam.org). Market research found that wealthy businessmen from Hanoi and HCMC were the main consumers. As these people had little global environmental awareness, Chi promoted the slogan 'The most charismatic and successful men create their own good fortune' (the inference being rather than use rhino horn to prove their wealth or status). Other public education efforts have sought to reinforce the fact that rhino horn has no beneficial medical properties. However, progress is slow; a 2015 survey found that 38% of Vietnamese still thought rhino horn could help treat diseases such as cancer and rheumatism.

Rhino horn actually consists of a form of keratin, similar to fingernails.

Vietnam banned unprocessed timber exports in 1992, which has produced a rise in the amount of forest cover. However, this has been bad news for its neighbours, because it simply means Vietnam buys its timber from Laos and Cambodia, where environmental enforcement is lax.

Hunting

Wildlife poaching has decimated forests of animals; snares capture and kill indiscriminately, whether animals are common or critically endangered. Figures are very difficult to ascertain, but a 2007 survey by wildlife trade monitoring organisation Traffic estimated that a million animals were illegally traded each year in Vietnam.

PanNature (www.nature.org.vn) is a Vietnamese NGO promoting solutions to environmental problems. It occasionally offers volunteer opportunities.

Some hunting is done by minority people simply looking to put food on the table, but there's a far bigger market (fuelled by domestic and Chinese traders) for *dac san* (bush meat) and traditional medicine. For many locals, a trip to the country involves dining on wild game, the more exotic the better, and there are bush-meat restaurants on the fringes of many national parks. A 2010 survey by the Wildlife Conservation Society found that 57 out of 68 restaurants in Dalat were offering wild game (including civet, porcupine and wild pig).

Attempts to curtail this trade at local and national level are thwarted by bribery, corruption and understaffing of the Forest Protection Department. ENV (Education for Nature-Vietnam) is a local NGO combating the illegal wildlife trade by lobbying politicians and providing educational programs in schools. It maintains files on restaurants offering bush meat and campaigns against the bear bile trade.

Industry & Pollution

Vietnam has a serious pollution problem. In Ho Chi Minh City, the air quality is punishing, while Hanoi is the most contaminated city in Southeast Asia. Motorbikes are the main culprits, all running on low-quality fuel that has choking levels of benzene, sulphur and microscopic dust (PM10). Particulate (dust, grime) matter in Hanoi is around 150 micrograms per cu metre, whereas the World Health Organisation recommends a limit of 20.

Water pollution affects many regions, particularly the cities and coastal areas (where groundwater has become saline due to over-exploitation). Manufacturers have flooded into Vietnam to build clothing, footwear and food-processing plants, but most industrial parks have no wastewater treatment plants. The result is that discharge has caused biological death for rivers like the Thi Van. Nationwide, only 14% of all city waste water is treated.

Toxic and industrial waste is illegally imported along with scrap for use as raw materials for production and for re-export. Enforcement is lax, though some violators have been fined.

ENV (Education for Nature-Vietnam; www.envietnam.org) works to foster greater understanding in Vietnam about wildlife, and the illegal consumption of products from endangered animals. If you see endangered animals for sale or listed on a restaurant menu, call its toll-free hotline (☎1800 1522).

Global Warming

Vietnam is ranked as one of the most vulnerable countries in the world in the face of climate change, because rising tides, flooding and hurricanes will likely inundate low-lying areas.

The National Centre for Hydro-Meteorology Forecasting reported that 246 tropical storms affected Vietnam between 1961 and 2010. While there were three storms in 1961, the number was 10 in 2008.

A sea-level rise of only a metre would flood more than 6% of the country and affect up to 10 million people. HCMC already experiences serious flooding every month, and the Saigon River only has to rise 1.35m for its dyke defences to be breached. If monsoons worsen, similar flooding will create havoc in the vast deltas of the Red River.

PARADISE IN PERIL

Unesco World Heritage site Halong Bay is one of Vietnam's crown jewels. A dazzling collection of jagged limestone karst islands emerging from a cobalt sea, its beauty is breathtaking.

This beauty has proved a blessing for the tourist industry, yet cursed Halong with an environmental headache. In 2014, 1.8 million people cruised the karsts. In order to accommodate everyone, the authorities have ripped up mangroves to build coastal roads and new docks. Inadequate toilet-waste facilities and diesel spills from cruise boats have long contaminated the bay.

A deep-water port in Hon Gai draws hundreds of container ships a year through an international shipping channel that cuts through the heart of Halong. The resulting silt and dust has cloaked the sea grasses and shallow sea bottom, making it a struggle for sea life to survive, and putting the entire marine ecosystem in peril.

Even more alarming are the gargantuan Cam Pha coal mines and cement factory, just 20km east of Halong City, from which tonnes of coal dust and waste leak into the bay.

There's been some recent progress. Until 2012, untreated water was dumped into rivers and ended up in the bay, but a new treatment plant on the Vang Dang River has eased the flow of pollutants. And in November 2015 authorities suspended the cruise licences of over 200 boats which had failed to install oil waste separator filters.

In the Mekong Delta, the nation's rice bowl, rivers up to 50km inland are seeing increased salinity. Near the mouth of the delta, salination of water supplies has been such that many families have switched from rice cultivation to shrimp farming.

Vietnam is the world's second-largest coffee producer. It's a vital cash crop in the southwest highlands where it's known as 'brown gold'. Around 97% of Vietnamese coffee is the cheaper, caffeine-packed robusta bean.

Ecocide: The Impact of War

The American War witnessed the most intensive attempt to destroy a country's natural environment the world has ever seen. Forty years later, Vietnam is still in recovery mode, such was the devastation caused. American forces sprayed 72 million litres of defoliants (including Agent Orange, loaded with dioxin) over 16% of South Vietnam to destroy the Viet Cong's natural cover.

Enormous bulldozers called 'Rome ploughs' ripped up the jungle floor, removing vegetation and topsoil. Flammable melaleuca forests were ignited with napalm. In mountain areas, landslides were deliberately created by bombing and spraying acid on limestone hillsides. Elephants, useful for transport, were attacked from the air with bombs and napalm. By the war's end, extensive areas had been taken over by tough weeds (known locally as 'American grass'). The government estimates that 20,000 sq km of forest and farmland were lost as a direct result of the American War.

Scientists have yet to conclusively prove a link between the dioxin residues of chemicals used by the USA and spontaneous abortions, stillbirths, birth defects and other human health problems. Links between dioxin and other diseases including several types of cancer are well established.

The Vietnam Association for Conservation of Nature & Environment (www.vacne.org.vn) acts as a bit of a clearing house for stories and projects related to Vietnam's environment.

Chemical manufacturers that supplied herbicides to the US military paid US$180 million to US war veterans, without admitting liability. However, the estimated four million Vietnamese victims of dioxin poisoning in Vietnam have never received compensation. Court cases brought by the Vietnamese Association of Victims of Agent Orange (http://vava.org.vn) have so far been rejected in the USA.

Journalists and other commentators have concluded that the Vietnamese government has been reluctant to pursue compensation claims for Agent Orange poisoning through the international courts because it has placed a higher priority on normalising relations with the USA.

In December 2014, President Barack Obama authorised funds for a clean-up of a dioxin-contaminated former US base at Danang airport. The Vietnamese government continues to lobby for US assistance so other affected areas can be decontaminated.

Survival Guide

Directory A–Z

Accommodation

Accommodation in Vietnam is superb value for money. Big cities and the main tourism centres have everything from hostel dorm beds to luxe hotels. In the countryside and visiting provincial towns, there's less choice; you'll usually be deciding between guesthouses and midrange hotels.

Cleanliness standards are generally good and there are very few real dumps – even remote rural areas have some excellent budget places. Communication can often be an issue (particularly off-the-beaten path where few staff speak English), but it's usually possible to reach an understanding. Perhaps because of this, service standards in Vietnam can be a little haphazard.

Prices are quoted in dong or US dollars based on the preferred currency of the particular property. Most rooms fall into a budget price category and dorm bed prices are given individually. Discounts are often available at quiet times of year. Some hotels (particularly those on the coast) raise their prices in the main tourist season (July and August) and for public holidays.

Passports are almost always requested on arrival at a hotel. It is not absolutely essential to hand over your passport, but at the very least you need to provide a photocopy of the passport details and visa.

Guesthouses & Hotels

Hotels are called *khach san* and guesthouses *nha khach* or *nha nghi*. Many hotels have a wide variety of rooms (a spread of between US$20 and US$60 is not unusual). Often the cheapest rooms are at the end of several flights of stairs or lack a window.

Budget hotels Guesthouses (usually family-run) vary enormously depending on the standards of the owner; often the newest places are in the best condition. Most rooms in this category are very well equipped, with US$12 to US$16 often bagging you in-room wi-fi, air-con, hot water and a TV. Some places even throw in a free breakfast, too. Towards the upper end of this category, minihotels – small, smart private hotels – usually represent excellent value for money. Few budget places have lifts (elevators), however.

Midrange hotels At the lower end of this bracket, many of the hotels are similar to budget hotels but with bigger rooms or balconies. Flash a bit more cash and the luxury factor rises exponentially, with contemporary design touches and a swimming pool and massage or spa facilities becoming the norm.

Top-end hotels Expect everything from faceless business hotels, colonial places resonating with history and chic boutique hotels in this bracket. Resort hotels are dotted along the coastline. Top beach spots such as Nha Trang and Mui Ne all have a range of sumptuous places. Villa-hotels (where your accommodation has a private pool) are becoming popular, while others even include complimentary spa facilities. You'll find ecolodges in the mountains of the north and around the fringes of national parks.

BOOK YOUR STAY ONLINE

For more accommodation reviews by Lonely Planet authors, check out http://lonelyplanet.com/hotels/vietnam. You'll find independent reviews, as well as recommendations on the best places to stay. Best of all, you can book online.

Homestays

Homestays are a popular option in parts of Vietnam. As the government imposes strict rules about registering

SLEEPING PRICE RANGES

The following price ranges refer to a double room with bathroom in high season. Unless otherwise stated, tax is included, but breakfast excluded, from the price.

$ less than US$25 (560,000d) a night

$$ US$25 (560,000d) to US$75 (1,680,000d)

$$$ more than US$75 (1,680,000d)

foreigners who stay overnight, all places have to be officially licensed.

Areas that are well set up include the Mekong Delta; the White Thai villages of Mai Chau, Ba Be, Moc Chau; parts of the central highlands; the Cham Islands; and the Bho Hoong village near Hoi An.

Some specialist tour companies and motorbike touring companies have developed excellent relations with remote villages and offer homestays as part of their trips.

Taxes

Most hotels at the top end levy a tax of 10% and a service charge of 5%, displayed as ++ ('plus plus') on the bill. Some midrange (and even the odd budget place) also try to levy a 10% tax, though this can often be waived.

Children

Children get to have a good time in Vietnam, mainly because of the overwhelming amount of attention they attract and the fact that almost everybody wants to play with them. However, this attention can sometimes be overwhelming, particularly for blonde-haired, blue-eyed babes. Cheek pinching, or worse still (though rare), groin grabbing for boys, are distinct possibilities, so keep them close.

Big cities have plenty to keep kids interested, though in most smaller towns and rural areas boredom may set in from time to time. There are some great beaches, but pay close attention to any playtime in the sea, as there are some big riptides running along the main coastline. Some popular beaches have warning flags and lifeguards, but at quieter beaches parents should test the current first. Seas around Phu Quoc Island are more sheltered.

Kids generally enjoy local cuisine, which is rarely too spicy: the range of fruit is staggering and spring rolls usually go down very well. Comfort food from home (pizzas, pasta, burgers and ice cream) is available in most places too.

Pack plenty of high-factor sunscreen before you go as it's not that widely available in Vietnam (and costs more than in many Western countries).

Babies & Infants

Baby supplies are available in the major cities, but dry up quickly in the countryside. You'll find cots in most midrange and top-end hotels, but not elsewhere. There are no safety seats in rented cars or taxis, but some restaurants can find a high chair.

Breastfeeding in public is quite common in Vietnam, but there are few facilities for changing nappies (diapers) other than using toilets and bathrooms. For kids who are too young to handle chopsticks, most restaurants also have cutlery.

The main worry throughout Vietnam is keeping an eye on what strange things infants are putting into their mouths. Their natural curiosity can be a lot more costly in a country where dysentery, typhoid and hepatitis are commonplace. Anti-bacterial hand gel (bring from home) is a great idea.

Keep their hydration levels up and slap on the sunscreen.

Customs Regulations

Enter Vietnam by air and the procedure usually takes a few minutes. If entering by land, expect to attract a bit more interest, particularly at remote borders.

Duty limits:

- 400 cigarettes
- 1.5 litres of spirit
- Large sums of foreign currency (US$5000 and greater) must be declared.

HOTELS FROM HELL

We hear about a lot less hotel scam stories these days but they do still occur occasionally; Hanoi is one city to take care in. This is what can happen: a hotel will get a good reputation and before you know it a copycat place with exactly the same name opens down the road. Dodgy taxi drivers work in tandem with these copycat hotels, ferrying unsuspecting visitors to the fake place. Check out your room before you check in if you have any concerns. Some Hanoi hotels will also harass you to book tours with them. That said, most guesthouse and hotel operators are decent and honest folk.

Electricity

The usual voltage is 220V, 50 cycles, but you'll (very rarely) encounter 110V, also at 50 cycles, just to confuse things. Electrical sockets usually accommodate plugs with two round pins.

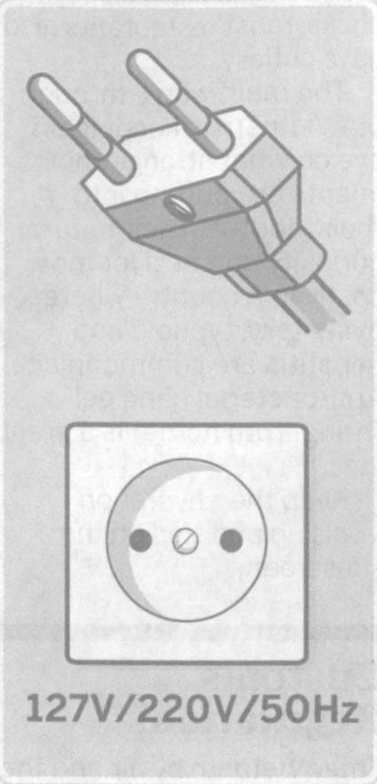

Embassies & Consulates

Generally speaking, embassies won't be that sympathetic if you end up in jail after committing a crime. In genuine emergencies you might get some assistance, but only if other channels have been exhausted.

If you have your passport stolen, it can take some time to replace it as some embassies in Vietnam do not issue new passports, which have to be sent from a regional embassy.

Australian Embassy (Map p70; ☎04-3774 0100; www.vietnam.embassy.gov.au; 8 Đ Dao Tan, Ba Dinh District, Hanoi)

Australian Consulate (Map p315; ☎08-3521 8100; www.hcmc.vietnam.embassy.gov.au; 20th fl, Đ 47 Ly Tu Truong, Vincom Center, Ho Chi Minh City)

Cambodian Embassy (Map p68; camemb.vnm@mfa.gov.kh; 71A P Tran Hung Dao, Hanoi)

Cambodian Consulate (Map p319; ☎08-3829 2751; camcg.hcm@mfa.gov.kh; 41 Đ Phung Khac Khoan, HCMC)

Canadian Embassy (Map p66; www.canadainternational.gc.ca/vietnam; 31 Đ Hung Vuong, Hanoi)

Canadian Consulate (Map p315; ☎08-3827 9899; hochi@international.gc.ca; 10th fl, 235 Đ Dong Khoi, HCMC)

Chinese Embassy (Map p66; ☎04-8845 3736; http://vn.china-embassy.org/chn; 46 P Hoang Dieu, Hanoi)

Chinese Consulate (Map p319; ☎08-3829 2457; http://hcmc.chineseconsulate.org; 175 Đ Hai Ba Trung, HCMC)

French Embassy (Map p68; ☎04-3944 5700; www.ambafrance-vn.org; P Tran Hung Dao, Hanoi)

French Consulate (Map p319; www.consulfrance-hcm.org; 27 Đ Nguyen Thi Minh Khai, HCMC)

German Embassy (Map p66; ☎04-3845 3836; www.hanoi.diplo.de; 29 Đ Tran Phu, Hanoi)

German Consulate (Map p319; ☎08-3829 1967; www.ho-chi-minh-stadt.diplo.de; 126 Đ Nguyen Dinh Chieu, HCMC)

Japanese Embassy (Map p70; ☎04-3846 3000; www.vn.emb-japan.go.jp; 27 P Lieu Giai, Ba Dinh District, Hanoi)

Japanese Consulate (Map p320; ☎08-3933 3510; www.hcmcgj.vn.emb-japan.go.jp; 261 Đ Dien Bien Phu, HCMC)

Laotian Embassy (Map p68; ☎04-3942 4576; www.embalaohanoi.gov.la; 22 P Tran Binh Trong, Hanoi)

Laotian Consulate (Map p315; ☎08-3829 7667; 93 Đ Pasteur, HCMC)

Netherlands Embassy (Map p62; ☎04-3831-5650; www.hollandinvietnam.org; 7th fl, BIDV Tower, 194 Đ Tran Quang Khai, Hanoi)

Netherlands Consulate (Map p319; ☎08-3823 5932; www.hollandinvietnam.org; Saigon Tower, 29 ĐL Le Duan, HCMC)

New Zealand Embassy (Map p62; ☎04-3824 1481; www.nzembassy.com/viet-nam; Level 5, 63 P Ly Thai To, Hanoi)

New Zealand Consulate (Map p315; ☎08-3822 6907; www.nzembassy.com; 8th fl, The Metropolitan, 235 Đ Dong Khoi, HCMC)

Singaporean Embassy (Map p66; ☎04-3848 9168; www.mfa.gov.sg/hanoi; 41-43 Đ Tran Phu, Hanoi)

Thai Embassy (Map p66; ☎04-3823 5092; www.thaiembassy.org; 3-65 P Hoang Dieu, Hanoi)

Thai Consulate (Map p320; ☎08-3932 7637; www.thaiembassy.org/hochiminh; 77 Đ Tran Quoc Thao)

UK Embassy (Map p62; ☎04-3936 0500; http://ukinvietnam.fco.gov.uk; 4th fl, Central Bldg, 31 P Hai Ba Trung, Hanoi)

UK Consulate (Map p319; ☎08-3829 8433; consularenquiries.vietnam@fco.gov.uk; 25 ĐL Le Duan, HCMC)

US Embassy (Map p70; ☎04-3850 5000; http://vietnam.usembassy.gov; 7 P Lang Ha, Ba Dinh District, Hanoi)

US Consulate (Map p319; ☎08-3822 9433; http://hochiminh.usconsulate.gov; 4 ĐL Le Duan, HCMC)

Food

Eating out is a real highlight of travel in Vietnam. For much, much more on the subject consult the Food & Drink chapter (p464).

Insurance

Insurance is a must for Vietnam, as the cost of major medical treatment is prohibitive. A travel insurance policy to cover theft, loss and medical problems is the best bet.

Some insurance policies specifically exclude such 'dangerous activities' as riding motorbikes, diving and even trekking. Check that your policy covers an emergency evacuation in the event of serious injury.

Worldwide travel insurance is available at www.lonelyplanet.com/bookings. You can buy, extend or claim anytime – even if you're already on the road.

If you're driving a vehicle, you need a Vietnamese insurance policy (p494).

Internet Access

Internet and wi-fi is very widely available throughout Vietnam. Something like 98% of hotels and guesthouses have wi-fi, only in very remote places (such as national parks) is it not standard. It's almost always free of charge, except in some five-star places. Many cafes and restaurants also have wi-fi.

Connection speeds in towns and cities are normally quite good, though not usually fast enough for gaming or streaming.

Cybercafes are also plentiful, usually costing 3000d to 8000d per hour.

Legal Matters

Civil Law

On paper it looks good, but in practice the rule of law in Vietnam is a fickle beast. Local officials interpret the law any way it suits them, often against the wishes of Hanoi. There is no independent judiciary. Not surprisingly, most legal disputes are settled out of court.

Drugs

The country has a very serious problem with heroin and methamphetamine use and the authorities clamp down hard.

Marijuana and, in the northwest, opium are readily available. Note that there are many plain-clothes police in Vietnam and if you're arrested, the result might be a large fine, a long prison term or both.

Police

Few foreigners experience much hassle from police and demands for bribes are very rare. That said, police corruption is an everyday reality for locals. If something does go wrong, or if something is stolen, the police can't do much more than prepare an insurance report for a negotiable fee – take an English-speaking Vietnamese with you to translate.

LGBT Travellers

Vietnam is a relatively hassle-free place for gay, lesbian and trans travellers. There are no official laws prohibiting same-sex relationships, or same-sex sexual acts in Vietnam, nor is there much in the way of individual harassment. VietPride (www.vietpride.com) marches have been held in Hanoi and HCMC since 2012. The Hanoi event now takes place over several days in late July/early August and includes film screenings, talks, parties and a bike rally.

In recent years two critically lauded Vietnamese films featuring gay characters have been released (p462).

In January 2015, a Law on Marriage and Family was passed which officially allows gay weddings (though their legal status has not yet been recognised). This has been welcomed as a positive step by activists, and Vietnam now has a more progressive governmental policies than many of its Asian neighbours.

Hanoi and Ho Chi Minh City both have gay scenes, but gay venues still keep a low profile. Most gay Vietnamese have to hide their sexuality from their families and friends and a lot of stigma remains.

Gay travellers shouldn't expect any problems in Vietnam. Checking into hotels as a same-sex couple is perfectly acceptable, though it's prudent not to flaunt your sexuality. As with heterosexual couples, passionate public displays of affection are considered a basic no-no.

Interestingly, the US Ambassador to Vietnam, Ted Osius, is openly gay and arrived with his husband and baby when appointed in December 2014.

Utopia (www.utopia-asia.com) has useful gay travel information and contacts in Vietnam. The gay dating app Grindr is popular in Vietnam.

PLANET OF THE FAKES

You'll probably notice a lot of cut-price Lonely Planet *Vietnam* titles available as you travel around the country. Don't be deceived, these are pirate copies. Sometimes the copies are OK, sometimes they're awful. The only certain way to tell is the price. If it's cheap, it's a copy.

EATING PRICE RANGES

The following price ranges refer to a typical meal (excluding drinks). Unless otherwise stated, taxes are included in the price.

Budget less than US$5 (107,000d)

Midrange US$5 (107,000d) to US$15 (323,000d)

Top end more than US$15 (323,000d)

PRACTICALITIES

Laundry You'll find laundry places in all the main tourist areas. Guesthouses also have cheap laundry services, but check that there is a dryer if the weather is bad.

Newspapers & Magazines *Vietnam News* is a propagandist English-language daily. Popular listings mags include the *Guide*, which covers the whole country, plus *AsiaLife* and *The Word* in HCMC and *Live Hoi An* in Hoi An. For national news, the website www.thanhniennews.com is a good resource.

Radio & TV *Voice of Vietnam* hogs the airwaves all day and is pumped through loudspeakers in many rural towns (and Hanoi). There are many TV channels and a steady diet of satellite/cable stuff.

Smoking Vietnam is a smoker's paradise (and a non-smoker's nightmare). People spark up everywhere, though there's an official ban against smoking in public places and on public transport. It's not socially acceptable to smoke on air-conditioned transport – so those long bus journeys are usually smoke-free.

Weights & Measures The Vietnamese use the metric system for everything except precious metals and gems, where they follow the Chinese system.

Maps

The road atlas *Tap Ban Do Giao Thong Duong Bo Viet Nam* is the best available, but the latest roads are not included. It's available in bookstores including Fahasa (which has shops in HCMC, Hanoi and Danang) and costs 220,000d.

Vietnamese street names are preceded by the words Pho, Duong and Dai Lo – on maps they appear respectively as P, Đ and ĐL.

It's also worth picking up a copy of the highly informative *Xin Chao Map of Hanoi*, the second edition was published in July 2015, which has tips and recommendations. You can order it at www.nancychandler.net.

Money

The Vietnamese currency is the dong (abbreviated to 'd'). US dollars are also widely used, though less so in rural areas.

For the last few years the dong has been fairly stable at around 22,000d to the dollar.

Where prices on the ground are quoted in dong, we quote them in dong. Likewise, when prices are quoted in dollars, we follow suit.

There's no real black market in Vietnam.

ATMs

ATMs are widespread in Vietnam and present in virtually every town in the country. You shouldn't have any problems getting cash with a regular Maestro/Cirrus debit card, or with a Visa or MasterCard debit or credit card. Watch out for stiff withdrawal fees, however (typically 25,000d to 50,000d), and withdrawal limits – most are around 2,000,000d; Agribank allows up to 6,000,000d and Commonwealth Bank up to 10,000,000d.

Bargaining

Some bargaining is essential in most tourist transactions. Remember that in Asia 'saving face' is important, so bargaining should be good-natured. Smile and don't get angry or argue. In some cases you will be able to get a 50% discount or more, at other times this may only be 10%. And once the money is accepted, the deal is done.

Cash

The US dollar remains king of foreign currencies and can be exchanged and used widely. Other major currencies can be exchanged at banks including Vietcombank and HSBC.

Check that any big dollar bills you take do not look too tatty, as no-one will accept them in Vietnam.

You cannot legally take dong out of Vietnam but you can reconvert reasonable amounts of it into US dollars on departure.

Most land border crossings now have some sort of official currency exchange, offering the best rates available in these remote parts of the country.

Credit Cards

Visa and MasterCard are accepted in major cities and many tourist centres, but don't expect budget guesthouses or noodle bars to take plastic. Commission charges (around 3%) sometimes apply.

If you wish to obtain a cash advance, this is possible at Vietcombank branches in most cities. Banks generally charge at least a 3% commission for this service.

Tipping

Tipping is not expected in Vietnam, but it is enormously appreciated. For a person who earns US$150 per month, a US$1 tip is significant. Upmarket hotels and some restaurants may levy a 5% service charge, but this may not make it to the staff.

Consider tipping drivers and guides. Typically, travellers on minibus tours will pool together to collect a communal tip to be split between the guide and driver.

It is considered proper to make a small donation at the end of a visit to a pagoda (roughly US$2), especially if a monk has shown you around; most pagodas have contribution boxes for this purpose.

Travellers Cheques

Travellers cheques are a total pain to cash in Vietnam. Few banks will touch them these days and expect a long wait if one agrees to. Try Asia Commercial Bank (ACB) or **Sinh Tourist** (☎08-3838 9597; www.thesinhtourist.com) offices.

Opening Hours

Vietnamese people rise early and consider sleeping in to be a sure indication of illness. Lunch is taken very seriously and virtually everything shuts down between noon and 1.30pm. Government workers tend to take longer breaks, so figure on getting nothing done between 11.30am and 2pm. Many government offices are open till noon on Saturday, but closed Sunday. Opening hours are only included when they differ from these standard hours.

Hours vary very little throughout the year.

Banks 8am to 3pm weekdays, to 11.30am Saturday

Offices and museums 7am or 8am to 5pm or 6pm; museums generally close on Monday and some take a lunch break

Restaurants 11.30am to 9pm

Shops 8am to 6pm

Temples and pagodas 5am to 9pm

Photography

Memory cards are pretty cheap in Vietnam, which is fortunate given the visual feast awaiting even the amateur photographer. Slide and monochrome film can be bought in Hanoi and HCMC, but don't count on it elsewhere.

Cameras are reasonably priced in Vietnam and all other camera supplies are readily available in major cities.

Sensitive Subjects

Avoid snapping airports, military bases and border checkpoints. Don't even think of trying to get a snapshot of Ho Chi Minh in his glass sarcophagus!

Photographing anyone, in particular hill-tribe people, demands patience and the utmost respect for the local customs. Photograph people with discretion and manners. It's always polite to ask first and if the person says no, don't take the photo. If you promise to send a copy of the photo, make sure you do.

Post

Every city, town and village has some sort of *buu dien* (post office).

Vietnam has a quite reliable postal service. For anything important, express-mail service (EMS), available in the larger cities, is twice as fast as regular airmail and everything is registered.

Private couriers such as FedEx, DHL and UPS are reliable for transporting documents or small parcels.

Public Holidays

If a public holiday falls on a weekend, it is observed on the Monday.

New Year's Day (Tet Duong Lich) 1 January

Vietnamese New Year (Tet) January or February – a three-day national holiday

Founding of the Vietnamese Communist Party (Thanh Lap Dang CSVN) 3 February – the date the party was founded in 1930

Hung Kings Commemorations (Hung Vuong) 10th day of the 3rd lunar month (March or April)

Liberation Day (Saigon Giai Phong) 30 April – the date of Saigon's 1975 surrender is commemorated nationwide

International Workers' Day (Quoc Te Lao Dong) 1 May

Ho Chi Minh's Birthday (Sinh Nhat Bac Ho) 19 May

Buddha's Birthday (Phat Dan) Eighth day of the fourth moon (usually June)

National Day (Quoc Khanh) 2 September – commemorates the Declaration of Independence by Ho Chi Minh in 1945

Safe Travel

All in all, Vietnam is an extremely safe country to travel in. The police keep a pretty tight grip on social order and we rarely receive reports about muggings, robberies or sexual assaults. Sure there are scams and hassles in some cities, particularly in

GOVERNMENT TRAVEL ADVICE

The following government websites offer travel advisories and information on current hot spots:

Australian Department of Foreign Affairs www.smarttraveller.gov.au

British Foreign Office www.fco.gov.uk

Global Affairs Canada www.dfait-maeci.gc.ca

NZ Foreign Affairs www.safetravel.govt.nz

US State Department http://travel.state.gov

Hanoi, HCMC and Nha Trang (and to a lesser degree in Hoi An). But perhaps the most important thing you can do is to be extra careful if you're travelling on two wheels on Vietnam's anarchic roads – traffic accident rates are woeful and driving standards are pretty appalling.

Sea Creatures

If you plan to spend your time swimming, snorkelling and scuba-diving, familiarise yourself with the various hazards. The list of dangerous sea creatures includes jellyfish, stonefish, scorpion fish, sea snakes and stingrays. However as most of these creatures avoid humans, the risk is very small.

Jellyfish tend to travel in groups, so as long as you look before you leap into the sea, avoiding them should not be too hard. Stonefish, scorpion fish and stingrays tend to hang out in shallow water along the ocean floor and can be very difficult to see. One way to protect against these nasties is to wear plastic shoes in the sea.

Undetonated Explosives

For more than three decades, four armies expended untold energy and resources mining, booby-trapping, rocketing, strafing, mortaring and bombarding wide areas of Vietnam. When the fighting stopped, most of this ordnance remained exactly where it had landed or been laid; American estimates at the end of the war placed the quantity of unexploded ordnance (UXO) at 150,000 tonnes.

Since 1975 more than 40,000 Vietnamese have been maimed or killed by this leftover ordnance. The central provinces are particularly badly affected, with more than 8000 incidents in Quang Tri alone.

While cities, cultivated areas and well-travelled rural roads and paths are safe for travel, straying from these areas could land you in the middle of danger. *Never* touch any rockets, artillery shells, mortars, mines or other relics of war you may come across. Such objects can remain lethal for decades. And don't climb inside bomb craters – you never know what undetonated explosive device is at the bottom.

You can learn more about the issue of landmines from the Nobel Peace Prize–winning International Campaign to Ban Landmines (www.icbl.org), or visit the websites of the Mines Advisory Group (www.maginternational.org) and Clear Path International (www.cpi.org) which both specialise in clearing landmines and UXO.

Telephone

A mobile phone with a local SIM card and a Skype/Viber (or similar) account will allow you to keep in touch economically with anyone in the world.

International Calls

It's usually cheapest to use a mobile phone to make international phone calls; rates can be as little as US$0.15 a minute.

Otherwise, you can call abroad from any phone in the country. Just dial 171 or 178, the country code and your number – most countries cost a flat rate of just US$0.60 per minute. Many budget hotels now operate even cheaper web-call services.

You'll also find many hotels have Skype and webcams set up for their guests.

Local Calls

Phone numbers in Hanoi, HCMC and Haiphong have eight digits. Elsewhere around the country phone numbers have seven digits. Telephone area codes are assigned according to the province.

Local calls can usually be made from any hotel or restaurant phone and are often free. Domestic long-distance calls are also quite reasonably priced.

Mobile Phones

Vietnam has an excellent, comprehensive cellular network. Call and data packages are extremely cheap by international standards. The nation uses GSM 900/1800, which is compatible with most of Asia, Europe and Australia but not with North America.

It's well worth getting a local SIM card if you're planning to spend any time in Vietnam. A local number will enable you to send texts (SMS) anywhere in the world for 500d to 2500d per message and make calls to most countries for between 3000d and 6000d a minute. 3G data packages start at just 50,000d for 1GB.

If you don't want to bring your flash handset from home, you can buy a cheap phone in Vietnam for as little as 300,000d, often with 150,000d of credit included. Get the shop owner (or someone at your hotel) to set up your phone in English or your native language. Three main mobile phone companies (Viettel, Vinaphone and Mobifone) battle it out in the local market, and they all

ALL CHANGE

In January 2015, the Vietnamese government announced that phone codes across the country (affecting 59 of Vietnam's 63 provinces) were to change. However, this plan was not implemented, and by December 2015 existing codes were still in operation.

have offices and branches nationwide.

If your phone has roaming, it is easy enough to use your handset in Vietnam, though it can be outrageously expensive, particularly if you use the internet.

Time

Vietnam is seven hours ahead of Greenwich Mean Time/Universal Time Coordinated (GMT/UTC). Because of its proximity to the equator, Vietnam does not have daylight-saving or summer time.

Toilets

The issue of toilets and what to do with used toilet paper can cause confusion. In general, if there's a wastepaper basket next to the toilet, that is where the toilet paper goes (many sewage systems cannot handle toilet paper). If there's no basket, flush paper down the toilet.

Toilet paper is usually provided, except in bus and train stations, though it's wise to keep a stash of your own while on the move.

There are still some squat toilets in public places and out in the countryside.

The scarcity of public toilets is more of a problem for women than for men. Vietnamese men often urinate in public. Women might find roadside toilet stops easier if wearing a sarong. You usually have to pay a few dong to an attendant to access a public toilet.

Tourist Information

Tourist offices in Vietnam have a different philosophy from the majority of tourist offices worldwide. These government-owned enterprises are really travel agencies whose primary interests are booking tours and turning a profit. Don't come here hoping for independent travel information.

Vietnam Tourism (www.vietnamtourism.com), the main state organisation, and Saigon Tourist (www.saigon-tourist.com) are examples of this genre, but nowadays most provinces have at least one such organisation. Travel agents, backpacker cafes and your fellow travellers are a much better source of information than these 'tourist offices'.

There are fairly helpful tourist offices in Hanoi and HCMC.

Travellers with Disabilities

Vietnam is not the easiest of places for travellers with disabilities, despite the fact that many Vietnamese are disabled as a result of war injuries. Tactical problems include the chaotic traffic and pavements that are routinely blocked by parked motorbikes and food stalls.

That said, with some careful planning it is possible to enjoy a trip to Vietnam. Find a reliable company to make the travel arrangements and don't be afraid to double-check things with hotels and restaurants yourself.

Some budget and many midrange and topend hotels have lifts. Note that bathroom doorways can be very narrow; if the width of your wheelchair is more than 60cm you may struggle to get inside.

Train travel is not really geared for travellers with wheelchairs, but open tour buses are doable. If you can afford to rent a private vehicle with a driver, almost anywhere becomes instantly accessible. As long as you are not too proud about how you get in and out of a boat or up some stairs, anything is possible, as the Vietnamese are always willing to help.

The hazards for blind travellers in Vietnam are acute, with traffic coming at you from all directions. Just getting across the road in cities such as Hanoi and HCMC is tough enough for those with 20:20 vision, so you'll definitely need a sighted companion!

The Travellers With Disabilities forum on Lonely Planet's Thorn Tree (www.lonelyplanet.com/thorntree) is a good place to seek the advice of other travellers. Alternatively, you could try organisations like Mobility International USA (www.miusa.org), the Royal Association for Disability Rights (http://disabilityrightsuk.org) or the Society for Accessible Travel & Hospitality (www.sath.org).

Visas

The (very complicated) visa situation has recently changed for many nationalities, and is fluid – always check the latest regulations. The government has relaxed visa exemption rules to include more countries and reduced visa fees in a bid to stimulate tourism.

Firstly, if you are staying more than 15 days and from a Western country, you'll still need a visa (or approval letter from an agent) in advance. If your visit is under 15 days, some nationalities are now visa exempt.

Note that travellers using a visa exemption cannot extend their stay at the end of the visa exemption period and must leave Vietnam; they cannot return again using a visa exemption within 30 days. So if you are from a non-visa exemption country (say the USA, Australia or New Zealand) or you wish to stay longer in Vietnam than your permitted exemption period, or you wish to enter and leave Vietnam multiple times, you will need to apply for a visa in advance.

Tourist visas are valid for either 30 days or 90 days. A single-entry 30-day visa

VISA-EXEMPTED NATIONALITIES

Citizens of the following countries do not need to apply in advance for a Vietnamese visa (when arriving by either air or land). Always double-check visa requirements before you travel as policies change regularly.

COUNTRY	DAYS
Myanmar, Brunei	14
Belarus, Denmark, Finland, France, Germany, Italy, Japan, South Korea, Norway, Russia, Spain, Sweden, UK	15
Philippines	21
Cambodia, Indonesia, Laos, Malaysia, Singapore, Thailand	30

costs US$20, a three-month multiple entry visa is US$70.

There are two methods of applying for a visa: via online visa agents, or via a Vietnamese embassy or consulate.

Online Visa Agents

This is now the preferred method for most travellers arriving by air, since it's cheaper, faster and you don't have to part with your passport by posting it to an embassy. It can only be used if you are flying into any of Vietnam's five international airports, not at land crossings. The process is straightforward, you fill out an online application form and pay the agency fee (around US$20). You'll then receive by email a Visa on Arrival approval letter signed by Vietnamese immigration which you print out and show on arrival (and then pay your visa fee). There are many visa agents, but we recommend you stick to well-established companies, these two are professional and efficient:

Vietnam Visa Choice (www.vietnamvisachoice.com) Online support from native English speakers and they guarantee your visa will be issued within the time specified.

Vietnam Visa Center (www.vietnamvisacenter.org) Competent all-rounder which offers a two-hour express service for last-minute trips.

Visas via an Embassy or Consulate

You can also obtain visas through Vietnamese embassy and consulates around the world. but fees are normally higher than using a visa agent, and (depending, on the country) the process can be slow. In Asia, Vietnamese visas tend to be issued in two to three working days in Cambodia, or Europe and North America it takes around a week.

Multiple-Entry Visas

It's possible to enter Cambodia or Laos from Vietnam and then re-enter without having to apply for another visa. However, you must hold a multiple-entry visa before you leave Vietnam.

If you arrived in Vietnam on a single-entry visa, multiple-entry visas are easiest to arrange in Hanoi or HCMC, but you will have to ask a visa or travel agent to do the paperwork for you. Agents charge about US$50 for the service and visa fees are charged on top of this – the procedure takes up to seven days.

Visa Extensions

If you've got the dollars, they've got the rubber stamp. Tourist visa extensions officially cost as little as US$10, and have to be organised via agents. The procedure can take seven days and you can only extend the visa for 30 or 90 days depending on the visa you hold.

You can extend your visa in big cities, but if it's done in a different city from the one you arrived in (oh the joys of Vietnamese bureaucracy!), it'll cost you around US$30. In practice, extensions work most smoothly in HCMC, Hanoi, Danang and Hue.

Volunteering

Opportunities for voluntary work are quite limited in Vietnam as there are so many professional development staff based here.

For information, chase up the full list of nongovernment organisations (NGOs) at the **NGO Resource Centre** (Map p70; ☎04-3832 8570; www.ngocentre.org.vn; Room 201, Building E3, 6 Dang Van Ngu, Trung Tu Diplomatic Compound, Dong Da, Hanoi), which keeps a database of all of the NGOs assisting Vietnam. Service Civil International (www.sciint.org) has links to options in Vietnam, including the Friendship Village (www.vietnamfriendship.org), established by veterans from both sides to help victims of Agent Orange. The Center for Sustainable Development Studies (http://csds.vn) addresses development issues through international exchange and non-formal education.

Or try contacting the following organisations if you want to help in some way.

KOTO (www.koto.com.au) helps give street children career opportunities in its restaurants in Hanoi or HCMC; a three-month minimum commitment is required.

International organisations offering placements in Vietnam include Voluntary Service Overseas (www.vsointernational.org) in the UK, Australian Volunteers International (www.australianvolunteers.com), Volunteer Service Abroad (www.vsa.org.nz) in New Zealand and US-based International

Volunteer HQ (www.volunteerhq.org), which has a wide range of volunteer projects in Hanoi. The UN's volunteer program details are available at www.unv.org.

Women Travellers

Vietnam is relatively free of serious hassles for Western women. There are issues to consider of course, but thousands of women travel alone through the country each year and love the experience. Most Vietnamese women enjoy relatively free, fulfilled lives and a career; the sexes mix freely and society does not expect women to behave in a subordinate manner.

East Asian women travelling in Vietnam may want to dress quite conservatively, especially if they look Vietnamese. Things have improved as more Vietnamese people are exposed to foreign visitors, but very occasionally some ill-educated locals may think an Asian woman accompanying a Western male could be a prostitute.

Many Vietnamese women dress modestly and expose as little body flesh as possible (partly to avoid the sun). Be aware that exposing your upper arms (by wearing a sleeveless top) can attract plenty of attention away from the beach.

Work

There's some casual work available in Western-owned bars and restaurants throughout the country. This is of the cash-in-hand variety, that is, working without paperwork. Dive schools and adventure sports specialists will always need instructors, but for most travellers the main work opportunities are teaching a foreign language.

Looking for employment is a matter of asking around – jobs are rarely advertised.

Teaching

English is by far the most popular foreign language with Vietnamese students. There's some demand for Mandarin and French too.

Private language centres (US$10 to US$18 per hour) and home tutoring (US$15 to US$25 per hour) are your best bet for teaching work. You'll get paid more in HCMC or Hanoi than in the provinces.

Government-run universities in Vietnam also hire some foreign teachers.

Transport

GETTING THERE & AWAY

Most travellers enter Vietnam by plane or bus, but there are also train links from China and boat connections from Cambodia via the Mekong River. Flights, tours and rail tickets can be booked online at lonelyplanet.com/bookings.

Entering Vietnam

Formalities at Vietnam's international airports are generally smoother than at land borders. That said, crossing overland from Cambodia and China is now relatively stress-free. Crossing the border between Vietnam and Laos can be slow.

Passport

Your passport must be valid for six months upon arrival in Vietnam. Many nationalities need to arrange a visa in advance.

Air

Airlines

The state-owned carrier **Vietnam Airlines** (www.vietnamairlines.com.vn) has flights to 17 countries, mainly in East Asia, but also to the UK, Germany, France and Australia. The airline has a modern fleet of Airbuses and Boeings, and has a good recent safety record.

Airports

There are five international airports in Vietnam. Others, including Hue, are officially classified as 'international' but have no overseas connections (apart from the odd charter).

Cam Ranh International Airport (☎058-398 9913) Located 36km south of Nha Trang, with flights to Hong Kong, Chengdu and Seoul.

Danang Airport (Map p200; ☎0511-383 0339) International flights to Lao airports including Pakse, Savannakhet and Vientiane; also Kuala Lumpur, Siem Reap, Singapore, Tokyo and airports in China including Hong Kong, Guangzhou and Nanning.

Noi Bai Airport (☎04-3827 1513; www.hanoiairportonline.com) Serves the capital Hanoi.

Phu Quoc International Airport (Map p390; www.phuquoc-airport.com) International flights include to Hanoi, HCMC and Singapore.

Tan Son Nhat International Airport (☎08-3848 5383; www.tsnairport.hochiminhcity.gov.vn/vn; Tan Binh District) For Ho Chi Minh City.

Tickets

It's hard to get reservations for flights to/from Vietnam during holidays, especially Tet, which falls between late January and mid-February.

Land

Vietnam shares land borders with Cambodia, China and Laos and there are plenty of border crossings open to foreigners with each neighbour.

CLIMATE CHANGE & TRAVEL

Every form of transport that relies on carbon-based fuel generates CO_2, the main cause of human-induced climate change. Modern travel is dependent on aeroplanes, which might use less fuel per kilometre per person than most cars but travel much greater distances. The altitude at which aircraft emit gases (including CO_2) and particles also contributes to their climate change impact. Many websites offer 'carbon calculators' that allow people to estimate the carbon emissions generated by their journey and, for those who wish to do so, to offset the impact of the greenhouse gases emitted with contributions to portfolios of climate-friendly initiatives throughout the world. Lonely Planet offsets the carbon footprint of all staff and author travel.

Border Crossings

Standard times that foreigners are allowed to cross are usually 7am to 5pm daily.

There are now legal money-changing facilities on the Vietnamese side of these border crossings, which can deal with US dollars and some other key currencies, including Chinese renminbi, Lao kip and Cambodian riel. Avoid black marketeers, as they have a well-deserved reputation for short-changing and outright theft.

Travellers at border crossings are occasionally asked for an 'immigration fee' of a dollar or two.

CAMBODIA

Cambodia and Vietnam share a long frontier with seven border crossings. One-month Cambodian visas are issued on arrival at all border crossings for US$30, but overcharging is common at all borders except Bavet.

Cambodian border crossings are officially open daily between 8am and 8pm.

CHINA

There are currently three borders where foreigners are permitted to cross between Vietnam and China: Huu Nghi Quan (the Friendship Pass), Lao Cai and Mong Cai. It is necessary to arrange a Chinese visa in advance. China time is one hour ahead.

LAOS

There are seven overland crossings between Vietnam and Laos. Thirty day Lao visas are available at all borders.

The golden rule is to try to use direct city-to-city bus connections between the countries, as potential hassle will be greatly reduced. If you travel step-by-step using local buses expect transport scams (eg serious overcharging) on the Vietnamese side. Devious drivers have even stopped in the middle of nowhere to renegotiate the price.

Transport links on both sides of the border can be hit-and-miss, so don't use the more remote borders unless you have plenty of time, and patience, to spare.

Bus

Bus connections link Vietnam with Cambodia, Laos and China. The most popular way to/from Cambodia is using international buses via the Moc Bai–Bavet border crossing. When it comes to Laos, many travellers take the long nightmare bus between Vientiane and Hanoi via the Cau Treo crossing, or the easier route from Savannakhet in southern Laos to Hue in central Vietnam via the Lao Bao border crossing.

VIETNAM BORDER CROSSINGS

Cambodia

CROSSING	VIETNAMESE TOWN	CONNECTING TOWN
Le Thanh–O Yadaw (p305)	Pleiku	Ban Lung
Moc Bai–Bavet (p355)	Ho Chi Minh City	Phnom Penh
Vinh Xuong–Kaam Samnor (p408)	Chau Doc	Phnom Penh
Xa Xia–Prek Chak (p401)	Ha Tien	Kep, Kampot
Tinh Bien–Phnom Den (p407)	Ha Tien, Chao Doc	Takeo, Phnom Penh

China

CROSSING	VIETNAMESE TOWN	CONNECTING TOWN
Lao Cai–Hekou (p143)	Lao Cai	Kunming
Mong Cai–Dongxing (p122)	Mong Cai	Dongxing
Dong Dang–Pingxiang (p123)	Lang Son	Nanning

Laos

CROSSING	VIETNAMESE TOWN	CONNECTING TOWN
Bo Y–Phou Keau (p307)	Kon Tum, Pleiku	Attapeu
Cau Treo–Nam Phao (p161)	Vinh	Lak Sao
Lao Bao–Dansavanh (p174)	Dong Ha, Hue	Sepon, Savannakhet
Nam Can–Nong Haet (p161)	Vinh	Phonsavan
Tay Trang–Sop Hun (p133)	Dien Bien Phu	Muang Khua

Vietnam Border Crossings

Two daily buses also link Hanoi with Nanning in China.

Passengers always have to get off buses at borders to clear immigration and customs.

Car & Motorcycle

It is theoretically possible to travel in and out of Vietnam by car or motorbike, but only through borders shared with Cambodia and Laos. However, bureaucracy makes this a real headache. It is generally easy enough to take a Vietnamese motorbike into Cambodia or Laos but very difficult in the other direction (and the permits are costly). It's currently not possible to take any vehicle into China.

Consult the forums on www.gt-rider.com for the latest cross-border biking information.

PAPERWORK

Drivers of cars and riders of motorbikes will need the vehicle's registration papers, liability insurance and an International Driving Permit. Most important is a *carnet de passage en douane*, which acts as a temporary waiver of import duty.

Train

Several international trains link China and Vietnam. A daily train connects Hanoi with Nanning (and on to Beijing!). The most scenic stretch of railway is between Hanoi and Kunming via Lao Cai; there are currently four daily trains from the Chinese border town of Hekou to Kunming. There are no railway lines linking Vietnam with Cambodia or Laos.

Readers have reported being able to book tickets for Chinese trains online using www.chinahighlights.com/china-trains; there's a small booking fee.

River

There's a river border crossing between Cambodia and Vietnam on the banks of the Mekong. Regular fast boats ply the route between Phnom Penh in Cambodia and Chau Doc in Vietnam via the Vinh Xuong–Kaam Samnor border. Several luxury riverboats with cabins run all the way to the temples of Angkor at Siem Reap in Cambodia.

CHINA GUIDEBOOKS CONFISCATED

Travellers entering China from Vietnam have periodically reported that Lonely Planet *China* guidebooks have been confiscated by border officials. The guidebook's maps show Taiwan as a separate country and this is a sensitive issue. If you're carrying a copy of Lonely Planet's *China* guide, consider putting a cover on the book, removing any potentially offensive maps and burying it deep in your bag.

GETTING AROUND

Air

Airlines in Vietnam

Vietnam has good domestic flight connections, with new routes opening up all the time, and very affordable prices (if you book early). Airlines accept bookings on international credit or debit cards. Note, however, that cancellations are quite common. It's safest not to rely on a flight from a regional airport to make an international connection the same day – travel a day early if you can. Vietnam Airlines is the least likely to cancel flights, but its fares are usually higher than rival airlines.

Jetstar Airways (☎1900 1550; www.jetstar.com) This budget airline has very affordable fares, and serves 16 airports in Vietnam.

Vasco (☎038 422 790; www.vasco.com.vn) Connects HCMC with the Con Dao Islands and the Mekong Delta. Owned by, and code-shares with, Vietnam Airlines.

VietJet Air (☎1900 1886; www.vietjetair.com) Serves 15 domestic airports.

Vietnam Airlines (www.vietnamairlines.com.vn) Excellent coverage of the entire nation.

Bicycle

Bikes are a great way to get around Vietnam, particularly when you get off the main highways. In the countryside, Westerners on bicycles are often greeted enthusiastically by locals who don't see many foreigners pedalling around.

Long-distance cycling is popular in Vietnam. Much of the country is flat or moderately hilly, and the major roads are in good shape. Safety, however, is a concern.

Bicycles can be transported around the country on the top of buses or in train baggage compartments if you run out of puff (usually US$1 for a short trip or US$1.50 per hour for longer trips).

Bicycle Types

Decent bikes can be bought at a few speciality shops in Hanoi and HCMC, but it's better to bring your own if you plan to cycle long distances. Basic cycling safety equipment and authentic spare parts are also in short supply. A bell or horn is mandatory – the louder the better.

Rentals

Hotels and some travel agencies rent bicycles for US$1 to US$3 per day, better-quality models cost from US$6. Cycling is the perfect way to explore smaller cities such as Hoi An, Hue or Nha Trang (unless it's the rainy season!). There are innumerable bicycle repair stands along

FARE'S FAIR?

For most visitors one of the most frustrating aspects of travelling in Vietnam is the perception that they are being ripped off. Here are some guidelines to help you navigate the maze.

Airfares Dependent on when you book and what dates you want to travel. No price difference between Vietnamese and foreigners.

Boat fares Ferries and hydrofoils have fixed prices, but expect to pay more for the privilege of being a foreigner on smaller local boats around the Mekong Delta and to places like the Cham Islands.

Bus fares More complicated. If you buy a ticket from the point of departure (ie the bus station), then the price is fixed and very reasonable. However, should you board a bus along the way, there's a good chance the driver or conductor will overcharge. In remote areas drivers may ask for four, or even 10, times what the locals pay. Local bus prices should be fixed and displayed by the door, but foreigners are sometimes overcharged on routes such as Danang–Hoi An.

Rail fares Fixed, although naturally there are different prices for different classes.

Taxis Mostly metered and very cheap, but very occasionally some taxis have dodgy meters that run fast.

Xe oms & cyclos Fares are definitely not fixed and you need to bargain. Hard.

the side of the road to get punctures and the like fixed.

Boat

Vietnam has an enormous number of rivers that are at least partly navigable, but the most important by far is the Mekong and its tributaries. Scenic day trips by boat are possible on rivers in Hoi An, Danang, Hue, Tam Coc and even HCMC.

Boat trips are also possible on the sea. Cruising the islands of Halong Bay is a must for all visitors to northern Vietnam. In central Vietnam the lovely Cham Islands (accessed from Hoi An) are a good excursion, while in the south, trips to the islands off Nha Trang and around Con Dao are also popular.

Bus

Vietnam has an extensive network of buses that reaches the far-flung corners of the country. Modern buses, operated by myriad companies, run on all the main highways. Out in the sticks expect seriously uncomfortable local services.

Most travellers never visit a Vietnamese bus station at all, preferring to stick to the convenient, tourist-friendly open-tour bus network.

Whichever class of bus you're on, bus travel in Vietnam is never speedy – reckon on just 50km/h on major routes (including Hwy 1) due to the sheer number of motorbikes, trucks and pedestrians competing for space.

Bus Stations

Cities can have several bus stations, and responsibilities can be divided according to the location of the destination (whether it is north or south of the city) and the type of service (local or long distance, express or non-express).

Bus stations can look chaotic but many now have ticket offices with official prices and departure times clearly displayed.

Deluxe Buses

Modern air-con buses operate between the main cities. This is the deluxe class and you can be sure of an allocated seat and enough space.

Some offer reclining seats, others have padded flat beds for really long trips. These sleeper buses can be a good alternative to trains, and costs are comparable.

Deluxe buses are non-smoking and some even have wi-fi (don't count on fast connections though). On the flipside, most of them are equipped with TVs (expect crazy kung-fu videos) and some with dreaded karaoke machines. Earplugs and eye masks are recommended.

Deluxe buses stop at most major cities en route, and for meal breaks.

Mai Linh Express (☎098 529 2929; www.mailinhexpress.vn) This reliable, punctual company operates clean, comfortable deluxe buses across Vietnam. Destinations covered include all main cities along Hwy 1 between Hanoi and HCMC, Hanoi to Haiphong, HCMC to Dalat, and cities in the central highlands.

The Sinh Tourist (☎08-3838 9597; www.thesinhtourist.com) An efficient company that has nationwide bus services, including sleepers. You can book ahead online. Look out for special promotional prices.

Local Buses

Short-distance buses depart when full. Don't count on many leaving after about 4pm.

These buses and minibuses drop off and pick up as many passengers as possible along the route; frequent stops make for a slow journey.

Conductors tend to routinely overcharge foreigners on these local services so they're not popular with travellers.

Open Tours

In backpacker haunts throughout Vietnam, you'll see lots of signs advertising 'Open Tour' or 'Open Ticket'. These are bus services catering mostly to foreign budget travellers. The air-con buses run between HCMC and Hanoi (and other routes) and passengers can hop on and hop off the bus at any major city along the route.

Prices are reasonable. A through ticket from Ho Chi Minh City to Hanoi costs between US$30 and US$75, depending on the operator and exact route. The more stops you add, the higher the price. Try to book the next leg of your trip at least a day ahead.

Buses usually depart from central places (often hostels popular with travellers), avoiding an extra journey to the bus station. Some open-tour buses also stop at sights along the way (such as the Cham ruins of Po Klong Garai).

The downside is that you're herded together with other backpackers and there's little contact with locals. Additionally, it's harder to get off the main 'banana pancake' trail as open-route buses just tend to run to the most popular places. Some open-tour operators also depend on kickbacks from sister hotels and restaurants along the way.

Buying shorter point-to-point tickets on the open-tour buses costs a bit more but you achieve more flexibility, including the chance to take a train, rent a motorbike or simply change your plans.

Nevertheless, cheap open-tour tickets are a temptation and many people go for them. Aside from the main north–south journey, the HCMC–Mui Ne–Dalat–Nha Trang route is popular.

If you are set on open-tour tickets, look for them at budget cafes in HCMC and Hanoi. **The Sinh Tourist** (☎08-3838 9597; www.thesinhtourist.com) has a good reputation, with computerised seat reservations and comfortable buses.

Reservations & Costs

Reservations aren't required for most of the frequent, popular services between towns and cities, but it doesn't hurt to purchase the ticket the day before. Always buy a ticket from the office, as bus drivers are notorious for overcharging.

On many rural runs foreigners are typically overcharged anywhere from twice to 10 times the going rate. As a benchmark, a typical 100km ride *should be* between US$2 and US$3.

Car & Motorcycle

Having your own set of wheels gives you maximum flexibility to visit remote regions and stop when and where you please. Car hire always includes a driver. Motorbike hire is good value and this can be self-drive or with a driver.

Driving Licence

The rules governing driving licences were changing in late 2015, and foreigners are now permitted to drive in Vietnam with an International Drivers' Permit (IDP). However, this must be combined with local insurance for it to be valid.

The reality on the ground has always been that foreigners are never asked for IDPs by police, and no rental places ever ask to see one. However this may change with the new law.

No car rental agencies allow you to self-drive, so all car rentals come with a driver.

Fuel

Fuel costs around 20,500d per litre of unleaded gasoline.

Even the most isolated communities usually have someone selling petrol by the roadside. Some sellers dilute fuel to make a quick profit – try to fill up from a proper petrol station.

Hire

The major considerations are safety, the mechanical condition of the vehicle, the reliability of the rental agency, and your budget.

CAR & MINIBUS

Self-drive rental cars are unavailable in Vietnam, which is a blessing given traffic conditions, but cars with drivers are popular and plentiful. Renting a vehicle with a driver-cum-guide is a realistic option even for budget travellers, provided there are enough people to share the cost.

ROAD DISTANCES (KM)

	Dalat	Hoi An	Sapa	Hue	Halong City	Hanoi
Hoi An	716					
Sapa	1868	1117				
Hue	830	138	1038			
Halong City	1653	911	545	823		
Hanoi	1488	793	380	658	165	
HCMC	310	942	2104	1097	1889	1724

Note: Distances are approximate

Hanoi, HCMC and the main tourist centres have a wide selection of travel agencies that rent vehicles with drivers for sightseeing trips. For the rough roads of northwestern Vietnam you'll definitely need a 4WD.

Approximate costs per day are between US$80 and US$120 for a standard car, or between US$120 and US$135 for a 4WD.

MOTORBIKE

Motorbikes can be rented from virtually anywhere, including cafes, hotels and travel agencies. Some places will ask to keep your passport until you return the bike. Try to sign some sort of agreement, clearly stating what you are renting, how much it costs, the extent of compensation and so on.

To tackle the mountains of the north, it is best to get a more powerful model such as a road or trail bike. Plenty of local drivers are willing to act as chauffeur and guide for around US$20 per day.

The approximate costs per day without a driver are between US$5 and US$7 for a semi-auto moped, between US$6 and US$10 for a fully automatic moped, or US$20 and up for trail and road bikes.

Insurance

If you're travelling in a tourist vehicle with a driver, the rental company organises insurance. If you're using a rental bike, the owners should have some insurance. If you're considering buying a vehicle Baoviet (www.baoviet.com.vn) has a third-party fire and theft coverage policy which includes liability for 87,000d.

Many rental places will make you sign a contract agreeing to a valuation for the bike if it is stolen. Make sure you always leave it in guarded parking where available.

Do not even consider renting a motorbike if you are daft enough to be travelling in Vietnam without travel insurance. The cost of treating serious injuries can be bankrupting for budget travellers.

Road Conditions & Hazards

Road safety is definitely not one of Vietnam's strong points. The intercity road network of two-lane highways is becoming more and more dangerous. High-speed, head-on collisions are a sickeningly familiar sight on main roads.

In general, the major highways are paved and reasonably well maintained, but seasonal flooding can be a problem. A big typhoon can create potholes the size of bomb craters. In some remote areas, roads are not surfaced and transform themselves into a sea of mud when the weather turns bad – such roads are best tackled with a 4WD vehicle or motorbike. Mountain roads are particularly dangerous: landslides, falling rocks and runaway vehicles can add an unwelcome edge to your journey.

EMERGENCIES

Vietnam does not have an efficient emergency-rescue system, so if something happens on the road, it could be some time before help arrives and a long way to even the most basic of medical facilities. Locals might help in extreme circumstances, but in most cases it will be up to you (or your guide) to get you to the hospital or clinic.

Road Rules

Basically, there aren't many or, arguably, any. Size matters and the biggest vehicle wins by default. Be particularly careful about children on the road. Livestock is also a menace; hit a cow on a motorbike and you'll both be hamburger.

HIRING A VEHICLE & DRIVER

Renting a car with a driver gives you the chance to design a tailor-made tour. Seeing the country this way is almost like independent travel, except that it's more comfortable, less time-consuming and allows for stops along the way.

Most travel agencies and tour operators can hook you up with a vehicle and driver (most of whom will *not* speak English). Try to find a driver-guide who can act as a translator and travelling companion and offer all kinds of cultural knowledge, opening up the door to some unique experiences. A bad guide can ruin your trip. Consider the following:

- Try to meet your driver-guide before starting out and make sure that this is someone you can travel with.
- How much English (French or other language) do they speak?
- Drivers usually pays for their own costs, including accommodation and meals, while you pay for the petrol. Check this is the case.
- Settle on an itinerary and get a copy from the travel agency. If you find your guide is making it up as they go along, use it as leverage.
- Make it clear you want to avoid tourist-trap restaurants and shops.
- Tip them if you've had a good experience.

The police almost never bother stopping foreigners on bikes. However, speeding fines are imposed and the police now have speed 'guns'. In any area deemed to be 'urban' (look out for the blue sign with skyscrapers), the limit is 50km/h. In cities, there is a rule that you cannot turn right on a red light.

Honking at all pedestrians and bicycles (to warn them of your approach) is not road rage but an essential element of safe driving – larger trucks and buses might as well have a dynamo-driven horn. There is no national seat-belt law.

Legally, a motorbike can carry only two people, but we've seen up to six on one vehicle! This law is enforced in major cities, but wildly ignored in rural areas.

Spare Parts

Vietnam is awash with Japanese (and Chinese) motorbikes, so it is easy to get spare parts for most bikes. But if you are driving something obscure, bring substantial spares.

Local Transport

Bus

Few travellers deal with city buses due to communication issues and the cheapness of taxis, *cyclos* and *xe om*. That said, the bus systems in Hanoi and HCMC are not impossible to negotiate – get your hands on a bus map.

Cyclo

The *cyclo* is a bicycle rickshaw. This cheap, environmentally friendly mode of transport is steadily dying out, but is still found in Vietnam's main cities.

Groups of *cyclo* drivers always hang out near major hotels and markets, and many speak at least broken English. To make sure the driver understands where you want to go, it's useful to bring a city map. Bargaining is imperative. Settle on a fare before going anywhere or you're likely to get stiffed.

Approximate fares are between 10,000d and 20,0000d for a short ride, between 20,000d and 40,000d for a longer or night ride, or around 40,000d per hour.

Travellers have reported being mugged by *cyclo* drivers in HCMC so, as a general rule, hire *cyclos* only during the day in that city. When leaving a bar late at night, take a metered taxi.

HELMET LAW

It is compulsory to wear a helmet when riding a motorbike in Vietnam, even when travelling as a passenger. Consider investing in a decent imported helmet if you are planning extensive rides on busy highways or winding mountain roads, as the local eggshells don't offer much protection. Better-quality helmets are available in major cities from US$30.

Taxi

Taxis with meters, found in most major cities, are very cheap by international standards and a safe way to travel around at night. Average tariffs are 12,000d to 15,000d per kilometre. However, dodgy taxis with go-fast meters do roam the streets of Hanoi and HCMC, and they often hang around bus terminals. Only travel with reputable or recommended companies.

Two nationwide companies with excellent reputations are Mai Linh (www.mailinh.vn) and Vinasun (www.vinasuntaxi.com).

Xe Om

The *xe om* (*zay*-ohm) is a motorbike taxi. *Xe* means motorbike, *om* means hug (or hold), so you get the picture. Getting around by *xe om* is easy, as long as you don't have a lot of luggage.

Fares are comparable with those for a *cyclo*, but negotiate the price beforehand. There are plenty of *xe om* drivers hanging around street corners, markets, hotels and bus stations. They will find you before you find them...

Tours

The quality of bottom-end budget tours being peddled in HCMC and Hanoi is often terrible. You tend to get what you pay for.

Handspan Travel Indochina (☎04 3926 2828; www.handspan.com) Expert locally owned company that offers a wide range of innovative, interesting tours to seldom-visited regions including Moc Chau and alternative destinations like Cao Bang in the north. Other options include jeep tours, mountain biking, trekking and kayaking.

Ocean Tours (☎04-3926 0463; www.oceantours.com.vn) Professional tour operator based in Hanoi, with Ba Be National Park and mountain-biking options, a great Thousand Island tour of Halong Bay, and excellent 4WD road trips around the northeast.

Buffalo Tours (Map p58; www.buffalotours.com) Offers diverse and customised trips, including a superb Halong Bay tour by seaplane and luxury junk.

Exo Travel (www.exotravel.com) Offers a wide range of tours, including cycling, trekking and community tourism. The 10-day Central Coast Cycle Ride between Hue and Nha Trang covers lots of great coastal scenery.

Sinhbalo Adventures (www.sinhbalo.com) Specialises in cycling tours to the Mekong Delta and beyond, plus trips to the Dalat region and southwestern highlands.

Grasshopper Adventures (www.grasshopperadventures.com) Well-planned cycling trips, from day-rides in the Mekong to an excellent seven-day Highlands & Coast of Vietnam trip.

Motorbike Tours

Specialised motorbike tours through Vietnam are a brilliant way to experience the nation and get off the main highways. Two wheels can reach the parts that four wheels sometimes can't, by traversing small trails and traffic-free back roads. A little experience helps, but many leading companies also offer tuition for first-timers. Mounting a bike to take on the peaks of the north is one of Vietnam's defining moments and should not be missed.

Foreign guides charge considerably more than local guides. Based on a group of four people, you can expect to pay from US$100 per person per day for an all-inclusive tour that provides motorbike rental, petrol, guide, food and accommodation.

Hoi An Motorbike Adventure (Map p204; ☎090 510 1930; www.motorbiketours-hoian.com; 111 Ba Trieu) A professional, established operator with a fine selection of tours, most shortish rides around the Hoi An area (from US$50). Options include a great off-road tour (US$125), and trips to Danang, Hue and a Co Tu minority village are also offered. Well-maintained classic-looking Minsk bikes are used, either self-drive or with driver.

Explore Indochina (☎09-1309 3159; www.exploreindochina.com) Using vintage Ural or Minsk bikes, these tours are expertly coordinated. The Karst Away trip (from US$1240) is a seven-day adventure around northeast Vietnam.

Offroad Vietnam (☎04-3926 3433; www.offroadvietnam.com) An experienced, well-organised operator which offers three types of trips: fully guided (all-inclusive), semi-guided (you and a guide), and self-guided (DIY) trips across northern and central Vietnam, mainly using Honda bikes. The Ha Giang tours (US$1192 for an eight-day tour) really get you off the beaten track.

Cuong's Motorbike Adventure (http://cuongs-motorbike-adventure.com) Adventurous tours across the north organised by experts with decades of experience. Urals (solo and with sidecar) and Hondas are used; jeep and 4WD trips are also offered.

Free Wheelin' Tours (Map p70; ☎04-3926 2743; www.free-wheelin-tours.com; 62 Đ Yen Phu, Ba Dinh; ⌚10am-7pm) Based in Hanoi, offering some great custom-made tours in northern Vietnam.

Moto Tours Asia (http://mototoursasia.com; from US$90 per day) Enjoys a good reputation for its trips in the north, with bike options from scooters to Royal Enfields.

Train

Operated by national carrier **Vietnam Railways** (Duong Sat Viet Nam; ☎04-3747 0308; www.vr.com.vn), the Vietnamese railway system is an ageing but dependable service, and offers a relaxing way to get around the nation. Travelling in an air-con sleeping berth sure beats a hairy overnight bus journey along Hwy 1.

Classes

Trains classified as SE are the smartest and fastest, while those referred to as TN are slower and older.

There are four main ticket classes: hard seat, soft seat, hard sleeper and soft sleeper. These are also split into air-con and non-air-con options. Presently, air-con is only available on the faster express trains. Some SE trains now have wi-fi (though connection speeds, like Vietnamese trains, are not the quickest). Hard-seat class is usually packed and tolerable for day travel, but expect plenty of cigarette smoke.

PRIVATE CARRIAGES

Comfortable, even luxurious private carriages tagged onto the back of trains offer a classy way of travelling between Lao Cai and Hanoi: those offered by **Orient Express Trains** (☎04-3929 0999; www.orientexpresstrain-sapa.com) and Victoria Hotels are renowned and very pricey, but there are at least six other options including **Livitrans** (www.livitrans.com; from US$52).

Livitrans also offers luxury carriages between Hanoi and Hue (US$75) and Danang (US$85), as do many other companies. **Golden Trains** (☎08-3825 7636; www.golden-train.com) connects HCMC with Nha Trang (US$35 to US$43 soft sleeper).

SLEEPERS

A hard sleeper has three tiers of beds (six beds per compartment), with the upper berth cheapest and the lower berth most expensive. Soft sleeper has two tiers (four beds per compartment) and all bunks are priced the same. Fastidious travellers will probably want to bring a sleeping sheet, sleeping bag and/or pillow case with them, although linen is provided.

Costs

Ticket prices vary depending on the train; the fastest trains are more expensive. Children under two are free; those between two and nine years of age pay 50% of adult fare. There are no discounts on the Hanoi–Lao Cai route.

Freight

Bicycles and motorbikes must travel in freight carriages, which will cost around 375,000d for a typical overnight trip. Sometimes it's not possible to travel on the same train as your bike, so remember to make a note of the train it's on and when it is expected to arrive.

Reservations

You can can buy tickets in advance from Vietnam Railways' booking site (http://dsvn.vn), however at the time

REUNIFICATION EXPRESS

Construction of the 1726km-long Hanoi–Saigon railway, the Transindochinois, began in 1899 and was completed in 1936. In the late 1930s, the trip from Hanoi to Saigon took 40 hours and 20 minutes at an average speed of 43km/h.

During WWII the Japanese made extensive use of the rail system, resulting in Viet Minh sabotage on the ground and US bombing from the air. After WWII, efforts were made to repair the Transindochinois, major parts of which were either damaged or had become overgrown.

During the Franco–Viet Minh War (1946–54), the Viet Minh again engaged in sabotage against the rail system. At night the Viet Minh made off with rails to create a 300km network of tracks (between Ninh Hoa and Danang) in an area wholly under their control – the French quickly responded with their own sabotage.

In the late 1950s the South, with US funding, reconstructed the 1041km track between Saigon and Hue. But between 1961 and 1964 alone, 795 Viet Cong (VC) attacks were launched on the rail system, forcing the abandonment of large sections of track (including the Dalat spur).

By 1960, North Vietnam had repaired 1000km of track, mostly between Hanoi and China. During the US air war against the North, the northern rail network was repeatedly bombed. Even now, clusters of bomb craters can be seen around virtually every rail bridge and train station in the north.

Following reunification in 1975, the government immediately set about re-establishing the Hanoi–Ho Chi Minh City rail link as a symbol of Vietnamese unity. By the time the Reunification Express trains were inaugurated on 31 December 1976, 1334 bridges, 27 tunnels, 158 stations and 1370 shunts (switches) had been repaired.

Today, the Reunification Express chugs along only slightly faster than the trains did in the 1930s, at an average speed of 50km/h. Chronic under-investment means that it's still mainly a single-track line, and carries less than 1% of all north–south freight.

Plans for a massive overhaul of the rail system to create a high-speed network have been shelved, but a gradual upgrade of the network is ongoing and it's hoped that this will raise maximum speeds up towards 90km/h by 2020.

of research only Vietnamese credit cards were accepted. However, you can book online using the travel agency Bao Lau (www.baolau.vn), which has an efficient website, details seat and sleeper-berth availability, and accepts international cards. E-tickets are emailed to you; there's a 40,000d commission per ticket.

You can reserve seats/berths on long trips 60 to 90 days in advance (fewer on shorter trips). Most of the time you can book train tickets a day or two ahead without a problem, except during peak holiday times. But for sleeping berths, it's wise to book a week or more before the date of departure.

Schedules, fares, information and advance bookings are available on Bao Lau's website. Vietnam Impressive (www.vietnamimpressive.com) is another dependable private booking agent and will deliver tickets to your hotel in Vietnam, free of charge (or can send them abroad for a fee).

Many travel agencies, hotels and cafes will also buy you train tickets for a small commission.

Routes

Aside from the main HCMC–Hanoi run, three rail-spur lines link Hanoi with the other parts of northern Vietnam. One runs east to the port city of Haiphong. A second heads northeast to Lang Son and continues across the border to Nanning, China. A third runs northwest to Lao Cai (for trains on to Kunming, China).

'Fast' trains between Hanoi and HCMC take between 32 and 36 hours.

Safety

Petty crime can be a problem on Vietnamese trains. Thieves can try to grab stuff as trains pull out of stations. Always keep your bag nearby and lock or tie it to something, especially at night.

Schedules

Many Reunification Express trains depart from Hanoi and HCMC every day. Train schedules change frequently, so check departure times on the Vietnam Railways website, Bao Lau's website or www.seat61.com, the international train website.

A bare-bones train schedule operates during the Tet festival, when most trains are suspended for nine days, beginning four days before Tet and continuing for four days afterwards.

Health

Health issues (and the quality of medical facilities) can vary enormously depending on where you are in Vietnam. The major cities are generally not high risk and have good facilities, though rural areas are another matter.

Travellers tend to worry about contracting infectious diseases in Vietnam, but serious illnesses are rare. Accidental injury (especially traffic accidents) account for most life-threatening problems. That said, a bout of sickness is a relatively common thing. The following advice is a general guide only.

BEFORE YOU GO

- Pack any medications in clearly labelled containers.
- Bring a letter from your doctor describing your medical conditions and medications.
- If carrying syringes or needles, have a physician's letter documenting their medical necessity.
- If you have a heart condition, bring a copy of a recent ECG.
- Bring extra supplies of any regular medication (in case of loss or theft).

Insurance

Even if you are fit and healthy, don't travel without health insurance – accidents do happen. If your health insurance doesn't cover you for medical expenses abroad, get extra insurance – check our website (www.lonelyplanet.com) for more information. Emergency evacuation is expensive – bills of US$100,000 are not unknown – so make sure your policy covers this.

Required Vaccinations

The only vaccination required by international regulations is yellow fever. Proof of vaccination will only be required if you have visited a country in the yellow-fever zone within six days of entering Vietnam.

Most vaccines don't produce immunity until at least two weeks after they're given, so visit a doctor four to eight weeks before departure.

Medical Checklist

Recommended, but not exhaustive, items for a personal medical kit:

- antibacterial cream, eg mupirocin
- antifungal treatments for thrush and tinea, eg clotrimazole or fluconazole
- antihistamines for allergies, eg cetirizine for daytime and promethazine for night
- antiseptic for cuts and scrapes, eg iodine solution such as Betadine
- DEET-based insect repellent
- diarrhoea 'stopper', eg loperamide
- first-aid items, such as scissors, plasters (such as Band-Aids), bandages, gauze, safety pins and tweezers
- paracetamol or ibuprofen for pain
- steroid cream for allergic/itchy rashes, eg 1% hydrocortisone
- sunscreen

Websites

There's a wealth of travel-health advice on the internet.

www.who.int/ith Publishes a superb book called *International Travel & Health*, which is available free online.

www.cdc.gov Good general information.

www.travelhealthpro.org.uk Useful health advice.

IN VIETNAM

Availability & Cost of Health Care

The significant improvement in Vietnam's economy has brought with it some major advances in public health. However, in remote parts, local clinics will only have basic supplies – if you become seriously ill in rural Vietnam, get to Ho Chi Minh City (HCMC), Danang or Hanoi as quickly as you can. For surgery or other extensive treatment, don't hesitate to fly to Bangkok, Singapore or Hong Kong.

Private Clinics

These should be your first port of call. They are familiar with local resources and can organise evacuations if necessary. The best medical facilities – in Hanoi, HCMC and Danang – have health-facility standards that come close to those in developed countries.

State Hospitals

Most are overcrowded and basic. In order to treat foreigners, a facility needs to obtain a special licence and so far only a few have been provided.

Self-Treatment

If your problem is minor (eg travellers' diarrhoea) this is an option. If you think you may have a serious disease, especially malaria, do not waste time – travel to the nearest quality facility to receive attention.

Buying medication over the counter is not recommended, as fake medications and poorly stored or out-of-date drugs are common. Check expiry dates on all medicines.

Infectious Diseases

Bird Flu

The bird flu virus rears its head from time to time in Vietnam. It occurs in clusters, usually among poultry workers. It's rarely fatal for humans. When outbreaks do occur, eggs and poultry are banished from the menu in many hotels and restaurants.

Dengue

This mosquito-borne disease is becoming increasingly problematic in Southeast Asia. Several hundred thousand people are hospitalised with dengue haemorrhagic fever in Vietnam every year, but the fatality rate is less than 0.3%. As there is no vaccine available, it can only be prevented by avoiding mosquito bites. The mosquito that carries dengue

RECOMMENDED VACCINATIONS

The World Health Organization (WHO) recommends the following vaccinations for travellers to Southeast Asia:

Adult diphtheria and tetanus Single booster recommended if you've had none in the previous 10 years.

Hepatitis A Provides almost 100% protection for up to a year; a booster after 12 months provides at least another 20 years' protection.

Hepatitis B Now considered routine for most travellers. Given as three shots over six months. A rapid schedule is also available, as is a combined vaccination with Hepatitis A. Lifetime protection occurs in 95% of people.

Measles, mumps and rubella Two doses of MMR are required unless you have had the diseases. Many young adults require a booster.

Typhoid Recommended unless your trip is less than a week and only to developed cities. The vaccine offers around 70% protection and lasts for two or three years.

Varicella If you haven't had chickenpox, discuss this vaccination with your doctor.

Long-Term Travellers

These vaccinations are recommended for people travelling for more than one month, or those at special risk:

Japanese B encephalitis Three injections in all. A booster is recommended after two years. A sore arm and headache are the most common side effects reported.

Meningitis Single injection.

Rabies Three injections in all. A booster after one year will provide 10 years of protection.

Tuberculosis Adults should have a TB skin test before and after travel, rather than the vaccination.

TAP WATER

Be very careful of what you drink. Tap water is heavily chlorinated in urban areas, but you should still avoid it. Stick to bottled water, which is available everywhere. Ice is generally safe in the cities and resorts, and is often added to drinks and coffee.

bites throughout the day and night, so use insect-avoidance measures at all times. Symptoms include a high fever, a severe headache and body aches (dengue was once known as 'breakbone fever'). Some people develop a rash and experience diarrhoea. There is no specific treatment, just rest and paracetamol – do not take aspirin as it increases the likelihood of haemorrhaging. See a doctor to be diagnosed and monitored.

Hepatitis A

A problem throughout the region, this food- and water-borne virus infects the liver, causing jaundice (yellow skin and eyes), nausea and lethargy. There is no specific treatment for hepatitis A – you just need to allow time for the liver to heal. All travellers to Vietnam should be vaccinated against hepatitis A.

Hepatitis B

The only serious sexually transmitted disease that can be prevented by vaccination, hepatitis B is spread by body fluids, including sexual contact. In some parts of Southeast Asia up to 20% of the population are carriers of hepatitis B, and usually are unaware of this. The long-term consequences can include liver cancer and cirrhosis.

HIV

The official figures on the number of people with HIV/AIDS in Vietnam are vague, but they are on the rise. Health-education messages relating to HIV/AIDS are visible all over the countryside, but the official line is that infection is largely limited to sex workers and drug users. Condoms are widely available throughout Vietnam.

Japanese B Encephalitis

This viral disease is transmitted by mosquitoes. It's very rarely caught by travellers but vaccination is recommended for those spending extended time in rural areas. There is no treatment; a third of infected people will die while another third will suffer permanent brain damage.

Malaria

For such a serious and potentially deadly disease, there is an enormous amount of misinformation concerning malaria. You must get expert advice as to whether your trip actually puts you at risk. Many parts of Vietnam, particularly city and resort areas, have minimal to no risk of malaria, including Danang, Hanoi, Ho Chi Minh City and Nha Trang. For most rural areas, however, the risk of contracting the disease far outweighs the risk of any tablet side effects. Travellers to isolated areas in high-risk regions such as Ca Mau and Bac Lieu provinces, and the rural south, may like to carry a treatment dose of medication for use if symptoms occur. Remember that malaria can be fatal. Before you travel, seek medical advice on the right medication and dosage for you.

Malaria is caused by a parasite transmitted by the bite of an infected mosquito. The most important symptom of malaria is fever, but general symptoms such as headache, diarrhoea, cough or chills may also occur. Diagnosis can only be made by taking a blood sample.

Two strategies should be combined to prevent malaria: mosquito avoidance and antimalarial medications.

MALARIA PREVENTION

- Choose accommodation with screens and fans (if not air-conditioned).
- Impregnate clothing with permethrin in high-risk areas.
- Sleep under a mosquito net.
- Spray your room with insect repellent before going out for your evening meal.
- Use a DEET-containing insect repellent on all exposed skin, particularly the ankle area. Natural repellents such as citronella can be effective but must be applied frequently.
- Use mosquito coils.
- Wear long sleeves and trousers in light colours.

MALARIA MEDICATION

There are various medications available.

Chloroquine & Paludrine The effectiveness of this combination is now limited in Vietnam. Generally not recommended.

Doxycycline A broad-spectrum antibiotic that has the added benefit of helping to prevent a variety of tropical diseases, including leptospirosis, tick-borne disease, typhus and melioidosis. Potential side effects include a tendency to sunburn, thrush in women, indigestion and interference with the contraceptive pill. It must be taken for four weeks after leaving the risk area.

Lariam (mefloquine) Receives a lot of bad press, some of it justified, some not. This weekly tablet suits many people. Serious side effects are rare but include depression, anxiety, psychosis and seizures. It's around 90% effective in Vietnam.

Malarone Side effects are uncommon and mild, most commonly nausea and headaches. It is the best tablet for scuba-divers and for those on short trips to high-risk areas.

A final option is to take no preventive medication but to have a supply of emergency medication (Malarone is usually recommended: four tablets once daily for three days) should you develop the symptoms of malaria. This is less than ideal, and you'll still need to get to a good medical facility within 24 hours of developing a fever.

Measles

Measles remains a problem in Vietnam, including the Hanoi area. Many people born before 1966 are immune as they had the disease in childhood. Measles starts with a high fever and rash but can be complicated by pneumonia and brain disease. There is no specific treatment.

Rabies

This uniformly fatal disease is spread by the bite or lick of an infected animal – most commonly a dog or monkey. Seek medical advice immediately after any animal bite and start post-exposure treatment. Having a pre-travel vaccination means the post-bite treatment is greatly simplified. If an animal bites you, gently wash the wound with soap and water, and apply an iodine-based antiseptic. If you are not vaccinated you will need to receive rabies immunoglobulin as soon as possible.

Schistosomiasis

Schistosomiasis (also called bilharzia) is a tiny parasite that enters your skin after you've been swimming in contaminated water. If you are concerned, you can be tested three months after exposure. Symptoms are coughing and fever. Schistosomiasis is easily treated with medications.

STDs

Condoms, widely available throughout Vietnam, are effective in preventing the spread of most sexually transmitted diseases. However, they may not guard against genital warts or herpes. If after a sexual encounter you develop any rash, lumps, discharge or pain when passing urine, seek immediate medical attention.

Tuberculosis

Tuberculosis (TB) is very rare in short-term travellers. Medical and aid workers, and long-term travellers who have significant contact with the local population should take precautions. Vaccination is usually only given to children under the age of five, but it is recommended that at-risk adults have pre- and post-travel TB testing. The main symptoms are fever, cough, weight loss, night sweats and tiredness.

Typhoid

This serious bacterial infection is spread via food and water. It gives a high, slowly progressive fever and headache. Vaccination is recommended for all travellers spending more than a week in Vietnam, or travelling outside of the major cities. Be aware that vaccination is not 100% effective so you must still be careful with what you eat and drink.

Typhus

Murine typhus is spread by the fleas of rodents whereas scrub typhus is spread via a mite. These diseases are rare in travellers. Symptoms include fever, muscle pains and a rash. You can avoid these diseases by following general insect-avoidance measures. Doxycycline will also help prevent them.

Travellers' Diarrhoea

Travellers' diarrhoea is by far the most common problem affecting travellers – between 30% and 50% of people will suffer from it within two weeks of starting their trip. In over 80% of cases, travellers' diarrhoea is caused by a bacteria, and therefore responds promptly to treatment with antibiotics. It can also be provoked by a change of diet, and your stomach may settle down again after a few days.

Treatment consists of staying hydrated, or you could take rehydration solutions.

Loperamide is just a 'stopper' and doesn't get to the cause of the problem. It is helpful if you have to go on a long bus ride, but don't take loperamide if you have a fever or blood in your stools.

Amoebic Dysentery

Amoebic dysentery is very rare in travellers. Symptoms are similar to bacterial diarrhoea (eg fever, bloody diarrhoea and generally feeling unwell). Treatment involves two drugs: tinidazole or metronidazole to kill the parasite and a second to kill the cysts.

Giardiasis

Giardia lamblia is a parasite that is relatively common in travellers. Symptoms include nausea, bloating, excess gas, fatigue and intermittent diarrhoea. 'Eggy' burps are often attributed solely to giardiasis, but they are not specific to this infection. The treatment of choice is tinidazole.

Environmental Hazards

Air Pollution

Air pollution, particularly vehicle pollution, is severe in Vietnam's major cities. If you have severe respiratory problems consult your doctor before travelling.

Food

Eating in restaurants is the biggest risk factor for contracting travellers' diarrhoea. Ways to avoid it include eating only freshly cooked food, and avoiding shellfish and buffets. Peel all fruit and try to stick to cooked vegetables. Eat in busy restaurants with a high turnover of customers.

Heat

Many parts of Vietnam are hot and humid throughout the year. Take it easy when you first arrive. Avoid dehydration and excessive activity in the heat. Drink rehydration solution and eat salty food.

Heat exhaustion Symptoms include feeling weak, headaches, irritability, nausea or vomiting, sweaty skin and a fast, weak pulse. Cool down in a room with air-conditioning and rehydrate with water containing a quarter of a teaspoon of salt per litre.

Heatstroke This is a serious medical emergency. Symptoms come on suddenly and include weakness, nausea, a temperature of over 41°C, dizziness, confusion and eventually collapse and loss of consciousness. Seek medical help and start cooling by following cooling treatment.

Prickly heat A common skin rash in the tropics. Stay in an air-conditioned area for a few hours and take cool showers.

Bites & Stings

Bedbugs These don't carry disease but their bites are very itchy. Move hotel, and treat the itch with an antihistamine.

Jellyfish In Vietnamese waters most are not dangerous, just irritating. Pour vinegar (or urine) onto the affected area. Take painkillers, and seek medical advice if you feel ill in any way. Take local advice if there are dangerous jellyfish around and keep out of the water.

Leeches Found in humid forest areas. They do not transmit any disease but their bites can be intensely itchy. Apply an iodine-based antiseptic to any leech bite to help prevent infection.

Snakes Both poisonous and harmless snakes are common in Vietnam, though very few travellers are ever bothered by them. Wear boots and avoid poking around dead logs and wood when hiking. First aid in the event of a snakebite involves pressure immobilisation via an elastic bandage firmly wrapped around the affected limb, starting at the bite site and working up towards the chest. The bandage should not be so tight that the circulation is cut off, and the fingers or toes should be kept free so the circulation can be checked. Immobilise the limb with a splint and carry the victim to medical attention. Do not use tourniquets or try to suck the venom out. Antivenom is available only in major cities.

Ticks Contracted during walks in rural areas. If you have had a tick bite and experience symptoms such as a rash (at the site of the bite or elsewhere), fever or muscle aches, you should see a doctor. Doxycycline prevents tick-borne diseases.

Skin Problems

Fungal rashes Common in humid climates. Moist areas that get less air, such as the groin, armpits and between the toes, are often affected. Treatment involves using an antifungal cream such as clotrimazole. Consult a doctor.

Cuts and scratches Minor cuts and scratches can become infected easily in humid climates and may fail to heal because of the humidity. Take meticulous care of any wounds: immediately wash in clean water and apply antiseptic.

Sunburn

- Even on a cloudy day, sunburn can occur rapidly.
- Always use a strong sunscreen (at least factor 30).
- Reapply sunscreen after swimming.
- Wear a hat.
- Avoid the sun between 10am and 2pm.

Women's Health

Supplies of sanitary products are readily available in urban areas. Birth-control options may be limited, so bring adequate stocks.

Pregnant women should receive specialised advice before travelling. The ideal time to travel is in the second trimester (between 16 and 28 weeks), during which the risk of pregnancy-related problems is at its lowest. Some advice:

Rural areas Avoid remote areas with poor transportation and medical facilities.

Travel insurance Ensure you're covered for pregnancy-related possibilities, including premature labour.

Malaria None of the more effective antimalarial drugs are completely safe in pregnancy.

Travellers' diarrhoea Many diarrhoea treatments are not recommended during pregnancy. Azithromycin is considered safe.

Language

Vietnamese, or *tiếng Việt* dee·úhng vee·uht, is the official language of Vietnam and spoken by about 85 million people worldwide, both in Vietnam and among migrant communities around the world. It belongs to the Mon-Khmer language family and has Muong (a hill-tribe language) as its closest relative.

Vietnamese pronunciation is not as hard as it may seem at first as most Vietnamese sounds also exist in English. With a bit of practice and reading our coloured pronunciation guides as if they were English, you shouldn't have much trouble being understood. Note that the vowel a is pronounced as in 'at', aa as in 'father', aw as in 'law', er as in 'her', oh as in 'doh!', ow as in 'cow', u as in 'book', uh as in 'but' and uhr as in 'fur' (without the 'r'). Vowel sounds can also be combined in various ways within a word – we've used dots (eg dee·úhng) to separate the different vowel sounds to keep pronunciation straightforward. As for the consonants, note that the ng sound, which is also found in English (eg in 'sing') can also appear at the start of a word in Vietnamese. Also note that d is pronounced as in 'stop', đ as in 'dog' and ğ as in 'skill'.

You'll notice that some vowels are pronounced with a high or low pitch while others swoop or glide in an almost musical manner. This is because Vietnamese uses a system of tones. There are six tones in Vietnamese, indicated in the written language (and in our pronunciation guides) by accent marks above or below the vowel: mid (ma), low falling (mà), low rising (mả), high broken (mã), high rising (má) and low broken (mạ). Note that the mid tone is flat. In the south, the low rising and the high broken tones are both pronounced as the low rising tone. Vietnamese words are considered to have one syllable, so word stress is not an issue.

The variation in vocabulary between the Vietnamese of the north and that of the south is indicated in this chapter by (N) and (S).

WANT MORE?

For in-depth language information and handy phrases, check out Lonely Planet's *Vietnamese Phrasebook* and *Hill Tribes Phrasebook*. You'll find them at **shop.lonelyplanet.com**, or you can buy Lonely Planet's iPhone phrasebooks at the Apple App Store.

BASICS

Hello.	*Xin chào.*	sin jòw
Goodbye.	*Tạm biệt.*	daạm bee·ụht
Yes.	*Vâng.* (N)	vuhng
	Dạ. (S)	yạ
No.	*Không.*	kawm
Please.	*Làm ơn.*	laàm ern
Thank you	*Cảm ơn.*	ğaảm ern
You're welcome.	*Không có chi.*	kawm ğó jee
Excuse me./ Sorry.	*Xin lỗi.*	sin lỗy

How are you?
Có khỏe không? ğáw kwẻ kawm

Fine, thank you. And you?
Khỏe, cám ơn. kwẻ ğaảm ern
Còn bạn thì sao? kwẻ ğòn baạn teè sow

What's your name?
Tên là gì? den laà zeè

My name is ...
Tên tôi là ... den doy laà ...

Do you speak English?
Bạn có nói được tiếng Anh không? baạn ğó nóy đuhr·ẹrk díng aang kawm

I (don't) understand.
Tôi (không) hiểu. doy (kawm) heẻ·oo

ACCOMMODATION

Where is a ...?	*Đâu có ... ?*	đoh ğó ...
hotel	*khách sạn*	kaák saạn
guesthouse	*nhà khách*	nyaà kaák

I'd like (a) ...	*Tôi muốn ...*	doy moo·úhn ...
single room	*phòng đơn*	fòm dern
double room (big bed)	*phòng giường đôi*	fòm zuhr·èrng đoy

How much is it per night/person?
Giá bao nhiêu một đêm/người? zaá bow nyee·oo mạwt đem/nguhr·eè

air-con	*máy lạnh*	máy laạng
bathroom	*phòng tắm*	fòm dúhm
fan	*quạt máy*	gwaạt máy
hot water	*nước nóng*	nuhr·érk nóm
mosquito net	*màng*	maàng
sheet	*ra trãi giường*	zaa chaĩ zuhr·èrng
toilet	*nhà vệ sinh*	nyaà vẹ sing
toilet paper	*giấy vệ sinh*	záy vẹ sing
towel	*khăn tắm*	kúhn dúhm

DIRECTIONS

Where is ...?
... ở đâu ? ... ẻr đoh

What is the address?
Địa chỉ là gì? đee·ụh cheẻ laà zeè

Could you write it down, please?
Xin viết ra giùm tôi. sin vee·úht zaa zùm doy

Can you show me (on the map)?
Xin chỉ giùm (trên bản dồ này). sin jeẻ zùm (chen baản dàw này)

Go straight ahead.
Thẳng tới trước. tủhng der·eé chuhr·érk

at the corner	*ở góc đường*	ẻr góp đuhr·èrng
at the traffic lights	*tại đèn giao thông*	dại đèn zow tawm
behind	*đằng sau*	đùhng sow
in front of	*đằng trước*	đùng chuhr·érk
near (to)	*gần*	gùhn
opposite	*đối diện*	đóy zee·ụhn
Turn left.	*Sang trái.*	saang chaí
Turn right.	*Sang phải.*	saang fai

EATING & DRINKING

I'd like a table for ...	*Tôi muốn đặt bàn cho ...*	doy moo·úhn đụht baàn jo ...
(two) people	*(hai) người*	(hai) nguhr·eè
(eight) o'clock	*vào lúc (tám) giờ*	vòw lúp (dúhm) zèr

KEY PATTERNS

To get by in Vietnamese, mix and match these simple patterns with words of your choice:

When's (the next bus)?
Khi nào là (chuyến xe buýt tới)? kee nòw laà (jwee·úhn sa bweét der·eé)

Where's (the station)?
(Nhà ga) ở đâu? (nyaà gaa) ẻr đoh

Where can I (buy a ticket)?
Tôi có thể (mua vé) ở đâu? doy ğó tẻ (moo·uh vá) ér đoh

I'm looking for (a hotel).
Tôi tìm (khách sạn). doy dìm (kaát saạn)

Do you have (a map)?
Bạn có (bản đồ) không? baạn ğó (baản đàw) kawm

Is there (a toilet)?
Có (vệ sinh) không? ğó (vẹ sing) kawm

I'd like (the menu).
Xin cho tôi (thực đơn). sin jo doy (tụhrk đern)

I'd like to (hire a car).
Tôi muốn (xe hơi). doy moo·úhn (sa her·ee)

Could you please (help me)?
Làm ơn (giúp đỡ)? laàm ern (zúp đẽr)

I have (a visa).
Tôi có (visa). doy ğó (vee·saa)

Do you have a menu in English?
Bạn có thực đơn bằng tiếng Anh không? baạn káw tụhrk đern bùhng díng aang kawm

What's the speciality here?
Ở đây có món gì đặc biệt? ẻr đay kó món zeè dụhk bee·ụht

I'd like ...
Xin cho tôi ... sin jo doy ...

Not too spicy, please.
Xin đừng cho cay quá. sin đùrng jo ğay gwaá

I'm a vegetarian.
Tôi ăn chay. doy uhn jay

I'm allergic to (peanuts).
Tôi bị dị ứng với (hạt lạc). doy beẹ zeẹ úhrng ver·eé (haạt laạk)

Can you please bring me ...?
Xin mang cho tôi...? sin maang jo doy ...

Can I have a (beer), please?
Xin cho tôi (chai bia)? sin jo doy (jai bee·uh)

Cheers!
Chúc sức khoẻ! júp súhrk kwả

Thank you, that was delicious.
Cám ơn, ngon lắm. ğaám ern ngon lúhm

The bill, please.
Xin tính tiền. sin díng dee·ùhn

Key Words

bottle	*chai*	jai
bowl	*bát/ chén* (N/S)	baát/ jén
breakfast	*ăn sáng*	uhn saáng
chopsticks	*đôi đũa*	đoy·ee đoõ·uh
cold	*lạnh*	laạng
dessert	*món tráng*	món chaáng
dinner	*ăn tối*	uhn dóy
fork	*cái dĩa/ nĩa* (N/S)	ğaí deẽ·uh/ neẽ·uh
glass	*cốc/ly* (N/S)	káwp/lee
hot (warm)	*nóng*	nóm
knife	*con dao*	ğon zow
lunch	*ăn trưa*	uhn chuhr·uh
plate	*đĩa*	đeẽ·uh
restaurant	*nhà hàng*	nyaà haàng
snack	*ăn nhẹ*	uhn nyạ
spicy	*cay*	ğay
spoon	*cái thìa*	ğaí tee·ùh
with	*với*	ver·eé
without	*không có*	kawm ğó

Meat & Fish

beef	*thịt bò*	tịt bò
chicken	*thịt gà*	tịt gaà
crab	*cua*	ğoo·uh
eel	*lươn*	luhr·ern
fish	*cá*	kaá
frog	*ếch*	ék
goat	*thịt dê*	tịt ze
pork	*thịt lợn/ heo* (N/S)	tịt lẹrn/ hay·o
prawns/shrimp	*tôm*	dawm
snail	*ốc*	áwp
squid	*mực*	mụhrk

Fruit & Vegetables

apple	*táo/bơm* (N/S)	dów/berm
banana	*chuối*	joo·eé
cabbage	*bắp cải*	búhp ğai
carrot	*cà rốt*	ğaà záwt
coconut	*dừa*	zuhr·ùh
corn	*ngô/bắp* (N/S)	ngow/búp
cucumber	*dưa leo*	zuhr·uh lay·o
eggplant	*cà tím*	ğaà dím
grapes	*nho*	nyo
green beans	*đậu xanh*	đọh saang
green pepper	*ớt xanh*	ért saang
lemon	*chanh*	chaang
lettuce	*rau diếp*	zoh zee·úhp
lychee	*vải*	vai
mandarin	*quýt*	gweét
mango	*xoài*	swaì
mushrooms	*nấm*	núhm
orange	*cam*	ğaam
papaya	*đu đủ*	đoo đỏo
peas	*đậu bi*	đọh bee
pineapple	*dứa*	zuhr·úh
potato	*khoai tây*	kwai day
pumpkin	*bí ngô*	beé ngaw
strawberry	*dâu*	zoh
sweet potato	*khoai lang*	kwai laang
tomato	*cà chua*	ğaà joo·uh
watermelon	*dưa hấu*	zuhr·uh hóh

Other

chilli sauce	*tương ớt*	duhr·erng ért
eggs	*trứng*	chúhrng
fish sauce	*nước mắm*	nuhr·érk múhm
flat rice noodles	*phở*	fẻr
fried rice	*cơm rang thập cẩm* (N) *cơm chiên* (S)	ğerm zaang tụhp ğũhm ğerm jee·uhn
rice	*cơm*	ğerm
salad	*sa lát*	saa laát
soup	*canh*	ğaang
steamed rice	*cơm trắng*	ğerm chaáng
ice	*đá*	đaá
pepper	*hạt tiêu*	haạt dee·oo
salt	*muối*	moo·eé
sugar	*đường*	dur·èrng
thin rice noodles	*bún*	bún
yellow egg noodles	*mì*	meè

Drinks

beer	*bia*	bi·a
coffee	*cà phê*	ğaà fe
iced lemon juice	*chanh đá*	jaang đaá
milk	*sữa*	sũhr·uh
mineral water	*nước khoáng* (N) *nước suối* (S)	nuhr·érk kwaáng nuhr·érk soo·eé

Numbers

1	*một*	mạwt
2	*hai*	hai
3	*ba*	baa
4	*bốn*	báwn
5	*năm*	nuhm
6	*sáu*	sóh
7	*bảy*	bảy
8	*tám*	dúhm
9	*chín*	jín
10	*mười*	muhr·eè
20	*hai mươi*	hai muhr·ee
30	*ba mươi*	ba muhr·ee
40	*bốn mươi*	báwn muhr·ee
50	*năm mươi*	nuhm muhr·ee
60	*sáu mươi*	sów muhr·ee
70	*bảy mươi*	bảy muhr·ee
80	*tám mươi*	daám muhr·ee
90	*chín mươi*	jín muhr·ee
100	*một trăm*	mạwt chuhm
1000	*một nghìn* (N) *một ngàn* (S)	mạwt ngyìn mọt ngaàn

orange juice	*cam vắt*	ğaam vúht
red wine	*rượu vang đỏ*	zee·oọ vaang đỏ
soy milk	*sữa đậu nành*	sũhr·uh đọh naàng
tea	*chè/trà* (N/S)	jà/chaà
white wine	*rượu vang trắng*	zee·oọ vaang chaáng

EMERGENCIES

Help!
Cứu tôi! — ğuhr·oó doy

There's been an accident!
Có tai nạn! — ğó dai naạn

Leave me alone!
Thôi! — toy

I'm lost.
Tôi bị lạc đường. — doi beẹ laạk đuhr·èrng

Where is the toilet?
Nhà vệ sinh ở đâu? — nyaà vẹ sing ẻr đoh

Please call the police.
Làm ơn gọi công an. — laàm ern gọy ğawm aan

Please call a doctor.
Làm ơn gọi bác sĩ. — laàm ern gọy baák seẽ

I'm sick.
Tôi bị đau. — doy beẹ đoh

It hurts here.
Chỗ bị đau ở đây. — jãw beẹ đoh ẻr đay

I'm allergic to (antibiotics).
Tôi bị dị ứng với (thuốc kháng sinh). — doy beẹ zeẹ úhrng ver·eé (too·úhk kaáng sing)

SHOPPING & SERVICES

I'd like to buy ...
Tôi muốn mua ... — doy moo·úhn moo·uh ...

Can I look at it?
Tôi có thể xem được không? — doy ğó tẻ sam đuhr·ẹrk kawm

I'm just looking.
Tôi chỉ ngắm xem. — doy jeẻ ngúhm sam

I don't like it.
Tôi không thích nó. — doy kawm tík nó

How much is this?
Cái này giá bao nhiêu? — ğaí này zaá bow nyee·oo

It's too expensive.
Cái này quá mắc. — ğaí này gwaá múhk

Do you accept credit cards?
Bạn có nhận thẻ tín dụng không? — baạn kó nyụhn tả dín zụm kawm

There's a mistake in the bill.
Có sự nhầm lẫn trên hoá đơn. — ğó sụhr nyùhm lũhn chen hwaá đern

I'm looking for a/the ...	*Tôi tìm ...*	doy dìm ...
bank	*ngân hàng*	nguhn haàng
market	*chợ*	jẹr
tourist office	*văn phòng hướng dẫn du lịch*	vuhn fòm huhr·érng zũhn zoo lịk

TIME & DATES

What time is it?
Mấy giờ rồi? — máy zèr zòy

It's (eight) o'clock.
Bây giờ là (tám) giờ. — bay zèr laà (dúhm) zèr

morning	*buổi sáng*	boỏ·ee saáng
afternoon	*buổi chiều*	boỏ·ee jee·oò
evening	*buổi tối*	boỏ·ee dóy
yesterday	*hôm qua*	hawm ğwaa
today	*hôm nay*	hawm nay
tomorrow	*ngày mai*	ngày mai

Monday	*thứ hai*	túhr hai
Tuesday	*thứ ba*	túhr baa
Wednesday	*thứ tư*	túhr duhr
Thursday	*thứ năm*	túhr nuhm

Friday	*thứ sáu*	túhr sóh
Saturday	*thứ bảy*	túhr bảy
Sunday	*chủ nhật*	jỏo nhụht
January	*tháng giêng*	taáng zee·uhng
February	*tháng hai*	taáng hai
March	*tháng ba*	taáng baa
April	*tháng tư*	taáng tuhr
May	*tháng năm*	taáng nuhm
June	*tháng sáu*	taáng sóh
July	*tháng bảy*	taáng bảy
August	*tháng tám*	taáng dúhm
September	*tháng chín*	taáng jín
October	*tháng mười*	taáng muhr·eè
November	*tháng mười một*	taáng muhr·eè mạwt
December	*tháng mười hai*	taáng muhr·eè hai

TRANSPORT

Public Transport

When does the (first)... leave/arrive?	*Chuyến ... (sớm nhất) chạy lúc mấy giờ?*	jwee·úhn ... (sérm nyúht) jạy lúp máy zèr
boat	*tàu/ thuyền*	dòw/ twee·ùhn
bus	*xe buýt*	sa beét
plane	*máy bay*	máy bay
train	*xe lửa*	sa lủhr·uh

I'd like a ... ticket.	*Tôi muốn vé ...*	doy moo·úhn vá ...
1st class	*hạng nhất*	haạng nyúht
2nd class	*hạng nhì*	haạng nyeè
one way	*đi một chiều*	đee mạt jee·oò
return	*khứ hồi*	kúhr haw·eè

I want to go to ...
Tôi muốn đi ... doy moo·úhn đee ...

How long does the trip take?
Chuyến đi sẽ mất bao lâu? jwee·úhn đee sã múht bow loh

What time does it arrive?
Mấy giờ đến? máy zèr đén

bus station	*bến xe*	bén sa
railway station	*ga xe lửa*	gaa sa lủhr·uh
the first	*đầu tiên*	đòw dee·uhn
the last	*cuối cùng*	ğoo·eé ğùm
the next	*kế tiếp*	ğé dee·úhp
ticket office	*phòng bán vé*	fòm baán vá
timetable	*thời biểu*	ter·eè beẻ·oo

Driving & Cycling

I'd like to hire a ...	*Tôi muốn thuê ... (N)*	doy moo·úhn twe ...
	Tôi muốn mướn ... (S)	doy moo·úhn muhr·érn ...
car	*xe hơi*	sa her·ee
bicycle	*xe đạp*	sa đạp
motorbike	*xe moto*	sa mo·to

Is this the road to ...?
Con đường này có dẫn đến ...? ğon đuhr·èrng này gó zũhn đén ...

How many kilometres to ...?
... cách đây bao nhiêu ki-lô-mét? ... ğaák đay bow nyee·oo kee·law·mét

Where's a service station?
Trạm xăng ở đâu? chạm suhng ẻr doh

Please fill it up.
Làm ơn đổ đầy bình. laàm ern đỏ đày bìng

I'd like ... litres.
Tôi muốn ... lít. doy moo·úhn ... léet

diesel	*dầu diesel*	zòh dee·sel
highway	*xa lộ*	saa lạw
leaded petrol	*dầu xăng có chì*	zòh suhng ğó jeè
map	*bản đồ*	baản đàw
unleaded petrol	*dầu xăng*	zòh suhng

(How long) Can I park here?
Chúng tôi có thể đậu xe được (bao lâu)? júm doy ğó tẻ dọh sa đuhr·ẹrk (bow loh)

I need a mechanic.
Chúng tôi cần thợ sửa xe. júm doy ğùhn tẹr sủhr·uh sa

The car/motorbike has broken down (at ...)
Xe bị hư (tại ...). sa beẹ huhr (daị ...)

The car/motorbike won't start.
(Xe hơi/Xe moto) không đề được. (sa her·ee/sa mo·to) kawm đè đuhr·ẹrk

I have a flat tyre.
Bánh xe tôi bị xì. baáng sa doy beẹ seè

I've run out of petrol.
Tôi bị hết dầu/xăng. doy beẹ hét zòh/suhng

I've had an accident.
Tôi bị tai nạn. doy beẹ dai nạn

GLOSSARY

A Di Da – Buddha of the Past
Agent Orange – toxic, carcinogenic chemical herbicide used extensively during the American War
am duong – Vietnamese equivalent of Yin and Yang
American War – Vietnamese name for what is also known as the Vietnam War
Annam – old Chinese name for Vietnam, meaning 'Pacified South'
ao dai – Vietnamese national dress worn by women
apsaras – heavenly maidens
ARVN – Army of the Republic of Vietnam (former South Vietnamese army)

ba mu – midwife. There are 12 'midwives', each of whom teaches newborns a different skill necessary for the first year of life: smiling, sucking, lying on their stomachs, and so forth
ban – mountainous village
bang – congregation (in the Chinese community)
bar om – literally 'holding' bars associated with the sex industry. Also known as 'karaoke om'.
buu dien – post office

cai luong – Vietnamese modern theatre
Cao Daism – indigenous Vietnamese religion
Cham – ethnic minority descended from the people of Champa
Champa – Hindu kingdom dating from the late 2nd century AD
Charlie – nickname for the Viet Cong, used by US soldiers
chua – pagoda
chu nho – standard Chinese characters (script)
Cochinchina – the southern part of Vietnam during the French-colonial era
com pho – rice and rice-noodle soup
crémaillère – cog railway
cyclo – pedicab or bicycle rickshaw

Dai The Chi Bo Tat – an assistant of *A Di Da*
dan bau – single-stringed zither that generates an astounding magnitude of tones
dan tranh – 16-stringed zither
den – temple
Di Lac Buddha – Buddha of the Future
dikpalaka – gods of the directions of the compass
dinh – communal meeting hall
DMZ – Demilitarised Zone, a strip of land that once separated North and South Vietnam
doi moi – economic restructuring or reform, which commenced in Vietnam in 1986
dong – natural caves. Also Vietnamese currency.
dong son – drums

ecocide – term used to describe the devastating effects of the herbicides sprayed over Vietnam during the American War

fléchette – experimental US weapon. An artillery shell containing thousands of darts.
Funan – see *Oc-Eo*

garuda – half human-half bird
gom – ceramics

hai dang – lighthouse
hat boi – classical theatre in the south
hat cheo – Vietnamese popular theatre
hat tuong – classical theatre in the north
ho ca – aquarium
Ho Chi Minh Trail – route used by the North Vietnamese Army and Viet Cong to move supplies to the south
Hoa – ethnic Chinese, one of the largest single minority groups in Vietnam
hoi quan – Chinese congregational assembly halls
huong – perfume
huyen – rural district

Indochina – Vietnam, Cambodia and Laos. The name derives from Indian and Chinese influences.

kala-makara – sea-monster god
kalan – a religious sanctuary
khach san – hotel
Khmer – ethnic Cambodians
Khong Tu – Confucius
kich noi – spoken drama
Kinh – Vietnamese language
Kuomintang – Chinese Nationalist Party, also known as KMT. The KMT controlled China between 1925 and 1949 until defeated by the communists.

li xi – lucky money distributed during the Vietnamese Lunar New Year
liberation – 1975 takeover of the South by the North. Most foreigners call this 'reunification'.
Lien Xo – literally, Soviet Union. Used to call attention to a foreigner
linga – stylised phallus which represents the Hindu god Shiva

manushi-buddha – Buddha who appeared in human form
moi – derogatory word meaning 'savages', mostly used by ethnic Vietnamese to describe hill-tribe people
Montagnards – term meaning highlanders or mountain people, sometimes used to refer to the ethnic minorities who inhabit remote areas of Vietnam
muong – large village unit made up of *quel* (small stilt-houses)

naga – Sanskrit term for a mythical serpent being with divine powers; often depicted forming a kind of shelter over the Buddha
nam phai – for men
napalm – jellied petrol (gasoline) dropped and lit from aircraft; used by US forces with devastating repercussions during the American War

nguoi thuong – the current government's preferred term for highland people

nha hang – restaurant

nha khach – hotel or guesthouse

nha nghi – guesthouse

nha rong – large stilt house, used by hill tribes as a kind of community centre

nha tro – dormitory

NLF – National Liberation Front, the official name for the VC

nom – Vietnamese script, used between the 10th and early 20th centuries

nu phai – for women

nui – mountain

nuoc mam – fish sauce, added to almost every main dish in Vietnam

NVA – North Vietnamese Army

Oc-Eo – Indianised Khmer kingdom (also called Funan) in southern Vietnam between the 1st and 6th centuries

Ong Bon – Guardian Spirit of Happiness and Virtue

OSS – US Office of Strategic Services. The predecessor of the CIA.

pagoda – traditionally an eight-sided Buddhist tower, but in Vietnam the word is commonly used to denote a temple

phong thuy – literally, 'wind and water'. Used to describe geomancy. Also known by its Chinese name, feng shui.

PRG – Provisional Revolutionary Government, the temporary Communist government set up by the VC in the South. It existed from 1969 to 1976.

quan – urban district

Quan Cong – Chinese God of War

Quan The Am Bo Tat – Goddess of Mercy

quoc am – modern Vietnamese literature

quoc ngu – Latin-based phonetic alphabet in which Vietnamese is written

rap – cinema

Revolutionary Youth League – first Marxist group in Vietnam and predecessor of the Communist Party

roi can – conventional puppetry

roi nuoc – water puppetry

ruou (pronounced xeo) – rice wine

RVN – Republic of Vietnam (the old South Vietnam)

salangane – swiftlet

sao – wooden flute

saola – antelope-like creature

shakti – feminine manifestation of Shiva

song – river

SRV – Socialist Republic of Vietnam (Vietnam's official name)

Strategic Hamlets Program – program (by South Vietnam and the USA) of forcibly moving peasants into fortified villages to deny the VC bases of support

sung – fig tree

Tam Giao – literally, 'triple religion'. Confucianism, Taoism and Buddhism fused over time with popular Chinese beliefs and ancient Vietnamese animism.

Tao – the Way. The essence of which all things are made.

Tay ba lo – backpacker

Tet – Vietnamese Lunar New Year

thai cuc quyen – Vietnamese for t'ai chi

Thich Ca Buddha – the historical Buddha Sakyamuni, whose real name was Siddhartha Gautama

thong nhat – reunification. Also a commonly used term for the Reunification Express train.

thuoc bac – Chinese medicine

toc hanh – express bus

Tonkin – the northern part of Vietnam during the French-colonial era. Also the name of a body of water in the north (Tonkin Gulf).

truyen khau – traditional oral literature

UNHCR – UN High Commissioner for Refugees

VC – Viet Cong or Vietnamese Communists

Viet Kieu – overseas Vietnamese

Viet Minh – League for the Independence of Vietnam, a nationalistic movement that fought the Japanese and French but later became communist dominated

VNQDD – Viet Nam Quoc Dan Dang. Largely middle -class nationalist party.

xang – petrol

xe Honda loi – wagon pulled by a motorbike

xe lam – tiny three-wheeled trucks used for short-haul passenger and freight transport

xe loi – wagon pulled by a motorbike in the Mekong Delta region

xe om – motorbike taxi, also called *Honda om*

xich lo – *cyclo*, from the French *cyclo-pousse*

Behind the Scenes

SEND US YOUR FEEDBACK

We love to hear from travellers – your comments keep us on our toes and help make our books better. Our well-travelled team reads every word on what you loved or loathed about this book. Although we cannot reply individually to postal submissions, we always guarantee that your feedback goes straight to the appropriate authors, in time for the next edition. Each person who sends us information is thanked in the next edition – the most useful submissions are rewarded with a selection of digital PDF chapters.

Visit **lonelyplanet.com/contact** to submit your updates and suggestions or to ask for help. Our award-winning website also features inspirational travel stories, news and discussions.

Note: We may edit, reproduce and incorporate your comments in Lonely Planet products such as guidebooks, websites and digital products, so let us know if you don't want your comments reproduced or your name acknowledged. For a copy of our privacy policy visit lonelyplanet.com/privacy.

OUR READERS

Many thanks to the travellers who used the last edition and wrote to us with helpful hints, useful advice and interesting anecdotes:

A Aida Soldevila , Alex Jones, Alfonso Tedeschi, Alison Lewis, Amy Baxter, Andrew Wood, Angeline Schoor, Anna Staudigl, Antonia Diaz, Arundhati Katju **B** Bill Batcheller, Bill Weir, Bonnet Jean-Baptiste, Brandon Caesar, Bryan Brennan **C** Carole Moore, Cornay Sinac **D** Daniel Kingston, David Cutaia, David English, Delphine Charlet, Douglas Bratten, Duc Le, Dustin Gerding **E** Eline Bongers, Emily McGill **F** Fabiola Frattini, Felicity Bush, Florin Teodorescu, Frank Knab **G** Garry Grass, Giles Denby, Ginny Tong, Gordon Blues **H** Harriet & Bryony Perks, Holly Hutchinson, Huw Jones **J** Jack Tattis, James Morrison, Jane Edwards, Janneke Blom, Jasper Rautenberg, Jay Sherrerd, Jeffrey Eng, Josephine Van As, Jvala Schelling **K** Karlie Drutz, Kilian Friese **L** Lesli Uebel, Liz Cornwell, Liz Rushton, Loeiz Lagadec, Lucy Marris **M** Mar Mosquera, Marcus Wood, Markus Pusnik, Martin Woodford, Massimo Corona, Matt Yates, Megan Harcourt, Michael A. Jensen, Michael Hromadka, Michael Meryash **N** Nadine Tapfer, Nguyen Tanh, Nick Comer **O** Ozzy Unsworth **P** Patricia & John Livesley, Peter Aston, Peter Calingaert, Peter Heading **R** Rehahn Croquevielle, Réhahn Croquevielle, Riad El-Bdour, Richard Ackermann, Robert Hoke, Robert Moss, Rogier van den Heuvel, Ruth Webber **S** Sabine Höhn, Selma Askin, Sina Afshar, Sophie Sykes, Steven Cras, Susan Prolman **T** Ted Kaynor, Theo Muth, Tia Bullen, Tim Bird, Tim Schmitt, Tina Trenkner, Tony Chan, Torben Retboll **W** William Tinkler, Wouke Eindhoven **Y** Yee Foo, Yves Le Saux

AUTHOR THANKS

Iain Stewart

So many people have helped me over the years, shape and create this guide. I'd particularly like to single out Nick and Slo in HCMC, the Mui Ne posse, Dave in Con Dao, all the Nha Trang crew and Nick Ray. Caroline Mills' contacts and contributions greatly helped me along the way and cheers to Vinh Vu of Handspan, Ben and Bich, Howard and Deb, Chien in Hanoi and Neil Fraser, Mark and Dzung in Hoi An. Thanks also to Laura Crawford for her support and all the LP editorial and production staff.

Brett Atkinson

Cam ơn to Kien Tran and my extended Hanoi family, and around Phong Nha, thanks to Ben, Bich and the team. In Dong Ha, thanks to Tam for surprising local flavours, and cheers to Mark, Leanne, Neil, and Caroline in Hoi An, and to Tony in Danang. Nick Ross, Ariele Gold and (especially) Mark Zazula were great contacts in HCMC, and thanks to all the Lonely Planet editors and cartographers. Final thanks to Carol and my family in New Zealand.

Anna Kaminski

I would like to thank Laura for entrusting me with these chapters, fellow scribes for advice along the way, and also the following: Kelly McCartney for the serendipitous meeting on a plane, Thu and friends for the wonderful outing in Cao Lanh, Sherry and Brijiu for the company in Chau Doc, Hieu in Can Tho (and on Pirate Island), the good people of Mango Home Riverside, Murray Guesthouse and Villa Vista for all your help and advice, Curtis and Thuy in Dalat, Andy in Ha Tien, Mr The and Mr Hiep for the careful driving, and Mr An for introducing me to the culture of the Bahnar.

Jessica Lee

On the road, thanks to Shu, Mr Tung, Dong and Linh and huge thanks to my road-tripping buddy Kien. Also, thanks to fellow author Brett for some great advice and tips. Back home, shout out to the amazing Shannon Wang who tossed her entire plans out the window at extremely short notice, to house sit for me so that I could research this book.

Benedict Walker

Big thanks to my friends in Vietnam, Kien and family, Sophie, Fabiola and my old pal Zoe Butt: you're an inspiration, girl. To Mum for keeping me sane when my bag disappeared and for always keeping the faith. To Jess at LP for lending a hand and the wonderful Laura Crawford for opening so many doors. This book is for aunty Bonnie, my book lady, for sticking around when I hit the road and still being here when I got back. If you're an angel by the time this hits shelves, keep an eye on me please!

ACKNOWLEDGMENTS

Climate map data adapted from Peel MC, Finlayson BL & McMahon TA (2007) 'Updated World Map of the Köppen-Geiger Climate Classification', *Hydrology and Earth System Sciences*, 11, 1633–44.

Cover photograph: Temple of Literature, Hanoi; Jon Arnold, AWL ©

Illustrations pp180–1 and pp428–29 by Michael Weldon.

THIS BOOK

This 13th edition of Lonely Planet's *Vietnam* guidebook was researched and written by Iain Stewart, Brett Atkinson, Anna Kaminski, Jessica Lee, Nick Ray and Benedict Walker. The previous edition was written and researched by Iain Stewart, Brett Atkinson, Damian Harper and Nick Ray.

This guidebook was produced by the following:

Destination Editor Laura Crawford

Product Editors Alison Ridgway, Katie O'Connell

Regional Senior Cartographers Valentina Kremenchutskaya, Diana Von Holdt

Book Designer Mazzy Prinsep

Assisting Editors Carolyn Bain, Michelle Bennett, Andrea Dobbin, Carly Hall, Victoria Harrison, Lauren O'Connell, Kristin Odijk, Jeanette Wall

Assisting Layout Designer Virginia Moreno

Cover Researcher Naomi Parker

Thanks to Carolyn Boicos, Jane Grisman, Jenna Myers, Kathryn Rowan, Dianne Schallmeiner, Ellie Simpson, Lauren Wellicome

Index

Map Pages **000**
Photo Pages **000**

Map Pages **000**
Photo Pages **000**

T

U

V

W

X

Y

Map Pages **000**
Photo Pages **000**

Map Legend

Sights
- Beach
- Bird Sanctuary
- Buddhist
- Castle/Palace
- Christian
- Confucian
- Hindu
- Islamic
- Jain
- Jewish
- Monument
- Museum/Gallery/Historic Building
- Ruin
- Shinto
- Sikh
- Taoist
- Winery/Vineyard
- Zoo/Wildlife Sanctuary
- Other Sight

Activities, Courses & Tours
- Bodysurfing
- Diving
- Canoeing/Kayaking
- Course/Tour
- Sento Hot Baths/Onsen
- Skiing
- Snorkelling
- Surfing
- Swimming/Pool
- Walking
- Windsurfing
- Other Activity

Sleeping
- Sleeping
- Camping

Eating
- Eating

Drinking & Nightlife
- Drinking & Nightlife
- Cafe

Entertainment
- Entertainment

Shopping
- Shopping

Information
- Bank
- Embassy/Consulate
- Hospital/Medical
- Internet
- Police
- Post Office
- Telephone
- Toilet
- Tourist Information
- Other Information

Geographic
- Beach
- Gate
- Hut/Shelter
- Lighthouse
- Lookout
- Mountain/Volcano
- Oasis
- Park
- Pass
- Picnic Area
- Waterfall

Population
- Capital (National)
- Capital (State/Province)
- City/Large Town
- Town/Village

Transport
- Airport
- Border crossing
- Bus
- Cable car/Funicular
- Cycling
- Ferry
- Metro/MRT/MTR station
- Monorail
- Parking
- Petrol station
- Skytrain/Subway station
- Taxi
- Train station/Railway
- Tram
- Underground station
- Other Transport

Note: Not all symbols displayed above appear on the maps in this book

Routes
- Tollway
- Freeway
- Primary
- Secondary
- Tertiary
- Lane
- Unsealed road
- Road under construction
- Plaza/Mall
- Steps
- Tunnel
- Pedestrian overpass
- Walking Tour
- Walking Tour detour
- Path/Walking Trail

Boundaries
- International
- State/Province
- Disputed
- Regional/Suburb
- Marine Park
- Cliff
- Wall

Hydrography
- River, Creek
- Intermittent River
- Canal
- Water
- Dry/Salt/Intermittent Lake
- Reef

Areas
- Airport/Runway
- Beach/Desert
- Cemetery (Christian)
- Cemetery (Other)
- Glacier
- Mudflat
- Park/Forest
- Sight (Building)
- Sportsground
- Swamp/Mangrove